barbri

OUTLINES FOR
MULTISTATE

FOUNDER AND SENIOR ADVISOR
PROFESSOR RICHARD J. CONVISER

EDITORS
CHRISTINA J. GUARISCO, ESQ.
STEVEN J. LEVIN, ESQ.
COURTNEY D. LORENTZ, ESQ.
ROGER W. MESLAR, ESQ.
MAUREEN A. MITCHELL, ESQ.
ANGEL M. MURPHY, ESQ.
PAUL T. PHILLIPS, ESQ.
RACHEL M. SCHINDELAR, ESQ.
ANDREW T. SUSZEK, ESQ.

DIRECTOR OF PUBLISHING
ELIZABETH GOODMAN DUKE

TABLE OF CONTENTS

MS

CIVIL PROCEDURE

CIVIL PROCEDURE—FEDERAL
TABLE OF CONTENTS

CIVIL PROCEDURE—FEDERAL

I. INTRODUCTION

This outline is designed to acquaint you with commonly tested areas within the fields of federal jurisdiction and procedure. These are: personal jurisdiction, subject matter jurisdiction, venue, discovery, and joinder of multiple parties.

A. PERSONAL JURISDICTION

Personal jurisdiction refers to the ability of a court to exercise power over a particular defendant or item of property. It may be categorized as in personam, in rem, or quasi in rem. The primary limitations on a court's power to exercise personal jurisdiction are found in the United States Constitution and state statutes.

B. SUBJECT MATTER JURISDICTION

The subject matter jurisdiction of the federal courts is limited to that authorized by the Constitution as implemented by federal statute and decisional law. In general, it may be categorized as follows:

1. Diversity of Citizenship Jurisdiction

Diversity of citizenship jurisdiction under 28 U.S.C. section 1332 is grounded historically in the desire to protect out-of-state parties from local prejudice. Its main requirement is that there be complete diversity between opposing parties. Each plaintiff must be of diverse citizenship from each defendant. Also, the amount in controversy must exceed $75,000.

2. Federal Question Jurisdiction

Federal question jurisdiction under section 1331 presents fewer specific difficulties. The principal problem in this area is to determine when an action "arises under" federal law. A secondary problem is to know what types of actions are within the exclusive jurisdiction of the federal courts under other specific statutes.

3. Removal Jurisdiction

Removal jurisdiction allows defendants to remove an action brought in a state court to a federal court if the federal court would have had original jurisdiction over the action.

4. Supplemental Jurisdiction

The doctrine of supplemental jurisdiction is codified under section 1367 and includes, under a single name, the concepts of "ancillary" and "pendent" jurisdiction. In any form, supplemental jurisdiction allows a federal court to entertain certain claims over which it would have no independent basis of subject matter jurisdiction, i.e., claims that do not satisfy diversity or federal question jurisdiction requirements. It is important to note that supplemental jurisdiction operates only after a claim has invoked federal subject matter jurisdiction, after the case is properly in federal court. Supplemental jurisdiction operates to bring additional claims into that case that arise from the same transaction or occurrence as the original claim, but it cannot be used to get the case into federal court in the first instance.

C. VENUE

Venue is the designation of the proper geographic district in which to bring an action. Venue will depend on where the cause of action arose and on the nature of the parties (i.e., whether corporate or natural persons).

D. DISCOVERY

Discovery issues principally revolve around the scope of the examination allowed in discovery, the uses of depositions at trial, and the available methods of enforcing discovery rights.

E. MULTIPLE PARTIES

Multiple party questions concern whether various types of joinder are permitted under federal law and, if so, whether there is a jurisdictional basis for a particular attempted joinder. The majority of the issues that arise in this area are grounded in the interpretation or application of statutes and the Federal Rules of Civil Procedure ("Federal Rules"), and also require knowledge of subject matter jurisdictional bases, especially supplemental jurisdiction.

II. PERSONAL JURISDICTION

A. OVERVIEW

There are two branches of jurisdiction: subject matter jurisdiction and personal jurisdiction. *Subject matter jurisdiction* involves the court's power over a particular *type of case*. *Personal jurisdiction* involves the ability of a court having subject matter jurisdiction to exercise power over a *particular defendant or item of property*. This section discusses personal jurisdiction.

1. Limitations on Personal Jurisdiction

The exercise of personal jurisdiction generally must be authorized by statute *and* constitutional.

a. Statutory Limitations

States have the power to decide over whom their courts may exercise jurisdiction. Therefore, the first place to look to determine whether the court has properly exercised personal jurisdiction usually is state law. If no state statute grants the court the power over the parties before the court, the court lacks personal jurisdiction.

b. Constitutional Limitations

The Due Process Clause of the Constitution places two restrictions on the exercise of personal jurisdiction. First, the defendant must have such contacts with the forum state that the exercise of jurisdiction would be fair and reasonable. Second, the defendant must be given appropriate notice of the action and an opportunity to be heard. Exercise of personal jurisdiction over a defendant in violation of these constitutional requirements is not valid, even if a statute purports to grant the court jurisdiction.

c. Personal Jurisdiction in Federal Courts

The main jurisdictional problem in state courts arises when the defendant over whom power is sought lives in another state. Since the federal borders encompass all states, one might expect that federal courts would encounter problems of personal jurisdiction only when the defendants were foreign nationals. However, Rule 4 of the Federal Rules provides that, absent some special federal statute, each federal court must analyze personal jurisdiction *as if it were a court of the state in which it is located*. Thus, in most cases, the assessment of whether the court has personal jurisdiction over the defendant will be exactly the same in federal court as it is in state court. Rule 4 also authorizes jurisdiction without regard to state long arm statutes over third-party defendants and parties required to be joined under the compulsory joinder rules, provided the party is served within 100 miles from the place where the summons was issued. (*See* VIII.B.3., *infra*.)

2. Three Types of Personal Jurisdiction

a. In Personam Jurisdiction

In personam jurisdiction exists when the forum has power over the person of a particular defendant. (Jurisdiction over a plaintiff is generally not an issue because the plaintiff accedes to the court's jurisdiction by bringing suit in that court.) In these cases, the court may render a money judgment against the defendant or may order the defendant to perform acts or refrain from acting. Such a judgment creates a personal obligation on the defendant and is entitled to full faith and credit in all other states; i.e., if a defendant is ordered to pay a sum of money to a plaintiff, the plaintiff may enforce the judgment against the defendant's property in any other state where that property is located.

b. In Rem Jurisdiction

In rem jurisdiction exists when the court has power to adjudicate the rights of all persons in the world with respect to a ***particular item*** of property. This jurisdiction is limited to situations where the property is located within the physical borders of the state and where it is necessary for the state to be able to bind all persons regarding the property's ownership and use. This occurs with respect to actions for condemnation (eminent domain cases), forfeiture of property to the state (e.g., when the property is used for the unlawful transportation of narcotics), and settlement of decedents' estates.

c. Quasi In Rem Jurisdiction

One type of quasi in rem jurisdiction exists when the court has power to determine whether particular individuals own specific property within the court's control. Unlike in rem jurisdiction, however, it does not permit the court to determine the rights of all persons in the world with respect to the property. A second type of quasi in rem jurisdiction permits the court to adjudicate disputes other than ownership based on the presence of the defendant's property in the forum (*see* E.2.a.2), *infra*, regarding applicable constitutional limitations).

1) Defendant Is Not Bound Personally

The basis of a court's power to exercise quasi in rem jurisdiction is the property within the state. (*See* E., *infra*.) The judgment does not bind the defendant ***personally*** and cannot be enforced against any other property belonging to the defendant.

B. STATUTORY LIMITATIONS ON IN PERSONAM JURISDICTION

Each state is free to prescribe its own statutory bases for personal jurisdiction. Of course, the exercise of jurisdiction in a given case must also satisfy the constitutional requirements. (*See* C., *infra*.) Most states have statutes granting their courts in personam jurisdiction in the following four situations:

(i)　Where the defendant is present in the forum state and is personally served with process;

(ii)　Where the defendant is domiciled in the forum state;

(iii)　Where the defendant consents to jurisdiction; and

(iv)　Where the defendant has committed acts bringing him within the forum state's long arm statutes.

Each of these bases of in personam jurisdiction will be discussed in detail below.

1. Physical Presence at Time of Personal Service

Most states grant their courts in personam jurisdiction over any defendant who can be served with process within the borders of the state, no matter how long he was present (i.e., even if merely passing through). The Supreme Court has upheld this type of jurisdiction, allowing a transient defendant to be served with process for a cause of action unrelated to his brief presence in the state. [Burnham v. Superior Court, 495 U.S. 604 (1990)]

2. State Law Exceptions to Traditional Rule

Even though jurisdiction through presence at the time of service has been upheld under the Constitution, state statutes and court decisions have limited the power of their courts in certain situations.

a. Service by Fraud or Force Invalid

If a plaintiff brings a defendant into a state by fraud or force to serve process, most courts will find the service invalid. [*See, e.g.*, Copas v. Anglo-American Provision Co., 73 Mich. 541 (1889)]

b. Immunity of Parties and Witnesses

Most states likewise grant immunity from personal jurisdiction to nonresidents who are present in the state solely to take part in a judicial proceeding, or who are passing through the state on their way to a judicial proceeding elsewhere.

3. Domicile

Most states grant their courts in personam jurisdiction over persons who are domiciliaries of the state, even when the defendant is not physically within the state when served with process.

a. Defined

Domicile refers to the place where a person maintains her permanent home. If a person has legal capacity, her domicile is the place she has chosen through presence (even for a moment), coupled with the intention to make that place her home. If a person lacks capacity, domicile is determined by law (e.g., infant is domiciliary of custodial parent's home state).

b. Citizenship

A United States citizen, even though domiciled abroad, is subject to personal jurisdiction in the United States. The scope of this basis for jurisdiction is unclear, because states have never attempted to enact laws or rules enabling their courts to obtain jurisdiction solely on the basis of citizenship.

4. **Consent**
   Virtually every state provides for in personam jurisdiction through the defendant's consent. Such consent may be express or implied or through the making of a general appearance.

   a. **Express Consent**
      A party's express consent to the jurisdiction of local courts, whether given before or after suit is commenced, serves as a sufficient basis for in personam jurisdiction.

      1) **By Contract**
         A person can, by contract, give advance consent to jurisdiction in the event a suit is brought against him.

      2) **By Appointment of Agent to Accept Service of Process**
         A person can, by contract, appoint an agent in a particular state to receive service in that state in an action against him. The terms of the contract determine the extent of the agent's power and, thus, the scope of the jurisdiction conferred.

         a) **Appointment Required by State**
            When the state heavily regulates a type of business (e.g., sale of securities) to protect its citizens, it can require a nonresident engaged in that business to appoint an agent for service of process in the state. *Note:* The state cannot require every nonresident businessperson to appoint such an agent, because the state lacks power to exclude individuals from the state. However, a state can require nonresident corporations to make such an appointment before doing business in the state.

   b. **Implied Consent**
      When the state has substantial reason to regulate the in-state activity of a nonresident of the state, it may provide that by engaging in such activity, the nonresident thereby appoints a designated state official as his agent for service of process. Thus, for example, the Supreme Court has upheld statutes that use such implied consent to subject a nonresident motorist to jurisdiction in any state in which he has an accident. [Hess v. Pawloski, 274 U.S. 352 (1927)]

   c. **Voluntary Appearance**
      A defendant may consent to jurisdiction by a voluntary appearance, i.e., by contesting the case without challenging personal jurisdiction. Generally, any sort of appearance provides a sufficient basis for jurisdiction, but many states allow *"special appearances"* through which a defendant can object to the court's exercise of jurisdiction. The defendant usually must make this special appearance—by stating grounds for his objection to jurisdiction—in his initial pleading to the court; otherwise, the defendant will be deemed to have consented to jurisdiction.

5. **Long Arm Statutes**
   Virtually all states grant their courts in personam jurisdiction over nonresidents who perform or cause to be performed certain acts within the state or who cause results within the state by acts performed out of the state. In personam jurisdiction is granted regardless of whether the defendant is served within or outside the forum, but is limited to causes of action arising from the acts performed or results caused within the state.

a.   Unlimited Long Arm Statutes

        A few states, such as California, have long arm statutes that give their courts power over any person or property over which the state can constitutionally exercise jurisdiction. (*See* C., *infra*.) These are known as unlimited long arm statutes.

    b.   Limited (or Specific) Long Arm Statutes

        Most states, however, have long arm statutes that specify in detail the situations in which their courts can exercise jurisdiction.

        1)   Limitations in Tort Cases

            Some statutes permit jurisdiction when a "tort" occurs within the state, while others require a "tortious act." The latter language has caused problems where an out-of-state manufacturer puts his products into the stream of commerce knowing that some items will end up in the forum state. When the gravamen of the complaint is negligent manufacture, some courts have read "tortious act" narrowly and confined jurisdiction to the place of manufacture; others have read it to mean "the place the tort occurred," interpreting that to be the place of injury.

        2)   Limitations in Contract Cases

            Many statutes permit jurisdiction if the cause of action arises out of the "transaction of business" in the state. Some states require the defendant or his agent to have been physically present in the state at the time the transaction took place, but others have taken a broader view—e.g., New York has upheld jurisdiction over a California resident who made telephone bids from California on paintings being sold in New York.

        3)   Limitations in Property Actions

            Many state statutes permit jurisdiction over a nonresident defendant when the cause of action arises from ownership of property within the state—as in the case of a tort action based on negligent maintenance of realty or a contract action regarding the sale of the property. Some statutes include chattels, while others are confined to realty.

        4)   Limitations in Marital Dissolution Cases

            All states provide that when a married couple last lived together in the state and one spouse then abandons the other, the remaining spouse may obtain personal jurisdiction over the absent spouse for divorce or legal separation proceedings. States vary on whether the plaintiff spouse must be living in the state at the time of abandonment (or other cause for dissolution) or whether jurisdiction may be acquired whenever the plaintiff has acquired domicile in the state.

C.   CONSTITUTIONAL LIMITATIONS ON IN PERSONAM JURISDICTION

    Once it is determined that a state has a statute that allows the court to exercise in personam jurisdiction over the parties before it, the constitutionality of the exercise must next be determined. There are two components of the constitutional aspect: contacts with the forum and notice.

    1.   Sufficient Contacts with the Forum

a. **Traditional Rule: Physical Power**
Traditionally, jurisdiction over a person (or res) was a consequence of the state's physical power to carry out its judgment; i.e., it was based on the power to arrest the person to force compliance with a judgment. Accordingly, the Supreme Court upheld exercises of jurisdiction whenever the defendant was served with process within the forum state. [*See* Pennoyer v. Neff, 95 U.S. 714 (1878)] The Court later expanded the states' physical power to extend not only to those defendants who were served within the state, but also to those defendants who consented to the state's power or who were domiciled in the state, regardless of where they were served.

b. **Modern Due Process Standard: Contact, Relatedness, and Fairness**
The concept of power by which a state could enforce its judgments was greatly expanded by the Supreme Court in *International Shoe Co. v. Washington*, 326 U.S. 310 (1945). No longer was power controlled solely by whether one of the traditional bases of presence, residence, or consent was present. Instead, the focus became whether sufficient minimum contacts exist between the defendant and the forum so that maintenance of the suit against the defendant does not offend "traditional notions of fair play and substantial justice." The Supreme Court has listed a series of factors by which to assess the constitutionality of personal jurisdiction. In general, the factors fall under three headings: contact, relatedness, and fairness.

1) **Contact**
International Shoe requires that the defendant have "such minimum contacts" with the forum that the exercise of jurisdiction would be fair and reasonable. In considering whether there are such contacts, a court will look to two factors: purposeful availment and foreseeability.

a) **Purposeful Availment**
Defendant's contact with the forum must result from her purposeful availment with that forum. The contacts cannot be accidental. Defendant must reach out to the forum in some way, such as to make money there or to use the roads there. The court must find that through these contacts the defendant *purposefully availed* herself "of the privilege of conducting activities within the forum state, thus invoking the benefits and protections of its laws." [Hanson v. Denckla, 357 U.S. 235 (1958)]

Examples: 1) Defendants, Michigan residents, entered into a franchise contract with a Florida corporation. The agreement required, among other things, that fees be sent to the franchisor's home office in Florida, and provided that Florida law would govern any dispute. The Court held that the defendants could be sued in Florida; their contact with Florida resulted from their purposeful availment of that state. [Burger King v. Rudzewicz, 471 U.S. 462 (1985)]

2) Defendant manufactures widgets in Alabama and markets them to customers in Mississippi. Plaintiff, a resident of Mississippi, purchases a widget from Defendant. Defendant accepts the order and ships the widget to Plaintiff in

Mississippi. If the widget explodes and injures Plaintiff, she can probably sue Defendant in Mississippi. Defendant purposefully availed itself of the market in Mississippi. [*See* International Shoe Co. v. Washington, *supra*]

Compare: 1) Father, in New York, agreed to give up custody of Daughter to Mother in California. Mother sued Father in California for additional support. Father's only contact with California was letting Daughter go there. The Court held that California could not obtain in personam jurisdiction over Father because, in acting in the interest of family harmony, Father could not be said to have purposefully availed himself of the benefits and protections of California laws. [Kulko v. Superior Court, 436 U.S. 84 (1978)]

2) Defendant, a New York car dealer, was sued in Oklahoma based on an injury that Plaintiff received from an accident in Oklahoma. The only basis for jurisdiction over Defendant was the sale of the allegedly defective car in New York by Defendant, who knew no more than that any vehicle sold might be driven elsewhere. The Court found that there was no purposeful availment of the privileges or protections of Oklahoma. [World-Wide Volkswagen Corp. v. Woodson, 444 U.S. 286 (1980)]

(1) "Stream of Commerce" Cases
There is great difficulty in assessing purposeful availment in "stream of commerce" cases. Stream of commerce cases typically arise when Defendant manufactures its product in State A (or even Country A) and sells them to a second party in State B, thereby placing the product in the stream of commerce. The product eventually winds up in another state (State C) and causes an injury therein. The question is whether Defendant ***purposefully availed itself*** of State C. The Supreme Court has addressed such a scenario twice, but it has failed to reach a consensus both times. [Asahi Metal Industry Co. v. Superior Court, 480 U.S. 102 (1987); J. McIntyre Machinery, Ltd. v. Nicastro, 564 U.S. 873 (2011)] For bar exam purposes, the important points to remember are:

(i)   ***Merely placing an item in the stream of commerce***, by itself, ***is not a sufficient basis*** for personal jurisdiction.

(ii) ***It is unresolved*** whether (probably unlikely that) placing an item in the stream of commerce ***with the knowledge or hope*** that it will wind up in a particular state would be a sufficient basis for personal jurisdiction. If you encounter such a question on the exam, you should scour the question for facts showing an ***intentional targeting*** (purposeful availment) of the forum. (*See* (iii), below.) If there is no targeting, you should discuss the connections the defendant has with the forum, and fairness to the defendant, while mentioning the state's interest in providing a forum for its citizens and noting that the question has not been definitively resolved. Your conclusion will be less important than the discussion.

(iii) ***Placing an item in the stream of commerce***, with the knowledge or hope that it will end up in the forum state, and coupled with some ***other act that shows the intent*** to serve a particular state (e.g., modifying its product to comply with state law, maintaining a sales office within the state, etc.), ***is a sufficient basis*** for personal jurisdiction.

(2) Internet Cases

The Supreme Court has not set out a specific test or standard for assessing purposeful availment based on the defendant's Internet activity. Many courts will look at whether the defendant has a passive website that allows people to view only content, an active website that allows people to order and download products, or something in between. The maintenance of a website for only informational purposes, without more activity in the forum, is insufficient to exercise jurisdiction over the defendant for all causes of action (i.e., general jurisdiction), but it may be sufficient for a claim arising from the maintenance of the website itself and brought under the state's long arm statute (thus invoking specific jurisdiction) if the defendant is specifically targeting readers in the forum. On the other hand, maintenance of an active website alone would be sufficient for the exercise of general jurisdiction (i.e., a claim unrelated to the website activities) if the "at home" test is satisfied. Specific jurisdiction hinges on whether the defendant was purposefully directing his activities to the forum. [*See, e.g.*, Snowney v. Harrah's Entertainment, Inc., 35 Cal. 4th 1054 (2006)—Nevada hotel subject to personal jurisdiction in California when it specifically targeted California consumers by providing rate information to and accepting reservations on its website, by touting its proximity to California, and by providing driving directions from California]

b) Foreseeability

In addition to purposeful availment, the contact requirement of *International Shoe* requires that it be foreseeable that the defendant's activities make her amenable to suit in the forum. The defendant must know or reasonably anticipate that her activities in the forum render it foreseeable that she may be "haled into court" there.

Example: A national magazine is probably subject to in personam jurisdiction for libel cases in every state in which the magazine is marketed. Its publishers may reasonably anticipate causing injury in every state in which the magazine is sold, and thus should reasonably anticipate being haled into court in each state. [Keeton v. Hustler Magazine, 465 U.S. 770 (1984); Calder v. Jones, 465 U.S. 783 (1984)]

2) Relatedness of Claim to Contact

One important factor is whether the claim asserted against the defendant arises in some way from the defendant's contacts with the forum. If it does, the court is more likely to find that jurisdiction is fair and reasonable. This assessment requires the court to determine the nature and quality of the defendant's contacts with the state. Some authorities consider this factor to be part of the "contact" or the "fairness" assessment; others consider it, as we do here, to be part of the "relatedness" assessment. The important point is that you address the issue in your answer, whether under the contact, relatedness, or fairness prong of the analysis.

a) Claim Arising from Activity in the State (Specific Jurisdiction)

If the defendant's in-state activity is based on isolated acts committed within the jurisdiction, personal jurisdiction over the defendant will be proper only for causes of action arising from *that in-state activity*; i.e., the court will have "specific jurisdiction." When there are multiple claims or parties involved, each claim of each plaintiff must arise from some in-state activity for there to be specific jurisdiction.

Example: Eighty-six plaintiffs from California and 592 plaintiffs from other states sued Bristol-Myers Squib, a pharmaceutical company incorporated in Delaware and headquartered in New York, in California, alleging that the drug Plavix injured them. None of the non-California plaintiffs alleged any connection to California with regard to their treatment. Because there was no activity in California as to the nonresident plaintiffs, the court lacked personal jurisdiction over Bristol-Myers Squibb as to the claims of the *non-California* plaintiffs, even though Bristol-Myers Squibb was subject to personal jurisdiction in California with respect to the California plaintiffs. [Bristol-Myers Squibb Co. v. Superior Court, 137 S. Ct. 1773 (2017)]

Note: In such a situation, there also could be a lack of statutory authorization because no state would authorize personal jurisdiction over a defendant who commits an out-of-state act that produces an out-of-state injury. However, California has an unlimited long arm statute, so the statutory authorization issue essentially rolled into the constitutional issue.

Note also: The court specifically stated its ruling does not apply to class actions.

b) "At Home" in the State (General Jurisdiction)

General jurisdiction—in personam jurisdiction for *any* cause of action against the defendant, regardless of where the cause of action arose—requires that a defendant be "*at home*" in the jurisdiction. A person is "at home" in the state in which he is domiciled, and a corporation is "at home" in the state in which it was incorporated and the state in which it has its principal place of business. [Goodyear Dunlop Tires Operations, S.A. v. Brown, 564 U.S. 915 (2011); Daimler AG v. Bauman, 571 U.S. 117 (2014); BNSF Railway Co. v. Tyrrell, 137 S. Ct. 1549 (2017)] A number of states have statutes that authorize personal jurisdiction over a defendant that conducts systematic and continuous activity ("doing business") within the state. Such "authorization" statutes must be read with this constitutional requirement in mind.

Note: Remember that the discussion here is about **general** jurisdiction, **not** specific jurisdiction. If a plaintiff is injured in State A by a defendant, he may still sue in State A regardless of whether the defendant is "at home" in State A, because there will very likely be specific (long arm) jurisdiction. Should you need to discuss general jurisdiction, make sure to discuss whether the defendant is "at home" in the state, as discussed above.

3) Fairness

In addition to the defendant's having relevant contacts with the forum, *International Shoe* requires that the exercise of jurisdiction not offend "traditional notions of fair play and substantial justice." The Court has listed several factors relevant to assessing whether jurisdiction would be fair. It is possible that an especially strong showing of fairness might make up for a lesser amount of contact (although minimum contacts are always required). Note, however, that fairness is not a factor for the exercise of general jurisdiction.

a) Convenience

A defendant will often complain that the forum is inconvenient. The Supreme Court has emphasized, however, that the Constitution does not require that the forum be the best of several alternatives. The forum is constitutionally acceptable unless it is "so gravely difficult and inconvenient that a party is unfairly put at a severe disadvantage in comparison to his opponent." [Burger King v. Rudzewicz, *supra*] This is a very difficult standard to meet, and the defendant usually will not be able to meet it simply by showing that the plaintiff has superior economic resources.

b) Forum State's Interest

The forum may have a legitimate interest in providing redress for its residents.

Examples: 1) Decedent, a California resident, purchased a life insurance policy by mail from a Texas company. Decedent regularly mailed his premiums from California to the Texas company, which had no other contacts with California. In a suit brought by the beneficiary of the life insurance policy, the Supreme Court held that California had personal jurisdiction over the Texas company. Among other things, the Court noted that California had a strong interest in protecting its citizens from alleged misfeasance by insurance companies. [McGee v. International Insurance Co., 355 U.S. 220 (1957)]

2) Asahi, a Japanese manufacturer of tire valves, shipped valves to a Taiwanese manufacturer of motorcycle tire tubes. The valves were incorporated into tires and sold in California, where a resident was injured by a defective tire. The Taiwanese manufacturer was sued in a California court, where it sought to implead Asahi. The main case was settled, leaving only

the indemnity claim by the tire manufacturer against Asahi pending. *Held:* Even though Asahi placed the defective goods in the stream of commerce knowing that some would be used in California, exercise of jurisdiction by the California court would be unreasonable considering the severe burdens of Asahi in defending in a foreign legal system, the slight interest of the Taiwanese manufacturer and California in the exercise of jurisdiction, and the international interest in not subjecting an alien corporation to United States jurisdiction. [Asahi Metal Industry Co. v. Superior Court, *supra*]

c) Other Factors

The Supreme Court has listed other factors relevant to the assessment of whether the exercise of jurisdiction would be fair and reasonable, but has not discussed these factors in detail: (i) the plaintiff's interest in obtaining convenient and effective relief, (ii) the interstate judicial system's interest in obtaining the most efficient resolution of controversies, and (iii) the shared interest of the states in furthering fundamental substantive social policies.

2. Notice

In addition to the requirement that the defendant have such minimum contacts with the forum to render the exercise of jurisdiction there fair and reasonable, due process also requires that a ***reasonable method be used to notify the defendant of a pending lawsuit*** so that she may have an opportunity to appear and be heard. Due process requires that notice be "reasonably calculated, under all the circumstances, to apprise interested parties of the pendency of the action and afford them an opportunity to present their objections." [Dusenbery v. United States, 534 U.S. 161 (2002)—*quoting* Mullane v. Central Hanover Bank & Trust Co., 339 U.S. 306 (1950)]

a. Traditional Methods of Personal Service Satisfy Due Process Notice Requirements

Any of the traditional methods of personal service satisfy due process notice require-ments. These include personal delivery to the defendant; leaving papers with a respon-sible person at the defendant's residence or place of business; delivery to an agent appointed to accept service; or delivery by registered mail, return receipt requested. (*See* VIII.B., *infra*, for discussion of methods of service of process.)

b. Requirement that Agent Notify Defendant

If an agent is appointed by contract, in a case where the plaintiff chose the agent for his own benefit, or the agent is appointed by operation of law (as under a nonresident motor vehicle statute), the failure of the agent to notify the defendant will prohibit jurisdic-tion—since the defendant will in fact be deprived of an opportunity to be heard. (This is not true when the defendant voluntarily selects his own agent, since any failure of the agent can and will be attributed to the principal.)

c. Requirements for Cases Involving Multiple Parties or Unknown Parties

In *Mullane v. Central Hanover Bank & Trust Co., supra,* an action was brought against a number of trust beneficiaries scattered throughout the world. The Supreme Court held that the Constitution did not require personal service on each beneficiary since the cost would have been prohibitive. However, every beneficiary had to be notified by the ***best practical means*** available. Thus, those whose addresses were known or could reasonably be ascertained had to be notified by ordinary mail, while those whose names or addresses were unknown could be notified by publication. Such methods of notice are valid only if all defendants have substantially identical interests.

d. Knowledge that Notice by Mail Was Not Received
Although *Mullane v. Central Hanover Bank & Trust Co., supra,* does not require actual notice, if a party knows that the notice by mail was not received, he may not proceed in the face of such knowledge if practicable alternatives to apprise the defendant of the action exist.

Example: In *Jones v. Flowers*, 547 U.S. 220 (2006), the state sent a certified letter to a homeowner to inform him that he was delinquent on taxes and that failure to pay would make his property subject to public sale. By statute, the taxpayer was required to keep his address updated. The letter was returned "unclaimed," after which the state took no further steps (such as using first class mail or posting notice on the property) to notify the taxpayer. The Court held that taking no further steps to provide notice with the knowledge that notice had not been received violated due process.

D. IN REM JURISDICTION
As stated in II.A.2.b., *supra*, in rem actions adjudicate rights of all persons with respect to property located in the state. An in rem judgment does not bind the parties personally, but is binding as to the disposition of the property in the state.

1. Statutory Limitations
Most states have statutes providing for in rem jurisdiction in actions for condemnation, title registration, confiscation of property (such as vehicles used to transport narcotics), forfeiture of a vessel, distribution of the assets of an estate, and a grant of divorce when only the complaining spouse is present and subject to personal jurisdiction. In the last case, the "property" is the marital status of the complainant.

2. Constitutional Limitations

a. Nexus
In in rem actions the basis of jurisdiction is the presence of the property in the state. The state has a great interest in adjudicating the rights of all the world regarding this property. Therefore, the presence of the property in the state is constitutionally sufficient for the exercise of jurisdiction over the property.

1) No Jurisdiction If Property Not Located in State
A court has no in rem power over property outside the state; e.g., in settling a decedent's estate, the court has no in rem power over property in other jurisdictions.

2) No Jurisdiction If Property Brought in by Fraud or Force
The exercise of in rem power is prohibited when the property is brought into the state by fraud or force.

b. Notice

The early view held that attachment of property, when supplemented by publication of notice in a local newspaper or by posting of notice on the property, would give all interested persons sufficient notice of the action. However, such procedures are no longer adequate, and the requirements of *Mullane v. Central Hanover Bank & Trust Co., supra,* apply to in rem actions. Thus, persons whose interests are affected and whose addresses are known must at least be notified by ordinary mail. [Walker v. City of Hutchinson, 352 U.S. 112 (1956)]

E. QUASI IN REM JURISDICTION

Quasi in rem jurisdiction permits a court without in personam jurisdiction to determine certain disputes between a plaintiff and defendant regarding property when the property is located in the forum state. (*See* II.A.2.c., *supra.*)

1. Statutory Limitations

There are two types of quasi in rem jurisdiction. The first type (type I) involves disputes between parties over their rights in property within the state. The second type (type II) involves disputes *unrelated* to the in-state property and has been severely limited by the Supreme Court. In quasi in rem cases, the plaintiff is unable to obtain personal jurisdiction over the defendant, but the defendant has property in the state that the plaintiff attaches. The court then adjudicates the dispute between the parties on the basis of its power over the property. Since the court's sole basis of jurisdiction is the property, *any judgment against the defendant can be satisfied only out of that property*.

2. Constitutional Limitations

a. Nexus

Before 1977, a state clearly had power over all persons and property found within its borders. A defendant with no other connections with the state could be sued in the state for *any* dispute simply because he owned property there. However, in 1977, the Supreme Court held that the *minimum contacts standard* is applicable to *every* exercise of jurisdiction. The Court further found that the mere presence of property within a state is not itself sufficient to permit a court to exercise quasi in rem jurisdiction over property in a quasi in rem action. [Shaffer v. Heitner, 433 U.S. 186 (1977)]

1) Quasi In Rem Type I

Thus, when the dispute involves the rights of the parties in the property itself (quasi in rem type I), jurisdiction based upon the presence of the property in the state is proper. The close connection between the litigation and the property provides the necessary minimum contacts.

2) Quasi In Rem Type II

When the dispute is unrelated to the ownership of property (quasi in rem type II), jurisdiction cannot be based solely on the presence of property in the forum state; there must be minimum contacts between the defendant and the forum. However, if the defendant has minimum contacts with the forum, it is also likely that a court could exercise *in personam* jurisdiction over a defendant under the forum's long arm statute, thus removing the limit on recovery to the defendant's in-state property. As a result, use of quasi in rem jurisdiction type II will be rare.

Example: A, a Maine resident, flies to Ohio and enters into a contract with B, an Ohio resident. All performance is to occur in Ohio. A flies home. B breaches. A does not want to fly to Ohio to sue B, but he discovers that B has a boat docked in Maine. Traditionally, A could have sued on his contract claim in Maine by attaching the boat (his remedy being limited by the value of the boat). Today, he would have to show minimum contacts between B and Maine.

3) Procedural Requirements

To obtain quasi in rem jurisdiction, a plaintiff must "bring the asset before the court" by attachment (or garnishment). This will inhibit the sale or mortgage of the defendant's interest, since a new owner must take subject to the decision of the court. Serious questions have been raised as to whether such a pretrial interference with a defendant's property rights is constitutional unless the defendant is afforded a hearing on the necessity of such procedures. Most commentators think the process is valid, but the Supreme Court has thus far avoided the issue.

b. Notice

As in in rem cases, quasi in rem cases require the best practical notice. Therefore, posting of notice or notice by publication will be insufficient where the addresses of persons affected by the action are known or reasonably ascertainable. The federal statute for the enforcement of liens or other claims to real or personal property requires personal service if practicable and service by publication if personal service is not practicable. If the defendant is not personally served, he may appear within one year of final judgment, and the court must set aside the judgment on payment of costs as the court deems just. [28 U.S.C. §1655]

III. DIVERSITY OF CITIZENSHIP JURISDICTION

A. INTRODUCTION

The federal courts have been given subject matter jurisdiction over controversies between citizens of different states, even though the controversies do not involve questions of federal substantive law, in order to protect an out-of-state party from possible local bias in state courts.

B. DIVERSITY AMONG THE PARTIES

1. Complete Diversity When Action Is Commenced

a. Multiple Parties—Complete Diversity

Diversity jurisdiction requires "complete diversity," meaning that no plaintiff may be a citizen of the same state as any defendant. If one defendant and one plaintiff are co-citizens of the same state, complete diversity is lacking and there is no diversity jurisdiction.

Example: A, B, and C bring an action against X, Y, and Z. A and B are citizens of New York; X and Y are citizens of Florida; and C and Z are citizens of Texas. Since no diversity exists between C and Z, the requirement of *complete* diversity is not satisfied, and, as structured, the case cannot be brought in federal court under diversity jurisdiction.

1) **But Note**

The rule of complete diversity does not require that every party be of diverse citizenship from every other party. It requires only that no plaintiff be a co-citizen with any defendant. Thus, two plaintiffs who are both citizens of Missouri may invoke diversity of citizenship jurisdiction against three defendants, all three of whom are citizens of Kansas.

2) **Interpleader Exception**

a) **Federal Interpleader Statute—Minimal Diversity**

The federal interpleader statute [28 U.S.C. §1335] requires only that among the parties there be "two or more adverse claimants, of diverse citizenship." Thus, "minimal diversity" is sufficient to confer jurisdiction under the statute. If there is diversity between *any two* of the claimants, all other claimants may be citizens of the same state. (Also, section 1335 only requires that the money or property at issue be valued at $500 or more.)

b) **Interpleader Under Federal Rules—Complete Diversity**

Interpleader pursuant to Rule 22 of the Federal Rules, on the other hand, requires the usual diversity between all the plaintiffs (stakeholders) and all the defendants (claimants).

b. **"Alienage" Jurisdiction**

Most bar exam questions in this general area involve basic diversity of citizenship jurisdiction, in which the dispute involves "citizens of different states," as discussed immediately above. However, section 1332(a)(2) grants subject matter jurisdiction over "alienage" cases, in which the dispute is between a citizen of a U.S. state and an "alien"—meaning a citizen or subject of a foreign country. Jurisdiction is denied, however, if the case is between a citizen of a state and a citizen of a foreign country who has been admitted to the United States for permanent residence and domiciled in the same state as the U.S. citizen. Also note that the U.S. Constitution does not provide for federal jurisdiction over cases *by* an alien *against* an alien; there must be a citizen of a U.S. state on one side of the suit to qualify for alienage jurisdiction.

Examples: 1) A, a citizen of Venezuela, sues B, a citizen of New York. This dispute would invoke alienage jurisdiction (assuming the amount in controversy requirement was also met), because it is between a citizen of a state and a citizen of a foreign country.

2) A, a citizen of Venezuela, sues B, a citizen of France. This dispute would *not* invoke alienage jurisdiction, because it is *not* between a citizen of a state and a citizen of a foreign country. There is no citizen of a state involved here.

3) A, a citizen of New York, sues B, a permanent resident alien domiciled in New York. Alienage jurisdiction would be denied because B has the same U.S. domicile as A.

1) **Aliens as Additional Parties**

28 U.S.C. section 1332(a)(3) grants jurisdiction in a case between citizens of different states in which citizens or subjects of a foreign country are additional parties. The foreign parties are disregarded for jurisdictional purposes. The restriction in example 3) above does not apply—it applies *only* to section 1332(a)(2) actions. Although not entirely clear from case law, there appears to be no subject matter jurisdiction when there are U.S. citizens on one side of the action and aliens on both sides.

c. **Diversity When Action Is Commenced**

Diversity of citizenship (or alienage) must exist as of the time the suit is instituted. [Grupo Dataflux v. Atlas Global Group, 541 U.S. 567 (2004)] It need not exist at the time the cause of action arose, and it is not defeated if, after commencement of the action, a party later becomes a citizen of the same state as one of his opponents.

2. **Questions of Citizenship**

a. **State Citizenship of an Individual—Domicile**

The determination of the state of citizenship of a natural person depends on the permanent home to which he intends to return. The concept is the same, except in name, as domicile. A new state citizenship may be established by (i) *physical presence* in a new place and (ii) the *intention to remain there*, i.e., no present intent to go elsewhere. The citizenship of a child is that of her parents. In most cases, the citizenship of a party will be determined by the court, but it may be left to the jury.

b. **Citizenship of a Corporation—Possible Multiple Citizenships**

For diversity purposes, a corporation's citizenship is defined by 28 U.S.C. section 1332. Under this statute, a corporation is deemed to be a citizen of *every* state and foreign country in which it is incorporated and the *one* state or foreign country in which it has its principal place of business. The Supreme Court has held that a corporation's "principal place of business" is the state from which the corporation's high level officers direct, control, and coordinate the corporation's activities (i.e., its "nerve center," which will usually be the corporation's headquarters). [Hertz Corp. v. Friend, 559 U.S. 77 (2010)] Thus, many corporations have *two* citizenships—their state of incorporation *and* the state in which their principal place of business is located. Although rare, it also is possible for a corporation to have more than two state citizenships because a corporation may be incorporated in more than one state. It is impossible, however, for a corporation to have more than one principal place of business. If an opposing party is a citizen of any of the corporate party's states of citizenship, there is no diversity.

1) **Special Rule for Direct Actions**

The rules of corporate citizenship are subject to a special rule in direct action cases. When a plaintiff sues an insurer on a policy or contract of liability insurance, and does not also join the insured, the insurer (whether incorporated or not) is treated as a citizen of all of the following: (i) the state or foreign country in which the insurer is incorporated (if it is), (ii) the state or foreign country in which the insurer has its principal place of business, and (iii) the state or foreign country of which the *insured* is a citizen.

2) Incorporation or Principal Place of Business in Foreign Country
Because a corporation is a citizen of both its place of incorporation and its principal place of business, and either of those places may be in a foreign country, a corporation might simultaneously be an alien and a citizen of a U.S. state. The fact that a corporation is an alien will defeat jurisdiction in a suit involving solely another alien, even though the corporation may also have U.S. state citizenship. (*See* 1.b., *supra.*)

c. Unincorporated Associations

1) Citizenship
In claims based on federal law for or against an unincorporated association, the association has entity capacity, but the question of its citizenship is normally irrelevant because the court will have federal question jurisdiction. When diversity jurisdiction is involved, an unincorporated association:

(i) May sue or be sued in its own name if local state law so permits; or

(ii) Is an aggregate of individuals if local state law follows the common law rule.

In either case, the unincorporated association's citizenship is that of *each and every one* of its members.

2) Class Action
If the association is large, a class action is possible. If a class action is brought, the relevant citizenship is that of the *named members* who sue or are sued on behalf of the members of the association. (*See* f., *infra.*)

3) Partnerships
The citizenship of a general partnership is that of each and every general partner, and the citizenship of a limited partnership is that of each and every partner, both limited and general. [Carden v. Arkoma Associates, 494 U.S. 185 (1990)]

4) Limited Liability Companies
Although limited liability companies ("LLCs") are formed in a manner similar to corporations, they are treated as unincorporated associations for citizenship purposes. Thus, an LLC is a citizen of all states of which its members are citizens. [*See, e.g.,* Belleville Catering Co. v. Champaign Market Place LLC, 350 F.3d 691 (7th Cir. 2003)]

d. Business Trusts
The *trustees* of a business trust are the real parties in interest and their citizenship, not that of the individual shareholders, determines whether there is diversity. [Navarro Savings v. Lee, 446 U.S. 458 (1980)]

e. Legal Representatives
A legal representative of an infant, an incompetent, or an estate of a decedent is deemed to be a citizen of the same state as the infant, incompetent, or decedent.

f.   Class Actions

If suit is brought by several named persons on behalf of a class under Rule 23, diversity is determined on the basis of the citizenship of the ***named members*** of the class who are suing. Thus, there is considerable room for maneuvering to create diversity if the class has members who are citizens of several different states. The Class Action Fairness Act (*see* VIII.G.2.d., *infra*) also expands the federal court's jurisdiction over class actions.

g.   Nonresident United States Citizens

A United States citizen ***domiciled abroad*** is not a citizen of any state and also is not an alien. (Alien status depends on nationality, not domicile.)

3.   Collusion and Devices to Create or Defeat Diversity

The federal court does not have jurisdiction if a party "by assignment or otherwise, has been improperly or collusively made or joined to invoke jurisdiction." [28 U.S.C. §1359]

a.   Assignment of Claims

The assignment of a claim to another party for collection only is clearly within this section. [Kramer v. Caribbean Mills, Inc., 394 U.S. 823 (1969)] Thus, the assignment would be ignored in determining whether diversity exists. *But note:* There is no collusion if an absolute assignment of a claim is made and the assignor retains no interest in the assigned claim.

b.   Class Actions

No rule prevents achieving diversity by the adroit selection of named plaintiffs to bring a proper class action on behalf of others. The naming of only members of the class who are not co-citizens of the defendants will create diversity even though other unnamed members of the class are co-citizens who would defeat diversity if named.

c.   Voluntary Change of State Citizenship

A plaintiff can create diversity by changing his state citizenship after the cause of action accrued but before suit is commenced, but the change must be genuine. In other words, a true change of citizenship can create or destroy diversity. The party's ***motive*** for changing citizenship is ***irrelevant***.

4.   Realignment According to Interest

a.   May Create or Destroy Diversity

In determining whether diversity exists, the court will look beyond the nominal designation of the parties in the pleadings and realign them according to their true interests in the dispute. Thus, realignment may create diversity or destroy it.

b.   Shareholder Derivative Actions

Taking the view that the shareholder's alignment of the corporation as a party plaintiff or defendant is not controlling insofar as diversity jurisdiction is affected by the citizenship of the corporation, the federal courts have established the rule (at least when alignment of the corporation in a shareholder's derivative suit is not specifically provided for by state law) that the corporation is to be aligned as a party ***defendant.*** Federal diversity jurisdiction is determined in accordance with that alignment when, with respect to the claim sought to be enforced by the shareholder's derivative suit, the corporation is "antagonistic" to the shareholder. [*See* Smith v. Sperling, 354 U.S. 91 (1957)]

5.   "Supplemental" Jurisdiction

Occasionally, a claim may be joined that could not, by itself, invoke federal question jurisdiction or diversity jurisdiction (because, for example, it is a state claim between parties who are citizens of the same state or because it does not involve the requisite amount in controversy). (*See* C., *infra*.) The federal court may nonetheless entertain such claims under its supplemental jurisdiction. (This type of supplemental jurisdiction used to be known as "ancillary jurisdiction.") Supplemental jurisdiction requires that the supplemental claim arise from a common nucleus of operative fact as the claim that invoked original (diversity or federal question, usually) federal subject matter jurisdiction. Some courts consider the common nucleus test to mean that the claims must arise from the same transaction or occurrence, but the growing trend is that the common nucleus test is broader than that.

6.   Joinder or Subsequent Addition of Parties

The Federal Rules permit numerous methods by which multiple claims or parties may be joined or added to the case. A claim by or against such a party, like any claim in federal court, must satisfy some basis of federal subject matter jurisdiction, such as diversity of citizenship or federal question. If the claim does not satisfy either of those, and it arises from a common nucleus of operative fact (*see* above), the party asserting the claim might invoke supplemental jurisdiction. Joinder of claims or parties is also discussed in VIII.G., *infra*.

a.   Restriction on the Use of Supplemental Jurisdiction in Diversity Cases

For cases that are in federal court based *solely* on diversity, supplemental jurisdiction may not be used to support:

(i)   Claims by *plaintiffs* against persons made parties under Rules 14 (impleader), 19 (compulsory joinder), 20 (permissive joinder), or 24 (intervention);

(ii)   Claims by persons proposed to be joined as *plaintiffs* under Rule 19; and

(iii)   Claims by persons seeking to intervene as *plaintiffs* under Rule 24;

When the exercise of supplemental jurisdiction would be inconsistent with the requirements for complete diversity.

[28 U.S.C. §1367(b)]

b.   Intervention of Right

Intervention of right is given under Rule 24(a) when: (i) the intervenor claims an interest relating to the property or transaction that is the subject of the action; (ii) the disposition of the action may adversely affect that interest; and (iii) the current parties do not adequately represent the intervenor's rights. Under the supplemental jurisdiction statute, there appears to be no supplemental jurisdiction for claims by or against intervenors (with limited exceptions unlikely to be tested). Thus, such a claim could proceed only if there were an independent basis of jurisdiction, e.g., diversity or federal question.

c.   Permissive Intervention

Under Rule 24(b), permissive intervention may be permitted in the court's discretion when the intervenor's action and the main action have a claim or defense involving a *common question of law or fact*. The claim by a permissive intervenor must invoke either diversity of citizenship or federal question jurisdiction.

d.   Substitution of Parties

Substitution under Rule 25 involves changes in parties to a lawsuit necessitated by death, incompetency, etc., of an original party after an action has been commenced. The citizenship of the substituted party is disregarded; that of the original party controls. Substitution should be distinguished from an *amendment* that allows "replacement" of an original party by the party in whom or against whom the action properly lies. A "replacement" party must be diverse to the party or parties on the opposing side.

Example: A v. B. A dies and the administrator of his estate is substituted as plaintiff. Jurisdiction is not destroyed even though B and the administrator are co-citizens. However, if A sues B and subsequently discovers that C—not B—is the proper defendant, an amendment to the complaint by which B is replaced by C must show that diversity exists between A and C.

e.   Third-Party Practice—Impleader

A third-party claim under Rule 14 is the joinder by the defendant in the original action (who is usually called the third-party plaintiff) of another person not originally a party to the action (who is called the third-party defendant). The impleader claim asserts that the third-party defendant is or may be liable to the defendant for all or part of the plaintiff's claim against the defendant. In other words, an impleader claim is for indemnity or contribution.

Example: P sues D for $500,000 for personal injuries allegedly inflicted by joint tortfeasors D and X. Applicable law provides that joint tortfeasors have a right of contribution against each other. D may implead X into the pending case. D is seeking to deflect her liability on P's claim, in part, to X. (If X owed D indemnity for some reason, then D could implead X to deflect her entire liability on the underlying claim to X.)

Under Rule 14, after the third-party defendant is impleaded, he may assert a claim against the plaintiff in the pending case if the claim arises from the same transaction or occurrence as the underlying suit. In addition, under Rule 14, after the third-party defendant is impleaded, the plaintiff may assert a claim against him if it arises from the same transaction or occurrence as the underlying suit.

1)   Subject Matter Jurisdiction Required

Of course, every claim asserted in federal court must have a basis of subject matter jurisdiction.

Examples: 1) P, a citizen of Illinois, sues D, a citizen of Wisconsin, asserting a state law claim of more than $75,000. Thus, the case invokes diversity of citizenship jurisdiction and is properly brought in federal court. Now D impleads X, who is also a citizen of Illinois, on an indemnity claim of more than $75,000. That claim invokes diversity of citizenship jurisdiction, because it is asserted by a citizen of Wisconsin (D) against a citizen of Illinois (X) and exceeds $75,000. The fact that P is also a citizen of Illinois is irrelevant; the claim is not by or against her, so her citizenship does not affect the impleader claim. If P wanted to assert a claim against X in this situation, however, there would not be diversity because P and X are co-citizens of Illinois. In addition, the claim would not invoke supplemental jurisdiction, because in diversity of citizenship cases, the supplemental jurisdiction statute cannot be used to override the complete diversity rule. Thus, unless the claim by P against X invoked federal question jurisdiction, it could not be asserted in the pending case; it would have to be asserted in state court.

2) P, a citizen of Alabama, sues D, a citizen of Maine, asserting a state law claim of more than $75,000. Thus, the case invokes diversity of citizenship jurisdiction and is properly brought in federal court. Now D impleads X, who is also a citizen of Maine, on a state law contribution claim. The impleader claim does not invoke diversity of citizenship jurisdiction, because it is asserted by a citizen of Maine (D) against another citizen of Maine (X). It does not invoke federal question jurisdiction because it is based on state law. The claim invokes the ancillary form of supplemental jurisdiction, however, because it arises from a common nucleus of operative fact as the underlying case and is asserted by the defendant, not the plaintiff, thus avoiding the restriction on the use of supplemental jurisdiction in 28 U.S.C. section 1367(b).

f.   Cross-Claims

Rule 13(g) allows a party to assert a claim in a pending case against a co-party, but only if the claim arises from the ***same transaction or occurrence*** as the underlying dispute. So, in a lawsuit of A v. B and C, a claim by B against C (or C against B) that arises from the same transaction or occurrence as the underlying case would be a cross-claim.

1)   Subject Matter Jurisdiction Required

Cross-claims, like all claims in federal court, must invoke subject matter jurisdiction. Therefore, after determining that a cross-claim would be filed, assess whether that claim could invoke diversity of citizenship or federal question jurisdiction. If so, the claim may be asserted in federal court. ***However***, if a cross-claim does not invoke diversity of citizenship or federal question jurisdiction, the cross-claim could nonetheless be asserted in federal court through supplemental (ancillary) jurisdiction.

C.   JURISDICTIONAL AMOUNT: IN EXCESS OF $75,000

Actions brought in a federal court under the diversity statute must meet the jurisdictional amount requirement. The matter in controversy must be ***in excess of $75,000,*** exclusive of interest and costs. [28 U.S.C. §1332] The amount is determined from what is claimed in the complaint, disregarding potential defenses or counterclaims. Usually, all that is necessary is a ***good faith allegation*** that the amount of the damages or injuries in controversy ***exceeds***, exclusive of interest and costs, the sum of $75,000. Good faith means that there must be a legally tenable possibility that recovery will exceed the jurisdictional amount. The complaint can be dismissed only if it appears there is no legal possibility of a recovery exceeding the jurisdictional amount. Jurisdiction is not retroactively defeated by the fact that the amount actually recovered is less than the jurisdictional amount.

1. What Is "In Controversy"?

a. Collateral Consequences of the Judgment

Does the collateral effect of the judgment sought by the plaintiff bring into controversy the value of other claims that may be governed by the judgment? The Supreme Court has held that the collateral effects of a judgment may ***not*** be considered.

Examples: 1) If an insured asserts a claim for installments due under a disability policy, only the installments due may be considered, even though the judgment may control the insured's rights to payment of future installments. However, if the insurance company sues to cancel the contract for fraud, the value of the entire contract is brought into controversy.

2) If a bondholder sues to collect amounts due on coupons that have matured, only the amount of the coupons is in controversy, even though the judgment will determine the validity of the entire bond issue. However, if the issuer of the bonds seeks a declaratory judgment that the bonds are properly issued, the value of the entire bond issue would be in controversy.

b. Interest and Costs

The statute excludes interest and costs in determining the jurisdictional amount. However, attorneys' fees that are recoverable by contract or by statute are considered part of the matter in controversy rather than as costs. Similarly, interest that constitutes a part of the claim itself, as distinguished from interest payable by virtue of a delay in payment, is part of the jurisdictional amount.

Example: Plaintiff sues on a three-year note with face value of $70,000 and interest at 5% (an additional $10,500). Since the interest on the note is part of the claim, the jurisdictional amount is satisfied. [*See, e.g.,* Brainin v. Melikian, 396 F.2d 153 (3d Cir. 1968)] But if the interest accrued between maturity and filing, the additional interest after maturity is not part of the claim.

c. Equitable Relief

There may be difficulty calculating an amount in controversy for a claim for equitable relief, given that the claimant does not seek money damages. For example, suppose P sues D for an injunction ordering D to remove part of D's house that blocks P's view. What is the value of the injunction and, therefore, the claim? Some courts look at the issue from the ***plaintiff's viewpoint***, and ask what the value of the harm caused by the blocked view is. Other courts look at the issue from the ***defendant's viewpoint***, and ask what it would cost the defendant to comply with the injunction if it were ordered. Some courts conclude that the amount in controversy requirement is satisfied if the amount under ***either*** test—plaintiff's viewpoint or defendant's viewpoint—exceeds $75,000.

d. Punitive Damages

If a punitive damage claim is permitted under state substantive law, it may be used in making the dollar amount requirement because there is "no legal certainty" that the amount will not be recovered.

2. Aggregation of Separate Claims

a. One Plaintiff Against One Defendant

For purposes of meeting the jurisdictional amount, the plaintiff may aggregate all her claims against a single defendant. This aggregation is permitted regardless of whether the claims are legally or factually related to each other.

b. One Plaintiff Against Several Defendants

A plaintiff who has an action against several defendants cannot aggregate claims based on separate liabilities. Thus, if P had a claim of $50,000 against D-1 and a separate claim of $30,000 against D-2, she may not aggregate those claims. Note, however, that there is no aggregation problem if plaintiff asserts a joint claim against multiple defendants. With a joint claim, courts look to the total value of the claim.

Example: P sues alleged joint tortfeasors X, Y, and Z for damages of $76,000. This claim satisfies the amount in controversy requirement. Because this is a claim based on *joint liability,* any of the three defendants might be held liable for the total amount of the claim. This is not a case of trying to aggregate three separate claims. Because of joint liability, courts see this as one claim. Because it exceeds $75,000, it meets the amount requirement.

c. Several Plaintiffs Against One Defendant

Several plaintiffs can aggregate their claims only where they are seeking "to enforce a single title or right in which they have a common or undivided interest . . . . "

Example: If joint owners of real estate file suit to quiet title, the right asserted is held jointly and the amount in controversy is the total value of the land. However, if several victims of the same accident sue for personal injuries, their claims are separate and distinct from one another and aggregation is not allowed.

This rule has special importance in class actions, in which the rule is that the claims of the class members cannot be aggregated if their rights are "separate" rather than "joint" or "common." One class representative's claim must exceed $75,000, and the court will have supplemental jurisdiction over the claims that do not exceed $75,000. [Snyder v. Harris, 394 U.S. 332 (1969)]

3. Supplemental Jurisdiction over Claims Not Exceeding $75,000 in Diversity Cases

Claims that do not meet the amount in controversy requirement for diversity of citizenship jurisdiction may invoke supplemental jurisdiction if they arise from a common nucleus of operative fact as a claim that invoked diversity of citizenship. However, the supplemental jurisdiction *cannot* be used to override the complete diversity rule. [Exxon Mobil Corp. v. Allapattah Services, 545 U.S. 546 (2005)]

Example: P-1, a citizen of California, asserts a claim for $100,000 against D, a citizen of Arizona. That claim invokes diversity of citizenship jurisdiction. In the same case, P-2 asserts a claim against the same D for $50,000. The claims by P-1 and P-2 arise from the same transaction and are based on state law. The claim by P-2 cannot invoke diversity of citizenship jurisdiction because it does not exceed $75,000. Nonetheless, the claim by P-2 can be heard in federal court under supplemental jurisdiction.

Compare: P-1, a citizen of California, asserts a claim for $100,000 against D, a citizen of Arizona. That claim invokes diversity of citizenship jurisdiction. In the same case, P-2, a citizen of Arizona, asserts a claim against the same D for $100,000. The claim by P-1 and the claim by P-2 arise from the same transaction and are based on state law. The claim by P-2 cannot invoke diversity of citizenship jurisdiction because it is by a citizen of Arizona against a citizen of Arizona, and supplemental jurisdiction cannot override the complete diversity requirement. Thus, that claim may be asserted only in state court.

4.   **Counterclaims**

A defendant's counterclaim [*see* Fed. R. Civ. P. 13] cannot be combined with the plaintiff's claim to reach the jurisdictional amount; e.g., if the plaintiff claims $20,000, there is no jurisdictional amount even though the defendant counterclaims for $100,000. Does a counterclaim itself have to meet the requirements of the jurisdictional amount?

a.   **Compulsory Counterclaim Need Not Meet Jurisdictional Amount**

A compulsory counterclaim (arising out of the *same* transaction or occurrence) does not need to meet the jurisdictional amount requirement. The court has *ancillary* (supplemental) jurisdiction over such a counterclaim just as it does over a third party claim under Rule 14 impleader.

b.   **Permissive Counterclaim Must Meet Jurisdictional Amount**

A defendant's permissive counterclaim (arising out of a *completely unrelated* transaction) must have an independent jurisdictional basis, and thus *must meet the jurisdictional amount* requirement. A growing body of case law holds that supplemental jurisdiction is available if there is some sort of factual relationship between the two claims.

c.   **No Removal to Federal Court Based on Counterclaim**

A plaintiff who claims $75,000 or less in a state court action who is met with a counterclaim for more than $75,000 may not remove the suit to federal court, regardless of whether the counterclaim is compulsory or permissive, because removal is permitted only to defendants. The weight of authority also holds that in a situation where the plaintiff has not met the jurisdictional amount, the *defendant* who must assert a compulsory counterclaim in the state suit *may not remove* the action, even though the counterclaim is over $75,000 and there is complete diversity. Thus, a plaintiff with a small claim can require a defendant with a large claim to litigate it in state court simply by being the first to file. *But note:* Even though this is the *traditional rule*, there is a *trend allowing removal.*

D.   ***ERIE* DOCTRINE AND THE LAW APPLIED UNDER DIVERSITY JURISDICTION**

A federal court, in the exercise of its diversity jurisdiction, is required to apply the *substantive law of the state* in which it is sitting, including that state's conflict of law rules. [Erie Railroad v. Tompkins, 304 U.S. 64 (1938); Klaxon Co. v. Stentor Electric Manufacturing Co., 313 U.S. 487 (1941)] However, the federal courts apply *federal procedural law*.

1. **Federal Statutes or Federal Rules of Civil Procedure**

   To determine whether federal law should be applied, the first question to ask is whether there is a federal law (e.g., statute, Federal Rule of Civil Procedure) on point. If there is, the federal statute or federal rule will apply, provided that it is valid. (Since the Supreme Court reviews and sends proposed rules to Congress prior to enactment, it is very unlikely that a Federal Rule would be held invalid.) Of course, if there is a federal constitutional provision (e.g., right to jury trial in cases over $20), it applies.

   Example: Federal Rule 4 permits substituted service of process. Suppose that state law (of the state in which the federal court sits) does not permit substituted service. The court will apply the Federal Rule, because it is on point and is valid. A Federal Rule of Civil Procedure is valid if it is "arguably procedural." [Hanna v. Plumer, 380 U.S. 460 (1965)]

   a. **Caution**

      Sometimes it is difficult to determine whether a federal statute or rule is on point. For example, Federal Rule 3 provides that a case is commenced when the complaint is filed. Many people thought that the rule thus was a directive that the statute of limitations would be tolled from the date of filing the complaint. The Supreme Court held, however, that Rule 3 did not address tolling at all, and thus did not constitute a federal directive on the tolling question. [Walker v. Armco Steel, 446 U.S. 740 (1980)]

   b. **Recent Application**

      In *Shady Grove Orthopedic Associates v. Allstate Insurance Co.*, 559 U.S. 393 (2010), a plaintiff brought a diversity jurisdiction class action under a New York law for recovery of interest on claims paid late by insurance companies. A New York statute would have denied class action status to claims seeking such recovery. A majority of the Court held that Federal Rule of Civil Procedure 23 governed regarding class action status and refused to apply the New York statute. Under the Rules Enabling Act, a Federal Rule is valid if it deals with "practice or procedure" and does not "abridge, enlarge, or modify" a substantive right. A majority in *Shady Grove* concluded that Rule 23 is valid. Only four Justices concluded, however, that a Rule's validity is determined solely by referring to its terms (ignoring the state provision) and asking whether it is "arguably procedural." If so, according to those four Justices, the Federal Rule is valid.

2. **If There Is No Federal Statute or Rule on Point, Is the Issue Substantive or Procedural?**

   If there is no federal statute or rule on point, can a federal judge refuse to follow state law on a particular issue? The answer depends on whether the law on that issue is substantive or procedural. If it is a matter of substance, the federal judge must follow state law in a diversity case. If it is a matter of procedure, the federal judge may ignore state law.

   Example: In medical malpractice actions, some states require that an affidavit addressing the legitimacy of the claim from a qualified expert be attached to the complaint. Must such an affidavit be attached to a complaint filed in federal court based on diversity? Step one would be determining whether there is a federal directive on point. (There is no such directive.) Step two is determining whether the affidavit requirement is substantive or procedural.

a. Some Situations Are Clearly Established

In some instances, the characterization as substance or procedure is well established. For example, the Supreme Court has established that *statutes of limitations and rules for tolling statutes of limitations* are substantive for *Erie* purposes; therefore, a federal judge in a diversity case must follow state law on those issues. [Guaranty Trust Co. v. York, 326 U.S. 99 (1945)] *Choice of law rules* are also substantive for *Erie* purposes, and a federal judge in a diversity case must follow state law on that issue as well. [Klaxon v. Stentor Electric Manufacturing Co., 313 U.S. 487 (1941)] Finally, of course, *elements of a claim or defense* are substantive.

Note: There can be two issues presented in a conflict of laws problem. The first issue involves determining *whether federal or state law* applies. The second issue involves determining *which state's laws apply*. Both questions are often resolved using "substantive" and "procedural" language, but a determination that a law is "substantive" for the federal vs. state question does *not* mean that *has to be* "substantive" for the state vs. state question.

b. Law Is Unclear in Other Situations

Outside these areas, when there is no federal directive on point, it is often difficult to determine whether an issue is substantive or procedural for *Erie* purposes. The Supreme Court has given different "tests" at different times on this point, and has failed to integrate the tests comprehensively. One such test is *outcome determination*, which holds that an issue is substantive if it substantially affects the outcome of the case. [Guaranty Trust Co. v. York, *supra*] Another test is *balance of interests*, in which the court weighs whether the state or federal judicial system has the greater interest in having its rule applied. [Byrd v. Blue Ridge Electric Cooperative, Inc., 356 U.S. 525 (1958)] Yet another test is *forum shopping deterrence*, which directs that the federal judge should follow state law on the issue if failing to do so would cause litigants to flock to federal court. [Hanna v. Plumer, *supra*]

3. Statutes Involving Both Substance and Procedure

Sometimes, a state statute or rule may be both substantive *and* procedural. In one case, the state tort reform law relaxed the standard for granting a new trial, making it easier to grant a new trial than under the basic federal standard. Also, the state *appellate* court was charged with the responsibility to consider whether a new trial should be ordered. In a diversity case under this state law, the standard for granting a new trial was held to be substantive, so the federal court had to apply the state standard for granting a new trial. However, the requirement that the appellate court consider whether a new trial should be ordered was held to be procedural, so a federal *trial* court would determine whether a new trial should be ordered, using the aforementioned state standard, rather than an appellate court. [Gasperini v. Center for Humanities, Inc., 518 U.S. 415 (1996)—in diversity case, federal trial court applied New York "excessive damages" standard for new trial rather than federal "shock the conscience" standard]

4. **Interpreting State Law**

The federal court is bound to apply the substantive state law that would be applied by the highest court of the state. If the state courts have not decided the issue that is before the federal court, or if the decisions on point are old and no longer current with the decisions of other jurisdictions, the federal court may consider the law of other jurisdictions in reaching its decision. However, the focus of the federal court is to *determine what decision the highest court of the state would reach* if confronted with the issue.

a. **De Novo Review of District Court's Decision**

On appeal, the federal appellate court reviews the federal trial judge's decision as to state law *de novo*. [*See* Salve Regina College v. Russell, 499 U.S. 225 (1991)]

b. **Subsequent State Court Decisions**

If the highest state court renders a decision on an issue after the federal court has made its determination, the decision of the district court may be changed to conform to the new decision of the highest state court until the disposition of the final federal appeal. [*See* Thomas v. American Home Products, Inc., 519 U.S. 913 (1996)]

E. **FEDERAL COMMON LAW**

1. **When Federal Courts Create Federal Common Law Rules**

Although *Erie* held that federal courts cannot create "federal general common law" rules to govern state-law claims, *Erie* did not change the authority of federal courts to create "federal common law."

a. **Interpretation of Federal Statute or Constitution**

The federal courts create substantive rules of federal law when interpreting the meaning of federal statutes or the federal Constitution.

b. **Creating Rules to Fill Gaps in Federal Regulatory Schemes**

The federal courts may also create substantive rules of federal law based on the determination that Congress has expressly or by implication authorized the federal courts to do so for the purpose of filling in gaps or silences in a federal regulatory statute.

1) **Formulating Uniform Federal Standard**

In some instances, the federal courts have determined that a uniform judge-made standard is necessary as a matter of federal common law. Examples of such cases include suits involving the rights and obligations of the United States, admiralty cases, border disputes between states, and disputes involving relations with foreign states. But ordinarily, in the absence of congressional authorization to formulate substantive rules of decision, federal common law will not be created outside these areas.

Example: Even though no federal statute supplies a rule of decision, *Clearfield Trust Co. v. United States*, 318 U.S. 744 (1943), held that rules for the negotiability of checks payable by the United States should be governed by uniform judge-made federal law rather than by state law.

2) **Borrowing State Standard**

When borrowing a legal rule from state law authority, a federal court may select a rule that is used by a majority of state courts. Or, if there is little need for federal uniformity, and if the parties might expect that state law would apply, then the borrowed rule may be the one that would be applied under the law of the state forum.

Example: In *De Sylva v. Ballentine*, 351 U.S. 570 (1956), the Court held that the meaning of the term "children" in the federal copyright statute should be defined in accordance with ordinary usage under state law, and that it would be up to the federal courts to determine which state's definition would be applicable.

2. **When Federal Courts Create Federal Implied Rights of Action**

In some decisions, federal courts have exercised the authority to provide judicial recognition for "implied" remedies in the form of causes of action that are not specified in federal statutes or federal constitutional provisions that establish particular rights.

a. **Implied Right of Action Based on Federal Statute**

Initially, federal courts looked to several factors in determining whether an unspecified remedy could be viewed as "implied" in a statute. These factors looked to the questions of whether the plaintiff belonged to a class for whose special benefit the statute was enacted, whether evidence of legislative intent supported an implied remedy, whether such a remedy would be consistent with the underlying purposes of the legislative scheme, and whether a remedy should not be implied because the cause of action was one traditionally relegated to state law. This approach led to the recognition, for example, of an implied cause of action under the nondiscrimination provision of Title IX (a law prohibiting discrimination on the basis of gender in schools receiving federal funds).

1) **Need for Affirmative Congressional Intent**

More recently, federal courts have required a showing of affirmative congressional intent for implied remedies in federal statutes, the absence of which led to the judicial rejection of an implied cause of action under the nondiscrimination provisions of Title VI of the Civil Rights Act.

b. **Implied Right of Action Based on Constitution**

The federal courts have recognized several implied causes of action for damages against federal officials for the violation of particular constitutional rights. These rights include the Fourth Amendment protection from unreasonable searches and seizures, the Equal Protection right to nondiscrimination in employment on the basis of gender under the Fifth Amendment, and the right of a prisoner to not be deprived of medical treatment under the Eighth Amendment's prohibition on cruel and unusual punishment. In other cases, federal courts have declined to recognize additional implied remedies based on the existence of alternate federal statutory remedies. Note that the violation of federal constitutional rights by a federal official is not cognizable under 42 U.S.C. section 1983 (which provides for a cause of action for constitutional deprivations performed under color of law because section 1983 applies only to defendants who are state or local officials).

F. EXCEPTIONS TO DIVERSITY OF CITIZENSHIP JURISDICTION

For historical reasons, even though the requirements for diversity of citizenship jurisdiction are satisfied, federal courts will not exercise jurisdiction over domestic relations or probate proceedings.

1. Domestic Relations

The federal court will not take jurisdiction over actions "involving the issuance of a divorce, alimony or child custody decree." [Akenbrandt v. Richards, 504 U.S. 689 (1992)] Note that this exception is quite narrow. Federal courts may maintain actions upon state court decrees, such as those for alimony. They also may hear cases involving intra-family torts. They refuse only cases involving issuance of decrees of divorce, alimony, or child custody.

2. Probate Proceedings

Federal courts will not entertain cases to probate a decedent's estate. To fall within this exception to diversity of citizenship jurisdiction, however, the claim asserted ***must involve actual probate or annulment of a will or seek to reach property in the custody of a state probate court***. [Marshall v. Marshall, 547 U.S. 293 (2006)]

Example: The federal court had jurisdiction over a claim for damages for alleged tortious interference with testator's efforts to create a trust benefiting the plaintiff (who was Anna Nicole Smith). [Marshall v. Marshall, *supra*]

G. MULTIPARTY, MULTIFORUM TRIAL JURISDICTION ACT

The Multiparty, Multiforum Trial Jurisdiction Act applies to accidents meeting the statutory definition. The principal points are these:

1. Requirements

a. The Action

The Act grants jurisdiction to federal district courts of civil actions that (i) arise "from a ***single accident,*** (ii) ***where at least 75 natural persons have died*** in the accident (iii) ***at a discrete location.***" [28 U.S.C. §1369(a)]

b. Minimal Diversity

Such jurisdiction attaches based on ***minimal diversity of citizenship***; thus, all that is required is that at least one plaintiff be of diverse citizenship from at least one defendant.

c. One Additional Condition

In addition, however, ***one of three other conditions*** must be satisfied: either (i) a defendant "resides" in a different state from the place where "a substantial part" of the accident took place (even if the defendant also resides where the accident took place); (ii) any two defendants "reside" in different states; or (iii) substantial parts of the accident took place in different states.

2. Intervention

Anyone "with a claim arising from the accident" is ***permitted to intervene*** as a plaintiff, even if she could not have maintained an action in the district where the case is pending. [28 U.S.C. §1369(d)]

3. **Service of Process**
    Finally, the Act provides for *nationwide service of process*. [28 U.S.C. §1697]

IV. FEDERAL QUESTION JURISDICTION

A. INTRODUCTION
It is difficult to formulate a summary of the case holdings as to when an action "arises under" federal law. The best one can do, perhaps, is the following: A case arises under federal law if the plaintiff is alleging a right or interest that is substantially founded on federal law, which consists of federal common law, federal constitutional law, federal statutory law, treaty law, and federal administrative regulations.

B. FEDERAL QUESTION MUST APPEAR IN THE COMPLAINT
The federal question must appear as part of the *plaintiff's cause of action* as set out in a well-pleaded complaint. It is therefore sometimes necessary to determine whether certain allegations are proper in pleading the cause of action, and whether the federal element is essential to the plaintiff's case.

1. **Defendant's Answer or Defense Is Irrelevant**
    The content of the defendant's answer is not relevant; the existence of a defense based on federal law will not give federal question jurisdiction. Likewise, the court may not look to a counterclaim asserted by the defendant to determine whether the plaintiff's complaint states a federal question claim. [Holmes Group, Inc. v. Vornado Air Circulation System, Inc., 535 U.S. 826 (2002)]

2. **Anticipation of a Defense**
    Similarly, a complaint does not create federal question jurisdiction if it alleges federal issues only in anticipation of some defense.
    Example: A sues B for specific performance of a contract and alleges that B's refusal to perform is based on B's erroneous belief that federal law prohibits his perfor-mance. No federal question jurisdiction exists because the federal question presented by the plaintiff's complaint is merely in anticipation of B's defense. [Louisville & Nashville Railroad v. Mottley, 211 U.S. 149 (1908)]

C. IMPLIED FEDERAL RIGHT OF ACTION
It is not essential that the federal statute expressly provide for a civil cause of action for an alleged violation. Thus, federal question jurisdiction was held to exist in an action involving an alleged violation of the Fourth and Fifth Amendments [Bell v. Hood, 327 U.S. 678 (1946)] and an alleged violation of the Securities Exchange Acts of 1934 [J. I. Case v. Borak, 377 U.S. 426 (1964)], although neither the Constitution nor the act involved created a "remedy" for the wrongs complained of. However, not all federal provisions creating duties are held to create an implied private right of action. [Cort v. Ash, 422 U.S. 66 (1975)]

D. FEDERAL CORPORATIONS
Federal question jurisdiction does not arise merely from the fact that a corporate party was incorporated by an act of Congress *unless* the United States *owns more than one-half* of the

corporation's capital stock, in which case it is treated as a federal agency that can sue or be sued on that basis in federal court. [28 U.S.C. §1349]

E. SUPPLEMENTAL (PENDENT) JURISDICTION OVER STATE CLAIMS

As previously discussed (*supra,* III.B.5.), claims sometimes can invoke supplemental jurisdiction when the supplemental claim arises from a common nucleus of operative fact as the original claim, whether the case got into federal court by diversity of citizenship or federal question jurisdiction. Supplemental jurisdiction in federal question cases is discussed here.

1. Supplemental (Pendent) Claims

In some cases, the plaintiff will have both federal and state claims against the defendant. Although there may be no diversity, the federal court has ***discretion*** to exercise supplemental (pendent) jurisdiction over the claim based on state law if the two claims "derive from a common nucleus of operative fact" and are such that a plaintiff "would ordinarily be expected to try them all in one judicial proceeding." [United Mine Workers of America v. Gibbs, 383 U.S. 715 (1966)] Essentially, this means that the two claims must arise from the same transaction or occurrence. The supplemental jurisdiction statute [28 U.S.C. §1367(a)] adopts this standard for the grant of supplemental jurisdiction.

Example: P, a citizen of Arkansas, asserts two claims against D, who is also a citizen of Arkansas, in federal court. Importantly, both claims arise from a common nucleus of operative fact. Claim #1 is for violation of a federal statute, and thus invokes federal question jurisdiction. Claim #2 is based on state law, and thus does not invoke federal question jurisdiction (because it is based on state, not federal, law). Also, Claim #2 does not invoke diversity of citizenship (because P and D are citizens of the same state). Nonetheless, Claim #2 invokes supplemental jurisdiction because it arises from a common nucleus of operative fact as the claim that invoked federal question jurisdiction.

a. Effect of Dismissal of Federal Claim on Supplemental (Pendent) Claim

The court may exercise supplemental (pendent) jurisdiction over the state claim even though the federal claim is dismissed on the merits. However, the state claim should probably also be dismissed (without prejudice) if the federal claim is dismissed before trial. Indeed, the supplemental jurisdiction statute provides that the court may refuse supplemental jurisdiction if the federal claim is dismissed, if the state claims are complex or novel, or if the state claims predominate substantially over federal claims. Note also that a federal court may not award relief against a state official based solely on a state law claim. [Pennhurst State School & Hospital v. Halderman, 465 U.S. 89 (1984)]

2. Pendent Parties

Pendent party jurisdiction is relevant in cases in which the plaintiff sues more than one defendant, there is federal jurisdiction over the claim against one defendant, and the claim against the second defendant does not invoke federal question or diversity of citizenship jurisdiction. Under the supplemental jurisdiction statute, the claim against the second defendant might invoke supplemental jurisdiction if it arises from a common nucleus of operative fact as the claim against the first defendant.

Example: P asserts a federal question claim against D-1 and joins a transactionally related state law (not federal question) claim against D-2. P and D-2 are citizens of the same state. The claim against D-2 does not invoke federal question jurisdiction (because it is based upon state law) and does not invoke diversity of citizenship jurisdiction (because P and D-2 are citizens of the same state). The claim against D-2 invokes supplemental jurisdiction, however, because it arises from a common nucleus of operative fact as the claim that invoked federal question jurisdiction and is asserted by the plaintiff in a federal question case.

Conversely, pendent party jurisdiction can arise when multiple plaintiffs assert claims against one defendant.

Example: P-1 asserts a federal question claim against D. In the same case, P-2 asserts a state law claim against D. P-2 and D are citizens of the same state. The claim by P-2 invokes supplemental jurisdiction if it arises from a common nucleus of operative fact as the federal question claim by P-1 against D.

F.   SPECIFIC STATUTORY GRANTS

1.   Amount in Controversy

There is no amount in controversy requirement in federal question cases, with the narrow exception for cases brought against defendants ***other than*** the United States, its agencies, or employees under section 23(a) of the Consumer Product Safety Act. That section authorizes action by any person who sustains injury by reason of a knowing violation of a consumer product safety rule, or any other rule issued by the Commission. In such actions, at least $10,000 must be in controversy. [15 U.S.C. §2072]

2.   Exclusive Jurisdiction

Congress has expressly provided that the jurisdiction of the federal courts shall be exclusive of state courts in:

a.   Bankruptcy Proceedings [28 U.S.C. §1334]

b.   Patent and Copyright Cases [28 U.S.C. §1338]

c.   Many Cases Where United States Is Involved
Cases involving fines, penalties, or forfeitures under the laws of the United States; crimes against the United States; tort suits against the United States; or customs review. (Because of the doctrine of sovereign immunity, there is no jurisdiction in the courts to hear lawsuits against the United States unless the United States has consented to be sued.)

d.   Cases with Consuls and Vice-Consuls as Defendants [28 U.S.C. §1351]

e.   Antitrust Cases
Although 28 U.S.C. section 1337 does not expressly make federal jurisdiction exclusive in actions arising under laws regulating interstate commerce, the federal antitrust statutes are interpreted to place the remedy exclusively in the federal courts. [Freeman v. Bee Machine Co., 319 U.S. 448 (1943)]

f.   Admiralty Cases—Caveat

28 U.S.C. section 1333 grants exclusive jurisdiction in cases of admiralty and maritime jurisdiction, but since the same section has a clause "saving to suitors in all cases all other remedies," the result is that federal jurisdiction is exclusive only in limitation of liability proceedings and in maritime actions in rem.

g.   Foreign State—Caveat

28 U.S.C. section 1441(d) permits a foreign state (or agency thereof), if sued in state court, to remove the action to federal court.

h.   Postal Matters [28 U.S.C. §1339]

i.   Internal Revenue [28 U.S.C. §1340]

j.   Securities Exchange Act [15 U.S.C. §78aa]

V.   VENUE

A.   SUBJECT MATTER JURISDICTION DISTINGUISHED

Subject matter jurisdiction and venue are very often confused. Subject matter jurisdiction is the ***power*** of the court to adjudicate the matter before it, whereas venue relates to the ***proper geographic district*** in which to bring the action. [28 U.S.C. §1390] Subject matter jurisdiction is a question of power or authority; venue is a question of geography. Subject matter jurisdiction cannot be conferred by agreement; venue can be. A court can have subject matter jurisdiction without having proper venue.

Example: Smith, a citizen of Georgia, brings a personal injury suit arising in Florida against Jones, a citizen of New York. Suit is brought in the federal district court in California. The amount in controversy exceeds $75,000. Under section 1332, the district court has diversity jurisdiction, but venue is improper and the case is subject to transfer or dismissal.

B.   GENERAL RULES

1.   General Rules for Most Civil Actions

Venue in civil actions in the federal courts is proper in:

(i)   A judicial district in which ***any defendant resides***, if all defendants are residents of the state in which the district is located;

(ii)   A judicial district in which ***a substantial part of the events or omissions giving rise to the claim occurred***, or ***a substantial part of property that is the subject of the action is situated***; or

(iii)   If there is no district anywhere in the United States which satisfies (i) or (ii), a judicial district in which ***any defendant is subject to the court's personal jurisdiction*** with respect to such action.

[28 U.S.C. §1391]

Note: Unlike past federal practice and the existing practice in many states, local actions (e.g., those involving real property) and transitory actions (e.g., tort actions) are treated under the same venue provision in federal court.

2. **Special Venue Provisions**
    There are many venue provisions applicable only to specified types of actions. One is worth noting: Where the defendant is the United States or an agency thereof, or an officer, employee, etc., of the United States acting in his official capacity, a civil action may be brought where: (i) a defendant resides; (ii) a substantial part of the events or omissions giving rise to the action occurred, or a substantial part of property that is the subject of the action is situated; or (iii) the plaintiff resides if no real property is involved in the action. [28 U.S.C. §1391(e)]

C. **RESIDENCE**

1. **Natural Persons**
    For venue purposes, a natural person, including an alien lawfully admitted for permanent residence in the United States, is deemed to reside in the judicial district in which that person is domiciled. [28 U.S.C. §1391(c)(1)]

2. **Business Entities**
    An entity with the capacity to sue and be sued in its common name under applicable law, whether or not incorporated, is deemed to reside, if a defendant, in any judicial district in which the defendant *is subject to the court's personal jurisdiction* with respect to the civil action in question. [28 U.S.C. §1391(c)(2)]

    a. **Note for Corporations**
        In a state having more than one judicial district and in which a *corporate* defendant is subject to personal jurisdiction at the time the action is commenced, the corporation is deemed to reside in any district in that state within which the corporation's contacts would be sufficient to subject the corporation to personal jurisdiction if the district were a state. If there is no such district, the corporation is deemed to reside in the district within which it has the most significant contacts. [28 U.S.C. §1391(d)]

3. **Nonresident of United States**
    A defendant who is not a resident of the United States—whether a U.S. citizen or an alien— may be sued in any judicial district. The joinder of such a defendant, however, is disregarded in determining where the action may be brought with respect to any other defendants. [28 U.S.C. §1391(c)(3)]

D. **IMPROPER VENUE MAY BE WAIVED**
    Unlike jurisdiction over the subject matter, venue may be waived by the parties. Venue is considered to be waived unless timely objection (in a pre-pleading motion or, where no such motion is made, in the answer) is made to the improper venue.

E. **TRANSFER**

1. **Original Venue Proper**
    Section 1404(a) allows transfer to another district where the action *"might have been*

brought" or "to which all parties have consented," even though venue has been properly laid in the court before which the motion to transfer is made. The policy behind section 1404 is that while venue may be correct, the parties or the witnesses might be greatly inconvenienced by the trial in the original forum. By balancing the relative convenience offered by the alternative forums, the original court has discretion to transfer the action to a court in which the action "might have been brought" in conformity with the rules governing: (i) subject matter jurisdiction, (ii) in personam jurisdiction over the defendant, and (iii) venue. Another alternative is transfer to a court to which all parties have consented (even if venue ordinarily would not be proper there). If the superior forum is in another judicial system, the court may dismiss or stay the action under the doctrine of forum non conveniens.

2.   Original Venue Improper

When a case is filed in an improper venue, a court must dismiss, or, in *"the interests of justice,"* transfer the case to a venue in which it could have been brought (i.e., subject matter jurisdiction, personal jurisdiction, and proper venue must exist). [28 U.S.C. §1406(a)] *Transfer* is more appropriate than dismissal except in extraordinary circumstances. Some courts have held that section 1406(a) applies when the original court is a proper venue but lacks personal jurisdiction over the defendant. This view seems contrary to the language and purpose of the statute.

3.   Effect of Forum Selection Clauses

A forum selection clause represents the parties' agreement as to the most proper forum, and it will be enforced by means of a motion to transfer "in the interests of justice" unless exceptional *public interest* factors dictate otherwise. [Atlantic Marine Construction Co. v. United States District Court for the Western District of Texas, 571 U.S. 49 (2013)]

4.   Original Court Lacks Personal Jurisdiction

The Supreme Court has held that the original court's lack of personal jurisdiction over the defendant does not affect its power to transfer a case under section 1406(a). [Goldlawr, Inc. v. Heiman, 369 U.S. 463 (1962)] There is also authority to support the conclusion that the same is true in transfers under section 1404(a). [*See, e.g.,* United States v. Berkowitz, 328 F.2d 358 (3d Cir. 1964)]

F.   LAW APPLICABLE UPON TRANSFER

1.   Original Venue Proper

A transfer solely on convenience grounds carries to the transferee court the originally applicable (under *Erie*) rules (including choice of law); i.e., the law of the state in which the transferor court sat unless transfer was ordered to enforce a forum selection clause. [Atlantic Marine Construction Co., *supra*]. This is true even where the plaintiff initiates a transfer for convenience after initially choosing the inconvenient forum. [Ferens v. Deere Co., 494 U.S. 516 (1990)]

Example: P sued D in a federal district court in Pennsylvania. Upon the transfer to Massachusetts, the district court judge there must apply the law that would have been applied in Pennsylvania. [Van Dusen v. Barrack, 376 U.S. 612 (1964)]

2.   Original Venue Improper

A transfer on the ground that the original choice of venue was improper generally results in a change of the law applicable under *Erie*; i.e, the law of the state in which the transferee court sits.

Example: P sued D in the federal district court in Maryland. Upon transfer to New York under section 1406(a), the law applied in the transferee court (New York) would be its own law.

VI.   REMOVAL JURISDICTION

A.   ORIGINAL JURISDICTION NECESSARY
Under section 1441(a), a defendant can remove an action that could have originally been brought by the plaintiff in the federal courts.

1.   When
The prevailing rule is that removal is tested only as of the date of removal. Some courts held under the statute as it existed before 1989 that original jurisdiction must have existed both at the time the suit was instituted in the state court and at the time of removal. [*In re* Carter, 618 F.2d 1093 (5th Cir. 1980)]

2.   Federal Defense Insufficient
A defendant cannot remove on the ground that she has a defense grounded in federal law, since the existence of a federal defense is insufficient to confer original federal question jurisdiction under section 1331.

3.   State Court Need Not Have Had Jurisdiction
By statute, the federal court *may* hear and decide a claim in a removed civil action even where the state court had no jurisdiction because the action is exclusively federal. [28 U.S.C. §1441(e)] Formerly, the federal court was required to dismiss.

B.   ONLY DEFENDANT MAY REMOVE; ALL MUST SEEK REMOVAL
Only defendants can exercise the right of removal. Thus, a plaintiff cannot remove on the ground that a counterclaim against him could have been brought independently in a federal court. If there is more than one defendant, *all defendants* who have been properly joined and served must join in or consent to the removal. (*Note:* The Class Action Fairness Act relaxes this rule for some class actions. *See* VIII.G.2.d., *infra*.)

C.   VENUE
Venue for an action removed under section 1441(a) lies in the federal district court "embracing the place where such [state] action is pending." In removal cases, section 1441(a) determines proper venue, not section 1391(a). Thus, in a properly removed case, venue is proper in the federal court of the state where the case was pending, even if venue would have been improper had the plaintiff originally filed the action in the federal district court of that state.

Example: Linda, a citizen of State A, sues Jim, a citizen of State B, in the state court in State Z in the amount of $2 million for negligent acts Jim committed in State B. Jim may remove the case to the federal district court of State Z because the court has diversity jurisdiction and Jim is not a citizen of State Z. Although under section 1391(a) venue would have been improper if Linda had filed her case in the State Z federal district court, under section 1441(a) venue is proper in the federal district court of State Z because it "embraces the place" where the state court action was pending.

D. DEFENDANT MAY REMOVE SEPARATE AND INDEPENDENT FEDERAL QUESTION CLAIM

If a case filed in state court contains a claim that would arise under federal law, and it is joined with state law claims that do not invoke diversity or supplemental jurisdiction, the entire case can be removed to federal court. The federal court, however, must then sever and remand the state law claims to state court. Only those defendants against whom a federal claim is asserted are required to join in the removal.

E. DISMISSAL OF NONDIVERSE PARTY ALLOWS REMOVAL

If no federal question is involved and diversity does not exist because a party is a co-citizen of an opposing party, removal will be permitted if the nondiverse parties are thereafter dismissed from the action and there is complete diversity between the remaining parties, subject to the limitations discussed below.

F. LIMITATIONS ON REMOVAL IN DIVERSITY OF CITIZENSHIP CASES

1. Defendant Citizen of Forum State

When the jurisdiction of the federal court is based *solely* on diversity and one of the defendants is a citizen of the state in which the state action was brought, the action is not removable. [28 U.S.C. §1441(a)(2)]

Example: Jones, a citizen of State A, sues Brown, a citizen of State B, and Smith, a citizen of State C, in the state court in State B. Although diversity jurisdiction would have existed originally (assuming the jurisdictional amount had been met), Brown and Smith cannot remove. Had Jones brought the action in the state court in State A, Brown and Smith could remove. [28 U.S.C. §1441(b)]

When the original jurisdiction of the district court would have been based on a federal question, the defendants can remove without regard to the citizenship of the parties.

2. One Year Rule

A case may not be removed on the basis of diversity of citizenship jurisdiction more than one year after it was commenced in state court. [28 U.S.C. §1446(b)] Note also that a case must be removed no later than 30 days after the defendant discovers, through service of an amended pleading, order, etc., that the case has become removable (*see* G.2., *infra*). Because most cases will be removable, if at all, at commencement of the action, the one year deadline generally will not be difficult to meet. The provision may be important, however, if the case is not removable at the outset, but becomes removable later. The one year rule does not apply to removals based on federal question jurisdiction, nor does it apply if the district court finds that *the plaintiff has acted in bad faith* (e.g., by fraudulently joining a nondiverse party or by intentionally failing to disclose the true amount in controversy) *in order to prevent a defendant from removing the action*.

Examples: 1) A (a citizen of State A) sues B (a citizen of State B) in state court in State A, seeking damages of $100,000. The case is removable at its commencement, since the case meets the requirements of diversity of citizenship jurisdiction and no defendant is a citizen of the forum. B must remove the case within 30 days of being served with process.

2) P (a citizen of State A) sues D1 (a citizen of State B) and D2 (a citizen of State A) in state court in State C, seeking damages of $250,000. The case is not removable at its commencement, since it does not satisfy the complete diversity rule for diversity of citizenship jurisdiction. However, if P later voluntarily dismisses the claim against D2, the case becomes removable. D1 must then remove within 30 days. But if more than a year has passed since the state case was commenced, D1 cannot remove on the basis of diversity of citizenship.

G. PROCEDURE FOR REMOVAL

1. Notice of Removal

A defendant seeking removal must file a notice of removal—containing a short and plain statement of the grounds for removal and signed under Rule 11—in the federal district court in the district and division within which the action is pending. A copy of the notice should be sent to the other parties *and* to the state court. Once this is done, the state court can no longer deal with the case. If the state court attempts to do so, the federal court can enjoin the state court's action.

a. Allegation of Amount in Controversy

In cases seeking nonmonetary relief, or in cases in which the plaintiff (under state law) is not required to state an amount in controversy or in which recovery may be in excess of the damages stated, the defendant may state that the amount in controversy exceeds $75,000, and the district court may keep the case if it finds, by a preponderance of the evidence, that the amount does exceed $75,000.

2. Thirty Day Rule

Generally, a defendant must file a notice of removal within 30 days "after receipt by or service on that defendant of the initial pleading or summons." [28 U.S.C. §1446(b)] The statute is intended to address different state approaches to the order of filing a case and serving process. For instance, in some states, the defendant is served with a summons but not a copy of the complaint. For such defendants, the 30-day removal period would start to run upon formal receipt of the complaint. If defendants are served at different times, and a later served defendant initiates timely removal, the earlier served defendant may join in the removal even though his 30-day period for initiating removal may have expired.

Example: P files an action against B in state court. P faxes a "courtesy copy" of the complaint to B, but does not have formal process (a summons and complaint) served for two weeks. D removes the case within 30 days after being served with process, but more than 30 days after receiving the faxed copy of the complaint. Was removal timely? Yes. The 30 days ran from service of process on the defendant. [Murphy Brothers v. Michetti Pipe Stringing, Inc., 526 U.S. 344 (1999)]

A defendant also may file a notice of removal within 30 days of receipt of an amended pleading, motion, order, or other court paper (such as discovery or other state court pleadings) that shows *that a nonremovable case (or an apparently nonremovable case) is in fact removable*. [28 U.S.C. §1446(b)(3)] This provision is significant in states that either prohibit the plaintiff from alleging or do not require the plaintiff to allege a specific amount of damages and in cases in which a nondiverse defendant has been dismissed. In such cases, the 30-day window to remove may begin much later than after the service of the initial pleading.

3. Procedure After Removal

After removal, the case proceeds according to the federal rules of procedure. Repleading is not necessary unless the court so orders. If the defendant has not answered, she must answer or present the other defenses or objections available to her under the Federal Rules within 21 days after being served, or within seven days after filing the petition for removal, whichever period is longer. Amendments may be made to pleadings filed before removal.

4. Right to Jury Trial

a. Demand for Jury Trial

The right to a jury trial in a case removed to a federal court may be waived unless a timely demand for a jury trial is filed. If, at the time of removal, all necessary pleadings have been served, a trial by jury will be granted to a party so entitled. The removing party must file a demand for jury trial within 14 days after the notice of removal is filed. The nonremoving party generally must file for jury trial within 14 days after service on her of the notice of filing for removal.

b. Demand Not Required

A party who, *prior to removal*, has made an express demand for trial by jury in accordance with state law, need not make a demand after removal. In addition, if *state law* applicable in the court from which the case is removed does not require the parties to make an express demand in order to claim trial by jury, they need not make such demand after removal unless the court directs they do so.

5. Remand

A plaintiff can file a motion to have the case remanded (sent back) to the state court. If the plaintiff bases this motion on a defect other than subject matter jurisdiction (e.g., a defect in removal procedures), the motion must be brought within 30 days of removal. The court must remand, however, whenever it is shown that there was no federal subject matter jurisdiction. If the court erroneously fails to remand, but the subject matter defect is cured before trial begins, failure to remand does not require that the federal judgment be vacated. [Caterpillar Inc. v. Lewis, 519 U.S. 61 (1996)] The federal court has discretion to remand a case to state court once all federal claims have been resolved, leaving only state claims over which there would be no diversity jurisdiction. [Carnegie-Mellon University v. Cohill, 484 U.S. 343 (1988)] Appellate review of remand orders is generally barred [28 U.S.C. §1447(d)]; however, appeal is allowed where a case involving civil rights is remanded to state court. Remand orders can also be reviewed by means of a mandamus if the remand represented a refusal to exercise plainly proper jurisdiction. [Thermtron v. Hermansdorfer, 423 U.S. 336 (1976)]

a. Subject Matter Jurisdiction Generally Considered First

Ordinarily, a federal court will determine whether it has subject matter jurisdiction before it considers the merits of the case. [Steel Co. v. Citizens for Better Environment, 523 U.S. 83 (1998)] However, the Supreme Court has held that when the subject matter jurisdiction issue is complicated, and the personal jurisdiction issue is fairly easy, a federal court does not abuse its discretion by addressing the personal jurisdiction issue first. [Ruhrgas AG v. Marathon Oil Co., 526 U.S. 574 (1999)]

H. SPECIFIC TYPES OF ACTIONS

1. Removable
Statutes allow removal of certain actions against *federal officers* when they were allegedly acting under color of law [28 U.S.C. §1442] and *federal employees* for torts by motor vehicle committed in the scope of employment [28 U.S.C. §2679(d)]; actions involving *international banking*; and criminal or civil actions where the defendant will be denied a right protected under federal *civil rights* statutes [28 U.S.C. §1443], but only if the denial is inevitable under state law [Georgia v. Rachel, 384 U.S. 780 (1966)]. Not all of these special types of cases could have been brought originally in the federal courts.

2. Nonremovable
Actions under the Federal Employers Liability Act ("FELA") are not removable; nor are actions for less than $10,000 against carriers for losses to certain shipments in interstate commerce or workers' compensation proceedings. [28 U.S.C. §1445]

a. All Writs Act Not a Basis for Removal
Some courts permitted removal of a case under the All Writs Act, 28 U.S.C. section 1651 (permitting federal courts to "issue all writs necessary or appropriate in aid of their respective jurisdictions and agreeable to the usages and principles of law"), even if the case did not invoke federal subject matter jurisdiction. However, the Supreme Court held that the All Writs Act does not provide an independent basis for removal jurisdiction; a case thus must satisfy some independent basis of subject matter jurisdiction, such as diversity of citizenship or federal question jurisdiction. [Syngenta Crop Protection, Inc. v. Henson, 537 U.S. 28 (2002)]

VII. CONFLICT OF JURISDICTION BETWEEN STATE AND FEDERAL COURTS

A. FULL FAITH AND CREDIT EXTENDED TO FEDERAL COURTS
The Constitution's Full Faith and Credit Clause—which requires a state to recognize the legislative acts and judicial decisions of its sister states—is applicable only where a state court judgment is sought to be enforced in another state. However, an implementing federal statute provides that this Clause is extended to the federal courts. Therefore, recognition of judgments is required between state and federal courts *and* between federal courts.

B. INJUNCTIONS AGAINST PENDING STATE PROCEEDINGS
Potentially, a case also could be filed in state court by one party and in federal court by the other party. In such a case, federal court is prohibited from enjoining *pending* state court proceedings unless *expressly* authorized by statute (e.g., the interpleader provision expressly authorizes injunctions against state court proceedings), or "where necessary in aid of its jurisdiction, or to protect or effectuate its judgments." [28 U.S.C. §2283] The case coming to a final decision first will have preclusive effect on the other. (*See* XI.B., *infra*.)

C. INJUNCTIONS AGAINST THREATENED STATE CRIMINAL PROSECUTIONS

Threatened state criminal prosecutions (i.e., where state court proceedings have not already been instituted) will be enjoined only when necessary *to prevent irreparable harm* which is clear and imminent *and* where *appellate remedies in the criminal case are clearly inadequate to provide relief.* Such injunctions are almost invariably denied, except where a federal right of free speech or assembly or a federally protected civil right is threatened by the state criminal proceeding, and it is shown that the prosecution is in bad faith or is for the purpose of harassment. Relief by declaratory judgment will ordinarily be denied if an injunction would be denied.

D. INJUNCTIONS AGAINST STATE TAX PROCEDURES

28 U.S.C. section 1341 prohibits injunctions against the assessment, levy, or collection of state taxes "where there is a plain, speedy and efficient remedy . . . in the courts of such State." [*See* Rosewell v. LaSalle National Bank, 450 U.S. 503 (1980)]

VIII. THE FEDERAL RULES OF CIVIL PROCEDURE

A. COMMENCEMENT OF THE ACTION

Rule 3 provides that an action is commenced by *filing a complaint* with the court. Filing a complaint before the statute of limitations has run will satisfy the statute of limitations in federal question cases and in diversity cases where the state rule is similar. However, the Supreme Court has held that a state rule that an action is commenced for purposes of the statute of limitations *only upon service of process* must be applied in diversity cases. [Walker v. Armco Steel Corp., 446 U.S. 740 (1980)]

B. SERVICE OF PROCESS

1. Who May Serve

Rule 4 authorizes any person who is at least 18 years old and not a party to the action to serve the summons and complaint (together known as "process"). A party may request that service be made by a United States marshal.

2. How Service Is Made

An individual may be served by (i) personal service, (ii) service left at the defendant's usual place of abode with one of suitable age and discretion residing therein, or (iii) service upon an authorized agent of the defendant. A minor or incompetent person must be served in accordance with the rules of the state in which service is to be made. A corporation, partnership, or association may be served by serving an officer, a managing or general agent, or an authorized agent of the corporation. Alternatively, service may be made under state rules or by mail under the waiver of service provision. Service within the United States ordinarily must be made within 90 days of the complaint being filed; however, the court must extend this period for good cause shown. [Fed. R. Civ. P. 4]

a. Service Under State Rules

Rule 4 provides that service—other than on a minor, incompetent person, or a person whose waiver has been filed—may alternatively be made as provided by the rules of the state in which the federal court sits or the state in which service is to be effected, regardless of the basis of subject matter jurisdiction. Hence, federal courts can use state long arm provisions.

b. Waiver of Service (Service by Mail)
The plaintiff may also request the defendant to waive service of process. To request a waiver of service, the plaintiff must mail the defendant certain items, the most important of which are a formal request to waive service (that also informs the defendant of the consequences of failing to waive service), two copies of the waiver form, and a copy of the complaint. The defendant generally has 30 days (60 days if outside the United States) from the date that the request was sent to return the waiver.

1) Effect of Waiver
A defendant who waives formal service of process has *60 days* (90 days if outside the United States) from the date the request was sent, instead of the usual 21 days (*see* F.3.b., *infra*) to answer the complaint. The waiver of service does *not* waive the defendant's right to object to venue and jurisdiction.

2) Effect of Failure to Waive
If the defendant does not waive service of process, the plaintiff must serve him using one of the methods described in 2., *supra*. However, a defendant who is located in the United States is liable for the cost of such service if he does not have good cause for failing to waive service.

3. Parties Served Outside State
The court will acquire personal jurisdiction over parties served outside the state:

a. Under statute and rules for extraterritorial service of the state in which the federal court sits (domiciliaries, long arm jurisdiction, and in rem jurisdiction);

b. If they are third-party defendants [Fed. R. Civ. P. 14] or required to be joined for just adjudication [Fed. R. Civ. P. 19], if served within 100 miles from the place where the summons was issued (but within the United States);

c. If out-of-state service is permitted by federal statute (e.g., interpleader); and

d. *For cases that involve a federal question*, when a defendant is served with process (or waiver thereof), provided that the defendant is *not subject to general jurisdiction in any state court*, that the defendant has *sufficient contacts with the United States* to warrant the application of federal law, and that the exercise of jurisdiction is *not prohibited by statute*.

4. Parties Served in Foreign Country
Unless a federal law provides differently, a court will acquire personal jurisdiction over a party served in a foreign country:

a. As provided in an *international agreement*;

b. In absence of an agreement, as provided by *the foreign country's law or as directed by a foreign official* in response to a letter of request (but the method must be reasonably calculated to provide notice);

c. Unless it is prohibited by the foreign country's law, ***by personal service or by mail***, signed return receipt requested. (However, a corporation may not be served by personal service, and a minor or incompetent person may not be served by either of these methods); or

d. ***Any method the court orders*** (so long as the method is not prohibited by international agreement).

5. Immunity from Process

The federal courts recognize the immunity from service of process of parties, witnesses, and attorneys who enter a state to appear in another action. In addition, if a party was induced by the plaintiff's fraud or deceit to enter a state so that he could be served, the service is invalid and the court does not acquire personal jurisdiction.

C. TIME PERIODS

1. Counting Time

Under Rule 6(a), when a time period is expressed in days, the day of the event that triggers the period is excluded, and the last day of the period is included, when determining on what day an action must be taken. Intermediate Saturdays, Sundays, and legal holidays are included, except that if the last day of the period falls on a Saturday, Sunday, or legal holiday, the due date becomes the next workday. Three days are added to the period when service of the paper is made by mail, by leaving the paper with the clerk, or by other means to which the parties have consented.

2. Extensions of Time

Rule 6(b) gives the district court power to extend the period within which actions under the Federal Rules must be performed (e.g., when a paper is delivered late in the day). However, certain time periods may never be extended. The following motions must be filed, with no extensions, ***within 28 days after entry of judgment***: a renewed motion for judgment as a matter of law, a motion to amend judgment, a motion for a new trial, a motion to amend findings of fact in a nonjury case, and a grant of a new trial on the court's initiative.

D. INTERLOCUTORY INJUNCTIONS

An injunction is an equitable remedy by which a person is ordered to act or to refrain from acting in a specified manner. Interlocutory injunctions are granted to maintain the status quo until a trial on the merits may be held.

1. Preliminary Injunction

A preliminary injunction is sought by a party prior to a trial on the merits of the complaint. A preliminary injunction may not be issued without notice to the adverse party. [Fed. R. Civ. P. 65(a)]

a. Requirements for a Preliminary Injunction

A preliminary injunction ordinarily will be granted when: (i) the plaintiff will suffer ***irreparable harm*** if the injunction is not granted; (ii) the harm to the plaintiff if the injunction is not granted ***outweighs*** the harm to the defendant if the injunction is granted; (iii) the plaintiff shows that he is ***likely to be successful on the merits***; and (iv) the ***public interest*** favors granting the injunction. Irreparable harm is the most important factor. If the party seeking injunctive relief has an adequate remedy at law (e.g., money damages will adequately compensate the party), the injunction will be denied.

2. **Temporary Restraining Order**

A temporary restraining order ("TRO") is granted by a court when it is necessary to prevent irreparable injury to a party, and the injury will result before a preliminary injunction hearing can be held.

a. **Requirements for Ex Parte Temporary Restraining Orders**

Generally, notice of the hearing for the issuance of the TRO must be given before a TRO is issued. However, a court may grant a TRO *without notice of the hearing to the adverse party* if three requirements are met [Fed. R. Civ. P. 65(b), (c)]:

1) **Specific Facts Showing Immediate and Irreparable Injury**

The moving party must give specific facts in an affidavit or in the verified complaint to establish that immediate and irreparable injury will result to the moving party before the adverse party can be heard in opposition.

2) **Efforts to Give Notice**

The moving party must certify in writing all efforts she made to give notice of the hearing to the adverse party and the reasons why notice should not be required.

3) **Security**

The moving party must provide some security, the amount of which is determined by the court, to pay for any costs and damages incurred by the adverse party if he was wrongfully enjoined or restrained. The United States, its officers, and its agencies are not required to give security.

b. **Notice of Hearing vs. Actual Notice**

Although a TRO may be issued without notice of the hearing, due process requires that a person must receive actual notice (through service of process or otherwise) of the TRO (or any other injunction for that matter) before he may be held in contempt for violating it. [*See* Fed. R. Civ. P. 65(d)]

c. **Time Limit**

The TRO will expire within 14 days unless the restrained party consents to an extension or good cause is shown for an extension for a like period. If the TRO is extended beyond 28 days from its issuance, it is considerd to be a preliminary injunction for purposes of appeal.

E. **PROVISIONAL REMEDIES**

"Provisional remedies" provide for the pretrial seizure of property for the purpose of securing satisfaction of a judgment that may be entered in the case. Federal Rule 64 specifically authorizes the use of provisional remedies but notes that the remedy's precise name and the precise procedure to be used will be governed by state law. Some of the more common remedies (which are also listed in Rule 64) are:

(i) *Garnishment*—A court order directing that money or property in the hands of a third party (e.g., wages) be seized;

(ii) *Attachment*—A process by which another's property is seized in accordance with a writ or judicial order for the purpose of securing a judgment yet to be entered. (*See* II.E.2.a.3), *supra*, and II.E.2.b., *supra*, for some restrictions on the use of attachment.); and

(iii) *Replevin*—A process by which the plaintiff takes possession of and holds disputed property during the lawsuit (possession pendente lite).

Procedure will vary from state to state, but the party seeking the remedy generally must make out a prima facie case on the underlying claim and show that the property will likely not be available after trial if relief is not granted.

F. PLEADINGS
Pleadings serve the function of giving *notice* to the opposing parties.

1. Complaint
Each claim for relief should contain:

(i) A short statement of the grounds for the court's jurisdiction;

(ii) A short statement of the claim showing that the pleader is entitled to relief; and

(iii) A demand for judgment for relief, which may be in the alternative.

The federal pleading rules generally require only that a pleader put the other side on notice of the claim being asserted; detailed assertions of facts underlying the claim generally are not required. However, the Supreme Court in recent years has required that the plaintiff state facts supporting a *plausible* (not just possible) claim. [Bell Atlantic Corp. v. Twombly, 550 U.S. 544 (2007); Ashcroft v. Iqbal, 556 U.S. 662 (2009)]

2. Pre-Answer Motions

a. Rule 12(b)
Prior to filing an answer, the defendant may, if he chooses, file a motion and raise any or all of the following defenses:

(i) Lack of subject matter jurisdiction;

(ii) Lack of personal jurisdiction;

(iii) Improper venue;

(iv) Insufficient process;

(v) Insufficient service of process;

(vi) Failure to state a claim upon which relief can be granted (i.e., even if plaintiff's allegations are taken as true, relief could not be granted); or

(vii) Failure to join a party needed for a just adjudication (includes necessary and indispensable parties).

The first defense may be raised at any time—even for the first time *on appeal*. The defendant must raise defenses (ii) through (v) *at the time he files a motion or his answer (or an amendment as of right thereto)*—whichever is first. If he does not, the defendant waives these defenses. The last two defenses (if limited to failure to join an "indispensable party") can be made *at any time prior to trial or "at trial."* The defendant may choose not to file a motion and instead raise these defenses in his answer. A motion to dismiss for failure to state a claim that raises issues outside of the pleadings will be treated as a motion for summary judgment.

b. **Motion for More Definite Statement**

A party may move for a more definite statement *before responding* (by filing an answer or reply) to a pleading (a complaint) that is so vague or ambiguous that a responsive pleading cannot reasonably be framed. The opposing party has 14 days after notice of an order to obey unless the court fixes a different time. If not obeyed, the court may strike the pleading or issue any other appropriate order. [Fed. R. Civ. P. 12(e)]

c. **Motion to Strike**

Before responding to a pleading or, if no responsive pleading is permitted, within 21 days after service of the pleading, a party may move to have stricken any insufficient defense, or any redundant, immaterial, impertinent, or scandalous matter. Such motion may also be made upon the court's initiative at any time. [Fed. R. Civ. P. 12(f)]

And note: An objection of failure to state a legal defense to a claim is not waived merely because a Rule 12(f) motion is not made. Such a defense can be made by motion for judgment on the pleadings, or at the trial. [Fed. R. Civ. P. 12(h)]

3. Answer

a. **Must Contain Denials or Admissions and Any Affirmative Defenses**

The answer must contain a *specific* denial or admission of each averment of the complaint, or a *general* denial with specific admissions to certain averments. Where the defendant is without knowledge or information sufficient to form a belief, a statement to that effect constitutes a denial. A *failure to deny* constitutes an *admission.* The answer must also state any *affirmative defenses* the defendant may have, such as statute of limitations, Statute of Frauds, res judicata, etc.

b. **Time**

If no Rule 12 motion is made, a defendant who was formally served with a summons and complaint must present an answer within *21 days* after service; a defendant to whom the complaint was mailed and who waives formal service must answer within *60 days* after the request for waiver was mailed to her. If a Rule 12 motion is made and the court does not fix another time, the responsive pleading is to be served within *14 days* of the court's denial or postponement of the motion. The answer is due within *14 days* of service of a more definite statement if the court grants a Rule 12(e) motion (*see* 2.b., *supra.*) The same timing rules apply to answers to counterclaims and cross-claims.

c. **Counterclaims**

Claims that the defendant may have against the plaintiff may be pleaded in the answer as counterclaims. If a counterclaim arises out of the *same transaction or occurrence* as one of the plaintiff's claims, it is a *compulsory* counterclaim and must be pleaded or it will be barred. Any other counterclaim is permissive and may be asserted (assuming there is subject matter jurisdiction) even though there is no connection at all between it and the plaintiff's claim.

d. Effect of Failure to Answer—Default and Default Judgment

A *default* is simply a notation in the case file by the clerk that there has been no answer filed within the time permitted by the rules. A *default judgment* is a judgment, with the same effect as any other judgment, that is entered because the defendant did not oppose the case.

1) Default

If a party against whom a judgment for relief is sought has failed to plead or otherwise defend, and that fact is made to appear by affidavit or otherwise, the clerk must enter the default of that party. Once the default has been entered, the party may not proceed with the action until the default has been set aside by the court. [Fed. R. Civ. P. 55]

2) Default Judgment

A defendant against whom a default is entered loses the right to contest liability. However, the amount of damages must still be determined before a default judgment may be entered, and the defaulting party can be heard at the hearing for damages. A default judgment may be entered against a minor or incompetent person only if she has a personal representative who has appeared in the case.

a) Default Judgment Entered by the Clerk

On request of the plaintiff, supported by an affidavit as to the amount due, the clerk may sign and enter judgment for that amount and costs against the defendant if: (i) the plaintiff's claim against the defaulted defendant is for a *sum certain*; (ii) the default was entered because the *defendant failed to appear*; (iii) the defaulted defendant is *not an infant or incompetent person*; and (iv) the damages amount requested is not greater than the amount requested in the complaint. [Fed. R. Civ. P. 54(c), 55(b)(1)]

3) Notice Required

If the defendant has "appeared," even though he has not answered, he must be notified of the request for a default judgment by first-class mail at least seven days before the hearing on the application for a default judgment. Appearance includes any actual formal appearance before the court and any other action that clearly indicates that the defendant intends to contest the case on the merits (e.g., the defendant's continued settlement negotiations). [Fed. R. Civ. P. 55(b)(2)]

4) Setting Aside a Default or a Default Judgment

An entry of default may be set aside for "good cause shown." Although not specifically required by the rules, a majority of courts will require that the defendant have a meritorious defense. A default judgment may be set aside as provided in Rule 60 (relief from judgments) (*see* IX.A., *infra*).

4. **Inconsistent Claims or Defenses**

A party may set out as many alternative claims or defenses as he may have regardless of consistency.

5. **Special Pleading**

The general rule of pleading is for short and plain statements, but there are certain rules for special circumstances. [*See* Fed. R. Civ. P. 9] Note that in some of these situations (notably concerning fraud, mistake, and special damages), the Federal Rules require a party to state more detail than simply a short and plain statement. These situations requiring greater specificity are narrow, however, and the Supreme Court has emphasized that courts have no power to impose such rigorous pleading requirements outside the areas addressed by Federal Rule or statute. [Swierkiewicz v. Sorema N.A., 534 U.S. 506 (2002)—lower court erred by requiring detailed pleading of employment discrimination claim; Leatherman v. Tarrant County, 507 U.S. 163 (1993)—lower court erred by requiring detailed pleading of civil rights case against municipality]

a. **Capacity**

Capacity or authority to sue or be sued *need not be alleged*. A person wishing to challenge a party's capacity has the duty to raise the issue by specific negative averment, including such particulars as are within his knowledge.

b. **Fraud or Mistake**

Circumstances that establish fraud or mistake must be stated with *particularity*. By statute (the Private Securities Litigation Reform Act), plaintiffs in federal securities fraud cases must plead with particularity facts relating to the defendant's acting with the required scienter.

c. **Conditions of the Mind**

Malice, intent, knowledge, or other conditions of the mind may be averred *generally*.

d. **Conditions Precedent**

The performance of conditions precedent may be alleged *generally*. Denial of performance or occurrence must be made specifically and with particularity.

e. **Official Document or Act**

When dealing with an official document or act, it is *sufficient* to aver that it was issued or the act was *done in compliance with the law*.

f. **Judgment**

It is *not necessary to aver jurisdiction* when a domestic or foreign court or a board or officer renders a judgment or decision.

g. **Timing**

Time and place averments are *material* for the purpose of testing the sufficiency of a pleading.

h. **Special Damages**

Elements of special damages must be *specifically* stated.

6. Reply

A reply *by the plaintiff* to the defendant's answer is required *only* if the court orders the plaintiff to file one. A plaintiff need not reply to an affirmative defense; he is deemed to deny or avoid the allegation of the defense. [Fed. R. Civ. P. 7, 12]

7. Amendment and Supplemental Pleadings

a. Amendment

As a matter of course, a pleading may be amended *once* within 21 days of serving it or, if the pleading is one to which a responsive pleading is required, 21 days after service of a responsive pleading or a pre-answer motion. Thereafter, a pleading may be amended only by the written consent of the adverse party or by leave of the court upon motion. Leave of the court is "freely given when justice so requires." [Fed. R. Civ. P. 15]

1) Relation Back

For statute of limitations purposes, an amendment to a pleading that arises from the same conduct, transaction, or occurrence that was set forth (or was attempted to be set forth) in the original pleading generally is deemed filed on the date that the original pleading was filed. (In other words, the filing of the amendment *relates back* to the filing date of the original pleading.) Amendments also relate back if relation back is permitted by the law that provides the statute of limitations applicable to the action. [Fed. R. Civ. P. 15(c)] Of course, the original complaint must have been filed within the applicable statute of limitations period.

2) Changing Party

An amendment changing the party or the naming of the party against whom a claim is asserted relates back if the amendment *concerns the same conduct, transaction, or occurrence* as the original pleading *and* if, within the period for filing a complaint and serving process, the party to be brought in by amendment:

(i) Has *received such notice of the action that she will not be prejudiced in maintaining her defense* on the merits; and

(ii) Knew or should have known that, *but for a mistake concerning the proper party's identity*, the action would have been brought against her.

[Fed. R. Civ. P. 15(c)(1)(C)] The Supreme Court has emphasized that it is the knowledge of the party to be brought in by amendment (not of the plaintiff) that is relevant. [Krupski v. Costa Crociere S.p.A., 560 U.S. 538 (2010)] And again, the original complaint must have been filed within the applicable statute of limitations period.

3) Conform to Evidence

A pleading may be amended during or after trial, or even after judgment, to conform to the evidence, reflect an issue actually tried by the express or implied consent of the parties, or permit the raising of new issues at trial. However, a party may not raise a new claim or defense for which the opposing party had no opportunity to prepare and which would result in prejudice in maintaining his action or defense. [Fed. R. Civ. P. 15(b)]

4) Due Process Limitation

Amendments to pleadings must satisfy due process. For example, in *Nelson v. Adams U.S.A. Inc.,* 529 U.S. 460 (2000), the trial court permitted a post-verdict amendment to add a defendant, and simultaneously entered judgment against that new defendant. The Supreme Court held that this procedure violated the new defendant's due process rights. The Federal Rules are meant to provide an opportunity for an added defendant to respond to a claim, and do not permit such "swift passage from pleading to judgment in the pleader's favor."

b. Supplemental Pleadings

Supplemental pleadings relate to matters *occurring after* the date of the original pleading. The permission of the court, upon motion, is required. Permission may be granted even though the original pleading is defective in its statement of a claim for relief or a defense. [Fed. R. Civ. P. 15(d)]

8. Rule 11

a. Certification upon Presenting Paper to Court

In federal civil cases, the attorney (or unrepresented party), by presenting to the court a pleading, written motion, or other paper, certifies that to the best of her knowledge, information, and belief formed after an inquiry reasonable under the circumstances:

(i) The paper is not presented for any *improper purpose* (harassment, delay, etc.);

(ii) The legal contentions therein are *warranted by existing law* or a nonfrivolous argument for the *modification of existing law* or the establishment of a new law;

(iii) The allegations and factual contentions either have, or upon further investigation or discovery are likely to have, *evidentiary support*; and

(iv) Denials of factual contentions are *warranted on the evidence* or, where specified, are reasonably based on a lack of information and belief.

The certification applies anew each time an attorney or unrepresented party "later advocates" a position contained in a pleading, motion, etc. Thus, a paper that was not sanctionable when first presented may become sanctionable if the attorney or party later advocating a position contained in the paper has since learned or should have learned that the position no longer has merit.

b. Sanctions

The court has discretion to impose sanctions, "limited to what is sufficient to deter repetition of such conduct," against a party who presents a paper to the court in violation of the above requirements, either on the court's own initiative or on motion of the opposing party. When appropriate, sanctions may be imposed against parties, attorneys, or law firms, and may consist of nonmonetary directives or monetary penalties including payment of expenses and attorneys' fees incurred because of the improper paper. However, a monetary sanction may not be imposed on a represented party for violation of a.(ii), *supra*.

1) Court's Initiative
A court on its own initiative may enter an order describing the matter that appears to violate Rule 11 and direct the proponent to show cause why sanctions should not be imposed.

2) Party's Motion
A party who believes that his opponent has presented a paper in violation of Rule 11 may serve a motion for sanctions on the party. If the party does not withdraw or correct the matter within 21 days, the moving party may then file the motion for sanctions with the court.

G. JOINDER

1. Joinder of Parties

a. Capacity
An individual's capacity to sue or be sued is determined by the law of her domicile; the capacity of an organization (e.g., an association or partnership) is determined by the law of the state where the federal court sits, except that a partnership or unincorporated association always has capacity where a substantive federal right is asserted by or against it.

b. Compulsory Joinder (Indispensable Parties)
In certain situations, a plaintiff must join all interested parties or face dismissal of the lawsuit. The dismissal is usually sought under Rule 12(b), and the issue may be raised any time up until judgment. [Fed. R. Civ. P. 19] Analysis of a compulsory joinder issue follows a three-step process:

(i) *Should* the absentee be joined?

(ii) *Can* the absentee be joined?

(iii) If not, *should the action proceed in his absence* (i.e., is the absentee *"indispensable"*)?

1) Should the Absentee Be Joined?
The absentee should be joined as a party when:

(i) *Complete relief cannot be accorded* among the other parties to the lawsuit without the absentee being made a party; or

(ii) *The absentee has such an interest in the subject matter* of the lawsuit that a decision in his absence will:

    i. As a practical matter, *impair or impede his ability to protect the interest*; or

    ii Leave any of the other parties subject to *a substantial risk of incurring multiple or inconsistent obligations.*

2) Can the Absentee Be Joined?

Assuming that the absentee should be joined under the analysis above, the next question is whether he can be joined, i.e., whether the court can obtain *personal* jurisdiction over the absentee and whether the court will still have *subject matter* jurisdiction over the action after joinder of the absentee. (28 U.S.C. section 1367 does not permit supplemental jurisdiction over claims by or against parties joined under Rule 19, so joinder of a party who would destroy diversity is not possible under the compulsory joinder rules.) If the court has personal jurisdiction over the absentee, and his joinder will not destroy diversity or venue, he *must* be joined.

3) Should the Action Proceed Without the Absentee?

If the absentee cannot be joined (e.g., plaintiff cannot serve process on the absentee), the court must determine whether *"in equity and good conscience"* the action *should proceed* among the parties before it, *or should be dismissed*, the absentee thus being regarded as *indispensable*. The decision requires consideration of:

(i) The extent of *prejudice to the absentee or available parties* of a judgment;

(ii) The extent to which the *prejudice can be reduced or avoided* by means of protective provisions in the judgment, the shaping of relief, or other measures;

(iii) The *adequacy of a judgment* rendered without the absentee; and

(iv) Whether the plaintiff will have *an adequate remedy (e.g., in another forum) if the case is dismissed* for nonjoinder.

Note: The Supreme Court has held that a joint tortfeasor subject to joint and several liability is not a person needed for just adjudication. [Temple v. Synthes Corp., 498 U.S. 5 (1990)]

c. Permissive Joinder—Requirements

Parties may join as plaintiffs or be joined as defendants whenever:

(i) Some claim is made by each plaintiff and against each defendant relating to or arising out of the *same series of occurrences or transactions; and*

(ii) There is a *question of fact or law common* to all the parties.

Example: It is very common for all persons injured in an automobile accident to join as plaintiffs. The common issue is the defendant's negligence; the other issues of contributory negligence and damages are tried individually for each plaintiff.

The court is given wide discretion to order separate trials where joinder would be unfair to a party not sufficiently involved in all the claims. Note that the court still must have subject matter jurisdiction over the claim.

2. Joinder of Claims

The policy of the Federal Rules is to permit the adjudication of all claims between the parties and all claims arising out of a single transaction. A plaintiff can join any number and type of claims against a defendant; when multiple plaintiffs or multiple defendants are involved, it is essential only that at least one of the claims arise out of a transaction in which all were involved.

a. Successive Claims

Rule 18(b) permits the plaintiff to join two claims when success on the first is a prerequisite to the second, such as a claim for money damages and a suit to set aside a conveyance that was fraudulent because of the debt asserted in the first claim.

b. Jurisdiction

When jurisdiction is based on the diversity of citizenship between the plaintiff and defendant, the plaintiff may aggregate all claims she has against the defendant to satisfy the jurisdictional amount. When jurisdiction is based on a "federal question" claim, and diversity jurisdiction is not available, a nonfederal claim can be joined only if the court has supplemental (pendent) jurisdiction over it. The court will have supplemental (pendent) jurisdiction over the claim if it is regarded as part of the same case or controversy as the federal claim.

Example: Plaintiffs claimed that the defendant appropriated plaintiffs' literary work in such a way as to (i) infringe federal law copyright, and (ii) constitute state law unfair competition. There was federal pendent jurisdiction over the state claim. [Hurn v. Oursler, 289 U.S. 238 (1933)]

c. Class Actions

1) Prerequisites

Rule 23 takes a functional approach to the class action device. Named representatives will be permitted to sue on behalf of a class if:

a) The class is so *numerous* that joinder of all members is *impracticable*;

b) There are *questions of law or fact* common to the class;

c) The *named parties' interests are typical* of the class;

d) The named representatives will ensure the *fair and adequate representation* of the interests of absent members of the class [Fed. R. Civ. P. 23(a)]; and

e) The action meets the definition of *any* of the following three types of class actions found in Rule 23(b):

(1) Separate actions by class members would create a *risk of inconsistent results* or, as a practical matter, *would impair the interests of other absent members of the class*; or

(2) A defendant has acted or refused to act on grounds applicable to the class and *injunctive or declaratory relief is appropriate* for the class as a whole (e.g., employment discrimination claims; but note that in *Wal-Mart Stores, Inc. v. Dukes*, 564 U.S. 338 (2011), the Supreme Court rejected an effort to recover monetary relief in such a class action); or

(3) There are *questions of fact or law common to members* of the class that *predominate* over individual issues and a class action is superior to the alternative methods of adjudication.

2) Consideration in Treating Case as a Class Action

The court should determine at an early practicable time whether the action may be maintained as a class action, i.e., whether to "certify" a class, but may determine at any time thereafter that the action is not an appropriate one for class action treatment. In determining whether to treat the case as a class action, the court should consider, inter alia, the following factors: (i) the interest of individual control, (ii) the extent and nature of litigation elsewhere on the same subject, (iii) the desirability of having the whole package in this court, and (iv) the difficulties in managing the class action.

a) Court Must Define Class Claims, Issues, or Defenses

The court, in certifying a class, must "define the class and the class claims, issues, or defenses."

b) Appointment of Class Counsel

The court must appoint class counsel for every certified class and expressly mandates that the attorney must fairly and adequately represent the interests of the class. [Fed. R. Civ. P. 23(g)(1)]

3) Effect of Judgment

All members of a class will be *bound* by the judgment rendered in a class action *except* those in a "common question" class action [Fed. R. Civ. P. 23(b)(3)] who notify the court that they do not wish to be bound ("opting out"). Members of Rule 23(b)(1) and 23(b)(2) classes cannot opt out. Note that if the substantive claim of the individual representing the class is mooted, this *does not* render the class action moot. [United States Parole Commission v. Geraghty, 445 U.S. 388 (1980)—release from prison of named plaintiff in class action suit challenging parole procedure did not moot entire class action suit]

a) Personal Jurisdiction Over Absent Class Members Not Required

The minimum contacts requirements that must be met for the assertion of personal jurisdiction need not be satisfied to bind absent members of the plaintiff class in a Rule 23(b)(3) ("common question") suit who chose not to opt out. [Phillips Petroleum Co. v. Shutts, 472 U.S. 797 (1985)] This allows a state or federal court to bind persons to a class action judgment under Rule 23(b)(3) even though they have no contact at all with the state.

4) Notice

a) Notice Required in Common Question Suits

Notice to all members of the class *of the pendency* of the class action is required under Rule 23 only in *"common question" suits* [Fed. R. Civ. P. 23(b)(3)], so that class members can opt out. The notice must state (i) the nature of the action, (ii) the definition of the class, (iii) the class claims, issues, or defenses, and (iv) the binding effect of a class judgment. Notice may be by first-class mail, electronic means, or other appropriate means.

b) Notice Discretionary in Other Types of Class Action Suits
Notice to members of the class of the pendency of the class action in other class suits is discretionary with the court. [*See* Eisen v. Carlisle & Jacquelin, 417 U.S. 156 (1974); Oppenheimer v. Sanders, 437 U.S. 340 (1978)]

Note: Notice of **dismissal or settlement** is a separate notice that must be given to class members of all types of class actions. (*See* 6)a), *infra.*)

5) Jurisdiction

a) Diversity Action
In class actions founded on diversity, only the ***citizenship of the named representatives*** of the class is taken into account to establish diversity. The Supreme Court held that the amount in controversy requirement is satisfied in a class action that invokes diversity of citizenship if ***any named representative's*** claim exceeds $75,000. The class action may proceed in federal court ***even if class members' claims do not exceed $75,000***. The claims by the class members that do not exceed $75,000 invoke supplemental jurisdiction. [Exxon Mobil Corp. v. Allapattah Services, III.C.3., *supra*]

b) Federal Question Action
If the class asserts a claim arising under federal law, it can invoke federal question jurisdiction. In that sort of case, of course, the citizenship of the parties and the amount in controversy are irrelevant. (*See* IV., *supra*.)

6) Court Approval of Dismissal or Settlement
The court must approve the dismissal or settlement of a class action. The class must satisfy the requirements for certification under Rule 23(a) and (b) before a court can approve a class settlement (*see* 1), above).

a) Notice of Dismissal or Settlement
Moreover, notice of the proposed dismissal or settlement must be given to all members of the class in a manner as directed by the court. [Fed. R. Civ. P. 23(e)] This notice is required in all types of class actions, unless the judgment will not bind the class. The purpose of notice to class members is to allow them to object to the proposed dismissal or settlement when the court holds a "fairness hearing" to determine whether to approve the dismissal or settlement. (*See* below.)

b) Procedures for Settlements of Class Action Suits
Rule 23(e) requires a settlement hearing (usually called a "fairness hearing") if the judgment will bind the class and permits settlement only if the court finds the terms to be fair, reasonable, and adequate, considering such factors as whether:

(i) The class representative and class counsel have fairly and adequately represented the class;

(ii) The settlement was negotiated at arm's length;

(iii) The relief provided to the class is adequate in light of the risks and delays of further litigation, the effectiveness of distributing relief to the class, and attorneys' fees; and

(iv) The settlement treats all class members equitably.

The court must make a finding supporting its conclusion that the settlement meets that standard. Parties seeking approval of a settlement must inform the court of any collateral agreements made in connection with the class settlement.

(1) "Opt Out" Provision
The court may refuse to approve a settlement of a Rule 23(b)(3) class action if members are not provided a new opportunity to opt out. Thus, members who received notice of the pendency of the class action (*see* 4), above) but declined to opt out may be permitted a second opportunity to opt out, essentially to reject the terms of the settlement and proceed on their own.

(2) Court Approval Required for Payment in Connection with Objection
The court also must approve, after a hearing, any payments or other consideration made to a party so that she will forgo an objection or appeal.

c) Appeal of Approval of Settlement
A class member who objects to the approval of settlement may bring an appeal of the approval of settlement [Devlin v. Scardelletti, 536 U.S. 1 (2002)]

7) Appeal of Class Action Certification Decision
Although a court's order granting or denying the certification of a class is not a final judgment in the case, a party may seek review of the decision in the court of appeals under Rule 23(f). (*See* X.C.6., *infra*.) The court's decision on the type of notice to give may not be immediately appealed.

d. Class Action Fairness Act
The Class Action Fairness Act ("CAFA") relaxes federal jurisdictional requirements for *some* class actions in an effort to make it easier for class action plaintiffs to file in federal court and for class action defendants to remove class actions from state to federal court. (Congress had concluded that some state courts had certified class actions inappropriately and that greater access to federal courts would protect defendants from such perceived abuses.)

1) Subject Matter Jurisdiction Under the CAFA
Under the CAFA, subject matter jurisdiction is established if:

a) *Any* class member (not just the representative, but anyone in the plaintiff class) is of diverse citizenship from *any* defendant;

b) The amount in controversy *in the aggregate* (i.e., adding all the class claims together) *exceeds $5 million*; and

c) There are at least *100 members* in the proposed class or classes.

2) **Removal Under the CAFA**
Additionally, in a case falling under the CAFA, *any* defendant, rather than *all* defendants, may remove the case from state to federal court. Moreover, there is no in-state defendant limitation on removal—the case may be removed under the CAFA even if a defendant is a citizen of the forum.

3) **Excluded Actions**

a) **Primary Defendants Are States or Governmental Entities**
There is no federal court jurisdiction under the CAFA if the primary defendants are states, state officials, or other governmental entities against whom the court may be foreclosed from ordering relief.

b) **Claims Based on Securities Laws or Regarding Corporate Governance**
There is no federal court jurisdiction under the CAFA over a class action that *solely* involves a claim under *federal securities laws*, or that relates to the *internal affairs of a corporation and is based on the laws of the state of incorporation*.

4) **Local Considerations May Defeat Jurisdiction**
The CAFA has some provisions designed to defeat federal jurisdiction in class actions that are relatively local in nature. These provisions contain some unclear terms.

a) **Mandatory Decline of Jurisdiction**
A district court *must* decline jurisdiction provided by the CAFA if: (i) *more than two-thirds* of the members of the proposed plaintiff class *are citizens of the state in which the action was filed*; (ii) *a defendant* from whom *"significant relief"* is sought is *a citizen of that state*; (iii) the *"principal injuries"* were incurred *in the state in which the action was filed*; and (iv) no similar class action has been filed within *the prior three years*.

b) **Discretionary Decline of Jurisdiction**
A district court *may* decline jurisdiction provided by the CAFA if *more than one-third but less than two-thirds* of the proposed plaintiff class are *citizens of the state in which the action was filed* and the *"primary defendants" are also citizens of that state*. In that case, the court considers a variety of factors, including whether the claims involve matters of national interest, whether the claims will be governed by the law of the state in which it was filed, and whether the state has a "distinct nexus" with the class members, the alleged harm, or the defendants.

5) **Protections Under the CAFA**
The CAFA adds a number of protections that apply to settlements in *all* class actions in federal court.

a) **Coupon Settlements**
Sometimes, class action settlements provide that the class members are to receive coupons good for purchase of further goods or services from the defendant. The court may approve such a settlement only after *holding a hearing* and *making a finding that the settlement is fair*, and it may also require that *unclaimed coupons be distributed to charitable organizations*. If attorneys' fees in such cases are to be based on the value of the settlement to the class, they must be limited to the value of the coupons actually redeemed by class members, rather than the total amount available to class members. Alternatively, attorneys' fees can be based on the amount of time class counsel reasonably expended on the action.

b) **Protection Against Loss by Class Members**
In some consumer class actions, some class members have actually lost money, because attorneys' fee awards required them to pay the lawyers more than they received from the settlement. A court may approve a settlement that would have that effect only if it makes a written finding that nonmonetary benefits to the class member *substantially outweigh* the monetary loss.

c) **Protection Against Discrimination Based on Geographic Location**
The court may not approve a settlement that provides larger payouts for some class members than others solely because the benefitted class members are located closer to the court.

d) **Notification of Federal and State Officials**
Settling defendants are required to give notice of proposed settlements to identified federal and state officials. Final approval of the proposed settlement may not be issued until at least 90 days after the notice is served. A class member who demonstrates that required notice was not provided may choose not to be bound by the settlement.

e. **Shareholder Derivative Suits**

1) **Minority Shareholder Allegations**
Under Rule 23.1, a minority shareholder, suing on behalf of other minority shareholders to enforce some right of the corporation which the corporation refuses to assert, *must allege* in a *verified* complaint that:

(i) She was *a shareholder at the time* of the transaction complained of (or received her shares thereafter by operation of law);

(ii) The action is not a *collusive* effort to confer jurisdiction on the court that it would otherwise lack; and

(iii) She made a *demand on the directors* and, if required by state law, on the shareholders, or the reasons why she did not make such demands. For this requirement, facts must be pleaded with particularity.

Rule 23.1, like Rule 23, requires that the class representative be able to fairly and adequately represent the class.

2) Corporation Named as Defendant
The corporation must be named as a defendant if those who control the corporation are antagonistic to the action sought by the plaintiffs. If not so named, the court will align the corporation as a defendant to reflect the antagonism.

3) Jurisdictional Amount and Venue
The judgment runs to the corporation; therefore, the jurisdictional amount looks to the damages allegedly suffered by the corporation. By statute, venue is proper wherever the corporation could have sued the same defendants (i.e., usually in the state of its incorporation). [28 U.S.C. §1401]

4) Court Approval
The court must approve the dismissal or settlement of a derivative suit.

f. Interpleader

1) Purpose Is to Avoid Double Liability
Interpleader permits a person in the position of a stakeholder to require two or more claimants to litigate among themselves to determine which, if any, has the valid claim where separate actions might result in double liability on a single obligation. Interpleader is available under Rule 22 and under the Federal Interpleader Statute. [28 U.S.C. §1335]

2) Rights of Plaintiff Stakeholder
The plaintiff stakeholder does not have to admit liability to any claimant and the claims do not have to have common origin. Once the court has allowed interpleader, a trial by jury is available to determine the issues of fact.

3) Jurisdiction

a) Rule 22 Interpleader
If Rule 22 interpleader is relied on, the normal rules as to subject matter jurisdiction apply. Therefore, there must be either a federal question claim, or complete diversity between the stakeholder and the claimants and more than $75,000 in controversy.

b) Federal Interpleader Statute
Under the Federal Interpleader Statute, on the other hand, the jurisdictional requirements are less restrictive. The federal statute permits jurisdiction where the amount in controversy is $500 or more and where there is diversity between *any two* contending claimants. Venue lies where any claimant resides, and process may be served anywhere in the United States under the statute (but not under Rule 22). The plaintiff stakeholder must deposit the amount in controversy (or a bond) with the court.

g. Intervention
Intervention may be granted to a party of right or permissively. [Fed. R. Civ. P. 24]

1) Intervention of Right

Intervention of right is available whenever the applicant claims an interest in the property or transaction that is the subject matter of the action, and the disposition of the action without her may impair her ability to protect that interest (unless her interest is already represented). The possible *stare decisis* effect of a judgment may be sufficient "interest" to authorize intervention of right. Traditionally, intervention of right invoked ancillary jurisdiction, so that no independent basis of subject matter jurisdiction was required over claims by or against the intervenor of right. Under the supplemental jurisdiction statute, however, it appears that there is *no* supplemental jurisdiction (with limited excpetions that are unlikely to be tested) over claims by or against one seeking to intervene in a diversity action. The United States has a right of intervention in all cases where the constitutionality of a United States statute is raised.

2) Permissive Intervention

Permissive intervention is available when the applicant's claim or defense and the main action have a question of fact or law in common; no direct personal or pecuniary interest is required. A claim in permissive intervention must not destroy complete diversity (if it does, intervention will be denied), and *must be supported by its own jurisdictional ground*. Permissive intervention is discretionary with the court.

3) Caveat

In all cases of intervention, the application must be timely, a matter within the court's discretion.

h. Third-Party Practice (Impleader)

1) Claims for Indemnity or Contribution

A defending party may implead a nonparty, but only if the nonparty is or may be liable to her for any part of a judgment that the plaintiff may recover against her. Usually, such an impleader claim will be for indemnity or contribution. If the indemnity or contribution claim by the defending party against the third-party defendant does not meet the requirements for diversity of citizenship or federal question jurisdiction, it will invoke supplemental (ancillary) jurisdiction, because such claims will meet *the "common nucleus of operative fact" requirement of supplemental (ancillary) jurisdiction*. (*See* III.B.5., 6.e., *supra*.) Thus, the defending party may assert an indemnity or contribution claim in federal court even if there is no diversity between the defending party and the third-party defendant and the third-party claim is based on state law. Furthermore, *venue need not be proper* for the third-party defendant.

2) Non-Indemnity or Non-Contribution Claims

As part of the third-party complaint, the third-party plaintiff (i.e., the original defending party) may join *other* (non-indemnity or non-contribution) claims she may have against the third-party defendant. *If these other claims cannot invoke diversity of citizenship or federal question jurisdiction, they would also need to invoke supplemental (ancillary) jurisdiction* (*see* III.B.5., 6.e., *supra*), although it is less likely that the "common nucleus" test could be met.

3) Severance of Third-Party Claims
In any event, *even if jurisdiction exists*, the court *may sever any third-party claim* to be tried separately *if it is just to do so* (e.g., if addition of those claims would lead to unfair prejudice to one of the parties).

4) Response of Impleaded Party
After he is joined by the third-party complaint, the third-party defendant may assert defenses to the plaintiff's original claim, as well as defenses to the third-party liability asserted against him.

5) Impleading Insurance Companies
In some states, a defendant may not implead its own insurance company, but if the insurance company denies coverage and refuses to defend, then the defendant may implead the company and have that issue decided in the same case.

i. Cross-Claims
Co-parties may assert claims against each other that arise out of the same transaction or occurrence as the main action by filing cross-claims. Since a cross-claim is, by definition, transactionally related to the existing action, it is commonly considered to come within the court's supplemental jurisdiction at least if the claim is by a defendant against a co-defendant.

H. DISCOVERY

1. Duty of Disclosure
Rule 26 requires parties to disclose certain information to other parties without waiting for a discovery request. However, Rule 26 also has provisions allowing stipulation of the parties or court order to modify some disclosure requirements.

a. Types of Disclosure Required
Before making her disclosures, a party has an obligation to make a reasonable inquiry into the facts of the case. Rule 26 requires parties to disclose all information "then reasonably available" that is not privileged or protected as work product. A party is not relieved from her obligation to disclose merely because she has failed to complete her investigation or because another party has not made his disclosures or has made inadequate disclosures. Three types of disclosure are required: *initial* disclosures, disclosure of *expert testimony*, and *pretrial* disclosures.

1) Initial Disclosures
Without waiting for a discovery request, a party must provide to other parties (unless stipulation or court order provides otherwise):

(i) The names, addresses, and telephone numbers of individuals likely to have discoverable information that the disclosing party may use to support its claims or defenses, unless the use would be solely for impeachment;

(ii) Copies or descriptions of documents, electronically stored information, and tangible things that are in the disclosing party's possession or control and that the disclosing party may use to support its claims or defenses, unless the use would be solely for impeachment;

    (iii) A computation of damages claimed by the disclosing party and copies of materials upon which the computation is based; and

    (iv) Copies of insurance agreements under which an insurer might be liable for all or part of any judgment that might be entered.

These disclosures must be made *within 14 days* after the meeting of the parties required by Rule 26(f) (discussed at I.1., *infra*) unless a different time is set by court order or by stipulation.

a)   Exemptions from Initial Disclosure Requirement
Initial disclosures are not required in particular types of cases, such as actions to review an administrative record, actions to enforce an arbitration award, pro se litigation brought by prisoners, actions to quash or enforce subpoenas, or habeas corpus petitions. [Fed. R. Civ. P. 26(a)(1)(B)]

2)   Disclosure of Expert Testimony
A party must also disclose to other parties the identities of expert witnesses expected to be used at trial. If the expert witness has been specially retained to provide expert testimony, or if the expert's duties as the party's employee regularly involve giving expert testimony, the disclosure must be accompanied by a report prepared and signed by the expert witness stating her qualifications, the opinions to be expressed, and the basis for those opinions, along with a list of cases in which he has testified in the past four years and his compensation, among other items. Otherwise, no report is required, and instead these disclosures are required: the identity of the expert, the subject matter on which the expert is expected to present evidence, and a summary of the facts and opinions to which the witness is expected to testify. This disclosure must be made at the time directed by the court or, in the absence of any directions or any stipulations among the parties, at least 90 days before trial; if the evidence is intended solely to rebut another party's disclosure of expert testimony, it must be made within 30 days after disclosure of the evidence being rebutted.

3)   Pretrial Disclosures
At least 30 days before trial, a party must disclose to the other parties and file with the court a list of (i) the witnesses she expects to call at trial, (ii) the witnesses she will call if the need arises, (iii) the witnesses whose testimony will be presented by means of a deposition and a transcript of pertinent portions of the deposition, and (iv) documents or exhibits she expects to offer or might offer if needed. Evidence or witnesses that would be used solely for impeachment need not be disclosed. Within 14 days after this disclosure, a party may serve objections to use of the depositions at trial and to the admissibility of disclosed documents and exhibits. Such objections are waived if not made at this point, except for objections that the

evidence is irrelevant, prejudicial, or confusing under Federal Rules of Evidence 402 and 403.

2. **Discovery of Electronically Stored Data**

The Rules require parties to discuss the discovery and preservation of electronically stored data and to report to the court on those discussions. Electronically stored information need not be produced if the responding party identifies it as from a source not reasonably accessible because of undue burden or cost. On motion to compel or for a protective order, that party must show to the court's satisfaction that its assertion is justified. Even then, the court may order the information produced for good cause, but it may also impose conditions such as cost-shifting or cost-sharing. [Fed. R. Civ. P. 26(b)(2)(B)]

a. **Format for Producing Electronic Documents**

A requesting party may specify the form or forms for producing electronically stored information, and the responding party must use that form unless it objects (but the party must still produce other items to which it has no objections). The court will determine if the objection is valid. If the request does not specify the form for producing electronically stored information, the responding party may use any form in which the information is maintained or a form that is reasonably usable by the requesting party. [Fed. R. Civ. P. 34(b)]

b. **Destruction of Electronically Stored Information**

Rule 37(e) creates remedies for discovering parties and sanctions against parties who fail to take *reasonable steps* to preserve electronically stored information *when litigation is reasonably foreseeable.* (If reasonable steps were taken, or if litigation was not reasonably foreseeable, no sanctions may be imposed for the destruction of discoverable information.) Additionally, if unpreserved electronically stored information *can be restored or adequately replaced through additional discovery,* no other remedial measures need be imposed. If the information cannot be restored or replaced, and the discovering party is prejudiced by the lack of information, the court may order remedial measures *no greater than necessary to cure the prejudice,* taking into consideration the importance of the information to the case and the expenses resulting from restoring or replacing the information. *If the disclosing party acted with intent to deprive the discovering party of the information,* the court *may* (i) presume the lost information was unfavorable to the party; (ii) instruct the jury that it may or must presume the information was unfavorable to the party; or (iii) dismiss the action or enter a default judgment. The imposition of these measures is discretionary with the court.

3. **Scope of Disclosure and Discovery**

a. **In General**

Unless the court limits discovery by order, discovery may be had of *"any nonprivileged matter that is relevant to any party's claim or defense"* and proportional to the needs of the case, considering the importance of the issues at stake in the action, the amount in controversy, the parties' relative access to information, the parties' resources, the importance of the discovery in resolving the issues, and whether the burden or expense of the proposed discovery outweighs its likely benefits. "Any matter" encompasses both documentary evidence and individuals with knowledge of any discoverable matter.

Furthermore, information need not be admissible at trial to be discoverable. [Fed. R. Civ. P. 26(b)(1)]

b. **Trial Preparation Materials**

Work product of a party or a representative of a party (e.g., a lawyer) made *in anticipation of litigation*, is discoverable only upon showing *"substantial need"* and to *avoid "undue hardship"* in obtaining materials in an alternative way. If the court orders the disclosure of work product, it must take steps to avoid the disclosure of mental impressions, conclusions, opinions, or legal theories of the disclosing party. However, a party may obtain, without a court order and without showing need and hardship, a copy of any statement or recording previously made by *that party*. Draft reports and draft disclosures of "trial" experts are work product. Confidential communications between such experts and counsel for the party are generally protected as trial preparation materials, except for communications relating to the expert's compensation or to facts or data the attorney provided to the expert. [Fed. R. Civ. P. 26(b)]

1) **Procedure for Claiming Work Product**

When a party claims that certain discoverable information is privileged trial preparation material, he still must disclose the existence of the material in sufficient detail to the opposing party so that the opposing party may assess the claim of privilege.

c. **Inadvertent Disclosure of Trial Preparation or Privileged Materials**

If a party inadvertently discloses trial preparation or privileged material to opposing parties, he may still invoke a claim of work-product protection or any privilege by notifying the opposing parties of the inadvertent disclosure and the basis for the claim of work product or privilege. Once so notified, the opposing party may not use or disclose the trial preparation or privileged material until the claim is resolved, and he must take reasonable steps to retrieve the material if he disclosed it to others.

d. **Experts**

A party may depose experts who are expected to be called at trial (*testifying experts*). If a report from the expert is required, the deposition may take place only after the report is provided. The opinions of experts who are retained in anticipation of litigation but who are not expected to testify at trial (*consulting experts*) may be discovered only upon a showing of exceptional circumstances under which it is impracticable to obtain facts or opinions by other means. [Fed. R. Civ. P. 26(b)(4)]

e. **Protective Orders**

Protective orders may be obtained under Rule 26(c) to limit the nature and scope of examination or to terminate examination if discovery is abused. The court also may allocate the expenses of discovery among the parties.

f. **Supplementation of Disclosures and Discovery Responses**

A party *must* timely supplement required disclosures and prior responses to interrogatories, requests for production, or requests for admissions if she learns that the information disclosed was materially incomplete or incorrect and the new information has not been made known to the other party in discovery or in writing. The duty to supplement also applies to an expert's reports and information from any deposition of an expert. [Fed. R. Civ. P. 26(e)]

4. Types of Discovery

a. Pre-Action Depositions

Prior to a lawsuit being filed, or while an appeal is pending, a potential party or party to an appeal may ask the court to order the deposition of any person in order *to perpetuate her testimony*. To do so, the potential party must file a verified petition in the federal court for the judicial district in which *any expected adverse party resides*.

1) Contents of Petition

The request for a court order is included within the petition itself. The petition also must show that, among other things, the petitioner *expects to be a party* to an action cognizable in a court in the United States but is *presently unable* to bring it or cause it to be brought. All expected adverse parties must be named.

2) Notice and Appointed Counsel

At least 21 days before the hearing date for the court order, the potential party must serve each expected adverse party with a copy of the petition and a notice of hearing. The manner of service is the same as for an original petition (*see* VIII.B., *supra*). If the expected adverse party cannot be so served, the court must appoint counsel for that party.

3) Court Order

If the court finds that ordering a deposition may prevent a failure or delay of justice, it will issue an order that specifies the person being deposed, the subject matter of the deposition, and the manner of the deposition.

b. Depositions

A party may not take more than *10 depositions*, nor may she depose the same person more than once, without leave of court or stipulation of the parties.

1) Oral Deposition of a Witness, Including a Party-Witness

A common form of discovery is the oral deposition under Rule 30. If the deponent is not available at trial, the deposition may be used in lieu of her appearance as a witness. The deposition may be recorded by sound, sound and visual, or steno-graphic means. Depositions may be taken by telephone or through other remote electronic devices. All parties may pose questions to the deponent. A deposition may not exceed "one day of seven hours" absent court order or stipulation to the contrary.

a) Compulsory Appearance of Witnesses

####### (1) Subpoena Not Needed for Parties

It is not necessary to serve a subpoena on an adverse party or an officer, director, or managing agent of a party to compel appearance; the notice of deposition is sufficient to compel attendance. For organizations, the notice may name the organization and state with "reasonable particularity" the matters to be covered. The organization then designates individuals to testify. [Fed. R. Civ. P. 30(b)(6), 37]

(2) Nonparties Should Be Subpoenaed

If the witness to be deposed is not a party to the action, he should be subpoenaed. The subpoena may be served by any person who is not a party and is not less than 18 years old. Service is made by delivering a copy of the subpoena with any necessary fees to the person named in the subpoena. A nonparty organization may be required by subpoena to designate individuals to testify, as in (1), *supra*. A subpoena may command a person to appear only (i) within 100 miles from where he resides, works, or regularly transacts business in person; or (ii) within the state where he resides, works, or regularly transacts business in person so long as he would not incur substantial expense. A subpoena is enforceable in the court it was issued or the court in which the action is pending on transfer from the issuing court. [Fed. R. Civ. P. 30, 45]

(3) Costs When Notifying Party Fails to Attend

When the party who notices the deposition does not appear (in person or by an attorney) to take the deposition, and the other party does appear, the latter can obtain his costs of attending, including reasonable attorneys' fees.

2) Deposition of Witnesses on Written Questions

Rule 31 provides for written questions to witnesses (including parties) and is designed to facilitate the depositions of witnesses living a great distance from the parties. All parties can pose questions to the deponent, which must be served on all parties before the deposition.

c. Interrogatories to the Parties

Rule 33 provides for written interrogatories to other parties and written answers by the party to whom the interrogatories are directed. The party must respond not only with facts which she herself knows, but also with facts that are available to her. The party may also be asked to give opinions, even on the application of law to facts. Initially, the requesting party may not serve more than *25 interrogatories including subparts* without court order or stipulation, and leave may be granted to serve additional ones.

1) Option to Produce Business Records

If the answer to an interrogatory may be ascertained from the responding party's business records (including electronically stored information), and the burden of ascertaining the answer will be essentially the same for the parties, the responding party may (i) specify the records that must be reviewed, in sufficient detail to enable the requesting party to locate and identify them as readily as the responding party could; and (ii) give the interrogating party a reasonable opportunity to examine and audit the records and to make copies, compilations, abstracts, or summaries.

d. Production of Physical Material; Inspection

Rule 34 provides (i) for the production by a *party* (or, if accompanied by a subpoena, a nonparty) of physical material, including documents and electronically stored information, relevant to the pending action; and (ii) that a party be required to permit entry onto land for relevant testing. Notice must be given to all other parties before a nonparty subpoena issues. A subpoena is limited to production at a place within 100 miles of where the person resides, works, or regularly transacts business in person.

e. Physical and Mental Examinations

1) Order for Examination

Rule 35 provides for an independent physical or mental examination of a party when that party's physical or mental condition is in controversy. Such exam is available only if ordered by the court, on showing of good cause. Traditionally, the Rule has allowed exams only by "physicians." Now, however, it allows exams by a "suitably licensed or certified examiner," which would include, for example, doctors, dentists, occupational therapists, and any others required to be licensed and qualified to comment on a physical or mental condition.

2) Report of Findings

The person examined may request a copy of the examiner's report, but if that person so requests or takes a deposition of the examiner, she waives any privilege and must produce, upon demand, copies of her own doctor's reports of any other examinations of the same condition.

f. Requests for Admission

Any party may serve on any other party a written request for admission as to the truth or genuineness of any matter or document described in the request. The matters will be considered admitted unless the party upon whom the request was served returns a sworn statement denying the truth of the matters set forth in the request, or explaining why she cannot admit or deny them. Alternatively, the party upon whom the request was served can file written objections to those requests that she has a legal basis for not answering. A party may be asked to admit matters that are genuine issues for trial. The admission is for the purpose of the pending action only and may not be used against the party in any other proceeding. [Fed. R. Civ. P. 36]

5. Enforcing Disclosure and Discovery

a. Motion for an Order Compelling Disclosure or Discovery

On notice and motion, a party may seek an order compelling discovery from the court. (An evasive or incomplete response to discovery essentially is treated as a failure to make discovery.) The movant must certify that he has, in good faith, conferred or attempted to confer with the person or party failing to make discovery in an effort to avoid court intervention. If the motion is to compel a party to make discovery, the motion must be filed in the court in which the action is pending; if the order is sought against a nonparty, the motion must be made in the court in which discovery will be taken. [Fed. R. Civ. P. 37(a)]

1) Motion Granted or Discovery Is Provided After Filing

If the motion is granted, or if the discovery is provided after the motion was filed (and, of course, after the movant conferred or attempted to confer to resolve the dispute), the court must, after giving an opportunity to be heard, require the party or deponent whose conduct necessitated the motion, the party or attorney advising that conduct, or both, to pay the moving party's reasonable expenses incurred in making the motion, including attorney's fees, unless the nondisclosure was *substantially justified or other circumstances exist that make an award of expenses unjust*.

2) Motion Denied

If the motion is denied, the court may issue a protective order and must, after giving an opportunity to be heard, require the movant and/or the attorney filing the motion to pay the opposing party's or deponent's reasonable expenses, including attorney's fees, incurred in opposing the motion unless the motion *was substantially justified or other circumstances exist that make an award of expenses unjust*.

3) Motion Granted In Part and Denied In Part

If the motion is granted in part and denied in part, the court may issue a protective order and/or, after giving an opportunity to be heard, apportion the reasonable expenses for the motion.

b. Failure to Comply with a Court Order

A party or deponent may be held in contempt of court for failing to obey a court order (except for an order for a mental or physical examination). There are further sanctions that may be available against a party. The court in which the action is pending may: (i) take designated facts as true for the purposes of the action; (ii) prohibit the nondisclosing party from supporting designated claims or defenses; (iii) strike pleadings; (iv) stay the proceedings until the order is obeyed; (v) dismiss the action in whole or in part; (vi) render a default judgment against the nondisclosing party; and/or (vii) order the party and/or his attorney to pay reasonable expenses, including attorney's fees. [Fed. R. Civ. P. 37(b)]

c. Failure to Disclose or Supplement an Earlier Response

If a party fails to provide information or identify a witness, the party is not allowed to use that information or witness to supply evidence in a motion, or at a hearing or at trial, *unless* the failure was *substantially justified or harmless*. In addition to or instead of this sanction, the court, on motion, may (i) order payment of the reasonable expenses, including attorney's fees, caused by the failure; (ii) inform the jury of the party's failure; and (iii) impose other appropriate sanctions. A motion to compel is not required for these sanctions. [Fed. R. Civ. P. 37(c)(1)]

d. Failure to Admit

If a party fails to admit a fact that is the subject of a request for admissions, and the requesting party later proves the matter true, the requesting party may move that the party who failed to admit pay the reasonable expenses, including attorney's fees, incurred in making that proof. The court must order payment of expenses unless: (i) the request was held objectionable; (ii) the admission sought was of no substantial importance; (iii) the party failing to admit had a reasonable ground to believe that it might prevail on the matter; or (iv) there was other good reason for the failure to admit. A motion to compel is not required for this sanction. [Fed. R. Civ. P. 37(c)(2)]

    e.   **Party's Failure to Attend His Own Deposition, Serve Answers to Interrogatories, or Respond to a Request for Inspection**

If a party, after being served with proper notice, fails to attend his own deposition, or if a party fails to provide *any* response to interrogatories or a request for inspection, the requesting party may, instead of moving to compel, apply for immediate sanctions against the nondisclosing party. However, the movant (requesting party) must certify that he made a good faith attempt to resolve the discovery dispute. That a request is objectionable does not serve as a defense *unless* the nondisclosing party has a pending motion for a protective order. Permissible sanctions are the same as those described above. [Fed. R. Civ. P. 37(d)]

6.   **Use of Depositions at Trial or Hearing**

Subject to the rules of evidence, a deposition may be used (at trial or in a hearing) against any party who was present at the deposition or had notice of it:

   (i)   *To impeach* the testimony of the deponent as a witness;

   (ii) For any purpose if the court finds that the deponent (including a party-deponent) is *dead,* at a distance greater than *100 miles* from the place of trial (unless the absence was procured by the party offering the deposition), *unable to testify* because of age, sickness, or imprisonment, or the party offering the deposition could not procure the witness's attendance by subpoena;

   (iii) For any purpose if, on notice and motion, the judge permits the deposition to be so used due to exceptional circumstances; or

   (iv) For any purpose if the *deponent is an adverse party.*

[Fed. R. Civ. P. 32]

7.   **Errors and Irregularities in Depositions**

Rule 32 governs the waiver of errors and irregularities in the taking of depositions.

    a.   **As to Notice**

Errors and irregularities relating to the notice of deposition are waived unless written objection is promptly served on the party giving notice.

    b.   **As to Manner of Taking**

Errors of any kind which could have been obviated if promptly presented are waived unless *seasonable* objection is made at the time of taking the deposition (applies to form of questions, oath, conduct of parties, etc.).

    c.   **As to Completion and Return**

Errors and irregularities as to the completion and return of the deposition are waived unless a motion to suppress is made with reasonable promptness after the error was or should have been discovered (applies to signing, sealing, certification, and transmittal).

d.   As to Form of Written Questions

    Objections to the form of written questions are waived unless served on the party propounding them within the time for serving succeeding questions and within five days after service of the last questions authorized.

I.   PRETRIAL CONFERENCES

1.   Rule 26(f) Conference of Parties—Planning for Discovery

As soon as practicable, and in any event before the Rule 16(b) scheduling conference (*see* below), the parties must confer to consider *their claims and defenses, the possibility of settlement, initial disclosures, any issues concerning the preservation of evidence, and a discovery plan*. The parties must submit to the court a proposed discovery plan within 14 days after the conference addressing the timing and form of required disclosures, the subjects on which discovery may be needed, the timing of and limitations on discovery, and relevant orders that may be required of the court.

2.   Rule 16(b) Scheduling Conference

The court must (except in classes of cases exempted by local rule) hold a scheduling conference among the parties or counsel. The scheduling order will limit the time for *joinder, motions*, and *discovery*. The order may also include dates for *pretrial conferences, a trial date*, and *any other appropriate matters*. This schedule cannot be modified except by leave of court upon a showing of good cause. [Fed. R. Civ. P. 16(b)]

3.   Pretrial Conferences

The court may also hold pretrial conferences as necessary to expedite trial and foster settlement. A *final pretrial conference*, if any, is held as close to the time of trial as reasonable, and is for the purpose of formulating a plan for the trial, including the admission of evidence. This conference is to be attended by at least one of the lawyers for each side who will actually be conducting the trial, and by any unrepresented parties. After a pretrial conference, an order must be entered that *controls the subsequent course of events* in the case. Thus, the final pretrial conference order is a blueprint for the trial, usually listing witnesses to be called, evidence to be presented, factual and legal issues needing resolution, and like matters. It is thus said to supersede the pleadings and may be modified only to prevent manifest injustice.

4.   Sanctions

A party or counsel may be sanctioned for failure to attend a conference or obey an order entered pursuant to a conference, for being substantially unprepared to participate in a conference, or for acting in bad faith. The court has a broad range of available sanctions including contempt, striking pleadings, and prohibiting the introduction of evidence. In addition, the court must require the disobedient party or counsel to pay expenses incurred (including attorneys' fees) by other parties, unless the court finds that circumstances make such an award unjust.

J.   ALTERNATIVE DISPUTE RESOLUTION

Alternative dispute resolution ("ADR") is a process in which a neutral person resolves a dispute or helps the parties to resolve their dispute. Examples of these processes include contractual arbitration, judicial arbitration, and mediation.

1. **Contractual Arbitration**

   The Federal Arbitration Act ("FAA") governs written arbitration agreements involving interstate or international commerce and preempts conflicting state law. [9 U.S.C. §§1 *et seq.*]

   a. **Procedure**

      A written agreement to arbitrate a dispute is valid and enforceable unless a contractual ground for revocation exists (e.g., fraud in the inducement of the arbitration clause, illegality or unconscionability of the arbitration clause). Court proceedings are stayed until the arbitration proceedings are completed. The appointment of the arbitrator usually will be provided for in the arbitration agreement. At the arbitration proceeding, the arbitrator can subpoena witnesses and require them to bring documentary evidence to the hearing. After the arbitrator renders the award, a party can move to have the court confirm the award. The opposing party may move to vacate the arbitration award on the grounds below. If the award is confirmed, it is considered to be final and binding, and it is enforceable as a court judgment.

      1) **Judicial Review of Award**

         An arbitration award may be vacated, even on appeal, only on narrow statutory grounds, such as *fraud or evident partiality of the arbitrator, the arbitrator's refusal to delay proceedings for sufficient cause, or the arbitrator's failure to follow the arbitration agreement to such a degree as to affect the outcome.* A party may also move to modify the award *to correct miscalculations, to modify awards that go beyond the scope of the arbitration agreement, or to correct minor imperfections of form.* Additionally, an arbitration award also may be overturned when it represents a *manifest disregard of the law*, a judicially created and extremely deferential standard that requires the complaining party to show that the arbitrator knew the applicable law but chose to disregard it.

2. **Judicial Arbitration**

   "Judicial arbitration" is a dispute-resolution process conducted by a neutral person under the auspices of the court in an attempt to resolve the action without trial. Judicial arbitration may be employed by federal courts under local district court rules. At the federal level, participation in arbitration procedures is voluntary, and even then certain actions (cases involving a violation of constitutional rights, certain civil rights actions, and cases alleging an amount in controversy of more than $150,000) may not be referred to ADR even if the parties consent. Within 30 days of the arbitration award, a party may reject the award and request trial de novo. Any evidence that the case was arbitrated is generally excluded. [28 U.S.C. §§654 *et seq.*]

3. **Mediation**

   Mediation involves the use of a neutral person to help parties to a dispute reach a mutually acceptable agreement. The mediator does not have decisionmaking power; his role is to facilitate the process by which the parties reach their own voluntary agreement. In federal court, mediation is accomplished by local district rule. By local rule, mediation may be made mandatory for certain cases. [28 U.S.C. §§651, 652]

K. TRIAL

1. **Jury Trial Problems**

   Rule 38 requires a party who desires a jury trial (on some or all fact issues) to file a written demand with the court and serve it on the parties. (Such demand may be indorsed upon a pleading of the party.) Failure to make such a demand within 14 days after the service of the last pleading directed to the jury-triable issue constitutes a *waiver* by that party of any right to trial by jury. A court may, within its discretion, order a trial by jury if the plaintiff's waiver was not intentional. In the absence of compelling reasons to the contrary, a court should grant relief from waiver if the issue is one normally tried by a jury. [Cox v. Masland & Sons, Inc., 607 F.2d 138 (5th Cir. 1979)] A jury demand may be withdrawn only if *all* parties consent.

a. Right to Jury Trial

1) The Seventh Amendment preserves the right to a jury trial in federal courts of facts in all "suits of common law" where the amount in controversy exceeds $20. The determination is historical and turns initially on whether the claim or relief was available at law or in equity in 1791. The Supreme Court has demonstrated a clear *preference for jury trial* in doubtful cases by holding that:

2) If legal and equitable claims are joined in one action involving common fact issues, the *legal claim should be tried first to the jury* and then the equitable claim to the court (the jury's finding on fact issues will bind the court in the equitable claim);

3) If a procedure formerly available only in equity, such as a class suit, interpleader, or derivative action, is now permitted under the Federal Rules for determining a "legal" claim, a *jury should try the fact issues*;

4) If damages are claimed as part of an action seeking an injunction, the defendant *cannot be denied a jury on the damages issues* on the ground that they are "incidental" to the equitable relief; and

5) If a new claim is created that did not exist at common law, a right to a jury trial will exist if the claim is similar to a claim for common law rights and remedies, unless the statute creating the right provides otherwise. [*See, e.g.,* Feltner v. Columbia Pictures Television, Inc., 523 U.S. 340 (1998)—statutory damages under Copyright Act to be tried to jury]

b. Jury Trials in Diversity Cases

1) Right to a Jury Trial
The federal court *must permit a jury trial* in any diversity "suit at common law" even though the state court would deny a jury (the Seventh Amendment prevails over state law in *Erie* situations); and a federal court will generally *follow the federal practice* of submitting issues of fact to the jury even though the state law assigns the issue to the court. [Byrd v. Blue Ridge Electric Cooperative, Inc., III.D.2.b., *supra*] If the state rule requires submission of a fact issue to the jury, the federal court may nonetheless direct a verdict under the usual standards or otherwise follow a federal practice that calls for the court to be the trier of fact. Likewise, state law is disregarded in determining the sufficiency of the evidence to create a jury issue; i.e., the directed verdict standards are always federal.

2) Motion for New Trial Based on Excessiveness of Verdict
The Supreme Court has required federal trial courts to apply a state standard when considering a motion for a new trial based on excessiveness of the verdict. [Gasperini v. Center for Humanities, Inc., III.D.3., *supra*] Under the Seventh Amendment, federal appellate review of whether a trial court properly denied a motion to set aside a verdict as excessive is limited to whether the trial court abused its discretion in denying the motion. In contrast, a jury's determination of the amount of a punitive damage award is reviewed de novo on appeal. [Cooper Industries, Inc. v. Leatherman Tool Group, Inc., 532 U.S. 424 (2001)]

c. Jury Size
In federal civil cases, a jury must begin with at least six jurors and not more than 12 jurors. [Fed. R. Civ. P. 48]

d. Jury Selection

1) Jury Venire
Jury selection process begins with individual potential jurors being summoned to appear in court. At this stage, the potential jurors together are called a "venire," and the jurors who will actually hear the case are chosen from the venire. The venire must be a reasonable cross-section of the community.

2) Voir Dire
Typically, the potential jurors will be asked to fill out a questionnaire to discover if the juror has some potential bias in the case (e.g., whether the juror knows any of the parties or attorneys involved in the case, whether the juror has been involved in a similar case, whether the juror owns stock in one of the parties, etc.). The juror likely will be asked questions individually also. This process is known as "voir dire."

3) Jury Challenges
If the questioning of a potential juror reveals that the juror is biased, that juror may be excused *for cause*. Bias may be actual or implied. Actual bias *may* be inferred by the juror's *deliberately* lying during voir dire. Implied (or presumed) bias arises when it is very unlikely that an average person in the juror's shoes would be impartial. Examples of implied bias include when the juror is closely related to one of the parties or attorneys, when the juror is employed by one of the parties, when the juror was the victim of a similar crime or suffered a similar injury, or when the juror has a financial stake in one of the parties. In such cases, the juror must be excused, even if the juror states that she can be fair and impartial.

e. Jury Instructions
At the close of the evidence, or sooner at the court's direction, a party may file proposed instructions. A party must timely object to a proposed instruction. Ordinarily, the judge will inform the parties of the instructions she intends to give, and the party will be given an opportunity to object outside of the jury's presence before the instruction is actually given.

f. Jury Deliberations
Jurors may take into the jury room *all papers or exhibits in evidence and their own*

notes. Instructions, pleadings, or other matters are generally improper for use in the jury room, except when they are formally admitted into evidence. A jury may not engage in experiments in the jury room, and jurors may not make private studies of documents or items outside of the jury room. Jurors may not view property or places involved in the case, except by court order. Jurors **must not communicate with any nonjuror** regarding the trial; in fact, **any** private communication between jurors and counsel or parties is serious misconduct that may lead to a new trial. It is error for a juror, in the jury room, to state facts not in evidence; however, jurors are entitled to evaluate evidence presented in light of their general knowledge and experience.

g. Jury Verdicts

The jury verdict must be unanimous unless the parties agree otherwise. The trial court has discretion to decide the type of verdict to be used (e.g., general vs. special; *see* below). [Fed. R. Civ. P. 49] Jurors cannot decide a verdict by flipping a coin or averaging (although averaging may be proper as a starting point for discussion). A juror may be excused for good cause (e.g., illness) without causing a mistrial, so long as at least six jurors participate in reaching the verdict unless the parties agree otherwise.

1) General Verdict

In a general verdict, the jury finds for the plaintiff or defendant and gives the amount of damages or relief due. A general verdict implies that all essential issues were found in favor of the prevailing party.

2) Special Verdict

In a special verdict, a jury is asked to make a finding on all material conclusions of fact, and the court applies the law. The procedure for a special verdict is to submit to the jury a series of questions regarding each ultimate fact. The court then makes legal conclusions based on those facts. Each question must deal with a single fact only and must not assume the existence of facts in dispute. A party waives objections to the form of the questions if she does not object when they are given. If the court fails, on request, to submit an issue to the jury, the case will be reversed unless the omission was harmless. If no request was made, a jury trial on the issue is generally held to be waived, and the court will decide it. [*See* Fed. R. Civ. P. 49]

3) General Verdict with Written Questions

Sometimes, a jury is asked to give a general verdict and also to answer specific written questions concerning certain ultimate facts in the case. The purpose is to ensure that the jury properly considered the important issues. The questions must be submitted with the general verdict to test the verdict's validity. [*See* Fed. R. Civ. P. 49(b)]

4) Erroneous Verdicts and Inconsistent Findings

Inconsistent determinations in a verdict make the verdict erroneous if the determinations are irreconcilable (e.g., when a verdict is rendered against a person vicariously liable and the principal wrongdoer is exonerated). Any clear compromise verdict is also erroneous, as is any verdict that simply finds for the plaintiff "for actual damages suffered." When a verdict is erroneous, the jury may be asked to reconsider it, or a new trial may be ordered. When answers to special interrogatories are consistent with each other, but one or more is inconsistent with the general verdict, the court may (i) enter judgment in accord with the special interrogatories; (ii) have the jury reconsider its answers or verdict; or (iii) order a new trial. When the answers to the special interrogatories are inconsistent with each other and one or more is inconsistent with the general verdict, judgment cannot be entered, and the court must either have the jury reconsider its answers and verdict, or the court may order a new trial. A jury may completely change its answers or verdict when redeliberation is ordered.

5) Juror Misconduct

A new trial is appropriate if a juror *gave false testimony on voir dire or concealed material facts relating to his qualifications to serve*. A verdict will not be set aside if the alleged misconduct was harmless.

2. Consolidation and Separate Trials

Rule 42(a) allows the court to consolidate actions then before it when the actions have a common question of law or fact. Rule 42(b) allows the court to order separate trials of any claim, cross-claim, counterclaim, or other issues when such separation will foster judicial economy.

3. Involuntary Dismissals

On the defendant's motion or on its own motion, a court may order an involuntary dismissal against a plaintiff for failure to: (i) prosecute; (ii) comply with the Federal Rules; or (iii) comply with a court order. [Fed. R. Civ. P. 41(b)] An involuntary dismissal is with prejudice, meaning that it operates as adjudication on the merits, unless the court orders otherwise.

4. Voluntary Dismissals

The plaintiff can give up his case voluntarily by way of a voluntary dismissal, either with or without leave of court. [Fed. R. Civ. P. 41(a)]

a. Without Leave of Court

If the defendant has not answered or filed a motion for summary judgment, the plaintiff may dismiss her case by filing a notice of dismissal. A dismissal by notice is without prejudice unless the plaintiff has previously dismissed any federal or state court action on the same claim, in which case the dismissal by notice is with prejudice. (This is known as the "two dismissal rule.") The parties may also stipulate to a voluntary dismissal at any time. A stipulated dismissal is without prejudice unless the stipulation states otherwise. The plaintiff is charged with costs only if she files the action again after the dismissal.

b. With Leave of Court

When a voluntary dismissal without leave of court is not available (i.e., there has been an answer or a motion for summary judgment), the court has discretion to grant dismissal on such terms and conditions as the court deems proper. The dismissal is without prejudice unless the court specifies otherwise. If there is a *counterclaim pending in the action*, there can be *no dismissal* over the defendant's objection *unless the counterclaim remains pending*.

5. Offer of Judgment

Under Rule 68, a party defending against a claim or counterclaim may serve, at least 14 days before trial, *a formal offer to have a judgment entered against it on specified terms with costs then accrued*, thereby settling the case out of court. A defending party may also serve an offer of judgment after it has been determined to be liable to another party, but before actual damages have been set; such an offer must be made at least 14 days before the hearing on damages. If the claiming party rejects the offer, and the ultimate judgment is less favorable to him, he must pay costs incurred after the offer was made. So long as the offer does not explicitly or implicitly *exclude* costs, it is a valid offer. Evidence of an unaccepted offer is not admissible except in a proceeding to determine costs. Unlike the practice in a number of states, Rule 68 allows only defending parties to make a formal offer to have a judgment entered voluntarily.

6. Summary Judgment

a. Standard

Summary judgment may be granted if, from the pleadings, affidavits, and discovery materials, it appears that there is *no genuine dispute of material fact* and the moving party is entitled to judgment as a matter of law. [Fed. R. Civ. P. 56] The court may not decide disputed fact issues on a motion for summary judgment; if there is a genuinely disputed material fact (meaning a dispute backed by evidence on both sides of the issue), the case must go to trial.

b. Applicable to All Civil Actions

Rule 56 applies to all parties and civil actions that are subject to the Federal Rules including actions by and against the United States, and to all types of claims that appear in a civil action (counterclaim, cross-claim, declaratory judgment, injunction, and interpleader).

c. Time

Unless local rule or court order dictates otherwise, a party may file a motion for summary judgment any time until 30 days after close of all discovery. [Fed. R. Civ. P. 56(b)] If a motion is premature, the court may defer ruling on it.

d. Partial

Summary judgment may be partial (as well as complete).
Example: Summary judgment may be rendered on the issue of liability alone although there is a genuine issue as to the amount of damages.

e. Support

The motion may be supported or opposed with affidavits or other declarations made under penalty of perjury, depositions, sworn pleadings, admissions, answers to interrogatories, or other materials in the record.

f. Affidavits

1) Affidavits or declarations must: (i) be made on *personal knowledge*; (ii) set forth such facts as would be *admissible* in evidence; and (iii) show the affiant is *competent to testify*.

2) A party *may object* that the material cited to support or dispute a fact *cannot be presented in a form that would be admissible* in evidence.

3) If a party fails to support an assertion of fact or fails properly to address another party's assertion of fact, the court may *consider the fact undisputed* for purposes of the motion, *grant summary judgment* if appropriate, *give an opportunity to address the fact*, or issue any other appropriate order.

4) When the party opposing the motion shows by affidavit or declaration that he cannot present facts, he *may state the reasons* for their unavailability or declarations. The court may then *deny* the motion, *order a continuance* to permit affidavits to be obtained or depositions to be taken, or *make such other order* as is just.

5) When affidavits or declarations are made in *bad faith*, the court may:

    a) Order the party using them to *reimburse* the other party for those expenses that the affidavits caused him, including attorneys' fees.

    b) Adjudge in *contempt* the offending party or attorney.

g. Nonappealability
The denial of a motion for summary judgment is generally not appealable.

h. Relationship to Motion to Dismiss
A motion pursuant to Rule 12(b)(6) to dismiss a complaint for failure to state a claim upon which relief can be granted differs from a motion for summary judgment in that the former is addressed only to the *legal sufficiency of the complaint*.

i. Relationship to Motion for Judgment on the Pleadings
A motion for judgment on the pleadings presents the moving party's contention that *on the face of the pleadings*, he is entitled to judgment. Theoretically, matters outside the pleadings are irrelevant to a decision on either of these motions. However, a party making such a motion and accompanying it with an affidavit or other matters outside the pleadings may in reality be making a motion for summary judgment, putting the wrong label on the motion. The court is expressly authorized to treat such a motion as one for summary judgment and to conduct subsequent proceedings thereon in accordance with the rule on summary judgment, giving the parties full opportunity to present material made relevant by that rule.

7. Motion for Judgment as a Matter of Law (Formerly Directed Verdict)
Historically, a judge could direct a particular verdict whenever the evidence—viewed in the light most favorable to the party against whom the verdict was directed (including legitimate inferences in that party's favor) and without considering the credibility of witnesses—was such that reasonable persons could come to only one conclusion. Today, this can be done pursuant to a party's *motion for judgment as a matter of law* ("JMOL"). The motion may be made by any party any time before submission of the case to the jury, and the moving party must specify the judgment sought and the law and facts on which the party is entitled to judgment. The motion may be granted only after the nonmoving party *"has been fully heard"* on the matter. To grant the motion, the court must find that *"a reasonable jury would not have a legally sufficient basis* to find for the [nonmoving] party on that issue." [Fed. R. Civ. P. 50(a)]

8. **Renewed Motion for Judgment as a Matter of Law (Formerly Judgment Notwithstanding the Verdict ("JNOV"))**

    Historically, a party against whom judgment was entered could move for JNOV if the judgment was based upon a verdict that reasonable persons could not have reached and if the moving party had sought a directed verdict at the close of all the evidence. Now, the motion for JNOV is called a *renewed motion for judgment as a matter of law*. It must be filed no later than 28 days after entry of judgment and the party making the renewed motion must have moved for judgment as a matter of law *at some time during the trial*. In theory, a party may raise only those issues raised in the motion for a JMOL. The standard is the same as for the motion for judgment as a matter of law. [Fed. R. Civ. P. 50(b)]

9. **Motion for New Trial**

    A motion for a new trial must be filed no later than 28 days after judgment is entered. Within that period, the court may order a new trial on its own motion. [Fed. R. Civ. P. 59]

    a. **Reasons for Granting New Trial**

        The court may grant a new trial because of an error during the trial (usually going to the admissibility of evidence or the propriety of the instructions), because the verdict is against the weight of the evidence (limited to cases where the judge finds the verdict seriously erroneous), because of juror misconduct, or because the verdict is excessive or inadequate.

        1) **Remittitur**

            If the trial judge believes that the jury's compensatory damages award is so excessive as to "shock the conscience" (or in a diversity case if the award meets the state standard for excessiveness), the judge may order a new trial or may offer the alternative of remittitur. When offered remittitur, the plaintiff is given the choice between accepting an award less than that given her by the jury or submitting to a new trial. Note that the court cannot simply lower the award given by the jury. It must offer the plaintiff the alternative of a lower award or a new trial. [Hetzel v. Prince Williams County, 523 U.S. 208 (1998)]

        2) **Additur**

            If the trial judge believes that the jury's compensatory damages are inadequate, she may *not* offer the defendant the choice of accepting a higher award or submitting to a new trial. "Additur" has been held to violate the Seventh Amendment (which is not applicable to the states). However, inadequate damages may be a basis for a new trial.

    b. **Renewed Motion for Judgment as a Matter of Law with Motion for New Trial**

        When a renewed motion for judgment as a matter of law and a motion for a new trial are made *in the alternative* and the renewed motion is granted, the court must rule hypothetically on the new trial motion so that no remand is required if the ruling on the judgment as a matter of law is subsequently reversed on appeal.

10. **Effect of Failure to Move for a Renewed Judgment as a Matter of Law or for a New Trial**

    If a party fails to move for either a renewed judgment as a matter of law or for a new trial on the basis of insufficiency of the evidence, that party is precluded from raising the question of evidentiary sufficiency on appeal. [Unitherm Food Systems, Inc. v. Swift-Eckrich, Inc., 546 U.S. 394 (2006)]

11. Judgment on Partial Findings

In a ***nonjury*** trial, the judge may enter a judgment as a matter of law against a party on any issue whenever there are ***sufficient facts to resolve the issue***, provided that the ***party has been fully heard*** on the issue. If the issue is dispositive of a claim or defense, the judge may enter judgment as a matter of law against a party on that claim or defense. The judge may also wait until the close of all evidence to render judgment. Because the judge is acting as the trier of fact, she decides issues of disputed facts, and she may consider the credibility of witnesses. The judgment must be supported by findings of fact and conclusions of law. [Fed. R. Civ. P. 52]

IX. ATTACK ON THE JUDGMENT AT THE TRIAL COURT LEVEL

A. RELIEF FROM JUDGMENT OR ORDER

1. Clerical Mistakes

A clerical error is one arising from oversight or omission, and may occur in judgments, orders, or other parts of the record. The court can correct clerical errors ***on its own motion or the motion of any party***. [Fed. R. Civ. P. 60(a)] There is no time limit for the correction of clerical errors, and the court order correcting the error dates back to the time judgment was entered. As a result, the battle over what constitutes a clerical error is acute.

2. Motions to Amend Prior Orders or Renew Prior Motions

Motions to amend a final order (i.e., one that disposes of the litigation) may be brought under Federal Rule 59(e) when: (i) new evidence has been discovered that was not previously available; (ii) there has been an intervening change in controlling law; (iii) there is a need to correct a clear error of law or fact; or (iv) there is a need to prevent manifest injustice. Such a motion must be brought within 28 days of the order; otherwise, the party must seek relief from judgment under Rule 60 or appeal. It should be noted that an order that does not dispose of all parties and claims is not a final order and may be modified under Federal Rule 54(b).

3. Other Grounds for Relief from Judgment

On motion and just terms, the court may relieve a party from a final judgment or order on the following grounds:

(i) ***Mistake, inadvertence, surprise, or excusable neglect***;

(ii) ***Newly discovered evidence*** that by due diligence ***could not have been discovered*** in time to move for a new trial;

(iii) ***Fraud, misrepresentation, or other misconduct*** of an adverse party;

(iv) The judgment is ***void***;

(v) The judgment has been *satisfied, released, or discharged*; a *prior judgment* on which it is based has been *reversed or otherwise vacated*; or it is *no longer equitable* that the judgment should have prospective application; or

(vi) *Any other reason* justifying relief from the operation of the judgment.

For grounds (i), (ii), and (iii), the motion must be made within a reasonable time not to exceed one year; for the other grounds, the motion must be made within a reasonable time. [Fed. R. Civ. P. 60(b)] *Note:* Ground (iv) does not apply simply because the judgment was erroneous; such errors are to be remedied on appeal. Ground (iv) applies only if there was a fundamental flaw such as lack of jurisdiction or deprivation of due process by failure to give notice or opportunity to be heard. [United Student Aid Funds, Inc. v. Espinoza, 559 U.S. 260 (2010)]

B. INDEPENDENT ACTION IN EQUITY TO SET ASIDE THE JUDGMENT

A court, in its discretion, may entertain an independent action to relieve a party from a judgment or order. The plaintiff must show that he is likely to win if a new action is allowed. The only advantage of an independent action is that it will not be barred by the specific time limits outlined in A., above. However, the aggrieved party must act promptly once he knows or should know of the ground for relief. An independent action will be rejected if a motion to set aside the judgment has been rejected on the merits.

X. FINAL JUDGMENT AND APPELLATE REVIEW

A. JUDGMENT

1. Relief that May Be Given

Except in default cases, the court is not limited to the demand for relief in the pleadings and may give *any relief* that is appropriate based on the evidence. Thus, damages may exceed the plaintiff's demand and an injunction may be entered although not requested. Interest on a money judgment is awarded at the rate provided under state law from the date of judgment.

2. Judgment on Multiple Claims or Parties

When multiple claims or multiple parties are involved in an action, the court may enter a final judgment as to fewer than all of the claims or parties only on an *express determination that there is no just reason for delay* and an entry of judgment. *Unless* the trial judge makes such an *express determination*, the order determining the merits of fewer than all of the claims or dismissing fewer than all of the parties is *not a final judgment and is not appealable*. This is in accord with the traditional policy against piecemeal appeals. [Fed. R. Civ. P. 54(b)]

3. Final Decision on Merits May Be Valid Despite Lack of Subject Matter Jurisdiction

Occasionally, lack of subject matter jurisdiction is not raised until the decision is final and all appeals are completed. The question then is whether the decision may be collaterally attacked—i.e., be set aside in an independent proceeding or treated as invalid in a later case. The factors that must be balanced in making this determination are: (i) lack of jurisdiction is clear; (ii) jurisdiction depends on a question of law, not fact; (iii) the court is of limited, not general, jurisdiction; (iv) the question of jurisdiction was not litigated; and (v) strong policy exists against the court acting beyond its jurisdiction.

B. TIME FOR APPEALS

Under Rules 3 and 4 of the Federal Rules of Appellate Procedure, an appeal may be taken by filing a notice of appeal with the district court *within 30 days* from the entry of the judgment appealed from (60 days where the United States is a party to the action). However, if a *timely* (within 28 days) renewed motion for judgment as a matter of law, a motion for new trial, or a motion to set aside or amend the judgment is made, the running of the 30 days is terminated. Upon the entry of an order based on such post-trial motions, a new 30 day period begins to run. A notice of appeal filed during the pendency of such a post-trial motion will become effective on final disposition of the motion by the trial court.

1. Extension of Time for Appeal

Upon a showing of excusable neglect, made within 30 days after the time to appeal has expired, the district court may extend the time for filing a notice of appeal by 30 days from the time it would otherwise have run, or 14 days from the date of the order granting the extension, whichever is later. The court also may reopen the time to appeal for a period of 14 days when (i) the party did not timely receive notice of entry of judgment; (ii) the motion for extension is filed within 180 days of the judgment or within 14 days of receiving notice of judgment, whichever is earlier; and (iii) the opposing party will not be prejudiced.

C. REVIEWABLE ORDER

Generally, *only final orders* are reviewable on appeal. A final order is one that disposes of the whole case on its merits, by rendering final judgment not only as to all the parties but as to all causes of action involved. [Cunningham v. Hamilton County, 527 U.S. 198 (1999)—order imposing sanctions on attorney is not a final order even when the attorney no longer represents a party to the case] However, certain interlocutory orders are *also reviewable*:

1. Interlocutory Orders as of Right

a. Injunction

A party may appeal as of right any order granting, continuing, modifying, refusing, dissolving, or refusing to dissolve or modify an injunction.

b. Receivers

A party may appeal as of right any order appointing a receiver, or refusing to wind up or take steps to accomplish purposes of receiverships (e.g., directing sales or other disposals of property).

c. Admiralty

An order finding liability but leaving damages to be assessed later in admiralty cases may be appealed.

d. Patent Infringement

A patent infringement order where only an accounting is wanting may be appealed.

e. **Property Possession**

A party may appeal as of right any order whereby possession of property is changed or affected, such as orders dissolving writs of attachment and the like.

2. **Interlocutory Appeals Act**

Review under the Interlocutory Appeals Act [28 U.S.C. §1292] is *discretionary* and may be available when: (i) the trial judge certifies that the interlocutory order involves a controlling question of law, as to which there is substantial ground for difference of opinion, and immediate appeal from the order may materially advance the ultimate termination of the litigation; and (ii) the court of appeals then agrees to allow the appeal. A party obtaining such a certificate from the trial judge must, within *10 days,* apply to the court of appeals, where two out of three judges must agree to hear the appeal.

3. **Fewer than All Claims or Parties**

(*See* A.2., *supra.*)

4. **Collateral Order Rule**

If the claim or issue is separable from and collateral to the main suit and is too important to require deferring appellate review, it may be classified as a judgment in a separate ("collateral") proceeding and thus be appealable. [Puerto Rico Aqueduct & Sewer Authority v. Metcalf & Eddy, Inc., 506 U.S. 139 (1993)—governmental entity's claim of Eleventh Amendment immunity from suit denied; issue appealable immediately under collateral order rule because failure to permit interlocutory appeal would effectively eviscerate Eleventh Amendment immunity from suit in federal court by requiring entity to litigate to final judgment before appealing]

5. **Review of Nonappealable Orders by Writ**

In exceptional cases, nearly all jurisdictions allow some circumvention of the final judgment rule through the appellate writs of mandamus and prohibition. Mandamus commands a trial judge to act, and prohibition commands the judge to refrain from acting. The writs are available only if an appeal will be insufficient to correct a problem and the trial court's actions constitute a serious abuse of power that must be immediately corrected.

6. **Certification of Class Actions**

A district court's order granting or denying certification of a class action can be appealed within 14 days of entry of the order. [Fed. R. Civ. P. 23(f)] The court of appeals has complete discretion in deciding whether to hear the appeal. If the court decides to hear the appeal, proceedings are *not stayed* at the district court unless the district court or court of appeals so orders.

D. STANDARDS OF REVIEW

1. **On Matters of Law**

On appeal, when it is alleged that the trial judge erred on a pure matter of law, the appellate court may substitute its judgment for that of the trial judge. This is called a de novo review.

2. **On Questions of Fact**

In a bench trial, the trial judge will make findings of fact (*see* VIII.K.11., *supra*). The trial judge's findings of fact will not be disturbed on appeal unless they were "clearly erroneous." [Fed. R. Civ. P. 52(a)(6)] A factual determination by the jury is afforded even greater weight on appeal. Findings of fact by a jury will be affirmed on appeal if, while viewing the evidence in the light most favorable to affirming the jury's verdict, a reasonable jury could have reached the same conclusion. (This is similar to the standard a trial judge faces when deciding whether to grant a judgment as a matter of law; *see* VIII.K.7., *supra*.)

3.   On Mixed Questions of Law and Fact

Mixed questions of law or fact are reviewed de novo. It is often difficult to determine whether the question is purely factual, purely legal, or mixed. Generally speaking, whether a set of facts meets a legal definition (e.g., whether the use of copyrighted material is "fair use" under copyright law) is considered to be a mixed question of law and fact.

4.   On Discretionary Matters

Many decisions a trial judge makes are left to her discretion (e.g., whether to consolidate or sever cases, whether to grant leave to amend a pleading, etc.). On appeal, the standard of review is whether the judge "abused her discretion" in making her decision. This means that the judge's ruling will not be overturned on appeal unless is it plainly wrong or without an appropriate basis.

E.   STAY PENDING APPEAL

Stays are governed generally by Rule 62.

1.   Execution

No execution on judgments is allowed for 30 days after entry except injunctions or receiverships, which are not held up unless otherwise ordered by a court. If the case follows the usual route to appeal, the appellate court ordinarily will continue the stay or issue a new stay.

2.   Bond

A bond or other security is required in sufficient size to satisfy the judgment, costs, interest, and damages for delay, should the appeal be dismissed or affirmed. Upon filing such a bond, an appellant has a stay pending appeal.

3.   Injunction Order

a.   Power of Trial Court

When appeal is taken from an interlocutory or final judgment granting, dissolving, or denying an injunction, the court may suspend, modify, restore, or grant an injunction during the pendency of the appeal upon such bond or other security as it considers sufficient to protect the adverse party.

b.   Power of Appellate Court

An appellate court has similar power to grant a stay or injunction pending appeal, or to vacate one granted by the trial court, or to make any order appropriate to preserve the status quo or the effectiveness of the judgment subsequently to be entered. Ordinarily such a stay or injunction pending appeal must be sought in the trial court before the appellate court will entertain it.

F.   SUPREME COURT JURISDICTION

1. **Court of Appeals Cases**
   Cases in the courts of appeals may be reviewed by the Supreme Court:

   (i) ***By certiorari*** granted upon petition of any party to any civil or criminal case, before or after rendition of judgment or decree; or

   (ii) ***By certification*** by the court of appeals of any question of law in any civil or criminal case as to which it desires instructions. Upon such certification, the Supreme Court may give binding instructions or may require the entire record to be sent to it for decision of the entire case.

   [28 U.S.C. §1254]

2. **Cases from Highest State Court**
   Final judgments rendered by the highest court of a state in which a decision could be had may be reviewed by the Supreme Court ***by certiorari*** in the following circumstances:

   (i) Where the validity of a ***treaty or federal statute*** is drawn into question; or

   (ii) Where the validity of a ***state statute*** is drawn into question on the ground that it is repugnant to the federal Constitution or to a treaty or federal statute; or

   (iii) Where any ***title, right, privilege, or immunity*** is claimed under the federal Constitution or treaty or federal statute.

   [28 U.S.C. §1257] Only the Supreme Court may hear appeals coming from the state court system.

XI. EFFECTS OF JUDGMENT ON FUTURE CASES

A. CLAIM PRECLUSION (RES JUDICATA)

1. **Definition**
   Once a ***final*** judgment ***on the merits*** has been rendered on a particular cause of action, the claimant is barred by claim preclusion (res judicata) from asserting the ***same cause*** of action in a later lawsuit.

2. **Terminology Used to Describe Effect—"Merger" and "Bar"**
   When the ***claimant wins*** the earlier lawsuit, the cause of action is said to have been "***merged***" into the judgment. When the ***defendant wins,*** the claimant is said to be "***barred***" by the earlier adverse judgment. Both terms simply mean that the ***claimant cannot sue again*** on the same cause.

3. **Requirements for "Merger" and "Bar"**
   Before merger or bar apply, it must be shown that (i) the earlier judgment is a ***valid, final judgment*** "***on the merits***"; (ii) the cases are brought by the ***same claimant*** against the ***same defendant***; and (iii) the ***same "cause of action"*** (or "claim") is involved in the later lawsuit.

4. **Valid, Final Judgment**

    Claim preclusion (res judicata) flows from the entry in an earlier case of a valid, final judgment "on the merits." A judgment is valid as long as it is not void (e.g., for lack of subject matter jurisdiction). Whether a judgment is final for these purposes is generally the same as whether it is final for purposes of taking an appeal. (*See* X.C., *supra.*)

5. **"On the Merits"**

    Usually, the more difficult issue is whether the valid, final judgment is considered "on the merits" for purposes of claim preclusion. Often, a judgment will be based on actual litigation between the parties, but it can also be a default judgment entered as a penalty against a party (such as a dismissal for willful violation of discovery orders) or an involuntary dismissal closely related to the merits (such as for failure to state a claim upon which relief may be granted). In contrast, other involuntary dismissals not involving the merits (such as those based on lack of jurisdiction, improper venue, or failure to join an indispensable party) are not a judgment on the merits and do not have claim preclusive effect. Although Federal Rule 41(b) indicates that all dismissals are to operate "as an adjudication on the merits" unless based on jurisdiction, improper venue, or failure to join an indispensable party, the Supreme Court has held that Rule 41(b) does ***not*** govern whether the judgment is "on the merits" for purposes of claim preclusion. [Semtek, Inc. v. Lockheed Martin Corp., 531 U.S. 497 (2001)] Thus, jurisdictions may take different views of whether a particular dismissal—e.g., dismissal because the statute of limitations has run—is deemed "on the merits" for purposes of claim preclusion.

6. **Same Claimant Versus Same Defendant**

    Traditionally, claim preclusion applies only if the earlier case and the latter case are brought by the same claimant against the same defendant. It is not enough that the same litigants were also parties in the previous case; they must have been in the same configuration of one asserting a claim against the other.

    Examples: 1) In Case One, A sues Z to recover damages for personal injuries suffered in an automobile collision between the two. A valid, final judgment on the merits is entered. Now A sues Z again, this time to recover damages for property damage inflicted in the same wreck. Assuming that both cases involve the same "cause of action" (discussed immediately below), claim preclusion would apply, because both cases were brought by A against Z.

    2) In Case One, A sues Z to recover damages for personal injuries suffered in an automobile collision between the two. A valid, final judgment on the merits is entered. Now Z sues A to recover for her personal injuries suffered in the same wreck. Claim preclusion ***does not apply.*** Here, the second case is brought ***by Z against A, while the first case was brought by A against Z.***

    Note: Z may be barred from asserting her claim because of the compulsory counterclaim rule, but not because of claim preclusion. The compulsory counterclaim rule requires a defending party to assert against the claimant ***in the pending case*** any claims arising from the same transaction or occurrence as the claimant's claim. (*See* VIII.F.3.c., *supra.*)

7. **"Cause of Action"**

    While various tests have been used to define "cause of action," the modern approach is to require assertion of all claims arising out of the same transaction or occurrence that is the subject matter of a claim asserted by the claimant.

a. Common Examples

1) Accidents

The claimant seeks to recover separate damages from the same accident in separate actions. The claimant may not seek damages for neck injuries in one action and leg injuries in another. Likewise, most courts would not permit the claimant to sue for personal injuries and property damage in separate actions. However, if the claimant is insured for property damage and, after payment of the claim, the claimant assigns her cause of action for property damage to the insurance company, most courts would consider the property damage claim and personal injury claim as two separate causes of action.

2) Installment Obligations

In the situation of a series of obligations, such as installment payments on a debt or lease, the claimant is required to sue on all installments due at the time of suit, but not later installments. But if the contract has an acceleration clause that makes all installments due if earlier ones are not paid, the claimant must sue for all installments (unless the acceleration clause is optional and the claimant elects not to exercise the option). This rule does not apply if the installment obligations are represented by separate notes; in such cases, suit as each note comes due represents suit on a separate cause of action.

B. ISSUE PRECLUSION (COLLATERAL ESTOPPEL)

1. Definition

A judgment binds the plaintiff or defendant (or their privies) in subsequent actions on different causes of action between them (or their privies) as to *issues actually litigated* and *essential to the judgment* in the first action. This conclusive effect of the first judgment is called issue preclusion (or collateral estoppel). Note that issue preclusion is narrower than claim preclusion. Claim preclusion focuses on something relatively large—the scope of a "*cause of action*." If it applies, the result is usually to bar the claimant from asserting a second case. Issue preclusion, in contrast, focuses on something relatively narrow—*an issue* that was litigated and determined in the first case, and that is relevant in a second case. With issue preclusion, the issue is deemed established in the second case without need to proffer evidence on it.

2. Requirements

a. Final Judgment

The traditional view is that the final judgment requirement for issue preclusion (collateral estoppel) is very similar to the final judgment requirement for claim preclusion. (*See* A.4.-5., *supra*.) However, recent decisions have relaxed the final judgment rule for issue preclusion. A judgment may be "final" even if it is subject to post-trial motions or appeals. Several factors may be weighed in determining whether to give preclusive effect to a judgment not entered as final, such as whether the prior decision was adequately deliberated, whether the court's decision is supported by reasoned opinion, and whether the prior decision was subject to appeal or is on appeal.

b.   Issue Actually Litigated and Determined
The issue on which issue preclusion applies must actually have been litigated and determined in the previous case. Thus, if a *default* or *consent* judgment is entered, there is generally no issue preclusion as to the fact issues that would have been tried had the case gone forward.

c.   Issue Was Essential to the Judgment

1)   It must be clear exactly how the issue was decided by the trier of fact.
      Example: P sues for personal injuries based on D's negligence. D pleads contributory negligence as a defense. If the jury renders a general verdict for D, the decision will have no issue preclusive effect in a subsequent case involving either P or D's negligence, because there is no way of knowing whether the jury found that D was not negligent or that P was contributorily negligent, or both.

      Compare: However, if the jury found for P for the full amount of his injuries, it clearly had to decide that D was negligent and P was not. Thus, both issues could have issue preclusive effect in a later case.

2)   The judgment must depend on the issue of fact decided.
      Example: If, in a personal injury action, the jury specially finds that neither P nor D was negligent—thereby rendering a verdict for D—the finding that P was not negligent was *not* essential to judgment and will have no issue preclusive effect in a later suit.

3)   Note that the "essential fact" rule tends to reduce the number of cases in which issue preclusion can be applied, thus eliminating some of the burden from the first suit.

d.   Due Process and Mutuality Considerations

1)   *Against* **Whom Is Issue Preclusion Used?**
      Issue preclusion may be asserted *only against* someone who was a party (or in privity with a party) to the previous case (the case in which the issue was actually litigated and determined). This requirement is imposed by due process, and thus is the rule in every jurisdiction.

2)   *By* **Whom Is Issue Preclusion Used?**
      Under the traditional "mutuality" rule, only someone who was a party (or in privity with a party) in the previous case can use issue preclusion. This requirement is not imposed by due process, however, and has been subject to modification in certain circumstances to allow nonparties to take advantage of a prior judgment.

3)   **Exceptions to Mutuality When Judgment Used Defensively**
      When a nonparty wishes to utilize a prior judgment *to avoid liability* in a subsequent suit, there are often compelling reasons for allowing her to do so. *Fairness* to the party being bound will also be considered.

Example: If P unsuccessfully sues a person primarily liable (e.g., an employee), P's later suit against a person secondarily liable (e.g., against the employer for the employee's acts) will be barred by issue preclusion in virtually all courts. Similarly, if P unsuccessfully sues a person secondarily liable, there is little reason why the person primarily liable should be subjected to a separate suit, and most courts so hold.

4) Exceptions to Mutuality When Judgment Used Offensively—Consider Fairness

Courts have been very reluctant to permit a nonparty to use issue preclusion to aid him (as a plaintiff) to obtain relief.

Example: Suppose one of many passengers in a public vehicle successfully sues the driver for injuries received in an accident, and other passengers wish to utilize the judgment to establish liability. While a few courts have permitted such use, others refuse. They fear a situation in which 10 plaintiffs each sue and lose, and the 11th plaintiff wins, and all other potential plaintiffs seek to ignore the first 10 suits and rely solely on the 11th; application of issue preclusion in such a situation is considered **unfair and demeaning to the legal system**.

However, the United States Supreme Court, in *Parklane Hosiery Co. v. Shore,* 439 U.S. 322 (1979), upheld the use of issue preclusion offensively. In the first action, brought by the Securities and Exchange Commission, the defendant was held to have violated the federal securities laws. The second suit, brought by a private plaintiff against the same defendant, alleged damages resulting from the same violation established in the first action. The Court allowed the latter plaintiff to rely on issue preclusion to establish the existence of the violation since under all the circumstances it **was fair** to the defendant to do so. Thus, in cases of **nonmutual** issue preclusion used **offensively**, the key often is whether such use is **fair and equitable**.

C. CLAIM AND ISSUE PRECLUSION IN SPECIAL SITUATIONS

1. Judgments for Specific Performance
Rules of bar and issue preclusion apply in actions brought for specific performance and the like. However, **merger does not apply** because such a judgment, unlike one for money, cannot be enforced by bringing a suit on the judgment. Thus, if the defendant fails to obey the first judgment, the claimant may sue again.

2. In Rem Judgments
If a court exercises in rem jurisdiction over some property or status within its control, and if proper notice has been given to all interested persons, the judgment as to title or status is **binding on all persons**.

3. Quasi In Rem Judgments
A quasi in rem judgment determines the rights of the parties only in the specific property

before the court. *No personal judgment* is granted against anyone, and *no other property is affected*.

D. WHICH PERSONS ARE BOUND BY A JUDGMENT?

1. Parties Are Bound

Parties are persons named as parties who have the power to control the action or who, if they lack capacity, are represented by guardians. *Nonparties* normally are *not bound*. Even where the lawsuit raises an issue as to performance or rights, nonparties normally are not bound by the judgment; e.g., an assignor who has no control over the suit and no interest in the outcome, or an employee who allegedly was negligent, where the suit is filed only against the employer.

2. Privies to Parties Are Bound by Issue Preclusion

Persons who control the litigation and who will be affected by the outcome are bound by issue preclusion as to *all issues litigated*. For example, if the owner of a patent assumes control of an infringement suit brought by her licensee against a competitor, and the court holds the patent invalid, the owner is barred on that issue should she sue the same competitor. The owner has had her day in court.

3. Represented Parties May Be Bound by Claim Preclusion

Persons whose interests are represented and privities also may be bound by claim preclusion. For example, *beneficiaries* are bound by an action brought or defended on their behalf by the fiduciary, provided the fiduciary is operating within her authority. *Holders of future interests* are bound. *Unborn or unascertained* persons having future interests in property are bound by judgments as to the property if their interests are identical to those of parties to the action, or if a special representative is appointed for them. This rule reflects public policy favoring free marketability of property. *Members of a class* are bound by a valid class action judgment. *Successors in interest* are bound. *Transferees of property* are in privity with prior owners and thus are bound by a prior judgment concerning the property. This rule protects the public as to security of titles.

Note, however, that one is not barred from asserting a claim simply because she is asserting the same claim that a previous claimant has already litigated.

Example: Citizen A sues to challenge a tax as unconstitutional and loses. Citizen B is not barred from suing to challenge the same tax on the same basis unless Citizen A and Citizen B are in privity or Citizen A represented Citizen B in bringing the first suit. [Richards v. Jefferson County, 517 U.S. 793 (1996)]

In *vicarious liability* situations (employer-employee, principal-agent, insurer-insured) a judgment exonerating either generally is held to preclude an action on the same claim against the other.

Example: P sues Principal claiming injuries as a result of Agent's negligence. P alleges Agent was acting in the course and scope of agency at the time of harm. A judgment in favor of Principal on the ground that Agent was not negligent would in some jurisdictions preclude suing Agent thereafter on the theory that Agent was negligent in causing the harm. If P first sued Agent and Agent was found not negligent, P should thereafter be barred from suing Principal for the negligence of Agent causing the harm.

E. WHICH CHOICE OF LAW RULES APPLY TO PRECLUSION QUESTIONS?

Preclusion questions—whether claim preclusion or issue preclusion—always involve at least two cases. One case has gone to a valid, final judgment on the merits. Preclusion law determines whether that judgment (in "case one") precludes litigation of any matters in a pending case ("case two"). (By the way, note that "case one" was not necessarily filed first; it is "case one" because it went to judgment first.) A choice of law issue arises when case two is brought in a different jurisdiction than case one; i.e., what law does the court in case two use to determine whether the judgment in case one is entitled to claim or issue preclusion?

1. Case One Decided in State Court

When case one has been decided in state court, the court in case two (whether state or federal) generally will apply the claim or issue preclusion law of the jurisdiction that decided case one.

Example: Judgment is entered in a case in Kansas. A second case is brought in Missouri. To decide whether that case is subject to claim or issue preclusion, the judge in Missouri should generally apply Kansas law on claim or issue preclusion.

2. Case One Decided in Federal Court Under Diversity Jurisdiction

What if case one was decided in a federal court under diversity jurisdiction? Here, the Supreme Court held that the court in case two should apply federal law (because a federal court decided case one). However, it also held that usually the federal law in such an instance would be the state law of the state in which the federal court sat.

Example: After plaintiff files suit in a California state court, defendant removes the case to federal court based on diversity jurisdiction. Plaintiff's federal court case is then involuntarily dismissed because it is barred by California's statute of limitations. Plaintiff files the same claims in state court in Maryland (which has a longer statute of limitations). In determining whether to dismiss the case under claim preclusion, the Maryland state court should look to federal law. But, despite the language of Federal Rule 41(G), federal law would adopt the California law (unless "state law is incompatible with federal interests"). Because California law would allow the plaintiff to file in a jurisdiction with a longer statute of limitations, the Maryland court should not dismiss under claim preclusion. [Semtek, Inc. v. Lockheed Martin Corp., A.5., *supra*]

CONSTITUTIONAL LAW

barbri

CONSTITUTIONAL LAW

TABLE OF CONTENTS

CONSTITUTIONAL LAW

PART ONE: POWERS OF THE FEDERAL GOVERNMENT

I. THE JUDICIAL POWER

A. ARTICLE III

The federal government is a government of limited powers, which means that for federal action to be legitimate, it must be authorized. The Constitution is the instrument that authorizes the federal government to act. Thus, whenever a question involves action by an entity of the federal government, the action will be valid only if it is authorized by the Constitution. The Constitution authorizes a federal court system in Article III, which provides that federal courts shall have judicial power over all *"cases and controversies"*:

1. Arising under the Constitution, laws, or treaties of the United States;

2. Affecting ambassadors, other public ministers, and consuls;

3. Of admiralty and maritime jurisdiction;

4. In which the United States is a party;

5. Between two or more states;

6. Between a state and citizens of another state;

7. Between citizens of different states;

8. Between citizens of the same state claiming lands under grants of different states; and

9. Between a state or citizens thereof and foreign states, citizens, or subjects.

B. POWER OF JUDICIAL REVIEW

1. Review of Other Branches of Federal Government

The Constitution does not explicitly state that the Supreme Court may determine the constitutionality of acts of other branches of government. However, judicial review of other branches of the federal government was established in *Marbury v. Madison,* 5 U.S. 137 (1803) (per Marshall, C.J.); the Constitution is "law" and it is the province and duty of the judiciary to declare what the law is.

a. Separation of Powers and Finality of Court Decisions

The Constitution separates governmental powers among the branches of government. This separation of powers doctrine prohibits the legislature from interfering with the courts' *final* judgments. However, Congress may change federal statutes and may direct federal courts to apply those changes in all cases in which a final judgment has not been rendered.

> *Example:* The Supreme Court inferred a limitations period under an ambiguous federal securities law. Because new Supreme Court rulings generally apply to all pending cases, the limitations period imposed by the Court resulted in the dismissal of many pending cases as time-barred. Congress amended the securities law to provide (i) a different limitations period and (ii) a special motion for reinstating the cases dismissed as time-barred by the Supreme Court's ruling. Because the dismissed cases were final judgments, the statute providing for the reinstatement violated the separation of powers doctrine under the Constitution. [Plaut v. Spendthrift Farm, Inc., 514 U.S. 211 (1995)]

2. Federal Review of State Acts

Federal review of state acts (executive, legislative, or judicial) was established by the Marshall Court in a series of decisions. Clear basis exists here in the Supremacy Clause of Article VI, which states that the Constitution, Laws, and Treaties of the United States take precedence over state laws and that the judges of the state courts must follow federal law, anything in the constitution or laws of any state to the contrary notwithstanding. [Fletcher v. Peck, 10 U.S. 87 (1810)]

C. FEDERAL COURTS

Only the actions of Article III courts are the subject of our outline, but you should know that there are two types of federal courts.

1. Article III Courts

Article III courts are those established by Congress pursuant to the provisions of Article III, Section 1. Congress has power to delineate the jurisdictional limits, both original and appellate, of these courts, although it is bound by the standards of judicial power set forth in Article III as to subject matter, parties, and the requirement of "case or controversy." Thus, Congress cannot require these courts to render advisory opinions or perform administrative or nonjudicial functions.

2. Article I Courts

Congress has created certain other courts, however, by way of implementing its various legislative powers; e.g., United States Tax Court, courts of the District of Columbia. Judges of such Article I courts do not have life tenure or protection from salary decrease as do Article III court judges. Article I courts are sometimes vested with ***administrative as well as judicial*** functions, and the congressional power to create such "hybrid" courts has been sustained by the Supreme Court. [Glidden v. Zdanok, 370 U.S. 530 (1962)]

a. Limitation

Congress may not take cases of the type traditionally heard by Article III courts and assign jurisdiction over them to Article I courts. [Northern Pipeline Construction Co. v. Marathon Pipe Line Co., 458 U.S. 50 (1982)—broad grant of jurisdiction to bankruptcy courts, including jurisdiction over contract claims, violates Article III]

D. JURISDICTION OF THE SUPREME COURT

1. Original (Trial) Jurisdiction

Under Article III, Section 2, the Supreme Court has original jurisdiction "in all cases affecting Ambassadors, other public Ministers and Consuls, and those in which a State shall be a Party." This provision is self-executing: Congress may ***neither restrict nor enlarge*** the Supreme Court's original jurisdiction, but Congress may give concurrent jurisdiction to lower federal courts and has done so regarding all cases except those between states.

2. Appellate Jurisdiction

Article III, Section 2 further provides that "in all other Cases before mentioned [i.e., arising under the Constitution, Act of Congress, or treaty], the Supreme Court shall have appellate jurisdiction, both as to Law and Fact, with such Exceptions, and under such Regulations as the Congress shall make."

a. Statutory Application of Appellate Jurisdiction

Congress has provided two methods for invoking Supreme Court appellate jurisdiction: ***appeal*** (where jurisdiction is mandatory), and ***certiorari*** (where jurisdiction is within the Court's discretion). Very few cases fall within the Court's mandatory appeal jurisdiction; thus, appellate jurisdiction is almost completely discretionary.

1) Writ of Certiorari (Discretionary)

The Supreme Court has complete discretion to hear cases that come to it by writ of certiorari. A case will be heard if four justices agree to hear it. The following cases may be heard by certiorari:

a) Cases from the ***highest state courts*** where (i) the constitutionality of a federal statute, federal treaty, or state statute is called into question; or (ii) a state statute allegedly violates federal law [28 U.S.C. §1257]; and

b) All cases from ***federal courts of appeals*** [28 U.S.C. §1254].

2) Appeal (Mandatory)

The Supreme Court must hear those few cases that come to it by appeal. Appeal is available only as to decisions made by three-judge federal district court panels that grant or deny injunctive relief. [28 U.S.C. §1253]

b. Limitations on Statutory Regulation

Ex parte McCardle, 74 U.S. 506 (1868), has been read as giving Congress full power to regulate and limit the Supreme Court's appellate jurisdiction. However, ***possible*** limitations on such congressional power have been suggested:

1) Congress may eliminate specific avenues for Supreme Court review as long as it does not eliminate all avenues. For example, in *McCardle,* two statutes had allowed the Supreme Court to grant habeas corpus to federal prisoners. The Supreme Court upheld the constitutionality of the repeal of one of the statutes because the other statute remained as an avenue for Supreme Court habeas corpus review.

2) Although Congress may eliminate Supreme Court review of certain cases within the federal judicial power, it must permit jurisdiction to remain in ***some*** lower federal court.

3) If Congress were to deny **all** Supreme Court review of an alleged violation of constitutional rights—or go even further and deny a hearing before any federal judge on such a claim—this would violate due process of law.

E. CONSTITUTIONAL AND SELF-IMPOSED LIMITATIONS ON EXERCISE OF FEDERAL JURISDICTION—POLICY OF "STRICT NECESSITY"

Even if a federal court has jurisdiction over the subject matter of a case, it still might refuse to hear the case. Whether the court will hear the case (i.e., whether the case is justiciable) depends on whether a "case or controversy" is involved, and on whether other limitations on jurisdiction are present.

1. No Advisory Opinions

The Supreme Court's interpretation of the "case and controversy" requirement in Article III bars rendition of "advisory" opinions. Thus, federal courts will not render decisions in *moot* cases, *collusive* suits, or cases involving challenges to governmental legislation or policy whose enforcement is neither actual nor threatened.

a. Compare—Declaratory Judgments

Federal courts can hear actions for declaratory relief. A case or controversy will exist if there is an actual dispute between parties having adverse legal interest. Complainants must show that they have engaged in (or wish to engage in) specific conduct and that the challenged action poses a ***real and immediate danger*** to their interests. However, the federal courts will not determine the constitutionality of a statute if it has never been enforced and there is no real fear that it ever will be. [Poe v. Ullman, 367 U.S. 497 (1961)—anticontraceptive law not enforced for 80 years despite open public sales]

2. Ripeness

To avoid issuing advisory opinions, federal courts require that a dispute has matured sufficiently to warrant a decision. Courts avoid getting involved in abstract disagreements over government policies, preferring to wait until a policy has been formalized and can be felt in a concrete way. When considering a question of ripeness, a federal court considers two main factors: (i) the fitness of the issues for judicial decision, and (ii) the hardship to the parties of withholding court consideration. [Pacific Gas and Electric Co. v. State Energy Resources Conservation and Development Commission, 461 U.S. 190 (1983)]

a. Fitness of Issue for Judicial Decision

Generally, an issue is not fit for judicial decision if it relies on uncertain or contingent future events that may not occur as anticipated.

Example: The city of Los Angeles adopts rules regarding the type of trucks that can be used at the Port of Los Angeles. A trucking association challenges the rules in court. During the litigation, the city does not enforce the rules, which are eventually upheld. The trucking association then files an action seeking to prevent the city from retroactively enforcing the rules. The court dismisses the action for lack of ripeness because the court had no way of knowing whether the city would attempt to enforce the rules retroactively. [American Trucking Associations, Inc. v. Los Angeles, 569 U.S. 641 (2013)]

1) **Immediate Impact of Future Events**

A court will hold that an issue is fit for judicial decision even if it relies on uncertain or contingent future events when the future events have an immediate impact.

Example: A state passes a law requiring all children to attend a public school beginning in three years. A private school challenges the law. A court holds that the challenge is ripe, even though enforcement cannot start for another three years because the private school can show that its enrollment is already declining because parents are making decisions based on the pending enforcement of the law. [Pierce v. Society of the Sisters of the Holy Names of Jesus and Mary, 268 U.S. 510 (1925)]

b. **Hardship to the Parties of Withholding Consideration**

A court will find that an action is ripe for review if a party would have to risk substantial hardship to provoke enforcement of law.

Example: A state passes a law preventing aliens from owning property. An alien who is in the market to purchase land but has not yet done so files an action to prevent enforcement of the law. A court finds the action ripe because to force the alien to purchase land before suing would require him to risk a substantial hardship (the forfeiture of the land). [Terrace v. Thompson, 263 U.S. 197 (1923)]

3. **Mootness**

A federal court will not hear a case that has become moot; a ***real, live controversy*** must exist ***at all stages of review***, not merely when the complaint is filed. [*See, e.g.,* DeFunis v. Odegaard, 416 U.S. 312 (1974)—dismissing as moot a white law student's challenge to state's affirmative action program, since the student, although originally passed over for minority applicants with allegedly poorer records, had been admitted to law school while litigation was pending, was about to graduate by the time the case reached the Supreme Court, and would receive the same law degree whether or not the affirmative action program was invalidated]

a. **Exception—Capable of Repetition But Evading Review**

Where there is a reasonable expectation that the same complaining party will be subjected to the same action again and would again be unable to resolve the issue because of the short duration of the action (i.e., where the controversy is capable of repetition yet evading review), the controversy will not be deemed moot. [*See* Weinstein v. Bradford, 423 U.S. 147 (1975)]

Examples: 1) Issue concerns events of short duration (e.g., pregnancy, elections, divorce actions); and

2) Defendant voluntarily stops the offending practice, but is free to resume it.

b. **Class Actions**

A class representative may continue to pursue a class action even though the representative's controversy has become moot, as long as the claims of others in the class are still viable. [United States Parole Commission v. Geraghty, 445 U.S. 388 (1980)]

c. Distinguish Ripeness

Ripeness and mootness are related concepts in that the court will not hear a case unless there is a live controversy. Ripeness bars consideration of claims *before* they have been developed; mootness bars their consideration *after* they have been resolved.

4. Standing

The Supreme Court will not decide a challenge to a government or private action unless the person who is challenging the action has "standing" to raise the issue. A person has standing only if she can demonstrate a concrete stake in the outcome of the controversy.

a. Components

A plaintiff will be able to show a sufficient stake in the controversy only if she can show an *injury in fact*—caused by the defendant—that will be *remedied* by a decision in her favor (i.e., causation and redressability).

1) Injury in Fact

To have standing, a person must be able to assert an injury in fact, which requires both: (i) a *particularized injury*—an injury that affects the plaintiff in a personal and individual way; and (ii) a *concrete injury*—one that exists in fact. It is not enough to show merely that a federal statute or constitutional provision has been violated (and that we all suffer when that happens). [Spokeo, Inc. v. Robins, 136 S. Ct. 1540 (2016)]

Examples: 1) The Fair Credit Reporting Act requires consumer reporting agencies to follow reasonable procedures to assure accuracy of consumer credit reports. The act also imposes liability on any person who willfully fails this requirement with respect to any individual. Defendant maintains an online credit reporting service. Plaintiff searched his own name in defendant's service, discovered inaccuracies, and brought suit against defendant in federal court for violation of the statute. To find that plaintiff has standing, it is not enough that the plaintiff has alleged that the Act may have been violated, but neither is it fatal that the plaintiff was not harmed when he found the inaccuracies, provided the court finds that a violation would cause a real risk of harm to the plaintiff. [Spokeo, Inc. v. Robins, *supra*]

2) A Communist Party member would have standing to challenge a statute making it a crime to be a member of the Communist Party because the member's freedom of association is directly infringed, but a non-Party member would have no standing.

a) Injury Need Not Be Economic

The injury does not always have to be economic. In some cases, the Court has found that an individual is harmed because the alleged illegal act or unconstitutional action has an impact on the person's well-being.

Example: Law students were allowed to challenge an Interstate Commerce Commission rate-setting policy on the ground that such policies discouraged recycling and thereby diminished the quality of each student's physical environment. If the ICC rate-setting policy violated congressional statutes, the elimination of those rate-setting policies would have an impact on the students' physical environment. [United States v. SCRAP, 412 U.S. 669 (1973)]

2) **Causation**

There must be a causal connection between the injury and the conduct complained of—i.e., the injury must be traceable to the challenged conduct of the defendant and not be attributable to some independent third party not before the court.

Example: Plaintiffs claiming that a municipality's zoning policies prevented low-income persons from finding housing in the municipality were denied standing because they failed to show a substantial probability that they would be able to afford housing in the municipality even absent the zoning policies. [Warth v. Seldin, 422 U.S. 490 (1975)]

3) **Redressability**

In determining whether a litigant has a sufficient injury to establish standing, courts ask whether a ruling favorable to the litigant would eliminate the harm to him. If a court order declaring an action to be illegal or unconstitutional (and ending that action) would not eliminate the harm to the litigant, then that individual does not have the type of specific injury that would grant him standing to challenge the action.

Examples: 1) The Supreme Court held that mothers do not have standing to challenge the government's refusal to enforce criminal laws that would require the fathers of their children to pay child support. The enforcement of the criminal laws against a father who is guilty of nonsupport would not necessarily result in the father's providing support to the mother and her children.

2) Indigents have no standing to challenge an Internal Revenue Service policy that allows hospitals to receive favorable tax treatment even though they refuse to provide free or subsidized care for indigents. The indigents could not demonstrate that a different IRS policy would cause hospitals to provide them with free care.

4) **Required at All Stages**

Standing must be met at all stages of litigation, including on appeal. [Hollingsworth v. Perry, 133 S. Ct. 2652 (2013)]

Example: A district court held unconstitutional a state constitutional amendment that defined marriage as a union between a man and a woman. After trial, the court enjoined state officials from enforcing the provision, and the state officials elected not to appeal. The proponents of the state constitutional amendment sought to appeal. Since the proponents were not ordered to do or refrain from doing anything, they have no injury other than a generalized grievance in vindicating the validity of a generally applicable state law.

Such an interest does not give the proponents a concrete stake in the outcome. Therefore, they lack standing to bring the appeal. [Hollingsworth v. Perry, *supra*]

b.   Common Standing Issues

1)   Congressional Conferral of Standing

Congress has no power to completely eliminate the case or controversy requirement, because the requirement is based in the Constitution. [*See* United Food & Commercial Workers Union Local 751 v. Brown Group, Inc., 517 U.S. 544 (1996)] However, a federal statute may create new interests, injury to which may be sufficient for standing.

2)   Standing to Enforce Government Statutes—Zone of Interests

In some instances a plaintiff may bring suit to force government actors to conform their conduct to the requirements of a specific federal statute. Even in such cases, the person must have an "injury in fact." Often, the Court asks whether the injury caused to the individual or group seeking to enforce the federal statute is within the "zone of interests" that Congress meant to protect with the statute. If Congress intended the statute to protect such persons, and intended to allow private persons to bring federal court actions to enforce the statute, the courts are likely to be lenient in granting standing to those persons.

Example: Persons who sold data processing services to private businesses had standing to challenge a ruling by the Comptroller of Currency that allowed national banks to make data processing services available to other banks and bank customers. These plaintiffs had an injury in fact because the Comptroller's ruling would hurt their future profits. The plaintiffs were determined to be within the "zone of interests" protected by the federal statutes limiting the authority of the Comptroller and national banks.

3)   Standing to Assert Rights of Others

To have standing, the claimant must have suffered or may presently suffer a direct impairment of his *own* rights. A plaintiff may, however, *assert third-party rights* where he himself has suffered injury and:

(i)   *Third parties find it difficult to assert their own rights* (the NAACP was permitted to assert the freedom of association rights of its members in attacking a state law requiring disclosure of membership lists because its members could not file suit without disclosing their identities) [NAACP v. Alabama, 357 U.S. 449 (1958)]; or

(ii)   *The injury suffered by the plaintiff adversely affects his relationship with third parties*, resulting in an indirect violation of their rights (a vendor of beer was granted standing to assert the constitutional rights of males under 21 in attacking a state law prohibiting sale of beer to them but not to females under 21) [Craig v. Boren, 429 U.S. 190 (1976)].

a) **Limitation—Family Law Issues**

A divorced father sought to challenge on First Amendment grounds, on behalf of his daughter, the saying of the Pledge of Allegiance at her public school because the Pledge includes the words "under God." A state court order gave the girl's mother final authority over decisions regarding the girl's health, education, and welfare. The mother objected to the lawsuit, and neither the mother nor the daughter objected to the Pledge. The Court held that the father lacked standing to bring the claim. [Elk Grove Unified School District v. Newdow, 542 U.S. 1 (2004)]

4) **Standing of Organizations**

An organization (unincorporated association, corporation, union, etc.) has standing to challenge action that causes injury to *the organization itself*. An organization also has standing to challenge actions that cause an injury in fact to *its members if* the organization can demonstrate the following three facts:

(i) There must be an *injury in fact to the members* of the organization that would give individual members a right to sue on their own behalf;

(ii) The injury to the members must be *related to the organization's purpose*; *and*

(iii) *Neither the nature of the claim nor the relief requested requires participation of the individual members* in the lawsuit.

[Hunt v. Washington Apple Advertising Commission, 432 U.S. 333 (1977)]

Example: The American Dental Association ("ADA") is composed entirely of dentists; its purpose is to promote the professional well-being of dentists. Assume that most ADA members make between $100,000 and $200,000 per year. The ADA would not have standing to challenge a change in the federal income tax rates that will disadvantage all persons making between $100,000 and $200,000 on the basis that the statute deprives all persons (in the income category) of property without due process, because that claim is not related to the organization's purpose—the representation of dentists as such. But the ADA probably could bring a lawsuit challenging a state regulation of dental practices if the regulation injures ADA members, as long as the injury to ADA members does not vary.

5) **No Citizenship Standing**

As stated above, if an injury is too generalized, there can be no standing. Thus, people have no standing merely "as citizens" to claim that government action violates federal law or the Constitution. Congress cannot change this rule by adopting a statute that would allow persons to have standing merely as citizens (where they otherwise have no direct, personal claim) to bring suit to force the government to observe the Constitution or federal laws. [Lujan v. Defenders of Wildlife, 504 U.S. 555 (1992)]

a) **Compare—Tenth Amendment Violation Claims**
A person can have standing to allege that federal action violates the Tenth Amendment by interfering with the powers reserved to the states, assuming the person can show injury in fact and redressability. [Bond v. United States, 564 U.S. 211 (2011)]

6) **Taxpayer Standing**

a) **Generally No Standing to Litigate Government Expenditures**
A taxpayer, of course, has standing to litigate her tax bill (e.g., whether she really owes X dollars). However, people generally do not have standing as taxpayers to challenge the way tax dollars are spent by the state or federal government, because their interest is too remote. Nor do taxpayers have standing to challenge a law granting tax credits to persons who contribute to organizations that provide scholarships to students attending private schools. [Arizona Christian School Tuition Organization v. Winn, 563 U.S. 125 (2011)] Note that such tax credits do not fall under the Establishment Clause exception below—even to the extent that the credits are available for contributions used for religious school scholarships—because the program does not involve the transfer of government funds; thus, there is no injury for standing purposes.

b) **Exception—Congressional Measures Under Taxing and Spending Power that Violate Establishment Clause**
There is an exception to the general rule: A federal taxpayer has standing to challenge federal appropriation and spending measures if she can establish that the challenged measure:

(i) Was enacted under *Congress's* taxing and spending power (*see* II.A.2., 3., *infra*); and

(ii) Exceeds some specific limitation on the power.

To date, the only limit that the Supreme Court has found on the taxing power is the Establishment Clause. (*See* XXII.D., *infra*.)

Note: The measure challenged must arise under the taxing and spending power. Thus, there was no standing to challenge a federal government transfer of surplus property under the Property Clause that allegedly violated the Establishment Clause. [Valley Forge Christian College v. Americans United for Separation of Church and State, 454 U.S. 464 (1982)] Neither was there standing to challenge expenditures of executive branch general funds that allegedly violated the Establishment Clause. [Hein v. Freedom From Religion Foundation, 551 U.S. 587 (2007)]

7) **Legislators' Standing**
Legislators may have standing to challenge the constitutionality of government action if they have a sufficient "personal stake" in the dispute and suffer sufficient "concrete injury." [Raines v. Byrd, 521 U.S. 811 (1997)]

Example: A state's lieutenant governor cast the deciding vote to break a tie in the state senate. Legislators who had voted against the prevailing position had standing to challenge the right of the lieutenant governor to vote because his vote completely nullified theirs and caused the specific legislative enactment to go into effect. [Coleman v. Miller, 307 U.S. 433 (1939)]

Compare: Members of Congress had **no** standing to challenge the Line Item Veto Act authorizing the President to cancel (veto) certain spending and tax law measures that are part of a bill that he signs into law. *Rationale:* Rather than causing a "personal" and "concrete" injury, the challenged statute caused only a type of "institutional" injury to all members of Congress equally. [Raines v. Byrd, *supra*]

8) Assignee Standing

An assignee of a legal claim has standing even if the assignee has agreed to remit any proceeds recovered from the litigation back to the assignor, if this is done pursuant to an ordinary business agreement made in good faith. [Sprint Communications Co., L.P. v. APCC Services, Inc., 554 U.S. 269 (2008)—a paid collection agent has standing to bring the claims of an assignor even though the collection agent will submit any recovery back to the assignor]

5. Adequate and Independent State Grounds

The Supreme Court will hear a case from a state court only if the state court judgment turned on federal grounds. The Court will refuse jurisdiction if it finds **adequate and independent** nonfederal grounds to support the state decision.

a. "Adequate"

The nonfederal grounds must be "adequate" in that they are fully dispositive of the case, so that even if the federal grounds are wrongly decided, it would not affect the outcome of the case. Where that is the case, the Supreme Court's review of the federal law grounds for the state court's decision would have no effect on the judgment rendered by the state court, so that the Supreme Court, in effect, would be rendering an advisory opinion.

b. "Independent"

The nonfederal grounds must also be "independent": If the state court's interpretation of its state provision was based on federal case law interpreting an identical federal provision, the state law grounds for the decision are not independent.

c. Where Basis Is Unclear

If it is unclear whether the state court decision turned on federal or state law, the Supreme Court may dismiss the case or remand it to the state court for clarification. However, the Court will usually assume that there is no adequate state ground unless the state court expressly stated that its decision rests on state law.

Example: When a state supreme court relied on *Terry v. Ohio* and other federal cases to suppress evidence from a search and did not cite a single state case to support its holding, although it referred to its state constitution in the opinion, the Supreme Court concluded that the state court had rested its decision on federal law, and therefore refused to dismiss the appeal based on adequate and independent state grounds. [*See* Michigan v. Long, 463 U.S. 1032 (1983)]

6. Abstention

a. Unsettled State Law
When a federal constitutional claim is premised on an *unsettled question of state law*, the federal court should stay its hand ("abstain" temporarily), so as to give state courts a chance to settle the underlying state law question and thus potentially avoid the needless resolution of a federal constitutional issue. [Railroad Commission of Texas v. Pullman, 312 U.S. 496 (1941)]

b. Pending State Proceedings
Generally, federal courts will *not enjoin pending state criminal proceedings*. [Younger v. Harris, 401 U.S. 37 (1971)]

1) Pending
State court proceedings are pending if begun before the federal court begins proceedings on the merits. Hence, the order of filing charges is irrelevant. "Proceedings of substance" must occur first in federal court before an injunction will issue. [Hicks v. Miranda, 422 U.S. 332 (1975)]

2) Civil and Administrative Proceedings
Federal courts should abstain from enjoining pending state administrative or civil proceedings when those proceedings involve an important state interest.
Examples: 1) A federal court should not enjoin a pending state civil action to remove a child from the child's parents due to alleged child abuse.

2) A federal court should not enjoin: (i) a state court order holding a person or corporation in contempt for failing to pay a civil judgment; or (ii) a state court judgment that permits a plaintiff to execute a lien against a defendant's property. [Juidice v. Vail, 430 U.S. 327 (1977); Pennzoil Co. v. Texaco, Inc., 481 U.S. 1 (1987)]

3) Exception
An order enjoining state proceedings will be issued in cases of *proven harassment* or *prosecutions taken in bad faith* (without hope of a valid conviction).

7. Political Questions
The Court will not decide political questions.

a. Definition
Political questions are:

(i) Those issues committed by the Constitution to another branch of government; or

(ii) Those inherently incapable of resolution and enforcement by the judicial process.

Examples: Political questions include:

1) Questions regarding the conduct of foreign relations or issues as to when hostilities have stopped;

2) Questions relating to which group of delegates should be seated at the Democratic National Convention [O'Brien v. Brown, 409 U.S. 1 (1972)];

3) The procedures used by the Senate to "try" impeachments (e.g., the Court refused to rule on the constitutionality of the Senate's delegation of the duty to take evidence and testimony to a committee of senators prior to the Senate deciding whether to vote for conviction on an impeachment of a federal judge) [Nixon v. United States, 506 U.S. 224 (1993)];

4) What constitutes a "republican form of government" guaranteed to the state by Article IV, Section 4 [Pacific States Telephone & Telegraph Co. v. Oregon, 223 U.S. 118 (1912)];

5) Whether the number of votes a candidate for Congress received is sufficient to elect him [Roudebush v. Hartke, 405 U.S. 15 (1972)]; and

6) Questions regarding partisan legislative reapportionment (i.e., partisan gerrymandering)—these are effectively nonjusticiable [*see* League of United Latin American Citizens v. Perry, 548 U.S. 399 (2006)].

b.   Compare—"Nonpolitical Controversy"
Presidential papers and communications are generally considered to be privileged and protected against disclosure in the exercise of the executive power. But where these documents are necessary to the continuation of criminal proceedings, the question of production is *justiciable and not political*. [United States v. Nixon, 418 U.S. 683 (1974)]

8.   Eleventh Amendment Limits on Federal Courts
The Eleventh Amendment is a jurisdictional bar that modifies the judicial power by prohibiting a federal court from hearing a private party's or foreign government's claims against a state government. [*See* Hans v. Louisiana, 134 U.S. 1 (1890)]

a.   What Is Barred?
The Eleventh Amendment's jurisdictional bar extends to the following:

(i)   Actions against state governments *for damages*;

(ii)   Actions against state governments for injunctive or declaratory relief *where the state is named as a party*;

(iii)   Actions against state government officers where the effect of the suit will be that *retroactive damages* will be paid from the state treasury or where the action is the functional equivalent of a *quiet title action* that would divest the state of ownership of land; and

(iv)   Actions against state government officers *for violating state law*.

1) Compare—Sovereign Immunity

The Court has also held that the following are barred by the doctrine of *sovereign immunity:*

a) Suits against a state government in state court, even on federal claims, without the defendant state's consent [Alden v. Maine, 527 U.S. 706 (1999)— provision in federal Fair Labor Standards Act creating a private cause of action in state courts against state employers who violate the Act violates sovereign immunity]; and

b) Adjudicative actions against states and state agencies before federal administrative agencies. [Federal Maritime Commission v. South Carolina State Ports Authority, 535 U.S. 743 (2002)]

b. What Is Not Barred?

1) Actions Against Local Governments

The Eleventh Amendment protects only state governments. Local governments (e.g., cities or counties) are not protected.

2) Actions by the United States Government or Other State Governments

Actions by the United States Government or other state governments are not barred.

3) Bankruptcy Proceedings

The Eleventh Amendment does not apply to federal laws that are exercises of Congress's Article I power to create bankruptcy laws, and thus does not bar actions of the United States bankruptcy courts that have a direct impact on state finances. [Tennessee Student Assistance Corp. v. Hood, 541 U.S. 440 (2004); Central Virginia Community College v. Katz, 546 U.S. 356 (2006)]

c. Exceptions to Eleventh Amendment

1) Certain Actions Against State Officers

The Supreme Court allows the following actions to be brought against *state officials* despite the Eleventh Amendment:

a) **Actions Against State Officers for Injunctions**

A federal court may enjoin a state officer to refrain from future actions that violate federal law or to take prospective actions to comply with constitutional mandates. [*Ex parte* Young, 209 U.S. 123 (1908)]

b) **Actions Against State Officers for Monetary Damages from Officer**

A federal court may hear an action for damages against a state officer for violations of *federal law if* the monetary damages are to be paid out of the officer's own pocket. *Rationale:* By acting outside the scope of federal law, the officer is stripped of his representative capacity—the action is not one against a state, but rather is against an individual.

c) **Actions Against State Officers for Prospective Payments from State**
   A federal court may hear an action for damages against a state officer where the effect of the action will be to force the state to pay money in the future to comply with the court order. [*Ex parte* Young, *supra*] However, federal court jurisdiction is barred if the action will result in retroactive damages to be paid from the state treasury. [Edelman v. Jordan, 415 U.S. 651 (1974)]

   Example: P sues the State Commissioner of the Department of Public Welfare for failing to comply with federal welfare regulations. The federal court can order future compliance with the federal regulations, even if this will result in costing the state a large amount of money in the future. However, the federal court cannot award back payments of amounts previously improperly withheld, because the order would require payment from the state treasury for retroactive relief. [Edelman v. Jordan, *supra*]

 2) **Congressional Removal of Immunity Under the Fourteenth Amendment**
  Congress can remove the states' Eleventh Amendment immunity under its power to ***prevent discrimination under the Fourteenth Amendment.*** For example, the Equal Pay Act—based on the Fourteenth Amendment—can serve as a basis for federal suits against a state by its employees. [Fitzpatrick v. Bitzer, 427 U.S. 445 (1976)]

  a) **Compare—Article I Powers**
   Unlike its power under the Fourteenth Amendment, Congress's legislative powers under Article I (*see* II., *infra*) do ***not*** include the power to abrogate state immunity under the Eleventh Amendment. [Seminole Tribe of Florida v. Florida, 517 U.S. 44 (1996)] However, the Supreme Court has held that states may not assert sovereign immunity in proceedings arising under the bankruptcy law. [Central Virginia Community College v. Katz, *supra*]

 d. **Summary**
  For most bar exam questions, a key principle to remember is this: The Eleventh Amendment will prohibit a federal court from hearing a claim for damages against a state government (although not against state officers) unless:

  1) The state has consented to allow the lawsuit in federal court;

  2) The plaintiff is the United States or another state; or

  3) Congress has clearly granted federal courts the authority to hear a specific type of damage action under the Fourteenth Amendment (e.g., under a civil rights statute).

II. LEGISLATIVE POWER

A. ENUMERATED AND IMPLIED POWERS
The Constitution grants Congress a number of specific powers, many of which are enumerated

in Article I, Section 8. It also grants Congress auxiliary power under the Necessary and Proper Clause.

1. **Necessary and Proper "Power"**

    The Necessary and Proper Clause grants Congress the power to make all laws necessary and proper (i.e., appropriate) for carrying into execution *any* power granted to *any* branch of the federal government.

    Example: Congress has the power to charter banks since that power is appropriate to executing Congress's enumerated powers to tax, borrow money, regulate commerce, etc. [McCulloch v. Maryland, 17 U.S. 316 (1819)]

    Note: The Necessary and Proper Clause is not itself a basis of power; it merely gives Congress power to execute specifically granted powers. Thus, if a bar exam question asks what is the best source of power for a particular act of Congress, the answer should not be the Necessary and Proper Clause, standing alone.

    a. **Limitation**

        Congress cannot adopt a law that is expressly prohibited by another provision of the Constitution.

2. **Taxing Power**

    Congress has the power to lay and collect taxes, imposts, and excises, but they must be uniform throughout the United States. [Art. I, §8] Capitation or other direct taxes must be laid in proportion to the census [Art. I, §9, cl. 4], and direct taxes must be apportioned among the states [Art. I, §2, cl. 3].

    a. **Determining What Is a Tax**

        The determination of whether a legislative enactment imposes a tax does not depend on the label Congress gives it, but rather on its function. [National Federation of Independent Business v. Sebelius, 567 U.S. 519 (2012)—law requiring individuals to purchase health insurance or to pay an additional amount of money to the IRS when they pay their income tax, the amount of which varies by household income, joint vs. single filing status, number of dependents, etc., and which is estimated to bring $4 billion annually into federal coffers, functionally is a tax regardless of the fact that Congress labeled it a "penalty"]

    b. **Uniformity**

        Requirement of uniformity in the levy of indirect taxes (generally, this means any kind of "privilege" tax, including duties and excises) has been interpreted by the Court to mean *geographical uniformity* only—i.e., identical taxation of the taxed Article in every state where it is found. [Fernandez v. Wiener, 326 U.S. 340 (1945)]

    c. **Direct Taxes—Must Be Apportioned**

        A "direct" tax (imposed directly on property or on the person) has seldom been employed by Congress because of the cumbersome *apportionment requirement*; taxes on income from real or personal property were initially held "direct" by the Court, but the resulting need for apportioning such taxes was obviated by the Sixteenth Amendment (income tax amendment).

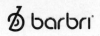

d. **Taxes Are Generally Valid**
Absent a specific restriction such as those above, be very hesitant to rule against a tax measure on the exam. A tax measure will be upheld if it bears some ***reasonable relationship to revenue production*** or if Congress has the ***power to regulate*** the taxed activity.
Example: Special excise tax levied on dealers in illegal narcotics is valid because it raises revenue. [United States v. Doremus, 249 U.S. 86 (1919)]

3. **Spending Power**
Congress may spend to "provide for the common defense and general welfare." [Art. I, §8] This spending may be for ***any public purpose***—not merely the accomplishment of other enumerated powers. However, nonspending regulations are not authorized. Remember that the Bill of Rights still applies to this power; i.e., the federal government could not condition welfare payments on an agreement not to criticize government policies.

a. **Regulation Through Spending**
Note that Congress can use its spending power to "regulate" areas, even where it otherwise has no power to regulate the area, by requiring entities that accept government money to act in a certain manner (i.e., attaching "strings" to government grants). (*See* VI.A.2.b., *infra.*)

4. **Commerce Power**
Article I, Section 8, Clause 3 empowers Congress to "regulate commerce with foreign nations and among the several states, and with the Indian tribes."

a. **Definition of Commerce**

1) **Includes Basically All Activity Affecting Two or More States**
Chief Justice Marshall, in *Gibbons v. Ogden,* 22 U.S. 1 (1824), defined commerce as "every species of commercial intercourse . . . which concerns more states than one" and included within the concept virtually every form of activity involving or affecting two or more states.

2) **Includes Transportation or Traffic**
The Court has consistently regarded transportation or traffic as commerce, whether or not a commercial activity is involved.
Example: Interstate transportation of liquor for personal consumption, women for immoral purposes (not necessarily prostitution), and interstate transportation of stolen motor vehicles are all interstate commerce.

a) **Vehicular Transportation Not Required**
Any ***transmission across state lines***, such as electricity, gas, telegraph, telephone, TV, radio, and mail transmission (including educational materials and sale of insurance), will constitute interstate commerce.

b. **"Substantial Economic Effect"**
The Supreme Court has sustained congressional power to regulate any activity, local or interstate, that either in itself ***or in combination with other activities*** has a ***"substantial economic effect upon,"*** or ***"effect on movement in,"*** interstate commerce.

Example: The classic case is the Court's holding that Congress can control a farmer's ***production*** of wheat ***for home consumption***. [Wickard v. Filburn, 317 U.S. 111 (1942)] *Rationale:* Cumulative effect of many instances of such production could be felt on the supply and demand of the interstate commodity market.

1) Power Not Unlimited

The Supreme Court has recently made clear that the power of Congress to regulate commerce, although very broad, does have limits so as not to obliterate the distinction between what is national and what is local. To be within Congress's power under the Commerce Clause, a federal law must either:

(i) ***Regulate the channels*** of interstate commerce;

(ii) ***Regulate the instrumentalities*** of interstate commerce and persons and things in interstate commerce; or

(iii) ***Regulate activities that have a substantial effect*** on interstate commerce.

a) Intrastate Activity

When Congress attempts to regulate ***intrastate*** activity under the third prong, above, the Court will uphold the regulation if it is of ***economic or commercial activity*** and the court can conceive of a ***rational basis*** on which Congress could conclude that the activity ***in aggregate*** substantially affects interstate commerce. [Gonzales v. Raich, 545 U.S. 1 (2005)—upholding regulation of intrastate cultivation and use of marijuana (permitted by state law for medicinal purposes) because it was part of a comprehensive federal program to combat interstate traffic in illicit drugs] If the regulated intrastate activity is not commercial or economic, the Court generally will not aggregate the effects and the regulation will be upheld only if Congress can show a direct ***substantial economic effect*** on interstate commerce, which it generally will not be able to do. [*See, e.g.,* United States v. Lopez, 514 U.S. 549 (1995)—federal statute barring possession of a gun in a school zone is invalid; United States v. Morrison, 529 U.S. 598 (2000)—federal civil remedy for victims of gender-motivated violence is invalid]

(1) Activity vs. Inactivity

The Commerce Clause gives Congress power only to regulate existing commercial activity; it does not give Congress power to compel activity, even if failure to undertake the activity may affect interstate commerce. [National Federation of Independent Business v. Sebelius, 2.a., *supra*]

5. War and Related Powers

Article I, Section 8 gives Congress the power to declare war, raise and support armies, provide for and maintain a navy, make rules for the government and regulation of the armed forces, and organize, arm, discipline, and call up the militia. Of course, several other congressional powers may have direct or indirect application to military purposes: tax and spending power, commerce power, Senate's treaty consent power, maritime power, investigatory power, etc.

a. **Economic Regulation**

1) **During War**

Regulatory power of Congress, especially in economic matters and mobilization of troops, in support of war effort is *pervasive* (although theoretically limited by the Bill of Rights); thus, the Court has sustained national price and rent control, as well as conscription and regulation of civilian/military production and services.

2) **Postwar**

To a considerable extent, this pervasive regulatory power may be validly extended into post-wartime periods both to *remedy wartime disruptions* [e.g., Woods v. Cloyd W. Miller Co., 333 U.S. 138 (1948)—rent controls] and to cope with *"cold war" exigencies*. Legislation in the field of veterans' rights and limitations thereon may be extended indefinitely as long as veterans or their relatives may survive.

b. **Military Courts and Tribunals**

The constitutional basis of courts of military justice (trial and review of offenses by military personnel, including courts-martial and reviewing agencies and tribunals) is not Article III, but rather Article I, Section 8, Clause 14 (congressional power to make rules for government and regulation of armed forces), buttressed by the Necessary and Proper Clause.

1) **Judicial Review**

The regular federal (or state) courts have *no general power to review* court-martial proceedings. However, in habeas corpus cases, the Article III courts, including the Supreme Court, may make a limited inquiry into the military court's jurisdiction of the person and offense or the validity of the court's legislative creation.

2) **Court-Martial of Enemy Civilians and Soldiers Permitted**

Military courts may try enemy civilians as well as enemy military personnel, at least during wartime.

a) **Suspension of Habeas Corpus for Enemy Combatants**

Congress does not have the power to deny habeas corpus review to all aliens detained as enemy combatants absent a meaningful substitute for habeas corpus review. A meaningful substitute would allow prisoners to (i) challenge the President's authority to detain them indefinitely, (ii) contest the military commission's findings of fact, (iii) supplement the record on review with exculpatory evidence discovered after the military commission's proceedings, and (iv) request release. [Boumediene v. Bush, 553 U.S. 723 (2008)]

3) **Court-Martial of American Soldiers Permitted**

Military courts have jurisdiction over *all* offenses (not just service connected offenses) committed by persons who are members of the armed services, both when charged and at the time of the offense. [Solorio v. United States, 483 U.S. 435 (1987), *overruling* O'Callahan v. Parker, 395 U.S. 258 (1969)]

4) Court-Martial of American Civilians Generally Prohibited
The Supreme Court has denied Congress the power to authorize the court-martial trial of American civilians as long as actual warfare has not forced courts to shut down, even though martial law has been declared [*Ex parte* Milligan, 71 U.S. 2 (1866)]; even though the civilians accused may have been members of the armed forces when committing the alleged offense [Toth v. Quarles, 350 U.S. 11 (1955)] or are dependents of military personnel accompanying the latter overseas [Reid v. Covert, 354 U.S. 1 (1957)] or are civilian employees of the military forces at overseas bases and installations; such trials by court-martial violate the Fifth and Sixth Amendments, particularly the right to trial by jury.

c. Calling Forth the Militia
Under the Militia Clauses [Art. I, §8, cl. 15, 16], Congress has the power to authorize the President to order members of National Guard units into federal service—even in circumstances that do not involve a national emergency (e.g., for training outside of the United States). The President need not obtain the consent of the governor of a unit's home state to call it into such service. [Perpich v. Department of Defense, 496 U.S. 334 (1990)]

6. Investigatory Power
The power to investigate to secure information as a basis for potential legislation or other official action (such as impeachment or trying impeachments) is a well-established implied power. It is a *very broad power*, in that an investigation need not be directed toward enactment of particular legislation, but the following limitations on its use do exist.

a. Authorized Investigation
The investigatory inquiry must be expressly or impliedly authorized by the congressional house concerned, i.e., by statute or resolution creating or directing the investigating committee or subcommittee.

b. Witnesses' Rights

1) Fifth Amendment
The privilege against compulsory self-incrimination (the Fifth Amendment) is available to witnesses, whether formal or informal, unless a statutory immunity co-extensive with the constitutional immunity is granted.

2) Relevance
Written or oral information elicited by the investigative body must be "pertinent" to the subject of the inquiry.

3) Procedural Due Process
Witnesses are generally entitled to procedural due process, such as presence of counsel and right of cross-examination; but it is not yet clear whether such rights are constitutionally required or whether some of them are required merely by house rule or statute.

c. Enforcement of Investigatory Powers
Congress can hold a subpoenaed witness in contempt for refusing to appear or answer before Congress.

7. **Property Power**

Congress has the power to "dispose of and make all needful rules and regulations respecting the territory or other property belonging to the United States." [Art. IV, §3] Many other congressional powers (war, commerce, postal, fiscal, etc.) obviously would be unworkable if the ancillary ***power to acquire and dispose of property of all kinds***—real, personal, and intangible—were not also implied from the main grants.

Example: The Property Clause empowers Congress to even protect wildlife wandering onto federally owned lands. [Kleppe v. New Mexico, 426 U.S. 529 (1976)]

a. **No Limits on Disposition of Property**

There is no express limitation on Congress's power to dispose of property owned by the United States. The power extends to all species of property, such as leasehold interests and electrical energy, as well as ordinary realty and personalty. Moreover, disposal may involve direct competition with private enterprise and has never been invalidated on that ground.

b. **Eminent Domain**

Acquisition of property for a public purpose by eminent domain is indirectly recognized by the Fifth Amendment: ". . . nor shall private property be taken for public use, without just compensation." Federal taking must be for the purpose of ***effectuating an enumerated power*** under some other provision of the Constitution.

8. **No Federal Police Power**

Congress has no general police power (i.e., power to legislate for the health, welfare, morals, etc., of the citizens). Thus, on the bar exam the validity of a federal statute cannot rely on "the police power." However, Congress can exercise police power-type powers as to the District of Columbia pursuant to its power to legislate over the capital [Art. I, §8, cl. 17] and over all United States possessions (e.g., territories, military bases, Indian reservations) pursuant to the property power.

9. **Bankruptcy Power**

Article I, Section 8, Clause 4 empowers Congress "to establish uniform laws on the subject of bankruptcies throughout the United States." This power has been interpreted by the Supreme Court as nonexclusive; i.e., state legislation in the field is superseded only to the extent that it conflicts with federal legislation therein.

10. **Postal Power**

Article I, Section 8, Clause 7 empowers Congress "to establish post offices and post roads."

a. **Exclusive**

The postal power has been interpreted as granting Congress a postal monopoly. Neither private business nor the states may compete with the Federal Postal Service absent Congress's consent. [Air Courier Conference of America v. American Postal Workers Union, 498 U.S. 517 (1991)]

b. **Scope of Power**

Congress may validly classify and place ***reasonable restrictions*** on use of the mails, ***but it may not deprive*** any citizen or group of citizens of the general mail "privilege" or regulate the mail in such a way as to abridge freedom of speech or press (except under valid standards, such as "obscenity") or violate the ban of the Fourth Amendment against unreasonable search and seizure.

11. Power Over Citizenship
Article I, Section 8, Clause 4 empowers Congress "to establish a uniform rule of naturalization."

a. Exclusion of Aliens
Congress's power to exclude aliens is broad.

1) Nonresident Aliens
Aliens have no right to enter the United States and *can be refused entry* because of their political beliefs. [Kleindienst v. Mandel, 408 U.S. 753 (1972)]

2) Resident Aliens
Resident aliens are entitled to *notice and hearing* before they can be deported.

b. Naturalization and Denaturalization—Exclusive Control of Congress
Congress has exclusive power over naturalization and denaturalization. The Supreme Court has held that this grant gives Congress plenary power over aliens (*see* XVIII.D.2.a., *infra*).

1) No Loss of Citizenship Without Consent
Under the Fourteenth Amendment, Congress may not take away the citizenship of any citizen—native-born or naturalized—without his consent.
Example: The Court held unconstitutional a statute that provided for loss of citizenship upon voting in a foreign election. [Afroyim v. Rusk, 387 U.S. 253 (1967)]

a) Proof of Intent
A citizen's intent to relinquish citizenship may be expressed by words or conduct—and Congress may provide that such intent may be proven by a preponderance of the evidence. [Vance v. Terrazas, 444 U.S. 252 (1980)]

2) Rights of Children of Citizens
A person born in another country to United States citizen parents does not have a constitutional right to become a United States citizen. Congress can grant citizenship to children born abroad conditioned on their return to live in the United States within a specified period of time or for a specified number of years. Such a child who fails to return to the United States loses his grant of citizenship because he has failed to meet the statutory condition precedent to his final grant of citizenship.

12. Admiralty Power
Although congressional power to legislate in maritime matters is not expressed in the Constitution, the Supreme Court has implied it from the exclusive jurisdiction given the federal courts in this field by Article III, Section 2, supported by the Necessary and Proper Clause of Article I, Section 8.

a. **Exclusive Power**
The congressional power is plenary and exclusive, except to the extent that Congress may leave (and has left) some maritime matters to state jurisdiction.

b. **Navigable Waterways**
The federal admiralty power attaches to all navigable waterways—actually or potentially navigable—and to small tributaries that affect navigable waterways. The federal maritime power is not limited to tidewaters or interstate waters.

13. **Power to Coin Money and Fix Weights and Measures**
Congress has the power to coin money and fix the standard of weights and measures under Article I, Section 8, Clause 5.

14. **Patent/Copyright Power**
Congress has the power to control the issuance of patents and copyrights under Article I, Section 8, Clause 8.

B. DELEGATION OF LEGISLATIVE POWER

1. **Broad Delegation Allowed**
Congress has broad discretion to delegate its legislative power to executive officers and/ or administrative agencies [A.L.A. Schechter Poultry Corp. v. United States, 295 U.S. 495 (1935)], and even delegation of rulemaking power to the courts has been upheld [Mistretta v. United States, 488 U.S. 361 (1989)].

Example: Congress can delegate the power to establish sentencing guidelines for criminal cases to a sentencing commission located in the federal courts and made up, in part, of federal judges, as long as the tasks delegated do not undermine the integrity of the judiciary or usurp the powers of the other branches. [Mistretta v. United States, *supra*]

2. **Limitations on Delegation**

a. **Power Cannot Be Uniquely Confined to Congress**
To be delegable, the power must not be uniquely confined to Congress; e.g., the power to declare war cannot be delegated, nor the power to impeach.

b. **Clear Standard**
It is said that delegation will be upheld only if it includes intelligible standards for the delegate to follow. However, as a practical matter almost anything will pass as an "intelligible standard" (e.g., "upholding public interest, convenience, or necessity").

c. **Separation of Powers Limitations**
While Congress has broad power to delegate, the separation of powers doctrine restricts Congress from keeping certain controls over certain delegates. For example, Congress cannot give itself the power to remove an officer of the executive branch by any means other than impeachment (e.g., if Congress delegates rulemaking power to an executive branch agency (e.g., the FCC), it may not retain the power to fire the agency head). (*See* III.B.1.c.2)a), *infra*.) Similarly, Congress cannot give a government employee who is

subject to removal by Congress (other than by impeachment) purely executive powers. (*See* III.B.1.c.2)b), *infra*.)

Example: A federal statute transferred the authority to control two D.C. area airports from the federal government to a local authority. However, the statute reserved to a review board a veto power over the local authority's decisions. The review board was comprised of nine members of Congress. The statute violates the separation of powers doctrine in one of two ways: (i) If the review board's power is considered to be legislative, the statute created an unconstitutional legislative veto (*see* D., *infra*). (ii) If the review board's power is considered to be executive, the separation of powers doctrine prohibits members of Congress from exercising it. [Metropolitan Washington Airports Authority v. Citizens for Abatement of Aircraft Noise, 501 U.S. 252 (1991)]

d. Important Liberty Interests
If the delegate interferes with the exercise of a fundamental liberty or right, the burden falls upon the delegate to show that she has the power to prevent the exercise of the right and her decision was in furtherance of that particular policy.

Example: In *Kent v. Dulles,* 357 U.S. 116 (1958), the Secretary of State was required to issue a passport to a Communist because he could not show that Congress gave him the power to encroach upon the fundamental right to travel simply because the applicant was a Communist.

e. Criminal vs. Civil Punishment
The legislature may delegate its authority to enact regulations, the violation of which are crimes, but prosecution for such violations must be left to the executive and judicial branches. [*See* United States v. Grimaud, 220 U.S. 506 (1911)] However, agencies may enact and impose civil penalties (i.e., fines labeled as civil fines) without prosecution in court. [Helvering v. Mitchell, 303 U.S. 391 (1938)]

C. THE SPEECH OR DEBATE CLAUSE—SPECIAL IMMUNITY FOR FEDERAL LEGISLATORS
Article I, Section 6 provides that "For any speech or debate in either House [members of Congress] shall not be questioned in any other place."

1. Persons Covered
The immunity extends to aides who engage in acts that would be immune if performed by a legislator. [Gravel v. United States, 408 U.S. 606 (1972)]

Note: The Speech or Debate Clause does *not extend to state legislators* who are prosecuted for violation of federal law. [United States v. Gillock, 445 U.S. 360 (1980)]

2. Scope of Immunity
Conduct that occurs in the regular course of the legislative process and the motivation behind that conduct are immune from prosecution.

a. Bribes Excluded
Taking of a bribe is not an act in the regular course of the legislative process and is therefore actionable. [United States v. Brewster, 408 U.S. 501 (1972)]

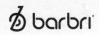

b. Speeches Outside Congress
Speeches and publications made outside Congress are not protected.

c. Defamatory Statements
Republication in a press release or newsletter of a defamatory statement originally made in Congress is not immune. [Hutchinson v. Proxmire, 443 U.S. 111 (1979)]

D. SEPARATION OF POWERS—THE REQUIREMENT OF BICAMERALISM AND PRESENTMENT
To pass a law, Congress must use bicameralism (passage of a bill by both houses of Congress) followed by presentment to the President for signature or veto. Attempts by Congress to create laws or control the enforcement of laws without bicameralism and presentment are invalid. [Immigration & Naturalization Service v. Chadha, 462 U.S. 919 (1983)]

Examples: 1) Congress granted to the Immigration & Naturalization Service ("INS") the power to deport or suspend from deportation illegal aliens. INS decisions to suspend deportations had to be submitted to Congress. Either house could pass a resolution overriding the decision. This "legislative veto" provision is unconstitutional because it allowed Congress to act without presentment. [Immigration & Naturalization Service v. Chadha, *supra*]

2) By statute, Congress grants to the President the power to send military troops into combat, without Congress's prior approval, whenever the United States or its territories are attacked. The statute, however, reserves to the Senate the power to force the President to withdraw the troops. The statute does not provide for presidential veto of the Senate's decision to withdraw. This statute is unconstitutional because the congressional action does not require bicameralism or presentment.

3) Congress passes a resolution in both houses to declare the second Tuesday of November "National Elk Appreciation Day." The resolution is not sent to the President for signature or veto. It has no binding impact but is entered into the official congressional record. This resolution is valid without presentment because it is nonbinding and does not create or control the enforcement of any laws.

III. THE EXECUTIVE POWER

A. VESTED IN PRESIDENT
The entire "executive power" is vested in the President by Article II, Section 1 of the Constitution. Various executive functions may be and are delegated within the "executive branch" by the President or by Congress.

B. DOMESTIC POWERS

1. Appointment and Removal of Officers

a. Appointment
Under Article II, Section 2, the President is empowered "with the advice and consent of the Senate" to appoint "all *ambassadors*, other *public ministers* and consuls, *judges of*

the Supreme Court, and all *other officers of the United States*, whose appointments are not herein otherwise provided for . . . but the Congress may by law vest the appointment of such inferior officers, as they think proper, in the President alone, in the courts of law, or in the heads of departments."

1) **Appointment of "Independent Counsel" (Special Prosecutor)**
A special prosecutor with the limited duties of investigating a narrow range of persons and subjects (e.g., to investigate alleged misconduct of a government employee) is an inferior officer. Therefore, under the Appointment Clause, Congress is free to vest the power to appoint a special prosecutor in the judiciary. [Morrison v. Olson, 487 U.S. 654 (1988)]

2) **No Appointments by Congress**
Although Congress may appoint its own officers to carry on *internal legislative tasks* (i.e., its staff), it may not appoint members of a body with administrative or enforcement powers; such persons are "officers of the United States" and must, pursuant to Article II, Section 2, be appointed by the President with senatorial confirmation unless Congress has vested their appointment in the President alone, in federal courts, or in heads of departments. [Buckley v. Valeo, 424 U.S. 1 (1976)]

b. **Recess Appointments**
The Recess Appointments Clause of the Constitution gives the President the power to make appointments for vacancy without Senate approval during any Senate recess of "sufficient duration." Under the Clause, the Senate is in recess only when it states it is in recess. If the Senate does not declare a recess and it holds pro forma sessions, the Senate is not in recess and the President has no power to make appointments without Senate approval. [NLRB v. Canning, 134 S. Ct. 2550 (2014)]

c. **Removal**
As to removal of appointees, the *Constitution is silent* except for ensuring tenure of all Article III judges "during good behavior."

1) **By President**
Under the Court's decisions, the President probably can remove high level, purely executive officers (e.g., Cabinet members) at will, without any interference from Congress. However, after *Morrison v. Olson, supra,* it appears that Congress may provide statutory limitations (e.g., removal for good cause) on the President's power to remove all other executive appointees.

2) **By Congress**

a) **Limitation on Removal Power**
Congress cannot give itself the power to remove an officer charged with the execution of laws except through impeachment. A congressional attempt through legislation to remove from government employment specifically named government employees is likely to be held invalid as a bill of attainder.

b) Limitation on Powers of Removable Officers

Congress cannot give a government employee who is subject to removal from office by Congress any powers that are truly executive in nature. For this reason, Congress could not give to the Comptroller General (who could be removed from office not only by impeachment but also by a joint resolution of Congress) the function of establishing the amount of automatic budget reductions that would be required if Congress failed to make budget reductions necessary to insure that the federal budget deficit did not exceed a legislatively established maximum amount. [Bowsher v. Synar, 478 U.S. 714 (1986)]

2. Pardons

The President is empowered by Article II, Section 2, "to grant reprieves and pardons for offenses against the United States, *except in cases of impeachment*." This power has been held to apply before, during, or after trial, and to extend to the offense of criminal contempt, but not to civil contempt, inasmuch as the latter involves the rights of third parties. The pardon power *cannot be limited by Congress*, and includes power to commute a sentence on any conditions the President chooses, as long as they are not independently unconstitutional. [Schick v. Reed, 419 U.S. 256 (1974)]

3. Veto Power

a. Congress May Override Veto by Two-Thirds Vote

Every act of Congress must be approved by the President before taking effect, unless passed over his disapproval by two-thirds vote of *each house*. [Art. I, §7]

b. President Has Ten Days to Veto

The President has 10 days (excepting Sundays) to exercise his veto power. If he fails to act within that time:

(i) The bill becomes law if Congress is still in session; or

(ii) The bill is automatically vetoed if Congress is not in session (a "*pocket veto*"). [Pocket Veto Case, 279 U.S. 655 (1929)]

Note: Brief recesses during an annual session create no pocket veto opportunity. [Wright v. United States, 302 U.S. 583 (1938)]

c. Line Item Veto Unconstitutional

The veto power allows the President only to approve or reject a bill in toto; he cannot cancel part (through a line item veto) and approve other parts. *Rationale:* The President's veto power does not authorize him to amend or repeal laws passed by Congress. [Clinton v. City of New York, 524 U.S. 417 (1998)]

4. Power as Chief Executive

The President's power over internal (i.e., within the United States) affairs as the chief executive is unclear. Clearly the President has some power to direct subordinate executive officers, and there is a long history of presidents issuing executive orders. Perhaps the best guide for determining the validity of presidential actions regarding internal affairs can be based on Justice Jackson's opinion in *Youngstown Sheet & Tube v. Sawyer*, 343 U.S. 579 (1952):

(i) Where the President acts with the express or implied authority of Congress, his authority is at its maximum and his actions likely are valid;

(ii) Where the President acts where Congress is silent, his action will be upheld as long as the act does not take over the powers of another branch of the government or prevent another branch from carrying out its tasks [*see, e.g.,* United States v. Nixon, I.E.7.b., *supra*—President's invocation of executive privilege was invalidated because it kept federal courts from having evidence they needed to conduct a fair criminal trial]; and

(iii) Where the President acts against the express will of Congress, he has little authority and his action likely is invalid.

Example: Hamdan was captured in the Afghanistan war, sent to Guantanamo Bay, and then tried for war crimes by a military commission that had been created by an Executive Order issued after the 9/11 terrorist attack. Citing Justice Jackson's *Youngstown* concurrence, the Court held that the military commission could not proceed, because the executive order authorizing the commission went beyond the limitations that Congress had placed on the President. The Court found that the Executive Order was authorized by an act of Congress that was interpreted as limiting the President's power to convene commissions to those that comply with the Constitution, laws, and rules of war, and that the commission here violated the laws and rules of war in several respects (e.g., it did not require a sufficient showing of the facts justifying the commission's jurisdiction; it did not provide the accused and his attorney sufficient access to the evidence). [Hamdan v. Rumsfeld, 548 U.S. 557 (2006)]

a.   No Power to Impound and the Take Care Clause

It follows from the above that the President has no power to refuse to spend appropriated funds when Congress has expressly mandated that they be spent. [Kendall v. United States *ex rel.* Stokes, 37 U.S. 524 (1838)] Some authorities base this result on Article II, Section 3, Clause 4—the Take Care Clause—which provides that the President "shall take care that the laws be faithfully executed . . . ."

C.   POWER OVER EXTERNAL AFFAIRS

1.   War

Although lacking the power to declare or initiate a "formal" war, the President has extensive military powers (essentially an external field, although applicable to civil war as well and to many domestic affairs caught up in military necessities).

a.   Actual Hostilities

The President may act militarily under his power as **commander in chief** of the armed forces and militia (when federalized), under Article II, Section 2, in actual hostilities against the United States without a congressional declaration of war. But **Congress** may limit the President under its power to enact a **military appropriation every two years**. (A military appropriation may not be for more than two years.)

b. **Military Government**
This power includes the establishment of military governments in occupied territories, including military tribunals.

2. Foreign Relations

The President's power to represent and act for the United States in day-to-day foreign relations is paramount. He has the power to appoint and receive ambassadors and make treaties (with the advice and consent of the Senate), and to enter into executive agreements. His power is broad even as to foreign affairs that require congressional consent.

a. **Power to Recognize Foreign States**
The power to recognize foreign states lies exclusively with the president. [*See* Zivotofsky v. Kerry, 135 S. Ct. 2076 (2015)—legislation requiring the secretary of state, upon request, to designate "Israel" and not "Jerusalem" as the place of birth on the passport of a U.S. citizen born in Jerusalem infringes on the long-time executive branch policy of favoring recognition of Jerusalem]

b. **Standard of Review—Rational Basis at Most**
Generally, courts defer to the President and Congress regarding foreign affairs. When reviewing whether an act violates a constitutional right, courts apply rational basis review.

Example: A statute gave the President broad discretion to decide immigration policy. After making campaign statements suggesting he wanted to ban Muslims from entering the United States, the President issued an executive order limiting immigration from several countries, most of which were majority-Muslim, purportedly on the ground that the order was necessary to prevent terrorists from entering the United States. When challenged as a violation of the Establishment Clause, the Supreme Court upheld the order, using rational basis review, because the stated purpose of the rule was proper and the order was rationally related to the purpose. [Trump v. Hawaii, 138 S. Ct. 2392 (2018)]

3. Treaty Power

The treaty power is granted to the President "by and with the advice and consent of the Senate, provided ***two-thirds of the Senators*** present concur." [Art. II, §2, cl. 2]

a. **Supreme Law**
Like other federal law, treaties are the "supreme law of the land." Any state action or law in conflict with a United States treaty is invalid (regardless of whether it is a state law or a state constitutional provision).

1) **Self-Executing vs. Non-Self-Executing Treaties**
Some treaties are expressly or impliedly self-executing (i.e., they are effective without any implementation by Congress). Others are not effective unless and until Congress passes legislation to effectuate their ends. If a treaty is not self-executing, it is not treated as the supreme law of the land until Congress acts to effectuate it, but the treaty itself can serve as an independent basis for Congress's power to adopt the required legislation (i.e., Congress need not point to one of its enumerated powers, such as the commerce power, as the basis for the legislation).

a) **President Has No Power to Implement Non-Self-Executing Treaties**
Based on the *Youngstown* analysis (B.4., *supra*), the President generally does not have any independent power to issue a "memorandum" ordering compliance with a non-self-executing treaty that has not been the subject of effectuating legislation by Congress. [Medellin v. Texas, 552 U.S. 491 (2008)—President had no power to enforce provisions of the Vienna Convention (a non-self-executing international treaty) by issuing a memorandum requiring states to grant habeas corpus petitions to reconsider convictions of criminals who are foreign nationals and who were not informed at the time of their arrest of their right to notify their consulate of their detention]

2) **Conflict with Congressional Acts**
Valid treaties are on a "supremacy parity" with acts of Congress; a conflict between an act of Congress and a treaty is resolved by order of adoption—*the last in time prevails*.

3) **Conflict with Constitution**
Treaties are not co-equal with the Constitution. For example, no treaty (or executive agreement) could confer on Congress authority to act in a manner inconsistent with any specific provision of the Constitution. [Reid v. Covert, 354 U.S. 1 (1957)]

b. **Other Limitations**
Other substantive limitations on the treaty power have not been judicially established; but in one case the Court expressed in dictum the view that a treaty could not upset the basic structure of the United States's federalism, or wield a power barred to the national government by the Constitution, or cede any part of a state to a foreign nation without the state's consent. The Court has *never held a treaty unconstitutional* (*Reid v. Covert, supra,* invalidated an executive agreement for violating the Fifth Amendment), but it is conceivable that the treaty power extends only to subjects plausibly bearing on our relations with other countries.

4. **Executive Agreements**
The President's power to enter into agreements (i.e., executive agreements) with the heads of foreign countries is not expressly provided for in the Constitution; nevertheless, the power has become institutionalized. Executive agreements can probably be on any subject as long as they do not violate the Constitution. They are very similar to treaties, except that they do not require the consent of the Senate.

a. **Conflicts with Other Governmental Action**
Executive agreements that are not consented to by the Senate are not the "supreme law of the land." Thus, *conflicting federal statutes and treaties* will prevail over an executive agreement, regardless of which was adopted first. However, executive agreements prevail over conflicting state laws.

b. **Example—Power to Settle Claims of United States Citizens**
The President, with the implicit approval of Congress, has power to settle claims of United States citizens against foreign governments through an executive agreement. [Dames & Moore v. Regan, 453 U.S. 654 (1981)]

D. EXECUTIVE PRIVILEGE/IMMUNITY

1. Executive Privilege

The executive privilege is not a constitutional power, but rather is an inherent privilege necessary to protect the confidentiality of presidential communications.

a. Extent of the Privilege

Presidential *documents and conversations* are *presumptively privileged*, but the privilege must yield to the need for such materials as evidence in a criminal case to which they are relevant and otherwise admissible. This determination must be made by the trial judge after hearing the evidence.

1) National Security Secrets

Military, diplomatic, or sensitive national security secrets are given great deference by the courts.

2) Criminal Proceedings

In criminal proceedings, presidential communiques will be available to the prosecution, where a need for such information is demonstrated. [United States v. Nixon, B.4., *supra*]

3) Civil Trials

The Court has avoided ruling on the scope of executive privilege in a civil case. Nevertheless, in *Cheney v. United States District Court*, 542 U.S. 367 (2004), the Court noted that the need for information in a criminal case is "weightier," and the Executive's withholding of information in a civil trial would not impair the judiciary's ability to fulfill its responsibility to resolve cases as much as in a criminal trial. Thus, it appears that an Executive branch decision to withhold information will be given more deference in a civil trial than in a criminal trial.

4) Screening Papers and Recordings of Former President

A federal statute requiring the Administrator of General Services to screen presidential papers is valid, notwithstanding the privilege. [Nixon v. Administrator of General Services, 433 U.S. 425 (1977)]

5) Screening by Judge in Chambers

The court will determine in an *in-camera* inspection which communications are protected and which are subject to disclosure.

2. Executive Immunity

a. Absolute Immunity for President

The President has *absolute immunity from civil damages* based on any action that the President took within his *official responsibilities* (even if the action was only arguably within the "outer perimeter" of presidential responsibility). [Nixon v. Fitzgerald, 457 U.S. 731 (1982)] However, the President has *no* immunity from private suits in federal courts based on *conduct that allegedly occurred before taking office*. [Clinton v. Jones, 520 U.S. 681 (1997)] *Rationale:* The immunity is intended only to enable the President to perform his *designated functions* without fear of personal liability.

b. Immunity May Extend to Presidential Aides

Presidential aides share in this immunity only if they are exercising discretionary authority for the President in "sensitive" areas of national concern, such as foreign affairs. Other aides are entitled only to a qualified immunity (a "good faith" defense). [Harlow v. Fitzgerald, 457 U.S. 800 (1982)]

Example: The Attorney General does not share the President's absolute immunity for authorizing a warrantless wiretap on "national security" grounds. The Attorney General would have a defense to a lawsuit regarding such a wiretap if it was shown that he was able to act in good faith because his actions were not violating clearly established or well-settled statutory or constitutional rights. [Mitchell v. Forsyth, 472 U.S. 511 (1985)]

E. IMPEACHMENT

1. Persons Subject to Impeachment

The President, Vice President, and all civil officers of the United States are subject to impeachment.

2. Grounds

The grounds for impeachment are treason, bribery, high crimes, and misdemeanors.

3. Impeachment by the House

A *majority vote* in the House is necessary to invoke the charges of impeachment.

4. Conviction by the Senate

A *two-thirds vote* in the Senate is necessary to convict.

PART TWO: THE FEDERAL SYSTEM

IV. RELATIVE SPHERES OF FEDERAL AND STATE POWER

A. EXCLUSIVE FEDERAL POWERS

1. Power of States Expressly Limited

Some powers are exclusively federal because of express constitutional limitation on or prohibition of the states' exercise thereof—such as the treaty power, coinage of money, and duty on imports.

2. Inherent Federal Powers

Others are exclusively federal in view of their nature—such as declaration of war, federal citizenship, naturalization, and borrowing money on the credit of the United States. Any state exercise of these powers would basically subvert the federal system. On the exam, *do not* allow states to take actions that might touch upon *foreign relations*.

Examples: 1) In *Zschernig v. Miller,* 389 U.S. 429 (1968), the Court held invalid state statutes that sought to withhold the proceeds of local decedents' estates from heirs living in nations that (i) discriminate against Americans in their probate laws, (ii) impede the transmission of funds to the United States, or (iii) confiscate property inherited by their citizens. The Court concluded that such laws are so potentially disruptive of a nationally conducted foreign policy that they are invalid notwithstanding the traditional commitment of probate law to the states.

2) California adopted an act to aid Holocaust victims that, among other things, required any California insurer that sold insurance policies in Europe between 1920 and 1945 to disclose certain information about those policies. The President of the United States also entered into an agreement with Germany regarding Holocaust victims' claims and informed California that its law would impede the effectiveness of that agreement. Nevertheless, California announced that it would enforce its law. Several insurance companies and a trade association brought suit to enjoin enforcement of the act. *Held:* The act interferes with the President's power over foreign affairs and is preempted on that ground. [American Insurance Association v. Garamendi, 539 U.S. 396 (2003)]

B.   EXCLUSIVE STATE POWERS

Whereas the federal government has only those powers granted to it by the Constitution, the state governments are governments of "unlimited" powers, having all powers not prohibited to them by the Constitution. This is recognized by the Tenth Amendment, which provides that all powers not delegated to the federal government by the Constitution are reserved to the states (or to the people). However, given the expansive interpretation of federal powers (e.g., the commerce power; *see* II.A.4., *supra*), little state power is exclusive.

C.   CONCURRENT FEDERAL AND STATE POWER—SUPREMACY CLAUSE

Most governmental power is concurrent, belonging to both the states and the federal government. Thus, it is possible for states and the federal government to pass legislation on the same subject matter. When this occurs, the Supremacy Clause provides that the federal law is supreme, and the state law is rendered void if it is preempted. State law may be preempted expressly or impliedly.

1.   Express Preemption

A federal law may expressly provide that the states may not adopt laws concerning the subject matter of the federal legislation. Note, however, that an express preemption clause will be narrowly construed. [*See* Altria Group, Inc. v. Good, 555 U.S. 70 (2008)]

Example: A federal law [15 U.S.C. §1334(b)] provides that: "no requirement or prohibition based on smoking and health shall be imposed under state law with respect to the advertising or promotion of any cigarettes" that are labeled in conformity with federal law. A smoker brought a state law consumer fraud claim against a cigarette company, claiming that the company's advertisements that its cigarettes were "light" and contain less tar and nicotine were fraudulent. The cigarette company argued that its advertisements were in conformity with federal law and, therefore, the state law claim was preempted by the federal law. *Held:* The state law claim is not preempted. The state consumer protection law is based on a duty not to deceive rather than on smoking or health, and the federal law preempts only state laws based on smoking or health. [Altria Group, Inc. v. Good, *supra*]

2.   Implied Preemption

Even if federal law does not expressly prohibit state action, state laws will nevertheless be held impliedly preempted if they actually conflict with federal requirements, they prevent achievement of federal objectives, or Congress has preempted the entire field.

a. **Actual Conflict Between State and Federal Law Requirements**
A valid act of Congress or federal regulation supersedes any state or local action that actually conflicts with the federal rule—whether by commanding conduct inconsistent with that required by the federal rule, or by forbidding conduct that the federal rule is designed to foster.
Example: Federal law [42 U.S.C. §1983] gives state and federal courts jurisdiction to hear claims for violations of federal rights committed by persons acting under color of state law. New York determined that the majority of suits seeking money damages from corrections officers under section 1983 are frivolous and therefore divested its trial courts of jurisdiction to hear such cases. *Held:* The state's policy of shielding corrections officers from suits under section 1983 violates the Supremacy Clause. State courts must hear federal claims. They may apply their own procedural rules as they do to state claims, but they cannot exclude a class of federal claims from being heard in state court. [Haywood v. Drown, 556 U.S. 729 (2009)]

b. **State Prevents Achievement of Federal Objective**
State law will also be held impliedly preempted if it interferes with achievement of a federal objective. This is true even if the state or local law was enacted for some valid purpose and not merely to frustrate the federal law.
Example: A purpose of the federal bankruptcy laws is to give bankrupts a fresh start, free of their old debts. A state law providing for suspension of the driver's license of persons who have failed to pay off auto accident judgments, regardless of the judgment debtor's discharge in bankruptcy, interferes with the federal objective and will fail. [Perez v. Campbell, 402 U.S. 637 (1971)]

c. **Field Preemption**
A state or local law may also be found to be preempted if it appears that Congress intended to "occupy" the entire field, thus precluding *any* state or local regulation. The courts will look at the federal regulatory scheme to deduce Congress's intent. For example, if the federal laws are comprehensive or a federal agency is created to oversee the field, preemption will often be found.
Example: Because Congress has enacted extensive regulatory laws concerning registration of aliens and employment of aliens who are in the country unlawfully, states may not make laws concerning these matters (not even a law making it a misdemeanor to fail to comply with federal immigration laws). Neither may a state authorize its officers to arrest a person without a warrant whom the officer has probable cause to believe has committed a public offense that makes the person removable from the United States—because such a law goes beyond the situations in which federal law provides for warrantless arrests for removable offenses. However, a state law requiring officers conducting a stop or detention to verify the detainee's immigration status if the officers have reasonable

suspicion to believe the detainee is an alien unlawfully present in the United States is not necessarily preempted, at least absent a showing that this practice will delay release of the detainees. [Arizona v. United States, 567 U.S. 387 (2012)]

3. Presumption Against Preemption

The Supreme Court has stated that in all preemption cases, especially any involving a field traditionally within the power of the states (e.g., regulations involving health, safety, or welfare), it will start with the **presumption** that the historic state police powers are **not** to be superseded unless that was the **clear and manifest purpose of Congress**. [Wyeth v. Levine, 555 U.S. 555 (2009)]

Example: A person who was injured by a prescription drug that was improperly administered brought a state law tort suit against the drug's manufacturer, claiming that the drug's label did not provide adequate warnings. The label was approved by the Food and Drug Administration ("FDA") pursuant to its power to regulate prescription drugs. The drug company claimed that the state tort action was preempted. *Held:* Congress did not intend to preempt the state court action here. The Court held that while Congress enacted the legislation here to protect consumers, it did not provide a remedy for consumers injured by unsafe drugs. Also, Congress had not enacted an express preemption provision within the statute for prescription drugs although it did enact an express preemption provision for medical devices. Moreover, there is no conflict between the FDA approval of a warning label and the state tort failure to warn claim here because the FDA regulation allowed companies to strengthen warnings without preapproval and, thus, the company was free to provide stronger warnings. [*See, e.g.,* Wyeth v. Levine, *supra*]

D. ABSENCE OF FEDERAL AND STATE POWERS

Some powers are denied to both Congress and the states. For example, the Supreme Court has held that the Qualifications Clauses [Art. I, §2, cl. 2; §3, cl. 3], setting the qualifications to serve in Congress, are exclusive and cannot be altered by Congress or the states. [United States Term Limits, Inc. v. Thornton, 514 U.S. 779 (1995)—state-imposed term limit for members of Congress invalidated; *and see* Cook v. Gralike, 531 U.S. 510 (2001)—state law instructing each member of its congressional delegation to support a constitutional amendment for term limits, and providing that failure to do so be noted on the ballot, was held invalid because it imposes a substantive qualification rather than regulates the "manner" in which elections are held]

E. INTERSTATE COMPACT CLAUSE

The Constitution provides that states may enter into agreements or compacts with other states upon the consent of Congress. [Art. I, §10, cl. 3] However, not all agreements between states are "compacts" requiring congressional consent. The Compact Clause reaches only interstate agreements that **increase the political power** of the states at the expense of federal supremacy (e.g., an agreement whereby one state cedes territory to another state). [*See* United States Steel Corp. v. Multistate Tax Commission, 434 U.S. 452 (1978)—congressional consent not required for multistate tax compact because the compact does not give member states any powers they could not exercise in its absence] The Supreme Court has the power to interpret such compacts—the member states do not have final authority over interpretation. [West Virginia *ex rel.* Dyer v. Sims, 341 U.S. 22 (1951)]

V. INTERSOVEREIGN LITIGATION

A. SUITS BY THE UNITED STATES AGAINST A STATE
The United States may sue a state without its consent.

B. SUITS BY STATE AGAINST UNITED STATES—UNITED STATES MUST CONSENT
Public policy forbids a state from suing the United States without its consent. Congress can pass legislation that permits the United States to be sued by a state in given situations.

C. FEDERAL OFFICER AS DEFENDANT

1. Limitation
Suits against a federal officer are *deemed to be brought against the United States* itself *if* the judgment sought would be satisfied out of the public treasury or would interfere with public administration and, therefore, are not permitted.

2. Specific Relief Against the Individual Officer
Specific relief against an officer as an individual will be granted if the officer acted ultra vires:

a. Beyond his statutory powers; or

b. The valid power was exercised in an unconstitutional manner.

D. SUITS BY ONE STATE AGAINST ANOTHER
One state may sue another state without the latter's consent. The Supreme Court has *exclusive original jurisdiction*.

VI. INTERGOVERNMENTAL TAX AND REGULATION IMMUNITIES

A. FEDERAL TAXATION AND REGULATION OF STATE OR LOCAL GOVERNMENTS
The Tenth Amendment provides that powers not delegated to the United States by the Constitution, nor prohibited to the states, are reserved to the states. This reservation of power is often cited as a restriction on Congress's power to regulate the states.

1. Tax or Regulation Applying to State and Private Entities—Valid
The Supreme Court will not likely strike down on Tenth Amendment grounds a tax or regulation that subjects states or local governments to regulations or taxes that apply to *both* the public sector and the private sector. It has held that in such cases, the states' interests are best protected by the states' representation in Congress. [Garcia v. San Antonio Metropolitan Transit Authority, 469 U.S. 528 (1985)]

Example: Congress can require state and local governments to follow the provisions of the Federal Fair Labor and Standards Act requiring minimum wages for all employees. [Garcia v. San Antonio Metropolitan Transit Authority, *supra*]

2. Tax or Regulation that Applies Only to States
However, the Tenth Amendment does limit Congress's power to regulate the states alone

by requiring the states to act in a particular way. Congress may not compel states to enact or enforce a regulatory program. [New York v. United States, 505 U.S. 144 (1992)—federal statute requiring states to either regulate radioactive waste or take title to it is beyond Congress's power] Similarly, if Congress passes a tax that does not apply to private businesses but merely taxes state government entities, there is a possibility that the Court would use the Tenth Amendment to prohibit the tax.

a. **Exception—Civil Rights**

Congress *may* use its power under the Fourteenth and Fifteenth Amendments to restrict state activities that it determines would violate the civil liberties of persons within the state.

Examples: 1) Congress may invalidate state laws establishing a literacy test as a prerequisite to voting in state elections. [Oregon v. Mitchell, 400 U.S. 112 (1970)]

2) Congress may restrict changes in state voting laws that have the effect of diminishing the voting power of racial minorities even though the change in state law was not purposeful racial discrimination that would violate Section 1 of the Fifteenth Amendment. [Rome v. United States, 446 U.S. 156 (1980)]

b. **Exception—Spending Power Conditions**

Congress may also "regulate" states through the spending power by imposing ***conditions on the grant of money to state or local governments*** (sometimes referred to as grants with strings attached). Such conditions will not violate the Tenth Amendment merely because Congress lacked the power to directly regulate the activity that is the subject of the spending program if the conditions:

(i) Are *clearly stated;*

(ii) ***Relate to the purpose*** of the program; and

(iii) Are ***not unduly coercive.***

Example: A federal law that would withhold 5% of the federal highway funds otherwise allocable to a state if the state did not set a 21 years' minimum age for the drinking of alcohol was upheld where the funds withheld amounted to less than one-half of 1% of the state's total budget. [South Dakota v. Dole, 483 U.S. 203 (1987)]

1) **What Is "Unduly Coercive"?**

There is a limit to the conditions the Supreme Court will tolerate. A condition that goes beyond mere "incentive" and turns into "compulsion" or "undue influence" violates principles of federalism. However, the Court has not set out a brightline test for making this determination. [National Federation of Independent Business v. Sebelius, II.A.2.a., *supra*—law that threatens to withhold from states current Medicare funding if they do not greatly expand Medicare programs amounts to a "gun to the head," given that the law threatens to withhold about 10% of an average state's total budget]

3. **Commandeering State Officials**

The Supreme Court has held that the Tenth Amendment prohibits Congress from adopting a statute that "commandeers" state officials by ***requiring states to regulate their own citizens***. [Printz v. United States, 521 U.S. 898 (1997)—striking portions of a federal gun law that required state law enforcement officers to collect from gun dealers reports regarding prospective handgun purchasers and to conduct background checks on them] However, the Court has allowed Congress to ***regulate the states by prohibiting them from performing certain acts***. [*See* Reno v. Condon, 528 U.S. 141 (2000)—upholding federal act that bars states (as well as private resellers) from disclosing personal information required on drivers' license applications]

B. STATE TAXATION AND REGULATION OF FEDERAL GOVERNMENT

1. **No Direct Tax on Federal Instrumentalities**

A state tax levied directly against the property or operation of the federal government without the consent of Congress is invalid.

2. **Nondiscriminatory, Indirect Taxes**

Nondiscriminatory, indirect taxes on the federal government or its property are permissible if they ***do not unreasonably burden*** the federal government.

Examples: 1) State income taxes on salaries of federal employees are valid. However, a state tax that imposes a higher tax on federal employees (or retired federal employees) than on state or local government employees (or retired employees) would violate the principle of intergovernmental tax immunity, unless Congress had approved this discriminatory tax. [Davis v. Michigan Department of Treasury, 489 U.S. 803 (1989)]

2) Private contractors, ***acting as purchasing agents*** for the federal government, cannot be compelled to pay state sales or use taxes on materials purchased on behalf of the federal government. However, state sales or use taxes are valid where the contractor is working for the federal government on a "cost-plus" basis. These extra costs are not characterized as direct taxes.

3. **State Regulation of Federal Government**

The states have no power to regulate the activities of the federal government unless Congress consents to the regulation. Thus, instrumentalities and agents of the federal government are immune from state regulations relating to performance of their federal functions.

Examples: 1) A state may not require a post office employee to obtain a state driver's license in order to drive a mail truck. [Johnson v. Maryland, 254 U.S. 51 (1920)]

2) A state may not require a contractor to obtain a state license to build facilities on an Air Force base, located within the state, pursuant to a government contract. [Leslie Miller, Inc. v. Arkansas, 352 U.S. 187 (1956)]

VII. PRIVILEGES AND IMMUNITIES CLAUSES

A. INTRODUCTION

There are two Privileges and Immunities Clauses: the Fourteenth Amendment Privileges or Immunities Clause and the Interstate Privileges and Immunities Clause of Article IV. The Fourteenth Amendment clause protects attributes of United States citizenship and is rarely applicable. The Article IV provision prevents some discrimination by states against nonresidents, and is usually more relevant on the bar exam.

B. ARTICLE IV—PRIVILEGES OF STATE CITIZENSHIP

Article IV, Section 2, the Interstate Privileges and Immunities Clause, provides that "[t]he Citizens of each state shall be entitled to all Privileges and Immunities of citizens in the several states." Thus, it prohibits discrimination by a state against nonresidents.

1. Corporations and Aliens Not Protected

Corporations and aliens are *not citizens* of a state for purposes of the Privileges and Immunities Clause.

2. Only "Fundamental Rights" Protected

The Interstate Privileges and Immunities Clause prohibits discrimination by a state against nonresidents of the state when the discrimination concerns "fundamental rights"—i.e., rights relating to important *commercial activities* (such as pursuit of a livelihood) or *civil liberties*. However, the Clause applies only if the discrimination is *intentionally protectionist* in nature. [*See* McBurney v. Young, 569 U.S. 221 (2013)—state law limiting Freedom of Information Act requests to state citizens did not violate the Privileges and Immunities Clause when it interfered with a nonresident's vocation of obtaining property records for clients, because there was no evidence that the discrimination was protectionist in nature] The following protectionist measures have been struck down:

a. *Statute charging nonresident commercial fishermen substantially more for commercial fishing license* than resident commercial fishermen ($2,500 vs. $25) [Toomer v. Witsell, 334 U.S. 385 (1948); *cf.* Baldwin v. Montana Fish & Game Commission, 436 U.S. 371 (1978)—vast difference between resident and nonresident *recreational* hunting license constitutional since no essential commercial activity involved];

b. *Statute giving resident creditors priority* over nonresident creditors as to assets of foreign corporations in receivership proceedings [Blake v. McClung, 172 U.S. 239 (1898)];

c. *Statute or court rule requiring state residency to be licensed* to practice law within the state [Supreme Court of Virginia v. Friedman, 487 U.S. 59 (1988)];

d. *State income tax only on nonresidents* who earn money within the state [Austin v. New Hampshire, 420 U.S. 656 (1975)]; and

e. *State law requiring private sector employers to give hiring preference to residents* absent a closely related substantial justification (*see* below) [Hicklin v. Orbeck, 437 U.S. 518 (1978)], but states *may* require a person to be a resident to hold *government employment* [McCarthy v. Philadelphia Civil Service Commission, 424 U.S. 645 (1976) (per curiam)].

3. **Substantial Justification Exception**
   A state law discriminating against nonresidents may be valid if the state has a substantial justification for the different treatment. In effect, it must show that nonresidents either cause or are part of the problem it is attempting to solve, and that there are *no less restrictive means* to solve the problem. Stated another way, the law must be necessary to achieve an important government purpose.

   Example: The Court held that a city ordinance requiring 40% of employees of contractors and subcontractors working on city construction projects to be city residents was an apparent violation of the Article IV Privileges and Immunities Clause because it gave a preference in private sector employment to city residents. However, the Court found that it could not make a final determination as to *whether the preference was justified* in this case because the record from the lower courts did not allow it to evaluate the city's argument that the preference was necessary *to counteract grave economic and social ills* in urban environments caused by spiraling unemployment and declines in the population base of such cities. [United Building & Construction Trades Council v. Mayor of Camden, 465 U.S. 208 (1984)]

4. **Note—Relationship to Commerce Clause**
   Although the Article IV Privileges and Immunities Clause and the Commerce Clause may apply different standards and produce different results, they tend to mutually reinforce each other. Consequently, they both have to be considered in analyzing bar exam questions.

C. **FOURTEENTH AMENDMENT—PRIVILEGES OF NATIONAL CITIZENSHIP**
   The Fourteenth Amendment Privileges or Immunities Clause prohibits states from denying their citizens the privileges and immunities of national citizenship, such as the right to petition Congress for redress of grievances, the right to vote for federal officers, the right to enter public lands, the right to interstate travel, and any other right flowing from the distinct relation of a citizen to the United States Government.

   1. **Corporations Not Protected**
      Corporations are *not citizens* of the United States and are *not protected*.

   2. **Bill of Rights Not Included**
      The *Slaughterhouse Cases,* 83 U.S. 36 (1873), held that the fundamental rights protected against federal abuse (first 10 Amendments) are *not privileges or immunities of national citizenship* within the meaning of the Fourteenth Amendment; nor are such other basic rights as the right to live, work, and eat. Thus, the guarantees of the Bill of Rights are protected from state action only by the Due Process and Equal Protection Clauses of the Fourteenth Amendment.

   3. **Right to Travel and the Privileges or Immunities Clause**
      The right to travel, which is protected by the Fourteenth Amendment, includes the right of newly arrived citizens to enjoy the same privileges and immunities as are enjoyed by other citizens of the state.

Example: A California statute limiting the welfare benefits of first year residents was held unconstitutional under the Fourteenth Amendment Privileges or Immunities Clause. The statute provided that citizens who had lived in California for less than one year could receive only the benefits they would have received in their prior state of residence. The Court noted that the right to travel includes the right to be treated equally in a new state of residence. [Saenz v. Roe, 526 U.S. 489 (1999)]

PART THREE: STATE REGULATION OR TAXATION OF COMMERCE

VIII. REGULATION OF FOREIGN COMMERCE

A. LIES EXCLUSIVELY WITH CONGRESS

For all practical purposes, the power to regulate foreign commerce lies exclusively with Congress. "Foreign" commerce has been held to include traffic on the high seas, even though both terminal ports are within the United States. [Japan Line, Ltd. v. County of Los Angeles, 441 U.S. 434 (1979)]

B. MINOR EXCEPTIONS WHERE STATE REGULATION PERMITTED

The Supreme Court, however, has recognized a few minor exceptions; thus, the states are free to regulate local aspects of port pilotage and navigation of ships in foreign commerce (e.g., aspects such as safety of handling); and in one case the Court permitted state regulation of excursion boat traffic between Detroit and a Canadian island (state barred racial discrimination among boat passengers) since no Canadians or Canadian products or services were involved. [Bob-Lo Excursion Co. v. Michigan, 333 U.S. 28 (1948)]

IX. REGULATION OF INTERSTATE COMMERCE

A. REGULATION OF COMMERCE BY CONGRESS

As already seen, Congress's power over interstate commerce is very broad and pervasive. However, the power is *nonexclusive*—it is shared with the states to some degree.

1. Power of Congress to Supersede or Preempt State Regulation

Recall that the Supremacy Clause makes federal law supreme. (*See* IV.C., *supra*.) Thus, if a state law regulating commerce conflicts with a federal law, the state law will be void. Moreover, if Congress desires, it may preempt an entire area of regulation, thus preventing states from making any laws concerning the area preempted. (*See* IV.C.3., *supra*.)

2. Power of Congress to Permit or Prohibit State Regulation

Although Congress's commerce power is nonexclusive, the states' power to regulate interstate commerce is restricted by the negative implications of the Commerce Clause, even absent federal legislation—the states generally may *not* discriminate against interstate commerce. (*See* below.) Nevertheless, Congress is not so restricted; it may allow the states to adopt legislation that would otherwise violate the Commerce Clause.

Example: A state imposed a 3% tax on out-of-state insurance companies for all premiums received from insuring residents of the state. No similar tax was placed on in-state insurance companies. Although such a tax would ordinarily be held invalid under the Commerce Clause—because it discriminates against interstate commerce—the tax here was upheld because Congress had adopted an act permitting the states to regulate insurance in any manner, as long as the state regulation did not conflict with a federal statute specifically regulating insurance. [Prudential Insurance Co. v. Benjamin, 328 U.S. 408 (1946); *and see* Northeast Bancorp, Inc. v. Board of Governors, 472 U.S. 159 (1985)]

Note: As indicated above, Congress may also prohibit the states from adopting legislation that would otherwise be permitted under the Commerce Clause.

a.   Limitation
While Congress may permit states to adopt regulations that would otherwise violate the Commerce Clause, such consent will not obviate other constitutional objections to the regulation. Thus, Congress may not give states the power to restrict civil liberties. (*See* X.A.1.b.2)a), *infra.*)

B.   STATE REGULATION OF COMMERCE IN THE ABSENCE OF CONGRESSIONAL ACTION
If Congress has not enacted laws regarding the subject, a state or local government may regulate local aspects of interstate commerce if the regulation:

(i)   Does *not discriminate* against out-of-state competition to benefit local economic interests; and

(ii)   Is *not unduly burdensome* (i.e., the incidental burden on interstate commerce does not outweigh the legitimate local benefits produced by the regulation).

If either test is not met, the regulation will be held void for violating the Commerce Clause (sometimes called the "*Dormant Commerce Clause*" or "*Negative Commerce Clause*" under such circumstances).

1.   Discriminatory Regulations

a.   Generally Invalid
State or local regulations that discriminate against interstate commerce to protect local economic interests are almost always invalid.

b.   Examples

1)   Regulations Protecting Local Businesses
Laws designed to protect local businesses against interstate competition generally will be invalidated.

Examples: 1) A state cannot place a surcharge on out-of-state milk to make that milk as expensive as (or more expensive than) milk produced in the state.

2) A state cannot exempt local businesses or products from taxation or regulation that it seeks to apply to out-of-state businesses or products that come into the state.

3) A law requiring all locally produced solid waste to be processed at a local waste processing business was held to violate the Commerce Clause because it was a trade barrier against competition from out-of-state waste processors. [C&A Carbone, Inc. v. Town of Clarkstown, 511 U.S. 383 (1994)]

2) **Regulations Requiring Local Operations**
If a state law requires a business to perform specific business operations in the state to engage in other business activity within the state, the law will normally be held invalid as an attempt to discriminate against other states where the business operations could be performed more efficiently.

Example: If a state required all businesses that produce melons in the state and all businesses that purchase melons from local producers to wrap or package the melons in the state (before the melons were exported from the state), the law would be invalid as an attempt to force businesses to locate their packaging operations in the state.

3) **Regulations Limiting Access to In-State Products**
A state law that makes it difficult or impossible for out-of-state purchasers to have access to in-state products (other than products owned by the state itself) is likely to be held invalid.

Examples: 1) A state cannot prohibit in-state owners of "ground water" from selling and exporting the water they own to persons in other states.

2) A state cannot require in-state companies to sell products at a lower price to in-state residents than to out-of-state residents.

4) **Regulations Prohibiting Out-of-State Wastes**
A state may not prohibit private landfill or waste disposal facilities from accepting out-of-state garbage or waste or surcharge such waste [Philadelphia v. New Jersey, 437 U.S. 617 (1978); Chemical Waste Management v. Hunt, 504 U.S. 334 (1992)] unless Congress authorizes such discrimination [New York v. United States, VI.A.2., *supra*—federal statute allowing states to impose surcharge on certain out-of-state nuclear wastes upheld]. This rule applies even to hazardous wastes. [Oregon Waste Systems, Inc. v. Department of Environmental Quality, 511 U.S. 93 (1994)]

c. **Exceptions**

1) **Necessary to Important State Interest**
A discriminatory state or local law may be valid if it furthers an important, noneconomic state interest (e.g., health or safety) and there are ***no reasonable alternatives*** available.

Example: A state could prohibit the importation of live baitfish (such as minnows) into the state because the state could demonstrate that it had no other way of effectively avoiding the possibility that such baitfish might bring certain parasites into the state or, in other ways, have a detrimental effect on the state's wild fish population. [Maine

v. Taylor, 477 U.S. 131 (1986)] However, a state could not prohibit the export of live baitfish to out-of-state purchasers because the sale of such fish to out-of-state purchasers would not impair any interest of the state, except the interest of protecting local purchasers of baitfish from competition by out-of-state purchasers. [Hughes v. Oklahoma, 441 U.S. 322 (1979)]

2) State as Market Participant

The Commerce Clause does not prevent a state from preferring its own citizens when the state is acting as a market participant (e.g., buying or selling products, hiring labor, giving subsidies).

Examples: 1) A state may purchase scrap automobiles from its citizens at a higher-than-market rate and refuse to pay nonresidents the same amount. [Hughes v. Alexandria Scrap Corp., 426 U.S. 794 (1976)]

2) Under the market participant exception to the Commerce Clause, a city may require that all construction *projects funded by the city* be performed by contractors using a workforce composed of at least 50% bona fide residents of the city. [White v. Massachusetts Council of Construction Employers, 460 U.S. 204 (1983)]

a) Limitation—Interstate Privileges and Immunities Clause

While a state or local government does not violate the *Commerce Clause* by preferring its own citizens while acting as a market participant, there is no market participant exception to the Interstate Privileges and Immunities Clause. Thus, a regulation that interferes with private sector employment, such as the one in example 2), above, may violate the Privileges and Immunities Clause unless the regulating entity can show a substantial justification for the regulation. (*See* VII.B.3., *supra.*)

b) Limitation—"Downstream" Restrictions

While a state may choose to sell only to state residents, it may not attach conditions to a sale that would discriminate against interstate commerce.

Example: Alaska violated the Commerce Clause when it imposed a contractual requirement on purchasers of state-owned timber that the timber be processed in Alaska before being shipped out of state. [South-Central Timber Development, Inc. v. Wunnicke, 467 U.S. 82 (1984)—plurality opinion]

3) Favoring Government Performing Traditional Government Functions

The Supreme Court applies a more lenient standard when a law favors government action involving the performance of a traditional government function (such as waste disposal). Discrimination against interstate commerce in such a case is permissible because it is likely motivated by legitimate objectives rather than by economic protectionism.

Examples: 1) A county flow control ordinance that favored a state-created public waste facility by requiring waste haulers to bring the wastes to the state facility rather than to private facilities is valid.

[United Haulers Association, Inc. v. Oneida-Herkimer Solid Waste Management Authority, 550 U.S. 330 (2007)]

2) A state may exempt from state taxation interest on its own bonds and bonds of its municipalities while taxing bonds of other states and their subdivisions. [Department of Revenue of Kentucky v. Davis, 553 U.S. 328 (2008)—issuing debt securities to pay for public projects is a "quintessentially public function" with a venerable history]

2. Nondiscriminatory Laws—Balancing Test

Sometimes a nondiscriminatory state or local law that regulates commerce may impose a burden on interstate commerce; e.g., a state law regulating the size of trucks within that state may burden interstate commerce because interstate trucking operations will be subject to the law when their trucks enter the state. A nondiscriminatory law will be invalidated only if the burden on interstate commerce outweighs the promotion of legitimate (not discriminatory) local interests. This is a case-by-case balancing test. Thus, some regulations of trucks will be upheld, because they do not impose an undue burden on interstate commerce, whereas other truck regulations will be invalidated, because they would make it extremely difficult for interstate trucking operators to have their trucks travel into or through the state.

a. Absence of Conflict with Other States

State and local laws regulating commerce are more likely to be upheld when there is little chance that states would have conflicting regulations of the same subject matter.

Example: A state could validly apply a state law prohibiting racial or gender discrimination in the hiring of personnel to an airline doing business in the state because the law was not discriminatory against out-of-state businesses, it promoted a legitimate interest, and no other state could validly require or permit racial or gender discrimination by airlines.

b. State Control of Corporations

A different standard may apply to statutes regulating the internal governance of a corporation adopted by the state of incorporation. Because of the states' long history of regulating the internal governance of corporations that they create, and because of their strong interest in doing so, even a statute that heavily impacts interstate commerce may be upheld.

Example: To protect shareholders of corporations incorporated in Indiana from hostile takeovers, the Indiana legislature adopted a "control share acquisition statute." The statute provided that once a person acquires shares that take him across a specified ownership threshold (e.g., one-third ownership of all voting shares), he may not vote those shares unless the other shareholders consent. Even though most hostile takeover bids originate from outside the state, the Supreme Court found that the statute did not violate the Commerce Clause because its aim was to protect current shareholders, it did not discriminate between takeover bidders based on their state of origin, and there is no chance that the state law would conflict with the laws of other states because the internal governance of a corporation is regulated only by the state in which the corporation is incorporated. [CTS Corp. v. Dynamics Corp. of America, 481 U.S. 69 (1987)]

C. TWENTY-FIRST AMENDMENT—STATE CONTROL OVER INTOXICATING LIQUOR

1. Intrastate Regulations

The Twenty-First Amendment, which repealed prohibition, gives state governments wide latitude over the importation of liquor and the conditions under which liquor is sold or used within the state. However, state liquor regulations that constitute only an economic preference for local liquor manufacturers may violate the Commerce Clause. The Commerce Clause prohibits both outright economic favoritism for local businesses and attempts to regulate out-of-state transactions in order to guarantee the competitive position of in-state businesses.

Examples:　1) A state law that prohibits out-of-state wineries from shipping wine directly to in-state consumers, but permitting in-state wineries to do so if licensed, discriminates against interstate commerce. [Granholm v. Heald, 544 U.S. 460 (2005)]

2) A state law that requires out-of-state distillers or sellers of alcoholic beverages to affirm that the price the distiller/seller is charging liquor retailers or wholesalers in the state is no greater than the price the distiller/seller is charging in other states violates the Commerce Clause. Such a price affirmation law directly interferes with and burdens interstate commerce. The Twenty-First Amendment does not authorize this type of state interference with commerce. [Brown-Forman Distillers Corp. v. New York State Liquor Authority, 476 U.S. 573 (1986); Healy v. The Beer Institute, Inc., 491 U.S. 324 (1989)]

2. Interstate Regulations

Transitory liquor (liquor bound for out-of-state destinations) is subject to the Commerce Clause. Thus, a state prohibition on transporting liquor through the state would probably be held unconstitutional as violating the Commerce Clause.

3. Federal Power

The Twenty-First Amendment does not prohibit Congress from controlling economic transactions involving alcoholic beverages under the federal commerce power. Thus, federal antitrust law can prohibit a practice of liquor dealers that has the effect of fixing minimum prices. [324 Liquor Corp. v. Duffy, 479 U.S. 335 (1987)] Similarly, as mentioned above, Congress may, without violating the Twenty-First Amendment, "regulate" liquor distribution by imposing conditions on the grant of federal funds given under the spending power. [South Dakota v. Dole, VI.A.2.b., *supra*]

D. BAR EXAM APPROACH

Whenever a bar exam question involves a state regulation that affects the free flow of interstate commerce, you should proceed as follows:

First, see if the question refers to *any federal legislation* that might be held either to: (i) *supersede* the state regulation or *preempt* the field, or (ii) *authorize* state regulation otherwise impermissible.

Second, if neither of these possibilities is dispositive of the question, ask if the state legislation either *discriminates* against interstate or out-of-state commerce or places an *undue burden* on the free flow of interstate commerce. If the legislation is discriminatory, it will be invalid unless (i) it furthers an important state interest *and* there are no reasonable nondiscriminatory alternatives, or (ii) the state is a market participant. If the legislation does not discriminate but burdens interstate commerce, it will be invalid if the burden on commerce outweighs the state's interest. Consider whether there are less restrictive alternatives.

X. POWER OF STATES TO TAX INTERSTATE COMMERCE

A. GENERAL CONSIDERATIONS

The same general considerations applicable to state regulation of commerce (*supra*) apply to taxation. Pursuant to the Commerce Clause, Congress has complete power to authorize or forbid state taxation affecting interstate commerce. If Congress has not acted, look to see whether the tax *discriminates* against interstate commerce. If it does, it is invalid. If it does not, assess whether the burden on interstate commerce outweighs the benefit to the state. Three tests must be met: (i) there must be a *substantial nexus* between the taxpayer and the state; (ii) the tax must be *fairly apportioned*; and (iii) there must be a *fair relationship* between the tax and the services or benefits provided by the state.

1. Discriminatory Taxes

Unless authorized by Congress, state taxes that discriminate against interstate commerce violate the Commerce Clause. Such taxes may also be held to violate the Interstate Privileges and Immunities Clause (*see* VII.B., *supra*) if they also discriminate against nonresidents of the state [Austin v. New Hampshire, 420 U.S. 656 (1975)], as well as the Equal Protection Clause if the discrimination is not rationally related to a legitimate state purpose [WHYY, Inc. v. Borough of Glassboro, 393 U.S. 117 (1968)—denial of tax exemption solely because taxpayer was incorporated in another state is invalid].

a. Finding Discrimination

1) Tax Singles Out Interstate Commerce
If a state tax singles out interstate commerce for taxation, the Court ordinarily will not "save" the tax by finding other state taxes imposed only on local commerce (which might arguably eliminate the "apparent" discrimination against interstate commerce).

Example: The Supreme Court invalidated an Ohio statute that gave a tax credit against the Ohio motor vehicle fuel sales tax (paid by fuel dealers) for each gallon of ethanol sold as a component of gasohol if, but only if, the ethanol was produced in Ohio or in a state that granted a similar tax advantage to ethanol produced in Ohio. The Supreme Court found that this tax credit system constituted discrimination against interstate commerce. [New Energy Co. of Indiana v. Limbach, 486 U.S. 269 (1988)]

However, state taxes that single out interstate commerce are considered ***nondiscriminatory*** if the particular statutory section or scheme ***also*** imposes the same type of tax on ***local*** commerce (e.g., sales and use taxes, discussed *infra*).

2) Tax with In-State Subsidy

A seemingly uniform tax may be ruled to be discriminatory if the proceeds from the tax are "earmarked" for subsidies to in-state businesses.

Example: A state imposed a tax on all milk dealers, but the tax law provided that revenue from the tax would be put into a fund that would be used to pay subsidies to in-state dairy farmers. This assessment-subsidy system violates the Commerce Clause because it operates identically to a tax placed only on sales of milk produced outside the state. [West Lynn Creamery, Inc. v. Healy, 512 U.S. 186 (1994)]

3) Double Taxation on Out-of-State Income

A state must grant a credit against a local tax for income taxed by another state.

Example: Maryland's personal income tax on residents includes both a state and a county tax. Residents who pay taxes to another state for income earned in that state are allowed a credit against the state tax but not the county tax. Such a tax scheme violates the Dormant Commerce Clause because it leads to double taxation on out-of-state income and discriminates in favor of intrastate over interstate economic activity. [Comptroller of Treasury of Maryland v. Wynne, 135 S. Ct. 1787 (2015)]

b. Choosing the Proper Clause

While a state or local tax that discriminates against interstate commerce generally violates the Commerce Clause, the Clause is not always the strongest argument against the tax.

1) Interstate Privileges and Immunities Clause

If a state or local tax discriminates against a ***natural person who is a nonresident***, the Article IV Interstate Privileges and Immunities Clause is the strongest argument against the tax's validity, because it is more direct than a Commerce Clause argument.

2) Equal Protection

a) Where Congress Approves the Discrimination

Although the Supreme Court normally uses the Commerce Clause to invalidate discriminatory legislation, it may also find that such discrimination violates the Equal Protection Clause. This is important where Congress has given the states the power to do something that would otherwise violate the Commerce Clause: Congress can give states the power to take actions that otherwise would violate the Commerce Clause, but it ***cannot*** approve state actions that would violate equal protection. Thus, if Congress has approved a type of state tax that discriminates against out-of-state businesses, that state tax will not be in violation of the Commerce Clause, but it might be found to be a violation of equal protection.

Example: In *Metropolitan Life Insurance Co. v. Ward,* 470 U.S. 869 (1985), the Court invalidated a state tax on insurance companies that imposed a higher tax on out-of-state insurance companies than was paid by in-state companies. The Court found that federal statutes exempted state regulation of insurance businesses from Commerce Clause restrictions but found that the tax violated equal protection because it did not relate to a legitimate interest of government (i.e., the state does not have a legitimate interest in discriminating against out-of-state businesses simply to protect local economic interests from competition).

b) **Taxes Based on Suspect Classifications or Infringing on Fundamental Rights**

The Court may use equal protection analysis rather than Commerce Clause analysis to strike state taxes that are imposed on the basis of a *suspect classification* or that burden a *fundamental right*. A state tax system giving tax exemptions only to long-time residents of the state and denying a similar tax exemption to newer residents will be held to violate the Equal Protection Clause.

Example: The Court invalidated a state property tax provision that gave an exemption from the property tax only to those Vietnam-era veterans who had been residents of the state before May 1976. [Hooper v. Bernalillo County Assessor, 472 U.S. 612 (1985)]

2. **Nondiscriminatory Taxes**

The Court reviews nondiscriminatory state and local taxes affecting interstate commerce and balances the state need to obtain the revenue against the burden the tax imposes on the free flow of commerce—an approach similar to the one used for examining nondiscriminatory regulations to see whether they impose an undue burden on interstate commerce (*see* IX.B.2., *supra*).

a. **Factors**

The Court generally considers three factors in determining whether the nondiscriminatory tax is valid:

1) **Substantial Nexus**

A state tax will be valid under the Commerce Clause only if there is a substantial nexus between the activity or property taxed and the taxing state. A substantial nexus exists when the business that must collect the tax *avails itself* of the privilege of doing business in the state. A physical presence in the state is *not* necessary.

Example: Internet retailers that annually sold more than $100,000 of goods to or engaged in more than 200 transactions with South Dakota customers had a substantial nexus with South Dakota even though the retailers had no physical presence in the state. [South Dakota v. Wayfair, Inc., 138 S. Ct. 2080 (2018)]

2) Fair Apportionment

A state or local tax affecting interstate commerce will be valid under the Commerce Clause only if it is fairly apportioned according to a rational formula (i.e., the tax should be based on the extent of the taxable activity or property in the state). Otherwise the activity or property would be subject to cumulative tax burdens.

Examples: 1) State A imposes a 1% tax on gross receipts of all businesses within the state. Harvester is located in State A but makes a number of sales out of state. The tax is invalid as to Harvester's out-of-state sales since it potentially subjects those sales to cumulative burdens—the tax by the seller's state and a similar tax by the buyer's state—without apportioning the tax.

2) Chooch is a resident of State A. It owns railroad cars used in interstate commerce. The cars are in State A three months each year and State B three months each year. For a State B property tax on the railroad cars to be valid, it must fairly apportion the tax, so that the cars will not be subjected to a similar tax by State A, thus cumulating Chooch's tax burden.

Note: The taxpayer has the burden of proving an unfair apportionment.

3) Fair Relationship

A state or local tax affecting interstate commerce will be valid under the Commerce Clause only if the tax is fairly related to the services or benefits provided by the state.

Example: A state may levy a tax on passengers enplaning at a state airport if the tax is related to the benefits that the passengers receive from the state (e.g., the airport facilities). [*See* Evansville-Vanderburgh Airport Authority District v. Delta Airlines, Inc., 405 U.S. 707 (1972)]

B. USE TAX

Use taxes are taxes imposed on the users of goods purchased out of state.

1. Permissible in Buyer's State

Use taxes are not considered to discriminate against interstate commerce even though they single out interstate commerce for taxation (i.e., they are imposed only on goods purchased outside the state), as long as the use tax rate is not higher than the sales tax rate. *Rationale:* The purpose of such a tax is to *equalize* the tax on in-state and out-of-state goods rather than to give in-state goods an advantage. [*See* Henneford v. Silas Mason Co., 300 U.S. 577 (1937)]

2. State May Force Seller to Collect Use Tax

Often, states force the user to come forward and pay the state the use tax owed. However, a state may force a nonresident, interstate seller to *collect* the use tax from the local buyer and remit it to the state *if* the seller has the substantial nexus required by the Commerce Clause. (*See* A.2.a.1), *supra.*)

C. **SALES TAXES**
Sales taxes are taxes imposed on the seller of goods for sales consummated within the state. They generally do not discriminate against interstate commerce; rather the issue usually involves whether there is a substantial nexus (*see* A.2.a.1), *supra*) between the taxpayer and the taxing state, or whether the tax is properly apportioned.

D. **AD VALOREM PROPERTY TAXES**
Ad valorem property taxes are taxes based on a percentage of the assessed value of the property in question. Such taxes are generally valid. However, a Commerce Clause issue arises when the property taxed moves in interstate commerce. Goods in transit are *totally exempt* from taxation. Once the goods come to a halt in a state (i.e., obtain a *taxable situs*), they may be taxed. Then, the issue usually revolves around whether the tax imposes an undue cumulative burden (i.e., apportionment).

1. **No Tax on Commodities in the Course of Interstate Commerce**
Commodities in the course of interstate commerce are *entirely exempt* from local taxation—since each state could otherwise exact a toll as the goods passed through, imposing an intolerable burden on interstate commerce. [Standard Oil v. Peck, 342 U.S. 382 (1952)] Thus, states may not levy an ad valorem property tax on commodities being shipped in interstate commerce, even if the goods happen to be in the state on tax day.

a. **When Is Property "in the Course of" Interstate Commerce?**
Only property "in the course of" interstate commerce is immune from local property taxation.

1) **When Does Interstate Transportation Begin?**
Interstate transportation begins when (i) the cargo is delivered to an interstate carrier (the shipper thereby relinquishing further control), *or* (ii) the cargo actually starts its interstate journey. Goods merely being prepared for transit are *not* in the course of interstate commerce.

2) **Effect of a "Break" in Transit**
Once started, a shipment remains in the course of interstate commerce unless actually diverted. Breaks in the continuity of transit will not destroy the interstate character of the shipment, unless the break was *intended to end or suspend* (rather than temporarily interrupt) the shipment.

3) **When Does Interstate Shipment End?**
The interstate shipment usually ends when it *reaches its destination*, and thereafter the goods are *subject to local tax*.

b. **No Apportionment Required**
The validity of state taxes on goods in interstate commerce is strictly a Commerce Clause question; i.e., either the goods are "in the course of" interstate commerce and exempt from tax or they are not. There is no need for apportionment.

2. **Tax on Instrumentalities Used to Transport Goods Interstate**
The validity of ad valorem property taxes on instrumentalities of commerce (airplanes,

railroad cars, etc.) depends on (i) whether the instrumentality has acquired a *"taxable situs"* in the taxing state (i.e., whether there are *sufficient "contacts" with the taxing state* to justify the tax), and (ii) since the physical situs of the instrumentalities may change from state to state during the year, whether the *value* of the instrumentality has been properly *apportioned according to the amount of "contacts"* with each taxing state. (The taxable situs ("nexus") is required by the Due Process Clause to establish the state's power to tax at all, and apportionment is required by the Commerce Clause to prevent an intolerable burden on interstate commerce.)

a. **Taxable Situs ("Nexus")**
In general, an instrumentality has a taxable situs in a state if it receives *benefits or protection* from the state. [Braniff Airways v. Nebraska Board of Equalization and Assessment, 347 U.S. 590 (1954)—airplanes have taxable situs in nondomiciliary state where airline company owned no property but made 18 regularly scheduled flights per day from rented depot space, even though same aircraft did not land every day] Note that an instrumentality *may have more than one taxable situs*, upon each of which states can impose a tax subject to the required apportionment (*infra*).

b. **Apportionment Requirement**
If an instrumentality has only one situs, the domiciliary state can tax at full value. If the instrumentality has more than one taxable situs, a tax apportioned on the value of the instrumentality will be upheld if it fairly approximates the average physical presence of the instrumentality within the taxing state. [Union Tank Line Co. v. Wright, 249 U.S. 275 (1919)] The *taxpayer has the burden* of proving that an instrumentality has acquired a taxable situs outside his domiciliary state.

1) **Proper Apportionment**
The following methods have been upheld:

(i) Using the proportion of *miles traveled* within the taxing state to the total number of miles traveled by the instrumentalities in the entire operation. [Ott v. Mississippi Valley Barge Line Co., 336 U.S. 169 (1949)]

(ii) Computing the *average number of instrumentalities* (tank cars) *physically present* in the taxing state on any one day during the tax year and taxing that portion at full value—i.e., as if in the state all year. [Johnson Oil Refining Co. v. Oklahoma, 290 U.S. 158 (1933)]

Note: Because different states may use different apportionment formulas to tax the same property, there may still be some double taxation of the same instrumentalities. However, the double taxation should be minimal if proper apportionment formulas have been used.

E. **PRIVILEGE, LICENSE, FRANCHISE, OR OCCUPATION TAXES**
Privilege, license, franchise, and occupation taxes are cumulatively known as "doing business" taxes. States generally can impose such taxes—on companies engaged exclusively in interstate commerce, as well as on interstate companies engaged in local commerce—for the privilege of doing business within the state. Such taxes may be measured by a flat amount or by a proportional

rate based on revenue derived from the taxing state. In either case, the tax must meet the basic requirements—the activity taxed must have a **substantial nexus to the taxing state**; and the tax must be **fairly apportioned**, must **not discriminate** against interstate commerce, and must **fairly relate to services provided** by the state. [Complete Auto Transit, Inc. v. Brady, 430 U.S. 274 (1977)—*overruling* Spector Motor Service v. O'Connor, 340 U.S. 602 (1951)]

Examples: 1) A privilege tax for doing business, based on the gross income derived from transporting goods within the state, can be applied to a trucking company that delivers goods coming from outside the state. [Complete Auto Transit, Inc. v. Brady, *supra*]

2) An occupation tax on all businesses, based on gross income derived within the state, can be applied to a stevedoring company operating within the state that loads and unloads ships carrying goods in interstate commerce. [Department of Revenue v. Association of Washington Stevedoring Cos., 435 U.S. 734 (1978)—*overruling* Joseph v. Carter & Weekes Stevedoring Co., 330 U.S. 422 (1947)]

1. **Taxpayer Has Burden of Proof**

The taxpayer has the burden of showing that the state's apportionment formula is unfair. However, a state tax that discriminates against interstate commerce will be held invalid regardless of whether the taxpayer can show that an actual, unfair multiple burden is imposed on his business.

XI. POWER OF STATES TO TAX FOREIGN COMMERCE

A. **IMPORT-EXPORT CLAUSE**

Article I, Section 10, Clause 2 provides: "No state shall, without the Consent of the Congress, lay any Imposts or Duties on Imports or Exports, except what may be absolutely necessary for executing its inspection Laws . . . ."

1. **State Taxation of "Imports" Prohibited Absent Congressional Consent**

The Import-Export Clause prohibits the states from imposing any tax on imported goods as such or on commercial activity connected with imported goods *as such* (i.e., taxes discriminating against imports), except with congressional consent. [Brown v. Maryland, 25 U.S. 419 (1827)]

2. **State Taxation of "Exports" Prohibited**

The Import-Export Clause prohibits the states from imposing any tax on goods after they have entered the "export stream."

B. **COMMERCE CLAUSE**

The Commerce Clause gives Congress the exclusive power to regulate foreign commerce and thus inherently limits a state's power to tax that commerce. Therefore, a state tax applied to foreign commerce must meet all of the Commerce Clause tests that apply to state taxation of interstate commerce. (*See* X.A., *supra*.) And even if a state tax meets those tests, the tax is invalid if it would (i) create a substantial risk of international multiple taxation or (ii) prevent the federal government from "speaking with one voice" regarding international trade or foreign affairs issues. [Barclays Bank PLC v. Franchise Tax Board, 512 U.S. 298 (1994)]

PART FOUR: INDIVIDUAL GUARANTEES AGAINST GOVERNMENTAL OR PRIVATE ACTION

XII. LIMITATIONS ON POWER AND STATE ACTION REQUIREMENT

A. CONSTITUTIONAL RESTRICTIONS ON POWER OVER INDIVIDUALS

The Constitution provides individuals with a number of rights that restrict the power of the government (e.g., the right to speak freely). Some rights/restrictions are applicable only to the federal government, some are applicable only to state and local governments, and some are applicable to all governmental bodies. A few even apply to private action. Several constitutional provisions also give Congress the power to adopt legislation to protect individual rights.

Note: The Constitution sets the **minimum level** of protection for individuals. States generally are free to grant broader protections than those granted in the United States Constitution.

1. Bill of Rights

The Bill of Rights (first 10 Amendments to the Constitution) is the most important source of limitations on the federal government's power. By its terms, the Bill is not applicable to the states, although most of its safeguards have been held to be applicable to the states through the Fourteenth Amendment Due Process Clause.

a. Rights Applicable to States

The Supreme Court has stated that only those safeguards in the Bill of Rights that are "essential to liberty" are applicable to the states through the Fourteenth Amendment. Included in this concept are: **all the First Amendment** guarantees (speech, press, assembly, right to petition, free exercise, and nonestablishment of religion); the **Second Amendment** right to bear arms; the **Fourth Amendment** (unreasonable search and seizure); some **elements of the Fifth Amendment** (privilege against self-incrimination; compensation for taking of private property for public use); the **Sixth Amendment** (speedy and public trial by impartial jury, notice and right of confrontation, compulsory process, and right to legal counsel in all serious criminal proceedings); and the **Eighth Amendment** (cruel and unusual punishment, excessive bail, and excessive fine provisions are **assumed** to be incorporated but there is no precise ruling).

b. Rights Not Applicable to States

There are three provisions of the Bill of Rights that have not yet been incorporated into the Due Process Clause:

(i) The **Third Amendment** prohibition against quartering troops in a person's home;

(ii) The **Fifth Amendment** right to a grand jury indictment in criminal cases; and

(iii) The **Seventh Amendment** right to a jury trial in civil cases.

[*See* McDonald v. Chicago, 561 U.S. 742 (2010)] The **Tenth Amendment**, by its terms, limits the federal government's power over states, and so is inapplicable to the states.

2. Thirteenth Amendment

The Thirteenth Amendment provides that neither slavery nor involuntary servitude shall exist in the United States.

a. No Requirement of State Action

The amendment contains no language limiting its effect to governmental action (e.g., "no *state* shall . . . "); thus, it is applicable even to ***private action***.

b. Involuntary Servitude

The Court has defined involuntary servitude as forcing someone to perform work—whether compensated or not—through the use or threatened use of physical injury or restraint (such as imprisonment), or through the use or threat of legal sanction. Psychological and other forms of coercion alone are generally inadequate to show involuntary servitude. [*See* United States v. Kozminski, 487 U.S. 931 (1988)] The Thirteenth Amendment does not prohibit all forms of labor that one person is compelled to perform for the benefit of another: It does not apply to compulsory military service, civic obligations such as jury duty, convicted prisoners who must perform work as part of their criminal sentence, or even recipients of medical scholarships who are required to work *pro bono*. However, courts are reluctant to order specific performance of a personal service contract because the order would be tantamount to involuntary servitude.

c. Congressional Power

The enabling clause of the Thirteenth Amendment gives Congress the power to adopt appropriate legislation, and the Supreme Court apparently will uphold legislation proscribing almost any private racially discriminatory act that can be characterized as a ***"badge or incident of slavery."***

Examples: The Supreme Court has upheld legislation:

> 1) Prohibiting private parties from refusing to rent or sell housing to a person because of race [Jones v. Alfred H. Mayer Co., 392 U.S. 409 (1968)];
>
> 2) Prohibiting private, nonsectarian schools from refusing to admit nonwhite children [Runyon v. McCrary, 427 U.S. 160 (1976)]; and
>
> 3) Prohibiting a private employer from discriminating in hiring on the basis of race [Patterson v. McLean Credit Union, 491 U.S. 164 (1989)].

Note: The above are examples of where Congress used its power to adopt statutes prohibiting "badges of slavery"; the proscribed activities would not necessarily be held to violate the Thirteenth Amendment absent the legislation.

3. Fourteenth Amendment

The Fourteenth Amendment ***prohibits states*** (not the federal government or private persons) from depriving any person of life, liberty, or property without due process and equal protection of the law. As discussed above, this amendment is a most important source of limitations on the states' power over individuals, because, through the Due Process Clause, most of the protections of the Bill of Rights are applicable to the states.

Note: The meaning of due process and equal protection will be discussed later in this outline.

a. **Requirement of State Action**

The Fourteenth Amendment applies only if there is action by a state or local government, government officer, or private individual whose behavior meets the requirements for state action (*see* B., below).

b. **Scope of Congressional Power**

Section 5 of the Fourteenth Amendment is an enabling clause giving Congress the power to adopt **appropriate legislation** to enforce the rights and guarantees provided by the Fourteenth Amendment. Under Section 5, Congress may **not** expand existing constitutional rights or create new ones—it may only enact laws to prevent or remedy violations of rights already recognized by the courts. To adopt a valid law, Congress must point to a history or pattern of state violation of such rights and adopt legislation that is **congruent and proportional** (i.e., narrowly tailored) to solving the identified violation. Note, however, that when Congress is dealing with a type of discrimination that the Supreme Court reviews using heightened scrutiny (i.e., race, national origin, or gender—*see* XVIII.D., E., *infra*), Congress will generally have more power to act.

Examples: 1) The Americans With Disabilities Act ("ADA") includes provisions that, among other things, prohibit states from discriminating against disabled persons in hiring practices and requires states to make reasonable accommodations for disabled employees. Under the Fourteenth Amendment Equal Protection Clause, the Court has recognized a right of disabled people to be free from irrational state discrimination. In adopting the ADA, Congress did not identify a history or pattern of irrational employment practices by the states. Even if there were such a pattern, the provisions here were not congruent and proportional to remedying irrational discrimination; they are overinclusive, because they prohibit states from making employment decisions that are constitutional under the rational basis test. [Board of Trustees of University of Alabama v. Garrett, 531 U.S. 356 (2001)] Under similar reasoning, the Supreme Court has held that Congress has no power under Section 5 to broadly restrict **age discrimination by state employers**. [Kimel v. Florida Board of Regents, 528 U.S. 62 (2000)]

2) The Supreme Court held that there is no violation of the First Amendment, applicable to the states through the Fourteenth Amendment, where a state law incidentally burdens a religious practice. [Employment Division v. Smith, XXII.C.3., *infra*] In response, Congress adopted a statute, purportedly under Section 5, providing that a state may not burden religious practices absent a compelling interest. The statute was held unconstitutional because it sought to expand substantive First Amendment rights beyond those recognized by the Supreme Court. [City of Boerne v. Flores, 521 U.S. 507 (1997)]

Compare: The Court has held that Congress **has** power under Section 5 to provide that state governments may be sued for violating Title II of the ADA (which prohibits state and local government discrimination against people with disabilities in government programs, services, or activities) when the discrimination involves access to the courts. *Rationale:* The right of meaningful access to judicial proceedings is a "fundamental right" under the Due Process Clause, and is thus subject to "heightened judicial scrutiny" much more demanding than "rational basis." This heightened scrutiny makes it "easier for Congress to show a pattern of state constitutional violations." [Tennessee v. Lane, 541 U.S. 509 (2004)]

4. Fifteenth Amendment

The Fifteenth Amendment is a limitation on both the ***states and the federal government***. It prohibits them from denying any citizen the right to vote on account of race or color. As indicated above, the Fifteenth Amendment contains an enabling clause that allows Congress to adopt legislation protecting the right to vote from discrimination.

a. Limitations

Fifteenth Amendment legislation can be limited by other constitutional principles. For example, the Supreme Court found that the Tenth Amendment and principles of equal sovereignty among the states require Congress to have extraordinary justification to adopt legislation requiring some, but not all, states to obtain federal approval before changing any voting law. [Shelby County v. Holder, 570 U.S. 529 (2013)—subjecting states to pre-clearance based on formula containing decades-old data unconstitutional]

5. Commerce Clause

The Supreme Court has allowed Congress to use the Commerce Clause to limit the power of individuals over other individuals—by adopting legislation barring private racial discrimination in activities "connected with" interstate commerce. Recall that under the affectation doctrine, almost any activity can be said to be connected with interstate commerce. (*See* II.A.4.a.1), *supra.*)

a. Civil Rights Act

Provisions of the Civil Rights Act of 1964 ***barring discrimination in places of public accommodation*** are proper and valid exercises of commerce power.

b. Extent of Commerce Power

The reach of the commerce power is broad. Any business that is ***open to interstate travelers*** or that ***uses products shipped in interstate commerce*** is covered. [Daniel v. Paul, 395 U.S. 298 (1969)—private resort held to be a public place of accommodation encompassed within the Act because drinks and entertainment facilities had been purchased and shipped through interstate commerce]

6. Rights of National Citizenship

The Supreme Court has also allowed Congress to limit the power of private individuals to infringe upon others' rights of national citizenship (e.g., the right of interstate travel, the right to assemble to petition Congress for redress), without pointing to any specific constitutional source for the power. [Griffin v. Breckenridge, 403 U.S. 88 (1971)]

B. STATE ACTION REQUIREMENT

As indicated above, the Constitution generally prohibits only governmental infringement of constitutional rights. Thus, to find some action unconstitutional, it is generally necessary to attribute the action to the state, which includes government agencies and officials acting under the color of state law. However, this does not mean that the act must be directly by a government actor; "state action" can be found in the actions of seemingly private individuals who (i) perform exclusive public functions, or (ii) have significant state involvement in their activities.

1. Exclusive Public Functions

The Supreme Court has found that certain activities are so ***traditionally*** the ***exclusive*** prerogative of the state that they constitute state action even when undertaken by a private individual or organization. To date, only running a town and running an election for public office have been found to be such exclusive public functions.

Examples: 1) The owner of a "company town" with ***all*** of the attributes of a public town (e.g., homes, sidewalks, streets, police and fire protection, etc.) cannot deny a person's First Amendment right to distribute religious literature in the town, since the company town is equivalent to a town. [Marsh v. Alabama, 326 U.S. 501 (1946)] However, the owner of a shopping mall can deny people their First Amendment right to picket, since a mall does not have all of the attributes of a town. [Hudgens v. NLRB, 424 U.S. 507 (1976)]

    2) Running elections is an exclusive public function, so if a private organization runs a preprimary that has a substantial effect on who is ultimately elected, its actions will be state action. [Terry v. Adams, 345 U.S. 461 (1953)—county political group whose candidate almost always runs unopposed in primary and general election cannot discriminate]

a. Must Be Traditional and Exclusive Function

To be state action, the activity must be ***both*** a ***traditional*** and ***exclusive*** government function. Thus, the Court has held that a warehouseman authorized by statute to sell goods stored with him for unpaid charges is not exercising state action when he makes the sale, because while resolution of private disputes is a traditional public function, it is not exclusive—the bailor had state law remedies to check abuses by the warehouseman. [Flagg Brothers v. Brooks, 436 U.S. 149 (1978)] State action exists, and due process guarantees apply, ***only if*** the creditor uses judicial or executive agencies to secure properties in the possession of the debtor.

2. Significant State Involvement—Facilitating Private Action

"State action" also exists whenever a state ***affirmatively*** facilitates, encourages, or authorizes acts of discrimination by its citizens. Note, however, that there must be some sort of affirmative act by the state approving the private action; it is not enough that the state permits the conduct to occur.

a. Instances of Significant State Involvement

1) Official Encouragement

Purportedly private action will be given state action status if the action is encouraged or sanctioned by the state.

a) **Judicial Approval**
State court enforcement of *restrictive covenants prohibiting sale or lease of property to blacks* constitutes state action even in civil proceedings between private parties. [Shelley v. Kraemer, 334 U.S. 1 (1948)]

(1) **Peremptory Challenges**
The use of peremptory challenges, even by a private party, constitutes state action, both because jury selection is a traditional public function and because there is overt, significant participation by the government (the judge) in the jury selection process. Thus, private litigants and defendants are prohibited from using peremptory challenges in a discriminatory manner. [*See* Edmonson v. Leesville Concrete, 500 U.S. 614 (1991); Georgia v. McCollum, 505 U.S. 42 (1992)]

b) **Official Acts**
State action may be found in the absence of an unconstitutional statute or ordinance if it appears that the state sanctions constitutional violations by its own officers.

(1) **Discriminatory Law Enforcement**
The Court reversed a conviction of sit-in demonstrators where no statute or ordinance required segregation but the mayor and police had announced publicly that they would invoke trespass and breach of the peace laws to enforce a local custom of racial separation in eating places. [Lombard v. Louisiana, 373 U.S. 267 (1963)]

(2) **Apparent Legal Authority**
Even if a state forbids officers from acting in a certain way (e.g., depriving persons of their constitutional rights), the forbidden action may still constitute state action if the state puts the actor in a position to commit the unconstitutional act.

Example: A sheriff beat a prisoner to death in an effort to secure a confession. Both the state and the sheriff were held liable. The actions of the sheriff involved "state action" because the sheriff *acted under "the color of state law*—the state in effect cloaked him with the apparent legal authority." [Screws v. United States, 325 U.S. 91 (1945)]

(3) **Public Defenders**
A public defender *does not act for the state* when he represents an indigent client. Therefore, negligence or malpractice by the public defender is not a denial of due process because the public defender's actions are not "state actions." [Polk County v. Dodson, 454 U.S. 312 (1981)]

2) **State Authorization**
In *Reitman v. Mulkey,* 387 U.S. 369 (1967), the Court invalidated a state constitutional provision that *repealed* all existing *state laws banning discrimination* in

the sale or lease of property and prohibited reenactment of such laws in the future because such laws "authorize" private discrimination.

3) The State as Lessor for a Racially Discriminatory Lessee
In *Burton v. Wilmington Parking Authority,* 365 U.S. 715 (1961), Delaware was held responsible under the Fourteenth Amendment Equal Protection Clause for the exclusion of blacks from a coffee shop which was located in a public building. The shop was constructed by and leased from the state. The *maintenance* of the facility was *paid for with public funds* and Delaware was able to charge a higher rent because it allowed the restaurant owner to cater to the prejudices of its white customers.

4) Administration of Private Discriminatory Trust by Public Officials
State action exists where city personnel maintain a park, "open to all except blacks," under a private trust. [Evans v. Newton, 382 U.S. 296 (1966)]

5) Entwinement of State and Private Entities
The fact that a state entity helps formulate and adopts the rules of a private entity, and chooses to follow the order of the private entity pursuant to those rules, does not convert the private entity's action into state action. However, a state may be so entwined with a private organization that the organization's actions will be considered state action. [Brentwood Academy v. Tennessee Secondary School Athletic Association, 531 U.S. 288 (2001)]

Example: The National Collegiate Athletic Association ("NCAA") is a voluntary association of public and private universities that establishes rules for its members regarding collegiate sports. Pursuant to its rules, the NCAA urged a member college to suspend its coach for recruiting violations. The coach cannot successfully sue the NCAA for violating his constitutional rights because there is no state action. [National Collegiate Athletic Association v. Tarkanian, 488 U.S. 179 (1988)]

Compare: An association that regulates high school sports within a single state: (i) to which most public high schools belong; (ii) whose governing body is made up mostly of public school officials; (iii) whose meetings are held during regular school hours; (iv) whose employees may join the state retirement system; and (v) which is funded by gate receipts from the regulated sports is so entwined with the state that its action can be considered state action. [Brentwood Academy v. Tennessee Secondary School Athletic Association, *supra*]

b. Instances of Insignificant State Involvement

1) Heavily Regulated Businesses and/or Granting of a Monopoly to a Utility

a) Electric Company
State action will not be found merely because the state has granted a monopoly to a business or heavily regulates it.

Example: In *Jackson v. Metropolitan Edison,* 419 U.S. 345 (1974), ***no state action*** was found where an electric company terminated the user's service without notice and hearing. The state had not directed or ordered the termination and the fact that the company was heavily regulated and the state commission had approved private utility regulations authorizing such termination was not enough.

b) **Nursing Home**
A nursing home operated by a private corporation did ***not exercise state action*** when it discharged Medicaid patients, even though its operation was extensively regulated by the government. [Blum v. Yaretsky, 457 U.S. 991 (1982)]

c) **School**
A school operated by a private corporation did ***not*** exercise state action when it discharged teachers (allegedly in violation of their First Amendment rights) even though the school had contracts with the state to educate or care for many of its students and it received almost all of its operating funds from the government. [Rendell-Baker v. Kohn, 457 U.S. 830 (1982)]

2) **Licensing and Provision of Essential Services**
Granting a liquor license and providing essential services (police, fire, water, power, etc.) to a ***private club*** that imposes racial restrictions on its members and guests are ***not*** sufficient to constitute state action. [Moose Lodge v. Irvis, 407 U.S. 163 (1972)]

3) **Congressional Grant of Corporate Charter and Exclusive Name**
Congressional grant of a corporate charter and exclusive use of a name is not sufficient to constitute state action. [San Francisco Arts & Athletics, Inc. v. United States Olympic Committee, 483 U.S. 522 (1987)—congressional charter and grant of exclusive name "Olympic" does not clothe United States Olympic Committee with state action]

4) **No Government Duty to Protect Individuals from Harm by Private Persons**
The mere refusal of government agents to protect a victim from harm by a private person will not result in a finding that the harm was attributable to "state action," at least when state law does not give the victim a right to government protection. [DeShaney v. Winnebago County Department of Social Services, 489 U.S. 189 (1989)—government not responsible for harm inflicted on a child by his father, even though government social worker had reason to believe the child was being abused and did nothing to protect the child] However, if government employees enter into an agreement or conspiracy with private persons to cause harm to a victim, the victim's injuries are the result of state action; the private persons, as well as the government employees with whom they conspired, will have violated the victim's constitutional rights. [Screws v. United States, a.1)b)(2), *supra*; Dennis v. Sparks, 449 U.S. 24 (1980)]

C. TIPS FOR BAR EXAM

1. State Must Be "Significantly Involved" in Private Entity
The state must be "significantly involved" in the private entity. Merely granting a license or providing essential services is insufficient.

2. No Constitutional Mandate to Outlaw Discrimination
States are not constitutionally required to outlaw discrimination. The Constitution forbids only their encouraging or authorizing it.

XIII. RETROACTIVE LEGISLATION

A. CONTRACT CLAUSE—IMPAIRMENT OF CONTRACT
The Contract Clause limits the ability of states to enact laws that *retroactively* impair contract rights. It does not affect contracts not yet made.

1. Not Applicable to Federal Government
There is no comparable clause applicable to the federal government, although a flagrant contract impairment would be forbidden by the Due Process Clause of the Fifth Amendment.

2. Only Applicable to State Legislation
The provision applies only to state *legislation*, not court decisions. [*See* Tidal Oil v. Flanagan, 263 U.S. 444 (1924)]

3. Basic Impairment Rules

a. Private Contracts
The Contract Clause prevents only *substantial impairments* of contract (i.e., destruction of most or all of a party's rights under a contract). However, not all substantial impairments are invalid. In determining whether legislation is valid under the Contract Clause, use a three-part test:

(i) Does the legislation substantially impair a party's rights under an existing contract? If it does not, the legislation is valid under the Contract Clause. If it does, it will be valid *only if* it:

(ii) Serves an important and legitimate public interest; and

(iii) Is a reasonable and narrowly tailored means of promoting that interest.

Examples: 1) A Minnesota statute that imposed a moratorium on mortgage foreclosures during a severe depression did not violate the Contract Clause. [Home Building & Loan Association v. Blaisdell, 290 U.S. 398 (1934)]

2) A state statute that restricted underground coal mining to protect a variety of public and private uses of surface land (and buildings) and that left the owners of subsurface mining rights with some reasonable value in, or return from, their investment does not violate the Contract Clause.

[Keystone Bituminous Coal Association v. DeBenedictis, 480 U.S. 470 (1987)]

b. Public Contracts—Stricter Scrutiny

Public contracts (i.e., those in which the state or political subdivision is a party) are tested by the same basic test detailed above; however, they will likely receive stricter scrutiny, especially if the legislation reduces the contractual burdens on the state. When applying the three-part test, note the following:

(i) There is no substantial impairment if the state has reserved the power to *revoke, alter, or amend* either in the contract itself or in a statute or law the terms of which should be considered to be incorporated into the contract [Dartmouth College v. Woodward, 17 U.S. 518 (1819)];

(ii) In determining whether the law serves as a legitimate public interest, note that the state cannot be obligated by contract to refrain from exercising its police powers necessary to protect the health and safety of its residents; and

(iii) To be narrowly tailored, the law should not constitute an unnecessarily broad repudiation of contract obligations.

Example: In *Allied Structural Steel Co. v. Spannaus,* 438 U.S. 234 (1978), the Court invalidated state pension reform legislation which increased the obligation of companies under preexisting pension plans to employees who previously had terminated their work for the company or who previously had retired from employment with the company. Because the legislation constituted a substantial impairment of contract by changing the compensation for work already completed and because it was not necessary to remedy an important social problem in the nature of an emergency, it was held to be a violation of the Contract Clause.

B. EX POST FACTO LAWS

1. Two Ex Post Facto Clauses

Neither the state nor the federal government may pass an ex post facto law. [Art. I, §9—federal prohibition; Art. I, §10—state prohibition] An ex post facto law is *legislation* that *retroactively* alters the *criminal law* (not civil regulation, such as denial of professional licenses) in a *substantially prejudicial* manner so as to deprive a person of any right previously enjoyed *for the purpose of punishing the person for some past activity.*

a. What Is "Criminal"

If a law's *purpose* is civil rather than punitive, it is not an ex post facto law unless its *effect* is so *clearly* punitive as to negate the legislature's intention.

Example: A law requiring any sex offender within the state to register and provide his name, address, place of employment, vehicle information, etc., to law enforcement authorities and authorizing law enforcement authorities to make some of this information public is not an ex post facto law, even if noncompliance can be punished criminally, and even if some of the law is contained in the state's criminal code. The goal of such a law is not to punish or stigmatize. Rather, legislatures have found that sex offenders pose a high risk of reoffending, and the release of the information required under the act is intended to protect the public from sex offenders. [Smith v. Doe, 538 U.S. 84 (2003)]

b. Retroactive Alterations

A statute retroactively alters a law in a substantially prejudicial manner if it:

(i) Makes criminal an act that *was innocent when done*;

(ii) Prescribes *greater punishment* for an act than was prescribed for the act when it was committed; or

(iii) *Reduces the evidence* required to convict a person of a crime from what was required at the time that the act was allegedly committed.

Example: A statute of limitations reflects a legislative judgment that after a certain time, no quantum of evidence is sufficient to convict. Thus, a law that revives the possibility of a criminal prosecution after the previously applicable statute of limitations has expired is an unconstitutional ex post facto law. [Stogner v. California, 539 U.S. 607 (2003)]

2. Distinguish—Procedural Changes

Mere procedural changes in state law will not necessarily trigger the Ex Post Facto Clause. A modified law can be applied to a crime committed before the law's modification if the defendant had notice of the possible penalty and the modified law does not increase the burden on the defendant.

Example: Florida had a death penalty statute that was invalidated by the Supreme Court because the statute restricted discretion in sentencing. Before a new statute was enacted, D committed a murder. Florida then passed a new death penalty provision that complied with Supreme Court criteria. The new provision was applied at D's trial, and he was sentenced to death. This was not a prohibited ex post facto law, since the earlier statute (although unconstitutional) gave D notice of the possible penalty and the new provision made it *less likely* that the death penalty would be imposed in a given case. [Dobbert v. Florida, 432 U.S. 282 (1977)]

3. Indirect "Application" to Courts

Although the Ex Post Facto Clauses prohibit only retroactive *legislation*, the Supreme Court has held that due process prohibits courts from retroactively interpreting criminal law in an unexpected and indefensible way. [Rogers v. Tennessee, 532 U.S. 451 (2001)—state supreme court's abolition of common law "year and a day rule" (which prohibits prosecution for murder if the victim dies more than a year after an attack) was not unexpected and indefensible because medical science has undermined the rule's usefulness and the rule has already been abolished in most jurisdictions]

C. BILLS OF ATTAINDER

A bill of attainder is a legislative act that *inflicts punishment without a judicial trial* upon individuals who are designated either by name or in terms of past conduct. Past conduct acts to define who those particular persons are.

1.   **Two Clauses**
     Both the *federal and state governments* are prohibited from passing bills of attainder.

2.   **Two Requirements Preclude Finding of Bill of Attainder**
     These provisions *require both judicial machinery* for trial and punishment of crime and
     definition of criminal conduct in such general terms as not to ensnare within the definition
     a single individual or small group for punishment because of past behavior.
     Example: The Court found a provision in the Landrum-Griffin Act, making it a crime
                      for a member of the Communist Party to act as an officer or employee of a
                      labor union, to be legislative punishment for a party membership, and hence a
                      bill of attainder. [United States v. Brown, 381 U.S. 437 (1965)]

3.   *Nixon* **Case**
     In *Nixon v. Administrator of General Services,* 433 U.S. 425 (1977), Congress passed legisla-
     tion to authorize government control of the presidential papers and tape recordings of former
     President Nixon. The Supreme Court held that this was *not a bill of attainder.* The circum-
     stances of the Nixon resignation made him a unique "class of one" as to the need to control
     his papers. The act was held "*nonpunitive*" and in pursuance of *important public policy.*

4.   **Draft Registration Case**
     In *Selective Service System v. Minnesota Public Interest Research Group,* 468 U.S. 841
     (1984), the Court upheld a federal statute denying financial aid for higher education to male
     students between the ages of 18 and 26 who had failed to register for the draft. The law
     required applicants for the aid to file a statement with their institutions of higher learning
     certifying their compliance. Failure to register within 30 days of one's 18th birthday was a
     felony, but the regulations allowed men who failed to register in a timely manner to qualify
     for aid by registering late. The Court found that this was *not a bill of attainder.* The law
     reasonably *promoted nonpunitive goals* and was *not a legislative punishment* taken on the
     basis of any irreversible act, since aid was awarded to those who registered late. The Court
     also found that the statute did not violate the Fifth Amendment privilege against self-incrim-
     ination.

D.   **DUE PROCESS CONSIDERATIONS**
     Under the Due Process Clauses of the Fifth and Fourteenth Amendments, retroactive legislation
     or other governmental action may be, but is not necessarily, a violation of the Constitution. The
     question of whether a retroactive law (that does not violate the Contracts, Ex Post Facto, or Bill
     of Attainder Clauses) violates due process is a *substantive due process* issue. If the law does not
     relate to a fundamental civil right, the retroactive law should be upheld if it is rationally related to
     a legitimate government interest.
     Examples: 1) A retroactive tax law will be upheld as long as the retroactive aspects of the law
                      are rationally related to legitimate government interests. [United States v. Carlton,
                      512 U.S. 26 (1994)—upholding retroactive modification of the estate tax]

                      2) Retroactive legislation affecting *merely a remedy* does not violate due process
                      (e.g., repealing or extending a statute of limitations), unless it would oust an
                      already vested property interest. [Chase Securities Corp. v. Donaldson, 325 U.S.
                      304 (1945)—permissible to revive a previously dead cause of action]

XIV. PROCEDURAL DUE PROCESS

A. BASIC PRINCIPLE

The Due Process Clauses of the Fifth Amendment (applicable to the federal government) and the Fourteenth Amendment (applicable to the states) provide that the government shall not take a person's life, liberty, or property without due process of law. Due process contemplates fair process/procedure, which requires at least an opportunity to present objections to the proposed action to a fair, neutral decisionmaker (not necessarily a judge).

1. When Is Individualized Adjudication Required?

There is a right to procedural due process only when the government acts to deprive an *individual* of life, liberty, or property (*see* below). There is no right to individualized adjudication when the government acts generally, even if the action will result in burdening individuals' life, liberty, or property interests.

Example: A state legislature need not provide individuals with an opportunity for a hearing when adopting the general requirements for obtaining a driver's license (e.g., age, residence, ability, etc.), but it must provide individualized process to determine whether a particular person meets the requirements.

2. Intentional Deprivation vs. Negligent Deprivation

Fair process is required for *intentional* acts of the government or its employees. If an injury is caused to a person through the mere *negligence* of a government employee, there is no violation of the Due Process Clause. [Daniels v. Williams, 474 U.S. 327 (1986); Davidson v. Cannon, 474 U.S. 344 (1986)]

a. "Deprivation"

A "deprivation" of life, liberty, or property requires more than a mere denial of certain kinds of remedies. Only when the government affords *no* remedy or *inadequate* remedies may a deprivation of life, liberty, or property result. [Florida Prepaid Postsecondary Education Expense Board v. College Savings Bank, 527 U.S. 627 (1999)]

3. Fair, Neutral Decisionmaker—Judge Bias

The Due Process Clause requires a judge to recuse himself when he has *actual bias* (e.g., he has a direct, personal, substantial, pecuniary interest in a case) or when there is merely a *serious risk of actual bias*. A serious risk of actual bias exists when "under a realistic appraisal of psychological tendencies and human weakness," the judge's interest poses such a risk of actual bias or prejudice that it must be forbidden. [Caperton v. A. T. Massey Coal Co., 556 U.S. 868 (2009)]

Example: The chairman of a company spent over $3 million to support an attorney's campaign to be elected to the state supreme court after a $50 million verdict was entered against the chairman's company, knowing that the supreme court would eventually hear the appeal of the verdict. The $3 million was more than the total amount spent by all of the other supporters of the attorney, and the attorney won by fewer than 50,000 votes. When the case was appealed, the winner of the verdict asked the newly elected justice to recuse himself. Under these circumstances, recusal was required. [Caperton v. A. T. Massey Coal Co., *supra*]

4. **Protection vs. Creation**
    The due process provisions do not create property or liberty interests; their purpose is to provide ***procedural safeguards against arbitrary deprivation***. Hence, the Fourteenth Amendment Due Process Clause does not, for example, give out-of-state attorneys the right to appear in state courts without meeting a state's bar admission requirements. [Leis v. Flynt, 439 U.S. 438 (1979)]

B. **IS LIFE, LIBERTY, OR PROPERTY BEING TAKEN?**
    Older Supreme Court cases indicated that due process protects "rights," but not "privileges." This approach is no longer followed; rather the Court will determine whether a ***legitimate*** liberty or property interest is being taken.

1. **Liberty**
    The term "liberty" is not specifically defined. It includes more than just freedom from bodily restraints (e.g., it includes the right to contract and to engage in gainful employment). A deprivation of liberty occurs if a person:

    (i)   Loses significant freedom of action; ***or***

    (ii) Is denied a freedom provided by the Constitution or a statute.

    Examples of liberty interests include:

    a. **Commitment to Mental Institution**

        1) **Adults**
            Adults are entitled to an ***adversary hearing*** before they are indefinitely committed to a mental institution against their will. The state must prove the basis for commitment by "clear and convincing" evidence. However, after a person has been acquitted of criminal charges on the basis of an insanity defense, the acquitted defendant can be committed if a court finds by a "preponderance of the evidence" that the person should be committed to a mental health care facility. [Jones v. United States, 463 U.S. 354 (1983)]

        2) **Minor Children**
            Minor children have a substantial liberty interest in not being confined unnecessarily for medical treatment. Thus, they are entitled to a ***screening by a "neutral factfinder"*** before commitment to a mental institution. Mere parental consent to commitment is not enough. [Parham v. J.R., 442 U.S. 584 (1979)]

    b. **Injury to Reputation**
        Injury to reputation in itself is not a deprivation of liberty or property. [Paul v. Davis, 424 U.S. 693 (1976)] However, if governmental acts (such as a statement of reasons given for termination of public employment) so injure a person's reputation that he will have ***lost significant employment or associational opportunities***, there is a loss of liberty.

    c. **Exercise of Fundamental Constitutional Rights**
        The Due Process Clause protects a person's freedom to engage in activities that involve

fundamental constitutional rights, such as the right to speak and associate, the right to travel, and the right to vote.

1)   Application—Government Employee's Freedom of Speech
A public employee may not be discharged for engaging in ***constitutionally protected speech***. (*See* XXI.C.1., *infra*.) If a government employee is discharged for her speech or writing, a hearing must be held to determine whether the speech was protected. If so, the employee cannot be fired. [*See* Givhan v. Western Line Consolidated School District, 439 U.S. 410 (1979)—Court held that teacher could not be fired for privately communicating her grievances about working conditions or opinions concerning public issues to her employer]

2.   Property
"Property" includes more than personal belongings and realty, chattels, or money, but an abstract need or desire for (or a unilateral expectation of) the benefit is not enough. There must be a ***legitimate claim*** or "***entitlement***" to the benefit under state or federal law. [Board of Regents v. Roth, 408 U.S. 564 (1972); Leis v. Flynt, *supra*] Examples of property interests include:

a.   Public Education
There is a property interest in public education when school attendance is required. Thus, a significant suspension (e.g., 10 days) requires procedural due process. [Goss v. Lopez, 419 U.S. 565 (1975)]

b.   Welfare Benefits
One has a property interest in welfare benefits if she has previously been determined to meet the statutory criteria. [Goldberg v. Kelly, 397 U.S. 254 (1970)]

c.   Continued Public Employment
If there is a state statute or ordinance that creates a public employment contract, or there is some clear practice or mutual understanding that an employee can be terminated only for "cause," then there is a property interest [Arnett v. Kennedy, 416 U.S. 134 (1974)]; but if the employee holds his position only at the "will" of the employer, there is no property interest in continued employment [Bishop v. Wood, 426 U.S. 341 (1976)].

C.   WHAT TYPE OF PROCESS IS REQUIRED?
While all intentional governmental deprivations of life, liberty, or property require fair process, what constitutes fair process in terms of the timing and scope of the hearing varies according to the circumstances of the deprivation. The Court will weigh:

(i)   The importance of the ***individual interest*** involved;

(ii)   The value of specific ***procedural safeguards*** to that interest; and

(iii) The ***governmental interest*** in fiscal and administrative efficiency.

[Mathews v. Eldridge, 424 U.S. 319 (1976)] In all situations, the Court will probably require ***fair procedures*** and an ***unbiased decisionmaker***. Normally, the person whose interest is being deprived should also receive **notice** of the government's action and have an **opportunity to respond before** termination of the interest. However, the court may allow a post-termination hearing in situations where a pre-termination hearing is highly impracticable. The Court has made the following rulings with regard to specific types of deprivations:

1. **Welfare Benefits**

   Due process requires an **evidentiary hearing prior to termination** of welfare benefits. It need not be a judicial or quasi-judicial trial if there is adequate post-termination review; but the recipient must have timely and adequate **notice** of the reasons for the proposed termination, the right to confront adverse witnesses, and the right to present his own arguments and evidence orally. Counsel need not be provided, but must be permitted. Finally, the decision must be based solely on evidence adduced at the hearing and must be rendered by an impartial decisionmaker (thus disqualifying any participant in the termination proposal under review). [Goldberg v. Kelly, *supra*]

2. **Disability Benefits**

   No prior evidentiary hearing is required for termination of disability benefits, as long as there is *prior notice* to the recipient, an opportunity to respond in writing, and a *subsequent evidentiary hearing* (with retroactive payment if the recipient prevails). *Rationale*: Disability benefits (unlike welfare benefits) are not based on financial need and hence are not vital. [Mathews v. Eldridge, *supra*]

3. **Public Employment**

   A public employee who is subject to removal only for "cause" (and who, therefore, has a property interest in his job) generally must be given **notice** of charges against him that are to be the basis for his job termination, and a **pre-termination opportunity to respond** to those charges. The employee does not have to be given a full, formal hearing before his termination, as long as there is a fair system of pre-termination notice, an opportunity to respond (to the person making the termination decision), and a **subsequent evidentiary hearing** regarding the termination (with reinstatement if the employee prevails). [Cleveland Board of Education v. Loudermill, 470 U.S. 532 (1985)] *But note:* If there is a **significant reason** for not keeping the employee on the job, he may be suspended without pay and without an opportunity to respond, as long as there is a prompt post-suspension hearing with reinstatement and back pay if the employee prevails. [Gilbert v. Homar, 520 U.S. 924 (1997)—police officer suspended after being arrested and formally charged with a felony]

4. **Public Education—Disciplinary Suspension**

   Although no formal evidentiary hearing is required before a student may be temporarily suspended (for 10 days or less), due process usually requires **notice** of the charges and an **opportunity to explain**. However, if the student's presence poses a danger to persons or property, or threatens to disrupt the academic process, such notice and hearing may *follow* removal as soon as practicable. [Goss v. Lopez, *supra*]

   a. **Corporal Punishment in Public School**

      This may involve constitutionally protected "liberty." However, the traditional common law tort remedies for excessive punishment satisfy procedural due process, and a prior hearing is not required. [Ingraham v. Wright, 430 U.S. 651 (1977)]

5. Public Education—Academic Dismissal

No prior evidentiary hearing is required when a student is dismissed for "academic" deficiencies rather than for "disciplinary" reasons. Due process is satisfied if the student is adequately informed of the deficiency and given an opportunity to respond. [Board of Curators v. Horowitz, 435 U.S. 78 (1978)]

6. Creditors' Remedies

Pretrial remedies, such as attachment of property or garnishment of wages, that are merely designed to provide a plaintiff with some guarantee that there will be assets to satisfy a judgment against the defendant if the plaintiff eventually wins the case *should not be issued by a court without notice* to the defendant and a *hearing prior to the issuance* of the order. A court may issue a temporary order of this type if: (i) there are exigent circumstances that justify the order; and (ii) the defendant is given a hearing after the order is issued but prior to trial. [Sniadach v. Family Finance Corp., 395 U.S. 337 (1969); Connecticut v. Doehr, 501 U.S. 1 (1991)] However, laws authorizing creditors to garnish assets, or a conditional seller to seize or sequester property, will be upheld *without prior notice* to the debtor *if*:

a. The creditor posts a security bond;

b. The application is made to a judge, is not conclusory, and documents narrowly confined facts susceptible of summary disposition; *and*

c. Provision is made for an early hearing at which the creditor must show probable cause.

7. Driver's License

The state generally must afford a *prior hearing* before a driver's license is suspended or terminated. [Bell v. Burson, 402 U.S. 535 (1971)] However, a post-suspension hearing satisfies due process where a statute mandates suspension of a driver's license for refusing to take a breathalyzer test upon arrest for drunk driving. [Mackey v. Montrym, 443 U.S. 1 (1979)]

8. Parental Status Litigation and Hearing

a. **Termination of Parental Status**

Due process does *not require the appointment of counsel* for indigent parents in every case in which the state seeks to terminate parental status (i.e., take children from their parents), *but* only when "fundamental fairness" requires the appointment. [Lassiter v. Department of Social Services, 452 U.S. 18 (1981)] To terminate parental rights, the state must prove its allegations of parental neglect or misconduct by "clear and convincing evidence." [Santosky v. Kramer, 455 U.S. 745 (1982)]

b. **Paternity Actions**

A state may allow paternity to be established in a support proceeding brought by a mother or child by a *preponderance of evidence*—no greater burden of proof is required by the Due Process Clause. [Rivera v. Minnich, 483 U.S. 574 (1987)] However, due process requires the state to *pay for blood tests* that might exculpate an indigent defendant in a paternity action if the *state is responsible for the lawsuit* (the suit is brought by a state agency or the state requires the mother to bring the civil paternity suit). [Little v. Streater, 452 U.S. 1 (1981)]

c. **Hearings for Men Who Seek to Establish Paternity**

1) **Unmarried Father Living with Mother**

If the father of a nonmarital child is a part of a "family unit" that includes the child, the relationship between the father and child will be protected by due process. [Stanley v. Illinois, 405 U.S. 645 (1972)—state cannot take child from father after mother dies, unless state has a fair process to determine whether the parental relationship should be severed]

2) **Father Who Never Tried to Establish Paternity**

The father of a nonmarital child who has never attempted to establish a legal or personal relationship with the child has no right to notice prior to the adoption of the child by other persons. [Lehr v. Robertson, 463 U.S. 248 (1983)]

3) **Mother Married to Another Man**

The Supreme Court has upheld a statute that presumed that a child born during wedlock was the husband's child where the statute allowed an alleged biological father to have a hearing regarding visitation rights, but the Court did not rule on whether a biological father could be denied visitation under these circumstances without a hearing. [Michael H. v. Gerald D., 491 U.S. 110 (1989)]

9. **Detention of Citizen Enemy Combatants**

Due process requires that a *citizen held in the United States* as an "enemy combatant" have a meaningful opportunity to contest the factual basis for his detention before a neutral decisionmaker. However, due process does not forbid some tailoring of the proceedings to alleviate burdens that they may impose on Executive authority during an ongoing military conflict. This may include accepting some use of hearsay, permitting government rebuttable presumptions, and *perhaps* use of a properly authorized and constituted military tribunal. [Hamdi v. Rumsfeld, 542 U.S. 507 (2004)—effect of views of five Justices in two separate opinions]

Example: Hamdi, an American citizen, was captured in Afghanistan, classified as an "enemy combatant" for allegedly taking up arms with the Taliban, and transported to a naval brig in Charleston, SC. Hamdi's father brought a habeas corpus petition on his behalf. The appellate court held that because Hamdi was caught in a combat zone, he had no right to refute the government's charges. The Supreme Court reversed, holding that Hamdi was at least entitled to some hearing to contest the factual basis for his detention before a neutral decisionmaker. [Hamdi v. Rumsfeld, *supra*]

10. **Notice of Adversary Proceedings**

When the government seeks to use a judicial or administrative process to take or terminate property interests, it *must give notice* to those persons whose property interests may be taken by that process. The form of notice must be reasonably designed to insure that those persons will in fact be notified of the proceedings.

Example: Personal notice or notice by mail must be given to both mortgagor and mortgagee before a "tax sale" of property for unpaid taxes. [Mennonite Board of Missions v. Adams, 462 U.S. 791 (1983)]

11. **Civil Forfeitures**

Procedural due process limits the government's ability to seize property allegedly subject to forfeiture (which most often occurs when the government claims that the property was connected to, or was the product of, criminal activity). Absent exceptional circumstances, the government must provide the owner of *real property* notice and an opportunity for some type of hearing *prior* to seizing real property. [United States v. James Daniel Good Real Property, 510 U.S. 43 (1993)] However, the government might be able to seize *personal property prior* to providing the owner a hearing, since personal property can be hidden or destroyed. [Calero-Toledo v. Pearson Yacht Leasing Co., 416 U.S. 663 (1974)]

12. **Deprivation of Property After Criminal Conviction**

When facts have been established in a *prior proceeding* with appropriate procedural due process, such as a criminal trial, a new hearing *is not required* for every deprivation of property based on the previously established facts.

Example: State law prohibits any person who has been convicted of perjury from practicing law. An attorney is convicted of perjury. The state's attorney licensing commission revokes the attorney's license to practice law without a hearing. The revocation does not violate the Due Process Clause because procedural due process interests usually protected by a hearing were afforded during the criminal trial.

D. **DUE PROCESS RIGHTS ARE SUBJECT TO WAIVER**

Due process rights are subject to waiver. However, the Supreme Court has not clearly defined the standard for determining whether someone has validly waived the right to a hearing before governmental deprivation of liberty or property. Presumably, any such waiver must be *voluntary*. Additionally, it is possible that a waiver will be valid only if it is made *knowingly* (with an understanding of the nature of the rights being waived).

E. **ACCESS TO COURTS—INDIGENT PLAINTIFFS**

There may often be a fee for government services, including a fee for use of courts (e.g., a filing fee). Whether the government must waive such fees for indigents depends on the nature of the rights involved.

1. **Fundamental Rights—Waiver Required**

The Supreme Court has required a waiver of government fees when the imposition of a fee would deny a fundamental right to the indigent. (Fundamental rights are examined in the substantive due process and equal protection sections of this outline.)

Examples: 1) The government cannot deny an indigent the right to marry or divorce because of the indigent's inability to pay a marriage license fee or a divorce court filing fee.

2) The government must waive even a reasonable filing fee for candidates for electoral office if it can be shown that the candidate cannot afford to pay the filing fee. The right to be a candidate is connected to the fundamental right of individuals to vote for candidates of their choice.

3) The government may not require an indigent to pay the cost of a transcript in order to appeal from termination of her parental rights. [M.L.B. v. S.L.J., 519 U.S. 102 (1996)]

2. **Nonfundamental Rights—Waiver Not Required**

When there is no fundamental right regulated by the imposition of a fee, the government can refuse to grant the service to those persons who cannot pay the required fee.

Examples: 1) The federal government can refuse to grant access to bankruptcy courts to persons who cannot pay a filing fee. There is no fundamental right to receive a bankruptcy discharge from debts.

2) A state can limit judicial review of welfare termination hearings to those persons who pay a $25 fee.

XV.   THE "TAKING" CLAUSE

A.   IN GENERAL

The Fifth Amendment prohibits governmental taking of private property "for public use without just compensation." The prohibition is applicable to the states through the Fourteenth Amendment [Chicago Burlington & Quincy Railroad v. Chicago, 166 U.S. 226 (1897)], and taking questions often arise in connection with states' exercise of their police power (i.e., the power to legislate for the health, welfare, safety, etc., of the people).

1. **Not a Grant of Power**

The Fifth Amendment is not a grant of power, but rather is a limitation on power (i.e., a taking must be for a public purpose and compensation must be paid). The power for a taking must arise out of some other source (e.g., the police power).

2. **Scope of Taking**

The concept of a governmental taking probably originally contemplated only physical appropriations of property. Today, however, the term also encompasses some governmental action that significantly damages property or impairs its use (e.g., frequent flyovers by airplanes near airport [United States v. Causby, 328 U.S. 256 (1946)]). Moreover, even personal property and intangibles may be the subject of a taking. [*See* Horne v. Department of Agriculture, 135 S. Ct. 2419 (2015)—raisin growers must be paid just compensation for being required to set aside a portion of their crops for the government pursuant to federal regulations, even if the growers retain a contingent interest in the reserved portion; *and see* Ruckelshaus v. Monsanto Co., 467 U.S. 986 (1984)—government requirement that trade secret be disclosed may be a taking where government takes and discloses the secret in such a way that it diminishes the secret's economic value and interferes with reasonable, investment-backed expectations of its holders]

B.   "PUBLIC USE" LIMITATION LIBERALLY CONSTRUED

The Court will not review underlying policy decisions, such as general desirability for a particular public use or the extent to which property must be taken therefor. A use will be held to be "public" as long as it is rationally related to a legitimate public purpose, e.g., health, welfare, safety, moral, social, economic, political, or aesthetic ends. The government may even authorize a taking by private enterprise, as long as the taking will redound to the public advantage (e.g., railroads and public utilities).

Example: A city adopted an integrated development plan to revitalize its ailing economy by buying up privately held land in its riverfront area, developing some land into parks, and transferring the rest to developers who would open marinas, stores, etc. Pursuant to the plan, the city bought up land from willing sellers and initiated condemnation proceedings against owners who refused to sell. The recalcitrant owners brought suit against the city, claiming that the use for which the city was condemning the land (i.e., to transfer the land to private developers) was not a public use. The Supreme Court held that a taking is for public use so long as the government acts out of a reasonable belief that the taking will benefit the public, and taking private property to promote economic development has long been accepted as a public use. [Kelo v. City of New London, 545 U.S. 469 (2005)]

C. "TAKING" VS. "REGULATION"

While the government must fairly compensate an owner when her property is taken for public use, it need not pay compensation for mere regulation of property. Thus, whether government action amounts to a taking or is merely regulation is a crucial issue. The question is one of degree; there is no clear cut formula for determining whether there has been a taking. The following guidelines have emerged.

1. Actual Appropriation or Physical Invasion

A taking will almost always be found if there is an actual appropriation or destruction of a person's property or a permanent physical invasion by the government or by authorization of law.
Examples: A taking was found in the following situations:

1) Ordinance requiring landlords to allow installation of cable TV in their rental units but limiting to $1 the fee landlords could charge for this access. [Loretto v. Teleprompter Manhattan CATV Corp., 458 U.S. 419 (1982)]

2) Statute *abolishing* rights of descent and devise of property (although government has broad authority to regulate this area). [Hodel v. Irving, 481 U.S. 704 (1987)]

3) Requirement that public be given free access to a privately developed waterway. [Kaiser Aetna v. United States, 444 U.S. 164 (1979)]

a. Exception—Emergencies

A taking is less likely to be found in emergency situations, even where there is destruction or actual occupation of private property.
Examples: 1) No compensation was required when the state ordered the destruction of cedar trees that threatened to spread disease to apple orchards. [Miller v. Schoene, 276 U.S. 272 (1928)]

2) No compensation was required when federal troops destroyed oil facilities to prevent them from falling into enemy hands. [United States v. Caltex, Inc., 344 U.S. 149 (1952)]

b. Damage from Temporary Interference with Use

Government action that amounts to a temporary appropriation or physical invasion of property may also amount to a taking. For example, temporary flooding caused by government release of dammed up waters can amount to a taking. [Arkansas Game and Fish Commission v. United States, 568 U.S. 23 (2012)]

2. **Use Restrictions**

a. **Denial of All Economic Value of Land—Taking**

If a government regulation denies a landowner of *all* economic use of his land, the regulation is equivalent to a physical appropriation and is thus a taking unless principles of nuisance or property law that existed when the owner acquired the land make the use prohibitable. [Lucas v. South Carolina Coastal Council, 505 U.S. 1003 (1992)—state's zoning ordinance, adopted after owner purchased lots, amounted to a taking because the ordinance prohibited owner from erecting any permanent structures on his lots]

1) **Temporary Denials of All Economic Use**

Temporarily denying an owner of all economic use of property does not constitute a per se taking. Instead, the Court will carefully examine and weigh all the relevant circumstances—the planners' good faith, the reasonable expectations of the owners, the length of the delay, the delay's actual effect on the value of the property, etc.—in order to determine whether "fairness and justice" require just compensation. [Tahoe-Sierra Preservation Council, Inc. v. Tahoe Regional Planning Agency, 535 U.S. 302 (2002)—finding no taking where there was a 32-month moratorium on land development in the Lake Tahoe Basin while a comprehensive land-use plan was being developed for the area]

b. **Decreasing Economic Value**

Generally, regulations that merely decrease the value of property (e.g., prohibit its most beneficial use) do not necessarily result in a taking, *as long as they leave an economically viable use for the property*. The Court considers (i) the social goals sought to be promoted; (ii) the diminution in value to the owner; and (iii) whether the regulation substantially interferes with distinct, investment-backed expectations of the owner. [Penn Central Transportation Co. v. New York, 438 U.S. 101 (1978)]

Example: The Court upheld a "landmark" zoning ordinance that prohibited altering the external appearance of Grand Central Station. It found historic preservation to be an important government interest and that certain rights granted to the landmark owners mitigated their loss. [Penn Central Transportation Co. v. New York, *supra*]

1) **Building/Development Permits—Exaction of Occupation Rights**

Municipalities often attempt to condition building or development permits on a landowner's (i) conveying title to part, or all, of the property to the government or (ii) granting the public access to the property (e.g., an easement across the property). Such exactions constitute an uncompensated taking unless (i) the government can show that the condition relates to a legitimate government interest (nexus) and (ii) the adverse impact of the proposed building/development on the area is roughly proportional to the loss caused to the property owner from the forced transfer of occupation rights (proportionality). [Nollan v. California Coastal Commission, 483 U.S. 825 (1987); Dolan v. City of Tigard, 512 U.S. 374 (1994)]

Example: City agreed to approve a permit to expand plaintiff's retail store and pave a parking lot on the condition that plaintiff dedicate land for (i) a public greenway and (ii) a bike path. The Supreme Court found that City did not show a sufficient relationship between the dedications and the impact that the expansion would have on the area. [Dolan v. City of Tigard, *supra*]

a) Permit Denials

The government's demand for property with respect to a land-use permit application must satisfy the *Nollan/Dolan* requirements, above, even when the government denies a permit. A refusal to issue a permit based on a refusal to dedicate land under terms that do not satisfy the nexus and/or proportionality requirements of *Nollan* and *Dolan* constitutes a taking. [Koontz v. St. Johns River Water Management District, 133 S. Ct. 2586 (2013)]

2) Utility Rate Regulation

There is no taking where the government sets rates that utility companies can charge, as long as the rates are not set so low that they are unjust and confiscatory. [Duquesne Light Co. v. Barasch, 488 U.S. 299 (1989)]

3) Zoning Ordinances

The Court has long held that governments may adopt zoning ordinances that regulate the way real property may be used, pursuant to the police power (e.g., limiting development in a particular area to single-family homes, restricting buildings to a particular height, etc.). Such regulations generally do not amount to a taking—even if they deny an owner the highest and best use of her property—unless they: (i) amount to a physical appropriation, as in *Loretto*, (ii) deny an owner of all economic use, as in *Lucas*, or (iii) unreasonably interfere with distinct, investment-backed expectations as set out in *Penn Central*. [*See* Lingle v. Chevron, 544 U.S. 528 (2005)]

3. Remedy—Inverse Condemnation

When a government acts under the power of eminent domain to take property for public use, it will condemn the property and pay the owner just compensation, as discussed below. When property is taken by occupation or regulation without condemnation proceedings, the landowner can bring an action for inverse condemnation. If the court determines that the government action amounted to a taking, the government will be required to either:

(i) *Pay the property owner compensation* for the taking (*see* below); or

(ii) *Terminate the regulation and pay the owner for damages* that occurred while the regulation was in effect (i.e., temporary taking damages).

[First English Evangelical Lutheran Church of Glendale v. County of Los Angeles, 482 U.S. 304 (1987)]

a. Who May Sue

The right to claim a "taking" is *not* limited to persons who held title to the property at the time a challenged use restriction was imposed. A person who purchases property after a regulation is in place still may bring a taking claim. [Palazzolo v. Rhode Island, 533 U.S. 606 (2001)]

D. "JUST COMPENSATION"

The owner is entitled to the *fair market value* of her property *at the time of the taking*—not the value it would have if put to its highest and best use. The measure is based on the *loss to the owner*, not the gain to the taker. Increases in value to the owner's remaining property as a result of the taking cannot be used to offset damages. Due process guarantees notice and hearing, administrative or judicial, on the amount of compensation, but the hearing need not precede the taking.

1. "Worthless" Property

Because just compensation is measured by the loss to the owner and not by the gain to the taker, property that is "worthless" to the owner can be the subject of a taking, but no compensation need be paid when it is taken.

Example: A state law required attorneys to keep clients' funds in trust accounts on behalf of their clients and to pay to the client any interest earned on the funds. If a client's funds were too small to earn enough interest to exceed the costs of distributing the interest, the attorneys were required to pay the interest over to a legal aid charity. Although this requirement constitutes a taking, no compensation is due because the clients have not suffered a pecuniary loss. [Brown v. Legal Foundation of Washington, 538 U.S. 216 (2003)]

XVI. INTRODUCTION TO SUBSTANTIVE DUE PROCESS AND EQUAL PROTECTION

A. RELATIONSHIP BETWEEN SUBSTANTIVE DUE PROCESS AND EQUAL PROTECTION

The Due Process Clauses and the Equal Protection Clause guarantee the fairness of laws— substantive due process guarantees that laws will be reasonable and not arbitrary, and equal protection guarantees that similarly situated persons will be treated alike. Both guarantees require the Court to review the *substance of the law* rather than the procedures employed.

1. Substantive Due Process

Generally where a law limits the liberty of *all* persons to engage in some activity, it is a due process question.

2. Equal Protection

Where a law treats a person or class of persons differently from others, it is an equal protection question. [*See* Village of Willowbrook v. Olech, 528 U.S. 562 (2000)—equal protection claims may be brought by a class with as few as one member] However, an at-will government employee who claims to be a victim of arbitrary discrimination cannot use the "class of one" theory to make an equal protection claim. [Engquist v. Oregon Department of Agriculture, 553 U.S. 591 (2008)]

3. **Examples**

If a law prohibits all persons from purchasing contraceptive devices, there is a due process issue; if the law prohibits only purchases by unmarried persons, there is an equal protection issue. A state's refusal to have any publicly funded schools raises a due process issue; a state law that establishes separate schools for children of different races raises an equal protection issue.

4. **Note—Clauses Not Necessarily Mutually Exclusive**

Since both clauses protect against unfairness, both may be appropriate challenges to the same governmental act, and a discussion of both may be appropriate in an essay answer. On the MBE, however, the examiners will probably not include both as alternatives in the same question. The above approaches can be used as a rough guideline of when each clause applies.

Example: Petitioners challenged state laws limiting marriage as between one man and one woman and refusing to recognize same-sex marriages from outside the state. The Court held that the fundamental liberties protected by ***both*** the Due Process and Equal Protection Clauses extend to certain personal choices central to individual dignity and autonomy, including intimate choices defining personal identity and beliefs. This includes the right of same-sex couples to marry. [Obergefell v. Hodges, 135 S. Ct. 1039 (2015)]

B. WHAT STANDARD OF REVIEW WILL THE COURT APPLY?

The Court employs one of three tests in reviewing laws under these clauses, depending on the circumstances.

1. **Strict Scrutiny (Maximum Scrutiny)**

The Court uses the strict scrutiny standard when a suspect classification or fundamental right (these terms will be discussed *infra*) is involved. Under the strict scrutiny standard, a law will be upheld only if it is ***necessary*** to achieve a ***compelling*** government purpose. The Court will always consider whether less burdensome means for accomplishing the legislative goal are available. Most governmental action examined under this test fails.

a. **Burden of Proof on Government**

When the strict scrutiny standard is applied, the ***government*** will have the burden of proving that the law is necessary. The Court will not allow a loose fitting law (i.e., if a law reaches more people or conduct than is necessary (overinclusive) or does not reach all of the people or conduct sought to be regulated (underinclusive), it will likely be struck down).

b. **Alternative Strict Scrutiny Language**

The Supreme Court's language sometimes varies when expressing the strict scrutiny standard. It commonly uses language such as "narrowly tailored to achieve a compelling government purpose" or "necessary to achieve an overriding government purpose" in addition to "necessary to achieve a compelling government purpose." For bar exam purposes, these varying iterations all have the same meaning.

2. **Intermediate Scrutiny**

The Court uses intermediate scrutiny when a classification based on gender or legitimacy is involved. Under the intermediate scrutiny standard, a law will be upheld if it is *substantially* related to an *important* government purpose.

a. Burden of Proof Probably on Government
It is unclear who has the burden of proof when the Court uses the intermediate standard, but in most cases, it appears to be the government.

3. Rational Basis (Minimal Scrutiny)
The rational basis standard is used whenever the other two standards are not applicable (i.e., most legislation). Under the rational basis standard, a law will be upheld if it is *rationally related to a legitimate* interest. It is difficult to fail this test, so most governmental action examined under this standard is upheld unless it is *arbitrary* or *irrational*.

a. Burden of Proof on Challenger
Under the rational basis standard, laws are presumed valid. Therefore, the challenger has the burden of proof. This is a very difficult burden to meet, given the deference the Court gives to legislatures under the rational basis standard. (*See* below.)

b. Deference to Legislature
Under the rational basis standard, the Court will usually defer to a legislature's decision that a law is rational. Loose fitting laws are permissible here: The law need not be the best law that could have been written to achieve the legislative goal. Indeed, it need not go far at all toward a conceivable legislative goal; the Court will uphold a law taking a "first step" toward any legitimate goal, even if the Court thinks the law is unwise.

Example: City decided that advertisements on motor vehicles are traffic hazards, so it banned such advertisements except for those on vehicles advertising the owner's own product. Even though the excepted advertisements were no less distracting than the banned ones, the Court upheld the "first step" law. [Railway Express Agency v. New York, 336 U.S. 106 (1949)]

XVII. SUBSTANTIVE DUE PROCESS

A. CONSTITUTIONAL SOURCE—TWO CLAUSES
There are two separate clauses protecting substantive due process:

(i)   The Due Process Clause of the Fifth Amendment (applies to the federal government); and

(ii) The Due Process Clause of the Fourteenth Amendment (applies to state and local governments).

As indicated above, *the same tests* are employed under each clause.

B. APPLICABLE STANDARDS

1. Fundamental Right—Strict Scrutiny
Where a law limits a fundamental right, strict scrutiny will be applied, and the law (or other

governmental action) will be upheld only if the government can prove that the action is necessary to promote a *compelling or overriding interest*. Fundamental rights include:

a.   Right to travel;

b.   Privacy;

c.   Voting; and

d.   All First Amendment rights.

2. All Other Cases—Mere Rationality

In all other cases, the mere rationality test is applied, and the law will be upheld unless the challenger can prove that the action is *not rationally related to any conceivable legitimate end of government*. Examples include the following:

a. Business and Labor Regulations
The Court will sustain all varieties of business regulation; e.g., "blue sky" laws, bank controls, insurance regulation, price and wage controls, unfair competition and trade practice controls, etc.

b. Taxation
Taxation is also invariably *sustained*. However, discriminatory taxes might still be invalidated.

c. Lifestyle
There is, as yet, *no recognized right* to lead a certain lifestyle. Thus, the Supreme Court will uphold laws: prohibiting drugs ("hard" or "soft"), requiring motorcyclists to wear helmets, or requiring police officers to have short hair. [Kelley v. Johnson, 425 U.S. 238 (1976)]

d. Zoning
Regulation of the ownership or use of property has also been liberally tolerated by the Court.

1) Statutes Forbidding Nuisances or Promoting Community's Preferred Lifestyle
Statutes forbidding certain uses as nuisances have been sustained, as have all kinds of statutes designed to promote the public's enjoyment of space and safety or to promote a community's preferred lifestyle and character. For example, the Supreme Court held that a Long Island suburb could zone out all groups of three or more persons unrelated by blood, adoption, or marriage. [Village of Belle Terre v. Boraas, 416 U.S. 1 (1974)]

2) Cannot Prohibit Traditionally Related Families from Living Together
However, you should know that the Supreme Court held that zoning regulations that prohibit members of traditional families from living together (i.e., zoning excluding cousins or grandchildren) violate due process. [Moore v. City of East Cleveland, 431 U.S. 494 (1977)]

e. **Punitive Damages**

The Supreme Court has held that punitive damages do not necessarily violate due process. However, "grossly excessive" damages—those that are unreasonably high to vindicate the state's interest in punishment—are invalid. [TXO Production Corp. v. Alliance Resources Corp., 509 U.S. 443 (1993)]

1) **Factors Considered**

In assessing whether punitive damages violate due process, the key issue is whether the defendant had *fair notice of the possible magnitude* of the punitive damages. In assessing such notice, the Court will look to:

(i) The *reprehensibility* of the defendant's conduct (e.g., whether the defendant caused physical harm rather than merely economic harm, whether the defendant acted with reckless disregard for harm, whether the conduct was repeated rather than isolated, and whether the harm resulted from intentional malice or deceit rather than from an accident);

(ii) The *disparity between* the actual or potential *harm suffered* by the plaintiff and the *punitive award;* and

(iii) The *difference between the punitive damages award and the criminal or civil penalties* authorized for comparable misconduct.

[BMW of North America, Inc. v. Gore, 517 U.S. 559 (1996)]

2) **Rule of Thumb**

Except for particularly egregious conduct—especially when the conduct resulted in only a small amount of compensatory damages—punitive damages should not exceed *nine times the compensatory damages.* [State Farm Mutual Auto Insurance Co. v. Campbell, 538 U.S. 408 (2003)—punitive damages of 145 times compensatory damages violate due process]

f. **Compare—Vagueness Doctrine**

Under the Due Process Clause of the Fourteenth Amendment, a law can be held unconstitutional if it fails to provide minimal guidelines to govern law enforcement officers so as to discourage arbitrary and discriminatory enforcement. [Kolender v. Lawson, 461 U.S. 352 (1983); City of Chicago v. Morales, 527 U.S. 41 (1999)—holding unconstitutional on vagueness grounds an ordinance that allowed officers to disperse suspected gang members when they were "loitering," which was defined as remaining in any one place with no *apparent purpose*]

C. **A FEW IRREBUTTABLE PRESUMPTIONS MAY BE INVALID**

If the government "presumes facts" against a person so that she is not qualified for some important benefit or right, the irrebuttable presumption may be unconstitutional. Although the Court often characterizes this as a due process question, it is more accurately an equal protection question because the government is creating an arbitrary classification. In any case, if the presumption affects a fundamental right (e.g., right to travel) or a suspect or quasi-suspect classification (e.g., gender), it will likely be invalid under strict scrutiny or intermediate scrutiny analysis, because the administrative convenience created by the presumption is not an important enough interest to justify the burden on the right or class. If some other classification or right is involved, the presumption will likely be upheld under the rational basis standard.

Examples: 1) A state may not presume a teacher incapable of continuous service in the classroom merely because she is four or five months' pregnant or has a child under age three. [Cleveland Board of Education v. LaFleur, 414 U.S. 632 (1974)]

2) The government may presume that a marriage entered into within nine months of a wage earner's death was simply to secure Social Security benefits. [Weinberger v. Salfi, 422 U.S. 749 (1975)]

D.   FAIR NOTICE

A fundamental principle of our legal system is that laws that regulate people or entities must give fair notice of conduct that is forbidden or required. A regulation that fails to give fair notice violates the Due Process Clause. [*See, e.g.,* Federal Communications Commission v. Fox Television Stations, Inc., 567 U.S. 239 (2012); *and see* XX.A.3.b., *infra*]

XVIII.   EQUAL PROTECTION

A.   CONSTITUTIONAL SOURCE

The Equal Protection Clause of the Fourteenth Amendment has ***no counterpart in the Constitution applicable to the federal government***; it is limited to state action. Nevertheless, it is clear that grossly unreasonable discrimination by the federal government violates the ***Due Process Clause of the Fifth Amendment***. [Bolling v. Sharpe, 347 U.S. 497 (1954)—racial discrimination in the public schools of the District of Columbia held a violation of due process] Thus, there are really two equal protection guarantees. The Court usually applies the same standards under either constitutional provision.

Example: The Supreme Court struck down a federal law defining "marriage" and "spouse" to exclude same-sex couples as applied to residents of a state that recognized same-sex marriage. The Court found that the liberty protected by the Due Process Clause of the Fifth Amendment contains within it a prohibition against denying any person the equal protection of laws. And a law that discriminates against some married couples recognized by a state in favor of other married couples violates equal protection. It should be noted that the Court did not rely on any of the traditional due process or equal protection tests (i.e., strict scrutiny, intermediate scrutiny, or rational basis) in arriving at the holding. [United States v. Windsor, 570 U.S. 744 (2013)]

B.   APPLICABLE STANDARDS

As indicated above, the Court will apply one of three standards when examining governmental action involving classifications of persons. If a ***suspect classification or fundamental right*** is involved, the strict scrutiny standard will be applied and the action will be struck down unless the government proves that it is necessary to achieve a compelling interest. If a ***quasi-suspect classification*** is involved, the Court will likely require the government to prove that the action is substantially related to an important government interest. If ***any other classification*** is involved, the action will be upheld unless the challenger proves that the action is not rationally related to a legitimate government interest.

C. PROVING DISCRIMINATORY CLASSIFICATION

The mere fact that legislation or governmental action has a discriminatory effect is not sufficient to trigger strict scrutiny or intermediate scrutiny. There must be *intent* to discriminate on the part of the government. Intent can be shown in three ways: (i) facial discrimination; (ii) discriminatory application; or (iii) discriminatory motive.

1. Facial Discrimination

A law may include a classification on its face. This type of law, by its own terms, makes an explicit distinction between classes of persons (perhaps by race or gender). In such cases the courts merely have to apply the appropriate standard of review for that classification. (The standards for racial classifications and gender classifications are described below.)

a. Facial Discrimination Absent Racial Language

In a few cases, the Supreme Court has held that a law used a racial classification "on its face" even though the language of the law did not include racial language. In these cases, the Supreme Court found that the law could not be explained except in racial terms.

Example: The Court found that a state law establishing districts for the election of Representatives to the United States Congress should be deemed to use a racial classification on its face because one bizarrely shaped district could not be explained except in terms of establishing a district where minority race voters would control the outcome of the election. The Court did not rule on the question of whether this racial classification was narrowly tailored to a compelling interest, such as remedying proven past discrimination, because that question had not been addressed in the lower courts. [Shaw v. Reno, 509 U.S. 630 (1993)]

Note: If a legislative districting map could be explained in terms other than race, the Court would not find that the law constituted racial discrimination on its face. In such a case, the persons attacking legislative districts as being based on racial classification would have to show that district lines were drawn for a racially discriminatory purpose. [Hunt v. Cromartie, 532 U.S. 234 (2001)—"Hunt II"]

2. Discriminatory Application

In some instances, a law that appears to be neutral on its face will be applied in a different manner to different classes of persons. If the persons challenging the governmental action can prove that the government officials applying the law had a discriminatory purpose (and used discriminatory standards based on traits such as race or gender), the law will be invalidated.

Examples: 1) A law prohibited operating a laundry in wooden buildings, but gave a government agency discretion to grant exemptions. It was shown that most such laundries were owned by people of Chinese descent, but the agency granted exemptions only to non-Asian applicants. The law was deemed to involve racial or national origin classification and was invalidated as applied. [Yick Wo v. Hopkins, 118 U.S. 356 (1886)]

2) Laws allow attorneys to move to strike potential jurors from a jury either for cause or without cause (a peremptory strike). In either case, there is an

equal protection violation when it is proved that an attorney excluded a person from a jury on account of the person's race or sex. [*See* Batson v. Kentucky, 476 U.S. 79 (1986); J.E.B. v. Alabama *ex rel.* T.B., 511 U.S. 127 (1994)] Note that because striking potential jurors from a jury significantly involves the state, even attorneys representing private parties are prohibited from discriminatory strikes. (*See* XII.B.2.a.1)a)(1), *supra*.)

3. Discriminatory Motive

Sometimes a government action will appear to be neutral on its face and in its application, but will have disproportionate impact on a particular class of persons (such as a racial minority or women). Such a law will be found to involve a classification (and be subject to the level of scrutiny appropriate to that classification) only if a court finds that the law-making body enacted or maintained the law for a ***discriminatory purpose***. In such cases, the court should admit into evidence statistical proof that the law has a disproportionate impact on one class of persons. However, mere statistical evidence will rarely be sufficient in itself to prove that the government had a discriminatory purpose in passing a law. Statistical evidence may be combined with other evidence of legislative or administrative intent to show that a law or regulation is the product of a discriminatory purpose.

Examples: 1) A police department used results from a written test as a criterion for hiring police officers. Members of identifiable racial minorities consistently got low scores on the test, although there was no proof that the test was written or otherwise employed for the purpose of disadvantaging minority applicants. Because of the absence of nonstatistical proof of discriminatory purpose, there was no equal protection violation. [Washington v. Davis, 426 U.S. 229 (1976)]

2) A state law gave a preference in the hiring and promotion of civil service employees to persons who were honorably discharged from the United States military. The foreseeable and actual impact of this law was to disadvantage the female population of job applicants, because the majority of veterans are men. Because there was no proof (other than the statistical impact of the law) that the legislature enacted the law for the purpose of hurting women (as opposed to the purpose of aiding veterans), the law was upheld.

3) A statistical study showing that black defendants in capital cases are much more likely to receive the death penalty than are white defendants in a state will not in itself establish that a particular black defendant was denied equal protection by being sentenced to death for murder in that state. The statistical study is insufficient to prove purposeful discrimination. [McCleskey v. Kemp, 481 U.S. 279 (1987)]

D. SUSPECT CLASSIFICATIONS

1. Race and National Origin

If governmental action classifies persons based on exercise of a fundamental right or involves a suspect classification (race, national origin, or alienage), strict scrutiny is applied. The result is invalidation of almost every case where the classification would burden a person because of her status as a member of a racial or national origin minority.

Example: A state could not deny custody of a child from a previous marriage to a white mother merely because her new husband was black, where the mother was otherwise found to be an appropriate parent. Racial prejudice against mixed race couples does not justify taking a child from his mother. [Palmore v. Sidoti, 466 U.S. 429 (1984)]

a.   School Integration
Recall that only intentional discrimination will be found to create discriminatory classifications calling for strict scrutiny (*see* C., *supra*); thus, only intentional segregation in schools will be invalidated under equal protection.

Example: No equal protection violation was found where a school system established attendance zones in a racially neutral manner, but racial imbalance occurred because of housing patterns. [Keyes v. School District No. 1, 413 U.S. 189 (1973)]

1)   Remedying Intentional School Segregation
If it is proven that a school board has engaged in the racial districting of schools, the board must take steps to eliminate the effects of that discrimination (e.g., busing students). If the school board refuses to do so, a court may order the school district to take all appropriate steps to eliminate the discrimination.

a)   Order Limited
A court may not impose a remedy that goes beyond the purpose of remedying the vestiges of past segregation. Thus, it is impermissible for a court to impose a remedy whose purpose is to attract nonminority students from outside the school district when there is no evidence of past segregation outside the district. [Missouri v. Jenkins, 515 U.S. 70 (1995)—state not required to fund salary increases and remedial programs to create magnet schools to attract suburban students to urban schools]

b.   "Benign" Government Discrimination—Affirmative Action
Government action—whether by federal, state, or local governmental bodies—that *favors* racial or ethnic minorities is subject to strict scrutiny, as is government action discriminating *against* racial or ethnic minorities. [Adarand Constructors, Inc. v. Pena, 515 U.S. 200 (1995)—*overruling* Metro Broadcasting, Inc. v. Federal Communications Commission, 497 U.S. 547 (1990), which applied intermediate standard to federal discrimination]

Note: Prior to its ruling in *Adarand, supra,* the Supreme Court upheld a federal requirement that 10% of federal grants for public works be set aside for minority businesses. [Fullilove v. Klutznick, 448 U.S. 448 (1980)] In *Adarand*, the Court reserved judgment on whether a *Fullilove*-type program would survive strict scrutiny. Some commentators have suggested that it might, because the Court might give Congress more deference than the states based on Congress's power under the Enabling Clause of the Fourteenth Amendment (*see* XII.A.3., *supra*), but the continued validity of *Fullilove* is, at best, uncertain.

1)   Remedying Past Discrimination
The government has a compelling interest in remedying past discrimination

against a racial or ethnic minority. Thus, if a court finds that a governmental agency has engaged in racial discrimination, it may employ a race-conscious remedy tailored to end the discrimination and eliminate its effects. A remedy of this type is permissible under the Equal Protection Clause because it is narrowly tailored to further a compelling interest (the elimination of the illegal or unconstitutional discrimination).

Example: When it has been proven that a public employer engaged in persistent racial discrimination, a court may order relief that establishes a goal for the hiring or promotion of minority persons so as to eliminate the effects of the past discrimination. [United States v. Paradise, 480 U.S. 149 (1987)]

2) **Where There Has Been No Past Discrimination by Government**

Even where a state or local government has not engaged in past discrimination, it may have a compelling interest in affirmative action. However, the governmental action must be *narrowly tailored* to that interest. [City of Richmond v. J.A. Croson Co., 488 U.S. 469 (1989)]

a) **Remedial Justifications**

(1) **Local Private Discrimination**

Remedying past private discrimination *within* the governmental agency's jurisdiction is a compelling interest, but there is no compelling interest in remedying the general effects of societal discrimination. Thus, for a city to give a preference to minority race applicants for city construction contracts, it must identify the past unconstitutional or illegal discrimination against minority-owned construction businesses that it is now attempting to correct. [City of Richmond v. J.A. Croson Co., *supra*]

Example: In *United Jewish Organizations v. Carey,* 430 U.S. 144 (1977), the Court upheld New York's revised voting district plan, based solely on racial statistics, because the revisions were made to insure that minorities that had previously been discriminated against in New York would be represented in the legislature.

(2) **Diversity in Primary and Secondary Public Education**

A school board may not assign students to a public primary or secondary school on the basis of race unless necessary to achieve a compelling interest, such as remedying past unconstitutional (i.e., intentional) discrimination. A majority of the Court has not found diversity itself to be a sufficiently compelling interest. [*See* Parents Involved in Community Schools v. Seattle School District No. 1, 551 U.S. 701 (2007)]

(3) **Diversity in Post-Secondary Public Education**

The Supreme Court has treated post-secondary educational institutions (e.g., public colleges and universities) differently. It has held that courts should defer to a public university's judgments that diversity is itself a compelling interest in post-secondary education. [Grutter v. Bollinger, 539 U.S. 306 (2003); Gratz v. Bollinger, 539 U.S. 244 (2003)] Thus, the Court held that race and ethnicity could be used as a factor (although not a predominant factor) in determining whether a particular student should be admitted. However, while the Court is willing to grant a public university deference as to the importance of diversity in a student body, it has held that courts should not give universities deference on the issue of whether a particular scheme for assuring diversity is narrowly tailored to that purpose. Strict scrutiny applies, so to pass constitutional muster, a university must show that no workable race-neutral alternatives would assure the diversity sought. Further, the Court indicated that because a school's use of racial preferences is permissible at one particular time does not mean the school can continue to rely on the same policy without "refinement." Universities must continually reassess their need for race-conscious admissions and engage in "constant deliberation and continued reflection" regarding these policies. [Fisher v. University of Texas at Austin, 136 S. Ct. 2198 (2016)]

b) States May Eliminate Race-Based Preferences
States are not required to have affirmative action programs for admission to their universities. Moreover, states may eliminate existing race-based preferences, including by voter initiative. The Court upheld the constitutionality of a Michigan initiative providing that the state and its political subdivisions could not discriminate or give preference based on race or gender in education, contracting, or employment. [Schuette v. Coalition to Defend Affirmative Action (BAMN), 572 U.S. 291 (2014)]

c. Discriminatory Legislative Apportionment
Race can be considered in drawing up new voting districts, but it *cannot be the predominant factor*. If a plaintiff can show that a redistricting plan was drawn up predominantly on the basis of racial considerations (as opposed to the more traditional factors, such as compactness, contiguity, and community interest), the plan will violate the Equal Protection Clause *unless* the government can show that the plan is *narrowly tailored* to serve a *compelling state interest*. [Miller v. Johnson, 515 U.S. 900 (1995)— while eradicating the effects of past discrimination would be a compelling state interest, the redistricting here was driven by the Justice Department's policy of maximizing the number of districts where racial minority members are the majority, which is not a compelling interest]

d. Private Affirmative Action
Private employers, of course, are not restricted by the Equal Protection Clause, since the Clause applies only to the government, and private employers lack state action. Nevertheless, Congress has adopted statutes regulating private discrimination by employers pursuant to its power under the enabling provisions of the Thirteenth and Fourteenth Amendments and the Commerce Clause. Thus, if an exam question asks whether private employer discrimination is valid, the answer generally cannot be based on equal protection.

2. Alienage Classifications

a. Federal Classifications

The standard for review of federal government classifications based on alienage is not clear, but they never seem to be subject to strict scrutiny. Because of Congress's plenary power over aliens, these classifications are valid if they are *not arbitrary and unreasonable*. Thus, federal Medicare regulations could establish a five-year residency requirement for benefits that eliminated many resident aliens. [Mathews v. Diaz, 426 U.S. 67 (1976)]

b. State and Local Classifications

State/local laws are *subject to strict scrutiny* if based on alienage. A "compelling state interest" must be shown to justify disparate treatment. For example, a state law requiring United States citizenship for welfare benefits, civil service jobs, or a license to practice law will be struck down because there is no compelling interest justifying the requirement.

1) Exception—Participation in Self-Government Process

If a law discriminates against alien participation in the functioning of the state government, the *rational basis* standard is applied.

Examples: 1) A state cannot require a notary public to be a citizen. A notary's responsibilities are essentially clerical and do not fall within the exception for positions related to participation in the governmental process, and there is no compelling government interest justifying such a requirement. [Bernal v. Fainter, 467 U.S. 216 (1984)]

2) A state can validly refuse to hire aliens as police officers and *primary* and *secondary* school teachers (because such teachers influence the attitudes of young minds toward government, the political process, and citizenship, as well as provide an example for civic virtues) and for all other positions that have a direct effect on the functioning of government. [Ambach v. Norwick, 441 U.S. 68 (1979); Cabell v. Chavez-Salido, 454 U.S. 432 (1982)]

c. Undocumented Aliens

1) Punitive Laws Against "Illegal" Alien Adults

The Supreme Court has *not* held that undocumented ("illegal") aliens are a suspect classification. Thus, a state law that denies benefits to (or imposes burdens on) persons who are in the United States without the permission of the federal government might be upheld under the rational basis test as long as the law was not totally arbitrary.

2) Education Rights of Alien Children

The Supreme Court has found that undocumented aliens are "persons" within the protection of the Fourteenth Amendment and that it would be fundamentally unfair to punish children for the crimes of their parents (i.e., illegally coming into the United States). Moreover, the Court found that refusing to educate children of undocumented aliens would hinder their lives in a way that would work a punishment on them. Therefore, the Court held that it is not rational for a state to deny children of undocumented aliens a free public education unless the state can show that the denial furthers a substantial state interest. Moreover, the Court held that the cost saved in not educating such children is not a sufficient interest. [Plyler v. Doe, 457 U.S. 202 (1982)]

a) Compare—Children Living Apart from Parents

The Supreme Court upheld a state statute that permitted a school district to deny tuition-free education to any child (whether or not he is a United States citizen) who lived apart from his parent or lawful guardian if the child's presence in the school district was for the "primary purpose" of attending school in the district. The state does not have to consider such a child to be a bona fide resident of the school district. [Martinez v. Bynum, 461 U.S. 321 (1983)]

E. QUASI-SUSPECT CLASSIFICATIONS

Classifications based on gender or legitimacy are almost always suspect. When analyzing government action based on such classifications, the Court will apply the intermediate standard and strike the action unless it is **substantially related** to an **important** government interest.

1. Gender

The Court has expressly held that the **government** bears the burden of proof in gender discrimination cases and that an **"exceedingly persuasive justification"** is required in order to show that gender discrimination is substantially related to an important government interest. [United States v. Virginia, 518 U.S. 515 (1996)]

a. Intentional Discrimination Against Women

Gender classifications that **intentionally** discriminate against women will generally be invalid under the intermediate standard, because the government is unable to show the "exceedingly persuasive justification" that is required.

Examples: 1) A statute giving the husband, as head of the household, the right to unilaterally dispose of property jointly owned with his wife violates equal protection. [Kirchberg v. Feenstra, 450 U.S. 455 (1981)]

2) A statute giving preference to males over females to act as administrator of an estate violates equal protection. [Reed v. Reed, 404 U.S. 71 (1971)—ease in determining who should serve is not an important interest]

Compare: 1) A state law that excluded from state disability insurance benefits "disabilities" arising from normal pregnancy and childbirth was upheld on a holding that it did not constitute a gender classification and so did not constitute intentional discrimination. [Geduldig v. Aiello, 417 U.S. 484 (1974)]

2) A state statute granting a hiring preference to veterans was upheld even though the result would disadvantage women since most veterans

are men. The Court found that the purpose of the statute was to help veterans, not to discriminate against women. [Personnel Administrator of Massachusetts v. Feeney, 442 U.S. 256 (1979)]

1) Government Interest Must Be Genuine

The "important government interest" advanced to justify categorization on the basis of gender must be *genuine*—not hypothesized for the purpose of litigation defense. Neither may the government's justification rely on *overbroad generalizations* about males and females that will create or perpetuate the legal, social, and economic inferiority of women. [United States v. Virginia, *supra*]

Example: When a state military school's policy of admitting only men was challenged, the state justified the policy, claiming that: (i) offering a diversity of educational approaches within the state (e.g., some schools having men only, some having women only, and some having both) yields important educational benefits, and (ii) females *generally* would not be able to meet the school's physical requirements and would not do well under the school's adversative approach to education. The Supreme Court found these arguments unavailing. There was no evidence that the single-sex school in question was established or had been maintained with a view toward fostering a diversity of educational opportunities, and there was some evidence that *some* women could meet the school's physical requirements and thrive under the school's adversative approach. [United States v. Virginia, *supra*]

b. Affirmative Action Benefiting Women

Classifications benefiting women that are designed to *remedy past discrimination* against women will generally be upheld.

Examples: 1) Social Security and tax exemptions that entitle women to greater benefits to make up for past discrimination in the workplace are valid. [Califano v. Webster, 430 U.S. 313 (1977)]

2) A Navy rule granting female officers longer tenure than males before mandatory discharge for nonproduction is valid to make up for past discrimination against females in the Navy. [Schlesinger v. Ballard, 419 U.S. 498 (1975)]

c. Intentional Discrimination Against Men

Intentional discrimination against men generally is invalid. However, a number of laws have been held valid as being substantially related to an important government interest.

1) Invalid Discrimination

The following have been held invalid under the Equal Protection Clause:

a) *Denial to admit males to a state university or nursing school* [Mississippi University for Women v. Hogan, 458 U.S. 718 (1982)];

b) Law that provides that *only wives are eligible for alimony* [Orr v. Orr, 440 U.S. 268 (1979)];

c) Law that permits ***unwed mother, but not unwed father, to stop adoption*** of offspring [Caban v. Mohammed, 441 U.S. 380 (1979)]; and

d) Law providing a ***higher minimum drinking age for men*** than for women [Craig v. Boren, 429 U.S. 190 (1976)].

2) Valid Discrimination
The following have been upheld under the Equal Protection Clause despite their discriminatory intent:

a) Law punishing males but not females for ***statutory rape*** (sexual intercourse with a minor) [Michael M. v. Superior Court, 450 U.S. 464 (1981)—classification was found to be substantially related to important interest of preventing pregnancy of minors];

b) ***Male-only draft registration*** [Rostker v. Goldberg, 453 U.S. 57 (1981)—classification was found to be substantially related to important interest of preparing combat troops]; and

c) A law granting ***automatic United States citizenship to nonmarital children born abroad to American mothers***, but requiring American fathers of children born abroad to take specific steps to establish paternity in order to make such children United States citizens. [Nguyen v. Immigration and Naturalization Service, 533 U.S. 53 (2001)—promotes the important governmental interest of avoiding proof of paternity problems, which are more difficult to resolve for fathers]

2. Legitimacy Classifications
Distinctions drawn between marital and nomarital children are also reviewed under the intermediate scrutiny standard. Such classifications "must be ***substantially related*** to an ***important*** governmental objective." [Clark v. Jeter, 486 U.S. 456 (1988)]

a. No Punitive Purpose
When the Court examines a classification based on illegitimacy, it gives greater attention to the purpose behind the distinction. It will not uphold discriminatory legislation intended to punish the offspring of illicit relationships.

1) Inheritance from Father
A state statute cannot absolutely exclude nomarital children from inheriting from their intestate fathers. [Trimble v. Gordon, 430 U.S. 762 (1977)]

Note: However, to promote efficient disposition of property at death (an important government interest), a state can require that the paternity of the father be proved before his death, since the requirement is substantially related to the important interest. [Lalli v. Lalli, 439 U.S. 259 (1978)]

2) Statute of Limitations on Paternity Suits May Be Discriminatory
The Supreme Court struck down a state statute that required nomarital children to bring paternity suits within six years of their birth while allowing marital children

to seek support from parents at any time. The Court found that the law was not related to the state interest of preventing stale or fraudulent claims. [Clark v. Jeter, *supra*]

b. Immigration Preference to Legitimate Children—Permissible
Due to the plenary power over immigration, the Court upheld a federal law granting immigration preferences to marital children. [Fiallo v. Bell, 430 U.S. 787 (1977)]

F. OTHER CLASSIFICATIONS

All other classifications are reviewed under the rational basis standard and will be upheld unless they bear no rational relationship to any conceivable legitimate government interest. Nevertheless, if the government has no interest in denying a benefit or imposing a burden on a group of persons other than a societal fear or dislike of them, the classification will not meet the standard.

Examples: 1) The Court struck down a zoning ordinance that allowed denial of a special use permit to a group of unrelated, mentally retarded persons who wished to share a residential home or apartment building. Retarded persons are not a suspect or quasi-suspect class and the right to housing is not a fundamental right; thus the Court applied the rational basis standard. It found that the sole reason the permit was denied was the applicants' mental condition and that the government has no legitimate interest in prohibiting mentally retarded persons from living together. [Cleburne v. Cleburne Living Center, Inc., 473 U.S. 432 (1985)]

2) Several municipalities passed ordinances banning discrimination in housing, employment, etc., based on sexual orientation. In response, the state voters adopted a state constitutional amendment prohibiting any state or local action protecting the status of persons based on their homosexual or bisexual orientation. *Held:* A state constitutional provision that identifies persons by a single trait and then denies them the right to seek *any* specific protections from the law—no matter how local or widespread the injury—is so unprecedented as to imply animosity toward such persons and is thus not related to any legitimate state interest. [Romer v. Evans, 517 U.S. 620 (1996)]

1. Age Not Suspect
Age is not a suspect class. Thus, government action based on age will be upheld if there is a conceivable rational basis for the classification. [*See, e.g.,* Massachusetts Board of Retirement v. Murgia, 427 U.S. 307 (1976)—police officer can be forced to retire at age 50, even though he is as physically fit as a younger officer; Gregory v. Ashcroft, 501 U.S. 452 (1991)—a state constitution that requires state judges to retire at age 70 does not violate the Equal Protection Clause]

2. Wealth Not Suspect
The Court has never held that wealth alone is a "suspect classification." However, the lack of wealth, or the inability to pay a governmentally required fee, cannot be the sole basis upon which a person is deprived of a *fundamental* constitutional right.

Example: The government will be required to waive a marriage license fee or divorce court fee for a person who cannot afford to pay that fee. Marriage and divorce rights are part of the right of privacy.

a. **Abortions**
The Supreme Court upheld the governmental refusal to pay for abortions. The Court found that a woman does not have a fundamental constitutional right to obtain abortion services; rather, a woman has a fundamental right to make her decision to have an abortion without government interference.

b. **Education**
The Supreme Court has not yet held education to be a fundamental right. The Court has not found that children are denied equal protection when the government provides greater educational opportunities for children who can afford to pay for access to the best state-operated schools. In fact, the Court has upheld the use of a property tax to fund local schools where the tax system resulted in children in districts with a high tax base getting a significantly better education than children in tax districts that could not afford significant taxes for education. [San Antonio Independent School District v. Rodriguez, 411 U.S. 1 (1973)] The Court has also upheld a statute that authorizes some school districts in the state to charge user fees for bus transportation to the local public schools. [Kadrmas v. Dickinson Public Schools, 487 U.S. 450 (1988)]

XIX. FUNDAMENTAL RIGHTS

A. **INTRODUCTION**
Certain fundamental rights are protected under the Constitution. If they are denied to everyone, it is a substantive due process problem. If they are denied to some individuals but not to others, it is an equal protection problem. The applicable standard in either case is strict scrutiny. Thus, to be valid the governmental action must be *necessary* to protect a *compelling interest*.

B. **RIGHT OF PRIVACY**
Various privacy rights, including marriage, procreation, contraception, and childrearing, are fundamental rights. Thus, regulations affecting these rights are reviewed under the *strict scrutiny* standard and will be upheld only if they are *necessary* to a *compelling interest*.

1. **Marriage**
Although not all cases examining marriage regulations clearly use the compelling interest standard, a law prohibiting a class of adults from marrying is likely to be invalidated unless the government can demonstrate that the law is narrowly tailored to promote a compelling or overriding or, at least, important interest.

Note: The Court has indicated that there is a "marital zone of privacy" [*see* Griswold v. Connecticut, 381 U.S. 479 (1965)], so it will likely grant broader protection to private sexual relations between married persons than it does concerning nonmarried persons.

a. **Same-Sex Marriage**
The Court has held that the fundamental liberties guaranteed by the Fourteenth Amendment require every state to issue marriage licenses to two people of the same sex and recognize same-sex marriages validly performed elsewhere. However, the Court did not expressly hold that same-sex marriage is a fundamental right, nor did it address the

standard of review (presumably, strict scrutiny). [Obergefell v. Hodges, 135 S. Ct. 1039 (2015)]

b.   Special Test in Prisoners' Rights Cases
A statute or regulation that restricts the constitutional rights of prison inmates will be upheld as long as the statute or regulation "is reasonably related to legitimate penological interests."

Example: Even under this lenient standard, a prison regulation that prohibited an adult prisoner from establishing a legal marriage relationship with another adult unless the prison superintendent approved the marriage was held invalid, because the regulation was not reasonably related to any asserted penological interest. [Turner v. Safley, 482 U.S. 78 (1987)]

2.   Procreation
Individuals have a fundamental right to reproduce that cannot be limited by the state. [Skinner v. Oklahoma, 316 U.S. 535 (1942)—invalidating a mandatory sterilization program as unconstitutional]

3.   Use of Contraceptives
A state cannot prohibit distribution of nonmedical contraceptives to adults except through licensed pharmacists, nor prohibit sales of such contraceptives to persons under 16 who do not have approval of a licensed physician. [Carey v. Population Services International, 431 U.S. 678 (1977)]

4.   Abortion
The Supreme Court has held that the right of privacy includes the right of a woman to have an abortion under certain circumstances without undue interference from the state. [Roe v. Wade, 410 U.S. 113 (1973)] However, because the Court has held that the states have a compelling interest in protecting the health of both the woman and the fetus that may become a child, it is difficult to apply the normal "strict scrutiny" analysis to abortion regulations (since these two compelling interests may conflict with each other and with the woman's privacy right). Moreover, the Supreme Court has actively been changing the rules regarding abortions and the Justices have not come to agreement on any applicable standard. In the Court's latest announcement, the plurality opinion adopted two rules: a pre-viability rule and a post-viability rule.

a.   Pre-Viability Rule—No Undue Burdens
Before viability (i.e., a realistic possibility of maintaining the fetus's life outside the womb), a state may adopt regulations protecting the mother's health and the life of the fetus only if the regulation does not impose an "undue burden" or substantial obstacle to the woman's right to have an abortion. The Court has not specifically defined what will constitute an undue burden, stating that a state can adopt a statute designed to persuade a woman to choose childbirth over abortion as long as the statute is reasonably related to that purpose and does not put a *substantial* obstacle to abortion in the woman's path. A statute will not impose a substantial obstacle or an undue burden simply because it has the incidental effect of making it more difficult or more expensive to obtain an abortion. [Planned Parenthood of Southeastern Pennsylvania v. Casey, 505 U.S. 833 (1992)]

1) **Informed Consent—No Undue Burden**
States can require abortions to be performed by licensed physicians, and it is not an "undue burden" to require the *physician* to provide the woman with truthful information about the nature of the abortion procedure, the health risks of abortion and childbirth, and the probable gestational age of the fetus. [Planned Parenthood of Southeastern Pennsylvania v. Casey, *supra*]

2) **Waiting Period—No Undue Burden**
Requiring a 24-hour waiting period between the time the woman gives her informed consent and the time of the abortion does not amount to an undue burden. [Planned Parenthood of Southeastern Pennsylvania v. Casey, *supra*]

3) **Parental Consent—No Undue Burden**
A state may require a minor to obtain her parents' (one or both) consent to have an abortion (or give notice to them even if their consent is not required) if there is a "bypass procedure" whereby the minor may obtain the abortion (without notice to or consent of her parents) with the consent of a judge. The judge is required to make a prompt decision as to (i) whether the minor is sufficiently mature to make her own abortion decision, and (ii) if she is not sufficiently mature, whether having an abortion without notice to her parents is in her best interests. [Hodgson v. Minnesota, 497 U.S. 417 (1990); Ohio v. Akron Center for Reproductive Health, 497 U.S. 502 (1990); Planned Parenthood of Southeastern Pennsylvania v. Casey, *supra;* Lambert v. Wicklund, 520 U.S. 292 (1997)]

4) **Compare—Spousal Consent Is Undue Burden**
It is an undue burden to require a woman to sign a statement that she has notified her spouse that she is about to undergo an abortion. [Planned Parenthood of Southeastern Pennsylvania v. Casey, *supra*]

5) **"Physician Only" Requirement—No Undue Burden**
A law restricting the performance of abortions to licensed physicians does not impose an undue burden on a woman seeking an abortion. [Mazurek v. Armstrong, 520 U.S. 968 (1997)—*per curiam*]

6) **Compare—Admitting Privileges Requirement Is Undue Burden**
A law requiring that physicians who perform abortions have admitting privileges at a nearby hospital imposes an undue burden on the right to abortion. [Whole Woman's Health v. Hellerstedt, 136 S. Ct. 2292 (2016)]

7) **"Partial-Birth Abortion" Ban—No Undue Burden**
A federal law (the Partial-Birth Abortion Ban Act of 2003) prohibiting "intact D&E" (a type of abortion procedure in which a live fetus is partially delivered, killed, and then fully removed from the woman's body) does not *on its face* impose an undue burden where other abortion procedures are available (e.g., a D&E not involving partial live delivery), the law includes specific anatomical standards and an exception to protect the woman's life, and there is uncertainty within the medical profession whether banning the intact D&E procedure creates a significant health risk for women. Although the Court generally upheld the statute,

it also held that the statute could not be applied in situations wherein the woman's health would be endangered. [Gonzales v. Carhart, 550 U.S. 124 (2007)—*distinguishing* Stenberg v. Carhart, 530 U.S. 914 (2000)—which invalidated a state partial-birth abortion ban that did not contain clearly defined anatomical standards nor provide any health exception]

8) Other Regulations Uncertain

Prior to *Planned Parenthood of Southeastern Pennsylvania v. Casey, supra,* the Supreme Court upheld a requirement that abortions be performed in a clinic or medical facility with all of the basic medical equipment that would be found in a hospital surgery room. The Court also upheld a requirement that tissue from an aborted fetus be sent to a pathologist. These holdings surely are still valid. But the Court struck down certain other regulations (e.g., requiring early term abortions to be approved by another doctor or hospital committee). Whether these regulations would be found to be undue burdens is uncertain.

b. Post-Viability Rule—May Prohibit Abortion Unless Woman's Health Threatened

Once the fetus has become viable, the state's interest in the fetus's life can override the woman's right to choose an abortion, but it does not override the state's interest in the woman's health. Thus, after viability the state can prohibit a woman from obtaining an abortion unless an abortion is necessary to protect the mother's life or health. However, viability is itself a medical question, and a state cannot unduly interfere with the attending physician's judgment as to the reasonable likelihood that the fetus can survive outside the womb. [Colautti v. Franklin, 439 U.S. 379 (1979)]

c. Remedy

When a court is faced with a statute restricting access to abortions that may be applied in an unconstitutional manner so as to harm the mother's health, it should *not* invalidate the statute in its entirety if the statute has valid applications. Instead, the court should attempt to fashion narrower declaratory and injunctive relief against the unconstitutional application. [Ayotte v. Planned Parenthood of Northern New England, 546 U.S. 320 (2006)]

Example: Court should not have invalidated an entire statute requiring minors to give parents notice before obtaining an abortion merely because the statute did not include an exception for cases where the minor's health is at stake; rather, it should be "declared invalid to the extent that it reaches too far, but otherwise left intact." [Ayotte v. Planned Parenthood of Northern New England, *supra*]

d. Financing Abortions

Neither federal nor local governments are required to grant medical benefit payments for abortions to indigent women, even if they grant benefits to indigent women for childbirth services. [Maher v. Roe, 432 U.S. 464 (1977); Harris v. McRae, 448 U.S. 297 (1980)] Moreover, a state may prohibit the public funding of abortions by prohibiting the use of public facilities for abortions and prohibiting any public employee acting within the scope of her public employment from performing or assisting in the performance of abortions. [Webster v. Reproductive Health Services, 492 U.S. 490 (1989)]

5. **Obscene Reading Material**
   The right of privacy encompasses the freedom to read obscene material in your home, except for child pornography. [Stanley v. Georgia, 394 U.S. 557 (1969); Osborne v. Ohio, 495 U.S. 103 (1990)] It does not, however, include the right to sell, purchase, receive, or transport obscene material. [Paris Adult Theatre v. Slayton, 413 U.S. 49 (1973)]

6. **Rights of Parents**
   Parental rights are fundamental rights. They include the companionship, care, custody, and management of children. [Santosky v. Kramer, 455 U.S. 745 (1982)]

   a. **Education**
      Although the state may prescribe reasonable educational standards, it may ***not*** require that all children be educated in public schools. [Pierce v. Society of the Sisters of the Holy Names of Jesus and Mary, 268 U.S. 510 (1925)] Neither may the state forbid education in a language other than English. [Meyer v. Nebraska, 262 U.S. 390 (1923)]

   b. **Visitation**
      A state law was found to be overbroad and in violation of parents' rights where it (i) authorized the courts to grant "any person" (including grandparents) a right to visit a child upon finding that this would be in the child's best interests, and (ii) did not allow the judge to give significant weight to the parent's offer of meaningful visitation opportunity and the traditional presumption that a fit parent will act in the child's best interests. [Troxel v. Granville, 530 U.S. 57 (2000)]

7. **Keeping Extended Family Together**
   The right of privacy includes the right of family members—even extended ones—to live together. Thus, a zoning ordinance cannot prohibit extended families from living in a single household since there is no compelling interest to justify such a rule. [Moore v. City of East Cleveland, 431 U.S. 494 (1977)]

8. **Intimate Sexual Conduct**
   The state has no legitimate interest in making it a crime for ***fully consenting adults*** to engage in ***private*** intimate sexual conduct that is not commercial in nature. Although the Court has not said what standard of review applies, it has indicated that a statute regulating such conduct cannot pass even the rational basis test because of the lack of a legitimate government interest. [Lawrence v. Texas, 539 U.S. 558 (2003)—a state law making it a crime for members of the same sex to engage in sodomy violates the Due Process Clause]

9. **Freedom from Collection and Distribution of Personal Data**
   The right of privacy does not prevent the state from accumulating and computerizing the names and addresses of patients for whom dangerous drugs are prescribed. [Whalen v. Roe, 429 U.S. 589 (1977)] And the state can republish the recording of an official act, such as an arrest. [Paul v. Davis, 424 U.S. 693 (1976)]

C. **RIGHT TO VOTE**
   The right of all United States citizens over 18 years of age to vote is mentioned in the Fourteenth, Fifteenth, Nineteenth, Twenty-Fourth, and Twenty-Sixth Amendments. It extends to all national and state government elections, including primaries. The right is fundamental; thus, restrictions

on voting, other than on the basis of age, residency, or citizenship, are *invalid* unless they can pass strict scrutiny.

1. Restrictions on Right to Vote

a. Residency Requirements

Relatively short residency requirements restricting the right to vote (e.g., 30 days) are valid because there is a compelling interest in ensuring that only bona fide residents vote. However, longer residency requirements will probably be held invalid (e.g., one year) because they discriminate against newer residents without a compelling reason, and thus violate the Equal Protection Clause. Such residency requirements might also violate the right to travel interstate. (*See* D.1.b.1), *infra*.) Note also that Congress may override state residency requirements in *presidential* elections. [Oregon v. Mitchell, 400 U.S. 112 (1970)]

1) Members of Armed Forces

The right to vote cannot automatically be denied to members of the armed forces stationed at a particular locality. They must be given an opportunity to prove their bona fide residency. [Carrington v. Rash, 380 U.S. 89 (1965)]

2) Compare—Nonresidents

Laws that prohibit nonresidents from voting are generally valid as long as they have a rational basis. [*See* Holt Civic Club v. City of Tuscaloosa, 439 U.S. 60 (1978)—upholding denial of right to vote in city elections to persons outside of city limits, but within the city's police and licensing jurisdiction]

b. Identification

A state may require in-person voters to show a government-issued voter ID. This is an "evenhanded" protection of the integrity of the electoral process and is justified by "sufficiently weighty" interests of detecting voter fraud and protecting public confidence in elections. [Crawford v. Marion County Election Board, 553 U.S. 181 (2008)]

c. Property Ownership

Conditioning the right to vote, to be a candidate, or to hold office on property ownership is usually invalid under the Equal Protection Clause, since property ownership is not necessary to any compelling governmental interest related to voting. [*See, e.g.,* Kramer v. Union Free School District, 395 U.S. 621 (1969)—requirement of owning property or having children in schools to vote in school board elections struck] However, certain special purpose elections (e.g., water storage district elections) can be based on property ownership. (*See* below.)

d. Poll Taxes

Poll taxes are prohibited under the Twenty-Fourth Amendment, and the Supreme Court has held that they also violate equal protection because wealth is not related to the government's interest in having voters vote intelligently. [Harper v. Virginia Board of Elections, 383 U.S. 663 (1966)]

e. Primary Elections

1) State Regulation of Party Primaries

States may exercise some control over primary elections, but such regulation is subject to restrictions under the First Amendment (freedom of political association) and the Fourteenth Amendment (Equal Protection Clause). Thus, to prevent interparty "raiding," the Supreme Court has held that states can require a person to have been registered with a party for a reasonable time before that party's primary election in order to be eligible to vote in the primary. [Rosario v. Rockefeller, 410 U.S. 752 (1973)—11 months' registration upheld; Kusper v. Pontikes, 414 U.S. 51 (1973)—23 months not upheld] However, if a political party wishes to open its primary elections to anyone, whether or not registered with the party, the state cannot prohibit this because the state interest here is overridden by the right of political association. [Tashjian v. Republican Party of Connecticut, 479 U.S. 208 (1986)]

2) States May Subsidize Primaries of Major Parties

States may subsidize the primaries of major parties without similarly defraying the costs of mechanisms through which minor parties qualify candidates for the general election [American Party of Texas v. White, 415 U.S. 767 (1974)—upholding law requiring new or small parties to proceed by petition or convention at their own expense rather than by publicly funded primary], as long as new or small parties are given some effective way to qualify for the general election [Williams v. Rhodes, 393 U.S. 23 (1968)—unduly burdensome petition requirements for new or small parties struck down as not justified].

2. Dilution of Right to Vote

a. One Person, One Vote Principle

The Equal Protection Clause of the Fourteenth Amendment has been interpreted to prohibit state dilution of the right to vote, and Article I has been interpreted to place the same type of restriction on the federal government.

1) Establishing Voting Districts

Whenever a governmental body establishes voting districts for the election of representatives, the number of persons in each district may not vary significantly. This is commonly referred to as the one person, one vote principle.

a) Congressional Elections—Almost Exactly Equal

States establish the districts for congressional elections. However, the Supreme Court requires *almost exact mathematical equality* between the *congressional* districts within a state; thus, deviations of even a few percentage points between the congressional districts within a state may result in the invalidation of the congressional district plan.

(1) Compare—Apportionment Among the States

Congress apportions representatives among the states "according to their respective number." [Art. I, §2] Congress's good faith choice of method in so apportioning the representatives commands far more deference than state districting decisions and is *not* subject to the same precise mathematical standard as state plans. [United States Department of Commerce v. Montana, 503 U.S. 442 (1992)]

b) **State and Local Elections—Variance Not Unjustifiably Large**
The variance in the number of persons included in districts for the purpose of electing representatives to a *state or local governmental body* must not be unjustifiably large, but the districts need not be within a few percentage points of each other: If a state can show that the deviation from mathematical equality between districts is reasonable and tailored to promote a legitimate state interest, the law establishing the districts may be upheld. [Mahan v. Howell, 410 U.S. 315 (1973)—16% variance in district populations was upheld in light of state's interest in preserving political subdivisions, although 30% variance would be excessive]

c) **Districts Can Be Measured Using Total Population**
States need not measure the equality of their districts by counting only persons eligible to vote. It is sufficient to count the total population. [Evenwel v. Abbott, 136 S. Ct. 1120 (2016)—representatives serve all the residents of their districts, not merely those eligible to vote; The one person, one vote principle is best served by taking the entire population into consideration]

d) **Scope**
The one person, one vote principle applies to almost every election where a person is being elected to perform normal governmental functions. [Hadley v. Junior College District, 397 U.S. 50 (1970)—trustees for junior college district] However, there are a few exceptions to note:

(1) **Exception—Appointed Officials and Officials Elected "At Large"**
The apportionment requirement is inapplicable to appointed officials. Neither is it applicable in at-large systems of election, because in such a system there are no electoral districts to violate the one person, one vote principle. However, if an at-large voting system were established or maintained for the purpose of suppressing the voting power of minority race voters, it would be unconstitutional.

(2) **Exception—Special Purpose Government Units (Water Storage Districts)**
The government can limit the class of persons who are allowed to vote in an election of persons to serve on a special purpose government unit *if* the government unit has a special impact on the class of enfranchised voters. To date, the Supreme Court has found only "water storage districts" to be so specialized that their governing boards are not subject to the one person, one vote principle. [Salyer Land Co. v. Tulare Lake Basin Water Storage District, 410 U.S. 719 (1973); Ball v. James, 451 U.S. 355 (1981)—apportionment rules do not apply to water district even if the district is major supplier of electricity in the state]

2) **Standardless Recount**
Counting uncounted ballots in a presidential election without standards to guide

ballot examiners in determining the intent of the voter violates the Fourteenth Amendment Equal Protection Clause. [Bush v. Gore, 531 U.S. 98 (2000)]

b. Gerrymandering

1) Racial Gerrymandering

As indicated above, race (and presumably other suspect classifications) cannot be the predominant factor in drawing the boundaries of a voting district unless the district plan can pass muster under strict scrutiny. [*See* Miller v. Johnson, XVIII.D.1.c., *supra*] Moreover, a district's bizarre shape can be used to show that race was the predominant factor in drawing the district's boundaries [*see* Shaw v. Reno, XVIII.C.1.a., *supra*], although a bizarre shape is not necessary to such a finding. Note that the person challenging the reapportionment has the burden of proving the race-based motive. [Shaw v. Hunt, 517 U.S. 899 (1996)]

2) Political Gerrymandering

The Court has *never* ruled that a legislative redistricting map should be overturned on the basis of political gerrymandering, and a number of Justices have suggested that political gerrymandering is a nonjusticiable issue. [Vieth v. Jubelirer, 541 U.S. 267 (2004); *and see* League of United Latin American Citizens v. Perry, I.E.7.a., *supra*, 548 U.S. 399 (2006)—refusing to find a constitutional violation when there was mid-decade redistricting for partisan political reasons]

c. Multi-Member Districts

A state is generally free to have some multi-member districts together with some single-member districts, as long as the number of members representing a district is proportional to its population. However, single-member or multi-member districts will be held to violate equal protection (even though they meet the one person, one vote principle) if the district lines were drawn on the basis of unconstitutional criteria, such as to suppress the voting power of racial minorities or an identifiable political group.

d. States May Use Independent Commissions to Draw Districts

To avoid gerrymandering, states may use independent commissions to adopt congressional districts, rather than allowing the state legislature to redistrict. [Arizona State Legislature v. Arizona Independent Redistricting Commission, 135 S. Ct. 2652 (2015)]

3. Candidates and Campaigns

a. Candidate Qualifications

1) Fee Must Not Preclude Indigents as Candidates

States may not charge candidates a fee that results in making it impossible for indigents to run for office. An unreasonably high filing fee (which was not tailored to promote a substantial or overriding state interest) might be held totally invalid so that no candidate would have to pay the fee. A reasonable, valid fee would have to be waived for an indigent candidate who could not pay the fee.

2) Restrictions on Ability of Person to Be a Candidate

Restrictions on the ability of persons to be candidates must be examined to see if they violate either the First Amendment right of political association or the Fourteenth Amendment Equal Protection Clause. Such regulations are judged on a sliding scale of scrutiny. (*See* XXI.B., *infra.*)

Example: The Court invalidated a March deadline for filing a nominating petition for independent candidates for a November election where the state allowed the major political parties to name their candidates later in the year. [Anderson v. Celebrezze, 460 U.S. 780 (1983)]

Note: A state may require candidates to show reasonable support (signatures or votes) to qualify to have their names placed on the ballot. [Munro v. Socialist Workers Party, 479 U.S. 189 (1986)—upholding requirement of receipt of at least 1% of the votes cast in the primary election]

3) Required Resignation of Office Is Permissible

A state may require state officials to resign their office if they enter an election for another government office. [Clements v. Fashing, 457 U.S. 957 (1982)]

b. Campaign Funding, Contributions, and Expenditures

Government *may* allocate more public funds to the two "major" parties than to "minor" parties for political campaigns, and may withhold public funding from candidates who do not accept reciprocal limits on their total campaign expenses; but such expenses cannot otherwise be limited, unlike campaign contributions to political candidates, which may be limited if government chooses. (XXI.B., *infra.*)

4. Extraordinary Majorities—Referendum Elections

The government may require a supermajority vote for voter referendums, even though such a requirement might give a minority disproportionate power. [Gordon v. Lance, 403 U.S. 1 (1971)—upholding 60% requirement for referendum approval; Town of Lockport v. Citizens for Community Action, 430 U.S. 259 (1977)—upholding requirement that new county charter be approved by separate majorities of city and noncity voters]

5. Replacement of Incumbent Legislators

A state may validly give to a political party the right to name an interim appointee to the legislature to fill out the unexpired term of a legislator from that political party who left office. No voter is denied equal protection by this system. [Rodriguez v. Popular Democratic Party, 457 U.S. 1 (1982)]

D. RIGHT TO TRAVEL

1. Interstate Travel

a. Nature of the Right

Individuals have a fundamental right to travel from state to state, which encompasses the right: (i) to leave and enter another state, and (ii) to be treated equally if they become permanent residents of that state. [Saenz v. Roe, VII.C.3., *supra*—striking down California law that limited welfare benefits for new residents to what they would have received in their prior state of residence]

b. **Standard of Review**

When a state uses a durational residency requirement (a waiting period) for dispensing benefits, that requirement normally should be subject to the "strict scrutiny" test. This means that the government must show that the waiting period requirement is tailored to promote a compelling or overriding interest. However, in some right to travel cases, the Court has not been clear as to whether it is using this strict scrutiny, compelling interest standard of review. The important point to note for the bar exam is that state residency requirements should not be upheld merely because they have some theoretical rational relationship to an arguably legitimate end of government.

1) **Examples**

Because of the ad hoc nature of these rulings, we will list four examples of Supreme Court decisions in this area:

a) A one-year waiting period before a person may receive subsistence welfare payments is *invalid*. Similarly, a law providing that persons residing in the state for less than a year may receive welfare benefits no greater than those paid in the state of prior residence is also invalid. [Saenz v. Roe, *supra*]

b) A one-year waiting period for state subsidized medical care is *invalid*.

c) A one-year waiting period to get a divorce is *valid*.

d) A state may require a voter to register to vote in a party primary 10 months before the primary election (to avoid interparty "raiding"). However, a 23-month registration period would be *invalid*.

c. **Distinctions Between Old and New Residents**

Some state laws that have an adverse impact on new residents do not involve a waiting period. For example, a state may attempt to dispense state benefits on the basis of the length of time a person has resided in the state. A state law that distinguishes between residents of the state on the sole basis of their length of residency will serve no legitimate state interest. This type of law should be *stricken* under the rational basis test because it has *no rational relationship* to any legitimate state interest.

Examples: 1) A state statute that dispensed differing amounts of state money to residents of the state based on each resident's length of residence was held invalid.

2) A state statute that grants an annual property tax exemption to a veteran of military service only if he resided in the state before a specific date (May 1976) is invalid.

3) A state law that grants a hiring preference (for civil service employment) to a veteran only if he was a resident of the state prior to joining the armed services is invalid.

2. **International Travel**

The Supreme Court has not yet declared that the right to international travel is fundamental, although the right appears to be ***protected from arbitrary federal interference*** by the Due Process Clause of the Fifth Amendment. The Court has held that this right is not violated when the federal government refuses to pay Social Security benefits to persons who leave the country. The test here is "mere rationality, not strict scrutiny." [Califano v. Aznavorian, 439 U.S. 170 (1978)] Congress may give the executive branch the power to revoke the passport of a person whose conduct in another country presents a danger to United States foreign policy. [Haig v. Agee, 453 U.S. 280 (1981)] The Treasury Department, with congressional authorization, could restrict travel to and from Cuba without violating the Fifth Amendment. [Regan v. Wald, 468 U.S. 222 (1984)]

E. RIGHT TO REFUSE MEDICAL TREATMENT

The Supreme Court had held that the right to refuse medical treatment is a part of an individual's "liberty" that is protected by the Fifth and Fourteenth Amendment Due Process Clauses. However, the Supreme Court has not ruled that this aspect of liberty is a "fundamental right" and ***has not*** explained which standard of review should be used. Nevertheless, the Court has ruled on the validity of several types of legislation.

1. Vaccination

An individual can be made to submit to vaccination against contagious diseases because of the governmental and societal interest in preventing the spread of disease. [Jacobson v. Massachusetts, 197 U.S. 11 (1905)]

2. Refusal of Medical Treatment

The Supreme Court has assumed (without deciding) that a mentally competent adult has the right to refuse lifesaving medical treatment (including lifesaving nutrition). [Cruzan v. Director, Missouri Department of Health, 497 U.S. 261 (1990)]

a. Compare—No Right to Assisted Suicide

There is no general right to commit suicide; thus, a state may ban persons from giving individuals assistance in committing suicide. [Washington v. Glucksberg, 521 U.S. 702 (1997)] It is not irrational to permit competent persons to refuse life-sustaining treatment but prohibit physicians to assist in suicide because there is a logical, rational, and well-established distinction between letting someone die and making someone die. [Vacco v. Quill, 521 U.S. 793 (1997)]

b. Compare—Criminal Defendants

Under the Due Process Clause, the government may ***involuntarily*** administer antipsychotic drugs to a mentally ill defendant facing serious criminal charges in order to make him competent to stand trial if: (i) the treatment is medically appropriate, (ii) the treatment is substantially unlikely to cause side effects that may undermine the fairness of the trial, and (iii) considering less intrusive alternatives, the treatment is necessary to further important governmental trial-related interests. [Sell v. United States, 539 U.S. 166 (2003)]

PART FIVE: FIRST AMENDMENT FREEDOMS

The First Amendment prohibits Congress from establishing a religion or interfering with the exercise of religion, abridging the freedom of speech or the press, or interfering with the right of the people to assemble. These prohibitions have been made applicable to the states through the Fourteenth Amendment. The freedoms, however, are not absolute, and exam questions often focus on their boundaries. The following material will outline the scope of each freedom.

XX. FREEDOM OF SPEECH AND ASSEMBLY

A. GENERAL PRINCIPLES

The freedoms of speech and assembly protect the free flow of ideas, a most important function in a democratic society. Thus, whenever the government seeks to regulate these freedoms, the Court will weigh the importance of these rights against the interests or policies sought to be served by the regulation. When analyzing regulations of speech and press, keep the following guidelines in mind:

1. Government Speech

The Free Speech Clause restricts government *regulation of private speech*; it does not require the government to aid private speech nor restrict the government from expressing its views. The government generally is free to voice its opinions and to fund private speech that furthers its views while refusing to fund other private speech, absent some other constitutional limitation, such as the Establishment Clause or Equal Protection Clause. Because government speech does not implicate the First Amendment, it is not subject to the various levels of scrutiny that apply to government regulation of private speech (*see infra*). [Pleasant Grove City, Utah v. Summum, 555 U.S. 460 (2009)] Generally, government speech and government funding of speech will be upheld if it is *rationally related to a legitimate state interest*.

Examples: 1) The government may choose to aid a union representing government employees by providing for payroll deductions of general union dues while refusing to allow payroll deductions that will be used by unions to fund political activities. The decision not to collect funds for political activities is rationally related to a legitimate government interest (i.e., avoiding the appearance of favoritism), and thus the refusal to collect such funds is constitutional. [Ysursa v. Pocatello Education Association, 555 U.S. 353 (2009)]

2) The government may fund family planning services but except from funding services that provide abortion information. [Rust v. Sullivan, 500 U.S. 173 (1991)]

3) The government may refuse to fund artists whose work it finds offensive. [National Endowment for the Arts v. Finley, 524 U.S. 569 (1998)]

4) The government may reject proposed specialty license plate designs submitted by private individuals while accepting others. Since license plates are issued by the state and bear the state name, this is a form of government speech, and states are entitled to refuse to issue plates featuring certain messages or images. [Walker v. Texas Division, Sons of Confederate Veterans, 135 S. Ct. 2239 (2015)]

a. **Limitation**

Spending programs may not impose conditions that limit First Amendment activities of fund recipients outside of the scope of the spending program itself. For example, while the government could prohibit the use of federal funds to advocate for or support abortion [Rust v. Sullivan, *supra*], it could not require recipients of federal funds given to organizations to combat HIV/AIDS to agree in their funding documents that they oppose prostitution. [Agency for International Development v. Alliance for Open Society International, Inc., 133 S. Ct. 2321 (2013)]

b. **Public Monuments**

A city's placement of a ***permanent*** monument in a public park is government speech and thus is not subject to Free Speech Clause scrutiny. This is true even if the monument is privately donated. By displaying the monument, the government is disseminating a message, and the message is not necessarily the message of the donor(s). As a corollary, the government cannot be forced to display a permanent monument with a message with which the government disagrees, and the government's refusal to display a proffered monument likewise is not subject to Free Speech Clause scrutiny.

Example: A city with a Ten Commandments monument in its park was not required to display a religious monument of another religion (the "Seven Aphorisms" of the Summum faith). The Ten Commandments monument, although privately donated, was deemed government speech. When the government is the speaker, it may engage in content-based choices. [Pleasant Grove City, Utah v. Summum, *supra*] (*Note:* While an Establishment Clause issue was not raised in *Summum,* a concurring opinion suggested that the Ten Commandments monument did not violate the Establishment Clause because it was one of 15 monuments in the park recognizing the historical roots and morals of the community. [*And see* Van Orden v. Perry, XXII.D.2.c., *infra*])

c. **Compare—Government Funding of Private Messages**

In contrast to government funding of speech for the purpose of promoting its own policies (such as the family planning services involved in *Rust v. Sullivan, supra*), when the government chooses to fund private messages, it generally must do so on a viewpoint neutral basis. [*See* Rosenberger v. Rector and Visitors of the University of Virginia, 515 U.S. 819 (1995)—state university exclusion of religious magazine from program financially supporting many other types of student publications violates the First Amendment]

1) **Exception—Funding of the Arts**

From a financial standpoint, the government cannot fund all artists, and choosing among those it will fund and those it will not inevitably must be based on the content of the art. [National Endowment for the Arts v. Finley, *supra*]

d. **Trademark Protection**

Trademark protection is ***not*** government speech, thus, ***it is*** subject to strict scrutiny. Trademarks are private speech because they are produced by private individuals and merely protected by government.

> *Example:*   As part of a statutory scheme to grant trademark protection, Congress adopts a rule prohibiting the registration of derogatory or disparaging trademarks. A rock band adopted the derogatory term "Slants" as its name in an effort to reclaim the term. The federal government's denial of the band's trademark application on the grounds that the trademark was derogatory was unconstitutional because the rule was viewpoint based and its enforcement would allow the government to suppress speech from certain viewpoints. [Matal v. Tam, 137 S. Ct. 1744 (2017)]

2. Content vs. Conduct

A regulation seeking to forbid communication of specific ideas (i.e., a *content* regulation) is less likely to be upheld than a regulation of the *conduct* incidental to speech.

a. Content

It is presumptively unconstitutional for the government to place burdens on speech because of its content. To justify such content-based regulation of speech, the government must show that the regulation (or tax) is *necessary* to serve a *compelling* state interest and is narrowly drawn to achieve that end. [Simon & Schuster, Inc. v. Members of the New York State Crime Victims Board, 502 U.S. 105 (1991)—striking a law requiring that proceeds to criminals from books and other productions describing their crimes be placed in escrow for five years to pay claims of victims of the crimes]

> *Example:*   A state may not prohibit the sale or rental of violent video games to minors. Such a prohibition is content-based, and the Supreme Court found that the prohibition was not narrowly tailored to serve a compelling interest. It found the law both underinclusive, because psychological studies show that such games have only a small effect on youth violence, and overinclusive, because only some parents object to them. The Court also declined to add violence as an additional area of unprotected speech (*see* below). [Brown v. Entertainment Merchants Association, 564 U.S. 786 (2011)]

1) Exception—Unprotected Categories of Speech

The Supreme Court has previously determined that certain categories of speech (e.g., obscenity, defamation, and "fighting words"; *see* C., *infra*) generally are proscribable despite the First Amendment. Even in these cases, however, the Court is less likely to uphold a prior restraint (i.e., a regulation prohibiting speech before it occurs) than a punishment for speech that has already occurred.

a) Falsity in and of Itself Does Not Make Speech Unprotected

A statute criminalizing speech merely because it is false is a content regulation. And while some categories of false speech are unprotected (e.g., defamation, false advertising, fraud, and perjury), those categorical exceptions are based on the harm caused. Speech is not unprotected merely for being false. [United States v. Alvarez, 567 U.S. 709 (2012)—Stolen Valor Act making it a crime to falsely claim to have received military decorations is unconstitutional; while the government may have a compelling interest in maintaining the integrity of military honors, nothing indicates that the law here is necessary to that purpose]

2) Content-Neutral Speech Regulations

While content-based regulation of speech is subject to strict scrutiny, content-neutral speech regulations generally are subject to *intermediate scrutiny*—they will be upheld if the government can show that: (i) they advance *important* interests unrelated to the suppression of speech, and (ii) they *do not burden substantially more speech than necessary* or are *narrowly tailored* to further those interests. [Turner Broadcasting System, Inc. v. FCC, 512 U.S. 622 (1994)]

b. Conduct

The Court has allowed the government more leeway in regulating the conduct related to speech, allowing it to adopt content-neutral, *time*, *place*, *and manner* regulations. Regulations involving public forums (i.e., forums historically linked with the exercise of First Amendment freedoms) must be *narrowly tailored* to achieve an *important* government interest (e.g., a prohibition against holding a demonstration in a hospital zone). Regulations involving nonpublic forums must have a reasonable relationship to a legitimate regulatory purpose (e.g., a law prohibiting billboards for purposes of traffic safety).

3. Reasonableness of Regulation

a. Overbroad Regulation Invalid

Since the purpose of the freedoms of speech and assembly is to encourage the free flow of ideas, a regulation will not be upheld if it is overbroad (i.e., prohibits *substantially* more speech than is necessary). If a regulation of speech or speech-related conduct punishes a *substantial amount of protected speech,* judged in relation to the regulation's plainly legitimate sweep, the regulation is *facially invalid* (i.e., it may not be enforced against anyone—not even a person engaging in activity that is not constitutionally protected) unless a court has limited construction of the regulation so as to remove the threat to constitutionally protected expression. [Virginia v. Hicks, 539 U.S. 113 (2003)] If a regulation is not substantially overbroad, it can be enforced against persons engaging in activities that are not constitutionally protected.

Examples: 1) The Supreme Court struck down as overbroad an ordinance that prohibited speech that *"in any manner"* interrupts a police officer in the performance of her duties. [Houston v. Hill, 482 U.S. 451 (1987)]

2) An airport authority rule that bans "*all* First Amendment activities" within the "central terminal area" is invalid as being substantially overbroad. [Board of Airport Commissioners v. Jews for Jesus, 482 U.S. 569 (1987)]

3) A law banning *all* door-to-door solicitations will be struck as being overbroad [Martin v. City of Struthers, 319 U.S. 141 (1943)], but a law requiring solicitors to obtain a homeowner's consent to solicit is valid. [Breard v. City of Alexandria, 341 U.S. 622 (1951)]

4) An ordinance that prohibited *all* canvassers from going onto private residential property to promote *any* cause without first obtaining a permit was overbroad. While the government may have an interest in

preventing fraud from door-to-door solicitation, the permit requirement here went beyond cases where fraud was likely to occur, and applied to religious proselytization, advocacy of political speech, and enlisting support for unpopular causes. [Watchtower Bible and Tract Society of New York, Inc. v. Village of Stratton, 536 U.S. 150 (2002)]

5) A city ordinance that prohibits homeowners from displaying *any sign* on their property except "residence identification" or "for sale" signs is invalid because the ordinance bans virtually all residential signs. [Ladue v. Gilleo, 512 U.S. 43 (1994)]

b. **Void for Vagueness Doctrine**

If a criminal law or regulation fails to give persons reasonable notice of what is prohibited, it may violate the Due Process Clause. This principle is applied somewhat strictly when First Amendment activity is involved in order to avoid the chilling effect a vague law might have on speech (i.e., if it is unclear what speech is regulated, people might refrain from speech that is permissible for fear that they will be violating the law). Vagueness issues most often arise in relation to content regulations, but the same principles would apply to time, place, and manner restrictions.

Examples: 1) A municipal ordinance that prohibited vagrants was held void for vagueness when it defined vagrants as "rogues and vagabonds . . . lewd, wanton, and lascivious persons . . . persons wandering or straying around from place to place without any lawful purpose or object . . . ." [Papachristou v. City of Jacksonville, 405 U.S. 156 (1972)]

2) A statute that prohibits attorneys representing clients in a pending case from making statements that would have a substantial likelihood of prejudicing a trial, but that also allows attorneys to make public statements regarding the "general nature of the defense" they will present at trial, is void for vagueness, because it does not give fair notice of the types of trial-related statements that are punishable. [Gentile v. State Bar, 501 U.S. 1030 (1991)]

1) **Burden on Challenger**

The person challenging the validity of the regulation has the burden of showing substantial overbreadth. [Virginia v. Hicks, *supra*]

2) **Funding Speech Activity**

Greater imprecision is allowed when the government acts as a patron in funding speech activity than when enacting criminal statutes or regulatory schemes, because speakers are less likely to steer clear of forbidden areas when only a subsidy is at stake. [National Endowment for the Arts v. Finley, 1., *supra*— requirement that NEA consider standards of "decency" and "respect for values of American people" is not invalid on its face]

c. **Cannot Give Officials Unfettered Discretion**

A regulation cannot give officials broad discretion over speech issues; there must be *defined standards* for applying the law. The fear, of course, is that the officials will use their discretionary power to prohibit dissemination of ideas that they do not agree with. This issue usually arises under licensing schemes established to regulate the time, place, and manner of speech. To be valid, such licensing schemes must be related to an important government interest, contain procedural safeguards (*see* D.2., *infra*), and not grant officials unbridled discretion.

Example: County required persons desiring to hold a parade, march, or rally to first obtain a permit from the county administrator. The administrator was empowered to charge up to $1,000 for the permit, but could adjust the fee to meet the necessary expenses of administration and police protection. This scheme is invalid because it gives the administrator unbridled discretion despite the $1,000 limit. It also is unconstitutional because it is a content-based restriction (the administrator theoretically would adjust the costs based on the popularity of the subject at issue—an unpopular subject would require greater police protection). [Forsyth County, Georgia v. Nationalist Movement, 505 U.S. 123 (1992)]

1) **Unlimited Discretion—Void on Face**

If a statute gives licensing officials unbridled discretion, it is *void on its face*, and speakers need not even apply for a permit. They may exercise their First Amendment rights even if they could have been denied a permit under a valid law, and they may not be punished for violating the licensing statute. [Lovell v. City of Griffin, 303 U.S. 444 (1938)]

Examples: 1) An ordinance vesting officials with the power to grant or deny parade permits based on their judgment as to the effect of the parade on community "welfare" or "morals" is unconstitutional on its face. [Shuttlesworth v. Birmingham, 394 U.S. 147 (1969)] Similarly, ordinances giving officials broad discretion as to who may place magazine racks on public property or who may obtain licenses to solicit door to door are invalid. [City of Lakewood v. Plain Dealer Publishing Co., 486 U.S. 750 (1988); Lovell v. City of Griffin, *supra*]

2) A statute prohibiting excessively loud sound trucks is valid [Kovacs v. Cooper, 336 U.S. 77 (1949)], but an ordinance giving officials discretion as to who may use sound trucks is invalid [Saia v. New York, 334 U.S. 558 (1948)].

2) **Statutes Valid on Face**

If the licensing statute is valid on its face because it contains adequate standards, a speaker may not ignore the statute, but must seek a permit. If he is denied a permit, even if he believes the denial was incorrect, he must then seek reasonably available administrative or judicial relief. Failure to do so precludes later assertion that his actions were protected by the First Amendment. [Poulos v. New Hampshire, 345 U.S. 395 (1953)]

4. **Scope of Speech**

a. **Includes Freedom Not to Speak**

The freedom of speech includes not only the right to speak, but also the right to refrain from speaking or endorsing beliefs with which one does not agree—the government may not compel an individual personally to express a message with which he disagrees.

Examples: 1) A state *cannot force school children to salute* or say a pledge to the flag. [West Virginia State Board of Education v. Barnette, 319 U.S. 624 (1943)]

2) A motorist *could not be punished* for blocking out the portion of his automobile license plate bearing the motto "Live Free or Die"; as long as he left the license plate in a condition that served its auto identification purpose, he did not have to display a slogan endorsed by the state. [Wooley v. Maynard, 430 U.S. 705 (1977)]

3) A state may not require private parade organizers to include in their parade groups with messages with which the organizers disagree. [Hurley v. Irish-American Gay, Lesbian & Bisexual Group of Boston, 515 U.S. 557 (1995)]

4) A state cannot force all licensed clinics that offered pregnancy-related services to provide a government-drafted notice about the availability of abortion and contraception. [National Institute of Family and Life Advocates v. Becerra, 138 S. Ct. 2361 (2018)]

1)   Mandatory Financial Support
Although the government may not compel a person to express a message, the government may tax people and use the revenue to express a message with which people disagree.

a)   Government Speech
The Court has held that compelled support of government speech does *not* raise First Amendment concerns. [Johanns v. Livestock Marketing Association, 544 U.S. 550 (2005)—beef producers can be required to pay an assessment to support generic advertising of beef approved by a semi-governmental producers' board and ultimately by the Secretary of Agriculture—even if they think generic advertising is a waste of money—because the advertisements are governmental speech]

b)   Compare—Private Speech
On the other hand, people *cannot* be compelled to subsidize *private* messages with which they disagree.
Example: Non-union members *cannot* be forced to pay a proportionate share of union dues on the ground that they too benefit from collective bargaining agreements because such a requirement would force the non-union members to financially support political views that they might not endorse. [Janus v. American Federation of State, County, and Municipal Employees, 138 S. Ct. 2448 (2018)]

(1)   Exception—University Activity Fees
The government can require public university students to pay a student

activity fee even if the fee is used to support political and ideological speech by student groups whose beliefs are offensive to the student, as long as the program is viewpoint neutral (*see* B.2.a., *infra*). [Board of Regents v. Southworth, 529 U.S. 217 (2000)]

2) State Can Require Shopping Center to Permit Persons to Exercise Speech Rights

Note that the freedom not to speak does not prohibit a state's requiring a large shopping center (that is open to the public) to permit persons to exercise their speech rights on shopping center property—at least as long as the particular message is not dictated by the state and is not likely to be identified with the owner of the shopping center. [Pruneyard Shopping Center v. Robins, 447 U.S. 74 (1980)]

b. Includes Symbolic Conduct

Speech includes not only verbal communication, but also conduct that is undertaken to communicate an idea. Of course, not all regulation of symbolic conduct is prohibited. The Court will uphold a conduct regulation if: (i) the regulation is within the constitutional power of the government; (ii) it furthers an important governmental interest; (iii) the governmental interest is *unrelated to suppression of speech*; and (iv) the incidental burden on speech is no greater than necessary. [United States v. O'Brien, 391 U.S. 367 (1968)—upholding a prohibition against burning draft cards to protect the government's important interest in facilitating the smooth functioning of the draft system] Note, however, that a regulation is *not* invalid simply because there is some imaginable alternative that might be less burdensome on speech. [Rumsfeld v. Forum for Academic and Institutional Rights, 547 U.S. 47 (2006)—statute requiring schools of higher education to grant the military access to recruit on campus is not invalid merely because the military could take out ads in newspapers, on television, etc.]

Example: A state may prohibit public nudity, even as applied to nude dancing at bars and places of adult entertainment. Although nude dancing is marginally within the protections of the First Amendment—because it involves the communication of an erotic message—the government has a "substantial" interest in combating crime and other "secondary effects" caused by the presence of adult entertainment establishments that is unrelated to the suppression of free expression. [Barnes v. Glen Theatre, Inc., 501 U.S. 560 (1991); City of Erie v. Pap's A.M., 529 U.S. 277 (2000)—city council made findings regarding secondary effects]

Compare: 1) A prohibition against students wearing armbands to protest the war in Vietnam was struck because it had no regulatory interest other than prohibiting the communicative impact of the conduct. [Tinker v. Des Moines Independent Community School District, 393 U.S. 503 (1969)]

2) A prohibition against mutilating a United States flag (except in cases of proper disposal of a soiled flag) was held invalid as an attempt to restrain speech; the Court found that no imminent breach of the peace was likely to result, and the government has no other interest in prohibiting such burnings. [United States v. Eichman, 496 U.S. 310 (1990)]

c. **Excludes Freedom to Bar Military Recruitment**
Requiring schools of higher education to allow military recruiters to recruit on campus or risk losing federal funding does not implicate free speech rights. This is so even if the schools disagree with the military's ban against homosexuals. School recruitment receptions are not inherently expressive from the schools' standpoint; they are merely a way to help students obtain jobs. Schools are not being asked to say or refrain from saying anything, and neither are they being asked to associate with the military in any significant way. Moreover, there is little chance that a person would attribute the military's positions to the schools. Therefore, there is no First Amendment violation. [Rumsfeld v. Forum for Academic and Institutional Rights, *supra*]

5. **Prison Speech**
A regulation concerning the activities of prison inmates, including *any* First Amendment speech activities, is governed by a different standard in order to facilitate prison order: The regulation will be upheld if it is *reasonably related to legitimate penological interests.* [Shaw v. Murphy, 532 U.S. 223 (2001)] Thus, a restriction on *incoming* mail will be upheld if it is rational; a restriction on *outgoing* mail must be narrowly tailored because there is less of a penological interest involved. [*See* Thornburgh v. Abbott, 490 U.S. 401 (1989)]

B. **TIME, PLACE, AND MANNER RESTRICTIONS—REGULATION OF CONDUCT**
All speech is conveyed through physical action (e.g., talking, writing, distributing pamphlets, etc.), and while the freedom of belief is absolute, the freedom to convey beliefs cannot be. The extent to which government may regulate speech-related conduct depends on whether the forum involved is a public forum, a designated public forum, a limited public forum, or a nonpublic forum.

1. **Public Forums and Designated Public Forums**
Public property that has historically been open to speech-related activities (e.g., *streets, sidewalks, public parks* and *the Internet*) is called a public forum. Public property that has not historically been open to speech-related activities, but which the government has thrown open for such activities on a permanent or temporary basis, by practice or policy (e.g., school rooms that are open for after-school use by social, civic, or recreation groups), is called a designated public forum. The government may regulate speech in public forums and designated public forums with reasonable time, place, and manner regulations.

a. **Test**
To be valid, government regulations of speech and assembly in public forums and designated public forums must:

(i) Be *content neutral* (i.e., subject matter neutral and viewpoint neutral);

(ii) Be *narrowly tailored* to serve an *important* government interest; and

(iii) Leave open *alternative channels* of communication.

Remember: Even if a regulation meets the above conditions, it might still be struck down on other grounds (e.g., overbreadth, vagueness, unfettered discretion; *see* A.3., *supra*).

1) Content Neutral

The regulation cannot be based on the content of the speech—i.e., it must be subject matter neutral and viewpoint neutral—absent substantial justification (*see* C., *infra*).

Examples: 1) The Court held invalid an ordinance allowing peaceful **labor** picketing near schools, but prohibiting all other picketing, since it was a content-based restriction. [Police Department of City of Chicago v. Mosely, 408 U.S. 92 (1972)]

                             2) A law may not forbid only those signs within 500 feet of a foreign embassy that are critical of the foreign government. [Boos v. Barry, 485 U.S. 312 (1988)]

2) Narrowly Tailored

The regulation must be narrowly tailored (i.e., it may not burden **substantially** more speech than is necessary to further the significant government interest). However, the regulation **need not be the least restrictive means** of accomplishing the goal.

Example: A law requiring persons performing at a city's theater to use the city's sound equipment is narrowly tailored to the city's interest in preventing excessive noise. [Ward v. Rock Against Racism, 491 U.S. 781 (1989)]

Compare: 1) An ordinance that prohibited **all** canvassers from going onto private residential property to promote **any** cause without first obtaining a permit was not narrowly tailored to the interest of preventing fraud because it included too much speech that was not likely to give rise to fraud (e.g., religious proselytization, advocacy of political speech, and enlisting support for unpopular causes). [Watchtower Bible and Tract Society of New York, Inc. v. Village of Stratton, A.3.a., *supra*]

                             2) A ban on **all** leafletting was not narrowly tailored to the state's interest in controlling litter because it would suppress too much speech. [Schneider v. New Jersey, 308 U.S. 147 (1939)]

                             3) Banning registered sex offenders from **all** social media websites was not narrowly tailored to the state's interest in preventing sex crimes. [Packingham v. North Carolina, 137 S. Ct. 1730 (2017)]

Note: A regulation that is not narrowly tailored might also fail on overbreadth grounds. (*See* A.3.a., *supra*.)

3) Important Interest

The regulation must further an important government interest. Such interests include: traffic safety, orderly crowd movement, personal privacy, noise control, litter control, aesthetics, etc.

4) Alternative Channels Open

The law must leave open alternative channels of communication; i.e., other reasonable means for communicating the idea must be available.

b. Examples—Residential Areas

1) Targeted Picketing

The Supreme Court upheld a statute that prevented focused residential picketing (i.e., picketing in front of a single residence). The street/sidewalk involved was a public forum, but the ordinance passed the three-part test: (i) it was content neutral because it regulated the location and manner of picketing rather than its message; (ii) it was narrowly tailored to the important interest of protecting a homeowner's privacy (because it applied only to focused picketing); and (iii) alternative means of communications were available because the protesters could march *through* the neighborhood in protest. [Frisby v. Schultz, 487 U.S. 474 (1988)]

2) Charitable Solicitations

Charitable solicitations for funds in residential areas are within the protection of the First Amendment. However, they are subject to reasonable regulation.

Example: A state cannot require professional fundraisers (before making an appeal for funds) to disclose to potential donors the percentage of contributions collected over the previous year that were actually turned over to the charity. The disclosure is not necessary to promote the state interest of protecting the public from fraud. However, the state can require a fundraiser to disclose her professional status. [Riley v. National Federation of the Blind of North Carolina, 487 U.S. 781 (1988)] In *Riley,* the Court also invalidated a restriction on the fees that professional fundraisers could charge a charity, because the particular statute was not narrowly tailored to protect either the public or the charities.

Compare: States have a significant interest in preventing fraudulent charitable solicitations. This interest justifies charging a telemarketing firm with fraud for telling persons solicited that the firm pays "a significant amount of each donation" to the charity, when in fact the firm keeps 85% of gross receipts. [Illinois *ex rel.* Madigan v. Telemarketing Associates, Inc., 538 U.S. 600 (2003)]

3) Permits

A state may not require persons to obtain permits in order to canvass door to door for noncommercial or nonfundraising purposes. [Watchtower Bible and Tract Society of New York, Inc. v. Village of Stratton, *supra*]

c. Example—Buffer Zones

Laws and injunctions restricting expression within so-called "buffer zones" are often found in the context of cases dealing with demonstrations on streets and sidewalks outside abortion clinics. These laws typically set boundaries of a specified number of feet from clinic entrances within which anti-abortion protestors may not approach women entering the clinics, in order to ensure unobstructed access and maintain public safety and the free flow of vehicular and pedestrian traffic.

1) **Content-Neutral/Important Government Interest**
    The Supreme Court has for the most part found buffer-zone laws to be reasonable, content-neutral regulations of speech that further the important state interest of preserving access to healthcare facilities and maintaining public order.
    Example: The Court upheld the constitutionality of a state law prohibiting persons within 100 feet of a clinic from approaching within eight feet of those seeking access to the clinic for purposes of oral protest, education, or counseling. [Hill v. Colorado, 530 U.S. 703 (2000)—statute upheld against challenge by petitioners who wished to "counsel" women as they enter abortion clinics]

2) **Narrowly Tailored**
    Under the second prong of the time, place, and manner test, buffer-zone laws will be upheld only if they burden no more speech than necessary to achieve the purpose of protecting access to healthcare facilities and maintaining order on public rights-of-way. Moreover, the right of access does not amount to a right to be free from all communication in the vicinity of a facility that might be unwelcome. Court decisions in this area tend to be very fact-specific, and the Court has indicated it is more likely to find a buffer-zone law narrowly tailored if the state has first tried less-restrictive measures to address the problems created by anti-abortion protests.
    Example: A targeted injunction establishing a 36-foot buffer zone between specific protesters and abortion clinic entrances was upheld where previous measures had failed to achieve the goal of ensuring public order and safety. [Madsen v. Women's Health Center, 512 U.S. 753 (1994)]

    Compare: 1) An injunction providing for a "floating buffer zone" of 15 feet between protesters and persons entering and leaving an abortion clinic was held to violate the First Amendment. The floating zone barred all verbal and written communication from a normal conversational distance on public sidewalks, and thus burdened more speech than necessary to ensure ingress and egress from the clinic. [Schenck v. Pro-Choice Network of Western New York, 519 U.S. 357 (1997)]

    2) Anti-abortion pamphleteers challenged a state law that made it a crime for anyone except clinic patients and workers to "enter or remain in" an area within 35 feet of entrances to abortion clinics. The Court held that this provision of the law violated the Free Speech Clause because it was not narrowly tailored to achieve the interests of public safety and access to healthcare facilities. The law burdened more speech than necessary because only one clinic in the state was the site of disruptive abortion demonstrations one day a week; the state had not first tried "less intrusive" measures

(e.g., enforcing an unchallenged section of the law prohibiting harassment and intimidation, or seeking a targeted injunction as in *Madsen, supra*); and the asserted rationale that the law made the jobs of police "easier" was not sufficient to justify such a sweeping restriction on speech. [McCullen v. Coakley, 134 S. Ct. 2518 (2014)]

d. Example—Designated Public Forum

Schools generally are not public forums. However, if a public school or university allows private organizations and members of the public to use school property for meetings when school programs or classes are not in session, the property is a designated public forum for that time, and the school cannot deny a religious organization permission to use the property for meetings merely because religious topics will be discussed. Such a restriction would be content discrimination. [Widmar v. Vincent, 454 U.S. 263 (1981); Lamb's Chapel v. Center Moriches Union Free School District, 508 U.S. 384 (1993)]

e. Injunctions

Injunctions that restrict First Amendment activity in public forums are treated differently from generally applicable ordinances because injunctions present a greater risk of censorship and discriminatory application. The test to be used to determine whether an injunction that restricts speech or protest is constitutional depends on whether the injunction is content neutral.

1) Content Based—Necessary to a Compelling Interest

If the injunction is content based, it will be upheld only if it is necessary to achieve a compelling government interest.

2) Content Neutral—Burdens No More Speech than Necessary

If the injunction is content neutral, it will be upheld only if it burdens no more speech than is necessary to achieve an *important* government purpose.

2. Limited Public Forums and Nonpublic Forums

Other than streets, sidewalks, parks, and designated public forums, most public property is considered to be a limited public forum (e.g., government property opened up for a specific speech activity, such as a school gym opened on a particular night to host a debate on a particular community issue) or a nonpublic forum. The government can regulate speech in such forums to *reserve them for their intended use*. Regulations will be upheld if they are:

(i) *Viewpoint neutral*; and

(ii) *Reasonably related to a legitimate government purpose*.

a. Viewpoint Neutral

Regulations on speech in nonpublic forums need not be content neutral; i.e., the government may allow speech regarding some subjects but not others. However, such regulations must be *viewpoint* neutral; i.e., if the government allows an issue to be presented in a nonpublic forum, it may not limit the presentation to only one view.

Example: If a high school newspaper is a nonpublic forum, a school board could decide to prohibit articles in the paper regarding nuclear power. However, it may not allow an article in favor of nuclear power and prohibit an article against nuclear power.

Similarly, the government may discriminate based on the identity of the speaker in nonpublic forums (e.g., a school board might limit speakers to licensed teachers).

b. Reasonableness

Regulation of speech and assembly in nonpublic forums need only be rationally related to a legitimate governmental objective.

Example: A city bus is not a public forum. The city, therefore, may constitutionally sell space for signs on the public buses for commercial and public service advertising while refusing to sell space for political or public issue advertising in order to minimize the appearance of favoritism and the risk of imposing on a captive audience. [Lehman v. Shaker Heights, 418 U.S. 298 (1974)]

c. Significant Cases

1) Military Bases

Military bases are not public forums; thus, on-base speech and assembly may be regulated, even during open houses where the public is invited to visit. [*See* United States v. Albertini, 472 U.S. 675 (1985)] However, if the military leaves its streets open as thoroughfares, they will be treated as public forums. [Flower v. United States, 407 U.S. 197 (1972)]

2) Schools

Generally, schools and school-sponsored activities are not public forums. Thus, speech (and association) in schools may be reasonably regulated to serve the school's educational mission.

Examples: 1) Schools can control the content of student speeches or student newspapers for legitimate pedagogical concerns. [*See, e.g.,* Bethel School District No. 403 v. Fraser, 478 U.S. 675 (1986)—student suspended for sexually explicit speech at school assembly] Similarly, a school may prohibit student speech that may be interpreted as advocating or celebrating the use of illegal drugs ("BONG HiTS 4 JESUS") during a school-supervised activity (e.g., a field trip). [Morse v. Frederick, 551 U.S. 393 (2007)]

    2) To be given access to the platform of official school recognition and school funding, a public law school may require extracurricular student groups to accept all students regardless of their "status or beliefs." [Christian Legal Society v. Martinez, 561 U.S. 661 (2010)—school could deny funding to group that limited membership to persons who were willing to sign a statement of faith based on Christianity and excluded persons who supported homosexuality and premarital sex; *and see* XXI.D., *infra*]

3) A state association that regulates interscholastic high school sports of schools that *voluntarily join* may prohibit certain recruiting statements to middle-school students for athletic programs. Even if the message involves a matter of public concern, the rule is *necessary* for managing an effective high school athletic league. [Tennessee Secondary School Athletic Association v. Brentwood Academy, 551 U.S. 291 (2007)]

Compare: A school was forbidden to prohibit the wearing of black armbands in the school (to protest government policies), because that prohibition was designed to suppress communication, i.e., not related to regulatory interest. [Tinker v. Des Moines Independent Community School District, A.4.b., *supra*]

3) Government Workplace or Charity

Neither a government workplace (including a court building and its grounds) nor a government controlled charity drive constitutes a public forum.

Examples: 1) The government may conduct an annual fundraising drive that includes some charities but excludes others on some ideologically neutral basis (e.g., all charities that lobby). However, it cannot exclude a charity merely because it disagrees with the organization's political views. [Cornelius v. NAACP Legal Defense and Educational Fund, Inc., 473 U.S. 788 (1985)]

2) A state may develop a system for meeting with and hearing the views of a select group of its employees (e.g., union representatives) while denying the ability to voice opinions at such restricted meetings to other government employees. [Minnesota State Board v. Knight, 465 U.S. 271 (1984)]

Compare. In a public forum, the government cannot restrict the ability to participate in public speech on the basis of union membership. Thus, the Court has held that a teacher cannot be constitutionally prohibited from speaking at a meeting of the school board that was open to the public. [City of Madison Joint School District No. 8 v. Wisconsin Employment Relations Commission, 429 U.S. 167 (1976)]

4) Postal Service Property

Although sidewalks generally are public forums, sidewalks on postal service property are not public forums. [United States v. Kokinda, 497 U.S. 720 (1990)]

5) Signs on Public Property

The Supreme Court has upheld a city ordinance prohibiting posting signs on public property (including sidewalks, crosswalks, street lamp posts, fire hydrants, and telephone poles), even if the sign is temporary in nature and could be removed without damage to the public property. [Members of City Council v. Taxpayers for Vincent, 466 U.S. 789 (1984)]

6) Airport Terminals

Airport terminals operated by a public authority are *not* public forums. Thus, it is reasonable to ban *solicitation* within airport terminals, since it presents a risk of fraud to hurrying passengers. [International Society of Krishna Consciousness v. Lee, 505 U.S. 672 (1992)] However, it is *not* reasonable to ban *leafletting* within multipurpose terminals having qualities similar to a shopping mall [Lee v. International Society of Krishna Consciousness, 505 U.S. 830 (1992)]; although such leafletting can still be subject to reasonable time, place, and manner regulations (*see* B.1., *supra*).

7) Candidate Debates on Public Television

A public television station debate for congressional candidates from major parties or who have strong popular support is not a "public forum" because such debates are not open to a class of speakers (e.g., all candidates), but rather to selected members of the class. Exclusion of candidates who are not from a major party and who lack popular support is permissible because these criteria are (i) viewpoint neutral and (ii) reasonable in light of the logistics for an educationally valuable debate. [Arkansas Educational Television Commission v. Forbes, 523 U.S. 666 (1998)]

8) Mailboxes

A letter/mailbox at a business or residence is *not* a public forum. Thus, the government may prohibit the placing of unstamped items in post boxes to promote efficient mail service. [United States Postal Service v. Council of Greenburgh Civic Association, 453 U.S. 114 (1981)]

9) Polling Places

A polling place is *not* a public forum since a polling place is, at least on Election Day, government-controlled property set aside for the sole purpose of voting and as such is a special enclave, subject to greater restrictions. A state may reasonably decide that the interior of the polling place should reflect that distinction by excluding some forms of advocacy from the polling place. [Minnesota Voters Alliance v. Mansky, 138 S. Ct. 1876 (2018)]

C. UNPROTECTED SPEECH—REGULATION OR PUNISHMENT BECAUSE OF CONTENT

Restrictions on the content of speech must be necessary to achieve a compelling government interest. As indicated above, very few restrictions on the content of speech are tolerated. The Court allows them only to prevent grave injury. The following is a list of the only reasons for which the Court has allowed content-based restrictions on speech (i.e., the following are categories of unprotected speech):

(i) It creates a *clear and present danger* of imminent lawless action.

(ii) It constitutes *"fighting words"* as defined by a narrow, precise statute.

(iii) The speech, film, etc., is *obscene*. (This category includes "child pornography.")

(iv) The speech constitutes **defamation**, which may be the subject of a civil "penalty" through a tort action brought by the injured party in conformity with the rules set out *infra*.

(v) The speech violates regulations against **false or deceptive advertising—commercial speech is protected** by the First Amendment and it cannot be proscribed simply to help certain private interests.

(vi) The government can demonstrate a **"compelling interest"** in limitation of the First Amendment activity.

Recall that even if a regulation falls within one of the above categories, it will not necessarily be held valid; it might still be held to be void for vagueness or overbreadth. (*See* A.3., *supra*.)

1. **Clear and Present Danger of Imminent Lawlessness**
   A state cannot forbid advocating the use of force or of law violation unless such advocacy (i) *is directed to producing or inciting imminent lawless action*, and (ii) *is likely to produce or incite such action*. [Brandenberg v. Ohio, 395 U.S. 444 (1969)]
   Example: The "clear and present danger" test has been applied to hold that a state may not punish as contempt out-of-court utterances critical of a judge, absent special circumstances showing an extremely high likelihood of serious interference with the administration of justice. [*See* Wood v. Georgia, 370 U.S. 375 (1962)]

   a. **Allows for Sanctions Against Speech**
      The test allows for sanctions against speech causing demonstrable danger to important government interests. Disclosure of United States intelligence operations and personnel is "clearly not protected" speech. [Haig v. Agee, 453 U.S. 280 (1981)]

   b. **Compelling Justification Test**
      A similar test—one of "compelling justification"—was employed to hold unconstitutional the Georgia legislature's refusal to seat Julian Bond, an elected black representative, where Bond's speeches, critical of United States policy on Vietnam and the draft, led the legislature to doubt his fitness and his ability to take the oath of office in good faith. [Bond v. Floyd, 385 U.S. 116 (1966)]

2. **Fighting Words**

   a. **True Threats**
      The First Amendment does not protect "true threats"—statements meant to communicate an intent to place an individual or group in fear of bodily harm. [Virginia v. Black, 538 U.S. 343 (2003)—a state may ban cross burning done with an intent to intimidate; because of cross burning's long history as a signal of impending violence, the state may specially regulate this form of threat, which is likely to inspire fear of bodily harm]

   b. **States May Ban Words Likely to Incite Physical Retaliation**
      States are free to ban the use of "fighting words," i.e., those personally abusive epithets that, when addressed to the ordinary citizen, are inherently likely to incite immediate physical retaliation. [Chaplinsky v. New Hampshire, 315 U.S. 568 (1942)]

Chaplinsky has, however, been narrowly read. Thus, in *Cohen v. California,* 403 U.S. 15 (1971), the Court held that the state may not punish the defendant for wearing a jacket bearing the words "Fuck the Draft," pointing out that "while the four-letter word displayed by Cohen in relation to the draft is commonly employed in a personally provocative fashion, in this instance, it was clearly not directed to the person of the hearer."

c. **Statutes Regulating Fighting Words Tend to Be Overbroad or Vague**
While this classification of punishable speech continues to exist *in theory*, the Court rarely upholds punishments for the use of such words. Statutes that attempt to punish fighting words will tend to be overbroad or vague; the statute will define the punishable speech as "opprobrious words," "annoying conduct," or "abusive language." Such statutes will fail, as their imprecise terms could be applied to protected (nonfighting words) speech. Such a statute could not be used to punish a person for saying to a police officer, "White son of a bitch, I'll kill you." [Gooding v. Wilson, 405 U.S. 518 (1972); Lewis v. City of New Orleans, 415 U.S. 130 (1974)]

d. **Statutes Cannot Be Viewpoint-Based—Limits Hate Crime Legislation**
Although the general class of "fighting words" is proscribable under the First Amendment, the Supreme Court generally will not tolerate in fighting words statutes restrictions that are designed to punish only certain viewpoints (i.e., proscribing fighting words only if they convey a particular message). [R.A.V. v. City of St. Paul, 505 U.S. 377 (1992)—ordinance that applies only to those fighting words that insult or provoke violence on the basis of race, religion, or gender is invalid]

1) **Compare—Punishing Racially Motivated Conduct**
The First Amendment does not protect conduct simply because it happens to be motivated by a person's views or beliefs. Thus, a state can increase a convicted defendant's sentence for aggravated battery based on the fact that the defendant selected the victim of his crime because of the victim's race. [Wisconsin v. Mitchell, 508 U.S. 476 (1993)] However, punishment may not be increased merely because of the defendant's abstract beliefs. [Dawson v. Delaware, 503 U.S. 159 (1992)—unconstitutional to increase defendant's sentence merely because it was proved that he belongs to an organization that advocates racism]

3. **Obscenity**
Obscenity is *not protected* speech. [Roth v. United States, 354 U.S. 476 (1957)] The Court has defined "obscenity" as a description or depiction of sexual conduct that, taken *as a whole*, by the *average person*, applying *contemporary community standards*:

(i) Appeals to the *prurient interest* in sex;

(ii) Portrays sex in a *patently offensive* way; and

(iii) *Does not have serious literary, artistic, political, or scientific value*—using a national, reasonable person standard, rather than the contemporary community standard. [Miller v. California, 413 U.S. 15 (1973); Pope v. Illinois, 481 U.S. 497 (1987)]

a. **Elements**

1) **Appeal to Prurient Interest**
The dominant theme of the material considered as a *whole* must appeal to the prurient interest in sex of the average person. The Supreme Court has found this to include that which appeals to *shameful or morbid interests* in sex, but not that which incites *lust* (insofar as lust may include a *normal* interest in sex). [Brockett v. Spokane Arcades, Inc., 472 U.S. 491 (1985)] Mere portrayals of nudity do not appeal to the prurient interest and are not obscene.

   a) **Average Person**
   Both sensitive and insensitive adults may be included in determining contemporary community standards, but children may not be considered part of the relevant audience.

   b) **Material Designed for Deviant Group**
   Where the allegedly obscene material is designed for and primarily disseminated to a clearly defined deviant sexual group (e.g., sadists), rather than to the public at large, the prurient appeal requirement is satisfied if the *dominant theme* of the material, taken as a whole, *appeals to the prurient interest of that group*. [Mishkin v. New York, 383 U.S. 502 (1966)]

2) **Patently Offensive**

   a) **Community Standard**
   The material must be patently offensive in affronting contemporary community standards regarding the description or portrayal of sexual matters.

   b) **National Standard Not Required**
   A statewide standard is permissible but not mandatory. A juror may draw on knowledge of the community or vicinity from which he comes, and the court may either direct the jury to apply "community standards" without specifying the "community," or define the standard in more precise geographic terms. [Hamling v. United States, 418 U.S. 87 (1974); Jenkins v. Georgia, 418 U.S. 153 (1974)]

3) **Lacking in Serious Social Value**
The fact that the material may have some redeeming social value will not necessarily immunize it from a finding of obscenity. It must have serious literary, artistic, political, or scientific value, using a national standard. [Pope v. Illinois, *supra*]

4) **Standard May Be Different for Minors**
The state can adopt a specific definition of obscenity applying to materials sold to minors, even though the material might not be obscene in terms of an adult audience. [Ginsberg v. New York, 390 U.S. 629 (1968)] However, government may not prohibit the sale or distribution of material to adults merely because it is inappropriate for children.

Example: Because of the present lack of "gateway" technology that would permit speakers on the Internet to block their communications, a federal statute's bar on transmitting "indecent" or "patently offensive" messages to minors effectively amounts to a total ban and thus violates the First Amendment right of adults to receive such materials. [Reno v. American Civil Liberties Union, 521 U.S. 844 (1997)]

Compare: To prevent minors from getting harmful material, the government *may* condition its support of Internet access in public libraries on their installing software to block obscenity and child pornography—at least when the library will unblock filtered material on any adult user's request. [United States v. American Library Association, Inc., 539 U.S. 194 (2003)]

a) Pictures of Minors

To protect minors from exploitation, the government may prohibit the sale or distribution of *visual* depictions of sexual conduct involving minors, even if the material would not be found obscene if it did not involve children. [New York v. Ferber, 458 U.S. 747 (1982)] The government may also prohibit *offers* to provide (and requests to obtain) material depicting children engaged in sexually explicit conduct when the prohibition requires scienter and does not criminalize a substantial amount of protected speech. Such offers of material that is unlawful to possess have no First Amendment protection. [United States v. Williams, 553 U.S. 285 (2008)]

b) Compare—Simulated Pictures of Minors

The government may not bar visual material that only appears to depict minors engaged in sexually explicit conduct, but that in fact uses young-looking adults or computer-generated images. [Ashcroft v. Free Speech Coalition, 535 U.S. 234 (2002)] A holding otherwise would bar speech that is not obscene under the *Miller* test and that does not involve the exploitation of children as in *Ferber*.

b. Question of Fact and Law

1) Jury Question

The determination of whether material is obscene is a question of fact for the jury. Of course, the judge can grant a directed verdict if the evidence is such that a reasonable, unprejudiced jury could not find that all parts of the test have been met.

2) Independent Review by Appellate Court

Appellate courts will conduct an independent review of constitutional claims, when necessary, to assure that the proscribed materials "depict or describe patently offensive 'hard core' sexual conduct." [Jenkins v. Georgia, *supra*]

3) Evidence of Pandering

In close cases, evidence of "pandering"—commercial exploitation for the sake of prurient appeal—by the defendant may be probative on whether the material is obscene. Such evidence may be found in the defendant's advertising, his instructions to authors and illustrators of the material, or his intended audience. In effect, this simply accepts the purveyor's own estimation of the material as relevant. [Ginzburg v. United States, 383 U.S. 463 (1966)]

4)   Evidence—Similar Published Materials Not Automatically Admissible
The state need not produce expert testimony. Evidence that similar materials are available on community newsstands, or that the publication has acquired a second-class mailing privilege, does not necessarily show that the material is not obscene and hence is not automatically admissible. Nor is there any automatic right to have other materials held not to be obscene admitted into evidence. [Hamling v. United States, *supra*]

c.   Statutes Must Not Be Vague

1)   Sweeping Language
Attempts to define obscenity broadly have encountered difficulties before the Court.
Examples: 1) A statute banning publication of news or stories of "bloodshed or lust so massed as to become vehicles for inciting crime" is unconstitutionally vague and uncertain. [Winters v. New York, 333 U.S. 507 (1948)]

2) The Court held invalid a statute prohibiting the sale of any book "tending to the corruption of the morals of youth." [Butler v. Michigan, 352 U.S. 380 (1957)]

2)   Construction May Save Vague Statute
A state statute will be upheld if it meets the tests as construed by the courts of the state. Thus, a seemingly vague obscenity statute may be saved by a state supreme court opinion that limits it to a proscription of depictions of specific types of sexual conduct. [Ward v. Illinois, 431 U.S. 767 (1977)]

d.   Land Use Regulations
A land use (or zoning) regulation may limit the location or size of adult entertainment establishments (i.e., businesses that focus on sexual activities) if the regulation is designed to reduce the secondary effects of such businesses (e.g., rise in crime rates, drop in property values and neighborhood quality, etc.). However, regulations may not ban such establishments altogether. [City of Los Angeles v. Alameda Books, Inc., 535 U.S. 425 (2002)]
Example: A city ordinance limiting adult entertainment establishments to one corner of the city occupying less than 5% of the city's area was deemed constitutional. [City of Renton v. Playtime Theatres, Inc., 475 U.S. 41 (1986)]

e.   Liquor Regulation
The Twenty-First Amendment grants states more than the usual regulatory authority

with respect to intoxicating beverages. Therefore, regulations prohibiting explicit live sexual entertainment and films in establishments licensed to sell liquor by the drink, even though proscribing some forms of visual presentation that would not be obscene under *Miller,* do not violate the First Amendment as long as they are not "irrational."

f. Display

The Court has suggested that the state *may regulate* the display of certain material, to prevent it from being so obtrusive that an unwilling viewer cannot avoid exposure to it. [Redrup v. New York, 386 U.S. 767 (1967)]

g. Private Possession of Obscenity

Private possession of obscenity at home cannot be made a crime because of the constitutional right of personal privacy. [Stanley v. Georgia, 394 U.S. 557 (1969)] However, the protection does not extend beyond the home. Thus, importation, distribution, and exhibition of obscene materials can be prohibited.

1) Exception—Child Pornography

The state may make private possession of child pornography a crime, even private possession for personal viewing in a residence. [Osborne v. Ohio, 495 U.S. 103 (1990)]

4. Defamatory Speech

When a person is sued for making a defamatory statement, the First Amendment places restrictions on the ability of the government (through its tort law and courts) to grant a recovery where the person suing is a *public official or public figure*, or where the defamatory statement involves an issue of *public concern*. In these cases, the plaintiff must prove not only the elements of defamation required by state law, but also that the statement was *false* and that the person making the statement was at *fault* to some degree in not ascertaining the truth of the statement.

a. Falsity

At common law, a defamatory statement was presumed to be false; to avoid liability for an otherwise defamatory statement on the ground that it was true, the defendant had to assert truth as an affirmative defense. The Supreme Court has rejected this presumption in all public figure or public concern cases. In these cases, the plaintiff must prove by clear and convincing evidence that the statement was false. [Philadelphia Newspapers, Inc. v. Hepps, 475 U.S. 767 (1986)]

1) Requirement of Factual Statement

To be defamatory, the false statement must be viewed by a reasonable person as a statement of fact, rather than as a statement of opinion or a parody. Furthermore, a public figure cannot circumvent the First Amendment restrictions by using a different tort theory to collect damages for a published statement about him that is not a false statement of fact.

Example: Even though a publisher may have intended to cause psychological distress to a public figure by publishing statements about him that were derogatory, the public figure cannot receive a judgment for "emotional distress" damages if a reasonable person who read or viewed the publication would not understand it to contain a statement of fact about that public figure. [Hustler Magazine Inc. v. Falwell, 485 U.S. 46 (1988)]

Note: The fact that a publisher labels a statement as "opinion" will not provide First Amendment protection if the statement would reasonably be understood to be a statement of fact. [Milkovich v. Lorain Journal Co., 497 U.S. 1 (1990)]

b.   Fault

At common law, a defendant who had no reason to know that the statement he was making was false and defamatory could still be liable for defamation. Now, however, a plaintiff in a public figure or public concern case must prove fault on the part of the defendant. The degree of fault required is higher when the plaintiff is a public official or public figure than when the plaintiff is a private person suing on a matter of public concern.

1)   Public Official or Public Figure—Actual Malice Required

A public official may not recover for defamatory words relating to his official conduct or a matter of public concern without clear and convincing evidence that the statement was made with "actual malice" (defined below). [New York Times v. Sullivan, 376 U.S. 254 (1964)] This rule has since been extended to public figure plaintiffs. (Note that while the Supreme Court has not specifically held that all statements regarding public officials or public figures necessarily involve matters of public concern, a case to the contrary should be rare.)

a)   Actual Malice Defined

Actual malice was defined by the Supreme Court in *New York Times v. Sullivan* as:

(i)   *Knowledge* that the statement was false, *or*

(ii)   *Reckless disregard* as to its truth or falsity.

The plaintiff must show that the defendant was subjectively aware that the statement he published was false or that he subjectively *entertained serious doubts* as to its truthfulness.

(1)   Actual Malice in False Quotation Cases

Proof that a defamation plaintiff was inaccurately quoted does not, by itself, prove actual malice, even if the quotation was intentionally altered by the defendant. If the published "quotation" is substantially accurate, the plaintiff may not collect damages. To show actual malice, the public figure plaintiff must prove that the defendant's alteration of the quotation materially changed the meaning of the actual statements made by the plaintiff. [Masson v. New Yorker Magazine, Inc., 501 U.S. 496 (1991)]

(2)   Permitted Inquiries by Plaintiff

In attempting to prove knowing or reckless disregard of the truth, the plaintiff may inquire into the state of mind of those who edit, produce, or publish (i.e., conversations with editorial colleagues). [Herbert v. Lando, 441 U.S. 153 (1979)]

(3) Petition Clause Does Not Protect Defamatory Statement Made with Actual Malice

The First Amendment guarantees individuals the right to "petition government for a redress of grievances." However, this right to petition the government does not grant absolute immunity to persons who make defamatory statements about public officials or public figures in their communications with government officials. The defamed individual may prevail by meeting the *New York Times* requirements. [McDonald v. Smith, 472 U.S. 479 (1985)]

b) Two Ways to Become a Public Figure

(1) General Fame or Notoriety

A person may be a public figure for all purposes and all contexts if he achieves "*general fame or notoriety* in the community and pervasive involvement in the affairs of society," although "a citizen's participation in community and professional affairs" does not render him a public figure for all purposes.

(2) Involvement in Particular Controversy

A person may "*voluntarily inject* himself or be drawn into a particular controversy to influence the resolution of the issues involved" and thereby become a public figure for a limited range of issues. [Gertz v. Robert Welch, Inc., 418 U.S. 323 (1974)]

Note that *Gertz* appears to allow for the possibility of a person's being an involuntary public figure for a limited range of issues, although such a case would be "exceedingly rare."

c) Examples of Persons Not Deemed Public Figures

(1) Spouse of Wealthy Person

Marriage to an extremely wealthy person and divorcing such a person does not amount to voluntarily entering the public arena, even though press conferences are held by the plaintiff, because going to court is the only way she could dissolve her marriage. [Time, Inc. v. Firestone, 424 U.S. 448 (1976)]

(2) Person Engaging in Criminal Conduct

A person who engages in *criminal conduct* does not automatically become a public figure even when the defamatory statements relate solely to his conviction. [Wolston v. Reader's Digest Association, 443 U.S. 157 (1979)]

(3) Scientist in Federally Funded Program
A behavioral scientist engaged in *federally funded* animal research studies is not a public figure because he applies for federal grants and *publishes* in professional journals. [Hutchinson v. Proxmire, 443 U.S. 111 (1979)]

2) Private Individual Suing on Matter of Public Concern—At Least Negligence Required
When a private individual is defamed, there is less of a need to protect freedom of speech and press and more of a need to protect private individuals from injury from defamation because they do not have opportunities as effective for rebuttal as public figures. Accordingly, defamation actions brought by private individuals are subject to constitutional limitations only when the defamatory statement involves a matter of public concern. And even in those cases, the limitations are not as great as those established for public officials and public figures. [Gertz v. Robert Welch, Inc., *supra*] When the defamatory statement involves a matter of public concern, *Gertz* imposes two restrictions on private plaintiffs: (i) it prohibits liability without fault, and (ii) it restricts the recovery of presumed or punitive damages.

a) No Liability Without Proof of at Least Negligence
The plaintiff must show that the defendant was negligent in failing to ascertain the truth of the statement. If the plaintiff establishes negligence but not actual malice, which is a higher degree of fault, he also has to provide competent evidence of "actual" damages. (This changes the common law rule that damages would be presumed by law for injury to reputation and did not need to be proved by the plaintiff.) Actual damages may be awarded not only for economic losses but also for injury to the plaintiff's reputation in the community and for personal humiliation and distress.

b) Presumed or Punitive Damages Allowed Only If Actual Malice Established
If the plaintiff establishes that the defendant made the statement with actual malice, the actual damage requirement is extinguished. The plaintiff can recover whatever damages are permitted under state law (usually presumed damages and even punitive damages in appropriate cases). In other words, there is no constitutional protection for statements made with actual malice, even though a matter of public concern is involved.

c) What Is a Matter of Public Concern?
The courts decide on a case-by-case basis whether the defamatory statement involves a matter of public concern, looking at the content, form, and context of the publication. [Dun & Bradstreet, Inc. v. Greenmoss Builders, Inc., 472 U.S. 749 (1985)]

Example: In *Dun & Bradstreet,* the Court determined that a credit agency's erroneous report of plaintiff's bankruptcy, distributed to five subscribers, was speech solely in the private interest of the speaker and its specific business audience. Therefore, because a matter of public concern was not involved, the First

Amendment restrictions did not apply and the state court award of presumed and punitive damages was upheld.

d) Intentional Infliction of Emotional Distress

Damage actions by private individuals for intentional infliction of emotional distress are subject to the First Amendment rights of defendants if the speech relates to a matter of public concern, despite its "outrageous" and "particularly hurtful" quality. [Snyder v. Phelps, 562 U.S. 443 (2011)—peaceful picketing accompanied by signs critical of government policy regarding the political and moral conduct of the United States and homosexuality in the military that was conducted in a public place near, but not visible from, nor disruptive of, a military funeral is protected speech]

3) Private Individual Suing on Matter Not of Public Concern

The Supreme Court has not imposed constitutional restrictions on defamation actions brought by private individuals that do not involve a matter of public concern. Hence, presumed and punitive damages can be recovered even if actual malice is not established.

c. Procedural Issues

1) Federal Summary Judgment Standard

When ruling on a motion for summary judgment in a federal court defamation action in a case involving an issue of public concern, a judge must apply the clear and convincing evidence standard (i.e., the judge should grant the motion *unless* it appears that the plaintiff could meet his burdens of proving falsity and actual malice at trial by clear and convincing evidence). However, the Supreme Court has not clearly held that state courts must follow this practice under similar circumstances.

2) Judicial Review

An appellate court must review a defamation case by conducting an independent review of the record to determine if the finder of fact (the jury) could have found that the malice standard was met in the case. [Harte-Hanks Communications, Inc. v. Connaughton, 491 U.S. 657 (1989)]

d. Recovery for Depiction in a False Light

To recover damages for depiction in a false light (as opposed to a defamatory injury to reputation) arising out of comments directed at activities of public interest, an individual must establish *falsity* and *actual malice* whether or not he qualifies as a public figure under *Time, Inc. v. Hill,* 385 U.S. 374 (1967). However, it is *assumed* that the Court would now modify this to mirror the *Gertz* negligence rule for private plaintiffs.

e. True Privacy Actions

1) Publishing True Fact of Public Record

A newspaper or broadcaster cannot be sued for publishing a true fact once it is lawfully obtained from the public record or otherwise released to the public. [Cox

Broadcasting Corp. v. Cohn, 420 U.S. 469 (1975)—rape victim's name already in court records open to the public; The Florida Star v. B.J.F., 491 U.S. 524 (1989)—rape victim's name inadvertently given to the press by police]

2) Publishing Name of Juvenile Charged with Crime
A state cannot require judicial approval before the media can print the name of a juvenile charged with murder where the name of the juvenile was obtained through legal means (reporter heard name of defendant over police frequency radio and questioned witnesses to the crime). [Smith v. Daily Mail Publishing Co., 443 U.S. 97 (1979)]

3) Publishing Information on Judge's Competency
A state cannot make it a crime to publish information, released in a confidential proceeding, concerning the competency of members of the state judiciary. [Landmark Communications v. Virginia, 435 U.S. 829 (1978)]

f. Commercial Privacy—Disclosing a Private Performance Can Violate "Right to Publicity"
In *Zacchini v. Scripps-Howard Broadcasting Co.,* 433 U.S. 562 (1977), the Court held that state law could award damages to an entertainer who attempted to restrict the showing of his act to those who paid admission, when a television station broadcast his entire act. Here the "human cannonball" had his entire 15-second act broadcast over his objection.

g. Copyright Infringement
The First Amendment does not require an exception to copyright protection for material written by a former President or other public figures. Magazines have no right to publish such copyrighted material beyond the statutory fair use exception. [Harper & Row Publishers v. Nation Enterprises, 471 U.S. 539 (1985)]

5. Some Commercial Speech
False advertising is not protected by the First Amendment, although commercial speech in general does have some First Amendment protection. In determining whether a regulation of commercial speech is valid, the Supreme Court asserts that it uses a four-step process. However, it may be easiest to think about this as an initial question followed by a three-step inquiry. *First,* determine whether the commercial speech concerns a lawful activity and is not misleading or fraudulent. Speech proposing an unlawful transaction (e.g., "I will sell you this pound of heroin for X dollars") and fraudulent speech may be outlawed. If the speech regulated concerns a *lawful activity* and is *not misleading or fraudulent*, the regulation will be valid only if it:

(i)   Serves a *"substantial"* government interest;

(ii)   *"Directly advances"* the asserted interest; and

(iii)   Is *narrowly tailored* to serve the substantial interest. This part of the test does *not* require that the "least restrictive means" be used. Rather, there must be a *reasonable fit* between the legislation's end and the means chosen. [Board of Trustees of State University of New York v. Fox, 492 U.S. 469 (1989)]

[Central Hudson Gas v. Public Service Commission, 447 U.S. 557 (1980)]

Examples: 1) A city could not prohibit the use of newsracks on sidewalks for the distribution of commercial publications (such as free publications advertising products or real estate for sale) if the city allowed sidewalk newsracks for the distribution of newspapers. There is no "reasonable fit" between the category of commercial speech and any substantial interest. Commercial newsracks do not cause any physical or aesthetic harm different from that caused by newspaper newsracks. [Cincinnati v. Discovery Network, Inc., 507 U.S. 410 (1993)]

2) Similarly, a law prohibiting beer bottle labels from displaying alcohol content was held invalid because, although the government has a substantial interest in preventing "strength wars," the government did not show that the label prohibition advanced this interest in a material way. [Rubin v. Coors Brewing Co., 514 U.S. 476 (1995)]

3) The Court struck down a statute prohibiting pharmacies from selling information about doctors and the medications they prescribe "for marketing or promoting a prescription drug" without the prescriber's consent. The statute also prohibited pharmaceutical companies from using such information in marketing drugs without the prescriber's consent. This is a content-based, viewpoint-based, and speaker-based restriction and is subject, at the least, to the scrutiny applied in commercial speech cases. Even assuming that the state has a substantial interest in protecting prescription confidentiality, the law is not narrowly tailored because it allows pharmacies to disclose prescriber information to anyone for any reason other than marketing. [Sorrell v. IMS Health, Inc., 564 U.S. 552 (2011)]

a.   Complete Bans

Complete bans on truthful advertisement of lawful products are very unlikely to be upheld due to a lack of tailoring. Thus, the Court has **struck down** total bans against advertising:

(i)   Legal abortions;

(ii)   Contraceptives;

(iii)   Drug prices;

(iv)   Attorneys' services; and

(v)   Liquor prices.

Note that the Twenty-First Amendment—giving states the power to regulate liquor commerce within their borders—does not give states power to override First Amendment protections.

1)   Commercial Sign Regulation

It is unclear whether billboards may be totally banned from a city. However, they can be regulated for purposes of traffic safety and aesthetics.

a) **Blockbusting**
A town could not prohibit the use of outdoor "for sale" signs by owners of private homes as a way of reducing the effect of "blockbusting" real estate agents (i.e., encouraging homeowners to sell at reduced prices because of the threat of a sudden influx of minorities). [Linmark Associates v. Willingboro Township, 431 U.S. 85 (1977)]

b. **Required Disclosures**
Commercial speech is protected largely because of its value to consumers. Thus, the government may require commercial advertisers to make certain disclosures if they are not unduly burdensome and they are reasonably related to the state's interest in preventing deception. [*See, e.g.*, Milavetz, Gallop & Milavetz, P.A. v. United States, 559 U.S. 229 (2010)—advertisements by lawyers (and others) as debt relief agencies may be required to include information about their legal status and the nature of the assistance provided, as well as the possibility of the debtor's filing for bankruptcy]

c. **Special Attorney Advertising Rules**
The Court has upheld prohibitions against in-person solicitation by attorneys for pecuniary gain [Ohralik v. Ohio State Bar, 436 U.S. 447 (1978)—state interest in protecting laypersons from fraud and overreaching is substantial, and prohibition here is narrowly tailored and directly advances that interest] and sending mail solicitations to accident victims and their relatives within 30 days following an accident [Florida Bar v. Went For It, Inc., 515 U.S. 618 (1995)—state interest in protecting lawyers' reputation is substantial, and ban here is narrowly tailored and directly advances that interest].

D. PRIOR RESTRAINTS
A prior restraint is a court order or administrative system that keeps speech from occurring (e.g., a licensing system, a prohibition against using mails, an injunction). Prior restraints are not favored in our political system; the Court would rather allow speech and then punish it if it was unprotected. However, the Court will uphold prior restraints if some special harm would otherwise result. As with other restrictions on speech, a prior restraint must be narrowly tailored to achieve some compelling or, at least, significant governmental interest. The Court has also required that certain procedural safeguards be included in any system of prior restraint.

1. **Sufficiency of Governmental Interest**
The Supreme Court has not adopted a brightline standard for determining when a prior restraint is justified, but it has said that the government's burden is heavy. For exam purposes, you should ask whether there is some ***special societal harm*** that justifies the restraint.

a. **National Security**
National security is certainly a sufficient harm justifying prior restraint. Thus, a newspaper could be prohibited from publishing troop movements in times of war. [Near v. Minnesota, 283 U.S. 697 (1931)] However, the harm must be more than theoretical. Thus, the Court refused to enjoin publication of *The Pentagon Papers* on the basis that publication might possibly have a detrimental effect on the Vietnam War. [New York Times v. United States, 403 U.S. 713 (1971)]

b. Preserving Fair Trial

Preserving a fair trial for an accused might be a sufficient basis for prior restraint. However, the restraint will be upheld only if it is the only sure way of preserving a fair trial. [Nebraska Press Association v. Stewart, 427 U.S. 539 (1976)]

1) Compare—Grand Jury Prior Restraint

A state law prohibiting a grand jury witness from ever disclosing the testimony he gave to the grand jury (even after the grand jury term had ended) violates the First Amendment. Such a law is not narrowly tailored to a compelling interest, since any such interest that the government may have in protecting the grand jury process can be protected by a nonpermanent prohibition. [Butterworth v. Smith, 494 U.S. 624 (1990)]

c. Contractual Agreements

The Supreme Court has held that prior restraint is permissible where the parties have contractually agreed to the restraint. [Snepp v. United States, 444 U.S. 507 (1980)—CIA agent contractually agreed to give agency a prepublication review of any item related to his employment]

d. Military Circumstances

The Supreme Court has held that the interests of maintaining discipline among troops and efficiency of operations on a military base justify a requirement that persons on a military base obtain the commander's permission before circulating petitions.

e. Obscenity

The Court has held in a number of cases that the government's interest in preventing the dissemination of obscenity is sufficient to justify a system of prior restraint.

2. Procedural Safeguards

The Supreme Court has held that no system of prior restraint will be upheld unless it provides the persons whose speech is being restrained certain procedural safeguards. The safeguards arose in the context of movie censorship for obscenity, but the court has held that similar safeguards must be provided in all prior restraint cases:

(i) The standards must be "*narrowly drawn, reasonable, and definite,*" so as to include only prohibitable speech (e.g., improper to permanently enjoin witness from disclosing grand jury testimony; government interest can be protected by nonpermanent injunction [Butterworth v. Smith, *supra*]);

(ii) If the restraining body wishes to restrain dissemination of an item, it must *promptly seek an injunction* (e.g., improper to allow 50 days before seeking injunction [Teitel Film Corp. v. Cusack, 390 U.S. 139 (1968)]); and

(iii) There must be a *prompt and final judicial determination* of the validity of the restraint (e.g., improper to leave an injunction in place pending an appeal that could take up to a year; government must either lift the injunction or expedite the appeal [National Socialist Party v. Village of Skokie, 432 U.S. 43 (1977)]).

A number of other cases, especially in the area of movie censorship, also provide that the **government bears the burden** of proving that the speech involved is unprotected. [Freedman v. Maryland, 380 U.S. 51 (1965)]

Example: A federal statute authorized the Postmaster General (i) to deny use of the mails and postal money orders for materials found to be obscene in an administrative hearing, and (ii) to obtain a court order, upon a showing of probable cause, to detain incoming mail pending completion of the administrative hearing. The Court found that this denial of use of the mails violated the First Amendment: The procedures did not require the government to initiate proceedings to obtain a final judicial determination of obscenity, failed to assure prompt judicial review, and failed to limit any restraint in advance of a final judicial determination to preserving the status quo for "the shortest fixed period compatible with sound judicial resolution." [Blount v. Rizzi, 400 U.S. 410 (1971)]

3. **Obscenity Cases**

Much of the case law in the area of prior restraint has arisen in connection with banning obscenity.

a. **Seizure of Books and Films**

As with any seizure by the government, seizures of books and films may be made only upon probable cause that they contain obscenity or are otherwise unlawful. (*See* Criminal Procedure outline.)

1) **Single Seizures**

Seizures of a single book or film (to preserve it as evidence) may be made only with a warrant issued by a neutral and detached magistrate. And even here, a prompt post-seizure determination of obscenity must be available. If other copies of a seized film are not available to the exhibitor, he must be allowed to make a copy so that he may continue showing the film until a final determination has been made. [Heller v. New York, 413 U.S. 483 (1973)] Of course, if the materials are available for sale to the general public, an officer may enter into the establishment and purchase the book or film to use it as evidence in a later prosecution without obtaining a warrant. [Maryland v. Macon, 472 U.S. 463 (1985)]

2) **Large Scale Seizures**

"Large scale" seizures of allegedly obscene books and films—"to destroy them or block their distribution or exhibition"—must be **preceded** by a **full adversary hearing** and a judicial determination of obscenity. [Fort Wayne Books, Inc. v. Indiana, 489 U.S. 46 (1989)]

3) **Forfeiture of Business**

The First Amendment does not prohibit forfeiture of a defendant's adult entertainment business after the defendant has been found guilty of violating the Racketeer Influenced and Corrupt Organizations Act and criminal obscenity laws, even though the business assets included nonobscene books and magazines, where the entire business was found to be part of the defendant's racketeering activity. [Alexander v. United States, 509 U.S. 544 (1993)]

b. **Injunction**

After seizing material, the government may enjoin its further publication only after it is determined to be obscene in a *full judicial hearing*. [Kingsley Books, Inc. v. Brown, 354 U.S. 436 (1957)]

c. **Movie Censorship**

The Court has noted that movies are different from other forms of expression, and that time delays incident to censorship are less burdensome for movies than for other forms of expression. Thus, the Court allows governments to establish censorship boards to screen movies *before* they are released in the community, as long as the procedural safeguards mentioned above are followed. The censor bears the burden of proving that the movie is unprotected speech.

d. **Burden on Government**

When the government adopts a content-based, prior restraint of speech, the government has the burden of proving that the restriction is the least restrictive alternative to accomplish its goal. [Ashcroft v. American Civil Liberties Union, 542 U.S. 656 (2004)—upholding a preliminary injunction against enforcement of a statute requiring age verification for access to Internet websites with sexually explicit material, and criminalizing the failure to obtain age verification, because less restrictive alternatives (e.g., parents installing filters) are available]

E. **FREEDOM OF THE PRESS**

As a general rule, the press has no greater freedom to speak than does the public. However, a number of issues have arisen in the freedom of press context.

1. **Publication of Truthful Information**

Generally, the press has a right to publish information about a matter of public concern, and this right can be restricted only by a sanction that is narrowly tailored to further a state interest of the highest order. The right applies even if the information has been unlawfully obtained in the first instance, as long as (i) the speech relates to a matter of public concern, (ii) the publisher did not obtain it unlawfully or know who did, and (iii) the original speaker's privacy expectations are low. [Bartnicki v. Vopper, 532 U.S. 514 (2001)]

Example: During heated collective bargaining negotiations between a teachers' union and a school board, an unknown person intercepted a cell phone call between a union negotiator and the union's president. The tape was forwarded to a radio commentator, who played it on the radio. The commentator was sued for damages under civil liability provisions of state and federal wiretap laws that prohibited intentional disclosure of the contents of an electronically transmitted conversation when one has reason to know that the conversation was intercepted unlawfully. The Supreme Court held that the statute violated the First Amendment as applied under these circumstances. [Bartnicki v. Vopper, *supra*]

2. **Access to Trials**

The First Amendment guarantees the public and press a right to attend criminal trials. But the right may be outweighed by an overriding interest articulated in findings by the trial judge. [Richmond Newspapers v. Virginia, 448 U.S. 555 (1980)—no majority opinion]

The right probably applies to civil trials, although the Supreme Court has not conclusively resolved that issue.

a. **Access to Voir Dire Examination**

The First Amendment guarantee of public and press access to criminal trials also includes access to proceedings involving the voir dire examination of potential jurors. In *Press-Enterprise Co. v. Superior Court,* 464 U.S. 501 (1984), the Court found that a trial court could not constitutionally close voir dire examination of potential jurors without consideration of alternatives to closure even though, in some circumstances, there may be a compelling interest in restricting access to such proceedings to protect the privacy of potential jurors or the fairness of the trial.

b. **Access to Other Pretrial Proceedings**

Pretrial proceedings are presumptively subject to a First Amendment right of access for the press and public. Thus, a law requiring that all preliminary hearings be closed to the press and public violates the First Amendment. [El Vocero de Puerto Rico (Caribbean International News Corp.) v. Puerto Rico, 508 U.S. 147 (1993)—per curiam] If the prosecution and defense counsel seek to have a judge close pretrial proceedings, the judge would have to make specific findings on the record demonstrating (i) that closure was essential to preserve "higher" or "overriding" values, and (ii) that the closure order was narrowly tailored to serve the higher or overriding value. [Press-Enterprise Co. v. Superior Court, 478 U.S. 1 (1986)]

If the prosecution seeks to have a pretrial hearing or trial closed to the public and the defendant objects to the closure, there will be a Sixth Amendment violation if the judge excludes the public and the press from the hearing or trial without a clear finding that a closure order was necessary to protect an overriding interest.

c. **Compelling Interest in Protecting Children**

The government has a compelling interest in protecting children who are victims of sex offenses. Portions of trials wherein such children testify may be closed to the public and press, but only if the trial court makes a finding that such closure is necessary to protect the child in the individual case. A state statute, however, violates the First Amendment if it requires closure of the trial during testimony of a child victim of a sex offense without a finding of necessity by the trial judge. [Globe Newspaper Co. v. Superior Court, 457 U.S. 596 (1982)]

d. **Protective Order in Publishing Information Gained in Pretrial Discovery**

The Supreme Court has upheld a state trial court "protective order" prohibiting a newspaper defendant in a defamation suit from publishing, disseminating, or using information gained through pretrial discovery from the plaintiff in any way except where necessary for preparation for trial. [*See* Seattle Times Co. v. Rhinehart, 467 U.S. 20 (1984)]

3. **Requiring Members of the Press to Testify Before Grand Juries**

In *Branzburg v. Hayes,* 408 U.S. 665 (1972), the Court held that requiring a journalist to appear and testify before state or federal grand juries **does not abridge freedom of speech or press**, despite the claim that such a requirement would so deter the flow of news from confidential sources as to place an unconstitutionally heavy burden on the First Amendment interest in the free flow of information to the public. The Court's opinion refused to create—and even rejected—a conditional privilege not to reveal confidential sources to a grand jury conducting a good faith inquiry. This position was affirmed in *New York Times v. Jascalevich,* 439 U.S. 1331 (1978).

4. Interviewing Prisoners

Although the First Amendment protects prisoners, and especially those corresponding with them by mail, from a sweeping program of censorship [Procunier v. Martinez, 416 U.S. 396 (1974)], it does not permit journalists to insist upon either interviewing specified prisoners of their choice [Pell v. Procunier, 417 U.S. 817 (1974)] or inspecting prison grounds [Houchins v. KQED, Inc., 438 U.S. 1 (1978)].

5. Business Regulations or Taxes

Press and broadcasting companies can be subject to general business regulations (e.g., antitrust laws) or taxes (e.g., federal or state income taxes). Thus, a tax or regulation applicable to both press and non-press businesses will be upheld, even if it has a special impact on a portion of the press or broadcast media, as long as it is not an attempt to interfere with First Amendment activities. However, no tax or regulation impacting on the press or subpart of the press may be based on the content of the publication absent a compelling justification.

Examples: 1) State tax on publisher's use of more than $100,000 of paper and ink products annually violates the First Amendment. [Minneapolis Star & Tribune v. Minnesota Commissioner of Revenue, 460 U.S. 575 (1983)]

2) State sales tax or "receipts tax" on the sale of general interest magazines that exempts newspapers and religious, professional, trade, and sports journals from the tax violates the First Amendment. [Arkansas Writers' Project, Inc. v. Ragland, 481 U.S. 221 (1987)]

3) A state sales tax that exempted the sales of newspapers and magazines from the tax but did not give a similar exemption to the sale of broadcast services (cable or subscription television) did not violate the First Amendment. The tax was not based on the content of broadcasts and did not target a small category of publishers. The tax was applicable to all cable or satellite television sales. (There is no comparable sale of "free TV" such as network broadcasts.) [Leathers v. Medlock, 499 U.S. 439 (1991)]

6. Monetary Damages for Failure to Keep Identity Confidential

When a reporter or publisher promises a "source person" to keep his identity confidential and then publishes the source person's name, state contract law or promissory estoppel law may allow the source person to recover from the reporter or publisher any damages caused by the publication of his identity. [Cohen v. Cowles Media Co., 501 U.S. 663 (1991)]

7. Broadcasting Regulations

Radio and television broadcasting may be more closely regulated than the press. *Rationale:* Due to the limited number of frequencies available, broadcasters have a special privilege—and, consequently, a special responsibility to give suitable time to matters of public interest and to present a suitable range of programs. The paramount right is the ***right of viewers and*** *listeners* to receive information of public concern, rather than the right of broadcasters to broadcast what they please.

a. **Fairness Doctrine**

Accordingly, the Court has upheld, under a regulatory "fairness doctrine" (which is no longer enforced), FCC orders requiring a radio station to offer free broadcasting time (i) to opponents of political candidates or views endorsed by the station, and (ii) to any person who has been personally attacked in the course of a broadcast, for a reply to the attack. [Red Lion Broadcasting Co. v. FCC, 395 U.S. 367 (1969)]

1) **Compare—Grant of Equal Newspaper Space**

A statute granting political candidates a right to equal space to reply to criticism by the newspaper *violates* First Amendment freedom of the press. Decisions respecting size and content of a newspaper are forbidden to government. [Miami Herald Publishing Co. v. Tornillo, 418 U.S. 241 (1974)]

b. **Newspaper Ownership of Radio or TV Station**

Similarly, to promote the diversity of information received by the public, the FCC may forbid ownership of a radio or television station by a daily newspaper located in the same community. [FCC v. National Citizens Committee, 436 U.S. 775 (1978)]

c. **Prohibiting Indecent Speech**

Because of a broadcast's ability to invade the privacy of the home, the First Amendment does not forbid imposing civil sanctions on a broadcaster for airing a full monologue (in contrast to isolated use of a few such words) of "patently offensive sexual and excretory speech," even though it is not "obscene"—at least at those times when children are likely to be listening. [FCC v. Pacifica Foundation, 438 U.S. 726 (1978)]

d. **Political Advertisements**

The First Amendment does *not* require broadcasters to accept political advertisements.

e. **Elimination of Editorial Speech from Stations Receiving Public Grants**

Congress violated the First Amendment when it forbade any noncommercial educational station receiving a grant from the Corporation for Public Broadcasting from engaging in "editorializing." [FCC v. League of Women Voters, 468 U.S. 364 (1984)] This was the *suppression of speech* because of its content; the elimination of editorial speech from stations receiving public grants of this type was not narrowly tailored to promote an overriding government purpose regarding the regulation of broadcasting in general or noncommercial broadcasters in particular. Congress could deny persons receiving the federal funds the right to use those funds for editorial activities, but it could not condition the receipt of those funds upon a promise not to engage in any such speech.

8. **Cable Television Regulation**

While generally regulations of newspapers are subject to strict scrutiny, and regulations of the broadcast media are subject to less critical review, regulations of cable television transmissions are subject to review by a standard somewhere between these two. *Rationale:* The physical connection to a viewer's television set makes the cable subscriber a more captive audience than a newspaper reader and distinguishes cable from newspapers, which cannot prevent access to competing newspapers. On the other hand, unlike broadcast media, which is limited to a small number of frequencies (*see* 7., *supra*), there is no practical limitation on the number of cable channels; thus, the government's interest in protecting viewers' rights is weaker with regard to cable. [Turner Broadcasting System, Inc. v. FCC, A.2.a.2), *supra*]

Example: A law requiring cable operators to carry local stations is subject to "intermediate scrutiny" since it is content neutral (*see* A.2.a.2), *supra*). Since a "must carry" provision directly serves the important interest of preserving economic viability of local broadcasters and promotes the dissemination of information to noncable viewers, it is constitutional. [Turner Broadcasting System, Inc. v. FCC, *supra*]

a. **Compare—Content-Based Cable Broadcast Regulations**

A content-based cable broadcast regulation will be upheld only if it passes muster under the strict scrutiny test. [United States v. Playboy Entertainment Group, Inc., 529 U.S. 803 (2000)—law requiring cable operators to limit "sexually oriented" programs to after 10 p.m. is invalid because of the less restrictive alternative of enabling each household to block undesired channels]

9. **Internet Regulation**

The strict standard of First Amendment scrutiny, rather than the more relaxed standard applicable to broadcast regulation, applies to regulation of the Internet. *Rationale*: In contrast to broadcasting, there is no scarcity of frequencies (*see* 7., *supra*) on the Internet and little likelihood that the Internet will unexpectedly invade the privacy of the home (*see* 7.c., *supra*). [Reno v. American Civil Liberties Union, C.3.a.4), *supra*]

XXI.   FREEDOM OF ASSOCIATION AND BELIEF

A. **NATURE OF THE RIGHT**

Although the First Amendment does not mention a right of freedom of association, the right to join together with other persons for expressive or political activity is protected by the First Amendment. However, the right to associate for expressive purposes is ***not absolute***. It may be infringed to serve a ***compelling government interest***, unrelated to the suppression of ideas, that cannot be achieved through means significantly less restrictive of associational freedoms, at least when the infringement would not significantly affect an association's right to express its viewpoints. However, in some cases, as noted below, a more lenient standard will apply.

Examples: 1) A state's interest in ending invidious discrimination justifies prohibiting private clubs that are large and basically unselective in their membership, or that are often used for business contacts, from discriminating on the basis of race, creed, color, national origin, or sex—at least when it is not shown that this would impede the individual members' ability to engage in First Amendment activity. [New York State Club Association, Inc. v. New York City, 487 U.S. 1 (1988); Board of Directors of Rotary Club International v. Rotary Club of Duarte, 481 U.S. 537 (1987); Roberts v. United States Jaycees, 468 U.S. 609 (1984)]

2) A federal statute making it a crime to provide "material ***support*** or resources" of any kind to a ***foreign terrorist*** organization with ***knowledge*** of its being

designated a foreign terrorist organization by the federal government does not violate the freedom of association (or speech). The statute does not forbid mere membership or association with the organization, only material support (which was defined in the statute). Moreover, given the difficulty of obtaining information about terrorist threats, any burden that the statute places on a person's freedom of association is justified. [Holder v. Humanitarian Law Project, 561 U.S. 1 (2010)]

Compare: 1) A state antidiscrimination law may not bar the Boy Scouts from excluding an openly gay assistant scoutmaster from membership. Forced inclusion would **significantly burden** the right of expressive association of the Boy Scouts, since one of the **sincerely held** purposes of the Scouts is to instill certain moral values in young people, including the value that "homosexual conduct is not morally straight." [Boy Scouts of America v. Dale, 530 U.S. 640 (2000)]

2) A city ordinance that restricted admission to certain dance halls to persons between the ages of 14 and 18 was constitutional; it did not have to be justified with a compelling interest because the associational activity of meeting in a dance hall is not an activity within the protection of the First Amendment. [Dallas v. Stanglin, 490 U.S. 19 (1989)]

B. ELECTORAL PROCESS

Laws regulating the electoral process might impact on First Amendment rights of speech, assembly, and association. The Supreme Court uses a **balancing test** in determining whether a regulation of the electoral process is valid: If the restriction on First Amendment activities is severe, it will be upheld only if it is narrowly tailored to achieve a compelling interest, but if the restriction is reasonable and nondiscriminatory, it generally will be upheld on the basis of the states' important regulatory interests. [Burdick v. Takushi, 504 U.S. 428 (1992)—upholding prohibition against write-in candidates]

1. Ballot Regulation

a. Signature Requirements

The Court has found that the interest of running an efficient election supports a requirement that candidates obtain a reasonable number of signatures to get on the ballot. [Munro v. Socialist Workers Party, 479 U.S. 189 (1986)—1%] Similarly, a state's interest in promoting transparency and accountability in elections is sufficient to justify public disclosure of the names and addresses of persons who sign ballot petitions. [Doe v. Reed, 561 U.S. 186 (2010)] However, the Court struck down a severe ballot restriction requiring new political parties to collect twice as many signatures to run for county office as for state office. [Norman v. Reed, 502 U.S. 279 (1992)]

b. Primary Voting Regulations

A state may enforce a party rule requiring that a person be registered as a member of the party within a reasonable amount of time prior to a primary to be able to vote. [Rosario v. Rockefeller, 410 U.S. 752 (1973)] It may also require that voters in a party's primary be registered either in the party **or as independents.** *Rationale:* The burden on the party's associational rights is **not severe.** Thus, strict scrutiny does not apply and the state's important regulatory interests (e.g., in preserving political parties as viable identifiable groups, preventing party raiding, etc.) are sufficient to justify the restriction. [Clingman v. Beaver, 544 U.S. 581 (2005)] However, a state may not prohibit a party from allowing independent voters to vote in the party's primary if the party wishes to allow independent voters to participate; such a requirement constitutes a severe burden on the associational rights of the party and can be justified only if it is narrowly tailored to serve a compelling interest. [Tashjian v. Republican Party of Connecticut, 479 U.S. 208 (1986)]

c. **Single Party Limitation**

A state law that prohibits an individual from appearing on the ballot as the candidate of more than one party does ***not*** impose a severe burden on the association rights of political parties. The state's interest in ballot integrity and political stability are "sufficiently weighty" to justify the law. [Timmons v. Twin Cities Area New Party, 520 U.S. 351 (1997)]

d. **"Nonpartisan" Blanket Primary**

A state primary ballot law providing that candidates ***self-identify*** their party preference and that the two top vote getters advance to the general election does not ***on its face*** violate the association rights of political parties. *Rationale:* (i) The law does not state that any candidate is a party's nominee, (ii) there was no evidence that voters would be confused by the self-identifications, and (iii) the state may design a ballot that will make this clear. [Washington State Grange v. Washington State Republican Party, 552 U.S. 442 (2008)]

2. **Party Regulation**

The state has less interest in governing party activities than in governing elections in general. Thus, the Court has held invalid a statute prohibiting the governing committee of a political party from endorsing or opposing candidates in primary elections. [Eu v. San Francisco County Democratic Central Committee, 489 U.S. 214 (1989); *and see* California Democratic Party v. Jones, 530 U.S. 567 (2000)—state cannot require political parties to allow nonparty members to vote in the party's primary election] Similarly, it has held invalid state regulations concerning the selection of delegates to a national party convention and the selection of candidates at such elections. [Cousins v. Wigoda, 419 U.S. 477 (1975); Democratic Party v. LaFolette, 450 U.S. 107 (1981)]

a. **Judicial Candidate Selection**

A state law that permits political parties to choose nominees for state judgeships at state conventions does not violate the freedom of association rights of candidates for judgeships simply because the historic domination of party leaders results in strongly favoring those that they support. *Rationale:* This process "has been a traditional means of choosing party nominees." [New York State Board of Elections v. Lopez Torres, 552 U.S. 196 (2008)]

3. **Limits on Contributions**

A statute limiting election campaign contributions is not tested under a strict scrutiny standard; rather, it must be "closely drawn" to match a "sufficiently important interest"—an intermediate scrutiny standard. [McConnell v. Federal Election Commission, 540 U.S. 93 (2003)]

a. **To Political Candidate**

Laws limiting the amount of money that a person or group may contribute to a political candidate are ***valid***, since the government has a sufficiently important interest in stopping the fact (or appearance) of corruption that may result from large contributions. Moreover, such laws do not substantially restrict freedom of expression or freedom of association (as long as the contributor may spend his money directly to discuss candidates and issues). [Buckley v. Valeo, 424 U.S. 1 (1976)]

1) **Equalizing Large Expenditures**

A law increasing contribution limits for a candidate whose wealthy opponent achieves an advantage by spending personal funds (exceeding $350,000) violates the First Amendment. *Rationale*: Although Congress may raise contribution limits for both candidates in situations of this kind, "penalizing" a self-financing candidate who robustly expresses the right to advocate his own election cannot be justified by leveling opportunities for candidates of different personal wealth. [Davis v. Federal Election Commission, 554 U.S. 724 (2008)]

b. **To Ballot Referendum Committee**

The government may ***not*** limit contributions to a political committee that supports or opposes a ballot referendum (as opposed to one that supports a political candidate). Such a limitation on contributions to influence referendum elections violates the freedoms of speech and association. [Citizens Against Rent Control v. Berkeley, 454 U.S. 290 (1981)]

c. **Disclosure of Contributors or Recipients of Money**

The government may require a political party or committee to disclose the names of contributors or recipients of money to or from the party or committee. However, if the party or committee can show a "reasonable probability" that disclosure will cause harm to the party, committee, or private individuals, they have a First Amendment right to refuse to make such disclosures. [Brown v. Socialist Workers '74 Campaign Committee, 459 U.S. 87 (1982)]

d. **Aggregate Contribution Limits Unconstitutional**

The government may not limit the ***aggregate*** amount one person or entity contributes to political candidates or committees during an election even though it may limit the amount given to a single candidate. Aggregate limits violate the First Amendment's protection of political speech because unlike individual contribution limits, they do not further the government's interest in preventing *quid pro quo* corruption or the appearance of such, and they seriously restrict participation in the democratic process. Spending large sums of money in connection with elections, but not in an effort to control the exercise of a specific officeholder's duties, does not give rise to such corruption, nor does the possibility that the contributor may garner "influence over or access to" elected officials or political parties. [McCutcheon v. Federal Election Commission, 572 U.S. 185 (2014)]

4. **Limits on Expenditures**

As discussed above, the government ***may*** limit the amount that a person is permitted to ***contribute*** to another's campaign. However, the government ***may not*** limit the amount that a person *expends* on his own campaign. [Buckley v. Valeo, *supra*] Neither may the government limit the amount that a person spends to get a candidate elected, as long as the expenditures are not contributed directly to the candidate nor coordinated with that of the candidate—i.e., the expenditures must be independent of the candidate and not disguised contributions. Thus, corporations, unions, etc., may spend whatever they desire to get a candidate elected. [*See, e.g.,* Citizens United v. Federal Election Commission, 558 U.S. 310 (2010)]

5. **Compare—Regulations of Core Political Speech**
   Regulation of "core political speech" must be distinguished from regulation of the process surrounding elections. Regulation of "core political speech" will be upheld only if it passes muster under strict scrutiny. [McIntyre v. Ohio Elections Commission, 514 U.S. 334 (1995)]

   a. **Prohibiting Any Election Day Campaigning**
      A state law prohibiting *any* campaigning on election day has been held *invalid* as applied to a newspaper urging people to vote in a certain way. The right to comment on political issues is one of the most essential elements of free speech, and such conduct by newspapers would pose little danger to conducting elections. [Mills v. Alabama, 384 U.S. 214 (1966)]

      1) **Compare—Hundred-Foot Limit**
         A law prohibiting campaign activity within 100 feet of a polling place is *valid*. Even though the law is content based and concerns an essential element of free speech, it is *necessary* to serve the *compelling* interest of preventing voter intimidation and election fraud. [Burson v. Freeman, 504 U.S. 191 (1992)]

   b. **Prohibiting Anonymous Campaign Literature**
      Laws prohibiting distribution of anonymous campaign literature involve core political speech and have been stricken because they were not narrowly tailored to a compelling state interest. [McIntyre v. Ohio Elections Commission, *supra*; Buckley v. American Constitutional Law Foundation, 525 U.S. 182 (1999)]

   c. **Prohibiting Judge Candidates from Announcing Their Views**
      A rule prohibiting candidates for judicial election from announcing their views on disputed legal and political issues violates the First Amendment. This is both a content-based restriction and a restriction on core political speech. In either case, it can be justified only if it is necessary to a compelling state interest. Two state interests were suggested to support the rule here: It is necessary to maintain an impartial judiciary and it is necessary to preserve the appearance of impartiality. The Court found that the rule is "woefully underinclusive" and so is not tailored at all toward achieving these goals. For example, it allows candidates to show bias toward political parties while it prohibits them from stating an opinion about political issues. The Court also found that finding judges without any preconceptions in favor of particular legal views is not a compelling interest because it would be both impossible to find such a person and undesirable. [Republican Party of Minnesota v. White, 536 U.S. 765 (2002)]

   d. **Distinguishing Political Speech from Candidate Advocacy**
      An ad concerning a political issue, even if sponsored by a corporation, run during an election campaign will be considered to be core political speech—rather than candidate

advocacy—unless it is susceptible of no reasonable interpretation other than one as an appeal to vote for or against a particular candidate. [Federal Election Commission v. Wisconsin Right to Life, Inc., 551 U.S. 449 (2007)—ad urging voters to contact their senators to encourage them to end a filibuster of federal judicial nominations was core political speech—and could not be banned—even when one of the senators was running for re-election]

e. Solicitation of Campaign Funds by Judicial Candidates

A state may ban personal solicitation of campaign funds by judicial candidates. *Rationale*: If judicial candidates personally ask for money, individuals might feel obligated to donate in the hopes of garnering a favor from the candidates or from fear of retribution for not donating. The ban withstands strict scrutiny because it "advances the state's compelling interest in preserving public confidence in the integrity of the judiciary, and it does so through means narrowly tailored to avoid unnecessarily abridging speech." [Williams-Yulee v. Florida Bar, 135 S. Ct. 1656 (2015)]

C. BAR MEMBERSHIP AND PUBLIC EMPLOYMENT

The government often requires persons who accept government jobs to submit to loyalty oaths and refrain from certain conduct (e.g., campaigning). Such regulations often impact upon the freedom of speech and association.

1. Restraints on Speech Activities of Government Employees

Under the First Amendment, speech generally cannot be regulated or punished based on the content of the speech unless the regulation or punishment is necessary to achieve a compelling government interest. However, special rules apply when the government seeks to punish a government employee for speech or speech-related activities.

a. Speech Made Pursuant to Official Duties

A government employer may punish a government employee's speech whenever the speech is made on the job and pursuant to the employee's official duties. This is true even if the speech touches on a matter of public concern. [Garcetti v. Ceballos, 547 U.S. 410 (2006)]

Example: P, a district attorney, reviewed a case, concluded that there were irregularities in an underlying search warrant, contacted his supervisors, and suggested dismissing the case. P's supervisors nevertheless proceeded with the prosecution. At a hearing challenging the warrant, P again raised his concerns about the warrant, but the court rejected the challenge. P claims that he was then subjected to retaliatory employment actions because of his testimony and sued his employer for violating his First Amendment rights. P's employer denied undertaking any retaliatory actions, but even if such actions did occur, no First Amendment violation could occur here because the speech was undertaken as part of P's job—a government employer may evaluate an employee based on any writing or speech that the employee undertakes as part of his official duties. [Garcetti v. Ceballos, *supra*]

b. Other Speech

If speech is not made pursuant to an employee's official duties, two tests apply. If a government employee's speech does ***not involve a matter of public concern***, the courts give the government employer a wide degree of deference and allow the employer to punish the employee if the speech was disruptive of the work environment. However, if a ***matter of public concern is involved***, courts must balance the employee's rights as a citizen to comment on a matter of public concern against the government's interest as an employer in efficient performance of public service.

Examples: 1) A teacher cannot be fired for writing a letter to a newspaper attacking the school superintendent's handling of proposals to raise new revenue for the school—a matter of public concern. [Pickering v. Board of Education, 391 U.S. 563 (1968)]

                2) The Court held invalid the firing of a clerical employee from a constable's office for expressing her disappointment that an assassination attempt on President Reagan did not succeed, because in context the statement could not be understood to be an actual threat or an action that would interfere with the running of the office; rather, the Court viewed it as a commentary on the public issue of the President's policies. [Rankin v. McPherson, 483 U.S. 378 (1987)]

Compare: The Court upheld the firing of an attorney for circulating in the office a petition regarding transfer policies. [Connick v. Myers, 461 U.S. 138 (1983)]

1)   Petition Clause Claims Treated Similarly

A government employee's right under the First Amendment to petition the government for redress is governed by the principles discussed above. Thus, unless a government employee's grievance relates to a matter of public concern, it is not a constitutionally protected activity, and the employee may not bring a constitutional tort suit (under 42 U.S.C. section 1983) alleging that his employer took retaliatory actions in violation of the employee's right to petition. [Duryea v. Guarnieri, 564 U.S. 379 (2011)]

c.   Participation in Political Campaigns

The federal government ***may*** prohibit federal executive branch employees from taking an active part in political campaigns. The rationale is twofold: to further nonpartisanship in administration and to protect employees from being coerced to work for the election of their employers. [United Public Workers v. Mitchell, 330 U.S. 75 (1947)]

d.   Bans on Receiving Honoraria

A provision of the Ethics in Government Act banning government employees from accepting an honorarium for making speeches, writing articles, or making appearances was held to violate the First Amendment when applied to "rank and file" employees. Such a rule deters speech within a broad category of expression by a massive number of potential speakers and thus can be justified only if the government can show that the employees' and their potential audiences' rights are outweighed by the necessary impact the speech would have on actual operation of the government. The government failed to cite any evidence of misconduct related to honoraria by the rank and file employees, and so failed to meet the burden here. [United States v. National Treasury Employees Union, 513 U.S. 454 (1995)]

e. **Patronage**

The First Amendment freedoms of political belief and association forbid the hiring, promotion, transfer, firing, or recall of a public employee because of the person's political views or political party affiliation unless the hiring authority demonstrates that party affiliation or beliefs are appropriate requirements for the effective performance of the public office involved, e.g., "policymaking" or "confidential" nature of work. [Rutan v. Republican Party of Illinois, 497 U.S. 62 (1990)]

2. Loyalty Oaths

It is permissible for the federal government to require employees and other public officers to take loyalty oaths. However, such oaths will not be upheld if they are overbroad (i.e., prohibit constitutionally protected activities) or are vague so that they have a chilling effect on First Amendment activities.

a. **Overbreadth**

1) **Knowledge of Organization's Aim Required**

Public employment cannot be denied to persons who are simply members of the Communist Party because only knowing membership with "specific intent to further unlawful aims" is unprotected by the First Amendment. [Keyishian v. Board of Regents, 385 U.S. 589 (1967)]

2) **Advocacy of Doctrine Protected**

A political party may not be denied a place on the ballot for refusing to take a loyalty oath that it does not advocate violent overthrow of the government as an abstract doctrine. The First Amendment forbids "statutes regulating advocacy that are not limited to advocacy of action." [Communist Party v. Whitcomb, 414 U.S. 441 (1974)]

b. **Vagueness**

1) **Oaths Upheld**

Compare the following oaths that have been upheld:

a) **To Support the Constitution**

An oath that required public employees and bar applicants to "support the Constitution of the United States" and the state constitution has been upheld. [Connell v. Higgenbotham, 403 U.S. 207 (1971)]

b) **To Oppose the Overthrow of the Government**

An oath required of all state employees "to oppose the overthrow of the government . . . by force, violence, or by an illegal or unconstitutional method" has also been upheld. The Court read this oath as akin to those requiring the taker simply to "support" the Constitution, "to commit themselves to live by the constitutional processes of our system." Moreover, the oath provided fair notice, because its violation could be punished only by a prosecution for perjury, which required proof of knowing falsity. [Cole v. Richardson, 405 U.S. 676 (1972)]

2) Oath Not Upheld

A loyalty oath for public employees that they "promote respect for the flag and . . . reverence for law and order" is void for vagueness, since a refusal to salute the flag on religious grounds might be found in breach thereof. [Baggett v. Bullitt, 377 U.S. 360 (1964)]

3. Disclosure of Associations

Forcing disclosure of First Amendment activities as a condition of public employment, bar membership, or other public benefits may have a chilling effect. Thus, the state cannot force every prospective government employee to disclose *every* organizational membership. Such a broad disclosure has **insufficient relation** to loyalty and professional competence, and the state has available **less drastic means** to achieve its purpose. [Shelton v. Tucker, 364 U.S. 479 (1960)] The state may inquire only into those activities that are relevant to the position. If the candidate fails to answer relevant questions, employment may be denied. [Konigsberg v. State Bar of California, 366 U.S. 36 (1961)]

a. Fifth Amendment Limitation

If the job candidate refuses to answer on a claim of the privilege against self-incrimination, denial of the job violates the Fifth and Fourteenth Amendments. [Spevack v. Klein, 385 U.S. 511 (1967)] However, if individuals are ordered by appropriate authorities to answer questions "specifically, directly, and narrowly relating to their official duties," and they refuse to do so by claiming the privilege against self-incrimination, they may be denied the job or discharged without violating the Fifth Amendment, if they were given immunity from the use of their answers or the fruits thereof in a criminal prosecution. [Lefkowitz v. Turley, 414 U.S. 70 (1973); Gardner v. Broderick, 392 U.S. 273 (1968)]

4. Practice of Law

Regulation of the legal profession may conflict with the freedom of association rights of certain groups because it may impair their ability to band together to advise each other and utilize counsel in their common interest.

a. Countervailing State Interest Required

To overcome a group's right to exercise its First Amendment rights, the state must show a substantial interest, such as evidence of objectionable practices occurring or an actual or clearly threatened conflict of interest between lawyer and client.

Examples: 1) The NAACP encouraged, instructed, and offered to represent parents of black children to litigate against school segregation. This was held to be protected political expression. The state's ban on solicitation of legal business was inapplicable because the NAACP sought no monetary gain. [NAACP v. Button, 371 U.S. 415 (1963)]

2) A railroad labor union recommended a specific lawyer to pursue rights of members injured on the job, and also obtained a fee from a

lawyer for performing investigative services. This was held protected. [Brotherhood of Railroad Trainmen v. Virginia, 377 U.S. 1 (1964)]

D.   SCHOOL SPONSORSHIP OF EXTRACURRICULAR CLUBS

The Supreme Court has held that the compelling interest test does not apply to infringement cases involving public school sponsorship of extracurricular clubs; instead, the test used in limited-public-forum-speech cases applies—sponsorship of associations can be subject to regulation that is **viewpoint neutral** and **reasonably related to a legitimate government interest.** (*See* XX.B.2.c.2), *supra*.)

Example: A public law school officially recognized student groups and gave them funding from mandatory student activity fees only if the groups accepted all students regardless of their "status or beliefs" (i.e., the "all comers" policy). A group that required students to sign a statement of faith based on Christian beliefs and denied membership to persons who supported homosexuality and premarital sex sought an exemption from the "all comers" policy and was denied. The group sued the school, claiming that the policy violated members' associational rights. *Held:* The "all comers" policy is constitutional. It is viewpoint neutral in that it draws no distinctions on point of view. Moreover, it is reasonably related to school purposes such as encouraging tolerance and providing leadership, educational, and social opportunities to all students. [Christian Legal Society v. Martinez, XX.B.2.c.2), *supra*]

XXII.   FREEDOM OF RELIGION

A.   CONSTITUTIONAL PROVISION

The First Amendment provides "Congress shall make no law respecting an establishment of religion, or prohibiting the free exercise thereof."

B.   APPLICABILITY TO THE STATES

Both the Establishment and Free Exercise Clauses of the First Amendment apply to the states under the Fourteenth Amendment.

C.   FREE EXERCISE CLAUSE

1.   No Punishment of Beliefs

The Free Exercise Clause prohibits the government from punishing (denying benefits to, or imposing burdens on) someone on the basis of the person's **religious beliefs.** It is sometimes said that the government can engage in such activity only if it is necessary to achieve a compelling interest; sometimes the rule is stated as a total prohibition of such government actions. In any case, the Supreme Court has never found an interest that was so "compelling" that it would justify punishing a religious belief.

a.   What Constitutes Religious Belief?

The Supreme Court has not defined what constitutes a religious belief. However, it has made clear that religious belief does not require recognition of a supreme being [Torcaso v. Watkins, 367 U.S. 488 (1961)], and need not arise from a traditional, or even an organized, religion [*see* Frazee v. Illinois Department of Employment Security,

489 U.S. 829 (1989)]. One possible definition is that the "belief must occupy a place in the believer's life parallel to that occupied by orthodox religious beliefs." [United States v. Seeger, 380 U.S. 163 (1965)—interpreting statutory, rather than constitutional, provision] In any case, the Court has never held an asserted religious belief to be not religious for First Amendment purposes.

1) Courts May Not Find Religious Beliefs to Be False

The courts may not declare a religious belief to be "false." For example, if a person says he talked to God and that God said the person should solicit money, he cannot be found guilty of fraud on the basis that God never made such a statement. However, the court may determine whether the person is sincerely asserting a belief in the divine statement. [United States v. Ballard, 322 U.S. 78 (1944), *as described in* Employment Division v. Smith, 494 U.S. 872 (1990)]

b. States Must Act with Religious Neutrality

A state action might violate the Free Exercise Clause when the applicable law is neutral with respect to religion on its face if, during adjudication of a case, a state actor made disparaging remarks about religion to justify the state action. [Masterpiece Cakeshop, Ltd. v. Colorado Civil Rights Commission, 138 S. Ct. 1719 (2018)—overturning a civil rights commission decision that a Christian baker discriminated against a gay couple by refusing to bake a wedding cake because a member of the commission said similar religion-supported arguments were used to justify slavery and the Holocaust]

c. Religious Oaths for Governmental Jobs Prohibited

The *federal* government may not require any federal office holder or employee to take an oath based on a religious belief as a condition for receiving the federal office or job, because such a requirement is prohibited by Article VI of the Constitution. State and local governments are prohibited from requiring such oaths by the Free Exercise Clause. [Torcaso v. Watkins, *supra*]

d. States May Not Exclude Clerics from Public Office

A state may not exclude clerics (persons who hold an office or official position in a religious organization) from being elected to the state legislature, or from other governmental positions, because that exclusion would impose a disability on these persons based upon the nature of their religious views and their religious status. [McDaniel v. Paty, 435 U.S. 618 (1978)]

2. No Punishment of Religious Conduct Solely Because It Is Religious

The Supreme Court has stated that the Free Exercise Clause prohibits the government from punishing conduct merely because it is religious or displays religious belief (e.g., the state cannot ban the use of peyote only when used in religious ceremonies). [Employment Division v. Smith, *supra*—dicta] A law that is designed to suppress actions only because the actions are religiously motivated is not a neutral law of general applicability. Such a law will be invalid unless it is necessary to promote a compelling interest.

Example: A city law that prohibited the precise type of animal slaughter used in the ritual of a particular religious sect violated the Free Exercise Clause because the Court found that the law was designed solely to exclude the religious sect from the city. The law was not a neutral law of general applicability; nor was the law necessary to promote a compelling interest. [Church of the Lukumi Babalu Aye, Inc. v. Hialeah, 508 U.S. 520 (1993)]

Compare: A state law that excluded pursuit of a degree in **devotional theology** from a college scholarship program for all students did **not** violate the Free Exercise Clause. Although a school **could** provide such scholarships without violating the Establishment Clause (*see infra*), the Free Exercise Clause does not require such scholarships. The exclusion from scholarship eligibility does not show animus toward religion, but rather merely reflects a decision not to fund this activity. Moreover, the burden that the exclusion imposes on religion is modest, and there is substantial historical support against using tax funds to support the ministry. [Locke v. Davey, 540 U.S. 712 (2004)]

a.   **No Exclusion from Government Benefits Programs Solely Because an Organization Is Religious**

A state may not limit eligibility for a governmental benefit to nonreligious organizations. Even if a state has no obligation to create a benefit, once it has done so, it may not ban religious groups from receiving the benefit merely because they are religious.

Example: A state creates a program to provide free playground upgrade materials to playgrounds that apply and meet certain criteria. Because the state's constitution bans state funds from being used for the benefit of religious organizations, such organizations are excluded from the program. The state's denial of a church playground's application violated the Free Exercise Clause. [Trinity Lutheran Church of Columbia, Inc. v. Comer, 137 S. Ct. 2012 (2017)]

3.   **States Can Regulate General Conduct—Criminal Laws and Other Regulations**

Of course, states may prohibit or regulate conduct in general, and this is true even if the prohibition or regulation happens to interfere with a person's religious practices. The Free Exercise Clause cannot be used to challenge a law of general applicability unless it can be shown that the law was motivated by a desire to interfere with religion. [Employment Division v. Smith, *supra*]

a.   **Generally No Exemptions Required**

The Free Exercise Clause does not require exemptions from criminal laws or other governmental regulations for a person whose religious beliefs prevent him from conforming his behavior to the requirements of the law. In other words, a law that regulates the conduct of all persons can be applied to prohibit the conduct of a person despite the fact that his religious beliefs prevent him from complying with the law.

1)   **Federal Statutory Exemption—Outside the Scope of Exam**

The Religious Freedom Restoration Act ("RFRA") allows a person to challenge federal laws of general applicability as burdening his religious beliefs and practices. If there is a substantial burdening of religious free exercise, under RFRA the government must meet strict scrutiny. In *Burwell v. Hobby Lobby, Inc.*, 134 S. Ct. 2751 (2014), the Court found that a federal requirement that businesses include contraceptive coverage in their insurance coverage for employees violates RFRA for close corporations whose owners object to this on religious grounds.

However, RFRA is statutory in nature and is outside the scope of a constitutional law question.

b.   Examples

The Supreme Court has held that no religious exemption was required from the following religiously neutral regulations, even though certain groups objected because the regulation interfered with conduct inspired by sincerely held religious beliefs:

1)   Prohibition against **use of peyote** [Employment Division v. Smith, *supra* — challenged by person whose religious beliefs require use of peyote during religious ceremony];

2)   **Denial of tax exempt status to schools that discriminate** on the basis of race [Bob Jones University v. United States, 461 U.S. 574 (1983)—challenged by religious school whose tenets require certain separations of races];

3)   Requirement that employers comply with **federal minimum wage laws** [Tony and Susan Alamo Foundation v. Secretary of Labor, 471 U.S. 290 (1985)—challenged by employer that argued minimum wages interfere with members' religious desires to work without compensation];

4)   Requirement that employers pay **Social Security taxes** [United States v. Lee, 455 U.S. 252 (1982)—challenged by person whose religious beliefs prohibited payment and receipt of Social Security type payments]; and

5)   **Sales and use taxes** [Jimmy Swaggart Ministries v. Board of Equalization of California, 493 U.S. 378 (1990)—challenged as applied to sales of goods and literature by religious group].

c.   Cases in Which Exemptions Were Required

1)   Ministerial Exemption

The Supreme Court has held that religious organizations must be granted an exemption from suits alleging employment discrimination by ministers against their religious organizations. The government may not interfere with a decision of a religious group to fire one of its ministers. Imposing an unwanted minister would infringe on the Free Exercise Clause, which protects a religious group's right to shape its own faith through appointments. And allowing the government to determine who will minister within a faith also violates the Establishment Clause by interfering with ecclesiastical decisions. Moreover, this ministerial exception is not limited to the head of a religious congregation; it can extend to others in positions considered by the congregation to be ministerial. [Hosanna-Tabor Evangelical Lutheran Church and School v. Equal Employment Opportunity Commission, 565 U.S. 171 (2012)—ministerial exemption applied to parochial school teacher considered to be "called," who trained by taking a number of college level courses and was given a diploma with the title "Minister of Religion," who occasionally led school worship, and whom the congregation prayed for as a minister]

2) **Unemployment Compensation Cases—Some Exemptions Required**

Many state unemployment compensation programs make payments only to persons who are involuntarily unemployed (i.e., were fired or laid off rather than resigned), and who are available for work (i.e., willing to accept offered employment). Here, however, unlike other areas of regulation, the Supreme Court has held that the states must grant religious exemptions. Thus, if a person resigns from a job or refuses to accept a job because it conflicts with her religious beliefs, the state must pay her unemployment compensation if she is otherwise entitled.

Examples: 1) A state cannot deny unemployment compensation merely because the applicant quit a job rather than work on a "holy day" on which religious beliefs forbid work. [Sherbert v. Verner, 374 U.S. 398 (1963)]

2) A state cannot deny unemployment compensation merely because the applicant quit his job rather than work on production of military equipment after his factory converted from nonmilitary to military production. [Thomas v. Review Board, 450 U.S. 707 (1981)]

a) **Need Not Belong to Formal Religious Organization**

A person does not have to be a member of a formal religious organization to receive the above exemptions from unemployment compensation requirements. All that is required is that the person *sincerely hold* religious beliefs that prevent him from working on a certain day or on military products. [Frazee v. Illinois Department of Employment Security, 1.a., *supra*]

b) **Limitation—Criminal Prohibitions**

The unemployment compensation cases do not give individuals a right to disregard criminal laws due to their religious beliefs. Thus, unemployment compensation laws may disqualify persons fired for "misconduct" (which includes any violation of criminal law).

Example: A person was fired from his job as a counselor at a private drug abuse clinic when it was discovered that he used peyote (at times when he was not at work) for religious reasons. All use of peyote was illegal in the state (even if the use was part of a religious ceremony). The Supreme Court held that unemployment compensation could properly be denied here. [Employment Division v. Smith, *supra*]

3) **Right of Amish Not to Educate Children**

The Supreme Court has required an exemption for the Amish from a neutral law that required school attendance until age 16, because a fundamental tenet of Amish religion forbids secondary education. The Court found that the Amish are productive and law-abiding, and ruled that the right to educate one's children (*see* XIX.B.7., *supra*) and the Free Exercise Clause outweighed the state's interest here. [Wisconsin v. Yoder, 406 U.S. 205 (1972)]

D. **ESTABLISHMENT CLAUSE**

The Establishment Clause, along with the Free Exercise Clause, compels the government to pursue a course of neutrality toward religion. Government action challenged under the Establishment Clause will be found invalid unless the action:

(i)   Has a *secular purpose*;

(ii) Has a *primary effect* that neither advances nor inhibits religion; *and*

(iii) Does not produce *excessive government entanglement* with religion.

[Lemon v. Kurtzman, 403 U.S. 602 (1971)—the *"Lemon"* test] (Note that some recent cases have simply focused on whether the action is neutral as between the religious and nonreligious when there is no endorsement of a particular religion.) The Establishment Clause cases can be grouped into four categories: (i) cases preferring one religious sect over others; (ii) a limited group of cases unconnected to financial aid or education; (iii) cases involving financial aid to religiously affiliated institutions; and (iv) cases concerning religious activities in public schools. The details regarding the Supreme Court rulings are given below.

1.   **Sect Preference**
     Government action that prefers one religious sect over others violates the Establishment Clause, at least if such action is not necessary to achieve a compelling interest. The Court generally will not even resort to the *Lemon* test in such a case, although such action would fail the first two prongs of the *Lemon* test, because if the government is favoring one religious sect, it is acting with the purpose of and having the primary effect of aiding that religion.
     Example: A state law created a public school district whose boundaries were intentionally set to match the boundaries of a particular Jewish neighborhood (so that several handicapped students would not have to be sent outside their neighborhood to attend special education classes that the state required and which the students' private school could not adequately provide). The Supreme Court found the law unconstitutional. [Board of Education v. Grumet, 512 U.S. 687 (1994)]

2.   **Cases Unconnected to Financial Aid or Education**
     In cases unconnected to financial aid or education, a good rule of thumb is that a law favoring or burdening religion or a specific religious group in particular will be invalid, but a law favoring or burdening a larger segment of society that happens to include religious groups will be upheld.
     Example: The government may not delegate governmental power to religious organizations because such action would involve excessive governmental entanglement. [Larkin v. Grendel's Den, Inc., 459 U.S. 116 (1982)—statute gave church-affiliated schools power to veto nearby liquor licenses]

     Compare: The IRS may deny tax exemptions claimed for religious donations when the sums were paid to the church *in exchange for services* (e.g., classes) since this is a general rule that applies to all charities. [Hernandez v. Commissioner of Internal Revenue, 490 U.S. 680 (1989)]

     a.   **State Legislature Can Employ a Chaplain**
          Despite the principle of separation of church and state, the Court has held that a state

legislature could employ a chaplain and begin each legislative day with a prayer. [Marsh v. Chambers, 463 U.S. 783 (1983)] This decision was based on the history of legislative prayer in America; it does not modify the "Religious Activities in Public Schools" rulings examined below.

b.   Town Board Can Begin Town Meetings with a Prayer
Extending *Marsh v. Chambers, supra*, the Court has held that a town board may begin its meetings with prayers led by clergy members listed in the town's congregation directory, even if the clergy is predominately Christian. The Court found the practice is consistent with the tradition of legislative prayer and does not discriminate against minority faiths nor coerce the participation of nonadherents, and therefore does not violate the Establishment Clause. The Constitution requires only that the town is equitable in drawing from available clergy, not that it ensure equal representation of all faiths. [Town of Greece v. Galloway, 134 S. Ct. 1811 (2014)]

c.   Displays of Ten Commandments on Public Property
If a display of the Ten Commandments is shown to have a ***"predominantly religious purpose,"*** it violates the Establishment Clause; otherwise, the Ten Commandments may be displayed. [McCreary County v. ACLU, 545 U.S. 844 (2005)]

Example: Two counties posted large copies of the Ten Commandments in their courthouses. After complaints based on the Establishment Clause, each county adopted a resolution calling for a more extensive exhibit showing that the Commandments are Kentucky's "precedent legal code" and noting the state legislature's acknowledgment of Christ as the "Prince of Ethics." The displays were then modified to add smaller copies of other historic texts with religious references (e.g., the "endowed by their creator" clause of the Declaration of Independence). A district court found the displays invalid under the *Lemon* test because they lacked any secular purpose. The counties again modified the displays—without any guiding resolutions—to include eight equally sized items around the Ten Commandments (including the Bill of Rights and a picture of Lady Justice) and the title "Foundations of American Law and Government." The ACLU moved to enjoin these displays, claiming that their purpose was still religious rather than secular. Given the displays' history, the Supreme Court agreed, finding that the taint from the earlier displays had not been dissipated even though, on their faces, the most current displays appeared not to have a religious purpose. [McCreary County v. ACLU, *supra*]

Compare: A monument of the Ten Commandments on a 22-acre State Capitol ground displaying 17 monuments and 21 historical markers commemorating the state's "people, ideals, and events that compose its identity" communicated not only a religious message but also a secular moral message, and its setting suggested that the state intended the secular message to predominate. [Van Orden v. Perry, 545 U.S. 677 (2005)]

d.   Some Holiday Displays Are Permissible
If the ***government*** maintains a holiday-Christmastime display that does not appear to

endorse religion, the display will survive review under the three-part Establishment Clause test. If a government's holiday display includes religious symbols (e.g., a nativity scene or a menorah) as well as other holiday decorations (e.g., a Christmas tree or a Santa Claus figure), the courts will hold that the display: (i) has a secular purpose (based on the history of government recognition of holidays); (ii) has a primary nonreligious effect (it does not endorse religion); and (iii) does not create excessive entanglement between government and religion. If the display includes only the religious symbols (e.g., only a nativity scene), it will violate the Establishment Clause because it has a religious effect (it "endorses" religion). [County of Allegheny v. ACLU, 492 U.S. 573 (1989)]

e. Absolute Right Not to Work on a Sabbath Impermissible

The state may not force employers to grant all employees an absolute right to refrain from working on their sabbath, because the primary effect of such a law is to advance religion. [Estate of Thornton v. Caldor, 472 U.S. 703 (1985)] However, a state may require employers to make reasonable efforts to accommodate employee religious practices.

f. Exemptions from Antidiscrimination Laws

The federal government may exempt religious organizations from the federal statutory prohibition against discrimination in employment on the basis of religion, at least regarding their nonprofit activities. Thus, a janitor can be discharged from his employment at a gymnasium owned by a religious organization (which was open to the public and run as a nonprofit facility) because he was not a member of that religious organization. [Corporation of the Presiding Bishop of the Church of Jesus Christ of Latter-Day Saints v. Amos, 483 U.S. 327 (1987)]

3. Cases Involving Financial Benefits to Church-Related Institutions

A statute authorizing governmental aid to a religiously affiliated institution (hospital, school, etc.) must be tested under the general test detailed above (secular purpose, primary effect, and excessive entanglement). However, the Supreme Court applies these tests with greater strictness when the government aid is going to a religiously affiliated grade school or high school than it does when the aid is going to another type of religiously affiliated institution (such as a college or hospital).

a. Recipient-Based Aid

The government may give aid in the form of financial assistance to a defined class of persons as long as the class is defined without reference to religion or religious criteria. Such a program is valid even if persons who receive the financial assistance are thereby enabled to attend a religiously affiliated school.

Examples: 1) The Supreme Court upheld a state program that made education subsidy payments directly to a blind or disabled student even though a student used his aid to study at a Christian college for the purpose of becoming a pastor or missionary. The class of persons who received the aid was defined without reference to any religious criteria; only an incidental benefit would go to the religiously affiliated college or vocational training institution. The aid program thus passed review under the purpose, effect, and entanglement tests. [Witters v. Washington Department of Services, 474 U.S. 481 (1986)]

2) The Court held that the Establishment Clause would not prevent a public school district from paying for a sign language interpreter for a deaf student at a religious high school under a religiously neutral program of aid to all handicapped school children in both public and private schools. [Zobrest v. Catalina Foothills School District, 509 U.S. 1 (1993)]

3) The Supreme Court upheld a program that provided tuition vouchers to parents of poor children in kindergarten through the eighth grade which could be used to pay for attending participating public or private schools of their parents' choice, even though a very high percentage of the recipients chose to attend religiously affiliated schools. The program was part of a larger program that also created publicly funded magnet schools and community schools that were independent from the local school district. The Court found that the program did not have the purpose or effect of advancing religion. Its purpose was secular—to provide educational assistance to poor children in a failing public school system. Its primary effect was to provide poor children with funds to attend other schools. Any benefit to the religious schools resulted from parents choosing to send their children to those schools and was not attributable to the government. [Zelman v. Simmons-Harris, 536 U.S. 639 (2002)]

1) **Compare—Tuition Tax Deductions or Credits Limited to Religious School Tuition**
A state may not use a system of statutory grants, tax credits, or tax deductions to reimburse parents or students for tuition paid *only to religiously affiliated schools*. However, a tax deduction to all students or parents based on the actual expenditures for attending any public or private school (including religious schools) has been upheld. [Mueller v. Allen, 463 U.S. 388 (1983)]

It would appear that a valid tax deduction statute must allow a deduction for: (i) expenditures for public as well as private schools; and (ii) some expenditures other than tuition (such as expenditures for school supplies or books) so that public school students or their parents may benefit from the deduction.

b. **Aid to Colleges, Hospitals, Etc.**
The Court will uphold a government grant of aid to the secular activity of a religiously affiliated hospital or college (such as a grant to build a new hospital ward or a laboratory-classroom building) as long as the government program requires that the aid be used only for *nonreligious purposes*, and the recipient so agrees in good faith. [Tilton v. Richardson, 403 U.S. 672 (1971); Bradfield v. Roberts, 175 U.S. 291 (1899)]
Example: The Adolescent Family Life Act—which provides for grants of government funds to a variety of public and private (including religiously affiliated) agencies to provide counseling and educational services to young people regarding sexual activity—has been upheld. The Act has a secular purpose (dealing with problems of teenage pregnancy). The Act does not on its face advance religion because a religiously affiliated

organization could contractually be required to use the funds for nonreligious counseling. And the Act does not give rise to excessive entanglement because there is no reason to assume that a significant percentage of the funds would be granted to pervasively sectarian institutions. [Bowen v. Kendrick, 487 U.S. 589 (1988)]

c.   **Aid to Religiously Affiliated Grade Schools or High Schools**
Programs of aid to these institutions are subject to the same three-part test as are all other laws under the Establishment Clause. Most of the time, such programs will have a secular purpose—to aid in education. However, if significant aid is given to the religious school, the program may be deemed to have a primary effect that advances religion. If the government program has detailed administrative or legislative regulations that are designed to ensure that the aid does not result in a primary effect of advancing religion, the law may be stricken as giving rise to an excessive entanglement between government and religion.

1)   **Aid Upheld**
The Supreme Court has upheld state programs that:

a)   Provide state-approved **textbooks** to **all** students [Board of Education v. Allen, 392 U.S. 236 (1968)] (but note that the state may not loan textbooks to students attending schools that discriminate on the basis of race, since this would violate the Fourteenth Amendment [Norwood v. Harrison, 413 U.S. 455 (1973)]);

b)   Lend religiously neutral instructional materials (e.g., library books, computers) to parochial schools as well as to public and other nonprofit private schools, where the program did not define recipients by reference to religion and the **challenger did not prove** that the neutral aid was used for religious indoctrination. [Mitchell v. Helms, 530 U.S. 793 (2000)—*overruling* Meek v. Pittenger, 421 U.S. 349 (1975)];

c)   Provide **transportation to and from school** to **all** students [Everson v. Board of Education, 330 U.S. 1 (1947)];

d)   Reimburse private schools for the expenses of **compiling state-required data**, such as student attendance records, or administering and grading **standardized** state educational achievement tests [Committee for Public Education and Religious Liberty v. Regan, 444 U.S. 646 (1980)]; and

e)   Provide **"auxiliary services"** (e.g., remedial education, guidance, or job counseling) to all disadvantaged children at their school, including children at parochial schools [Agostini v. Felton, 521 U.S. 203 (1997)].

2)   **Aid Invalidated**
The Supreme Court has struck down the following state programs, either because they had a primary effect that advanced religion or because they involved excessive entanglement between government and religion:

a) Programs paying a portion of private school ***teachers' salaries*** (for their secular classes), since the primary effect would be to advance religion and a system to ensure that the money/teachers not be used for religious purposes would involve excessive entanglements. [Lemon v. Kurtzman, D., *supra*]; and

b) Programs reimbursing private schools for ***writing achievement tests*** (this would have the primary effect of advancing religion since the schools could write tests advancing their religious mission) [Levitt v. Community for Public Education, 413 U.S. 472 (1973)].

d. Tax Exemption for Religious, Charitable, or Educational Property
An exemption from property taxation for "real or personal property used exclusively for religious, educational, or charitable purposes" does not violate the Establishment Clause. Neither the purpose nor the effect of such an exemption is the advancement or the inhibition of religion, and it constitutes neither sponsorship nor hostility, nor excessive government entanglement with religion. The "government does not transfer part of its revenue to churches but simply abstains from demanding that the church support the state . . . ." [Walz v. Tax Commission, 397 U.S. 664 (1970)]

e. Tax Exemption Available Only to Religions
Although religious schools or religious associations may be included in tax exemptions available to a variety of secular and religious organizations, a tax exemption that is available only for religious organizations or religious activities violates the Establishment Clause. [Texas Monthly, Inc. v. Bullock, 489 U.S. 1 (1989)—an exemption from the sales and use tax for religious magazines or books (but no other publications) violates the Establishment Clause]

4. Religious Activities in Public Schools

a. Prayer and Bible Reading
Prayer and Bible reading in school are invalid as establishments of religion [Engel v Vitale, 370 U.S. 421 (1962); Abington School District v. Schempp, 374 U.S. 203 (1963)] It does not matter whether participation is voluntary or involuntary, and neither does it matter that the prayer period is designated as a period of silent prayer or meditation. [Wallace v. Jaffree, 472 U.S. 38 (1985)] This rule extends to prohibit public school officials from having clerics give invocation and benediction prayers at graduation ceremonies. [Lee v. Weisman, 505 U.S. 577 (1992)] Similarly, a school policy authorizing students to elect whether to have a student invocation before varsity games, to select a student to deliver it, and to decide its content *violates* the Establishment Clause. Unlike student speeches at an open public forum (*see* d., below), this policy's purpose is to encourage religious messages. [Santa Fe Independent School District v. Doe, 530 U.S. 290 (2000)]

b. Posting Ten Commandments in Classroom Is Invalid
Posting the Ten Commandments on the walls of public school classrooms plainly serves a religious purpose and is invalid, despite the legislature's statement that it was for a secular purpose. [Stone v. Graham, 449 U.S. 39 (1980)]

c. **Released-Time Programs**

1) **In Public School Building**
Programs in which regular classes end an hour early one day a week and religious instruction is given in public school classrooms to students who request it are invalid. [McCollum v. Board of Education, 333 U.S. 203 (1948)]

2) **Nonpublic Building Used**
Programs in which participating children go to religious classes conducted at religious centers away from the public school do not violate the Establishment Clause. [Zorach v. Clauson, 343 U.S. 306 (1952)]

d. **Accommodation of Religious Students—On-Campus Meetings**
As discussed at XX.B.1.d.., *supra*, under the Free Speech Clause, if a public school allows members of the public and private organizations to use school property when classes are not in session, it cannot deny a religious organization permission to use the property for meetings merely because religious topics will be discussed. Such an "equal access rule" does not violate the Establishment Clause because the primary purpose of such programs is secular (to accommodate all interests), people are not likely to assume that the government endorses the religious ideas discussed, and there is no excessive government entanglement, at least where the meetings are not run by school personnel. [Good News Club v. Milford Central School, 533 U.S. 98 (2001)]

e. **Curriculum Controls**
A government statute or regulation that modifies a public school curriculum will violate the Establishment Clause if it fails the secular purpose test, primary effect test, or excessive government entanglement test.

Example: A state statute that prohibited the teaching of human biological evolution in the state's public schools was held to violate the Establishment Clause because the Supreme Court found that the legislature had a religious purpose for enacting the statute. [Epperson v. Arkansas, 393 U.S. 97 (1968)] Similarly, the Court invalidated a state statute that prohibited instruction regarding "evolution science" (the theory of human biological evolution) in the public schools unless that instruction was accompanied by instruction regarding "creation science," because the Court found that the legislature enacted this statute for the purpose of promoting religion. [Edwards v. Aguillard, 482 U.S. 578 (1987)]

CONTRACTS AND SALES

CONTRACTS AND SALES

TABLE OF CONTENTS

CONTRACTS AND SALES

I. WHAT IS A CONTRACT?

A. GENERAL DEFINITION

A contract is a promise or set of promises, for the breach of which the law gives a remedy, or the performance of which the law in some way recognizes as a duty.

B. COMMON LAW VS. ARTICLE 2 SALE OF GOODS

Generally, the common law governs contracts. However, special rules have been developed for contracts involving the sale of *goods*, and those rules are contained in Article 2 of the Uniform Commercial Code ("UCC"). Article 2 has adopted much of the common law of contracts, but where the common law and Article 2 differ, Article 2 prevails in a contract for the sale of goods.

1. "Sale" Defined

A sale is a contract in which title to *goods* passes from the seller to the buyer for a price. [UCC §2-106(1)]

2. "Goods" Defined

Article 2 defines "goods" as all *things movable* at the time they are identified as the items to be sold under the contract. [UCC §2-105(1)] Thus, Article 2 applies to sales of most tangible things (e.g., cars, horses, hamburgers), but does not apply to the sale of real estate, services (e.g., a health club membership), or intangibles (e.g., a patent), or to construction contracts. Goods associated with real estate (e.g., minerals, growing crops and uncut timber, and fixtures removed from the land) *may* fall under Article 2 under certain circumstances.

3. Contracts Involving Goods and Nongoods

If a sale involves both goods and services (e.g., a contract to paint a portrait), a court will determine which aspect is dominant and apply the law governing that aspect to the whole contract. However, if the contract divides payment between goods and services, then Article 2 will apply to the sale portion and the common law will apply to the services portion.

4. Merchants vs. Nonmerchants

A number of the rules in Article 2 depend on whether the seller and/or buyer are merchants. Article 2 generally defines "merchant" as one who regularly deals in goods of the kind sold or who otherwise by his occupation holds himself out as having knowledge or skill peculiar to the practices or goods involved. [UCC §2-104(1)] For many of the Article 2 provisions dealing with general business practices (e.g., Statute of Frauds, confirmatory memos, firm offers, modification), almost anyone in business can be deemed a merchant because they have knowledge of the business practices. However, a few Article 2 provisions (e.g., the implied warranty of merchantability) are narrower and require a person to be a merchant with respect to goods of the kind being sold. To be subject to any of the merchant rules, the merchant must be acting in his mercantile capacity; i.e., he must be acting in his business, rather than personal, capacity.

Example: Martha sells computers for Acme Corp. On Monday, Martha places Acme Corp.'s annual coffee order with the coffee service. Later that day, she offers to sell her car to her neighbor for $5,000. Martha is a merchant with respect to the coffee order, but she is not a merchant with respect to the offer to sell her car. In the first instance, she is acting in her mercantile capacity (i.e., as part of her business). In the second, she is engaging in a transaction in her personal life.

5. Good Faith and Fair Dealing
Every contract within the UCC imposes an obligation of good faith in its performance and enforcement. [UCC §1-304] The UCC's definition of "good faith" is honesty in fact and the observance of reasonable commercial standards. [UCC §1-201(20)] The common law also imposes a duty of good faith and fair dealing on each party to a contract with respect to performance and enforcement. A breach of this duty is a question of fact, but it usually involves exercising discretion in a way that deprives the other party of the fruits of the contract.

Example: Pursuant to a written contract giving both parties the power terminate the contract without cause, CarCo employs Sam to sell cars on commission, with the commission to be paid when the customers take delivery of their cars. One month, Sam earned $100,000 in potential commissions, with the bulk of his customers taking delivery at the end of the month. To avoid paying the commissions, CarCo terminated Sam's employment on the 28th of the month. Although CarCo was within its contractual rights in terminating Sam, it was acting in bad faith. CarCo terminated the employment to escape paying money that was rightfully due. Thus, Sam is entitled to recover the commission [*See* Fortune v. National Cash Register, 373 Mass. 96 (1977)]

C. TYPES OF CONTRACTS

1. As to Formation
Contracts are frequently described as express, implied, or quasi. Only the first two are actually contracts, and they differ only in the manner in which they are formed.

a. Express Contract
Express contracts are formed *by language*, oral or written.

b. Implied in Fact Contract
Implied contracts are formed by manifestations of assent other than oral or written language, i.e., *by conduct* (e.g., if a person sits in a barber's chair and the barber cuts his hair, a contract has been formed by the parties' conduct).

c. Quasi-Contract or Implied in Law Contract
Quasi-contracts are *not contracts* at all. They are constructed by courts to *avoid unjust enrichment* by permitting the plaintiff to bring an action in restitution to recover the amount of the benefit conferred on the defendant. (*See* VIII.C., *infra.*) Their only relationship to genuine contracts is historical.

2. As to Acceptance

a. Bilateral Contracts—Exchange of Mutual Promises
The traditional bilateral contract is one consisting of the exchange of mutual promises, i.e., a promise for a promise, in which each party is both a promisor and a promisee.

Example: Sidney promises to sell Blackacre to Bertram for $6,000, and Bertram promises to purchase Blackacre at that price.

b. Unilateral Contracts—Acceptance by Performance
The traditional unilateral contract is one in which the offeror requests performance rather than a promise. Here, the offeror-promisor promises to pay upon the *completion of the requested act* by the promisee. Once the act is completed, a contract is formed. In such contracts, there is one promisor and one promisee.
Example: Susan promises to pay Charles $5 if he will deliver a textbook to Rick. Charles is not obligated to deliver the book, but if he does in fact deliver it, Susan is obligated to pay him the $5.

c. Modern View—Most Contracts Are Bilateral

1) Acceptance by Promise or Start of Performance
Under Article 2 and the Restatement (Second) of Contracts, unless clearly indicated otherwise by the language or circumstances, *all* offers are "indifferent" offers, which means that they may be accepted by promising or beginning performance. (*See* II.D.3.b., *infra*.)
Example: Acme Co. orders specifically manufactured goods from Barnes Manufacturing Co. Recognizing the speed with which the order must be filled, Barnes begins to manufacture the ordered item shortly after the order is received. This constitutes an acceptance of the offer if Barnes gives Acme notice of its beginning of performance within a reasonable time, and it creates an implied promise on the part of Barnes to complete manufacture.

2) Unilateral Contracts Limited to Two Circumstances
Under Article 2 and the Second Restatement, a traditional unilateral contract (i.e., a contract that can be formed only by full performance) occurs in only two situations: (i) where the offeror clearly (unambiguously) indicates that *completion of performance is the only manner of acceptance*—the offeror is the master of the offer and may create the offer in this fashion; and (ii) where there is an *offer to the public*, such as a reward offer, which so clearly contemplates acceptance by performance rather than a promise (not to mention the total ineffectiveness of a promise in such a situation) that only the performance requested in the offer will manifest acceptance.

3. As to Validity

a. Void Contract
A void contract is one that is totally *without any legal effect* from the beginning (e.g., an agreement to commit a crime). It *cannot be enforced by either party*.

b. Voidable Contract
A voidable contract is one that one or both parties may *elect to avoid* (e.g., by raising a defense that makes it voidable, such as infancy or mental illness).

c. **Unenforceable Contract**
An unenforceable contract is an agreement that is otherwise valid but which may not be enforceable due to *various defenses* extraneous to contract formation, such as the statute of limitations or Statute of Frauds.

D. CREATION OF A CONTRACT

When a suit is brought in which one party seeks to enforce a contract or to obtain damages for breach of contract, a court must first decide whether there was in fact a contract. In making this determination, a court will ask the following three basic questions:

1. Was there *mutual assent*?

2. Was there *consideration* or some substitute for consideration?

3. Are there any *defenses* to creation of the contract?

II. MUTUAL ASSENT—OFFER AND ACCEPTANCE

A. IN GENERAL

Mutual assent is often said to be an agreement on the "same bargain at the same time"—"a meeting of the minds." The process by which parties reach this meeting of the minds generally is some form of negotiation, during which, at some point, one party makes a proposal (an offer) and the other agrees to it (an acceptance). An actual subjective meeting of the minds is not necessary. Rather, courts use an *objective measure*, by which each party is bound to the *apparent intention* that he manifested to the other(s).

B. THE OFFER

An offer creates a power of acceptance in the offeree and a corresponding liability on the part of the offeror. For a communication to be an offer, it must create a *reasonable expectation* in the offeree that the offeror is willing to enter into a contract on the basis of the offered terms. In deciding whether a communication creates this reasonable expectation, you should ask the following three questions:

(i) Was there an expression of a *promise, undertaking, or commitment* to enter into a contract?

(ii) Were there *certainty and definiteness* in the essential terms?

(iii) Was there *communication* of the above to the offeree?

1. Promise, Undertaking, or Commitment

For a communication to be an offer, it must contain a promise, undertaking, or commitment to enter into a contract, rather than a mere invitation to begin preliminary negotiations; i.e., there must be an *intent* to enter into a contract. The criteria used to determine whether a communication is an offer include the following:

a. Language

The language used may show that an offer was or was not intended. Technical language such as "I offer" or "I promise" is useful to show that an offer was made, but it is not necessary. Also, certain language is generally construed as merely contemplating an invitation to deal, preliminary negotiations, or "feelers," rather than being an offer. This includes phrases such as "I quote," "I am asking $30 for," and "I would consider selling for." No mechanical formula is available. For example, price quotes, which are generally considered invitations to deal, can be offers if made in response to an inquiry that contains a quantity term.

b. **Surrounding Circumstances**
The circumstances surrounding the language will be considered by courts in determining whether an offer exists. For example, where the statement is made in jest, anger, or by way of bragging, and the statement is reasonably understood in this context, it will have no legal effect. However, where the statement is subjectively intended to be in jest but reasonably understood by the hearer to have been made seriously, the statement is an offer because it is interpreted objectively (i.e., according to a reasonable person's expectations).

c. **Prior Practice and Relationship of the Parties**
In determining whether certain remarks constitute an offer rather than preliminary negotiations, a court will look to the prior relationship and practice of the parties involved.

d. **Method of Communication**

1) **Use of Broad Communications Media**
The broader the communicating media (e.g., publications), the more likely it is that the courts will view the communication as merely the *solicitation of an offer*. (Note that there is an exception as to reward offers.)

2) **Advertisements, Etc.**
Advertisements, catalogs, circular letters, and the like containing price quotations are *usually* construed as mere *invitations for offers*. They are announcements of prices at which the seller is willing to receive offers. Typically, these are not considered offers because they usually are indefinite as to quantity and other terms, and addressed to the general public. If an advertisement addressed to the general public were considered an offer, it might be overaccepted; i.e., the number of acceptances may exceed the number of items for sale. However, in certain situations, courts have treated advertisements as offers if the language of the advertisement can be construed as containing a promise, the terms are certain and definite, and the offeree(s) is clearly identified. Price quotations also may be considered offers if given in response to an inquiry.
Example: Defendant store advertised a particular coat worth $140 for $1 on a "first come, first served" basis. *Held:* Valid offer to first person accepting on this basis as nothing was left open for negotiation.

e. **Industry Custom**
The courts will also look to generally accepted custom in the industry in determining whether the proposal qualifies as an offer.

2. Definite and Certain Terms

An offer must be definite and certain in its terms. The basic inquiry is whether enough of the essential terms have been provided so that a contract including them would be *capable of being enforced*. The principle is that the parties make their own contract; the courts do not make it for them. What is essential for the requisite certainty in an offer depends on the kind of contract contemplated. Typically, the following are important: (i) the *identity of the offeree*; (ii) the *subject matter*; and (iii) the *price* to be paid. However, a promise generally will be enforceable even if it does not spell out every material term, as long as it contains some *objective standard* for the court to use to supply the missing terms. (*See* b.2), *infra.*)

a. Identification of the Offeree

To be considered an offer, a statement must sufficiently identify the offeree or a class to which she belongs to justify the inference that the offeror intended to create a power of acceptance.

Examples: 1) In the example above with the $140 coat selling for $1, the "first come, first served" language eliminates any identification problem.

2) Harvey promises a reward to the person who captures a wanted fugitive. Although the offeree is unidentified and indeed unidentifiable at the time the offer is made, the performance of the requested act constitutes both an identification of the offeree and an acceptance.

b. Definiteness of Subject Matter

The subject matter of the deal must be certain, because a court can enforce a promise only if it can tell with reasonable accuracy what the promise is.

1) Requirements for Specific Types of Contracts

a) Real Estate Transactions—Land and Price Terms Required

An offer involving realty must identify the *land* and the *price* terms. The land must be identified with some particularity but a deed description is not required (e.g., "my house in Erewhon" is sufficient if the seller has only one house in Erewhon). Most courts will *not* supply a missing price term.

b) Sale of Goods—Quantity Term Required

In a contract for the sale of goods, the *quantity* being offered must be certain or capable of being made certain.

(1) "Requirements" and "Output" Contracts

In a requirements contract, a buyer promises to buy from a certain seller all of the goods the buyer requires, and the seller agrees to sell that amount to the buyer. In an output contract, a seller promises to sell to a certain buyer all of the goods the seller produces, and the buyer agrees to buy that amount from the seller. Although no specific quantity is mentioned in offers to make these contracts, the offers are sufficiently definite because the quantity is *capable* of being made certain by reference to objective, extrinsic facts (i.e., the buyer's actual requirements or the seller's actual output).

(a) **Quantity Cannot Be Unreasonably Disproportionate**
It is assumed that the parties will act in good faith; hence, there may not be a tender of or a demand for a quantity *unreasonably disproportionate* to (i) any stated estimate, or in the absence of a stated estimate (ii) any normal or otherwise comparable prior output or requirements.

(b) **Established Business vs. New Business**
A number of courts have sometimes refused to enforce such agreements if the promisor did not have an established business. The courts in these cases reason that, due to the lack of any basis for estimating quantity, the agreement is illusory or the damages too speculative. Article 2 avoids this problem by reading a "good faith" agreement into the contract; i.e., the promisor must operate his plant or conduct his business in good faith and according to commercial standards of fair dealing in the trade so that his output or requirements will approximate a reasonably foreseeable figure.

(2) **Reasonable Range of Choices**
An offer allowing a person to specify an item within a reasonable range of choices may be sufficiently definite to result in a contract if accepted.
Example: Seller states to Buyer: "I will sell you any of these motorcycles for $1,000. Pick one." These words will result in a contract when Buyer's choice is made and manifested.

c) **Employment and Other Services**
In contracts for employment, if the *duration* of the employment is not specified, the offer, if accepted, is construed as creating a contract terminable at the will of either party. For other services, the *nature of the work* to be performed must be included in the offer.

2) **Missing Terms**
The fact that one or more terms are left open does *not prevent the formation* of a contract if it appears the parties *intended to make a contract* and there is a *reasonably certain basis* for giving a remedy. In such a case, the majority of jurisdictions and Article 2 hold that the *court can supply reasonable terms* for those that are missing. [*See* UCC §§2-204, 2-305] These terms will be supplied, however, only where they are consistent with the parties' intent as otherwise expressed. Note that the more terms the parties leave open, the less likely it is that they intended to enter into a binding agreement.

a) **Price**
Except in contracts for real property, the failure to state the price does not prevent the formation of a contract if the parties intended to form a contract without the price being settled. For example, if parties enter into a contract for services and the price is not included in the offer, a court might imply the service provider's usual price for the services, the normal price for such services in the area, etc.

(1) Article 2 Gap Filler

Article 2 includes some very specific "gap fillers" for situations where certain terms are not included in a contract for the sale of goods. Under Article 2, the price will be a *reasonable price at the time of delivery* if:

(i) Nothing is said as to price;

(ii) The price is left to be agreed to by the parties and they fail to agree; or

(iii) The price is to be fixed by some external factor or third party and it is not so set.

[UCC §2-305(1)]

(2) Price Fixed by Party Under Article 2

Under Article 2, a contract will be formed even if the parties agree that one of the parties will fix the price in the future (e.g., "price to be set by seller at time of delivery"). However, the party to whom the contract gives the right to fix the price must act in *good faith*. If that party does not fix the price in good faith, the other party may either cancel the contract or fix a reasonable price herself. [UCC §2-305(3)]

b) Time

If an agreement does not specify the time in which an act is to be performed, the law implies that it is to be performed *within a reasonable time*.

3) Distinguish—Vague Terms

If a material term is vague or ambiguous, it is not an offer at common law or under the UCC. The presumption that the parties' intent was to include a reasonable term goes to supplying *missing* terms. However, the presumption *cannot* be made if the parties have *included* a term that makes the contract too vague to be enforced. The problem then is that the parties have manifested an intent that cannot be determined.

Examples: 1) An agreement to divide profits "on a liberal basis" is too vague to be enforced.

2) An agreement to purchase a parcel of land for "$8,000 or less" is also too vague.

a) Vagueness Can Be Cured by Part Performance

Where part performance supplies the needed clarification of the terms, it can be used to cure vagueness.

b) Uncertainty Can Be Cured by Acceptance

If uncertainty results because the offeree is given a choice of alternative performances, the offer becomes definite when the offeree communicates her choice. (*See* previous example about choice of motorcycle for $1,000.)

c) **Focus on Contract**
In short, the **contract** (as distinguished from the offer) must be definite and certain in its terms—hence, even if the offer lacks certainty, the problem can be cured if there is some way in which the offer is capable of being made certain, e.g., by part performance or acceptance.

4) **Terms to Be Agreed on Later**
Often, an offer will state that some term is to be agreed on at a future date. If the term is a **material** term, the offer is **too uncertain**. The courts will not supply a reasonable term, as the parties have provided otherwise. However, as discussed above, Article 2 permits a reasonable **price** term to be supplied by the court under these circumstances if the other evidence indicates that the parties intended to form a contract.

3. **Communication to Offeree**
To have the power to accept, the offeree must have **knowledge** of the offer. Therefore, the proposal must be communicated to her.

Example: Chauncey returned Bowater's lost briefcase unaware that Bowater had placed an advertisement offering a $20 reward for its return. Because the offer had not been communicated to Chauncey, there could not be mutual assent. Hence, there is no contract.

C. TERMINATION OF OFFER
The power of acceptance created by an offer ends when the offer is terminated. The mutual assent requirement obviously cannot be met where the termination occurs before acceptance is effective. Thus, you must establish whether the offer has been terminated, and if so, in what fashion.

1. **Termination by Acts of Parties**

a. **Termination by Offeror—Revocation**
A revocation is the retraction of an offer by the offeror. A revocation terminates the offeree's power of acceptance if it is communicated to her **before she accepts**.

1) **Methods of Communication**

a) **Revocation by Direct Communication**
Revocation directly communicated to the offeree by the offeror terminates the offer.

(1) **Revocation by Publication**
Offers made by publication may be terminated by publication of revocation **through comparable means**.
Example: An offer published in *The New York Times* may be revoked by publication in *The New York Times*. It may not be revoked by publication in *Reader's Digest* or by a TV spot.

b) **Revocation by Indirect Communication**
The offer may be effectively terminated if the offeree **indirectly** receives: (i)

correct information, (ii) from a reliable source, (iii) of acts of the offeror that would indicate to a reasonable person that the offeror no longer wishes to make the offer.

Example: Offeree, before attempting to accept Offeror's offer to sell Greenacre, was informed by a reliable third party that Offeror had sold Greenacre to another. *Held:* Offeror revoked the offer.

2) Effective When Received

A revocation is generally effective when *received* by the offeree. Where revocation is by publication, it is effective when *published.*

a) When a Communication Is Received

At common law, a written communication is considered to have been "received" when it comes into the possession of the person addressed (or of someone authorized by him to receive it) or when it is deposited in some place authorized as the place for this or similar communications to be deposited. [Restatement (Second) of Contracts §68] The communication *need not be read* by the recipient to be effective. Similarly, under the UCC, a person receives notice when (i) it comes to his attention, or (ii) it is delivered at a place of business through which the contract was made or another location held out by that person as the place for receipt of such communications. An organization receives a communication at the time it is brought (or should have been brought) to the attention of the individual conducting the transaction. [UCC §1-202] Note that these rules do not restrict the communication or notice to a writing; thus, courts will likely apply the same rules to phone messages.

3) Limitations on Offeror's Power to Revoke

Offers can be revoked at will by the offeror, even if he has promised not to revoke for a certain period, except under certain situations where the offeror's power to terminate the offer is limited.

a) Options

An option is a distinct contract in which the *offeree gives consideration* for a promise by the offeror not to revoke an outstanding offer.

Example: An offeror offers to sell her farm—Blackacre—to an offeree for $1 million and promises to keep the offer open for 90 days if the offeree pays the offeror $1,000 to keep the offer open. If the offeree pays the offeror the $1,000, an option contract is formed and the offeror must keep the offer open for 90 days.

Compare: An offeror offers to sell her farm—Blackacre—to an offeree for $1 million and promises to keep the offer open for 90 days. Because there is no consideration (*see infra*) to make enforceable the promise to keep the offer open, the offeror may terminate her offer at any time despite her promise.

(1) Timely Acceptance Under Option Contract

An offer must be accepted within the time specified or, if no time is specified, within a reasonable time. Often, an option contract specifies that the offer must be accepted within the option period; i.e., the offer terminates when the option expires. In the absence of specific language stating when the offer terminates, the power of acceptance arguably survives the option period, but courts often treat the option period as the offer period so that at the end of that time, the option expires and the offer lapses.

Example: As in the above example, a farmer offers to sell her farm to a buyer for $1 million and promises to keep the offer open for 90 days if the buyer pays $1,000 to keep the offer open. The buyer pays the $1,000 but does not buy the farm during the 90-day period. On the 92nd day, the farmer sells the farm to someone else. Most courts would find that the option holder can no longer accept the offer, even if the farmer has not revoked it. The option period and offer period are treated as one and the same.

b) Merchant's Firm Offer Under Article 2

Under Article 2, there are circumstances in which a promise to keep an offer open is enforceable even if no consideration has been paid to keep the offer open. Under Article 2:

(i) If a *merchant*;

(ii) Offers to buy or sell goods in a *signed writing*; and

(iii) The writing *gives assurances that it will be held open* (e.g., "this offer will be held open for 10 days," "this offer is firm for 10 days," "I shall not revoke this offer for 10 days");

(iv) The offer *is not revocable* for lack of consideration during the time stated, or if no time is stated, for a reasonable time (but in no event may such period exceed *three months*).

[UCC §2-205] *Note:* As with the Statute of Frauds requirements (IV.F., *infra*), the signed writing requirement for a merchant's firm offer may be satisfied by an electronic record (e.g., e-mail, fax) and an electronic signature. [*See* Uniform Electronic Transactions Act §7 (1999)]

(1) Form Supplied by Offeree

If the term assuring that the offer will be held open is on a form supplied by the offeree, it must be separately signed by the offeror. [UCC §2-205]

c) Detrimental Reliance

Where the offeror could reasonably expect that the offeree would rely to her detriment on the offer, and the offeree does so rely, the offer will be held *irrevocable as an option contract for a reasonable length of time*. [Restatement (Second) of Contracts §87] The case law indicates that this may be limited to those situations in which the offeror would *reasonably contemplate reliance* by the offeree in *using the offer before it is accepted*.

Example: A general contractor solicited bids from various subcontractors before making its own irrevocable offer on a construction project. For the subcontractor to be held to its offer, the subcontractor must reasonably have foreseen the possible use of its subcontracting bid in the making of the general contractor's irrevocable offer.

d) Beginning Performance in Response to True Unilateral Contract Offer

An offer for a true unilateral contract becomes *irrevocable once performance has begun.* Note that the unilateral contract will not be formed until the total act is complete. However, once the offeree begins to perform, she is given a *reasonable time to complete performance*, during which time the offer is irrevocable. Note also that the offeree is *not bound* to complete performance—she may withdraw at any time prior to completion of performance.

Example: Matt offers to pay Lisa $1,000 if she will paint his house, insisting that the acceptance occur only by the act of painting the house rather than through Lisa's promise. Lisa begins to paint the house. Matt attempts to revoke the offer. Matt's attempt at revocation is ineffective because Lisa must have a reasonable time in which to complete the act of painting. If Matt refuses to allow Lisa to continue to paint, Matt will be in breach of contract and will be liable for damages.

(1) Preparations to Perform

The rules limiting the offeror's power to revoke an offer for a unilateral contract apply only if the offeree has *embarked* on performance. They do not apply when the offeree is only *preparing* to perform. Note, however, that substantial preparations to perform *may constitute detrimental reliance* sufficient to make the offeror's promise binding to the extent of the detrimental reliance. [Restatement (Second) of Contracts §§45, 87, 90]

Example: Matt offers to pay Lisa $1,000 if she will paint his house, insisting that the acceptance occur only by the act of painting. Lisa immediately drives to the local hardware store; expends $100 purchasing paint brushes, drop cloths, and masking tape to enable her to paint the house; and returns. On her return, Matt tells Lisa that he has changed his mind and does not want his house painted after all. Matt's revocation of his offer is valid because Lisa's acts did not constitute the beginning of performance, but rather were merely done in preparation to perform. However, Lisa will have an action against Matt to recover the $100 she spent in detrimental reliance on his offer.

(2) Offeror Refuses to Accept Performance
What happens if performance is tendered by the offeree but refused by the offeror? If the offeror's cooperation is necessary for performance, his withholding of it upon the tender of performance is the equivalent of commencing performance. [Restatement (Second) of Contracts §45]

e) Beginning Performance—Offer Indifferent as to Manner of Acceptance
As noted above, most offers are indifferent as to the manner of acceptance, and, thus, a bilateral contract may be formed ***upon the start of performance*** by the offeree. (*See* I.C.2.c.1), *supra.*) Therefore, once the offeree ***begins performance,*** the contract is complete and ***revocation*** becomes ***impossible.*** *But note:* Notification of the start of performance may be necessary. (*See* D.3.b., *infra.*)

b. Termination by Offeree

1) Rejection

a) Express Rejection
An express rejection is a statement by the offeree that she does not intend to accept the offer. Such a rejection will terminate the offer. [Restatement (Second) of Contracts §36]

b) Counteroffer as Rejection
A counteroffer is an offer made by the ***offeree*** to the offeror that contains the same subject matter as the original offer but differs in its terms. A counteroffer serves as a rejection of the original offer ***as well as a new offer.*** [Restatement (Second) of Contracts §39] This usually happens in two situations:

(i) Counteroffer combined with express rejection, e.g., "Not at that price, but I'll take it at $200."

(ii) Acceptance conditional upon additional terms, e.g., "I'll take it at that price, but only if it is also equipped with air conditioning."

Note: Article 2 provides for exceptions to the above general treatment in the "battle of forms" provision. (*See* D.5.b., *infra.*)

(1) Distinguish—Mere Inquiry
Distinguish between a counteroffer (which constitutes a rejection) and a mere inquiry. An inquiry will not terminate the offer when it is consistent with the idea that the offeree is still keeping the original proposal under consideration. The test is whether a ***reasonable person*** would believe that the original offer had been rejected.
Examples: 1) The offeree says to the offeror, "Would you consider lowering your price by $5,000?" This, without more, is merely an inquiry, not a rejection.

2) The offeree says to the offeror, "I couldn't possibly pay your asking price but could pay $5,000 less." This is more than a mere inquiry because of the certitude involved and will be treated as a counteroffer.

c) Effective When Received
A rejection is effective when *received* by the offeror.

d) Revival of Offer
If an offer is rejected, the offeror may restate the same offer and create a new power of acceptance. Some courts refer to this as the revival of the original offer. It is more precise to suggest that a new offer, although the same as the original offer, has been made.

e) Rejection of Option
Because an option is a contract to keep an offer open, a rejection of or a counteroffer to an option does *not* constitute a termination of the offer. The offeree is still free to accept the original offer within the option period unless the offeror has *detrimentally relied* on the offeree's rejection. [Restatement (Second) of Contracts §37]

2) Lapse of Time

a) Must Accept Within Specified or Reasonable Time
The offeree must accept the offer within the time period specified or, if no time period is specified, within a reasonable time. If she does not do so, then she will have allowed the offer to terminate. (*Note:* Where the offer's terms are unclear as to time, e.g., "by return mail," the time limit is what a reasonable person in the offeree's position would have assumed.)

b) Look to When Offer Is Received by Offeree
If the offer provides that it will expire within a particular time period, that period commences when the offer is received by the offeree. If the offer is delayed in transmission and this fact *is or should have been apparent to the offeree*, the offer terminates at the time it would have expired had there been no delay. All relevant facts must be considered in determining whether this knowledge is present. These include, e.g., date of letter, postmark, and any subsequent statements made by the offeror.

2. Termination by Operation of Law

a. Termination by Death or Insanity of Parties
If either of the parties dies or is adjudicated insane prior to acceptance, the offer is terminated. It is *not* necessary that the death or insanity be *communicated* to the other party. [Restatement (Second) of Contracts §48] (*Compare:* Supervening mental incapacity of the offeror without an adjudication of incapacity will terminate an offer only if the offeree is aware of the incapacity.) Note, however, that the offer will *not* terminate in this fashion if the rules limiting an offeror's power to terminate are applicable (e.g., an option contract).

b.   Termination by Destruction of Subject Matter
Destruction of the subject matter terminates the offeree's power of acceptance.
[Restatement (Second) of Contracts §36]

c.   Termination by Supervening Legal Prohibition of Proposed Contract
If the subject matter of the proposed contract becomes illegal, the offer will terminate.
[Restatement (Second) of Contracts §36]
Example: Lucky Lou offers Vegas Vernon a share in his casino business. Prior to acceptance, a law is passed banning casinos. The offer is automatically terminated.

D.   THE ACCEPTANCE
An acceptance is a manifestation of assent to the terms of an offer. Through this manifestation of assent, the offeree exercises the power given her by the offeror to create a contract.

1.   Who May Accept

a.   Party to Whom Offer Is Addressed or Directed
Generally, only the person to whom an offer is addressed has the power of acceptance. This is so even if the offer does not call for personal performance or special financial responsibility on the part of the offeree. One may also have the power of acceptance if she is a member of a class to which an offer has been directed. If the offer is made to the general public, anyone may qualify as an offeree. If the offer requests performance from an unlimited number of persons, performance by anyone knowing of the offer will cut off the power of every other person to accept, provided that the offeror desires only one performance and there is no indication that he is willing to pay more than once.

b.   Offeree's Power of Acceptance Cannot Be Assigned
Unlike rights under an existing contract, the offeree's power of acceptance ***cannot be assigned***.

1)   Exception—Option Contracts
An exception exists for the right to accept under an option contract, because the power to accept is itself a contract right in these contracts, and contract rights generally are assignable (*see* IX.C.1.b., *infra*).

2.   Offeree Must Know of Offer
The offeree must know of the offer in order to accept, and this is true whether the offer is for a bilateral or unilateral contract.
Examples: 1) Alex sends Becky a letter offering to sell her Blackacre for $500,000. That same day, without knowledge of Alex's letter, Becky sends Alex a letter offering to buy Blackacre from him for $500,000. No contract is formed because neither party knew of the other's letter when sending his or her own letter.

2) Cindy offers to pay $1,000 to the person who finds her missing dog. Dee finds a dog in her yard, reads its tags, and returns the dog to Cindy without knowledge of Cindy's offer. Most courts hold that no contract is formed here.

3. **Acceptance of Offer for Unilateral Contract**

If an offer provides that it may be accepted only by performance (i.e., an offer for a unilateral contract), note the following particular rules.

a. **Completion of Performance**

Most courts hold that an offer to form a unilateral contract is not accepted until performance is completed. The beginning of performance may create an option so that the offer is irrevocable. (*See* C.1.a.3)d), *supra.*) However, the offeree is not obligated to complete performance merely because he has begun performance, as only complete performance constitutes an acceptance of the offer.

b. **Notice**

Generally, the offeree is ***not*** required to give the offeror notice that he has begun the requested performance, but is required to notify the offeror within a reasonable time after performance has been completed. If a required notice is not given, a contract is formed, but the offeror's duties are discharged for failure of an implied condition subsequent (*see* VI.D.2.c., *infra*). However, no notice is required if:

(i) The offeror ***waived notice***; or

(ii) The offeree's ***performance would normally come to the offeror's attention*** within a reasonable time.

Example: Joe tells Susan he will pay her $1,000 if she paints the house that he is living in. Susan need not formally notify Joe that she has painted his house, as her performance would be obvious to him.

Compare: In writing, Joe tells Susan that if she lends Tina $1,000 for one year, he will repay the loan if Tina fails to pay. Joe becomes contractually bound on his promise the instant Susan loans Tina the money, but Joe will be discharged from this contractual obligation unless Susan notifies him of her acceptance (i.e., her making the loan to Tina) within a reasonable time.

1) **Compare—Article 2**

Article 2 has a slightly different rule regarding notice, although the end result is basically the same. It provides that when a contract is accepted by the beginning of performance, if the offeree fails to notify the offeror of the acceptance (i.e., the ***beginning*** of performance rather than the completion of performance) within a reasonable time, the offeror may treat the offer as having ***lapsed before acceptance*** (i.e., no contract was ever formed, as opposed to the Restatement view that a contract was formed but performance is excused by failure of a condition). [UCC §2-206(2)]

4. **Acceptance of Offer for Bilateral Contract**

Recall that unless an offer specifically provides that it may be accepted only through performance, it will be construed as an offer to enter into a bilateral contract and may be accepted either by a promise to perform or by the ***beginning of performance*** (compare offers for true unilateral contracts, which may be accepted only by full performance).

a. Generally, Acceptance Must Be Communicated

Generally, acceptance of an offer to enter into a bilateral contract must be communicated to the offeror.

1) Exception—Waiver in Offer

If an offer provides that acceptance need not be communicated, then no communication of the acceptance is required.

Example: Alex applies for life insurance on a form that provides that the policy will become effective immediately upon approval by the insurance company's home office. The insurance contract is formed when the home office approves Alex's application.

2) Silence as Acceptance

Although the offeree cannot be forced to speak under penalty of having her silence treated as an acceptance, if the offeree silently takes offered benefits, the courts will often find an acceptance. This is especially true if prior dealings between the parties, or trade practices known to both, create a commercially reasonable expectation by the offeror that silence represents an acceptance. In such a case, the offeree is under a duty to notify the offeror if she does not intend to accept. [Restatement (Second) of Contracts §69]

a) Offered Services

When the recipient of services knows or has reason to know that the services are being rendered with the expectation of compensation and *by a word* could prevent the mistake, he may be held to have accepted the offer if he fails to speak. [*See* Restatement (Second) of Contracts §69, comment b]

Example: At Homeowner's request, Landscaper prepared a proposal for planting trees in Homeowner's yard. Homeowner stated that of the trees proposed she preferred beech trees. As beech trees were in short supply, Landscaper said he would check the availability and get back to her. Landscaper e-mailed Homeowner that he had secured the beech trees and would need to plant them within the week as a hard freeze was coming. Landscaper stated that if he did not hear back, he was going ahead with the planting. Homeowner read the e-mail but did not respond. Just in advance of the freeze, Landscaper planted the trees. Homeowner watched the work from her window. When it was done, Homeowner refused to pay, arguing there was no contract. Because Homeowner knew that Landscaper was rendering services with the expectation of payment and Homeowner, by a word, could have prevented the mistake, she will be held to have accepted the offer.

b. Method of Acceptance

Unless otherwise provided, an offer is construed as inviting acceptance in *any reasonable manner* and by any medium reasonable under the circumstances. Any objective manifestation of the offeree's counterpromise is usually sufficient.

Example: Nikki **telephones** an offer to Skip that is to remain open for five days. Two days later, Skip **e-mails** an acceptance, or two days later Skip **mails** an acceptance. Whether there has been a proper acceptance depends on whether the use of e-mail or mail was reasonable under the circumstances.

1) Act as an Acceptance
The offeror is the master of her offer and may require an act to signify acceptance.

Example: Jennifer offers to purchase Steve's car for $1,000, specifying that Steve accept the offer by wearing a yellow shirt to lunch next Tuesday. Steve can accept the offer only by acting as requested. If Steve simply tenders the automobile, most courts would construe the tender as a rejection and counteroffer. Also, recall that Steve must know of the offer to accept. If he simply wears a yellow shirt without knowing of Jennifer's offer, there is no acceptance and no bilateral contract.

2) Offers to Buy Goods for Current or Prompt Shipment
Under Article 2, an offer to buy goods for current or prompt shipment is construed as inviting acceptance either by a **promise to ship** or by **current or prompt shipment** of conforming or nonconforming goods. (*See* 5.a., *infra.*)

c. Acceptance Must Be Unequivocal
Traditional contract law insisted on an absolute and unequivocal acceptance of each and every term of the offer (the "mirror image rule"). At common law, any different or additional terms in the acceptance make the response a **rejection and counteroffer**.

Example: Adam offers to lease a warehouse to Jamie by handing Jamie a signed copy of his standard lease agreement. Jamie reads over the lease, adds a clause providing that disputes will be settled by arbitration, signs the lease, and hands it back to Adam. Adam hands the keys over to Jamie. By adding the arbitration clause to the lease, Jamie rejected Adam's offer and made a counteroffer. By handing Jamie the keys to the warehouse, Adam accepted Jamie's counteroffer.

1) Distinguish—Statements that Make Implicit Terms Explicit
Statements by the offeree that make implicit terms explicit do not prevent acceptance.

Example: The statement by an offeree, "I accept provided you convey marketable title," is a valid acceptance because the obligation to convey marketable title is implicit in the offer to sell.

2) Distinguish—"Grumbling Acceptance"
A "grumbling acceptance" (i.e., an acceptance accompanied by an expression of dissatisfaction) is an effective acceptance as long as it stops short of actual dissent.

Example: "I think it's highway robbery at that price, but I guess I'll have to accept" is a valid acceptance.

3) **Distinguish—Request for Clarification**
A request for clarification does not necessarily amount to a rejection and counter-offer.
Example: "The $1,000 price—that includes shipping, doesn't it?" is not a counteroffer.

5. Acceptance Under Article 2

a. Offers to Buy Goods for Current or Prompt Shipment
As noted above, an offer to buy goods for current or prompt shipment may be accepted by either a promise to ship or by a shipment of conforming or nonconforming goods.

1) **Shipment of Nonconforming Goods**
The shipment of nonconforming goods is an acceptance creating a bilateral contract as well as a *breach* of the contract unless the seller seasonably notifies the buyer that a shipment of nonconforming goods is offered only as an *accommodation*. The buyer is not required to accept accommodation goods and may reject them. If he does, the shipper is not in breach and may reclaim the accommodation goods, because her tender does not constitute an acceptance of the buyer's original offer.

Examples: 1) Craig orders 1,500 blue widgets from Susy. Susy ships 1,500 black widgets but does not notify Craig that the goods are offered only as an accommodation. Susy's shipment is both an acceptance of Craig's offer and a breach of the resulting contract. Craig may sue for any appropriate damages.

2) In the example above, Susy, before the goods arrive, notifies Craig that black widgets have been sent as an accommodation. The shipment is a counteroffer and, if Craig accepts delivery, there will be a contract for the purchase of black widgets.

3) Craig orders 1,500 blue widgets from Susy. Susy sends Craig an email promising to ship the widgets within two days. Upon checking her stock, Susy discovers that she has only 1,000 blue widgets. She ships the 1,000 blue widgets along with 500 black widgets and a letter explaining that the black widgets are offered only as an accommodation. Craig may sue for damages. Susy accepted Craig's order via email, promising to ship 1,500 blue widgets. This is not a case of acceptance by shipment.

b. Battle of the Forms

1) **Mirror Image Not Required**
Article 2 has abandoned the mirror image rule, providing instead that the proposal of additional or different terms by the offeree in a definite and timely acceptance does *not* constitute a rejection and counteroffer, but rather is *effective as an acceptance*, unless the acceptance is *expressly* made conditional on assent to the additional or different terms. (*See* 3), *infra*.)

Example: Harry sends Sally an e-mail offering to sell her his car for $1,000. Sally e-mails back, "I accept; deliver it to my house by noon tomorrow." At common law, no contract would be formed here because Sally's acceptance added a delivery term. Under Article 2, a contract is formed and whether or not Harry is required to deliver the car to Sally's house by noon of the next day is determined by the rules discussed below.

Compare: Same facts as above, but Sally's e-mail says, "I accept, but only if you agree to deliver the car to my house by noon tomorrow." No contract is formed here because Sally's acceptance was expressly conditioned on assent to the new terms.

2) Terms Included

a) Contracts Involving a Nonmerchant—Terms of Offer Govern

If any party to the contract is not a merchant, the additional or different terms are considered to be mere proposals to modify the contract that do ***not*** become part of the contract unless the offeror expressly agrees.

Example: Paul sends a letter offering to sell his car to Stephanie for $1,200. Stephanie sends Paul a letter stating: "I accept and want you to put new tires on it." This is a contract, but Paul is not bound to put new tires on the car.

b) Contracts Between Merchants—Additional Terms Usually Included

If *both* parties to the contract are merchants, ***additional*** terms in the acceptance will be included in the contract unless:

(i) They ***materially alter*** the original terms of the offer (e.g., they change a party's risk or the remedies available);

(ii) The offer ***expressly limits acceptance*** to the terms of the offer; or

(iii) The ***offeror has already objected*** to the particular terms, or ***objects within a reasonable time*** after notice of them is received.

Note: Whether an alteration is material is a fact question.

Example: Sellco emails an offer to sell to Buyco 1,500 widgets at $10 each. Buyco replies, "We accept, 5% discount for paying within 30 days." The parties have formed a contract and it probably includes a 5% discount for payment within 30 days (assuming that the discount is not material).

Compare: Buyco emails Sellco an order for 1,500 widgets at $10 each. Sellco replies, "We accept. Warranties are limited to the express warranties in these attached documents. These warranties are in lieu of the implied warranty of merchantability." The parties have formed a contract. However, the warranty disclaimer is a material alteration that will not be included in the terms of the contract.

(1) Note—Different Terms May or May Not Be Included

There is a split of authority over whether terms in the acceptance that are *different* from (as opposed to in addition to) the terms in the offer will become part of the contract. Some courts treat different terms like additional terms and follow the test set out above in determining whether the terms should be part of the contract. Many courts follow the *"knockout rule,"* under which conflicting terms in the offer and acceptance are knocked out of the contract because each party is assumed to object to the inclusion of such terms in the contract. Under the knockout rule, gaps left by knocked-out terms are filled by the UCC (e.g., when the date of delivery differs in the offer and the acceptance, the UCC provides that delivery must be made within a reasonable time). Even though it is possible for a contract to be formed despite the fact that the acceptance has different terms, there must still be a meeting of the minds. Differences between the offer and acceptance as to price, quantity, or quality indicate there is no meeting of the minds, and thus there is no contract.

Example: Sellco offers to sell to Buyco 1,500 widgets at $10 each *plus freight*. Buyco replies, "I accept. The price is $10.10 each *including freight*." There is a contract, assuming that the actual cost of freight is not materially different from $150, as the offer was to sell the widgets for $10 plus (actual) freight costs and the acceptance was to purchase the widgets at $10.10 each including freight costs (the extra 10¢ apparently being to cover freight costs). Under the approach treating different terms like additional terms, the buyer's acceptance will control (i.e., the buyer is obligated to pay $15,150 for the widgets and no additional freight charges) unless the seller objects. If the seller does object, there is a contract on the seller's original terms. However, under the knockout rule, the different freight terms will be knocked out. The price will be $10 plus the reasonable cost of freight at the time of delivery according to the UCC.

c) Merchant's Confirmatory Memo

A merchant's memo confirming an oral agreement (IV.F.3.f.2), *infra*) that contains different or additional terms is also subject to the battle of the forms provisions. [UCC §2-207(1)]

3) Effect of Conditional Acceptance

When an acceptance is made expressly conditional on the acceptance of new terms, it is a rejection of the offer. The conditional acceptance is essentially a new offer, and the original offeror may form a contract by expressly assenting to the new terms. However, the offer that results from a conditional acceptance cannot be accepted by performance. If the parties ship or accept goods after a conditional acceptance, a contract is formed by their conduct, and the new terms are not included. The contract consists of all terms on which their writings agree, plus supplementary terms supplied by the UCC. [UCC §2-207(1), (3)]

> *Example:* Same facts as the example in b.1) *supra*, except that after Sally's e-mail making her acceptance conditional on Harry's consent to the delivery term, Harry does not reply but delivers the car to Sally's house two days later. Sally accepts the delivery. Harry is not in breach because Sally's conditional acceptance was not a counter-offer that could be accepted by performance. When Sally conditioned her acceptance on consent to the delivery term, there was no contract. The contract was not formed until Harry delivered the car and Sally accepted it. The contract was formed by performance and its terms are those to which the parties agreed (i.e., $1,000 for the car) plus the terms supplied by their course of performance (delivery two days later at Sally's house) and the UCC.

c. Moment of Mutual Assent Uncertain

In situations in which it cannot be determined with certainty which specific communication was the offer and which the acceptance but the parties act as though there is a contract, the UCC considers this a binding contract even though the moment of its making is uncertain. [UCC §2-204(2)]

6. Bilateral Contracts Formed by Performance

Sometimes in business, a contract is not formed by the parties' communications, either because: (i) the mirror image rule has not been satisfied; or (ii) in a contract for the sale of goods, the original offeror's form contains a clause objecting in advance to any new or inconsistent term and the offeree sends a response with new or different terms that states it is not an acceptance unless the original offeror agrees to these terms. Clearly, no contract is formed at this point. But, as is sometimes the case, if the parties begin to perform as if they formed a contract, a contract is formed. *Rationale:* At common law, the last communication sent to the party who performed is considered a counteroffer and the performance is considered acceptance of the counteroffer. In contracts for the sale of goods, Article 2 specifically provides that conduct by both parties that recognizes the existence of a contract is sufficient to establish the contract. [UCC §2-207(3)]

7. When Acceptance Effective—The Mailbox Rule

Acceptance by mail or similar means creates a contract at the ***moment of dispatch***, provided that the mail is properly addressed and stamped, ***unless:***

(i) The ***offer stipulates*** that acceptance is not effective until received; or

(ii) An ***option contract*** is involved (an acceptance under an option contract is effective only upon ***receipt*** [Restatement (Second) of Contracts §63]).

Note: Because in most states a revocation is effective only upon receipt (*see* C.1.a.2), *supra*), under the mailbox rule if the offeree dispatches an acceptance ***before he receives a revocation*** sent by the offeror, a contract is formed. This is true even though the acceptance is dispatched after the revocation is dispatched and received after the revocation is received.

a. **Effect of Offeree Sending Both Acceptance and Rejection**

Because a rejection is effective only when received, an offeree sending both an acceptance and rejection could create problems for the offeror if the mailbox rule were applicable; e.g., a contract would be created when the acceptance was dispatched even if the offeror received the rejection and relied on it before receiving the acceptance.

1) **Offeree Sends Rejection, Then Acceptance—Mailbox Rule Does Not Apply**

If the offeree sends a rejection and then sends an acceptance, the mailbox rule does not apply. Whichever one is *received first* is effective.

2) **Offeree Sends Acceptance, Then Rejection—Mailbox Rule Generally Applies**

If the offeree sends the acceptance first, the mailbox rule applies; i.e., a contract is created upon dispatch of the acceptance. However, if the offeror received the rejection first and *changed his position in reliance* on it, the offeree will be *estopped* from enforcing the contract.

b. **Acceptance by Unauthorized Means**

An acceptance transmitted by unauthorized means or improperly transmitted by authorized means may still be *effective if it is actually received* by the offeror while the offer is still in existence.

Examples: 1) Bailey makes an offer to Janet specifying that acceptance should be by email. Janet mails Bailey her acceptance. The acceptance will not be effective upon dispatch of the letter but only upon receipt by Bailey, if the offer is still open.

2) Janet, in a situation where the mailbox rule otherwise applies, incorrectly addressed the envelope in mailing back the acceptance. It will be effective upon receipt if the offer is still open.

E. **AUCTION CONTRACTS**

The UCC contains some special rules regulating auction sales. [*See* UCC §2-328] They are:

1. **Goods Auctioned in Lots**

In a sale by auction, if goods are put up in lots, each lot is the subject of a separate sale.

2. **When Sale Is Complete**

A sale by auction is complete when the auctioneer so announces by the *fall of the hammer* or in another customary manner. Where a bid is made while the hammer is falling in acceptance of a prior bid, the auctioneer may, in his discretion, reopen the bidding or declare the goods sold under the bid on which the hammer was falling.

3. **Auction With Reserve or Without Reserve**

An auction sale is with reserve unless the goods are explicitly put up without reserve. "*With reserve*" means the *auctioneer may withdraw the goods* at any time until he announces completion of the sale. In an auction without reserve, once the auctioneer calls for bids on an article or lot, that article or lot cannot be withdrawn unless no bid is made within a reasonable time. In either case, a bidder may retract his bid until the auctioneer announces completion of the sale, but a bidder's retraction does not revive any previous bid.

4. A Bid on Seller's Behalf

Except at a forced sale, if the auctioneer knowingly receives a bid on the seller's behalf, or the seller makes or procures such a bid (in order to drive up the price of the goods), and notice has not been given that liberty for such bidding is reserved, the winning bidder may at his option avoid the sale or take the goods at the price of the *last good faith bid* prior to the completion of the sale.

III. CONSIDERATION

A. INTRODUCTION

The majority of agreements that qualify as legally enforceable contracts contain a bargained-for change in legal position between the parties, i.e., valuable consideration. While substitute doctrines may permit enforcement of an agreement, only the presence of *valuable consideration on both sides* of the bargain will make an executory bilateral contract fully enforceable from the moment of formation. Simply stated, consideration is the price for enforceability in the courts.

B. ELEMENTS OF CONSIDERATION

Basically, two elements are necessary to constitute consideration: (i) there must be a *bargained-for exchange* between the parties; and (ii) that which is bargained for must be considered of *legal value* or, as it is traditionally stated, it must constitute a benefit to the promisor *or* a detriment to the promisee. At the present time, the *detriment* element is emphasized in determining whether an exchange contains legal value.

Example: Jeff promises to sell his used television to Kristen for $100 in exchange for Kristen's promise to pay $100. Both elements of consideration are found in this example. First, Jeff's promise was bargained for. Jeff's promise induced a detriment in the promisee, Kristen. Kristen's detriment induced Jeff to make the promise. Second, both parties suffered detriments. The detriment to Jeff was the transfer of ownership of the television, and the detriment to Kristen was the payment of $100 to Jeff.

1. Bargained-For Exchange

This element of consideration requires that the promise induce the detriment *and* the detriment induce the promise (*see* preceding example). Unless both of these elements are present, the "bargained-for exchange" element of consideration is not present. If either of the parties intended to make a gift, he was not bargaining for consideration, and this requirement will not be met.

a. Act or Forbearance by Promisee Must Be of Benefit to Promisor

It is not enough that the promisee incurs detriment; the detriment must be the *price* of the exchange, and not merely fulfillment of certain conditions for making the gift. The test is whether the act or forbearance by the promisee would be of any benefit to the promisor. In other words, if the promisor's motive was to induce the detriment, it will be treated as consideration; if the motive was no more than to state a condition of a promise to make a gift, there is no consideration.

Example: "Come to my house and I will give you my old television." The promisee suffers a detriment by going to the promisor's house, as she did not have to go there at all. However, the promise of the television was probably not made to induce the promisee to come to the promisor's house. Hence, there is no consideration.

b. **Economic Benefit Not Required**
The benefit to the promisor need not have economic value. Peace of mind or the gratification of influencing the mind of another may be sufficient to establish bargained-for consideration, provided that the promisee is not already legally obligated to perform the requested act.
Example: Father tells Daughter, "I'll give you $1,000 if you stop smoking." Father's emotional gratification from influencing his daughter's health suffices as consideration.

c. **"Past" or "Moral" Consideration**

1) **General Rule—Not Sufficient Consideration**
If something was already given or performed before the promise was made, it will not satisfy the "bargain" requirement. The courts reason that it was not given in exchange for the promise when made.
Example: A loose piece of molding fell from a building and was about to hit Sam. Sherry, seeing this, pushed Sam out of the molding's path and was herself struck by it and seriously injured. Sam later promised Sherry that he would pay her $100 per month for life. There is no consideration because Sherry did not bargain for Sam's promise.

2) **Exceptions**
There is substantial disagreement with the general rule. Thus, the courts have sought to avoid its application by creating exceptions.

a) **Debt Barred by a Technical Defense**
If a past obligation would be enforceable except for the fact that a technical defense to enforcement stands in the way (e.g., statute of limitations), the courts will enforce a new promise if it is *in writing* or has been *partially performed*. However, the court will enforce the contract only to the extent of the new promise.
Example: Debtor owed Creditor $2,000, but the statute of limitations had run on the debt. Debtor won some money in her state lottery and wrote to Creditor, explaining that she had just won some money and promising to pay Creditor $1,000. The promise to pay is enforceable—at least to the extent of the $1,000— despite the lack of new consideration.

b) **Promise to Pay Arising Out of Past Material Benefit—Material Benefit Rule**
Under a modern trend, *some* courts will enforce a promise if it is based on a material benefit that was previously conferred by the promisee on the promisor and if the promisee did not intend to confer the benefit as a gift. This includes situations in which the promisee performed an act at the

promisor's request or performed an unrequested act during an emergency (such as in the example in b.1), above). The Second Restatement follows this rule but adds that the promise is unenforceable to the extent it is disproportionate to the benefit conferred. [Restatement (Second) of Contracts §86]

2. Legal Value

a. Adequacy of Consideration

Courts of law normally will *not* inquire into the adequacy of consideration (i.e., the relative values exchanged). If a party wishes to contract to sell an item of high market value for a relatively low price, so be it. However, ***courts of equity*** may inquire into the relative values and deny an ***equitable remedy*** (such as an order for specific performance) if they find a contract to be unconscionable.

1) Token Consideration

If the consideration is only token (i.e., something entirely devoid of value), it will usually not be legally sufficient. The courts reason that this indicates a gift rather than bargained-for consideration.

2) Sham Consideration

Parties to a written agreement often recite that it was made in consideration of $1 or some other insignificant sum. Frequently, this recited sum was not in fact paid and, indeed, it was never intended to be paid. Most courts hold that evidence may be introduced to show that the consideration was not paid and no other consideration was given in its stead.

3) Possibility of Value

Where there is a possibility of value in the bargained-for act, adequacy of consideration will be found even though the value never comes into existence.

Example: Alex and Becky are siblings. They agree that whatever their grandmother leaves them in her will they will pool it together and divide it evenly. There is consideration even though the grandmother may leave everything to one of the siblings or nothing at all.

b. Legal Detriment and Benefit

1) Legal Detriment to Promisee

Legal detriment will result if the promisee does something he is under no legal obligation to do or refrains from doing something that he has a legal right to do. It is important to remember that the detriment to the promisee need not involve any actual loss to the promisee or benefit to the promisor.

Example: Uncle promises Nephew $5,000 if he will refrain from drinking, smoking, swearing, and gambling until he reaches age 21. Nephew's refraining is a legal detriment, and because it was bargained for, Uncle must pay the $5,000 if Nephew so refrains. [*See* Hamer v. Sidway, 124 N.Y. 538 (1891)]

Note: Remember that the promisor must have sought to induce the detrimental act by his promise. (*See* television set example under B.1.a., *supra.*)

2) **Legal Benefit to Promisor**

A legal benefit to the promisor is simply the reverse side of legal detriment. In other words, it is a forbearance or performance of an act by the promisee which the promisor was not legally entitled to expect or demand, but which confers a benefit on the promisor.

c. **Preexisting Legal Duty Not Consideration**

Traditionally the promise to perform, or the performance of, an existing legal duty *is not consideration*.

Examples: 1) Mike contracts to build a garage for Richard for $15,000. Mike discovers that he cannot make a profit at that price and tells Richard that he will not build the garage unless Richard promises to pay him $16,000. Because Richard does not have time to find a new contractor before winter and he does not want his new car exposed to snow, he agrees to pay Mike the $16,000. When Mike finishes the garage, Richard pays Mike $15,000. Mike cannot enforce the promise for the additional $1,000 because he was under a preexisting duty to build the garage.

2) Smith offers a $10,000 reward for recovery of his kidnapped daughter. Jones, a police officer assigned to this case, recovers the daughter. Jones's performance of her official duty is not sufficient consideration.

1) **Exception—New or Different Consideration Promised**

If the promisee has given something in addition to what she already owes in return for the promise she now seeks to enforce, or has in some way agreed to vary her preexisting duty, such as by accelerating performance, there is consideration. It is important to note that it is usually immaterial how slight the change is, because courts are anxious to avoid the preexisting duty rule.

2) **Exception—Voidable Obligation**

A promise to perform a voidable obligation (i.e., ratification) is enforceable despite the absence of new consideration. Thus, an infant's (i.e., minor's) ratification of a contract upon reaching the age of majority is enforceable without new consideration, as is a defrauded person's promise to go through with the tainted contract after learning of the fraud.

3) **Exception—Preexisting Duty Owed to Third Party**

Traditionally, when a preexisting duty was owed to a third party, courts held that the new promise did not constitute consideration. However, the modern view adopted by the Second Restatement and the majority of jurisdictions states that the new promise **constitutes consideration**. [*See* Restatement (Second) of Contracts §73]

Example: Saul Pimon contracts with Pam Promotor to sing at a concert in New York for $25,000. Later, when Pimon threatens to cancel, Dud Dooright, a Pimon fan, offers to pay Pimon an additional $5,000 if he sings at the concert. Pimon appears and sings as agreed. Under the traditional view, Pimon cannot enforce Dooright's promise to pay the additional $5,000, but under the majority view Pimon can enforce the promise because Pimon did not owe a duty to Dooright under the original contract.

4) Exception—Honest Dispute as to Duty

If the scope of the legal duty owed is the subject of honest dispute, then a modifying agreement relating to it will ordinarily be given effect. The compromise by each party is a detriment.

5) Exception—Unforeseen Circumstances

Under the modern view, which appears to be the view adopted by the National Conference of Bar Examiners for MBE purposes, a promise modifying a contract that has not been fully performed on either side is binding without consideration if the modification is *fair and equitable in view of circumstances not anticipated* when the contract was made (e.g., contractor unexpectedly hits bedrock). [*See* Restatement (Second) of Contracts §89] Under the majority view, however, mere unforeseen difficulty in performing is *not* a substitute for consideration. But if the unforeseen difficulty *rises to the level of impracticability*, such that the duty of performance would be discharged (*see* VI.E.5., *infra*), most states will hold that the unforeseen difficulty is an exception to the preexisting legal duty rule.

6) Exception—Modification of Contract for the Sale of Goods

At common law, a contract modification generally is *unenforceable* unless it is supported by new consideration. Article 2 does not follow this rule. Under Article 2, contract modifications sought in *good faith* are binding without consideration. A good faith modification is based on a legitimate commercial reason outside the control of the party seeking the modification. Modifications extorted from the other party are in bad faith and are unenforceable. [*See* UCC §2-209, comment 2]

Example: Paintco has agreed to sell to Retailco 15,000 gallons of paint at a price of $5 per gallon, to be delivered in 500-gallon installments each month for 30 months. After 15 months, the price of materials rises so that Paintco is losing 50¢ per gallon. Paintco had at the inception of the contract made a profit of 25¢ per gallon. Paintco tells Retailco the circumstances and asks if Retailco will agree to pay $5.75 per gallon for the remaining deliveries. Retailco agrees and the proper writing is executed. The modification was no doubt sought in good faith and is binding even though Paintco gave Retailco no new consideration. If Paintco had asked for an increased price because she believed that it was too late for Retailco to purchase elsewhere and Retailco would pay the higher price to get the paint, the modification would be in bad faith and would be unenforceable.

7) Existing Debts

One of the recurring problems in the preexisting duty area concerns promises regarding existing debts. When the amount due is undisputed, *payment of a smaller sum* than due will *not* be sufficient consideration for a promise by the creditor to discharge the debt. Neither a legal detriment nor a benefit would be present.

But again, bear in mind that courts will attempt to avoid this result by application of the above exceptions. Thus, for example, if the consideration is in any way *new or different* (e.g., payment before maturity or to one other than the creditor; payment in a different medium, e.g., stock instead of cash; or payment of a debt that is subject to an honest dispute), then sufficient consideration may be found.

d. Forbearance to Sue

The promise to refrain from suing on a claim may constitute consideration. If the claim is *valid*, the forbearance to sue is, of course, sufficient consideration. If the claim is *invalid* and the claimant is aware of this fact, he has no such right; his suit is no more than the wrongful exercise of a power. But even if the claim is invalid, in law or in fact, if the claimant reasonably and in good faith believes his claim to be valid, forbearance of the legal right to have his claim adjudicated constitutes detriment and consideration.

C. MUTUAL AND ILLUSORY PROMISES—THE REQUIREMENT OF MUTUALITY

Consideration must exist on both sides of the contract; that is, promises must be mutually obligatory. There are many agreements in which one party has become bound but the other has not. Such agreements lack mutuality, i.e., at least one of the promises is "illusory." If so, consideration fails.

Example: Acme Co. promises to buy from Batcher, Inc. "such ice cream as I may wish to order from Batcher, Inc." Acme's promise is illusory, because it is still free to buy from anyone else it chooses, or not to buy at all.

However, the requisite mutuality will be found to exist in certain situations even though the promisor has some choice or discretion. Notable among these are the following:

1. Requirements and Output Contracts

"Requirements" contracts (promises to buy "all that I will require") and "output" contracts (promises to sell "all that I manufacture") are enforceable. (*See* II.B.2.b.1)b)(1), *supra*.) Consideration exists, as the promisor is suffering a legal detriment; he has parted with the legal right to buy (or sell) the goods he may need (or manufacture) from (or to) another source. [UCC §2-306]

2. Conditional Promises

Conditional promises are *enforceable*, no matter how remote the contingency, *unless* the "condition" is entirely within the promisor's control.

Example: Alice promises to deliver goods to Charles "only if her son comes into the business." Valid consideration exists. If the promise were "only if I decide to take my son into the business," a court might find no consideration.

a. Promise Conditioned on Satisfaction

A promise conditioned on the promisor's satisfaction is not illusory because the promisor is constrained by good faith (for contracts involving personal taste) and a reasonable person standard (for contracts involving mechanical fitness, utility, or marketability). (*See* VI.D.3.a., *infra*.)

3. **Right to Cancel or Withdraw**

Although reservation of an unqualified right to cancel or withdraw at any time may be an illusory promise, the consideration is valid if this right is in *any way restricted*, e.g., the right to cancel upon 60 days' notice. Note that Article 2 implies a requirement of reasonable notice even if it is not specified in the contract. [UCC §2-309(3)]

4. **Exclusivity Agreements—Best Efforts Implied**

A court may find an implied promise furnishing mutuality in appropriate circumstances (such as exclusive marketing agreements). The courts generally will find an implied promise to use best efforts and sustain agreements that might otherwise appear illusory.

Example: Y Corp. was granted exclusive rights to sell Dominick's dresses in return for one-half the profit. The agreement was silent as to any obligation on the part of Y Corp. *Held:* Y Corp. impliedly promised to use its best efforts to sell Dominick's dresses. [*See* UCC §2-306(2)]

5. **Voidable Promises**

Voidable promises are not held objectionable on "mutuality" grounds. [Restatement (Second) of Contracts §78]

Example: Victor entered into a contract with Baby Jane, an infant. Baby Jane's power to disaffirm her contractual obligation will not prevent her promise from serving as consideration.

6. **Unilateral/Option Contracts**

Unilateral contracts, enforceable because one has begun performance, or option contracts, enforceable because one has purchased time to decide (e.g., whether to purchase land), are not held objectionable on "mutuality" grounds.

7. **Suretyship Promises**

A suretyship contract involves a promise to pay the debt of another. A suretyship contract is not enforceable unless it is supported by consideration. If a surety is compensated, the requirement of consideration is not much of an issue, because the compensation will serve as consideration for the surety's promise. If, however, the surety is gratuitous (i.e., the surety is not paid for his services), the consideration requirement may cause problems. The timing becomes important in determining whether adequate consideration is present in a gratuitous surety situation.

a. **Surety Makes Promise Before (or at the Same Time as) Creditor Performs or Promises to Perform—Consideration Present**

If the gratuitous surety makes his promise to pay *before* (or at the *same time* as) the creditor performs or promises to perform, the *creditor's* performance or promise will serve as consideration for the surety's promise, because the creditor has incurred a detriment in exchange for the surety's promise.

Example: Beth sees a car on Sam's used car lot that she wants, but she does not have enough money to pay for the car. Sam tells Beth that he will sell her the car for $500 and a two-year promissory note for the remainder if Beth can get her father to co-sign the note with her. Beth's father agrees. The three parties meet, Beth and her father sign the note, and Sam signs over title of the car to Beth. Beth's father is bound as a surety because the consideration passed from Sam at the same time Beth's father made his promise.

b. Surety Makes Promise After Creditor Performs or Promises to Perform— Generally No Consideration to Support Surety's Promise

If a gratuitous surety does not make his promise until *after* the creditor has performed or made an absolute promise to perform, there is no consideration to support the surety's promise because of the preexisting legal duty rule—the creditor has not incurred any new detriment in exchange for the surety's promise. Thus, the surety's promise is unenforceable.

Example: Beth sees a car on Sam's used car lot that she wants, but she does not have enough money to pay for the car. Sam tells Beth that she can have the car for $500 and a two-year promissory note for the remainder. Beth agrees. Sam signs the title of the car over to Beth, and Beth gives Sam $500 and a promissory note for the remainder. A few days later, Sam discovers that Beth works only part-time and will likely have trouble making payments on her current income. He calls Beth and asks her to get a surety on the note. Beth's father sends Sam a letter promising to pay whatever Beth owes if she defaults. Beth's father is not bound as surety because there is no consideration to support his promise.

1) Exception—Obtaining Surety Is Condition Precedent

If the contract between the debtor and the creditor makes obtaining a surety a condition precedent to the creditor's performance, so that the creditor would be justified in refusing to perform the contract until a surety is obtained, the surety's promise is binding if the creditor performs in reliance on the surety's promise.

2) Exception—Additional Consideration

As with other contracts, if the creditor gives additional consideration in exchange for the surety's promise, the surety will be bound.

8. Right to Choose Among Alternative Courses

A promise to choose one of several alternative means of performance is illusory unless *every alternative* involves *some legal detriment* to the promisor. However, if the power to choose rests with the *promisee* or some *third party* not under the control of the promisor, the promise is enforceable as long as *at least one alternative* involves some legal detriment.

Example: Smith, an English professor, tells Jack that in return for Jack's promise to pay $250, Smith will either (i) give Jack swimming lessons, (ii) paint Jack's portrait, or (iii) teach his English class (of which Jack is a member) on a regular basis during the next term, the choice to be entirely Smith's. Because alternative (iii) represents a *preexisting duty* owed by Smith to the university under his contract of employment, it involves no legal detriment, and Smith's promise does not constitute valuable consideration for Jack's promise to pay $250.

Compare: Had Smith allowed Jack's mother (or Jack) to select the performance, there would be a legal detriment and valuable consideration—even if alternative (iii) were selected.

a. **Selection of Valuable Alternative Cures Illusory Promise**
Even if a promisor retains the power to select an alternative without legal detriment, his *actual* selection of an alternative involving legal detriment would cure the illusory promise.

Example: In the above example (in which Smith was allowed to select a means of performance), if Smith had *actually* chosen alternative (i) or (ii), his illusory promise would have been cured.

D. PROMISSORY ESTOPPEL OR DETRIMENTAL RELIANCE
Consideration is not necessary if the facts indicate that the promisor should be estopped from not performing. A promise is enforceable if necessary to prevent injustice if:

(i) The promisor should reasonably *expect to induce action or forbearance*; and

(ii) *Such action or forbearance is in fact induced*.

If the elements for promissory estoppel are present, some jurisdictions will award expectation damages (i.e., what was promised under the contract), but the Second Restatement provides that the remedy "*may be limited as justice requires*." Thus, a jurisdiction following the Second Restatement might award only reliance damages (i.e., whatever the promisee spent in reliance on the promise), which usually is something less than expectation damages, but theoretically can exceed them.

Examples: 1) Alberto Alum promises to bequeath State University $5 million for a new School of Management building. State University puts up a plaque announcing the new building and hires an architect to design it. If Alberto Alum does not bequeath the money, expectation damages would be $5 million, but State University would likely recover only the cost of the plaque and the architect's fees under the Second Restatement approach.

2) Tom offers to give Betty $15,000 if she will buy herself a new car. Betty buys a car for $13,000. The expectation damages are $15,000, but Tom is liable to Betty for only $13,000 under the Second Restatement approach.

IV. REQUIREMENT THAT NO DEFENSES EXIST

A. INTRODUCTION
Even if an agreement is supported by valuable consideration or a recognized substitute, contract rights may still be unenforceable because there is a defense to formation of the contract, because there is a defect in capacity (making the obligations voidable by one of the parties), or because a defense to enforcement of certain terms exists.

B. ABSENCE OF MUTUAL ASSENT

1. Mutual Mistake as to Existing Facts
A mutual mistake is generally a mistaken assumption *shared* by both parties. Thus, when both parties entering into a contract are mistaken *about existing facts* (not future happenings) relating to the agreement, the contract may be voidable by the adversely affected party if:

(i)   The mistake concerns a ***basic assumption*** on which the contract is made (e.g., the parties think they are contracting for the sale of a diamond but in reality the stone is a cubic zirconia);

(ii)   The mistake has a ***material effect*** on the agreed-upon exchange (e.g., the cubic zirconia is worth only a hundredth of what a diamond is worth); and

(iii)   The party seeking avoidance ***did not assume the risk*** of the mistake.

a.   Not a Defense If Party Bore the Risk

Mutual mistake is not a defense if the party asserting mistake as a defense bore the risk that the assumption was mistaken. This commonly occurs when one party is in a position to better know the risks than the other party (e.g., contractor vs. homeowner) or where the parties knew that their assumption was doubtful (i.e., when the parties were consciously aware of their ignorance). In other words, to be a defense it must be a mistake, not a mere uncertainty.

Examples: 1) Homeowner contacts Builder regarding the cost of installing an inground pool. Builder bids $15,000 and Homeowner accepts. While digging the hole for the pool, Builder encounters an unexpected slab of granite. Blasting away the granite will add 20% to Builder's costs, making the contract unprofitable. Builder will be held to have assumed the risk.

2) Roger finds a stone that appears to be valuable and shows it to his friend Betsy. The two do not know what the stone is but think it is a topaz. Roger agrees to sell the stone to Betsy for $100. The parties subsequently discover that the stone is a diamond worth $1,000. Roger cannot void the contract on mutual mistake grounds because the parties knew that their assumption about the stone was doubtful.

Compare: Roger finds a stone that appears to be valuable. Because Roger is not an expert as to gems, he takes it to Jeweler. Jeweler, in good faith, tells Roger that the stone is a topaz worth very little and offers to buy it for $100. Roger accepts, but subsequently discovers that the stone actually is a diamond worth $1,000. Roger can rescind the contract on mutual mistake grounds. Roger's reliance on an expert's opinion shows that Roger did not intend to assume the risk of not knowing about the stone.

1)   Mistake in Value Generally Not a Defense

If the parties to a contract make assumptions as to the value of the subject matter, mistakes in those assumptions will generally not be remedied—even though the value of the subject matter is generally a basic assumption and the mistake creates a material imbalance—because both parties usually assume the risk that their assumption as to value is wrong. However, it is possible for the facts to show that the adversely affected party did not assume the risk in determining value.

Example: Roger finds a stone that appears to be valuable and shows it to his friend Betsy. The two properly determine that the stone is a topaz. Roger believes the topaz is worth $500, and Betsy believes the topaz is worth $50, but Roger agrees to sell it to Betsy for $200. The parties subsequently discover that the topaz is worth $600. Roger cannot void the contract because he knew that the parties did not know the true value of the stone, and so assumed the risk that their valuation was incorrect.

Compare: Same facts as above, but because Roger and Betsy did not know the value of a topaz, they took it to Jeweler, who told them the stone was worth $200. Subsequently, Roger discovers that Jeweler knows nothing about topaz stones and determines that the stone was worth $600. Roger can void the contract for mutual mistake and force Betsy to return the stone because here the facts show that the parties did not intend to assume the risk of determining value (because they sought out an expert to determine the true value).

2. Unilateral Mistake

Unilateral mistakes arise most commonly when one party makes a mechanical error in computation. If only one of the parties is mistaken about facts relating to the agreement, the mistake will *not* prevent formation of a contract. However, if the nonmistaken party *knew or had reason to know of the mistake* made by the other party, the contract is voidable by the mistaken party. As is the case with mutual mistake, for the contract to be voidable, the mistake must have a *material effect* on the agreed upon exchange and the mistaken party must not have borne the risk of the mistake. Materiality is determined by the overall impact on both parties. Ordinarily this is proven by showing the exchange is much less desirable to the mistaken party and more advantageous to the nonmistaken party.

Example: Seller agrees to sell Buyer a number of different items of hardware. Seller computes the total price at $15,000, and Buyer agrees to pay this amount. Subsequently, Seller discovers that he made an error in computation and the price should be $17,000. In this situation, the preferred analysis is that there *is* a contract at $15,000, assuming that Buyer was *reasonably unaware of the unilateral computation error*. Note also that the error was not an error in the offer; the mistake was *antecedent* to the offer by Seller. When Seller stated the offer at $15,000, he meant $15,000.

Compare: Homeowner asks four contractors to submit bids to build a two-car garage on Homeowner's property. When Homeowner receives the bids they are: $17,000, $19,000, $19,500, and $9,000. The last bid was due to a typographical error. Homeowner will not be able to snap up the $9,000 offer because he should have known, based on the other bids, that the $9,000 bid probably contained an error.

a. Unilateral Mistake May Be Canceled in Equity

There is authority in a number of cases that contracts with errors, such as mistakes in *computation*, may be canceled in equity, assuming that the nonmistaken party has *not relied* on the contract. There is also modern authority indicating that a unilateral mistake that is *so extreme* that it outweighs the other party's expectations under the agreement will be a ground for cancellation of the contract.

b. **Error in Judgment**

An error in judgment by one of the parties as to the value or quality of the work done or goods contracted for will **not** result in a voidable contract, even if the nonmistaken party knows or has reason to know of the mistake made by the other party.

Examples: 1) Seller offers to sell her car to Buyer for $500, and Buyer accepts. Buyer knows that Seller's car has a market value of $1,500 and that this fact is unknown to Seller. The contract is enforceable.

2) Seller advertises a particular dredge for sale. After an employee of Buyer inspects the dredge, Buyer offers $35,000 for it, which Seller accepts. Prior to the delivery of the dredge, Buyer discovers that the dredge will not perform certain operations in shallow water, which was the central purpose Buyer intended for the dredge. The contract is not voidable by Buyer because Buyer's unilateral mistake was a mistake in judgment about goods contracted for.

3. **Mistake by the Intermediary (Transmission)**

When there is a mistake in the transmission of an offer or acceptance by an intermediary, the prevailing view is that the message **as transmitted** is operative unless the other party knew or should have known of the mistake.

Example: Harry put his home up for sale at the price of $340,000. After viewing the home, Sally called her attorney and asked him to prepare an offer to purchase the home for $313,000. The attorney misunderstood Sally and prepared an offer for $330,000 and transmitted the offer to Harry. Harry accepted. Assuming that the attorney had the power to bind Sally, a contract was formed to buy the house for $330,000, despite the attorney's mistake in transmitting the price.

Compare: Same facts as above, but Sally asked her attorney to prepare an offer for $318,000 and the attorney misunderstood and submitted an offer for $380,000. Here, Sally probably would not be bound because Harry probably should have known of the error as the offer substantially exceeded his asking price.

4. **Misunderstanding—Ambiguous Contract Language**

Contract language with at least two possible meanings leads to different results depending on the awareness of the parties. Most often there is no contract because there is no meeting of the minds.

a. **Neither Party Aware of Ambiguity—No Contract**

If neither party was aware of the ambiguity at the time of contracting, there is **no contract unless** both parties happened to intend the same meaning.

Example: Buyer agrees to purchase cotton from Seller when the cotton is delivered by a ship named Peerless. This is the total expression of the agreement. It is subsequently determined that Buyer contemplated a ship named Peerless that was to dock in September while Seller contemplated a ship named Peerless that was to dock in December. Neither party was aware that there were two ships named Peerless. Their subsequent expression of the ship each intended indicates that they did not intend the same ship at the time of contracting. Therefore, there is no contract. [*See* Raffles v. Wichelhaus, 159 Eng. Rep. 375 (1864)]

b. **Both Parties Aware of Ambiguity—No Contract**

If both parties were aware of the ambiguity at the time of contracting, there is *no contract unless* both parties in fact intended the same meaning.

c. **One Party Aware of Ambiguity—Contract**

If one party was aware of the ambiguity and the other party was not at the time of contracting, a *contract* will be enforced according to the intention of the party who was unaware of the ambiguity.

Example: Collector agrees to purchase a Picasso sketch from Gallery. It is subsequently determined that Gallery has two sketches and that Gallery intended to sell one of these to Collector while Collector intended to buy the other one. Collector did not know that Gallery owned two sketches; Gallery, of course, knew that it did. Here, there is a contract for the sketch that Collector had in mind because this is a situation in which one party knew of the ambiguity (Gallery) while the other party did not (Collector).

d. **Subjective Intention of Parties Controls**

While the objective test is used in contract law generally, the latent ambiguity situation is unique in that the courts look to the subjective intention of the parties. This is because the objective test simply does not work in this situation. The objective manifestations of the parties appear to be perfectly clear but subsequent facts indicate the latent ambiguity. It is then necessary to receive evidence of what each party subjectively thought at the time of contracting.

5. **Misrepresentation**

a. **Fraudulent Misrepresentation (Fraud in the Inducement)**

A misrepresentation is a false assertion of fact. It is fraudulent if it is intended to induce a party to enter into a contract and the maker knows or believes the assertion is false or knows that he does not have a basis for what he states or implies with the assertion. A fraudulent assertion can be inferred from conduct; i.e., concealment or sometimes even nondisclosure may be considered a misrepresentation. If a party induces another to enter into a contract by using *fraudulent misrepresentation* (e.g., by asserting information she knows is untrue), the contract is *voidable* by the innocent party if she *justifiably relied* on the fraudulent misrepresentation. This is a type of *fraud in the inducement*.

Example: Buyer agreed to buy a painting from Seller because Seller told her that the painting previously had been owned by Bubbles Springfield, a famous rock star. In fact, Seller knew that Springfield had never owned the painting. Buyer's promise is voidable if she justifiably relied on Seller's misrepresentation.

1) **Distinguish—Fraud in the Factum**

If one of the parties was tricked into giving assent to the agreement under circumstances that prevented her from appreciating the significance of her action, the agreement cannot be enforced; it is *void*.

Example: Joe Rocket, a famous football player, signs autographs after each game. After one game, a fan handed him a paper to sign that was in reality the last page of a contract. The contract is void due to fraud in the factum because Rocket was tricked into signing it.

b.   Material Misrepresentation

Whether or not a misrepresentation is fraudulent, the contract is *voidable* by the innocent party if the innocent party *justifiably relied* on the misrepresentation and the misrepresentation was *material*. A misrepresentation is material if: (i) it would induce a reasonable person to agree, or (ii) the maker knows that for some special reason it is likely to induce the particular person to agree, even if a reasonable person would not.

Example: Same facts as in the painting example in a., above, except that Seller truly believed that the painting had once belonged to Springfield. Because a famous prior owner would likely make a reasonable person agree to buy a painting, the misrepresentation is material. Therefore, Buyer's promise is voidable if she justifiably relied on Seller's misrepresentation.

c.   Concealment and Nondisclosure

An action intended to prevent another from learning a fact is the equivalent of asserting that a fact does not exist. Similarly, if a party frustrates an investigation by the other party or falsely denies knowledge of a fact, it can be considered a misrepresentation. Note, however, that nondisclosure without concealment usually is not a misrepresentation. A party is not required to tell everything he knows to the other party, but if the nondisclosure is either *material or fraudulent*, the contract is voidable for misrepresentation. [*See* Restatement (Second) of Contracts §§159 - 164]

d.   Justified Reliance

A party's reliance on a misrepresentation must be justified for the contract to be voidable; i.e., he is not entitled to relief if the reliance was unreasonable under the circumstances. However, the mere fact that the misrepresentation could have been revealed by the exercise of reasonable care does not mean reliance was unjustified. For example, a party's failure to read a contract or use care in reading it will not necessarily preclude him from avoiding the contract.

Example: Able and Baker agree that Able will mow Baker's lawn weekly for $50. Able draws up a contract, hands it to Baker, and states that it is the written version of their agreement. In fact, the writing states that Baker will pay Able $60 per week for the mowing. Baker signs the contract without reading it, despite having an opportunity to do so. Baker can void the contract.

e.   Innocent Party May Rescind Agreement

The innocent party need not wait until she is sued on the contract, but may take affirmative action in equity to *rescind* the agreement. The right to rescind the agreement exists even if the terms are fair or beneficial to the misled party. The right to void or rescind such a contract may be lost, however, if the party so induced affirms the contract in question.

f. Remedies for Fraud
In addition to rescission, remedies for material misrepresentation or fraud include all remedies available for breach (*see* VIII., *infra*). In a contract for the sale of goods, neither rescission nor the return of the goods is inconsistent with a claim for damages. [UCC §2-721] Note that the time period to bring an action for fraud does not run until the party knows or should have known of the fraud.

C. ABSENCE OF CONSIDERATION
If the promises exchanged at the formation stage lack the elements of bargain or legal detriment, *no contract* exists. In this situation, one of the promises is always illusory.

D. PUBLIC POLICY DEFENSES—ILLEGALITY
If either the *consideration or the subject matter* of a contract is illegal, this will serve as a defense to enforcement. Contracts may be illegal because they are inconsistent with the Constitution, violate a statute, or are against public policy as declared by the courts.

1. Some Typical Cases of Illegality
Some of the most common areas in which problems of illegality have arisen are:

a. Agreements in restraint of trade;

b. Gambling contracts;

c. Usurious contracts;

d. Agreements obstructing administration of justice;

e. Agreements inducing breach of public fiduciary duties; and

f. Agreements relating to torts or crimes.

2. Effect of Illegality

a. Generally Contract Is Void
Illegal consideration or subject matter renders a contract void and unenforceable. In a close case, a court may sever an illegal clause from the contract rather than striking down the entire contract.

b. Effect Depends on Timing of Illegality
If the subject matter or consideration was illegal at the time of the offer, there was *no valid offer*. If it became illegal after the offer but before acceptance, the supervening illegality operates to *revoke the offer*. If it became illegal after a valid contract was formed, the supervening illegality operates to *discharge the contract* because performance has become impossible (*see* VI.E.5.a., *infra*).

c. Compare—Illegal Purpose
If the contract was formed for an illegal *purpose* but neither the consideration nor the subject matter is illegal (e.g., a contract to rent a plane when the renter's purpose is to smuggle drugs out of Colombia), the contract is only *voidable* (rather than void) by the party who (i) did not know of the purpose; or (ii) knew but did not facilitate the purpose

and the purpose does not involve "serious moral turpitude." If both parties knew of the illegal purpose and facilitated it, or knew and the purpose involves serious moral turpitude, the contract is *void* and unenforceable. [Restatement (Second) of Contracts §182]

3. Limitations on Illegality Defense

a. Plaintiff Unaware of Illegality
If the plaintiff contracted without knowledge that the agreement was illegal and the defendant acted with knowledge of the illegality, the innocent plaintiff may recover on the contract.

b. Parties Not in Pari Delicto
A person may successfully seek relief if he was not as culpable as the other.
Example: Punter, a casual bettor, may recover against Booker, a professional bookie. (Some courts reach this result on the theory that the criminal proscription was designed to protect a class to which Punter belongs.)

c. Licensing—Revenue Raising vs. Protection
If a contract is illegal solely because a party does not have a required license, whether the contract will be enforceable depends on the reason for the license:

1) Revenue Raising—Contract Enforceable
If the license is required merely to raise revenue (e.g., a city requires all vendors at a fair to pay a $25 license fee), the contract generally is enforceable.

2) Protection of Public—Contract Not Enforceable
If the license is required to ensure that the licensee meets minimum requirements to protect the public welfare (e.g., a license to practice law, medicine, accounting, etc.), the contract is void. This means that even if the unlicensed party performs perfectly under the contract, the party cannot collect any damages.

E. DEFENSES BASED ON LACK OF CAPACITY

1. Legal Incapacity to Contract
Individuals in certain protected classes are legally incapable of incurring binding contractual obligations. Timely assertion of this defense by a promisor makes the contract *voidable* at his election.

a. Contracts of Infants (Minors)

1) Who Is an Infant?
The age of majority in most jurisdictions is 18. However, in many states, married persons under age 18 are considered adults.

2) Effect of Infant's Contract
Infants generally lack capacity to enter into a contract binding on themselves. However, contractual promises of an adult made to an infant are binding on the adult. In other words, a contract entered into between an infant and an adult is *voidable by the infant but binding on the adult*.

3) Disaffirmance

An infant may choose to disaffirm a contract any time before (or shortly after) reaching the age of majority. If a minor chooses to disaffirm, she must return anything that she received under the contract *that still remains* at the time of disaffirmance. However, there is no obligation to return any part of the consideration that has been squandered, wasted, or negligently destroyed.

a) Exceptions

Most states have created a small number of statutory exceptions to the rule that minors can disaffirm their contracts (e.g., student loan agreements, insurance contracts, agreements not to reveal an employer's proprietary information, etc.).

b) Contracts for Necessaries

"Necessaries" generally includes food, shelter, clothing, medical care, medicines, and other items necessary for the minor's subsistence, health, or education. A minor may disaffirm a contract for necessaries but in most states will be liable in restitution for the value of benefits received.

4) Affirmance upon Majority

An infant may affirm, i.e., choose to be bound by his contract, upon reaching majority. He affirms either expressly or by conduct, e.g., *failing to disaffirm* the contract *within a reasonable time after reaching majority.*

b. Mental Incapacity

One whose mental capacity is so deficient that he is incapable of understanding the nature and significance of a contract may disaffirm when lucid or by a later appointed legal representative. He may likewise affirm during a lucid interval or upon complete recovery, even without formal restoration by judicial action. In other words, a contract made by a mentally incompetent person is *voidable*. As in the case of infants, mentally incompetent persons are liable in quasi-contract for necessaries furnished to them.

Note: Once a mentally incompetent person has been adjudicated and placed under a guardianship, that person no longer has any ability to contract as the guardian has complete control of the incompetent person's property. Thus any attempted contracts by an incapacitated person who is under a guardianship would be *void*.

c. Intoxicated Persons

One who is so intoxicated that he does not understand the nature and significance of his promise may be held to have made only a *voidable* promise if the other party had reason to know of the intoxication. The intoxicated person may affirm the contract upon recovery. Once again, there may be quasi-contractual recovery for necessaries furnished during the period of incapacity.

2. Duress and Undue Influence

Contracts induced by duress (e.g., "sign the contract or I'll break your legs") or undue influence are *voidable* and may be rescinded as long as not affirmed.

a. Duress

There are two types of duress. In the first, a party is physically forced to sign against her will; e.g., a stronger person grabs her hand and signs the contract with the victim's hand or the victim signs the contract at gunpoint. With this type of physical-compulsion duress, the contract is void. The much more common type of duress arises when a party's assent to a contract is induced by an improper threat by the other party that leaves the victim no reasonable alternative. In these cases, the contract is voidable by the victim. [*See* Restatement (Second) of Contracts §175] Examples of this type of duress include threats of bodily harm to the victim or her family and threats to bring unfounded criminal or civil charges.

Example: Able tells Baker that Baker must sign a business contract with Able in which all provisions greatly favor Able. Able states that if Baker fails to sign, Able will hire someone to hurt Baker's teenage daughter. Baker signs the agreement. The contract is voidable at Baker's option.

1) Economic Duress Generally Not a Defense

Generally, taking advantage of another person's economic needs is not a defense. However, withholding something someone wants or needs will constitute economic duress if:

(i) The party threatens to commit a wrongful act that would seriously threaten the other contracting party's property or finances; and

(ii) There are no adequate means available to prevent the threatened loss.

Example: Barry buys his dream home for $700,000. A few years later, Barry loses his job, stops making mortgage payments, and is threatened with foreclosure. Because of the economy, houses are not selling in Barry's neighborhood, so his friend Freida offers to buy Barry's house for the $500,000 that he owes on it. Before the closing, Barry finds a job and does not want to sell the house. Barry is bound; his economic duress is not a defense.

Compare: Barry buys his dream home for $700,000. A few years later, Barry's boss, Freida, tells Barry that if he will not sell her his house for $500,000, she will fire him from his job. Barry agrees to the sale, but before closing finds a new job. The economic duress here would probably be a defense.

b. Undue Influence

Undue influence is unfair persuasion of a party who is under the domination of the person exercising the persuasion or who by virtue of the relationship between them is justified in assuming that that person will not act in a manner inconsistent with his welfare. [Restatement (Second) of Contracts §177] The elements of undue influence are often described as undue susceptibility to pressure by one party and excessive pressure by the other. Other factors considered are the unfairness of the resulting bargain and the availability of independent advice.

F. STATUTE OF FRAUDS

In most instances, an oral contract is valid. However, certain agreements, by statute, must be evidenced by a ***writing signed by the party sought to be bound.***

1. Writing Requirement

The Statute of Frauds does not require a formal written contract. Among other things, the writing could be a receipt, a letter, a check with details in the memo line, or a written offer that was accepted orally. The Statute requires only one or more writings, signed by the party to be charged, that: (i) reasonably identify the subject matter of the contract, (ii) indicate that a contract has been made between the parties, and (iii) state with reasonable certainty the essential terms of the unperformed promises. [Restatement (Second) of Contracts §131]

Example: Becky Baker calls Sam Supplier and orders 2,000 pounds of flour for use in her bakery at Sam's price of 70¢ a pound. As will be discussed *infra,* this contract is within the Statute of Frauds and is unenforceable by either party without some writing evidencing the material terms. Later the same day, Becky receives a flyer from another supplier indicating that their price for flour is 65¢ per pound. Becky immediately emails Sam Supplier the following note: "Please cancel my order for 2,000 pounds of flour. /s/ Becky Baker." Becky's attempted cancelation of the contract is a sufficient writing under the Statute of Frauds to make the contract enforceable, at least against her.

a. Electronic Record Satisfies Writing Requirement

Whenever a law, such as the Statute of Frauds, requires a record to be in writing, an electronic record satisfies that law. [Uniform Electronic Transactions Act ("UETA") §7(c)] Thus, the writing requirement may be satisfied by an e-mail.

b. Essential or Material Terms

If a writing does not contain the essential terms of the agreement, it does not satisfy the Statute and the contract cannot be enforced. There is no definitive list of essential terms. They vary depending on the situation. What is essential depends on the agreement, its context, and the subsequent conduct of the parties, including the dispute that has arisen. There must be enough in the writing to enable a court to enforce the contract. If an element is contained in the writing, evidence is admissible to explain the particulars. If, however, a term is missing and cannot be supplied by implication or rule of law, evidence will not be admitted to add it. The essential terms normally include the identity of the parties, description of the subject matter, and the terms necessary to make the contract definite (*see* II.B.2., *supra*). For example, writings evidencing land sale contracts must contain a description of the land and the price, and those for employment contracts must state the length of employment. For the sale of goods, the UCC requires only some signed writing indicating that a contract has been made and specifying the quantity term.

2. Signature Requirement

The signature requirement is liberally construed by most courts. A signature is any mark or symbol made with the intention to authenticate the writing as that of the signer. It need not be handwritten; it can be printed or typed. Under the UCC, even a party's initials or letterhead may be sufficient.

a. **Electronic Signature**

The signature requirement may be satisfied by an electronic signature. [UETA §7(d)] As with paper signatures, whether a record is "signed" is a question of fact. No specific technology is necessary to create a valid signature. If the requisite intent is present, one's name as part of an e-mail may suffice as a signature, as may the firm name on a facsimile (fax).

3. **Agreements Covered**

a. **Executor or Administrator Promises Personally to Pay Estate Debts**

A promise by an executor or administrator to pay the estate's debts out of *his own funds* must be evidenced by a writing.

b. **Promises to Pay Debt of Another (Suretyship Promises)**

1) **Must Be a Collateral Promise**

A promise to answer for the debt or default of another must be evidenced by a writing. The promise may arise as a result of a tort or contract, but it must be collateral to another person's promise to pay, and not a primary promise to pay.

Example: "Give him the goods, and if he does not pay, I will." This promise is a collateral promise and must be evidenced by a writing. But if the promise is, "Give him the goods, and I will pay for them," the promise is a primary promise and need not be evidenced by a writing.

2) **Main Purpose Must Not Be Pecuniary Interest of Promisor**

If the main purpose or leading object of the promisor is to serve a pecuniary interest of his own, the contract is *not within the Statute of Frauds* even though the effect is still to pay the debt of another.

Example: Ernie contracted with ABC Co. to have some machines custom-made for his factory. He promised ABC Co.'s supplier that if it would continue to deliver materials to ABC, Ernie would guarantee ABC Co.'s payment to the supplier. This promise need not be in writing because Ernie's main purpose in guaranteeing payment was to assure that ABC Co. had adequate supplies to build his machines.

c. **Promises in Consideration of Marriage**

A promise the consideration for which is marriage must be evidenced by a writing. This applies to promises that induce marriage by offering something of value (other than a return promise to marry—e.g., "if you marry my son, I will give the two of you a house").

d. **Interest in Land**

A promise creating an interest in land must be evidenced by a writing. This includes not only agreements for the sale of real property, but also other agreements pertaining to land.

1) What Is an Interest in Land?

In addition to agreements for the *sale of real property*, the following items are among the more important interests in land generally covered by the Statute:

a) *Leases for more than one year;*

b) *Easements of more than one year;*

c) *Mortgages* and most other security liens;

d) *Fixtures;* and

e) *Minerals (or the like) or structures* if they are to be severed by the *buyer.* If they are to be severed by the seller, they are not an interest in land but rather are goods. If the subject matter is growing crops, timber to be cut, or other things attached to realty capable of severance without material harm to the realty, it is a contract for the sale of goods (*see* f., *infra*). [UCC §2-107]

2) Items That Do Not Create an Interest in Land

Even though the end result of some contracts may involve land, they still do not come within this portion of the Statute. For example, a contract to build a building or a contract to buy and sell real estate and divide the profits does not create an interest in land.

3) Effect of Performance on Contracts

Full performance by the seller will take the contract out of the Statute of Frauds. Part performance by the buyer may also remove the contract from the Statute. (*See* 5.a.1), *infra*.)

e. Performance Not Within One Year from Date of Contract

A promise that by its terms *cannot* be performed within one year is subject to the Statute of Frauds. Part performance does not satisfy the Statute of Frauds in this case.

1) Effective Date

The date runs from the *date of the agreement* and not from the date of performance.

Example: Maria entered into an employment agreement whereby she was to perform services from April 1, 2014, until March 31, 2015. The agreement was entered into on March 15, 2014. It must be evidenced by a writing.

2) Contracts Not Within the Statute

The following contracts do not fall within this provision of the Statute:

a) Possibility of Completion Within One Year

If the contract is *possible* to complete within one year, it is not within the one-year prong of the Statute of Frauds, even though actual performance may extend beyond the one-year period.

Example: Carlo makes the following oral statement to Nellie: "Be my nurse until I recover and I will pay you a small salary now, but leave you a large estate in my will." The contract need not be evidenced by a writing because Carlo could recover within one year.

b) **Right to Terminate Within Year**

If a contract that cannot be performed within one year allows both parties the right to terminate within a year, there is a *split* as to whether the right to terminate takes the contract out of the one-year prong of the Statute of Frauds. The majority view is that nonperformance is not performance within one year, and so the contract is still within the Statute of Frauds. The minority Second Restatement view suggests that because the contract is terminable by either party within a year, it is outside the Statute.

Example: Susan contracts to employ Linda for two years. Part of their agreement allows either party to terminate on 30 days' notice. Under one view, this contract would be within the Statute of Frauds (excusable nonperformance is still not performance within a year). The Second Restatement view makes this contract enforceable because giving the 30 days' notice is an alternative form of performance that can occur within one year.

c) **Lifetime Contracts**

A contract measured by a lifetime (e.g., a promise to "employ until I die" or "work until I die") is not within the Statute because it is capable of performance within a year, since a person can die at any time.

d) **Performance by One Party**

Even if a contract cannot be performed within one year, if it has been *fully performed on one side*, most courts will find that it is enforceable even though it is oral. Even if a court were to find that it was not enforceable, the performing party can sue for restitution for the reasonable value of the benefit conferred.

f. **Goods Priced at $500 or More**

A contract for the sale of goods for a price of $500 or more is within the Statute of Frauds and generally must be evidenced by a signed writing to be enforceable. Note that a writing is sufficient even though it omits or incorrectly states a term, but the contract is *not enforceable beyond the quantity of goods shown in the writing*.

Examples: 1) To meet the Statute of Frauds requirement, Constructo offers a notation made on Widgetco's office pad and signed by Widgetco's president reading: "Sold to Constructo, widgets." The writing is probably not sufficient because no quantity term is given.

2) Facts the same as above, but the memorandum reads: "Sold to Constructo, 1,500 widgets." The memorandum is sufficient to support a contract for up to 1,500 widgets. If the actual agreement was for 15,000

widgets, the agreement would be enforceable only to the extent of 1,500 widgets. However, if the actual agreement was for only 150 widgets, the actual agreement may be shown.

1) When Writing Not Required
There are three situations described in UCC section 2-201(3) in which contracts are enforceable without the writing described above:

a) Specially Manufactured Goods
If goods are to be specially manufactured for the buyer and are not suitable for sale to others by the seller in the ordinary course of his business, the contract is enforceable if the seller has, under circumstances that reasonably indicate that the goods are for the buyer, made a *substantial beginning* in their manufacture or *commitments* for their purchase before notice of repudiation is received. [UCC §2-201(3)(a)]

b) Admissions in Pleadings or Court
If the party against whom enforcement is sought admits in pleadings, testimony, or otherwise in court that the contract for sale was made, the contract is enforceable without a writing (but in such a case the contract is not enforced beyond the quantity of goods admitted). [UCC §2-201(3)(b)]

c) Payment or Delivery of Goods
If goods are either received and accepted or paid for, the contract is enforceable. However, the contract is not enforceable beyond the quantity of goods accepted or paid for. Thus, if only some of the goods called for in the oral contract are accepted or paid for, the contract is only partially enforceable. If an indivisible item is partially paid for, most courts hold that the Statute of Frauds is satisfied for the whole item.

Examples: 1) Ketty and Lydia orally agree that Lydia will purchase 150 widgets from Ketty at a price of $10 each. Lydia gives Ketty a check for $70. The contract is enforceable for seven widgets only.

2) Joe orally contracts to buy a car from Suzette for $15,000. Joe gives her a $1,000 down payment. Although Joe has only partially paid for the car, most courts would hold that the contract is enforceable.

2) Merchants—Confirmatory Memo Rule
In contracts between merchants, if one party, within a reasonable time after an oral agreement has been made, sends to the other party a *written* confirmation of the understanding that is sufficient under the Statute of Frauds to bind the sender, it will also bind the recipient if: (i) he has reason to know of the confirmation's contents; and (ii) he does not object to it in writing within 10 days of receipt. [UCC §2-201(2)]

4. Effect of Noncompliance with the Statute
Under the majority rule, noncompliance with the Statute of Frauds renders the contract

unenforceable at the option of the party to be charged (i.e., the party being charged may raise the lack of a sufficient writing as an affirmative defense). If the Statute is not raised as a defense, it is waived.

5. **Situations in Which the Contract Is Removed from the Statute of Frauds**

   a. **Performance**

      1) **Land Sale Contracts**
         If a seller conveys to the buyer (i.e., fully performs), he can enforce the buyer's oral promise to pay. Likewise, the buyer may seek to specifically enforce an oral land sale contract under the doctrine of *part performance*. Part performance that *unequivocally* indicates that the parties have contracted for the sale of land takes the contract out of the Statute of Frauds. What constitutes sufficient part performance varies among jurisdictions. Most require *at least two* of the following: (i) payment (in whole or in part), (ii) possession, and/or (iii) valuable improvements.

         a) **Specific Performance Only**
            A purchaser of an interest in land may enforce an oral contract in this manner only in equity (i.e., he may sue only for specific performance, not damages).

      2) **Sale of Goods Contracts**
         Part performance is sufficient to take a sale of goods contract out of the Statute of Frauds when: (i) the goods have been specially manufactured, or (ii) the goods have been either paid for or accepted. If a sales contract is only partially paid for or accepted, the contract is enforceable *only to the extent of the partial payment or acceptance*.

      3) **Services Contracts—Full Performance Required**
         As noted above, an oral contract that cannot be completed within one year but has been fully performed by one party is enforceable.

   b. **Equitable and Promissory Estoppel**
      Estoppel (*see* III.D., *supra*) is sometimes applied in cases where it would be inequitable to allow the Statute of Frauds to defeat a meritorious claim. When a defendant *falsely and intentionally* tells a plaintiff that the contract is not within the Statute or that he will reduce their agreement to a writing, or when his conduct foreseeably induces a plaintiff to change his position in reliance on an oral agreement, courts may use the doctrine to remove the contract completely from the Statute of Frauds.

   c. **Judicial Admission**
      If the party asserting the Statute of Frauds defense admits in pleadings or testimony that there was an agreement, it is treated as though the Statute is satisfied. The contract will be enforced without a writing.

6. **Remedies If Contract Is Within Statute**
   If a contract is within the Statute of Frauds and there is noncompliance with the Statute with no applicable exception, in almost all cases a party can sue for the *reasonable value* of the

services or part performance rendered, *or* the *restitution* of any other benefit that has been conferred. (*See* VIII.C., *infra,* for a detailed discussion.) This recovery would be in *quantum meruit* rather than a suit on the contract. The rationale is that it would be unjust to permit a party to retain benefits received under the failed contract without paying for them.

7. Contract Made by Agent

The problem: A given contract is required under state law to be evidenced by a writing. An agent now purports to enter into such a contract on behalf of her principal. Must the agent's authority also be in writing? Most states would answer no, except for contracts involving interests in real property. A few states would answer yes as to all such contracts pursuant to the states' *equal dignities* statutes. However, even where written authority would otherwise be required, written authority may be dispensed with if the agent contracted in the presence and under the direction of the principal or if the principal later ratified the contract in writing.

G. UNCONSCIONABILITY

The concept of unconscionability allows a court to *refuse to enforce a provision or an entire contract* (or to modify the contract) to avoid "unfair" terms. It is sometimes said that there are two types of unconscionability: substantive unconscionability (i.e., unconscionability based on price alone) and procedural unconscionability (i.e., unconscionability based on unfair surprise or unequal bargaining power). However, few cases recognize substantive unconscionability based on unfair price alone. Instead, the cases have dealt mostly with procedural unconscionability.

1. Common Instances of Procedural Unconscionability

a. Inconspicuous Risk-Shifting Provisions

Standardized printed form contracts often contain a material provision that seeks to shift a risk normally borne by one party to the other. Examples of such provisions are:

(i) *Confession of judgment* clauses, which are illegal in most states;

(ii) *Disclaimer of warranty* provisions; and

(iii) *"Add-on" clauses* that subject all of the property purchased from a seller to repossession if a newly purchased item is not paid for.

Typically, such clauses are found in the fine print ("boilerplate") in printed form contracts. Courts have invalidated these provisions because they are *inconspicuous* or *incomprehensible* to the average person, even if brought to his actual attention.

b. Contracts of Adhesion—"Take It or Leave It"

Courts will deem a clause unconscionable and unenforceable if the signer is unable to procure necessary goods, such as an automobile, from any seller without agreeing to a similar provision. The buyer has no choice.

c. Exculpatory Clauses

An exculpatory clause releasing a contracting party from liability for his own *intentional* wrongful acts is usually found to be unconscionable because such a clause is against public policy in most states. Exculpatory clauses for *negligent* acts may be found to be unconscionable if they are inconspicuous (as discussed above), but commonly are upheld if they are in contracts for activities that are known to be hazardous (e.g., a contract releasing a ski hill operator for liability for negligence often will be upheld).

d. Limitations on Remedies

A contractual clause limiting liability for damages to property generally will **not** be found to be unconscionable unless it is inconspicuous. However, if a contract limits a party to a certain remedy and that remedy **fails of its essential purpose**, a court may find the limitation unconscionable and ignore it. Note that under the UCC any limitation on consequential damages for personal injury caused by consumer goods is prima facie unconscionable. [*See* UCC §2-719]

Example: An automobile dealership sells a car and the contract provides that the dealer's liability for defects in the car is limited to repair or replacement. Generally, such a clause is **not** unconscionable. However, if a particular customer brings his car back numerous times for the same problem and the dealer is unable to effectively fix the car, the remedy fails of its essential purpose, and a court may ignore the limiting clause and allow the normal remedies for breach.

2. Timing

Unconscionability is determined by the circumstances as they existed *at the time the contract was formed*.

3. Effect If Court Finds Unconscionable Clause

If a court finds as a matter of law that a contract or any clause of the contract was unconscionable **when made**, the court may: (i) refuse to enforce the contract; (ii) enforce the remainder of the contract **without** the unconscionable clause; or (iii) **limit the application of any clause** so as to avoid an unconscionable result. [*See, e.g.,* UCC §2-302]

V. DETERMINING THE TERMS OF THE CONTRACT

A. INTRODUCTION

Once you have determined that a contract exists, the next thing you must do is determine its terms.

B. GENERAL RULES OF CONTRACT CONSTRUCTION

There are a number of general rules of construction applied by the courts when interpreting contracts. The following are among the more frequently invoked:

1. Construed as a Whole

Contracts will be construed as a "whole"; specific clauses will be subordinated to the contract's general intent.

2. Ordinary Meaning of Words

The courts will construe words according to their "ordinary" meaning unless it is clearly shown that they were meant to be used in a technical sense.

3. **Inconsistency Between Provisions**

If provisions appear to be inconsistent, written or typed provisions will prevail over printed provisions (which indicate a form contract).

4. **Preference to Construe Contract as Valid and Enforceable**

It is important to note that the courts generally will try to reach a determination that a contract is valid and enforceable. Hence, they will be inclined to construe provisions in such a fashion as to make them operative. Obviously, this general policy will not be carried so far as to contravene the intention of the parties.

5. **Ambiguities Construed Against Party Preparing Contract**

Ambiguities in a contract are construed against the party preparing the contract, absent evidence of the intention of the parties. This is particularly true when there is no evidence of fraud, mutual mistake, duress, or knowledge by one party of unilateral mistake; and both parties are represented by counsel.

6. **Course of Performance**

Where a contract involves *repeated occasions for performance* by either party and the other party has the opportunity to object to such performance, any course of performance accepted or acquiesced to is relevant in determining the meaning of the contract. [UCC §1-303(a), (d)]

7. **Course of Dealing**

The parties' course of dealing may be used to explain a contract. A course of dealing is a sequence of conduct concerning *previous transactions* between the parties to a particular transaction that may be regarded as establishing a common basis of their understanding. [UCC §1-303(b), (d)]

8. **Usage of Trade**

A usage of trade may also be used to explain a contract. A usage of trade is a *practice or method of dealing*, regularly observed in a particular business setting so as to justify an expectation that it will be followed in the transaction in question. [UCC §1-303(c), (d)]

9. **Priorities of Conflicting Rules**

Express terms are given greater weight than course of performance, course of dealing and usage of trade. Course of performance is given greater weight than course of dealing or usage of trade, and course of dealing is given greater weight than usage of trade.

C. **PAROL EVIDENCE RULE—SUPPLEMENTING, EXPLAINING, OR CONTRADICTING TERMS**

In interpreting and enforcing a contract, questions often arise as to whether the written instrument is the complete embodiment of the parties' intention. Where the parties to a contract express their agreement in a *writing* with the *intent* that it embody the final expression of their bargain, the writing is an "*integration*." Any other expressions—written or oral—made *prior to* the writing, as well as any oral expressions *contemporaneous with* the writing, are *inadmissible to vary* the terms of the writing.

Example: Buyer is interested in purchasing a new car from Dealer. He settles on a particular car, and Buyer and Dealer begin to negotiate the terms of the sale. During the negotiations, Dealer tells Buyer that if he agrees to buy the car "today," Dealer will provide free car washes for as long as Buyer owns the car. The two parties finally come to an agreement on price and sign a written contract. The written contract contains a clause providing that it is the full agreement between the parties. However, it does not provide for free car washes. Absent an applicable exception, the parol evidence rule would prevent Buyer from introducing evidence in court of the oral agreement concerning car washing services that was made prior to the execution of the written contract.

1. **Purpose**

    Its name notwithstanding, the parol evidence rule is not generally regarded as a rule of evidence, but rather as a rule of *substantive contract law*. It is designed to carry out the apparent intention of the parties and to facilitate judicial interpretation by having a single clean source of proof (the writing) on the terms of the bargain.

2. **Is the Writing an "Integration"?**

    The question of whether a writing is an "integration" of all agreements between the parties can be broken down into two further subquestions:

    (i)   Is the writing intended as a *final* expression?

    (ii) Is the writing a *complete* or *partial* integration?

    a. **Is the Writing Intended as a Final Expression?**

        Writings that evidence a purported contract are not necessarily the "final" expression of that contract. Thus, for example, the parties might only have intended such writings to be preliminary to a final draft. If so, the parol evidence rule will not bar introduction of further evidence. Any relevant evidence is admissible to show that the parties did not intend the writing to be final. Note that the *more complete* the agreement appears to be on its face, the more likely it is that it was intended as an *integration*.

    b. **Is the Writing a Complete or Partial Integration?**

        After establishing that the writing was "final," one should determine if the integration was "complete" or only "partial." If complete, the writing may not be contradicted or supplemented; if partial, it cannot be contradicted, but it may be supplemented by proving up consistent additional terms. As with the finality component, whether an integration is complete or partial depends on the intent of the parties. All relevant evidence is admissible for the purpose of making the determination, even the evidence whose admissibility is challenged. The UCC presumes all writings are partial integrations unless there is evidence that the parties intended a writing to be the complete agreement. [UCC §2-202(b)]

        1) **Effect of Merger Clause**

            A merger clause is a statement in a writing reciting that the agreement is the complete agreement between the parties. The presence of a merger clause is often determinative in large commercial contracts in which both parties are represented by lawyers. The modern trend, however, is to consider the clause as one factor in determining the integration issue.

c. Who Makes Decision?

The *majority view* is that the question as to whether an agreement is an integration is decided by the *judge*, not the jury. If the judge decides that the writing was an integration of all agreements between the parties, he will exclude evidence of prior written or oral terms, or contemporaneous oral terms, that seek to vary the terms of the integrated writing. Otherwise, he may admit the offered extrinsic evidence. Then, if there is a jury, it will make its own determination as to whether this extrinsic evidence was part of the agreement.

3. Evidence Outside Scope of Rule

Because the rule prohibits admissibility only of extrinsic evidence that seeks to vary, contradict, or add to an "integration," other forms of extrinsic evidence may be admitted where they will not bring about this result, i.e., they will fall outside the scope of the parol evidence rule.

a. Validity Issues

A party to a written contract can attack the agreement's validity. The party acknowledges (concedes) that the writing reflects the agreement but asserts, most frequently, that the *agreement never came into being* because of any of the following:

1) Formation Defects

Formation defects (e.g., fraud, duress, mistake, and illegality) may be shown by extrinsic evidence.

2) Conditions Precedent to Effectiveness

Where a party asserts that there was an oral agreement that the written contract would not become *effective* until a condition occurred, all evidence of the understanding may be offered and received. This would be a condition precedent to effectiveness. The rationale is that you are not altering a written agreement by means of parol evidence if the written agreement never came into being. It should be borne in mind that parol evidence of such a condition precedent will not be admitted if it contradicts the express language of the written contract.

Example: Giorgio and Susan sign what appears to be a complete contract, but agree orally that the agreement is not to become binding unless Susan can secure financing, or until her home office approves, or the like. The nonhappening of the stipulated event may be shown because the parol evidence rule does not come into play until a binding contract exists.

Note that parol evidence is not admissible to show a condition that limits or modifies a duty under an *existing or formed* contract.

b. Collateral Agreements and Naturally Omitted Terms

Parol evidence is often said to be admissible if the alleged parol agreement is collateral to the written obligation (i.e., related to the subject matter but not part of the primary promise) and does not conflict with it. This "collateral agreement" doctrine is hard to apply because it is conclusory. The Restatements of Contracts include a similar concept with a more definitive approach: the naturally omitted terms doctrine. The doctrine allows evidence of terms that would naturally be omitted from the written agreement. A term would naturally be omitted if:

(i) It *does not conflict* with the written integration; and

(ii) It concerns a subject that similarly situated parties *would not ordinarily be expected to include* in the written instrument.

[Restatement (First) of Contracts, §240; Restatement (Second) of Contracts, §216|

Example: Seller offered to sell his sister his ranch. The deed gave Seller an option to repurchase, but the parties orally agreed that the option could not be transferred to a third party. Oral evidence of the agreement was not barred by the parol evidence rule. The court held that when family members are contracting, they would not ordinarily be expected to put such a term into the written contract. [*See* Masterson v. Sine, 68 Cal. 2d 222 (1968)]

c. **Interpretation**
If there is uncertainty or ambiguity in the written agreement's terms or a dispute as to the *meaning* of those terms, parol evidence can be received to aid the fact-finder in reaching a correct interpretation of the agreement. If the meaning of the agreement is plain, parol evidence is inadmissible.

d. **Showing of "True Consideration"**
The parol evidence rule will not bar extrinsic evidence showing the "true consideration" paid.
Example: A contract states that $10 has been given as full and complete consideration. Extrinsic evidence will be admitted, by way of a defense, to show that this sum has never been paid.

e. **Reformation**
If a party to a written agreement alleges facts (e.g., mistake) entitling him to reformation of the agreement (*see* VIII.E., *infra*), the parol evidence rule is inapplicable. Why? Because the plaintiff is asserting as a cause of action that despite the apparently unambiguous terms of the written agreement, those terms do not in fact constitute the agreement between the parties.

f. **Subsequent Modifications**
Parol evidence can be offered to show subsequent modifications of a written contract, because the parol evidence rule applies only to prior or contemporaneous negotiations. In short, the parties may show that they have altered the integrated writing after its making.

g. **Additional Terms Under Article 2**
As noted above, under Article 2 a party cannot contradict a written contract but he may add *consistent additional terms* unless: (i) there is a merger clause, or (ii) the courts find from all of the circumstances that the writing was intended as a complete and exclusive statement of the terms of the agreement. [*See* UCC §2-202] Article 2 also

provides that a written contract's terms may be *explained* or *supplemented* by evidence of course of performance, course of dealing, and usage of trade—regardless of whether or not the writing appears to be ambiguous.

D. ARTICLE 2 PROVISIONS ON INTERPRETING CONTRACTS

1. Supplemental ("Gap-Filler") Terms

Recall that the key to forming a contract for the sale of goods is the quantity term (*see* II.B.2.b.1)b), *supra*). If other terms are missing from the agreement, Article 2 has gap-filler provisions to fill in the missing term(s).

a. Price

If: (i) nothing has been said as to price; (ii) the price is left open to be agreed upon by the parties and they fail to agree; or (iii) the price is to be fixed in terms of some standard that is set by a third person or agency and it is not set, then the price is a *reasonable price at the time for delivery*. [UCC §2-305]

b. Place of Delivery

If the place of delivery is not specified, the place is the *seller's place of business*, if he has one; otherwise, it is the seller's home. However, if the goods have been identified as the ones to satisfy the contract and the parties know that they are in some other place, then that is the place of delivery. [UCC §2-308]

c. Time for Shipment or Delivery

If the time for shipment or delivery is not specified, shipment/delivery is due in a *reasonable time*. [UCC §2-309]

d. Time for Payment

If the time for payment is not specified, payment is due at the *time and place at which the buyer is to receive the goods*. [UCC §2-310]

e. Assortment

If a contract provides that an assortment of goods is to be delivered (e.g., blouses in various colors and sizes) and does not specify which party is to choose, the assortment is to be *at the buyer's option*. If the party who has the right to specify the assortment does not do so seasonably, the other party is excused from any resulting delay and may either proceed in any reasonable manner (e.g., choose a reasonable assortment) or treat the failure as a breach. [UCC §2-311]

2. Delivery Terms and Risk of Loss

All contracts for the sale of goods require delivery of the goods. Often, delivery consists merely of allowing the buyer to take the goods with him (e.g., a purchase of groceries from the grocery store). However, circumstances often require some other type of delivery (e.g., delivery of 100 cases of cereal to the grocery store requires shipment). A contract's delivery terms are important because they determine when risk of loss passes from the seller to the buyer if the goods are damaged or destroyed.

a. Noncarrier Case

A noncarrier case is a sale in which it appears that the parties did not intend that the goods would be moved by a common carrier (e.g., when you buy groceries). In such a case, if the *seller is a merchant*, risk of loss passes to the buyer only when she *takes physical possession* of the goods. If the *seller is not a merchant*, risk of loss passes to the buyer upon *tender of delivery*. [*See* UCC §2-509(3)]

Examples: 1) Merchant Seller sells goods to Buyer who is to pick them up at noon on Monday. Seller has the goods ready for Buyer at that time, but Buyer does not arrive. The goods are destroyed at 1:30 p.m. that day. Risk of loss falls on the merchant seller because the buyer had not actually picked up the goods.

2) Nonmerchant Seller sells goods to Buyer and the parties agree that the goods will be picked up by Buyer at noon on Monday. Seller has the goods ready for Buyer at that time, but Buyer does not arrive. The goods are destroyed at 1:30 p.m. that day. Risk of loss falls on Buyer because Seller tendered delivery at noon when he had the goods ready for pickup by Buyer.

b.   Carrier Cases

A carrier case is a sale in which it appears that the parties intended the goods to be moved by a carrier (e.g., when you order a book from an Internet website). There are two types of carrier cases: shipment contracts and destination contracts. Whether a contract is a shipment contract or a destination contract depends on the delivery terms used in the contract.

1)   Shipment Contract

If the contract authorizes or requires the seller to ship the goods by carrier but does not require him to deliver them at a particular destination, it is a shipment contract and risk of loss passes to the buyer when the goods are *delivered to the carrier*. The UCC presumes a contract is a shipment contract in the absence of a contrary agreement. A "ship to" address does not overcome this presumption. [UCC §2-509(1)(a)]

Example: Seller in New York sells 10,000 tons of steel to Buyer in California. The contract authorizes shipment by carrier but does not require Seller to tender the goods in California. Risk passes to Buyer when the goods are placed in possession of the carrier. If the goods are damaged in transit, the loss falls on Buyer.

a)   Seller's Duties Under Shipment Contract

In a shipment contract, the seller has the following duties:

(1)   Make a *reasonable contract* with the carrier on behalf of the buyer (considering the nature of the goods and other relevant circumstances);

(2)   *Deliver the goods to the carrier;*

(3)   *Promptly notify* the buyer of the shipment; and

(4)   Provide the buyer with *any documents* needed to take possession of the goods.

2) Destination Contracts

If the contract requires the seller to deliver the goods at a particular destination, the risk of loss passes to the buyer when the goods are ***tendered to the buyer at the destination***. [UCC §2-509(1)(b)] Specifying a destination in this context means more than just indicating an address for shipment. Otherwise, all contracts would be destination contracts. A contract that contains neither an F.O.B. term nor any other term explicitly allocating the risk of loss is a shipment contract.

Example: If, in the last example, the contract provided that the goods must be tendered in California, risk of loss during transit to California would have been on Seller.

3) Common Delivery Terms

A number of abbreviations are often used in commercial contracts to set out the shipping terms. When used, these abbreviations determine whether the contract is a shipment or a destination contract. If the contract contemplates delivery by a carrier and no delivery term is used, the contract is a shipment contract.

a) F.O.B.

F.O.B. stands for "free on board." The letters F.O.B. are always followed by a location, and the risk of loss passes to the buyer at the named location. The seller bears the risk and expense of getting the goods to the named location. These contracts can be either shipment contracts or destination contracts, depending on the location named.

Examples: 1) Seller in New York sells 10,000 widgets to Buyer in California, "F.O.B. New York," or "F.O.B. Seller's materials yard." This is a shipment contract and risk of loss and expenses of shipment must be borne by the buyer during shipment.

2) Same facts as above, but the contract is "F.O.B. California" or "F.O.B. Buyer's warehouse." This is a destination contract and Seller must bear the risk of loss and expenses of shipping to the named destination.

b) F.A.S.

F.A.S. stands for "free alongside." The term is generally used only when goods are to be shipped by boat. The risk of loss passes to the buyer once the goods are delivered to the dock.

c. Effect of Breach on Risk of Loss

1) Defective Goods

If the buyer has a right to reject the goods, the risk of loss does not pass to the buyer until the defects are ***cured*** or she ***accepts*** the goods in spite of their defects. [UCC §2-510(1)] Note that a buyer generally has the right to reject for any defect. (*See* VII.C., *infra*.)

Example: Buyer has ordered blue widgets from Seller, F.O.B. Seller's plant. Seller ships blue-black widgets, giving Buyer a right to reject. The widgets are damaged in transit. The risk of loss falls on Seller, although the risk would have been on Buyer if blue widgets had been shipped.

2) **Revocation of Acceptance**

If the buyer rightfully revokes acceptance, the *risk of loss* is treated as having rested *on the seller from the beginning* to the extent of any deficiency in the buyer's insurance coverage, the risk of loss at issue being that between the time of acceptance and the time of revocation of acceptance. [UCC §2-510(2)] However, revocation of acceptance is rightful only if it occurs "before any substantial change in condition of the goods which is not caused by their own defects." [UCC §2-608(2)] Thus, there can be no revocation of acceptance after a casualty loss to the goods.

d. **Risk in Sale or Return and Sale on Approval Contracts**

1) **Sale or Return**

For the purpose of determining the risk of loss, a sale or return contract (e.g., the buyer takes goods for resale but may return them if she is unable to resell them) is treated as an ordinary sale and the above rules apply. If the goods are returned to the seller, the *risk remains on the buyer* while the goods are in transit. [UCC §2-327(2)]

Example: A magazine distributor delivers 1,000 magazines to a newsstand. The parties agree that the buyer need only pay for any magazines that are not returned to the seller within 40 days. This is a sale or return, and the buyer has the risk of loss until the seller receives any returned magazines.

2) **Sale on Approval**

In a sale on approval (i.e., the buyer takes goods for use but may return them even if they conform to the contract), the risk of loss does not pass to the buyer until she *accepts*. Acceptance may take place by failure to return or notify the seller of an intention to return within the required time. If the buyer decides not to take the goods, return is *at the seller's risk*. [UCC §2-327(1)]

Example: A door-to-door vacuum seller offers to leave a vacuum with a homeowner for 30 days on approval—and the homeowner is not obligated to buy unless completely satisfied at the end of the 30-day period. This is a sale on approval. The risk of loss remains with the seller during the approval period. Thus, if the vacuum is destroyed during the trial period, the buyer is not liable to the seller for its price.

e. **Goods Destroyed Before Risk of Loss Passes**

If goods that were *identified when the contract was made* are destroyed (i) without fault by either party and (ii) before the risk of loss passes to the buyer, the contract is avoided (i.e., the seller's performance is excused). If the goods were not identified until after the contract was made, the seller in this situation would have to prove impracticability (*see* VI.E.5.b., *infra*) to be discharged.

3. **Insurable Interest and Identification**

As noted above, a buyer often bears the risk of loss before receiving the goods purchased. To aid buyers in this situation (and a few others), Article 2 gives buyers a special property interest in goods as soon as they are identified as the ones that will be used to satisfy the contract (e.g., as soon as the seller sets them aside for the buyer). This special property interest is insurable, so that a buyer may obtain insurance for goods while they are being shipped to prevent loss in case of damage or destruction during shipment. [*See* UCC §2-501]

4. **Bilateral Contracts Formed by Performance**

Recall that a contract may be formed by the parties' performance where the mirror image rule is not satisfied and under certain circumstances under Article 2's "battle of the forms" provision [UCC §2-207]. (*See* II.D.5.b., *supra*.) In such cases, under Article 2, the contract includes all of the terms on which the writings of both parties agree. Any necessary missing terms are filled in by the supplemental terms provided for in Article 2. [UCC §2-207(3)]

a. **Compare—Common Law Last Shot Rule**

The rule is different in common law contracts. At common law, the contract will include the terms of the last communication sent to the party who performed. *Rationale:* That communication was a rejection of any prior offer and a counteroffer, and the performance was an acceptance of the terms in that counteroffer.

5. **Warranties**

Contracts for the sale of goods automatically include a warranty of title (in most cases). They also may include certain implied warranties and express warranties.

a. **Warranty of Title and Against Infringement**

1) **Warranty of Title**

Any seller of goods warrants that the title transferred is good, that the transfer is rightful, and that there are no liens or encumbrances against the title of which the buyer is unaware at the time of contracting. [UCC §2-312] This warranty arises automatically and need not be mentioned in the contract.

2) **Warranty Against Infringement**

A *merchant seller* regularly dealing in goods of the kind sold also automatically warrants that the goods are delivered free of any patent, trademark, copyright, or similar claims. But a *buyer who furnishes specifications* for the goods to the seller must hold the seller harmless against such claims. If this warranty is breached and the buyer is sued, she must give the seller notice of the litigation within a reasonable time or lose her right to any remedy. In such a case, the seller can give the buyer notice of his wish to defend the lawsuit and, if the seller agrees to bear all expenses and satisfy any adverse judgment, the buyer must let him defend or lose any rights against him arising out of the breach. [UCC §2-607(3), (5)]

b. **Implied Warranty of Merchantability**

1) **When Given**

Implied in every contract for sale by *a merchant who deals in goods of the kind sold*, there is a warranty that the goods are merchantable. The serving of food or drink for consumption on the premises is a sale of goods subject to the warranty of merchantability. [UCC §2-314(1)]

2) **Elements of Warranty of Merchantability**
To be merchantable, goods must at least:

(i) *Pass without objection* in the trade under the contract description;

(ii) In the case of fungible goods, *be of fair average quality* within the description;

(iii) *Be fit for the ordinary purposes* for which such goods are used;

(iv) Be, within the variations permitted by the agreement, *of even kind, quality, and quantity* within each unit and among all units involved;

(v) *Be adequately contained, packaged, or labeled* according to the contract; and

(vi) *Conform to any promises or affirmations of fact made on the label.* Other warranties of merchantability may arise from the course of dealing or usage of trade.

[UCC §2-314(2)] The most important test is "*fit for the ordinary purposes for which such goods are used*," and a failure to live up to this test is the usual claim in a merchantability suit.

3) **Seller's Knowledge of Defect Not Relevant**
As in all implied warranty cases, it makes no difference that the seller himself did not know of the defect or that he could not have discovered it. Implied warranties are not based on negligence but rather on *absolute liability* that is imposed on certain sellers.

c. **Implied Warranty of Fitness for a Particular Purpose**
A warranty will also be implied in a contract for the sale of goods whenever (i) *any seller*, merchant or not, *has reason to know the particular purpose* for which the goods are to be used and that the *buyer is relying* on the seller's skill and judgment to select suitable goods; and (ii) the *buyer in fact relies* on the seller's skill or judgment. [UCC §2-315] The comment to section 2-315 says, "A particular purpose differs from the ordinary purpose for which goods are used in that it envisages a specific use by the buyer which is peculiar to the nature of his business whereas the ordinary purposes for which goods are used are those envisaged in the concept of merchantability."

Examples: 1) Seller, who as a hobby prepared an automobile for dirt track racing, sold it to Buyer for racing purposes. Buyer was a novice in racing. The steering mechanism collapsed in a turn during a race. The mechanism would not have collapsed in ordinary driving. There was a breach of warranty of fitness for "particular purposes" if the seller had reason to know that the buyer was relying on him to provide a suitable racing vehicle.

2) Seller, a law student, sells his used automobile to Buyer. The steering mechanism collapses during an ordinary Sunday afternoon drive. There is no breach of a warranty of fitness for particular purposes because the element of selection based on Seller's purported skill is not present.

3) Note that in both of the above examples, if the seller knew that the automobile had a particular defect and did not disclose this fact to the buyer, he might be subject to liability because of a lack of good faith. Section 1-304 provides that every contract or duty within the UCC imposes an obligation of good faith in its performance or enforcement.

d. Express Warranties

Any affirmation of fact or promise made by the seller to the buyer, any description of the goods, and any sample or model creates an express warranty if the statement, description, sample, or model is part of the ***basis of the bargain***. For the statement, description, sample, or model to be a part of the basis of the bargain, it need only come at such a time that the ***buyer could have relied*** on it when she entered into the contract. The buyer does not need to prove that she actually did rely, although the seller may negate the warranty by proving that the buyer as a matter of fact did not rely. It is not necessary that the seller intended the affirmation of fact, description, model, or sample to create a warranty. [UCC §2-313]

1) Distinguish—Statements of Value or Opinion

A statement relating merely to the value of the goods, or a statement purporting to be only the seller's opinion or commendation of the goods, does not create an express warranty.

Examples: 1) "Chevrolet cars are better." No warranty.

                2) "You will like this." No warranty.

Compare: A number of courts have held that such statements as "this tractor is in A-1 condition" or "this automobile is in top mechanical condition" do create express warranties that are breached if the statement is not a proper characterization of the condition of the thing sold.

e. Disclaimer of Warranties

1) Warranty of Title

The title warranty can be disclaimed or modified only by specific language or by circumstances which give the buyer notice that the seller does not claim title or that he is selling only such rights as he or a third party may have (e.g., a sheriff's sale).

2) Implied Warranties

The implied warranties of merchantability and fitness for a particular purpose can be disclaimed by either specific disclaimers or general methods of disclaimer.

a) Specific Disclaimers

Article 2 provides specific methods for disclaiming the implied warranties of merchantability and fitness. Use of these methods is the best way for a seller to ensure that a disclaimer is effective.

(1) Disclaimer of Warranty of Merchantability
The warranty of merchantability can be specifically disclaimed or modified only by *mentioning merchantability*. If the sales contract is in writing, the disclaimer must be *conspicuous*. [UCC §2-316(2)]

(2) Disclaimer of Warranty of Fitness for a Particular Purpose
The warranty of fitness for a particular purpose can be specifically disclaimed only by a *conspicuous writing*. A written disclaimer, according to the statute, is sufficient if it says, for example, "[t]here are no warranties which extend beyond the description on the face hereof." [UCC §2-316(2)]

(3) "Conspicuous" Defined
A term is conspicuous when it is "so written, displayed, or presented that a reasonable person against whom it is to operate ought to have noticed it." Language in the body of a writing is conspicuous if: (i) it is in larger type than surrounding text; (ii) it is in a contrasting type, font, or color; or (iii) it is set off from the text by marks that call attention to it. [UCC §1-201(b)(10)] The court, not the jury, decides any fact question as to conspicuousness.

b) Other Methods of Disclaiming Implied Warranties
The UCC also provides several more general methods for disclaiming implied warranties. These methods are more dependent on the circumstances than the specific methods, and so are less certain to be effective than specific disclaimers.

(1) By "As Is" or Similar Language
Unless the circumstances indicate otherwise, the implied warranties of merchantability and fitness can be disclaimed by expressions such as "as is," "with all faults," or other expressions that in common understanding call the buyer's attention to the fact that there are no implied warranties. Although nothing in the UCC specifically requires this type of disclaimer to be conspicuous, many courts have found that a hidden or fine-print disclaimer of this type is not effective.

(2) By Examination or Refusal to Examine
When the buyer, before entering into the contract, has examined the goods or a sample or model as fully as she desires or has refused to examine, there is no warranty as to defects that a reasonable examination would have revealed to her.

(3) By Course of Dealing, Etc.
Implied warranties may also be disclaimed by the course of dealing, course of performance, or usage of trade.

3) **Express Warranties**

As discussed above, any affirmation of fact or promise, description of the goods, model, or sample will create an express warranty. If there are also words or conduct negating the express warranty, problems of interpretation will arise. The UCC provides that words or conduct relevant to the creation of express warranties and words or conduct tending to negate such warranties shall wherever possible be construed as consistent with each other, but "***negation or limitation is inoperative to the extent that such construction is unreasonable.***" [UCC §2-316] Practically every sale will involve some description of the goods, and the comment to section 2-313 suggests that the ***basic obligation*** created by this description cannot be read out of the contract by a disclaimer clause.

Example: Seller sells to Buyer something that Seller describes as an "automobile" being sold "as is," and with sufficient disclaimers of all implied warranties. The thing delivered is an automobile body without an engine, a transmission, or wheels. While an automobile with very substantial defects would have fulfilled this contract, what was delivered was not an "automobile" at all. Seller's description "automobile" created an express warranty that an automobile would be delivered, and the disclaimer did not negate this basic obligation.

Of course, the language of disclaimer in the example would substantially reduce the quality of the automobile that must be delivered.

a) **Parol Evidence Rule**

The parol evidence rule might be an obstacle to a buyer to whom an express warranty was made when the contract contains a broad disclaimer of warranties. In a typical situation, the seller makes an express warranty verbally, but the written contract contains no such warranty and instead contains a clause disclaiming all warranties not set forth in the contract. Here, the parol evidence rule could prevent the buyer from introducing evidence of the verbal warranty. *But note:* The buyer can often avoid the rule by a showing that he did not intend that the writing be the complete and exclusive expression of the parties' agreement (*see* V.C.2., *supra*) or that the disclaimer is unconscionable under the circumstances (*see* 6), *infra*).

4) **Limitations on Damages**

Parties may include in their contract a clause limiting the damages available in the case of breach of warranty (e.g., "remedy for breach of warranty is limited to repair or replacement of the defective goods"). However, such a limitation generally will not be upheld if it is unconscionable (e.g., causes the remedy to fail of its essential purpose; *see* IV.G.1.d., *supra*). Moreover, warranty disclaimers that limit damages for personal injury caused by a breach of warranty on consumer goods are prima facie unconscionable.

5) **Timing—Disclaimers and Limitations in the Box**

To be effective, a disclaimer of warranty or limitation on remedies must be agreed to during the bargaining process. Thus, although a few courts hold otherwise, most hold that a warranty disclaimer or limitation on remedy included inside the packaging of goods is not effective against the buyer. However, there are ways around this (e.g., the outside of the box could indicate that the sale is subject to the conditions stated inside the box; a registration card within the box can indicate that by registering, the owner agrees to all of the conditions set out in the documents in the box (modifying the contract), etc.).

a) Compare—"Clickwrap"

Computer software often comes with terms that appear on the user's computer screen during the installation process, and the purchaser must click to agree to the terms before installing. Such limitations and disclaimers typically are upheld on the rationale that the purchaser can return the software if he disagrees with the conditions.

6) Unconscionability and Warranty Disclaimers

Some courts will, in addition to determining whether disclaimers have met the formal requirements discussed above, test warranty disclaimers by the conscionability standards of UCC section 2-302. Such things as lack of bargaining position, lack of choice, and failure to understand would be relevant in determining whether a disclaimer is unconscionable. (*See* IV.G., *supra*.)

f. Buyer's Damages for Breach of Warranty

1) In General—Difference Between Goods Tendered and as Warranted

Generally, the measure of damages for breach of any warranty is the difference between the value of the goods accepted and the value of the goods as warranted, measured at the time and place of acceptance. When, however, there are special circumstances that show proximate damages of a different amount, that amount is the proper measure. [UCC §2-714(2)] In addition, the buyer can recover appropriate incidental and consequential damages. (*See* VIII.B.1.a.3)-4), *infra*.)

2) Breach of Warranty of Title

In the case of a breach of warranty of title, the buyer may rescind the contract, revoke acceptance of the goods, or sue for damages. In these cases, the goods are reclaimed by the true owner or lien holder, thus dispossessing the purchaser. The value of the goods accepted is deemed to be nothing; so the damages are the value of the goods as warranted. Often, but not always, that is the same as the purchase price.

a) Special Circumstances—Appreciation and Depreciation

As noted above, damages may be measured differently if there are special circumstances. A great appreciation or depreciation in the value of the goods from the time of delivery until the purchaser is dispossessed of the property is usually considered such a special circumstance. In that case, the value is measured at the time of the dispossession rather than at the time of acceptance.

Examples: 1) Buyer purchases a painting for $10,000 from Seller, who in turn purchased the painting from Gallery. Unbeknownst to any of the parties, the person who sold the painting to Gallery had stolen it. Several years after Buyer's purchase, Owner, the painting's true owner, sues Buyer and recovers the painting, which is now worth $100,000. The appreciation is a special circumstance, so Buyer's damages will be the value of the painting at dispossession—$100,000. [*See* Menzel v. List, 24 N.Y.2d 91 (1969)]

2) Buyer purchases a used truck for $5,000 from Seller's used car dealership. After driving it for one year, Buyer is pulled over in a routine traffic stop. The police inform Buyer the truck is stolen and impound it. When taken by the police, the truck was worth $4,200. Having use and possession of the truck for a substantial period of time is a special circumstance, and Buyer is entitled only to the value of the truck on the date it was impounded. [*See* City Car Sales v. McAlpin, 380 So. 2d 865 (Ala. 1979); Schneidt v. Absey Motors, Inc., 248 N.W.2d 792 (N.D. 1976)]

g. To Whom Do Warranties Extend?

Article 2 provides alternative provisions for determining to whom warranty liability extends beyond the initial buyer. [UCC §2-318] Most states have adopted **Alternative A**, which provides that the seller's warranty liability extends to any natural person who is in the **family** or **household** of the buyer or who is a **guest** in the buyer's home if it is reasonable to expect that the person may use, consume, or be affected by the goods and that person suffers **personal injury** because of a breach of warranty. The seller cannot escape the effect of this section by contract. (The comments say that beyond this, the section is neutral and is not intended to enlarge or restrict the developing case law on whether the seller's warranties given to his buyer who resells extend to other persons in the distributive chain.) Alternative B extends a seller's express or implied warranty liability to **any natural person** reasonably expected to use, consume, or be affected by the goods and who suffers **personal injury** because of a breach of warranty. The broadest alternative, Alternative C, extends warranty liability to **any person** reasonably expected to use, consume, or be affected by the goods and who is **injured** by breach of the warranty (this includes property damage). The seller may not exclude or limit the operation of the section with respect to **personal injury**.

E. MODIFICATION OF CONTRACT TERMS

1. Consideration

Under general contract law, a final contract cannot be modified unless the modification is supported by new consideration. The modern view, however, permits modification without consideration if: (i) the modification is due to circumstances that were unanticipated by the parties when the contract was made and (ii) it is fair and equitable. [*See* Restatement (Second) of Contracts §89] *The bar examiners have indicated that they are looking for the modern view on the MBE.* The UCC is even more liberal with regard to modification. Under the UCC, promises of new and different terms by the parties to a sales contract are valid without consideration, but good faith is required to make a modification enforceable.

2. **Writing**

A written contract can be modified orally. However, the modification must be in writing if the contract as modified falls within the Statute of Frauds. Thus, for a sale of goods contract, if the contract *as modified* is for $500 or more, it must be evidenced by a writing; if the contract *as modified* is for less than $500, no writing is necessary. [UCC §2-209]

Examples: 1) Seller agrees to sell Buyer his car for $525 and the parties put the contract in writing to satisfy the Statute of Frauds. Subsequently, Buyer discovers that he can afford to spend only $475 on a car. Buyer calls Seller and tells Seller of his trouble. Seller agrees to lower the price to $475. A writing is no longer necessary, and either party can enforce the oral modification.

2) Mary phones Paul and asks Paul for his price on widgets. Paul informs Mary that he currently is selling widgets for $3 each. Mary asks Paul to send her 150 widgets. Paul agrees, and tells Mary that he will ship them the next day. The contract is enforceable without a writing. A few hours later, Mary phones Paul back and asks Paul whether he could send her 200 widgets instead of 150. Paul agrees. The contract as modified is not enforceable absent a written memorandum satisfying the Statute of Frauds. The original contract remains enforceable.

a. **Provisions Prohibiting Oral Modification Not Effective at Common Law**

The common law rule is that even if a written contract expressly provides that it may be modified only by a writing, the parties can orally modify the contract.

b. **UCC Recognizes No-Modification Clauses**

Under the UCC, even if a contract is not within the Statute of Frauds, if it explicitly provides that it may not be modified or rescinded except by a signed writing, that provision will be given effect. [UCC §2-209]

1) **Contract Between Merchant and Nonmerchant**

If a contract is between a merchant and a nonmerchant and the provision requiring written modification is on the merchant's form, the provision will not be given effect unless it is *separately signed* by the nonmerchant.

2) **Waiver**

If the parties attempt to orally modify a contract that requires written modification (either because of a contract clause or the Statute of Frauds), it is technically ineffective as a modification, but can operate as a waiver. Such a waiver will be found whenever the other party has changed position in reliance on the oral modification.

a) **Retraction of Waiver**

A party who makes a waiver affecting an executory (not yet performed) portion of the contract may retract the waiver if she notifies the other party that strict performance of the waived terms is required. The waiver may not be retracted, however, if the other party detrimentally relied on it. [UCC §2-209(5)]

Example: A contract between Buyer and Seller for 800 widgets contains a clause requiring all modifications to be in writing. The parties orally agree to reduce the number to 400 widgets. Buyer later decides he wants 800 widgets after all. If Seller relied on the oral modification in making contracts with other parties for widgets and does not have stock available, Buyer cannot retract the waiver. If, however, Seller did not change his position in reliance on the waiver, Buyer may retract the waiver and enforce the contract for the full 800 widgets.

3. Parol Evidence Rule Does Not Apply

As noted above, parol evidence is admissible to show subsequent oral modifications of a written contract.

VI. PERFORMANCE AND EXCUSE OF NONPERFORMANCE

A. INTRODUCTION

Having established that there is a contract and having determined what are the terms of the contract, the next issue to consider is what performance is due and whether any nonperformance is excused.

B. PERFORMANCE AT COMMON LAW

A party's basic duty at common law is to **substantially perform** all that is called for in the contract.

C. PERFORMANCE UNDER ARTICLE 2

Article 2 generally requires a **perfect tender**—the delivery and condition of the goods must be exactly as promised in the contract. Note the following:

1. Obligation of Good Faith

As noted in I.B.5., *supra*, in performance or enforcement of a contractual duty, Article 2 requires all parties to act in good faith, which is defined as "honesty in fact and the observance of reasonable commercial standards of fair dealing." [UCC §1-201(2)] This obligation cannot be waived by the parties.

2. Seller's Obligation of Tender and Delivery

a. Noncarrier Cases

Recall that a noncarrier case is a sale in which it appears that the parties did not intend that the goods be moved by carrier. (*See* V.D.2.a., *supra*.)

1) Tender of Delivery

In a proper tender of delivery, the seller must put and hold conforming goods at the buyer's disposition for a time sufficient for the buyer to take possession. The seller must **give the buyer notice** reasonably necessary to enable her to take possession of the goods. The **tender must be at a reasonable hour.** [UCC §2-503(1)]

2) Place of Delivery

In the absence of an agreement otherwise, the place of delivery is the **seller's place** *of business*, or if he has none, his residence. However, if at the time of contracting, the goods are, to the knowledge of both parties, at some other place, that place is the place of delivery. [UCC §2-308]

b. Carrier Cases

Recall that a carrier case is a sale in which, due either to the circumstances or to the express terms of the agreement, it appears that the parties intended that a carrier be used to move the goods. (*See* V.D.2.b., *supra*.)

1) Shipment Contracts—Where Seller Has Not Agreed to Tender at Particular Destination

In the absence of an agreement otherwise, the seller need not see that the goods reach the buyer, but need only:

a) Put the goods into the hands of a reasonable carrier and make a reasonable contract for their transportation to the buyer;

b) Obtain and promptly tender any documents required by the contract or usage of trade or otherwise necessary to enable the buyer to take possession; and

c) Promptly notify the buyer of the shipment.

2) Destination Contracts—Where Seller Has Agreed to Tender at Particular Destination

If the contract requires the seller to tender delivery of the goods at a particular destination, the seller must, at the destination, put and hold conforming goods at the buyer's disposition. He must also give the buyer any notice of tender that is reasonably necessary and provide her with any documents of title necessary to obtain delivery. Tender of documents through ordinary banking channels is sufficient. [UCC §2-503]

3. Buyer's Obligation to Pay—Right to Inspect

a. Delivery and Payment Concurrent Conditions

In *noncarrier cases*, unless the contract provides otherwise, a sale is for cash and the price is due concurrently with tender of delivery. However, unless otherwise agreed, when goods are shipped *by carrier*, the price is due only at the time and place at which the buyer receives the goods. Therefore, in a shipment case, the price is due when the goods are put in the hands of the carrier, and in a destination contract, the price is due when the goods reach the named destination.

b. Payment by Check

Tender of payment by check is sufficient unless the seller demands legal tender and gives the buyer time to get cash. If a check is given, the buyer's duty to pay is suspended until the check is either paid or dishonored. If the check is paid, the buyer's duty to pay is discharged. If the check is dishonored, the seller may sue for the price or recover the goods. [UCC §2-511]

c. Installment Contracts

In an installment contract (i.e., one that requires or authorizes delivery in separate installments), the seller may demand payment for each installment if the price can be so apportioned, unless a contrary intent appears. [UCC §2-307]

d. Buyer's Right of Inspection

Unless the contract provides otherwise, the buyer has a right to inspect the goods before she pays. Expenses of inspection must be borne by the buyer but may be recovered from the seller if the goods do not conform and are rejected. A buyer may inspect at any reasonable time and in any reasonable manner. [UCC §2-513]

Note: If the contract between the parties provides for payment C.O.D. or otherwise indicates that the buyer has promised to pay without inspecting the goods, there is no right of inspection prior to payment. If payment is due before inspection, the fact that the goods are defective does not excuse nonpayment unless the defect appears without inspection or there is fraud in the transaction. [UCC §§2-512, 2-513]

Examples: 1) Buyer in California and Seller in New York contract for sale of steel to be shipped to California. Nothing is said as to payment. Buyer has a right to inspect the goods before payment.

2) Same situation as above, except that the contract provides for payment of cash on delivery. Buyer must pay when the steel is delivered, and she does not have a right of inspection prior to payment.

3) Same situation as last example, except that the goods are defective. To put Seller in breach, Buyer must pay, unless the defect appears without inspection.

D. CONDITIONS—HAS THE DUTY TO PERFORM BECOME ABSOLUTE?

A contract may provide that a party does not have a duty to perform unless some condition is fulfilled. In such a case, the party's failure to perform will normally be *justified* if the condition was not fulfilled.

1. Distinction Between Promise and Condition

It is important to understand that there is a difference between whether a party is bound under a contract and whether a party who is bound has come under a duty to perform. A person is bound if there has been an offer, an acceptance, and an exchange of consideration. However, the contract may provide (impliedly or explicitly) that a party who is bound does not come under a duty to perform unless or until some specified condition occurs. In looking at the terms of a contract, a distinction has to be drawn between an absolute promise on the one hand and a condition on the other.

a. Definitions

1) Promise

A promise is a commitment to do or refrain from doing something. If a promise is unconditional, the failure to perform according to its terms is a breach of contract.

2) Condition

In this context, the term "condition" normally means *either*: (i) an event or state of the world that must occur or fail to occur *before* a party has a duty to perform under a contract; or (ii) an event or state of the world the occurrence or nonoccurrence of which *releases* a party from its duty to perform under a contract. In other words, a condition is a provision, the fulfillment of which creates or extinguishes a duty to perform under a contract. A condition is a *"promise modifier."* There can be no breach of promise until the promisor is under an immediate duty to perform. He may insert conditions on his promise to prevent that duty of immediate performance from arising until the conditions are met.

a)   **Failure of Condition vs. Breach of Contract**
       The failure of a contractual provision that is only a condition is *not a breach of contract*, but it discharges the liability of the promisor whose obligations on the conditional promise never mature.

       Example: Gene agrees to sell his horse to Roy, the contract providing
                         that delivery of possession will take place on June 1. On May
                         25, the horse dies. Was delivery of possession of the horse a
                         condition? If so, its failure to occur will discharge Roy's duty
                         to pay; however, Roy will not have a cause of action against
                         Gene for nondelivery. Or was it a promise by Gene, the breach
                         of which will give to Roy both an action against Gene for
                         breach of contract and release him from his duty to pay?

       An unexcused failure to perform a *promise* is always a breach of contract and always gives rise to liability, however minimal. On the other hand, nonfulfillment of a *condition* is *not* a breach of contract and does not give rise to liability.

b)   **Excuse of Performance**
       Breach of a *promise* by one party may or may not excuse the other party's duty to perform under the contract (*see* 6.b., *infra*). Nonfulfillment of a *condition* normally will excuse a duty to perform that was subject to the condition.

c)   **Interrelation of Conditions and Promises**
       If a party's *promise* to perform is subject to a condition, there can be no breach of contract by that party until the condition has been fulfilled.

b.   **Interpretation of Provision as Promise or Condition**
      As the above example indicates, it is of considerable importance whether any given contractual provision is to be interpreted as a promise or condition. The basic test is one of *"intent of the parties."* The courts employ several basic criteria in reaching a determination as to intent.

1)   **Words of Agreement**
       Words such as "provided," "if," and "when" usually indicate that an express condition rather than a promise was intended. Words such as "promise" and "agree" usually indicate a promise. However, words by themselves might not be determinative. Both the specific words of the phrase and the words of the rest of the agreement (thus the context of the entire contract) will be examined by the courts in drawing a conclusion.

2) Prior Practices

The prior practices of the contracting parties, particularly with one another, will be taken into consideration.

3) Custom

The custom with respect to that business in the community will be examined.

4) Third-Party Performance

If performance is to be rendered by a third party, it is more likely to be a condition than an absolute promise.

5) Courts Prefer Promise in Doubtful Situations

In doubtful situations, most courts will hold that the provision in question is a *promise*. The underlying rationale is that this result will serve to support the contract, thereby preserving the expectancy of the parties. This preference is particularly significant in situations where the breaching party has **substantially performed**, because if the provision is treated as a **condition**, the nonbreaching party is completely discharged from her obligation; whereas, if the provision is treated as a **promise**, the nonbreaching party must perform, although she may recover for the damage she has suffered as a result of the breach.

Example: Stan contracts to build a house for Natasha using pipe of Reading manufacture. In return, Natasha agrees to pay Stan $100,000. Without Stan's knowledge, a subcontractor mistakenly uses pipe of Cohoes manufacture, which is identical in quality and is virtually indistinguishable from Reading pipe. The substitution is not discovered until the house is completed, when replacement of the pipe would require substantial destruction of the house. Natasha refuses to pay Stan. The installation of Reading pipe was a promise, not a condition, of the contract; therefore, Stan has a claim against Natasha for $100,000, subject to her claim against him for breach of duty to use Reading pipe. To treat it as a condition would be unfair to Stan, because he would be penalized in an amount far greater than the amount of the damage suffered by Natasha.

Note: When seeking to establish the reasonable expectations of the parties, one should determine whether the performance of the stipulation goes to the "very root" of the contract's consideration. If so, it is probably a condition rather than a promise.

6) Reference to Time

A provision that states that a duty is to be performed "when" an event occurs raises an issue of whether the event is a condition or is intended to merely mark the passage of time. Courts prefer the time interpretation, which reduces the obligee's risk of forfeiture, unless the event is within the obligee's control. [*See* Restatement (Second) of Contracts §227]

Example: A subcontractor's contract with the general contractor provides that the general contractor will pay the subcontractor's fee when the general contractor is paid by the landowner. Absent language such as "on condition that," this contract language is interpreted as a time for payment, not a condition. Payment by the landowner is not within the subcontractor's control. Therefore, the general contractor must pay the subcontractor within a reasonable time regardless of whether the landowner pays the general contractor.

c. Provision Both Promise and Condition

1) Condition May Imply a Promise

When the occurrence of a condition is within the benefiting party's control, that party impliedly promises to act in good faith and use reasonable effort to cause the condition to occur.

Example: Buyer and Seller enter into an agreement for the sale of Blackacre. The written contract provides that the contract is contingent on Buyer obtaining a 30-year mortgage at 5%. Buyer changes his mind about the purchase and does not apply for any mortgages. Because of his lack of good faith reasonable effort to obtain a mortgage, Buyer's duty to perform under the contract will not be excused by the failure of the condition.

2) Express Promise and Condition

In some cases, a provision may be both a promise and a condition—i.e., a party may commit (promise) to bring about a given state of events, and the contract containing that commitment may also expressly state that the other party's duty to perform under the contract is conditioned on the occurrence of the state of events.

Example: Carrier promises to get Manufacturer's goods to Los Angeles by October 1, and the contract expressly provides that Manufacturer will have no duty to pay Carrier unless the goods arrive by that time. Getting the goods to Los Angeles by October 1 is both a promise by Carrier and a condition to Manufacturer's liability.

2. Classification of Conditions

a. Condition Precedent

A condition precedent is one that must occur *before* an absolute duty of immediate performance arises in the other party.

Example: Sal and Mary agree that "in consideration of Mary's promise to repay principal plus 8% interest, Sal hereby promises to loan Mary $50,000 for one year, provided that on July 1, the market value of Mary's country home is not less than $100,000." On July 1, Mary's country home is appraised at a market value of $80,000. Sal refuses to make the loan, and Mary sues. Sal wins because his duty to loan the $50,000 is subject to an express condition precedent. Because the condition was not satisfied, Sal's contingent liability never matured.

b. Conditions Concurrent

Conditions concurrent are those that are capable of occurring *together*, and that the parties are bound to perform at the same time (e.g., tender of deed for cash). Thus, in effect, each is a condition "precedent" to the other.

Example: Smith and Jones agree that "in consideration of Jones's promise to pay the sum of $500, Smith promises to convey his 1970 Buick." Having signed this agreement, Jones never tenders the $500 and Smith does not tender the car. Neither party is in breach of contract. The contract is silent regarding the time and place of performance, but the promises exchanged as consideration can obviously be performed at the same time and place. Hence, tender of the promised performance by each party is a constructive condition concurrent to liability of the other. Because both parties failed to tender performance, neither obligation matured.

c. **Condition Subsequent**

A condition subsequent is one the occurrence of which ***cuts off*** an already existing absolute duty of performance.

Example: Will and Grace enter the following contract: In consideration of Will's conveying his painting to her, Grace promises to pay Will $5,000 on July 1. Grace further promises to permit Will to retain the painting for purposes of exhibition during the months of July and August, provided security precautions for the safety of the painting are approved by Captain Smith. On July 1, Grace pays Will $5,000, and Will begins to exhibit the painting. On July 10, Captain Smith inspects security at the exhibition and declares it to be inadequate. Grace immediately asserts her right to possession, but Will refuses to surrender the painting. Grace is entitled to immediate possession of the painting. Her allowing Will to retain the painting for exhibition was subject to an express condition subsequent based on Captain Smith's approval of security precautions. Because the condition subsequent has ripened, Grace's conditional obligation to allow Will to retain the painting is extinguished.

3. **Express Conditions**

The term "express condition" normally refers to an ***explicit contractual provision***. It is an express statement in the contract providing that either (i) a party does not have a duty to perform unless some event occurs or fails to occur; or (ii) if some event occurs or fails to occur, the obligation of a party to perform one or more of his duties under the contract is suspended or terminated. Conditions of satisfaction are common express conditions.

a. **Promisor's Satisfaction as Condition Precedent**

Many contracts include an express condition that a party will pay only if "satisfied" with the other party's performance. Because it is a condition, the promisor is under no duty to pay unless she is satisfied. The issue is how the promisor's satisfaction is to be measured; i.e., whether the performance must meet with promisor's ***actual personal*** satisfaction, or must only be a performance that would meet with the satisfaction of a ***reasonable person***. The provision requiring the promisor's satisfaction is construed according to the ***subject matter*** of the contract.

1) **Mechanical Fitness, Utility, or Marketability**

In contracts involving mechanical fitness, utility, or marketability (e.g., construction or manufacturing contracts), a condition of satisfaction is fulfilled by a performance that would satisfy a ***reasonable person***. It is therefore immaterial that the promisor was not personally satisfied if a reasonable person would have accepted and approved the performance tendered.

2) Personal Taste or Judgment

If the contract involves personal taste or personal judgment, a condition of satisfaction is fulfilled only if the promisor is *personally satisfied*. For example, contracts for portraits, dental work, or tailoring all require the promisor's personal satisfaction.

a) Lack of Satisfaction Must Be Honest and in Good Faith

Even if a condition requires personal satisfaction, it will fail to be fulfilled only if the promisor's lack of satisfaction is honest and in good faith. Therefore, if the promisor refuses to examine the promisee's performance, or otherwise rejects the performance in bad faith, the condition of satisfaction will be *excused*.

b. Satisfaction of Third Person as Condition

In many contracts, an express condition requires the satisfaction of a third person rather than a party to the contract. In particular, construction contracts often include a condition requiring the satisfaction of the owner's architect or engineer. When the satisfaction of a third person is a condition, most courts take the position that the condition requires the *actual personal satisfaction* of the third person. As in the case where a party's personal satisfaction is required, however, a condition that requires a third person's personal satisfaction will be excused if the third person's dissatisfaction is not *honest and in good faith*.

c. When Purpose of Condition Is to Benefit One Party

When it is clear that the purpose of a condition is to protect or benefit only one of the parties, the other party's duty will not be subject to the condition.

Example: A buyer and seller enter into a contract under which the buyer will purchase the seller's property if the buyer is able to obtain a loan at 6% interest. The buyer is only able to obtain a loan at 7% but wants to go through with the purchase. The condition was clearly inserted for the buyer's benefit. Courts will not allow the seller to use the condition to excuse his duty and avoid the contract.

4. Constructive (Implied) Conditions

Sometimes it is implied that the duty to render performance under a contract is conditional upon the occurrence of some event or state of the world, even though the contract does not explicitly so state. In that case, there is said to be an "implied" or "constructive" condition that the relevant event or state of the world must occur before the performance of one or both parties comes due.

a. Constructive Conditions of Performance

By far the most important and common implied condition is that the duty of each party to render performance is conditioned on the *other party* either rendering *his* performance or making a tender of his performance.

Example: Owen and Pete make a contract under which Pete will paint Owen's house by May 30, and Owen will pay Pete $8,000 on June 1. It is an implied condition to Owen's duty to pay $8,000 that Pete shall have painted the house. If Pete fails to paint Owen's house by June 1, it has a dual effect: (i) it is a breach of contract for which Pete will be liable in damages, and (ii) it is a nonfulfillment of an implied condition to Owen's duty to pay, so Owen does not have a duty to pay Pete.

b. Constructive Conditions of Cooperation and Notice

Constructive conditions of cooperation and notice are common. Under a constructive condition of cooperation, the obligation of one party to render performance is impliedly conditioned on the other party's cooperation in that performance. Also, it is often a condition to one party's performance of a duty under a contract that the other party give him *notice* that the performance is due. A condition of notice is most commonly applied where a party could not reasonably be expected to know a fact that triggered the duty to perform unless such notice was given.

Examples: 1) Seller promises to deliver certain goods to the "No. 2 loading dock" of Buyer's factory. It is an implied condition to Seller's duty to deliver the goods that such a loading dock exists, that the dock is reasonably accessible for making a delivery, and that Buyer permits Seller to make the delivery at the dock.

2) Landlord leases a building to Tenant and promises to maintain and repair the interior of the building as necessary. It is an implied condition to Landlord's promise to repair that Tenant will give her reasonable notification of the need for repairs and will permit her to enter to make the repairs. Tenant therefore cannot sue Landlord for failure to make a needed repair unless he has first notified Landlord that the repair is required, and given Landlord an opportunity to make the repair.

c. Order of Performance

The courts will also imply conditions relating to the time for performing under the contract.

1) Simultaneous Performance Possible—Conditions Concurrent

If both performances can be rendered at the same time, they are constructively concurrent; thus, each is a condition "precedent" to the other. Hence, absent excuse, each party must first tender his own performance if he wishes to put the other under a duty of immediate performance resulting in breach if he fails to perform.

Example: Lulu agrees to sell Hank her old tractor for $4,000. Because Lulu can sign over title and Hank can hand over money at the same time, the conditions are constructively concurrent.

2) One Performance Takes Time—Conditions Precedent

If one performance will take a period of time to complete while the other can be rendered in an instant, completion of the longer performance is a constructive condition precedent to execution of the shorter performance.

Example: Lulu agrees to paint Hank's barn for $400. In absence of a contract provision to the contrary, Lulu must paint the barn before Hank must pay.

5. **Effect of Condition—Equitable Remedy**

If a contract is not enforceable due to the failure or occurrence of a condition, and one of the parties has fully or partially performed, he can usually recover under unjust enrichment theories (*see* VIII.C., *infra*), although the measure of damages in that case may be less advantageous than the contract price.

6. **Have the Conditions Been Excused?**

A duty of immediate performance with respect to a conditional promise does not become *absolute* until the conditions (i) have been *performed*, or (ii) have been *legally excused*. Thus, in analyzing a question, if the facts do not reveal performance of the applicable condition precedent or concurrent, look to see whether the condition has been excused. Excuse of conditions can arise in a variety of ways.

a. **Excuse of Condition by Hindrance or Failure to Cooperate**

If a party having a duty of performance that is subject to a condition (i.e., she is the party protected by the condition) prevents the condition from occurring, the condition will be excused if such prevention is *wrongful*. Note, however, that it is not necessary to prove bad faith or malice. Courts construe the requirement simply to mean that the other party would not have reasonably contemplated or assumed the risk of this type of conduct.

Example: Franz agrees to paint Worthington's portrait. Worthington's promise to pay for the portrait is conditional upon her being satisfied with it. Worthington refuses to even look at the portrait. Because of her refusal, the condition is excused and her promise to pay becomes absolute.

Note: It appears fairly well settled today that a condition will be excused not only by "active" noncooperation but by "passive" noncooperation as well.

b. **Excuse of Condition by Actual Breach**

An actual breach of the contract when performance is due will excuse the duty of counterperformance. Note, however, that counterperformance will be excused at common law *only* if the *breach is material*. A minor breach may suspend this duty, but it will not excuse it. Even if the minor breach may be cured, it will not suffice to excuse conditions. Rather, the courts will make the nonbreaching party whole by either giving him damages or otherwise mitigating his promised performance so as to account for the breach. (As to rules determining materiality of breaches, *see* VII.B., *infra*.)

c. **Excuse of Condition by Anticipatory Repudiation**

Anticipatory repudiation occurs if a promisor, prior to the time set for performance of his promise, indicates that he will not perform when the time comes. If the requirements set forth below are met, this anticipatory repudiation will serve to excuse conditions.

1) **Executory Bilateral Contract Requirement**

Anticipatory repudiation applies only if there is a bilateral contract with *executory (unperformed) duties on both sides*. If the nonrepudiating party has nothing further to do at the moment of repudiation, as in the case of a unilateral contract or a bilateral contract fully performed by the nonrepudiator, the doctrine of anticipatory repudiation does not apply. The nonrepudiator must wait until the time originally set for performance by the repudiating party. Until such time, the repudiator has the option to change his mind and withdraw the repudiation and perform in accordance with the contract. [*Accord:* UCC §2-611]

Example: Winston promises to pay Salem $2,000 on November 15 as consideration for Salem's car, the latter to be delivered on October 20. Salem delivers the car to Winston on October 20; on November 3, Winston repudiates. Because Salem does not have any more duties to perform, he will not have a cause of action until November 15.

2)   Requirement that Anticipatory Repudiation Be Unequivocal

An anticipatory repudiation stems from the words or conduct of the promisor *unequivocally* indicating that he cannot or will not perform when the time comes. This statement must be positive.

Example: Wright states to Jones, "Business has not been going well and I have doubts about whether I will be able to perform my contract with you." This is *not* an anticipatory repudiation; mere expressions of doubt or fear will not suffice (although such expressions may establish prospective inability to perform, discussed below).

3)   Effect of Anticipatory Repudiation

In the case of an anticipatory repudiation, the nonrepudiating party has four alternatives:

(i)   Treat the anticipatory repudiation as a total repudiation and *sue immediately*;

(ii)   Suspend his own performance and *wait to sue* until the performance date;

(iii)   Treat the repudiation as an offer to rescind and *treat the contract as discharged*; or

(iv)   Ignore the repudiation and *urge the promisor to perform*. Note that by urging the promisor to perform, the nonrepudiating party is not waiving the repudiation—she can still sue for breach and is excused from performing unless the promisor retracts the repudiation. Not only is the nonrepudiating party excused from performing, but she should suspend her performance. If she continues to perform in spite of the repudiation, she may be precluded from claiming damages for any loss that could have been avoided. (*see* VIII.B.7, *infra*). [Restatement (Second) Contracts §257 cmt. a]

Note: UCC section 2-610 provides substantially identical alternatives to a nonrepudiating party when there is an anticipatory repudiation in the case of the sale of goods.

4)   Retraction of Repudiation

A repudiating party may at any time before his next performance is due withdraw his repudiation unless the other party has *canceled, materially changed* her *position* in reliance on the repudiation, or otherwise indicated that she considers the ***repudiation final.*** Withdrawal of the repudiation may be in any manner that clearly indicates intention to perform, but must include any assurances justifiably demanded. [*See* UCC §2-611]

d. Excuse of Condition by Prospective Inability or Unwillingness to Perform
Prospective failure of condition occurs when a party has reasonable grounds to believe that the other party will be unable or unwilling to perform when performance is due.

Example: John contracts with Barbara to buy her house for $150,000. Payment is due on August 1. On July 10, John goes into bankruptcy (or Barbara transfers title to the house to Emily). Prospective inability to perform has occurred.

1) Distinguish from Actual and Anticipatory Repudiation
Prospective inability or unwillingness to perform is not an anticipatory repudiation because such a repudiation must be ***unequivocal***, whereas prospective failure to perform involves conduct or words that merely raise doubts that the party will perform. (In short, the distinction between anticipatory repudiation and prospective inability to perform is one of degree.)

2) What Conduct Will Suffice?
Any conduct may suffice for a finding that there is prospective inability or unwillingness to perform. Note that in judging this conduct, a ***reasonable person*** standard will be applied.

3) Effect of Prospective Failure
The effect of this prospective failure is to allow the innocent party to suspend further performance on her side until she receives ***adequate assurances*** that performance will be forthcoming. If she fails to obtain adequate assurances, she may be excused from her own performance and may treat the failure to provide assurances as a repudiation. (This same basic right is provided in UCC section 2-609—*see* VIII.A.2.c., *infra.*)

4) Retraction of Repudiation
As with anticipatory repudiation, retraction is possible if the defaulting party regains his ability or willingness to perform. However, this fact must be communicated to the other party in order to be effective. If the other party has already changed her position in reliance on the prospective failure, an attempted retraction may be ineffective.

e. Excuse of Condition by Substantial Performance
The performance of one contractual promise is usually a condition precedent to the duty of immediate performance of the return promise (*see* 4., *supra*). Technically, if the promise has not been completely performed, the other performance is not yet due. This can cause forfeiture if the breach is minor, because the promisee can receive almost complete performance with no duty to perform in return. To avoid this harsh result, the courts have adopted the "substantial performance" and "divisibility" concepts.

1) Rule of Substantial Performance

Generally, the condition of complete performance may be excused if the party has rendered substantial performance. In this case, the other party's duty of counter-performance becomes absolute. It should be noted, however, that courts generally apply this doctrine only where a ***constructive*** (implied in law) condition is involved. They will not apply it where there is an ***express*** condition for fear this would defeat the express intent of the parties.

2) Substantial Performance Arises If Breach Is Minor

Rules for determining substantiality of performance are the same as those for determining materiality of breach. (*See* VII.B.2., *infra*.) In other words, the test is whether the breach of contract by the performing party is material or minor. If it is material, then performance ***has not*** been substantial; if it is minor, performance ***has*** been substantial.

3) Inapplicable Where Breach "Willful"

Most courts will not apply the substantial performance doctrine if the breach was "willful." (This is so even though willfulness is only one of the six factors usually relied on in determining materiality of a breach. *See* VII.B.2., *infra*.) Trivial defects, however, even if willful, will be ignored by the courts as de minimis.

4) Damages Offset

Even though the party who has substantially performed is able to enforce the contract, the other party will be able to mitigate by deducting damages suffered due to the first party's incomplete performance.

5) Generally Inapplicable to Contracts for the Sale of Goods

For contracts for the sale of goods, the UCC's "***perfect tender rule***" gives the buyer the right to reject goods that do not conform to the contract in any manner, with a few exceptions (*see* VII.C., *infra*). [UCC §2-601]

f. Excuse of Condition by "Divisibility" of Contract

Divisibility, like the doctrine of substantial performance, is a concept designed to mitigate the harsh result of a potential forfeiture.

1) Rule of "Divisibility"

If a party performs one of the units of a divisible contract, he is entitled to the agreed-on equivalent for that unit even if he fails to perform the other units. It is not a condition precedent to the other party's liability that the whole contract be performed. However, the other party has a cause of action for failure to perform the other units and may withhold his counterperformance for those units.

Example: Cambridge Construction Co. is to build 10 houses for $800,000, at $80,000 per house, for Beth. Because the building takes a long time and payment can be rendered in one instant, the substantial completion of 10 houses would normally be a constructive condition precedent to payment. Completion of seven houses would leave Cambridge without any remedy on the contract itself (whatever rights it might have as a defaulting party would be by way of quasi-contractual relief). The divisibility doctrine allows Cambridge to sue for the pro rata price each time it completes a house.

2) **What Is a "Divisible" Contract?**
Obviously, the rule applies only if there is a finding that the contract is "divisible" (as compared to "entire"). ***Three tests*** must be ***concurrently*** satisfied in order to make this finding.

(i) The ***performance of each party is divided into two or more parts*** under the contract;

(ii) The ***number of parts due from each party is the same***; and

(iii) The ***performance of each part by one party is agreed on as the equivalent of the corresponding part*** from the other party, i.e., each performance is the quid pro quo of the other.

[Restatement (Second) of Contracts §240]

a) **Interpretation**
Decisions on divisibility are questions of interpretation. The underlying consideration is one of fairness. Generally, the courts will construe contracts as divisible so as to avoid hardships and forfeitures that might otherwise result.

b) **Contract Expressly Indivisible**
If the contract by its own terms is expressly indivisible, the court may not construe it as otherwise.

3) **Sales of Goods—Installment Contracts**
Like the common law, Article 2 assumes that a contract is not divisible unless it authorizes deliveries in several lots, in which case the contract is called an installment contract. In installment contracts, the price, if it can be apportioned, may be demanded for ***each lot*** unless a contrary intent appears. [UCC §§2-307, 2-612]

g. **Excuse of Condition by Waiver or Estoppel**
One having the benefit of a condition under a contract may indicate by ***words or conduct*** that she will not insist on that condition's being met. Consideration is not required for a valid waiver of condition. The courts, in certain circumstances, will enforce this expression on the basis that the party has "waived" the condition or is "estopped" from asserting it.

1) **Estoppel Waiver**
Whenever a party indicates that she is "waiving" a condition before it is to happen, or she is "waiving" some performance before it is to be rendered, and the person addressed ***detrimentally relies*** on the waiver, the courts will hold this to be a binding (estoppel) waiver. Note, however, that the promise to waive a condition may be retracted at any time ***before*** the other party has changed his position to his detriment.

2) Election Waiver

When a condition does not occur or a duty of performance is broken, the beneficiary of the condition or duty must make an election; she may: (i) terminate her liability, *or* (ii) continue under the contract. If she chooses the latter course, she will be deemed to have waived the condition or duty. This election waiver requires neither consideration nor estoppel (although estoppel elements are often present). Note that, unlike an estoppel waiver, an election waiver ***cannot be withdrawn***— even if the other party has not relied on it.

Example: Frederick contracted with Karen to sell her a new MP3 player in "perfect working order." In fact, the player when delivered had some minor mechanical troubles that Karen was apprised of at the time. Karen, nonetheless, elects to accept the player. She will be deemed to have waived the "perfect working order" condition.

3) Conditions that May Be Waived

If *no consideration* is given for the waiver, the condition must be ***ancillary or collateral*** to the main subject and purpose of the contract for the waiver to be effective. In other words, one cannot "waive" entitlement to the entire or substantially entire return performance. This would amount to a new undertaking that is really a gift in the disguise of a waiver.

Example: Robinson, a contractor, breaches a promise to build a garage for Hortense at a price of $6,000. Hortense says, "Even though you have not built the garage, I shall pay you the $6,000, waiving the constructive condition of performance." This waiver will not be enforceable; Robinson did not give consideration for the waiver, and the condition concerned the main subject and purpose of the contract.

4) Waiver in Installment Contracts

In an ***installment contract***, if a waiver is not supported by consideration, the beneficiary of the waived condition can insist on strict compliance with the terms of the contract for future installments (so long as there has been no detrimental reliance on the waiver) by giving notice that he is revoking the waiver.

Example: Carrie, a boutique owner, entered into an installment contract with Jimmy Shoos. Jimmy was to deliver 20 pairs of shoes to Carrie every week, payment due in cash on delivery ("C.O.D.") of each shipment. Once the deliveries started, Jimmy allowed Carrie to mail him a check one week after delivery for the first three deliveries, rather than demanding payment at the time the shoes were delivered. Jimmy will be held to have waived the C.O.D. term because he did not demand immediate payment for the first three shipments, but Jimmy may insist on compliance with the original terms for any future deliveries (so long as Carrie is given notice and has not detrimentally relied on the waiver).

5) Right to Damages for Failure of Condition

It is important to note that a waiver severs only the right to treat the failure of the condition as a total breach excusing counterperformance. However, the waiving party does **not** thereby waive her right to damages. Thus, for instance, in the example above involving delivery of the MP3 player in "perfect working order," the waiving party still has her right to damages for the defects in the player—she merely waived her right to treat the failure as a total breach excusing counterperformance.

   h.   Excuse of Condition by Impossibility, Impracticability, or Frustration
       Conditions may be excused by impossibility, impracticability, or frustration of purpose. (*See* E.5., *infra*.)

E. HAS THE ABSOLUTE DUTY TO PERFORM BEEN DISCHARGED?

Once it is determined that a party is under an immediate duty to perform, the duty to perform must be discharged.

   1.   Discharge by Performance
       The most obvious way to discharge a contractual duty is, of course, by full and complete performance.

   2.   Discharge by Tender of Performance
       Good faith tender of performance made in accordance with contractual terms will also discharge contractual duties. Note that to tender performance the party must offer to perform and possess the ***present ability*** to perform; a mere promise of performance will not suffice.

   3.   Discharge by Occurrence of Condition Subsequent
       The occurrence of a condition subsequent will serve to discharge contractual duties.

   4.   Discharge by Illegality
       If the subject matter of the contract has become illegal due to a subsequently enacted law or other governmental act, performance will be discharged. This is often referred to as "supervening illegality."

       Example: Jim and Beam enter into a partnership contract to operate a tavern in the city of Clover. Subsequently, the Clover legislature enacts a prohibition law. The contract is discharged.

       Note: If the illegality existed at the time the agreement was made, no contract was formed because of the illegality. (*See* IV.D., *supra*.)

   5.   Discharge by Impossibility, Impracticability, or Frustration
       The occurrence of an unanticipated or extraordinary event may make contractual duties impossible or impracticable to perform or may frustrate the purpose of the contract. Where the nonoccurrence of the event was a ***basic assumption*** of the parties in making the contract and ***neither*** party has expressly or impliedly ***assumed the risk*** of the event occurring, contractual duties may be discharged. Although discussed separately below, for MBE purposes, the bar examiners use the term "impracticability" as encompassing both impossibility and impracticability.

       Remember that the promisor's duty to perform serves as a condition precedent to the other party's duty to perform. Hence, if these duties should be excused by impossibility, impracticability, or frustration, the other party's contractual duties will also be discharged.

a. **Discharge by Impossibility**
Contractual duties will be discharged if it has become impossible to perform them.

1) **Impossibility Must Be "Objective"**
For this rule to operate, the impossibility must be "objective"; i.e., the duties could not be performed by anyone. "Subjective" impossibility will not suffice, i.e., where the duties could be performed by someone but not the promisor.

2) **Timing of Impossibility**
The impossibility must arise *after* the contract has been entered into. If the facts giving rise to impossibility already existed when the contract was formed, the question is not really one of "discharge of contractual duties." Rather, it is a "contract formation" problem, namely, whether the contract is voidable because of mistake.

3) **Effect of Impossibility**
If a contract is discharged because of impossibility, each party is excused from duties arising under the contract that are yet to be fulfilled. Either party may sue for rescission and receive restitution of any goods delivered, payments made, etc.

4) **Partial Impossibility**
If the performance to be rendered under the contract becomes only partially impossible, the duty may be discharged *only to that extent*. The remainder of the performance may be required according to the contractual terms. This is so even though this remaining performance might involve added expense or difficulty.

5) **Temporary Impossibility**
Temporary impossibility *suspends* contractual duties; it does not discharge them. When performance once more becomes possible, the duty "springs back" into existence. Note, however, that a duty will not "spring back" into existence if the burden on either party to the contract would be substantially increased or different from that originally contemplated.

6) **Part Performance Prior to Impossibility—Quasi-Contractual Recovery**
If part performance has been rendered by either party prior to the existence of the facts leading to impossibility, that party will have a right to recover in quasi-contract at the contract rate or for the reasonable value of his performance if that is a more convenient mode of valuation. (Note that such recovery will also be available when contract duties are discharged by impracticability or frustration, discussed below.)

7) **Specific Situations**

a) **Death or Physical Incapacity**
Death or the physical incapacity of a person *necessary* to effectuate the contract serves to discharge it.
Example: Helmut agrees to teach German to Max. Helmut's death or physical incapacity would discharge the contract. Max's death

or physical incapacity would similarly discharge the contract. (The death or physical incapacity may also be that of a third person. Thus, for example, if Helmut had contracted with Max to teach German to Max's son, the death or physical incapacity of the son would also serve to discharge the contract.)

Note: Most fact situations on this point involve personal service contracts. Check to see whether the services involved are *"unique."* If the services are the kind that could be delegated (*see* IX.C.2.b., *infra*), the contract is **not** discharged by the incapacity of the person who was to perform them.

b) **Supervening Illegality**
As we have seen, supervening illegality may serve to discharge a contract. Many courts treat such supervening illegality as a form of impossibility.

c) **Subsequent Destruction of Contract's Subject Matter or Means of Performance**
If the contract's subject matter is destroyed or the designated means for performing the contract are destroyed, contractual duties will be discharged. Note, however, that this destruction must not have been the fault of either party. Substantial damage to the subject matter will generally be construed by the courts as the equivalent of "destruction."
Example: Olivia hires Charlie to replace the shingles on the roof of her house. When Charlie has completed 90% of the work, the house is hit by lightning and is destroyed by fire. The contract will be discharged for impossibility because there no longer is a house needing reshingling. Charlie will be able to recover for the work done in quasi-contract. (*See* VIII.C., *infra*.)

(1) **Compare—Contracts to Build**
A contractor's duty to **construct** a building is **not** discharged by destruction of the work in progress. *Rationale:* Construction is not rendered impossible; the contractor can still rebuild. However, if the destruction was not caused by the contractor, most courts will excuse the contractor from meeting the original deadline.
Example: Olivia hires Charlie to build her a garage. When Charlie has completed 90% of the work, the garage is hit by lightning and is destroyed by fire. Charlie will not be discharged from his contractual duty to build the garage because it is not impossible to rebuild the garage.

(2) **Specificity Required**

(a) **Subject Matter**
Note that destruction of the subject matter will render a contract impossible only if the very thing destroyed is necessary to fulfill the contract. If the thing destroyed is not actually necessary, impossibility is not a defense.

Example: Linda contracts to sell her car to John. Subsequently, the car is destroyed through no fault of either party. The contract will be discharged because of impossibility because the only car that could fulfill the obligation no longer exists.

Compare: John orders a new car from his local Kia dealer. While the car that the dealer ordered for John is being delivered from the factory, it is destroyed in a crash. The contract is not discharged for impossibility because it is not impossible for the dealer to get another Kia that will satisfy the contract.

(b) Specificity of Source

As with the destruction of the subject matter, destruction of a source for fulfilling the contract will render the contract impossible only if the source is the one source specified by the parties.

Example: Jackson contracts to sell Daley 100 tons of iron ore from the Blarney Iron Mine, which Jackson owns. A nearby dam breaks and floods the mine. Jackson will be discharged from the contract for impossibility.

Compare: Jackson, who owns the Blarney Iron Mine, contracts to sell Daley 100 tons of iron ore. A nearby dam breaks and floods Jackson's mine. Jackson will not be discharged from the contract because the contract did not specify that the iron ore was to come from Jackson's mine. Thus, iron ore from any other mine can fulfill the contract.

(3) If Risk of Loss Has Already Passed to Buyer

The rules relating to discharge because of destruction of the subject matter *will not apply* if the risk of loss has already passed to the buyer. The usual situations involve contracts for the sale of goods under the UCC and contracts for the sale of land where equitable conversion has taken place. In such cases, the seller may enforce the contract and the buyer will have to pay.

b. Discharge by Impracticability

Modern courts will also discharge contractual duties where performance has become impracticable.

1) Test for Impracticability

The test for a finding of impracticability is that the party to perform has encountered:

(i)   *Extreme and unreasonable* difficulty and/or expense; and

(ii) Its nonoccurrence was a *basic assumption* of the parties.

In effect, the courts will allow relief against performance where subjective impossibility is found. It should be noted, however, that a mere change in the degree of difficulty or expense due to such causes as increased wages, prices of raw materials, or costs of construction, unless well beyond the normal range, does **not** amount to impracticability, because these are the types of risks that a fixed-price contract is intended to cover. Thus, the fact that something is more expensive—even much more expensive—is not impracticability. [Restatement (Second) of Contracts §261]

2) **Contracts for the Sale of Goods**

Article 2 generally follows the above rules for impossibility and impracticability. If performance has become impossible or commercially impracticable, the seller will be *discharged to the extent of the impossibility or impracticability*. [UCC §2-615]

a) **Allocation of Risk**

Generally, the seller assumes the risk of the occurrence of such unforeseen events and must continue to perform. However, if it is fair to say that the parties would not have placed on the seller the risk of the extraordinary occurrence, the seller will be discharged.

b) **Events Sufficient for Discharge**

Events sufficient to excuse performance include a *shortage of raw materials* or the inability to convert them into the seller's product because of contingencies such as war, strike, embargo, or unforeseen shutdown of a major supplier. Catastrophic local crop failure (as opposed to a mere shortage) also is sufficient for discharge. However, mere increases in costs are rarely sufficient for discharge unless they change the nature of the contract.

Example: Assume StoneOil contracted with Manuco to sell Manuco one million gallons of Persian Gulf crude oil. If a war subsequently breaks out in the Gulf, and supplies of Gulf oil are interrupted, StoneOil is discharged. However, if instead a war breaks out between Israel and Egypt and the Suez Canal is blocked, thus forcing StoneOil to ship the oil around the Cape of Good Hope, StoneOil will probably not be discharged merely because of the increase in the cost of shipping. [*See* Transatlantic Financing Co. v. United States, 363 F.2d 312 (D.C. Cir. 1966)]

Note: There is no bright line test for determining when a rise in price changes the nature of the contract, but increases in costs of more than 50% have been held to be insufficient. [*See, e.g.,* Iowa Light & Power Co. v. Atlas Corp., 467 F. Supp. 129 (N.D. Iowa 1978)]

c) **Seller's Partial Inability to Perform**

If the seller's inability to perform as a result of the unforeseen circumstance is only partial, he *must allocate deliveries* among his customers and, at his option, may include in the allocation regular customers not then under contract. The seller must reasonably notify his buyers of any delay or reduction in deliveries because of unforeseen circumstances. A buyer who receives such a notification may refuse any particular delivery affected, and if the deficiency substantially impairs the whole contract, she may treat the contract as at an end.

3) Temporary or Partial Impracticability
The rules spelled out above for temporary and partial impossibility are equally applicable to temporary and partial impracticability.

c. Discharge by Frustration
Frustration will exist if the purpose of the contract has become valueless by virtue of some supervening event not the fault of the party seeking discharge. (Recall the *Coronation Cases* if you studied them.) If the purpose has been frustrated, a number of courts will discharge contractual duties even though performance of these duties is still possible. The elements necessary to establish frustration are as follows:

(i) There is some *supervening act* or event leading to the frustration;

(ii) At the time of entering into the contract, the parties *did not reasonably foresee* the act or event occurring;

(iii) The *purpose* of the contract has been completely or almost completely *destroyed* by this act or event; and

(iv) The purpose of the contract was realized by *both parties* at the time of making the contract.

Example: Sports, Inc. contracted to rent a sports stadium for a boxing match to be held on August 1 in the town of Greensville. On July 31, a sudden hurricane resulted in tremendous damage in Greensville, causing it to be classified as a "disaster area." No one could get in or out of the area. Sports, Inc.'s promise to rent the stadium (which was still intact) was discharged by frustration of purpose (a hurricane was not anticipated by the parties and it completely destroyed the value of the contract).

Note: Article 2's rules on impracticability apply equally to frustration situations.

d. Distinguish Uses of Defenses of Impossibility/Impracticability and Frustration
A seller of land, goods, or services will raise impossibility or impracticability as a defense that discharges performance. By contrast, the party who is supposed to pay (usually the buyer) will raise frustration of purpose as a defense discharging performance. Paying money is never impracticable.

Example: Caretaker is hired to tend to the mansion on Blackacre and signs a three-year employment contract to that effect at a rate of $30,000 per year. In the second year of Caretaker's contract, the mansion is destroyed by fire and the employer stops paying Caretaker. Caretaker sues the employer for breach and the employer countersues Caretaker. Caretaker will raise the defense of discharge by impossibility because the subject matter of the contract was destroyed. The employer will raise the defense of discharge by frustration of purpose for the same reason. The employer cannot claim impossibility because he is still able to pay money.

6. Discharge by Rescission
Rescission will serve to discharge contractual duties. Rescission may be either mutual or unilateral.

a. Mutual Rescission
The contract may be discharged by an *express agreement* between the parties to rescind. The agreement to rescind is itself a binding contract supported by consideration, namely, the giving up by each party of her right to counterperformance from the other. The reasons for entering into such an agreement are immaterial absent duress or fraud.

1) Contract Must Be Executory
For a contract to be effectively discharged by rescission, the duties must be executory on *both* sides.

a) Unilateral Contracts
If the contract is unilateral (i.e., only one party owes an absolute duty), a contract to mutually rescind where one party still has a duty to perform will be ineffective. The courts reason that the original promisor, who has not suffered a legal detriment, has not given consideration. Thus, for an effective rescission in a unilateral contract situation where the offeree has already performed, the rescission promise must be supported by one of the following:

(1) An offer of *new consideration* by the nonperforming party;

(2) Elements of *promissory estoppel*, i.e., detrimental reliance; or

(3) Manifestation of an *intent* by the original offeree to make a *gift* of the obligation owed her.

b) Partially Performed Bilateral Contracts
A mutual agreement to rescind will usually be enforced when a bilateral contract has been partially performed. Whether the party who has partially performed will be entitled to compensation will depend on the terms of the rescission agreement. The party seeking such compensation must affirmatively prove his right to the compensation in order to recover.

2) Formalities
Mutual rescission may be made *orally*. This is so even though the contract to be rescinded expressly states that it can be rescinded only by a written document. Several *exceptions* should be noted, however:

a) Subject Matter Within Statute of Frauds
If the subject matter of the contract to be rescinded falls within the Statute

of Frauds (e.g., transfer of land), then the rescission should generally be in writing. Some courts, however, hold that even when the Statute of Frauds comes into play, the oral rescission will still be enforceable if it is "executed" or promissory estoppel is present.

b) Contracts for the Sale of Goods

In addition to the Statute of Frauds requirement with respect to contracts for the sale of goods, Article 2 requires a written rescission or modification if the original contract to be rescinded or modified expressly requires a written rescission. [UCC §2-209(2)]

3) Contracts Involving Third-Party Beneficiary Rights

If the rights of third-party beneficiaries have already **vested** (*see* IX.B.2., *infra*), the contract may **not** be discharged by mutual rescission.

b. Unilateral Rescission

Unilateral rescission results when one of the parties to the contract desires to rescind it but the other party desires that the contract be performed according to its terms. For unilateral rescission to be granted, the party desiring rescission must have adequate legal grounds. Most common among these are mistake, misrepresentation, duress, and failure of consideration. If the nonassenting party refuses to voluntarily grant rescission, the other party may file an action in equity to obtain it. (*See* VIII.D., *infra*.)

7. Partial Discharge by Modification of Contract

If a contract is subsequently modified by the parties, this will serve to discharge those terms of the original contract that are the subject of the modification. It will **not** serve to discharge the **entire contract**. To have such a partial discharge, the following requirements must usually be met.

a. Mutual Assent

The modifying agreement must have been mutually assented to. Note, however, that under the doctrine of **reformation** (VIII.E., *infra*), either of the parties to the contract may bring an equity action to have a contract's terms modified if the writing, through mistake or misrepresentation, does not incorporate the terms orally agreed on.

b. Consideration

Generally, consideration is necessary to modify a contract. However, the courts usually find consideration to be present because each party has limited his right to enforce the original contract as is. Check the facts to see whether the modification would operate to the benefit of one of the parties only. If so, it may be unenforceable without some consideration being given to the other party. (*See* discussion of the preexisting legal duty rule, III.B.2.c., *supra*.)

1) Requirement Where Modification Is Only "Correction"

No consideration is necessary where the effect of the modification is merely to correct an error in the original contract.

2) Contracts for the Sale of Goods

No consideration is needed for the modification of a contract for the sale of goods under Article 2, as long as the modification is sought in good faith. [UCC §2-209(1)]

8. **Discharge by Novation**

A novation occurs when a new contract substitutes a new party to receive benefits and assume duties that had originally belonged to one of the original parties under the terms of the old contract. A novation will serve to discharge the old contract. The elements for a valid novation are as follows:

(i) A *previous* valid contract;

(ii) An *agreement* among all parties, including the new party (or parties) to the new contract;

(iii) The *immediate extinguishment* of contractual duties as between the original contracting parties; and

(iv) A valid and enforceable *new* contract.

Example: John contracts to sell his house to Jane for $150,000. Before the closing date, John, Jane, and Joanna execute a new agreement wherein all rights and duties in connection with the transaction are transferred by Jane to Joanna. The original John-Jane contract will be discharged by novation.

9. **Discharge by Cancellation**

The destruction or surrender of a written contract will not usually by itself discharge the contract. If, however, the parties manifest their *intent* to have these acts serve as a discharge, it will usually have this effect if consideration or one of its alternatives is present.

10. **Discharge by Release**

A release and/or contract not to sue will serve to discharge contractual duties. The release or contract not to sue usually must be in *writing* and supported by *new consideration* or *promissory estoppel* elements. [*Compare* UCC §1-306—governing the sale of goods and requiring an authenticated record (such as a writing) but *not* requiring consideration]

11. **Discharge by Substituted Contract**

A contract may be discharged by a substituted contract. This occurs when the parties to a contract enter into a second contract that *immediately revokes* the first contract.

a. **Revocation May Be Express or Implied**

The second contract may revoke the first contract either expressly or impliedly. The first contract will be impliedly revoked if the second contract's terms are inconsistent with the terms of the first contract.

b. **Intent Governs**

Whether a second contract will constitute a substituted contract depends on whether the parties intend an immediate discharge or a discharge only after performance of the second contract. If an immediate discharge is intended, there is a substituted contract. If the parties intend the first contract to be discharged only after performance of the second contract, there is an executory accord (*see* 12.a., *infra*) rather than a substituted contract.

12. Discharge by Accord and Satisfaction
A contract may be discharged by an accord and satisfaction.

a. Accord
An accord is an agreement in which one party to an existing contract agrees to accept, in lieu of the performance that she is supposed to receive from the other party to the existing contract, some other, different performance.

Example: Mel owes Alice $1,000 under a contract. Mel promises to give his car to Alice in settlement of the debt, and Alice agrees to accept the car in settlement of the debt. This agreement is an accord.

1) Requirement of Consideration
In general, an accord must be supported by consideration. Where the consideration is of a lesser value than the originally bargained-for consideration in the prior contract, it will be sufficient if the new consideration is of a **different type** or if the claim is to be paid to a **third party**.

Example: Fred owes Barney $700 under an existing contract. Fred offers Barney a new TV set worth $500 in lieu of the existing debt. Barney accepts. This new consideration is sufficient to form a valid accord, even though it is worth less than the consideration originally owed, because it is of a different type.

a) Partial Payment of Original Debt
One frequently encountered problem involves the offer of a smaller amount than the amount due under an existing obligation in satisfaction of the claim, i.e., partial payment of an original debt. The **majority view** is that this will suffice for an **accord and satisfaction** if there is a **"bona fide dispute"** as to the claim or there is otherwise some alteration, even if slight, in the debtor's consideration. (*See* discussion of the preexisting legal duty rule, III.B.2.c., *supra*.)

2) Effect of Accord
The accord, taken alone, will not discharge the prior contract. It merely **suspends** the right to enforce it in accordance with the terms of the accord contract.

3) Distinguish Modification
Sometimes an accord is difficult to distinguish from a modification. In an accord, the parties to an existing obligation agree to accept a **different future performance** in satisfaction of the obligation. If the performance is carried out (satisfaction), the duty under the original contract is discharged; but if it is not carried out, the original contract remains enforceable. In a modification, the parties to an existing obligation agree to a **different agreement**. The duties of the parties change immediately, and the original terms are no longer in effect. An accord and satisfaction most often arises when payment or performance is overdue or there is a dispute as to the performance due. A modification typically occurs before performance is due.

b. **Satisfaction**

Satisfaction is the performance of the accord agreement. Its effect is to discharge not only the original contract but also the accord contract as well.

c. **Effect of Breach of Accord Agreement Before Satisfaction**

What happens when the accord agreement is not followed by an immediate satisfaction, and one of the parties breaches the accord agreement?

1) **Breach by Debtor**

If the breach is by the debtor, the creditor may sue either on the original undischarged contract *or* for breach of the accord agreement.

2) **Breach by Creditor**

If the accord agreement is breached by the creditor, i.e., he sues on the *original* contract, the debtor has two courses of action available:

a) She may raise the accord agreement as an equitable defense and ask that the contract action be dismissed.

b) As an alternative, she may *wait until she is damaged*, i.e., the creditor is successful in his action on the original contract, and then bring an action at law for damages for breach of the accord contract.

d. **Checks Tendered as "Payment in Full"**

If a monetary claim is *uncertain* or is subject to a *bona fide dispute*, an accord and satisfaction may be accomplished by a *good faith* tender and acceptance of a check when that check (or an accompanying document) *conspicuously states* that the check is tendered in *full satisfaction* of the debt. [UCC §3-311]

13. **Discharge by Account Stated**

An account stated is a contract between parties whereby they agree to an amount as a *final balance due* from one to the other. This final balance encompasses a number of transactions between the parties and serves to merge all of these transactions by discharging all claims owed. In other words, all rights as to the individual, original transactions are discharged and the new agreement is enforceable. For an agreement to qualify as an account stated, the parties must have had *more than one prior transaction* between them.

a. **Writing Generally Not Required**

It is not necessary that the account stated be in writing. However, if one or more of the original transactions was subject to the Statute of Frauds, a writing will usually be required.

b. **Account May Be Implied**

It is also not required that an account stated be "express." It may be implied.

Example: Cindy and Dave have entered into a number of transactions. Cindy presents Dave with a bill for $1,000 covering all of these previous transactions. Dave does not object to this amount within a reasonable period of time. It will be held that there is an account stated.

14. Discharge by Lapse

Where the duty of each party is a condition concurrent to the other's duty, it is possible that on the day set for performance, neither party is in breach and their contractual obligations lapse.

a. Time When Lapse Becomes Effective

If the contract states that time is "of the essence," the lapse will occur immediately; otherwise the contract will lapse after a reasonable time.

Example: Sally contracts with Bobby to sell 100 widgets to her for $1,000 on November 15. On November 15, Sally does not tender the widgets and Bobby does not tender the $1,000. Ten months afterward, Sally attempts to put Bobby in breach by tendering the widgets. Sally will not have a claim, as the contractual obligations of both parties have been discharged by lapse.

15. Effect of Running of Statute of Limitations

If the statute of limitations on an action has run, it is generally held that an action for breach of contract may be barred. Note, however, that only *judicial remedies* are barred; the running of the statute *does not discharge the duties.* (Hence, if the party who has the advantage of the statute of limitations subsequently agrees to perform, new consideration will not be required.)

VII. BREACH

A. WHEN DOES A BREACH OCCUR?

If it is found that (i) the promisor is under an absolute duty to perform, and (ii) this absolute duty of performance has not been discharged, then this failure to perform in accordance with contractual terms will amount to a breach of the contract. The nonbreaching party who sues for breach of contract must show that she is *willing and able* to perform but for the breaching party's failure to perform.

B. MATERIAL OR MINOR BREACH—COMMON LAW CONTRACTS

Once you have determined that there is a breach of contract, the next determination to be made in a common law contract situation is whether that breach is material or minor.

1. Effect of Breaches

a. Minor Breach

A breach of contract is minor if the obligee gains the substantial benefit of her bargain despite the obligor's defective performance. Examples would be insignificant delays in completing performance or small deficiencies in the quality or quantity of performance when precision is not critical. The effect of a minor (immaterial) breach is to provide a remedy for the immaterial breach to the aggrieved party. The aggrieved party is *not relieved* of her duty of performance under the contract.

b. Material Breach

If the obligee does not receive the *substantial benefit of her bargain* as a result of failure to perform or defective performance, the breach is considered material. If the breach is material, the consequences are more severe. The nonbreaching party (i) may treat the contract as at an end, i.e., any duty of counterperformance owed by her will be discharged, and (ii) will have an ***immediate right*** to all remedies for breach of the entire contract, including total damages.

c. Minor Breach Coupled with Anticipatory Repudiation

If a minor breach is coupled with an anticipatory repudiation (*see* VI.D.6.c., *supra*), the nonbreaching party may treat it as a material breach; i.e., she may sue immediately for total damages and is permanently discharged from any duty of further performance. Indeed, the courts hold that the aggrieved party must not continue on, because to do so would be a failure to mitigate damages. The UCC modifies this to permit a party to complete the manufacture of goods to avoid having to sell unfinished goods at the lower salvage value. (*See infra.*)

d. Material Breach of Divisible Contract

In a divisible contract, recovery is available for substantial performance of a divisible part even though there has been a material breach of the entire contract.

2. Determining Materiality of Breach

a. General Rule

Whether a breach is material or minor is a fact question. To make this determination, the courts generally apply the following six criteria [Restatement of Contracts §275]:

1) Amount of Benefit Received

Look to the extent to which the nonbreaching party will receive substantially the benefit she could have anticipated from full performance. The greater the extent, the less material the breach.

2) Adequacy of Damages

Look to the extent to which the injured party may be adequately compensated in damages. The greater the extent, the less material the breach.

3) Extent of Part Performance

Look to the extent the party failing to perform completely has already performed or made preparations to perform. The greater the extent, the less material the breach.

4) Hardship to Breaching Party

Look to the extent of hardship on the breaching party should the contract be terminated. If a finding of materiality and termination of the contract would cause great hardship to the breaching party, the breach is less likely to be found to be material.

5) Negligent or Willful Behavior

Look to the extent of negligent or willful behavior of the party failing to perform. The greater the extent, the more material the breach.

6) Likelihood of Full Performance

Look to the extent of likelihood the party who has failed to perform will perform the remainder of his contract. The greater the extent, the less material the breach.

b. Failure of Timely Performance

The basic question here is whether the parties to the contract must perform on time. Assuming that the defaulting party had a duty of immediate performance when his failure to perform occurred, then his failure to perform on time will always be a breach of contract. There are, however, additional specific rules for determining the materiality of breach by failure of timely performance.

1) Nature of Contract or Time of the Essence Provision

Unless the nature of the contract is such as to make performance on the exact day agreed upon of vital importance (e.g., contract for use of a wedding chapel), or the contract by its terms provides that time is of the essence, failure by a promisor to perform at the stated time will not be material. Merely providing a date for performance does not make time of the essence.

a) Time of the Essence

Traditionally, courts have held that if the contract contains a "time is of the essence" provision, any delay is a material breach of contract. The modern trend, however, is for the court to consider all of the circumstances, including the time of the essence clause, in determining whether performance at the time specified is important. For example, if the parties sign a preprinted form contract that contains a "time is of the essence" clause and there are no surrounding circumstances indicating that performance on that date is of vital importance, a court could find that delayed performance is only a minor breach. [*See* Restatement (Second) of Contracts §242(c)]

2) When Delay Occurs

Delay at the onset of performance before the delaying party has rendered any part of his agreed-on performance is more likely to be considered material than delay where there has been part performance.

3) Mercantile Contracts

In mercantile contracts, timely performance as agreed is important, and unjustified delay is material.

4) Land Contracts

More delay in land contracts is required for materiality than in mercantile contracts.

5) Availability of Equitable Remedy

In equity, the courts generally are much more lenient in tolerating considerable delay. Hence, they will tend to find the breach immaterial and award compensation for the delay where possible.

c. **Material Breach and Substantial Performance**
Whether performance is "substantial" depends on the quantity and quality of the performance. If the performance is "substantial," the breach is not material.

C. PERFECT TENDER RULE—SALE OF GOODS

Article 2 generally does not follow the common law substantial performance doctrine. Instead, it follows the perfect tender rule—if *goods or their delivery fail to conform to the contract in any way*, the buyer generally may reject all, accept all, or accept any commercial units and reject the rest.

1. Commercial Unit Defined

A "commercial unit" is one that by commercial usage is treated as a single whole for the purpose of sale, and division of which materially impairs its value (e.g., place setting of dishes). A commercial unit may be a single article (e.g., a machine) or a set of articles (e.g., a suite of furniture), a quantity (e.g., a bale, a gross), or any other unit treated in use or in the relevant market as a single whole. [UCC §2-105(6)] The test for "commercial unit" is "not only what unit has been the basis of contract, but also whether the partial acceptance produces so materially an adverse effect upon the remainder as to constitute bad faith." [UCC §2-601, comment 1]

Example: Widgets are always sold in units of 100. Buyer orders 500 widgets. They arrive but are found to be defective. Buyer keeps 25 and rejects 475. Buyer is probably required to reject in units of 100 and the rejection of the 75 above 400 is probably wrongful.

2. Right to Reject Cut Off by Acceptance

A buyer's right to reject under the perfect tender doctrine generally is cut off by acceptance. Under Article 2, a buyer accepts when:

(i) After a reasonable opportunity to inspect the goods, she *indicates to the seller that they conform* to requirements or that she will keep them even though they fail to conform;

(ii) She *fails to reject* within a reasonable time after tender or delivery of the goods or fails to seasonably notify the seller of her rejection; or

(iii) She does any *act inconsistent with the seller's ownership*.

[UCC §2-606]

a. **Notice**
If in connection with rejection the buyer fails to state that the goods have a particular defect that is ascertainable by reasonable inspection, she *cannot rely on that defect* to justify rejection or to show seller's breach *if*:

(i)   The *seller could have cured* the defect if he had been told about it; or

(ii) ***Between merchants*** when the ***seller has***, after rejection, ***made a request*** in writing for a full and final written statement of all defects upon which the buyer proposes to rely.

[UCC §2-605]

Example: Buyer has ordered blue widgets. Buyer rejects because the shipment did not contain the widget wrench that, under the contract, went with each widget. Buyer does not give the reason for rejection. If Seller had known the reason, he could have had the necessary number of widget wrenches at Buyer's business within hours. That probably would have constituted an adequate cure. If so, Buyer's rejection is unjustified; she will not be able to rely on the absence of the wrenches as a reason for rejection or as the basis for a claim for damages.

3. Buyer's Responsibility for Goods After Rejection

a. Buyer Must Hold Goods with Reasonable Care

After rejecting goods in her physical possession, the buyer has an obligation to hold them with reasonable care at the seller's disposition for a time sufficient to permit the seller to remove them. If the seller has no agent or place of business within the market area where the goods are rejected, a ***merchant*** buyer has an obligation to obey any reasonable instructions as to the rejected goods (i.e., she must arrange to reship the goods to a destination designated by the seller or resell on request of the seller, if reasonable). [UCC §2-602]

b. When Seller Gives No Instructions on Disposal of Goods

If a seller gives no instructions within a reasonable time after notification of rejection, the buyer may ***reship*** the goods to the seller, ***store*** them for the seller's account, or ***resell*** them for the seller's account. The buyer has a ***security interest*** in rejected goods in her possession for ***any part of the price already paid*** and for expenses reasonably incurred in connection with handling them after rejection. [UCC §2-604]

c. When Buyer Resells Goods

If the buyer does resell rejected goods, she is entitled to have her expenses of selling and any commission ordinarily paid in the trade or, if there is none, a reasonable commission not exceeding 10%. [UCC §2-603(2)]

4. Buyer's Right to Revoke Acceptance

Once goods are accepted, the buyer's power to reject the goods generally is terminated and the buyer is obligated to pay the price less any damages resulting from the seller's breach. However, under limited situations, a buyer may revoke an acceptance already made. A proper revocation of acceptance has the effect of a rejection.

a. When Acceptance May Be Revoked

The buyer may revoke her acceptance of goods if the goods have a defect that ***substantially impairs*** their ***value*** to her ***and***:

(i) She accepted them on the ***reasonable belief that the defect would be cured*** and it has not been; or

(ii)   She accepted them because of the *difficulty of discovering defects* or because of the *seller's assurance that the goods conformed* to the contract.

[UCC §2-608]

b.   Other Requirements for Revocation of Acceptance
Revocation of acceptance must occur:

1)   *Within a reasonable time* after the buyer discovers or should have discovered the defects; and

2)   *Before any substantial change in the goods occurs* that is not caused by a defect present at the time the seller relinquished possession. [UCC §2-608(2)]
Example: If the buyer receives defective goods and due to her own fault damages the goods in some other way, she can no longer revoke acceptance, because the damage is a substantial change in the goods not caused by the seller. Similarly, if the buyer receives damaged goods and then resells the goods, she cannot revoke acceptance and her only remedy is to recover damages for the defect (*see* VIII.B.2.a.2), *infra*). If the buyer sells some but not all of the defective units, she can revoke acceptance (within a reasonable time) of any unsold unit.

5.   Exceptions to the Perfect Tender Rule

a.   Installment Contracts
The right to reject when a contract is an installment contract (i.e., when there is to be more than one delivery) is much more limited than in a single delivery contract situation. Installment contracts follow a rule akin to the common law substantial performance doctrine. In an installment contract situation, an installment can be rejected only if the nonconformity *substantially impairs* the value of that installment *and cannot be cured* (*see* below). In addition, the whole contract is breached only if the nonconformity *substantially impairs* the value of the *entire contract*.
Example: Steve and Becky enter into a contract under which Steve is to deliver to Becky 100 blue widgets on the first day of each month, and Becky is to pay Steve $275 by the 10th of each month. Steve makes a perfect delivery the first two months and Becky makes the required payments. On the first day of the third month, Steve sends only 90 widgets. The 10-widget shortfall would be a basis for rejection under the perfect tender rule, but because this is an installment contract, Becky cannot reject the installment unless she can show that the 10-widget shortfall substantially impairs the value of that installment, and she cannot cancel the entire contract unless she can show that the shortfall substantially impairs the value of the entire contract.

b.   Seller's Right to Cure

1)   Single Delivery Contracts

a) **Seller Can Cure by Notice and New Tender Within Time for Performance**

If the buyer has rejected goods because of defects, the seller may within the time originally provided for performance "cure" by giving *reasonable notice* of her intention to do so and making a *new tender of conforming goods* which the buyer must then accept. [UCC §2-508]

Example: Buyer ordered blue widgets for delivery during the first 15 days of June. The widgets are delivered on June 9, but the widget wrenches required by the contract are missing. Seller can cure this defect by giving reasonable notice of his intention to provide and subsequently providing wrenches for the widgets by June 15. If he does, Buyer must accept, or Buyer will breach the contract.

b) **Seller's Right to Cure Beyond Original Contract Time**

Ordinarily, the seller has no right to cure beyond the original contract time. However, in cases where the buyer rejects a tender of nonconforming goods that the seller *reasonably* believed would be acceptable "with or without money allowance," the seller, upon a reasonable notification to the buyer, has a *further reasonable time* beyond the original contract time within which to make a conforming tender. A seller will probably be found to have had reasonable cause to believe that the tender would be acceptable if the seller can show that (i) trade practices or prior dealings with the buyer led the seller to believe that the goods would be acceptable, or (ii) the seller could not have known of the defect despite proper business conduct (e.g., packaged goods purchased from a supplier).

Examples: 1) In the last example above, widgets are delivered without wrenches on June 15. Seller and Buyer have had a number of contracts over the years for the sale of widgets in which the wrench was a part of the contract. On several occasions, Seller has not been able to deliver the wrenches, and on each occasion, Buyer has accepted the widgets with a reduction in price and purchased the wrenches from another source. This time Buyer rejects the widgets. Seller will have a reasonable time after June 15 within which to cure by furnishing the wrenches.

2) Barry ordered 100 barrels of grade A oil from Sonya to be delivered on or before January 1. On January 1, Sonya delivered to Barry 100 barrels of oil that she had purchased from her supplier, Refineco. Upon delivery, Barry opened a barrel and found that the oil was grade B oil. Barry immediately rejected the delivery. Sonya checked with Refineco and discovered that Refineco had made a packaging error and could replace the oil within two days. Assuming two days is a reasonable time under the circumstances (e.g., if Barry does not need the oil immediately), Sonya will have a right to cure even though the time for performance has passed.

> **2) Installment Contracts**
>
> Article 2 provides that a defective shipment in an installment contract cannot be rejected *if the defect can be cured*. Ordinarily, defects in the particular goods themselves cannot be cured, so the buyer can reject them, but then might be required to accept substitute goods under the provisions discussed above. Note that a deficiency in quantity may be cured by an additional delivery, and a delivery of too much may be cured by acceptance or return of a part. [UCC §2-612]

D. ANTICIPATORY REPUDIATION

Recall that an anticipatory repudiation (*see* VI.D.6.c., *supra*) can be treated as an immediate breach of contract.

E. BREACH OF WARRANTY

At common law, the rule was caveat emptor—let the buyer beware. Once goods were accepted, the seller's obligations were discharged. However, as we have seen, today sellers give warranties as to the condition of the goods that apply even after acceptance. Failure to live up to these warranties constitutes a breach of warranty, for which a remedy is available.

VIII. REMEDIES

A. NONMONETARY REMEDIES

There are two broad branches of remedies available in breach of contract situations: nonmonetary and monetary. The primary nonmonetary remedy for exam purposes is specific performance, but Article 2 has a number of other specific nonmonetary remedies for certain situations involving contracts for the sale of goods.

1. Specific Performance

If the *legal remedy is inadequate*, the nonbreaching party may seek specific performance, which is essentially an order from the court to the breaching party to perform or face contempt of court charges. The legal remedy (damages) generally is inadequate when the *subject matter of the contract is rare or unique*. The rationale is that if the subject matter is rare or unique, damages will not put the nonbreaching party in as good a position as performance would have, because even with the damages the nonbreaching party would not be able to purchase substitute performance.

a. Available for Land and Rare or Unique Goods

Specific performance is always available for land sale contracts because all land is considered to be unique. It is also available for goods that are rare or unique at the time performance is due (e.g., rare paintings, gasoline in short supply because of oil embargoes, etc.).

b. Not Available for Service Contracts

Specific performance is not available for breach of a contract to provide services, even if the services are rare or unique. This is because of problems of enforcement (it would be difficult for the court to supervise the performance) and because the courts feel it is tantamount to involuntary servitude, which is prohibited by the Constitution.

1) Injunction as Alternate Remedy

In contrast, a court may ***enjoin*** a breaching employee from working for a competitor throughout the duration of the contract if the services contracted for are rare or unique. This is allowed because less court supervision is required for a negative injunction than for a specific performance decree, and the prohibition against working (as opposed to the requirement of working) does not run afoul of the Constitution. The rationale for this approach is that an employee providing rare or unique services expressly or impliedly covenants that she will not work for a competitor during the contract term.

c. Covenant Not to Compete

Most courts will grant an order of specific performance to enforce a contract not to compete if: (i) the services to be performed are unique (thus rendering money damages inadequate); and (ii) the covenant is reasonable. To be reasonable:

(i)   The covenant must be reasonably necessary to protect a ***legitimate interest*** of the person benefited by the covenant (i.e., an employer or the purchaser of the covenantor's business);

(ii)   The covenant must be reasonable as to its ***geographic scope and duration*** (i.e., it cannot be broader than the benefited person's customer base and typically cannot be longer than one or two years); and

(iii)   The covenant ***must not harm the public***.

Example: A locksmith agrees to sell his shop to a competitor and agrees not to open a new locksmith shop within 75 miles of his old shop within the next year. The covenant not to compete probably will be upheld.

d. Equitable Defenses Available

Because specific performance is an equitable remedy, it is subject to equitable defenses. The most frequently claimed equitable defenses are laches, unclean hands, and sale to a bona fide purchaser.

1) Laches

The equitable defense of laches arises when a party delays in bringing an equitable action and the delay prejudices the defendant (e.g., the delay has substantially increased the cost or difficulty of performance). Note that mere delay itself is not a ground for this defense.

2) Unclean Hands

The unclean hands defense arises when the party seeking specific performance is guilty of some wrongdoing in the transaction being sued upon (e.g., the defendant entered into the contract because of the plaintiff's lies). Note that the wrongdoing must be related to the transaction being sued upon; it is not sufficient that the plaintiff has defrauded other persons in similar transactions.

3) Sale to a Bona Fide Purchaser

If the subject matter of a goods or land contract has already been sold to another who purchased for value and in good faith (i.e., a bona fide purchaser), the right to specific performance is cut off.

Example: Store contracts to sell a specific Van Gogh painting to Ben. Before Store delivers the painting to Ben, Carla, who is unaware of Ben's contract with Store, offers to buy the same Van Gogh from Store. Store accepts Carla's offer and gives the painting to Carla. Ben may not obtain specific performance.

2. Nonmonetary Remedies Under Article 2

a. Buyer's Nonmonetary Remedies

1) Cancellation

If a buyer rightfully rejects goods because they do not conform to the contract, one of her options is simply to cancel the contract.

2) Buyer's Right to Replevy Identified Goods

a) On Buyer's Prepayment

If a buyer has made at least *part payment* of the purchase price of goods that have been identified under a contract and the seller *has not delivered* the goods, the buyer may *replevy* the goods from the seller in two circumstances:

(i) The seller becomes *insolvent* within 10 days after receiving the buyer's first payment; or

(ii) The goods were purchased for *personal, family, or household purposes.*

In either case, the buyer must *tender* any unpaid portion of the purchase price to the seller. [UCC §2-502]

b) On Buyer's Inability to Cover

In addition, the buyer may replevy undelivered, identified goods from the seller if the buyer, after reasonable effort, is *unable to secure adequate substitute goods* (i.e., cover). [UCC §2-716(3)]

Example: Buyer and Seller enter into a contract for the delivery of 10,000 widgets on December 31. Seller, who has identified goods to the contract (e.g., seller has set aside 10,000 widgets on his loading dock), refuses to deliver. Buyer makes reasonable efforts to find widgets from another source, but the earliest delivery date he can arrange is March 15. The widgets are needed for Buyer's manufacturing operations in February and March. Buyer can replevy the goods from Seller. However, if the widgets were not to be used by Buyer until June, widgets for March 15 delivery would probably be reasonable substitute goods and Buyer could not recover the widgets from Seller.

3) Buyer's Right to Specific Performance

A right closely related to the buyer's right to replevy is her right to specific performance "where the goods are unique or in other proper circumstances." [UCC §2-716(1)] The court may order specific performance *even where the goods have not yet been identified* to the contract by the seller. The comments to section 2-716 say that inability to cover is "strong evidence of other circumstances." Thus, buyers in inability-to-cover situations have their choice of replevin or specific performance remedies. Of course, a specific performance remedy is always discretionary with the court, and unclean hands, laches, etc., might bar an equity action but would not affect a replevin recovery. In any case, keep in mind that *replevin will lie only for identified goods*, while specific performance may be decreed even though the goods have not previously been identified.

b.   Seller's Nonmonetary Remedies

1)   Seller's Right to Withhold Goods
If the buyer fails to make a payment due on or before delivery, the seller may withhold delivery of the goods. The seller may also withhold goods when the goods are sold on credit and, before the goods are delivered, the seller discovers that the buyer is insolvent. However, in such a case, the seller must deliver the goods if the buyer tenders cash for their payment. [UCC §2-702]

2)   Seller's Right to Recover Goods

a)   Right to Recover from Buyer on Buyer's Insolvency
If a seller learns that a buyer has received delivery of goods on credit while insolvent, the seller may reclaim the goods upon demand made within 10 days after the buyer's receipt of the goods. However, the 10-day limitation does not apply if a misrepresentation of solvency has been *made in writing* to the particular seller *within three months* before delivery. Note that the seller's right to reclaim the goods is subject to the rights of a buyer in the ordinary course or any other good faith purchaser. [UCC §2-702]

b)   Right to Recover Shipped or Stored Goods from Bailee

(1)   On Buyer's Insolvency
The seller may stop delivery of goods in the possession of a carrier or other bailee when he discovers the buyer to be insolvent. Of course, the seller must deliver the goods if the buyer tenders cash for their payment. [UCC §2-705(1)]

(2)   On Buyer's Breach
The seller may stop delivery of carload, truckload, planeload, or larger shipments of goods when the buyer breaches the contract or when the seller has a right to withhold performance pending receipt of assurances. (*See* c., *infra,* on the right to demand assurances.) [UCC §2-705(1)]

(3)   When Goods May Not Be Stopped
The seller may stop delivery of the goods to the buyer *until* the buyer receives: (i) the goods or a negotiable document of title covering the

goods; or (ii) an acknowledgment from a bailee other than the carrier that it is holding the goods for the buyer. [UCC §2-705(2)]

(4) Obligation of Carrier or Bailee
The seller's notification must come in time to give the person in possession a *reasonable time to stop delivery*. If a negotiable document covers the goods, the carrier or bailee is not obligated to obey a stop order until the document is surrendered.

3) Seller's Ability to Force Goods on Buyer Limited
The seller's ability to force goods on a buyer is limited to an action for price when the seller is unable to resell the goods to others at a reasonable price. (*See* B.2.b.2), *infra*.)

c. Right to Demand Assurances
Under Article 2, actions or circumstances that increase the risk of nonperformance by a party to the contract but do not clearly indicate that performance will not be forthcoming, may *not* be treated immediately as an anticipatory repudiation (*see* VI.D.6.c., *supra*). Instead, if there are *reasonable grounds for insecurity* with respect to the other party's performance, a party may demand assurances that the performance will be forthcoming at the proper time. The demand for assurances must be made *in writing*. Until the party receives adequate assurances, he may suspend his own performance. [UCC §2-609] If the proper assurances are not given within a reasonable time (i.e., within 30 days after a justified demand for assurances), he may then treat the contract as repudiated. What constitutes an adequate assurance depends on the facts of the case.

Examples: 1) Seller hears a rumor, in fact false, that Buyer is in financial trouble. Seller reasonably believes that the rumor may have foundation in fact. He is justified in making a demand for assurances and withholding any goods for which he has not been paid. Buyer, within a reasonable time, sends a financial report from her banker showing good financial condition. This is adequate assurance and Seller must resume performance.

2) Same facts as above except that Buyer *is* in bad financial condition. Adequate assurance may require a third party of good credit to back up Buyer.

3) Same facts as above. Buyer does not give any assurances. Seller may treat the failure to give assurances as a repudiation of the contract.

B. MONETARY REMEDY—DAMAGES
The most frequently sought remedy for breach of contract is an action at law for damages. Damages can be recovered only to the extent they can be proved with reasonable certainty and could not be avoided with reasonable effort. In cases of willful breach, courts are more likely to be flexible in determining the plaintiff's damages alternatives.

1. Types of Damages

a. Compensatory Damages
The purpose of contract damages is to give compensation for the breach—i.e., to *put*

the nonbreaching party in the position she would have been in had the promise been performed so far as money can do this. The most common measure of this is the value of the breaching party's performance that was lost (expectation damages), plus incidental and consequential damages, less any loss or cost saved by not having to perform. [Restatement (Second) of Contracts §347]

1) **"Standard Measure" of Damages—Expectation Damages**

   In most cases, the plaintiff's standard measure of damages will be based on an "expectation" measure, i.e., sufficient damages for her to buy a *substitute performance*. This is also known as *"benefit of the bargain"* damages.

2) **Reliance Damage Measure**

   If the plaintiff's expectation damages will be too speculative to measure (e.g., the plaintiff cannot show with sufficient certainty the profits she would have made if the defendant had performed the contract), the plaintiff may elect to recover those damages she has suffered based on her reasonable reliance on the contract. Reliance damages award the plaintiff the cost of her performance; i.e., they are designed to *put the plaintiff in the position she would have been in had the contract never been formed*.

   Example: J-Mart gives Sam a "dealer franchise" to sell J-Mart's products in a stated area for one year. In preparation for performance, Sam spends money on advertising, hiring sales personnel, and acquiring premises that cannot be used for other purposes. J-Mart then repudiates before performance begins. If it cannot be established with reasonable certainty what profit Sam would have made if the contract had been performed (i.e., Sam's expectation damages), Sam can recover as reliance damages his expenditures in preparation for performance.

3) **Consequential Damages**

   Consequential damages are special damages and reflect losses over and above standard expectation damages. These damages result from the nonbreaching party's particular circumstances. Usually, consequential damages are lost profits resulting from the breach. These damages may be recovered only if *at the time the contract was made*, a *reasonable person* would have *foreseen* the damages as a probable result of a breach. Foreseeability is the key issue for consequential damages. To recover consequential damages, the plaintiff must show that the breaching party knew or had reason to know of the special circumstances giving rise to the damages.

   Example: Alex and Becky make a written contract under which Alex is to recondition by a stated date a used machine owned by Becky so that it will be suitable for sale by Becky to Cindy. Alex knows when they make the contract that Becky has contracted to sell the machine to Cindy but knows nothing of the terms of Becky's contract with Cindy. Because Alex delays in returning the machine to Becky, Becky is unable to sell it to Cindy and loses the profit that she would have made on that sale. Becky's loss of reasonable profit was foreseeable by Alex as a probable result of the breach at the time the contract was made. [Restatement (Second) of Contracts §351]

Compare: Suppose in the above example that the profit that Becky would have made was extraordinarily large because Cindy promised to pay an exceptionally high price as a result of a special need for the machine. Again Alex is aware of the contract with Cindy but unaware of its terms. Alex is not liable for Becky's loss of profit beyond what would ordinarily result from such a contract. The exceptionally high price paid by Cindy was not foreseeable by Alex as a probable result of the breach at the time the contract was made. [Restatement (Second) of Contracts §351]

Note that in contracts for the sale of goods, ***only a buyer*** may recover consequential damages.

4)   Incidental Damages
Compensatory damages may also include incidental damages. Incidental damages are most commonly associated with contracts for the sale of goods and typically include expenses reasonably incurred by a buyer in inspection, receipt, transportation, care, and custody of goods rightfully rejected and other expenses reasonably incident to the seller's breach, and by the seller in storing, shipping, returning, and reselling the goods as a result of the buyer's breach.

5)   Certainty Rule
The plaintiff must prove that the losses suffered were certain in their nature and ***not speculative***. Traditionally, if the breaching party prevented the nonbreaching party from setting up a new business, courts would not award lost profits from the prospective business as damages, because they were too speculative. However, modern courts may allow lost profits as damages if they can be made more certain by observing similar businesses in the area or other businesses previously owned by the same party.

b.   Punitive Damages
Punitive damages, awarded to punish a defendant for wrongful conduct, are generally ***not*** awarded in contract cases.

c.   Nominal Damages
Nominal (token) damages (e.g., $1) may be awarded where a breach is shown but no actual loss is proven.

d.   Liquidated Damages
The parties to a contract may stipulate what damages are to be paid in the event of a breach. These liquidated damages must be in an amount that is reasonable in view of the actual or anticipated harm caused by the breach.

1)   Requirements for Enforcement
Liquidated damage clauses will be enforceable if the following two requirements are met:

(i)   Damages for contractual breach must have been ***difficult to estimate or ascertain at the time the contract was formed***.

    (ii)   The amount agreed on must have been a ***reasonable forecast*** of compensatory damages in the case of breach. The test for reasonableness is a comparison between the amount of damages prospectively probable at the time of contract formation and the liquidated damages figure. If the liquidated damages amount is unreasonable, the courts will construe this as a ***penalty*** and will not enforce the provision.

a)   UCC Rule

The UCC allows a court to consider actual damages to validate a liquidated damages clause. Even if the clause was not a reasonable forecast of damages at the time of the contract formation, it will be valid if it was reasonable in light of the subsequent actual damages. [UCC §2-718(1)]

2)   Recoverable Even If No Actual Damages

If the above requirements are met, the plaintiff will receive the liquidated damages amount. Most courts hold this is so even if no actual money or pecuniary damages have been suffered. Should one or both of the above requirements not be met, the provision fails and the plaintiff will recover only those damages that she can ***prove***.

3)   Effect of Electing Liquidated or Actual Damages

Should a contract stipulate that the plaintiff may elect to recover liquidated damages set by a clause or actual damages, the liquidated damages clause may be unenforceable.

2.   Contracts for Sale of Goods

a.   Buyer's Damages

1)   Seller Does Not Deliver or Buyer Rejects Goods or Revokes Acceptance

The buyer's basic damages where the seller does not deliver or the buyer properly rejects or revokes her acceptance of tendered goods consist of the difference between the contract price and either the market price or the cost of buying replacement goods (i.e., ***cover***), plus incidental and consequential damages (*see* above), if any, less expenses saved as a result of the seller's breach. In the case of a seller's anticipatory repudiation, the buyer's damages are measured as of the time she learns of the breach.

a)   Difference Between Contract Price and Market Price

If the buyer measures damages by the difference between contract price and market price, market price usually is determined as of the time the buyer learns of the breach and at the place of tender. [UCC §2-713] Note that the ***buyer's damages*** are measured as of the ***time she learns of the breach***, while the ***seller's damages*** are measured as of the ***time for delivery***. (*See* b.1)a), *infra*.)

b) **Difference Between Contract Price and Cost of Replacement Goods— "Cover"**

Cover is the usual measure of damages for a buyer. Typically, if a buyer is not sent the goods contracted for, he will go out into the marketplace to buy replacement goods. If the buyer chooses the cover measure (i.e., difference between contract price and cost of buying replacement goods), the buyer must make a *reasonable contract* for substitute goods *in good faith* and *without unreasonable delay*. [UCC §2-712]

Example: Seller and Buyer have a contract for the sale of 10,000 widgets at $1 per widget. Seller does not deliver. At the time and place for determining market price, the average price of widgets is $1.05. However, Buyer made a replacement contract within a reasonable time and in good faith at a price of $1.07. Buyer can recover $700 based on her replacement costs. If, on the other hand, Buyer could have bought substitute widgets for $1.03 while the general market price was $1.05, but she chose not to cover, she could recover $500 based on the difference between contract and market prices, rather than being limited to her cover costs.

2) **Seller Delivers Nonconforming Goods that Buyer Accepts**

a) **Warranty Damages**

If the buyer accepts goods that breach one of the seller's warranties, the buyer may recover as damages "loss resulting in the normal course of events from the breach." The basic measure of damages in such a case is the difference between the *value of the goods as delivered* and the *value they would have had if they had been according to contract*, plus incidental and consequential damages. [UCC §2-714] (*See* V.D.5.f., *supra*.)

b) **Notice Requirement**

To recover damages for any defect as to accepted goods, the buyer must, *within a reasonable time after she discovers or should have discovered the defect*, notify the seller of the defect. If she does not notify the seller within a reasonable time, she loses her right to sue. "Reasonable time" is, of course, a flexible standard.

3) **Seller Anticipatorily Breaches Contract**

Under section 2-713, the measure of damages when the seller anticipatorily breaches the contract is the difference between the *market price at the time the buyer learned of the breach* and the *contract price*.

4) **Consequential Damages**

As noted above, a seller is liable for consequential damages arising from his breach if: (i) he had reason to know of the buyer's general or particular requirements, and (ii) the subsequent loss resulting from those needs could not reasonably be prevented by cover. Particular needs must be made known to the seller, but general requirements usually need not be. [UCC §2-715(2)]

a) Goods for Resale
If the buyer is in the business of reselling the goods, the seller is deemed to have knowledge of the resale.

b) Goods Necessary for Manufacturing
If a seller knows that the goods he provides are to be used in the manufacturing process, he should know that his breach would cause a disruption in production leading to a loss of profits.

b. Seller's Damages

1) Buyer Refuses to Accept Goods or Anticipatorily Breaches Contract
The seller's basic damages when the buyer refuses to accept goods or repudiates are either the difference between the contract price and the market price or the difference between the contract price and the resale price of the particular goods, plus incidental (but *not* consequential) damages, if any, less expenses saved as a result of the breach. If damages based on the difference between the contract price and market or resale price do not put the seller in as good a position as performance would have, then the seller may recover lost profits plus incidental damages. [UCC §§2-706, 2-708, 2-710] In the case of a buyer's anticipatory breach, the seller's damages are measured as of the actual time for performance, unless the suit comes to trial before the time for performance, in which case damages are measured as the time the seller learned of the breach.

a) Difference Between Contract Price and Market Price
The market price is measured as of the time and at the place for *delivery*.

b) Difference Between Contract Price and Resale Price
This is the usual measure of a seller's damages. If the seller chooses to resell, he must do so under the provisions of section 2-706, which requires a *good faith, commercially reasonable sale* that may be either private or public (auction). In the case of a private sale, the breaching buyer must be given reasonable notice of intention to resell. In the case of an auction sale, the sale must be at a usual market for such goods if such a market is reasonably available. Notice of the sale must be given to the breaching buyer unless the goods are perishable or threaten to decline rapidly in value. Only existing and identified goods may be sold, unless there is a market in futures for the particular goods. The seller may buy the goods at an auction sale.

c) Damages Based on Lost Profits
The previous two measures of damages might not give adequate compensation for the buyer's breach in situations where the seller can obtain or manufacture as many goods as he can sell (e.g., a car dealership). In such a case, the seller is known as a *lost volume seller*, because although he is able to resell the goods for the same or similar price as in the initial contract, he loses *volume* of business: But for the buyer's breach, the seller would have made *two* sales instead of one. Generally, lost profit is measured by the contract price with the breaching buyer minus cost to the seller.

Example:	Seller, a distributor of widgets, can get all of the widgets he needs for sale. He makes a contract to sell 10,000 widgets to Buyer at a price of $1 per widget. Buyer repudiates the contract. Seller resells the widgets he had identified to Buyer's contract to Z for $1 per widget. If damages are measured by the difference between the contract price and resale price, Seller will be denied recovery. However, assuming Seller paid 85¢ per widget for these widgets, his lost profit on the Buyer deal is $1,500 ($10,000 less $8,500), because even if Buyer had not breached, Seller would have been able to supply Z with widgets. Because Buyer's breach did not *enable* Seller to make the sale to Z, and because the sale to Z would have been made in any event, the only way to make Seller whole is to allow him to recover his lost profits, i.e., $1,500. If Seller would have incurred sales commissions of $500 and delivery expenses of $100 if Buyer had taken the goods, but does not now incur those expenses, the saved expenses reduce the recovery. Therefore, the recovery would be $900 ($1,500 less saved expenses of $600).
Compare:	Seller and Buyer enter into a contract for the sale of a particular painting by van Gogh at a price of $25,000. Seller paid $15,000 for the painting two years earlier. Buyer repudiates. Seller resells to Z at $24,000. Seller's measure of damages is $1,000 plus incidental damages. Seller cannot get the $10,000 lost profit measure (i.e., the difference between the contract price and what Seller paid for the painting) because there is only one painting, and Seller could not have made the sale to Z but for Buyer's repudiation.

2) Action for Price

If the buyer has accepted the goods and has not paid, or has not accepted the goods, and the seller is *unable to resell* them at any reasonable price, or if the goods have been lost or damaged at a time the risk of loss was on the buyer (*see* V.D.2., *supra*), the seller may maintain an action against the buyer for the full contract price. [UCC §2-709]

3. Contracts for Sale of Land

The standard measure of damages for breach of land sale contracts is the difference between the contract price and the fair market value of the land.

4. Employment Contracts

In employment contracts, check to see whether the breach was by the employer or the employee.

a. Breach by Employer

Irrespective of when the breach occurs—i.e., before performance, after part performance, or after full performance, the standard measure of the employee's damages is the *full contract price*.

b. Breach by Employee

If an employee materially breaches an employment contract, the employer is entitled to recover the cost of replacing the employee (i.e., the wages the employer must pay to a replacement employee minus the breaching employee's wages). The breaching employee may offset money owed for work done to date.

c. Employment at Will

Many employment relationships can be characterized as employment at will, which means employment may be terminated at any time for any reason. Thus termination of at-will employment by either party does not result in breach. A position characterized as "permanent" creates an employment-at-will relationship.

5. Construction Contracts

If construction contracts are involved, check to see whether the owner or the builder is breaching.

a. Breach by Owner

If the owner has breached, check to see when the breach occurred.

1) Breach Before Construction Started

If the breach occurred before construction started, the builder is entitled to the *profits* he would have derived from the contract.

2) Breach During Construction

If the breach occurs during construction, the builder is entitled to any *profit* he would have derived from the contract *plus* any *costs* he has incurred to date. The formula is also stated as the contract price minus the cost of completion. Either formula will give the same result.

3) Breach After Construction Completed

If the breach occurs after construction has been completed, the builder is entitled to the full *contract price plus interest* thereon.

b. Breach by Builder

If the breach is by the builder, check to see when it occurred.

1) Breach Before Construction Started

If the builder breaches before construction, the owner's measure of damages is the *cost of completion*, i.e., the amount above the contract price that it will cost to get the building completed *plus* reasonable compensation for any delay in performance.

2) Breach During Construction

If the builder breaches after partially performing, the owner is entitled to the *cost of completion plus reasonable compensation for any delay* in performance. If, however, completion would involve undue economic waste, the measure of damages will be the difference between the value of what the owner *would have received* if the builder had properly performed the contract and the value of what the owner *actually received*.

Example: Homeowner and Builder enter into a contract to build a house. The contract provides, among other things, that all of the plumbing pipes will be copper. After the plumbing is installed throughout the house, but before construction of the house is completed, Homeowner discovers that the pipes installed were made of polyvinyl chloride ("PVC"), and not copper. Homeowner insists that Builder remove the entire plumbing system and replace the PVC pipes with copper pipes. The house with PVC pipes would be valued at $500 less than it would have been had copper pipes been installed. However, it would cost Builder $10,000 in labor and materials to rip out the PVC pipes and replace them with copper pipes. *Result:* Builder would not be compelled to replace the pipes, and Homeowner's damages would be $500, which may be offset against the amount owed to Builder.

3) Breach by Late Performance

If the builder completes performance, but it is late, the owner has a right to damages for any loss incurred by not being able to use the property when performance was due, e.g., loss of reasonable rental value when property could have been leased. However, if damages for this "lost use" are not easily determined or were not foreseeable at the time the contract was entered into, the owner can recover only the *interest* on the value of the building as a capital investment.

c. Restoration and Economic Waste

Usually, when a building contract is not properly performed, the owner is entitled to the cost of fixing the defect. However, as noted in the pipes example above, unless there is special significance attached to use of a particular item (e.g., the owner is the CEO of the particular brand of copper pipe specified) and that significance is communicated to the builder, a court will not order a remedy that results in undue economic waste. Moreover, courts are split on the result when a party contracts to restore property and willfully refuses to do so because it is much more costly than any diminution in value of the property.

Example: Farmer and GasCo enter into a two-year contract that permits GasCo to explore Farmer's property and extract any natural gas it finds in exchange for a fixed sum and a promise to restore the land to its pre-exploration status upon completion of the two-year term. At the end of the term, GasCo determines that it will cost $200,000 to restore the property. Although it cannot be used for farming, the land has lost only $5,000 in value. Courts are split on whether GasCo must pay the $200,000 to restore the property or only the $5,000 loss in value. GasCo will argue that to pay the $200,000 is economic waste. Farmer will argue that it bargained for the restoration and GasCo will be unjustly enriched if it does not have to follow through—giving GasCo a $195,000 windfall at Farmer's expense.

6. Contracts Calling for Installment Payments

If a contract calls for payments in installments and a payment is not made, there is only a partial breach. The aggrieved party is limited to recovering only the missed payment, not the entire contract price. However, the contract may include an ***acceleration clause*** making the entire amount due on any late payment, in which case the aggrieved party may recover the entire amount. [Restatement (Second) of Contracts §243(3)]

7. Avoidable Damages (Mitigation)

Under the common law, the nonbreaching party cannot recover damages that could have been avoided with reasonable effort. Thus, she must refrain from piling up losses after she receives notice of the breach; she must not incur further expenditures or costs, and she must make reasonable efforts to cut down her losses by procuring a substitute performance at a fair price. Should she not do so, she will not be allowed to recover those damages that might have been avoided by such mitigation after the breach. Generally, a party may ***recover the expenses of mitigation***. Note the following specific contract situations:

a. Employment Contracts

If the breaching employer can prove that a comparable job in the same locale was available, then contract damages against that breaching employer for lost wages will be reduced by the wages that the plaintiff would have received from that comparable job.

b. Manufacturing Contracts

Generally, in a contract to manufacture goods, if the person for whom the goods are being manufactured breaches, the manufacturer is under a duty to mitigate by ***not continuing work*** after the breach. However, if the facts are such that completion of the manufacturing project will decrease rather than increase damages, the manufacturer has a right to continue.

Example:　　Partly manufactured goods may be without value because they cannot be sold. The nonbreaching manufacturer may complete production and recover for his expenses in doing so, because finished goods usually can be resold, and the damages will be decreased as a result.

c. Construction Contracts

A builder does not owe a duty to avoid the consequences of an owner's breach, e.g., by securing other work, but does have a duty to mitigate by ***not continuing work*** after the breach. Again, however, if completion will decrease damages, it will be allowed.

d. Contracts for Sale of Goods

Under Article 2, the rule of mitigation generally does not apply. An injured buyer is not required to cover, and an injured seller is not required to resell. Market damages are always available if the buyer does not cover or the seller does not resell. Recall, however, that the seller generally cannot bring an action against the buyer for the ***full contract price*** (rather than market or resale damages) unless the goods cannot be resold at a reasonable price or were damaged or lost when the risk of loss was on the buyer. (*See* 2.b.2), *supra.*)

C. RESTITUTION

As an alternative to the contract damages discussed above, restitution may be available in a contract-type situation. Restitution is not really part of contract law, but rather is a distinct concept. Restitution is based on preventing ***unjust enrichment*** when one has conferred a benefit on another without gratuitous intent. Restitution can provide a remedy not only when a contract exists and has been breached, but also when a contract is unenforceable, and in some cases when no contractual relationship exists at all between the parties.

1. **Terminology**

When a contract is unenforceable or no contract between the parties exists, an action to recover restitutionary damages often is referred to as an action for an *implied in law* contract, an action in *quasi-contract*, or an action for *quantum meruit*.

2. **Measure of Damages**

Generally, the measure of restitution is the *value of the benefit conferred*. Although this is usually based on the benefit received by the defendant (e.g., the increase in value of the defendant's property or the value of the goods received), recovery may also be measured by the "detriment" suffered by the plaintiff (e.g., the reasonable value of the work performed or the services rendered) if the benefits are difficult to measure or the "benefit" measure would achieve an unfair result.

Example: Homeowner hires Painter to paint Homeowner's house in exchange for $5,000. When the job is 70% complete, Homeowner orders Painter to stop because Homeowner does not like the new color. The value of the work performed thus far is $4,000. Although the value of Homeowner's house might not have been increased by the partially finished paint job, Painter may recover in a restitutionary action the $4,000 value of the services rendered.

3. **Specific Applications**

   a. **When Contract Breached**

   When a contract has been breached and the nonbreaching party has not fully performed, he may choose to cancel the contract and sue for restitution to prevent unjust enrichment. Note that if the plaintiff has fully performed, he is *limited to his damages under the contract*. This may be less than he would have received in a restitutionary action because a restitutionary remedy is not limited to the contract price (*see* example below).

   1) **"Losing" Contracts**

   A restitutionary remedy often is desirable in the case of a "losing" contract (i.e., a contract in which the actual value of the services or goods to be provided under the contract is higher than the contract price), because normal contract expectation damages or reliance damages would be for a lesser amount.

   Example: Owner and Contractor enter into a contract under which Contractor is to remodel Owner's kitchen for $30,000, to be paid on completion. It turns out Contractor underestimated the cost of the remodel by failing to take into account increasing supply costs. Contractor estimated that the job would end up costing him $33,000. When the remodel was nearly complete, Owner told Contractor that he was out of funds for home improvements and could not pay him. Contractor ceased work on the job. At that point, Contractor had spent $32,000 on the remodel. Contractor may recover the $32,000 in restitution, even though his contract damages would have been only $30,000.

2) **Breach by Plaintiff**

Typically, the plaintiff will be seeking restitution because the defendant breached the contract. However, under some circumstances, a plaintiff may seek restitution even though the plaintiff is the party who breached. If the breach was intentional, some courts will not grant the breaching party restitution; modern courts, however, will permit restitutionary recovery but limit it to the contract price less damages incurred as a result of the breach.

Example: Client hires Attorney to represent Client in a contract dispute. Attorney prepares the case, but withdraws without good cause. The case is settled favorably for Client. Modern courts will allow Attorney to recover for the value of the services he rendered to Client, up to the contract price, reduced by the reasonable amount Client had to expend to hire another attorney.

a) **Restitution of Advance Payments or Deposit If Buyer of Goods in Breach**

Article 2 has very specific rules concerning whether and how much a breaching buyer can recover of advance payments. If the buyer has paid part of the purchase price in advance and then breaches the contract, he can usually recover some of the payments.

(1) **General Offset Provision**

When the buyer breaches, the seller may keep advance payments totaling 20% of the purchase price or $500, whichever is less. The balance must be returned to the buyer. [UCC §2-718(2)(b)]

(2) **Effect of Liquidated Damages Provision**

If there is a valid liquidated damages clause, the seller is required to refund only the excess of the buyer's payments over the amount of liquidated damages. [UCC §2-718(2)(a)]

(3) **Seller's Right to Greater Damages**

The general offset rule above applies only if the seller cannot prove greater actual damages. If the seller can prove damages in excess of 20% of the price or $500, he may recover them. Even if he cannot prove actual damages beyond the offset, he is additionally entitled to incidental damages and the value of any benefits received by the buyer. [UCC §2-718(3)]

b. **When Contract Unenforceable—Quasi-Contract Remedy**

Restitution may be available in a *quasi-contract* action when a contract was made but is unenforceable and unjust enrichment otherwise would result.

Examples: 1) Aristotle hires Derek to sign autographs in Aristotle's sporting goods store one day next month and gives Derek half of his $1,000 fee upon making the contract. Derek then dies and so is discharged from his obligation to perform. Aristotle can recover the $500 from Derek's estate as restitution in quasi-contract.

2) Owner hires Contractor to repair Owner's house. After Contractor has completed half of the repair work, the house is destroyed by a tornado. Although the parties will be discharged for impossibility, Contractor will be able to recover in restitution for the valuable improvements made to the house before it was destroyed.

3) Landlord promises to sell Tenant five acres of a 1,000-acre tract that Tenant is leasing, but the contract fails to state which five acres. Tenant plants fruit trees on the five acres that he thinks were intended. Tenant cannot enforce the promise because it does not specify which five acres were intended, but he can recover restitution in a quasi-contract action for the value of the fruit trees.

c. When No Contract Involved—Quasi-Contract Remedy
Restitution may also be available in a *quasi-contract* action when there is no contractual relationship between the parties if:

(i) The plaintiff has **conferred a benefit** on the defendant by rendering services or expending properties;

(ii) The plaintiff conferred the benefit with the **reasonable expectation of being compensated** for its value;

(iii) The defendant **knew or had reason to know** of the plaintiff's expectation; and

(iv) The defendant would be **unjustly enriched** if he were allowed to retain the benefit without compensating the plaintiff.

Example: Doctor witnesses an automobile accident and rushes to aid an unconscious victim. Doctor can recover the reasonable value of his services.

Note: Where the parties are in a *close relationship* to one another, it is usually presumed that the benefits were given gratuitously and the party claiming relief bears the burden of showing that they were conferred with an expectation of being paid therefor.

D. RESCISSION
Rescission is a remedy whereby the original contract is considered voidable and rescinded. The parties are left as though a contract had never been made.

1. Grounds
The grounds for rescission must have occurred either before or at the time the contract was entered into. The grounds are:

a. *Mutual mistake* of a material fact (*see* IV.B.1., *supra*);

b. Unilateral mistake if the *other party knew* or should have known of the mistake;

c. Unilateral mistake if *hardship to the mistaken party is so extreme* it outweighs the other party's expectations under the contract;

d. ***Misrepresentation of fact or law*** by either party as to a material factor in the negotiations that was relied upon; and

e. ***Other grounds***, such as duress, undue influence, illegality, lack of capacity, and failure of consideration.

2. **Defenses**

Generally all equitable defenses (e.g., laches, unclean hands) are available in a rescission action. Note that the plaintiff's negligence is not a defense.

3. **Additional Relief**

If the plaintiff has paid money to the defendant, she is entitled to restitution in addition to rescission.

E. **REFORMATION**

Reformation is the remedy whereby the writing setting forth the agreement between the parties is changed so that it conforms to the original intent of the parties.

1. **Grounds**

a. **Mistake**

To reform a contract because of mistake, there must be: (i) an agreement between the parties, (ii) an agreement to put the agreement in writing, and (iii) a variance between the original agreement and the writing.

b. **Misrepresentation**

If a writing is inaccurate because of a misrepresentation, the plaintiff can choose between reformation and avoidance. To qualify for reformation, the misrepresentation must relate to the content or the legal effect ***of the record***. The court will reform the writing to reflect the ***expressed*** intent of the parties. Misrepresentations as to the subject matter of the agreement are not grounds for reformation because the court will not remake the parties' bargain. Rescission and damages are the proper remedy for that.

Example: Seller owns Blackacre, which is encumbered by a mortgage. Seller and Buyer agree that Buyer will purchase Blackacre subject to the mortgage. Buyer does not agree to assume the mortgage. If Seller inserts a clause under which Buyer agrees to assume the mortgage and Buyer signs without knowledge of this, Buyer is entitled to reformation. [*See* Bradshaw v. Provident Trust Co., 158 P. 274 (Or. 1916)]

2. **Negligence Does Not Bar Reformation**

Failure to read the record of the agreement does not preclude a party from obtaining reformation. In nearly every case in which the record does not reflect the agreement, either one or both parties have failed to read it.

3. **Clear and Convincing Evidence Standard**

The variance between the antecedent agreement and the writing must be established by clear and convincing evidence.

4. **Parol Evidence Rule and Statute of Frauds Do Not Apply**

The parol evidence rule is not applied in reformation actions. Likewise, the majority rule is that the Statute of Frauds does not apply—but many courts will deny reformation if it would add land to the contract without complying with the Statute of Frauds.

5. **Defenses**

In addition to the general equitable defenses, the existence of a bona fide purchaser for value is also a defense to reformation. If the subject matter of the contract is sold to a bona fide purchaser, reformation will not be allowed. Similarly, reformation is not permitted if the rights of third parties will be unfairly affected.

F. **STATUTE OF LIMITATIONS UNDER UCC**

States have enacted differing statutes of limitation for contracts actions in general, and some have specific limitations periods for specific types of contracts. For sales contracts, however, the UCC provides for a *four-year statute* of limitations. [UCC §2-725]

1. **Parties May Agree to Shorter Period**

The parties to a sales contract may shorten the limitations period by agreement to *no lessthan one year*, but they may not lengthen the period.

2. **Accrual of Action**

The statutory period begins to run when the cause of action accrues. The cause of action accrues when a party can bring suit, i.e., when the breach occurs. The statutory period begins to run regardless of whether the aggrieved party knows about the breach. [UCC §2-725(2)]

3. **Breach of Warranty Actions**

For a breach of warranty action, the breach occurs and the limitations period begins to run upon *delivery* of the goods. This is true even if the buyer does not discover the breach until much later.

a. **Warranty Extends to Future Performance**

If there is an express warranty that explicitly extends to future performance of the goods, the four-year period does not begin to run until the buyer should have discovered the breach.

Example: Buyer purchases a lawnmower from Seller. In the contract, Seller specifically warrants that all parts will be free from defect for five years. Two years after the sale, one of the blades breaks in two. The four-year period begins to run on the day the blade broke.

b. **Implied Warranties Breached on Delivery**

Because implied warranties cannot "explicitly" extend to future performance, they are breached, if at all, upon delivery.

IX. RIGHTS AND DUTIES OF THIRD PARTIES TO THE CONTRACT

A. **INTRODUCTION**

The general rule is that a contract operates to confer rights and impose duties only on the parties to the contract and on no other person. However, two important exceptions exist: (i) contractual rights involving third-party beneficiaries, and (ii) contractual rights or duties that are transferred to third parties. In the first situation, the original contract will confer the rights and duties on the third party; in the second situation, the original contract does not confer any rights or obligations on the third party, but subsequently one of the parties has sought to transfer his rights and/or duties under the contract to a third party (i.e., assignment of rights, delegation of duties).

B. THIRD-PARTY BENEFICIARIES

The basic situation to be dealt with here is: A enters into a valid contract with B that provides that B will render some performance to C. A is the promisee, B is the promisor, and C is a third party. Three main problems must be focused on:

(i)   Is C an intended third-party beneficiary?

(ii)   Can A and B alter the contract's terms to deprive C of her rights? That is, when do C's rights vest?

(iii) What are the rights of A and C against B; of C against A?

1. Which Third-Party Beneficiaries Can Sue?

a. Intended Beneficiaries Can Sue

Only intended third-party beneficiaries have contract rights. As the term "intended third-party beneficiary" suggests, whether a person is an intended beneficiary depends on the intent of the parties.

Example: Rich agrees to pay Erwin $1,000 to paint Paula's house, and Erwin agrees. Paula is an intended third-party beneficiary and has contract law rights even though she is not a party to the contract.

b. Incidental Third-Party Beneficiaries Have No Contract Rights

Incidental third-party beneficiaries benefit from the contract, but that is not the primary purpose of the contract. These beneficiaries have no contract rights.

Example: Rich agrees to pay Erwin $1,000 to paint Rich's house, and Erwin agrees. Rich's unpainted house has affected the property value of his neighbor Paula. Paula's property value will increase when Rich's house is painted; thus, she will benefit from the contract. Here, however, Paula has no contract rights. She is merely an incidental beneficiary; the purpose of the contract was to benefit Rich.

c. Determining the Promisee's Intention

1) Language of Contract

Often, but not always, whether a party is the intended beneficiary of a contract can be determined from the language of the contract itself. The issue is whether the purpose of the promisee was to confer a right on another directly.

Example: Alex offers to sell his car to Becky if Becky pays Cindy the $1,000 purchase price. Cindy is a third-party beneficiary because the contract appears to have been intended to directly benefit her.

> *Compare:* Alex promises Becky that he will give her a brand new General Motors car if she will work for him for three months. General Motors probably is not an intended beneficiary even though it is named in the contract (*see* factors to consider, below).

2) Factors

The courts generally look at the following *factors* in resolving the question of intention:

a) Is the third party expressly *designated* in the contract? If so, it is more likely that it is primarily for her benefit. But note that it is not necessary that the third-party beneficiary be named, or even identifiable, at the time the contract is made; she need only be identifiable at the time performance is due.

b) Is *performance to be made directly* to the third party? If so, it is more likely that the contract is primarily for her benefit.

c) Does the third party have any *rights* under the contract (e.g., the right to designate when and where performance is to be made)? If so, it is more likely that the contract is primarily for her benefit.

d) Does the third party stand in such a *relationship* to the promisee that one could infer that the promisee wished to make an agreement for the third party's benefit? If so, it is more likely that the contract is primarily for her benefit.

d. Creditor or Donee Beneficiary

There are two basic categories of "intended" beneficiaries who may sue on the promise: creditor and donee beneficiaries. The distinction between the two is based on the promisee's purpose in extracting the commitment from the promisor.

1) Creditor Beneficiary

If the promisee's purpose in extracting the promise was to discharge an obligation owed to the third party, the third party is a creditor beneficiary.

2) Donee Beneficiary

If the promisee's purpose in extracting the promise was to confer a gift on the third party, the third party is a donee beneficiary.

2. When Do the Rights of the Beneficiary Vest?

An "intended" beneficiary can enforce a contract only after his rights have vested. This becomes important when the original parties to the contract take actions (e.g., rescission, modification, etc.) that affect the third-party beneficiary. The general rule for *both* creditor and donee beneficiaries is that their rights vest when the beneficiary:

(i) Manifests *assent* to the promise in a manner invited or requested by the parties;

(ii) Brings *suit* to enforce the promise; or

(iii) Materially *changes position* in justifiable reliance on the promise.

[Restatement (Second) of Contracts §311]

a. **Significance of Vesting**

Before the intended third-party beneficiary's rights vest, the promisor and promisee are free to modify their contract—including removing the third-party beneficiary altogether—without consulting the third party. Once the third-party beneficiary's rights have vested, the promisor and promisee cannot vary his rights without his consent.

3. **What Are the Rights of the Third-Party Beneficiary and the Promisee?**

a. **Third-Party Beneficiary vs. Promisor**

If the promisor fails to perform, the third-party beneficiary may sue the promisor on the contract, subject to defenses as follows:

1) **Promisor's Defenses Against Promisee**

Because the third-party beneficiary's rights are derivative, the promisor may raise any defense against the third-party beneficiary that he would have against the promisee, including: lack of assent, lack of consideration, illegality, impossibility, and failure of a condition.

2) **Promisee's Defenses Against Third-Party Beneficiary If Promise Not Absolute**

Whether the promisor can use any of the defenses that the promisee would have against the third-party beneficiary depends on whether the promisor made an absolute promise to pay (e.g., "I will pay T $500 in exchange for your services") or only a promise to pay what the promisee owes the beneficiary (e.g., "I will pay T whatever you owe him in exchange for your services"). In the former case, the promisor *cannot* assert the promisee's defenses; in the latter case, the promisor *can* assert the promisee's defenses.

b. **Third-Party Beneficiary vs. Promisee**

If the promisor fails to perform vis-à-vis the third-party beneficiary, whether the third-party beneficiary may sue the promisee depends on whether the third-party beneficiary is a donee beneficiary or a creditor beneficiary. A *donee beneficiary* generally may *not* sue the promisee because generally there is no right to sue for nondelivery of a gift. (*But see* exception below.) However, a *creditor beneficiary* can sue the promisee on the underlying obligation that the promisor's performance was meant to discharge.

Example: Suppose Alex offers to sell his car to Becky if Becky pays Cindy the $1,000 purchase price. Alex informs Cindy of the arrangement and she nods with approval, thus vesting her rights. Alex transfers his car to Becky, but Becky does not pay the $1,000 to Cindy. If Alex intended the $1,000 to be a gift to Cindy, she cannot sue Alex for Becky's failure to pay. But if Alex owed Cindy a debt and the $1,000 was meant to satisfy the debt, Cindy may sue Alex on the unsatisfied obligation that he owed her.

Note: The rights of a creditor beneficiary are cumulative. She need not elect between suing the promisor and suing her own debtor (i.e., the promisee). She may *sue both*. Of course, she may obtain but *one satisfaction*.

1) **Exception—Detrimental Reliance**

If the *promisee tells* the donee beneficiary of the contract and should *foresee reliance* by the beneficiary, and the beneficiary *reasonably relies* to her detriment, the beneficiary can sue the promisee directly under a promissory estoppel/detrimental reliance theory (*see* III.D., *supra*), even though the beneficiary cannot sue the promisee as a third-party beneficiary.

Example: Alex contracts to rent his house to Becky for one year, but the contract provides that Becky is to make the first three payments to Alex's cousin Cindy. Alex then calls Cindy and tells her that she will be able to buy the new furniture that she has wanted because Becky will be making his first three payments to Cindy. Cindy rushes out and buys new furniture. Alex decides not to rent the house to Becky. Cindy can sue Alex under a promissory estoppel/detrimental reliance theory but not as a third-party beneficiary under the contract.

c.   Promisee vs. Promisor

1)   Donee Beneficiary Situation
If the promisor fails to perform and the contract involves a donee beneficiary, it was once said that the promisee could not sue the promisor at law. The rationale was that because the donee beneficiary had no cause of action against the promisee, there was no damage suffered. Today, however, the **majority view** is that the **promisee has a cause of action**. Because the promisee hardly ever suffers any actual damage, however, she will usually receive only nominal damages. Hence, most courts have resolved this problem by allowing **specific performance** in this situation.

2)   Creditor Beneficiary Situation
If the promisor fails to perform as to a creditor beneficiary and a promisee has had to pay the beneficiary on the existing debt, the promisee **may recover** against the promisor. If the debt has not yet been paid by the promisee to the third party, the promisee can compel the promisor to pay in a **specific performance** action.

C.   ASSIGNMENT OF RIGHTS AND DELEGATION OF DUTIES
The basic fact situation to be dealt with here is: X enters into a valid contract with Y. This contract does not contemplate performance to or by a third party. Subsequently, one of the parties seeks to transfer her rights and/or duties under the contract to a third party.

1.   Assignment of Rights
A transfer of a right under a contract is called an "assignment." The main issues regarding assignments are:

(i)   What rights may be assigned?

(ii)   What is necessary for an effective assignment?

(iii) Is the assignment revocable or irrevocable?

(iv)   What are the rights and liabilities of the various parties?

(v) What problems exist if there have been successive assignments of the same rights?

a. Terminology

X and Y have a contract. Y assigns her rights under the contract to Z. Y is the assignor, Z is the assignee, and X is the obligor.

b. What Rights May Be Assigned?

1) General Rule

Generally, ***all*** contractual rights may be assigned. However, several ***exceptions*** to this rule exist.

2) Exceptions

a) Assigned Rights Would Substantially Change Obligor's Duty

If an assignment of rights would substantially change the obligor's duty, the assignment will be barred.

(1) Personal Service Contracts

If the assignment of rights would result in the obligor having to perform personal services for someone other than the original obligee, the attempted assignment will be invalid. For the purposes of assignment, the test as to what constitutes personal services is whether the performance so involves the personality or personal characteristics of the obligor that it would be unfair to require the obligor to perform for a third person. Examples of personal services that cannot be assigned include those of a lawyer, physician, architect, and author. In contrast, repair and construction contracts usually are not considered to involve personal services, so a contractor may be required to render his performance to an assignee.

(2) Requirements and Output Contracts

Although at common law rights under requirements and output contracts were not assignable, under Article 2, they are assignable as long as the assignee does not disproportionately alter the contemplated quantity. Likewise, the buyer's duty to purchase goods under an output contract and the seller's duty to sell goods under a requirements contract can always be delegated, unless they fall within the general restrictions on delegation listed at 2.b., *infra,* because the other party's rights are not affected.

b)   Rights Assigned Would Substantially Alter Obligor's Risk
When the obligor's risk would be substantially altered by any attempted assignment, the assignment will fail.

Example: Kwan owns a summer home that is insured by Acme Insurance Co. against loss due to fire. Kwan sells the building to Lincoln, who intends to convert it into a restaurant. Kwan may not, without the consent of Acme, assign his rights under the policy to Lincoln.

c)   Assignment of Future Rights
The assignment of a *right expected to arise* under a contract of employment not then existing operates only as a promise to assign the right when it arises, i.e., when the expected future contract is in fact entered into.

Contrast this with *future rights in existing contracts*, which are generally *assignable* even though the right might not yet have vested.

d)   Assignment Prohibited by Law
A right may not be assigned if the assignment is prohibited by law. Such public policy against assignment may be embodied either in a statute or in case precedent. For example, many states have laws prohibiting, or at least limiting, wage assignments.

e)   Express Contractual Provision Against Assignment

(1)   Assignment of "the Contract"
Absent circumstances suggesting otherwise, a clause prohibiting the assignment of "the contract" will be construed as barring *only the delegation* of the assignor's *duties*. [Restatement (Second) of Contracts §322; UCC §2-210(4)]

Example: Sam and Betty enter into a contract wherein Betty will purchase 100 books from Sam, a book collector, for $5,000. The contract provides that "this contract shall not be assigned." Subsequently, Sam assigns to Charlie his right to receive the $5,000 from the contract. Sam has not breached the contract because he merely assigned his right to receive payment; he did not delegate his duty to deliver the books.

(2)   Assignment of Rights Under the Contract
A clause prohibiting the assignment of *contractual rights* generally does not bar assignment, but merely gives the obligor the right to sue for breach if an assignment is made. [Restatement (Second) of Contracts §322] In other words, the assignor has the *power but not the right* to assign.

(a)   Factors that Make Assignment Ineffective
Notwithstanding the general rule, if the clause provides that any

attempt to assign will be *"void,"* assignment will be ineffective (i.e., the assignor has neither the power nor the right to assign). Also, if the assignee has *notice* of the nonassignment clause, assignment will be ineffective.

c. Effect of Assignment—Real Party in Interest

The effect of an assignment is to establish privity of contract between the obligor and the assignee while extinguishing privity between the obligor and assignor. The assignee then replaces the assignor as the real party in interest, and she alone is entitled to performance under the contract. Once the obligor has knowledge of the assignment, he must render performance to or pay the assignee. If the obligor renders performance to or pays the assignor, he does so at his own risk. Typically, one of the parties (usually the assignee) will notify the obligor of the assignment.

d. What Is Necessary for an Effective Assignment?

1) Requirement of Writing

A writing is usually *not required* to have an effective assignment, so an oral assignment is generally effective. However, there are situations where an assignment *must* be in writing:

a) Wage assignments;

b) Assignments of an interest in land; and

c) Assignments intended as security interests under Article 9 of the UCC

2) Requirement of Adequate Description

The right being assigned must be adequately described.

3) Requirement of Present Words of Assignment

The assignor must also manifest an intent to transfer his rights under the contract *completely and immediately* to the assignee. Whether such intent is present will be determined by looking to the terms of the transfer itself, i.e., the test is objective, not subjective. It is not necessary to use the word "assign"; any generally accepted words of transfer will suffice (e.g., "convey," "sell," "transfer," etc.).

4) No Requirement of Consideration

Consideration is *not required*; a gratuitous assignment is effective.

Note: It is important to remember, however, that even though neither a writing nor consideration is generally required, the lack thereof will affect revocability. (*See* f., *infra*.)

e. Partial Assignments

Contract rights may be transferred to one assignee or split up and transferred to two or more. Similarly, the assignor may transfer some rights under the contract and retain others.

f.   Is the Assignment Revocable or Irrevocable?
When, if ever, do the rights of the assignee "vest" so that the assignment becomes irrevocable? Assignments are divided into two categories: assignments for value and gratuitous assignments.

1)   Assignments for Value Are Irrevocable
An assignment is for value if it is: (i) done for *consideration*, or (ii) taken as security for or payment of a *preexisting debt*. Assignments for value cannot be revoked.

2)   Gratuitous Assignments Are Revocable
An assignment not for value, i.e., a "gratuitous" assignment, is generally *revocable*.

a)   Exceptions to Rule of Revocability
In certain situations, however, a gratuitous assignment will be held irrevocable.

(1)   Performance by Obligor
If the obligor has already performed, the assignment will be irrevocable.

(2)   Delivery of Token Chose
If a token chose (tangible claim) involving the rights to be assigned (e.g., stock certificates, savings account passbook, etc.) has been delivered, the assignment will be irrevocable.

(3)   Assignment of Simple Chose in Writing
If the assignment involves a simple chose, i.e., an intangible claim not embodied by any token (or the great majority of ordinary contract rights), setting it forth in a writing will make the assignment irrevocable.

(4)   Estoppel
The theory of estoppel may prevent the assignor from revoking a gratuitous assignment if: (i) the assignor should reasonably foresee that the assignee will change her position in reliance on the assignment; and (ii) such detrimental reliance does in fact occur.

b)   Methods of Revocation
A gratuitous revocable assignment may be terminated in a number of ways:

(1)   *Death* of the assignor;

(2)   *Bankruptcy* of the assignor;

(3)   *Notice* of revocation communicated by the assignor to either the assignee or the obligor;

(4)   The *assignor takes performance* directly from the obligor; or

(5)   *Subsequent assignment* of the same right by the assignor to another.

c) **Effect of Revocation**

Once an assignment is revoked, the privity between the assignor and the obligor is restored, and the assignor is once again the real party in interest.

3) **Effect of "Irrevocable" Assignment**

One should note that the term "irrevocable" as applied to an assignment may be misleading. The effect of such irrevocability is to remove from the assignor the right to revoke or make a subsequent assignment of the same right to a third party. However, in many situations, even though the assignor no longer has this *right*, he still has the *power* to do so. He would, of course, be liable for a breach of contract. *Exception:* An exception exists for assignments accompanied by *delivery of a token chose*. In this case, the assignor loses both the right *and* the power to revoke or further assign.

g. **What Are the Rights and Liabilities of the Various Parties?**

1) **Assignee vs. Obligor**

As the assignee is the real party in interest, she may enforce her rights against the obligor *directly*.

a) **What Defenses Does Obligor Have Against Assignee?**

An assignee's rights against the obligor may be subject to any defenses that the obligor had against the assignor. This rule is similar to the rule discussed *supra* for promisors who are being sued by third-party beneficiaries.

Example: Opie, a mechanic, enters into a contract to purchase a car from Andy for $2,000, payment to be made in 30 days. Opie then performs some repair work for Andy and bills Andy $200. Andy tells Opie to subtract the $200 from the $2,000 that Opie owes Andy. The following week, Andy assigns his right to collect from Opie to his landlord, Lori. If Lori brings suit against Opie to collect the entire $2,000, Opie can raise the $200 setoff as a defense.

(1) **Exception—Personal Defenses Arising After Assignment**

If the obligor's defense is unrelated to the contract itself (i.e., it is a personal defense against the assignor, such as a setoff or counterclaim), the defense is not available against the assignee if it arose *after* the obligor had notice of the assignment.

Example: Same facts as in the example in a), above, but Opie performed the work for Andy after Andy asked Opie to pay the $2,000 due under the purchase agreement to Lori. Andy may *not* raise the setoff as a defense against Lori because it arose too late.

(a) **Test**

Is the defense *inherent* in the contract itself (e.g., failure of consideration) *or* is it a defense *unrelated* to the contract, the right of which has been assigned? As to defenses inherent in the contract itself, these defenses are always available against the assignee because they came into existence when the contract was made. As to setoffs, counterclaims, and the like, such defenses are good against the assignee only if they came into existence before the obligor had notice or knowledge of the assignment.

(2) Estoppel

The estoppel doctrine may operate to prevent the obligor from asserting a defense that might otherwise exist against the assignor.

Example: Jim and Harold entered into a contract. Subsequently, Harold sought to assign his rights under the contract to Zorba. Zorba inquired of Jim whether he had any defenses against Harold. Jim replied in the negative. Thereupon, Zorba paid Harold valuable consideration for the assigned rights. Jim may be estopped to raise any defenses existing at the time of his statement to Zorba.

b) Modification of the Contract

Generally, an assignee succeeds to the contract as it stands at the time of the assignment. This means that the assignee takes subject to any modifications, oral or written, made before the assignment. What about modifications after the assignment? Suppose that after the obligor has received *notice* of the assignment, the obligor and assignor attempt to *modify* the contract. Will the modification affect the assignee's rights?

(1) Post-Assignment Modification Generally Has No Effect on Rights of Assignee

Generally, such a modification of the contract will *not* affect the rights of the assignee. This is so even when the modification is undertaken in good faith.

(2) UCC Position

The UCC provides that such a modification of an assigned right to payment that *has not yet been fully earned by performance* is effective against the assignee if made in *good faith*. However, the modification will cause a breach of an assignment contract that prohibits such modifications. [UCC §9-405]

c) Defenses of Assignor Not Available

The obligor will not be able to raise by way of defense any defenses that the assignor might have against the assignee.

2) Assignee vs. Assignor

a) Assignor's Warranties

In every assignment *for value*, the assignor impliedly warrants that:

(i) He has the right to make the assignment; i.e., the assignor has made *no prior assignment* of the right;

(ii) The right exists and is *not subject to limitations or defenses* other than those stated or apparent at the time of the assignment; and

(iii) He will *do nothing to defeat or impair* the assigned right; e.g., he will not attempt a subsequent assignment.

[Restatement (Second) of Contracts §333] Breach of any of these warranties gives rise to a cause of action. For example, if the assignor wrongfully exercises his *power* to revoke the irrevocable assignment, the assignee may proceed against him. Also, the assignee may seek to recover against the assignor if the obligor successfully asserts a defense she had against the assignor in an action by the assignee, thereby defeating the assigned right—provided the assignee had no notice of the defense at the time of the assignment.

b) Obligor Incapable of Performance
The assignor will *not* be liable to the assignee if the obligor is incapable of performing, e.g., is insolvent.

c) Rights of Sub-Assignees
Sub-assignees do not have any rights against the original assignor. The courts reason that there is no privity of contract. However, the assignee who "sub-assigns" becomes the assignor with respect to that assignment and can be held liable thereon.

3) Do Third Parties Have Any Equities Relating to Assignment?
If third parties have any equities in the subject matter of the assignment, the assignee will take subject to them if she has notice; she will not be subject to such equities if she is a bona fide purchaser without notice of the assigned interest.

h. What Problems Exist If There Have Been Successive Assignments of the Same Rights?
The problem: X assigns to Y a right to the payment of $500 owed him by Smith. Subsequently, X assigns this same right to Z. Who prevails—Y or Z?

1) Revocable Assignments
If the first assignment made is *revocable*, a subsequent assignment will serve to *revoke* it (i.e., the subsequent assignee prevails).

2) Irrevocable Assignments

a) First Assignee Has Priority
The general rule is that if the assignor makes two assignments of the same right and the first assignment is *irrevocable*, the *first* assignee has priority.

b) Exceptions
In certain situations, a second assignee who *pays value* and takes *without notice* of the earlier irrevocable assignment will prevail.

(1)   Judgment Against Obligor

        If the subsequent assignee gets the *first judgment* against the obligor, she will prevail.

        (2)   Payment of Claim

        If the later assignee gets *first payment* from the obligor on the assigned claim, her rights will be superior.

        (3)   Delivery of Token Chose

        If the subsequent assignee gets the *first delivery of a token chose* from the assignor, she will prevail.

        (4)   Novation

        The second assignee will prevail if she obtains a novation that supersedes the obligation running to the assignor in favor of the new one running to her. This assumes that the obligor had *no knowledge* of the prior assignment at the time of the novation.

        (5)   Estoppel

        If the subsequent assignee is able to set up an estoppel against the first assignee, she will have priority, e.g., the first assignee permits the assignor to retain a document that would indicate to a reasonable person that the assignor was sole owner of the right. (Estoppel could, of course, operate the other way as well. Thus, if the subsequent assignee has actual knowledge of the earlier assignment, she will be estopped to assert her claim as against the earlier assignee even though she would, under any of the other rules above, normally succeed.)

    3)   UCC Rules

    Basically, the UCC has approached the successive assignments problem by imposing *filing requirements*. [UCC §9-310] If the filing provision is applicable to the transaction, generally the assignee who is the first to file will prevail. [UCC §9-322]

2.   Delegation of Duties

A transfer of contractual duties is called a "delegation." The main issues regarding delegations are:

(i)   What duties may be delegated?

(ii)   How does one make a valid delegation?

(iii)   What are the rights and liabilities of the various parties where there has been a valid delegation?

a.   Terminology

X and Y have a contract. Y delegates duties thereunder to Z. Y is the *obligor* because Y is the one with the duty to perform the obligation. Y also is the *delegator* (sometimes called the delegant) because Y delegated the duty. Z is the *delegate* (sometimes called the delegatee) because Z is the one to whom the duty was delegated. X is called the *obligee*, because X is the one for whom Y or Z is obligated to perform.

b. What Duties May Be Delegated?

1) General Rule
As a general rule, *all contractual duties* may be delegated to a third person.

2) Exceptions
There are several exceptions to the general rule.

a) Duties Involving Personal Judgment and Skill
If the duties involve personal judgment and skill, they may not be delegated.
Example: A talent agency cannot delegate its duty to select performers for a certain show to some other agency. It is immaterial that the other agency may have a better reputation and may have more performers under contract than the delegator. A court will not make such inquiries at all.

b) "Special Trust" in Delegator
Where a special trust has been reposed in the delegator, he may not delegate his duties (e.g., relationship of attorney and client, physician and patient, etc.).

c) Change of Obligee's Expectancy
If performance by the delegate will materially change the obligee's expectancy under the contract, the duty may not be delegated.

d) Contractual Restriction on Delegation
If a contract restricts either party's right to delegate duties, such a provision will usually be given *strict effect*.

c. What Is Necessary for Effective Delegation?
In general, no special formalities are required to have a valid delegation. The delegation may be either *written or oral*. However, the delegator must manifest a *present intention* to make the delegation. There is no need that the word "delegate" be used; any generally accepted words of transfer may be used.

d. What Are Rights and Liabilities of Parties?

1) Obligee
The obligee must accept performance from the delegate of all duties that may be

delegated. She need not accept performance from the delegate of those duties that may not be delegated.

2) **Delegator**

The delegator will *remain liable* on his contract, even if the delegate expressly assumes the duties. However, as between the delegator and the delegate, the delegation places the primary responsibility to perform on the delegate. The delegator becomes secondarily liable, as a surety, for performance of the duty. Note that if an obligee expressly consents to the transfer of duties, it could be construed as an offer of novation (*see* below) rather than a delegation.

3) **Delegate**

The liability of a delegate turns largely on the question of whether there is a mere "delegation" or that plus an "assumption of duty."

a) **Delegation**

Delegation is the creation of a *power* in another to perform the delegator's contract duty. The nondelegating party to the contract (the obligee) cannot compel the delegate to perform, as the latter has not promised to perform.

b) **Assumption**

An assumption occurs when the delegate promises that she will perform the duty delegated and the *promise* is *supported by consideration* or its equivalent. This creates a third-party beneficiary situation in which the nondelegating party to the contract can compel performance or bring suit for nonperformance.

Example: Tom promises Becky that he will paint her fence for $100. Tom then asks Huck if he would paint the fence for $50 if Tom provides Huck with all of the paint and supplies needed. Huck agrees. Becky is a third party beneficiary of the contract between Tom and Huck and may enforce Huck's promise to paint.

c) **Result When Duties Delegated with Assignment of Rights**

What happens if a delegation of duties is made in connection with an assignment of rights under the same contract out of which the duties arise, but the delegate has nonetheless not expressly assumed the duties? The majority of courts, the Restatement, and the UCC hold that unless a contrary intention appears, words assigning "the contract" or "all my rights under the contract" are to be construed as including an *assumption* of the duties; i.e., they imply a promise by the assignee to assume the duties of performance.

D. **NOVATION DISTINGUISHED FROM OTHER THIRD-PARTY SITUATIONS**

Note the difference between novation and the other third-party situations discussed above. Novation *substitutes a new party* for an original party to the contract. It requires the *assent of all parties* and *completely releases* the original party. The consent of the remaining party may be express or by implication of the acceptance of performance by the new party with knowledge that a novation is intended.

E. POWER OF PERSON OTHER THAN OWNER TO TRANSFER GOOD TITLE TO A PURCHASER

1. Entrusting

Entrusting goods to a merchant *who deals in goods of that kind* gives him the power (but not the right) to transfer all rights of the entruster to a *buyer in the ordinary course of business*. [UCC §2-403] Entrusting includes both delivering goods to the merchant and leaving purchased goods with the merchant for later pickup or delivery. Buying in the ordinary course means buying in good faith from a person who deals in goods of the kind without knowledge that the sale is in violation of the ownership rights of third parties.

Examples: 1) Amy leaves her watch with Jeweler for repairs. Jeweler sells the watch to Zoe, who does not know that Jeweler has no right to sell. Zoe gets good title as against Amy. Amy's only remedy is to sue Jeweler for damages.

        2) Amy leaves her watch with Jeweler for repairs. Jeweler borrows money from the bank, giving specific items of inventory, including Amy's watch, as pledged collateral. Amy can recover the watch from the bank. The bank is not a *buyer*.

2. Voidable Title Concept

The UCC continues the pre-Code concept of voidable title. [*See* UCC §2-403] That is, if a sale is induced by fraud, the seller can rescind the sale and recover the goods from the fraudulent buyer. However, the defrauded seller may not recover the goods from a *good faith purchaser for value* who bought from the fraudulent buyer. The UCC specifies four particular situations in which the bona fide purchaser for value cuts off the rights of the true owner; in several of these instances the result under pre-Code law is changed.

Under the UCC, the *good faith purchaser for value cuts off the defrauded seller's rights*, even though:

(i)   The seller was deceived as to the identity of the buyer;

(ii)   The delivery was in exchange for a check later dishonored;

(iii)   The sale was a "cash sale"; or

(iv)   The fraudulent conduct of the buyer is punishable as larceny.

The rights of a defrauded seller are cut off both by a buyer and by a person who takes a *security interest* in the goods.

3. Thief Generally Cannot Pass Title

If a thief steals goods from the true owner and then sells them to a buyer, the thief is *unable* to pass title to the buyer (because his title is *void*). *Rationale:* A seller can transfer only the title he has or has power to transfer. Therefore, even a good faith purchaser for value generally cannot cut off the rights of the true owner if the seller's title was void. [UCC §2-403(1)]

Example: Thief stole a painting from Owner and sold it to Buyer. Later, Owner discovered that Buyer had her painting. Owner may recover the painting from Buyer, even if Buyer purchased the painting in good faith and for value.

a.   **Exceptions**

A thief may pass title in limited circumstances, such as where the buyer has made *accessions* (i.e., valuable improvements) to the goods or the true owner is estopped from asserting title (e.g., if the true owner expressly or impliedly represented that the thief had title).

CRIMINAL LAW

CRIMINAL LAW

TABLE OF CONTENTS

CRIMINAL LAW

INTRODUCTION: GENERAL APPROACH

The Multistate Examination directs examinees to answer questions according to "the generally accepted view" unless otherwise noted. In Criminal Law, the examiners may tell you the law to apply if there is no prevailing view. For example:

(i) The call of a question might tell you that the common law applies or that the state follows the Model Penal Code ("M.P.C.") approach; hence, you should be familiar with both the common law rules and the important M.P.C. distinctions discussed in this outline.

(ii) A fact pattern may also include a statute that you are to apply to the facts; the outline discusses typical statutes on a variety of chapters that may be the subject of examination questions.

(iii) Finally, a question might reference a well-known legal doctrine (e.g., the Wharton rule or the *M'Naghten* test); you should review those doctrines in the outline as well.

Note that if the examiners do not tell you whether the common law or a statutory version of the crime applies, it likely means that specific elements of the crime are not relevant to the question—for example, the question may concern whether voluntary intoxication is a defense to a crime, in which case the relevant factor is what type of mental state the crime requires, not other elements of the crime that may vary from jurisdiction to jurisdiction.

I. JURISDICTION AND GENERAL MATTERS

A. JURISDICTION
As used in this section, jurisdiction means the authority of a sovereign to ***create*** substantive criminal law. The authority of a court to ***enforce*** criminal laws is also an aspect of jurisdiction, but is more properly treated as a matter of criminal procedure.

1. Federal Criminal Jurisdiction
The power of the federal government to create crimes falls into the following broad categories:

a. Power over Federally Owned or Controlled Territory
The federal government has extensive power to enact general criminal codes governing conduct in the District of Columbia, the territories, and federal enclaves (e.g., naval yards, federal courthouses, national parks, etc.).

b. Power over Conduct Occurring Within a State
In contrast, federal power to criminalize conduct within a state is limited by the requirement that each statute be founded upon an express or implied constitutional grant of authority.

c. Power over United States Nationals Abroad
Federal criminal statutes may, by express provision, reach conduct by citizens while on foreign soil.

d. Power over Conduct on Ships or Airplanes
Federal "maritime jurisdiction" extends to conduct by all persons aboard American ships or aircraft when on or over the high seas or even in foreign waters or ports.

2. State Criminal Jurisdiction
Unlike the federal government, every state has inherent authority by virtue of its "police power" to regulate its internal affairs for the protection or promotion of the health, safety, welfare, and morals of its citizens.

a. Situs of the Crime
At common law, and in those states that have not expanded jurisdiction by statute, only the state in which the situs of the crime is located has jurisdiction over the crime. "Situs" is generally defined as the place where the proscribed act (or omission) takes place, if the crime is defined in these terms; or the place of the harmful result, if the crime includes a result as a material element.
Example: A libelous statement may be made a crime where it is published, not where it is written, because the crime of libel proscribes the act of publication rather than the act of writing the libelous statement.

b. Modern Bases for Jurisdiction
A person is subject to prosecution in a state for an offense that he commits within or outside that state, by his own conduct or that of another for which he is legally accountable, under the following conditions:

1) When the ***offense is committed wholly or partly within the state*** ("partly within the state" includes occurrences within the state of either (i) conduct that is an element of the offense, or (ii) a result constituting such an element—e.g., in homicide, the "result" is either the physical contact causing death or the death itself); or

2) When there is ***conduct outside the state that constitutes an attempt or conspiracy*** to commit an offense within the state ***plus an act inside the state***; or

3) When there is ***conduct within the state constituting an attempt, solicitation, or conspiracy to commit, in another jurisdiction, an offense*** under the laws of both the state and such other jurisdiction; or

4) When an offense based on the ***omission of performance of a duty*** imposed by the law of a state is committed within that state, regardless of the location of the offender at the time of the omission.

B. SOURCES OF CRIMINAL LAW

1. Common Law Crimes
A common law crime is one created and enforced by the judiciary in the absence of a statute defining the offense.

a. No Federal Common Law Crimes
Federal criminal law is governed entirely by statute. Although there are no federal

common law crimes, Congress has provided for common law crimes in the District of Columbia.

b. **Traditional Approach—Common Law Crimes Retained**
From the colonial period forward, American criminal law included the English common law of crimes, unless repealed expressly or impliedly by statute.

c. **Modern Trend—Common Law Crimes Abolished**
In recent years, a great many states have enacted comprehensive criminal codes and, in doing so, most have abolished common law crimes, either explicitly or by implication. However, jurisdictions that have abolished common law crimes have not necessarily abolished common law *defenses* to crime, such as insanity and necessity, where their statutes do not expressly provide for these defenses.

2. **Constitutional Crimes**
The Constitution defines treason as levying war against the United States, adhering to enemies of the United States, or giving them aid and comfort. No person can be convicted of treason unless two witnesses testify to the same overt act, or unless the defendant confesses.

3. **Administrative Crimes**
A legislature may delegate to an administrative agency the power to prescribe rules, the violation of which may be punishable as a crime. Note, however, that the legislature may not delegate the power to determine which regulations shall carry criminal penalties; nor may it delegate the power of adjudication (i.e., the determination of guilt or innocence). With the proliferation of administrative agencies, this source of criminal law is becoming increasingly important.
Example: Violation of the antifraud rules adopted by the Securities and Exchange Commission may result in severe criminal liability.

4. **The Model Penal Code**
Although not a source of law, the Model Penal Code ("M.P.C.") was a scholarly endeavor to compile a comprehensive and coherent body of criminal law. Since its publication in 1962, the M.P.C. has greatly influenced the drafting of state criminal statutes. Due to its enlightened position on many different issues, the M.P.C. may be the single most important source of general criminal law.

C. **THEORIES OF PUNISHMENT**
Historically, several theories have been advanced to justify criminal punishment.

1. **Incapacitation (Restraint)**
While imprisoned, a criminal has fewer opportunities to commit acts causing harm to society.

2. **Special Deterrence**
Punishment may *deter the criminal* from committing future crimes.

3. **General Deterrence**
Punishment may *deter persons other than the criminal* from committing similar crimes for fear of incurring the same punishment.

4. Retribution

Punishment is imposed to vent society's sense of outrage and need for revenge.

5. Rehabilitation

Imprisonment provides the opportunity to mold or reform the criminal into a person who, upon return to society, will conform her behavior to societal norms.

6. Education

The publicity attending the trial, conviction, and punishment of some criminals serves to educate the public to distinguish between good and bad conduct and to develop respect for the law.

D. CLASSIFICATION OF CRIMES

At common law, all crimes were divided into three classes: treason, felonies, and misdemeanors. Several additional means of classifying crimes are now frequently employed either by the courts or by state statutory schemes.

1. Felonies and Misdemeanors

Most states now classify as *felonies* all crimes punishable by *death or imprisonment exceeding one year.* Under such modern schemes, *misdemeanors* are crimes punishable by *imprisonment for less than one year or by a fine* only. At common law, the only felonies were murder, manslaughter, rape, sodomy, mayhem, robbery, larceny, arson, and burglary; all other crimes were considered misdemeanors.

2. Malum In Se and Malum Prohibitum

A crime *malum in se* (wrong in itself) is one that is *inherently evil,* either because criminal intent is an element of the offense, or because the crime involves "moral turpitude." By contrast, a crime *malum prohibitum* is one that is wrong only because it is *prohibited by legislation*.

Example: Battery, larceny, and drunken driving are mala in se, whereas hunting without a license, failure to comply with the Federal Drug Labeling Act, and driving in excess of the speed limit are mala prohibita.

3. Infamous Crimes

At common law, infamous crimes are all crimes involving fraud, dishonesty, or the obstruction of justice. Under modern law, this concept has been expanded to include most felonies.

4. Crimes Involving Moral Turpitude

The concept of moral turpitude—committing a base or vile act—is often equated with the concept of malum in se. Conviction of a crime involving moral turpitude may result in the deportation of an alien, the disbarment of an attorney, or the impeachment of a trial witness.

E. PRINCIPLE OF LEGALITY—VOID-FOR-VAGUENESS DOCTRINE

The Due Process Clause of the federal Constitution, found in the Fifth and Fourteenth Amendments, has been interpreted by the Supreme Court to require that no criminal penalty be imposed without fair notice that the conduct is forbidden. The "void-for-vagueness" doctrine, which has been held to require particular scrutiny of criminal statutes capable of reaching speech protected by the First Amendment, incorporates two considerations:

1. **Fair Warning**

   A statute must give a person of ordinary intelligence fair notice that his contemplated conduct is forbidden by the statute.

2. **Arbitrary and Discriminatory Enforcement Must Be Avoided**

   A statute must not encourage arbitrary and erratic arrests and convictions.

F. CONSTITUTIONAL LIMITATIONS ON CRIME CREATION

In addition to the constitutional requirement that a criminal statute be sufficiently specific to provide fair warning and prevent arbitrary enforcement, Article I of the federal Constitution places two substantive limitations on both federal and state legislatures.

1. **No Ex Post Facto Laws**

   The Constitution expressly prohibits ex post facto laws. The Supreme Court has defined an ex post facto law as one that operates retroactively to:

   (i)   *Make criminal an act* that when done was not criminal;

   (ii) *Aggravate a crime or increase the punishment* therefor;

   (iii) *Change the rules of evidence* to the detriment of criminal defendants as a class; or

   (iv) *Alter the law of criminal procedure* to deprive criminal defendants of a substantive right.

   [Calder v. Bull, 3 U.S. (3 Dall.) 386 (1798)]

2. **No Bills of Attainder**

   Bills of attainder are also constitutionally prohibited. A bill of attainder is a legislative act that inflicts punishment or denies a privilege *without a judicial trial*. Although a bill of attainder may also be an ex post facto law, a distinction can be drawn in that an ex post facto law does not deprive the offender of a judicial trial.

G. INTERPRETATIONS OF CRIMINAL STATUTES

1. **Plain Meaning Rule**

   When the statutory language is plain and its meaning clear, the court must give effect to it even if the court feels that the law is unwise or undesirable. An exception to this rule exists if the court believes that applying the plain meaning of a statute will lead to injustice, oppression, or an absurd consequence.

2. **Ambiguous Statutes Strictly Construed in Favor of Defendant**

   The rule of lenity requires that an ambiguous criminal statute must be strictly construed in favor of the defendant. Ambiguity should be distinguished from vagueness. An ambiguous statute is one susceptible to two or more equally reasonable interpretations. A vague statute is one that is so unclear as to be susceptible to no reasonable interpretation.

3. *Expressio Unius, Exclusio Alterius*

   According to this maxim, the expression of one thing impliedly indicates an intention to exclude another.

Example: A criminal statute defines bigamy as the act of remarriage by one who has a living spouse. The statute expressly provides an exception for one whose spouse disappeared more than seven years before. Can a person remarry if the spouse has been gone for less than seven years provided he or she believes in good faith that the spouse is dead? Most jurisdictions answer no. The fact that the statute provides one exception impliedly excludes all others.

4. The Specific Controls the General, the More Recent Controls the Earlier

If two statutes address the same subject matter but dictate different conclusions, the more specific statute will be applied rather than the more general. The more recently enacted statute will control an older statute.

Examples: 1) If one statute prohibits all forms of gambling and another permits charity-sponsored raffles, the latter will control a church raffle.

2) A 1980 statute banning advertising of cigarettes will govern a 1975 statute providing a limit on advertising expenditure by cigarette manufacturers.

5. Effect of Repeal

At common law, in the absence of a saving provision, the repeal or invalidation of a statute operates to bar prosecutions for earlier violations, provided the prosecution is pending or not yet under way at the time of the repeal. However, a repeal will not operate to set free a person who has been prosecuted and convicted and as to whom the judgment has become final.

a. Saving Provision

Many of the new comprehensive codes include a provision to the effect that crimes committed prior to the effective date of the new code are subject to prosecution and punishment under the law as it existed at the time the offense was committed.

H. MERGER

1. Common Law Rule

a. Merger of Misdemeanor into Felony

At common law, if a person engaged in conduct constituting both a felony and a misdemeanor, she could be convicted only of the felony. The misdemeanor was regarded as merged into the felony.

b. No Merger Among Offenses of Same Degree

If the same act or a series of acts that were all part of the same transaction constituted several felonies (or several misdemeanors), there was no merger of any of the offenses into any of the others.

2. Modern Rule

There is generally no merger in American law, with the following limited *exceptions*:

a. "Merger" of Solicitation or Attempt into Completed Crime

One who solicits another to commit a crime (where solicitation itself is a crime) cannot be convicted of both the solicitation and the completed crime (if the person solicited does complete it). Similarly, a person who completes a crime after attempting it may not be convicted of both the attempt and the completed crime. Conspiracy, however, does not merge with the completed offense (e.g., one can be convicted of robbery and conspiracy to commit robbery).

1) **"Merger" of More than One Inchoate Crime**
    Under the M.P.C., a defendant may not be convicted of more than one inchoate crime when his conduct was designed to culminate in the commission of the same crime. For example, if a defendant conspired to commit burglary and then actually attempted to commit burglary, she could not be convicted of both conspiracy and attempt because her conduct was designed to culminate in a single crime—burglary.

b. **"Merger" of Lesser Included Offenses into Greater Offenses**
    Lesser included offenses "merge" into greater offenses, in the sense that one placed in jeopardy for either offense may not later be retried for the other. Nor may one be convicted of both the greater offense and a lesser included offense. A lesser included offense is one that consists entirely of some, but not all, elements of the greater crime. This rule is sometimes labeled a rule of merger, but it is also clearly required by the constitutional prohibition against double jeopardy.

    Examples: 1) D allegedly possessed certain narcotics. On the basis of this, she is charged with (i) illegal possession of narcotics, (ii) illegal possession of narcotics for sale, and (iii) possession of a drug not in a properly stamped container. May she be convicted of all three offenses? *Held:* No. She may not be convicted of simple possession and possession for sale. She may be convicted of possession for sale and possession in an improper container, because neither is a lesser included offense of the other. Each requires proof of something the other does not, i.e., intent to sell and use of an improper container.

    2) D is convicted of operating a motor vehicle without the owner's consent. She is then charged with stealing the vehicle based upon the same incident. Operating the vehicle without the owner's consent is a lesser included offense of theft, because theft requires proof of everything necessary to prove operation of a vehicle without consent of the owner *plus* the intent to steal. May D be prosecuted for theft? *Held*: No. Conviction for a lesser included offense bars prosecution for the greater offense. [Brown v. Ohio, 432 U.S. 161 (1977)]

    3) D is convicted of felony murder based on proof that his accomplice shot and killed a store clerk during an armed robbery. He is then charged with and convicted of armed robbery based on the same incident. *Held:* Because the armed robbery was the underlying felony for the felony murder conviction, it is a lesser included offense of the felony murder and the subsequent prosecution is barred. [Harris v. Oklahoma, 433 U.S. 682 (1977)]

3. **Developing Rules Against Multiple Convictions for Parts of Same "Transaction"**
    Many jurisdictions are developing prohibitions against convicting a defendant for more than

one offense where the multiple offenses were all part of the same "criminal transaction." In some states, this is prohibited by statute. In others, courts adopt a rule of merger or of double jeopardy to prohibit it.

a.   No Double Jeopardy If Statute Provides Multiple Punishments for Single Act
Imposition of cumulative punishments for two or more statutorily defined offenses, specifically intended by the legislature to carry *separate punishments*, arising from the same transaction, and constituting the same crime, does not violate the Double Jeopardy Clause prohibition against multiple punishments for the same offense when the punishments are imposed at a single trial. [Missouri v. Hunter, 459 U.S. 359 (1983)]

Example: D robs a store at gunpoint. D can be sentenced to cumulative punishments for armed robbery and "armed criminal action" under a "use a gun, go to jail" statute.

II.   ESSENTIAL ELEMENTS OF CRIME

A.   ELEMENTS OF A CRIME
Culpability under Anglo-American criminal law is founded upon certain basic premises that are more or less strictly observed by legislatures and courts when formulating the substantive law of crimes. Consequently, the prosecution is generally required to prove the following elements of a criminal offense:

(i)   *Actus Reus* (guilty act): A physical act (or unlawful omission) by the defendant;

(ii)   *Mens Rea* (guilty mind): The state of mind or intent of the defendant at the time of his act;

(iii) *Concurrence*: The physical act and the mental state existed at the same time; and

(iv)   *Harmful Result and Causation*: A harmful result caused (both factually and proximately) by the defendant's act.

Virtually all crimes require a physical act and may require some sort of intent. Many crimes also require proof of certain *attendant circumstances* without which the same act and intent would not be criminal. For example, the crime of receipt of stolen property requires that the property received has in fact been stolen. If the defendant receives property (the act) that he believes to have been stolen (the mental element), when in fact the property has not been stolen, the absence of this required circumstance renders the defendant not liable for receipt of stolen property. Other crimes require result and causation. Homicide, for example, requires that the victim die and that the defendant's act be the cause of death.

B.   PHYSICAL ACT
For there to be criminal liability, the defendant must have either performed a voluntary physical act or failed to act under circumstances imposing a legal duty to act. For this purpose, an act is defined as a *bodily movement*. A thought is not an act. Therefore, bad thoughts alone cannot constitute a crime. Note, however, that speech, unlike thought, is an act that can cause liability (e.g., perjury, solicitation).

1. **Act Must Be Voluntary**
   The defendant's act must be voluntary in the sense that it must be a ***conscious exercise of the will***. *Rationale:* An involuntary act will not be deterred by punishment. The following acts are ***not*** considered "voluntary" and therefore cannot be the basis for criminal liability:

   a. Conduct that is ***not the product of the actor's determination***.
      Example: A shoves B into C, with the result that C falls to his death. Can B be held criminally liable for C's death? No.

   b. ***Reflexive or convulsive*** acts.

   c. Acts performed while the defendant was either ***unconscious or asleep unless*** the defendant knew that she might fall asleep or become unconscious and engaged in dangerous behavior.

2. **Omission as an "Act"**
   Although most crimes are committed by affirmative action rather than by nonaction, a defendant's ***failure to act*** will result in criminal liability provided ***three requirements*** are satisfied.

   a. **Legal Duty to Act**
      The defendant must have a legal duty to act under the circumstances. A legal duty to act can arise from the following sources:

      1) A ***statute*** (e.g., filing an income tax return or reporting an accident).

      2) A ***contract*** obligating the defendant to act, such as one entered into by a lifeguard or a nurse.

      3) The ***relationship*** between the defendant and the victim, which may be sufficiently close to create a duty.
         Examples: 1) A parent has the duty to prevent physical harm to his or her children.

         2) A spouse has the duty to prevent harm to his or her spouse.

      4) The ***voluntary assumption of care*** by the defendant of the victim. Although in general there is no common law duty to help someone in distress, once aid is rendered, the Good Samaritan may be held criminally liable for not satisfying a reasonable standard of care.
         Examples: 1) A, while hiking, sees B drowning in a river. Although A is a good swimmer, he takes no steps to save B, who drowns. Was A's failure to act an "act" upon which liability could be based? No, because A had no duty to act. Note that the answer would be the same even if A recognized B as a person whom he disliked and took great pleasure in watching B drown.

         2) If A began to swim out toward B and only after reaching B decided that B was someone not worth saving, A would have violated his duty to act by unreasonably abandoning a rescue effort that was voluntarily undertaken.

5) The *creation of peril* by the defendant.

Example: Believing that B can swim, A pushes B into a pool. It becomes apparent that B cannot swim, but A takes no steps to help B. B drowns. Was A's failure to attempt a rescue an "act" on which liability can be based? Yes.

b. Knowledge of Facts Giving Rise to Duty

As a general rule, the duty to act arises when the defendant is aware of the facts creating the duty to act (e.g., the parent must know that his child is drowning before his failure to rescue the child will make him liable). However, in some situations the law will impose a duty to learn the facts (e.g., a lifeguard asleep at his post would still have a legal duty to aid a drowning swimmer).

c. Reasonably Possible to Perform

It must be reasonably possible for the defendant to perform the duty or to obtain the help of others in performing it.

Example: A parent who is unable to swim is under no duty to jump in the water to attempt to save his drowning child.

3. Possession as an "Act"

Criminal statutes that penalize the possession of contraband generally require only that the defendant have control of the item for a long enough period to have an opportunity to terminate the possession. Possession need not be exclusive to one person, and possession also may be "constructive," meaning that actual physical control need not be proved when the contraband is located in an area within the defendant's "dominion and control."

a. State of Mind Requirement

Absent a state of mind requirement in the statute, the defendant must be aware of his possession of the contraband, but he need not be aware of its illegality or true nature. However, many statutes and the M.P.C. add a "knowingly" state of mind element to possession crimes (*see* C.6., *infra.*). Under such statutes, the defendant ordinarily must know the identity or nature of the item possessed. On the other hand, a defendant may not consciously avoid learning the true nature of the item possessed; knowledge may be inferred from a combination of suspicion and indifference to the truth.

C. MENTAL STATE

1. Purpose of Mens Rea Requirement

The reason that mens rea is normally required is to distinguish between inadvertent or accidental acts and acts performed by one with a "guilty mind." The latter type of act is more blameworthy and, arguably, can be deterred. However, in some cases (strict liability crimes), mens rea is not required.

2. Specific Intent

If the definition of a crime requires not only the doing of an act, but the doing of it with a specific intent or objective, the crime is a "specific intent" crime.

a. Significance

It is necessary to identify specific intent for two reasons:

1) **Need for Proof**
The existence of a specific intent cannot be conclusively imputed from the mere doing of the act, and the prosecution must produce evidence tending to prove the existence of the specific intent. That said, *the manner* in which an act was done may provide circumstantial evidence of intent.

Example: A shoots B. The fact that A shot B does not show that A had the intent to shoot and kill B. However, if A bought a revolver and ammunition shortly before shooting B, carefully loaded the revolver, took careful aim at B, and fired several times, that evidence may circumstantially prove A's intent to kill B.

2) **Applicability of Certain Defenses**
Some defenses, such as voluntary intoxication and unreasonable mistake of fact, apply only to specific intent crimes.

b. **Enumeration of Specific Intent Crimes**
The major specific intent crimes and the intent they require are as follows:

1) *Solicitation*: Intent to have the person solicited commit the crime;

2) *Attempt*: Intent to complete the crime;

3) *Conspiracy*: Intent to have the crime completed;

4) *First degree premeditated murder* (where so defined by statute): Premeditated intent to kill;

5) *Assault*: Intent to commit a battery;

6) *Larceny and robbery*: Intent to permanently deprive another of his interest in the property taken;

7) *Burglary*: Intent at the time of entry to commit a felony in the dwelling of another;

8) *Forgery*: Intent to defraud;

9) *False pretenses*: Intent to defraud; and

10) *Embezzlement*: Intent to defraud.

3. **Malice—Common Law Murder and Arson**
Although the intents required for the "malice" crimes—common law murder and arson—sound similar to specific intent (e.g., the "intent to kill" for murder), these crimes are *not* open to the specific intent defenses. The common law created this special mental state category especially to deny to murder and arson the specific intent defenses. To establish malice in these cases, the prosecution need only show that the defendant recklessly disregarded an obvious or high risk that the particular harmful result would occur.

4. **General Intent—Awareness of Factors Constituting Crime**
Generally, all crimes require "general intent," which is an awareness of all factors

constituting the crime; i.e., the defendant must be aware that she is acting in the proscribed way and that any attendant circumstances required by the crime are present. (Note that the defendant need not be certain that these attendant circumstances exist; it is sufficient that she is aware of a high likelihood that they exist.)

Example: To commit the crime of false imprisonment (*see* VII.D., *infra*), the defendant must be aware that she is confining a person, and that the confinement has not been specifically authorized by law or validly consented to by the person confined.

a. Inference of Intent from Act

A jury can infer the required general intent merely from the doing of the act. It is not necessary that evidence specifically proving the general intent be offered by the prosecution.

5. Strict Liability Offenses

A strict liability offense is one that does not require awareness of all of the factors constituting the crime. Generally, the requirement of a state of mind is not abandoned with respect to all elements of the offense, but only with regard to one or some of the elements. The major significance of a strict liability offense is that ***defenses that would negate state of mind***, such as mistake of fact, are ***not available***.

a. Identification of Strict Liability Offenses

Strict liability offenses, also known as public welfare offenses, are generally "regulatory" offenses (i.e., offenses that are part of a regulatory scheme) that implicate public health or safety. They generally involve a relatively low penalty and are not regarded by the community as involving significant moral impropriety. Note that the mere fact that a statute is silent on the question of mental state does not necessarily mean that the offense is a strict liability offense. If no mental state is expressly required by the statute, the courts may still interpret the statute as requiring some mens rea, especially if the statute appears to be a codification of a traditional common law offense or if the statute imposes a severe penalty.

Example: Federal legislation prohibits the transfer of firearms not registered under federal law. Is it a defense that the defendant was ignorant of the fact that a firearm was not registered? *Held:* No, because this is a strict liability offense. Awareness of the fact of nonregistration is not necessary, although it is necessary that the defendant have been aware of the fact that she was possessing a firearm.

Compare: Federal legislation requires registration of any fully automatic machinegun. The statute is silent on the question of mental state and provides a penalty of up to 10 years' imprisonment. *Held:* Defendant may assert as a defense that he was not aware that the weapon in his possession was automatic. The type of statute and the harsh penalty indicate that Congress did not intend to dispense with the mens rea requirement. [*Staples v. United States*, 511 U.S. 600 (1994)]

b. Constitutionality

The majority view is that strict liability offenses are constitutional. *Exception:* The

Supreme Court struck down as a violation of due process a Los Angeles municipal ordinance imposing strict liability for failure to register as a felon. The key factor in the court's decision was the absence of "circumstances which might move one to inquire as to the necessity of registration." *Note:* The scope of this holding is limited to statutes making criminal the failure to register.

6. Model Penal Code Analysis of Fault

The M.P.C. advocates the elimination of the ambiguous common law distinction between general and specific intent. Instead, the M.P.C. proposes four categories into which the mental component of a criminal offense (i.e., the element of fault) can be characterized. Because consistent use of these categories leads to analytical clarity, they have been incorporated into several state criminal codes. They likewise provide a convenient way of analyzing problems on the exam that incorporate statutes.

a. Purposely, Knowingly, or Recklessly

When a statute requires that the defendant act purposely ("intentionally"), knowingly, or recklessly, a subjective standard is being used; i.e., the question is what was actually going on in the defendant's mind.

1) Purposely

A person acts purposely with respect to his conduct when it is his conscious object to engage in certain conduct or cause a certain result, e.g., burglary.

2) Knowingly

A person acts knowingly with respect to the nature of his conduct when he is aware that his conduct is of that nature or that certain circumstances exist. He is deemed to be aware of these circumstances when he is aware of a high probability that they exist and deliberately avoids learning the truth. He acts knowingly with respect to the result of his conduct when he knows that his conduct will necessarily or very likely cause such a result. Conduct performed knowingly frequently satisfies the mental state of a statute that requires willful conduct (*but note:* some criminal statutes define willfulness as requiring that a defendant act knowingly and intentionally).

3) Recklessly

A person acts recklessly when he ***consciously disregards a substantial and unjustifiable risk*** that circumstances exist or that a prohibited result will follow, and this disregard constitutes a ***gross deviation from the standard of care*** that a reasonable person would exercise in the situation. An act performed recklessly is also performed wantonly. Recklessness requires that the actor take an unjustifiable risk and that he know of and consciously disregard the risk. Mere realization of the risk is not enough. He must know that injury might result (if he knows that it is ***certain*** to result, he acts ***knowingly***). Thus, recklessness involves both objective ("unjustifiable risk") and subjective ("awareness") elements.

b. Negligence

A person acts negligently when he ***fails to be aware of a substantial and unjustifiable risk*** that circumstances exist or a result will follow, and such failure constitutes a ***substantial deviation from the standard of care*** that a reasonable person would exercise under the circumstances. To determine whether a person acted negligently, an *objective standard* is used. However, it is not merely the reasonable person standard that is used in torts; the defendant must have taken a *very unreasonable risk* in light of the usefulness of his conduct, his knowledge of the facts, and the nature and extent of the harm that may be caused.

Example: D held himself out to the public as a doctor even though he was not a licensed physician. He treated a sick woman by wrapping her in kerosene-soaked flannels for three days. The woman died. *Held:* D is guilty of manslaughter. His good intentions were irrelevant. By objective standards, he took an unjustifiable risk.

1) Violation of Statute or Ordinance as Evidence of Negligence
Violation of a state statute, municipal ordinance, or administrative regulation may—as in tort law—be evidence of liability.

Example: A, driving in excess of the speed limit, hits and kills B, a pedestrian. A's speeding violation may be admissible as evidence of his negligence in a prosecution for manslaughter.

c. Analysis of Statutes Using Fault Standards

1) State of Mind Applies to All Material Elements of Offense
Often a statute will establish a culpable state of mind without indicating whether it is required for all the material elements of the offense. In that case, the specified state of mind applies to all material elements of the offense unless a contrary purpose appears in the statute.

Example: Under a statute imposing criminal liability on anyone who "knowingly makes a sale of an intoxicating beverage to a minor," the M.P.C. would require knowledge for each material element of the offense. Thus, if the defendant can show that she did not know that a sale took place, that the beverage was intoxicating, or that the purchaser was a minor, she will be able to avoid liability.

2) General State of Mind Requirement—Recklessness
If the statute defining the offense (other than a strict liability offense) does not include a state of mind requirement, the defendant must have acted with at least recklessness with regard to each material element of the offense.

a) Higher Degree of Fault Suffices
Under the M.P.C.'s hierarchy of fault levels, a showing of a higher state of mind automatically satisfies a lower mental state requirement of a statute. Thus, a showing that the defendant acted purposely or knowingly will satisfy the general requirement of recklessness.

b) Other Levels of Fault Must Be Specified
Because a standard of recklessness is assumed where the state of mind is not specified, if a lower standard of negligence will satisfy liability, or if a higher standard of knowledge or purpose is required, those standards must be indicated in the language of the statute.

Example: Under a statute creating criminal liability for anyone who "sells intoxicating beverages to one whom he should know to be a minor," the material elements include the act of selling and the attendant circumstances that the beverage be intoxicating and that the purchaser be a minor. Under the M.P.C. formula, a minimum standard for recklessness is required as the state of mind for the first two elements, while the third element of the statute specifies that only a negligence level of fault is required.

7. Vicarious Liability Offenses

A vicarious liability offense is one in which a person without personal fault may nevertheless be held vicariously liable for the criminal conduct of another (usually an employee). The criminal law doctrine of vicarious liability is analogous to the tort doctrine of respondeat superior. *Note:* Unlike strict liability, which dispenses with the mens rea requirement but retains the requirement that the defendant have personally engaged in the necessary acts or omissions, vicarious liability dispenses with the personal actus reus requirement but retains the need for **mental fault on the part of the employee**.

a. Limitation on Punishment

Because the imposition of criminal liability for faultless conduct is contrary to the basic premise of criminal justice that crime requires fault on the part of the accused, at least one state court has held that imprisonment in such cases violates the due process guarantees of the state constitution. The current trend in the legislatures is to limit vicarious liability to **regulatory crimes** and to limit punishment to **fines**.

b. Implying Vicarious Liability from Underlying Strict Liability Offense

Despite some decisions to the contrary, the mere fact that the underlying offense is clearly a strict liability offense should **not** imply a legislative intent to impose vicarious liability.

Example: A statute makes it a crime "for anyone to serve an alcoholic beverage to a minor." Although a bartender may be strictly liable under this statute regardless of her belief that the customer was legally old enough to drink, this statute should not be construed to impose liability on the tavern owner who neither was present at the time the minor was served nor authorized the actions of the bartender.

8. Enterprise Liability—Liability of Corporations and Associations

a. Common Law—No Criminal Liability

At common law, a corporation could not commit a crime because it was unable to form the necessary criminal intent.

b. Modern Statutes—Vicarious Criminal Liability

Modern statutes often provide for the liability of corporations and sometimes even unincorporated associations (e.g., partnerships). This liability is, by necessity, vicarious. Under such provisions, corporations may be held liable under the following conditions:

1) **Act Within Scope of Office**

Except where the law specifically provides otherwise, the conduct giving rise to corporate liability must be performed by an agent of the corporation acting on behalf of the corporation and within the scope of his office or employment.

2) **"Superior Agent Rule"**

Some jurisdictions limit corporate criminal liability to situations in which the conduct is performed or participated in by agents sufficiently high in the corporate hierarchy to presume that their acts reflect corporate policy.

c. **Model Penal Code**

Under the M.P.C., a corporation may be guilty of a criminal offense provided the offense:

1) Consists of the *failure to discharge a specific duty* imposed by law on the corporation;

2) Is defined by a statute in which a *legislative purpose to impose liability* on corporations plainly appears; or

3) Was "authorized, requested, commanded, performed, or recklessly tolerated *by the board of directors or by a high managerial agent* acting on behalf of the corporation within the scope of his office or employment."

d. **Individual Liability Independent of Enterprise Liability**

The person who, in the name of the corporation, performs (or causes to be performed) the conduct that is an element of the offense is legally accountable and subject to punishment to the same extent as if the conduct were performed in his name or on his own behalf. Similarly, the fact that the corporation is liable does not prevent the conviction of the individual who committed the offense.

9. **Transferred Intent**

If a defendant intended a harmful result to a particular person or object and, in trying to carry out that intent, caused a similar harmful result to another person or object, her intent will be transferred from the intended person or object to the one actually harmed. Any defenses or mitigating circumstances that the defendant could have asserted against the intended victim (e.g., self-defense, provocation) will also be transferred in most cases. The doctrine of transferred intent most commonly applies to homicide, battery, and arson. It does *not* apply to *attempt*.

Example: A shoots at B, intending to kill him. Because of bad aim, she hits C, killing him. Is A guilty of C's murder? *Held:* Yes. Her intent to kill B will be transferred to C. Note that A may also be guilty of the attempted murder of B.

Compare: A shoots twice at B, thinking that B was C, whom she had wanted to kill. She wounds not only B, but also D, a bystander. Is A guilty of the attempted murder of B and D? *Held:* A is guilty of the attempted murder of B, because her mistake as to B's identity is a mistake of fact that does not negate her intent to kill the person in front of her (B). There is no transferred intent issue in that scenario. However, most courts would hold that she is not guilty of the attempted murder of D.

10. **Motive Distinguished**

The motive for a crime is distinct from the intent to commit it. A motive is the reason or explanation underlying the offense. It is generally held that *motive is immaterial* to substantive criminal law. A good motive will not excuse a criminal act. On the other hand, a lawful act done with bad motive will not be punished.

Example: An impoverished woman steals so that her hungry children may eat. Despite her noble *motive*—feeding her children—the woman could be held criminally liable for her acts because her *intent* was to steal.

D. CONCURRENCE OF MENTAL FAULT WITH PHYSICAL ACT REQUIRED

The defendant must have had the intent necessary for the crime at the time he committed the act constituting the crime. In addition, the intent must have prompted the act.

Example: A decides to kill B. While driving to the store to purchase a gun for this purpose, A negligently runs over B and kills him. Is A guilty of murder? No, because although at the time A caused B's death he had the intent to do so, this intent did not prompt the act resulting in B's death (i.e., A's poor driving).

Compare: With the intent to kill B, A strangles B to the point of unconsciousness, but does not actually kill B. Thinking B is dead, A buries B, and B dies as a result. Is A guilty of murder, even though the death-causing act of burying B was done without the intent to murder? Yes, in a majority of jurisdictions. Most courts would find that the two acts were part of a single transaction with a common intent.

E. CAUSATION

Some crimes (e.g., homicide) require a harmful result and causation. For a full discussion of causation, *see* VII.C.5., *infra*.

III. ACCOMPLICE LIABILITY

A. PARTIES TO A CRIME

1. **Common Law**

The common law distinguished four types of parties to a felony: *principals in the first degree* (persons who actually engage in the act or omission that constitutes the criminal offense); *principals in the second degree* (persons who aid, command, or encourage the principal and are present at the crime); *accessories before the fact* (persons who aid, abet, or encourage the principal but are *not* present at the crime); and *accessories after the fact* (persons who assist the principal after the crime).

a. **Significance of Common Law Distinctions**

At common law, the distinctions between the parties had a great deal of procedural significance. For example, an accessory could not be convicted unless the principal had already been convicted, although both could be convicted in a joint trial if the jury determined the principal's guilt first. Most modern jurisdictions have abandoned this requirement, and an accessory can be convicted even if the principal has evaded apprehension or has been tried and acquitted.

2. Modern Statutes

Most jurisdictions have abolished the distinctions between principals in the first degree, principals in the second degree, and accessories before the fact (accessories after the fact are still treated separately). Under the modern approach, all "parties to the crime" can be found guilty of the criminal offense. For convenience, this section will designate the actual perpetrator of the criminal act as the principal and the other parties to the crime as accomplices.

a. Principal

A principal is one who, with the requisite mental state, ***actually engages in the act or omission*** that causes the criminal result. Also, anyone who acts through an innocent, irresponsible, or unwilling agent is classified as a principal.

Example: A gives a poisonous drink to B to give to C. B does so; C drinks it and dies. If B did not know that the drink was poisonous, or if B was mentally ill or under duress, A, not B, is the principal. Note that the principal need not be present when the harm results.

b. Accomplice

An accomplice is one who (i) with the intent to assist the principal and the intent that the principal commit the crime (ii) actually aids, counsels, or encourages the principal before or during the commission of the crime.

c. Accessory After the Fact

An accessory after the fact is one who receives, relieves, comforts, or assists another, knowing that he has committed a felony, in order to ***help the felon escape arrest, trial, or conviction.*** The crime committed by the principal must be a ***felony*** and it must be ***completed*** at the time the aid is rendered. Today, the crime is usually called "harboring a fugitive," "aiding escape," or "obstructing justice."

1) Penalty

Typically the punishment for this crime bears no relationship to the principal offense; five years is the most common maximum sentence. Exemptions are usually provided for close relatives of the principal offender (the common law exempted only the spouse).

B. MENTAL STATE—DUAL INTENT REQUIRED

In order to be convicted of a substantive crime as an accomplice, the accomplice must have (i) ***the intent to assist the principal*** in the commission of a crime; and (ii) ***the intent that the principal commit*** the substantive offense. When the substantive offense has recklessness or negligence as its mens rea, most jurisdictions would hold that the intent element is satisfied if the accomplice (i) ***intended to facilitate*** the commission of the crime; and (ii) ***acted with recklessness or negligence*** (whichever is required by the particular crime).

1. Provision of Material

In the absence of a statute, most courts would hold that mere ***knowledge*** that a crime would result from the aid provided is insufficient for accomplice liability, at least where the aid involves the sale of ordinary goods at ordinary prices. However, procuring an illegal item or selling at a higher price because of the buyer's purpose may constitute a sufficient "stake in the venture" for a court to find intent to aid.

Example: A tells B that he wants to buy a can of gasoline from B to burn a house down. B sells A the gasoline and A burns down the house. B is not liable as an accomplice to arson (unless it was illegal to sell gasoline in cans or B charged A twice his usual price because of what A was using the gasoline for).

C.   SCOPE OF LIABILITY

An accomplice is responsible for the crimes he did or counseled *and* for any other crimes committed in the course of committing the crime contemplated, as long as the other crimes were *probable or foreseeable.*

Example: A commands B to burn C's house, and B does so. The fire spreads to X's house, and it was foreseeable that it would do so. A is an accomplice to the burning of X's house.

1.   Inability to Be Principal No Bar to Liability as Accomplice

One who may not be convicted of being a principal may be convicted of being an accomplice.

Example: At common law, a woman may not be convicted of rape as a principal, but she may be convicted of that crime as an accomplice.

2.   Exclusions from Liability

Under some circumstances, a person who would otherwise be liable as an accomplice is not subject to conviction, either because of a legislative intent to exempt him or because he has a special defense.

a.   Members of the Protected Class

If the statute is intended to protect members of a limited class from exploitation or overbearing, members of that class are presumed to be immune from liability, even if they participate in the crime in a manner that would otherwise make them liable.

Example: A is charged with transporting B, a woman, in interstate commerce for immoral purposes; B is charged as an accomplice, on the ground that she encouraged and assisted A. Is B guilty? *Held:* No. The statute was intended to protect women, and thus the woman transported cannot be convicted.

b.   Necessary Parties Not Provided For

If a statute defines a crime in a way that necessarily involves more than one participant and provides for the liability of only one participant, it is presumed that the legislative intent was to immunize the other participant from liability as an accomplice. The rule is most often applied to statutes making the sale of certain items a criminal offense.

Example: A asked B to sell her some heroin. B did so. Both were apprehended. B was charged as a principal for the sale of narcotics; A was charged as an accomplice. Is A subject to conviction? *Held:* No. Since the statute prohibiting sale does not mention the liability of the buyer, the presumed legislative intent is to exempt her.

c. **Withdrawal**

One who has rendered encouragement or aid to another may avoid liability as an accomplice if he voluntarily withdraws from the crime before it is actually committed by the principal. What is necessary for an effective withdrawal *depends upon what the person initially did*.

(i) If the person merely *encouraged* the commission of the crime, withdrawal requires that he *repudiate* this encouragement.

(ii) If the person assisted by *providing some material* to the principal, withdrawal requires at least that the person attempt to *neutralize this assistance*, e.g., by doing everything possible to retrieve the material provided.

If it is impossible to withdraw by these methods, an alternative means of withdrawing is to *notify authorities* or take some other action to prevent the commission of the offense. In any case, the withdrawal must occur *before* the chain of events leading to the commission of the crime becomes unstoppable.

Example: B expresses a desire to kill C. A encourages him to do so, and provides him with a gun. Later, A changes his mind. He seeks B out, and tells B that his earlier position was wrong and that B should not kill C. He also gets his gun back. Nevertheless, B obtains another gun and kills C. Is A liable as an accomplice? *Held:* No, since he did all that was possible to render his encouragement and assistance ineffective before B's plan to kill C became unstoppable.

IV. INCHOATE OFFENSES

A. IN GENERAL

The inchoate offenses are solicitation, attempt, and conspiracy. An inchoate offense is committed prior to and in preparation for what may be a more serious offense. It is a complete offense in itself, even though the act to be done may not have been completed. At common law under the doctrine of merger, inchoate offenses were regarded as misdemeanors; if the principal offense was carried out, they were considered felonies. The doctrine of merger has been abandoned in many jurisdictions in cases involving a conspiracy, allowing an accused to be convicted of *both* conspiracy and the principal offense. However, an accused *cannot* be convicted of either attempt or solicitation *and* the principal offense.

B. SOLICITATION

At common law it was a misdemeanor to solicit another to commit a felony or an act that would breach the peace or obstruct justice. Modern statutes often retain the crime of solicitation, but some restrict it to the solicitation of certain serious felonies.

1. Elements

Solicitation consists of inciting, counseling, advising, inducing, urging, or commanding another to commit a crime with the specific *intent that the person solicited commit the crime* (general approval or agreement is insufficient). The offense is complete at the time the solicitation is made. It is not necessary that the person solicited agree to commit the crime or do anything in response. (If the person solicited committed the crime, the solicitor would be liable for the crime as a party; if the person solicited proceeded far enough to be liable for attempt, the solicitor would be a party to that attempt.)

2. **Attempt Distinguished**

Solicitation generally is not an attempt to commit the crime solicited. This distinction is important in jurisdictions where there is no crime of solicitation or where the crime of solicitation does not extend to as many offenses as does the crime of attempt.

3. **Defenses**

a. **Factual Impossibility Is No Defense**

It is not a defense that the solicitation could not have been successful, as where the person solicited was a police undercover agent. The culpability of the solicitor is measured by the circumstances as she believed them to be.

b. **Withdrawal or Renunciation Is No Defense**

Once the solicitation has been made, it is generally no defense that the solicitor changed her mind or countermanded her advice or urging. The M.P.C. recognizes renunciation as a defense if the defendant prevents the commission of the crime, such as by persuading the person solicited not to commit the crime.

c. **Exemption from Intended Crime Is a Defense**

If the solicitor could not be guilty of the intended crime because of a legislative intent to exempt her, she would have a defense. For example, a minor female could not be found guilty of solicitation of statutory rape by urging an adult male to have intercourse with her, because she could not be guilty of the completed crime.

C. CONSPIRACY

1. **Elements**

The elements of conspiracy at common law are as follows:

(i) An *agreement between two or more* persons;

(ii) An *intent to enter into an agreement*; and

(iii) An *intent to achieve the objective* of the agreement.

Under the traditional definition of conspiracy, the agreement itself was the culpable act (the actus reus). Today, a majority of states require an *overt act* in furtherance of the conspiracy, but mere preparation will usually suffice.

a. **Agreement Requirement**

The parties must agree to accomplish the same objective by mutual action. The agreement need not be express. The existence of an agreement may be shown by a concert of action on the part of the conspirators over a period of time under circumstances showing that they were aware of the purpose and existence of the conspiracy and agreed to participate in the common purpose. Where multiple crimes and multiple parties are involved, there are often problems in deciding whether there is a single conspiracy or several smaller conspiracies.

1) Object of the Agreement

At common law, it was not necessary that there be an agreement to commit a crime in order to find a criminal conspiracy. It was only necessary that the object of the agreement was something "unlawful" or that the parties intended to accomplish something lawful by "unlawful" means. "Unlawful" in this context covered a variety of noncriminal matters that were regarded as contrary to the public welfare. Most states, however, now provide that the object of the conspiracy must be *some crime or some felony* or the achievement of a *lawful object by criminal means*.

2) Multiple Crimes

Where the same parties perform a number of crimes over an extended period of time, is each individual crime the subject of a separate conspiracy or are all the crimes to be treated as arising out of one overriding conspiracy? If there is an initial agreement among the parties to engage in a *course of criminal conduct* constituting all the crimes, then there is only *one conspiracy*.

Example: A and B agree to commit one bank robbery each month for one year. Even though they plan to rob 12 banks, they are guilty of only one conspiracy.

3) Number of Conspiracies in Multiple Party Situations

In complex situations involving numerous parties, it is sometimes important to determine how many conspiracies existed and who conspired with whom. There are two general ways to characterize situations of this sort.

a) "Chain" Relationship—One Large Conspiracy

If there is a series of agreements, all of which are regarded as part of a single large scheme in which all of the parties to the subagreements are interested, the situation will be regarded as one large conspiracy involving all of the participants. The subagreements will be characterized as "links" in the overall "chain" relationship.

b) "Hub-and-Spoke" Relationships—Multiple Conspiracies

One participant may enter into a number of subagreements, each involving *different persons*. All of the agreements are similar in that they have *one common member*. However, if it is established that the *subagreements are reasonably independent of each other*—if, for example, the members of each agreement (other than the common member) have little or no interest in whether the other agreements succeed—the situation will be regarded as involving numerous different and independent conspiracies. The common member can be characterized as the "hub" (as of a wheel) and each subagreement as a "spoke." The common member is, of course, a member of each conspiracy. But the members of each "spoke" conspiracy are not members of the other "spoke" conspiracies and have not conspired with the members of those conspiracies.

Examples: 1) In a large narcotics ring, a smuggler brings heroin into the country and sells it to a wholesaler. The wholesaler sells it to numerous retailers. How many conspiracies? One, because this is a "chain" situation. Because the smuggler-wholesaler agreement and the wholesaler-retailers agreements were all part of a scheme in which all participants were interested, there is only one conspiracy.

2) Brown agreed with A, B, and C to help each of them make fraudulent loan applications. Each application was to be an independent action and the applicants in one situation had no interest in whether the other fraudulent applications were successful. How many conspiracies? Three: Brown with A, Brown with B, and Brown with C. Since the subagreements were not part of an overall scheme in which A, B, and C all were interested, this is a "hub-and-spoke" situation. A has not conspired with B and C, but only with Brown.

4) Requirement of Two or More Parties

Since conspiracy, by definition, requires an agreement between two or more persons, a question arises whether a person may be convicted of conspiracy when his alleged co-conspirator is only feigning agreement (e.g., the alleged co-conspirator is an undercover police officer).

a) Modern Trend—"Unilateral" Approach

The modern trend follows the Model Penal Code's "unilateral" approach to conspiracy, which requires that only *one* party have genuine criminal intent. Accordingly, under the unilateral approach, a defendant can be convicted of conspiracy if he conspires with one person only and that individual is a police officer working undercover.

b) Traditional Rule—"Bilateral" Approach

At common law, a conspiracy requires at least two "guilty minds," i.e., persons who are actually committed to the illicit plan. Under this "bilateral" approach, if one person in a two-party agreement is only feigning agreement, the other party cannot be convicted of conspiracy. This requirement of two guilty minds gives rise to a number of problems.

(1) Husband and Wife

At common law, a husband and wife could not conspire together because the law viewed them as one person. They could, however, be guilty of conspiracy with a third person. This distinction has been abandoned in virtually all states today.

(2) Corporation and Agent

Since a corporation can act only through an agent, it has been held that there can be no conspiracy between the corporation and a single agent acting on behalf of the corporation. There is a split of authority as to whether the agents can be deemed co-conspirators. Note that a corporation may be a party to a conspiracy with other corporations or individuals who are not agents of the corporation.

c) **Wharton-Type Problems**

(1) **Wharton Rule**
Where two or more people are necessary for the commission of the substantive offense (e.g., adultery, dueling, sale of contraband), the "Wharton rule" (named after its author) states that there is *no crime of conspiracy unless more parties participate in the agreement than are necessary for the crime*. Some courts hold that, if the Wharton rule applies, there can never be a conviction for conspiracy. Others hold that, if the rule applies, it prohibits conviction for both conspiracy and the crime that the parties agreed to commit.

Example: A and B agree to meet at dawn to engage in a duel. They are apprehended before daybreak, however. Dueling is a crime in the jurisdiction, and A is charged with conspiracy to commit dueling. Does A have a defense? Yes. The Wharton rule applies and prevents liability.

Compare: The Wharton rule does not apply to agreements with "*necessary parties not provided for*" (*see* III.C.2.b., *supra*). Thus, where a state statute prohibiting the sale of narcotics imposes criminal liability only on the seller and not on the buyer, both the buyer and seller may be guilty of conspiracy to sell narcotics (even though both parties are necessary for commission of the substantive offense).

(2) **Agreement with Person in "Protected Class"**
If members of a conspiracy agree to commit an act that violates a statute that was designed to protect persons within a given class, *a person within that class* cannot be guilty of the crime itself. (*See* III.C.2.a., *supra*.) Moreover, she *cannot be guilty of a conspiracy* to commit that crime. It follows, then, that between two people, the person *not* in the protected class cannot be guilty of criminal conspiracy on the basis of an agreement with the person in the protected class.

Example: A, a woman, and B, a man, agreed on a scheme in which A would be transported over state lines for purposes of prostitution. Is B guilty of criminal conspiracy? No. The act of transporting women over state lines for immoral purposes violates a statute (the Mann Act) that was designed to protect women; thus, A could not be guilty of a violation of the Act and cannot be guilty of conspiracy to violate the Act. Therefore, B cannot be guilty of criminal conspiracy because there were not two guilty parties to the agreement.

d) Effect of Acquittal of Other Conspirators

A conspiracy requires two guilty parties at common law. Thus, in most courts, the acquittal of *all* persons with whom a defendant is alleged to have conspired precludes conviction of the remaining defendant. This rule does *not* apply where the other parties are not apprehended, are charged with lesser offenses, or are no longer being prosecuted (*nolle prosequi*).

b. Mental State—Specific Intent

Conspiracy is a *specific intent* crime. There are two different intents that are necessary: intent to agree and intent to achieve the objective of the conspiracy.

    1) Intent to Agree

It is very difficult to separate the intent to agree from the act of agreement. Hence, most courts do not even try. For bar exam purposes, the only thing that is important to remember is that the intent to agree can be *inferred* from conduct.

    2) Intent to Achieve Objective

The defendant must intend to achieve the objective of the conspiracy. This intent must be established as to *each* individual defendant. Under the common law approach, a minimum of two persons must intend to achieve the same purpose; i.e., there must be a "meeting of guilty minds."

Example: A, B, and C agree to steal D's car, but only A and B intend to keep it permanently; C intends to return it to D. Only A and B are guilty of conspiracy to commit larceny, because only they had the intent to permanently deprive D of his car. If only A so intended, and both B and C intended to return the car, then A could not be liable for conspiracy to commit larceny.

    3) Intent to Facilitate a Conspiracy

A person who acts with the intent to facilitate a conspiracy may thereby become a member of the conspiracy. However, *intent cannot be inferred from mere knowledge*. Therefore, a merchant who sells a good in the ordinary course of business that he knows will be used to further a conspiracy does not thereby join the conspiracy. On the other hand, a merchant may be held to have joined the conspiracy if the good sold is a specialty item that cannot easily be obtained elsewhere or if the merchant otherwise has a stake in the criminal venture (e.g., by raising the price of the good because of the buyer's purpose).

    4) "Corrupt Motive" Not Required

The majority rule is that the parties to a conspiracy need not have been aware that their plan was an illegal one. A minority of courts have held to the contrary, however, reasoning that a requirement of evil motive flows implicitly from the word conspiracy. According to the "corrupt motive" doctrine, which operates as an exception to the general rule that ignorance of the law will not excuse criminal liability, the parties to a conspiracy must have known that their objective was criminal. The corrupt motive doctrine is usually limited to offenses that are malum prohibitum (*see* I.D.2., *supra*).

5) Conspiracy to Commit "Strict Liability" Crimes

Conspiracy is a specific intent crime. Therefore, in most jurisdictions, a conspiracy to commit a "strict liability" crime (for which intent is not required) requires intent.

Example: A and B agree on a scheme to persuade C, a 12-year-old girl, to have intercourse with one of them. They believe she is 21, but this would not be a defense to the completed crime of statutory rape. Can they be convicted of conspiracy to commit statutory rape? No, because conspiracy to commit statutory rape requires knowledge of the victim's age even though the completed crime does not.

c. Overt Act

At common law, the conspiracy was complete when the agreement with the requisite intent was reached. This is still the law in some states. Most states, however, require that an ***act in furtherance of the conspiracy*** be performed. If an overt act is required, any act in pursuit of the conspiracy will suffice, even an act of mere preparation. The act may be performed by any one of the conspirators.

Example: A, B, and C agreed to rob a bank. A, unbeknownst to B and C, rents a car to be used in the getaway. If an overt act is required, the renting of a car is sufficient.

1) Attempt Distinguished

In attempt cases, the law requires that there be a ***substantial step*** toward commission of the crime, whereas the overt act for conspiracy requires only an act of mere preparation. The reason for this is that the secret activity in conspiracy cases is potentially more dangerous to society and, since a group is involved, it is more difficult for one person to stop the activity once the agreement has been made.

2. Termination of Conspiracy

Since acts or declarations of co-conspirators are admissible only if made in furtherance of the conspiracy, it becomes critically important to determine when the conspiracy ends. This is also important for statute of limitations purposes.

a. Acts of Concealment

Since most criminals attempt to conceal the fact that they have committed a crime, courts have generally taken the view that ***evidence of overt acts of concealment is not sufficient to make the act of concealment part of the conspiracy***. In other words, there must be direct evidence that the parties specifically agreed, prior to commission of the crime, that they would act in a certain way to conceal the fact that they had committed the crime.

Example: Suppose the statute of limitations for tax evasion is six years. If A and B conspire to commit tax evasion, does their conspiracy end at the time of the commission of the fraud, or does it extend for the six years during which time A and B presumably endeavor to keep their crime a secret? The answer depends upon whether at the time of the agreement to commit tax evasion there was also a specific subsidiary agreement to conceal the crime until the statute of limitations had run. If there was no such specific agreement, as, for example, if A and B were not aware of the statute of limitations, then the conspiracy does not extend beyond the completion of the act of evasion.

b. **Government Frustration of Conspiracy's Objective**
The government's defeat of the conspiracy's ultimate objective does not automatically terminate the conspiracy. [United States v. Jimenez-Recio, 537 U.S. 270 (2003)]
Example: Police stop A, who was transporting illegal drugs in his vehicle. Instead of simply arresting A, the police instead decide to set up a "sting" operation. They drive the vehicle to a preset location, and instruct A to contact B, a drug dealer, in accordance with A and B's original plan. B tells A that he will call C and D and have them pick up the vehicle with the drugs. C and D do so. C and D can be convicted of conspiracy to distribute illegal drugs. The fact that the government defeated the conspiracy's objective does not terminate the conspiracy, and impossibility is no defense to a charge of conspiracy (*see* below).

3. **Liability of One Conspirator for Crimes Committed by Other Conspirators**
One conspirator may, by virtue of his participation in the scheme, meet the requirements for "aiding and abetting" the commission of crimes by his co-conspirators and therefore be liable for those crimes as an accomplice. Even if the conspirator did not have the sufficient mental state for accomplice liability, a separate doctrine provides that each conspirator may be liable for the crimes of all other conspirators if *two requirements* are met:

(i) The *crimes were committed in furtherance* of the objectives of the conspiracy; and

(ii) The crimes were "a natural and probable consequence" of the conspiracy, i.e., *foreseeable*.

This doctrine applies only if the conspirator has not made a legally effective withdrawal from the conspiracy before the commission of the crime by the co-conspirator. (*See* 4.b., *infra.*)

4. **Defenses**

a. **Factual Impossibility Is No Defense**
Factual impossibility is *not a defense* to conspiracy. Even if it was factually impossible to achieve the ultimate objective of the conspiracy, the defendants can be found guilty of the conspiracy itself.
Example: A and B agree to rape a woman whom they believe is asleep. In fact, she is dead. A and B may be convicted of conspiracy to rape.

b. **Withdrawal Is No Defense**
The general rule is that withdrawal from a conspiracy is *not a defense* to a charge of conspiracy, because the conspiracy is complete as soon as the agreement is made and an overt act is committed. The M.P.C. recognizes voluntary withdrawal as a defense if the defendant thwarts the success of the conspiracy (e.g., by informing the police).

1) **Defense to Subsequent Crimes of Co-Conspirators**
A person may limit his liability for subsequent acts of the other members of the conspiracy, including the target crime for which the conspiracy was formed, if

he withdraws. To withdraw, he must perform an affirmative act that ***notifies all members*** of the conspiracy, and such notice must be given in time for them to have the opportunity to abandon their plans. (Note that if he has also provided material assistance so as to be liable as an accomplice, he must attempt to neutralize the assistance (*see* III.C.2.c., *supra*).)

5. No Merger—Conviction for Conspiracy and Substantive Crime

Under the old rule, if the conspirators committed a substantive offense, the crime of conspiracy "merged" into the completed crime. While the members of the agreement could be convicted of the substantive offense, they could not be convicted of the conspiracy. This is no longer the law in most jurisdictions. (*See* the discussion of merger in I.H., *supra*.) Now, if the conspirators are successful, they can be ***convicted of both criminal conspiracy and the substantive offense***.

6. State Codifications

While at common law a conspiracy was defined as a combination or agreement between two or more persons to accomplish some criminal or unlawful purpose, or to accomplish a lawful purpose by unlawful means, recent state codifications require that the object of the conspiracy be a specifically proscribed offense. Yet many states essentially codify the expansive common law notion by making it a crime to conspire to commit acts injurious to the public welfare. The Supreme Court has indicated that such statutes are unconstitutionally vague unless construed narrowly.

7. Punishment

Because a defendant may be convicted of both conspiracy and the completed crime, most jurisdictions have enacted express penalty provisions for conspiracies. Some statutes make conspiracy a misdemeanor regardless of its objective; some provide a permissible maximum sentence regardless of the objective; and still others provide different maximums depending upon the objective. Note that because the punishment for conspiracy usually is not expressed as a fraction of the punishment for the completed crime, the punishment for conspiracy may be more severe than the punishment for the completed crime.

D. ATTEMPT

A criminal attempt is an act that, although done with the intention of committing a crime, falls short of completing the crime. An attempt therefore consists of two elements: (i) a specific intent to commit the crime, and (ii) an overt act in furtherance of that intent.

1. Intent

The defendant must have the intent to perform an act and obtain a result that, if achieved, would constitute a crime.

a. Attempt Requires Specific Intent

Regardless of the intent required for a completed offense, an attempt always requires a ***specific intent***. For example, attempted murder requires the specific ***intent to kill*** another person, even though the mens rea for murder itself does not necessarily require a specific intent to kill (*see* VII.C.2.a.1), *infra*).

b. **Attempt to Commit Crimes Requiring Recklessness or Negligence Is Logically Impossible**

A crime defined as the reckless or negligent production of a result cannot be attempted, because if there were an intent to cause such a result, the appropriate offense would be attempt to intentionally commit the crime rather than attempt to recklessly or negligently cause the harm.

c. **Attempt to Commit Strict Liability Crimes Requires Intent**

Although a strict liability crime does not require criminal intent, to attempt a strict liability crime the defendant must act with the intent to bring about the proscribed result.

2. **Overt Act**

The defendant must have committed an act ***beyond mere preparation*** for the offense. Several tests have been used to determine whether the act requirement for attempt liability has been satisfied:

a. **Traditional Rule—Proximity Test**

Traditionally, courts used a proximity approach; i.e., they have evaluated the act based on how close the defendant came to completing the offense. Under the typical proximity test, attempt requires an act that is dangerously close to success.

Example: Pointing a loaded gun at an intended victim and pulling the trigger is sufficient under the proximity test, but going to the store to purchase bullets or even driving to the intended victim's house is insufficient. [*See* People v. Rizzo, 246 N.Y. 334 (1927)]

b. **Majority Rule—Model Penal Code Test**

The M.P.C. and most state criminal codes require that the act or omission constitute a "substantial step in a course of conduct planned to culminate in the commission of the crime." In addition, an act will not qualify as a substantial step unless it is strong corroboration of the actor's criminal purpose.

3. **Defenses**

a. **Impossibility of Success**

Factual impossibility traditionally has been distinguished from legal impossibility, and should be distinguished for exam purposes.

1) **Legal Impossibility Is a Defense**

If the defendant, having completed all acts that he had intended, would have committed no crime, he cannot be guilty of an attempt to do the same when he fails to complete all of the intended acts. True legal impossibility is rare.

Example: Defendant was charged with attempted subornation of perjury for soliciting false testimony from a third party witness in a divorce proceeding brought by Wife on the grounds of adultery. The divorce complaint alleged one act of adultery. The witness's testimony, which was never offered at trial, would have falsely accused Husband of having extramarital relations on an occasion that was not alleged in the complaint. Because Wife's complaint made no mention of this event, the witness's testimony, had it been offered at trial, would have been immaterial to the resolution of the complaint. The materiality of false testimony is an essential element of the crime of perjury; therefore, if the witness had testified falsely as planned, Defendant could not have been convicted of subornation of perjury. In equal measure, then, she cannot be guilty of an attempt to do the same. [People v. Teal, 196 N.Y. 372 (1909)]

a) Effect of Statute or Case Abolishing Impossibility Defenses

Even a jurisdiction with a statute or case law purporting to do away with impossibility defenses will recognize the above type of legal impossibility. Such statutes ordinarily contain a provision that the defendant must be charged with the attempt *of a crime*, thus implicitly recognizing a true legal impossibility defense. Such statutes or cases generally have the effect of preventing factual impossibility from becoming a good defense by its being labeled as legal impossibility.

2) Factual Impossibility Is No Defense

It is no defense that the substantive crime is incapable of completion due to some *physical or factual condition*, unknown to the defendant.

Example: In an attempt to steal A's wallet, B sticks his hand in A's back pocket. The pocket, however, is empty. Can B be convicted of attempted larceny? Yes, the "emptiness" of A's back pocket describes its physical condition at the time B reached his hand in. This factual impossibility is no defense to liability.

a) Includes Impossibility Due to Attendant Circumstances

Impossibility is also no defense when the defendant engages in conduct while mistaken about certain attendant circumstances: Had the circumstances been as she believed they were, what she set out to do would be a crime. However, because the circumstances were otherwise, what she has set out to do will not be a crime. Courts traditionally have split on whether this is legal or factual impossibility, but the *better view* is that it is factual impossibility and not a defense.

Example: An adult police officer, while pretending to be a minor, arranges for a time and place for a sexual encounter with an adult defendant. When the defendant shows up for the encounter, he is arrested and charged with some form of attempted statutory rape crime, even though the "minor" is in reality an adult. Given that there is no minor involved, there is no way for the defendant to complete the substantive crime. May the defendant be convicted? The answer is "yes," given that the defendant has engaged in conduct that would have constituted some sort of statutory rape type crime had the defendant been able to complete the crime and had the circumstances been as he believed them to be.

3) **Distinguishing Between Factual and Legal Impossibility**

The bright-line division between legal and factual impossibility above is a bit of an artifice; courts are not as consistent in distinguishing the two. However, for exam purposes, you should use the "better view" outlined above and define legal impossibility narrowly. Ask yourself: "If the defendant were able to complete all of the acts that he intended to do, and if all of the attendant circumstances actually were as the defendant believed them to be, would the defendant have committed a crime?" The answer usually will be yes, in which case the impossibility is factual and not a defense. In the unusual case where the answer is no, the defendant most likely has a legal impossibility defense.

b. **Abandonment**

If a defendant has, with the required intent, gone beyond preparation, may she escape liability by abandoning her plans? The majority rule is that abandonment is *never a defense*. The M.P.C. approach, followed in a number of jurisdictions, is that *withdrawal will be a defense but only if:*

1) It is *fully voluntary* and not made because of the difficulty of completing the crime or because of an increased risk of apprehension; and

2) It is a *complete abandonment* of the plan made under circumstances manifesting a renunciation of criminal purpose, not just a decision to postpone committing it or to find another victim.

4. **Prosecution for Attempt**

A defendant charged with a completed crime may be found guilty of either the completed crime or an attempt to commit the crime as long as the evidence presented supports such a verdict. The reverse is not true. A defendant charged only with attempt may not be convicted of the completed crime.

5. **Punishment for Attempt**

Most states punish attempt less severely than the crime attempted. The most common statutory scheme permits a penalty up to one-half the maximum penalty for the completed crime, with a specific maximum set for attempts to commit crimes punishable by death or life imprisonment. Under the M.P.C. and some state statutes, an attempt may be punished to the same extent as the completed crime, except for capital crimes and the most serious felonies.

V. RESPONSIBILITY AND CRIMINAL CAPACITY

A. INSANITY

The insanity defense exempts certain defendants because of the existence of an abnormal mental condition at the time of the crime. The various formulations differ significantly on what effects a mental illness must have had to entitle the defendant to an acquittal. Note that insanity is a *legal term* rather than a psychiatric one. Furthermore, insanity is a generic term comprising many possible mental abnormalities, all of which have only one thing in common: they are recognized by law as dictating certain legal consequences. Usually, the cause of a defendant's mental illness or insanity is irrelevant in determining the legal consequences.

1. **Formulations of Insanity Defense**

   a. *M'Naghten* **Rule**

      1) **Elements**
         The traditional *M'Naghten* rule provides that a defendant is entitled to an acquittal if the proof establishes that:

         a) A ***disease*** of the mind

         b) ***Caused a defect*** of reason

         c) Such that the defendant ***lacked the ability at the time*** of his actions to either:

            (1) Know the ***wrongfulness*** of his actions; or

            (2) Understand the ***nature and quality*** of his actions.

      2) **Application**

         a) **Defendant with Delusions**
            If the defendant suffered from delusions (false beliefs), it is necessary to determine whether his actions would have been criminal if the facts had been as he believed them to be.
            Example: A, because of a mental illness, believed B wanted to kill him. A killed B. Is A entitled to an acquittal on insanity grounds under the *M'Naghten* rule? *Held:* No. Even if A's delusion had been accurate, he would not have been legally entitled to kill B simply because B wanted to kill him.

         b) **Belief that Acts Are Morally Right**
            A defendant is not entitled to an acquittal merely because he believes his acts are morally right, unless he has lost the capacity to recognize that they are regarded by society as wrong.

         c) **Inability to Control Oneself**
            Under the traditional interpretation given to the *M'Naghten* rule, it is irrelevant that the defendant may have been unable to control himself and avoid committing the crime. Loss of control because of mental illness is ***no defense***.

      3) **Evidence Admissible**
         In practice, the *M'Naghten* rule does not unduly restrict the evidence heard by juries. Most jurisdictions admit any evidence that reasonably tends to show the mental condition of the defendant at the time of the crime.

   b. **Irresistible Impulse Test**
      Under the irresistible impulse test, a defendant is entitled to an acquittal if the proof establishes that because of mental illness he was ***unable to control his actions or to***

conform his conduct to the law. Contrary to what the name irresistible impulse might imply, this inability need not come upon the defendant suddenly. Some jurisdictions apply both *M'Naghten* and the irresistible impulse test. Thus, a person is entitled to an acquittal if he meets either test.

c.   ***Durham*(or New Hampshire) Test**

Under the *Durham* rule, a defendant is entitled to an acquittal if the proof establishes that his crime was the "***product of mental disease or defect***." A crime is a "product of" the disease if it would not have been committed ***but for*** the disease. In this way, the *Durham* test is broader than either the *M'Naghten* or irresistible impulse tests; it was intended primarily to give psychiatrists greater liberty to testify concerning the defendant's mental condition. Although severely criticized for being unduly vague, the *Durham* rule was followed in the District of Columbia from 1954 until 1972, at which time the court of appeals replaced it with the A.L.I. test. (*See* below.) It remains the law only in New Hampshire.

d.   **American Law Institute ("A.L.I.") or Model Penal Code Test**

Under this test, the defendant is entitled to an acquittal if the proof shows that he suffered from a ***mental disease*** or defect and as a result ***lacked substantial capacity*** to either:

(i)   ***Appreciate the criminality*** (wrongfulness) of his conduct; or

(ii) ***Conform his conduct*** to the requirements of law.

This test combines the *M'Naghten* and the irresistible impulse tests by allowing for the impairment of both cognitive and volitional capacity.

2.   **Exclusion of "Psychopaths"**

Many formulations (including the A.L.I. test) expressly exclude the psychopathic criminal—the person who repeatedly commits crimes without experiencing guilt. This is usually accomplished by defining "mental illness" so as to exclude any abnormality evidenced only by repeated antisocial conduct. "Sociopathic" and "psychopathic" are synonymous.

3.   **Refusal to Participate in Psychiatric Examination**

If the defendant does not put his mental state in issue and does not plan to use an insanity defense, he may refuse to participate in a court-ordered psychiatric examination to determine competency to stand trial. If he does not refuse, he is entitled to the *Miranda* warnings prior to such an examination.

4.   **Procedural Issues Related to Insanity Defense**

Several important procedural matters are raised by the insanity defense.

a.   **Burdens of Proof**

1)   **Presumption of Sanity and Burden of Producing Evidence**

All defendants are presumed sane. The insanity issue is not raised, then, until the defendant comes forward with some evidence tending to show that he was insane under the applicable test. Depending upon the jurisdiction, this burden is carried either by a mere shred (or scintilla) of evidence, or by evidence sufficient to raise a reasonable doubt as to sanity.

2) Burden of Persuasion

In most states, the defendant must prove his insanity, generally by a preponderance of the evidence. In some jurisdictions and under the M.P.C., however, once the issue has been raised, the prosecution must prove the defendant was sane beyond a reasonable doubt. Federal courts require the defendant to prove insanity by clear and convincing evidence.

b. When Defense May Be Raised and Who May Raise It

1) Defense May Be Raised After Arraignment

The insanity defense may be raised at the arraignment when the plea is taken, but the defendant need not raise it then. A simple "not guilty" at that time does not waive the right to raise the defense at some future time. A minority of jurisdictions, however, require that the defendant give reasonable notice to the prosecution of an intent to raise the defense at trial.

2) Neither Prosecutor Nor Judge May Raise Defense for Competent Defendant

Neither a prosecutor nor a judge can assert the insanity defense when a competent defendant, who is adequately represented, has elected not to do so.

c. Pretrial Psychiatric Examination

1) Right to Support Services for Defense

Where a defendant has made a preliminary showing that it is likely he will be able to use the insanity defense, the state must provide a psychiatrist for the preparation of the defense. Where the state presents evidence that the defendant is likely to be dangerous in the future, the defendant is entitled to psychiatric examination and testimony in the sentencing proceeding. [Ake v. Oklahoma, 470 U.S. 68 (1985)]

2) No Privilege Against Self-Incrimination

At the present time, a defendant has no right to refuse to be examined by a psychiatrist appointed to aid the court in the resolution of his insanity plea. However, a defendant who does not put his mental state in issue is entitled to the *Miranda* warnings before he may be compelled to undergo a court-ordered competency examination; the defendant may then refuse to be examined.

5. Post-Acquittal Commitment to Mental Institution

a. Committed Until Cured

In most jurisdictions, acquittal by reason of insanity puts into operation a procedure by which the acquitted defendant may be committed to a mental institution until cured. In some jurisdictions, such commitment is possible only if it is proven that the defendant is presently mentally ill and dangerous. In others, commitment follows automatically.

b. Confinement May Exceed Maximum Period of Incarceration Carried by Offense

The confinement of an insanity acquittee in a mental hospital, based solely on the trial court's finding of insanity by a preponderance of the evidence, may last until he has regained his sanity or is no longer dangerous. This *does not deny due process* even if the result is confinement for a period longer than the maximum period of incarceration carried by his offense. Nor is the insanity acquittee entitled, at the end of the statutory maximum incarceration period, to a civil commitment hearing at which proof of his insanity would have to be established by clear and convincing evidence. [Jones v. United States, 463 U.S. 354 (1983)]

6. **Mental Condition During Criminal Proceedings**
In addition to being a defense to criminal liability, the abnormal mental condition of a defendant is relevant at two other stages of the legal proceeding.

   a. **Incompetency to Stand Trial**
   Under the Due Process Clause of the United States Constitution, a defendant may not be tried, convicted, or sentenced if, as a result of a mental disease or defect, he is *unable*:

      (i) *To understand the nature of the proceedings* being brought against him; or

      (ii) *To assist his lawyer* in the preparation of his defense.

   The Due Process Clause prevents a defendant from being declared incompetent without notice and a hearing. Many jurisdictions grant a right to a jury determination of competence. A finding of incompetence will suspend the criminal proceedings and invariably *result in commitment* until such time as the defendant regains competence. The Constitution may demand that the defendant's hospitalization be limited to a reasonable period of time necessary to decide whether there is a likelihood of recovery in the near future.

   b. **Incompetency at Time of Execution**
   A defendant may not be executed if he is incapable of understanding the nature and purpose of the punishment. Modern statutes often permit only the warden to raise this issue. Some expressly provide for a jury determination.

7. **Limits on Testimony Regarding Sanity Issue**
About half the states limit evidence on the issue of insanity to expert psychiatric testimony. The M.P.C. rejects this approach, and would allow any type of evidence relevant to the issue of whether the defendant had the mental state required for the particular crime charged.

8. **Diminished Capacity**
Some states recognize the defense of "diminished capacity," under which the defendant may assert that as a result of a mental defect (e.g., neurosis, obsessive compulsiveness, or dependent personality) short of insanity, he did not have the particular mental state (purpose, knowledge, recklessness, or negligence) required for the crime charged. Most states recognizing this defense limit it to specific intent crimes.

9. **Bifurcated Trial**
Some states, such as California, employ a two-stage trial process whenever the defense of insanity is raised. The first stage determines *guilt* (did the defendant actually perform the criminal act?); the second stage (which may be tried before a new jury at the judge's

discretion) determines *insanity* (was the defendant legally insane at the time he performed the act?).

B. INTOXICATION

Intoxication may be caused by *any substance*. Alcohol, drugs, and medicine are the most frequent. Evidence of intoxication may be raised whenever the intoxication negates the existence of an element of a crime. The law generally distinguishes between voluntary and involuntary intoxication.

1. Voluntary Intoxication

Intoxication is voluntary (self-induced) if it is the result of the intentional taking without duress of a substance known to be intoxicating. The person need not have intended to become intoxicated.

a. Defense to Specific Intent Crimes

Voluntary intoxication evidence may be offered, when the defendant is charged with a crime that requires *purpose* (*intent*) *or knowledge*, to establish that the intoxication prevented the defendant from formulating the requisite intent. Thus, voluntary intoxication may be a good defense to *specific intent* crimes, but will *not* be a defense to *general intent crimes*. The defense is not available if the defendant purposely becomes intoxicated in order to establish the defense.

b. No Defense to Strict Liability Crimes or Crimes Requiring Malice, Recklessness, or Negligence

Voluntary intoxication is not a defense to crimes requiring malice, recklessness, or negligence, or crimes of strict liability. Thus, voluntary intoxication is not a defense to common law murder, which requires a mens rea of "malice aforethought" (*see* VII.C.2.a.1), *infra*).

Example: After drinking heavily, A breaks into a house, wrongly thinking it is her own. When surprised by B, the owner, A reacts with force, beating B with her fists. While driving home, A is cited for speeding. Will A have a defense of intoxication: (i) to burglary? (Yes, if as a result she did not know that the house belonged to B or did not have the intent to commit a felony therein); (ii) to battery? (No, because as defined battery may be the result of recklessness); or (iii) to speeding? (No, because speeding is a strict liability offense).

1) Crimes that Require Recklessness

While crimes calling for recklessness require a conscious disregard of a substantial and unjustifiable risk (*see* II.C.6.a.3), *supra*), a person who was not consciously aware of the risk only because he was intoxicated will be deemed to have acted recklessly with regard to the risk.

c. Defense to First Degree Murder, But Not Second Degree Murder

It is generally held that voluntary intoxication may reduce first degree (premeditated) murder to second degree murder, but it will not reduce second degree murder to manslaughter. *Rationale:* In a jurisdiction that divides murder into degrees (*see* VII.C.3. *infra*), all murders are second degree murder unless the prosecution proves, e.g., deliberation and premeditation. Common law "depraved heart" murders would fall into the second degree category. Although voluntary intoxication may negate the defendant's ability to deliberate and premeditate (first degree murder), it cannot negate the criminal recklessness required for depraved heart murder (second degree murder).

2. **Involuntary Intoxication**

Intoxication is involuntary only if it results from the taking of an intoxicating substance (i) *without knowledge* of its nature, (ii) *under direct duress* imposed by another, or (iii) *pursuant to medical advice* while unaware of the substance's intoxicating effect.

Involuntary intoxication may be *treated as mental illness,* in which case a defendant is entitled to acquittal if, because of the intoxication, she meets whatever test the jurisdiction has adopted for insanity.

3. **Relationship to Insanity**

Intoxication and insanity are two separate defenses. However, continuous, excessive drinking or drug use may bring on actual insanity (e.g., delirium tremens). Thus, a defendant may be able to claim both an intoxication defense and an insanity defense.

C. INFANCY

1. **Common Law**

At common law, the defense of lack of capacity to commit a crime by reason of infancy gave rise to three presumptions. *Physical age* (not mental age) *at the time of the crime* (not at the time of the trial) governs.

a. **Under Seven—No Criminal Liability**

Under the age of seven, a child could not be held responsible for any crime (conclusive presumption of incapability of knowing wrongfulness of acts).

b. **Under Fourteen—Rebuttable Presumption of No Criminal Liability**

Children between the ages of seven and 14 were presumed incapable of knowing the wrongfulness of their acts, but this presumption was rebuttable by clear proof that the defendant appreciated the nature and quality of his act (e.g., conduct undertaken to conceal the crime). Note, however, that children under 14 were *conclusively* presumed incapable of committing *rape.*

c. **Over Fourteen—Adult**

Children age 14 or older were treated as adults.

2. **Modern Statutes**

a. **Some Have Abolished Presumptions**

A number of modern statutes have abolished the presumptions of the common law and have provided that no child can be convicted of a crime until a stated age is reached, usually 13 or 14. Other states, however, retain the common law presumptions.

b. **Juvenile Delinquency**

All states have enacted some type of juvenile delinquency laws or have set up special juvenile or family courts. These laws ordinarily provide that with respect to conduct that would be deemed criminal if committed by an adult, the juvenile court has exclusive jurisdiction over children under a certain age, and concurrent jurisdiction (with the criminal courts) over older children. In the "concurrent jurisdiction" situation, the child must be "charged" with delinquency in juvenile court unless the juvenile court waives jurisdiction and authorizes the trial of the child as an adult in criminal court. In most jurisdictions, the common law immunity rules for infants do not apply in juvenile court because the primary goal is rehabilitation rather than punishment. The M.P.C. follows this approach, providing that the juvenile court has exclusive jurisdiction over minors younger than 16 and concurrent jurisdiction over 16- and 17-year-old minors.

VI. PRINCIPLES OF EXCULPATION

A. JUSTIFICATION

Under certain circumstances, the commission of a proscribed act is viewed by society as justified and hence not appropriate for criminal punishment. Generally, the defendant must raise the issue of justifiable use of force by introducing *some* evidence ("more than a scintilla") tending to show justification as an affirmative defense. Once she has done this, the state may require the prosecution to prove that the use of force was not justified, or it may impose on the defendant the burden of proving this affirmative defense by a preponderance of the evidence.

1. Self-Defense

a. Nondeadly Force

As a general rule, an individual who is without fault may use *such force as she reasonably believes is necessary* to protect herself from the imminent use of unlawful force upon herself. (*See* discussion *infra* on reasonableness and unlawful force.) There is *no duty to retreat* before using nondeadly force, even if retreat would result in no further harm to either party.

b. Deadly Force

A person may use deadly force in self-defense if she (i) is without fault, (ii) is confronted with unlawful force, and (iii) reasonably believes that she is threatened with imminent death or great bodily harm.

1) Without Fault

A person who has initiated an assault or provoked the other party will be considered the aggressor. (*See* discussion *infra*.)

2) Unlawful Force

The attacker must be using unlawful force (i.e., force that constitutes a crime or a tort).

3) Threat of Imminent Death or Great Bodily Harm

The defendant must *reasonably* believe that she is faced with imminent death or great bodily harm if she does not respond with deadly force. The danger of harm must be a present one. There is no right to use deadly force if harm is merely threatened at a future time or the "attacker" has no present ability to carry out the threat.

Example: A, who has his arms tied behind his back, says to D, "I am going to kill you." D pulls out a gun and shoots A. No self-defense.

4) Retreat

Must a person retreat as far as possible before using deadly force, if such retreat is possible without the person endangering himself? For purposes of the examination, the ***majority rule*** is that there is ***no duty to retreat***. A person (other than the initial aggressor) may use deadly force in self-defense even if this could be avoided by retreating. Even in the minority of courts that follow a common law rule and impose a duty to retreat, retreat is only sometimes necessary. First, no retreat is necessary unless it can be made in complete safety. Second, no retreat is necessary in several special situations: (i) where the attack occurs in one's own home, (ii) where the attack occurs while the victim is making a lawful arrest; or (iii) where the assailant is in the process of robbing the victim.

Example: A is standing in a public park feeding the birds. B walks up to A, pulls a knife from his pocket, and—as he comes closer to A—says, "I am going to kill you." A pulls a gun from her pocket and shoots B, killing him. Does A have a defense of self-defense? Under the majority rule the answer would be yes, because A had no duty to retreat before using deadly force, as long as the force was necessary to defend herself against imminent attack. Even under the minority approach the answer might be yes, because even if A was under a general duty to retreat before using deadly force, here it did not appear that such retreat could have been done in complete safety.

c. Right of Aggressor to Use Self-Defense

Generally, one who is at fault for starting a confrontation has no right to use force in her own defense during that confrontation. But an aggressor can "regain" her right to use force in self-defense in two ways:

1) Withdrawal or Retreat

An aggressor who, in good faith, attempts to remove herself from the fight, and communicates to the other person her desire to remove herself, regains her right to use force in self-defense.

2) Sudden Escalation

If the victim of the initial aggression suddenly escalates a "minor" fight into one involving deadly force and does so without giving the aggressor the chance to withdraw or retreat, the aggressor may use deadly force in her own defense.

2. Defense of Others

There are two issues in determining whether a person who has used force to defend another person is criminally liable for her acts.

a. Relationship with Person Aided

Must there be some special relationship between the defendant and the person in whose defense she acted? The majority rule is no. One may use force in defense of any other person if the other requirements of the defense are met. A few jurisdictions require that the person whom the defendant aided must either have been a member of the defendant's family or the defendant's employee or employer.

b.   Status of Person Aided

A defendant has the defense of defense of others only if she reasonably believed that the person she assisted had the legal right to use force in his own defense. If in fact that person had no such legal right, does the defendant still have a defense? The better view is yes, because all that is necessary for the defense is the ***reasonable appearance of the right to use force***. In a minority of jurisdictions, however, the answer is no, because the defendant "steps into the shoes of the person she defends" and therefore has no defense if that person had no legal right to use force in self-defense.

3.   Defense of a Dwelling

a.   Nondeadly Force

A person is justified in the use of nondeadly force in defense of her dwelling when, and to the extent that, she reasonably believes that such conduct is necessary to prevent or terminate another's unlawful entry into or attack upon her dwelling.

b.   Deadly Force

One is generally justified in the use of deadly force in two situations:

1)   Tumultuous Entry Plus Personal Danger

Use of deadly force is justifiable where the entry was made or attempted in a riotous, violent, or tumultuous manner ***and*** the person reasonably believes that the use of force is necessary to prevent a personal attack upon herself or another in the dwelling.

2)   Felony

Use of deadly force is also justifiable where the person reasonably believes that such force is necessary to prevent the entry into the dwelling by a person who intends to commit a felony in the dwelling.

4.   Defense of Other Property

a.   Nondeadly Force

Nondeadly force may be used to defend property in one's possession from unlawful interference. In the case of real property, this means entry or trespass; in the case of personal property, this means removal or damage. The person must reasonably believe that force is needed, and the need to use force must reasonably appear imminent. Thus, force may not be used if a request to desist or refrain from the activity would suffice. In addition, the right is limited to property in one's possession. Force cannot be used to regain possession of property that he reasonably believes was wrongfully taken, unless the person using it is in "immediate pursuit" of the taker.

b.   Deadly Force May Not Be Used

Defense of property alone can never justify the use of deadly force. A person may use deadly force in the defense of property generally only in conjunction with another privileged use of force, e.g., self-defense, defense of others, or to effectuate an arrest.

5. Crime Prevention

a. Nondeadly Force
Generally, one is privileged to use force to the extent that he reasonably believes is necessary to prevent a felony, riot, or other serious breach of the peace, although some states (e.g., California) have extended this to the prevention of any crime.

b. Deadly Force
The traditional rule was that deadly force could be used to prevent the commission of any felony, but the modern view is that deadly force may be used only if it appears reasonably necessary to prevent a "dangerous felony" involving risk to human life. This would include robbery, arson, burglary of a dwelling, etc.

6. Use of Force to Effectuate Arrest

a. By Police Officer
The use of deadly force to apprehend a fleeing felon constitutes a seizure. The force used to effect a seizure must be reasonable. Deadly force is reasonable only when the felon threatens death or serious bodily harm and deadly force is necessary to prevent his escape. [Tennessee v. Garner, 471 U.S. 1 (1985)] For purposes of state criminal law, under this rule a police officer cannot use deadly force to apprehend an unarmed, nondangerous felon; but an officer may use deadly force to prevent a felon from escaping if the police officer has probable cause to believe that the felon poses a threat of serious bodily harm to the officer or others.

1) By Person Acting At Direction of Police Officer
A police officer may summon a bystander to assist him in making a lawful arrest. The bystander has the same authority as the officer to use force in making the arrest, and the bystander's good faith assistance is justified even if it later turns out that the officer was exceeding his authority.

b. By Private Person
A private person has the same right to use force to make an arrest as a police officer or one acting at the direction of a police officer, except that the private person has a defense to the use of *deadly force only if* the person harmed was *actually guilty* of the offense (i.e., felony) for which the arrest was made. It is not enough that it reasonably appeared that the person was guilty. A private person has a privilege to use *nondeadly force* to make an arrest if a crime was in fact committed and the private person has *reasonable grounds to believe* the person arrested has in fact committed the crime.

7. Resisting Arrest

a. Right to Resist Person Not Known to Be Police Officer
An individual may lawfully repel, with deadly force if necessary, an attack made by a police officer trying to arrest her if the individual does not know that the person is a police officer.

b. Right to Resist Known Police Officer
May a person resist arrest if the person attempting to make the arrest is known to be a police officer? The majority rule is that **_nondeadly force_** may be used to resist an improper arrest even if a known officer is making that arrest. A minority of courts and the M.P.C. take the position that force may not be used to resist one known to be a police officer.

8. Necessity
Conduct otherwise criminal is justifiable if the defendant reasonably believed that the conduct was necessary to avoid some harm to society that would exceed the harm caused by the conduct. The **_test is objective_**; a good faith belief in the necessity of one's conduct is insufficient. However, causing the death of another person to protect property is never justified.

Example: Throwing cargo overboard during a violent storm, if necessary to save the lives of the crew and other people on board a ship, would not constitute criminal damage to property. On the other hand, throwing some members of the crew overboard to save the cargo would never be justifiable.

The defense of necessity is not available if the defendant is at fault in creating a situation requiring her to choose between two evils. Finally, under the traditional common law view, the pressure producing the choice of evils had to come from natural forces; however, modern cases **_do not require that the necessity arise from natural forces_**.

9. Public Policy
A police officer (or one assisting her) is justified in using reasonable force against another, or taking property, provided the officer acts pursuant to a law, court order, or process requiring or authorizing her to so act.

Example: The public executioner is not guilty of murder when she carries out a lawfully imposed sentence of execution. If the sentence was not lawful, the executioner is still immunized from criminal liability by a reasonable belief that her conduct was required by law.

10. Domestic Authority
The parents of a minor child, or any person "in loco parentis" with respect to that child, may lawfully use reasonable force upon the child for the purpose of promoting the child's welfare. Whether or not the force is "reasonable" is judged by the totality of the circumstances, including the age, sex, and health of the child.

B. EXCUSE OF DURESS (ALSO CALLED COMPULSION OR COERCION)
A person is not guilty of an offense, **_other than intentional homicide_**, if he performs an otherwise criminal act under the threat of imminent infliction of death or great bodily harm, provided that he reasonably believes death or great bodily harm will be inflicted on himself or on a member of his immediate family if he does not perform such conduct. **_Threats to harm any third person_** may also suffice to establish the defense of duress. Traditionally, **_threats to property_** were not sufficient; however, a number of states, consistent with the M.P.C., do allow for threats to property to give rise to a duress defense, assuming that the value of the property outweighs the harm done to society by commission of the crime. Note that an act committed under duress is termed excusable rather than justifiable. The subtle distinction stems from the fact that criminal acts performed under duress are condoned by society rather than encouraged.

1. **Necessity Distinguished**

   Unlike necessity, duress *always* involves a human threat.

   Example: A points a gun at B and threatens to kill B if she does not break into C's house and steal food. B does as she is told. B may raise the defense of duress. If, however, B is a starving victim of a plane crash in a desolate area and commits the same act, she has the defense of necessity.

C. OTHER DEFENSES

1. **Mistake or Ignorance of Fact**

   a. **Mistake Must Negate State of Mind**

   Ignorance or mistake as to a matter of fact will affect criminal guilt only if it shows that the defendant did not have the state of mind required for the crime.

   Example: A, hunting in the woods, shoots at what he reasonably believes to be a deer. In fact, it is B, who is killed. A's mistake of fact establishes that he did not have the state of mind required for murder.

   Compare: A, hunting in the woods, shoots through the trees at a figure he believes to be his enemy B, intending to kill him. In fact, the figure is C, who is killed. A is guilty of murdering C despite his mistake of fact as to C's identity, because A's mistake does not negate his intent to kill a person.

   b. **Requirement that Mistake Be Reasonable**

   1) **Malice and General Intent Crimes—Reasonableness Required**

   If the mistake or ignorance is offered to negate the existence of general intent or malice, it must be a reasonable mistake or ignorance, i.e., the type of mistake or ignorance that a reasonable person would have made under the circumstances.

   2) **Specific Intent Crimes—Reasonableness Not Required**

   Any mistake of fact, reasonable or unreasonable, is a defense to a specific intent crime.

   Example: A, leaving a restaurant, takes an umbrella, believing that it was the one she had left there a week ago. In fact, it belongs to B. Is A guilty of larceny? *Held:* No; since A believed the umbrella was hers, she could not have intended to deprive B of his right to it. Therefore, she lacked the state of mind necessary for larceny. Since her mistake negates a specific intent, it is not material whether it was a reasonable mistake or not.

   c. **Strict Liability Crimes—Mistake No Defense**

   Since strict liability crimes require no state of mind, mistake or ignorance of fact is no defense to them.

2. **Mistake or Ignorance of Law**

   a. **General Rule—No Defense**

   It is not a defense to a crime that the defendant was unaware that her acts were prohibited by the criminal law or that she mistakenly believed that her acts were not prohibited. This is true even if her ignorance or mistake was reasonable.

b. Mistake or Ignorance of Law May Negate Intent

If the mental state for a crime requires a certain belief concerning a collateral aspect of the law, ignorance or mistake as to that aspect of the law *will negate the requisite state of mind*. This situation involves ignorance of some aspect of the *elements* of a crime rather than the *existence* of the statute making the act criminal.

Examples: 1) A is charged with violating a statute prohibiting the sale of a pistol to one known to be a convicted felon. A was unaware of the statute prohibiting this, but was aware that the person to whom the pistol was sold had been convicted of assault. A mistakenly believed, however, that assault was a misdemeanor; in fact, it was a felony. Is A guilty? *Held:* No. A's ignorance of the statute prohibiting the sale does not affect her liability, but the statute requires awareness that the buyer was a convicted felon. Since A believed the buyer to be only a convicted misdemeanant, she lacked the state of mind required for the crime.

2) B, who has had her car repossessed by a loan company, honestly believes she is still the lawful owner of the vehicle and is lawfully entitled to possession of it. She sees it sitting in a parking space in front of the loan company office and takes it. Even if B is wrong about her right to take the automobile, she is not guilty of larceny because she lacks the requisite intent to deprive another of his property.

c. Exceptions

1) Statute Not Reasonably Available

The defendant has a defense if the statute proscribing her conduct was not published or made reasonably available prior to the conduct.

2) Reasonable Reliance on Statute or Judicial Decision

The defendant has a defense if she acted in reasonable reliance on a statute or judicial decision, even though the statute is later declared unconstitutional or the decision is overruled. The defense is strongest when the decision relied on was rendered by the highest court in the jurisdiction.

3) Reasonable Reliance on Official Interpretation or Advice

At common law, it was no defense that the defendant relied on an erroneous official statement of the law contained in an administrative order or grant, or in an official interpretation by the public officer or body responsible for the interpretation, administration, or enforcement of the law. The emerging rule, advocated by the M.P.C., provides a defense when the statement is obtained from one "charged by law with responsibility for the interpretation, administration, or enforcement of the law."

4) Compare—Reasonable Reliance on Advice of Private Counsel

Unlike reasonable reliance on an official interpretation of the law (e.g., an opinion of the Attorney General), relying on the advice of one's own counsel is normally not allowed as a true affirmative defense to a crime. If, however, the reliance on the attorney negates an otherwise necessary mental state element (e.g., knowingly violating the law), such reliance can demonstrate that the government has not proved its case beyond a reasonable doubt.

3. Consent

a. May Negate Element of Offense
Consent of the victim is generally no defense. However, if it negates an element of the offense, consent is a complete defense.

Examples: 1) Showing that the victim consented to intercourse is a defense to a charge of forcible rape.

2) Showing that an adult person consented to traveling with the defendant is a defense to kidnapping.

For some crimes, the consent of the victim is of no relevance (e.g., consent of a victim of statutory rape has no legal significance). For other offenses, consent may be of limited effect (e.g., within limits, victim may consent to infliction of physical violence, and one inflicting it will therefore not be guilty of assault or battery).

b. Requirements of Consent as Defense
Whenever consent may be a defense, it must be established that:

1) The consent was voluntarily and *freely given* (without compulsion or duress);

2) The party was *legally capable* of consenting; and

3) *No fraud* was involved in obtaining the consent.

4. Condonation by Injured Party No Defense
Forgiveness by the injured party after the crime has been committed ordinarily does not operate as a defense to the commission of a crime, unless a statute establishes such a defense.

Example: Forgiveness by an assault victim would not bar a criminal prosecution of the perpetrator.

Compare: Some statutes provide that marriage of the parties will bar a prosecution for seduction.

5. Criminality of Victim No Defense
The nearly universal rule is that illegal conduct by the victim of a crime is no defense.

Example: A, knowing that B has amassed a fortune through illegal gambling, defrauds B in a real estate deal. Does B's unlawful gambling activity provide A with a defense to fraud? No.

6. Entrapment
Entrapment occurs if the intent to commit the crime originated not with the defendant, but rather with the creative activities of law enforcement officers. If this is the case, it is presumed that the legislature did not intend to cover the conduct and so it is not criminal. The defense of entrapment consists of two elements:

(i)   The *criminal design* must have *originated with law enforcement* officers; and

(ii) The defendant must *not* have been *predisposed* to commit the crime prior to the initial contact by the government.

If the defendant offers credible evidence on these two elements, in most jurisdictions the government must then show predisposition beyond a reasonable doubt.

a.   Offering Opportunity to Commit Crime Distinguished

It is not entrapment if the police officer merely provides the opportunity for the commission of a crime by one otherwise ready and willing to commit it.

Example: A, an undercover police agent, poses as a narcotics addict in need of a fix. B sells narcotics to A. Does B have the defense of entrapment? No. By posing as an addict, A merely provided an opportunity for B to commit the criminal sale.

b.   Inapplicable to Private Inducements

A person cannot be entrapped by a private citizen. Inducement constitutes entrapment only if performed by an officer of the government or one working for him or under his control or direction.

c.   Availability If Offense Denied

If a defendant denies her participation in the offense, she has elected not to pursue entrapment and is not entitled to raise the issue, even if the facts would otherwise permit her to do so. Under the modern trend, however, a defendant may raise the defense of entrapment even while denying participation in the offense. The Supreme Court has adopted this rule for federal offenses. [Mathews v. United States, 485 U.S. 58 (1988)]

d.   Practical Difficulties of Entrapment

In cases where there is extended inducement by the government, the issue becomes whether the defendant was predisposed to commit the offense or whether the intent to commit it was instilled by the officers. Predisposition must exist prior to the government's initial contact with the defendant. A mere "inclination" to engage in the illegal activity is not adequate proof of predisposition. [Jacobson v. United States, 503 U.S. 540 (1992)] However, even if predisposition is not proved, the introduction by the prosecution of potentially damaging evidence on the issue of the defendant's predisposition may cause a jury to convict on the basis of the extensive evidence of the defendant's culpable state of mind.

e.   Minority Rule—Objective Test

The minority rule would replace the entrapment elements set out above with a test based entirely on the nature of the police activity. Under this test, a defendant would be entitled to acquittal if the police activity was reasonably likely to cause an innocent (i.e., unpredisposed) person to commit the crime. The defendant's innocence or predisposition is irrelevant. Under this approach, the issue is decided by the judge rather than the jury.

f.   Provision of Material for Crime by Government Agent Not Entrapment

The Supreme Court has held that under federal law an entrapment defense cannot be based solely upon the fact that a government agent provided material for commission of the crime, even if the material provided was contraband. [United States v. Russell, 411 U.S. 423 (1973); Hampton v. United States, 425 U.S. 484 (1976)] A few states, however, make the provision of essential material—such as ingredients for drugs or the drugs themselves—entrapment.

VII. OFFENSES AGAINST THE PERSON

A. ASSAULT AND BATTERY

1. Battery
Battery is an unlawful application of force to the person of another resulting in either bodily injury or an offensive touching. Simple battery is a misdemeanor.

a. State of Mind—Specific Intent Not Required
A battery can be, *but need not be*, intentional. It is sufficient that the defendant caused the application of force with general intent, interpreted in most jurisdictions today as requiring no more than criminal negligence.

b. Indirect Application of Force Sufficient
The force need not be applied directly. Thus, it is sufficient if the force is applied by a force or substance put in motion by the defendant. For example, battery may be committed by causing a dog to attack the victim or by causing the victim to take a poisonous substance.

c. Aggravated Battery
Most statutes define certain acts as aggravated batteries and punish them as felonies. Among the most common are batteries in which:

1) A *deadly weapon* is used (any ordinary object may become a deadly weapon depending upon how it is used);

2) *Serious bodily injury* is caused; or

3) The *victim is a child, woman, or police officer.*

d. Consent as a Defense
Contrary to the general rule that consent of the victim is not a valid defense, some jurisdictions recognize consent as a defense to simple battery and/or certain specified batteries, e.g., a medical operation, or reasonable injuries incurred in consensual athletic contests.

2. Assault
In a majority of jurisdictions, an assault is either:

(i) An *attempt to commit a battery*; or

(ii) The *intentional creation*—other than by mere words—of a *reasonable apprehension* in the mind of the victim of imminent bodily harm.

A minority of jurisdictions limit assault to an attempt to commit a battery. Simple assault is a misdemeanor.

a.   Present Ability to Succeed
Some statutes define assault as an unlawful attempt to commit a battery coupled with a present ability to succeed. Lack of an ability to succeed precludes liability under such statutes.

Example: A points an unloaded gun at B. A pulls the trigger, thereby frightening B. Is A guilty of assault under a statute defining assault as "an attempt to commit a battery, coupled with the present ability to succeed"? No. Because the gun was unloaded, A could not have succeeded in committing a battery.

b.   Battery Distinguished
If there has been an actual touching of the victim, a battery has been committed. If there has been no such touching, the act may or may not constitute an assault, depending on the circumstances.

c.   Aggravated Assault
All jurisdictions treat certain "aggravated assaults" more severely than simple assault. Such aggravated assaults include, but are not limited to, assaults:

1)   With a *dangerous (or deadly) weapon*;

2)   With *intent to rape, maim, or murder*.

d.   Terminology
Some modern statutes eliminate the term "battery" and define assault to include a battery. Thus, in some states, the term "assault" may encompass a battery, an attempted battery, and the intentional creation of a reasonable apprehension of imminent bodily harm.

B.   MAYHEM

1.   Common Law
At common law, the felony of mayhem required either dismemberment (the removal of some bodily part) or disablement of a bodily part. The crime was enforced to preserve the King's right to his subjects' military service.

2.   Modern Statutes
Most states retain the crime of mayhem in some form, although the recent trend is to abolish mayhem as a separate offense and to treat it instead as a form of aggravated battery. Modern statutes have expanded the scope of mayhem to include permanent disfigurement. A few states require a specific intent to maim or disfigure.

C.   HOMICIDE

1.   Classifications of Homicides
At common law, homicides were divided into three classifications:

a.   *Justifiable* homicides (those commanded or authorized by law);

b. **Excusable** homicides (those for which there was a defense to criminal liability); and

c. **Criminal** homicides.

2. Common Law Criminal Homicides
At common law, criminal homicides were subdivided into three different offenses.

a. Murder
Murder is the unlawful killing of another **human being** with **malice aforethought**. Malice aforethought may be express or implied.

1) Malice Aforethought
In the absence of facts excusing the homicide or reducing it to voluntary manslaughter, malice aforethought exists if the defendant has any of the following states of mind:

(i) Intent to kill (express malice);

(ii) Intent to inflict great bodily injury;

(iii) Reckless indifference to an unjustifiably high risk to human life ("abandoned and malignant heart"); or

(iv) Intent to commit a felony (felony murder; *see infra*).

In the case of (ii), (iii), or (iv), the malice is "implied."

2) Deadly Weapon Rule
Intentional use of a deadly weapon authorizes a permissive inference of intent to kill. A deadly weapon is any instrument—or in some limited circumstances, any part of the body—used in a manner calculated or likely to produce death or serious bodily injury.

Example: The following persons may be held guilty of murder under the deadly weapon rule: (i) one who intentionally pilots a speedboat through a group of bathers; (ii) one who fires a bullet into a crowded room; and (iii) a professional boxer who beats up and kills a belligerent tavern owner.

b. Voluntary Manslaughter
Voluntary manslaughter is a killing that would otherwise be murder but is distinguishable from murder by the existence of adequate provocation—i.e., a killing in the heat of passion.

1) Elements of Adequate Provocation
At common law, provocation would reduce a killing to voluntary manslaughter only if it met four tests:

a) The provocation must have been one that would arouse **sudden and intense passion** in the mind of an **ordinary person** such as to cause him to lose his self-control;

b) The defendant must have **in fact** been **provoked**;

c) There **must not have been a sufficient time** between the provocation and the killing for the passions of a reasonable person to cool. (This is a factual question that depends upon the nature of the provocation and the attendant circumstances, including any earlier altercations between the defendant and the victim); and

d) The defendant **in fact** did not cool off between the provocation and the killing.

2) When Provocation Is Adequate
Adequate provocation is most frequently recognized in cases of:

a) Being subjected to a **serious battery** or a threat of **deadly force**; and

b) Discovering one's **spouse in bed with another person**.

3) Provocation Inadequate as a Matter of Law
At common law, some provocations were defined as inadequate as a matter of law. The most significant was "**mere words**." Modern courts tend to be more reluctant to take such cases from juries and are more likely to submit to the jury the question of whether "mere words" or similar matters constitute adequate provocation.

4) Imperfect Self-Defense
Some states recognize an "imperfect self-defense" doctrine under which a murder may be reduced to manslaughter even though:

a) The **defendant was at fault** in starting the altercation; or

b) The defendant **unreasonably but honestly believed** in the necessity of responding with deadly force.

c. Involuntary Manslaughter
Involuntary manslaughter is of two types.

1) Criminal Negligence (or Recklessness)
If death is caused by criminal negligence (or by "recklessness" under the M.P.C.), the killing is involuntary manslaughter. Criminal negligence requires a greater deviation from the "reasonable person" standard than is required for civil liability. (States that use a recklessness standard also require that the defendant have had a subjective awareness of the risk.)

2) "Unlawful Act" Manslaughter
A killing caused by an unlawful act is involuntary manslaughter. There are two subcategories of such acts:

a) "Misdemeanor-Manslaughter" Rule
A killing in the course of the commission of a misdemeanor is manslaughter, although most courts would require either that the misdemeanor be malum in

se (i.e., an inherently wrongful act), or if malum prohibitum, that the death be the foreseeable or natural consequence of the unlawful conduct.

b) Felonies Not Included in Felony Murder

If a killing was caused during the commission of a felony but does not qualify as a felony murder case, the killing will be at least involuntary manslaughter. The death also must be a foreseeable consequence of the felony. (*See* 4.c.3), *infra*.)

3. Statutory Modification of Common Law Classification

Modern statutes often divide murder into degrees, and the bar examination often contains questions based on statutes similar to them. Under such schemes, all murders are *second degree* murders (similar to common law murder) unless the prosecution proves any of the following, which would make the murder *first degree* murder:

a. Deliberate and Premeditated Killing

"Deliberate" means that the defendant made the decision to kill in a cool and dispassionate manner. "Premeditated" means that the defendant actually reflected on the idea of killing, if only for a very brief period.

b. First Degree Felony Murder

Many state statutes list specific felonies that may serve as the basis for felony murder. If a killing is committed during the commission of one of these enumerated felonies, the killing is usually first degree murder without the prosecution needing to show that the killing was either deliberate or premeditated. The felonies most commonly listed are burglary, arson, rape, robbery, and kidnapping, but other felonies that are inherently dangerous to human life are often specifically added.

1) Second Degree Felony Murder

Even if the state lists the felonies to be included under the doctrine, a separate statute (or case) may provide for criminal liability for a killing committed during the course of a felony that is *not* listed. Such killings typically will be classified as second degree murder.

2) Other State Variations

Some states may not list the felonies to be included under the felony murder doctrine at all. Other states that permit felony murder liability based on a felony that is not listed sometimes include the additional requirement that the felony be inherently dangerous to human life or that the felony be dangerous to human life as committed.

c. Others

Some statutes make killings performed in certain ways first degree murder. Thus, killing by lying in wait, poison, or torture may be first degree murder.

4. Felony Murder (and Related Matters)

As the definition of malice aforethought above makes clear, a killing—even an accidental one—committed during the course of a felony is murder. Malice is implied from the intent to commit the underlying felony.

a. **What Felonies Are Included?**

Under the common law, there were only a handful of felonies (*see* I.D.1., *supra*). Today, the criminal codes of states have created many more.

b. **Scope of the Doctrine**

When the felony murder doctrine is combined with conspiracy law, the scope of liability becomes very broad. If, in the course of a conspiracy to commit a felony, a death is caused, all members of the conspiracy are liable for murder if the death was caused in furtherance of the conspiracy and was a foreseeable consequence of the conspiracy.

c. **Limitations on Liability**

There are some limitations on liability under the broad felony murder doctrine.

1) **Commission of Underlying Felony**

To convict a defendant of felony murder, the prosecution must prove that he committed or attempted to commit the underlying felony. Thus, if the defendant has a *substantive defense* that negates an element of the underlying felony, he has a defense to felony murder. However, procedural defenses (such as a statute of limitations defense to the underlying felony) will not be a defense to felony murder in most states.

2) **Felony Must Be Independent of Killing**

The felony murder rule can be applied only where the underlying felony is independent of the killing. Thus, a felony such as manslaughter or aggravated battery will not qualify as the underlying felony for purposes of felony murder liability.

3) **Foreseeability of Death**

The majority rule is that death must have been a foreseeable result of the commission of the felony. However, it is important to note that *courts have been willing to find most deaths foreseeable.* A minority of courts do not apply a foreseeability requirement, requiring only that the felony be malum in se.

Example: A intentionally sets fire to a dwelling. B, a firefighter, dies in an effort to extinguish the blaze. C, the owner of the dwelling, dies of a heart attack while watching his largest possession being destroyed. Is A guilty of felony murder? Of B, yes. The death of a firefighter is a foreseeable consequence of setting a fire. Of C, no. The heart attack was unforeseeable.

4) **During the Commission of a Felony—Termination of Felony**

The death must have been "caused during" the commission or attempted commission of the felony, but the fact that the felony was technically completed before death was caused does not prevent the killing from being felony murder. Deaths caused while fleeing from the crime are felony murder. But once the felon has reached a *place of "temporary safety,"* the impact of the felony murder rule ceases and deaths subsequently caused are not felony murder.

5) **Killing of Co-Felon by Victims of Felonies or Pursuing Police Officers**

Is the defendant liable for a co-felon's death caused by resistance of the victim or police? The majority view is no. The so-called *Redline* view (the majority position) is that *liability for murder cannot be based upon the death of a co-felon* from resistance by the victim or police pursuit.

a) Compare—Killing of Innocent Party by Victim or Police

The "agency" theory of felony murder provides that for a felon to be held liable for felony murder, the killing must have been committed by the felon or his "agent" (i.e., an accomplice). Thus, if a bystander is accidentally killed by a police officer during a shootout at the crime scene, there would be no felony murder liability because a police officer caused the bystander's death. (There are limited exceptions in cases in which the victim was used as a shield or otherwise forced by the felon to occupy a dangerous place.) Under the "proximate cause" theory, felons are liable for the deaths of innocent victims caused by someone other than a co-felon, since they put into operation a series of events that caused the death of the innocent party.

d. Related Limits on Misdemeanor Manslaughter

Limits similar to those placed on felony murder are placed on involuntary misdemeanor manslaughter. If the misdemeanor involved is not malum in se, i.e., one that involves conduct that is inherently wrong, a death caused during the commission of a misdemeanor is manslaughter only if death was a foreseeable result of the commission of the misdemeanor. A minority of courts limit the doctrine to malum in se misdemeanors.

Example: K is driving on a good road in excellent weather, but is slightly exceeding the posted speed limit. V dashes from behind a bush into the street and is struck by K's car. V dies. Is K guilty of involuntary manslaughter, assuming that speeding is a misdemeanor? The best answer is no, because the misdemeanor was not malum in se and death was not a foreseeable result of its commission.

5. Causation

a. General Requirement—Must Be Cause-in-Fact and Proximate Cause

When a crime is defined to require not merely conduct but also a specified result of that conduct, the defendant's conduct must be both the cause-in-fact and the proximate cause of the specified result.

1) Cause-in-Fact

The defendant's conduct must be the cause-in-fact of the result; i.e., the result would not have occurred "*but for*" the defendant's conduct.

2) Common Law Requirement—"Year and a Day" Rule

The death of the victim must occur within one year and one day from the infliction of the injury or wound. If it does not occur within this period of time, there can be no prosecution for homicide, even if it can be shown that "but for" the defendant's actions, the victim would not have died as and when he did. The rule has been sharply criticized by the United States Supreme Court as "an outdated relic of the common law," and most of the states that have reviewed the rule have abolished it.

3) "Proximate" Causation

Problems of proximate causation arise only when the victim's death occurs because of the defendant's acts, but in a manner not intended or anticipated by the defendant. The question in such cases is whether the difference in the way death was intended or anticipated and the way in which it actually occurred breaks the chain of "proximate cause" causation.

a) All "Natural and Probable" Results Are Proximately Caused

The general rule is that a defendant is responsible for all results that occur as a "natural and probable" consequence of his conduct, even if he did not anticipate the precise manner in which they would occur. All such results are "proximately caused" by the defendant's act. This chain of proximate causation is broken only by the intervention of a "superseding factor."

b. Rules of Causation

1) Hastening Inevitable Result

An act that hastens an inevitable result is nevertheless a legal cause of that result.

Example: A terminates the life support system of B, resulting in B's death. B had only 24 hours to live. Can A be held liable for B's death? Yes. Note that society may not wish to condemn such an "act of mercy." Nevertheless, for purposes of causation analysis, A's act caused B's death.

2) Simultaneous Acts

Simultaneous acts by two or more persons may be considered independently sufficient causes of a single result.

3) Preexisting Condition

A victim's preexisting condition that makes him more susceptible to death does not break the chain of causation; i.e., the defendant "takes the victim as he finds him."

Example: A, with malice aforethought, shoots B in the leg. B bleeds to death before he can receive medical attention because he is a hemophiliac. A is liable for murder despite the fact that a person without hemophilia would not have died from the shooting.

c. Intervening Acts

As a general rule, an intervening act will shield the defendant from liability if the act is a mere coincidence or is outside the foreseeable sphere of risk created by the defendant's act.

Examples: 1) *Act of Nature:* A is driving negligently. To avoid A's swerving car, B takes an unaccustomed route home. B's car is struck by lightning, and B dies. Can A be charged with manslaughter? No. The fact that lightning struck B was a mere coincidence.

2) *Act by Third Party:* A, intending to kill B, merely wounds him. B receives negligent medical treatment at a nearby hospital. B dies. Can A be held liable for B's death? Yes. Despite improvements in medical

care, negligent care remains a *foreseeable risk.* A contrary result would follow if B died due to gross negligence or intentional mistreatment.

3) *Acts by the Victim:* A, intending to kill B, merely wounds him. B refuses medical treatment for religious reasons and dies. If modern medical knowledge could have saved B, can A be held liable for B's death? Most jurisdictions have held yes, because A's act directly created the risk of death and because the refusal of medical care may be found to be foreseeable. This rule may apply even if the victim acts affirmatively to harm himself. Suppose B, in unbearable pain, commits suicide. The suicide may be found to be a foreseeable consequence of A's actions. Thus, A would be liable for B's death.

6. **Born Alive Rule**
Traditionally, an infant had to be "born alive" to be a victim of a homicide crime, meaning that the infant must be completely expelled from his mother and show independent signs of vitality. A number of states have abrogated this rule by statute by extending protection to unborn children as potential victims of homicide crimes.

7. **Summary—Analytical Approach**
In analyzing any homicide situation, the following questions must be asked and answered:

a. Did the defendant have any of the *states of mind* sufficient to constitute malice aforethought?

b. If the answer to a. is yes, is there proof of anything that will, under any applicable statute, raise the homicide to *first degree murder*?

c. If the answer to a. is yes, is there evidence to reduce the killing to *voluntary manslaughter*, i.e., adequate provocation?

d. If the answer to a. is no, is there a sufficient basis for holding the crime to be *involuntary manslaughter*, i.e., criminal negligence or misdemeanor manslaughter?

e. Is there *adequate causation* between the defendant's acts and the victim's death? Was the defendant's act the *factual cause* of death? Is there anything to break the chain of *proximate causation* between the defendant's act and the victim's death?
Example: A came upon B, who was letting the air out of a tire on A's car. When A shouted at B, B picked up a rock and threw it at A, shouting obscenities. B ran off, but A went to his car, pulled a gun out, and shot at B, hitting him in the leg. B was taken to a hospital where he underwent surgery; the wrong gas was used as an anesthetic, and B died. Generally, wounds of this sort are not deadly. A testifies under oath that he merely intended to wound B as revenge for causing A the inconvenience of the flat tire. What is A's liability?

1) Even if A intended only to wound B with a bullet, this is intent to inflict great bodily injury and is sufficient for malice aforethought.

2)   If the statute makes premeditated killings first degree murder, A almost certainly did not premeditate.

3)   While B's shouted obscenities might not be adequate provocation, a jury could certainly find that throwing the rock was such provocation.

4)   If the answer to inquiry a. had been no, A's actions would have constituted criminal negligence.

5)   There is causation. But for A's shot, B would not have died. Negligent medical care is not a superseding intervening factor that will break the chain of proximate causation, unless it is "gross" negligence or intentional malpractice.

D.   FALSE IMPRISONMENT
The common law misdemeanor of false imprisonment consisted of:

(i)   Unlawful

(ii)   Confinement of a person

(iii)   Without his valid consent.

1.   Confinement
Confinement requires that the victim be compelled either to go where he does not wish to go or to remain where he does not wish to remain. It is not confinement to simply prevent a person from going where he desires to go, as long as alternative routes are available to him. The confinement may be accomplished by actual force, by threats, or by a show of force. The M.P.C. takes a similar approach in that the confinement must "interfere substantially" with the victim's liberty.

2.   "Unlawfulness"
Confinement is unlawful unless it is specifically authorized by law or by the consent of the person.

3.   Lack of Consent
Consent to the confinement precludes it from constituting false imprisonment, but the consent must be *freely given* by one with *capacity* to give such consent. Thus, consent is invalidated by coercion, threats, deception, or incapacity due to mental illness, substantial cognitive impairment, or youth.

E.   KIDNAPPING
At common law, the misdemeanor of kidnapping was the forcible abduction or stealing away of a person from his own country and sending him into another. Modern statutes and the M.P.C. generally expand the definition of kidnapping far beyond the common law definition, although it usually remains a form of aggravated false imprisonment.

1.   General Pattern
Kidnapping is often defined as confinement of a person that involves either:

a. Some *movement* (i.e., "asportation") of the victim; *or*

b. *Concealment* of the victim in a "secret" place.

2. Aggravated Kidnapping

Modern statutes often contain as a separate offense an aggravated kidnapping crime. Among the more common forms of this offense are:

a. Kidnapping for Ransom

The abduction or secretion of a person for the purpose of obtaining anything of value for the return of the person is often defined as aggravated kidnapping.

b. Kidnapping for Purpose of Commission of Other Crimes

Abduction or secretion for the purpose of committing other offenses, such as robbery, is sometimes defined as aggravated kidnapping.

c. Kidnapping for Offensive Purpose

Abduction or secretion with the intent of harming the person or of committing some sexual crime with him is sometimes defined as aggravated kidnapping.

d. Child Stealing

Leading, taking, enticing, or detaining a child with the intent to keep or conceal the child from a guardian or parent is often defined as aggravated kidnapping. Use of "enticement" covers the situation in which a child is persuaded by promises or rewards to come with the defendant or remain. The consent of a child to his detention or movement is not of importance, because the child is incapacitated by age from giving valid consent.

3. Required Movement

Although at common law extreme movement was required, most modern statutes require only some movement of the person; if such movement occurs, the extent of the movement is not material. Other statutes require no movement, making confinement (as used in false imprisonment) sufficient.

4. Secrecy

Generally, it is not necessary that kidnapping involve secrecy. Some statutes, however, require secrecy when the kidnapping is based on confinement rather than movement of the victim.

5. Consent

As with false imprisonment, free consent given by a person competent to give it precludes the confinement or movement of a person from being kidnapping. But a person may be incompetent to give such consent by reason of age (*see* above) or mental condition.

6. Relationship to Other Offenses

Statutes that define kidnapping as detention involving movement of the victim mean that it is arguable that kidnapping often occurs incident to the commission of other crimes, such as robbery or rape. Some courts—but not all—have held that in such situations kidnapping (in addition to the robbery or rape) is committed only if the movement of the victim substantially increases the risk to the victim over and above that necessarily involved in the other crime. If no such increased risk is involved, the defendant will be held to have committed only the robbery or rape.

VIII. SEX OFFENSES

A. RAPE

Traditionally, rape (a felony) was the unlawful carnal knowledge of a woman by a man, not her husband, without her effective consent. Today, a number of states have renamed "rape" as "sexual assault" and have made such statutes gender neutral.

1. Penetration Sufficient

Rape requires only the penetration of the female sex organ by the male sex organ. Emission is not necessary to complete the crime.

2. Absence of Marital Relationship

At common law and under the M.P.C., the woman must not have been married to the man who committed the act. Today, however, most states have either dropped this requirement where the parties are estranged or separated, or abolished it entirely.

3. Lack of Effective Consent

The intercourse must be without the victim's effective consent. Consent, even if given, may be ineffective in several situations.

a. Intercourse Accomplished by Force

If the intercourse is accomplished by actual force, no question concerning consent is raised.

b. Intercourse Accomplished by Threats

If intercourse is accomplished by placing the victim in fear of great and immediate bodily harm, it constitutes rape. Any consent obtained by such threats is ineffective. The failure of the victim to "resist to the utmost" does not prevent the intercourse from being rape if resistance is prevented by such threats.

c. Victim Incapable of Consenting

If the victim is incapable of consenting, the intercourse is rape. Inability to consent may be caused by unconsciousness, by the effect of drugs or intoxicating substances, or by the victim's mental condition. If the victim is so insane or cognitively impaired as to be incapable of giving consent, intercourse with her constitutes rape.

d. Consent Obtained by Fraud

Only in limited circumstances will intercourse with consent obtained by fraud constitute rape.

1) Fraud as to Whether Act Constitutes Sexual Intercourse

If the victim is fraudulently caused to believe that the act is not sexual intercourse, the act of intercourse constitutes rape.

Example: D persuaded V that what was actually an act of intercourse was medical treatment accomplished by surgical instruments. Was D guilty of rape? Yes.

2) Fraud as to Whether Defendant Is Victim's Husband

If the defendant fraudulently persuades the victim that he is her husband, is the intercourse rape? The best answer is no.

Example: D arranges for X to pretend to marry D and V. In fact, X has no authority to marry persons and there is no marriage. After the sham marriage, D has intercourse with V. Is D guilty of rape? The best answer is no because there was consent.

3) Other Fraud

Other kinds of fraud will not make the intercourse rape.

Example: D promises to marry V at a later time and thereby induces V to consent to intercourse. D never intended to marry V. Is D guilty of rape? No. (But D may be guilty of seduction (*see* F., *infra*).)

B. STATUTORY RAPE

1. Victim Below Age of Consent

Statutory rape is the crime of carnal knowledge of a person under the age of consent. Even if the victim willingly participated, the offense is nevertheless committed because consent is irrelevant. The age of consent varies from state to state, generally from 16 to 18.

2. Mistake as to Age

Will a defendant's reasonable mistake as to the victim's age prevent liability for statutory rape? For purposes of the examination, the best answer is no, since statutory rape is a *strict liability crime*. A second best answer, to be used only if no alternative making use of the best position is presented, is that a reasonable mistake as to age will prevent conviction if the defendant reasonably believed the victim was old enough to give an effective consent.

C. CRIMES AGAINST NATURE

An early (1533) English statute made sodomy—a generic term encompassing many different acts—a felony, so that it became part of the American common law of crime. However, because of recent court decisions, it is unlikely that a defendant could be successfully prosecuted for most of these crimes if the act was consensual. Bestiality, which is the carnal copulation with an animal by a human being (male or female), is probably the only crime that survives.

D. ADULTERY AND FORNICATION

Adultery and fornication were not common law crimes in England, but were punished by the church as ecclesiastical offenses. They are made misdemeanor offenses by statute in some states.

1. Adultery

Under modern statutes, any person who cohabits or has sexual intercourse with another not his spouse commits the misdemeanor offense of adultery if:

a. The behavior is *open and notorious; and*

b.   The person is *married* and the other person involved in such intercourse is not his spouse; or

   c.   The person is not married and knows the *other person* in such intercourse is *married*.

   2.   Fornication
   Fornication is sexual intercourse between or open and notorious cohabitation by unmarried persons.

E.   INCEST
Incest is a statutory offense, usually a felony, that consists of either marriage or a sexual act (intercourse or deviate sexual conduct) between persons who are too closely related.

   1.   Degree of Relationship
   No uniformity exists among the states. A majority restricts the crime to blood relations, although a significant number of states include some nonblood relatives.

   2.   Degree of Responsibility
   Some states make a distinction in penalties depending on the parties involved.

F.   SEDUCTION OR CARNAL KNOWLEDGE
A statutory felony in many states, the crime of seduction is committed when a male person induces an unmarried female of previously chaste character to engage in an act of intercourse on promise of marriage. The M.P.C. includes a section on seduction; it requires only that there be a false promise of marriage and does not require chastity or that the female be unmarried.

In many states, subsequent marriage of the parties is a defense, but there is no uniformity as to whether the marriage must be entered into before indictment, after sentence, or anywhere in between.

G.   BIGAMY
Bigamy is a traditional strict liability offense that consists of marrying someone while having another living spouse. At common law, a defendant is guilty of bigamy even if she reasonably believes that a purported divorce is valid or that her spouse is dead.

IX.   PROPERTY OFFENSES

This section deals with a number of property offenses. Many of these offenses have been consolidated into state theft statutes. But for purposes of the examination, the greatest challenge is in distinguishing among three property crimes: larceny, embezzlement, and false pretenses. There is no difference among the intents required for the three crimes. The major differences among these crimes are in the kind of misappropriation of the property.

A.   LARCENY
Larceny was the basic common law property offense. It has been significantly modified by statute in many American jurisdictions. Larceny consists of:

(i)   A taking (caption);

(ii) And carrying away (asportation);

(iii) Of tangible personal property;

(iv) Of another;

(v)   By trespass;

(vi) With intent to permanently (or for an unreasonable time) deprive the person of his interest in the property.

1. **Property that May Be the Subject of Larceny**
    Larceny can be committed only by the acquisition of *personal property* capable of being possessed and of some value.

    a. **Realty and Severed Material**
        Realty and its fixtures are *not* subjects of larceny. If something is severed from the realty and taken before it comes into possession of the landowner as personal property, larceny is not committed. If, however, the landowner gains possession of the severed material as personalty, a subsequent taking of it is larceny.
        Example: A went onto land owned by B and cut down 15 trees. She loaded 10 into her truck and drove off. B came onto the land, found the remaining five trees, and placed them in his shed. A returned and took them. Is A guilty of larceny of 15, 10, five, or no trees? *Held:* A is guilty of larceny of the five trees that came into B's possession after their severance from the realty.

    b. **Services**
        Traditionally, obtaining services wrongfully cannot give rise to larceny.

    c. **Intangibles**
        Intangibles cannot give rise to larceny.
        Example: A wrongfully obtains entrance to B's theater and observes a performance of a play. Has A committed larceny of that performance? *Held:* No. The right or ability to observe a play is intangible.

        Note that gas and electricity are considered to be personal property that may be stolen.

    d. **Documents and Instruments**
        Documents and instruments were, at common law, regarded as merged with the matter they represented. Thus, unless they had monetary value in themselves, they could not be the subject of larceny.
        Example: A takes a deed to certain realty and a contract for the sale of cattle from B's desk. Is A guilty of larceny? *Held:* No. The deed "merged" with the realty and the contract merged with the intangible contract right; thus, there was no larceny.

Modern statutes have expanded larceny to include written instruments embodying intangible rights.

2. Property "Of Another"

Larceny is a crime against property. All that is necessary is that the property be taken from someone who has a possessory interest superior to that of the defendant.

a. Requirement that Taking Be from One with "Possession"

For larceny, the property must be taken out of the victim's possession, which means that the property was not already in the defendant's possession. If the defendant had possession at the time of the taking (e.g., defendant is a bailee of the property), the resulting offense is not larceny, although it may be embezzlement. However, if the defendant has "custody" rather than "possession," her misappropriation of the property is larceny.

1) Custody vs. Possession

Possession involves much greater scope of authority to deal with the property than does custody. Generally, the defendant has possession if she was given discretionary authority over the property and has custody if she was given limited authority over the property. If the defendant has only custody of the property, then another person inevitably has a greater possessory interest over that property than the defendant.

Example: A, while in a store, asks B, the clerk, if she may take a certain suit of clothing home on approval. B consents. A then asks to see a watch to examine it; B gives it to her. A then absconds with both items. Have either of them been taken from B's possession? *Held:* The watch was taken from B's possession, because A had only the authority to look at it. The suit, on the other hand, was in A's possession at the time it was misappropriated, because of the extent of control B had given A over it.

2) Employees

Low level employees generally have only custody of their employers' property. They have possession, however, if the employer gives them especially broad powers over it or if the property is given directly to them by a third person, without the employer having intermediate possession.

3) Bailee and "Breaking Bulk"

Generally, a ***bailee has possession***. If, however, she opens closed containers in which the property has been placed by the bailor (i.e., she "breaks bulk"), the possession is regarded by use of a fiction as returning to the bailor. If a bailee misappropriates property ***after breaking bulk***, she takes it from the possession of the bailor and is guilty of ***larceny*** if she has the intent to steal.

b. Possession at the Time of the Taking

In determining whether someone has committed larceny, it is important to determine who had lawful possession of the property in question at the time of the taking. If a person has lawful possession when she takes the property, she is not guilty of larceny, even if she does not own the property. (But she may be guilty of embezzlement.) By contrast, a person can be guilty of larceny for taking her own property, if someone else had lawful possession at the time the owner takes it.

Example: A owns two cars but only uses one of them. She decides, therefore, to lease the unused car to B for one year. Six months into the one year lease, A decides she wants the car back. When B refuses to rescind the lease, A sneaks into B's driveway and drives the car away, using her extra key. A is guilty of larceny even though she is the owner of the car, since B had lawful possession of the vehicle when A took it.

c. Stolen Property

Stolen property can be the subject of larceny (i.e., a second thief is guilty of larceny when he takes property from a first thief).

d. Joint Property

At common law, larceny could not be committed by the taking of jointly held property by one of the joint owners.

e. Lost, Mislaid, and Abandoned Property

Lost or mislaid property is regarded as constructively in the possession of the owner, and thus if it is found and taken, it is taken from his possession and larceny might be committed. Abandoned property, however, has no owner and larceny cannot be committed by appropriating it.

3. Taking

It is essential that the defendant actually obtain control of the property.

a. Destruction or Movement Is Not Sufficient

Mere destruction or movement of the property is not sufficient to constitute a taking.

Example: D knocked a glass from X's hand. It fell and broke. Is D guilty of larceny? No. Although X may have lost possession, D never obtained control. The damage to the item is irrelevant.

b. Sufficient If Caused to Occur by Innocent Agent

Even if a defendant obtains control of the property through the act of an innocent agent, it is a taking.

Example: D, pointing out a cow in a nearby field, offers to sell it to X for $10. X gives D the money and then takes the cow. In fact, the cow belonged to Y. Is D guilty of larceny of the cow? Yes. She obtained control of it by virtue of X, an innocent agent of hers.

4. Asportation

Larceny requires asportation, i.e., that all parts or portions of the property be moved and that this movement—which need only be slight—be part of the carrying away process.

Example: A came upon two upside-down wheelbarrows in B's yard. She turned them both right side up, and moved one six inches toward the gate. Was she guilty of larceny of one, two, or no wheelbarrows? *Held:* Guilty of larceny of one. Merely turning the wheelbarrows over is not part of the carrying away movement; thus, it is not asportation. But merely moving the other wheelbarrow a short distance is enough, because that movement is part of carrying it away.

5. Taking Must Be "Trespassory"

The defendant must take the property from the custody or possession of another in a trespassory manner, i.e., without the consent of the person in custody or possession of the property.

a. Taking by Consent Induced by Misrepresentations—"Larceny by Trick"

If the victim consents to the defendant's taking custody or possession of the property, but this consent has been induced by a misrepresentation, the consent is not valid. The resulting larceny is often called "larceny by trick." A major difficulty is in distinguishing larceny by trick from false pretenses. (*See* C.1., *infra*.)

6. State of Mind Required—Intent to Permanently Deprive

Generally, larceny requires that at the time of the taking the defendant must have the intent to permanently deprive the person from whom the property is taken of his interest in the property. The intent has to exist at the moment of the taking of the property.

a. Sufficient Intent

1) Intent to Create Substantial Risk of Loss

If the defendant intends to deal with the property in a manner that involves a substantial risk of loss, this is sufficient for larceny.

2) Intent to Pledge Goods or Sell Them to Owner

It is larceny to take goods with the intent to sell them back to the owner or to pledge them, because this involves the substantial equivalent of permanent loss or the high risk of permanent loss.

b. Insufficient Intent

1) Intent to Borrow

If the defendant intends to return the property within a reasonable time and at the time of the taking has a substantial ability to do so, the unauthorized borrowing does not constitute larceny. Note that many states make it a crime to borrow a motor vehicle, even when the borrower fully intends to return it ("joyriding").

2) Intent to Obtain Repayment of Debt

It is not larceny to take money or goods of another if the defendant honestly believes that she is entitled to them as repayment for a debt of the other (although the goods must not be worth more than the amount of the debt). In these situations, the defendant believes the property is "hers" and therefore lacks an intent to deprive someone else of "his" property.

c. Possibly Sufficient

1) Intent to Pay for Property

If the property taken is not for sale, the fact that the defendant intends to pay the other for it does not negate the larceny. If the property is for sale and the defendant has a specific and realistic intent to repay the person, the taking is not larceny.

2) Intent to Claim Reward

If the defendant takes goods, intending to return them and hoping for a reward, this is not larceny. However, if she takes them not intending to return them unless she is assured of a reward, this is larceny because it creates a substantial risk of loss.

7. **Specialized Application of Larceny Doctrine**
There are several situations in which the application of the requirements for larceny is highly technical.

a. **Abandoned or Lost Property**
Property abandoned by its owner, i.e., discarded with the intent of giving up all rights in it, cannot be the subject of larceny. One who finds property that has merely been lost by its owner can, however, commit larceny of it. Two requirements exist:

(i) The finder must know or have reason to believe she *can find* out the *identity of the owner*; and

(ii) The finder must, at the moment she takes possession of the lost property, have the *intent* necessary for larceny.

If the finder takes custody of the lost property without the intent to steal, but later formulates this intent, she has not committed larceny. Nor has she committed embezzlement, since no trust relationship between the finder and the owner has been created. (*See* below.)

b. **Misdelivered Property**
One to whom property is delivered by mistake may, by accepting the property, commit larceny of it. Two requirements must be met:

1) The recipient must, at the time of the misdelivery, *realize the mistake* that is being made; and

2) The recipient must, at the time she accepts the delivery, have the *intent* required for larceny.

c. **"Container" Situations**

1) **Issue Is Whether Defendant Already Has Possession**
One subcategory of "misdelivery" cases presents special problems: The "container" cases, in which the defendant is charged with larceny of an item that she discovers within another item after she has legitimately taken possession of the larger item—or the container—from the victim. The difficult question is whether, at the time she appropriates the item, does she already have possession? If so, larceny is not committed because the property is not taken from the possession of another.

2) **Larceny May Depend on Whether Parties Intended to Transfer Container**
One solution to this problem is to distinguish among cases according to whether or not the parties intended the original transfer to be the transfer of a container, i.e., an item containing other items. If the parties intended to transfer a container,

the recipient is regarded as taking immediate possession of both the container and its contents. Her later misappropriation of the contents is not larceny, because it occurs at a time when she already has possession. If, however, both parties did not intend to transfer a container but rather regarded the items transferred as empty (or otherwise not involving a transfer of contained items), the recipient does not obtain possession of the contents until she discovers them. If at the time she discovers and appropriates them she has the intent to steal, she is guilty of larceny.

d. "Continuing Trespass" Situations

A trespassory taking of property without the intent required for larceny is not, of course, larceny. However, if a defendant takes property with a wrongful state of mind but without the intent to steal, and later, while still in possession of it, forms the intent to steal it, the trespass involved in the initial wrongful taking is regarded as "continuing" and the defendant is guilty of larceny. This doctrine has no application if the defendant's initial taking of the property, although trespassory, was not motivated by a wrongful state of mind.

Example: A took X's umbrella from X's possession without X's permission, intending to use the umbrella and return it the next day. The next morning when A awoke, she examined the umbrella carefully and decided to keep it. Is A guilty of larceny of the umbrella? Yes. The larceny took place when A formed the intent to steal it. Since her initial possession was wrongful, the trespass continued until she formed the intent to steal. On the other hand, if A had taken X's umbrella by mistake, and later decided to keep it after discovering her mistake, the doctrine would not apply because her initial taking was done with an innocent state of mind.

B. EMBEZZLEMENT

Embezzlement was not originally a common law crime. Intended to plug the gaps in the law of larceny, it was made a misdemeanor by statute in 1799 and is regarded as part of American common law. Modern statutes often distinguish between grand embezzlement (a felony) and petit embezzlement (a misdemeanor) based upon the value of the property embezzled. Although variously defined in different jurisdictions, embezzlement generally requires:

(i)   The fraudulent;

(ii) Conversion;

(iii) Of property;

(iv) Of another;

(v)   By a person in lawful possession of that property.

1. Distinguished from Larceny

a. Manner of Obtaining Property

In embezzlement, the misappropriation of the property occurs while the defendant has lawful possession of it. In larceny, it occurs generally at the time the defendant obtains wrongful possession of the property.

Example: A was foreman of a construction crew. One day, he took a tool used by the crew to his home. The next day, he was fired. On his way out, he took another tool. Was he guilty of embezzlement of one, two, or no tools? *Held:* Only of the first tool, which he converted while it was in his possession by virtue of his employment. He had no right to possession of the tools at the time he took the second.

b. Manner of Misappropriation

Larceny requires caption and asportation with the intent to permanently deprive. Embezzlement requires intentional conversion. (*See* below.)

2. Conversion

The conversion required by embezzlement requires only that the defendant deal with the property in a manner inconsistent with the trust arrangement pursuant to which he holds it. No movement or carrying away of the property is required. The conversion need not result in direct personal gain to the defendant.

Example: A trustee who siphons off trust fund money in order to donate to a favorite charity is as guilty of embezzlement as the trustee who uses the converted funds to pay his overdue gambling debts.

3. Property

Embezzlement statutes are often worded in terms of "property that may be subject to larceny"; i.e., real property and services may not be embezzled. Some relatively expansive statutes, however, make embezzlement of real property a crime.

Example: A, an agent with apparent authority to sell B's real estate, fraudulently transfers the title to a bona fide purchaser. Is A guilty of embezzlement? No, under the traditional embezzlement statute. Yes, under the more expansive statute.

4. Requirement that Property Be that "Of Another"

Embezzlement requires that the property converted be that of someone other than the converter. Therefore, a person who borrows money, converts the sum to his own use, and subsequently fails to repay it is not guilty of embezzlement.

5. Fraudulent Intent

A defendant must intend to defraud for a conversion to become embezzlement. This appears to be the functional equivalent of larceny's specific intent to permanently deprive.

a. Intent to Restore

If the defendant intended to restore the *exact* property taken, it is not embezzlement. But if he intended to restore *similar or substantially identical* property, it is embezzlement, even if it was money that was initially taken and other money—of identical value—that he intended to return.

b. Claim of Right

As in larceny, embezzlement is not committed if the conversion is pursuant to a claim of right to the property, as where it is retained for payment of a debt honestly believed to be owed. The fact that the defendant retained the property openly tends to establish a claim of right.

6. **Necessity for Demand for Return**

If it is clear that there has been a conversion of the property, the victim need not make a demand that it be returned. If, however, there is doubt as to the existence of a conversion, a demand by the owner for return and a refusal to return by the defendant may be necessary.

7. **Limitation to Property Entrusted**

Some states limit embezzlement to the fraudulent conversion of property "entrusted" or "delivered" to the embezzler. These states would not punish one who finds lost property and, while in lawful possession of it, fraudulently converts it.

C. FALSE PRETENSES

The offense of false pretenses was created by English statute in 1757, and consequently is part of the common law in those American states that use 1776 as the determining date. Like larceny and embezzlement, most jurisdictions distinguish grand false pretenses (a felony) from petit false pretenses (a misdemeanor). The offense of false pretenses generally consists of:

(i) Obtaining title;

(ii) To the property of another;

(iii) By a knowing (or, in some states, an intentional) false statement of past or existing fact;

(iv) With intent to defraud the other.

1. **"Larceny by Trick" Distinguished**

False pretenses differs from larceny by trick in what is obtained. If only *custody* of the property is obtained by the defendant, the offense is larceny by trick. If *title* is obtained, the offense is false pretenses. What is obtained depends upon what the victim intended to convey to the defendant.

Example: D asked X if X would sell a car and offered as payment what was purported to be a demand note signed by Y. D falsely represented that the note was one executed by Y; in fact, D himself had forged it. X agreed to sell the car but told D that the sale would not be final until she had collected the amount of the note from Y. X then permitted D to use the car until Y could be located. D drove off in the car. Has he committed larceny or false pretenses? Larceny, because X did not intend to transfer title to D. X intended only to transfer possession pending collection on the note.

Compare: Same facts as above, except the note purportedly signed by Y is due in 30 days rather than on demand. Based on Y's good credit, X agreed to convey full title to the car in exchange for the note. D drove off in the car. D has committed false pretenses rather than larceny.

2. **Misrepresentation Required**

There are several limits upon the misrepresentations required for false pretenses. (These also apply to larceny by trick.)

a. **False Representation Concerning Matter of Fact**

The defendant must have created a false impression as to the matter of fact. If his statements reasonably construed constitute only an opinion or a "puffing," they are not representations. It is not misrepresentation to fail to correct what is known to be a mistaken belief that the victim holds, *if* the defendant was not responsible for creating that belief, or the defendant has no fiduciary duty to the aggrieved party.

    b.   Misrepresentation of Past or Existing Fact
Traditionally, the defendant's misrepresentation must have related to a past or present fact, and false promises to do something in the future, even without the present intent to perform, were not sufficient. However, under the M.P.C. and the modern prevailing view, any false representation suffices for the crime of false pretenses, including a false promise to perform in the future.

3.   Requirement that Representation Be the "Cause" of Obtaining Property
The victim must actually be deceived by, or act in reliance on, the misrepresentation, and this must be a major factor (or the sole cause) of the victim passing title to the defendant.

4.   State of Mind Required
The defendant must have known the statement to be false when he made it; however, most states will find that the defendant "knew" of the falsity of any statements when, after being put on notice of the high probability of the statement's falsity, he deliberately avoided learning the truth. On the other hand, if he believes the statement to be true, he has not committed false pretenses (even if his belief was unreasonable). The defendant also must have intended that the victim rely on the misrepresentation. Subjecting the victim to a risk of loss will suffice for the intent to defraud.

    Example: A obtained money from B by representing that he was securing it by a first mortgage on certain property. He intended to pay back the loan. The mortgage actually given was, as A knew, only a second mortgage. Is A guilty of false pretenses? *Held:* Yes. He knowingly subjected B to a substantially greater risk of loss of the money than B was aware of. This was a sufficient intent to defraud.

5.   Related Crimes
Many states have enacted specific legislation covering certain conduct that resembles the crime of false pretenses but is sufficiently different to warrant separate consideration.

    a.   Bad Check Legislation
Almost all jurisdictions have created a new and separate statutory crime prohibiting the giving of a no-account or insufficient funds check with the intent to defraud.

    b.   Abuse or Misuse of Credit Card
Most jurisdictions have enacted legislation making it a misdemeanor to knowingly obtain property by means of a stolen, forged, canceled, revoked, or otherwise unauthorized credit card.

D.   ROBBERY
Robbery, a felony in all jurisdictions, consists of the following:

(i)   A taking;

(ii)   Of personal property of another;

(iii)   From the other's person or presence;

(iv)   By force or intimidation;

(v)   With the intent to permanently deprive him of it.

Thus, robbery is basically an aggravated form of larceny in which the taking is accomplished by force or threats of force.

1.   Force or Threats Necessary

If force is used, it obviously must be sufficient to overcome the victim's resistance. If threats are used, they must be threats of immediate death or serious physical injury to the victim, a member of her family, a relative, or a person in her presence at the time. A threat to do damage to property will not suffice, with the exception of a threat to destroy the victim's dwelling house.

2.   Property Must Be Taken from Person or Presence of Victim

The property must be taken from some location reasonably close to the victim, but it need not be taken from her person. Property is in the victim's presence if it is in her vicinity. Property in other rooms of the house in which the victim is located is in her presence.

3.   Force or Threats Must Be Used to Obtain Property or Immediately Retain It

The force or threats must be used either to gain possession of the property or to retain possession *immediately* after such possession has been accomplished.

Example: A reached into B's pocket without B's knowledge and removed B's wallet. B felt the wallet slip out, turned around, and grabbed A as he moved away. A struck B, rendering her unconscious, and ran. Is A guilty of robbery? *Held:* Yes. The force was used to prevent the victim from immediately apprehending A and regaining the property. Thus, it is sufficiently related to the taking.

4.   Aggravated Robbery

Statutes often create a form of aggravated robbery, usually defined as robbery accomplished with a deadly weapon.

E.   EXTORTION

Extortion is an offense that generally has been expanded by modern statutes far beyond its initial common law definition.

1.   Common Law Definition—Collection of Unlawful Fee

The common law misdemeanor of extortion consisted of the corrupt collection of an unlawful fee by an officer under color of his office.

2.   Modern Definition—Blackmail

In many modern statutes, extortion (or blackmail) is defined as obtaining property from another by means of certain oral or written threats. The prohibited threats often include threats to do physical harm to the victim or others, or threats to damage the victim's property. Under some statutes, the crime is completed when the threats are made with the intent to obtain money or something of value; the threat is the essence of the offense. Under other statutes, the money or property must actually be obtained by means of the threats.

a. Threats Need Not Involve Immediate or Physical Harm
Extortion may be committed by threats that are not sufficient for robbery. To constitute extortion, the threats do not need to involve immediate or physical harm.

b. Property Need Not Be in Victim's Presence
To constitute extortion, it is generally not necessary that the property be obtained from the victim's person or presence (as is necessary for robbery).

F. RECEIPT OF STOLEN PROPERTY
The common law misdemeanor of receipt of stolen property is substantially identical to the modern offense. The elements of the crime are:

(i) Receiving possession and control;

(ii) Of "stolen" personal property;

(iii) Known to have been obtained in a manner constituting a criminal offense;

(iv) By another person;

(v) With the intent to permanently deprive the owner of his interest in the property.

1. Possession
Manual possession of the property, while sufficient for "receiving," is not necessary. It is also receiving if: (i) the thief places the stolen property in a place that the defendant has designated; or (ii) for profit, the defendant arranges for a sale of the property by the thief to a third person.

2. "Stolen" Property
Most jurisdictions define "stolen" property broadly to include property obtained by commission of any of the property offenses. However, the property must have "stolen" status at the time it is received by the defendant. Thus, if stolen goods have been recovered by the police and are used in an undercover operation with the owner's permission, the goods are not stolen and the defendant cannot be guilty of receipt of stolen property; however, the defendant may be guilty of attempt to receive stolen goods (*see* IV.D.3.a.2)a), *supra*).

G. STATUTORY CHANGES IN PROPERTY ACQUISITION OFFENSES
Modern criminal codes and the M.P.C. have substantially altered the common law. Among the major changes are the following:

1. Consolidation of Offenses into Theft
There is a growing tendency to consolidate larceny, embezzlement, false pretenses, and receipt of stolen goods under the single heading: Theft. It is important to note that theft is a modern statutory crime, not a traditional common law offense.

2. **Expansion of Property Subject to Larceny (and Other Offenses)**
The things subject to the offenses have often been expanded to cover services, documents, and intangibles, as well as joint property.

3. **Rejection of Asportation for Larceny**
Some jurisdictions have rejected the requirement of asportation and require only that "control" of property be obtained.

4. **Rejection of Technicalities of Trespass Requirement**
A number of jurisdictions have replaced the detailed technicalities of the trespass requirement by a simplified requirement that the defendant have obtained unauthorized "control" over the property.

H. FORGERY
At common law, forgery and uttering a forged instrument are separate offenses.

1. **Forgery**
Forgery consists of the following:

   a. Making or altering;

   b. Of a false writing;

   c. With intent to defraud.

2. **Uttering a Forged Instrument**
Uttering consists of:

   a. Offering as genuine;

   b. An instrument that may be the subject of forgery and is false;

   c. With intent to defraud.

3. **Writings that Are Possible Subjects of Forgery**
Any writing that has ***apparent legal significance*** is a potential subject of forgery. Writing includes typewritten, printed, engraved, and similar material.

   Example: A drafts and signs what purports to be a letter of introduction from a local physician and a letter of recommendation from a firm represented as a former employer. Both are false. Has A committed one, two, or no forgeries? *Held:* One forgery. The recommendation has apparent legal significance, because one who recommends another may incur legal liability if his recommendation is false. Thus, it can be the subject of forgery. But the letter of introduction has only social significance, and cannot be the subject of forgery.

   Writings that derive their value from the mere fact of their existence—historical or artistic value—cannot be the subject of forgery.

   Example: A painted a picture and signed it "Rembrandt." She then sold it to X, representing it as an original "Rembrandt." Is A guilty of forgery? No, because the picture and signature derive their value from the fact of their existence. (*Note:* A did commit false pretenses by the sale.)

4. **Required Falsity—Writing Itself Must "Be a Lie"**
It is not sufficient that the writing contains a false statement. The writing must represent itself to be something that it is not.

Examples: 1) A, in charge of a warehouse, issues a warehouse receipt that represents that the warehouse has received certain grain. It has not. Is this forgery? *Held:* No. The warehouse receipt contains a misrepresentation. But it is what it purports to be, i.e., a warehouse receipt issued by one with authority to issue it.

2) B obtains blank receipts from A's warehouse, fills them in so they represent that certain grain has been received, and signs A's name. Is this forgery? *Held:* Yes. The instruments purport to be what they are not, i.e., warehouse receipts issued by one with authority to do so.

5. **Required "Making"**

a. **Entire Instrument or Material Alteration**
Forgery can be committed by the "making" of an entire instrument. It can also, however, be committed by altering an existing instrument, if the alteration is "material," that is, if it affects a legal right. Alteration may be in the form of changing some of the writing, adding to the existing writing, removing some of the existing writing, or improperly filling in blanks left by the signer.

b. **Fraudulently Obtaining Signature of Another**
If the defendant fraudulently causes a third person to sign a document that the third person does not realize he is signing, forgery has been committed. But if the third person realizes he is signing the document, forgery has not been committed even if the third person was induced by fraud to sign it.

6. **Required Intent—Intent to Defraud**
The defendant must have had the intent to defraud, although no one need actually have been defrauded. It is not necessary that she intended to do pecuniary harm; it is sufficient if she intended to harm another in any way.

I. MALICIOUS MISCHIEF
The common law misdemeanor of malicious mischief consists of:

(i) Malicious;

(ii) Destruction of, or damage to;

(iii) Property of another.

1. **Damage Required**
Destruction of the property is not required for malicious mischief. All that is necessary is that some physical damage be done that impairs the utility of the property or materially diminishes its value.

2. State of Mind Required—Malice
Malice requires no ill will or hatred. It does, however, require that the damage or destruction have been intended or contemplated by the defendant.

X. OFFENSES AGAINST THE HABITATION

A. BURGLARY
At common law, the elements of burglary are:

(i) A breaking;

(ii) And entry;

(iii) Of the dwelling;

(iv) Of another;

(v) At nighttime;

(vi) With the intent of committing a felony therein.

1. Breaking Required

a. Actual Breaking—Minimal Force Sufficient
Actual breaking requires some use of force to gain entry, but minimal force is sufficient; opening a closed but unlocked door constitutes a breaking. If force is used to enlarge an opening so that entry can be made, the traditional rule was that this did not constitute a breaking. Under the better view, however, a breaking has occurred because force was used to gain entry.
Example: D, intending to steal a valuable painting inside V's house, approaches V's door. The door is open about six inches. D pushes it fully open and enters. Is D guilty of burglary? The best answer is yes, since force— although only minor force—was used to gain entry.

b. Constructive Breaking
Constructive breaking consists of gaining entry by means of fraud, threat, or intimidation, or by use of the chimney.
Example: P wants to get into V's apartment to commit a felonious assault on V, but V's door is securely locked. P knocks and when V asks who it is, P responds, "I am a friend of your brother and he asked me to deliver this message to you." V then unlocks the door and invites P in. P enters. P has never met V's brother. Is P guilty of burglary? Yes. Since entry was obtained by fraud, this is constructive breaking.

c. Requirement of Trespass—Consent to Enter
A breaking requires a trespass, so that if the defendant had the consent of the resident to enter, his use of force to gain entry is not a breaking. The existence of consent to enter

during limited periods, however, will not prevent entry by force at other times from being a breaking. Moreover, if the consent was procured by fraud or threats, this is a constructive breaking.

d. Requirement that Breaking Be "Of the House"
The breaking must be to effect entry into the structure or some separately secured subportion of it. Thus, it is sufficient that the defendant broke to enter a closed closet or wall safe within a dwelling, but it is not enough if he merely breaks open a box or trunk within the dwelling.

e. Breaking to Exit Insufficient
The breaking *must be to gain entry*. It is not burglary to hide in a dwelling, with the intent to commit a felony, and then break to get out of the dwelling.

2. Entry Required
Entry is made by placing any portion of the body inside the structure, even momentarily. Insertion of a tool or inanimate object into the structure is entry if it is inserted for the purpose of accomplishing the felony. It is not sufficient if it is inserted for purposes of gaining entry.

Examples: 1) A approached B's dwelling and shot a bullet through his window, intending to kill B. Has A committed burglary? *Held:* Yes. He has inserted an inanimate object into the dwelling by breaking for the purpose of committing the felony.

2) Z intends to go into V's house and steal valuable jewels from a safe. He carefully cuts out a small portion of glass from a window and reaches in with his hand to unlock the window. At that point he is apprehended. Is Z guilty of burglary? Yes. His hand had "entered" the dwelling.

3. "Dwelling"—Used for Sleeping Purposes
A structure is a dwelling if it is used with regularity for sleeping purposes.

a. Used for Other Purposes—Still a Dwelling
A structure remains a dwelling even if it is also used for other purposes, such as conducting a business.

b. Temporary Absence of Inhabitants—Still a Dwelling
Temporary absence of those dwelling in a structure will not deprive it of its character as a dwelling. It is not a dwelling, however, before anyone has moved in, even if it was built for use as a dwelling, nor does it remain a dwelling after the last dweller has moved out with no intent to return.

4. "Of Another"—Occupancy Is Determinative
The requirement is that the structure be used as a dwelling by someone other than the defendant. Occupancy rather than ownership is material. An owner can commit burglary of his own structure if it is rented and used as a dwelling by others.

5. Requirement of Nighttime
Burglary could be committed only during the nighttime, defined as that period during which the countenance of a person could not be discerned by natural light.

6. **Required Intent—Intent to Commit a Felony at Time of Entry**
The defendant must have intended to commit a felony. It is not necessary that this be carried out. It is, however, essential that the intent exist at the time of entry; if the intent is formed after entry is completed, burglary is not committed.

7. **Modern Statutory Changes**
Modern statutes have modified the common law definition of burglary in a variety of ways that differ among jurisdictions. Some of the most common are as follows:

   a. **Abandonment of Requirement of Breaking**
   In many jurisdictions, it is sufficient that the defendant entered the structure, even if he did not break to gain entry.

   b. **Remaining in a Structure**
   It is often a burglary to remain concealed in a structure with the intent to commit an offense.

   c. **Broadening Structures that Can Be Burglarized**
   The description of structures that can be burglarized is often expanded beyond dwellings and sometimes beyond structures to include yards and cars.

   d. **Elimination of Nighttime Requirement**
   The requirement that entry be at nighttime is often abandoned, although burglary at nighttime is often assigned a more severe penalty than other burglaries. Nighttime is often defined by statute in terms of sunset and sunrise.

   e. **Intent to Commit Misdemeanor Theft**
   The intent necessary is often expanded to make it sufficient that the defendant intended to commit any theft, even if it was misdemeanor theft.

B. **ARSON**
At common law, arson consists of:

(i)   The malicious;

(ii) Burning;

(iii) Of the dwelling;

(iv) Of another.

1. **Requirement of a "Burning"**

   a. **Necessity of Fire**
   At common law, the required damage (*see* below) must be caused by *fire*; damage caused by an explosion does not constitute arson.

   b. **Damage Required—"Scorching" (Insufficient) vs. "Charring" (Sufficient)**
   Traditionally, destruction of the structure or even significant damage to it is not required

to complete the crime of arson. But mere blackening by smoke or discoloration by heat (scorching) is not sufficient. There must be some damage to the fiber of the wood or other combustible material; this is generally stated as the rule that "mere charring is sufficient."

2. **"Dwelling"**
At common law, dwelling was defined for arson as it was for burglary. (*See* above.) Most states by statute extend arson to structures other than dwellings. (*Note:* Questions on the Multistate Exam that are testing on other arson issues (e.g., malice) will often assume without saying that the jurisdiction's arson law applies to structures other than dwellings.)

3. **"Of Another"—Ownership Immaterial**
Arson, like burglary, is a crime against the habitation. Thus, the structure had to be used as a dwelling by another; ownership was not material, even if the defendant himself was the owner. (*Note:* At common law, the burning of one's house was the misdemeanor of "house-burning" if other dwellings were nearby.)

4. **State of Mind Required—Malice**
The burning does not have to be with ill will or for any particular motive. No specific intent is required. On the other hand, it is not sufficient that the burning was accidental, even if the defendant was negligent. All that malice requires is that the defendant have acted with the intent or knowledge that the structure would burn, or with *reckless disregard* of an obvious risk that the structure would burn.

5. **Related Offenses**

    a. **Houseburning**
    The common law misdemeanor of houseburning consists of:

        1) Malicious (as defined in arson);

        2) Burning;

        3) Of one's own dwelling;

        4) If the structure is situated either:

            a) In a city or town; or

            b) So near to other houses as to create a danger to them.

    b. **Arson with Intent to Defraud an Insurer**
    At common law, it was not arson to burn one's own dwelling for purposes of fraudulently collecting the insurance on it. But this is often made an offense by modern statutes.

6. **Modern Statutory Changes**
Like statutory changes for burglary, modern arson statutes (including the M.P.C.) have modified the common law rules, usually to expand potential criminal liability. Most states

have expanded the definition of arson to include damage caused by explosion, and expanded the types of property that may be destroyed to include commercial structures, cars, trains, etc.

XI. OFFENSES INVOLVING JUDICIAL PROCEDURE

A. PERJURY

A misdemeanor at common law, perjury consisted of the willful and corrupt taking of a false oath in regard to a material matter in a judicial proceeding.

1. Materiality

Materiality is an element of this offense, which must be alleged in the indictment and proved by the prosecution. The statement is material if it might affect some phase or detail of the trial, hearing, declaration, etc.

2. Contradictory Statements

If a witness has made two contradictory statements at the same proceeding and admits, before the end of the proceeding, that one of the statements is false, he cannot be prosecuted for having made the false statement. This is to encourage witnesses to correct any false statements they may have made before substantial damage is caused.

3. Civil Liability

In litigation brought under 42 U.S.C. section 1983 (Civil Rights Act), all witnesses—including police officers—are absolutely immune from civil liability based on their testimony (i.e., alleged perjury) in judicial proceedings. [Briscoe v. LaHue, 460 U.S. 325 (1983)]

B. SUBORNATION OF PERJURY

A separate offense at common law, subornation of perjury consists of procuring or inducing another to commit perjury. In some states, this is not part of the perjury statute.

C. BRIBERY

The common law misdemeanor of bribery consisted of the corrupt payment or receipt of anything of value in return for official action. Under modern statutes, it can be a felony, and it may be extended to classes of persons who are not public officials (e.g., athletes). Either the offering of a bribe or the taking of a bribe may constitute the crime.

1. Mutual Criminal Intent Unnecessary

It is not necessary that there be mutual criminal intent on the part of both the person tendering the bribe and the recipient.

2. Failure to Report a Bribe

Some statutes also make it a misdemeanor offense to fail to report a bribe.

D. COMPOUNDING A CRIME

At common law, the misdemeanor of compounding a crime consisted of entering into an agreement *for valuable consideration* to not prosecute another for a felony or to conceal the commission of a felony or whereabouts of a felon. Under modern statutes, the definition remains essentially the same, except that it refers to *any crime* (not only felonies). A few states make it a felony offense.

E. MISPRISION OF A FELONY

At common law, the misdemeanor of misprision of a felony consisted of the failure—by someone other than a principal or accessory before the fact—to disclose or report knowledge of the commission of a felony. Misprision was distinguished from compounding a crime in that no passage of consideration was required for the former. Today, most jurisdictions do not recognize the crime of misprision of a felony. In these jurisdictions, therefore, a person is under *no obligation to report a crime*.

CRIMINAL PROCEDURE

CRIMINAL PROCEDURE

TABLE OF CONTENTS

CRIMINAL PROCEDURE

I. INTRODUCTION

A. CONSTITUTIONAL RESTRAINTS ON CRIMINAL PROCEDURE

The development of numerous constitutional limitations upon the manner in which a criminal suspect may be arrested, convicted, and punished has rendered much of criminal procedure an inquiry into constitutional law.

B. INCORPORATION OF BILL OF RIGHTS INTO DUE PROCESS

The first eight amendments to the United States Constitution apply by their terms only to the federal government. However, the Supreme Court has incorporated many of these rights into the due process requirement binding on the states by virtue of the Fourteenth Amendment. Those portions of the Bill of Rights "fundamental to our concept of ordered liberty" have been so incorporated. [Duncan v. Louisiana, 391 U.S. 145 (1968)]

C. CONSTITUTIONAL REQUIREMENTS BINDING ON STATES

The following rights have been held binding on the states under the due process provisions of the Fourteenth Amendment:

(i) The Fourth Amendment *prohibition against unreasonable searches and seizures* [Wolf v. Colorado, 338 U.S. 25 (1949)], and the *exclusionary rule* requiring that the result of a violation of this prohibition not be used as evidence against the defendant [Mapp v. Ohio, 367 U.S. 643 (1961)];

(ii) The Fifth Amendment *privilege against compulsory self-incrimination* [Malloy v. Hogan, 378 U.S. 1 (1964)];

(iii) The Fifth Amendment *prohibition against double jeopardy* [Benton v. Maryland, 395 U.S. 784 (1969)];

(iv) The Sixth Amendment right to a *speedy trial* [Klopfer v. North Carolina, 386 U.S. 213 (1967)];

(v) The Sixth Amendment right to a *public trial* [*In re* Oliver, 333 U.S. 257 (1948)];

(vi) The Sixth Amendment right to *trial by jury* [Duncan v. Louisiana, 391 U.S. 145 (1968)];

(vii) The Sixth Amendment right to *confront witnesses* [Pointer v. Texas, 380 U.S. 400 (1965)];

(viii) The Sixth Amendment right to *compulsory process* for obtaining witnesses [Washington v. Texas, 388 U.S. 14 (1967)];

(ix) The Sixth Amendment right to *assistance of counsel* in felony cases [Gideon v. Wainwright, 372 U.S. 335 (1963)], and in misdemeanor cases in which imprisonment is imposed [Argersinger v. Hamlin, 407 U.S. 25 (1972)]; and

(x) The Eighth Amendment *prohibition against cruel and unusual punishment* [Robinson v. California, 370 U.S. 660 (1962)].

Note: The Constitution provides the floor of protection for criminal defendants. States are free to grant greater protection, and many do.

D. CONSTITUTIONAL RIGHTS NOT BINDING ON STATES
Two provisions of the Bill of Rights have not been held binding on the states.

1. Right to Indictment
The right to indictment by a grand jury for capital and infamous crimes has been held not to be binding on the states. [Hurtado v. California, 110 U.S. 516 (1884)]

2. Prohibition Against Excessive Bail
It has not yet been determined whether the Eighth Amendment prohibition against excessive bail creates a right to bail (or whether it simply prohibits excessive bail where the right to bail exists) and whether it is binding on the states. However, most state constitutions create a right to bail and prohibit excessive bail.

II. FOURTH AMENDMENT

A. IN GENERAL
The Fourth Amendment provides that people should be free in their persons from ***unreasonable*** searches and seizures.

1. Search
A search can be defined as a governmental intrusion into an area where a person has a reasonable and justifiable expectation of privacy.

2. Seizure
A seizure can be defined as the exercise of control by the government over a person or thing.

3. Reasonableness
What is reasonable under the Fourth Amendment depends on the circumstances. For example, certain searches and seizures are considered to be reasonable only if the government has first obtained a warrant authorizing the action, while other searches and seizures are reasonable without a warrant. The material that follows specifically outlines the requirements for searches and seizures under the Fourth Amendment.

B. ARRESTS AND OTHER DETENTIONS
Governmental detentions of persons, including arrests, certainly constitute seizures of the person, so they must be reasonable to comply with the Fourth Amendment. Whether a seizure of the person is reasonable depends on the scope of the seizure (e.g., is it an arrest or merely an investigatory stop?) and the strength of the suspicion prompting the seizure (e.g., an arrest requires probable cause, while an investigatory detention can be based on reasonable suspicion).

1. What Constitutes a Seizure of the Person?
Generally, it is obvious when police arrest or seize a person. When it is not readily apparent, the Supreme Court has indicated that a seizure occurs only when, under the ***totality of the circumstances***, a reasonable person would feel that he was not free to decline the officer's

requests or otherwise terminate the encounter. [Florida v. Bostick, 501 U.S. 429 (1991)] In this regard, police pursuit of a suspect is not a seizure in and of itself. To constitute a seizure, the Fourth Amendment requires a ***physical application of force*** by the officer or a ***submission*** to the officer's show of force. It is not enough that the officer merely ordered the person to stop. [California v. Hodari D., 499 U.S. 621 (1991)]

Example: Without a warrant or probable cause, at around 3 a.m. in January, six police officers went to Kaupp's home. At least three officers entered his room, awoke him, and told him that they wanted him to "go and talk" about a murder. Kaupp replied, "Okay" and was handcuffed and taken out of his house, shoeless and dressed only in his underwear. Kaupp was taken to the murder scene and then to the police station, where he confessed to playing a minor role in the crime. Kaupp's attorney sought to have Kaupp's confession suppressed as the fruit of an illegal arrest, but the court ruled that Kaupp was not arrested until after his confession—he consented to going to the police station by saying, "Okay" and was handcuffed only pursuant to a policy adopted to protect officers when transporting persons in their squad cars. Kaupp was convicted and sentenced to 55 years' imprisonment. The Supreme Court overturned the conviction on appeal, finding that Kaupp's "Okay" was merely an assent to the exercise of police authority, that a reasonable person would not know that the handcuffs were merely for the protection of the officers, and that it cannot seriously be suggested that under the circumstances a reasonable person would feel free to tell the officers when questioning started that he wanted to go home and go back to bed. [Kaupp v. Texas, 538 U.S. 626 (2003)]

Compare: Officers boarded a bus shortly before its departure and asked individuals for identification and consent to search their luggage. The mere fact that people felt they were not free to leave because they feared that the bus would depart does not make this a seizure of the person.

2.   **Arrests**

An arrest occurs when the police take a person into custody against her will for purposes of criminal prosecution or interrogation.

a.   **Probable Cause Requirement**

An arrest must be based on probable cause. Probable cause to arrest is present when, at the time of arrest, the officer has within her knowledge reasonably trustworthy facts and circumstances sufficient to warrant a reasonably prudent person to believe that the suspect has committed or is committing a crime for which arrest is authorized by law. [Beck v. Ohio, 379 U.S. 89 (1964)] Probable cause is based on the totality of the circumstances. [District of Columbia v. Wesby, 138 S. Ct. 577 (2018)]

Examples: D was in the front passenger seat of a car that the police stopped for speeding late at night. The driver consented to a search of the car. The police found almost $800 in the car's glove compartment and bags of cocaine hidden in the back seat. None of the men admitted ownership of these items. Under the circumstances, the police had probable cause to believe that D, alone or with the other occupants, committed the crime of possession of cocaine. [Maryland v. Pringle, 540 U.S. 366 (2004)]

The police had probable cause to arrest 21 partygoers who were engaged in various forms of debauchery in a seemingly abandoned house. "Taken together, the condition of the house and the conduct of the partygoers allowed the officers to make several 'common-sense' conclusions about human behavior…Most homeowners do not live in near-barren houses. And most homeowners do not invite people over to use their living room as a strip club, to have sex in their bedroom, to smoke marijuana inside, and to leave their floors filthy. The officers could thus infer that the partygoers knew their party was not authorized" and arrest the partygoers for unlawful entry. [District of Columbia v. Wesby, *supra*]

1) Mistaken Offense

An arrest is not invalid merely because the grounds stated for the arrest at the time it was made are erroneous, as long as the officers had other grounds on which there was probable cause for the arrest. [Devenpeck v. Alford, 543 U.S. 146 (2005)]

Example: Police officers pulled Defendant over on suspicion that he was impersonating an officer because his car had police-type lights. They found his answers to their questioning evasive. Upon discovering that Defendant was taping their conversation, they arrested him, erroneously thinking that the taping violated a state privacy law. *Held:* If the officers had probable cause to arrest Defendant for impersonating an officer, the arrest was valid; it does not matter that they lacked probable cause for the "offense" they stated at the time of the arrest. [Devenpeck v. Alford, *supra*]

b. Warrant Generally Not Required

In contrast to the rule for searches, police generally need not obtain a warrant before arresting a person in a ***public place***, even if they have time to get a warrant. [United States v. Watson, 423 U.S. 411 (1976)]

1) Felony

A police officer may arrest a person without a warrant when she has ***probable cause to believe*** that a felony has been committed and that the person before her committed it.

2) Misdemeanor

An officer may make a warrantless arrest for a misdemeanor ***committed in her presence***. A crime is committed in the officer's "presence" if she is aware of it through any of her senses.

Note: The police may make a warrantless misdemeanor arrest even if the crime for which the arrest is made cannot be punished by incarceration. [Atwater v. Lago Vista, 532 U.S. 318 (2001)]

3) Exception—Home Arrests Require Warrant

The police must have an arrest warrant to effect a nonemergency arrest of an individual in her own home. The officers executing the warrant may enter the suspect's home only if there is reason to believe the suspect is within it. [Payton v. New York, 445 U.S. 573 (1980)] All warrantless searches of homes are presumed unreasonable. The burden is on the government to demonstrate sufficient exigent circumstances to overcome this presumption. [Welsh v. Wisconsin, 466 U.S. 740 (1984)]

a) Homes of Third Parties

Absent exigent circumstances, the police executing an arrest warrant may not search for the subject of the warrant in the home of a third party without first obtaining a separate search warrant for the home. If the police do execute an arrest warrant at the home of a third party without obtaining a search warrant for the home, the arrest is still valid (*see* c., below), but evidence of any crime found in the home cannot be used against the owner of the home since it is the fruit of an unconstitutional search. [Steagald v. United States, 451 U.S. 204 (1981)] However, the arrestee will ***not*** be able to have such evidence suppressed unless he can establish a legitimate expectation of privacy in the home. (*See* C.3.a.1), *infra*.)

c. Effect of Invalid Arrest

An unlawful arrest, ***by itself***, has no impact on a subsequent criminal prosecution. Thus, if the police improperly arrest a person (e.g., at his home without a warrant), they may detain him if they have probable cause to do so [*see* New York v. Harris, 495 U.S. 14 (1990)], and the invalid arrest is not a defense to the offense charged [Frisbie v. Collins, 342 U.S. 519 (1952)]. Of course, evidence that is a fruit of the unlawful arrest may not be used against the defendant at trial because of the exclusionary rule.

3. Other Detentions

a. Investigatory Detentions (Stop and Frisk)

Police have the authority to briefly detain a person for investigative purposes even if they lack probable cause to arrest. To make such a stop, police must have a ***reasonable suspicion*** supported by ***articulable facts*** of criminal activity or involvement in a completed crime. [Terry v. Ohio, 392 U.S. 1 (1968)] *Note.* If the police also have reasonable suspicion to believe that the detainee is ***armed and dangerous***, they may also conduct a frisk (a limited search) to ensure that the detainee has no weapons (*see* C.5.e., *infra*).

1) Reasonable Suspicion Defined

The Court has not specifically defined "reasonable suspicion." It requires something more than a vague suspicion (e.g., it is not enough that the detainee was in a crime-filled area [Brown v. Texas, 443 U.S. 47 (1979)]), but full probable cause is not required. Whether the standard is met is judged under the ***totality of the circumstances***. [United States v. Sokolow, 490 U.S. 1 (1989)]

Examples: 1) Reasonable suspicion justifying a stop is present when: (i) a suspect who is standing on a corner in a high crime area (ii) flees after noticing the presence of the police. Neither factor standing alone is enough to justify a stop, but together they are sufficiently suspicious. [Illinois v. Wardlow, 528 U.S. 119 (2000)]

2) Police had reasonable suspicion—and therefore there was no Fourth Amendment violation—where they detained Defendant

at an airport while dogs sniffed his bags for drugs based on the following facts known by the police: (i) Defendant paid for airline tickets in cash with small bills; (ii) Defendant traveled under a name that did not match the name for the phone number he gave; (iii) Defendant traveled to a drug source city (Miami) and stayed for only 48 hours, while his flight time was 20 hours; (iv) Defendant appeared nervous; and (v) Defendant refused to check his bags. [United States v. Sokolow, *supra*] *Note:* The fact that these suspicious circumstances are part of a drug courier profile used by the police neither helps nor hurts the totality of the circumstances inquiry.

2) Source of Suspicion

Like probable cause, reasonable suspicion need not arise from a police officer's personal knowledge. The suspicion can be based on a flyer, a police bulletin, or a report from an informant. [United States v. Hensley, 469 U.S. 221 (1985)]

a) Informant's Tips

Where the source of suspicion of criminal activity is an informant's tip, the tip must be accompanied by *indicia of reliability*, including predictive information, sufficient to make the officer's suspicion reasonable.

Example: Police received an anonymous tip asserting that a woman was carrying cocaine and predicting that she would leave a specified apartment at a specified time, get into a specified car, and drive to a specified motel. After observing that the informant had accurately predicted the suspect's movements, it was reasonable for the police to think that the informant had inside knowledge that the suspect indeed had cocaine, thus justifying a *Terry* stop. [Alabama v. White, 496 U.S. 325 (1990)]

Compare: Police received an anonymous tip that a young black man in a plaid shirt standing at a particular bus stop was carrying a gun. When police arrived at the bus stop, they found a young black man there wearing a plaid shirt. They searched the man and found an illegal gun. Here there was not sufficient indicia of reliability in the tip to provide reasonable suspicion. The fact that the informant knows a person is standing at a bus stop does not show knowledge of any inside information; any passerby could observe the suspect's presence. Unlike the tip in *White,* the tip here did not provide predictive information and left police with no way to test the informant's knowledge and credibility. [Florida v. J.L., 529 U.S. 266 (2000)]

3) Duration and Scope

While investigatory stops generally are brief, they are not subject to a specific time limit. For a stop to be valid, the police must act in a *diligent and reasonable manner in confirming or dispelling their suspicions.* [United States v. Sharpe, 470 U.S. 675 (1985)—20-minute stop deemed reasonable where officers investigated their suspicions diligently and the suspect's evasive conduct prolonged the encounter]

a) Identification May Be Required

As long as the police have the reasonable suspicion required to make a *Terry* stop, they may require the detained person to identify himself (that is, state his name), and the detainee may be arrested for failure to comply with such a requirement. [Hiibel v. Sixth Judicial District Court, 542 U.S. 177 (2004)] In dicta, the Court suggested that it would recognize an exception to this rule under the Fifth Amendment right against self-incrimination (*see* XIV., *infra*) if by merely giving his name, the detainee may incriminate himself, but noted that such a case would be rare.

4) Development of Probable Cause

If during an investigatory detention, the officer develops probable cause, the detention becomes an arrest, and the officer can proceed on that basis. He can, for example, conduct a full search incident to that arrest.

5) What Constitutes a Stop?

If an officer merely approaches a person but does not detain her, no arrest or investigatory detention occurs. Not even reasonable suspicion is necessary in such cases. A seizure or stop occurs only if a reasonable person would believe she is not free to decline an officer's requests or otherwise terminate the encounter. (*See* B.1., *supra*.)

6) Property Seizures on Reasonable Suspicion

Police may briefly seize items upon reasonable suspicion that they are or contain contraband or evidence, but such seizures must be limited. [United States v. Place, 462 U.S. 696 (1983)—90-minute detention of luggage reasonably suspected to contain drugs unconstitutional]

b. Automobile Stops

Stopping a car is a seizure for Fourth Amendment purposes. Thus, generally, police officers may not stop a car unless they have *at least reasonable suspicion* to believe that a law has been violated. However, in certain cases where *special law enforcement needs* are involved, the Court allows police officers to set up roadblocks to stop cars without individualized suspicion that the driver has violated some law. To be valid, it appears that such roadblocks must:

(i) Stop cars on the basis of some *neutral, articulable standard* (e.g., every car or every third car); and

(ii) Be designed to serve purposes *closely related to a particular problem pertaining to automobiles and their mobility*.

[*See* Delaware v. Prouse, 440 U.S. 648 (1979); *and see* Indianapolis v. Edmond, 531 U.S. 32 (2000)]

Examples: 1) Because of the gravity of the drunk driving problem and the magnitude of the states' interest in getting drunk drivers off the roads, police may set up roadblocks to check the sobriety of all drivers passing by. [Michigan Department of State Police v. Sitz, 496 U.S. 444 (1990)]

2) Because of the difficulty of discerning whether an automobile is transporting illegal aliens, police may set up roadblocks near the border to stop every car to check the citizenship of its occupants. [United States v. Martinez-Fuerte, 428 U.S. 543 (1976); *and see* United States v. Villamonte-Marquez, 462 U.S. 579 (1983)—suspicionless boarding of boat in channel leading to open sea justified on similar grounds]

Compare: The police may not set up roadblocks to check cars for illegal drugs. The nature of such a checkpoint is to detect evidence of ordinary criminal wrongdoing unrelated to use of cars or highway safety. If suspicionless stops were allowed under these circumstances, all suspicionless seizures would be justified. [Indianapolis v. Edmond, *supra*]

1) Police Officer's Mistake of Law

A police officer's mistake of law that gives rise to reasonable suspicion does not invalidate a seizure as long as the mistake was ***reasonable***. [Heien v. North Carolina, 135 S. Ct. 530 (2014)—police officer's reasonable mistake that a vehicle must have two working brake lights, when in fact only one was required by law, did not invalidate the stop and subsequent arrests of defendants who were in a car with one working brake light]

2) Seizure of Occupants

An automobile stop constitutes a seizure not only of the automobile's driver, but also any passengers as well. *Rationale:* Such a stop curtails the travel of the passengers as well the driver, and a reasonable passenger in a stopped vehicle would not feel free to leave the scene without police permission. [Brendlin v. California, 551 U.S. 249 (2007)]

Example: Officer pulled Driver's car over for, admittedly, no valid reason. Upon approaching Driver's car and asking Driver for her license, Officer noticed that Passenger resembled a person wanted for parole violation. Officer confirmed his suspicion via radio and arrested Passenger. Upon searching Passenger, Officer discovered drug paraphernalia. *Held:* Passenger has standing to challenge the admissibility of the drug paraphernalia as the fruit of an unlawful seizure.

3) Distinguish—Informational Roadblocks

If the police set up a roadblock for purposes other than to seek incriminating information about the drivers stopped, the roadblock likely will be constitutional.

Example: The police set up a roadblock to ask drivers if they had any information about a deadly hit and run that occurred a week earlier, approximately where the roadblock was set up. D was arrested at the roadblock for driving under the influence of alcohol after he nearly ran over one of the officers stationed at the roadblock.

The Court held that the roadblock and arrest were constitutional. [Illinois v. Lidster, 540 U.S. 419 (2004)]

4) Police May Order Occupants Out

Provided that a police officer has lawfully stopped a vehicle, in the interest of officer safety, the officer may order the occupants (that is, the vehicle's driver *and* passengers) to get out. Moreover, if the officer reasonably believes that the detainee is armed and dangerous, she may conduct a frisk of the detainee. She may also search the passenger compartment of the vehicle to look for weapons, even after the driver and other occupants have been ordered out of the vehicle. [Pennsylvania v. Mimms, 434 U.S. 106 (1977); Maryland v. Wilson, 519 U.S. 408 (1997); Thornton v. United States, 541 U.S. 615 (2004)]

5) Pretextual Stops

If an officer has probable cause to believe that a traffic law has been violated, the officer may stop the suspect's automobile, even if the officer's ulterior motive is to investigate a crime for which the officer lacks sufficient cause to make a stop. [Whren v. United States, 517 U.S. 806 (1996)—police in a high drug crime area stopped D's automobile after observing D wait a long time at an intersection, abruptly turn without signaling, and speed off at an unreasonable speed; *and see* Arkansas v. Sullivan, 532 U.S. 769 (2001)] Furthermore, as long as the police do not extend the valid stop beyond the time necessary to issue a ticket and conduct ordinary inquiries incident to such a stop, it does not violate the Fourth Amendment to allow a narcotics detection dog to sniff the car. [Illinois v. Caballes, 543 U.S. 405 (2005); *and see* C.3.b.1)b), *infra*]

c. Detention to Obtain a Warrant

If the police have probable cause to believe that a suspect has hidden drugs in his house, they may, for a reasonable time, prohibit him from going into the house unaccompanied so that they can prevent him from destroying the drugs while they obtain a search warrant. [Illinois v. McArthur, 531 U.S. 326 (2001)—police kept suspect from reentering his trailer alone for two hours while an officer obtained a warrant]

d. Occupants of Premises Being Searched May Be Detained

Pursuant to the execution of a *valid warrant* to search for contraband, the police may detain occupants of the premises while a proper search is conducted. [Michigan v. Summers, 452 U.S. 692 (1981)]

e. Station House Detention

Police officers must have *full probable cause* for arrest to bring a suspect to the station against the suspect's will for questioning [Dunaway v. New York, 442 U.S. 200 (1969)] or for fingerprinting [Hayes v. Florida, 470 U.S. 811 (1985)].

4. Grand Jury Appearance

For all practical purposes, seizure of a person (by subpoena) for a grand jury appearance is *not within the Fourth Amendment's protection*. Even if, in addition to testifying, the person is to be asked to give handwriting or voice exemplars, there is no need for the subpoena to be based on probable cause or even objective suspicion. In other words, a person compelled to appear cannot assert that it was unreasonable to compel the appearance. However, the

Supreme Court has suggested that it is conceivable that such a subpoena could be unreasonable if it was extremely broad and sweeping or if it was being used for harassment purposes. [United States v. Dionisio, 410 U.S. 1 (1973); United States v. Mara, 410 U.S. 19 (1973)]

5. **Deadly Force**

There is a Fourth Amendment "seizure" when a police officer uses deadly force to apprehend a suspect. An officer may not use deadly force unless it is *reasonable* to do so under the circumstances. [Scott v. Harris, 550 U.S. 372 (2007)]

Example: It was reasonable for an officer to end a chase by bumping a suspect's car (which ultimately resulted in the suspect's becoming a paraplegic) where the suspect was driving at high speeds and weaving in and out of traffic. Under such circumstances, the suspect's conduct posed an immediate threat to his own life and the lives of innocent bystanders. [Scott v. Harris, *supra*]

Compare: It was unreasonable to shoot a fleeing burglar who refused to stop when ordered to do so where there was no evidence that the suspect was armed or posed any threat to the police or others. [Tennessee v. Garner, 471 U.S. 1 (1985)]

C. EVIDENTIARY SEARCH AND SEIZURE

Like arrests, evidentiary searches and seizures must be reasonable to be valid under the Fourth Amendment. Reasonableness here usually means that the police must have obtained a warrant before conducting the search, but there are six circumstances where a warrant is not required (*see* 5., *infra*).

1. **General Approach**

A useful analytical model of the law of search and seizure requires answers to the following questions:

a. Does the defendant have a *Fourth Amendment right*?

1) Was there *governmental conduct*?

2) Did the defendant have a *reasonable expectation of privacy*?

b. If so, did the police have a *valid warrant*?

c. If the police did not have a valid warrant, was the search within one of the six exceptions to the warrant requirement?

2. **Governmental Conduct Required**

The Fourth Amendment generally protects only against governmental conduct and not against searches by private persons. The term "government agents" here includes only the *publicly paid officials* and those *citizens acting at their direction* or behest; private security guards are not government agents unless deputized as officers of the public police.

Example: A private freight carrier opened a package and resealed it; police later reopened the package. The Supreme Court found that this was not a "search" under the Fourth Amendment because the police found nothing more than the private carrier had found. Moreover, the warrantless field test of a substance found in the package to determine whether it was cocaine was not a Fourth Amendment "seizure," even though the testing went beyond the scope of the original private search. [United States v. Jacobsen, 466 U.S. 109 (1984)]

3. **Physical Intrusion into Constitutionally Protected Area or Violation of Reasonable Expectation of Privacy**

There are two ways in which searches and seizures can implicate an individual's Fourth Amendment rights: (i) search or seizure by a government agent of a constitutionally protected area in which the individual had a reasonable expectation of privacy; or (ii) physical intrusion by the government into a constitutionally protected area to obtain information.

Example: The government's installation of a GPS tracking device on a vehicle, and the use of the device to monitor the vehicle's movements, constituted a physical intrusion into a constitutionally protected area (that is., it was a trespass as to the vehicle) and, as such, was a search governed by the Fourth Amendment. [United States v. Jones, 565 U.S. 400 (2012)]

a. **Standing**

It is not enough merely that *someone* has an expectation of privacy in the place searched or the item seized. The Supreme Court has imposed a standing requirement so that a person can complain about an evidentiary search or seizure only if it violates his *own* reasonable expectations of privacy. [Rakas v. Illinois, 439 U.S. 128 (1978)] Whether a person has a *reasonable expectation of privacy* generally is based on the *totality of the circumstances*, considering factors such as ownership of the place searched and location of the item seized. [Rawlings v. Kentucky, 448 U.S. 98 (1980)] The Court has held that a person has a reasonable expectation of privacy any time:

(i) She *owned or had a right to possession* of the place searched;

(ii) The *place searched was in fact her home*, whether or not she owned or had a right to possession of it; or

(iii) She was an *overnight guest* of the owner of the place searched [Minnesota v. Olson, 495 U.S. 91 (1990)].

1) **Search of Third-Party Premises**

Standing does not exist merely because a person will be harmed by introduction of evidence seized during an illegal search of a third person's property.

Example: A police officer peered through the closed window blind of Lessee's apartment and observed Lessee and defendants bagging cocaine. When defendants left the apartment, the officer followed them to their car and arrested them. The car and apartment were searched, and cocaine and a weapon were found. At trial, defendants moved to suppress all evidence, claiming that the officer's peeking through the window blind constituted an illegal search. It was determined that defendants had spent little time in Lessee's apartment and had come there solely to conduct a business transaction (that is, bagging the cocaine). *Held:* The defendants did not have a sufficient expectation of privacy in the apartment. They were there only for a few hours and were not overnight guests. Moreover, they were there for business purposes rather than social purposes, and there is a lesser expectation of privacy in commercial settings. Therefore, the defendants had no Fourth Amendment protections in the apartment and cannot challenge the search. [Minnesota v. Carter, 525 U.S. 83 (1999)]

2) No Automatic Standing to Object to Seizure of Evidence in Possessory Offense

Formerly, a defendant had automatic standing to object to the legality of a search and seizure any time the evidence obtained was introduced against her in a possessory offense. (This allowed a defendant to challenge the search without specifically admitting possession of the items.) Because a defendant at a suppression hearing may now assert a legitimate expectation of privacy in the items without his testimony being used against him at trial [*see* Simmons v. United States, V.D.3, *infra*], the automatic standing rule has been abolished as unnecessary [United States v. Salvucci, 448 U.S. 83 (1980)].

3) No Automatic Standing for Co-Conspirator

That a co-conspirator may be aggrieved by the introduction of damaging evidence does not give the co-conspirator automatic standing to challenge the seizure of the evidence; the co-conspirator must show that her own expectation of privacy was violated. [United States v. Padilla, 508 U.S. 77 (1993)]

b. Things Held Out to the Public

1) Generally—No Expectation of Privacy

A person does not have a reasonable expectation of privacy in objects held out to the public, such as *the sound of one's voice* [United States v. Dionisio, B.4., *supra*]; one's *handwriting* [United States v. Mara, B.4., *supra*]; *paint on the outside of a car* [Cardwell v. Lewis, 417 U.S. 583 (1974)]; *the smell of one's luggage or car* (e.g., drug sniffs by narcotics dogs) [United States v. Place, 462 U.S. 696 (1983); Illinois v. Caballes, B.3.b.5), *supra*]; *account records held by the bank* [United States v. Miller, 425 U.S. 435 (1976)]; *or magazines offered for sale* [Maryland v. Macon, 472 U.S. 463 (1985)]. However, one does have a reasonable expectation of privacy in one's *cell-site location information* (that is, personal location information derived from cell phone usage data) which is stored in the hands of third parties. [Carpenter v. United States, 585 U.S. ___ (2018)]

a) Compare—Squeezing Luggage

Although the Supreme Court has held that one does not have a reasonable expectation of privacy in the smell of one's luggage, one does have a reasonable expectation of privacy in luggage against physically invasive inspections. Squeezing luggage to discern its contents constitutes a search. [Bond v. United States, 529 U.S. 334 (2000)]

Example: After completing an immigration status check of passengers on a bus, Officer began walking toward the front of the bus and squeezing soft-sided luggage in the overhead compartment. Upon feeling what felt like a brick in Defendant's bag,

Officer searched the bag and found a "brick" of methamphet-amine. The Court held that while travelers might expect their luggage to be lightly touched or moved from time to time, they do not expect their luggage to be subjected to an exploratory squeeze. Therefore, Officer's conduct constitutes a search under the Fourth Amendment. [Bond v. United States, *supra*]

b) Dog Sniffs at Traffic Stops

As long as police officers have ***lawfully stopped*** a car and ***do not extend the stop*** beyond the time necessary to issue a ticket and conduct ordinary inquiries incident to such a stop, a dog sniff of the car does not implicate the Fourth Amendment. [Illinois v. Caballes, *supra*—Fourth Amendment was not violated when, during a routine traffic stop, a police officer walked a narcotics detection dog around defendant's car and the dog alerted to the presence of drugs, even though before the dog alerted, the officer did not have a reasonable and articulable suspicion that would justify a search; the sniff is not a search] However, police officers may not extend an otherwise-completed traffic stop, absent ***reasonable suspicion***, in order to complete a dog sniff. The key question is not whether the dog sniff occurs before the police issue the ticket, but rather whether the dog sniff adds time to the stop. [Rodriguez v. United States, 135 S. Ct. 1609 (2015)—it was a violation of the Fourth Amendment when a police officer issued the defendant a warning ticket, thereby completing the traffic stop, and then detained the defendant for seven to eight minutes to conduct a dog sniff]

Note: During a routine traffic stop, a dog "alert" to the presence of drugs can form the basis for probable cause to justify a search of the automobile. [Florida v. Harris, 568 U.S. 237 (2013)]

c) Dog Sniffs at Entry to Home

Although the entry to a home is within the curtilage protected by the Fourth Amendment against unreasonable searches (*see* below), a police officer may approach a home in hopes of speaking to its occupants—just like a private citizen, such as a neighbor or a delivery person. However, the scope of the license is limited. Police officers may not exceed the license by having a drug dog sniff around the entry or other areas within the curtilage. Such a physical intrusion into a constitutionally protected area constitutes a "search" within the meaning of the Fourth Amendment, and therefore requires a valid warrant or warrant exception. [Florida v. Jardines, 569 U.S. 1 (2013)—canine drug alert at defendant's front door could not be the basis of probable cause to obtain a search warrant; the sniff constituted an unconstitutional warrantless search]

2) "Open Fields" Doctrine

Furthermore, under the "open fields" doctrine, areas outside the "curtilage" (dwelling house and outbuildings) are subject to police entry and search—these areas are "held out to the public" and are unprotected by the Fourth Amendment. (The Court will consider the building's proximity to the dwelling, whether it is within the same enclosure—such as a fence—that surrounds the house, whether the building is used for activities of the home, and the steps taken by the resident to protect the building from the view of passersby.) [Oliver v. United States, 466 U.S. 170 (1984)] Even a building such as a barn may be considered to be outside the curtilage and therefore outside the protection of the Fourth Amendment. [United States v. Dunn, 480 U.S. 294 (1987)] In addition, the Fourth Amendment does not prohibit the warrantless search and seizure of garbage left for collection outside the curtilage of a home. [California v. Greenwood, 486 U.S. 35 (1988)]

3) Fly-Overs

The police may, within the Fourth Amendment, fly over a field or yard to observe with the naked eye things therein. [California v. Ciraolo, 476 U.S. 207 (1986)] Even a low (400 feet) fly-over by a helicopter to view inside a partially covered greenhouse is permissible. [Florida v. Riley, 488 U.S. 445 (1989)—plurality decision based on flight being permissible under FAA regulations] The police may also take aerial photographs of a particular site. [Dow Chemical Co. v. United States, 476 U.S. 227 (1986)]

a) Compare—Technologically Enhanced Searches of Homes

The Supreme Court has held that because of the strong expectation of privacy within one's home, obtaining by sense enhancing technology any information regarding the interior of a home that could not otherwise have been obtained without physical intrusion constitutes a search, at least where the technology in question is not in general public use. [Kyllo v. United States, 533 U.S. 27 (2001)—use of thermal imager on defendant's home from outside the curtilage to detect the presence of high intensity lamps commonly used to grow marijuana constitutes a search]

4) Automobiles

A police officer may constitutionally reach into an automobile to move papers to observe the auto's vehicle identification number. [New York v. Class, 475 U.S. 106 (1986)] However, the police may not covertly and trespassorily place a GPS tracking device on a person's automobile without a warrant. [United States v. Jones, 3., *supra*]

4. Searches Conducted Pursuant to a Warrant

To be reasonable under the Fourth Amendment, most searches by criminal law enforcement officers must be pursuant to a warrant. The warrant requirement serves as a check against unfettered police discretion by requiring police to apply to a neutral magistrate for permission to conduct a search. A search conducted without a warrant will be invalid (and evidence discovered during the search must be excluded from evidence) unless it is within one of the six categories of permissible warrantless searches (*see* 5., *infra*).

a. Requirements of a Warrant

To be valid, a warrant must:

1) Be issued by a *neutral and detached magistrate*;

2) Be *based on probable cause* established from facts submitted to the magistrate by a government agent upon oath or affirmation; and

3) *Particularly describe* the place to be searched and the items to be seized.

b. **Showing of Probable Cause**

A warrant will be issued only if there is probable cause to believe that seizable evidence will be found on the premises or person to be searched. [Carroll v. United States, 267 U.S. 132 (1925)] The officers requesting the warrant must submit to the magistrate an affidavit containing sufficient facts and circumstances to enable the magistrate to make an independent evaluation of probable cause (that is, the officers cannot merely present their conclusion that probable cause exists). [United States v. Ventresca, 380 U.S. 102 (1965)]

1) **May Be Anticipatory**

It is sufficient that there is reason to believe that seizable evidence will be found on the premises to be searched at a future date when the warrant will be executed; there need not be reason to believe that there is seizable material on the premises at the time the warrant is issued. [United States v. Grubbs, 547 U.S. 90 (2006)—warrant was properly issued when it "predicted" that seizable material would be found in defendant's home after police delivered to the home pornographic material that the defendant had ordered]

2) **Use of Informers—Totality of Circumstances Test**

If the officers' affidavit of probable cause is based on information obtained from informers, its sufficiency is determined by the *totality of the circumstances*. [Illinois v. Gates, 462 U.S. 213 (1983)] The affidavit need not contain any particular fact about the informer, as long as it includes enough information to allow the magistrate to make a common sense evaluation of probable cause (that is, that the information is trustworthy).

a) **Reliability, Credibility, and Basis of Knowledge**

Formerly, the affidavit had to include information regarding the reliability and credibility of the informer (e.g., she has given information five times in the past and it has been accurate) and her basis for the knowledge (e.g., she purchased cocaine from the house to be searched). These are still relevant factors, but are no longer prerequisites.

b) **Informer's Identity**

Generally, the informer's identity need *not* be revealed to obtain a search warrant [McCray v. Illinois, 386 U.S. 300 (1967)] (although if the informer is a material witness to the crime, her identity may have to be revealed at or before trial).

c) **Going "Behind the Face" of the Affidavit**

When a defendant attacks the validity of a search warrant, the Fourth Amendment permits her to contest the validity of some of the assertions in the affidavit upon which the warrant was issued. The defendant may go "behind the face" of the affidavit.

(1) **Three Requirements to Invalidate Search Warrant**

A search warrant issued on the basis of an affidavit that, on its face, is sufficient to establish probable cause will be invalid if the defendant establishes *all three* of the following:

(i) A *false statement* was included in the affidavit by the affiant (that is, the police officer applying for the warrant);

(ii) The affiant *intentionally or recklessly* included that false statement (that is, the officer either knew it was false or included it knowing that there was a substantial risk that it was false); and

(iii) The false statement was *material* to the finding of probable cause (that is, without the false statement, the remainder of the affidavit could not support a finding of probable cause). Thus, the mere fact that an affiant intentionally included a false statement in the affidavit apparently will not automatically render the warrant invalid under Fourth Amendment standards.

[Franks v. Delaware, 438 U.S. 154 (1978)]

(2) Evidence May Be Admissible Even Though Warrant Not Supported by Probable Cause
A finding that the warrant was invalid because it was not supported by probable cause will not entitle a defendant to exclude the evidence obtained under the warrant. Evidence obtained by police in *reasonable reliance* on a facially valid warrant may be used by the prosecution, despite an ultimate finding that the warrant was not supported by probable cause. [United States v. Leon, 468 U.S. 897 (1984); *and see* Massachusetts v. Sheppard, 468 U.S. 981 (1984)—technical defect in warrant insufficient basis for overturning murder conviction]

c. Warrant Must Be Precise on Its Face
The warrant must describe with reasonable precision the *place to be searched* and the *items to be seized*. If it does not, the warrant is unconstitutional, even if the underlying affidavit gives such detail. [Groh v. Ramirez, 540 U.S. 551 (2004)]
Examples: 1) A warrant authorizes the search of premises at 416 Oak Street for heroin. The structure at 416 Oak Street is a duplex. Is the warrant sufficiently precise? No. In a multi-unit dwelling, the warrant must specify which unit is to be searched. *But note:* If police reasonably believe there is only one apartment on the floor of a building, the warrant is not invalid if they discover, during the course of their search, that there are in fact two apartments on the floor. Indeed, any evidence police seize from the wrong apartment prior to the discovery of the error will be admissible. [Maryland v. Garrison, 480 U.S. 79 (1987)]

2) A was believed to have committed criminal fraud in regard to certain complex land transactions. A search warrant was issued authorizing the search for and seizure of numerous described documents and "other fruit, instrumentalities and evidence of the crime at this time unknown." Was the warrant sufficiently precise? Yes, given the complex nature of

the crime and the difficulty of predicting precisely what form evidence of guilt would take. [Andresen v. Maryland, 427 U.S. 463 (1976)]

d. Search of Third-Party Premises Permissible
The Fourth Amendment does not bar searches of premises belonging to persons not suspected of crime, as long as there is *probable cause* to believe evidence of someone's guilt (or something else subject to seizure) will be found. Thus, a warrant can issue for the search of the offices of a newspaper if there is probable cause to believe evidence of someone's guilt of an offense will be found. [Zurcher v. Stanford Daily, 436 U.S. 547 (1978)]

e. Neutral and Detached Magistrate Requirement
The magistrate who issues the warrant must be neutral and detached from the often competitive business of law enforcement.
Examples: 1) The state attorney general is not neutral and detached. [Coolidge v. New Hampshire, 403 U.S. 443 (1971)]

2) A clerk of court may issue warrants for violations of city ordinances. [Shadwick v. City of Tampa, 407 U.S. 345 (1972)]

3) A magistrate who receives no salary other than compensation for each warrant issued is not neutral and detached. [Connally v. Georgia, 429 U.S. 245 (1977)]

4) A magistrate who participates in the search to determine its scope is not neutral and detached. [Lo-Ji Sales, Inc. v. New York, 442 U.S. 319 (1979)]

f. Execution of a Warrant

1) Must Be Executed by the Police
Only the police (and not private citizens) may execute a warrant. Moreover, when executing a warrant *in a home*, the police may not be accompanied by a member of the media or any other third party unless the third party is there to aid in executing the warrant (e.g., to identify stolen property that might be found in the home). [Wilson v. Layne, 526 U.S. 603 (1999)—unreasonable to allow newspaper reporter and photographer to accompany police during execution of an arrest warrant in plaintiff's home] *Rationale:* To be reasonable, police action pursuant to a warrant must be related to the objectives of the warrant. The presence of reporters or other third parties not aiding in the execution of the warrant renders the search unreasonable. Note that while the First Amendment prohibition against abridging freedom of the press is an important right, it does not supersede the very important Fourth Amendment right of persons to be free of unreasonable searches.

2) Execution Without Unreasonable Delay
The warrant should be executed without unreasonable delay because probable cause may disappear.

3) Announcement Requirement

Generally, an officer executing a search warrant must knock and announce her authority and purpose and await admittance for a reasonable time or be refused admittance before using force to enter the place to be searched.

a) Sufficiency of Delay

If the officers executing a warrant have a reasonable fear that evidence, such as cocaine, will be destroyed after they announce themselves, a limited 15-20 second delay before using force to enter the house is reasonable. [United States v. Banks, 540 U.S. 31 (2004)]

b) "No Knock" Entry Possible

No announcement need be made if the officer has reasonable suspicion, based on facts, that knocking and announcing would be *dangerous or futile* or that it would *inhibit the investigation*, e.g., because it would lead to the destruction of evidence. [Richards v. Wisconsin, 520 U.S. 385 (1997)] Whether a "no knock" entry is justified must be made on a case-by-case basis; a blanket exception for warrants involving drug investigations is impermissible. [Richards v. Wisconsin, *supra*] *Note:* The fact that property damage will result from a "no knock" entry does not require a different standard—reasonable suspicion is sufficient. [United States v. Ramirez, 523 U.S. 65 (1998)]

c) Remedy

The Supreme Court has held that the exclusionary rule will not be applied to cases where officers violate the knock and announce rule. (*See* V.B.8., *infra*.)

4) Scope of Search

The scope of the search is limited to what is reasonably necessary to discover the items described in the warrant.

5) Seizure of Unspecified Property

When executing a warrant, the police generally may seize any contraband or fruits or instrumentalities of crime that they discover, whether or not specified in the warrant.

6) Search of Persons Found on the Premises

A search warrant does not authorize the police to search persons found on the premises who are not named in the warrant. [Ybarra v. Illinois, 444 U.S. 85 (1979)] If the police have probable cause to arrest a person discovered on the premises to be searched, however, they may search her *incident to the arrest*. Of course, if a police officer has reason to believe any person present is armed and dangerous, the officer may conduct a *Terry* pat down for weapons. (*See* 5.e., *infra*.)

7) Detention of the Occupants

A warrant to search for contraband implicitly carries with it the limited authority to detain occupants of the premises while the search is being conducted. [Michigan v. Summers, B.3.d., *supra*] However, such detentions are limited to persons in the immediate vicinity of the premises when the warrant is being executed. It does not give officers authority to follow, stop, detain, and search persons who left the premises shortly before the warrant was executed. [Bailey v. United States, 568 U.S. 186 (2013)]

5. Exceptions to Warrant Requirement

There are **six exceptions** to the warrant requirement; that is, six circumstances where a warrantless search by law enforcement officers is reasonable and therefore is valid under the Fourth Amendment. To be valid, a warrantless search must meet all the requirements of at least one exception.

a. Search Incident to a Lawful Arrest

The police may conduct a warrantless search incident to an arrest as long as it was made on probable cause. [*See* Virginia v. Moore, 553 U.S. 164 (2008)]

1) Constitutional Arrest Requirement

If an arrest violates the Constitution, then any search incident to that arrest also will violate the Constitution.

2) Any Arrest Sufficient

The police may conduct a search incident to arrest whenever they arrest a person, and this is true even if the arrest is invalid under state law, as long as the arrest was constitutionally valid (e.g., reasonable and based on probable cause). Although the rationale for the search is to protect the arresting officer and to preserve evidence, the police need not actually fear for their safety or believe that they will find evidence of a crime as long as the suspect is placed under arrest. [United States v. Robinson, 414 U.S. 218 (1973)]

a) Issuance of Traffic Citation—Insufficient Basis

For traffic violations, if the suspect is not arrested, there can be no search incident to arrest, even if state law gives the officer the option of arresting a suspect or issuing a citation. [Knowles v. Iowa, 525 U.S. 113 (1999)—a nonconsensual automobile search conducted after the suspect was issued a citation for driving 43 m.p.h. in a 25 m.p.h. zone was illegal, and contraband found during the search was excluded from evidence] *Rationale:* When a citation is issued, there is less of a threat to the officer's safety than there is during an arrest, and the only evidence that needs to be preserved in such a case (e.g., evidence of the suspect's speeding or other illegal conduct) has already been found.

3) Geographic Scope

Incident to a constitutional arrest, the police may search the person and areas into which he might reach to obtain weapons or destroy evidence (his **"wingspan"**). [Chimel v. California, 395 U.S. 752 (1969)] The arrestee's wingspan follows him as he moves. Thus, if the arrestee is allowed to enter his home, police may follow and search areas within the arrestee's wingspan in the home. [Washington v. Chrisman, 455 U.S. 1 (1982)] The police may also make a **protective sweep** of the area beyond the defendant's wingspan if they believe accomplices may be present. [Maryland v. Buie, 494 U.S. 325 (1990)]

a) **Automobiles**

After arresting the occupant of an automobile, the police may search the interior of the auto incident to the arrest *if* at the time of the search:

(i) The *arrestee is unsecured and still may gain access* to the interior of the vehicle; or

(ii) The police reasonably believe that *evidence of the offense for which the person was arrested* may be found in the vehicle.

[Arizona v. Gant, 556 U.S. 332 (2009)] *Gant* overturned a practice permitting a search incident to arrest of the entire interior of an auto whenever the person arrested had recently been in the auto. This practice was based on a broad interpretation of an earlier case, *New York v. Belton,* 453 U.S. 454 (1981).

Example: A police officer stopped a vehicle for speeding. Upon approaching the vehicle, he smelled burnt marijuana and saw an envelope on the floor marked with the street name of a certain type of marijuana. He ordered the car's four occupants out of the vehicle and arrested them for unlawful possession of marijuana. Having only one pair of handcuffs and no assistance, he could not secure the arrestees. He had them stand apart from each other and proceeded to search the vehicle. During the search, the officer discovered cocaine in a jacket in the vehicle. The search was a valid search incident to arrest either because an "unsecured" arrestee easily could have gained access to the vehicle, or because the officer could reasonably believe that the vehicle contained evidence of the drug charge on which he arrested the occupants. [New York v. Belton, *supra*]

Compare: The police arrested defendant for driving on a suspended license shortly after he stepped out of his car. Defendant was then handcuffed and placed in a squad car. The police then searched the passenger compartment of defendant's car and found cocaine in a jacket in the car. The search here was an *invalid* search incident to arrest. Because defendant was handcuffed and locked in a squad car, he could not likely gain access to the interior of his car in order to destroy evidence or procure a weapon. Nor did the police have any reason to believe that the car contained any evidence relevant to the charge of driving on a suspended license. [Arizona v. Gant, *supra*]

4) **"Technological Searches"**

In assessing whether a search incident to arrest involving things that did not exist when the Fourth Amendment was adopted (e.g., cell phones, blood alcohol tests), the court will balance the degree to which the search incident to arrest intrudes upon a person's privacy against the degree to which the search is needed to promote legitimate governmental interests. [Birchfield v. North Dakota, 136 S. Ct. 2160 (2016)]

a) **DUI Arrest Justifies Breath (But Not Blood) Test**
Contemporaneous with an arrest for intoxicated driving, police officers may administer a warrantless breath test to determine the arrestee's alcohol levels but may not administer a warrantless blood test. *Rationale:* Breath tests are minimally intrusive (that is, they require an arrestee simply to blow into a tube) and leave no biological sample of the defendant. Blood alcohol tests are significantly more intrusive (e.g., require piercing of the skin) and leave the government with a biological sample of the arrestee that can be mined later to extract information about the defendant beyond blood alcohol level). Because both tests are available, the less-intrusive test is sufficient to preserve evidence of an arrestee's intoxicated driving absent a warrant granted upon a showing of why the more intrusive test is needed. [Birchfield v. North Dakota, *supra*]

(1) **Violation of Implied Consent Law May Be Punished Civilly But Not Criminally**
As a corollary to the search rule above, while a state may impose civil penalties (such as loss of a driver's license) under an implied consent law (that is, a law providing that by driving on roads within the state, a driver impliedly consents to submit to a blood test if stopped for driving while intoxicated), it is not reasonable under the Fourth Amendment to impose a *criminal* penalty for refusing to submit to a blood test under an implied consent law. [Birchfield v. North Dakota, *supra*]

b) **Physical Attributes of Cell Phone May Be Searched But Not Data**
Upon arresting a person, police officers have a strong interest in assuring that the arrestee does not have dangerous materials. Thus, officers may inspect the physical attributes of a cell phone. However, they may not, without a warrant, search digital information on a cell phone seized from the arrestee. Such a search implicates greater individual privacy interests than a brief physical search, and a search of the data would not further the goal of the search incident to arrest exception, since data stored on a cell phone cannot itself be used as a weapon to harm an arresting officer or to effectuate the arrestee's escape. [Riley v. California, 134 S. Ct. 2473 (2014)]

5) **Must Be Contemporaneous with Arrest**
A search incident to an arrest must be contemporaneous in time and place with the arrest. [Preston v. United States, 376 U.S. 364 (1964); United States v. Chadwick, 433 U.S. 1 (1977)]

a) **Automobiles**
At least with regard to searches of automobiles, the term "contemporaneous" does not necessarily mean "simultaneous." Thus, for example, if the police have reason to believe that an automobile from which a person was arrested contains *evidence of the crime for which the arrest was made*, they may search the interior of the automobile incident to arrest after the arrestee has

been removed from the automobile and placed in a squad car; and this is so even if the arrestee was already outside of the automobile at the time he was arrested, as long as he was a recent occupant of the automobile. [*See* Thornton v. United States, 541 U.S. 615 (2004)]

6) Search Incident to Incarceration or Impoundment
The police may search an arrestee's personal belongings before incarcerating him after a valid arrest. [Illinois v. Lafayette, 459 U.S. 986 (1983)] Similarly, the police may search an entire vehicle—including closed containers within the vehicle—that has been impounded. [Colorado v. Bertine, 479 U.S. 367 (1987)]

a) DNA Tests
When officers make an arrest supported *by probable cause to hold for a serious offense* and they bring the suspect to the police station to be detained in custody, taking and analyzing a cheek swab of the arrestee's DNA is a legitimate police booking procedure that is a *reasonable* search under the Fourth Amendment. [Maryland v. King, 567 U.S. 1301 (2012)]

b. "Automobile" Exception
If the police have probable cause to believe that a vehicle such as an automobile contains contraband or fruits, instrumentalities, or evidence of a crime, they may search the vehicle without a warrant. [Carroll v. United States, 267 U.S. 132 (1925)] *Rationale:* Automobiles and similar vehicles are mobile and so will not likely be available for search by the time an officer returns with a warrant. Moreover, the Supreme Court has declared that people have a lesser expectation of privacy in their vehicles than in their homes. However, if a vehicle is parked within the curtilage (e.g., the driveway) of one's home, the police may not search the vehicle without a warrant. [Collins v. Virginia, 138 S. Ct. 1663 (2018)]

Note: Similarly, if the police have probable cause to believe that the car itself is contraband, it may be seized from a public place without a warrant. [Florida v. White, 526 U.S. 559 (1999)]

Example: On three occasions, the police observed Defendant selling cocaine from his car, giving the police probable cause to believe that Defendant's car was used to transport cocaine. Under state law, a car used to transport cocaine is considered to be contraband subject to forfeiture. Several months later, the police arrested Defendant on unrelated drug charges while he was at work and seized his car from the parking lot without a warrant, based on their prior observations. While inventorying the contents of the car, the police found cocaine and brought the present drug charges against Defendant. The cocaine was admissible into evidence. Even though the police did not have probable cause to believe that the car contained cocaine when it was seized, they did have probable cause to believe that it was contraband and therefore seizable, and inventory searches of seized items are proper (*see* 6.b., *infra*). [Florida v. White, *supra*]

1) Scope of Search
If the police have full probable cause to search a vehicle, they can search the *entire*

vehicle (including the trunk) and all containers within the vehicle that *might contain the object* for which they are searching. [United States v. Ross, 456 U.S. 798 (1982)] Thus, if the police have probable cause to believe that drugs are within the vehicle, they can search almost any container, but if they have probable cause to believe that an illegal alien is hiding inside the vehicle, they must limit their search to areas where a person could hide.

a) **Passenger's Belongings**
   The search is not limited to the driver's belongings and may extend to packages belonging to a passenger. [Wyoming v. Houghton, 526 U.S. 295 (1999)—search of passenger's purse upheld where officer noticed driver had syringe in his pocket] *Rationale:* Like a driver, a passenger has a reduced expectation of privacy in a vehicle.

b) **Limited Probable Cause—Containers Placed in Vehicle**
   If the police only have probable cause to search a container (recently) placed in a vehicle, they may search that container, but the search may not extend to other parts of the car. [California v. Acevedo, 500 U.S. 565 (1991)]
   Example: Assume police have probable cause to believe that a briefcase that D is carrying contains illegal drugs. Unless they arrest D, they may not make a warrantless search of the briefcase because no exception to the warrant requirement applies. They follow D, and he places the briefcase in a car. They may then approach D and search the briefcase, even though they could not search it before it was placed in the car. They may not search the rest of the car, however, because D has not had an opportunity to move the drugs elsewhere in the car. Presumably, if some time passes and D has an opportunity to move the drugs, the police will have probable cause to search the entire car.

2) **Motor Homes**
   The automobile exception extends to any vehicle that has the attributes of mobility and a lesser expectation of privacy similar to a car. For example, the Supreme Court has held that it extends to motor homes if they are not at a fixed site. [California v. Carney, 471 U.S. 386 (1985)]

3) **Contemporaneousness Not Required**
   If the police are justified in making a warrantless search of a vehicle under this exception at the time of stopping, they may tow the vehicle to the station and search it later. [Chambers v. Maroney, 399 U.S. 42 (1970)]
   Example: A vehicle search, based on probable cause, conducted three days after the vehicle was impounded is permissible. [United States v. Johns, 469 U.S. 478 (1985)]

c. **Plain View**
   The police may make a warrantless seizure when they:

   (i)   Are *legitimately on the premises*;

(ii) Discover **evidence, fruits or instrumentalities** of crime, or **contraband**;

(iii) See such evidence **in plain view**; and

(iv) **Have probable cause** to believe (that is, it must be immediately apparent) that the item **is** evidence, contraband, or a fruit or instrumentality of crime.

[Coolidge v. New Hampshire, 4.e., *supra*; Arizona v. Hicks, 480 U.S. 321 (1987)]

Examples: 1) Police may seize **unspecified property** while executing a search warrant.

2) Police may seize from a lawfully stopped automobile an opaque balloon that, based on knowledge and experience, the police have probable cause to believe contains narcotics, even though the connection with the contraband would not be obvious to the average person. [Texas v. Brown, 460 U.S. 730 (1983)]

Compare: While investigating a shooting in an apartment, Officer spotted two sets of expensive stereo equipment which he had reasonable suspicion (but not probable cause) to believe were stolen. Officer moved some of the components to check their serial numbers. Such movement constituted an invalid search because of the lack of probable cause. [Arizona v. Hicks, *supra*]

d. Consent

The police may conduct a valid warrantless search if they have a **voluntary** consent to do so. Knowledge of the right to withhold consent, while a factor to be considered, is not a prerequisite to establishing a voluntary consent. [Schneckloth v. Bustamonte, 412 U.S. 218 (1973)]

Example: After Deputy stopped Defendant for speeding, gave him a verbal warning, and returned his license, Deputy asked Defendant if he was carrying any drugs in the car. Defendant answered "no" and consented to a search of his car, which uncovered drugs. Defendant argued that his consent was invalid because he had not been told that he was free to go after his license was returned. The Supreme Court, applying the principles of *Schneckloth*, found that no such warning was necessary. Voluntariness is to be determined from all of the circumstances, and knowledge of the right to refuse consent is just one factor to be considered in determining voluntariness. [Ohio v. Robinette, 519 U.S. 33 (1996)]

Note: An officer's false announcement that she has a warrant negates the possibility of consent. [Bumper v. North Carolina, 391 U.S. 543 (1968)]

1) Authority to Consent

Any person with an **apparent equal right to use or occupy** the property may consent to a search, and any evidence found may be used against the other owners or occupants. [Frazier v. Cupp, 394 U.S. 731 (1969); United States v. Matlock, 415 U.S. 164 (1973)] The search is valid even if it turns out that the person consenting to the search did not actually have such right, as long as the police reasonably believed that the person had authority to consent. [Illinois v. Rodriguez, 497 U.S. 177 (1990)]

a) **Limitation—Where Party Is Present and Objects**

The police may not act on consent from an occupant if a co-occupant is present and objects to the search and the search is directed against the co-occupant. [Georgia v. Randolph, 547 U.S. 103 (2006)] If a co-occupant has objected to a search and is removed for a reason unrelated to the refusal (e.g., a lawful arrest), the police may act on consent of the occupant, even if the removed co-occupant had refused consent. [Fernandez v. California, 134 S. Ct. 1126 (2014)]

b) **Parents and Children**

A parent generally has authority to consent to a search of a child's room (even an adult child), as long as the parent has access to the room, but, depending on the child's age, might not have authority to consent to a search of locked containers within the child's room. [See, e.g., United States v. Block, 590 F.2d 535 (4th Cir. 1978)—mother had authority to consent to search of 23-year-old son's room but not a locked footlocker in the room] Whether a child has authority to consent to a search of a parent's house or hotel room is a question of whether it is reasonable to believe that the child had such authority. [See United States v. Gutierrez-Hermosillo, 142 F.3d 1225 (10th Cir. 1998)—14-year-old had authority to allow police into father's hotel room while father was present] Even a relatively young child probably has authority to consent to a search of the common areas of a home or her own room. [See, e.g., Lenz v. Winburn, 51 F.3d 1540 (11th Cir. 1995)—nine-year-old had authority to consent to entry into her home]

2) **Scope of Search**

The scope of the search is limited by the *scope of the consent*. However, consent extends to all areas to which a reasonable person under the circumstances would believe it extends.

Example: Police stopped D for a traffic violation, told him that they suspected him of carrying drugs, and asked for permission to search the car. D consented. The officers found a bag containing cocaine. At trial, D argued that his consent did not extend to any closed container (the bag). The Supreme Court held that because D knew the police were searching for drugs and did not place any restriction on his consent, it was reasonable for the police to believe that the consent extended to all areas where drugs might be found. [Florida v. Jimeno, 500 U.S. 248 (1991)]

e. **Stop and Frisk**

1) **Standards**

As noted above (*see* B.3.a., *supra*), a police officer may *stop* a person without probable cause for arrest if she has an articulable and *reasonable suspicion* of criminal activity. In such circumstances, if the officer also *reasonably believes* that the person may be ***armed and presently dangerous***, she may conduct a protective ***frisk***. [Terry v. Ohio, B.3.a., *supra*; United States v. Cortez, 449 U.S. 411 (1981)]

2) **Scope of the Intrusion**

   a) **Patdown of Outer Clothing**
   The scope of the frisk is generally limited to a patdown of the outer clothing for concealed instruments of assault. [Terry v. Ohio, *supra*] However, an officer may reach directly into an area of the suspect's clothing, such as his belt, without a preliminary frisk, when she has specific information that a weapon is hidden there, even if the information comes from an informant's tip lacking sufficient reliability to support a warrant. [Adams v. Williams, 407 U.S. 143 (1972)]

   b) **Automobiles**
   If a vehicle has been properly stopped, a police officer may order the driver out of the vehicle even without a suspicion of criminal activity. If the officer then reasonably believes that the driver or any passenger may be armed and dangerous, she may conduct a frisk of the suspected person. [Pennsylvania v. Mimms, 434 U.S. 106 (1978); Arizona v. Johnson, 555 U.S. 323 (2009)] Moreover, the officer may search the passenger compartment of the vehicle, even if the officer has ***not arrested*** the occupant and has ordered the occupant out of the vehicle, provided the search is ***limited to those areas in which a weapon may be placed*** or hidden and the officer possesses a reasonable belief that the occupant is dangerous. [Michigan v. Long, 463 U.S. 1032 (1983)]

   c) **Identification May Be Required**
   As long as the police have the reasonable suspicion required to make a *Terry* stop, they may require the detained person to identify himself (that is, state his name), and the detainee may be arrested for failure to comply with such a requirement except, perhaps, where the detainee may make a self-incrimination claim. [*See* Hiibel v. Sixth Judicial District Court, B.3.a.3)a), *supra*]

   d) **Time Limit**
   There is no rigid time limit for the length of an investigative stop. The Court will consider the purpose of the stop, the reasonableness of the time in effectuating the purpose, and the reasonableness of the means of investigation to determine whether a stop was too long. [United States v. Sharpe, 470 U.S. 675 (1985)]

3) **Admissibility of Evidence**
   If a police officer conducts a patdown within the bounds of *Terry*, the officer may reach into the suspect's clothing and seize any item that the officer reasonably believes, based on its "***plain feel***," is a ***weapon or contraband***. [Terry v. Ohio, *supra*; Minnesota v. Dickerson, 508 U.S. 366 (1993)—excluding from evidence cocaine that officer found during valid patdown because officer had to manipulate package to discern that it likely was drugs] Properly seized items are admissible as evidence against the suspect.

f.   Hot Pursuit, Exigent Circumstances, Evanescent Evidence, and Other Emergencies

1)   Hot Pursuit Exception

Police officers in hot pursuit of a *fleeing felon* may make a warrantless search and seizure. The scope of the search may be as broad as may reasonably be necessary to prevent the suspect from resisting or escaping. [Warden v. Hayden, 387 U.S. 294 (1967)] When the police have probable cause and attempt to make a warrantless arrest in a "public place," they may pursue the suspect into private dwellings. [United States v. Santana, 427 U.S. 38 (1976)]

2)   Exigent Circumstances—Destruction of Evidence

Police officers may enter a home without a warrant to prevent the destruction of evidence, even if the exigency arose because police officers knocked on the door and asked for entry, as long as the officers have reason to believe that evidence is being destroyed *and* the officers did not create the exigency through an actual or threatened Fourth Amendment violation. [Kentucky v. King, 563 U.S. 452 (2011)]

Example: Police officers set up a drug buy in a parking lot and tried to apprehend the seller. The seller disappeared down a corridor. At the end of the corridor were two apartment doors. The officers smelled marijuana by one door, knocked to announce their presence, heard scuffling, and assumed the occupants were destroying drugs. The officers barged in. The suspect was not there (they found him in the other apartment), but drugs were present in the apartment. The entry was valid under the exigent circumstances exception. [Kentucky v. King, *supra*]

3)   Evanescent Evidence Exception

Police officers may seize without a warrant evidence likely to disappear before a warrant can be obtained. [*See* Cupp v. Murphy, 412 U.S. 291 (1973)—scrapings of tissues from under a suspect's fingernails, which could be washed away] Whether such a warrantless search is reasonable is judged by the totality of the circumstances.

a)   Blood Alcohol Testing

The natural dissipation of alcohol in the bloodstream does *not* automatically constitute a sufficient exigency to justify a warrantless blood alcohol content ("BAC") test. As in the case of any evanescent evidence, a determination of whether a warrantless BAC test is reasonable depends on the totality of the circumstances. In particular, where police officers can reasonably obtain a warrant before a blood sample is drawn without significantly undermining the efficacy of the search, the Fourth Amendment requires that they do so. In general, establishing probable cause is relatively simple in drunk driving cases, and warrants can often be obtained expeditiously by telephone, e-mail, or video conferencing. Thus, warrantless BAC testing often will be found unreasonable. [*See* Missouri v. McNeely, 569 U.S. 141 (2013)]

4)   Emergency Aid Exception

Emergencies that threaten health or safety if not immediately acted upon will justify a warrantless search. This includes situations where the police see someone injured or threatened with injury. [*See, e.g.,* Brigham City v. Stuart, 547 U.S. 389 (2006)] Whether an emergency exists is determined objectively, from the officer's point of view. [Michigan v. Fisher, 558 U.S. 45 (2010)] (Some states refer to this as the community caretaker exception.)

Examples: 1) Police responded to a domestic disturbance call at a home. Upon arriving, they found blood on the hood of a pickup truck and windows broken out of the home. They saw defendant through an open window, screaming and with a cut on his hand. An officer asked if medical attention was needed, and defendant told the officer to get a warrant. The officer then opened the house door part way, and defendant pointed a gun at the officer. Evidence of the gun need not be suppressed as the fruit of an unlawful entry. The officer could have objectively believed that the defendant could have attacked a spouse or child who needed aid or that defendant was in danger himself. [Michigan v. Fisher, *supra*]

                  2) A warrantless search may be justified to find contaminated food or drugs [*see, e.g.,* North American Cold Storage v. City of Chicago, 211 U.S. 306 (1908)] or to discover the source of a fire while it is burning (but not after it is extinguished). [Michigan v. Tyler, 436 U.S. 499 (1978)]

Compare: The need to search a murder scene, without more, does not justify a warrantless search. [Mincey v. Arizona, 437 U.S. 385 (1978)]

6. **Administrative Inspections and Searches**

    a. **Warrant Required for Searches of Private Residences and Businesses**
Inspectors must have a warrant for searches of private residences and commercial buildings. [Camara v. Municipal Court, 387 U.S. 523 (1967); Michigan v. Clifford, 464 U.S. 287 (1984)—warrantless administrative search of fire-damaged residence by officials seeking to determine origin of fire violated owners' Fourth Amendment rights; owners retained reasonable expectation of privacy in the damaged structure, and the warrantless search was unconstitutional] However, the same standard of probable cause as is required for other searches is not required for a valid administrative inspection warrant. A showing of a general and ***neutral enforcement plan*** will justify issuance of the warrant, which is designed to guard against selective enforcement. [Marshall v. Barlow's, Inc., 436 U.S. 307 (1978)]

       1) **Exceptions Permitting Warrantless Searches**

          a) **Contaminated Food**
A warrant is not required for the seizure of spoiled or contaminated food. [North American Cold Storage v. City of Chicago, *supra*]

          b) **Highly Regulated Industries**
A warrant is not required for searches of businesses in highly regulated industries, because of the urgent public interest and the theory that the business

has impliedly consented to warrantless searches by entering into a highly regulated industry. Such industries include liquor [Colonnade Catering Corp. v. United States, 397 U.S. 72 (1970)], guns [United States v. Biswell, 406 U.S. 311 (1972)], strip mining [Donovan v. Dewey, 452 U.S. 594 (1981)], and automobile junkyards [New York v. Burger, 479 U.S. 812 (1987)], but not car leasing [G.M. Leasing Corp. v. United States, 429 U.S. 338 (1977)] or general manufacturing [Marshall v. Barlow's, Inc., *supra*].

b.   Inventory Searches

The police may search an arrestee's personal belongings in order to inventory them before incarcerating the arrestee. [Illinois v. Lafayette, 5.a.6), *supra*] Similarly, the police may search an entire vehicle—including closed containers within the vehicle—that has been impounded, as long as the search is part of an established department routine. [Colorado v. Bertine, 5.a.6), *supra*] Moreover, jail officials need not have reasonable suspicion that a person arrested for a minor offense possesses a concealed weapon or contraband to subject him to a strip search before admitting him to the general prison population. Deference must be given to the officials unless there is substantial evidence indicating that their response to a situation is exaggerated. The risks that an unsearched prisoner poses are great—from diseases to weapons to gang affiliations. Therefore, suspicionless strip searches are not an exaggerated response. [Florence v. Board of Chosen Freeholders, 566 U.S. 318 (2012)]

c.   Search of Airline Passengers

Courts have generally upheld searches of airline passengers prior to boarding. This seems to be regarded as somewhat akin to a consent or administrative search. One court, however, has held that a passenger must be permitted to avoid such a search by agreeing not to board the aircraft.

d   Public School Searches

A warrant or probable cause is not required for searches conducted by public school officials; only *reasonable grounds* for the search are necessary. This exception is justified due to the nature of the school environment. [New Jersey v. T.L.O., 469 U.S. 325 (1985)] The Court has also upheld a school district rule that required students participating in *any extracurricular activity* to submit to random urinalysis drug testing monitored by an adult of the same sex. [Board of Education v. Earls, 536 U.S. 822 (2002)]

1)   Reasonableness Standard

A school search will be held to be reasonable only if:

(i)   It offers a *moderate chance of finding evidence* of wrongdoing;

(ii)   The measures adopted to carry out the search are *reasonably related to the objectives of the search;* and

(iii) The search is *not excessively intrusive* in light of the age and sex of the student and nature of the infraction.

[New Jersey v. T.L.O., *supra;* Safford Unified School District #1 v. Redding, 557 U.S. 364 (2009)]

Example: A 13-year-old student was brought before her school's principal. The principal had found in the student's day planner several knives and lighters and a cigarette. He also found five painkillers (four prescription and one over-the-counter) that were banned at school absent permission. He told the student he had a tip that she was distributing such pills. The student said the knives, etc., belonged to a friend and denied knowledge of the painkillers. She allowed the principal's assistant to search her outer clothing and backpack. No contraband was found. The principal then sent the student to the school nurse, who had her remove her outer clothing and pull her underwear away from her body so if any drugs were hidden in them, they would fall out. No drugs were found, and the student brought an action, claiming that the search violated her constitutional rights. *Held:* Because only a few, nondangerous pills were involved and there was a lack of any specific reason to believe that the student might have been hiding pills in her underwear, the strip search was excessively intrusive. [Safford Unified School District #1 v. Redding, *supra*]

e. **Parolees**

The Supreme Court has upheld warrantless searches of a parolee and his home—even without reasonable suspicion—where a state statute provided that as a condition of parole, a parolee agreed that he would submit to searches by a parole officer or police officer at any time, with or without a search warrant or probable cause. The Court held that such warrantless searches are reasonable under the Fourth Amendment because a parolee has a diminished expectation of privacy under such a statute and the government has a heightened need to search parolees because they are less likely than the general population to be law-abiding. [*See* Samson v. California, 547 U.S. 843 (2006)]

f. **Government Employees' Desks and Files**

A warrantless search of a government employee's desk and file cabinets is permissible under the Fourth Amendment if it is reasonable in scope and if it is justified at its inception by a noninvestigatory, work-related need or a reasonable suspicion of work-related misconduct. [O'Connor v. Ortega, 480 U.S. 709 (1987)]

g. **Drug Testing**

Although government-required drug testing constitutes a search, the Supreme Court has upheld such testing without a warrant, probable cause, or even individualized suspicion when justified by *"special needs"* beyond the general interest of law enforcement.

Examples: 1) The government can require railroad employees who are involved in accidents to be tested for drugs after the accidents. [Skinner v. Railway Labor Executives' Association, 489 U.S. 602 (1989)]

2) The government can require persons seeking Customs positions connected to drug interdiction to be tested for drugs. There is a special

need for such testing because persons so employed will have ready access to large quantities of drugs. [National Treasury Employees Union v. Von Raab, 489 U.S. 656 (1989)]

3) The government can require public school students who participate in *any extracurricular activities* to submit to random drug tests because of the special interest schools have in the safety of their students. [Board of Education v. Earls, *supra*]

Compare: 1) Special needs do not justify a warrantless and nonconsensual urinalysis test to determine whether a pregnant woman has been using cocaine, where the main purpose of the testing is to generate evidence that may be used by law enforcement personnel to coerce women into drug programs. [Ferguson v. Charleston, 532 U.S. 67 (2001)]

2) The government may not require candidates for state offices to certify that they have taken a drug test within 30 days prior to qualifying for nomination or election—there is no special need for such testing. [Chandler v. Miller, 520 U.S. 305 (1997)]

7. Searches in Foreign Countries and at the Border

a. Searches in Foreign Countries
The Fourth Amendment does *not* apply to searches and seizures by United States officials in foreign countries and involving an alien, at least where the alien does not have a substantial connection to the United States. Thus, for example, the Fourth Amendment was held not to bar the use of evidence obtained in a warrantless search of an alien's home in Mexico. [United States v. Verdugo-Urquidez, 494 U.S. 259 (1990)]

b. Searches at the Border or Its Functional Equivalent
There is a diminished expectation of privacy at the border and its functional equivalents due to competing interests of national sovereignty. Searches there do not require a warrant, probable cause, or reasonable suspicion. A functional equivalent of the border might be a point near the border where several routes all leading to the border merge.

c. Roving Patrols

1) Stops
Roving patrols inside the United States border may stop an automobile for questioning of the occupants if the officer *reasonably suspects* that the automobile may contain illegal aliens, but the apparent Mexican ancestry of the occupants alone cannot create a reasonable suspicion. [United States v. Brignoni-Ponce, 422 U.S. 873 (1975)]

2) Searches
A roving patrol inside the border may not conduct a warrantless search unless the requirements of one of the *exceptions* to the warrant requirement, such as the "automobile" exception (probable cause) or consent, are met. [Almeida-Sanchez v. United States, 413 U.S. 266 (1973)]

d. Fixed Checkpoints

Border officials may stop an automobile at a fixed checkpoint inside the border for questioning of the occupants even ***without a reasonable suspicion*** that the automobile contains illegal aliens. [United States v. Martinez-Fuerte, B.3.b., *supra*] Officials may disassemble stopped vehicles at such checkpoints, even without reasonable suspicion. [United States v. Flores-Montano, 541 U.S. 149 (2004)] However, the Supreme Court has suggested that nonroutine, personal searches at the border (e.g., strip searches or body cavity searches) may require probable cause.

e. Opening International Mail

Permissible border searches include the opening of international mail, which postal regulations authorize when postal authorities have ***reasonable cause*** to suspect that the mail contains ***contraband***, although the regulations prohibit the authorities from reading any correspondence inside. [United States v. Ramsey, 431 U.S. 606 (1977)]

1) Reopening

Once customs agents lawfully open a container and identify its contents as illegal, their ***subsequent reopening*** of the container after it has been resealed and delivered to defendant is not a search within the meaning of the Fourth Amendment, unless there is a substantial likelihood that the container's contents have been changed during any gap in surveillance. [Illinois v. Andreas, 463 U.S. 765 (1983)]

f. Immigration Enforcement Actions

The Supreme Court held that the I.N.S., which has been replaced by the Citizenship and Immigration Services Division of the Department of Homeland Security, may do a "factory survey" of the entire work force in a factory, to determine citizenship of each employee, without raising Fourth Amendment issues. The "factory survey" is not "detention" or a "seizure" under the Fourth Amendment. [Immigration & Naturalization Service v. Delgado, 466 U.S. 210 (1984)] Furthermore, evidence illegally obtained, in violation of the Fourth Amendment, may be used in a civil deportation hearing. [Immigration & Naturalization Service v. Lopez-Mendoza, 468 U.S. 1032 (1984)]

g. Detentions

If the officials have a "reasonable suspicion" that a traveler is smuggling contraband in her stomach, they may detain her for a time reasonable under the circumstances. *Rationale:* Stopping such smuggling is important, yet very difficult; stomach smuggling gives no external signs that would enable officials to meet a "probable cause" standard in order to conduct a search. [United States v. Montoya de Hernandez, 473 U.S. 531 (1985)—16-hour detention upheld until traveler, who refused an X-ray, had a bowel movement]

8. Wiretapping and Eavesdropping

a. Fourth Amendment Requirements

Wiretapping and any other form of electronic surveillance that violates a reasonable expectation of privacy constitute a search under the Fourth Amendment. [Katz

v. United States, 389 U.S. 347 (1967)] In *Berger v. New York*, 388 U.S. 41 (1967), the Supreme Court indicated that for a valid ***warrant*** authorizing a wiretap to be issued, the following ***requirements*** must be met:

1)   A showing of ***probable cause*** to believe that a ***specific crime*** has been or is being committed must be made;

2)   The ***suspected persons*** whose conversations are to be overheard must be ***named***;

3)   The warrant must ***describe with particularity*** the conversations that can be overheard;

4)   The wiretap must be limited to a ***short period of time*** (although extensions may be obtained upon an adequate showing);

5)   ***Provisions*** must be made for the ***termination*** of the wiretap when the desired information has been obtained; and

6)   A ***return*** must be made to the court, showing what conversations have been intercepted.

b.   Exceptions

1)   "Unreliable Ear"
A speaker assumes the risk that the person to whom she is talking is unreliable. If the person turns out to be an informer wired for sound or taping the conversation, the speaker has no basis in the Fourth Amendment to object to the transmitting or recording of the conversation as a warrantless search. [United States v. White, 401 U.S. 745 (1971)]

2)   "Uninvited Ear"
A speaker has no Fourth Amendment claim if she makes no attempt to keep the conversation private. [Katz v. United States, *supra*]

c.   Judicial Approval Required for Domestic Security Surveillance
A neutral and detached magistrate must make the determination that a warrant should issue authorizing electronic surveillance, including internal security surveillance of domestic organizations. The President may not authorize such surveillance without prior judicial approval. [United States v. United States District Court, 407 U.S. 297 (1972)]

d.   Federal Statute
Title III of the Omnibus Crime Control and Safe Streets Act regulates interception of private "wire, oral or electronic communications." [18 U.S.C. §§2510-2520] All electronic communication surveillance (e.g., phone taps, bugs, etc.) must comply with the requirements of this federal statute, which exhibits a legislative decision to require more than the constitutional minimum in this especially sensitive area.

e.   Pen Registers
A pen register records only the numbers dialed from a certain phone. The Fourth

Amendment does not require prior judicial approval for installation and use of pen registers. [Smith v. Maryland, 442 U.S. 735 (1979)] Neither does Title III govern pen registers, because Title III applies only when the **contents** of electronic communications are intercepted. However, by statute [18 U.S.C. §§3121 *et seq.*], police must obtain a court order finding pen register information to be relevant to an ongoing criminal investigation before utilizing a pen register. Note, however, that information obtained in violation of the statute would not necessarily be excluded from evidence in a criminal trial; the statute merely provides a criminal penalty.

f. Covert Entry to Install a Bug Permissible

Law enforcement officers do not need prior express judicial authorization for a covert entry to install equipment for electronic surveillance, which has been approved in compliance with Title III. [Dalia v. United States, 441 U.S. 238 (1979)]

D. METHODS OF OBTAINING EVIDENCE THAT SHOCK THE CONSCIENCE

Due process of law requires that state criminal prosecutions be conducted in a manner that does not offend the "sense of justice" inherent in due process. Evidence obtained in a manner offending that sense is **inadmissible**, even if it does not run afoul of one of the specific prohibitions against particular types of misconduct.

1. Searches of the Body

Intrusions into the human body implicate a person's most deep-rooted expectations of privacy. Thus, Fourth Amendment requirements apply. Ultimately, the "reasonableness" of searches into the body depends on weighing society's need for the evidence against the magnitude of the intrusion on the individual (including the threat to health, safety, and dignity issues). [Winston v. Lee, 470 U.S. 753 (1985)]

a. Blood Tests

Taking a blood sample (e.g., from a person suspected of drunk driving) by commonplace medical procedures "involves virtually no risk, trauma, or pain" and is thus a **reasonable** intrusion. [Schmerber v. California, 384 U.S. 757 (1966)]

b. Compare—Surgery

But a surgical procedure under a general anesthetic (to remove a bullet needed as evidence) involves significant risks to health and a severe intrusion on privacy, and thus is **unreasonable**—at least when there is substantial other evidence. [Winston v. Lee, *supra*]

2. Shocking Inducement

If a crime is induced by official actions that themselves shock the conscience, any conviction therefrom offends due process.

Example: D appears before a state legislative commission. Members of the commission clearly indicate that the privilege against self-incrimination is available to D, although in fact D could be convicted for failure to answer. Can D's conviction for refusal to answer be upheld? No, because the crime was induced by methods that shock the conscience. [Raley v. Ohio, 360 U.S. 423 (1959)]

III. CONFESSIONS

A. INTRODUCTION

The admissibility of a defendant's confession or incriminating admission involves analysis under the Fourth, Fifth, Sixth, and Fourteenth Amendments. We have already discussed Fourth Amendment search and seizure limitations. The Fifth Amendment gives defendants rights against testimonial self-incrimination. The Sixth Amendment gives defendants rights regarding the assistance of counsel. The Fourteenth Amendment protects against involuntary confessions.

B. FOURTEENTH AMENDMENT—VOLUNTARINESS

For confessions to be admissible, the Due Process Clause of the Fourteenth Amendment requires that they be voluntary. Voluntariness is assessed by looking at the totality of the circumstances, including the suspect's age, education, and mental and physical condition, along with the setting, duration, and manner of police interrogation. [Spano v. New York, 360 U.S. 315 (1959)]

Examples: 1) A confession will be involuntary where it was obtained by physically beating the defendant. [Brown v. Mississippi, 297 U.S. 278 (1936)]

        2) D was being held for questioning. O, a young officer who was a friend of D, told D that if he did not obtain a confession, he would lose his job, which would be disastrous for his wife and children. D confessed, but the Court found the confession involuntary. [Leyra v. Denno, 347 U.S. 556 (1954)]

1. Must Be Official Compulsion

Only official compulsion will render a confession involuntary for purposes of the Fourteenth Amendment. A confession is not involuntary merely because it is the product of mental disease that prevents the confession from being of the defendant's free will. [Colorado v. Connelly, 479 U.S. 157 (1986)]

2. Harmless Error Test Applies

A conviction will not necessarily be overturned if an involuntary confession was erroneously admitted into evidence. The harmless error test applies, and the conviction will not be overturned if the government can show that there was other overwhelming evidence of guilt. [Arizona v. Fulminante, 499 U.S. 279 (1991)]

3. Can "Appeal" to Jury

A finding of voluntariness by the trial court does not preclude the defendant from introducing evidence to the jury of the circumstances of the confession in order to cast doubt on its credibility. [Crane v. Kentucky, 476 U.S. 683 (1986)]

C. SIXTH AMENDMENT RIGHT TO COUNSEL APPROACH

The Sixth Amendment provides that in all criminal prosecutions, the defendant has a right to the assistance of counsel. The right protects defendants from having to face a complicated legal system without competent help. It applies at all *critical stages* of a criminal prosecution after formal proceedings have begun. [Rothgery v. Gillespie, 554 U.S. 191 (2008)] The right is violated when the police deliberately elicit an incriminating statement from a defendant without first obtaining a waiver of the defendant's right to have counsel present. [*See* Fellers v. United States, 540 U.S. 519 (2004)] Since *Miranda*, below, the Sixth Amendment right has been limited to cases where *adversary judicial proceedings* have begun (e.g., *formal charges have been filed*).

[Massiah v. United States, 377 U.S. 201 (1964)] Thus, the right does not apply in precharge custodial interrogations.

Examples: 1) The Sixth Amendment right to counsel is violated when an undisclosed, paid government informant is placed in the defendant's cell, after defendant has been indicted, and deliberately elicits statements from the defendant regarding the crime for which the defendant was indicted. [United States v. Henry, 447 U.S. 264 (1980)] However, it is not a violation merely to place an informant in a defendant's cell—the informant must take some action, beyond mere listening, designed deliberately to elicit incriminating remarks. [Kuhlman v. Wilson, 477 U.S. 436 (1986)]

2) The right to counsel is violated when police arrange to record conversations between an indicted defendant and his co-defendant. [Maine v. Moulton, 474 U.S. 159 (1985)]

1. Stages at Which Applicable

The defendant has a Sixth Amendment right to be represented by privately retained counsel, or to have counsel appointed for him by the state if he is indigent, at the following stages:

(i) Post-indictment interrogation [Massiah v. United States, *supra*];

(ii) Preliminary hearings to determine probable cause to prosecute [Coleman v. Alabama, *infra*, VI.C.];

(iii) Arraignment [Hamilton v. Alabama, 368 U.S. 52 (1961)];

(iv) Post-charge lineups [Moore v. Illinois, IV.B.1.a., *infra*];

(v) Guilty plea and sentencing [Mempa v. Rhay, 389 U.S. 128 (1967); Moore v. Michigan, 355 U.S. 155 (1957); Townsend v. Burke, 334 U.S. 736 (1948)];

(vi) Felony trials [Gideon v. Wainwright, 372 U.S. 335 (1963)];

(vii) Misdemeanor trials when imprisonment is actually imposed or a suspended jail sentence is imposed [Scott v. Illinois, 440 U.S. 367 (1979); Alabama v. Shelton, 535 U.S. 654 (2002)];

(viii) Overnight recesses during trial [Geders v. United States, 425 U.S. 80 (1976)];

(ix) Appeals as a matter of right [Douglas v. California, 372 U.S. 353 (1963)]; and

(x) Appeals of guilty pleas and pleas of nolo contendere [Halbert v. Michigan, 545 U.S. 605 (2005); *and see* X.B.1.a., *infra*].

Note: There also is a Fifth Amendment right to counsel at all custodial police interrogations; *see infra*, D.1).

2. Stages at Which Not Applicable

The defendant does not have a constitutional right to be represented by counsel at the following stages:

a. Blood sampling [Schmerber v. California, II.D.1.a., *supra*];

b. Taking of handwriting or voice exemplars [Gilbert v. California, 388 U.S. 263 (1967)];

c. Pre-charge or investigative lineups [Kirby v. Illinois, 406 U.S. 682 (1972)];

d. Photo identifications [United States v. Ash, IV.B.1.c., *infra*];

e. Preliminary hearings to determine probable cause to detain [Gerstein v. Pugh, 420 U.S. 103 (1975)];

f. Brief recesses during the defendant's testimony at trial [Perry v. Leeke, 488 U.S. 272 (1989)];

g. Discretionary appeals [Ross v. Moffitt, 417 U.S. 600 (1974)];

h. Parole and probation revocation proceedings [Gagnon v. Scarpelli, 411 U.S. 778 (1973)]; and

i. Post-conviction proceeding (e.g., habeas corpus) [Pennsylvania v. Finley, 481 U.S. 551 (1987)] including petitions by death-row inmates [Murray v. Giarratano, 492 U.S. 1 (1989)].

3. **Offense Specific**

The Sixth Amendment right to counsel is "offense specific." Thus, if a defendant makes a Sixth Amendment request for counsel for one charge, he must make another request if he is subsequently charged with a separate, unrelated crime if he desires counsel for the second charge. Similarly, even though a defendant's Sixth Amendment right to counsel has attached regarding one charge, he may be questioned without counsel concerning an unrelated charge. [Illinois v. Perkins, 496 U.S. 292 (1990)]

Example: D was in jail on a battery charge. Because the police suspected D of an unrelated murder, they placed an undercover officer in D's cell. The officer elicited damaging confessions from D regarding the murder. The interrogation did not violate the Sixth Amendment because D had not been charged with the murder. [Illinois v. Perkins, *supra*] Neither did the interrogation violate D's Fifth Amendment right to counsel under *Miranda*. (*See* D.2.a., *infra*.)

a. **Test for "Different Offenses"**

The test for determining whether offenses are different under the Sixth Amendment is the *Blockburger* test (*see* XIII.C.1., *infra*). Under the test, two crimes are considered different offenses if each requires proof of an additional element that the other crime does not require. [Texas v. Cobb, 532 U.S. 162 (2001)]

4. **Waiver**

The Sixth Amendment right to counsel may be waived. The waiver must be knowing and voluntary. Moreover, the waiver does not necessarily require the presence of counsel, at least if counsel has not actually been requested by the defendant but rather was appointed by the court. [Montejo v. Louisiana, 556 U.S. 778 (2009)]

Example: Defendant was arrested, was given *Miranda* warnings (*see* D.1., *infra*), and confessed to a murder. He was then brought before a judge, who appointed counsel to represent Defendant. Later that day, police officers went to Defendant's cell and asked him to help them find the weapon he used to commit the murder. The police gave Defendant a fresh set of *Miranda* warnings and convinced him to write a letter apologizing to his victim's widow. Later, the appointed attorney met with Defendant. At trial, the attorney argued that the letter was taken in violation of Defendant's Sixth Amendment right to counsel. *Held:* Because Defendant had not requested the appointment of an attorney, his right to an attorney was not violated. [Montejo v. Louisiana, *supra*]

5. Remedy

If the defendant was entitled to a lawyer at trial, the failure to provide counsel results in ***automatic reversal of the conviction***, even without any showing of specific unfairness in the proceedings. [Gideon v. Wainwright, I.C., *supra*] Similarly, erroneous disqualification of privately retained counsel results in automatic reversal. [United States v. Gonzalez-Lopez, 548 U.S. 140 (2006)] However, at ***nontrial proceedings*** (such as a post-indictment lineup), the harmless error rule applies to deprivations of counsel. [United States v. Wade, 388 U.S. 218 (1967)]

6. Impeachment

A statement obtained in violation of a defendant's Sixth Amendment right to counsel, while not admissible in the prosecution's case-in-chief, may be used to impeach the defendant's contrary trial testimony. [Kansas v. Ventris, 556 U.S. 586 (2009)] This rule is similar to the rule that applies to *Miranda* violations. (*See* D.4.a., *infra*.)

Example: After Defendant was charged with murder and arrested for aggravated robbery, police placed an informant in his cell, telling the informant to keep his ears open. The informant told Defendant that he looked like he had something serious on his mind (which probably was sufficient to violate Defendant's Sixth Amendment right to counsel). Defendant responded that he had just shot a man in the head and taken his money. At trial, after Defendant testified that an accomplice had shot and robbed the victim, the informant then testified as to what he heard. *Held:* The informant's testimony was admissible for impeachment purposes. [Kansas v. Ventris, *supra*]

D. FIFTH AMENDMENT PRIVILEGE AGAINST COMPELLED SELF-INCRIMINATION—*MIRANDA*

The Fifth Amendment, applicable to the states through the Fourteenth Amendment, provides that no person "shall be compelled to be a witness against himself . . . ." This has been interpreted to mean that a person shall not be compelled to give self-incriminating testimony. The scope of what is considered to be "testimony" under the amendment will be discussed later (*see* XIV., *infra*). This section explains the applicability of the amendment to confessions.

1. The Warnings

In *Miranda v. Arizona*, 384 U.S. 436 (1966), the Fifth Amendment privilege against compelled self-incrimination became the basis for ruling upon the admissibility of a confession. The *Miranda* warnings and a valid waiver are ***prerequisites to the admissibility*** of any statement made by the accused during custodial interrogation. A person in custody must, prior to interrogation, be clearly informed that:

(i) He has the right to remain silent;

(ii) Anything he says can be used against him in court;

(iii) He has the right to the presence of an attorney; and

(iv) If he cannot afford an attorney, one will be appointed for him if he so desires.

Note: The Supreme Court has held that the holding of *Miranda* was based on the **requirements** of the Fifth Amendment as made applicable to the states through the Fourteenth Amendment, and therefore Congress cannot eliminate the *Miranda* requirements by statute. [Dickerson v. United States, 530 U.S. 428 (2000)—invalidating a statute that purportedly eliminated *Miranda*'s requirements that persons in custody and being interrogated be informed of the right to remain silent and the right to counsel]

a. Need Not Be Verbatim
Miranda requires that all suspects be informed of their rights without considering any prior awareness of those rights. The warnings need not be given verbatim, as long as the substance of the warning is there. [Duckworth v. Eagan, 492 U.S. 195 (1989)— upholding warning that included statement, "We [the police] have no way of giving you a lawyer, but one will be appointed for you, if you wish, if and when you go to court"] The failure to advise a suspect of his right to appointed counsel may be found to be harmless error. [Michigan v. Tucker, 417 U.S. 433 (1974); California v. Prysock, 453 U.S. 355 (1981)]

b. Rewarning Not Needed After Break
There is generally no need to repeat the warnings merely because of a break in the interrogation, **unless** the time lapse has been so long that a failure to do so would seem like an attempt to take advantage of the suspect's ignorance of his rights.

2. When Required
Anyone in police custody and accused of a crime, no matter how minor a crime, must be given *Miranda* warnings **prior to interrogation** by the police. [Berkemer v. McCarty, 468 U.S. 420 (1984)]

a. Governmental Conduct
Miranda generally applies only to interrogation by the publicly paid police. It does not apply where interrogation is by an informant who the defendant does not know is working for the police. [Illinois v. Perkins, *supra*—*Miranda* warnings need not be given before questioning by a cellmate covertly working for the police] *Rationale:* The warnings are intended to offset the coercive nature of police-dominated interrogation, and if the defendant does not know that he is being interrogated by the police, there is no coercive atmosphere to offset.

1) State-Ordered Psychiatric Examination
The Fifth Amendment privilege against self-incrimination forbids admission of

evidence based on a psychiatric interview of defendant who was not warned of his right to remain silent. [Estelle v. Smith, 451 U.S. 454 (1981)] The admission of such evidence may, however, constitute harmless error. [Satterwhite v. Texas, 486 U.S. 249 (1988)]

2) Limits on *Miranda*

Miranda suggested that every encounter between police and citizen was inherently coercive. Hence, interrogation would result in compelled testimony for Fifth Amendment purposes. However, the Supreme Court has been narrowing the scope of *Miranda*'s application.

a) Meeting with Probation Officer

Admission of rape and murder by a probationer to his probation officer was not compelled or involuntary, despite the probationer's obligation to periodically report and be "truthful in all matters." [Minnesota v. Murphy, 465 U.S. 420 (1984)]

b) Uncharged Witness at Grand Jury Hearing

The *Miranda* requirements **do not apply** to a witness testifying before a grand jury, even if the witness is under the compulsion of a subpoena. Such a witness who has not been charged or indicted does not have the right to have counsel present during the questioning, but he may consult with an attorney outside the grand jury room. A witness who gives false testimony before a grand jury may be convicted of perjury even though he was not given the *Miranda* warnings. [United States v. Mandujano, 425 U.S. 564 (1976); United States v. Wong, 431 U.S. 174 (1977)]

b. Custody Requirement

Determining whether custody exists is a two-step process: The first step (sometimes called the "freedom of movement test") requires the court to determine whether a reasonable person under the circumstances would feel that he was *free to terminate the interrogation and leave*. All of the circumstances surrounding the interrogation must be considered. If an individual's freedom of movement was curtailed in this way, the next step considers "whether the relevant environment presents the *same inherently coercive pressures* as the type of station house questioning at issue in *Miranda*." [Howes v. Fields, 565 U.S. 499 (2012)] Therefore, the more a setting resembles a traditional arrest (i.e., the more constrained the suspect feels), the more likely the Court will consider it to be custody. If the detention is voluntary, it does not constitute custody. [*See* Berkemer v. McCarty, *supra*; Oregon v. Mathiason, 429 U.S. 492 (1977)] If the detention is long and is involuntary, it will likely be held to constitute custody. [*See* Mathis v. United States, 391 U.S. 1 (1968)]

Example: D is in custody when he is awakened in his own room in the middle of the night by four officers surrounding his bed, who then begin to question him. [Orozco v. Texas, 394 U.S. 324 (1969)]

1) Test Is Objective

The initial determination of whether a person is in custody depends on the *objective* circumstances of the interrogation, not on the subjective views harbored by either the interrogating officers or the person being interrogated. Thus, a court would consider things like the location of the questioning (e.g., suspect's home, workplace, or school; crime scene; police car; police station); whether police officers had their guns drawn; the length of the questioning; the suspect's apparent youth; whether the suspect was told he could not leave; etc.

2) **Traffic Stops Generally Not Custodial**

Although a routine traffic stop curtails a motorist's freedom of movement, such a stop is presumptively temporary and brief, and the motorist knows that he typically will soon be on his way; therefore, the motorist should not feel unduly coerced. Thus, *Miranda* warnings normally need not be given during a traffic stop.

Example: Officer stopped Defendant for weaving in and out of traffic. When Officer noticed Defendant had trouble standing, he performed a field sobriety test, which Defendant failed. Without giving *Miranda* warnings, Officer then asked Defendant if he had been drinking, and Defendant admitted to recent drinking and drug use. The admission is admissible. [Berkemer v. McCarty, *supra*]

3) **Incarcerated Suspects**

The fact that a suspect is incarcerated does not automatically mean that any interrogation of the suspect is custodial. The test still is whether the person's freedom of action is limited in a significant way. [Howes v. Fields, *supra*]

Example: Defendant, a prisoner, was escorted from his cell to a conference room in which he was questioned by two corrections officers about pre-incarceration criminal activity. He was told repeatedly that he was free to leave at any time to go back to his cell. He was not restrained and sometimes the conference room door was open. On the other hand, he was not given *Miranda* warnings and the corrections officers were armed. On balance, for purposes of *Miranda*, Defendant was not in custody. [Howes v. Fields, *supra*]

c. **Interrogation Requirement**

"Interrogation" refers not only to express questioning, but also to any words or actions on the part of the police that the police should know are reasonably likely to elicit an incriminating response from the suspect. [Rhode Island v. Innis, 446 U.S. 291 (1980)] However, *Miranda* does not apply to **spontaneous statements** not made in response to interrogation, although officers must give the warnings before any follow-up questioning. Neither does *Miranda* apply to routine booking questions (e.g., name, address, age, etc.), even when the booking process is being taped and may be used as evidence. [Pennsylvania v. Muniz, 496 U.S. 582 (1990)—defendant failed sobriety test and had trouble answering booking questions]

Examples: 1) Police comments about the danger a gun would present to handicapped children, which resulted in a robbery suspect's leading them to a weapon, did not constitute interrogation when the officers were not aware that the suspect was peculiarly susceptible to an appeal to his conscience. [Rhode Island v. Innis, *supra*]

2) Allowing a suspect's wife to talk to the suspect in the presence of an officer who is taping the conversation with the spouses' knowledge does not constitute interrogation. [Arizona v. Mauro, 481 U.S. 520 (1987)]

1) Break in Interrogation—Questioning by Different Police Agencies
When a second police agency continues to question a suspect at a point when the first police department terminates its questioning, the impact of an earlier denial of rights by the first department carries over into the questioning by the second agency. [Westover v. United States, 384 U.S. 436 (1966)]

3. Right to Waive Rights or Terminate Interrogation
After receiving *Miranda* warnings, a detainee has several options: do nothing, waive his *Miranda* rights, assert the right to remain silent, or assert the right to consult with an attorney.

  a. Do Nothing
If the detainee does not respond at all to *Miranda* warnings, the Court will not presume a waiver [*see* Fare v. Michael, 442 U.S. 707 (1979)], but neither will the Court presume that the detainee has asserted a right to remain silent or to consult with an attorney. Therefore, the police may continue to question the detainee. [*See* Berghuis v. Thompkins, 560 U.S. 370 (2010)]

  b. Waive Rights
The detainee may waive his rights under *Miranda*. To be valid, the government must show by a preponderance of the evidence that the waiver was ***knowing and voluntary***. The Court will look to the totality of the circumstances in determining whether this standard was met. But it appears that if the government can show that the detainee received *Miranda* warnings and then chose to answer questions, that is probably sufficient. [*See* Berghuis v. Thompkins, *supra*—suspect scarcely said anything after receiving *Miranda* warnings, but was held to have voluntarily waived his right to remain silent when he responded "yes" to an incriminating question posed three hours into his interrogation]

    1) Police Deception of Detainee's Lawyer
If the *Miranda* warnings are given, a voluntary confession will be admissible even if the police lie to the detainee's lawyer about their intent to question the detainee or fail to inform the detainee that his lawyer is attempting to see him, as long as adversary judicial proceedings have not commenced. [Moran v. Burbine, 475 U.S. 412 (1986)]

  c. Right to Remain Silent
At any time prior to or during interrogation, the detainee may indicate that he wishes to remain silent. Such an indication must be explicit, unambiguous, and unequivocal (e.g., the detainee's failure to answer does not constitute an invocation of the right to remain silent). [Berghuis v. Thompkins, *supra*] If the detainee so indicates, all ***questioning related to the particular crime must stop***.

    1) Police May Resume Questioning If They "Scrupulously Honor" Request
The police may reinitiate questioning after the detainee has invoked the right to remain silent, as long as they "scrupulously honor" the detainee's request. This means, at the very least, that the police may not badger the detainee into talking and must wait a significant time before reinitiating questioning.

> *Example:* In the Supreme Court's only opinion directly on point, it allowed police to reinitiate questioning where: (i) the police *immediately ceased questioning* upon the detainee's request and did not resume questioning for several hours; (ii) the detainee was *rewarned* of his rights; and (iii) questioning was *limited to a crime that was not the subject of the earlier questioning*. [Michigan v. Mosley, 423 U.S. 96 (1975)]

d. Right to Counsel

At any time prior to or during interrogation, the detainee may also invoke a *Miranda* (i.e., Fifth Amendment) right to counsel. If the detainee invokes this right, *all questioning must cease* until the detainee is provided with an attorney or initiates further questioning himself. [Edwards v. Arizona, 451 U.S. 477 (1981)]

1) Police May Not Resume Questioning About Any Crime

Once the detainee invokes his right to counsel under *Miranda,* all questioning must cease; the police may not even question the detainee about a totally unrelated crime, as they can where the detainee merely invokes the right to remain silent. [*See* Arizona v. Roberson, 486 U.S. 675 (1988)] *Rationale:* The right to counsel under *Miranda* is a prophylactic right designed by the Court to prevent the police from badgering a detainee into talking without the aid of counsel, and this purpose can be accomplished only if *all* questioning ceases. [*See* McNeil v. Wisconsin, 501 U.S. 171 (1991)]

a) Compare—Detainee May Initiate Resumption of Questioning

The detainee may waive his right to counsel after invoking the right, and thus initiate resumption of questioning.

> *Example:* The detainee cut off interrogation by asking for an attorney, but then asked the interrogating officer, "What is going to happen to me now?" The officer explained that the detainee did not have to talk, and the detainee said he understood. The officer then described the charge against the detainee and gave him fresh *Miranda* warnings. The detainee then confessed after taking a polygraph test. The Court upheld admission of the confession into evidence, finding that the detainee had validly waived his rights. [Oregon v. Bradshaw, 462 U.S. 1039 (1983)]

b) Scope of Right—Custodial Interrogation

The Fifth Amendment right to counsel under *Miranda* applies whenever there is custodial interrogation.

c) Compare—Sixth Amendment Right "Offense Specific"

Recall that the Sixth Amendment right to counsel (*see* C., *supra*) attaches only after formal proceedings have begun. Moreover, whereas invocation of the Fifth Amendment right prevents all questioning, the Sixth Amendment right is "offense specific." (*See* C.3., *supra*.)

2) Request Must Be Unambiguous and Specific

A Fifth Amendment request for counsel can be invoked only by an *unambiguous* request for counsel *in dealing with the custodial interrogation*. [McNeil v. Wisconsin, *supra*; Davis v. United States, 512 U.S. 452 (1994)] The request must be sufficiently clear that a reasonable police officer in the same situation would understand the statement to be a request for counsel.

Examples: 1) The statement by the suspect being interrogated, "Maybe I should talk to a lawyer," is not an unambiguous request for counsel under the Fifth Amendment, and so does not prevent further questioning.

                    2) D was arrested and charged with robbery. At his initial appearance, he requested the aid of counsel. After D's appearance, the police came to D's cell, gave him *Miranda* warnings, and questioned D about a crime unrelated to the robbery. D made incriminating statements. D's Fifth Amendment right to counsel was not violated because D did not request counsel in dealing with the interrogation. His post-charge request for counsel at his initial appearance was a ***Sixth Amendment*** request for counsel, which is offense specific (*see* C.3., *supra*).

3)   Ambiguities Relevant Only If Part of Request

Once the detainee has expressed an unequivocal desire to receive counsel, no subsequent questions or responses may be used to cast doubt on the request and all questioning of the detainee must cease. Where the request is ambiguous, police may ask clarifying questions, but are not required to do so; rather, they may continue to interrogate the detainee until an unambiguous request is received. [Davis v. United States, *supra*] Note that if the detainee agrees to answer questions orally, but requests the presence of counsel before making any written statements, the detainee's oral statements are admissible. The detainee's agreement to talk constitutes a voluntary and knowing waiver of the right to counsel. [Connecticut v. Barrett, 479 U.S. 523 (1987)]

4)   Counsel Must Be Present at Interrogation

Mere consultation with counsel prior to questioning does not satisfy the right to counsel—the police cannot resume questioning the detainee in the absence of counsel. [Minnick v. Mississippi, 498 U.S. 146 (1991)] Of course, counsel need not be present if the detainee waives the right to counsel by initiating the exchange. (*See* 1)a), *supra*.)

Example: The detainee answered a few questions during interrogation, but then requested an attorney. He was allowed to meet with his attorney three times. Subsequently, in the absence of counsel, police resumed interrogating the detainee, and he made incriminating statements. The Court held that the statements must be excluded from evidence. [Minnick v. Mississippi, *supra*]

5)   Duration of Prohibition

The prohibition against questioning a detainee after he requests an attorney lasts the entire time that the detainee is in custody for interrogation purposes, plus 14 more days after the detainee returns to his normal life. After that point, the detainee can be questioned regarding the same matter upon receiving a fresh set of *Miranda* warnings. [Maryland v. Shatzer, 559 U.S. 98 (2010)—while in prison, detainee was questioned about alleged sexual abuse, invoked his right to counsel, and was released back into the general prison population (his normal life); police could reinitiate questioning after 14 days without first providing counsel]

6) Statements Obtained in Violation May Be Used to Impeach

As indicated above, if the detainee requests counsel, all questioning must cease unless counsel is present or the detainee initiates a resumption of questioning. If *the police* initiate further questioning, the detainee's statements cannot be used by the prosecution in its case in chief, but they can be used to *impeach the detainee's* trial testimony, as long as the court finds that the detainee voluntarily and intelligently waived his right to counsel. [Michigan v. Harvey, 494 U.S. 344 (1990)] Note, however, that such illegally obtained evidence cannot be used to impeach trial testimony of witnesses other than the detainee. [James v. Illinois, 493 U.S. 307 (1990)]

4. Effect of Violation

Generally, evidence obtained in violation of *Miranda* is inadmissible at trial.

a. Use of Confession for Impeachment

A confession obtained in violation of the defendant's *Miranda* rights, but otherwise voluntary, may be used to *impeach the defendant's testimony* if he takes the stand at trial, even though such a confession is inadmissible in the state's case in chief as evidence of guilt. [Harris v. New York, 401 U.S. 222 (1971); Oregon v. Hass, 420 U.S. 714 (1975)] However, a truly involuntary confession is *inadmissible* for any purpose. [Mincey v. Arizona, II.C.5.f.4), *supra*]

1) Silence

The prosecutor may not use the defendant's silence after receiving *Miranda* warnings to counter the defendant's insanity defense. [Wainwright v. Greenfield, 474 U.S. 284 (1986)]

2) May Be Harmless Error

A single question by the prosecutor about the defendant's silence may constitute harmless error when followed by an objection sustained by the judge and an instruction to jurors to disregard the question. [Greer v. Miller, 483 U.S. 756 (1987)]

b. Warnings After Questioning and Confession

If the police obtain a confession from a detainee without giving him *Miranda* warnings and then give the detainee *Miranda* warnings and obtain a subsequent confession, the subsequent confession will be inadmissible if the "question first, warn later" nature of the questioning was intentional (i.e., the facts make it seem like the police used this as a scheme to get around the *Miranda* requirements). [Missouri v. Seibert, 542 U.S. 600 (2004)] However, a subsequent valid confession may be admissible if the original unwarned questioning seemed unplanned and the failure to give *Miranda* warnings seemed inadvertent. [*See* Oregon v. Elstad, 470 U.S. 298 (1985)]

c.   **Nontestimonial Fruits of an Unwarned Confession**

If the police fail to give *Miranda* warnings and during interrogation a detainee gives the police information that leads to nontestimonial evidence, the evidence will be suppressed if the failure was purposeful, but if the failure was not purposeful, the evidence probably will not be suppressed. [*See* United States v. Patane, 542 U.S. 630 (2004)]

5.   **Public Safety Exception to *Miranda***

If *police interrogation* is reasonably prompted by *concern for public safety*, responses to the questions may be used in court, even though the suspect is in custody and *Miranda* warnings are not given. [New York v. Quarles, 467 U.S. 649 (1984)—suspect was handcuffed and asked where he had hidden his gun; the arrest and questioning were virtually contemporaneous, and the police were reasonably concerned that the gun might be found and cause injury to an innocent person]

IV. PRETRIAL IDENTIFICATION

A.   IN GENERAL

The purpose of all the rules concerning pretrial identification is to ensure that when the witness identifies the person at trial, she is identifying the person who committed the crime and not merely the person whom she has previously seen at the police station.

B.   SUBSTANTIVE BASES FOR ATTACK

    1.   **Sixth Amendment Right to Counsel**

        a.   **When Right Exists**

A suspect has a right to the presence of an attorney at any *post-charge lineup or showup.* [Moore v. Illinois, 434 U.S. 220 (1977); United States v. Wade, 388 U.S. 218 (1967)] At a lineup, the witness is asked to pick the perpetrator of the crime from a group of persons, while a showup is a one-to-one confrontation between the witness and the suspect for the purpose of identification.

        b.   **Role of Counsel at a Lineup**

The right is simply to have an attorney present during the lineup so that the lawyer can observe any suggestive aspects of the lineup and bring them out on cross-examination of the witness. There is no right to have the lawyer help set up the lineup, to demand changes in the way it is conducted, etc.

        c.   **Photo Identification**

The accused does *not* have the right to counsel at photo identifications. [United States v. Ash, 413 U.S. 300 (1973)] However, as in the case of lineups, the accused may have a due process claim regarding the photo identification. (*See* 2., *infra.*)

        d.   **Physical Evidence**

The accused does *not* have the right to counsel when the police take physical evidence such as handwriting exemplars or fingerprints from her.

2.   **Due Process Standard**

A defendant can attack an identification as denying due process when the identification is *unnecessarily suggestive* and there is a *substantial likelihood of misidentification*. It is clear that both parts of this standard must be met for the defendant to win, and that to meet this difficult test, the identification must be shown to have been extremely suggestive.

Examples: 1) A showup at a hospital did not deny the defendant due process when such a procedure was necessary due to the need of an immediate identification, the inability of the identifying victim to come to the police station, and the possibility that the victim might die. [Stovall v. Denno, 388 U.S. 293 (1967)]

2) A photo identification with only six snapshots did not violate due process where the procedure was necessary because perpetrators of a serious felony (robbery) were at large, and the police had to determine if they were on the right track, and the Court found little danger of misidentification. [Simmons v. United States, 390 U.S. 377 (1968)]

3) No substantial likelihood of misidentification was found in the showing of a single photograph to a police officer two days after the crime. [Manson v. Brathwaite, 432 U.S. 98 (1977)]

4) A fundamentally unfair procedure, such as when the perpetrator of the crime is known to be black and the suspect is the only black person in the lineup, would violate the due process standard.

C.   **THE REMEDY**

The remedy for an unconstitutional identification is *exclusion* of the in-court identification (unless it has an independent source).

1.   **Independent Source**

A witness may make an in-court identification despite the existence of an unconstitutional pretrial identification if the in-court identification has an independent source. The factors a court will weigh in determining an independent source include the opportunity of the witness to observe the criminal at the time of the crime, the witness's degree of attention, the accuracy of the witness's prior description of the criminal, the level of certainty demonstrated at the confrontation, and the time between the crime and the confrontation. [Neil v. Biggers, 409 U.S. 188 (1972); Manson v. Brathwaite, 432 U.S. 98 (1977)]

2.   **Hearing**

The admissibility of identification evidence should be determined at a suppression hearing in the absence of the jury, but exclusion of the jury is not constitutionally required. [Watkins v. Sowders, 449 U.S. 341 (1981)] The government bears the burden of proof as to the presence of counsel or a waiver by the accused, or as to an independent source for the in-court identification, while the defendant must prove an alleged due process violation.

D.   **NO RIGHT TO LINEUP**

The defendant is not entitled to any particular kind of identification procedure. The defendant may not demand a lineup.

E.   **NO SELF-INCRIMINATION ISSUE**

Because a lineup does not involve compulsion to give evidence *"testimonial"* in nature, a suspect has no basis in the Fifth Amendment privilege against compelled self-incrimination to refuse to participate in one. [United States v. Wade, B.1.a., *supra*]

V. EXCLUSIONARY RULE

A. IN GENERAL

The exclusionary rule is a judge-made doctrine that prohibits the introduction, at a criminal trial, of evidence obtained in violation of a defendant's Fourth, Fifth, or Sixth Amendment rights.

1. Rationale

The main purpose of the exclusionary rule is to deter the government (primarily the police) from violating a person's constitutional rights: If the government cannot use evidence obtained in violation of a person's rights, it will be less likely to act in contravention of those rights. The rule also serves as one remedy for deprivation of constitutional rights (other remedies include civil suits, injunctions, etc.).

2. Scope of the Rule

a. Fruit of the Poisonous Tree

Generally, not only must ***illegally obtained evidence*** be excluded, but also ***all evidence obtained or derived*** from exploitation of that evidence. The courts deem such evidence the tainted fruit of the poisonous tree. [Nardone v. United States, 308 U.S. 338 (1939); Wong Sun v. United States, 371 U.S. 471 (1963)]

Example: D was arrested ***without probable cause*** and brought to the police station. The police read D his *Miranda* warnings three times and permitted D to see two friends. After being at the station for six hours, D confessed. The confession must be excluded because it is the direct result of the unlawful arrest—if D had not been arrested illegally, he would not have been in custody and would not have confessed. [Taylor v. Alabama, 457 U.S. 687 (1982)]

Compare: Police ***have probable cause*** to arrest D. They go to D's home and improperly arrest him without a warrant, in violation of the Fourth Amendment (*see* II.B.2.b.3), *supra*). D confesses at home, and the police then take him to the station. D confesses again at the station. The home confession must be excluded from evidence because it is the fruit of the illegal arrest, but the station house confession is admissible because it is not a fruit of the unlawful arrest. Because the police had probable cause to arrest D, they did not gain anything from the unlawful arrest—they could have lawfully arrested D the moment he stepped outside of his home and then brought him to the station for his confession. Thus, the station house confession was not an exploitation of the police misconduct; i.e., it was not a fruit of the fact that D was arrested at home as opposed to somewhere else. [New York v. Harris, 495 U.S. 14 (1990)]

1) Limitations—Fruits Derived from *Miranda* Violations

The fruits derived from statements obtained in violation of *Miranda* (*see* III.D.1., *supra*) may be admissible despite the exclusionary rule. (*See* III.D.4.b., *supra*.)

b. Exception—Balancing Test

In recent cases, the Court has emphasized that in deciding whether to apply the exclusionary rule, lower courts must *balance* the rule's *purpose* (i.e., deterrence of police misconduct) *against its costs* (i.e., the exclusion of probative evidence). Therefore, exclusion of tainted evidence, including fruit of the poisonous tree, is *not* automatic; whether exclusion is warranted in a given case depends on "the culpability of the police and the potential of the exclusion to deter wrongful police conduct." [Herring v. United States, 555 U.S. 135 (2009)]

1) Independent Source

Evidence is admissible if the prosecution can show that it was obtained from a source independent of the original illegality.

Example: Police illegally search a warehouse and discover marijuana, but do not seize it. The police later return to the warehouse with a valid warrant based on information totally unrelated to the illegal search. If police seize the marijuana pursuant to the warrant, the marijuana is admissible. [Murray v. United States, 487 U.S. 533 (1988)]

2) Attenuation—Intervening Act or Circumstance

If the connection between unconstitutional police conduct and the evidence is remote or has been interrupted by some intervening circumstance, so that the causal link between the police misconduct and the evidence is broken, the evidence will not be suppressed. In such a case, suppression would not serve the purpose of deterring future misconduct and so the evidence is admissible under the "attenuation exception" to the exclusionary rule. The court will consider:

- The *temporal proximity* between the unconstitutional conduct and the discovery of the evidence (the closer the temporal proximity, the less likely the exception applies);

- The presence of *intervening circumstances*; and

- Most importantly, the *purpose and flagrancy* of the official misconduct.

[Brown v. Illinois, 422 U.S. 590 (1975)]

Example: 1) The attenuation exception was held to apply when a police officer unlawfully stopped a suspect without a warrant, discovered that there was an outstanding arrest warrant for the suspect, arrested the suspect, and found drugs on the suspect's person. The stop was made because the suspect had been seen leaving a home at which police officers had reason to believe drugs were being dealt. The stop was unlawful because: (i) the police officer making the stop did not know what time the suspect entered the home (and so lacked a sufficient basis to conclude the suspect was a short-term visitor who may have been consummating a drug transaction); and (ii) the officer demanded that the suspect talk to him rather than asked if the suspect would talk to him. Although the unlawful stop was in close temporal proximity to discovery of the drugs (favoring exclusion), the outstanding arrest warrant predated the unlawful stop and was unconnected to it, making the arrest a "ministerial act that was independently compelled by the pre-existing warrant" (i.e., an intervening circumstance, favoring admission of the evidence). Moreover, the officer's conduct was at worst negligent; the officer's error in judgment "hardly rises to a purposeful or flagrant violation of [the defendant's] Fourth Amendment rights." [Utah v. Strieff, 136 S. Ct. 2056 (2016)]

a) Intervening Act of Free Will

An intervening act of free will by the defendant will break the causal chain between the evidence and the original illegality and thus remove the taint. [Wong Sun v. United States, 371 U.S. 471 (1963)]

Example: The defendant was released on his own recognizance after an illegal arrest but later returned to the station to confess. This voluntary act of free will removed any taint from the confession. [Wong Sun v. United States, *supra*]

Compare: The reading of *Miranda* warnings, even when coupled with the passage of six hours and consultation with friends, was not sufficient to break the causal chain under the facts of *Taylor v. Alabama* (*see* 2.a., above).

3) Inevitable Discovery

If the prosecution can show that the police would have discovered the evidence whether or not they had acted unconstitutionally, the evidence will be admissible. [Nix v. Williams, 467 U.S. 431 (1984)]

4) Live Witness Testimony

It is difficult for a defendant to have live witness testimony excluded as the fruit of illegal police conduct, because a more direct link between the unconstitutional police conduct and the testimony is required than for exclusion of other evidence. The factors a court must consider in determining whether a sufficiently direct link exists include the extent to which the witness is freely willing to testify and the extent to which excluding the witness's testimony would deter future illegal conduct. [United States v. Ceccolini, 435 U.S. 268 (1978)]

5) In-Court Identification

The defendant *may not exclude* the witness's in-court identification on the ground that it is the fruit of an unlawful detention. [United States v. Crews, 445 U.S. 463 (1980)]

6) Out-of-Court Identifications

Unduly suggestive out-of-court identifications that create a substantial likelihood of misidentification can violate the Due Process Clause of the Fourteenth Amendment. Whether an identification procedure is unduly suggestive is judged on a case-by-case basis under the totality of the circumstances. However, the Court will not consider applying the exclusionary rule unless the unnecessarily suggestive circumstances were *arranged by the police*. If the police do not arrange the circumstances, applying the exclusionary rule would do nothing to deter police misconduct. [Perry v. New Hampshire, 132 S. Ct. 716 (2012)]

Example: Police responded to a call that a man was trying to break into cars in a parking lot. They apprehended Defendant with speakers and an amplifier in the parking lot. An officer went to the caller's apartment to investigate and asked the caller to describe the man she saw. She pointed out her window to Defendant, who was standing with an officer. Since the police did not arrange the unduly suggestive identification procedure, the trial judge did not have to make a preliminary inquiry into the reliability of the identification and could allow the jury to assess reliability. [Perry v. New Hampshire, *supra*]

B. LIMITATIONS ON THE RULE

1. Inapplicable to Grand Juries

A grand jury witness may not refuse to answer questions on the ground that they are based on evidence obtained from an unlawful search and seizure [United States v. Calandra, 414 U.S. 338 (1974)], unless the evidence was obtained in violation of the federal wiretapping statute [Gelbard v. United States, 408 U.S. 41 (1972)].

2. Inapplicable to Civil Proceedings

The exclusionary rule does not forbid one sovereign from using in civil proceedings evidence that was illegally seized by the agent of another sovereign. [United States v. Janis, 428 U.S. 433 (1976)] Moreover, the Supreme Court would probably allow the sovereign that illegally obtained evidence to use it in a civil proceeding. The exclusionary rule does apply, however, to a proceeding for forfeiture of an article used in violation of the criminal law, when forfeiture is clearly a penalty for the criminal offense. [One 1958 Plymouth Sedan v. Pennsylvania, 380 U.S. 693 (1965)]

Example: Evidence that is inadmissible in a state criminal trial because it was illegally seized by the police may be used by the IRS. [United States v. Janis, *supra*]

3. Inapplicable to Violations of State Law

The exclusionary rule does not apply to mere violations of state law. [*See* Virginia v. Moore, II.C.5.a., *supra*]

Example: Police arrested D for driving on a suspended license, searched him, and found cocaine on his person. Under state law, arrest was not authorized for driving on a suspended license, and D moved to suppress the evidence found during the search. *Held:* Because it is constitutionally reasonable for the police to arrest a person if the police have probable cause to believe that the person has committed even a misdemeanor in their presence (*see* II.B.2.b.2), *supra*), and the police here had probable cause to believe that D committed the offense of driving on a suspended license, D's arrest was constitutionally reasonable and, thus, did not violate the Fourth Amendment, the state law notwithstanding. [*See* Virginia v. Moore, *supra*]

4. Inapplicable to Internal Agency Rules

The exclusionary rule applies only if there is a violation of the Constitution or federal law;

it does not apply to a violation of only internal agency rules. [United States v. Caceres, 440 U.S. 741 (1979)]

5. Inapplicable in Parole Revocation Proceedings
The exclusionary rule does not apply in parole revocation proceedings. [Pennsylvania v. Scott, 524 U.S. 357 (1998)]

6. Good Faith Exception
The exclusionary rule does not apply when the police arrest or search someone erroneously but in good faith, thinking that they are acting pursuant to a valid arrest warrant, search warrant, or law. [United States v. Leon, 468 U.S. 897 (1984); Herring v. United States, A.2.b., *supra*] *Rationale:* One of the main purposes of the exclusionary rule is to deter improper police conduct, and this purpose cannot be served where police are acting in good faith.

a. Exceptions to Good Faith Reliance on Search Warrant
The Supreme Court has suggested four exceptions to the good faith defense for reliance on a defective search warrant. A police officer cannot rely on a defective search warrant in good faith if:

1) The affidavit underlying the warrant is so lacking in probable cause that no reasonable police officer would have relied on it;

2) The warrant is defective on its face (e.g., it fails to state with particularity the place to be searched or the things to be seized);

3) The police officer or government official obtaining the warrant lied to or misled the magistrate; or

4) The magistrate has "wholly abandoned his judicial role."

7. Use of Excluded Evidence for Impeachment Purposes
Some illegally obtained evidence that is inadmissible in the state's case in chief may nevertheless be used to impeach the defendant's credibility if he takes the stand at trial.

a. Voluntary Confessions in Violation of *Miranda*
An otherwise voluntary confession taken in violation of the *Miranda v. Arizona* requirements is admissible at trial for impeachment purposes. [Harris v. New York, 401 U.S. 222 (1971); Oregon v. Hass, 420 U.S. 714 (1975)] However, a truly involuntary confession is not admissible for any purpose. [Mincey v. Arizona, III.D.4.a., *supra*]

b. Fruit of Illegal Searches
The prosecution may use evidence obtained from an illegal search that is inadmissible in its direct case to impeach the defendant's statements made in response to proper cross-examination reasonably suggested by the defendant's direct examination [United States v. Havens, 446 U.S. 620 (1980)], but such illegally obtained evidence cannot be used to impeach the trial testimony of witnesses other than the defendant [James v. Illinois, 493 U.S. 307 (1990)].

8. Knock and Announce Rule Violations
Exclusion is not an available remedy for violations of the knock and announce rule

pertaining to the execution of a warrant. *Rationale:* The exclusionary remedy is too attenuated from the purposes of the knock and announce rule of protecting human life and limb, property, privacy, and dignity. Moreover, the cost of excluding relevant evidence because of claims that the knock and announce rule was violated is too high when compared to the deterrence benefit that will be gained. Finally, there are other deterrents to prevent officers from violating the rule, such as civil suits and internal police disciplinary sanctions. [Hudson v. Michigan, 547 U.S. 586 (2006)]

C. HARMLESS ERROR TEST

A conviction will not necessarily be overturned merely because improperly obtained evidence was admitted at trial; the harmless error test applies, so a conviction can be upheld if the conviction would have resulted despite the improper evidence. On appeal, the government bears the burden of showing **beyond a reasonable doubt** that the admission was harmless. [Chapman v. California, 386 U.S. 18 (1967); Milton v. Wainwright, 407 U.S. 371 (1972)] In a habeas corpus proceeding, if a petitioner claims a constitutional error, the petitioner must be released if the error had **substantial and injurious effect or influence** in determining the jury's verdict. [Brecht v. Abrahamson, 507 U.S. 619 (1993)] If the judge is in "grave doubt" as to the harm (e.g., where the record is evenly balanced as to harmlessness), the petition must be granted. [O'Neal v. McAninch, 513 U.S. 432 (1995)]

D. ENFORCING THE EXCLUSIONARY RULE

1. Right to Hearing on Motion to Suppress

The defendant is entitled to have the admissibility of evidence or a confession decided as a matter of law by a judge out of the hearing of the jury. [Jackson v. Denno, 378 U.S. 368 (1964)] It is permissible to let the jury reconsider the "admissibility" of the evidence if the judge finds it admissible, but there is no constitutional right to such a dual evaluation. [Lego v. Twomey, 404 U.S. 477 (1972)] And the defendant is not constitutionally entitled to have a specific finding of fact on each factual question. [LaValee v. Delle Rose, 410 U.S. 690 (1973)]

2. Burden of Proof

The government bears the burden of establishing admissibility by a preponderance of the evidence. [Lego v. Twomey, *supra*]

3. Defendant's Right to Testify

The defendant has the right to testify at the suppression hearing without his testimony being admitted against him at trial on the issue of guilt. [Simmons v. United States, 390 U.S. 377 (1968)]

VI. PRETRIAL PROCEDURES

A. PRELIMINARY HEARING TO DETERMINE PROBABLE CAUSE TO DETAIN ("*GERSTEIN* HEARINGS")

A defendant has a Fourth Amendment right to be released from detention if there is no probable cause to hold him. Thus, a defendant has a right to a determination of probable cause. A preliminary hearing is a hearing held after arrest but before trial to determine whether probable cause for detention exists. The hearing is an informal, ex parte, nonadversarial proceeding.

1. **When Right Applies**

   If probable cause has already been determined (e.g., the arrest is pursuant to a grand jury indictment or an arrest warrant), a preliminary hearing need not be held. If no probable cause determination has been made, a defendant has a right to a preliminary hearing to determine probable cause if *"significant pretrial constraints on the defendant's liberty"* exist. Thus, the right applies if the defendant is released only upon the posting of bail or if he is held in jail in lieu of bail. It does not apply if the defendant is released merely upon the condition that he appear for trial.

   Note: The fact that the defendant has been released does not preclude a finding of a significant constraint on liberty, because many conditions can be attached to liberty.

2. **Timing**

   The hearing must be held within a reasonable time, and the Court has determined that 48 hours is presumptively reasonable. [Riverside County v. McLaughlin, 500 U.S. 44 (1991)]

3. **Remedy**

   There is *no real remedy* for the defendant for the mere denial of this hearing, because an unlawful detention, without more, has no effect on the subsequent prosecution. However, if evidence is discovered as a result of the unlawful detention, it will be suppressed under the exclusionary rule.

B. PRETRIAL DETENTION

1. **Initial Appearance**

   Soon after the defendant is arrested, she must be brought before a magistrate who will advise her of her rights, set bail, and appoint counsel if necessary. The initial appearance may be combined with the *Gerstein* hearing, but will be held whether or not a *Gerstein* hearing is necessary. For misdemeanors, this appearance will be the trial.

2. **Bail**

   Most state constitutions or statutes create a right to be released on appropriate bail (either on personal recognizance or on a cash bond).

   a. **Due Process Concerns**

      Because denial of release on bail deprives a person of liberty, such denials must comply with the Due Process Clause. In upholding the Federal Bail Reform Act (which permits a court to detain an arrestee if the judge determines that no condition of release would ensure the arrestee's appearance or the safety of any person or the community), the Court held that denial of bail does not violate substantive due process (by imposing punishment before a defendant is found guilty), because the denial of bail is not punishment but a regulatory solution to the problem of persons committing crimes while out on bail. The Court also held that the federal act does not violate procedural due process because it provides detainees with a right to a hearing on the issue, expedited review, etc. [United States v. Salerno, 479 U.S. 1026 (1987)] Similar state statutes would likely be upheld, but a state statute that arbitrarily denies bail (e.g., by not allowing the detainee to present evidence or denying release to a whole class of detainees) would probably violate the Due Process Clause.

b. **Right to Be Free from Excessive Bail**

Where the right to release exists, state constitutions and state statutes—and perhaps the Eighth Amendment as well—prohibit "excessive" bail. This has traditionally been interpreted to require that bail be set no higher than is necessary to ensure the defendant's appearance at trial.

c. **Bail Issues Are Immediately Appealable**

In most jurisdictions and under federal law, a refusal to grant bail or the setting of excessive bail may be appealed immediately, as an exception to the final judgment rule for appeals. If not immediately appealable, the denial of bail can be reached by an immediate petition for a writ of habeas corpus. Once the defendant is convicted, an appeal of a pretrial bail decision is moot. [Murphy v. Hunt, 455 U.S. 478 (1982)]

d. **Defendant Incompetent to Stand Trial**

As to deprivation of pretrial liberty by commitment of one who is not competent to stand trial, the standards for commitment and subsequent release must be essentially identical with those for the commitment of persons not charged with crime; otherwise, there is a denial of equal protection. [Jackson v. Indiana, 406 U.S. 715 (1972)]

3. **Pretrial Detention Practices**

Pretrial detention practices that are reasonably related to the interest of maintaining jail security, such as double-bunking, prohibiting inmates from receiving from the outside food and personal items or books not mailed directly from the publisher, routine inspections while the detainees remain outside their rooms, and body cavity searches following contact visits, do not violate due process or the Fourth Amendment and without more do not constitute punishment. [Bell v. Wolfish, 441 U.S. 520 (1979)]

C. **PRELIMINARY HEARING TO DETERMINE PROBABLE CAUSE TO PROSECUTE**

A later preliminary hearing may be held to determine whether probable cause to prosecute exists. The accused has the *right to counsel* at this hearing [Coleman v. Alabama, 399 U.S. 1 (1970)], and both the prosecutor and the accused may present evidence for the record. The accused may waive the hearing. Either side may use this hearing to preserve testimony of a witness unavailable at trial (e.g., the witness testifies at the preliminary hearing and dies before trial) provided there was some opportunity to cross-examine the witness at the preliminary hearing. [Ohio v. Roberts, 448 U.S. 56 (1980)]

D. **GRAND JURIES**

The Fifth Amendment right to indictment by grand jury has not been incorporated into the Fourteenth Amendment, but some state constitutions require grand jury indictment.

1. **Charging Grand Juries**

Most states east of the Mississippi and the federal system use the grand jury as a regular part of the charging process. The charging grand jury *determines probable cause to prosecute* by returning the bill of indictment submitted by the prosecutor as a "true bill." Western states generally charge by filing an information, a written accusation of crime prepared and presented by the prosecutor. Informations also are used when the defendant waives her right to grand jury indictment.

2. **Special or Investigative Grand Juries**

   Special or investigative grand juries are used almost everywhere. This type of grand jury investigates, on its own motion, crime in the particular jurisdiction, and can initiate a criminal case by bringing an indictment.

3. **Grand Jury Proceedings**

   a. **Secrecy and Defendant's Lack of Access**

      Grand jury proceedings are conducted in secret. In most jurisdictions, a defendant has no right to notice that a grand jury is considering an indictment against her, to be present and confront witnesses at the proceeding, or to introduce evidence before the grand jury.

   b. **Particularized Need Required for Prosecutor's Access to Grand Jury Materials**

      The "particularized need" standard generally required under Rule 6(e) of the Federal Rules of Criminal Procedure in order to obtain access to grand jury materials must be shown by state attorneys general [Illinois v. Abbott, 460 U.S. 557 (1983)], as well as Justice Department attorneys [United States v. Sells Engineering, Inc., 463 U.S. 418 (1983)]. The disclosure of such materials to the Internal Revenue Service for the purpose of assessing tax liability, rather than for litigation, is not permitted. [United States v. Baggot, 463 U.S. 476 (1983)]

   c. **Subpoena Powers of Grand Jury**

      The grand jury may use its subpoena power to investigate the matters before it or to initiate criminal investigations of its own. Rather than returning an indictment, grand juries sometimes issue a report.

      1) **Government Need Not Prove Relevance**

         A grand jury subpoena may be quashed only if the opposing party can prove that there is no reasonable possibility that the material sought will be relevant to the grand jury investigation. The government has no initial burden of proving that the material is relevant. [United States v. R. Enterprises, Inc., 498 U.S. 292 (1991)]

      2) **Defamatory Reports**

         If the defendant or any other person believes that she has been defamed by a grand jury report, she may make a motion to seal the report.

   d. **No Right to Counsel or *Miranda* Warnings**

      A witness subpoenaed to testify before a grand jury does not have the right to receive the *Miranda* warnings, and the witness may be convicted of perjury despite the lack of warnings if she testifies falsely. A grand jury witness does not have the right to have an attorney present, but she may consult with an attorney outside the grand jury room. [United States v. Mandujano, III.D.2.a.2)b), *supra*; United States v. Wong, III.D.2.a.2) b), *supra*]

   e. **No Right to "Potential Defendant" Warnings**

      A witness who is under investigation and may well become a defendant is not entitled to a warning that she is a "potential defendant" when called to testify before the grand jury. [United States v. Washington, 431 U.S. 181 (1977)]

f.   No Right to Have Evidence Excluded

A grand jury may base its indictment on evidence that would not be admissible at trial [Costello v. United States, 350 U.S. 359 (1956)], and a grand jury witness may not refuse to answer questions on the grounds that they are based upon unconstitutionally obtained evidence [United States v. Calandra, 414 U.S. 338 (1974)]. Nor may an indicted defendant have the indictment quashed on the grounds that it is based upon illegally obtained evidence.

g.   No Right to Challenge Subpoena on Fourth Amendment Grounds

A suspect-witness (or any witness, for that matter) subpoenaed before a grand jury cannot attack the subpoena on the ground that the grand jury lacked "probable cause"— or any reason at all—to call her for questioning. No such attack can be made even if the subpoena also requires the witness to provide a handwriting exemplar, a voice sample, or otherwise cooperate with law enforcement officials in a manner not violating the self-incrimination privilege.

h.   Exclusion of Minorities

Minorities may not be excluded from grand jury service. A conviction resulting from an indictment issued by a grand jury from which members of a minority group have been excluded will be reversed without regard to the harmlessness of the error. [Vasquez v. Hillery, 474 U.S. 254 (1986)] Note that the defendant and the excluded members need not be of the same race. [Campbell v. Louisiana, 523 U.S. 392 (1998)]

i.   Dismissal Seldom Required for Procedural Defect

An indicted defendant is seldom entitled to dismissal of an indictment upon a showing that procedural error occurred during the grand jury proceedings. Generally, she is entitled to dismissal only upon a showing that the error substantially influenced the grand jury's decision to indict. [Bank of Nova Scotia v. United States, 487 U.S. 250 (1988)—defendant failed to show that prosecutorial misconduct before grand jury substantially influenced its decision to indict]

j.   Exculpatory Evidence

An indictment may not be dismissed by a federal court for a prosecutor's failure to present exculpatory evidence to the grand jury unless the prosecutor's conduct violates a preexisting constitutional, legislative, or procedural rule. [United States v. Williams, 504 U.S. 36 (1992)]

E.   SPEEDY TRIAL

1.   Constitutional Standard

A determination of whether the defendant's right to a speedy trial has been violated will be made by an evaluation of the totality of the circumstances. The following factors should be considered:

(i)   Length of the delay;

(ii)   Reason for the delay;

(iii) Whether the defendant asserted his right; and

(iv) Prejudice to the defendant.

[Barker v. Wingo, 407 U.S. 514 (1972)]

Example: A defendant who was arrested 8½ years after his federal indictment due solely to the government's neglect and who promptly asserted his right to a speedy trial claim was ***presumptively prejudiced*** so that an actual showing of prejudice was not necessary. [Doggett v. United States, 505 U.S. 647 (1992)]

a. Delays Caused by Assigned Counsel
Delays caused by counsel assigned by the court to the defendant should ordinarily be attributed to the defendant and not to the state. [Vermont v. Brillon, 556 U.S. 81 (2009)]

b. Delays at Sentencing Phase Ordinarily Not Relevant
The right to a speedy trial ordinarily does not apply once a defendant has been found guilty or has pleaded guilty. Therefore, the right does not apply to the sentencing phase of a criminal prosecution. [Betterman v. Montana, 136 S. Ct. 1609 (2016)]

2. Remedy—Dismissal
The remedy for a violation of the constitutional right to a speedy trial is dismissal with prejudice. [Strunk v. United States, 412 U.S. 434 (1973)]

3. When Right Attaches
The right to a speedy trial does not attach until the defendant has been ***arrested or charged***. It is very difficult to get relief for a pre-arrest delay under this standard, because the defendant must show prejudice from a delay, and good faith investigative delays do not violate due process. [United States v. Lovasco, 431 U.S. 783 (1977)]

A defendant is not entitled to speedy trial relief for the period between the dismissal of charges and later refiling. [United States v. MacDonald, 456 U.S. 1 (1982)] The only limitation on pre-arrest delay (other than general due process requirements) seems to be the statute of limitations for the particular crime.

a. Knowledge of Charges Unnecessary
The Speedy Trial Clause attaches even if the defendant does not know about the charges against him and is thus not restrained in any way. [Doggett v. United States, *supra*]

4. Special Problems
Two situations create special speedy trial problems:

a. Detainees
A defendant incarcerated in one jurisdiction who has a charge pending in another jurisdiction has a right to have the second jurisdiction exert reasonable efforts to obtain his presence for trial of these pending charges. Failure to exert such efforts violates his right to a speedy trial. [Smith v. Hooey, 393 U.S. 374 (1969)]

b. Indefinite Suspension of Charges
It is a violation of the right to a speedy trial to permit the prosecution to indefinitely

suspend charges, such as permitting the government to dismiss "without prejudice," which permits reinstatement of the prosecution *at any time*. [Klopfer v. North Carolina, 386 U.S. 213 (1967)—nolle prosequi that indefinitely suspended the statute of limitations violated speedy trial requirements]

F. PROSECUTORIAL DUTY TO DISCLOSE EXCULPATORY INFORMATION AND NOTICE OF DEFENSES

1. Prosecutor's Duty to Disclose Exculpatory Evidence

The government has a duty to disclose material, exculpatory evidence to the defendant. [Brady v. Maryland, 373 U.S. 83 (1963)] Failure to disclose such evidence—whether willful *or inadvertent*—violates the Due Process Clause and is grounds for reversing a conviction if the defendant can prove that:

(i) The evidence at issue is *favorable to the defendant* because it impeaches or is exculpatory; and

(ii) *Prejudice has resulted* (i.e., there is a *reasonable probability* that the result of the case would have been different if the undisclosed evidence had been presented at trial).

[Strickler v. Greene, 527 U.S. 263 (1999); United States v. Bagley, 473 U.S. 667 (1985)] *Note:* If the prosecution can show that the verdict is strongly supported by other evidence, sufficient prejudice will not be found.

Example: Defendant was convicted on the testimony of a single eyewitness. After trial, Defendant obtained police files containing statements of the eyewitness that contradicted his trial testimony and were favorable to Defendant. Since Defendant was convicted solely on the eyewitness's testimony, it is likely the result of the case would have been different had the statements been disclosed. Therefore, the failure to disclose violates *Brady*, and the conviction must be overturned and a new trial granted. [Smith v. Cain, 565 U.S. 73 (2012)]

a. Exception—Reports on Sexually Abused Minors

A defendant may not automatically obtain investigative reports made by a state agency in charge of investigating sexually abused minors because of the confidentiality of the minors' records. Such reports can be obtained only if they are *favorable* to the defendant and are *material* to guilt or punishment. [Pennsylvania v. Ritchie, 480 U.S. 39 (1987)]

b. Probably Must Be Relevant to Merits

The duty to disclose appears to extend only to evidence relevant to the prosecution's case in chief. Material going to a defense not on the merits probably need not be disclosed. [*See* United States v. Armstrong, 517 U.S. 456 (1996)—material relevant to defendant's claim that he was selected for prosecution because of his race need not be disclosed]

c. Duty Does Not Apply at Post-Conviction Proceedings

A prosecutor's obligation to disclose material, exculpatory evidence under *Brady* does not apply at post-conviction proceedings. [District Attorney's Office for the Third

Judicial District v. Osborne, 557 U.S. 52 (2009)—a convicted offender has no federal due process right to obtain post-conviction access to a state's evidence for DNA testing in the absence of any indication that available state post-conviction relief procedures are fundamentally unfair]

2. Notice of Alibi and Intent to Present Insanity Defense

a. Reciprocity Required
The prosecution may demand to know whether the defendant is going to plead insanity or raise an alibi as a defense. If the defendant is going to raise an alibi, he must list his witnesses. In return, the prosecution is required to list the witnesses it will call to rebut the defendant's defense. [Williams v. Florida, 399 U.S. 78 (1970); Wardius v. Oregon, 412 U.S. 470 (1973)]

b. Commenting on Failure to Present the Alibi
The prosecutor may not comment at trial on the defendant's failure to produce a witness named as supporting the alibi or on the failure to present the alibi itself. But the prosecutor may use the notice of an alibi to *impeach* a defendant who takes the stand and testifies to a different alibi.

G. COMPETENCY TO STAND TRIAL

1. Competency and Insanity Distinguished
Competency to stand trial must be carefully distinguished from the insanity defense, although both rest on a defendant's abnormality. Insanity is a defense to the criminal charge; a defendant acquitted by reason of insanity may not be retried and convicted, although she may be hospitalized under some circumstances. *Incompetency* to stand trial depends on a defendant's mental condition at the *time of trial*, unlike *insanity*, which turns upon a defendant's mental condition at the *time of the crime*. Incompetency is not a defense but rather a bar to trial. A defendant who is incompetent to stand trial cannot be tried. But if she later regains her competency, she can then be tried and—unless she has a defense—convicted. Note that a defendant who is competent to stand trial is competent to plead guilty.

2. Due Process Standard
Due process of law, as well as the state law of most jurisdictions, prohibits the trial of a defendant who is incompetent to stand trial. A defendant is incompetent to stand trial under the due process standard if, because of her present mental condition, she either:

(i) Lacks a rational as well as a factual *understanding of the charges and proceedings*; or

(ii) Lacks sufficient present *ability to consult with her lawyer* with a reasonable degree of understanding.

[Dusky v. United States, 362 U.S. 402 (1960)]

a. Forced "Cure"
Under the Due Process Clause, the government may *involuntarily* administer antipsychotic drugs to a mentally ill defendant facing serious criminal charges in order to make him competent to stand trial if: (i) the treatment is medically appropriate, (ii) the

treatment is substantially unlikely to cause side effects that may undermine the fairness of the trial, and (iii) considering less intrusive alternatives, the treatment is necessary to further important governmental trial-related interests. [Sell v. United States, 539 U.S. 166 (2003)]

3. **Trial Judge's Duty to Raise Competency Issue**

If evidence of a defendant's incompetency appears to the trial judge, the judge has a constitutional obligation to conduct further inquiry and determine whether in fact the defendant is incompetent. If a defendant is tried and convicted but it later appears she was incompetent to stand trial, the judge's failure to raise the issue or to request a determination of competency does not constitute a "waiver." [Pate v. Robinson, 383 U.S. 375 (1966)]

Example: During preliminary proceedings at X's trial for robbery, X, while in open court, speaks irrationally and repeatedly interrupts the proceedings by shouting to a nonexistent dog in the courtroom. What, if anything, must the trial judge do before proceeding to trial? The facts here clearly require the trial judge to investigate and determine X's competency to stand trial. The judge must hold a hearing and determine whether X is mentally ill and, if so, whether she can consult with her lawyer and understand the charges and proceedings. This must be done even if neither X nor her lawyer raises the issue.

4. **Burden Can Be Placed on Defendant**

A state can require a criminal defendant to prove that he is not competent to stand trial by a preponderance of the evidence; this does not violate due process. [Medina v. California, 505 U.S. 437 (1992)] However, requiring a defendant to prove incompetence by *clear and convincing evidence* violates due process. [Cooper v. Oklahoma, 517 U.S. 348 (1996)]

5. **Detention of Defendant**

a. **Based on Incompetency**

A defendant who has been found incompetent may be detained in a mental hospital for a brief period of time for evaluation and treatment. But she cannot be hospitalized indefinitely or for a long period of time simply because she has been found incompetent. This can be done only if independent "civil commitment" proceedings are begun and result in her commitment. [Jackson v. Indiana, 406 U.S. 715 (1972)]

b. **Based on Insanity**

A defendant who has made a successful insanity defense can be confined in a mental hospital for a term longer than the maximum period of incarceration for the offense. The insanity acquittee is not entitled to any separate civil commitment hearing at the expiration of the maximum sentence. [Jones v. United States, 463 U.S. 354 (1983)] However, a defendant acquitted by reason of insanity who is determined to have recovered sanity cannot be indefinitely committed in a mental facility merely because he is unable to prove himself not dangerous to others. [Foucha v. Louisiana, 504 U.S. 71 (1992)]

H. PRETRIAL PUBLICITY AND THE RIGHT TO A FAIR TRIAL

Excessive pretrial publicity prejudicial to the defendant may require change of venue or retrial.

Examples: 1) Defendant sought and was improperly denied a change of venue on the ground of local prejudice. His trial by a jury that was familiar with the material facts and had formed an opinion as to his guilt before the trial began (on the basis of unfavorable newspaper publicity) denied him due process. [Irvin v. Dowd, 366 U.S. 717 (1961)] However, due process will be satisfied if the judge asks the venirepersons whether they were exposed to pretrial publicity, and if so, whether it would affect their impartiality and ability to hear the case with an open mind. The judge does not have to ask about the specific source or content of the pretrial information. [Mu'Min v. Virginia, 500 U.S. 415 (1991)]

2) A new trial is required where defendant sought and was denied a change of venue after a televised interview in which defendant admitted that he had perpetrated the crimes with which he was charged, and the jury was drawn from the people who had seen the interview. [Rideau v. Louisiana, 373 U.S. 723 (1963)—jurors' claims that they could be neutral were inherently implausible]

3) Defendant's request for a change of venue because of pretrial publicity was denied because state law did not permit a change of venue in misdemeanor cases. *Held:* The law violates the right to trial by an impartial jury; a defendant must be given the opportunity to show that a change of venue is required in his case. [Groppi v. Wisconsin, 400 U.S. 505 (1971)]

VII. TRIAL

A. BASIC RIGHT TO A FAIR TRIAL

1. Order of Arguments

Trial begins with the opening argument of the prosecution followed by the opening argument of the defense. Closing arguments proceed in the following order: (i) the government argues, (ii) the defense argues, and (iii) the government rebuts. [Fed. R. Crim. Pro. 29.1]

2. Right to Public Trial

The Sixth and Fourteenth Amendments guarantee the right to a public trial. [*In re* Oliver, 333 U.S. 257 (1948); Herring v. New York, 422 U.S. 853 (1975)] However, the extent of this right varies according to the stage of the proceeding involved.

a. Preliminary Probable Cause Hearing

Preliminary hearings to determine whether there is probable cause on which to prosecute are presumptively open to the public and the press. [Press Enterprise Co. v. Superior Court, 478 U.S. 1 (1986)]

b. Suppression Hearings

The Sixth Amendment right to a public trial extends to *pretrial suppression hearings*. Such hearings may not be closed to the public unless:

(i) The party seeking closure shows an *overriding interest* likely to be prejudiced by a public hearing;

(ii) The closure is *no broader than necessary* to protect such an interest;

(iii) *Reasonable alternatives* to closure have been considered; and

(iv) *Adequate findings* to support closure are entered by the trial court.

[Waller v. Georgia, 467 U.S. 39 (1984)]

c. **Voir Dire of Prospective Jurors**
The right to a public trial includes voir dire of prospective jurors. Trial courts must make every reasonable effort to accommodate public attendance. [Presley v. Georgia, 558 U.S 209 (2010)—Sixth Amendment violated when judge did not allow defendant's uncle to remain in courtroom during voir dire, stating that prospective jurors could not mingle with the uncle and needed all of the rows of seats in the courtroom]

d. **Trial**
The press and the public have a right under the First Amendment to attend the trial itself, even when the defense and prosecution agree to close it. A judge may not exclude the press and the public from a criminal trial without first finding that closure is necessary for a fair trial. [Richmond Newspapers, Inc. v. Virginia, 448 U.S. 555 (1980)]

1) **Televising Permissible**
The state may constitutionally permit televising criminal proceedings over the defendant's objection. [Chandler v. Florida, 449 U.S. 560 (1981)]

3. **Right to an Unbiased Judge**
Due process is violated if the judge is shown to have *actual malice* against the defendant or to have had a *financial interest* in having the trial result in a verdict of guilty. Impermissible bias also is present when a judge earlier had significant, personal involvement as a prosecutor in a critical decision regarding the defendant's case. [Williams v. Pennsylvania, 136 S. Ct. 2383 (2016)—due process violation arose when state supreme court justice refused to recuse himself from capital defendant's post-conviction challenge when the justice had been the district attorney who gave his official approval to seek the death penalty in the case]

4. **Must Judge Be a Lawyer?**
A defendant in a minor misdemeanor prosecution has no right to have the trial judge be a lawyer, if upon conviction he has a right to trial de novo in a court with a lawyer-judge. [North v. Russell, 427 U.S. 328 (1976)] It is likely, however, that in serious crime cases the Supreme Court will require that the judge be law-trained.

5. **Right to Be Free of Trial Disruption**
Due process is violated if the trial is conducted in a manner or atmosphere making it unlikely that the jury gave the evidence reasonable consideration. Televising and broadcasting parts of a trial, for example, may interfere with courtroom proceedings and influence the jury by emphasizing the notoriety of the trial to such an extent that it infringes the defendant's right to a fair trial. [Estes v. Texas, 381 U.S. 532 (1965)]

6. **Trial in Prison Clothing**
It is unconstitutional for the state to *compel* the defendant to stand trial in prison clothing. If

the defendant does not wish to be tried in prison clothing, he must make a timely objection. [Estelle v. Williams, 425 U.S. 501 (1976)] Similarly, the Due Process Clause prohibits the use of visible shackles during the trial and penalty phase of a capital proceeding unless the court makes a specific finding that their use is justified by concerns about courtroom security or risk of escape. [Deck v. Missouri, 544 U.S. 622 (2005)]

7. Right to Have Jury Free from Unfair Influences
If the jury is exposed to influences favorable to the prosecution, due process is violated.
Example: During X's trial, two sheriffs, who were also prosecution witnesses, were in constant and intimate association with the jurors, eating with them, running errands for them, etc. Did the trial violate due process standards? Yes, since this association must have influenced the jurors' assessment of the credibility of the witnesses. [Turner v. Louisiana, 379 U.S. 466 (1965)]

8. No Right to Preservation of Potentially Exculpatory Evidence
Defendants have no right to have the police preserve all evidence for trial, at least where it is not certain that the evidence would have been exculpatory. Due process is violated, however, if the police *in bad faith* destroy evidence potentially useful to the defense at trial. [Arizona v. Youngblood, 488 U.S. 51 (1988)—no due process violation where police failed to preserve seminal fluid on sodomy victim's clothing; California v. Trombetta, 467 U.S. 479 (1984)—same result where police failed to preserve samples of defendant's breath]

B. RIGHT TO TRIAL BY JURY
The Sixth Amendment right to trial by jury applies to the states. [Duncan v. Louisiana, 391 U.S. 145 (1968)] The cases after *Duncan,* while zealously guarding the jury trial right, have permitted the states great latitude in the details of jury use and conduct because of (i) the view that many of the details of the jury were historical accidents, (ii) the belief that the jury will act rationally, and (iii) the cost.

1. Right to Jury Trial Only for "Serious" Offenses
There is no constitutional right to jury trial for petty offenses, but only for serious offenses. Also, there is no right to jury trial in juvenile delinquency proceedings. [McKeiver v. Pennsylvania, 403 U.S. 528 (1971)]

    a. What Constitutes a Serious Offense?
For purposes of the right to jury trial, an offense is serious if *imprisonment for more than six months* is authorized. If imprisonment of six months or less is authorized, the offense is presumptively petty, and there is no right to a jury trial. [Blanton v. City of North Las Vegas, 489 U.S. 538 (1989)] The presumption may be overcome by showing additional penalties, but a possibility of a $5,000 fine and five years' probation is not sufficient to overcome the presumption that the crime is petty. [United States v. Nachtigal, 507 U.S. 1 (1993)]

        1) Aggregation of Petty Offenses
The right to a jury trial does not arise when in a single proceeding, sentences for multiple petty offenses are imposed which result in an aggregate prison sentence of more than six months. [Lewis v. United States, 518 U.S. 322 (1996)]

b. Contempt

1) Civil Contempt—No Jury Trial Right
If a penalty is imposed for purposes of compelling future compliance with a court order and the witness can avoid further penalty by complying with the order (e.g., judge sentences witness to prison until she is willing to testify), the proceeding is one of "civil" contempt and no jury trial is required.

2) Criminal Contempt—"Six Months" Rule
When there is no statutorily authorized penalty for a crime, such as criminal contempt, the actual sentence governs the right to jury trial. Cumulative penalties totaling more than six months cannot be imposed in a *post-verdict contempt adjudication* without affording the defendant the right to a jury trial. [Codispoti v. Pennsylvania, 418 U.S. 506 (1974)]

3) Summary Contempt Punishment During Trial
If the judge summarily imposes punishment for contempt during trial, the penalties may aggregate more than six months without a jury trial. [Codispoti v. Pennsylvania, *supra*]

4) Appellate Modification Sufficient
An appellate court may reduce the sentence imposed for contempt to six months or less and thereby protect the conviction and sentence imposed without a jury from constitutional attack. [Taylor v. Hayes, 418 U.S. 488 (1974)]

5) Probation
A judge may place a contemnor on probation for a term of up to five years without affording him the right to jury trial as long as revocation of probation would not result in imprisonment for more than six months. [Frank v. United States, 395 U.S. 147 (1969)]

2. Number and Unanimity of Jurors

a. No Right to Jury of Twelve
There is no constitutional right to a jury of 12, but there must be *at least six* jurors to satisfy the right to jury trial under the Sixth and Fourteenth Amendments. [Ballew v. Georgia, 435 U.S. 223 (1978)]

b. No Absolute Right to Unanimity
There is no right to a unanimous verdict. The Supreme Court has upheld convictions based upon 11-1, 10-2, and 9-3 votes [Apodaca v. Oregon, 406 U.S. 404 (1972); Johnson v. Louisiana, 406 U.S. 356 (1972)], but probably would not approve an 8-4 vote for conviction. Six-person juries must be unanimous. [Burch v. Louisiana, 441 U.S. 130 (1979); Brown v. Louisiana, 447 U.S. 323 (1980)]

3. Right to Venire Selected from Representative Cross-Section of Community
A defendant has a right to have the venire from which the jury is selected be from a representative cross-section of the community. A defendant can complain of an exclusion of a significant segment of the community from the venire, even if he is not a member of that

excluded segment. [Taylor v. Louisiana, 419 U.S. 522 (1975); Holland v. Illinois, 493 U.S. 474 (1990)]

a.   Showing of Exclusion of Significant Group Sufficient
To make out a case for exclusion, the defendant need only show the underrepresentation of a distinct and numerically significant group. [Taylor v. Louisiana, *supra*]

b.   No Right to Proportional Representation on Particular Jury
The cross-sectional requirement applies only to the venire from which the jury is selected. A defendant does not have the right to proportional representation of all groups on his particular jury. [Holland v. Illinois, *supra*]

c.   Use of Peremptory Challenges for Racial and Gender-Based Discrimination
In contrast to striking potential jurors for cause, a prosecutor generally may exercise peremptory challenges for any rational *or irrational* reason. However, the Equal Protection Clause forbids the use of peremptory challenges to exclude potential jurors solely on account of their race or gender. [Batson v. Kentucky, 476 U.S. 79 (1989); J.E.B. v. Alabama, 511 U.S. 127 (1994)]

1)   Proving Strike Improper
An equal protection-based attack on peremptory strikes involves three steps: (i) The defendant must show *facts or circumstances that raise an inference* that the exclusion of potential jurors was based on race or gender. (ii) If such a showing is made, the prosecutor must then come forward with a *race-neutral explanation* for the strike. The reason for the strike need not be reasonable, as long as it is race-neutral. [Purkett v. Elem, 514 U.S. 765 (1995)—explanation that potential jurors were struck because of their long hair and beards was sufficient] (iii) The judge then determines whether the prosecutor's explanation was the genuine reason for striking the juror, or merely a pretext for purposeful discrimination. If the judge believes that the *prosecutor was sincere*, the strike may be upheld. [Purkett v. Elem, *supra*]

Example: That a stricken juror was young, had no ties to the community, and was disrespectful were sufficient grounds to support a peremptory strike. [Rice v. Collins, 546 U.S. 333 (2006)]

Compare: During voir dire in a murder case, an African-American college student voiced concern that the trial might interfere with his student teaching, which he needed to fulfill to graduate college. The student's dean was called and agreed to work with him on rescheduling. The prosecutor asked no further questions about the matter. Nevertheless, the prosecutor used a peremptory challenge to exclude the student. When the peremptory strike was challenged, the prosecutor explained that he was concerned that, because of the student's pressing educational needs, he would find the defendant guilty of a lesser charge to avoid a lengthy capital sentencing hearing. As a result of peremptory challenges and challenges for cause, no African-Americans were included in the final jury. *Held:* Because white jurors also stated that they had pressing needs but were not excluded, and because it is unlikely that one juror could shorten the trial (he would have to convince the other jurors to follow his lead), the prosecutor's rationale for the strike was just a pretext and should not have been upheld. [Snyder v. Louisiana, 552 U.S. 472 (2008)]

Note: The defendant need not be a member of the group excluded. [Powers v. Ohio, 499 U.S. 400 (1991)]

2) Defendants

It is also unconstitutional for a criminal *defendant* or the defendant's attorney to use peremptory challenges in a racially discriminatory manner. [Georgia v. McCollum, 505 U.S. 42 (1992)] The same rule probably applies to a defendant's peremptory strike based on gender.

d. Distinct and Significant Groups

A fair cross-section of the community must include minorities and women, and possibly other distinct and significant groups. A state may neither exclude women from jury duty nor automatically exempt them upon request. [Duren v. Missouri, 439 U.S. 357 (1979)]

4. Right to Impartial Jury

a. Right to Questioning on Racial Bias

A defendant is entitled to questioning on voir dire specifically directed to racial prejudice whenever race is inextricably bound up in the case. [Ham v. South Carolina, 409 U.S. 524 (1973)] In *noncapital* cases, the mere fact that the victim is white and the defendant is black is not enough to permit such questioning. [Ristaino v. Ross, 424 U.S. 589 (1976); Rosales-Lopez v. United States, 451 U.S. 182 (1982)] However, a *capital* defendant accused of an interracial crime is entitled to have prospective jurors informed of the victim's race and is entitled to voir dire questioning regarding the issue of racial prejudice. [Turner v. Murray, 476 U.S. 28 (1986)]

b. Juror Opposition to Death Penalty

In cases involving capital punishment, a state may not automatically exclude for cause all prospective jurors who express a doubt or scruple about the death penalty. [Witherspoon v. Illinois, 391 U.S. 510 (1968); Adams v. Texas, 448 U.S. 38 (1980)]

1) Standard—Impair or Prevent Performance

The standard for determining when a prospective juror should be excluded for cause is whether the juror's views would *prevent or substantially impair* the performance of his duties in accordance with his instructions and oath. [Wainwright v. Witt, 469 U.S. 412 (1985)] Thus, if a juror's doubts or scruples about the death penalty prevent or substantially impair the performance of his duties, he may be excluded from the jury, and the fact that this may result in a "death qualified" jury does not infringe on a defendant's constitutional rights. [Lockhart v. McCree, 476 U.S. 162 (1986)] However, if a juror has scruples about the death penalty, but could perform her duties and follow instructions, it is error to exclude the juror.

2) Improper Exclusion May Result in Reversal

A death sentence imposed by a jury from which a juror was improperly excluded is subject to automatic reversal. [Gray v. Mississippi, 481 U.S. 648 (1987)]

c. Juror Favoring Death Penalty

If a jury is to decide whether a defendant in a capital case is to be sentenced to death, the defendant must be allowed to ask potential jurors at voir dire if they would automatically give the death penalty upon a guilty verdict. A juror who answers affirmatively should be excluded for cause because such a juror has indicated the same type of inability to follow jury instructions (as to mitigating circumstances) as a juror who has indicated an inability to impose the death penalty under any circumstances (*see supra*). [Morgan v. Illinois, 504 U.S. 719 (1992)]

d. Use of Peremptory Challenge to Maintain Impartial Jury

Peremptory challenges are not constitutionally required. Therefore, if a trial court refuses to exclude a juror for cause whom the court should have excluded, and the defendant uses a peremptory challenge to remove the juror, there is no constitutional violation. [Ross v. Oklahoma, 487 U.S. 81 (1988); United States v. Martinez-Salazar, 528 U.S. 304 (2000)]

5. Inconsistent Verdicts

Inconsistent jury verdicts (e.g., finding defendant guilty of some counts but not guilty on related counts or one defendant guilty and a co-defendant not guilty on the same evidence) are not reviewable. A challenge to an inconsistent verdict would be based upon pure speculation because it is impossible to tell on which decision the jury erred. [United States v. Powell, 469 U.S. 57 (1984)]

6. Sentence Enhancement

If substantive law provides that a sentence may be increased beyond the statutory maximum for a crime if additional facts (other than prior conviction) are proved, proof of the facts must be submitted to the jury and proved beyond reasonable doubt; the defendant's right to jury trial is violated if the judge makes the determination. [Apprendi v. New Jersey, 530 U.S. 466 (2000)] Moreover, because mandatory minimum sentences increase the penalty for a crime, any fact that increases the mandatory minimum is an "element" that must be submitted to the jury. [Alleyne v. United States, 133 S. Ct. 2151 (2013)]

Examples: 1) The right to jury trial was violated where a statute allowed a defendant's sentence to be increased by 10 years if the sentencing judge found by a preponderance of the evidence that the crime was motivated by hate. [Apprendi v. New Jersey, *supra*]

2) Following a jury adjudication of a defendant's guilt of first degree murder, a trial judge is prohibited by the Sixth Amendment from determining whether aggravating factors justify imposition of the death penalty. The jury must make such a determination. [Ring v. Arizona, 536 U.S. 584 (2002)]

a. Guilty Pleas

The same general rule applies to sentencing enhancements after guilty pleas.

> *Example:* Defendant pleaded guilty to kidnapping. Based on the facts admitted, under state law Defendant's maximum penalty was 53 months' imprisonment, but the judge found that Defendant acted with deliberate cruelty—an additional factor that allowed adding time to the standard sentence range—and imposed a 90-month sentence. Because the facts supporting Defendant's exceptional sentence were neither admitted by him nor found by a jury, his sentence violated the Sixth Amendment right to a trial by jury. [Blakely v. Washington, 542 U.S. 296 (2004)]

b. Fines
Determination of fines must also be based on facts found by a jury. [Southern Union Co. v. United States, 567 U.S. 343 (2012)]

> *Example:* Defendant was found guilty of storing a hazardous liquid on its property. The maximum fine for the violation was $50,000 per day. The sentencing officer found that the liquid had been stored on the property for 762 days and imposed a fine of over $38 million. The fine violated Defendant's Sixth Amendment right to a jury; Defendant had a right to have a jury determine how many days the liquid was stored. [Southern Union Co. v. United States, *supra*]

c. Harmless Error Test Applies
In deciding whether to overturn a sentence for failure to submit a sentencing factor to the jury, the harmless error test is applied. [Washington v. Recuenco, 548 U.S. 212 (2006)]

d. Distinguish—Judge May Decide Whether Sentences Run Consecutively
The Supreme Court has refused to extend the *Apprendi/Blakely* doctrine to the decision of whether sentences for multiple crimes are to run consecutively or concurrently. A state legislature may give to its judges (rather than the jury) the power to make such a decision even though it is based on the facts of the case. *Rationale:* Historically, judges have been entrusted with such decisions. The framers of the Constitution probably did not intend the Sixth Amendment's right to a jury trial to supplant this practice. [Oregon v. Ice, 555 U.S. 160 (2009)]

C. RIGHT TO COUNSEL
A defendant has a right to counsel under the Fifth and Sixth Amendments. The Fifth Amendment right applies at all custodial interrogations (*see* III.D., *supra*). The Sixth Amendment right applies at all **critical stages** of a prosecution after formal proceedings have begun (*see* III.C., *supra*), including trial. This includes the right of a defendant who does not require appointed counsel to choose who will represent him. [*And see* Luis v. United States, 136 S. Ct. 1083 (2016)—government may not freeze assets of a defendant (to assure payment of penalties or retribution) unrelated to the crime charged, if this prevents the defendant from hiring counsel of choice to defend her]

1. Remedy
Recall that if the defendant was entitled to a lawyer at trial, the failure to provide counsel results in **automatic reversal of the conviction**, even without any showing of specific unfairness in the proceedings. Similarly, erroneous disqualification of privately retained counsel results in automatic reversal. However, at **nontrial proceedings** (such as a post-indictment lineup), the harmless error rule applies to deprivations of counsel. (*See* III.C.5., *supra*.)

2. Waiver of Right to Counsel at Trial and Right to Defend Oneself

A defendant has a right to represent himself *at trial* as long as his waiver is *knowing and intelligent* [Faretta v. California, 422 U.S. 806 (1975); Godinez v. Moran, 509 U.S. 389 (1993)] and he is *competent* to proceed pro se [Indiana v. Edwards, 554 U.S. 135 (2008)]. The Court has held that a waiver will be held to be voluntary and intelligent if the trial court finds—after carefully scrutinizing the waiver—that the defendant has a rational and factual understanding of the proceeding against him. The Court has not established the standard for determining whether the defendant is mentally competent. It has noted that a defendant may be mentally competent to stand trial and yet incompetent to represent himself, based on the trial judge's consideration of the defendant's emotional and psychological state.

Note: On appeal, a defendant has no right to represent himself. [Martinez v. Court of Appeal, 528 U.S. 152 (2000)]

3. Indigence and Recoupment of Cost

As indicated above, if the defendant is indigent, the state will provide an attorney. Indigence involves the present financial inability to hire counsel, but none of the right to counsel cases defines indigence precisely. In any case, judges generally are reluctant to refuse to appoint counsel because of the risk of reversal should the defendant be determined indigent. The state generally provides counsel in close cases of indigence, but it may then seek reimbursement from those convicted defendants who later become able to pay. [Fuller v. Oregon, 417 U.S. 40 (1974)]

4. Effective Assistance of Counsel

The Sixth Amendment right to counsel includes the right to effective counsel. The ineffective assistance claim is the most commonly raised constitutional claim. With this claim, the defendant seeks to secure not malpractice damages, but rather a reversal of his conviction and a new trial.

a. Effective Assistance Presumed

Effective assistance of counsel is *presumed* unless the adversarial process is so undermined by counsel's conduct that the trial cannot be relied upon to have produced a just result. [Strickland v. Washington, 466 U.S. 668 (1984)]

b. Right Extends to First Appeal

Effective assistance of counsel is also guaranteed on a first appeal as of right. [Evitts v. Lucey, 469 U.S. 387 (1985)]

c. Circumstances Constituting Ineffective Assistance

An ineffective assistance claimant must show:

(i) *Deficient performance* by counsel; and that

(ii) But for such deficiency, the *result of the proceeding would have been different* (e.g., defendant would not have been convicted or his sentence would have been shorter).

[Strickland v. Washington, *supra*] Typically, such a claim can be made out only by specifying particular errors of trial counsel, and cannot be based on mere inexperience, lack of time to prepare, gravity of the charges, complexity of defenses, or accessibility of witnesses to counsel. [United States v. Cronic, 466 U.S. 648 (1984)]

Examples: 1) The Sixth Amendment right to counsel was violated when an attorney failed to timely file a motion to suppress evidence [Kimmelman v. Morrison, 477 U.S. 365 (1986)]; or failed to file a timely notice of appeal [Evitts v. Lucey, 469 U.S. 387 (1985)].

2) Sixth Amendment rights were also violated in a death penalty case when trial counsel failed to fully investigate the defendant's life history and had reason to believe that the investigation would turn up mitigating circumstances [Wiggins v. Smith, 539 U.S. 510 (2003)], and when defense counsel failed to look at the case file of defendant's prior crime that the prosecution had indicated would be central to proving aggravating circumstances justifying imposition of the death penalty, even when family members and the defendant himself have suggested that no mitigating evidence is available [Rompilla v. Beard, 545 U.S. 374 (2005)].

3) Sixth Amendment rights were also violated when the defendant's lawyer knowingly introduced evidence from a psychologist that the defendant was statistically more likely to act violently because he is black [Buck v. Davis, 137 S. Ct. 759 (2017)—imposition of death penalty turned on jury's assessment of future dangerousness] and when a lawyer incorrectly advised his client that pleading guilty to a drug charge would not result in deportation, even though the client had little hope of winning at trial. The required different result is that the client would not have pleaded guilty but for the erroneous advice. [Lee v. United States, 137 S. Ct. 1958 (2017)]

Note: The Sixth Amendment safeguards a defendant's autonomy to decide whether to assert innocence in the guilt phase of a capital trial. Thus, when counsel admits his client's guilt in the face of the defendant's clearly articulated desire to maintain his innocence in this context, a new trial must be granted without any need to first to show prejudice. [McCoy v. Louisiana, 138 S. Ct. 1500 (2018)]

1) **Plea Bargain Cases**

The Sixth Amendment requires effective assistance at all critical stages of a prosecution. Because the plea stage is a critical stage, *Strickland* applies to plea bargain cases as well as cases that go to trial. In a plea bargain case, the defendant must show deficient performance and a reasonable possibility that the outcome of the plea process would have been different with competent advice. An attorney's failure to notify a defendant of a plea offer can constitute deficient performance if the defendant can show that had the plea agreement been communicated he likely would have accepted, and the plea likely would have been entered without the prosecutor's canceling it. [Missouri v. Frye, 566 U.S. 134 (2012)] Moreover, deficiencies in counsel at this stage are not obviated by the fact that the defendant subsequently has a fair trial (after turning down a plea offer). [Lafler v. Cooper, 566 U.S. 156 (2012)]

Example: Defendant was charged with assault with intent to murder. He was offered a sentence of 51 - 85 months in exchange for a guilty plea. His attorney advised him to reject the plea, erroneously suggesting that the state could not prove intent to kill, since the victim was shot below the waist. At trial, Defendant was found guilty and received the minimum 185 - 360 month sentence. Defendant's Sixth Amendment right to counsel was violated. [Lafler v. Cooper, *supra*]

2) Deportation Risk

It is constitutionally deficient for counsel not to inform a client whether his plea carries a risk of deportation. When the deportation risk is clear under the law, counsel has a duty to give correct advice. If the law is not straightforward, counsel must advise the client that pending criminal charges may carry a risk of deportation. [Padilla v. Kentucky, 559 U.S. 356 (2010)]

d. Circumstances Not Constituting Ineffective Assistance

Circumstances not constituting ineffective assistance include:

1) Trial Tactics

Courts will not grant relief for any acts or omissions by counsel that they view as trial tactics.

Examples: 1) It was not ineffective assistance in a capital murder trial to fail to obtain a client's affirmative consent to the strategy of going to trial and not challenging guilt (rather than pleading guilty) in hopes of having more credibility at sentencing. [Florida v. Nixon, 543 U.S. 175 (2005)]

2) It was not ineffective assistance when appointed counsel for an indigent defendant refused to argue nonfrivolous issues that the attorney had decided, in the exercise of her judgment, not to present. [Jones v. Barnes, 463 U.S. 745 (1983)]

3) It was not ineffective assistance when an attorney failed to present mitigating evidence or make a closing argument at a capital sentencing proceeding when counsel asserted that mitigating evidence had just been presented at trial, the defendant's mother and other character witnesses would not have been effective and might have revealed harmful information, and a closing argument would have allowed rebuttal by a very persuasive lead prosecutor. [Bell v. Cone, 535 U.S. 685 (2002)]

2) Failure to Raise Constitutional Claim that Is Later Invalidated

The failure of a defendant's counsel to raise a federal constitutional claim that was the law at the time of the proceeding but that was later overruled does not prejudice the defendant within the meaning of the Sixth Amendment and does not constitute ineffective assistance of counsel. [Lockhart v. Fretwell, 506 U.S. 364 (1993)]

5. **Conflicts of Interest**

Joint representation (that is, a single attorney representing co-defendants) is not per se invalid. However, if an attorney advises the trial court of a resulting conflict of interest at or before trial, and the court refuses to appoint separate counsel, the defendant is entitled to *automatic reversal*. [Holloway v. Arkansas, 435 U.S. 475 (1978); Cuyler v. Sullivan, 446 U.S. 335 (1980)] If the defendant does not object to joint representation in a timely manner, to obtain reversal the defendant must show that the attorney *actively* represented conflicting interests and thereby prejudiced the defendant. [Burger v. Kemp, 483 U.S. 776 (1987)]

a. **Conflict with Attorney Is Rarely Ground for Relief**

A defendant can rarely obtain relief by claiming a conflict of interest between himself and counsel. Conflicts between a defendant and his attorney are best analyzed as claims of ineffective assistance of counsel. To be successful, the defendant must demonstrate that the conflict with his attorney was so severe that the attorney could not effectively investigate or present the defendant's claims.

b. **No Right to Joint Representation**

While a defendant ordinarily has the right to counsel of her own choosing, a defendant has no right to be jointly represented with her co-defendants. Trial courts have the authority to limit joint representation to avoid potential and actual conflicts of interest. Even when all of the defendants waive any claim to conflicts of interest, the trial court can still prohibit the joint representation. [Wheat v. United States, 486 U.S. 153 (1988)]

6. **Right to Support Services for Defense**

Where a defendant has made a preliminary showing that he is likely to be able to use the insanity defense, the state must provide a psychiatrist for the preparation of the defense. Where a state presents evidence that the defendant is likely to be dangerous in the future, the defendant is entitled to psychiatric examination and testimony in the sentencing proceeding. [Ake v. Oklahoma, 470 U.S. 68 (1985)]

7. **Seizure of Funds Constitutional**

The right to counsel does not forbid the seizure—under the federal drug forfeiture statute [21 U.S.C. §853]—of drug money and property obtained with drug money, even when such money and property were going to be used by the defendant to pay his attorney of choice. [Caplin & Drysdale, Chartered v. United States, 491 U.S. 617 (1989)]

8. **Right Limited While Testifying**

A defendant has a general right to consult with his attorney during the course of trial; however, he has no right to consult with his attorney while he is testifying. Whether a defendant has a right to consult with his attorney during breaks in his testimony depends on the character of the break. Generally, the longer the break, the more likely the Court will find the right. [*Compare* Geders v. United States, III.C.1., *supra*—defendant must be allowed to talk with attorney during overnight break in defendant's testimony because ordinary trial tactics can be, and usually are, discussed during such breaks—*with* Perry v. Leeke, 488 U.S. 272 (1989)—sequestration during 15-minute break between defendant's direct testimony and cross-examination permissible because cross-examination of uncounseled witness more likely to lead to truth]

D. RIGHT TO CONFRONT WITNESSES

The Sixth Amendment grants to the defendant in a criminal prosecution the right to confront adverse witnesses. This right, held applicable to the states in *Pointer v. Texas*, 380 U.S. 400 (1965), seeks to ensure that:

(i)   The fact finder and the defendant *observe the demeanor* of the testifying witness; and

(ii) The defendant has the opportunity to *cross-examine* any witness testifying against him.

The defendant is entitled to a face-to-face encounter with the witness, but absence of face-to-face confrontation between the defendant and the accuser does not violate the Sixth Amendment when preventing such confrontation serves an important public purpose (such as insulating a child witness from trauma) and the reliability of the witness's testimony is otherwise assured. [Maryland v. Craig, 497 U.S. 836 (1990)]

1. Right Not Absolute

a. Disruptive Defendant
A defendant has no absolute right to confront witnesses, as a judge may remove a disruptive defendant. [Illinois v. Allen, 397 U.S. 337 (1970)]

b. Voluntarily Leaving Courtroom
A defendant has not been deprived of his right of confrontation if he voluntarily leaves the courtroom during the trial, and the trial continues in his absence. [Taylor v. United States, 414 U.S. 17 (1974)]

c. Government May Discourage Attendance
Government action that has an effect of discouraging a defendant's attendance at trial will not necessarily violate the right to attend and confront witnesses.

Example: Defendant attended his trial and testified in his own defense as the last witness. On summation, the prosecutor commented to the jury that they should consider that by choosing to testify last, defendant had an opportunity to listen to all of the other witnesses and adjust his testimony accordingly. After he was convicted, defendant claimed that the prosecutor's summation was unconstitutional because it used defendant's constitutionally protected right to attend trial as a tool to impeach his credibility and so would have the effect of discouraging attendance. The Supreme Court held that the right to attend may be burdened and upheld the conviction. [Portuondo v. Agard, 529 U.S. 61 (2000)]

2. Introduction of Co-Defendant's Confession
A right of confrontation problem develops with the introduction of a co-defendant's confession because of the inability of the nonconfessing defendant to compel the confessing co-defendant to take the stand for cross-examination at their joint trial.

a. General Rule—Confession Implicating Co-Defendant Prohibited
If two persons are tried together and one has given a confession that implicates the other, the right of confrontation prohibits the use of that statement, even with instructions to the jury to consider it only as going to the guilt of the "confessing" defendant.

[Bruton v. United States, 391 U.S. 123 (1968)] A co-defendant's confession is inadmissible even when it interlocks with the defendant's own confession, which is admitted. [Cruz v. New York, 481 U.S. 186 (1987)]

b. Exceptions
Such a statement may be admitted if:

1) All portions referring to the other defendant can be eliminated. *Note:* It is not sufficient merely to insert a blank or some other substitution for the name of the other defendant; the redaction must not indicate the defendant's involvement. [*Compare* Richardson v. Marsh, 481 U.S. 200 (1987)—after redaction, confession indicated that defendant and a third party (who was not a co-defendant) participated in the crime and contained no indication of co-defendant's involvement, *with* Gray v. Maryland, 523 U.S. 185 (1998)—redaction "me, deleted, deleted, and a few other guys killed" the victim held to clearly refer to co-defendant];

2) The confessing defendant takes the stand and subjects himself to cross-examination with respect to the truth or falsity of what the statement asserts. This rule applies even if he denies having ever made the confession. [Nelson v. O'Neil, 402 U.S. 622 (1973)] In effect, an opportunity at trial to cross-examine the hearsay declarant with respect to the underlying facts makes the declaration nonhearsay for purposes of the Confrontation Clause; or

3) The confession of the nontestifying co-defendant is being used to rebut the defendant's claim that his confession was obtained coercively. The jury must be instructed as to the purpose of the admission. [Tennessee v. Street, 471 U.S. 409 (1985)]

3. Prior Testimonial Statement of Unavailable Witness
Under the Confrontation Clause, prior testimonial evidence (e.g., statements made at prior judicial proceedings) may ***not*** be admitted unless:

(i) The declarant is ***unavailable***; and

(ii) The defendant had an ***opportunity to cross-examine*** the declarant at the time the statement was made.

[Crawford v. Washington, 541 U.S. 36 (2004)]
Example: Crawford and his wife, Sylvia, confronted Lee at his apartment after Lee allegedly attempted to rape Sylvia. A fight ensued and Crawford stabbed Lee. Crawford was charged with assault and attempted murder. At trial, Crawford testified that he thought that Lee had reached for something in his pocket before Crawford stabbed him and that the stabbing was in self-defense. To negate this claim, the prosecution introduced a recording of Sylvia's statement to the police indicating that Lee's hands may have been out and open while he was being stabbed. Under state law, Crawford has a privilege that prevents Sylvia from testifying at trial. Crawford objects to introduction of the recording. Although Sylvia's statement would be admissible under the

hearsay exception for statements made against penal interest—because she led Crawford to Lee's apartment and facilitated the assault—it is inadmissible under the Confrontation Clause because there was no opportunity for cross-examination here (i.e., Crawford was not present and able to examine Sylvia when the police were questioning her). [Crawford v. Washington, *supra*]

a. **What Is "Testimonial"?**
In *Crawford*, the Supreme Court did not provide a comprehensive definition of the term "testimonial," raising many questions for both state and federal judges as to the reach of the Court's ruling. However, the Court held that, at a minimum, the term includes testimony from a preliminary hearing, grand jury hearing, former trial, or police interrogation.

1) **Police Interrogation**
Statements made in response to police interrogation are nontestimonial when made under circumstances indicating that the primary purpose of the interrogation is to enable the police to respond to an ongoing emergency, but statements are testimonial when there is no ongoing emergency and the primary purpose of the interrogation is to establish or prove past acts.

Example: A domestic battery victim called 911 to report that she was being beaten. The operator asked whether the victim knew the name of her assailant, and the victim provided defendant's name. Defendant was apprehended and charged. The victim did not appear at defendant's trial, but the prosecutor sought to introduce the 911 tape. Defendant objected, claiming a Confrontation Clause violation. The Supreme Court held that the response to the question about the assailant's name was nontestimonial because it was given to enable the police to respond to an ongoing emergency. [Davis v. Washington, 547 U.S. 813 (2006)]

Compare: In a companion case to *Davis*, the police had responded to a domestic battery complaint. When they arrived at defendant's home, his wife—the complainant—met them at the door and told them that everything was fine. She nevertheless invited the officers into the home. While one officer kept defendant busy in the kitchen, the other officer questioned the wife and got her to fill out and sign a battery affidavit. Defendant was then arrested. The wife did not appear at defendant's trial but the prosecutor offered her affidavit of battery into evidence over defendant's Confrontation Clause objection. *Held:* The wife's statements were testimonial, as the affidavit was made as part of an investigation into past criminal conduct and no emergency was in progress when the police arrived. [Hammon v. Indiana, 547 U.S. 813 (2006)]

2) **Statements to Individuals Who Are Not Law Enforcement**
Statements to individuals other than law enforcement officers are subject to the Confrontation Clause. However, statements made to individuals who are not principally charged with uncovering and prosecuting crimes are significantly less likely

to be testimonial than statements given to police officers. [Ohio v. Clark, 135 S. Ct. 2173 (2015)]

Example: Defendant watched his girlfriend's children while she was out of town. Preschool teachers noticed that one of the children, a three-year-old boy, had injuries and asked him who caused them. The boy identified Defendant as his abuser. At Defendant's trial, the prosecution introduced the boy's statements to his teachers as evidence of Defendant's guilt, but the boy did not testify. Defendant moved to exclude the boy's statements under the Confrontation Clause. The Supreme Court held that the boy's statements were nontestimonial because the purpose of the conversation with his teachers was to protect the boy from further abuse rather than to gather evidence for Defendant's prosecution. [Ohio v. Clark, *supra*]

3) **Results of Forensic Lab Testing**

If results of forensic lab tests are offered for proof of the matter asserted, they are testimonial in nature and inadmissible unless the person who did the testing is made available for cross-examination. [Melendez-Diaz v. Massachusetts, 557 U.S. 305 (2009)] However, lab test results that are not offered for the proof of the matter asserted raise no Confrontation Clause issue. [Williams v. Illinois, 567 U.S. 50 (2012)]

Example: A report was offered into evidence that a white powder obtained from Defendant was cocaine. Such a report is offered to prove the truth of the matter asserted in the report. Therefore, it is testimonial and inadmissible under the Confrontation Clause unless the person who did the testing is made available for cross-examination. [Melendez-Diaz v. Massachusetts, *supra*]

Compare: At trial, an expert testified that the results of a DNA test of a sample from a crime victim performed at a private lab matched the DNA test of a sample obtained from Defendant and performed at a state forensic lab. The state forensic technician had testified as to her procedures. Since the expert was not testifying as to the truth of the private lab's results, but rather only that the lab's results matched the results from that state lab, the private lab results were not being offered to prove the truth of the matter asserted, so there was no Confrontation Clause issue as to the results. It has long been the rule that scientific experts can render opinions on facts they do not personally know but that are made known to them for purposes of litigation. [Williams v. Illinois, *supra*]

b. **Forfeiture by Wrongdoing**

A defendant can be held to have forfeited a Confrontation Clause claim by wrongdoing. However, the Court will not find a forfeiture by wrongdoing unless the wrongdoing was intended to keep the witness from testifying. [Giles v. California, 554 U.S. 353 (2008)]

Example: Defendant shot Victim, his ex-girlfriend, six times, and she died as a result. At Defendant's murder trial, he claimed that Victim threatened him first and was coming toward him to mount an attack. To rebut this claim, the prosecution offered testimony that Victim had made in a complaint to the police three weeks before her death, alleging that Defendant beat her and choked her. Defendant objected to introduction of Victim's statements to the police, claiming that their admission would violate his confrontation rights. *Held:* Absent a finding that Defendant killed Victim with the intent to keep her from testifying, the forfeiture by wrongdoing exception to the Confrontation Clause's requirements does not apply and it would, therefore, be improper to admit Victim's statements into evidence. [Giles v. California, *supra*]

E. BURDEN OF PROOF, SUFFICIENCY OF EVIDENCE, AND JURY INSTRUCTIONS

1. Burden of Proof

a. Proof Beyond a Reasonable Doubt
The Due Process Clause requires in all criminal cases that the state prove guilt beyond a reasonable doubt. [*In re* Winship, 397 U.S. 358 (1970)] The prosecution must have the burden of proving the elements of the crime charged. Thus, the Supreme Court has held that if "malice aforethought" is an element of murder, the state may not require the defendant to prove that he committed the homicide in the heat of passion, on the rationale that this would require the defendant to disprove the element of malice aforethought. [Mullaney v. Wilbur, 421 U.S. 684 (1975)] However, a state may impose the burden of proof upon the defendant in regard to an ***affirmative defense*** such as insanity [Leland v. Oregon, 343 U.S. 790 (1952)] or self-defense [Martin v. Ohio, 480 U.S. 228 (1987)].

Example: Under state law, in a prosecution for second degree murder, the state must prove intentional causing of death. A defendant is entitled to acquittal of second degree murder and conviction of manslaughter if he proves by a preponderance of the evidence that he acted under the influence of "an extreme emotional disturbance." May the burden of proving that be placed on the defendant? Yes, because it does not affect the state's obligation to prove all elements of the crime of second degree murder. [Patterson v. New York, 432 U.S. 197 (1977)]

b. Presumption of Innocence
Although not mentioned in the Constitution, the presumption of innocence is a basic component of a fair trial. A defendant does not have an absolute right to a jury instruction on the presumption of innocence, but the trial judge should evaluate the totality of the circumstances, including (i) the other jury instructions, (ii) the arguments of counsel, and (iii) whether the weight of the evidence was overwhelming, to determine whether such an instruction is necessary for a fair trial. [Kentucky v. Whorton, 441 U.S. 786 (1979)]

2. Presumptions
A permissive presumption allows, but does not require, the jury to infer an element of an offense from proof by the prosecutor of the basic fact, while the jury must accept a mandatory presumption even if it is the sole evidence of the elemental fact.

a. Permissive Presumptions—Rational Relation Standard
A permissive presumption must comport with the standard that there be a rational

connection between the basic facts that the prosecution proved and the ultimate fact presumed, and that the latter is more likely than not to flow from the former. [Ulster County Court v. Allen, 442 U.S. 140 (1979)]

b. Mandatory Presumptions Unconstitutional

A mandatory presumption or a presumption that shifts the burden of proof to the defendant violates the Fourteenth Amendment's requirement that the state prove every element of a crime beyond a reasonable doubt. [Sandstrom v. Montana, 442 U.S. 510 (1979)]

Examples: 1) A mandatory presumption was created by jury instructions in a "malice murder" trial which stated that the "acts of a person of sound mind and discretion are presumed to be the product of a person's will, but the presumption may be rebutted," and a "person of sound mind and discretion is presumed to intend the natural and probable consequences of his acts, but the presumption may be rebutted." These instructions are unconstitutional because they would lead a reasonable juror to conclude that the state's burden of proof on intent to kill may be inferred from proof of the defendant's acts unless the defendant proves otherwise. [Francis v. Franklin, 471 U.S. 307 (1985)]

2) In a criminal contempt proceeding for failure to pay child support, the state may not presume that the defendant was able to pay the amount due. One of the elements of contempt is the ability to comply with the court's order. Thus, the state may not presume ability to pay, but rather ability to pay must be proved beyond a reasonable doubt. [Hicks v. Feiock, 485 U.S. 624 (1988)]

3. Sufficiency of Evidence

The requirement of proof beyond a reasonable doubt in the Due Process Clause means that the sufficiency of the evidence supporting a criminal conviction in state court is, to some extent, a federal constitutional issue. Due process is violated if, viewing all the evidence in the light most favorable to the prosecution, no rational judge or jury would have found the defendant guilty of the crime of which he was convicted. [Jackson v. Virginia, 443 U.S. 307 (1979)]

a. Confessions Must Be Corroborated

A criminal conviction cannot rest entirely on an uncorroborated extrajudicial confession. If the defendant does not admit guilt in court, the prosecution must introduce extrinsic evidence that, at the least, tends to establish the trustworthiness of the admission. [Wong Sun v. United States, V.A.2.b.2)a), *supra;* Opper v. United States, 384 U.S. 84 (1954)]

4. Prior Act Evidence

Under the Due Process Clause, as a general constitutional rule, prior act evidence is admissible for various purposes if it is probative and relevant. Thus in a criminal trial evidence of prior bodily injury was admissible to show that a child victim had sustained repeated and/ or serious injuries by nonaccidental means (the "battered child syndrome") to infer that the victim's death was not accidental, even though there was no direct evidence linking the prior injuries to the defendant. [Estelle v. McGuire, 502 U.S. 62 (1991)]

5. **Right to Present Defensive Evidence**
Due process requires an opportunity to establish innocence.

Example: The arbitrary exclusion of a class of defense witnesses violates both due process and the right to compel the production of witnesses on one's own behalf.

a. **Application—Barring Claim that Third Party Committed Crime**
A state cannot impose a rule prohibiting a defendant from suggesting that a third party committed the crime whenever there is strong forensic evidence of the defendant's guilt. [Holmes v. South Carolina, 547 U.S. 319 (2006)] Proffered evidence can be excluded if it is shown to be flawed, but not merely because of the perceived strength of the prosecutor's case.

b. **Application—Exclusionary Rules of Evidence**
Even exclusionary rules of evidence that are valid on their face may combine to deprive a defendant of a fair opportunity to rebut the prosecution's case.

Examples: 1) Given the right to an acquittal if there is reasonable doubt on any element of a criminal charge, a defendant is denied a fair trial when the state's hearsay rule prevents him from showing that another person has confessed to the crime for which he is being tried, and where the state's rule against impeaching one's own witness prevents the defendant from even using the prior confession to cast doubt on the credibility of the confessor's unexpectedly damning testimony. [Chambers v. Mississippi, 410 U.S. 284 (1973)]

2) A state's per se rule excluding hypnotically refreshed testimony unconstitutionally infringes on a defendant's right to present testimony on his own behalf. A per se rule excludes even testimony that may be reliable. [Rock v. Arkansas, 483 U.S. 44 (1987)]

c. **Exclusion as Sanction**
A trial court may, however, exclude defense evidence as a sanction for the defendant's violation of discovery rules or procedures. For example, if the defendant's attorney fails to give advance notice that a witness will testify, the trial court may prohibit that witness from testifying. [Taylor v. Illinois, 484 U.S. 400 (1988)]

6. **Jury Instructions**
A judge is to give a jury instruction requested by the defendant or the prosecution if: the instruction (i) is correct, (ii) has not already been given, and (iii) is supported by some evidence. If an instruction fails any of the above tests, it need not be given merely because it is the defendant's theory of defense.

VIII. GUILTY PLEAS AND PLEA BARGAINING

A. GUILTY PLEA WAIVES RIGHT TO JURY TRIAL

A guilty plea is a waiver of the Sixth Amendment right to jury trial. Between 70% and 95% of all criminal cases are settled by guilty pleas.

B.   BASIC TRENDS

1.   Intelligent Choice Among Alternatives
The Court from 1970 to the present has indicated an unwillingness to disturb a guilty plea it views as an intelligent choice among the defendant's alternatives on the advice of counsel.

2.   Contract View
There is a trend toward the contract view of plea negotiation and bargaining. In this view, the plea agreement should be revealed in the record of the taking of the plea and its terms enforced against both the prosecutor and the defendant. [Ricketts v. Adamson, 483 U.S. 1 (1987)]

C.   TAKING THE PLEA

1.   Advising Defendant of the Charge, the Potential Penalty, and His Rights
The judge must determine that the plea is *voluntary and intelligent.* This must be done by addressing the defendant personally in open court *on the record.* [McCarthy v. United States, 394 U.S. 459 (1969); Boykin v. Alabama, 395 U.S. 238 (1969)] Specifically, the judge must be sure that the defendant knows and understands things like:

(i)   *The nature of the charge* to which the plea is offered and the *crucial elements* of the crime charged [Henderson v. Morgan, 426 U.S. 637 (1976)—plea involuntary if defendant not informed that intent is an element of the murder charge against him];

(ii)   The *maximum possible penalty* and any *mandatory minimum* (but the failure to explain special parole terms is not fatal [United States v. Timmreck, 441 U.S. 780 (1979)]); and

(iii) That he has a *right not to plead guilty* and that, if he does, he *waives the right to trial.*

a.   Attorney May Inform Defendant
The judge need not personally explain the elements of each charge to the defendant on the record. Rather, the constitutional prerequisites of a valid plea may be satisfied where the record accurately reflects that the nature of the charge and the elements of the crime were explained to the defendant by his own counsel. [Bradshaw v. Stumpf, 545 U.S. 175 (2005)]

b.   Unfairly Informed Defendant Not Bound
If counsel makes unfair representations to the defendant concerning the result of the defendant's pleading guilty, and the defendant can prove this, the defendant is not bound by her record answer, obtained at the plea taking, that her counsel made no such representations. [Blackledge v. Allison, 431 U.S. 63 (1977)]

2.   Remedy
The remedy for a failure to meet the standards for taking a plea is withdrawal of the plea and *pleading anew.*

3.   Factual Basis for Plea Not Constitutionally Required
There is no general requirement that the record contain evidence of the defendant's guilt or other factual basis for the plea. (*But see* D.1., below.)

D. COLLATERAL ATTACKS ON GUILTY PLEAS AFTER SENTENCE

Those pleas that are seen as an intelligent choice among the defendant's alternatives are immune from collateral attack.

Examples: 1) A plea is not involuntary merely because it was induced by a fear of the death penalty, which could be imposed only after a jury trial. Fear of the death penalty is like fear of any other penalty, which is the reason defendants plead guilty. [Brady v. United States, 397 U.S. 742 (1970)]

2) Fear of a coerced confession in the hands of the state will not support a collateral attack, and the defendant will be bound to his choice to plead guilty. If the defendant thought the confession was coerced, he should have made a motion to suppress; if he did not, the court will think it was because he believed he could not win. [McMann v. Richardson, 397 U.S. 759 (1970)]

3) Unconstitutional, systematic, racial exclusion in the indicting grand jury will not entitle the defendant to collateral relief. Here also, the Court views the choice not to object and to plead guilty as the result of the defendant's informed decision as to what course would be in his best interest. [Tollett v. Henderson, 411 U.S. 258 (1973)]

1. Plea Offered by Defendant Who Denies Guilt

When a defendant pleads guilty despite protesting his innocence, the plea will be seen as an intelligent choice by the defendant, and withdrawal of the plea will not be permitted when there is other strong evidence of guilt in the record. Admission of guilt is not a constitutional requisite to imposition of criminal penalty. [North Carolina v. Alford, 400 U.S. 25 (1970)]

2. Bases for an Attack on a Guilty Plea After Sentence

a. Plea Involuntary

Failure to meet the constitutional standards for taking a guilty plea will support a post-sentence attack on the plea.

b. Lack of Jurisdiction

The defendant may withdraw his plea if the court lacked jurisdiction to take the plea, or if prosecution for the offense for which the plea was offered is barred by double jeopardy. [Menna v. New York, 423 U.S. 61 (1975)]

c. Ineffective Assistance of Counsel

Ineffective assistance of counsel undercuts the assumption of an intelligent choice among the defendant's alternatives on the advice of counsel. Therefore, a defendant may successfully attack a guilty plea on the ground that he received ineffective assistance of counsel if, ***but for counsel's errors, the defendant probably would not have pleaded guilty*** and instead would have insisted on going to trial. [Hill v. Lockhart, 474 U.S. 52 (1985)]

d. Failure to Keep the Plea Bargain

See E.1., below.

E. PLEA BARGAINING

1. **Enforcement of the Bargain**

   A defendant who enters into a plea bargain has a right to have that bargain kept. The plea bargain will be *enforced against the prosecutor and the defendant, but not against the judge*, who does not have to accept the plea.

   a. **Prosecution**

   If the prosecution does not keep the bargain, the court should decide whether the circumstances require specific performance of the plea agreement or whether the defendant should be granted an opportunity to withdraw her guilty plea. [Santobello v. New York, 404 U.S. 257 (1971)] However, if the prosecutor withdraws a proposed plea bargain and the accused subsequently pleads guilty on other terms, the original offer cannot be specifically enforced despite the accused's attempt to "accept" the offer. [Mabry v. Johnson, 467 U.S. 504 (1984)]

   b. **Defendant**

   If the defendant does not live up to the plea agreement, his plea and sentence can be vacated.

   Example: D agrees to testify against a co-defendant in exchange for a reduction in charges from first to second degree murder. If D fails to testify, the prosecution can have D's plea and sentence vacated and reinstate the first degree murder charge. [Ricketts v. Adamson, B.2., *supra*]

2. **Power of the State to Threaten More Serious Charge**

   Consistent with the contract theory of plea negotiation, the state has the power to drive a hard bargain. A guilty plea is not involuntary merely because it was entered in response to the prosecution's threat to charge the defendant with a more serious crime if she does not plead guilty. [Bordenkircher v. Hayes, 434 U.S. 357 (1978)]

3. **Power to Charge More Serious Offense**

   The Supreme Court has held that there is no prosecutorial vindictiveness in charging a more serious offense when defendant demands a jury trial. [United States v. Goodwin, 457 U.S. 368 (1982)]

4. **Admission of Statements Made in Connection with Plea Bargaining**

   Under the Federal Rules of Evidence and of Criminal Procedure, statements made by a defendant in the course of unsuccessful plea negotiations are inadmissible at trial. However, such statements can be admitted *if* the defendant has knowingly and voluntarily waived the Federal Rules' exclusionary provisions. [United States v. Mezzanatto, 513 U.S. 196 (1995)]

5. **No Right to Impeachment or Affirmative Defense Evidence**

   Defendants are *not* entitled either to impeachment evidence or to evidence relevant to affirmative defenses prior to entering a plea agreement. Failure to provide such evidence does not make a plea involuntary. [United States v. Ruiz, 536 U.S. 622 (2002)]

F. **COLLATERAL EFFECTS OF GUILTY PLEAS**

1. **Conviction May Be Used in Other Proceedings**

   The Supreme Court has held that evidence of a defendant's conviction, based on a guilty plea in one state, may be introduced at trial in a second state for the purpose of proving a "specification" allowing imposition of the death penalty [Marshall v. Lonberger, 459 U.S. 422 (1983)], and a defendant is "convicted" within the meaning of the firearms disabilities provisions of the 1968 Gun Control Act when the defendant pleads guilty to a state charge punishable by more than one year, even if no formal judgment is entered and the record has been expunged. [Dickerson v. New Banner Institute, 460 U.S. 103 (1983)]

2. Does Not Admit Legality of Search
The Court has decided that a defendant's guilty plea neither admits the legality of the incriminating search nor waives Fourth Amendment claims in a subsequent civil damages action challenging the constitutionality of the incriminating search. [Haring v. Prosise, 462 U.S. 306 (1983)]

IX. CONSTITUTIONAL RIGHTS IN RELATION TO SENTENCING AND PUNISHMENT

A. PROCEDURAL RIGHTS IN SENTENCING

1. Right to Counsel
Sentencing is usually a "critical stage" of a criminal proceeding, thus requiring the assistance of counsel, as substantial rights of the defendant may be affected.

Examples: 1) The absence of counsel during sentencing after a plea of guilty, coupled with the judge's materially untrue assumptions concerning a defendant's criminal record, deprived the defendant of due process. [Townsend v. Burke, 334 U.S. 736 (1984)]

2) The absence of counsel at the time of sentencing where no sentence of imprisonment was imposed, but the defendant was put on probation, deprived the defendant of due process because certain legal rights (i.e., the right to appeal) might be lost by failing to assert them at this time. [Mempa v. Rhay, III.C.1., *supra*]

2. Right to Confrontation and Cross-Examination
The *usual* sentence may be based on hearsay and uncross-examined reports. [Williams v. New York, 337 U.S. 241 (1949)]

a. "New" Proceeding
Where a magnified sentence is based on a statute (e.g., one permitting indeterminate sentence) that requires new findings of fact to be made (e.g., that defendant is a habitual criminal, mentally ill, or deficient, etc.), those facts must be found in a context that grants the right to confrontation and cross-examination. [Specht v. Patterson, 386 U.S. 605 (1966)]

b. Capital Sentencing Procedures
It is clear that a defendant in a death penalty case must have more opportunity for confrontation than need be given a defendant in other sentencing proceedings. [Gardner v. Florida, 430 U.S. 349 (1977)—sentence of death based in part upon report not disclosed to defendant invalid]

B. RESENTENCING AFTER SUCCESSFUL APPEAL AND RECONVICTION

1. General Rule—Record Must Show Reasons for Harsher Sentence

If a judge imposes a greater punishment than at the first trial after the defendant has successfully appealed and then is reconvicted, she must set forth in the record the reasons for the harsher sentence based on "objective information concerning identifiable conduct on the part of the defendant occurring after the time of the original sentencing proceedings." [North Carolina v. Pearce, 395 U.S. 711 (1969)] The purpose of this requirement is to ensure that the defendant is not vindictively penalized for exercising his right to appeal.

Note: When a defendant successfully appeals, an exception to the Double Jeopardy Clause permits retrial. (*See* XIII.B.3., *infra*.)

2. Exceptions

a. Reconviction upon Trial De Novo

Some jurisdictions grant the defendant the right to a trial de novo as a matter of course after a trial in an inferior court. A trial de novo involves a fresh determination of guilt or innocence without reference to the lower conviction or fact of appeal. The rationale of *Pearce* does not apply when the defendant receives a greater sentence upon a trial de novo, because the new judge reduces the likelihood of vindictiveness. [Colten v. Kentucky, 407 U.S. 104 (1972)]

b. Jury Sentencing

Pearce does not apply to states that use jury sentencing, unless the second jury was told of the first jury's sentence. [Chaffin v. Stynchcombe, 412 U.S. 17 (1973)]

3. Recharging in a Trial De Novo

The prosecutor may not obtain an indictment for a more serious charge in a trial de novo, because of the possibility of prosecutorial vindictiveness and retaliation for exercising the statutory right to a trial de novo. [Blackledge v. Perry, 417 U.S. 21 (1974)]

C. SUBSTANTIVE RIGHTS IN REGARD TO PUNISHMENT

1. Criminal Penalties Constituting "Cruel and Unusual Punishment"

The Eighth Amendment prohibition against cruel and unusual punishment places several limitations upon criminal punishments.

a. Punishment Grossly Disproportionate to Offense

A penalty that is grossly disproportionate to the seriousness of the offense committed is cruel and unusual.

Examples: 1) D, convicted of falsifying a public record, received a sentence of 20 years' imprisonment at hard labor. Did this violate the Eighth Amendment? Yes, because the penalty was so disproportionate to the offense. [Weems v. United States, 217 U.S. 349 (1910)]

2) A sentence of life imprisonment without the possibility of parole imposed upon a recidivist following conviction of his seventh nonviolent felony, the uttering of a bad check, is significantly disproportionate to the

crime and is thus a violation of the Eighth Amendment. The unconstitutional taint is not eliminated by the possibility of commutation which, unlike parole, is granted on an ad hoc, standardless basis. [Solem v. Helm, 463 U.S. 277 (1983)]

Compare: 1) A mandatory life sentence for possession of a certain quantity of cocaine (650 grams—indicating that the defendant was a dealer) is ***not*** cruel and unusual, even though the statute did not allow consideration of mitigating factors (*compare* death penalty cases, below). [Harmelin v. Michigan, 501 U.S. 957 (1991)]

2) A California "three strikes" law requires imposition of an indeterminate life sentence after a person is found guilty of a felony if the person has previously been convicted of two or more serious or violent felonies. Defendant was convicted of stealing three golf clubs worth $399 each. Although the trial judge had discretion to treat the crime as either felony grand theft or a misdemeanor, she treated the theft as a felony and sentenced Defendant to 25 years to life because he had four previous serious felony convictions. *Held:* The sentence does not constitute cruel and unusual punishment. [Ewing v. California, 538 U.S. 11 (2003)]

b.   Proportionality—No Right to Comparison of Penalties in Similar Cases
The Eighth Amendment does not require state appellate courts to compare the death sentence imposed in a case under appeal with other penalties imposed in similar cases. [Pulley v. Harris, 465 U.S. 37 (1984)]

c.   Death Penalty

1)   For Murder
The death penalty is not inherently cruel and unusual punishment, but the Eighth Amendment requires that it be imposed only under a ***statutory scheme*** that gives the judge or jury reasonable ***discretion,*** full ***information*** concerning defendants, and ***guidance*** in making the decision. [Furman v. Georgia, 408 U.S. 238 (1972); Gregg v. Georgia, 428 U.S. 153 (1976)]

a)   Discretion
A jury must be allowed discretion to consider mitigating circumstances in death penalty cases. Thus, a statute cannot make the death penalty mandatory upon conviction of first degree murder [Woodson v. North Carolina, 428 U.S. 280 (1976)], or for the killing of a police officer or firefighter [Roberts v. Louisiana, 431 U.S. 633 (1977)], or for a killing by an inmate who is serving a life sentence [Sumner v. Shuman, 483 U.S. 66 (1987)]. Moreover, it is not sufficient to allow the jury to consider only some mitigating circumstances; they must be allowed to consider any aspect of the defendant's character or any circumstance of his crime as a factor in mitigation. [Penry v. Lynaugh, 492 U.S. 302 (1989)—death sentence reversed because jury was not allowed to consider defendant's intellectual disability and abused childhood in mitigation] In addition, a death sentence must be reversed if the jurors may have

been confused by jury instructions regarding their right to consider mitigating circumstances. [Mills v. Maryland, 486 U.S. 367 (1988)]

Examples: 1) A statute requires the jury to impose the death penalty if a defendant is convicted of specific crimes with aggravation, but also requires the trial judge to hear evidence of aggravating and mitigating circumstances before sentencing the defendant. The statute is constitutional. [Baldwin v. Alabama, 472 U.S. 372 (1985)]

2) A statute that instructs jurors to impose the death penalty if they find it probable that the defendant would commit criminal acts in the future, considering all aggravating or mitigating evidence presented at trial, was upheld against an argument that the instruction foreclosed consideration of the defendant's youth. The court found that consideration of future danger-ousness leaves open ample room for considering youth as a mitigating factor because "the signature qualities of youth are transient." [Johnson v. Texas, 509 U.S. 350 (1993)]

(1) Evidence Required for Mitigation Instruction
Nothing in the Constitution requires state courts to give mitigating circumstance instructions where the jury has heard no evidence on mitigating circumstances. [Delo v. Lashley, 507 U.S. 272 (1993)]

b) Information

(1) Instructions on Lesser Included Offenses
A defendant is not entitled to a jury instruction on every possible lesser included offense supported by the facts in a capital case [Schad v. Arizona, 501 U.S. 624 (1991)], but a statute cannot prohibit instructions on *all* lesser included offenses [Beck v. Alabama, 447 U.S. 625 (1980)]. *Rationale:* If the jurors are not instructed on any lesser included offense and believe that the defendant is guilty of a crime other than murder, they might impose the death penalty rather than let the defendant go unpunished. But if the jury is given instructions on a lesser included offense (e.g., second degree murder), they will not have to make an all or nothing choice, and so a resulting death penalty will stand.

(2) Victim Impact Statements
A "victim impact statement" (i.e., an assessment of how the crime affected the victim's family) may be considered during the sentencing phase of a capital case. *Rationale:* The defendant has long been allowed to present mitigating factors, so the jury must be allowed to counterbal-ance the impact on the victim's family in order to "assess meaning-fully the defendant's moral culpability and blameworthiness." [Payne v. Tennessee, 501 U.S. 808 (1991)]

(3) Life Imprisonment Without Parole
Where a capital defendant's future dangerousness is at issue, and the

only sentencing alternative to death is life imprisonment without possibility of parole, the Due Process Clause entitles the defendant to inform the jury of his parole ineligibility, through either a jury instruction or arguments by counsel. [Lynch v. Arizona, 136 S. Ct. 1818 (2016)]

c) Guidance

A statute providing for the death penalty may not be vague.

Example: A statute that permits imposition of the death penalty when a murder is "outrageously or wantonly vile, horrible, or inhuman in that it involved torture, depravity of mind, or an aggravated battery to the victim" is unconstitutionally vague. [Godfrey v. Georgia, 446 U.S. 420 (1980); Maynard v. Cartwright, 486 U.S. 356 (1988)]

Compare: A statute that imposes the death penalty where the murderer displayed "utter disregard for human life" provides sufficiently clear and objective standards for imposition of the death penalty where the state supreme court had construed the statute to apply only where the killing was committed by a "cold-blooded, pitiless slayer." [Arave v. Creech, 507 U.S. 463 (1993)]

d) Prior Crimes

Most states provide that prior crimes by the defendant, particularly those involving force or violence, are aggravating factors that either make the defendant eligible for the death penalty or are weighed by the jurors in reaching their decision on whether to impose the death penalty. If a death sentence is based in any part on a defendant's prior conviction, the sentence must be reversed if the prior conviction is invalidated. [Johnson v. Mississippi, 486 U.S. 578 (1988)]

e) Standard of Review

Where a death sentence has been affected by a vague or otherwise unconstitutional factor, the death sentence can still be upheld, but only if all aggravating and mitigating factors involved are reweighed by all of the judges to whom the sentence is appealed and death is still found to be appropriate. [Richmond v. Lewis, 506 U.S. 40 (1993)]

2) For Rape

The Eighth Amendment prohibits imposition of the death penalty for the crime of raping an adult woman, because the penalty is disproportionate to the offense. [Coker v. Georgia, 433 U.S. 584 (1977)] Nor may a death sentence be imposed for the rape of a child that was neither intended to result in, nor did result in, death. [Kennedy v. Louisiana, 554 U.S. 407 (2008)]

3) For Felony Murder

The death penalty may not be imposed for felony murder where the defendant, as an accomplice, "did not take or attempt or intend to take life, or intend that lethal force be employed." [Enmund v. Florida, 458 U.S. 782 (1982)] However, the death penalty may be imposed on a felony murderer who neither killed nor intended to kill where he participated in a major way in a felony that resulted in murder, and acted with *reckless indifference to the value of human life*. [Tison v. Arizona, 481 U.S. 137 (1987)—defendants helped prisoner escape and provided him with weapons]

4) Jury Responsibility for Verdict

It is unconstitutional to diminish the jury's sense of responsibility for its role in determining a death sentence. [Caldwell v. Mississippi, 472 U.S. 320 (1985)—prosecutor's comment to the jury that its verdict is reviewable and that the verdict is not the final decision is sufficient to diminish the jury's sense of responsibility; Ring v. Arizona, VII.B.6., *supra*—unconstitutional for judge to determine after jury verdict of guilt whether aggravating factors justify imposition of the death penalty]

a) Compare—Instruction Regarding Failure to Agree

Even at the defendant's request, the court need not instruct the jury of the consequences of its failure to agree on a verdict. [Jones v. United States, 527 U.S. 373 (1999)—Eighth Amendment was not violated where court denied defendant's request that jury be instructed that judge would impose sentence if jury could not unanimously agree]

5) Racial Discrimination

Statistical evidence that black defendants who kill white victims are more likely to receive the death penalty does not establish that the penalty was imposed as a result of unconstitutional discrimination. [McCleskey v. Kemp, 481 U.S. 279 (1987)]

6) Sanity Requirement

The Eighth Amendment prohibits states from inflicting the death penalty upon a prisoner who is insane (i.e., one who was sane at the time the crime was committed and was properly sentenced to death, but is insane at the time of execution). [Ford v. Wainwright, 477 U.S. 399 (1986)]

7) Intellectual Disability

It is cruel and unusual punishment to impose the death penalty on a person who is intellectually disabled. [Atkins v. Virginia, 536 U.S. 304 (2002)] The state determines, under its own standards, whether an individual is intellectually disabled. However, the states do not have unfettered discretion to define the full scope of the constitutional protection. [Hall v. Florida, 134 S. Ct. 1986 (2014)—a state statutory requirement of showing an IQ score of 70 or below before being permitted to introduce other evidence of intellectual disability is unconstitutional]

8) For Minors

Execution of persons who were under 18 years old at the time they committed their offense (including murder) violates the Eighth Amendment. [Roper v. Simmons, 543 U.S. 551 (2005)]

9) Lethal Injection

The mere possibility that the three-drug lethal injection protocol used by many states to carry out executions *might* be administered improperly and thus cause the condemned unnecessary pain does not make the procedure cruel and unusual punishment. It would be cruel and unusual only if the condemned can prove that there is a serious risk of inflicting unnecessary pain or that an alternative procedure is feasible, may be readily implemented, and in fact significantly reduces substantial risk of severe pain. [Baze v. Rees, 553 U.S. 35 (2008)]

d. "Status" Crimes

A statute that makes it a crime to have a given "status" violates the Eighth Amendment because it punishes a mere propensity to engage in dangerous behavior. But it is no violation of the amendment to make specific activity related to a certain status criminal.

Example: A statute makes it criminal to "be a common drunkard" and to appear in public in an intoxicated condition. May a chronic alcoholic be convicted of both of these? No. He may not be convicted of being a common drunkard, because this is a prohibited status crime. But he may be convicted of appearing in public while intoxicated, because this crime prohibits the act of "appearing." [Powell v. Texas, 392 U.S. 514 (1968)]

e. Minors

As indicated above, the Supreme Court has found the execution of a person who was a minor (under age 18) when he committed his offense to be cruel and unusual under the Eighth Amendment. The Court has also found an Eighth Amendment violation in a sentencing scheme that imposes mandatory life imprisonment without the possibility of parole on a person who was a minor when the crime was committed. [Miller v. Alabama, 567 U.S. 460 (2012)]

2. Recidivist Statutes

A mandatory life sentence imposed pursuant to a recidivist statute does *not* constitute cruel and unusual punishment, even though the three felonies that formed the predicate for the sentence were nonviolent, property-related offenses. [Rummel v. Estelle, 445 U.S. 263 (1980)] (There is an apparent conflict with *Solem v. Helm, supra,* C.1.a. While *Solem* is inconsistent with *Rummel,* the Supreme Court declined to distinguish *Rummel* in reaching its holding in *Solem.*)

3. Punishing the Exercise of Constitutional Rights

A punishment of greater length or severity cannot constitutionally be reserved by statute for those who assert their right to plead innocent and to demand trial by jury. [United States v. Jackson, 390 U.S. 570 (1968)—death penalty available only for federal kidnapping defendants who insist on jury trial; penalty of death in such circumstances cannot be carried out, but guilty pleas induced by such a scheme are not automatically involuntary]

4. Consideration of Defendant's Perjury at Trial

In determining sentence, a trial judge may take into account a belief that the defendant, while testifying at trial on his own behalf, committed perjury. This is important in evaluating the defendant's prospects for rehabilitation and does not impose an improper burden upon a defendant's right to testify. [United States v. Grayson, 438 U.S. 41 (1978)]

5. **Imprisonment of Indigents for Nonpayment of Fines Violates Equal Protection Clause**
Where the aggregate imprisonment exceeds the maximum period fixed by statute and results directly from an involuntary nonpayment of a fine or court costs, there is an impermissible discrimination and a violation of the Equal Protection Clause. [Williams v. Illinois, 399 U.S. 235 (1970)] It is also a violation of equal protection to limit punishment to payment of a fine for those who are able to pay it, but to convert the fine to imprisonment for those who are unable to pay it. [Tate v. Short, 401 U.S. 395 (1971)—30 days or $30]

a. **Imprisonment of Parolee for Nonpayment of Fine**
A trial court may not revoke a defendant's probation and imprison him for the remainder of the probation term for failure to pay a fine and make restitution without showing that the defendant actually was capable of payment or that there were no alternative forms of punishment available to meet the state's interest in punishment and deterrence. [Bearden v. Georgia, 461 U.S. 660 (1983)]

X. CONSTITUTIONAL PROBLEMS ON APPEAL

A. **NO RIGHT TO APPEAL**
There is apparently no federal constitutional right to an appeal. Several Supreme Court opinions suggest that all appeals could constitutionally be abolished.

B. **EQUAL PROTECTION AND RIGHT TO COUNSEL ON APPEAL**

1. **First Appeal**
If an avenue of post-conviction review (appellate or collateral) is provided, conditions that make the review less accessible to the poor than to the rich violate equal protection. [Griffin v. Illinois, 351 U.S. 12 (1956)—indigent entitled to free transcript on appeal]

Examples: 1) The Equal Protection Clause was violated where a statute requiring the payment of fees for a transcript of a preliminary hearing was applied to deny a free transcript to an indigent. [Roberts v. LaValle, 389 U.S. 40 (1968)]

2) Requiring reimbursement for costs of a trial transcription only of those incarcerated (not from those fined, given suspended sentence, or placed on probation) violates equal protection. [Rinaldi v. Yaeger, 384 U.S. 305 (1966)] But a state can distinguish between convicted and acquitted defendants in this context and require reimbursement only from those convicted. [Fuller v. Oregon, 417 U.S. 40 (1974)]

3) Illinois rule providing for trial transcript on appeal only in felony cases is an unreasonable distinction in violation of equal protection. Even in misdemeanor cases punishable by fine only, a defendant must be afforded as effective an appeal as a defendant who can pay, and where the grounds of the appeal make out a colorable need for a complete transcript, the burden is on the state to show that something less will suffice. [Mayer v. City of Chicago, 404 U.S. 189 (1971)]

a. **Right to Appointed Counsel**

Indigents must be given counsel at state expense during a first appeal granted to all as a matter of right. [Douglas v. California, III.C.1., *supra*] This rule also extends to appeals by defendants who plead guilty or nolo contendere and who must (under state law) seek leave of the court before bringing an appeal. [Halbert v. Michigan, III.C.1., *supra*] *Rationale:* Although such appeals are discretionary, they present the first (and likely only) chance for review on the merits that such defendants have. Mere failure to request appointment of counsel does not constitute waiver of the right to assistance of counsel on appeal.

b. **Attorney May Withdraw If Appeal Frivolous**

An appellate court can permit withdrawal of counsel who concludes that appeal would be frivolous. However, before doing so, the state must take steps to *ensure that the defendant's right to counsel is not being denied.*

Examples: 1) It is sufficient to (i) require counsel to file a brief referring to anything in the record that might arguably support an appeal (an *Anders* brief) and (ii) require the appellate court to determine that counsel has correctly concluded that appeal is frivolous. [Anders v. California, 386 U.S. 738 (1967)—striking California procedure that allowed counsel to withdraw upon filing a conclusory letter that simply stated the appeal had no merit]

2) It is sufficient to require counsel to (i) summarize the procedural and factual history of the case but (ii) remain silent on the merits of the case unless the appellate court directs otherwise. [Smith v. Robbins, 528 U.S. 259 (2000)—reasoning that this procedure ensures that a "trained legal eye" will search the record and provide some assistance to the reviewing court]

2. **Discretionary Appeals**

In a jurisdiction using a two-tier system of appellate courts with discretionary review by the highest court, an indigent defendant need not be provided with counsel during the second, discretionary appeal. Representation also need not be provided for an indigent seeking to invoke the United States Supreme Court's discretionary authority to review criminal convictions. [Ross v. Moffit, 417 U.S. 600 (1974)]

C. NO RIGHT TO SELF-REPRESENTATION

On appeal, a defendant has no right to represent himself. [Martinez v. Court of Appeal, 528 U.S. 152 (2000)]

D. RETROACTIVITY

If the Court announces a new rule of criminal procedure (i.e., one not dictated by precedent) in a case on direct review, the rule must be applied to *all other cases on direct review.* [Griffith v. Kentucky, 479 U.S. 314 (1987)] *Rationale:* It would be unfair to allow the one defendant whose case the Supreme Court happened to choose to hear to benefit from the new rule, while denying the benefit to other similarly situated defendants simply because they were not lucky enough to have their case chosen.

XI. COLLATERAL ATTACK UPON CONVICTIONS

A. AVAILABILITY OF COLLATERAL ATTACK

After appeal is no longer available or has proven unsuccessful, defendants may generally still attack their convictions collaterally, usually by beginning a new and separate civil proceeding involving an application for a writ of habeas corpus. This proceeding focuses on the lawfulness of a detention, naming the person having custody as the respondent.

B. HABEAS CORPUS PROCEEDING

1. No Right to Appointed Counsel

An indigent does not have the right to appointed counsel to perfect her petition for a writ of habeas corpus.

2. Burden of Proof

Because the proceeding for a writ of habeas corpus is civil in nature, the petitioner has the burden of proof by a *preponderance of the evidence* to show an unlawful detention.

3. State May Appeal

The state may appeal the granting of a writ of habeas corpus, and double jeopardy bars neither the appeal nor retrial after the granting of the writ.

4. Requirement of Custody

The state defendant must be "in custody," but it is sufficient if he is out on bail, probation, or parole. [Hensley v. Municipal Court, 411 U.S. 345 (1973)] Generally, the "in custody" requirement is *not* met by a petitioner whose sentence has expired, even if his prior conviction is used to enhance a later one [Maleng v. Cook, 490 U.S. 488 (1989)], but a petitioner who remains in jail on a *consecutive sentence* is in custody, even if the jail time for the crime being challenged has expired [Garlotte v. Fordice, 515 U.S. 39 (1995)].

XII. RIGHTS DURING PUNISHMENT—PROBATION, IMPRISONMENT, PAROLE

A. RIGHT TO COUNSEL AT PAROLE AND PROBATION REVOCATIONS

1. Probation Revocation Involving Resentencing

If revocation of probation also involves the imposition of a new sentence, the defendant is entitled to representation by counsel in all cases in which she is entitled to counsel at trial. [Mempa v. Rhay, *supra*, IX.A.1.]

2. Other Situations

If, after probation revocation, an already imposed sentence of imprisonment springs into application, *or* the case involves parole revocation, the right to counsel is much more limited.

There is a right to be represented by counsel only if, on the facts of the case, such representation is *necessary to a fair hearing*. Generally, it will be necessary if the defendant denies commission of the acts alleged or asserts an argument as to why revocation should not occur that is "complex or otherwise difficult to develop or present." In addition, each defendant must be told of her right to request appointment of counsel, and if a request is refused, the record must contain a succinct statement of the basis for the refusal. [Gagnon v. Scarpelli, 411 U.S. 778 (1973)]

B. PRISONERS' RIGHTS

1. Due Process Rights

Prison regulations and operations may create liberty interests protected by the Due Process Clause, but due process is violated only where the regulations and operations *impose "atypical and significant hardship"* in relation to the ordinary incidents of prison life. [Sandin v. Conner, 515 U.S. 472 (1995)]

Example: Assignment for an indefinite period to a "supermax" prison (i.e., a maximum security prison with highly restrictive conditions, designed to segregate the most dangerous prisoners from the general prison population), in which prisoners rarely have visitors, are deprived of almost any environmental or human contact, and from which there is no eligibility for parole, *is* "atypical and extreme hardship." [Wilkinson v. Austin, 545 U.S. 209 (2005)]

Compare: Disciplinary segregation for 30 days does not implicate a liberty interest that triggers due process protections. [Sandin v. Conner, *supra*]

2. No Fourth Amendment Protections in Search of Cells

Prisoners have no reasonable expectation of privacy in their cells, or in personal property in their cells, and hence no Fourth Amendment protection therein. [Hudson v. Palmer, 468 U.S. 517 (1984)] Additionally, prisoners have no right to be present when prison officials search their cells. [Block v. Rutherford, 468 U.S. 576 (1984)]

3. Right of Access to Courts

Prison inmates must have reasonable access to courts, and no unreasonable limitations may be put upon their ability to develop and present arguments. Inmates may not be prevented from consulting with other inmates, unless a reasonable substitute (such as a law library) is provided. [Bounds v. Smith, 430 U.S. 817 (1977); Johnson v. Avery, 393 U.S. 483 (1969)] No absolute bar against law students and other paraprofessionals interviewing inmates for lawyers may be imposed. [Procunier v. Martinez, 416 U.S. 396 (1974)]

Note: A prisoner's *Bounds* claim of inadequate prison legal resources must include a showing that the alleged deficiencies in the legal resources have resulted in a hindrance of access to court. [Lewis v. Casey, 518 U.S. 343 (1996)]

4. First Amendment Rights

Prison officials need some discretion to limit prisoners' First Amendment activities (e.g., speech and assembly) in order to run a safe and secure prison. Therefore, generally prison regulations *reasonably related to penological interests* will be upheld even though they burden First Amendment rights. [Turner v. Safley, 482 U.S. 78 (1987)] For example, prison officials have broad discretion to regulate incoming mail to prevent contraband and even sexually explicit materials from entering the prison. Officials may even open letters from a prisoner's attorney, as long as they do so in the prisoner's presence and the letters are not read. [*See* Thornburgh v. Abbott, 490 U.S. 401 (1989); Wolff v. McDonnell, 418 U.S. 539

(1974)] However, prison officials have less discretion to regulate outgoing mail, because it usually does not have an effect on prison safety. [Procunier v. Martinez, *supra*]

Example: Pennsylvania housed its most dangerous and recalcitrant inmates in a special unit in which inmates start at level 2 but can graduate to level 1 with good behavior. Level 2 prisoners are very restricted and are prohibited from receiving any newspapers, magazines, or photographs. A prisoner sued, claiming that these prohibitions deprived him of his First Amendment rights. The prison justified the ban as a tool to encourage better behavior and argued that it was limited in the privileges that it could take away, because these prisoners had already lost most of their privileges. Under these conditions, the prohibition serves a legitimate penological interest and is reasonably related to that interest. [Beard v. Banks, 548 U.S. 521 (2006)]

Note: As a matter of federal **statutory** law (the Religious Land Use and Institutionalized Persons Act of 2000), no state that accepts federal funding for its prisons (and all states do) may place a burden on the **religious exercise** of prisoners unless the burden furthers a **compelling government interest** (e.g., a restriction that is necessary to ensure safety or discipline) and does so by the least restrictive means. [Cutter v. Wilkinson, 544 U.S. 709 (2005)] However, this standard should **not be applied on the MBE**, as that exam focuses on Constitutional Criminal Procedure (i.e., the constitutional standard) rather than on federal statutory standards.

5. **Right to Adequate Medical Care**

"Deliberate indifference to serious medical needs of prisoners" constitutes cruel and unusual punishment in violation of the Eighth Amendment, as does severe overcrowding that results in inadequate medical care. [Brown v. Plata, 563 U.S. 493 (2011)] However, simple negligent failure to provide care—"medical malpractice"—does not violate the amendment. [Estelle v. Gamble, 429 U.S. 97 (1976)] And while prisoners have a liberty interest in refusing medication, they can be forced to take antipsychotic drugs if an unbiased and qualified decision-maker finds it necessary to protect the prisoner or others. [Washington v. Harper, 494 U.S. 210 (1990)]

C. **NO RIGHT TO BE FREE FROM DISENFRANCHISEMENT UPON COMPLETION OF SENTENCE**

There is no right to be free from state disenfranchisement upon conviction of a felony, even if this continues after completion of the sentence imposed. [Richardson v. Ramirez, 418 U.S. 24 (1974)]

XIII. DOUBLE JEOPARDY

A. **WHEN JEOPARDY ATTACHES**

The Fifth Amendment right to be free of double jeopardy for the same offense has been incorporated into the Fourteenth Amendment. [Benton v. Maryland, 395 U.S. 784 (1969)] The general rule is that once jeopardy attaches, the defendant may not be retried for the same offense.

1. **Jury Trials**

Jeopardy attaches in a jury trial at the **empaneling and swearing** of the jury. [Crist v. Bretz, 437 U.S. 28 (1978)]

2. Bench Trials

In bench trials, jeopardy attaches when the *first witness is sworn*.

3. Juvenile Proceedings

The *commencement* of an adjudicatory juvenile proceeding (i.e., a hearing at which the court begins to hear evidence regarding the charged act) bars a subsequent criminal trial for the same offense. [Breed v. Jones, 421 U.S. 519 (1975)]

4. Not in Civil Proceedings

Jeopardy generally does not attach in civil proceedings other than juvenile proceedings. [One Lot Emerald Cut Stones & One Ring v. United States, 409 U.S. 232 (1972)]

Example: After the defendant is acquitted of criminal charges of smuggling, the government may still seek forfeiture of the items that the defendant allegedly smuggled into the country. [One Lot Emerald Cut Stones & One Ring v. United States, *supra*]

B. EXCEPTIONS PERMITTING RETRIAL

Certain exceptions permit retrial of a defendant even if jeopardy has attached.

1. Hung Jury

The government may retry a defendant whose trial ends in a hung jury. Note that it does not matter that the jury had agreed that the defendant could not be found guilty of a more severe charge before hanging on a lesser charge—if the jury does not return a verdict, double jeopardy does not bar retrial on any of the charges. [Blueford v. Arkansas, 566 U.S. 599 (2012)]

Example: Defendant was tried for capital murder, first degree murder, manslaughter, and negligent homicide. The jury was instructed to consider the most serious crime first, and the lesser included crimes only if they agreed Defendant could not be found guilty of the greater charge. The jury reported to the judge that they agreed Defendant was not guilty of capital murder or first degree murder, but that they had reached an impasse on the lesser charges. The judge sent the jury back for further deliberations. When the jury later could not agree on a verdict, the judge declared a mistrial. The jury did not return a partial verdict—it merely reported on its progress. Therefore, Defendant can be re-charged with all of the crimes. [Blueford v. Arkansas, *supra*]

2. Mistrial for Manifest Necessity

A trial may be discontinued and the defendant reprosecuted for the same offense when there is a manifest necessity to abort the original trial [United States v. Perez, 22 U.S. 579 (1824); Illinois v. Somerville, 410 U.S. 458 (1973)] or when the termination occurs at the behest of the defendant on any grounds not constituting an acquittal on the merits [United States v. Scott, 437 U.S. 82 (1978)]. Thus, double jeopardy is not an absolute bar to two trials.

3. Retrial After Successful Appeal

The state may retry a defendant who has successfully appealed a conviction, unless the ground for the reversal was insufficient evidence to support the guilty verdict. [Burks v. United States, 437 U.S. 1 (1978)] On the other hand, retrial is permitted when reversal is based on the *weight*, rather than *sufficiency*, of the evidence [Tibbs v. Florida, 457 U.S. 31

(1982)], or where a case is reversed because of erroneously admitted evidence [Lockhart v. Nelson, 488 U.S. 33 (1988)].

Example: If, after weighing the evidence in the record, an appellate court reversed a conviction on appeal, holding that the record did not support a finding of guilt beyond a reasonable doubt, a retrial would be permitted. However, if the appellate court reversed, holding that even if all of the evidence is taken as true, it was not sufficient to prove all of the elements of the crime charged, a retrial would not be permitted.

a. Charges on Retrial

The Double Jeopardy Clause prohibits retrying a defendant whose conviction has been reversed on appeal for any offense more serious than that for which she was convicted at the first trial. This right is violated by *retrial for the more serious offense*, even if at the second trial the defendant is convicted only of an offense no more than that for which she was convicted at the first trial. [Price v. Georgia, 398 U.S. 323 (1970)]

Example: X is charged with murder. She is convicted of manslaughter and her conviction is reversed on appeal. She is again tried for murder and again convicted of manslaughter. May this conviction stand? No, because she could not be retried for anything more serious than manslaughter. This is not harmless error, because the charge of murder in the second trial may have influenced the jury toward conviction of manslaughter.

b. Sentencing on Retrial

The Double Jeopardy Clause generally does *not* prohibit imposition of a *harsher sentence* on conviction after retrial, and such a sentence is valid provided it does not run afoul of the vindictiveness concerns discussed at IX.B.1., *supra*.

1) Death Penalty Cases

When there is a formalized, separate process for imposing the death penalty (e.g., when guilt is first determined and then the jury is presented with evidence on whether to impose death), if at the first trial the jury finds that a death sentence is not appropriate, a death sentence cannot be imposed at a second trial. [Bullington v. Missouri, 451 U.S. 430 (1981)] However, if the jury makes no such finding (e.g., when a judge imposes a life sentence pursuant to a statute providing for such a sentence when the jury is deadlocked on sentencing), a death sentence can be imposed at a second trial. [Sattazahn v. Pennsylvania, 537 U.S. 101 (2003)—"the relevant inquiry . . . is not whether the defendant received a life sentence the first time around, but whether a first life sentence was an 'acquittal' based on findings sufficient to establish legal entitlement to the life sentence—that is, findings that the government failed to prove one or more aggravating circumstances beyond a reasonable doubt"] In any case, note that these special rules apply only to capital sentencing proceedings. [Monge v. California, 524 U.S. 721 (1998)]

4. Breach of Plea Bargaining

When a defendant breaches a plea bargain agreement, his plea and sentence can be vacated and the original charges can be reinstated. [Ricketts v. Adamson, VIII.E.1.b., *supra*]

5. Election to Try Multiple Offenses Separately

If a defendant could have been tried on multiple charges in a single trial, but the defendant elects to have the offenses tried separately, jeopardy does not attach to the first trial. [Currier v. Virginia, 138 S. Ct. 2144 (2018)]

C.   SAME OFFENSE

1.   General Rule—When Two Crimes Do Not Constitute Same Offense

Two crimes do not constitute the same offense if *each crime requires proof of an additional element* that the other crime does not require, even though some of the same facts may be necessary to prove both crimes. [Blockburger v. United States, 284 U.S. 299 (1932)]

Example: D is arrested after the car he is driving strikes and kills a pedestrian. D is tried on the charges of reckless homicide and driving while intoxicated. D can receive separate punishments for both of the offenses because each crime requires proof of an additional element not required by the other: the homicide charge requires proof of a death but not proof of intoxication, while the driving while intoxicated charge requires proof of intoxication but not proof of a death.

a.   Application of *Blockburger*

Under *Blockburger*, the following do ***not*** constitute the same offenses:

1)   Manslaughter with an automobile and hit-and-run;

2)   Reckless driving and drunk driving;

3)   Reckless driving and failure to yield the right of way; and

4)   Uttering a forged check and obtaining money by false pretenses by using the forged check.

2.   Cumulative Punishments for Offenses Constituting Same Crime

Imposition of cumulative punishments for two or more statutorily defined offenses, *specifically intended by the legislature to carry separate punishments*, even though constituting the "same" crime under the *Blockburger* test, *supra*, does not violate the prohibition of multiple punishments for the same offense of the Double Jeopardy Clause, when the punishments are *imposed at a single trial*. [Missouri v. Hunter, 459 U.S. 359 (1983)]

Example: D robs a store at gunpoint. D can be sentenced to cumulative punishments for both the robbery and for violating a "Use a gun, go to jail" statute.

Note: Absent a clear intention, it will be presumed that multiple punishments are not intended for offenses constituting the same crime under *Blockburger*. Also, imposition of multiple punishments is prohibited even if the sentences for the two crimes run concurrently. [Rutledge v. United States, 517 U.S. 292 (1996)]

3.   Lesser Included Offenses

a.   Retrial for Lesser Included Offense Barred

Attachment of jeopardy for the greater offense bars retrial for lesser included offenses. [Harris v. Oklahoma, 433 U.S. 682 (1977)]

Example: D is convicted of felony murder based on proof that he and an accomplice shot and killed a store clerk during an armed robbery. D cannot then be tried for the armed robbery because it is a lesser included offense of the felony murder. [Harris v. Oklahoma, *supra*]

b. Retrial for Greater Offense

Attachment of jeopardy for a lesser included offense bars retrial for the greater offense. [Brown v. Ohio, 432 U.S. 161 (1977)]

1) Exception—New Evidence

An exception to the double jeopardy bar exists if unlawful conduct that is subsequently used to prove the greater offense (i) has not occurred at the time of the prosecution for the lesser offense, or (ii) has not been discovered despite due diligence. [Garrett v. United States, 471 U.S. 773 (1985)] Similarly, retrial for murder is permitted if the victim dies after attachment of jeopardy for battery. [Diaz v. United States, 223 U.S. 442 (1912)]

2) Effect of Plea on Related Offense

A state may continue to prosecute a charged offense, despite the defendant's guilty plea to lesser included or "allied" offenses stemming from the same incident. [Ohio v. Johnson, 467 U.S. 493 (1984)—defendant charged with murder and manslaughter, and robbery and theft, arising from the same incident, can be prosecuted for murder and robbery after pleading guilty to manslaughter and theft over state's objection]

4. Conspiracy and Substantive Offense

A prosecution for *conspiracy* is not barred merely because some of the alleged *overt acts* of that conspiracy have already been prosecuted. [United States v. Felix, 503 U.S. 378 (1992)]

5. Prior Act Evidence

The introduction of evidence of a substantive offense as prior act evidence is not equivalent to *prosecution* for that substantive offense, and therefore subsequent prosecution for that conduct is not barred. [United States v. Felix, *supra*]

6. Conduct Used as a Sentence Enhancer

The Double Jeopardy Clause is not violated when a person is indicted for a crime the conduct of which was already used to enhance the defendant's sentence for another crime. [Witte v. United States, 515 U.S. 389 (1995)—defendant indicted for conspiring to import cocaine after the conduct of the conspiracy was used to enhance his earlier sentence when he pleaded guilty to possession of marijuana]

7. Civil Actions

The Double Jeopardy Clause prohibits only repetitive *criminal* prosecutions. Thus, a state generally is free to bring a civil action against a defendant even if the defendant has already been criminally tried for the conduct out of which the civil action arises. Similarly, the government may bring a criminal action even though the defendant has already faced civil trial for the same conduct. However, if there is clear proof from the face of the statutory scheme that its purpose or effect is to impose a criminal penalty, the Double Jeopardy

Clause applies. [Hudson v. United States, 522 U.S. 93 (1998)—finding no clear proof of such purpose or effect where a civil statute allowed a government agency to impose a fine and bar defendants from working in banking industry for improperly approving loans]

D. SEPARATE SOVEREIGNS

The constitutional prohibition against double jeopardy *does not apply* to trials by separate sovereigns. Thus, a person may be tried for the same conduct by both a state and the federal government [United States v. Lanza, 260 U.S. 377 (1922)] or by two states [Heath v. Alabama, 474 U.S. 82 (1986)], but not by a state and its municipalities [Waller v. Florida, 397 U.S. 387 (1970)].

E. APPEALS BY PROSECUTION

Even after jeopardy has attached, the prosecution *may appeal any dismissal* on the defendant's motion *not constituting an acquittal on the merits*. [United States v. Scott, 437 U.S. 82 (1978)] Also, the Double Jeopardy Clause does not bar appeals by the prosecution if a *successful appeal would not require a retrial*, such as when the trial judge granted a motion to set aside the jury verdict. [United States v. Wilson, 420 U.S. 332 (1975)]

1. Appeal of Sentence

Government appeal of a sentence, *pursuant* to a congressionally enacted *statute* permitting such review, does not constitute multiple punishment in violation of the Double Jeopardy Clause. [United States v. DiFrancesco, 449 U.S. 117 (1980)]

F. ISSUE PRECLUSION (COLLATERAL ESTOPPEL)

The notion of collateral estoppel is embodied in the guarantee against double jeopardy. A defendant may not be tried or convicted of a crime if a prior prosecution by that sovereignty resulted in a *factual determination inconsistent with one required for conviction*. However, this doctrine has limited utility because of the general verdict in criminal trials.

Examples: 1) Where three or four armed men robbed six poker players in the home of one of the victims and the defendant was charged in separate counts with robbery of each of the six players and was tried on one count and was acquitted for insufficient evidence in a prosecution in which identity was the single rationally conceivable issue in dispute, he may not thereafter be prosecuted for robbery of a different player. [Ashe v. Swenson, 397 U.S. 436 (1970)] A second trial would not have been barred if there had been dispute at the first trial regarding whether the alleged victim was robbed. The court did not adopt the "same transaction" test proposed by some justices, under which a defendant could not be more than once put in jeopardy for offenses arising out of the "same transactions."

2) Where the ultimate issue of identity of the person who mailed a package with a bomb that killed two persons was decided at the first trial at which defendant was acquitted, the defendant may not thereafter be convicted of the second murder, even if the jury in the first trial (for the first murder) did not have all the relevant evidence before it and the state acted in good faith. [Harris v. Washington, 404 U.S. 55 (1971)]

1. Inconsistent Verdicts

If the defendant has been charged with multiple counts and there is an inconsistency in the verdicts among the counts (e.g., the jury acquitted the defendant on some and deadlocked on others), the focus should be on what was decided rather than on what was not decided. That is, the issues necessarily decided in the acquittal will have preclusive effect even if the same issues were involved in the counts on which the jury deadlocked. [Yeager v. United States, 557 U.S. 110 (2009)] However, if the same jury returns irreconcilably inconsistent verdicts on the same issue, the defendant cannot show what the jury decided and so the inconsistent verdicts will have no preclusive effect. [Bravo-Fernandez v. United States, 137 S. Ct. 352 (2016)]

Example: Defendant was charged with several counts of fraud and insider trading. A necessary element in each count was that Defendant possessed material, nonpublic information and used it unlawfully. He was acquitted of the fraud charges but the jury failed to reach a verdict on the insider trading charges. Retrial is barred on the insider trading counts under the issue preclusion component of the Double Jeopardy Clause. The jury's failure to decide the insider trading counts does not affect the preclusive force of the acquittals on the fraud counts, even though both relied on the same factual elements. [Yeager v. United States, *supra*]

XIV. PRIVILEGE AGAINST COMPELLED SELF-INCRIMINATION

A. APPLICABLE TO THE STATES

As discussed above (*see* III.D., *supra*), the Fifth Amendment prohibits the government from compelling self-incriminating testimony. The Fifth Amendment prohibition against compelled self-incrimination was made applicable to the states through the Fourteenth Amendment in *Malloy v. Hogan*, 378 U.S. 1 (1964).

B. WHO MAY ASSERT THE PRIVILEGE

Only *natural persons* may assert the privilege, not corporations or partnerships. [Bellis v. United States, 417 U.S. 85 (1974)] The privilege is personal, and so may be asserted by a defendant, witness, or party only if the answer to the question might tend to incriminate him.

C. WHEN PRIVILEGE MAY BE ASSERTED

A person may refuse to answer a question whenever his response might furnish a link in the chain of evidence needed to prosecute him.

1. Proceedings Where Potentially Incriminating Testimony Sought

A person may assert the privilege in *any* proceeding in which testimony that could tend to incriminate is sought. The privilege must be claimed in civil proceedings to prevent the privilege from being waived for a later criminal prosecution. If the individual responds to the questions instead of claiming the privilege during a civil proceeding, he cannot later bar that evidence from a criminal prosecution on compelled self-incrimination grounds. [United States v. Kordel, 397 U.S. 1 (1970)]

2. Privilege Not a Defense to Civil Records Requirements

The government may require that certain records be kept and reported on where the records are relevant to an *administrative purpose*, unrelated to enforcement of criminal laws. Such records acquire a public aspect and are not protected by the Fifth Amendment.

Examples: 1) The government may require people to keep tax records and to report their income on tax forms, because this serves a legitimate administrative purpose. Thus, a person may be prosecuted for failure to file a tax form. However, there is a Fifth Amendment privilege to refuse to answer specific questions on such forms that might be incriminating (e.g., source of income). [United States v. Sullivan, 274 U.S. 259 (1927)] Therefore, if a person chooses to answer incriminating questions on such forms, the answers may be used against him in court, because they were not compelled. [Garner v. United States, 424 U.S. 648 (1976)]

2) A person charged with being an unfit parent in a proceeding to determine whether she should maintain custody of her child may be compelled to produce the child in court. Even though the production might be testimonial in nature (admits control), the state's interest here is civil (protecting the child) rather than punitive in nature. [Baltimore City Department of Social Services v. Bouknight, 493 U.S. 549 (1990)] Note, however, that the state might have to grant immunity to the parent for the production. (*See* H.1., *infra.*)

3) A person may not claim the privilege and fail to comply with a law requiring motorists to stop at the scene of an accident and leave their name and address. [California v. Byers, 402 U.S. 424 (1971)]

a. **Limitation—Criminal Law Enforcement Purpose**
If the registration requirement is directed not at the general public but at a ***select group inherently suspect of criminal activities*** and the inquiry is in an area permeated with criminal statutes, the person may assert the privilege to avoid prosecution for failure to comply with the requirement. [Albertson v. Subversive Activities Control Board, 382 U.S. 70 (1965)]

Example: The government may not require registration of a sawed-off shotgun [Haynes v. United States, 390 U.S. 85 (1968)], payment of a wagering excise tax [Grosso v. United States, 390 U.S. 62 (1968)], payment of an occupational tax for engaging in the business of accepting wagers [Marchetti v. United States, 390 U.S. 39 (1968)], individual registration as a member of the Communist Party [Albertson v. Subversive Activities Control Board, *supra*], or the registration of transfer of marijuana [Leary v. United States, 395 U.S. 6 (1969)] if compliance would require self-incrimination.

Note: Such cases as *Marchetti* and *Grosso* do not bar conviction for making false statements on the registration form; to avoid incriminating himself, the individual must instead claim the privilege. [United States v. Knox, 396 U.S. 77 (1969)]

3. **Privilege Not Applicable to Identification Request After *Terry* Stop**
Merely being required to furnish one's name after a *Terry* stop (*see* II.B.3.a., *supra*) generally does not violate the Fifth Amendment because disclosure of one's name generally poses no danger of incrimination. [*See* Hiibel v. Sixth Judicial District Court, II.B.3.a.3)a), *supra*]

D. METHOD FOR INVOKING THE PRIVILEGE

How the privilege may be invoked depends upon whether the person seeking to invoke it is a criminal defendant or simply a witness.

1. Privilege of a Defendant

A criminal defendant has a right not to take the witness stand at trial and not to be asked to do so. It is even impermissible to call the jury's attention to the fact that he has chosen not to testify. (*See* G.1., *infra*.)

2. Privilege of a Witness

In any other situation, the privilege does not permit a person to avoid being sworn as a witness or being asked questions. Rather, the person must listen to the questions and specifically invoke the privilege rather than answer the questions.

E. SCOPE OF PROTECTION

1. Testimonial But Not Physical Evidence

The Fifth Amendment privilege protects only testimonial or communicative evidence and not real or physical evidence. Thus, the state may require a person to produce *blood samples* [Schmerber v. California, III.C.2., *supra*], *handwriting exemplars* [Gilbert v. California, III.C.2., *supra*], or *voice samples* [United States v. Wade, IV.E., *supra*] without violating the Fifth Amendment, even though such evidence may be incriminating. In addition, a court may order a suspect to authorize foreign banks to disclose records of any accounts he may possess. Merely signing an authorization form is not testimonial if it does not require the suspect to acknowledge the existence of any account. For a suspect's communication to be considered testimonial, it must explicitly or implicitly relate a factual assertion or disclose information. [Doe v. United States, 487 U.S. 201 (1988)]

Likewise, admission into evidence of a defendant's *refusal to submit to a blood-alcohol test* does not offend the right against self-incrimination even though he was not warned that his refusal might be introduced against him. [South Dakota v. Neville, 459 U.S. 553 (1983)]

2. Compulsory Production of Documents

A person served with a subpoena requiring the production of documents tending to incriminate him generally has no basis in the privilege to refuse to comply, because the act of producing the documents *does not involve testimonial self-incrimination*. Thus, there is also no attorney-client privilege violation by production of the documents by the attorney, because the documents were not privileged under the Fifth Amendment in the hands of the client. However, if the document in the hands of the attorney is within the Fifth Amendment privilege, the attorney-client privilege would permit the attorney to refuse to comply with the subpoena. [Fisher v. United States, 425 U.S. 391 (1976)]

a. Corporate Records

A custodian of corporate records may not resist a subpoena for such records on the ground that the production would incriminate him in violation of the Fifth Amendment. The production of the records by the custodian is not considered a personal act, but rather an act of the corporation, which possesses no Fifth Amendment privilege. [Braswell v. United States, 487 U.S. 99 (1988)]

3. **Seizure and Use of Incriminating Documents**
The Fifth Amendment does not prohibit law enforcement officers from searching for and seizing documents tending to incriminate a person. The privilege protects only against being compelled to communicate information, not against disclosure of communications made in the past. [Andresen v. Maryland, II.C.4.c., *supra*]

4. **When Does Violation Occur?**
A violation of the Self-Incrimination Clause does not occur until a person's compelled statements are used against him in a criminal case. [Chavez v. Martinez, 538 U.S. 760 (2003)]

Example: While Martinez was being treated for a gunshot wound that he received in an altercation with the police, he was interrogated by an officer without having been given *Miranda* warnings. Although Martinez admitted to using heroin and that he had taken an officer's gun during the incident in which he was shot, he was never charged with a crime. Nevertheless, Martinez sued police officers for violating his Fifth Amendment right against compelled self-incrimination. *Held:* Because Martinez had not been charged with a crime, there was no Fifth Amendment violation because his statements were not used against him in a criminal case. [Chavez v. Martinez, *supra*]

F. RIGHT TO ADVICE CONCERNING PRIVILEGE

A lawyer may not be held in contempt of court for her good faith advice to her client to invoke the privilege and refuse to produce materials demanded by a court order. Because a witness may require the advice of counsel in deciding how to respond to a demand for testimony or evidence, subjecting the lawyer to potential contempt citation for her advice would infringe upon the protection accorded the witness by the Fifth Amendment. [Maness v. Meyers, 419 U.S. 449 (1975)]

G. PROHIBITION AGAINST BURDENS ON ASSERTION OF THE PRIVILEGE

1. **Comments on Defendant's Silence**
A prosecutor may not comment on a defendant's silence after being arrested and receiving *Miranda* warnings. The warnings carry an implicit assurance that silence will carry no penalty. [Greer v. Miller, 483 U.S. 756 (1987)] Neither may the prosecutor ordinarily comment on the defendant's failure to testify at trial. [Griffin v. California, 380 U.S. 609 (1965)] However, where the defendant does not testify at trial, upon timely motion she is constitutionally entitled to have the trial judge instruct the jury that they are to draw no adverse inference from the defendant's failure to testify. [Carter v. Kentucky, 450 U.S. 288 (1981)] Moreover, a judge may warn the jury not to draw an adverse inference from the defendant's failure to testify, without violating the Fifth Amendment privilege, even where the defendant objects to such an instruction. [Lakeside v. Oregon, 435 U.S. 333 (1978)]

   a. **Exception**
   The prosecutor can comment on the defendant's failure to take the stand when the comment is in response to defense counsel's assertion that the defendant was not allowed to explain his side of the story. [United States v. Robinson, 485 U.S. 25 (1988)]

   b. **Silence Before *Miranda* Warnings**
   Note that if a suspect chooses to remain silent *before* police read him his *Miranda* rights, that silence can be used against him in court. [Salinas v. Texas, 133 S. Ct. 2174 (2013)]

c. **Harmless Error Test Applies**

When a prosecutor impermissibly comments on a defendant's silence, the harmless error test applies. Thus, the error is not fatal where the judge instructs the jury to disregard a question on the defendant's post-arrest silence. [Greer v. Miller, *supra*] Similarly, the error is not fatal where there is overwhelming evidence against the defendant and the prosecutor comments on the defendant's failure to proffer evidence rebutting the victim's testimony. [United States v. Hasting, 461 U.S. 499 (1987)]

2. **Penalties for Failure to Testify Prohibited**

The state may not chill the exercise of the Fifth Amendment privilege against compelled self-incrimination by imposing penalties for the failure to testify or cooperate with authorities.

Example: The state may not fire a police officer [Garrity v. New Jersey, 385 U.S. 493 (1967)], take away state contracts [Lefkowitz v. Turley, 414 U.S. 70 (1973)], or prohibit a person from holding party office [Lefkowitz v. Cunningham, 431 U.S. 801 (1977)] for failure to cooperate with investigating authorities.

Compare: There was no Fifth Amendment violation where a prisoner was required to disclose all prior sexual activities, including activities that constitute uncharged criminal offenses, in order to gain entry into a sexual abuse treatment program, even though refusal resulted in transfer from a medium security facility to a maximum security facility and curtailment of visitation rights, prison work and earnings opportunities, and other prison privileges. [McKune v. Lile, 536 U.S. 24 (2002)]

H. ELIMINATION OF THE PRIVILEGE

1. **Grant of Immunity**

A witness may be compelled to answer questions if granted adequate immunity from prosecution.

a. **"Use and Derivative Use" Immunity Sufficient**

The Supreme Court has held that a grant of "use and derivative use" immunity is sufficient to extinguish the privilege. [Kastigar v. United States, 406 U.S. 441 (1972)] This type of immunity guarantees that the testimony obtained and evidence located by means of the testimony will not be used against the witness. This type of immunity is not as broad as "transactional" immunity, which guarantees immunity from prosecution for any crimes related to the transaction about which the witness testifies, because the witness may still be prosecuted if the prosecutor can show that her evidence was derived from a *source independent* of the immunized testimony.

b. **Immunized Testimony Involuntary**

Testimony obtained by a *promise of immunity* is, by definition, coerced and therefore involuntary. Thus, immunized testimony may not be used for impeachment of the defendant's testimony at trial. [New Jersey v. Portash, 440 U.S. 450 (1979)] Immunized testimony may be introduced to supply the context for a perjury prosecution. Any immunized statements, whether true or untrue, can be used in a trial for making false statements. [United States v. Apfelbaum, 445 U.S. 115 (1980)]

c.   **Use of Testimony by Another Sovereign Prohibited**
The privilege against self-incrimination prohibits a state from compelling incriminating testimony under a grant of immunity unless the testimony and its fruits cannot be used by the prosecution in a federal prosecution. Therefore, federal prosecutors may not use evidence obtained as a result of a state grant of immunity, and vice versa. [Murphy v. Waterfront Commission, 378 U.S. 52 (1964)]

2.   **No Possibility of Incrimination**
A person has no privilege against compelled self-incrimination if there is no possibility of incrimination, as, for example, when the statute of limitations has run.

3.   **Scope of Immunity**
Immunity extends only to the offenses to which the question relates and does not protect against perjury committed during the immunized testimony. [United States v. Apfelbaum, *supra*]

I.   WAIVER OF PRIVILEGE
The nature and scope of a waiver depends upon the situation.

1.   **Waiver by Criminal Defendant**
A criminal defendant, by taking the witness stand, waives the privilege to the extent necessary to subject her to any cross-examination proper under the rules of evidence.

2.   **Waiver by Witness**
A witness waives the privilege only if she discloses incriminating information. Once such disclosure has been made, she can be compelled to disclose any additional information as long as such further disclosure does not increase the risk of conviction or create a risk of conviction on a different offense.

XV.   JUVENILE COURT PROCEEDINGS

A.   IN GENERAL
Some—but not all—of the rights developed for defendants in criminal prosecutions have also been held applicable to children who are the subjects of proceedings to have them declared "delinquents" and possibly institutionalized.

B.   RIGHTS THAT MUST BE AFFORDED
The following rights must be given to a child during the trial of a delinquency proceeding:

   (i)   Written *notice* of the charges with sufficient time to prepare a defense;

   (ii)   The *assistance of counsel* (court-appointed if the child is indigent);

   (iii)   The *opportunity to confront* and cross-examine witnesses;

   (iv)   The *right not to testify* (and other aspects of the privilege against self-incrimination); and

(v) The right to have **"guilt"** (the commission of acts making the child delinquent) established by proof **beyond a reasonable doubt**.

[*In re* Gault, 387 U.S. 1 (1967); *In re* Winship, 397 U.S. 358 (1970)]

C. RIGHTS NOT APPLICABLE

1. Jury Trial
The Supreme Court has held inapplicable to delinquency proceedings the right to trial by jury. In the juvenile court context, jury trial is not necessary to assure "fundamental fairness." [McKeiver v. Pennsylvania, 403 U.S. 528 (1971)]

2. Pretrial Detention Allowable
A finding that a juvenile is a "serious risk" to society and likely to commit a crime before trial is adequate to support pretrial detention of the juvenile, and does not violate the Due Process Clause as long as the detention is for a strictly limited time before trial may be held. [Schall v. Martin, 467 U.S. 253 (1984)]

D. DOUBLE JEOPARDY AND "TRANSFER" OF JUVENILE TO ADULT COURT
In many jurisdictions, a juvenile court may, after inquiry, determine that a juvenile is not an appropriate subject for juvenile court processing and "transfer" the juvenile to adult court for trial as an adult on criminal charges. If the juvenile court begins to hear evidence on the alleged delinquent act, however, jeopardy has attached and the prohibition against double jeopardy prevents the juvenile from being tried as an adult for the same behavior. [Breed v. Jones, XIII.A.3., *supra*]

XVI. FORFEITURE ACTIONS

A. INTRODUCTION
State and federal statutes often provide for the forfeiture of property such as automobiles used in the commission of a crime. Actions for forfeiture are brought directly against the property and are generally regarded as quasi-criminal in nature. Certain constitutional rights may exist for those persons whose interest in the property would be lost by forfeiture.

B. RIGHT TO PRE-SEIZURE NOTICE AND HEARING
The owner of **personal** property (and others with interests in it) is not constitutionally entitled to notice and hearing before the property is seized for purposes of a forfeiture proceeding. [Calero-Toledo v. Pearson Yacht Leasing Co., 416 U.S. 663 (1974)] A hearing is, however, required before final forfeiture of the property. Where **real property** is seized, notice and an opportunity to be heard is required before the seizure unless the government can prove that exigent circumstances justify immediate seizure. [United States v. James Daniel Good Real Property, 510 U.S. 43 (1994)]

C. FORFEITURES MAY BE SUBJECT TO EIGHTH AMENDMENT
The Eighth Amendment provides that excessive fines shall not be imposed. The Supreme Court has held that this Excessive Fines Clause applies only to fines imposed as punishment, i.e., penal fines. The Clause does not apply to civil fines. Thus forfeitures that are penal are subject to the Clause, but forfeitures that are civil are not.

1. **Penal Forfeitures**

   Generally, a forfeiture will be considered penal only if it is provided for in a criminal statute. If it is penal and the Clause applies, a forfeiture will be found to be excessive only if it is *grossly disproportionate to the gravity of the offense.* [United States v. Bajakajian, 524 U.S. 321 (1998)]

   Example: The Court held that forfeiture of $357,144 for the crime of merely failing to report that that sum was being transported out of the country was grossly disproportionate, because the crime caused little harm (it would have been legal to take the money out of the country; the only harm was that the government was deprived of a piece of information). [United States v. Bajakajian, *supra*]

2. **Compare—Nonpenal Forfeitures**

   a. **Civil In Rem Forfeitures**

      Civil in rem forfeitures treat the property forfeited as a "wrongdoer" under a legal fiction; the action is against the property and not against an individual, and therefore this type of forfeiture is *not* subject to the Excessive Fines Clause.

   b. **Monetary Forfeitures**

      Monetary forfeitures (e.g., forfeiture of twice the value of illegally imported goods) have also been found to be remedial in nature where they are brought in civil actions. They are seen as a form of liquidated damages to reimburse the government for losses resulting from the offense. Therefore, they are not subject to the Eighth Amendment. [*See* United States v. Bajakajian, *supra*]

D. **PROTECTION FOR "INNOCENT OWNER" NOT REQUIRED**

   The Due Process Clause does *not* require forfeiture statutes to provide an "innocent owner" defense, e.g., a defense that the owner took all reasonable steps to avoid having the property used by another for illegal purposes, at least where the innocent owner *voluntarily entrusted* the property to the wrongdoer. [Bennis v. Michigan, 517 U.S. 292 (1996)—due process not violated by forfeiture of wife's car that husband used while engaging in sexual acts with a prostitute even though wife did not know of use] In justifying its holding in *Bennis*, the Court also noted that the statute was not absolute, because the trial judge had discretion to prevent inequitable application of the statute.

EVIDENCE

EVIDENCE

TABLE OF CONTENTS

EVIDENCE

I. GENERAL CONSIDERATIONS

A. DEFINING EVIDENCE LAW

The law of evidence is a system of rules and standards by which the admission of proof at the trial of a lawsuit is regulated. The material facts in the controversy are determined by proof that is filtered through the applicable rules of evidence. This proof includes testimony, writings, physical objects, and anything else presented to the senses of the jury.

B. SOURCES OF EVIDENCE LAW

In some states, evidence law is derived from a blend of common law rules and miscellaneous statutes. However, today, most jurisdictions have enacted modern evidence codes, which form a comprehensive set of statutes or rules covering all major areas of evidence law. The most important codification is the Federal Rules of Evidence. The Federal Rules govern on the Multistate Bar Examination.

C. FEDERAL RULES OF EVIDENCE

The Federal Rules of Evidence are applicable in all *civil and criminal* cases in the United States courts of appeal, district courts, Court of Claims, bankruptcy courts, admiralty courts, and in proceedings before United States magistrates. [Fed. R. Evid. 101 and 1101] For the most part, the Federal Rules have codified well-established principles of evidence law. Where the Federal Rules depart from the traditional rules of evidence, the adopted Federal Rule is likely to represent an important modern trend, which the states are likely to follow as they revise and codify existing law.

1. Not Applicable in Certain Proceedings

Except for rules relating to privilege, the Federal Rules of Evidence do not apply in:

a. The court's determination on a preliminary question of fact governing admissibility (*see* VIII.C.3.b.5)a), *infra*);

b. Grand jury proceedings; or

c. Certain other miscellaneous proceedings, including those involving sentencing, extradition, bail, and probation.

D. THRESHOLD ADMISSIBILITY ISSUES

A shorthand summary of evidence law might be stated in one sentence: *Material* and *relevant* evidence is admissible if *competent*.

1. Materiality: The Proposition to Be Proved

Materiality exists when the proffered evidence relates to one of the substantive legal issues in the case. The key questions to ask regarding materiality are: What issue is the evidence offered to prove? Is that legal issue material to the substantive cause of action or defense in the case? The answer to these questions and the determination of materiality depend upon the substantive legal issues framed by the pleadings. Thus, evidence is immaterial if the proposition for which it is offered as proof is not a legal issue in the case.

Example: In a workers' compensation proceeding, evidence of the claimant's contributory negligence would be immaterial since the workers' compensation statute abrogates it as a defense.

2. Relevance: Probativeness—The Link Between Proof and Proposition

Probativeness embraces the test of materiality and something more. Probative evidence *contributes to proving or disproving* a material issue. Assuming that the issue the evidence is offered to prove is a material one, is the evidence logically probative of that issue? Does the evidence tend to prove that issue? Does the evidence tend to make the material proposition (issue) more probably true or untrue than it would be without the evidence?

Example: Evidence that the defendant drove recklessly on a prior occasion is material because it speaks to the question of his negligence. However, it is not sufficiently probative of the issue of negligence on this particular occasion, and is therefore not relevant.

3. Federal Rules—Materiality and Probativeness Combined

In the Federal Rules of Evidence, as in most modern codes, the requirements of materiality and probativeness are combined into a single definition of relevance. Thus, Federal Rule 401 provides that "relevant evidence" means evidence tending to make the existence of any fact of consequence to the determination of the action (materiality) more probable or less probable than it would be without the evidence (probativeness). You should watch for both aspects of the relevance problem. Ask yourself (i) whether the fact sought to be proved is itself in issue under the pleadings and the substantive law, and also (ii) whether the evidence helps to prove the fact for which it is offered.

4. Competence

As mentioned above, material and relevant evidence is admissible if competent. Evidence is competent if it *does not violate an exclusionary rule*. Basically, then, if evidence is material and relevant, the only reason such evidence would not be admitted is if it is prohibited by a special exclusionary rule of evidence. Exclusionary rules that prevent admissibility of relevant and material evidence are founded upon one or more of the following:

a. Policies Related to Truth-Seeking

The need to ensure the reliability and authenticity of evidence is a truth-seeking policy. Examples of exclusionary rules that perform this truth-seeking function are the hearsay rule, the best evidence rule, and Dead Man statutes.

b. Policies External to Litigation

The need to protect extrajudicial interests of society is an external policy goal. Rules granting testimonial privileges, for example, admittedly hamper the in-court search for truth.

E. EVIDENCE CLASSIFICATIONS

1. Direct or Circumstantial

a. Direct Evidence Relies on Actual Knowledge

Direct evidence goes directly to a material issue without intervention of an inferential process. Evidence is direct when the very facts in dispute are communicated by those who have actual knowledge by means of their senses.

Example: On the issue of whether anyone had recently crossed a snow-covered bridge, the testimony of a witness that he saw a man crossing would be direct evidence.

b. Circumstantial Evidence Relies on Inference

Circumstantial evidence is indirect and relies on inference. It is evidence of a subsidiary or collateral fact from which, alone or in conjunction with a cluster of other facts, the existence of the material issue can be inferred.

Example: On the issue of whether anyone had recently crossed a snow-covered bridge, the testimony of a witness that he saw human footprints in the snow on the bridge would be circumstantial evidence.

2. Testimonial, Documentary, or Real

a. *Testimonial* evidence is oral evidence given under oath. The witness responds to the questions of the attorneys.

b. *Documentary* evidence is evidence in the form of a writing, such as a contract or a confession.

c. *Real* evidence is the term applied to evidence consisting of things as distinguished from assertions of witnesses about things. Real evidence includes anything conveying a firsthand sense impression to the trier of fact, such as knives, jewelry, maps, or tape recordings.

F. LIMITED ADMISSIBILITY

1. Admissible for One Purpose But Not Another

The use of admissible evidence is a frequently encountered problem. It often happens that evidence is admissible for one purpose but is not admissible for another purpose.

Example: At the trial of the accused for assault, defendant's prior conviction for robbery may be shown by the prosecution to impeach the credibility of testimony given by the accused as a witness. The prior conviction is not admissible on the issue of defendant's guilt on the assault charge.

2. Admissible Against One Party But Not Another

It is also possible that the evidence is admissible against one party but is not admissible against another party.

Example: A post-accident admission of a negligent employee truck driver may be admissible against the truck driver in an action for negligence. However, under certain circumstances it may not be admissible against a defendant employer who owned the truck.

3. Jury Must Be Properly Instructed

As a general rule, if evidence is admissible for one purpose, it is not excluded merely because of the danger that the jury may also consider it for another incompetent purpose. When evidence that is admissible as to one party or for one purpose but is not admissible as to another party or for another purpose is admitted, the court must, upon timely request, restrict the evidence to its proper scope and instruct the jury accordingly. [Fed. R. Evid. 105] If the court determines that even with a limiting instruction, the probative value of the evidence with respect to its legitimate purpose would be substantially outweighed by danger of unfair prejudice with respect to its incompetent purpose, the evidence may still be excluded (*see* II.C., *infra*).

II. RELEVANCE

A. INTRODUCTION
Relevance, in the sense of probativeness, has to do with the tendency of evidence to ***prove or disprove a material issue***, to render it more probably true, or untrue, than it would have been without the particular evidence. Relevance is concerned with the ***substance or content*** of the evidence, not with the form or manner in which it is offered (e.g., hearsay rule, best evidence rule). It can be stated, as a general proposition, that all relevant evidence is admissible if it is offered in an unobjectionable form and manner. (As usual, there are some exceptions to this generalization, since some perfectly relevant evidence that is in the proper form is excluded for policy reasons.)

B. DETERMINING RELEVANCE
Relevant evidence is evidence having ***any*** tendency to make the existence of any fact that is of consequence to the determination of an action more or less probable than it would be without the evidence. [Fed. R. Evid. 401] Note that this definition of relevance includes materiality, since it requires that the disputed fact be of consequence to the determination of the action. The basic questions to ask regarding relevancy are: "What proposition is the evidence being used to prove? Is this a material issue in the case? Is the evidence probative of that proposition?" This type of relevance is sometimes called "logical relevance."

1. General Rule—Must Relate to Time, Event, or Person in Controversy
Whenever testimony or exhibit evidence that relates to a time, event, or person other than the time, event, or person directly involved in the controversy being litigated is offered, the relevance of that evidence is suspect and should be examined more carefully. In most cases, a previous similar occurrence proves little or nothing about the one in issue. In addition, the risk of confusion and unfair prejudice usually outweighs the helpfulness of this type of evidence (*see* C., *infra*). Note that when considering the relevance of such evidence, one of the important factors to consider is its proximity in time to the current events. A circumstance that would be relevant had it occurred in close time proximity to the event in question is irrelevant if, instead, it was very remote.

Examples: 1) Defendant is alleged to have run a red light and hit a pedestrian in the crosswalk. Proof that defendant ran other red lights in the past has little probative value in proving the occurrence in question. The probative value of such proof is outweighed by the confusion and unfair prejudice that would result from its admission.

2) On the issue of the fair market value of property in a condemnation action, the relevance of the sale price of other property depends on how comparable

the other property is to the property being condemned, how close it is geographically, and how recent that sale was. Sale of a neighbor's comparable property six months ago is probably relevant, but the sale of the same property five years ago probably is not relevant.

3) In a murder prosecution, evidence that the accused had threatened the alleged victim the day before the killing may be very relevant. But compare a threat a week before; a month before; a year before; 10 years before.

2. **Exceptions—Certain Similar Occurrences Are Relevant**
    Despite the above rule, previous similar happenings and transactions of the parties and others similarly situated may be relevant if they are probative of the material issue involved, and if that probative value outweighs the risk that the evidence will confuse the jury or result in unfair prejudice. Of course, whenever a similar occurrence is offered to establish an inference about the subject occurrence, the quality of the inference depends on the similarity between the other happening and the one in issue. The following are examples of relevant similar occurrences.

    a. **Causation**
        Complicated issues of causation may often be established by evidence that concerns other times, events, or persons. For example, evidence that other homes in the same area were damaged by defendant's blasting operations is some evidence that the damage to plaintiff's home was caused by defendant's activities.

    b. **Prior False Claims or Same Bodily Injury**
        Evidence that a person has previously filed similar *tort claims* or has been involved in *prior accidents* is *generally inadmissible* to show the invalidity of the present claim. At best, such evidence indicates plaintiff's tendency toward litigation or accident-proneness. In either case, the probative value is outweighed by the risk of confusion of issues and undue prejudice.

        But if evidence is introduced that the party has made previous similar *false* claims, such evidence is usually relevant, under a common scheme or plan theory, to prove that the present claim is likely to be false. Likewise, where the prior claim was for an injury to the *same portion of plaintiff's body* that she claims was injured in the present case, evidence of the prior claim or injury may be relevant to prove that her present claim is false or exaggerated.

    c. **Similar Accidents or Injuries Caused by Same Event or Condition**
        Where similar accidents or injuries were caused by the same event or condition, evidence of those prior accidents or injuries is *admissible to prove*:

        (i)   That a defect or dangerous *condition existed*;

        (ii) That the defendant had *knowledge* of the defect or dangerous condition; and

        (iii) That the defect or dangerous condition was the *cause* of the present injury.

        Example: In an action for dust damage from a mill, it may be proper to introduce evidence that plaintiff's neighbors have previously suffered similar dust damage, in order to prove that the mill created dust, that the mill owners knew of the dust, and that the dust caused plaintiff's damage.

1) Absence of Similar Accidents
Many courts are reluctant to admit evidence of the absence of similar accidents to show absence of negligence or lack of a defect. However, where a structural condition is involved and that condition is unchanged, the court has discretion to admit evidence of absence of other complaints to show lack of a defect. Evidence of prior safety history and absence of complaints is admissible to show *defendant's lack of knowledge* of any danger.

d. Previous Similar Acts Admissible to Prove Intent
Similar conduct previously committed by a party may be introduced to prove the party's present motive or intent when such elements are relevant.
Example: In an action against a school board for excluding a black child from school, similar exclusions of black children will be admissible into evidence to show intent.

e. Rebutting Claim of Impossibility
The requirement that prior occurrences be similar to the litigated act may be relaxed when used to rebut a claim or defense of impossibility. For example, if defendant denies negligent speeding on the ground that his automobile could never go above 50 m.p.h., plaintiff may rebut by showing that on other occasions, even under different circumstances, the vehicle was traveling at 75 m.p.h.

f. Sales of Similar Property
Evidence of sales of similar personal or real property that are not too remote in time is *admissible to prove value*. However, unlike commonly sold items of personal property, each parcel of real property is considered unique. Thus, the problem of producing evidence of other transactions requires a preliminary finding that the character, usage, proximity, date of sale, etc., are sufficiently similar to the property in issue. Evidence of prices quoted in mere *offers* is *not admissible* because to determine the sincerity of these offers would lead to collateral disputes. However, offers by a party to the present action to buy or sell the property may be admissible as admissions.

g. Habit
Habit describes one's *regular* response to a *specific* set of circumstances (e.g., "she always takes a staircase two steps at a time"). In contrast, character describes one's disposition in respect to general traits (e.g., "she's always in a hurry"). Since habits are more specific and particularized, evidence of habit is relevant and can be introduced in circumstances when it is not permissible to introduce evidence of character. Thus, under Federal Rule 406, evidence of a person's habit may be admitted to prove that on a particular occasion the person acted in accordance with the habit.
Example: Evidence could be introduced to show that a driver habitually failed to stop at a certain stop sign as circumstantial evidence that she failed to stop at the time in question. In contrast, evidence cannot be introduced to show that a person is a careless driver since that is closer to character than habit.

Many states either do not admit evidence of habit to show that a particular act occurred, or else limit admissibility to those cases where there are no eyewitnesses. Federal Rule 406 admits habit evidence freely and abandons the "no eyewitness" requirement. Even where admissible, however, the habit must be shown to be a regular response to a repeated specific situation.

h. Industrial or Business Routine

Just as evidence of personal habit is relevant to show conduct, evidence that a business or firm had an established business routine is relevant as tending to show that a particular event occurred.

Example: Evidence of a regular mailing procedure, such as a custom of picking up letters from a certain table and mailing them, would be relevant as evidence to show that a particular letter left on the table was duly mailed.

i. Industrial Custom as Evidence of Standard of Care

1) Industrial Custom Distinguished from Business Routine

Custom of the industry should be distinguished from business routine. In the latter case, the particular conduct and habit of a party are being offered to show that the party acted in the same manner on the occasion in question. Custom of the industry is offered to prove the actions of other persons in the same industry in an attempt to show adherence to or deviance from an industry-wide standard of care.

2) Relevant to Standard of Care But Not Conclusive

When one of the issues in dispute is negligence arising out of inadequate safety devices or precautions, evidence of general custom or usage in the same kind of business under the same circumstances may be introduced by either party as tending to establish a standard by which reasonable or ordinary care may be judged. Although custom of the trade or business is admissible on the standard of care to be exercised, it is not conclusive.

C. DISCRETIONARY EXCLUSION OF RELEVANT EVIDENCE (PRAGMATIC RELEVANCE)

A trial judge has broad discretion to exclude relevant evidence if its probative value is *substantially* outweighed by the danger of *unfair prejudice*, *confusion of the issues*, *misleading the jury*, *undue delay*, waste of time, or needless presentation of cumulative evidence. [Fed. R. Evid. 403] "*Unfair surprise*" is listed as an additional basis for exclusion under some state rules, but it was omitted under the Federal Rules on the theory that surprise can be prevented by discovery and pretrial conference or mitigated by granting a continuance.

Certain items of evidence may be directed to a material issue in the case and may be very probative of that issue, but they are excluded because of predictable policies designed to ensure an orderly and efficient proceeding and to encourage certain public policy solutions to legal problems. For example, inflammatory matter, which may be very probative of the issues, will not be admitted because of the potential prejudicial effect on the jury.

D. EXCLUSION OF RELEVANT EVIDENCE FOR PUBLIC POLICY REASONS (POLICY-BASED RELEVANCE)
Certain evidence of questionable relevance is excluded by the Federal Rules because public policy favors the behavior involved. For example, the law encourages the repair of defective premises that cause injury, and consequently, evidence of the subsequent repair may not be admitted to prove antecedent negligence, even though it may be probative of the issue. Evidence excluded for public policy reasons is set forth below.

1. Liability Insurance

a. Inadmissible to Show Negligence or Ability to Pay
Evidence that a person was or was not insured against liability is ***not admissible*** upon the issue of whether she ***acted negligently*** or otherwise wrongfully. Nor is it admissible to show ***ability to pay*** a substantial judgment. [Fed. R. Evid. 411]

b. When Admissible
Proof that a person carried liability insurance may be admissible and relevant for other purposes. Issue identification is important in these cases, since proof of the fact that the defendant maintained insurance ***may be used***:

1) To Prove Ownership or Control
Evidence that the defendant maintained insurance may be admitted for the limited purpose of proving the defendant's ownership or control when ownership or control is disputed.
Example: P sues D and alleges that D owned the building in which P fell on a defective staircase, further alleging a cause of action for negligence. D denies all allegations, and thereby puts in issue the question of ownership of the premises. P may show that D had insured the premises as evidence of ownership, but the evidence will only be used for the limited purpose of proving that issue.

2) For Purposes of Impeachment
Evidence that the defendant is insured may be used for the limited purpose of impeaching a witness.
Example: An investigator testifies on behalf of defendant. Plaintiff may demonstrate the bias or interest of this witness by showing that she is employed by defendant's liability insurance company.

3) As Part of Admission
An admission of liability may be so coupled with a reference to insurance coverage that the reference to insurance cannot be severed without lessening its value as an admission of liability.
Example: "Don't worry; my insurance company will pay off."

2. Subsequent Remedial Measures

a. Inadmissible to Prove Negligence or Culpable Conduct
Evidence of repairs or other precautionary measures made following an injury is

inadmissible to prove negligence, culpable conduct, a defect in a product or its design, or a need for a warning or instruction. [Fed. R. Evid. 407] The purpose of the rule is to encourage people to make such repairs.

b. When Admissible

Although evidence of subsequent repairs is not admissible to prove negligence, etc., this evidence may still be admissible for other purposes. Some of these purposes are:

1) To Prove Ownership or Control

Evidence of subsequent repairs performed by the defendant may be introduced to prove ownership or control, since a stranger would hardly make repairs.

2) To Rebut Claim that Precaution Was Not Feasible

Evidence of repairs or other precautionary measures made following an accident is admissible to establish the feasibility of precautionary measures when such feasibility is disputed.

3) To Prove Destruction of Evidence

Evidence of subsequent remedial measures may be admitted to prove that the opposing party has destroyed evidence; e.g., repainting a fender to cover up evidence of a collision (spoliation).

3. Settlement Offers—Negotiations Not Admissible

Evidence of compromises or offers to compromise is inadmissible to prove or disprove the validity or amount of a disputed claim. Such evidence is also inadmissible to impeach through a prior inconsistent statement or a contradiction. [Fed. R. Evid. 408] *Rationale:* Public policy favors the settlement of disputes without litigation, and settlement would be discouraged if either side were deterred from making offers by the fear that they would be admitted in evidence.

The Federal Rules also exclude conduct or statements made in the course of negotiating a compromise, as well as the offer to compromise itself; therefore, admissions of fact made during compromise negotiations are inadmissible. This position encourages settlements by allowing complete candor between the parties in negotiations. However, conduct or statements made during compromise negotiations regarding a civil dispute with a governmental regulatory, investigative, or enforcement authority are not excluded when offered ***in a criminal case***. [Fed. R. Evid. 408] Note that Rule 408 does not protect preexisting information simply because it is presented to one's opponent during compromise negotiations; e.g., one may not immunize otherwise admissible information under the guise of disclosing it during compromise negotiations.

a. Must Be a Claim

Although the filing of a suit is not a prerequisite for this exclusionary rule, there must be some indication, express or implied, that a party is going to make some kind of claim. Thus, a party's volunteered admission of fact accompanying an offer to settle immediately following the incident is usually admissible because there has not been time for the other party to indicate an intent to make a claim.

b. Claim Must Be Disputed as to Liability or Amount
To trigger the exclusionary feature of Rule 408, the claim must be disputed as to liability or amount. Thus, if a party admits liability and the amount of liability but offers to settle (rather than litigate) for a lesser amount, every statement made in connection with that offer is admissible.

4. Payment of Medical Expenses Not Admissible
Similarly, evidence that a party paid (or offered to pay) the injured party's medical expenses is ***not admissible to prove liability*** for the injury. [Fed. R. Evid. 409] This rule is based upon the concern that such payment might be prompted solely by "humanitarian motives." However, unlike the situation with compromise negotiation (3., *supra*), ***admissions of fact*** accompanying offers to pay medical expenses ***are admissible***.

5. Withdrawn Guilty Pleas and Offers to Plead Guilty Not Admissible
Under the Federal Rules neither withdrawn guilty pleas, pleas of nolo contendere, offers to plead guilty, nor evidence of statements made in negotiating such pleas are admissible in any proceeding. [Fed. R. Evid. 410] Most jurisdictions concur. The ***evidentiary value*** of a withdrawn plea of guilty as an admission is deemed ***offset by the prejudicial effect*** of the evidence. Moreover, it is felt that the judge who permitted the withdrawal of the guilty plea must have decided that there was a good reason to withdraw it and, under these circumstances, the significance of the initial plea is minimal. Most courts exclude offers to plead guilty on reasoning similar to that advanced for not admitting offers to compromise as proof of liability in civil cases.

a. Waiver
The protection of Rule 410 for plea negotiations may be validly waived unless there is an affirmative indication that the defendant entered the waiver agreement unknowingly or involuntarily. [United States v. Mezzanatto, 513 U.S. 196 (1995)]

Example: Defendant, who was charged with a drug offense, wished to arrange a deal with the government in exchange for his cooperation. As a prerequisite to this discussion, Prosecutor required that Defendant (i) be completely truthful and (ii) agree that any statements made by him in the course of the plea negotiations could be used to impeach him if he testified in a contrary fashion at trial. Defendant agreed. If at some point thereafter the discussion breaks off and Defendant is tried on the charges, Prosecutor may use statements made in the plea negotiations to impeach Defendant. [United States v. Mezzanatto, *supra*]

E. CHARACTER EVIDENCE—A SPECIAL RELEVANCE PROBLEM
The rules regarding use of character evidence are affected by three major concerns. These are: (i) the purpose for which evidence of character is offered; (ii) the method to be used to prove character; and (iii) the kind of case, civil or criminal.

1. Purposes for Offer of Character Evidence

a. To Prove Character When Character Itself Is Ultimate Issue in Case
When a person's character itself is the ultimate issue in the case, character evidence must be admitted. Cases where character is itself one of the material propositions in issue are confined mostly to civil litigation and are rare even among civil actions.

b. **To Serve as Circumstantial Evidence of How a Person Probably Acted**

    It is the use of character as circumstantial evidence of how a person probably acted that raises the most difficult problems of relevance, especially in criminal cases.

  c. **To Impeach Credibility of Witness**

    The discussion of the use of character evidence to impeach the credibility of a witness is postponed for later discussion under the heading of "Credibility—Impeachment." (*See* VI.E., *infra*.)

2. **Means of Proving Character**

Depending upon the jurisdiction, the purpose of the offer, and the nature of the case, the following types of evidence may be used to prove character:

  a. **Evidence of Specific Acts as Demonstrating Character**

    Evidence of specific acts of the person in question as demonstrating that person's character is permitted only in a few instances, such as where character is itself one of the ultimate issues in the case. Note, however, that specific acts may be admissible if relevant for some other purpose (*see* 6.a., *infra*).

  b. **Opinion Testimony**

    Witnesses who know the person may testify regarding their opinions about the person's character.

  c. **Testimony as to Person's General Reputation in Community**

    Testimony by witnesses as to a person's general reputation in the community is in some sense hearsay, since reputation is really what people say about a person. On the other hand, because reputation is a general indication of character, and because it involves fewer side issues than either of the above methods, it is the most common means of showing character.

3. **Generally Not Admissible in Civil Cases**

Evidence of character to prove the conduct of a person in the litigated event is generally not admissible in a civil case. [Fed. R. Evid. 404(a)] The reasons given are that the slight probative value of character is outweighed by the danger of prejudice, the possible distraction of the jury from the main question in issue, and the possible waste of time required by examination of collateral issues.

Examples: 1) Defendant may not introduce evidence that she is generally a cautious driver to prove that she was not negligent on the day in question.

      2) Plaintiff may not introduce evidence that the defendant is usually a reckless driver to prove that she was negligent on the day in question.

Such circumstantial use of prior behavior patterns for the purpose of drawing the inference that, at the time and place in question, the actor probably acted in accord with her prior behavior pattern is not permitted. A person's ***general behavior patterns*** (as distinguished from her habits and business routines) are ***irrelevant*** and inadmissible in evidence.

a. **Exception—When Character Is Directly in Issue**

When proof of a person's character, as a matter of substantive law, is an essential element of a claim or defense in a civil action, it is said that character is "directly in issue." Although character is rarely an essential issue in a civil case, character evidence is admissible in such circumstances.

Examples: 1) In a defamation action, when D is being sued for calling P a thief and pleads as an affirmative defense that she spoke the truth (i.e., that P is indeed a thief), P's character is clearly in issue.

                       2) When an employer is charged with negligently retaining an employee "of unstable and violent disposition," the character of the employee is also in issue.

Compare: In a civil action for damages based on assault or battery, the defendant's claim that he acted in self-defense does not put either the plaintiff-victim's or the defendant's character for violence or peacefulness into issue. On the issue of who struck first, the substantive law does not require proof of either party's character.

When character is directly in issue, almost all courts will admit evidence of specific acts that show this character (e.g., in Example 1) above, D may offer evidence that on different occasions P has stolen things to show that he is a thief). Under the Federal Rules, any of the types of evidence (***reputation***, ***opinion***, ***or specific acts***) may be used to prove character when character is directly in issue. [Fed. R. Evid. 405(b)]

4. **Accused in a Criminal Case—Prosecution Cannot Initiate, But Accused Can**

The general rule is that the prosecution cannot initiate evidence of the bad character of the defendant merely to show that she is more likely to have committed the crime of which she is accused. However, the accused may introduce evidence of her good character to show her innocence of the alleged crime.

The rationale is that even though the evidence is of some relevance, the prosecution should not be permitted to show that the defendant is a bad person, since the jury might then decide to convict her regardless of her guilt of the crime charged. However, since the life or liberty of the defendant is at stake, she should be allowed to introduce evidence of her good character since it may have a tendency to show that she did not commit the crime charged.

a. **How Defendant Proves Character**

1) **Reputation and Personal Opinion Testimony**

A defendant puts her character in issue by calling a qualified witness to testify to the defendant's good reputation (or that he has heard nothing bad) *for the trait involved* in the case. Under Federal Rule 405, the witness may also give his personal opinion concerning that trait of the defendant. However, the witness may *not* testify to *specific acts of conduct* of the defendant to prove the trait in issue.

2) **Testifying Places Defendant's Credibility—Not Character—In Issue**

A defendant does not put her character in issue merely by taking the stand and giving testimony on the facts of the controversy. However, if the defendant takes the stand, she puts her credibility in issue and is subject to impeachment. (*See* "Credibility—Impeachment," VI.E., *infra*.)

b. How Prosecution Rebuts Defendant's Character Evidence

If the defendant puts her character in issue by having a character witness testify as to his opinion of the defendant or the defendant's reputation, the prosecution may rebut in the following manner:

1) Cross-Examination

The prosecution may test the character witness by cross-examination regarding the basis for his opinion or knowledge of the reputation that he has testified about. In most jurisdictions, one is allowed to inquire on cross-examination whether the reputation witness has *heard* of particular instances of the defendant's misconduct pertinent to the trait in question. The rationale is that since the reputation witness relates what he has heard, the inquiry tests the accuracy of his hearing and reporting. Since the character witness may now testify in the form of opinion as well as by reputation, it follows that the basis of the opinion can be exposed. Thus, under Federal Rule 405(a), cross-examination inquiry is allowable as to whether the opinion witness *knows* of, as well as whether he has *heard* of, specific instances of misconduct. The distinction in form between "Have you heard" and "Do you know" is eliminated by the statement in Rule 405(a), which provides that "on cross-examination of the character witness, the court may allow an inquiry into relevant specific instances of the person's conduct." Note that if the witness denies knowledge of these specific instances of conduct, the prosecutor *may not* prove them by extrinsic evidence; he is limited to inquiry on cross-examination.

2) Testimony of Other Witnesses as to Defendant's Bad Character

The prosecution may rebut the defendant's character evidence by calling its own character witnesses to testify to the defendant's bad reputation or their opinion of the defendant's character for the particular trait involved.

5. Victim in Criminal Case

a. Defendant's Initiative

The defendant may introduce reputation or opinion evidence of a bad character trait of the alleged crime victim when it is relevant to show the defendant's innocence. However, by specific exception, this rule does not extend to showing the bad character of rape victims.

Example: In an assault or murder prosecution where the defendant claims self-defense, she may introduce evidence of the victim's violent character as tending to show that the victim was the aggressor.

b. Prosecution Rebuttal

Once the defendant has introduced evidence of the alleged victim's bad character for a pertinent trait, the prosecution may counter with reputation or opinion evidence of (i) the *victim's good character* for the *same trait*, or (ii) the *defendant's bad character* for the *same trait*. [Fed. R. Evid. 404(a)]

Example: Defendant is charged with the murder of Victim. Defendant pleads self-defense and offers evidence that Victim was a violent person. Prosecutor can rebut such evidence with evidence that Victim was a nonviolent person and/or with evidence that Defendant is a violent person.

c.   **Homicide Cases—Victim's Character for Peacefulness to Rebut Self-Defense Claim**

In a ***homicide case*** in which the defendant pleads ***self-defense***, evidence of any kind that the victim was the first aggressor (e.g., eyewitness testimony that the victim struck first) opens the door to evidence that the victim had a good character for peacefulness. [Fed. R. Evid. 404(a)(2)] This evidence can be introduced regardless of whether the defendant has introduced character evidence of the victim's generally violent propensity. The rationale behind this rule is that the victim's death deprives the prosecution of the victim's testimony as to the identity of the first aggressor.

d.   **Rape Cases—Victim's Past Behavior Inadmissible**

In any civil or criminal proceeding involving alleged sexual misconduct, evidence offered to prove the sexual behavior or sexual disposition of the alleged victim is generally inadmissible. [Fed. R. Evid. 412(a)]

1)   **Exceptions in Criminal Cases**

In a criminal case, evidence of specific instances of sexual behavior by the victim offered to prove that a person other than the accused was the ***source of semen, injury, or other physical evidence*** is admissible. Also, specific instances of sexual behavior between the victim and the accused are admissible by the prosecution, or by the defense to prove ***consent***. Evidence of a victim's sexual behavior is also admissible when its exclusion would violate the defendant's constitutional rights. [Fed. R. Evid. 412(b)(1)]

2)   **Exceptions in Civil Cases**

In civil cases, evidence offered to prove the sexual disposition or behavior of the alleged victim is admissible if it is otherwise admissible under the Federal Rules and its probative value substantially outweighs the danger of harm to the victim and of unfair prejudice to any party. Evidence of an alleged victim's reputation is admissible only if it has been placed in controversy by the victim. [Fed. R. Evid. 412(b)(2)]

3)   **Procedure**

To offer evidence under the above exceptions, the party must file a motion 14 days before trial describing the evidence and its purpose, and must serve the motion on all parties and notify the victim. Before admitting the evidence, the court must conduct an in camera hearing and afford the victim and the parties a right to be heard. [Fed. R. Evid. 412(c)]

6.   **Specific Acts of Misconduct Generally Inadmissible**

The basic rule is that when a person is charged with one crime, extrinsic evidence of her other crimes or misconduct is inadmissible if such evidence is offered solely to establish a criminal disposition. Thus, this statement of Federal Rule 404(b) is merely another way of saying that the prosecution may not show the accused's bad character to imply criminal disposition. The danger again is that the jury may convict the defendant because of past crimes rather than because of her guilt of the offense charged.

a. **Admissible If Independently Relevant**

Evidence of other crimes or misconduct is admissible if these acts are relevant to some issue other than the defendant's character or disposition to commit the crime charged. While acknowledging that prior acts or crimes are not admissible to show conformity or to imply bad character, Federal Rule 404(b) goes on to say that such prior acts or crimes may be admissible for other purposes (e.g., to show motive, opportunity, intent, preparation, plan, knowledge, identity, absence of mistake, or lack of accident) whenever these issues are relevant in either a *criminal or a civil case*. Upon request by the accused, the prosecution in a criminal case must provide reasonable notice prior to trial (or during trial if pretrial notice is excused for good cause shown) of the general nature of any of this type of evidence the prosecution intends to introduce at trial.

Example: Husband is on trial for the alleged shooting murder of Wife. Husband claims an accident occurred as he was cleaning the gun. Prosecution may prove that six months ago Husband tried to stab Wife. This evidence is not offered to show that the defendant is the kind of violent man likely to have murdered his wife (i.e., general bad character or violent disposition); rather, it is offered to show absence of mistake, that the killing was probably not an accident.

1) **Examples of Relevant Misconduct**

a) **Motive**

The commission of a prior crime may be evidence of a motive to commit the crime for which the defendant is accused.

b) **Intent**

In many crimes, such as forgery, passing counterfeit money, larceny by trick, and receiving stolen property, intent is the gravamen of the crime. Evidence that defendant committed prior, similar wrongful acts is admissible to establish guilty knowledge and to negate good faith.

c) **Absence of Mistake or Accident**

There are cases in which the defense of accident or mistake may be anticipated. In these situations prosecution evidence of similar misconduct by the defendant is admissible to negate the possibility of mistake or accident. (*See* example above.)

d) **Identity**

Evidence, including misconduct, that connects this defendant to the crime (e.g., theft of gun used in later crime) is admissible. Similarly, evidence that the accused committed prior criminal acts that are so distinctive as to operate as a "signature" may be introduced to prove that the accused committed the act in question (modus operandi).

e) Common Plan or Scheme—Preparation
Evidence that the defendant recently stole some burglar tools is probative of the fact that she committed the burglary for which she is accused.

f) Other
Similar acts or related misconduct may be used to prove opportunity, knowledge, or any relevant fact other than the accused's general bad character or criminal disposition.

2) Quantum of Proof for Independently Relevant Acts of Misconduct
Under Federal Rule 404(b), independently relevant uncharged misconduct by the defendant will be admissible, without a preliminary ruling, as long as (i) there is *sufficient evidence to support a jury finding* that the defendant committed the prior act (i.e., the standard of Federal Rule 104); and (ii) its probative value on the issue of motive, intent, identity, or other independently relevant proposition is not substantially outweighed by the danger of unfair prejudice (i.e., the test of Federal Rule 403). [Huddleston v. United States, 485 U.S. 681 (1988)]

b. Prior Acts of Sexual Assault or Child Molestation
Evidence of a defendant's prior acts of sexual assault or child molestation is admissible in a civil or criminal case where the defendant is accused of committing an act of sexual assault or child molestation. The party who intends to offer this evidence must disclose the evidence to the defendant 15 days before trial (or later with good cause). [Fed. R. Evid. 413 - 415]

III. JUDICIAL NOTICE

A. JUDICIAL NOTICE OF FACT
Judicial notice is the *recognition of a fact as true without formal presentation of evidence*. In most instances the costly, time-consuming, and cumbersome process of formal proof is required to ensure fact-finding accuracy. However, self-evident propositions need not be subjected to this process, but instead may be judicially noticed. Judicial notice, like the presumption, is a judicial shortcut, a substitute for proof. The underlying policy considerations include expediting the trial and avoiding judicial disrepute where the lack of evidence might result in a conclusion contrary to well-known facts. For example, requiring proof that Washington, D.C., is the capital of the United States would require unnecessary time in a situation where a contrary conclusion would be ridiculous.

1. Facts Appropriate for Judicial Notice
The Federal Rule conforms to the existing state rules governing judicial notice. Federal Rule 201(b) defines a fact that may be noticed as one "not subject to reasonable dispute" because it (i) "is generally known within the trial court's territorial jurisdiction" (notorious facts); or (ii) "can be accurately and readily determined from sources whose accuracy cannot reasonably be questioned" (manifest facts). Judicial notice may be taken of such facts *at any time*, whether or not requested, and such notice is mandatory if a party requests and supplies the court with the necessary information. A party is entitled to be heard on the propriety of taking judicial notice and the tenor of the matter noted.

a. **Matters of Common Knowledge in the Community—Notorious Facts**

Judicial notice will be taken of the body of facts that well-informed persons generally know and accept. Though usually facts of common knowledge are known everywhere, it is sufficient for judicial notice if they are known in the community where the court is sitting.

Examples: A court sitting in New York City will take judicial notice that:

1) The streets in Manhattan are numbered east and west from Fifth Avenue and that the odd numbers are on the north side of the street.

2) Many people are subject to low blood pressure and poor circulation.

3) The ordinary period of human gestation is 280 days.

b. **Facts Capable of Certain Verification—Manifest Facts**

Some facts, while not generally known and accepted, are easily verified by resorting to easily accessible, well-established sources.

Examples: 1) Judicial notice will be taken of the time of the rising or setting of the sun and moon on a particular day since this fact, although not commonly known, can be estimated quickly and accurately by reference to an almanac.

2) The court will accept without proof that February 14, 1999, was a Sunday by reference to a calendar.

c. **Judicial Notice of Scientific Principles**

1) **Judicial Notice of Scientific Basis of Test Results**

Trial courts have increasingly taken judicial notice of scientific principles as a type of manifest fact. Once a particular scientific test or principle has become sufficiently well-established (i.e., generally accepted among the scientific community), courts no longer require proof (expert testimony) of the underlying basis of the test. The results of such a test are therefore admissible into evidence.

Example: A trial court will take judicial notice of the reliability of radar speed tests, ballistics tests, and paternity blood tests, and will admit the results of these tests into evidence upon a showing that the tests were properly conducted.

2) **Conclusiveness of Test Results**

Some scientific tests have achieved such universal acceptance that not only are the test results admissible into evidence, but the results are binding on the finder of fact in civil cases.

Example: Where a blood test indicates that the accused father could not have been the parent of the child, that result is conclusive on the issue of paternity, and other evidence on that issue will be excluded.

d. **Judge's Personal Knowledge**

What a judge knows personally is not the same as what he may judicially notice. A judge may have to ignore facts that he knows as a private person if those facts are neither commonly known in the community nor capable of certain verification by resort to easily accessible sources of indisputable accuracy.

2. Procedural Aspects of Judicial Notice

a. Requirement of a Request
In instances where the court does not take judicial notice of a fact on its own accord, the general rule is that a party must formally request (e.g., through pleadings or an oral motion) that notice be taken.

b. Judicial Notice by Appellate Court
Judicial notice may be taken for the first time on appeal. A reviewing court is required to take judicial notice of any matter that the trial court properly noticed or was obliged to notice.

c. Conclusiveness of Judicial Notice
Federal Rule 201(f) provides that a judicially noticed fact is conclusive in a civil case but not in a criminal case. The Federal Rule states that in a civil case, the court shall instruct the jury to accept as conclusive any fact judicially noticed; in a criminal case, on the other hand, the jury is instructed that it may, but is not required to, accept as conclusive any fact judicially noticed.

3. "Adjudicative" and "Legislative" Facts
The Federal Rules govern *only judicial notice of "adjudicative" facts* (i.e., facts that relate to the parties in a particular case), not "legislative" facts (i.e., policy facts that relate to legal reasoning and the lawmaking process). The drafters of Federal Rule 201 reasoned that "legislative" facts are a necessary part of the judicial reasoning process, so that a rule imposing a requirement of indisputability and a formal procedure for taking judicial notice of these matters would destroy the concept of judge-made law. [Advisory Committee Note to Rule 201] Therefore, "legislative" facts need not meet the requirements of Rule 201 that facts must be either of common knowledge or capable of indisputable verification to be judicially noticed.

B. JUDICIAL NOTICE OF LAW—MANDATORY OR PERMISSIVE
The judge's task of finding applicable law is accomplished by informal investigation of legal source materials. This process, unmentioned in the Federal Rules of Evidence, has been traditionally described in terms of the judge taking judicial notice of the law applicable to the case.

1. Classification Depends on Accessibility of Source Materials
Judicial notice of law is mandatory in some instances and permissive in others. This mandatory-permissive classification is explainable in terms of the likely accessibility of source materials for different types of laws. State public law is easily available in reported volumes and, therefore, it is reasonable to require the court to be aware of and to notice it. Descriptions of foreign law or private acts are usually less available and, therefore, the court is permitted—but not required—to judicially notice such laws. In some cases, the contents of such laws may have to be established by proof to the satisfaction of the judge.

2. **Mandatory Judicial Notice**
Most courts must take judicial notice without request of:

a. *Federal public law*—the United States Constitution, federal treaties, public acts of Congress, and federal case law.

b. *State public law*—the constitution, public statutes, and common law of the states.

c. *Official regulations*—the official compilation of codes and rules and regulations of the forum state and the federal government, except those relating to internal organization or management of a state agency.

3. **Permissive Judicial Notice**
Most courts may, upon being supplied with sufficient information, take judicial notice of municipal ordinances and private acts or resolutions of Congress and of the local state legislature. Similarly, the laws of foreign countries may be judicially noticed.

IV. REAL EVIDENCE

A. IN GENERAL

1. **Addressed Directly to Trier of Fact**
Real or demonstrative evidence is addressed directly to the trier of fact. The object in issue is presented for *inspection by the trier of fact*. Ordinarily the evidence is addressed to the sense of sight (e.g., exhibition of injured arm to jury to demonstrate extent of injury), but it may be directed to other senses as well (e.g., sound recording of factory noise played during a nuisance trial).

2. **Special Problems**
This form of proof, which allows the triers of fact to reach conclusions based upon their own perceptions rather than relying upon those of witnesses, frequently involves special problems. Often there is concern regarding *proper authentication* of the "object." Additionally, the possibility exists that physical production of the thing may be too *burdensome* or may inspire *prejudicial emotions* outweighing its probative value to the litigation.

B. TYPES OF REAL EVIDENCE

1. **Direct**
Real evidence may be direct evidence; i.e., it may be offered to prove the facts about the object as an end in itself. For example, in a personal injury case, evidence of a permanent injury could be introduced by an exhibition of the injury itself to the trier of fact.

2. **Circumstantial**
Real evidence may also be circumstantial; i.e., facts about the object are proved as a basis for an inference that other facts are true. For example, in a paternity case, the trier of fact may be shown the child for the purpose of showing that she is of the same race as the alleged

father. In this case, the trier of fact is being asked to draw an inference that, since the child and alleged father are of the same race, the paternal relationship exists.

3. Original
Real evidence may be original; i.e., it may have had some connection with the transaction that is in question at the trial. An example of this kind of evidence would be an alleged murder weapon.

4. Prepared
Real evidence may also be prepared; e.g., sketches or models may be made to be shown to the trier of fact. This category of real evidence is called "***demonstrative evidence***."

C. GENERAL CONDITIONS OF ADMISSIBILITY
Real evidence, like all other forms of evidence, must be ***relevant*** to the proposition in issue. The admissibility of real proof also depends on additional legal requirements, such as those that follow.

1. Authentication
The object must first be identified as being what the proponent claims it to be. Real evidence is commonly authenticated by recognition testimony or by establishing a chain of custody.

a. Recognition Testimony
If the object has significant features that make it identifiable upon inspection, a witness may authenticate the object by testifying that the object is what the proponent claims it is.

Examples:　1) If a prosecutor offers a knife into evidence and claims that the knife is the very weapon used in the murder, the object may be authenticated by a witness who testifies that he can identify the knife as the one found next to the deceased.

2) If a prosecutor offers a knife into evidence and claims that it is ***similar*** to the knife used in the murder, it may be authenticated by a witness who testifies that the offered knife is indeed similar to the one found next to the deceased.

3) A witness can testify that a photograph is a fair and accurate representation of that which it is purported to depict.

b. Chain of Custody
If the evidence is of a type that is likely to be confused or can be easily tampered with, the proponent of the object must present evidence of chain of custody. The proponent of the evidence must show that the object has been held in a substantially ***unbroken chain of possession***. The proponent need not negate all possibilities of substitution or tampering, but must show adherence to some system of identification and custody.

Example:　A custodial chain—from the taking, to the testing, to the exhibiting of the sample—must be established before evidence of a blood alcohol test will be admitted.

2. **Condition of Object; Useful Probativeness**

If the condition of the object is significant, it must be shown to be in substantially the *same condition at the trial*. Moreover, the object must be logically helpful or reliable in tending to prove the proposition in issue.

Example: Would it be helpful in a paternity proceeding to present the baby so that the trier of fact can ascertain physical resemblance to the alleged father?

3. **Legal Relevance**

Assuming the object has been properly identified and is probative, the discretion of the trial judge is called upon to decide whether some auxiliary policy or principle outweighs the need to admit the real evidence. Such policies limiting the use of real evidence frequently concern:

a. *Physical inconvenience* of bringing the object into the courtroom;

b. *Indecency or impropriety*; or

c. *Undue prejudice* where the probative value of the object or exhibit is outweighed by the danger of unfair prejudice.

D. **PARTICULAR TYPES OF REAL PROOF**

1. **Reproductions and Explanatory Real Evidence**

When properly authenticated, relevant photographs, movies, diagrams, maps, sketches, or other *reproductions are admissible* if their value is not outweighed by the danger of unfair prejudice. On the other hand, items used entirely for *explanatory purposes* (such as skeletons, anatomy charts, etc.) are permitted at a trial, but are usually *not admitted into evidence* and are not given to the jury during its deliberations. These items are not represented to be reproductions of the real thing, but are merely used as aids to testimony.

Example: A doctor may use a model of an average male skeleton to explain his testimony. The skeleton may be marked for identification in order to preserve the record, but it is not admitted into evidence.

Compare: If the skeleton was offered as a reproduction of the bone structure of the deceased, assuming there is no undue prejudice, it may be admitted into evidence on a showing that it accurately represents the bone structure of the deceased.

2. **Maps, Charts, Models, Etc.**

Maps, charts, models, etc., are usually admissible for the purpose of illustrating testimony. Since these are all reproductions, they must be authenticated by testimonial evidence showing that they are *faithful reproductions* of the object or thing depicted. As with other real evidence, introduction of these items is within the discretion of the court, and they may be excluded where they would be wasteful of time or where they would unduly impress the trier of fact with the importance of the material.

3. **Exhibition of Child in Paternity Suits**

Almost all courts permit exhibition of the child for the purpose of showing whether she is of the race of the putative father. The courts are divided with respect to the propriety of exhibiting the child in order to prove physical resemblance to the putative father, but a growing majority of courts refuse to permit exhibition of the child.

4. Exhibition of Injuries
The exhibition of injuries in a personal injury or criminal case is generally permitted, but the court has discretion to exclude this evidence if the exhibition would result in unfair prejudice.

5. Jury View of the Scene
Closely related to real and demonstrative evidence is the matter of jury views of premises and places at issue in the case. In the trial court's discretion, they are permitted, sparingly, in both civil and criminal cases. The importance of information that could be obtained by a view, and the ease with which photographs, diagrams, or maps could be substituted for such a view, will be pivotal considerations to the trial judge. Any significant changes of condition in the premises that are to be viewed will also affect the decision. The trial judge usually need not be present during a jury view. The parties and their attorneys are usually permitted to attend, but the view will be conducted by a disinterested court attaché and neither counsel nor the parties will be permitted to engage in any commentary.

6. Demonstrations
The court, in its discretion, may permit experiments or demonstrations to be performed in the courtroom.

a. Demonstrations Showing Effect of Bodily Injury
Demonstrations to show the effect of bodily injury are usually excluded where the exhibition would reveal hideous wounds, elicit cries of pain, or otherwise unduly dramatize the injury and inflame the minds of the jurors.

b. Demonstrations Under Sole Control of Witness Are Excluded
Demonstrations may also be excluded where they are under the sole control of the witness and thus not subject to effective cross-examination. For example, an injured plaintiff might attempt to demonstrate lack of locomotion by showing that he cannot move a limb. The demonstration itself cannot be effectively cross-examined. However, if testimony is given to the same effect, it may be impeached by contradictory evidence.

c. Scientific Experiments
The judge may permit scientific experiments to be performed in the courtroom provided:

1) The conditions are ***substantially similar*** to those that attended the original event, and

2) The experiment will ***not result in undue waste of time or confusion*** of the issues.

V. DOCUMENTARY EVIDENCE

A. IN GENERAL
Documentary evidence, like other kinds of evidence, ***must be relevant*** in order to be admissible.

In the case of writings, the authenticity of the document is one aspect of its relevancy. Of course, documentary evidence, even if fully authenticated and relevant, *may be excluded if it violates a rule of competency* such as the best evidence or hearsay rule. Whenever any problem or question concerns a document, you should consider three separate and distinct possible barriers to admissibility (authentication, best evidence, and hearsay).

B.   AUTHENTICATION

Before a writing or any secondary evidence of its content may be received in evidence, the writing must be authenticated by proof showing that the writing is what the proponent claims it is. The writing is usually not self-authenticating. It needs a testimonial sponsor or shepherding angel to prove that the writing was made, signed, or adopted by the particular relevant person. [Fed. R. Evid. 901 - 903]

1.   Quantum of Proof of Authenticity

Authentication of documentary or, for that matter, real evidence requires only enough evidence to support a finding that the matter is what its proponent claims it is. It is not required that the proponent establish its genuineness by a preponderance of the evidence as a condition to admissibility. All that is necessary under Federal Rules 104(b) and 901 is proof *sufficient to support a jury finding* of genuineness.

2.   Authentication by Pleadings or Stipulation

The genuineness of a document may be admitted through the discovery process, through stipulation at pretrial conference, or by a failure to deny an allegation in a pleading.

3.   Evidence of Authenticity

In general, a writing may be authenticated by any evidence that serves to establish its authenticity. The Federal Rules do not limit the methods of authentication, but rather list several examples of proper authentication. [Fed. R. Evid. 901]

a.   Admissions

A writing may be authenticated by evidence that the party against whom the writing is offered has either *admitted* its authenticity or *acted upon* the writing as authentic.

b.   Testimony of Eyewitness

A writing may be authenticated by testimony of one who *sees it executed* or *hears it acknowledged*. Modern statutes eliminate the common law necessity of producing a subscribing witness, unless specifically required by statute. [Fed. R. Evid. 903] If testimony of a subscribing witness is required (e.g., in authenticating a will), his denial or failure to recollect the execution of the writing does not preclude authentication by other evidence.

c.   Handwriting Verifications

A writing may also be authenticated by evidence of the genuineness of the handwriting of the maker.

1)   Nonexpert Opinion

A lay witness who has personal knowledge of the handwriting of the supposed writer may state his opinion as to whether the document is in that person's handwriting. (This is an exception to the opinion rule, *see* VI.C.1., *infra*.) Note, however, that a nonexpert cannot become familiar with the handwriting merely for the purpose of testifying.

2) Comparison of Writings

An expert witness or the trier of fact (e.g., jury) can determine the genuineness of a writing by comparing the questioned writing with another writing proved to be genuine. (Note that authentication by comparison is not limited to handwriting. Fingerprints, blood, hair, clothing fibers, and numerous other things can be authenticated by comparison with authenticated specimens.)

d. Ancient Documents

Under the Federal Rules, a document may be authenticated by evidence that it:

(i) Is at least *20 years old*;

(ii) Is in such condition as to be *free from suspicion* concerning its authenticity; and

(iii) Was *found in a place* where such writing, if authentic, would likely be kept.

[Fed. R. Evid. 901(b)(8)] Note that while documents may be authenticated if they are at least 20 years old, the related *hearsay exception* for ancient documents will only apply if the document was prepared before 1998 (*see* VII.D.8., *infra*).

1) Federal Rules Distinguished from Majority of Jurisdictions

The Federal Rules apply to *all writings*. However, most jurisdictions limit the ancient documents rule to *dispositive instruments* (e.g., deeds, wills, etc.). In addition, most courts require that such documents be over *30 years old*.

e. Reply Letter Doctrine

A writing may be authenticated by evidence that it was written in response to a communication sent to the claimed author. The content of the letter must make it unlikely that it was written by anyone other than the claimed author of the writing.

f. Circumstantial Evidence in General

The rules for ancient documents and reply letters, above, involve authentication by circumstantial evidence. A complete list of ways to authenticate by circumstantial evidence would be impossible. Any proof tending in reason to *establish genuineness* is sufficient. For example, authentication may be established by the content of the writing and a showing that it contains information known only to the purported author. Alternatively it may be demonstrated that the author had the disputed writing in his custody at a prior time under circumstances evidencing his belief in its genuineness.

g. Photographs

As a general rule, photographs are admissible only if identified by a witness as a portrayal of certain facts relevant to the issue and verified by the witness as a correct representation of those facts. It suffices if the witness who identifies the photograph is familiar with the scene or object that is depicted. In general, it is *not necessary to call the photographer* to authenticate the photograph.

1) Unattended Camera—Proper Operation of Camera

In some situations, a photograph will portray an event that was observed *only* by the camera (i.e., there is no witness who can testify to the relevant scene to authenticate the photograph). For example, an unmanned surveillance camera may produce a photograph of a burglar taken at a time when no other person was on the premises. Such a photograph may be admitted upon a showing that the camera was properly operating at the relevant time and that the photograph was developed from film obtained from that camera.

h. X-Ray Pictures, Electrocardiograms, Etc.

Unlike photographs, an X-ray picture cannot be authenticated by testimony of a witness that it is a correct representation of the facts. Therefore, a different procedure of authentication is necessary. First, it must be shown that the *process used is accurate* (as to X-rays, the court will usually take judicial notice of this). Then it must be shown that the *machine itself was in working order* and the *operator was qualified* to operate it. Finally, a *custodial chain* must be established to forestall the danger that the evidence has been substituted or tampered with.

4. Compare—Authentication of Oral Statements

Oral statements often require authentication as to the *identity of the speaker*. Although this is technically a "relevance" topic, the rules are the same as those that apply to the authenticity of documents.

a. When Necessary

Not all oral statements need to be authenticated; only where the identity of the speaker is important (e.g., admission by a party) is authentication required.

b. Methods of Authentication

1) Voice Identification

A voice, whether heard firsthand or through a device (e.g., a tape recording) may be identified by the opinion of anyone who has heard the voice at *any time*. Thus, in contrast to the rule for handwriting verification, a person can become familiar with a voice after litigation has begun and for the sole purpose of testifying.

2) Telephone Conversations

Statements made during a telephone conversation may be authenticated by one of the parties to the call who testifies to one of the following:

a) He recognized the other party's voice.

b) The speaker has knowledge of certain facts that only a particular person would have.

c) He called, for example, Mr. A's telephone number, and a voice answered, "This is Mr. A" or "This is the A residence." This authenticates the conversation as being with Mr. A or his agent.

d) He called the person's business establishment and talked with the person answering the phone about matters relevant to the business. This is sufficient to show that the person answering the phone held a position in the business.

5. Self-Authenticating Documents

Contrary to the general rule, which requires testimonial sponsorship, there are certain writings that are said to "prove themselves" or to be "self-identifying" on their face. Federal Rule 902 specifically provides that extrinsic evidence of authenticity is not required as to the following:

a. *Domestic public documents* that are signed and sealed;

b. *Foreign public documents* signed by a person authorized by the laws of that country;

c. *Certified copies of public records* (i.e., records, reports, and recorded documents);

d. *Official publications* (i.e., books, pamphlets, or other publications purporting to be issued by a public authority);

e. Printed materials purporting to be *newspapers or periodicals*;

f. *Trade inscriptions*, signs, tags, or labels purporting to have been affixed in the course of business and indicating ownership, control, or origin;

g. *Documents accompanied by a certificate of acknowledgment* executed in the manner provided by law by a *notary public* or other officer authorized by law to take acknowledgments;

h. *Commercial paper*, signatures thereon, and documents relating thereto, to the extent provided by general commercial law; and

i. *Business records,* records *generated by an electronic process,* and *data copied from an electronic device,* provided that:

1) The record is *certified* by a custodian or other qualified person; and

2) The offering party gives the adverse party *reasonable written notice* and makes the record and certification available for inspection so the adverse party has a fair opportunity to challenge them.

C. BEST EVIDENCE RULE

The best evidence rule is more accurately called the *"original document rule."* It may be stated as follows: In proving the terms of a writing (recording, photograph, or X-ray), where the terms are material, the original writing must be produced. Secondary evidence of the writing, such as oral testimony regarding the writing's contents, is permitted only after it has been shown that the original is unavailable for some reason other than the serious misconduct of the proponent. [Fed. R. Evid. 1002]

1. **Rule Expresses Preference for Originals**
    Simply stated, the rule applies to writings and expresses a preference for originals. It reflects the belief that the exact words of a writing, particularly in the case of operative or dispositive instruments such as contracts, deeds, or wills, should be presented to the court; that there is a hazard of inaccuracy in common methods of approximating the contents of a writing; and that oral testimony based on memory of the terms of the writing presents greater risk of error than oral testimony concerning other situations.

2. **Applicability of the Rule**
    For the most part, the rule applies to two classes of situations: (i) where the writing is a *legally operative or dispositive instrument* such as a contract, deed, will, or divorce decree; or (ii) where the *knowledge of a witness* concerning a fact results from having *read* it in the document.

    Examples: 1) Witness may not testify about the content of a written deed unless sufficient reason is given for not producing the original deed.

                        2) Witness who memorized mileage recorded on car sticker for a certain date, and who had no other source of knowledge on this significant litigated issue, may not testify as to the mileage without establishing a reason for the unavailability of the writing.

3. **Nonapplicability of the Rule**

    a. **Fact to Be Proved Exists Independently of Any Writing**
        Where the fact to be proved has an existence independent of any writing, the best evidence rule does not apply. Therefore, the rule does not apply to all events that happen to have been memorialized by documents. There are many writings that the substantive law does not regard as essential repositories of the facts recorded. These writings happen to record details of essentially nonwritten transactions. As to these, oral testimony may be given without production of, or explanation for the absence of, the original writings.

        Examples: 1) Witness may testify orally that he paid for goods received without producing the receipt that was given.

                            2) Facts such as birth, marriage, age, and death may be proved orally, although certificates evidencing these facts are in existence. However, since a divorce is effective only by a judicial decree, the best evidence rule requires that the fact of divorce be proved by the decree itself.

                            3) Testimony heard at a prior trial may be testified to in another case without production of the stenographic transcript of the prior testimony. One who heard the prior testimony can repeat it.

                            4) Admissions or confessions of a party may be testified to orally by anyone who heard them, even though the admissions or confessions were later reduced to writing.

        The above examples are in contrast to those writings that are considered as essential repositories of the facts recorded. Written contracts, deeds, wills, and judgments are viewed as such repositories—they are considered written transactions—and as such are within the rule.

b. Writing Is Collateral to Litigated Issue

Any narration by a witness is likely to include references to transactions consisting partly of written communications. The best evidence rule does not apply to writings of minor importance (i.e., ones that are collateral) to the matter in controversy. [Fed. R. Evid. 1004(d)] For example, an expert witness testifying on the value of a car is allowed to establish his status as a car dealer without production of his dealer's license. The test of "collateralness" is likely to take into account:

1) *Centrality* of the writing to the major issues of a litigation;

2) *Complexity* of the relevant features of the writing; and

3) Existence of a *genuine dispute* as to the contents of the writing.

c. Summaries of Voluminous Records

When it would be inconvenient to examine a voluminous collection of writings, recordings, or photographs in court, the proponent may present their contents in the form of a chart, summary, or calculation. [Fed. R. Evid. 1006] However, the originals or duplicates (*see* 4.c., *infra*) must be made available for examination and copying, and the judge may order them to be produced in court.

d. Public Records

The best evidence rule is modified so that a proponent may offer into evidence a copy of an official record or a copy of a document that has been recorded and filed. Such a copy must be *certified as correct* by the custodian of the document or other person authorized to do so, or *testified to be correct* by a person who compared it to the original. [Fed. R. Evid. 1005] The purpose of this exception is to prevent the loss or absence of public documents due to litigation.

4. Definitions of "Writings," "Original," and "Duplicate"

a. Writings, Recordings, and Photographs

The Federal Rules govern writings, recordings, and photographs. Writings and recordings are defined broadly as "letters, words, numbers, or their equivalent set down in any form." A photograph is defined as "a photographic image or its equivalent stored in any form." [Fed. R. Evid. 1001]

b. "Original"

An original is the writing or recording itself or any counterpart intended by the person executing it to have the same effect as an original. With respect to a photograph, "original" includes the negative or any print from it. For computer-stored data, the original is any printout or other output readable by sight.

Example: D types a letter to P that is defamatory of P. D sends the letter to P himself and a photocopy of the letter to the newspaper. In P's defamation action, the document legally operative to create tort liability is the "published" photocopy, not the letter sent to P.

c.   **Admissibility of Duplicates**
The Federal Rules define a duplicate as "a counterpart produced by a mechanical, photographic, chemical, electronic, or other equivalent process or technique that accurately reproduces the original." [Fed. R. Evid. 1001(e)] A duplicate is thus an *exact copy of an original* (e.g., a carbon copy or photocopy) made by mechanical means. Duplicates are *admissible* to the same extent as originals in federal courts, *unless* (i) a genuine question is raised about the original's authenticity, or (ii) under the circumstances, it would be unfair to admit the duplicate in place of the original. [Fed. R. Evid. 1003] The rationale for admitting duplicates under such a relaxed standard is that by definition these documents are exact copies of the original, and therefore their introduction into evidence would be objectionable only if some question existed as to the genuineness of the original.

5.   **Admissibility of Secondary Evidence of Contents**
If the proponent cannot produce the original writing or recording in court, he may offer secondary evidence of its contents in the form of copies (e.g., handwritten copies, which would not be considered duplicates because they are not exact copies), notes, or oral testimony about the contents of the original if a satisfactory explanation is given for the nonproduction of the original.

a.   **Satisfactory Foundation**
A valid excuse justifying the admissibility of secondary evidence would include:

1)   **Loss or Destruction of Original**
A proper foundation for the admissibility of secondary evidence is laid by a showing that the original has been lost and cannot be found despite diligent search, or was destroyed in good faith.

2)   **Original Outside Jurisdiction and Unobtainable**
If the document is within the jurisdiction, it must be subpoenaed. If not, some reasonable effort or request to the third party for production must be shown before secondary evidence will be admitted. A proper foundation is laid, however, if it is shown that the original is (i) in the possession of a third party, (ii) outside the jurisdiction, and (iii) unobtainable.

3)   **Original in Possession of Adversary Who, After Notice, Fails to Produce**
If the opponent has custody of the original, a showing of his custody, service of a timely notice to produce, and his failure to produce it in court will justify the admissibility of secondary evidence. Where the pleadings give notice to the opposite party that he will be charged with possession of the writing, service of the notice to produce is unnecessary.

b.   **No Degrees of Secondary Evidence**
The Federal Rules recognize no degrees of secondary evidence. Once a satisfactory explanation for nonproduction of the original is established, the party seeking to prove the contents of a writing, photograph, or recording may do so by any kind of secondary evidence ranging from handwritten copies to oral testimony. This abolition of degrees of secondary evidence is a departure from the rule existing in most American jurisdictions. [Fed. R. Evid. 1004]

c. **Testimony or Written Admission of Party**
A proponent may prove the contents of a writing, recording, or photograph through the testimony, deposition, or written admission of the party against whom it is offered, and need not account for the nonproduction of the original. [Fed. R. Evid. 1007] However, it is also generally held that the ***contents*** of a writing, photograph, etc., ***cannot be proved simply by out-of-court oral admissions*** of the party against whom such evidence is offered (unless of course the original is otherwise accounted for).
Example: Witness testifies, "I heard D say that the telegram he received stated . . . ." D's oral admissions outside court are inadmissible to prove the contents of the telegram. [Fed. R. Evid. 1007]

6. **Functions of Court and Jury**
Ordinarily, it is for the court to make the determinations of fact that determine the admissibility of duplicates, other copies, and oral testimony as to the contents of an original. However, the Federal Rules specifically reserve three questions of ***preliminary fact for the jury***:

(i) Whether the original ever existed;

(ii) Whether a writing, recording, or photograph produced at trial is an original; and

(iii) Whether the evidence offered correctly reflects the contents of the original.

[Fed. R. Evid. 1008]

VI. TESTIMONIAL EVIDENCE

A. **COMPETENCY OF WITNESSES**
Witnesses are not "authenticated" in the same sense as real or documentary evidence. However, they too must pass tests of basic reliability to establish their competence to give testimony. Unlike the authentication situation pertaining to real or documentary proof, witnesses are generally ***presumed to be competent*** until the contrary is demonstrated.

1. **Basic Testimonial Qualifications**
There are four basic testimonial attributes that every witness must have to some degree. These are the capacity to observe, to recollect, to communicate, and to appreciate the obligation to speak truthfully. These, along with sincerity, are the qualities at which the cross-examiner directs his skill.

A diminution of any of these capacities usually goes only to the weight of the testimony and serves to make the witness less persuasive. However, a witness can be so deficient in one or more of these basic qualifications that she will be deemed incompetent to testify at all. The problem of infancy is a good example for all aspects of the basic qualifications. A witness may be too young ***at the time of the event*** to be able to accurately perceive what happened or to be able to remember at the time of the trial. The witness may also be too young ***at the time of the trial*** to effectively relate or communicate or appreciate the obligation to tell the truth.

a. **Ability to Observe—Perception**
The issue of a witness's ability to observe may arise in the following manner: W testifies on direct to details of how an intersection automobile collision occurred. On cross-examination, W admits that her attention was directed to the intersection by the sound of the crash. The direct testimony regarding details of the accident occurring before the collision will be stricken.

b. **Ability to Remember—Memory**
An example of a witness incompetent for this reason would be one who is suffering from senility or amnesia.

c. **Ability to Relate—Communication**
The ability to relate concerns the ability of the witness to communicate effectively with the trier of fact.

d. **Appreciation of Oath Obligation**
The witness must have sufficient intelligence and character to know and desire to tell the truth. The witness may be sworn by oath or affirmation. However, unsworn testimony may be permissible if the witness (e.g., a child) appreciates the obligation to tell the truth.

2. **Federal Rules of Competency**

a. **Personal Knowledge and Oath Required**
Federal Rule 601 provides that "[e]very person is competent to be a witness unless these rules provide otherwise." The rules do not specify any mental or moral qualifications for witness testimony beyond these two limitations:

1) *The witness must have personal knowledge* of the matter he is to testify about (i.e., must have observed the matter and must have a present recollection of his observation). This requirement is met if there is evidence "sufficient to support a finding" that the witness is speaking on the basis of personal knowledge. Proof of personal knowledge may consist of the witness's own testimony. [Fed. R. Evid. 602]

2) *The witness must declare he will testify truthfully*, by oath or affirmation. [Fed. R. Evid. 603]

b. **Use of Interpreter**
If a witness requires an interpreter, the interpreter must be qualified and take an oath to make a true translation. [Fed. R. Evid. 604]

c. **Applicability of State Rules in Diversity Cases**
Federal Rule 601 provides that the competency of a witness shall be determined by state law in civil actions "regarding a claim or defense for which state law supplies the rule of decision."

3. **Modern Modifications of Common Law Disqualifications**
At common law there were several grounds upon which a person could be disqualified from

giving testimony. Persons were incompetent to testify if they had a financial interest in the suit, if they were the spouse of a party, if they lacked religious belief, if they had been convicted of a crime, or if they lacked mental capacity. These common law disqualifications have been almost entirely removed under the Federal Rules and in the vast majority of American jurisdictions.

a. Lack of Religious Belief

Lack of religious belief is no longer a basis for excluding a witness. Not only are a person's religious convictions irrelevant in determining the competence of a witness, but they may also not be shown or commented upon for the purpose of affecting the credibility of a witness.

b. Infancy

There is *no precise age* at which an infant is deemed competent or incompetent to testify under oath. The competence of an infant depends on the capacity and intelligence of the particular child. This test is an individual one, to be determined by the trial judge upon preliminary examination.

c. Insanity

An insane person, even one who has been adjudicated incompetent, *may testify*, provided he understands the obligation to speak truthfully and possesses the capacity to give a correct account of what he has perceived in reference to the issue in dispute.

d. Conviction of Crime

The common law disqualification of felons has been removed by statute in most states. However, conviction of a crime may be shown to *affect the credibility* of the competent witness.

e. Interest

The common law disqualification of parties or interested persons has been abolished in most states. The only remaining vestiges of this disqualification are the so-called Dead Man Acts, discussed later.

f. Judge as Witness

Federal Rule 605 provides that the presiding judge *may not testify as a witness* in the proceeding, and that no objection need be made to preserve the point. The basis for this disqualification is that when the judge is called as a witness, her role as a witness is inconsistent with her role as presiding judge, which requires her to maintain impartiality.

g. Juror as Witness

1) Cannot Testify During Case

Jurors are incompetent to testify before the jury in which they are sitting. [Fed. R. Evid. 606(a)] The rationale is that a juror-witness cannot impartially weigh her own testimony and cannot be thoroughly cross-examined for fear of creating antagonism.

2) Inquiry into Verdict or Indictment—Generally Cannot Testify
During an inquiry into the validity of a verdict or indictment, a juror is generally prohibited from testifying as to: (i) anything that occurred during the jury's deliberations; (ii) the effect of anything on that juror's or another juror's vote; or (iii) any juror's mental processes concerning the verdict or indictment. The court may not receive a juror's affidavit or evidence of a juror's statement on these matters. [Fed. R. Evid. 606(b)(1)]

a) Exceptions—Permitted Topics
A juror may testify as to:

(1) Whether any *extraneous prejudicial information* was improperly brought to the jury's attention;

(2) Whether any *outside influence* was improperly brought to bear on any juror;

(3) Whether there is a *mistake on the verdict form* (e.g., wrong damages amount or other clerical error); or

(4) Whether any juror made a *clear* statement that he *relied on racial stereotypes or animus* to convict a *criminal defendant*. The rationale for allowing this evidence is to permit the court to determine whether the defendant's Sixth Amendment right to a jury trial was violated. Not every comment indicating racial bias will qualify; there must be a showing that racial animus was a *significant motivating factor* in the juror's vote to convict. Whether that threshold showing has been satisfied is a matter committed to the discretion of the trial court in light of all the circumstances, including the content and timing of the alleged statements and the reliability of the evidence.

[Fed. R. Evid. 606(b)(2); Pena Rodriguez v. Colorado, 137 S. Ct. 855 (2017)—following discharge of the jury, two jurors told defense counsel that during deliberations a specific juror had expressed anti-Hispanic bias toward the defendant and the defendant's alibi witness]

4. Dead Man Acts
The last remaining vestige of true incompetency of a witness appears in the Dead Man Acts. These statutes exist in most jurisdictions and their provisions vary from state to state. Although there is *no Dead Man Act in the Federal Rules of Evidence*, state Dead Man Acts operate to disqualify witnesses in federal cases where state law provides the rule of decision (most diversity cases). For bar examination purposes, only generalized comments are appropriate, and there are common provisions to most Dead Man Acts that could appear in a multistate bar exam question.

a. Rationale
The Dead Man Acts generally provide that a party or person interested in the event, or his predecessor in interest, is incompetent to testify to a *personal transaction or*

communication with a deceased, when such testimony is offered against the representative or successors in interest of the deceased. The rationale of the statute is to *protect estates from perjured claims*. The assumption is that the survivor claimant may lie, since the deceased cannot talk back. Because death has silenced one party, the statute closes the mouth of the living person who, being interested in the litigation's outcome, wishes to testify on her own behalf against someone who is suing or defending in a representative capacity (e.g., executor, administrator, heir, legatee, devisee).

b. Common Elements

Most Dead Man Acts have the following common elements and applications:

1) Applicable to Civil Cases Only

The bar to competency created by a Dead Man Act applies only to civil cases and has no application in criminal cases.

2) Protected Parties

The statute is designed to protect those who claim directly under the decedent. They usually include an executor, administrator, heir, legatee, and devisee. If a protected party is on either side of the lawsuit (suing or defending), the statute applies to prevent an interested person from testifying on his own behalf.

Examples: 1) Plaintiff sues the executor of the estate for a debt owed by the decedent. The executor is a protected party and the act applies.

2) Executor sues defendant for negligence in causing the death of the decedent. Executor is a protected party and the act applies.

3) Heir sues executor, legatees, and devisees in a will contest. Heir is a protected party, as are the adverse parties. The act applies.

3) Interested Person

A person is "interested in the event" if he stands to gain or lose by the direct and immediate operation of the judgment, or if the judgment may be used for or against him in a subsequent action. Thus, in states where a spouse has an inchoate right in the other spouse's property, both spouses may be interested and incompetent to testify. Similarly, a shareholder of a corporation and the co-maker of a note may be disqualified under the rule.

a) Predecessor in Interest

Most Dead Man Acts disqualify not only the person interested, but also the predecessor in interest.

Example: If A assigns to B a claim against Decedent, and B sues the estate, both A and B are incompetent. B is interested in the event; A is the person from, through, or under whom B derived his interest.

b) Party Adverse to Protected Party

As a short rule of thumb, a party adverse to the protected party is always an interested person who will be rendered incompetent by the Dead Man

Act. For other nonparty witnesses, ask whether the witness has a *pecuniary interest in the outcome of the case* or is a predecessor in interest with the adverse party.

4) Exceptions and Waiver of the Act
There are numerous situations where the Dead Man Act either will not apply against an interested person or the protected party may waive its effect. Of course, if an exception applies or the statute is waived, the interested person is competent to testify. The following are common to most jurisdictions:

a) Facts Occurring After Death
An interested person may always testify to facts that occurred *after* the death of the deceased, since the protection of the rule is not needed.

b) "Door Openers"
The estate representatives and those claiming under the decedent may *waive the protection* of the statute. Common provisions for waiver include:

(1) If the protected party calls the interested person to testify about the transaction, the interested person may explain all matters about which he is examined.

(2) Where the testimony of the deceased given at a former trial or at a deposition is read in evidence, the interested person may explain all matters about which he is examined.

(3) Where there is a failure to make timely and proper objection. Objection is to the incompetency of the witness, not to the incompetency of the testimony.

(4) If the protected party or an agent of the deceased testifies to a transaction with an interested person, the interested person may testify about the same transaction.

B. FORM OF EXAMINATION OF WITNESS
The *judge may exercise reasonable control* over the examination of witnesses in order to aid the effective ascertainment of truth, to avoid wasting time, and to protect witnesses from harassment or undue embarrassment. [Fed. R. Evid. 611(a)] Questions that frequently arise concerning the form of examination of witnesses are: when may leading questions be used, what other types of questions are objectionable, and when and how may a witness use memoranda.

1. Leading Questions

a. Generally Objectionable
A question is leading and generally objectionable on direct examination when it suggests to the witness the fact that the examiner expects and wants to have confirmed. Questions calling for "yes" or "no" answers and questions *framed to suggest the answer desired* are usually leading.

Example: On direct examination plaintiff is asked, "Is it true or not that at the time in question, you were driving well within the speed limit?" The question is leading.

b.   When Permitted

Leading questions are permitted on ***cross-examination***. Trial judges will usually allow leading questions on ***direct examination*** in noncrucial areas ***if no objection is made:***

(i)   If used to elicit ***preliminary or introductory matter***;

(ii)   When the witness ***needs aid to respond*** because of loss of memory, immaturity, or physical or mental weakness; or

(iii)   When the witness is ***hostile*** and improperly uncooperative, an ***adverse*** party, or a person ***identified with an adverse party***.

[Fed. R. Evid. 611(c)]

2.   Improper Questions and Answers

The following types of questions are improper and are not permitted:

a.   Misleading

A question is misleading and thus is not permitted if it is one that cannot be answered without making an unintended admission.
Example: "Do you still beat your wife?"

b.   Compound

Questions that require a single answer to more than one question are not permitted.
Example: "Did you see and hear the intruder?"

c.   Argumentative

Argumentative questions, which are leading questions that reflect the examiner's interpretation of the facts, are improper.
Example: "Why were you driving so recklessly?"

d.   Conclusionary

A question that calls for an opinion or conclusion that the witness is not qualified or permitted to make is improper.
Example: "What did your friend think about that?" The witness could not know his friend's thoughts, and is not permitted to give his opinion as to his friend's thoughts.

e.   Assuming Facts Not in Evidence

An attorney is not allowed to ask a question that assumes a disputed fact is true when it has not been established in the case.
Example: In a case where there is no evidence that Defendant had been drinking, the following question is improper: "After Defendant finished his fifth beer, he got up and went to his car, didn't he?"

f. Cumulative

An attorney is generally not permitted to ask a question that has already been asked and answered. More repetition is allowed on cross-examination than on direct, but if it is apparent that the cross-examiner is not moving forward, the judge may disallow the question.

g. Harassing or Embarrassing

The trial judge, in her discretion, may disallow cross-examination that is unduly harassing or embarrassing.

h. Calls for a Narrative Answer

Some courts generally prohibit questions calling for a narrative answer, i.e., a question allowing a witness to answer by recounting relevant facts, rather than a series of specific questions requiring specific answers.

Example: Tell me what you did on the evening of September 22.

i. Calls for Speculation

An examining attorney may not ask a witness to speculate, i.e., theorize, as to a fact, because such testimony is not based on the witness's personal knowledge.

Example: Where decedent expressed a desire to become an engineer but did not do so, it was speculation for a witness to testify regarding decedent's lost income based on an engineer's salary.

j. Lack of Foundation

A witness must have personal knowledge as to the facts of his testimony. Insufficient personal knowledge may subject testimony to an objection for lack of foundation. Additionally, a party may object on the basis of lack of foundation for real evidence if the proponent has not shown that the evidence is what he purports it to be. (*See* IV.C.1., *supra*.)

k. Nonresponsive Answer

A witness's response must address only the specific question asked by the examining attorney; otherwise the testimony is subject to being stricken for nonresponsiveness.

Example: Q. Did you leave your house on September 22?

A. I went to the dentist and then to the grocery store. This answer is nonresponsive, as the question calls for a "yes" or "no" response.

3. Use of Memoranda by Witness

A witness cannot read her testimony from a prepared memorandum. However, a memorandum may be used in certain circumstances to refresh the recollection of the witness, to substitute for the witness's forgotten testimony upon authentication of the memorandum, or in cross-examination of the witness.

a. Present Recollection Revived—Refreshing Recollection

A witness may use any writing or thing for the purpose of refreshing her present recollection. She usually may not read from the writing while she actually testifies, since the writing is ***not authenticated***, is ***not in evidence***, and may be used solely to refresh her recollection. The writing is intended to help her to recall by jogging her memory. The sworn testimony must demonstrate a *present* recollection.

1) Inspection and Use in Cross-Examination
Under Federal Rule 612, whenever a witness has used a writing to refresh her memory *while on the stand*, an adverse party is entitled to have the writing produced at trial, inspect it, cross-examine the witness thereon, and introduce into evidence those portions that relate to the witness's testimony. If the witness has refreshed her memory *before trial* by looking at the writing, it is within the court's discretion to require production of the document and to permit inspection, cross-examination, and introduction of pertinent excerpts.

b. Past Recollection Recorded—Recorded Recollection
Where a witness states that she has insufficient recollection of an event to enable her to testify fully and accurately, even after she has consulted a memorandum or other record given to her on the stand, the *record itself may be read into evidence* if a proper foundation is laid for its admissibility. The foundation for receipt of the record into evidence must include proof that:

(i) The witness at one time had *personal knowledge* of the facts recited in the record;

(ii) The record was *made by the witness* or made *under her direction* or it was *adopted by the witness*;

(iii) The record was *timely made* when the matter was fresh in the mind of the witness;

(iv) The record *accurately reflects the witness's knowledge* (i.e., the witness must indicate that the record was accurate when it was made); and

(v) The witness has *insufficient recollection* to testify fully and accurately.

Records that meet these requirements are admissible under an *exception to the hearsay rule* (*see* VII.D.6., *infra*). Remember that, under the Federal Rule, if admitted, the record may be read into evidence and heard by the jury, but *the document itself is not received* as an exhibit unless offered by the adverse party. [Fed. R. Evid. 803(5)]

C. OPINION TESTIMONY
The word "opinion" used in this context includes all opinions, inferences, conclusions, and other subjective statements made by a witness. A basic premise of our legal system is that, in general, witnesses should testify as to facts within their personal knowledge and that the trier of fact should draw any conclusions therefrom. Therefore, the general policy of the law is to restrict the admissibility of opinion evidence, except in cases where the courts are sure that it will be necessary, or at least helpful. Of course, the difference between "fact" and "opinion" is a matter of degree. Therefore, there cannot be any clear-cut opinion rule.

1. Opinion Testimony by Lay Witnesses

a. General Rule of Inadmissibility
Opinions by lay witnesses are generally inadmissible. However, there are many cases where, from the nature of the subject matter, no better evidence can be obtained. In

these cases, where the event is likely to be perceived as a whole impression (e.g., intoxication, speed) rather than as more specific components, opinions by lay witnesses are generally admitted.

b. **When Admissible**
In most jurisdictions and under the Federal Rules, opinion testimony by lay witnesses is admissible when:

(i) It is rationally *based on the perception of the witness*;

(ii) It is *helpful to a clear understanding* of her testimony or to the determination of a fact in issue; and

(iii) It is *not based on scientific, technical, or other specialized knowledge* (if so based, the witness's testimony would need to meet the requirements for expert testimony stated in Rule 702, *see* 2.a., *infra*).

[Fed. R. Evid. 701]

Example: Think how much easier and clearer it is for a witness to say someone looked "drunk" than it is to describe her gait, speech, eyes, diction, breath, and manner. All these things can also be brought out, but the term "drunk" may be more meaningful than any of them.

Some jurisdictions are stricter and allow lay opinion testimony only in cases of "necessity" when it is difficult for the witness to express her perception in any form other than opinion.

c. **Procedure**
Unless waived by a failure to object, a proper foundation must be laid by showing that the witness had the opportunity to observe the event that forms the basis of her opinion. Additionally, the court in its discretion may require a witness to state the facts observed before stating her opinion.

d. **Situations Where Opinions of Lay Witnesses Are Admissible**

1) **General Appearance or Condition of a Person**
Testimony that a person was "elderly," "about 60 years old," "strong," "weak," or "ill" would be admissible, but testimony that a person is suffering from specific diseases or specific injuries—usually requiring knowledge of an expert—would not.

2) **State of Emotion**
A witness would be permitted to testify that a person appeared "angry," "was joking," or that two persons were "in love" or appeared to have a strong affection for each other.

3) **Matters Involving Sense Recognition**
A witness would be permitted to testify that an object was "heavy," "red," "bulky," or that a certain beverage tasted like whiskey.

4) Voice or Handwriting Identification

Lay opinion is permissible and often essential to identify telephone voices and handwriting. In these instances a foundation must first be laid to show familiarity with the voice or handwriting.

5) Speed of Moving Object

A witness may estimate in miles per hour the speed of a moving object but must first show some experience in observing the rate of speed of moving objects. Characterization that a vehicle was going "fast" or "very fast" has been permitted.

6) Value of Own Services

A witness may give her opinion as to the value of her own services.

7) Rational or Irrational Nature of Another's Conduct (Sanity)

In many jurisdictions, a witness is permitted to state her opinion as to the sanity of another person. Some states limit these opinions to testimony describing the acts of a person whose sanity is in question and allow the witness to state only whether those acts impressed her at the time as rational or irrational (e.g., "She acted like a madwoman").

8) Intoxication

A witness who has seen a person and is able to describe that person's actions, words, or conduct may express an opinion as to whether that person was or was not intoxicated. In many states, the details of the person's appearance must be given as a foundation for the opinion.

Example: In Defendant's trial on a charge of driving while intoxicated, Witness testifies for the prosecution that Defendant "smelled of alcohol, his speech was incoherent, his eyes glassy and bloodshot, he could not stand or walk without assistance, he was slumped over the wheel of his vehicle," and, finally, that he "was intoxicated."

e.   Situations Where Opinions of Lay Witnesses Are Not Admissible

1) Agency or Authorization

When agency or authorization is in issue, the witness generally may not state a conclusion as to her authorization. Rather, she must be asked by whom she was employed and the nature, terms, and surrounding circumstances of her employment.

2) Contract or Agreement

When the existence of an express contract is in issue, a witness generally may not state her opinion that an agreement was made. Rather, she must be asked about the facts, the existence or nonexistence of which establish whether a contract existed.

2.   Opinion Testimony by Expert Witnesses

a.   Requirements of Expert Testimony

The expert may state an opinion or conclusion, provided the following conditions are satisfied:

1) **Relevance and Reliability**

Expert testimony is admissible if: (i) the subject matter is one where scientific, technical, or other specialized knowledge would *help the trier of fact* understand the evidence or determine a fact in issue; (ii) the opinion is *based on sufficient facts* or data; (iii) the opinion is the product of *reliable principles and methods*; and (iv) the expert has *reliably applied* the principles and methods to the facts of the case. [Fed. R. Evid. 702]

   a) **Scientific Evidence—*Daubert* Factors**

   When determining the reliability of evidence based on a scientific theory or technique, federal courts consider a variety of factors, including: (i) whether the theory or technique has been tested; (ii) whether it has been subject to peer review and publication; (iii) its known or potential error rate; (iv) the existence and maintenance of standards controlling its operation; and (v) whether it is generally accepted in the scientific community. [*See* Daubert v. Merrell Dow Pharmaceuticals, Inc., 509 U.S. 579 (1993); Kumho Tire Co. v. Carmichael, 526 U.S. 137 (1999)]

2) **Witness Must Be Qualified as an Expert**

To testify as an expert, a person must have special knowledge, skill, experience, training, or education sufficient to qualify him as an expert on the subject to which his testimony relates. [Fed. R. Evid. 702]

3) **Expert Must Possess Reasonable Probability Regarding His Opinion**

The expert must possess reasonable certainty or probability regarding his opinion. If the opinion of the expert is a mere guess or speculation, it is inadmissible.

Example: It would be error to permit plaintiff's medical expert to testify that plaintiff's symptoms "suggested" diabetes and "indicated" that the disease was caused by the accident.

4) **Opinion Must Be Supported by Proper Factual Basis**

The expert's opinion may be based upon one or more of these three possible sources of information: (i) facts that the expert knows from his own observation; (ii) facts presented in evidence at the trial and submitted to the expert, usually by hypothetical question; or (iii) facts not in evidence that were supplied to the expert out of court, and which are of a type reasonably relied upon by experts in the particular field in forming opinions on the subject. Note that the expert may give opinion testimony on direct examination without disclosing the basis of the opinion, unless the court orders otherwise. However, the expert may be required to disclose such information on cross-examination. [Fed. R. Evid. 705]

   a) **Personal Observation**

   If the expert has examined the person or thing about which he is testifying, he may relate those facts observed by him and upon which he bases his opinion. [Fed. R. Evid. 703]

   Example: An expert may testify that he examined plaintiff's leg following the accident, and in his opinion the plaintiff sustained a compound fracture.

b) Facts Made Known to Expert at Trial

The expert's opinion may be based upon the evidence introduced at the trial. The expert may *listen to testimony* at trial, or counsel may relate the facts to the expert in the form of a *hypothetical question*. The hypothetical question may be based on facts derived from any of the three sources of information noted above.

c) Facts Made Known to Expert Outside Court

Under Federal Rule 703, the expert may base an opinion upon facts not known personally but supplied to him outside the courtroom (e.g., reports of nurses, technicians, or consultants). The Federal Rule further provides that such facts *need not be in evidence or even of a type admissible* in evidence, as long as the facts are of a kind *reasonably relied upon* by experts in the particular field. However, if the facts are of a type inadmissible in evidence, the proponent of the expert opinion must *not* disclose those facts to the jury unless the court determines that their probative value in assisting the jury to evaluate the expert's opinion *substantially* outweighs their prejudicial effect.

Example: A physician bases his expert opinion upon (i) a personal examination of the patient, (ii) statements by the patient as to her medical history, and (iii) medically germane statements by the patient's relatives. The results of the personal examination are admissible and may therefore be relied upon by the physician because they are relevant, material, based on personal knowledge, and not subject to any exclusionary rule. The statements of the patient are admissible through an exception to the hearsay rule. The statements by the relatives, though inadmissible hearsay, may properly form a basis for a physician's expert opinion testimony because they are the facts reasonably relied upon by physicians in making a diagnosis; however, these statements should not be disclosed to the jury without the court first finding that their probative value substantially outweighs prejudice.

b. Opinion May Embrace Ultimate Issue

Federal Rule 704(a) and the modern trend repudiate the traditional prohibition on opinions embracing the ultimate issue in the case. The rule provides: "An opinion is not objectionable just because it embraces an ultimate issue." Note, however, that to be admissible under the Federal Rules, the expert opinion must "help the trier of fact" to understand the evidence or determine a fact in issue. Thus, an expert's conclusion that "X had testamentary capacity" is still inadmissible because it is not helpful to the jury.

1) Exception—Criminal Defendant's Mental State

The Federal Rules *prohibit* ultimate issue testimony in one situation: In a criminal case in which the defendant's mental state constitutes an element of the crime or defense, an expert may not state an opinion as to whether the accused did or did not have the mental state in issue. [Fed. R. Evid. 704(b)]

c. **Authoritative Texts and Treatises**

An expert may be cross-examined concerning statements contained in any scientific publication, as long as the publication is established as reliable authority. For example, the witness may be asked, "Doesn't Dr. Killum, in his book on diseases of the pancreas, disagree with your conclusion here?" A publication may be established as reliable by: (i) the direct testimony or cross-examination admission of the expert, (ii) the testimony of another expert, or (iii) judicial notice. Thus, even if the expert refuses to recognize the text as authoritative, it can be used on cross-examination if its reliability is established by one of the other methods.

The Federal Rules have expanded the admissibility of learned texts and treatises beyond impeachment of experts. Statements from an established treatise may be read into the record as substantive evidence, and may even be introduced on direct examination of a party's own expert. [Fed. R. Evid. 803(18)—exception to hearsay rule; *see* VII.D.10., *infra*)] There are two important limitations: (i) an expert must be on the stand when a statement from a treatise is read into evidence; and (ii) the relevant portion is read into evidence but is not received as an exhibit (i.e., the jury never sees it).

D. CROSS-EXAMINATION

1. **Necessity for Cross-Examination**

Cross-examination of adverse witnesses is a matter of right in every trial of a disputed issue of fact. It is recognized as the ***most efficacious truth-discovering device***. The principal basis for excluding hearsay is that the declarant whose testimony is offered cannot be subjected to the test of cross-examination. If adequate cross-examination is prevented by the death, illness, or refusal of a witness to testify on cross-examination, the direct examination is rendered incompetent and will be stricken.

2. **Scope of Cross-Examination**

Although a party is entitled as of right to some cross-examination, the extent or scope of cross-examination, like the order of calling witnesses, is frequently a matter of judicial discretion. Cross-examination is hedged about by far fewer rules than is direct examination. On cross-examination, leading questions are permissible, as are, obviously, efforts at impeachment. The most significant restriction is that the scope of cross-examination cannot range beyond the subject matter of the direct examination. This restriction does not apply to inquiries directed toward impeachment of the witness.

a. **Restrictions on Scope**

Under Federal Rule 611(b) and in the majority of American jurisdictions, ***cross-examination is limited to***: (i) matters brought out on ***direct examination*** and the inferences naturally drawn from those matters, and (ii) matters affecting the ***credibility of the witness***.

b. **Significance of Restrictions**

The question of the proper scope of cross-examination is important since it affects the ***right to use leading questions***. And, in jurisdictions that do not allow a party to impeach his own witness, going beyond the scope of direct examination means that you have made the witness "your own witness" and therefore cannot impeach his testimony.

Further, if the party placing a witness on the stand is the holder of a privilege, the court may hold it waived to the extent that the other party may engage in cross-examination; therefore, the scope of cross-examination permitted may determine to what extent the cross-examining party may inquire into privileged material.

c. Collateral Matters

The general rule is that the cross-examiner is ***bound by the answers of the witness*** to questions concerning collateral matters. Thus, the cross-examiner cannot refute the response of the witness by producing extrinsic evidence. Indeed, some federal courts resolve the matter under Rule 403 by treating the evidence on the collateral matter as being substantially outweighed by time considerations and the danger of confusion of the issues. Certain matters of impeachment, however, are recognized as sufficiently important to merit development by extrinsic evidence (e.g., bias or interest of the witness may be shown by other evidence, even if denied by the witness on cross-examination). Other matters of impeachment are limited solely to inquiry on cross-examination (e.g., prior misconduct of the witness not resulting in conviction but affecting the witness's credibility). Once beyond recognized impeachment techniques, the test as to what is "collateral" is sufficiently vague to permit a wide exercise of discretion by the trial judge.

E. CREDIBILITY—IMPEACHMENT

Impeachment means the casting of an adverse reflection on the veracity of the witness. The primary method of impeachment is by cross-examination of the witness under attack, although witnesses are often impeached by extrinsic proof that casts doubt on credibility. In terms of relevance, any matter that tends to prove or disprove the credibility of the witness should be admitted here.

1. Accrediting or Bolstering

a. General Rule—No Bolstering Until Witness Impeached

A party may not bolster or accredit the testimony of his witness until the witness has been impeached.

Example: A prior statement made by W at the time of the event that is consistent with W's in-court testimony would not be admissible to show that W's memory of the event is excellent or that he told the same story twice and therefore is especially worthy of belief.

b. Exceptions

The rule against accrediting is subject to exception where timeliness may raise an inference on the substantive issues of the case.

1) Timely Complaint

In certain cases a party may prove that the witness made a timely complaint, in order to bolster the party's credibility.

Examples: 1) Evidence of a prompt complaint of a rape victim is admissible to bolster the complainant's credibility in a subsequent criminal prosecution.

2) Where a defendant in a criminal trial claims that a confession offered against him was obtained by coercion, he may show that he complained of mistreatment at the first suitable opportunity.

2) Prior Identification

Evidence of any prior statement of identification made by a witness is admissible not only to bolster the witness's testimony, but also as substantive evidence that the identification was correct. [Fed. R. Evid. 801(d)(1)(C); and *see* VII.B.1., *infra*]

2. Any Party May Impeach

Contrary to the traditional rule, under which a party could not impeach his own witness, the Federal Rules provide that the credibility of a witness may be attacked by any party, ***including the party calling him***. [Fed. R. Evid. 607] Even under the traditional rule, however, a party could impeach his own witness if the witness: (i) was an adverse party, (ii) was hostile, (iii) was one required to be called by law, or (iv) gave damaging surprise testimony.

3. Impeachment Methods—Cross-Examination and Extrinsic Evidence

A witness may be impeached either by ***cross-examination*** (by eliciting facts from the witness that discredit his own testimony) or by ***extrinsic evidence*** (by calling other witnesses or introducing documents that prove the impeaching facts).

Note: In the discussion that follows, "cross-examination" also includes a party impeaching his own witness on direct examination.

There are certain well-recognized, often-used impeachment methods. These traditional impeachment devices include: the use of prior inconsistent statements; a showing of bias or interest in the litigation; an attack on the character of the witness by showing convictions of crime, prior acts of misconduct, or poor reputation for veracity; a showing of sensory deficiencies; and proof of contradictory facts. The basic questions for each of these methods are: Is the examiner limited to impeachment by cross-examination alone, or may he produce extrinsic evidence? If extrinsic evidence is permissible, must a foundation first be laid by inquiry on cross-examination?

a. Prior Inconsistent Statements

For the purpose of impeaching the credibility of a witness, a party may show that the witness has, on another occasion, made statements that are inconsistent with some material part of his present testimony. Under the Federal Rules, an inconsistent statement may be proved by either cross-examination or extrinsic evidence. To prove the statement by extrinsic evidence, certain requirements must first be met: (i) a ***proper foundation*** must be laid; and (ii) the statement must be ***relevant*** to some issue in the case, i.e., it cannot be a "collateral matter."

1) Laying a Foundation

Generally, extrinsic evidence of the witness's prior inconsistent statement is admissible only if: (i) the ***witness*** is, at some point, given an ***opportunity to explain or deny*** the allegedly inconsistent statement; and (ii) the ***adverse party*** is, at some point, given an ***opportunity to examine the witness*** about the statement.

(These opportunities need not come before introduction of the statement under the Federal Rules.) This foundation requirement may be dispensed with, however, where "justice so requires" (as where the witness has left the stand and is not available when his prior inconsistent statement is discovered). Furthermore, this foundation is **not** required when the prior inconsistent statement qualifies as an opposing party's statement (*see* VII.B.2., *infra*). [Fed. R. Evid. 613(b)] Also, the courts generally agree that inconsistent statements by a hearsay declarant may be used to impeach the declarant despite the lack of a foundation (obviously, where the declarant is not a witness no foundation could be laid anyway). [Fed. R. Evid. 806]

2) Evidentiary Effect of Prior Inconsistent Statements

In most cases, prior inconsistent statements are hearsay, admissible only to impeach the witness. However, where the statement was made **under oath at a prior trial, hearing, or other proceeding, or in a deposition, it is admissible nonhearsay** (i.e., it may be considered as substantive proof of the facts stated!). (*See* VII.B.1., *infra*.)

b. Bias or Interest

Evidence that a witness is biased or has an interest in the outcome of a suit tends to show that the witness has a **motive to lie**. A witness may usually be impeached by extrinsic evidence of bias or interest, provided a proper foundation is laid. Note that evidence that is substantively inadmissible may be admitted for impeachment purposes if relevant to show bias or interest.

Examples: 1) It may be shown that a witness is being paid to testify, that a witness is financing the case, or that he otherwise has a financial interest in the outcome of the litigation.

2) Inferences of bias may be shown by evidence of family or other relationship, business relationship, or by conduct or expressions of the witness demonstrating a friendship toward a party.

3) In a criminal case, it is proper for the defense to ask a prosecution witness whether he has been promised immunity from punishment for testifying, whether an indictment is pending against him, or whether he is on parole. This evidence may show a motive for the witness to curry the favor of the state.

4) Hostility toward a party may be shown by adverse statements against the party, or by the fact that the witness had a fight or quarrel with him or has a lawsuit pending against him.

1) Foundation

Most courts require that before a witness can be impeached by extrinsic evidence of bias or interest, he must first be asked about the facts that show bias or interest on cross-examination. If the witness on cross-examination admits the facts claimed to show bias or interest, it is within the trial judge's discretion to decide whether extrinsic evidence may be introduced as further proof of bias or interest.

2) Justification for Bias

Even though it is shown that a witness is biased, no evidence may be admitted to show that he was justified in his bias. This might make him look more reasonable, but is not very relevant to whether his bias might make him less credible.

c. Conviction of Crime

Under certain circumstances, a witness may be impeached by proof of conviction of a crime. [Fed. R. Evid. 609] The fact that the witness (including a defendant who testifies in a criminal case) has been convicted of a crime may usually be proved by either eliciting an admission on direct or cross-examination or by the record of conviction.

1) Actual Conviction Required

This type of impeachment requires an actual conviction of a crime. The fact that the witness has been arrested or indicted may not be elicited here.

2) Type of Crime

a) Crime Involving Dishonesty or False Statement

Under the Federal Rules, a witness's character for truthfulness may be attacked (or impeached) by *any crime* (felony or misdemeanor) if it can be readily determined that conviction of the crime required proof or admission of an act of *dishonesty* or *false statement*. Federal courts interpret this category *narrowly* to encompass only offenses in the nature of crimen falsi (e.g., perjury, false statement, criminal fraud, embezzlement, false pretense). In most cases, the statutory elements will indicate whether an act of dishonesty or false statement was required. An indictment, statement of admitted facts, or jury instructions may also be used to show that the crime required proof of such an act. The trial court has *no discretion*—not even under Federal Rule 403—to disallow impeachment by such crimes.

b) Felony Not Involving Dishonesty or False Statement

A witness's character for truthfulness may also be attacked, under the Federal Rules, by *any felony* whether or not it involves dishonesty or a false statement. However, if the felony is one that does not involve dishonesty or false statement, the trial court may exercise discretion to exclude it under one of the following standards.

(1) Accused in Criminal Case

If, in a criminal case, the witness being impeached is the accused, the felony conviction will be admitted only if the government shows that its probative value as impeachment evidence outweighs its prejudicial effect.

(2) Witness Other than Accused in Criminal Case

In the case of any witness other than the accused in a criminal case, any felony conviction is admissible, but the court retains discretion under Rule 403 to exclude it if its probative value as impeachment evidence is *substantially outweighed* by the danger of unfair prejudice.

(3) Compare the Balancing Tests

Note that under Federal Rule 609, different balancing tests apply for the exercise of discretion. If the felony conviction is offered to impeach the accused in a criminal case, the discretionary standard (*supra*) favors exclusion, since the probative value of the felony (not involving dishonesty or false statement) must outweigh prejudice. In the case of *all* other witnesses, the balancing test favors admission, since the conviction will be excluded only if the danger of prejudice substantially outweighs its probative value.

3) Must Not Be Too Remote

Under the *Federal Rules*, a conviction is usually too remote and inadmissible if *more than 10 years* have elapsed since the date of *conviction* or the date of *release* from the confinement imposed for the conviction, whichever is the later date. In extraordinary circumstances, such convictions can be admitted, but only if the trial judge determines that the probative value of the conviction substantially outweighs its prejudicial effect, and the adverse party is given notice that the conviction is to be used as impeachment. [Fed. R. Evid. 609(b)]

4) Juvenile Adjudication Generally Not Admissible

Juvenile offenses are generally not admissible for impeachment purposes. However, under the Federal Rules, a judge has the discretion in a criminal case to admit evidence of a juvenile offense committed by a witness other than the accused if the evidence would be admissible to attack the credibility of an adult and if the evidence is necessary to a determination of the accused's guilt or innocence. [Fed. R. Evid. 609(d); Davis v. Alaska, 415 U.S. 308 (1974)]

5) Effect of Pardon Depends on Basis

In most states, a conviction may be shown even though the witness has subsequently been pardoned. Under the Federal Rules, however, the conviction may not be shown if the pardon was based on innocence or if the person pardoned has not been convicted of a subsequent crime punishable by death or imprisonment in excess of one year. [Fed. R. Evid. 609(c)]

6) Pending Appeal Does Not Affect Admissibility

In most jurisdictions and under the Federal Rules, a conviction may be used to impeach even though an appeal is pending, though the pendency of the appeal may also be shown. [Fed. R. Evid. 609(e)]

7) Constitutionally Defective Conviction Invalid for All Purposes

Where the prior felony conviction was obtained in violation of the defendant's Sixth Amendment rights (e.g., to have counsel, to confront witness, etc.), the conviction is generally invalid for all purposes—including impeachment.

8) Means of Proof—Extrinsic Evidence Permitted

A prior conviction may usually be shown by either an admission on *direct or cross-examination* of the witness or by *introducing a record* of the judgment. *No foundation need be laid*. Note, however, that when a witness is being cross-examined about previous convictions, the questions must be asked in good faith (i.e., with a reasonable belief as to the existence of the conviction). Improper questioning may be grounds for a mistrial.

a) Appealing Admission of Prior Conviction Evidence

While a party as a general rule may appeal the erroneous admission of evidence of a prior conviction, she may not do so if she introduced evidence of the conviction herself.

Example: After a defendant's motion to exclude prior conviction evidence was erroneously denied, the defendant introduced evidence of the conviction during her case-in-chief to take the sting out of her impeachment on cross-examination. She will not be permitted to claim on appeal that it was error to admit evidence of the prior conviction. [Ohler v. U.S., 529 U.S. 753 (2000)]

d. Specific Instances of Misconduct—Bad Acts

1) General Rule—Interrogation Permitted

The traditional majority view is that, subject to discretionary control of the trial judge, a witness may be interrogated upon cross-examination with respect to any immoral, vicious, or criminal act of his life that may *affect his character* and show him to be *unworthy of belief*. Inquiry into "bad acts" is permitted even though the witness was never convicted. Federal Rule 608 permits such inquiry, in the discretion of the court, only if the act of misconduct is *probative of truthfulness* (i.e., is an act of deceit or lying).

2) Counsel Must Inquire in Good Faith

The cross-examiner must act in good faith with some reasonable basis for believing that the witness may have committed the "bad act" inquired about.

Example: It would be error for the prosecution to inquire about an act when the prosecutor knows that the witness has been tried for the act and acquitted.

3) Extrinsic Evidence Not Permitted

Extrinsic evidence of "bad acts" is not permitted. A specific act of misconduct, offered to attack the witness's character for truthfulness, can be elicited *only on cross-examination* of the witness. If the witness denies the act, the cross-examiner cannot refute the answer by calling other witnesses or producing other evidence. It is not usually improper for the cross-examiner, acting in good faith, to continue the cross-examination after a denial in the hope that the witness will change his answer.

4) Cannot Reference Consequences of Bad Act

Federal Rule 608(b) bars any reference during interrogation to consequences (e.g., termination of employment, discipline) the witness may have suffered as a result of his prior bad act. *Rationale:* The Advisory Note to Rule 608 explains that such a consequence is, in essence, a third person's opinion that the witness committed the act. Therefore, asking the witness about the consequence on examination is the equivalent of presenting extrinsic evidence of the act (*see* above).

Example: An attorney cannot impeach a witness with the witness's prior act of embezzlement by asking, "Weren't you fired from your last job for embezzling money?" (However, the attorney may ask, "Didn't you embezzle money from your last employer?")

e. **Opinion or Reputation Evidence of Untruthfulness**

1) **By Proof of Reputation**
A witness may be impeached by showing that she has a poor reputation for truthfulness. The usual method of impeachment is to ask other witnesses about her general reputation for truth and veracity in the community in which she lives. The modern view is to allow evidence of reputation in business circles as well as in the community in which the witness resides.

2) **By Opinion Evidence**
Most states do not allow the impeaching witness to state her opinion as to the character of a witness for truth and veracity. However, the ***Federal Rules allow*** an impeaching witness to state her personal opinions, based upon acquaintance, as to the truthfulness of the witness sought to be impeached. [Fed. R. Evid. 608(a)]

f. **Sensory Deficiencies**
A witness may be impeached by showing that he had no knowledge of the facts to which he testified, or that his faculties of perception and recollection were so impaired as to make it doubtful that he could have perceived those facts. Such a showing can be made either ***on cross-examination or by the use of extrinsic evidence***.

1) **Defects of Capacity**

a) **Perceptive Disabilities**
It is, of course, proper to show deficiencies of the senses, such as deafness or color blindness, that would have substantially impaired the witness's ability to perceive the facts to which he testifies. It may also be shown that at the time the witness observed the events his perception was temporarily diminished (e.g., that he was sleepy or under the influence of alcohol or drugs).

b) **Lack of Memory**
A witness can be impeached by showing that he has a poor memory of the events about which he testifies. This is usually done on cross-examination by asking the witness about other related matters to suggest the inference that if his memory of related matters is poor, his recollection of the events to which he is testifying is doubtful.

c) **Mental Disorders**
Psychiatric evidence of a mental disorder that would affect a witness's credibility has been admitted by some courts (particularly in sex offense cases).

2) Lack of Knowledge

a) Expert Witnesses

The credibility of an expert witness may be attacked by cross-examining him as to (i) his general knowledge of the field in which he is claiming to be an expert, and (ii) his particular knowledge of the facts upon which his opinion is based.

b) Opinion Witnesses

The credibility of an opinion witness may be attacked by showing lack of knowledge. For example, a witness who gives opinion evidence on the value of land may be cross-examined regarding her knowledge of land values and may be asked about sales of other land.

c) Character Witnesses

As discussed earlier, when a character witness testifies to the good character of another (e.g., a defendant), the witness may be cross-examined regarding the basis of his statement that the defendant's character is good. In other words, the testimony of the character witness may be discredited by asking him about specific criminal or immoral acts committed by the defendant, on the theory that if the witness has no knowledge of these acts, he does not really know the defendant's character. [Fed. R. Evid. 405(a)]

In most courts, a character witness may testify only as to *reputation*. Therefore, on cross-examination, the only acceptable form of question is: "Have you *heard* that the defendant . . . ?" However, under the Federal Rules and in modern jurisdictions that permit character witnesses to testify as to their *opinions* of character, questions in the form, "Do you *know* . . . ?" would be proper.

g. Contradictory Facts

Extrinsic evidence of facts that contradict a witness's testimony may sometimes be admitted to suggest that a witness's mistake or lie on one point indicates erroneous or false testimony as to the whole. Extrinsic evidence of contradictory facts to impeach is permitted: (i) where the witness's testimony on a particular fact is a *material issue* in the case, (ii) where the testimony on a particular fact is *significant on the issue of credibility*, or (iii) where the witness volunteers testimony about a *subject as to which the opposing party would otherwise be precluded from offering* evidence. However, as discussed in 4., below, extrinsic evidence is not permitted to prove contradictory facts that are *collateral*, i.e., not relevant to any material issue in the case or insignificant on the issue of credibility.

Example: A defendant charged with cocaine possession testifies that he has never in his life handled or come into contact with illegal narcotics of any kind. The defendant could be impeached with extrinsic evidence that he was seen purchasing marijuana on two occasions prior to the cocaine incident.

4. Impeachment on Collateral Matter

Where a witness makes a statement not directly relevant to the issues in the case, the rule against impeachment (other than by cross-examination) on a collateral matter applies to bar the opponent from proving the statement untrue either by extrinsic contradictory facts or by a prior inconsistent statement. The purpose of the rule is to avoid the possibility of unfair surprise, confusion of issues, and undue consumption of time resulting from the attempt to prove and disprove facts that are not directly relevant.

Example: Plaintiff's witness testifies, "I saw the defendant run a red light on the way home from a video arcade." The witness could be impeached with extrinsic evidence that the defendant had a green light, but it would be "collateral" for the defendant to show that the witness was on his way home from a pool hall rather than a video arcade. It would not be "collateral," however, to show that the witness was on his way home from a dinner at the plaintiff's house, because that suggests **bias**, which is a separate basis for impeachment (*see* 3.b., *supra*).

5. Impeachment of Hearsay Declarant

There are many occasions in which out-of-court statements are admitted into evidence by means of exceptions and limitations to the general rule excluding hearsay. These statements are frequently admitted into evidence, even though the person who made the statement (the declarant) does not testify at the trial. The party against whom the statement has been admitted may wish to impeach the credibility of the declarant so that the jury will discount or assign less probative value to the statement. Under Federal Rule 806, the credibility of a declarant may be attacked (and if attacked, may be supported) by evidence that would be admissible if the declarant had testified as a witness. Of course, the declarant need not be given the opportunity to explain or deny prior inconsistent statements. In addition, the party against whom the out-of-court statement was offered may call the declarant as a witness and cross-examine him about the statement.

6. Rehabilitation

A witness who has been impeached may be rehabilitated on redirect examination or by extrinsic evidence.

a. Explanation on Redirect

For purposes of rehabilitation, the witness on redirect examination may explain or clarify facts brought out on cross-examination.

Example: A witness testifying for the prosecution in an organized crime murder trial admitted to making a prior inconsistent statement. On redirect, the witness is permitted to explain that he gave a prior untruthful statement favoring the defendant out of fear of being killed by the defendant's gang.

b. Good Reputation for Truthfulness

When the witness's general character for truthfulness and veracity has been attacked, the party for whom the impeached witness has testified may call other witnesses to testify to the good reputation for truthfulness of the impeached witness or to give their opinion as to the truthfulness of the impeached witness.

c. Prior Consistent Statement

1) **Generally Not Permitted**
A party may not ordinarily rehabilitate a witness by showing a prior consistent statement because it seldom enhances credibility.

2) **Exceptions**

a) **To Rebut Charge of Fabrication Based on Improper Motive**
Where the opposing counsel has impeached the credibility of a witness by making an express or an implied charge that the witness is lying or exaggerating because of some improper motive, counsel may introduce into evidence a prior consistent statement made by the witness *before* the onset of the alleged motive.
Example: Defense attorney intimated on cross-examination that the prosecution witness was biased against his client because of a fight they recently had. The prosecutor may introduce evidence of a statement the witness made, consistent with his testimony, before the fight occurred.

b) **When Witness Impeached on Other Non-Character Ground**
Where the opposing counsel has impeached the credibility of a witness on some non-character ground *other* than a charge of recent motive to lie or exaggerate (e.g., an alleged inconsistency or sensory deficiency), counsel may introduce into evidence a prior consistent statement made by the witness if, under the circumstances, it has a special tendency to rehabilitate the witness's credibility. Note, however, that a prior consistent statement cannot be used to rehabilitate a witness whose general character for truthfulness has been impeached (i.e., by criminal convictions, acts of misconduct, or reputation or opinion testimony regarding the witness's untruthfulness).
Examples: 1) On direct examination, a police officer testified that she was able to single out the defendant because of a prominent scar on the defendant's forehead. On cross-examination, defense counsel intimated that the officer's testimony was not credible because she made no mention of the scar in a handwritten report made immediately after the defendant's arrest. The prosecutor may introduce evidence that three days after the arrest, the officer included a statement about the scar in her formal typewritten report, because this tends to demonstrate that the omission in the handwritten report—the alleged inconsistency—was an insignificant oversight.

2) On direct examination, a witness testified that the defendant's car ran the red light. On cross-examination, defense counsel intimated that the witness's memory was faulty because, one year after the accident, the witness began treatment for a mental disorder that can affect one's memory. To rebut the insinuation of faulty memory, the plaintiff's counsel may introduce evidence that the witness told the police a few days after the accident that the defendant's car ran the red light.

3) Also Admissible as Substantive Evidence

Under Federal Rule of Evidence 801(d)(1)(B), a prior consistent statement that is admissible to rehabilitate a witness's credibility (as described in 2), above) is also admissible as substantive evidence of the truth of its contents. (*See* VII.B.1.b., *infra.*)

F. OBJECTIONS, EXCEPTIONS, OFFERS OF PROOF

1. Objections

Unless an objection is made by opposing counsel, almost any kind of evidence will be admitted. Failure to object is deemed a *waiver* of any ground for objection. The trial judge need not raise grounds for objection on her own, but may take notice of plain errors affecting substantial rights (e.g., admission of coerced confession not objected to by defense).

a. Objections to Trial Testimony

Objections should be made after the question, but before the answer, if it is apparent that the question calls for inadmissible matter (e.g., hearsay) or that the question is in improper form (e.g., leading). Otherwise, a motion to strike must be made as soon as the witness's answer emerges as inadmissible (e.g., "Q: What color was the automobile? A: My sister told me it was gray.").

b. Objections to Deposition Testimony

Objections to the *form* of a question (e.g., leading) are waived unless made during the deposition, thereby affording counsel an opportunity to correct the form of his question. An objection based on a *testimonial privilege* should also be made then, lest it be deemed waived. However, objections going to the substance of a question or answer (e.g., relevance, hearsay) can be postponed until the deposition is offered in evidence.

c. Specificity of Objections

An objection may be either *general* ("I object") or *specific* ("Object, hearsay"). The importance of whether an objection is general or specific lies in the extent to which each type preserves the evidentiary issue on appeal. The following rules apply:

1) General Objection Sustained

If a general objection is sustained and the evidence excluded, the ruling will be upheld on appeal if there was *any ground* for the objection. In the absence of specificity in the trial court, it will be assumed that the ruling was placed upon the right ground.

2) General Objection Overruled

If a general objection is overruled and the evidence admitted, the objection is not available on appeal unless the evidence was *not admissible under any circumstances* for any purpose.

3) Specific Objection Sustained

If a specific objection is sustained and the evidence is excluded, the ruling will be upheld on appeal only if the ground stated was the correct one, unless the evidence excluded was not competent and could not be made so.

d. **"Opening the Door"**
   One who introduces evidence on a particular subject thereby asserts its relevance and cannot complain, except on grounds other than relevance, if his adversary thereafter offers evidence on the same subject. And counsel need not "stand" on his overruled relevance objection; he can offer counterevidence without thereby abandoning his relevance objection.

  e. **Rule of Completeness—Writings and Recorded Statements**
   Where a party introduces part or all of a writing or recorded statement, an adverse party may require the introduction of *any other part—or any related writing or recorded statement*—that in fairness ought to be considered at the same time. [Fed. R. Evid. 106] The party who introduced the original writing or recorded statement cannot object to the introduction of the additional evidence on the ground of lack of competency or hearsay, etc.

  f. **Motion to Strike—Unresponsive Answers**
   Unresponsive answers are subject to a motion to strike by examining counsel, but not by opposing counsel. Examining counsel, in other words, can "adopt" an unresponsive answer if it is not objectionable on some other ground.

2. **Exceptions**
 The common law rule requiring a party to "except" from an adverse trial court ruling in order to preserve the issue for appeal has been abolished in most jurisdictions. In some states, however, a written motion for a new trial, specifying the grounds, may be required.

3. **Offers of Proof**
 On some occasions, error cannot be based on exclusion of evidence unless there has been an "offer of proof" that discloses the nature, purpose, and admissibility of the rejected evidence. There are three types of "offers of proof."

  a. **Witness Offer**
   Subsequent to a sustained objection by opposing counsel, the examining counsel proceeds with his examination of a witness on the stand, out of the jury's hearing, thus making his record by the question-and-answer method.

  b. **Lawyer Offer**
   Counsel himself states, in narrative form, what the witness would have testified had he been permitted to do so. The "witness offer" is generally preferred to the "lawyer offer" and can be required by the trial court, especially if opposing counsel denies that the witness would testify as narrated.

  c. **Tangible Offer**
   A marked, authenticated, and offered item of tangible evidence is its own offer of proof.

G. **TESTIMONIAL PRIVILEGES**
 Testimonial privileges, which permit one to refuse to disclose and prohibit others from disclosing certain sorts of confidential information in judicial proceedings, have two basic reasons for their existence: (i) *practicality*, and (ii) society's desire to *encourage certain relationships* by ensuring their confidentiality, even at the high price of losing valuable information.

Some of the testimonial privileges are frankly grounded on hardheaded practicality. The particular kind of disclosure could not be obtained, as a practical matter, even if there were no privilege. Many priests, even when confronted by a contempt of court citation, would refuse to breach the priest-penitent relationship. Society values some relationships sufficiently that it is willing to protect their confidential nature even at the expense of the loss of information relevant to the issues of a lawsuit. These relationships will be encouraged if confidentiality, when desired, is assured. To put it more concretely, persons might forgo needed medical attention or be less than candid with legal counsel were there no guarantee that communications made during the physician-patient and attorney-client relationships would be accorded confidential status in legal proceedings.

1.   Federal Common Law Privileges

The Federal Rules have no specific privilege provisions. Federal Rule 501 provides that the privilege of a witness or person shall be governed by the principles of the common law as they may be interpreted by the courts of the United States in the light of reason and experience. Federal courts currently recognize:

a.   The *attorney-client* privilege;

b.   *Spousal immunity*;

c.   The privilege for *confidential marital communications*;

d.   The *psychotherapist/social worker-client* privilege;

e.   The *clergy-penitent* privilege; and

f.   *Governmental* privileges.

Note, however, that in civil actions when state law supplies the rule of decision as to an element of a claim or defense, the state law applies with respect to testimonial privileges as well. Thus, in *diversity* cases, the *state law of privilege applies*.

2.   General Considerations

a.   Persons Who May Assert a Privilege

A privilege is personal, and may be asserted only by the party whose interest is sought to be protected or by someone authorized to assert it on the holder's behalf (e.g., guardian of incompetent holder). If the privilege is held by more than one person, each of them can claim the privilege. In certain cases, the person with whom the confidence was shared may claim it on the holder's behalf.

b.   Confidentiality

To be privileged, a communication must be shown to have been made in confidence. Many states, however, recognize a presumption that any disclosures made in the course of a relationship for which a privilege exists were made in confidence.

c.   Comment on Privilege Forbidden

No inference should be drawn from the fact that a witness has claimed a privilege. Thus, counsel for the parties and the judge are not permitted to make any comment or argument based on a claim of privilege.

d. Waiver

All types of privileges are waived by the following:

(i) *Failure to claim the privilege* by the holder herself or failure to object when privileged testimony is offered;

(ii) *Voluntary disclosure* of the privileged matter by the holder (or someone else with the holder's consent) unless the disclosure is also privileged; or

(iii) A *contractual provision* waiving in advance the right to claim a privilege.

A privilege is not waived where someone wrongfully disclosed information without the holder's consent. Similarly, a waiver of the privilege by one joint holder does not affect the right of another joint holder to claim the privilege.

e. Eavesdroppers

A privilege based on confidential communications is not abrogated because the communication is overheard by someone whose presence is unknown to the parties; i.e., the privilege still applies to the parties to the confidential communication. There is some question, however, as to whether the eavesdropper may testify. The traditional view is that the eavesdropper may testify to what he has overheard. But a significant number of modern cases and statutes assert that as long as the holder of the privilege was not negligent, there is no waiver of the privilege, and the eavesdropper is also prohibited from testifying.

3. Attorney-Client Privilege

The first testimonial privilege ever established was the attorney-client privilege. It is a common law privilege, although in some jurisdictions it has now been codified by statute. It carries with it fewer exceptions than any other privilege.

Essentially, communications between an attorney and client, made during professional consultation, are privileged from disclosure. In other words, a client has a privilege to refuse to disclose, and to prevent others from disclosing, confidential communications between herself (or her representative) and her attorney (or her attorney's representative). Objects and preexisting documents are not protected.

a. Attorney-Client Relationship

The attorney-client privilege requires that the attorney-client relationship exist at the time of the communications. The client, or her representative, must be seeking the professional services of the attorney at the crucial time. But note that retainer negotiations, involving disclosures made before the attorney has decided to accept or decline the case, are covered if the other requirements of the privilege are present.

1) Client

A "client," in the context of the typical formulation of the attorney-client privilege, can be an individual private citizen, a public officer, a corporation, or any other organization or entity, public or private, seeking professional legal services.

2) Representative of Client

A "representative of a client" is one having the ***authority to obtain legal services or to act on advice*** rendered by an attorney, on behalf of the client.

3) Attorney

An "attorney" is any person who is authorized or, in many jurisdictions, who is ***reasonably believed*** by the client to be authorized, to practice law in any state or nation.

4) Representative of Attorney

A "representative of an attorney" is one employed by the attorney to assist in the rendition of professional services, e.g., a clerk or secretary.

5) Corporation as Client

A corporation, as indicated above, can be a "client" within the meaning of the attorney-client privilege. The statements of ***any corporate officials or employees*** made to the attorney are protected if they were authorized or directed by the corporation to make such statements.

b. Confidential Communication

A communication is "confidential" if it was not intended to be disclosed to third persons, other than those to whom disclosure would be in furtherance of the rendition of legal services to the client or those who are necessary for the transmission of the communication. Communications made in the known presence and hearing of a stranger are not privileged.

1) Communications Through Agents

Communications made to third persons are confidential, and thus covered by the attorney-client privilege, if necessary to transmit information between the attorney and client. Examples include: communications by the client to the attorney's secretary or messenger; information (not documents) given to the attorney by the client's accountant; communications between the client's liability insurer and the attorney; and communications through an interpreter.

a) Examination by Doctor

When a client is examined by a doctor at the attorney's request, the communications involved between the client and doctor (and the doctor and attorney) are not covered by the physician-patient privilege because no treatment is contemplated. These communications are, however, covered by the attorney-client privilege because the examination is necessary to help the client communicate her condition to the attorney. Note that this privilege would be waived if the doctor were later called as an expert witness by the same client.

Example: P, a pedestrian, was struck by a car driven by D. P employs Attorney to bring a negligence suit against D to recover for the physical injuries P suffered in the accident. Attorney sends P to Dr. Z for an evaluation of the extent and permanence of P's injuries. Attorney does not intend to call Dr. Z as an expert witness at trial. At trial, D's attorney, believing that P may have admitted to some negligence of his own when describing his injury, calls Dr. Z to testify to his examination of P. If P objects, claiming attorney-client privilege, he may prevent Dr. Z from testifying.

2) No Privilege Where Attorney Acts for Both Parties

Where an attorney acts for both parties to a transaction, no privilege can be invoked in a lawsuit between the two parties (they obviously did not desire and could not expect confidentiality as between themselves in a joint consultation), but the *privilege can be claimed* in a suit between either or both of the two parties and *third persons* (multiple parties can desire and expect confidentiality as against the outside world).

c. Client as Holder of Privilege

The privilege, if it exists, can be claimed by the client, her guardian or conservator, the personal representative of a deceased client, or the successor, trustee, or similar representative of a corporation, association, etc. The person who was the attorney at the time of the communication can claim the privilege, but only on behalf of the client. The attorney's authority to do this is presumed in the absence of any evidence to the contrary.

d. Duration of Privilege

The attorney-client privilege applies indefinitely. Termination of the attorney-client *relationship* does not terminate the privilege. The privilege even continues to apply after the client's death. *Rationale:* Knowing that communications will remain confidential even after death encourages the client to communicate fully and frankly with her attorney. [Swidler & Berlin v. United States, 524 U.S. 399 (1998)]

e. Nonapplicability of the Privilege

There are four significant exceptions to the application of the attorney-client privilege:

1) Legal Advice in Aid of Future Wrongdoing

There is no privilege if the services of the attorney were sought or obtained as an aid in the planning or actual commission of something that the *client knew, or should have known, was a crime or a fraud*.

2) Claimants Through Same Deceased Client

There is no privilege regarding a communication relevant to an issue between parties, all of whom claim through the same deceased client—regardless of whether the claims are by testate or intestate succession or by inter vivos transaction.

3) Dispute Between Attorney and Client

There is no privilege for a communication that is relevant to an issue of *breach of duty* by the attorney to his client (malpractice) or by the client to her attorney (e.g., client's failure to pay her attorney's fee for professional services).

4) Client Puts Legal Advice in Issue

There is no privilege where the client asserts a claim or defense that puts the legal services at issue in the case. For example, a defendant who argues that she is not liable because she was following her attorney's advice must disclose the advice.

f.   Waiver of the Privilege

The privilege belongs solely to the client and she alone can waive it. If the client chooses to waive the privilege, her attorney may be compelled to testify.

g.   Attorney's Work Product

Documents prepared by an attorney for his *own use* in prosecuting his client's case are not protected by the attorney-client privilege. However, they may be protected by the attorney's "work product" rule. In *Hickman v. Taylor*, 329 U.S. 495 (1947), the United States Supreme Court held that the work product of a lawyer—in that case, statements of interviews with potential witnesses—is not subject to discovery except in cases of necessity.

h.   Limitations on Waiver of Attorney-Client Privilege and Work Product Rule

Federal Rule of Evidence 502 allows parties to disclose privileged material without risking waiver of the attorney-client privilege and work product rule as to undisclosed material. Additionally, the rule protects against waiver when the disclosure is the result of an innocent mistake.

1)   Disclosure in Federal Proceeding

A voluntary disclosure of privileged material made in a federal proceeding operates as a waiver of the attorney-client privilege or work product protection *only with respect to the disclosed material*. The waiver *does not* extend to undisclosed privileged material *unless*: (i) the waiver is *intentional*, (ii) both the disclosed and undisclosed material concern the *same subject matter*, and (iii) fairness dictates that all the material should be considered together *to avoid a misleading presentation of evidence*. [Fed. R. Evid. 502(a)] If the disclosure was *inadvertent* and the holder took reasonable steps to prevent disclosure and rectify the error (e.g., attempting to retrieve the mistakenly disclosed material), then there is *no waiver*. [Fed. R. Evid. 502(a), (b)]

2)   Disclosure in State Proceeding

A disclosure of privileged material made in a state proceeding is not an effective waiver in a subsequent federal proceeding if: (i) the disclosure would not operate as a waiver if it had been made in a federal proceeding, or (ii) the disclosure is not a waiver under that state's law. [Fed. R. Evid. 502(c)]

4.   Physician-Patient Privilege

The physician-patient privilege is a statutory privilege, which has not been adopted in all jurisdictions. However, in a substantial number of jurisdictions, a physician (and, in some jurisdictions, a dentist or nurse) is foreclosed from divulging in judicial proceedings information that he acquired while attending a patient in a professional capacity, which information was necessary to enable the physician to act in his professional capacity.

a.   Elements of Physician-Patient Privilege

1) **Professional Member of Relationship Must Be Present**
   If the professional member of the relationship is not present for purposes of treatment, and that fact is known to the patient, the relationship does not exist and no privilege attaches.

2) **Information Must Be Acquired While Attending Patient**
   The information must be acquired while attending the patient in the course of treatment; the privilege does not apply to information obtained by the professional in some other way.

3) **Information Must Be Necessary for Treatment**
   If information given by the patient deals with a nonmedical matter (e.g., details of an accident), the information is not privileged. Physicians have also been held competent to testify regarding facts that a lay witness might observe which are not induced by the professional relationship, such as the observable fact that the patient was ill, dates of treatment, or description of clothing worn by the patient.
   Example: A treating physician who removed the clothing of an unconscious accident victim will be permitted to testify that a heroin packet fell out of the patient's right sock.

b. **Nonapplicability of the Privilege**
   There are many exceptions and implied waivers of the physician-patient privilege, and the privilege is of little importance as a result. The privilege does not apply (or is impliedly waived) in the following situations:

1) **Patient Puts Physical Condition in Issue**
   The physician-patient privilege is not applicable in those situations creating the largest number of litigated cases, since a person cannot invoke the privilege where he himself has put his physical condition in issue, e.g., where he sues for personal injuries.

2) **In Aid of Wrongdoing**
   Like the attorney-client privilege, there is no privilege if the physician's services were sought or obtained in aid of the planning or commission of a crime or tort, or to escape detection or apprehension after the commission of a crime or tort.

3) **Dispute Between Physician and Patient**
   There is no privilege regarding a communication relevant to an issue of breach, by the physician or by the patient, of a duty arising out of the physician-patient relationship, e.g., malpractice, failure to pay one's bill.

4) **Agreement to Waive the Privilege**
   The patient may agree by contract (e.g., life insurance policy) to waive the privilege.

5) **Federal Cases Applying Federal Law of Privilege**
   In cases where state law does not supply the rule of privilege (i.e., most federal question cases), the federal courts *do not recognize* any physician-patient privilege. They do, however, recognize a psychotherapist-client privilege (*see* below).

c. **Criminal Proceedings**

There is a split of authority as to the applicability of the physician-patient privilege in criminal proceedings. In some states, the privilege applies in both civil and criminal cases. In a number of others, it cannot be invoked in criminal cases generally. In still other states, the privilege is denied in felony cases, and in a few states, it is denied only in homicide cases. Note that where a psychiatrist is involved, however, the applicable privilege is the psychotherapist-client privilege (below), which is more widely accepted in all proceedings than the physician-patient privilege.

d. **Patient Holds the Privilege**

The privilege belongs to the patient, and he may decide to claim or waive it.

5. **Psychotherapist/Social Worker-Client Privilege**

The United States Supreme Court recognizes a federal privilege for communications between a psychotherapist (psychiatrist or psychologist) or licensed social worker and his client. [Jaffee v. Redmond, 518 U.S. 1 (1996)—confidential communications between police officer and licensed social worker following a shooting were privileged] Thus, the federal courts and virtually all of the states recognize a privilege for this type of confidential communication. In most particulars, this privilege operates in the same manner as the attorney-client privilege (*supra*).

6. **Privileges Related to Marriage**

Under the early rule, spouses were absolutely incompetent to testify for or against each other during the period of marriage, and this incompetency had the same effect as the Dead Man Acts—neither spouse could speak out in court if the other spouse was a party. The prohibition against spousal testimony in favor of the party-spouse has been abandoned. However, there remains a rule of spousal immunity whereby a married person may not be compelled to testify *against* her spouse in a criminal case. Apart from this rule, a separate privilege exists in most jurisdictions that protects confidential communications during marriage. Thus, there are two separate privileges as follows: (i) the privilege not to testify against a spouse in a criminal case—spousal immunity, and (ii) the privilege for confidential marital communications.

a. **Spousal Immunity—Privilege Not to Testify in Criminal Cases**

When the privilege of spousal immunity is invoked, a married person whose spouse is the defendant in a criminal case *may not be called as a witness by the prosecution*, and a married person *may not be compelled to testify* against his spouse in *any* criminal proceeding. (This second part of the privilege exists even where the spouse is not a defendant, such as in grand jury proceedings.) The purpose of this immunity is to protect the marital relationship from the disruption that would follow from allowing one spouse to testify against the other.

1) **Federal Courts—Privilege Belongs to Witness-Spouse**

In federal courts, only the witness-spouse may invoke the privilege against adverse spousal testimony. Thus, one spouse *may* testify against the other in criminal cases, with or without the consent of the party-spouse, but the witness-spouse may not be compelled to testify, nor may she be foreclosed from testifying (except as to confidential communications, *infra*). [*See* Trammel v. United States, 445 U.S. 40 (1980)] Some states (e.g., California) follow the federal view.

2) Some State Courts—Privilege Belongs to Party-Spouse

In some state courts, the privilege belongs to the party-spouse. Thus the witness-spouse may not be compelled to testify, and she may be foreclosed from testifying if the party-spouse asserts the privilege.

3) Valid Marriage Required

There must be a valid marriage for the privilege to exist. No privilege exists if the marriage is void (e.g., because it is incestuous, bigamous, or a sham).

4) Immunity May Be Asserted Only During Marriage

The privilege lasts only during the marriage and terminates upon divorce or annulment. If a marriage exists, the privilege can be asserted even as to matters that took place *before* the marriage. Remember, however, that in federal court the privilege belongs to the witness. Therefore, an accused cannot use marriage to silence a federal court witness.

b. Privilege for Confidential Marital Communications

In any civil or criminal case, either spouse, whether or not a party, has a privilege to refuse to disclose, and to prevent another from disclosing, a confidential communication made between the spouses while they were married. The rationale is to encourage open communication and trust and confidence between spouses.

1) Both Spouses Hold Privilege

Both spouses jointly hold this privilege, and either can refuse to disclose the communication or prevent any other person from disclosing the confidential communication.

2) Elements of the Privilege

a) Marital Relationship

The communication must be made during a valid marriage. Divorce will *not* terminate the privilege retroactively, but communications after divorce are not privileged.

b) Reliance upon Intimacy

The communication must be made in reliance upon the intimacy of the marital relationship. Routine exchanges of a business nature, abusive language, and misconduct directed to the spouse are not privileged. If the communication was made in the *known* presence of a stranger, it is not privileged. The confidential communication need not be spoken but may be made by conduct intended as a communication.

c. Nonapplicability of Privileges

Neither the spousal immunity nor the confidential marital communications privilege applies in legal actions between the spouses; in cases involving crimes against the testifying spouse or either spouse's children (e.g., assault and battery, incest, bigamy, child abuse, etc.); or to communications in furtherance of a joint crime or fraud.

7. Privilege Against Self-Incrimination

Under the Fifth Amendment of the United States Constitution, a witness cannot be compelled to testify against himself. (For full discussion, *see* Criminal Procedure outline.) Thus, any witness may refuse to answer any question whose answer might incriminate him, and a criminal defendant may use the privilege to refuse to take the witness stand at all. The privilege belongs to the witness; a party cannot assert it on the witness's behalf.

a. "Incriminating" Defined

Testimony is incriminating if it ties the witness to the commission of a ***crime*** or would furnish a lead to evidence tying the witness to a crime; the testimony need not prove guilt. [Hoffman v. United States, 341 U.S. 479 (1951)] A witness cannot refuse to answer because of exposure to civil liability; it must be to avoid ***criminal*** liability.

b. When Privilege Applies

The privilege can be claimed at any state or federal proceeding, whether civil or criminal, at which the witness's appearance and testimony are compelled (e.g., by subpoena). The privilege can be invoked only by natural persons, not corporations or associations.

8. Clergy-Penitent Privilege

A person has a privilege to refuse to disclose, and to prevent others from disclosing, a confidential communication by the person to a member of the clergy in the clergy member's capacity as a spiritual adviser. A member of the clergy can be a minister, priest, rabbi, or other similar functionary of a religious organization, or reasonably believed to be so by the person consulting him. This common law privilege is very similar in its operation to the attorney-client privilege, *supra*.

9. Accountant-Client Privilege

This is a statutory privilege, found in a number of jurisdictions, which is similar to the attorney-client privilege, *supra*.

10. Professional Journalist Privilege

Whether a journalist may be forced to divulge her sources of information has been a much-litigated question and the subject of a trend of statutory authority. The Supreme Court has held that there is no constitutional protection for a journalist's source of information, so the existence of the privilege is ***limited to individual state statutes***, which have been recently growing in number.

Less than half of the states have enacted statutes protecting the journalist's source of information, and the protection ranges from an absolute privilege to one qualified by the need for disclosure in the public interest.

11. Governmental Privileges

a. Identity of Informer

The federal government, or a state or subdivision of a state, generally has a privilege to refuse to disclose the identity of a person who has furnished to a law enforcement officer information purporting to reveal the commission of a crime.

1) **Privilege Claimed by Government**
   The privilege can be claimed by an appropriate representative of the government, such as a prosecutor.

2) **No Privilege If Identity Otherwise Voluntarily Disclosed**
   No privilege exists if the identity of the informer or his interest in the subject matter of his communication has been voluntarily disclosed by a holder of the privilege, such as a prosecutor, or if the informer appears as a witness in the case.

3) **Judge May Dismiss If Informer's Testimony Crucial**
   If the government elects not to disclose the identity of an informer and there is a reasonable probability that the informer could provide testimony necessary to the fair determination of guilt or innocence, the judge, on his own motion or that of the accused, must dismiss the proceedings.

   b. **Official Information**
   This is a general catch-all privilege that attaches to certain communications made *by or to public officials*. Official information has been defined as information not open to the public, relating to the internal affairs of the government or its subdivisions. It applies to some fairly low-level communications made by or to officials (e.g., a judge's communications to his law clerk).

H. EXCLUSION AND SEQUESTRATION OF WITNESSES

Upon a party's request, the trial judge *must* order witnesses excluded from the courtroom so they cannot listen to the testimony of other witnesses. [Fed. R. Evid. 615] The trial judge may also do this on his own motion. However, Federal Rule 615 prohibits the exclusion of: (i) a *party* or a designated officer or employee of a party, (ii) a person whose *presence is essential* to the presentation of a party's claim or defense, or (iii) a person *statutorily authorized* to be present.

I. WITNESSES EXAMINED OR CALLED BY THE COURT

The court may examine any witness called by any party. Furthermore, the court may call a witness on its own or at a party's request. Each party is entitled to cross-examine the court's witness. *A party may object* to the court's examining or calling a witness either at that time or at the next opportunity when the jury is not present (to spare counsel the potential embarrassment of objecting to the judge's questions in front of the jury). [Fed. R. Evid. 614]

VII. THE HEARSAY RULE

A. STATEMENT OF THE RULE

The Federal Rules define hearsay as a statement, other than one made by the declarant while testifying at the current trial or hearing, offered in evidence to prove the truth of the matter asserted. [Fed. R. Evid. 801(c)] The rule against hearsay is probably the most important exclusionary rule of evidence. If a statement is hearsay, and no exception to the rule is applicable, the evidence must be excluded upon appropriate objection to its admission. [Fed. R. Evid. 802]

1. Reason for Excluding Hearsay

The reason for excluding hearsay is that the adverse party was *denied the opportunity to cross-examine the declarant*; i.e., the party had no chance to test the declarant's perception (how well did she observe the event she purported to describe), her memory (did she really remember the details she related), her sincerity (was she deliberately falsifying), and her ability to relate (did she really mean to say what now appears to be the thrust of her statement).

a. Cross-Examination of Declarant

Note that it is the declarant who made the statement that the adverse party was not able to cross-examine. Of course, the adverse party can cross-examine the witness who repeats the statement, but this does not help much where all the witness does is repeat a statement as to which the party needs to cross-examine the original declarant.

If W (witness on the stand) testifies as to what D (declarant making out-of-court statement) said about an event, and D's statement is *offered for its truth*, then the opportunity to cross-examine W is not enough. The party against whom W testifies has *no opportunity to test* the perception, the memory, the articulateness, or the veracity of D, the very witness whose account of the event the jury is being asked to believe. Of course, W is available for cross-examination, but W is only repeating what D said, and W is of little help in the attempt to question the accuracy of D's version.

b. Cross-Examination at Time Statement Made

Note too that the *declarant and witness can be the same person*. For example, a witness might state, "I don't remember anything about the accident, but I do remember that later that day I said to my wife, 'the black car went through the red light.'" Since the adverse party could not cross-examine the witness-declarant as to his perception, memory, sincerity, or ability to relate at the time the statement was made, the statement is hearsay. It is *contemporaneous* cross-examination that is required.

2. "Statement"

For purposes of the hearsay rule, a "statement" is a person's (i) oral or written assertion, or (ii) nonverbal conduct intended as an assertion. [Fed. R. Evid. 801(a)]

a. Oral Statements

"Statement" includes oral statements (i.e., where the witness testifies that somebody said " . . . ").

b. Writings

Any written document that is offered in evidence constitutes a "statement" for hearsay purposes.

c. Assertive Conduct

Conduct intended by the actor to be a substitute for words (e.g., the nod of the declarant's head indicating yes) is a "statement" within the meaning of the hearsay rule.

d. Nonassertive Conduct

Under the traditional common law definition of hearsay, "statement" included nonassertive conduct—sometimes called "Morgan hearsay." Nonassertive conduct is conduct the declarant *did not intend as an assertion* but which is being offered as an assertion.

However, under modern codes and the Federal Rules, evidence of nonassertive conduct is not hearsay. The rationale is that the likelihood of fabrication is less with nonassertive conduct than with assertive or verbal conduct.

Examples: 1) Consider the conduct of a deceased sea captain who, after examining every part of a ship, embarked on it with his family, when his conduct is being introduced on the question of the seaworthiness of the vessel. Although the sea captain did not intend his embarking on the vessel to serve as an assertion of anything, his conduct can be used to imply that he thought the ship was seaworthy and, since he knew his business, that the ship was in fact seaworthy.

2) Similarly, the fact that a doctor treated a person for plague is nonassertive conduct by the doctor that could be used to show that the person had plague.

3. "Offered to Prove the Truth of the Matter"

This is the most crucial component of the hearsay rule. The basic reason for rejecting hearsay evidence is that a statement offered to prove that which it asserts is true may not be trustworthy without the guarantees of cross-examination. However, where the out-of-court statement is introduced for any purpose other than to prove the truth of the matter asserted, there is no need to cross-examine the declarant, and so the statement is not hearsay.

Example: The witness on the stand testifies, "On April 2, Decla said to me, 'Yesterday I was in Buffalo.'" If the issue is whether Decla was in Buffalo on April 1, the testimony is hearsay. It is *not* hearsay if the issue is whether on April 2, Decla was capable of talking. On the latter issue, it is enough to cross-examine the witness.

The following are other examples of out-of-court statements that are not hearsay.

a. Verbal Acts or Legally Operative Facts

There are certain utterances to which the law attaches legal significance (e.g., words of contract, defamation, bribery, cancellation, permission). Evidence of such statements (sometimes called "legally operative facts") is not hearsay because the issue is simply whether the statements were made.

Examples: 1) In an action on a *contract*, words that constitute the offer, acceptance, rejection, etc., are not hearsay because they are offered only to prove what was said, and not that it was true.

2) Similarly, in a *defamation* action, the statement alleged to be a slander or libel may be admissible as nonhearsay. Thus if D said, "X is a thief," X will introduce D's statement not to show its truth—that he himself is a thief—but merely to show that the actionable statement was made.

b. Statements Offered to Show Effect on Listener or Reader

A statement that is inadmissible hearsay to prove the truth of the statement may nevertheless be admitted to show the statement's effect on the listener or reader.

Examples: 1) In a ***negligence case*** where knowledge of a danger is the issue, a third person's statement of warning is admissible for the limited purpose of showing ***knowledge or notice*** on the part of a listener. Thus, a statement to the defendant driver, "Your tire is about to burst," is admissible to show that the defendant had notice of the possible danger. Of course, it is inadmissible hearsay to show that the statement was true—i.e., that there was in fact a defect or dangerous condition.

2) H is on trial for the stabbing murder of W. H claims the killing was done by a bushy-haired, one-armed man whom H saw fleeing the scene. Policeman, P, testifies for the prosecution that H was arrested immediately after the killing and that a letter was found in H's possession. The letter states, "Your wife has been having an affair with your neighbor, Mr. Gigolo, for the last five years. Wise up!" The letter was signed, "A friend." Prosecutor offers this letter to establish H's motive for killing W. Is the letter hearsay? No! True, the letter is an out-of-court statement of "friend." But it is not offered to prove the truth of its contents. The letter is relevant to the issue of ***motive*** and would still be relevant to motive if, in fact, W had been faithful. The letter, true or not, is offered to show the probable effect it had on H when he read it.

c. **Statements Offered as Circumstantial Evidence of Declarant's State of Mind**
Statements by a declarant that serve as circumstantial evidence of the declarant's state of mind are not hearsay. Such statements are not offered to prove the truth of the matters asserted but only that the declarant ***believed*** them to be true. The most common examples of this type of nonhearsay are evidence of ***insanity*** and evidence of ***knowledge***.

Examples: 1) In a proceeding where the declarant's sanity is in issue, evidence is offered to show that the declarant had stated out of court, "I am John the Baptist." This statement would not be introduced as proof of its truth, but rather as circumstantial evidence of the declarant's insanity.

2) Evidence that before an accident an automobile driver stated, "My brakes are defective," is not admissible to prove that the brakes were defective, but is admissible to show that the declarant believed the brakes were defective but drove the car anyway.

1) **Compare—State of Mind Exception**
Statements that reflect directly (rather than circumstantially) on the declarant's state of mind are ***hearsay but are admissible*** under an exception to the hearsay rule (*see* D.3., *infra*). Many courts have used this "state of mind exception" to admit all declarations that reflect on the declarant's state of mind without regard to the fact that many could simply be admitted as nonhearsay. Although the ability to distinguish the two may be helpful for exam purposes, as a practical matter, the distinction makes little difference because the result (admissibility of the statements) is the same.

4. **Nonhuman Declarations**
There is no such thing as animal or machine hearsay. Hearsay involves an out-of-court

statement by a **person**. Therefore, a witness who testifies to the time of day (what the clock says) or to radar readings (what the machine says) is not testifying to hearsay. Data that is generated completely electronically is not hearsay. Similarly, the behavior of a drug-sniffing dog in identifying a suspect is not hearsay. The issues presented by these examples are ones of relevance or reliability of the mechanism or animal. For example, a witness may testify to the actions of a drug-sniffing dog in identifying a suspect if there is a foundation showing that the dog was properly trained and is reliable in identifying drug carriers.

5. **Illustrations of Hearsay and Nonhearsay**
   The following are specific examples of the application of the hearsay definition.

   a. **Hearsay**

      1) On the issue of whether the traffic light was red or green, the witness testifies that he was told by Decla that the light was green. (**Oral** hearsay.)

      2) On the issue of whether a glassine envelope contained heroin, the prosecution offers a crime laboratory report that the envelope contained heroin. (**Written** hearsay.)

      3) On the issue of whether Spano had been a resident of New York for one year prior to commencing his lawsuit, Spano offers the affidavit of Decla that Spano had lived in Buffalo for 10 years. (**Written** hearsay; under oath, but hearsay nonetheless.)

      4) On the issue of whether Yuckl was the child molester, a police officer testifies that when he asked the child-victim whether the perpetrator had a beard, the child nodded his head. (Hearsay by **assertive conduct**; nodding, which translates, "Yes, the man had a beard.")

      5) On the issue of whether the painting sold to Harvey was actually a genuine Picasso, there is offered a dealer's bill of sale describing the painting as a Picasso. (**Written** hearsay.)

   b. **Nonhearsay**

      1) In a contract action, the written, executed contract is offered. (Although an extra-judicial writing, it is not offered to prove the truth of matters asserted in it; **legally operative fact**.)

      2) In an action for fraud, on the issue of defendant's good faith in representing to plaintiff that a painting was a genuine Picasso, defendant offers a bill of sale from his art dealer describing the painting as a Picasso. (Offered to prove **defendant's good faith** in repeating a representation; not offered to prove that the painting was in fact a Picasso. The evidence, in other words, was offered to show the impact of the dealer's representation on the defendant's state of mind, i.e., his belief.)

      3) On the issue of whether landlord knew about a defective stair, a witness testifies that he heard Decla say to the landlord, "The stair is broken." (Offered to prove **notice**, not that the stair was in fact broken.)

4) On the issue of whether the complaining witness had a venereal disease, Grutz testifies for the prosecution that the complaining witness had not been placed in the venereal disease ward upon her admission to the girls' reformatory. (Nonhearsay under the Federal Rules, since it is **nonassertive conduct**.)

5) On the issue of whether a transfer of a share of stock from Decla to Bushmat was a sale or a gift, Bushmat testifies that Decla made a statement at the time of the transfer: "I'm giving you this share of stock as a birthday present." (**Legally operative** words of gift.)

6) Action for personal injuries by a guest in an automobile against its owner. On the issues of contributory negligence and assumption of risk, a witness testifies that an hour before the accident a mechanic said to the owner in the presence of the guest, "The tread on that left front tire is paper-thin. You're likely to have a blowout." (**Notice, knowledge**; not offered to establish that in truth the tread was thin.)

7) Action of P against D. Witness No. 1 testifies for P that D's car was going "over 70 miles an hour." To impeach Witness No. 1, D offers the testimony of Witness No. 2 that Witness No. 1 said a day after the accident that D was going "slowly." (Used solely to cast **doubt on credibility**; not offered to establish the truth of the assertion.)

6. Hearsay Within Hearsay

An out-of-court statement that incorporates other hearsay within it is known as "hearsay within hearsay." Hearsay within hearsay is admissible only if both the outer hearsay statement **and** the inner hearsay statement fall within an exception to the hearsay rule. [Fed. R. Evid. 805] Note that in the context of the hearsay within hearsay rule, a statement categorized as a hearsay exclusion (e.g., an opposing party's statement) functions as a hearsay exception.

Examples: 1) The prosecution in a homicide case introduces the following statement from Victim, made when she knew she was about to die: "Defendant did this to me. He said he used an undetectable poison." Victim's outer statement is admissible as a dying declaration (*see* C.4., *infra*), and Defendant's incorporated statement is admissible as a statement of an opposing party (*see* B.2., *infra*). Thus, Victim's statement is admissible.

2) The manager of a grocery store drafts a standard incident report after a customer, Bob, falls and injures himself. At trial, the store offers a portion of the report that says, "An hour later, I interviewed Anne, a shopper who witnessed Bob's fall. She said that Bob was running at high speed and tripped over his own feet." The report itself likely qualifies as a business record (*see* D.5., *infra*), but Anne's incorporated statement does not fall within any hearsay exception. Thus, the report is inadmissible.

B. STATEMENTS THAT ARE NONHEARSAY UNDER THE FEDERAL RULES

Federal Rule 801(d) removes from the definition of hearsay certain statements that would be hearsay under the common law definition. Since the following types of statements are **not hearsay**, they are admissible as substantive evidence (unless excluded for some independent reason).

1. **Prior Statements by Witness**

   Certain statements by a person who testifies at the trial or hearing, and is *subject to cross-examination* about the statements, are not hearsay. A witness is generally "subject to cross-examination" when she is placed on the stand, is under oath, and responds willingly to questions.

   a. **Prior Inconsistent Statement**

   A witness's prior inconsistent statement is not hearsay if it was made *under penalty of perjury* at a prior trial or proceeding, or in a deposition. [Fed. R. Evid. 801(d)(1)(A)] For example, a statement made by the witness during grand jury testimony, if inconsistent with her in-court testimony, would be admissible not only to impeach her credibility (VI.E.3.a., *supra*) but also as substantive proof.

   b. **Prior Consistent Statement**

   A prior consistent statement, regardless of whether made under oath, is not hearsay if it is offered under either of the following circumstances: (i) to rebut an express or implied charge that the witness is lying or exaggerating because of some motive, provided the prior consistent statement was made *before* the onset of the alleged motive to lie or exaggerate [Tome v. United States, 513 U.S. 150 (1995)]; or (ii) to rehabilitate a witness whose credibility has been impeached on some non-character ground *other* than a charge of recent motivation to lie or exaggerate, such as an alleged inconsistency or sensory deficiency. [Fed. R. Evid. 801(d)(1)(B); *see* VI.E.6.c., *supra*, for further discussion and examples]

   c. **Prior Statement of Identification**

   A witness's prior statement identifying a person as someone he perceived earlier is not hearsay. [Fed. R. Evid. 801(d)(1)(C)] This is true even if the witness currently lacks memory and cannot testify as to the basis of the prior identification. [United States v. Owens, 484 U.S. 554 (1988)] Photo identifications are within the scope of this rule. Note that the prior identification need not have been made at a formal proceeding or under oath, and its admissibility is not limited to rehabilitation of the witness.

2. **Statements by or Attributable to Opposing Party (Admissions by Party-Opponent)**

   Under the Federal Rules, a statement by an opposing party (traditionally known as an "admission by a party-opponent") is not hearsay. Simply put, any statement *made by a party* and *offered against that party* is not hearsay. The party who made the prior statement can hardly complain about not having had the opportunity to cross-examine himself. He said it. He is stuck with it. Let him explain it if he can.

   Note: Although an opposing party's statement will fall within this hearsay exclusion even if it does not "admit" anything, these statements are still commonly referred to as "admissions" by courts and commentators. Because the term "admissions" better distinguishes these statements from statements against interest (an exception to the hearsay rule, *see* C.3., *infra*), this outline will generally refer to these statements as admissions.

   a. **In General**

   A statement need not have been against interest at the time it was made to qualify as an admission (compare the statement against interest exception, C.3., *infra*). The statement may even be in the form of an opinion. Note that some states admit these statements under an exception to the hearsay rule.

1) **Personal Knowledge Not Required**

Lack of personal knowledge *does not necessarily exclude* a party's admission (e.g., president of defendant company said, "My company has investigated the matter thoroughly and the reports indicate that we were negligent"). In fact, an admission may be predicated on hearsay.

2) **Judicial and Extrajudicial Admissions**

Formal judicial admissions (in pleadings, responses to requests to admit, stipulations) are *conclusive*; informal judicial admissions made during testimony *can be explained*; extrajudicial (evidentiary) admissions are *not conclusive and can be explained*. A formal judicial admission in one proceeding may become an extrajudicial or evidentiary admission in another proceeding. (Plea of guilty to traffic infraction admissible in civil action on same facts.) A formal judicial admission that is withdrawn may in that same action become an informal admission (statements in original answer admissible though superseded by amendment). A withdrawn plea of guilty in a criminal case is not, however, admissible against a defendant in any civil or criminal proceeding. [Fed. R. Evid. 410]

3) **Adoptive Admissions**

A party may expressly or impliedly adopt someone else's statement as his own, thus giving rise to an adoptive admission. [Fed. R. Evid. 801(d)(2)(B)]

Example: Where Plaintiff claims an orthopedic abnormality in a suit against Defendant, Defendant may properly offer against Plaintiff Plaintiff's prior application for a chauffeur's license, which included a doctor's certificate stating that Plaintiff had "no orthopedic abnormality."

a) **Silence**

If a party fails to respond to accusatory statements where a reasonable person would have spoken up, his silence may be considered an implied admission. For silence to be an admission the following requirements must be met:

(i)   The party must have *heard and understood* the statement;

(ii)   The party must have been *physically and mentally capable of denying* the statement; and

(iii) A *reasonable person would have denied* the accusation under the same circumstances.

Note that failure to reply to an accusation or statement made by the police in a criminal case can *almost never* be used as an implied admission of a criminal act.

b. **Vicarious Admissions**

A declarant's statement may be attributable to a party because of the relationship between them. The question that remains is—what relationship must exist between the declarant and the party to make the former's statement admissible against the latter?

1) **Co-Parties—Insufficient Relationship**
Statements of a party are *not receivable against her co-plaintiffs or co-defendants* merely because they happen to be joined as parties to the action. If there are two or more parties, the admission of one is receivable against her but, in the absence of authority, not against her co-party.

2) **Authorized Spokesperson**
The statement of a person *authorized by a party to speak on its behalf* (e.g., statement by company's press agent) can be admitted against the party. [Fed. R. Evid. 801(d)(2)(C)]

3) **Principal-Agent**
Statements by an agent or employee concerning any matter within the scope of her agency or employment, made *during the existence of the agency or employment relationship*, are admissible against the principal. [Fed. R. Evid. 801(d)(2)(D)] Therefore, if a truck driver-employee has an accident while on the job and admits that she was negligent, this admission may be introduced against her employer even if she was not authorized to speak for the employer.

4) **Partners**
After a partnership is shown to exist, an admission of one partner, relating to matters *within the scope of the partnership business*, is binding upon her co-partners since, as to such matters, each partner is deemed the agent of the others.

5) **Co-Conspirators**
The Supreme Court has held that admissions of one conspirator, made to a third party *in furtherance of a conspiracy to commit a crime or a civil wrong*, at a time when the declarant was participating in the conspiracy, are admissible against co-conspirators. [United States v. Inadi, 475 U.S. 387 (1986)] The thought is that a conspiracy is analogous to a partnership—"partners in crime." The government need not demonstrate the unavailability of a nontestifying co-conspirator as a prerequisite to admission of the co-conspirator's out-of-court statements under Rule 801(d)(2)(E). Also, the court must use the co-conspirator's statement itself, together with other evidence, to determine whether the statement is admissible. [Fed. R. Evid. 801(d)(2)] In other words, the proponent is not required to establish the existence of the conspiracy, and the participation of the declarant and party, with evidence that is entirely independent of the statement itself.

6) **Privies in Title and Joint Tenants—State Courts Only**
Where one person succeeds to the same property rights formerly enjoyed by another, there is often such privity that the rights of the present owner may be affected by admissions of the former owner made before the owner parted with her interest. In most state courts, admissions of each joint owner are admissible against the other, and admissions of a former owner of real property made at the time she held title are *admissible against those claiming under* her (grantees, heirs,

devisees, or otherwise). These statements are not considered admissions under the Federal Rules, although they may be admissible under one of the hearsay exceptions (e.g., as a statement against interest).

7) **Preliminary Determination of Agency or Conspiracy—Court Must Consider Contents of Hearsay Statement**

Before a hearsay statement is admissible as a vicarious admission, the court must make a preliminary determination of the declarant's relationship with the party against whom the statement is being offered. When making a determination of (i) the declarant's authority to make the statement, (ii) the existence and scope of an agency relationship, or (iii) the existence of a conspiracy and participation by the declarant and the party, the *court must consider the contents of the offered statement*, but the statement alone is *not sufficient* to establish the required relationship or authority. [Fed. R. Evid. 801(d)(2)]

C. HEARSAY EXCEPTIONS—DECLARANT UNAVAILABLE

Certain kinds of hearsay are considered to have special guarantees of trustworthiness and are recognized exceptions to the hearsay exclusion. The Federal Rules treat the exceptions in two groups—those that require the declarant be unavailable, and those under which the declarant's availability is immaterial. This section covers the five important exceptions requiring the declarant's unavailability: (i) former testimony, (ii) statements against interest, (iii) dying declarations, (iv) statements of personal or family history, and (v) statements offered against party procuring declarant's unavailability.

1. "Unavailability" Defined

A declarant is unavailable if:

(i) He is *exempted* from testifying because the court rules that a *privilege applies*;

(ii) He *refuses to testify* concerning the statement despite a court order to do so;

(iii) He testifies to *not remembering* the subject matter;

(iv) He is *unable* to be present or testify because of *death or physical or mental illness*; or

(v) He is *absent* (e.g., beyond the reach of the trial court's subpoena) and the statement's *proponent* has been *unable to procure* his *attendance or testimony* by process or other reasonable means. If the declarant cannot attend the trial or hearing but is able to give deposition testimony, he is considered to be an available witness, except with respect to the "former testimony" and "forfeiture by wrongdoing" exceptions discussed in 2. and 6., below.

[Fed. R. Evid. 804(a)(1) - (5)] Note that a declarant is not unavailable if his "unavailability" was procured by the proponent of the statement or if the statement's proponent did not attempt to procure the declarant's attendance.

2. Former Testimony

The testimony of a now-unavailable witness given at a trial, hearing, or in a deposition taken in accordance with law is admissible in a subsequent trial as long as there is a sufficient similarity of parties and issues so that the opportunity to develop testimony or cross-examine at the prior hearing was meaningful. [Fed. R. Evid. 804(b)(1)] This exception is the clearest example of hearsay with special guarantees of trustworthiness, since the former testimony was given during formal proceedings and under oath by a witness subject to cross-examination.

a. **Identity of Parties**

The requirement of identity of parties does not mean that parties on both sides of the controversies must be identical. It requires only that the party *against whom* the testimony is offered or, in civil cases, the party's predecessor in interest was a *party in the former action*. "Predecessor in interest" includes one in a privity relationship with the party, such as grantor-grantee, testator-executor, life tenant-remainderman, and joint tenants. The requirement of identity of parties is intended merely to ensure that the party against whom the testimony is offered (or a predecessor in interest in a civil case) had an adequate opportunity and motive to cross-examine the witness.

b. **Identity of Subject Matter**

The former testimony is admissible upon any trial in the same or another action of the same subject matter. Again, the sole purpose of this requirement is to ensure that the party against whom the transcript of testimony is offered had an adequate opportunity to cross-examine the unavailable witness on the relevant issue. Obviously, the "cause of action" in both proceedings need not be identical. It is enough if the "subject matter" of the testimony is the same. In other words, the party against whom the testimony is offered must have had an opportunity and similar motive to develop declarant's testimony at the prior hearing.

c. **Opportunity to Develop Testimony at Prior Hearing**

The party against whom the former testimony is offered (or a predecessor in civil cases) must have had the opportunity to develop the testimony at the prior proceeding by direct, cross, or redirect examination of the declarant. Thus, the *grand jury testimony* of an unavailable declarant is *not admissible* as former testimony *against the accused* at trial. This is because grand jury proceedings do not provide the accused with the opportunity for cross-examination.

d. **Under Oath**

The former testimony must have been given under oath or sworn affirmation.

e. **Use in Criminal Proceedings**

It has been argued that the use in a criminal proceeding of former testimony from some prior trial violates the defendant's constitutional *right to confront and cross-examine* all adverse witnesses. However, the Supreme Court has rejected this argument, holding that there is *no violation* of an accused's right of confrontation, as long as:

1) The accused or his attorney was present and *had the opportunity to cross-examine* at the time the testimony was given (e.g., at a preliminary examination or a former trial for the same offense); *and*

2) The witness, whose former testimony is sought to be used, is now *unavailable*, despite bona fide efforts by the prosecution to produce him. [California v. Green, 399 U.S. 149 (1970)] *Note:* A greater showing of "unavailability" is required in

criminal cases than in civil cases. For example, a mere showing that a witness is incarcerated in a prison outside the state has been held insufficient to establish "unavailability" (because no showing that he could not be produced by prosecution). [Barber v. Page, 390 U.S. 719 (1968)]

3. Statements Against Interest

A statement of a person, now unavailable as a witness, may be admissible if it was against that person's pecuniary, proprietary, or penal interest when made. To be admissible under the statement against interest exception, the statement must have been so against the declarant's pecuniary or proprietary interest, or had so great a tendency to invalidate the declarant's claim against someone else or to expose the declarant to civil or criminal liability, that a reasonable person in the declarant's position would have made the statement only if she believed it to be true. [Fed. R. Evid. 804(b)(3)] The statement against interest differs most significantly from an opposing party's statement in that, under the statement against interest exception, the statement *must be against interest when made*, and the declarant whose statement is admitted may be a stranger to the litigation rather than a party.

a. Requirements of the Statement

To qualify as an exception to the hearsay rule, a statement against interest must meet the following requirements:

1) The statement must have been *against pecuniary, proprietary, or penal interest when made*, such that a *reasonable person* in the declarant's position would have made it only if she believed it to be true.

2) Declarant must have had *personal knowledge of the facts*.

3) Declarant must have been *aware that the statement is against her interest* and she must have had *no motive to misrepresent* when she made the statement.

4) Declarant must be *unavailable as a witness*.

b. Risk of Civil Liability

Under the Federal Rules, statements subjecting the declarant to civil liability are specifically admissible. [Fed. R. Evid. 804(b)(3)]

c. Risk of Criminal Liability

Many courts have been reluctant to admit evidence of statements that subject the declarant to penal liability for fear of opening a door to a flood of perjured testimony. The modern trend and the Federal Rules permit statements against penal interest. However, in *criminal cases*, the Federal Rules require that there be *corroborating circumstances* indicating the trustworthiness of such statements. [Fed. R. Evid. 804(b)(3)]

1) Third-Party Confession Allowed

States that do not allow statements against penal interest may not exclude the confession of a third party where to do so would deprive the accused of a *fair trial*. [Chambers v. Mississippi, 410 U.S. 284 (1973)]

2) Co-Defendant's Confession May Not Be Admissible

The confession of a co-defendant *implicating herself and the accused* may not be admissible because of *confrontation* problems. (*See* F.1., *infra*.)

d. "Statement" Means Single Remark

A "statement" against interest for purposes of the exception means a single self-inculpatory remark, not an extended declaration. Thus, if a person makes a declaration containing statements that are against his interest and statements that are not, the statements that are not against interest are not admissible, even though they are part of a broader narrative that is on the whole against the declarant's interest. [Williamson v. United States, 512 U.S. 594 (1994)]

Example: X confessed to receiving and transporting drugs, but in so doing implicated Y as the owner of the drugs. The statements implicating Y did not contain any information against X's interest, although the confession as a whole was clearly against X's penal interest. X refused to testify at Y's trial. X's statements implicating Y are not within the scope of the hearsay exception for statements against interest and are thus inadmissible. The exception covers only those remarks that inculpate the declarant, not the extended declaration. [*See* Williamson v. United States, *supra*]

4. Dying Declarations—Statements Under Belief of Impending Death

In a prosecution for *homicide or a civil action*, a statement made by the now-unavailable declarant while *believing his death was imminent* that concerns the *cause or circumstances* of what he believed to be his impending death is admissible. [Fed. R. Evid. 804(b)(2)] The declarant need not actually die, but he must be unavailable (*see* 1., *supra*) at the time the statement is offered.

Note that under the traditional view, still followed by some states, the statement was admissible only in homicide prosecutions (not civil actions), and then only if the declarant actually died.

a. Firsthand Knowledge Required

To fall within the dying declaration exception, the statement must be based on the declarant's firsthand knowledge of what happened. As under the general rule for lay opinion testimony, a statement framed as an opinion is not admissible unless based on the declarant's perceptions (e.g., unsupported speculation as to the assailant's identity or motive would not qualify). [*See* Advisory Committee Note to Rule 804]

5. Statements of Personal or Family History

Statements concerning birth, marriage, divorce, death, relationship, etc., are admissible under an exception to the hearsay rule. Hearsay statements concerning family history are often necessary to prove the facts of people's everyday lives. For example, most people rely on the hearsay statements of others for the knowledge of where they were born, who their relatives are, etc.

a. Statement Need Not Have Been Made Before Controversy

In most jurisdictions, the statement must have been made at a time when no controversy existed as to the matters stated—to ensure their reliability. However, the Federal Rules have dropped this requirement on the theory that the time at which the statement was made affects its weight rather than its admissibility. [Fed. R. Evid. 804(b)(4)]

b. Usually Declarant Must Be a Family Member
The now-unavailable declarant must be a member of the family in question or otherwise intimately associated with the family. Most jurisdictions require that the declarant be related by blood or marriage to the family whose history is involved. Some jurisdictions, and the Federal Rules, have extended this requirement to admit statements by declarants who are so intimately associated with the family that they are likely to have accurate information concerning the matters declared (e.g., the family doctor). [Fed. R. Evid. 804(b)(4)]

c. Personal Knowledge Required
The declarant's statements may be based either on her own personal knowledge of the facts involved or on her knowledge of family reputation.

d. Other Ways to Prove Pedigree
Personal and family history may be proven by use of other exceptions to the hearsay rule. For example, it may be proven by: vital statistics [Fed. R. Evid. 803(9)]; records of religious organizations [Fed. R. Evid. 803(11)]; marriage certificates and other certificates [Fed. R. Evid. 803(12)]; family records [Fed. R. Evid. 803(13)]; statements in property documents [Fed. R. Evid. 803(15)]; reputation [Fed. R. Evid. 803(19)]; and judgments [Fed. R. Evid. 803(23)]. For these exceptions, the declarant's availability is immaterial.

6. Statements Offered Against Party Procuring Declarant's Unavailability
The statements of a person (now unavailable as a witness) are admissible when offered against a party who has engaged or acquiesced in wrongdoing that procured the declarant's unavailability as a witness, if the party *intended to cause that result*. [Fed. R. Evid. 804(b)(6)] In effect, a party forfeits his right to object on hearsay grounds to the admission of an unavailable declarant's statements when the party's deliberate wrongdoing procured the unavailability of the declarant as a witness.

D. HEARSAY EXCEPTIONS—DECLARANT'S AVAILABILITY IMMATERIAL
The following exceptions do not require that the declarant be unavailable. The admissibility of these declarations proceeds upon the theory that the out-of-court declarations were made under circumstances that make them more reliable and therefore preferable to the actual in-court testimony of the declarant. Included in this group of exceptions are the following:

1. Excited Utterances
A declaration made by a declarant during or soon after a startling event is admissible. The declaration must be made under the stress of excitement produced by the startling event. The declaration must relate to the startling occurrence. [Fed. R. Evid. 803(2)] The spontaneousness of such a declaration and the consequent lack of opportunity for reflection and deliberate fabrication provide an adequate guarantee of its trustworthiness.

a. Startling Event Required
There must have been some occurrence startling enough to produce a nervous

excitement and thus render the declaration an unreflective and sincere expression of the declarant's impression. The declaration *must relate to the startling event*.

b. **Declaration Must Be Made While Under Stress of Excitement**
The declaration must have been made while the declarant was under the stress of the excitement (i.e., *before the declarant had time to reflect* upon it). The time element is the most important factor in determining whether the declaration was made under the stress of the excitement. If a declaration is made while the event is still in progress, it is easy to find that the excitement prompted the utterance. Declarations made shortly after the event have sometimes been excluded as mere narrative of past events. But when the declaration is made so near to the time of the occurrence as to negate any probability of fabrication, it is usually admissible.

2. **Present Sense Impressions**
A present sense impression is a statement that *describes or explains* an event or condition, and is made *while* or *immediately after* the declarant perceives the event or condition. A present sense impression is admissible as an exception to the hearsay rule.

a. **Safeguards**
Such a comment regarding a situation then before the declarant, i.e., the statement of a present sense impression, does not have the supposed safeguards of impulse, emotion, or excitement, but there are other safeguards of reliability. Statements of present sense impression are *safe from defects in memory*. There is usually little or *no time for calculated misstatement*. The statement will usually have been made to another person—the very witness who reports it—who would have *equal opportunity to observe* and to contradict or correct a misstatement.
Example: Decla said to N, "Look at that car go." W may testify that Decla made the statement in order to prove that the car was speeding.

3. **Present State of Mind**
A statement of the declarant's then-existing state of mind (e.g., motive, intent, or plan) or emotional, sensory, or physical condition is admissible. [Fed. R. Evid. 803(3)] The exception is based on the need to obtain evidence as to the declarant's internal state of mind or emotion. It must usually be made under circumstances of apparent sincerity. The statement is often offered to establish the *intent* of a person, either as a direct fact to be proved as such (domicile, criminal intent) or as a basis for a circumstantial inference that the intent was probably carried out.

Note: The operation of this exception for a declarant's statement of present physical condition is discussed separately in 4.a., below.

a. **Rationale**
The rationale is that (i) insofar as the declarant knows her own state of mind, there is no need to check her perception; (ii) since the statement is of present state of mind, there is no need to check her memory; and (iii) since state of mind is in issue, it must be shown some way—and very often, the declarant's own statement is the only way.

b. **When Admissible**

1) **State of Mind Directly in Issue and Material to the Controversy**

Declarations of existing state of mind are admissible when the declarant's state of mind is directly in issue and material to the controversy.

Example: In a case where the domicile of Edwina is material, Edwina's statement that "I plan to live in Colorado for the rest of my life" is admissible.

2) **Offered to Show Subsequent Acts of Declarant**

Declarations of existing state of mind are also admissible when the declarant's state of mind is not directly in issue—if they are declarations of intent offered to show subsequent acts of the declarant; i.e., a declaration of intent to do something in the future is admitted as circumstantial evidence tending to show that the intent was carried out. In *Mutual Life Insurance Co. v. Hillmon*, 145 U.S. 285 (1892), a hearsay written statement was admitted into evidence to prove the declarant did what he said he intended to do.

Examples: 1) The location of X on May 15 is relevant. W may testify that she heard X say on May 8 that "I intend to go to Denver next week."

2) In a prosecution of a husband for murder of his wife, the wife's prior statements that she intended to commit suicide are admissible.

c. **Statements of Memory or Belief Generally Not Admissible**

The hearsay statement is ***not admissible*** if it expresses a memory or belief of the declarant, and the statement is offered for the purpose of proving the ***truth of the fact remembered or believed***.

Example: Declarant's out-of-court statement, "I think I left the keys in the car," may not be introduced for the purpose of proving that he left the keys in the car.

Statements of memory or belief are ***admissible***, however, to prove facts remembered or believed concerning the validity or terms of ***declarant's will***.

4. **Declarations of Physical Condition**

There are two hearsay exceptions involving statements of physical condition: (i) statements of ***the declarant's present physical condition, regardless of the purpose*** for which the statement is made; and (ii) ***statements made for the purpose of obtaining medical diagnosis or treatment***. Thus, whether a declarant's statement will fall within one or the other of these exceptions depends on the purpose for which it was made.

a. **Statement of Declarant's Present Bodily Condition**

Generally, declarations of present bodily condition are admissible as an exception to the hearsay rule, even though they are not made to a physician. They may be made to a spouse, relative, friend, or any other person. Of course, declarations made to a physician are admissible. [Fed. R. Evid. 803(3)] Such declarations relate to symptoms, including the existence of pain. Because they are contemporaneous with the symptoms, they are more reliable than present testimony based upon recollection.

Example: Victim tells friend, "My ankle hurts so much it must be broken." The statement is admissible as a declaration of present pain, although it is not to be used to prove the ankle was in fact broken.

b.   Statement Made for Medical Diagnosis or Treatment—Includes Past Conditions
A statement that describes a person's *medical history*, *past or present symptoms*, or their *inception or general cause* is admissible as an exception to the hearsay rule if it was made for—and was *reasonably pertinent* to—medical diagnosis or treatment. [Fed. R. Evid. 803(4)] The rationale for this exception is that a declarant has a strong motive to tell the truth when seeking medical assistance.

1)   Cause or Source of Injury—Must Be Pertinent
Remember that the cause or source of the injury must be reasonably pertinent to diagnosis or treatment to be admissible under this exception. Statements assigning fault or identifying a perpetrator are generally not pertinent.
Example: The statement, "Doctor, I was hit by a truck" would likely be admitted under this exception, but "Doctor, the blue truck ran the red light" would not be admitted.

a)   Special Treatment for Statements by Child Abuse Victims
In child abuse cases, many federal courts will admit statements in which a child identifies his abuser in the course of medical treatment. The rationale is that the identity of the abuser is often critical to treating the child's psychological or emotional injuries (e.g., removing the abuser from the child's household). [*See* United States v. Renville, 779 F.2d 430 (8th Cir. 1985)]

2)   Declarant Seeking Help for Someone Else
Usually, the declarant is the patient and is seeking help for herself, but this is not required. Statements by family members and bystanders may be admitted under this exception as long as the statements were clearly made to obtain a diagnosis or treatment for the patient. (Note that the court may exclude the statement if there are concerns about its reliability.)

3)   Need Not Be Made to Physician
Although such statements are usually made to a doctor or nurse, this is not required. Statements to ambulance drivers, hospital staff, and even the declarant's own family members may be admitted under the exception as long as they are made for, and reasonably pertinent to, medical diagnosis or treatment.

4)   Statements Made to Doctor Employed to Testify—Admissible Under Federal Rules
Contrary to the majority state view, Rule 803(4) permits statements made to a doctor employed to testify in the case.

5.   Records of a Regularly Conducted Activity—Business Records
Any writing or record, whether in the form of an entry in a book or otherwise, made as a memorandum or record of any act, transaction, occurrence, or event is admissible in evidence as proof of that act, transaction, occurrence, or event, if made in the regular course of any business; and if it was the regular course of such business to make it at the time of the act, transaction, occurrence, or event or within a reasonable time thereafter.

a.   Rationale
The rationale for this exception lies in the belief that special reliability is provided by

the *regularity* with which business records are kept, their *use and importance* in the business, and the *incentive* of employees *to keep accurate records* or risk employment penalties. If a record qualifies as a business record, it may be admitted without calling the author of the record or the employee with personal knowledge of the recorded event. It makes no difference that the record is self-serving and offered in evidence by the party whose business made the record.

b.   Elements of Business Records Exception
Under the Federal Rules and modern statutes, the main requirements for admissibility of a business record are as follows:

1)   "Business"
Although traditionally called a "business record," the exception applies to records kept by any "business, organization, occupation, or calling, whether or not for profit." Thus, the definition would include records made by churches, hospitals, schools, etc. [Fed. R. Evid. 803(6)]

2)   Entry Made in Regular Course of Business
It must also appear that the record was made in the course of a regularly conducted business activity, and that it was customary to make the type of entry involved (i.e., that the entrant had a duty to make the entry).

a)   Business Activity
The record must have been maintained in conjunction with a business activity.

(1)   Hospital Records
Entries in hospital records are generally admissible to the extent that they are *related to the medical diagnosis or treatment* of the patient (the primary business of the hospital). For example, a patient's statement that she was injured on X's property would probably be inadmissible because whether she was injured on X's property or someone else's is unrelated to her medical treatment.

(2)   Police Reports
Police reports may qualify as business records in civil cases. Generally, police reports are not admissible against a criminal defendant under the business records exception. However, some jurisdictions admit police reports if they contain only routine information rather than observations or opinions of officers.

(3)   The Rule of *Palmer v. Hoffman*—Records Prepared for Litigation
A similar aspect of the "business activity" requirement was raised in the case of *Palmer v. Hoffman,* 318 U.S. 109 (1943). In that case, railroad personnel, in accordance with their regular practice, prepared a report concerning an accident in which the railroad was involved. The United States Supreme Court held that the report was not admissible at trial because it was prepared in anticipation of litigation, and railroading, not litigating, was the railroad's primary business.

(a) **Narrow Interpretation**
Many courts have interpreted the rule of *Palmer v. Hoffman* narrowly. These courts have generally *excluded* such a self-serving employee accident report only when the report was prepared *primarily* for litigation and the author of the report had a strong motive to misrepresent.

(b) **Federal Rules—Court's Discretion**
The Federal Rules have dealt with the problem of *Palmer v. Hoffman* by granting the trial court discretion to exclude any business record if the *source of information* or *methods or circumstances of preparation* indicate the record lacks trustworthiness. [Fed. R. Evid. 803(6)]

b) **Entrant Under Duty to Record**
For a record to have been made in the regular course of a business activity, the entrant must have had some duty to make the entry as part of her employment (i.e., records kept as a hobby do not qualify). This duty may be either public (statutory, etc.) or private (contractual—including duties imposed by an employer).

3) **Personal Knowledge**
The business record must consist of matters within the personal knowledge of the entrant *or* within the personal knowledge of someone with a business duty to transmit such matters to the entrant.

a) **Recorder Need Not Have Personal Knowledge of Event**
Most business records statutes do not require that the person making the entries have personal knowledge of the event. Indeed, where the one who has personal knowledge of the transaction (informant) and the one making the record (recorder) are both employees of the business, there is no problem. Once established as a business record, it is admissible without calling either the informant or the recorder, even though the recorder lacked personal knowledge. The integrity of the special reliability assumption is maintained because the informant was under a *business duty to report* accurately and the recorder was under a *business duty to properly record* the information.

b) **Informant Must Be Under Business Duty to Convey Information**
A problem arises, however, when the informant with personal knowledge is an outsider, having little or no connection with the business whose records are being offered in evidence. The well-known case of *Johnson v. Lutz*, 253 N.Y. 124 (1930), engrafted a limitation on the business records exception. It holds that an entry is admissible as a business record only when the record was made by the employee recorder on information obtained directly by him or imparted to him by an informant who was under a business duty to convey such information. Thus, a police report entry by a police officer was held inadmissible where the informant was a third person who was under no "business" duty to convey information (the "business" being law

enforcement). The statutory business records exception, in other words, was not intended to permit receipt in evidence of hearsay statements made by third persons not engaged in the business in question or under any duty in connection with it. Thus, the rationale is that the assumed reliability justifying the hearsay exception cannot be maintained if the information in the record was supplied by an outsider who had no business incentive to report accurately.

c) **Recorded Statement May Be Admissible Under Other Exceptions**
If, as in *Johnson v. Lutz*, the record-maker and the informant are not business related, the recorded statement of the informant may nonetheless be receivable with the help of some other exceptions to the hearsay rule. This involves a two-phase process. The business records exception serves as a vehicle for demonstrating the bare fact that the ***statement was made*** (i.e., it allows the paper record to substitute for the in-court testimony of the employees who received the information); the second phase involves reference to some ***independent ground of admissibility*** of the statement to establish the ***truth*** of assertions contained in it. A police report entry is receivable where the informant was a party and his statement would be admissible as an ***opposing party's statement***. Note too that certain police reports may be admissible under the public records exception (*see* 7.a., *infra*).

4) **Entry Made Near Time of Event**
The entry must have been made at or near the time of the transaction while the entrant's knowledge of the facts was still fresh.

5) **Authentication**
The authenticity of the record must be established. The usual method of authentication is to have the custodian or other qualified witness testify to the identity of the record and the mode of its preparation. However, a foundation witness is not necessary to authenticate the record (i.e., the record will be self-authenticating) if the custodian or other qualified person certifies in writing that the record meets the requirements of the business records exception and the adverse party receives reasonable written notice (*see* V.B.5.i., *supra*). [Fed. R. Evid. 803(6), 902(11)]

Normally, the original or first permanent record of the transaction must be introduced, but where the records to be introduced are voluminous, summaries or compilations may be admitted.

6) **Entrant Need Not Be Unavailable**
For the business record to be admissible, the person who made the entry need not be unavailable as a witness.

7) **May Be Excluded If Not Trustworthy—Burden on Opponent**
The court may exclude an otherwise qualifying business record if the opponent makes a showing that the source of information or the method or circumstances of preparation indicate a lack of trustworthiness.

c.   Use of Business Records as Evidence of No Transaction
At common law, business records were admitted only to prove the facts contained therein. They were not admissible for negative purposes—i.e., to show that no transaction had taken place. However, the modern trend allows business records to be used to prove the nonoccurrence or the nonexistence of a matter if it was the regular practice of the business to record all such matters. [Fed. R. Evid. 803(7)] For example, the lack of any entry showing payment in a business record may be evidence that in fact no payment was made.

6.   Recorded Recollection
Witnesses are permitted to refresh their memories by looking at almost anything—either before or while testifying. This is called *present recollection revived* (*see* VI.B.3.a., *supra*). However, if the witness's memory cannot be revived, a party may wish to introduce a memorandum that the witness made or adopted at or near the time of the event. Use of the record to prove the facts contained therein raises a hearsay problem; but if a proper foundation can be laid, the contents of the record may be introduced into evidence under the *recorded recollection* exception to the hearsay rule. The rationale is that a record made by an observer when the facts were still fresh in her mind is probably more reliable than her testimony on the stand—despite the fact that cross-examination is curtailed. For admissibility requirements, *see* VI.B.3.b., *supra*.

7.   Official Records and Other Official Writings

a.   Public Records and Reports
The exception for public records and reports is necessary to avoid having public officers leave their jobs constantly to appear in court and testify to acts done in their official capacity, especially since the entrant could probably add nothing to the record. Also, such records are presumed to be trustworthy because officials are under a duty to record properly that which they do.

1)   What May Be Admitted
Records, reports, statements, or data compilations, in any form, of a public office or agency are admissible to the extent that they set forth:

(i)   The activities of the office or agency;

(ii)   Matters observed pursuant to a duty imposed by law (excluding police observations in criminal cases); or

(iii)   In civil actions and proceedings and against the government in criminal cases, factual findings (including opinions and conclusions) resulting from an investigation made pursuant to authority granted by law.

[Fed. R. Evid. 803(8); Beech Aircraft Corp. v. Rainey, 488 U.S. 153 (1988)]
Examples: 1) A manual prepared by the office that processes Medicare claims, explaining which claims are properly payable under Medicare, is admissible against the defendant in a Medicare fraud case under Federal Rule 803(8)(A).

2) A police officer arrives at the scene of the accident. Several witnesses tell him that Dan drove through a stop sign and hit Vic, who was riding a bicycle. The police officer has had many years' experience in evaluating accident scenes. From the tire marks, he decides that Dan did indeed run the stop sign. In his report he includes the statements of the witnesses and his evaluation of the scene, including his conclusion that Dan ran the stop sign. Everything except the witnesses' statements can be admitted under Federal Rule 803(8)(C), including the officer's conclusion. The witnesses' statements can be admitted only if they fall within some other exception. Remember that the investigative report is admissible only in civil cases and only *against the government* in criminal cases. The report could not be offered against Dan in a criminal prosecution.

3) An Equal Employment Opportunity Commission investigator's report would be admissible in an action against an employer alleging discriminatory employment practices. As with the officer's report above, any hearsay statements will be excised unless they fall within an exception, but the investigator's conclusions and opinions are admissible.

2) Requirements for Admissibility

a) Duty to Record
The writing must have been made by, and within the scope of duty of, the public employee.

b) Entry Near Time of Event
The writing must have been made at or near the time of the act, condition, or event.

c) May Be Excluded If Not Trustworthy—Burden on Opponent
The court may exclude an otherwise qualifying public record if the opponent makes a showing that the source of information or other circumstances indicate a lack of trustworthiness.

b. Records of Vital Statistics
Records of births, deaths, and marriages are admissible if reported to a public office in accordance with a legal duty. [Fed. R. Evid. 803(9)]

c. Statement of Absence of Public Record
Evidence in the form of testimony or a certification from the custodian of public records (or any other qualified person) that she has diligently searched and failed to find a record is admissible to prove that a matter was not recorded, or, inferentially, that a matter did not occur. [Fed. R. Evid. 803(10)]

1) Limitation on Certifications in Criminal Cases

Because a criminal defendant has a right to confront and cross-examine the witnesses against him (*see* F., *infra*), he may demand the presence of the custodian or other official who prepared the certification. Thus, this type of testimonial certificate is admissible only if the prosecutor provides the defendant with written notice at least 14 days before trial and the defendant does not object in writing within seven days of receiving the notice (unless the court sets a different timeline).

d. Judgments

A certified copy of a judgment is always admissible proof that such judgment has been entered. The problem is to what extent the facts adjudicated in the former proceeding can be introduced to prove facts in the present case.

1) Prior Criminal Conviction—Felony Conviction Admissible

The traditional view, still followed by most state courts, is that a judgment of conviction is inadmissible. First, it is merely the "opinion" of the jury, and second, it is hearsay as proof of the fact asserted, i.e., the guilt of the defendant. Of course, under certain circumstances the conviction may be used for impeachment. The Federal Rules, however, specifically provide that a judgment of a felony conviction is ***admissible as an exception to the hearsay rule in both criminal and civil actions to prove any fact essential to the judgment***. For example, if a defendant was convicted of a felony assault, the injured party could use the judgment of conviction in a later civil suit against the same defendant to prove the happening of the assault. In the Rules, felony convictions are defined as crimes punishable by death or imprisonment in excess of one year. [Fed. R. Evid. 803(22)] The convictions that may be used are limited to felonies because persons may choose not to defend misdemeanor charges (e.g., traffic violations).

a) Admissible to Prove Fact Only Against Accused

In a criminal case, the government may use a prior conviction for this purpose only against the accused. Against persons ***other than the accused***, the government may use prior convictions ***only for impeachment***.

b) Rules Barring Character Evidence Still Apply

The hearsay exception for judgments of prior felony convictions is subject to the general rule that prohibits the admissibility of convictions as character evidence. (*See* II.E., *supra*.) The hearsay exception merely provides a means of proving the facts upon which a conviction is based when such facts are independently admissible either to prove specific acts of misconduct on the issue of a person's motive, intent, absence of mistake, etc., or as proof of prior acts of sexual assault or child molestation in cases alleging sexual assault or child molestation.

2) Prior Criminal Acquittal—Excluded

The exclusionary rule is still applied to records of prior acquittals. The reason is that a criminal acquittal may establish only that the state did not prove the defendant guilty beyond a reasonable doubt, whereas the evidentiary standard is lower in civil cases.

3) **Judgment in Former Civil Case**

    a) **Inadmissible in Criminal Proceeding**
A civil judgment is clearly inadmissible in a subsequent criminal proceeding because of the differing standards of proof.

    b) **Generally Inadmissible in Civil Proceeding**
The general rule is that civil judgments are also inadmissible in subsequent civil proceedings. However, there are certain statutory *exceptions* to the rule of inadmissibility. For example, under the Federal Rules, a prior civil judgment is admissible as proof of matters of personal, family, or general history, or boundaries of land, if it would be provable by reputation evidence (e.g., X may prove her citizenship by a judgment establishing that X's parents were citizens). [Fed. R. Evid. 803(23)]

8. Ancient Documents
Under the Federal Rules, statements in *any* authenticated document *prepared before January 1, 1998*, are admissible. [Fed. R. Evid. 803(16)]

9. Documents Affecting Property Interests
A statement in a document affecting an interest in property (e.g., deed, will, etc.) is admissible as a hearsay exception if the statement is relevant to the document's purpose. However, the exception will not apply if later dealings with the property are inconsistent with the truth of the statement asserted or the intent of the document. [Fed. R. Evid. 803(15)]

10. Learned Treatises
Many courts do not admit statements from standard scientific treatises or authoritative works as substantive proof, limiting admissibility to use as impeachment of the qualifications of the expert witness. The Federal Rules recognize an exception to the hearsay rule for learned treatises. Federal Rule 803(18) provides for the substantive admissibility of a learned treatise if the treatise is:

(i)   Called to the attention of the expert witness upon cross-examination or relied upon by her during direct examination; and

(ii)   Established as reliable authority by the testimony or admission of the witness, by other expert testimony, or by judicial notice.

Even under the Federal Rules, however, the relevant portion of the treatise is not actually shown to the jury; it is admissible by being read into the record.

11. Reputation
In addition to reputation testimony concerning a person's character [Fed. R. Evid. 803(21)], reputation evidence concerning someone's personal or family history [Fed. R. Evid. 803(19)] or concerning land boundaries or the community's general history [Fed. R. Evid. 803(20)] is admissible hearsay.

12. Family Records
Statements of fact concerning personal or family history contained in family Bibles,

genealogies, jewelry engravings, engravings on urns or burial markers, or the like are admissible hearsay. [Fed. R. Evid. 803(13)]

13. Market Reports
Market reports and other published compilations (lists, directories, etc.) are admissible if generally used and relied upon by the public or by persons in a particular occupation. [Fed. R. Evid. 803(17)]

E. RESIDUAL "CATCH-ALL" EXCEPTION OF FEDERAL RULES
The Federal Rules provide a general catch-all exception for hearsay statements not covered by specific exceptions. [Fed. R. Evid. 807] There are three requirements for a statement to be admitted under the catch-all exception:

1. "Trustworthiness" Factor
First of all, the statement must have "circumstantial guarantees of trustworthiness" that are equivalent to those of statements admitted under other hearsay exceptions.

2. "Necessity" Factor
The statement must be offered on a *material fact*, and must be *more probative* as to that fact than any other evidence which the proponent can reasonably produce so that the *"interests of justice"* will be served by its admission.

3. Notice to Adversary
Finally, the proponent must give notice in advance of trial to the adverse party as to the nature of the statement (including the name and address of the declarant) so that the adversary has an opportunity to prepare to meet it.

F. CONSTITUTIONAL ISSUES

1. The Confrontation Clause
In criminal cases, it may be argued that the use of hearsay evidence violates the accused's *right to "confront" and cross-examine* the witnesses against him. Note, however, that there generally is no Confrontation Clause problem if the hearsay declarant is present at the trial and is subject to cross-examination at that time.

a. Prior Testimonial Statement of Unavailable Witness
Under the Confrontation Clause, a hearsay statement will *not* be admitted (even if it falls within a hearsay exception) when:

(i) The statement is offered *against the accused in a criminal case*;

(ii) The declarant is *unavailable*;

(iii) The statement was *"testimonial"* in nature; *and*

(iv) The accused had *no opportunity to cross-examine* the declarant's "testimonial" statement prior to trial.

[Crawford v. Washington, 541 U.S. 36 (2004)] Note, however, that the statement may be admitted if the prosecution demonstrates that the defendant forfeited his Confrontation Clause objection by wrongdoing that prevented the declarant from testifying at trial (*see* b., below).

1) "Testimonial" Statement

The definition of a "testimonial" statement is still evolving, but the following applications have been established.

a) Statements Made in the Course of Police Interrogation

Whether a statement made in response to police interrogation is testimonial depends on its ***primary purpose***. In making this determination, courts objectively evaluate the circumstances of the encounter between the declarant and the police.

(1) To Aid in Ongoing Emergency—Not Testimonial

If the primary purpose of police interrogation is to enable the police to help in an ongoing emergency, statements made in the course of the interrogation are nontestimonial (e.g., statements made during a 911 call describing the circumstances and perpetrator of an ongoing incident of domestic violence). In determining whether an "ongoing emergency" existed at the time of the interrogation, courts consider various factors, including: (i) the nature of the dispute (public vs. private); (ii) whether the perpetrator is still at large; (iii) the scope of the threat to the victim and to the public; and (iv) the type of weapon involved. [Michigan v. Bryant, 562 U.S. 344 (2010)]

(2) To Establish or Prove Events for Later Prosecution—Testimonial

When the primary purpose of the interrogation is to establish or prove past events potentially relevant to a later criminal prosecution, statements are testimonial (e.g., statements made by victim to police shortly after a domestic violence incident, setting forth details of the incident). [Davis v. Washington, 547 U.S. 813 (2006)] On the other hand, statements by a young child abuse victim to a school teacher about the abuse are not testimonial—even though the teacher has a statutory duty to report the abuse to law enforcement authorities—because the primary purpose of the conversation is protection of the child, not prosecution of the perpetrator. [Ohio v. Clark, 135 S. Ct. 2173 (2015)]

b) Affidavits or Written Reports of Forensic Analysis

Affidavits, certificates, or other written reports that summarize the findings of forensic analysis and have the effect of accusing a targeted individual of criminal conduct (e.g., identifying narcotics seized from a suspect or matching a suspect to blood test results) are testimonial and thus may not be admitted into evidence unless the defendant has had an opportunity to cross-examine the author of the report. [Melendez-Diaz v. Massachusetts, 557 U.S. 305 (2009)] A confrontation violation cannot be avoided by offering the results of the analyst's report through the testimony of the analyst's supervisor who played no role in conducting the tests. [Bullcoming v. New Mexico, 131 S. Ct. 2705 (2011)] However, reports by a nontestifying analyst may be used for a nonhearsay purpose rather than to prove the truth of the report's contents. Specifically, no confrontation violation occurs if a forensic expert, while testifying as to her independent analysis of data, makes only a general reference to a nontestifying analyst's report (without reading the report to the jury) for the limited purpose of showing a partial basis for her opinion (*see* VI.C.2.a.4)c), *supra*). [Williams v. Illinois, 132 S. Ct. 2221 (2012)—expert referenced a nontestifying private analyst's profile of the defendant's DNA only to indicate that it *matched* a state analyst's profile of DNA found at the crime scene]

b. Confrontation Clause Rights May Be Forfeited by Wrongdoing
A defendant forfeits his Sixth Amendment right of confrontation by committing a wrongful act that was *intended to keep the witness from testifying* at trial. [Giles v. California, 554 U.S. 353 (2008)—unless the defendant killed the victim with the intent to make her unavailable to testify, he did not forfeit his confrontation rights with respect to allegations of domestic violence made by the victim to the police three weeks before he killed her]

c. The Right to Physically Face Witnesses
The Sixth Amendment guarantee of confrontation includes not only the right to cross-examine witnesses, but also the right to physically face them at trial. The Supreme Court held that right to be violated at a child sex abuse trial because a screen was erected in court between the defendant and two youthful complainants so they could not see the defendant as they testified. [Coy v. Iowa, 487 U.S. 1012 (1988)] However, the Court has also held that the right of confrontation is not absolute. A child witness in a sexual abuse case may testify via one-way closed circuit television without violating the defendant's confrontation rights *if the trial judge makes individual findings of probable trauma to the child* from testifying in the defendant's presence. [Maryland v. Craig, 497 U.S. 836 (1990)]

2. Due Process Rights
In addition, the Court has held that state hearsay rules and other exclusionary rules cannot be applied where the effect would be to deprive an accused of her Fourteenth Amendment due process right to a *fair trial* [Chambers v. Mississippi, 410 U.S. 284 (1973)], or deny her right to compulsory process [Rock v. Arkansas, 483 U.S. 44 (1987)].

VIII. PROCEDURAL CONSIDERATIONS

A. BURDENS OF PROOF
The term "burden of proof," as used by judges and lawyers at trial, encompasses two separate meanings or burdens. Thus, burden of proof can mean:

1. Burden of Producing or Going Forward with Evidence

a. Produce Sufficient Evidence to Raise Fact Question for Jury
This defines the burden of one party to introduce sufficient evidence to avoid judgment

against her as a matter of law. It is the burden of producing sufficient evidence to create a fact question of the issue involved, so that the issue may appropriately reach the jury. The burden of producing evidence is a critical mechanism for judicial control of the trial. Although the burden is usually cast upon the party who has pleaded the existence of the fact, the burden as to this fact may shift to the adversary when the pleader has discharged her initial duty.

b.   Prima Facie Case May Shift Burden of Production
Consider *Plaintiff v. Defendant* in a negligence action. Plaintiff offers evidence in her case-in-chief of Defendant's negligence. Defendant's motion for a nonsuit, made at the conclusion of Plaintiff's case, is denied. This denial reflects a judicial ruling that Plaintiff has made out a prima facie case of Defendant's negligence. Put another way, it means that Plaintiff has met her burden of going forward with evidence on the negligence issue.

Now assume that Defendant rests immediately after Plaintiff's case-in-chief without producing any rebuttal evidence. Plaintiff then moves for a directed verdict in her favor, claiming that Defendant was negligent as a matter of law. If this motion were granted, it would mean that (i) Plaintiff's evidence was sufficiently persuasive, (ii) the burden shifted to Defendant, and (iii) Defendant failed to meet his newly imposed burden of producing evidence of no negligence. If Plaintiff's motion were denied, it would mean only that Plaintiff met her initial burden but that it did not shift to Defendant; and, therefore, the burden of production having dropped out of the case, the matter is now for the jury. Once in the hands of the jury, the question is whether Plaintiff has met her burden of persuasion.

2.   Burden of Persuasion (Proof)

a.   Determined by Jury After All Evidence Is In
This is what is usually meant when the term "burden of proof" is used. This burden becomes a crucial factor only if the parties have sustained their burdens of production and only when all the evidence is in. When the time of decision comes, the jury must be instructed how to decide the issue if their minds remain in doubt. There are no tie games in the litigation process. Either the plaintiff or the defendant must win. If, after all the proof is in, the issue is equally balanced in the minds of the jury, then the party with the burden of persuasion must lose.

b.   Jury Instructed as to Which Party Has Burden of Persuasion
The burden of persuasion does not shift from party to party during the course of the trial simply because it need not be allocated until it is time for a decision by the trier of fact. The jury will be told which party has the burden of persuasion and what the quantum of proof should be. The jury is never told anything about the burden of going forward with evidence because that burden is a matter for the judge alone.

c.   Quantum or Measure of Proof
The trier of fact must be persuaded of the truth of disputed facts by one of the following standards, depending upon the nature of the action:

1) Preponderance of the Evidence

The preponderance of the evidence standard applies in most civil cases. This standard has been defined as meaning that the fact finder must be persuaded by the party to whom the burden on the issue has been allocated that the fact is *more probably true than not true*.

2) Clear and Convincing Proof

Some civil cases (an oral contract to make a will or issues of fraud) often require proof by "clear and convincing evidence." This standard requires the trier of fact to be persuaded that there is a *high probability* that the fact in question exists.

3) Beyond a Reasonable Doubt

This is the *highest standard* and applies to criminal cases. In a criminal prosecution, the guilt of the defendant must be established beyond a reasonable doubt.

B. PRESUMPTIONS

A presumption is a rule that requires that a particular inference be drawn from an ascertained set of facts. It is a form of substitute proof or evidentiary shortcut, in that proof of the presumed fact is rendered unnecessary once evidence has been introduced of the basic fact that gives rise to the presumption. Presumptions are established for a wide variety of overlapping policy reasons. In some cases, the presumption serves to correct an imbalance resulting from one party's superior access to the proof on a particular issue. In others, the presumption was created as a timesaver to eliminate the need for proof of a fact that is highly probable in any event. In other words, the inference from the basic fact to the presumed fact is so probable and logical that it is sensible to assume the presumed fact upon proof of the basic fact. In still other situations, the presumption serves as a social or economic policy device. It operates to favor one contention by giving it the benefit of a presumption and to correspondingly handicap the disfavored adversary.

Example: A common presumption is that the driver of a vehicle is the owner's agent. When plaintiff has been injured by the negligent operation of a vehicle, the nondriving owner-defendant will be liable for the negligence of the driver if the driver is the owner's agent. Plaintiff's burden of proving that the driver was the agent of the owner is aided by a presumption of agency that arises upon proof of ownership. The justification of this presumption of agency from ownership may be explained in terms of *fairness* in light of defendant's superior access to the evidence; in terms of *probability*, since it is unlikely that defendant's car was stolen by the driver; or in terms of a *social policy* of promoting safety or increasing available compensation for traffic victims by widening the responsibility of owners.

1. Effect—Shift Burden of Production

Federal Rule 301 provides that a presumption imposes on the party against whom it is directed the burden of going forward with evidence to rebut the presumption. However, this rule does not shift the burden of persuasion, which remains throughout the trial upon the party who had it originally.

Example: Plaintiff has the burden of going forward and the burden of persuasion on the issue of Edwina's death. Plaintiff introduces evidence sufficient to support the fact that Edwina has been absent without tidings for a period of seven years. The proof of this basic fact causes a presumption of the presumed fact—Edwina's death. Plaintiff has made out a prima facie case on Edwina's death.

More than that, if the defendant is silent and fails to offer proof in rebuttal (either of the presumed fact of death, or the basic fact of absence for a period of seven years), the jury will be instructed that they *must* find Edwina is dead if they believe the absence has been for seven years.

2. Rebutting a Presumption

A presumption is overcome or destroyed when the adversary produces some evidence contradicting the presumed fact. In other words, the *presumption is of no force or effect* when sufficient contrary evidence is admitted. This is the federal view adopted by Federal Rule 301, except where state law provides the rule of decision (*see* 6., *infra*).

Example: Plaintiff-victim of automobile driver's negligence sues owner. Plaintiff proves ownership, thus giving rise to the presumption that the driver was the agent of the owner. Defendant-owner testifies that the driver was not his agent, and his evidence could justify a jury finding that the driver was without authority from the owner. At this point, plaintiff's presumption is gone. He will have to sustain the burden of proving by a preponderance of the evidence that the driver was the agent of the owner, or his case will fail.

a. Amount of Contrary Evidence Necessary

The amount of contrary evidence that must be introduced to overcome the presumption has never been clearly articulated. Some cases require "enough evidence to support a finding of the nonexistence of the presumed fact." Others simply require "substantial evidence."

3. Distinguish True Presumptions from Inferences and Substantive Law

The true presumption with its mandatory rebuttable inference should not be confused with inferences and rules of substantive law.

a. Permissible Inferences

The permissible inference (prima facie case, or sometimes erroneously called "presumption of fact") will allow a party to meet the burden of production but *will not shift the burden* to the adversary. Examples of situations giving rise to permissible inferences are:

1) Res Ipsa Loquitur

A permissible inference of negligence arises where this type of accident ordinarily occurs because of the negligence of someone in the defendant's position.

2) Spoliation or Withholding Evidence

The intentional destruction or mutilation of relevant evidence may give rise to an inference that the destroyed evidence is unfavorable to the spoliator. An unfavorable inference may also arise when a party fails to produce evidence or witnesses within his control which he is naturally expected to produce.

3) Undue Influence

Where the attorney who drafted a will is its principal beneficiary to the exclusion of the natural objects of the testator's bounty, an inference of undue influence may be found.

b. **"Presumptions" in Criminal Cases**

1) **Accused Is Presumptively Innocent**

The accused in a criminal case is presumptively innocent until the prosecution proves every element of the offense beyond a reasonable doubt. Accordingly, it is clear that in criminal cases "presumptions" do not shift to the accused the burden of producing evidence, nor of persuading the fact finder. A "presumption" in a criminal case is truly nothing more than a *permissible inference*.

2) **Judge's Instructions on Presumed Facts Against Accused**

The trial judge in a criminal case is not free to charge the jury that it *must* find a "presumed" fact against the accused. When the existence of a presumed fact is submitted to the jury, the judge shall instruct the jury that it *may* regard the basic facts as sufficient evidence of the presumed fact, but that it is not required by law to do so. If the presumed fact establishes guilt, is an element of the offense, or negates a defense, its existence must be found (proved) beyond a reasonable doubt.

c. **Conclusive Presumptions**

This form of inference goes beyond the true presumption since it *cannot be rebutted* by contrary evidence. A "conclusive" presumption is really a rule of substantive law.

Example: In some states, it is conclusively presumed that a child under a certain age (e.g., seven years old) cannot commit a crime. No evidence to the contrary can rebut this presumption, and part of the proof of the case requires a showing that the accused is over the minimum age.

4. **Specific Presumptions**

The following are common rebuttable presumptions:

a. **Presumption of Legitimacy**

The law presumes that every person is legitimate. The presumption applies to all cases where legitimacy is in dispute. The mere fact of birth gives rise to the presumption. The presumption is destroyed by evidence of illegitimacy that is "clear and convincing." For example, the presumption is overcome by proof of a husband's impotency, proof of lack of access, or the negative result of a properly conducted blood grouping test.

b. **Presumption Against Suicide**

When the cause of death is in dispute, a presumption arises in *civil* (not criminal) cases that the death was not a suicide.

c. **Presumption of Sanity**

Every person is presumed sane until the contrary is shown. The presumption of sanity applies in *criminal as well as civil* cases.

d. **Presumption of Death from Absence**

A person is presumed dead in any action involving the property of such person, the contractual or property right contingent upon his death, or the administration of his estate, if:

1) The person is inexplicably absent for a continuous period of *seven years* (death is deemed to have occurred on the last day of the seven-year period); and

2) He *has not been heard from,* or of, by those with whom he would normally be expected to communicate.

e. Presumption from Ownership of Car—Agent Driver
Proof of ownership of a motor vehicle gives rise to the presumption that the owner was the driver or that the driver was the owner's agent.

f. Presumption of Chastity
There is a presumption that every person is chaste and virtuous.

g. Presumption of Regularity
The general presumption is that no official or person acting under an oath of office will do anything contrary to his official duty, or omit anything that his official duty requires to be done.

h. Presumption of Continuance
Proof of the existence of a person, an object, a condition, or a tendency at a given time raises a presumption that it continued for as long as is usual with things of that nature.

i. Presumption of Mail Delivery
A letter shown to have been properly addressed, stamped, and mailed is presumed to have been delivered in the due course of mail. The presumption is said to be based upon the probability that officers of the government will perform their duty.

j. Presumption of Solvency
A person is presumed solvent, and every debt is presumed collectible.

k. Presumption of Bailee's Negligence
Upon proof of delivery of goods in good condition to a bailee and failure of the bailee to return the goods in the same condition, there is a presumption that the bailee was negligent.

l. Presumption of Marriage
Upon proof that a marriage ceremony was performed, it is presumed to have been legally performed and that the marriage is valid. A presumption of marriage also arises from cohabitation.

5. Conflicting Presumptions
If two or more conflicting presumptions arise, the judge shall apply the presumption that is founded on the weightier considerations of policy and logic. For example, where the validity of a later marriage is attacked by evidence of a prior valid marriage, the presumption of the validity of the later marriage is deemed to prevail over the presumption of the continuance of the first marriage.

6. Choice of Law Regarding Presumptions in Civil Actions
Under the Federal Rules, the effect of a presumption respecting a fact that is an element of a

claim or defense as to which the rule of decision is supplied by state law is also governed by state law.

C. RELATIONSHIP OF PARTIES, JUDGE, AND JURY

1. Party Responsibility

Ours is an adversarial adjudicative process, and so the focus is on party responsibility or, perhaps what is more to the point, on lawyer responsibility. Very little happens in the litigation process unless some lawyer makes it happen by filing pleadings and motions, by initiating discovery, by entering into stipulations, by calling witnesses and offering exhibits at trial, or by interposing objections to the admission of evidence. In other words, the parties, through their lawyers, frame the issues in a litigation by making allegations, admissions, and denials in their pleadings, and by entering into binding stipulations. They assume the burden of proving the issues they have raised. And then, by deciding which witnesses to call to the stand and what tangible exhibits to introduce (and by deciding to what they will object), they control the flow of evidence. But the parties and their lawyers are not the only ones to be allocated important responsibilities in the adversary trial process.

2. Court-Jury Responsibility

Under our system, the trial court is more umpire than advocate. The trial judge's primary responsibility is to fairly superintend the trial; the judge is not permitted to become a partisan in it. As a general rule, questions of law are for the trial court to deal with, and questions of fact determination are for the jury, although trial judges frequently encounter the necessity of making preliminary fact determinations in connection with such matters as the admission or exclusion of evidence. (Of course, both types of questions—legal and factual are for the trial court in a nonjury case.)

3. Preliminary Determination of Admissibility

In most cases, the existence of some preliminary or foundational fact is an essential condition to the admissibility of proffered evidence. Thus, before a written contract may be received in evidence, it must be shown that the contract is genuine; and before testimony as to an alleged dying declaration may be admitted into evidence, it must be shown that the declaration was made under a sense of impending death. In some cases, the existence or nonexistence of the preliminary fact is determined by the jury, with the judge merely deciding whether the evidence of the foundational fact is sufficient to allow the jury to find its existence. In other cases, the question of the preliminary fact must be decided by the judge alone—in which case the evidence will not even be heard by the jury unless the judge first finds the preliminary or foundational fact.

a. Preliminary Facts Decided by Jury

The Federal Rules of Evidence distinguish preliminary facts to be decided by the jury from those to be decided by the judge, on the ground that the former questions involve the ***relevancy*** of the proffered evidence, while the latter questions involve the ***competency*** of evidence that is relevant. Rule 104(b) of the Federal Rules of Evidence defines preliminary facts to be decided by the jury as those where the answer to the preliminary question determines whether the proffered evidence is relevant at all. For example, if a statement is proffered to show notice to X, the jury must decide whether X heard it. If X did not, the statement is irrelevant for that purpose; but the decision is left ultimately to the jury, because if the jury does not believe X heard it, they will not use it anyway.

1) **Role of the Judge**

Before the judge allows the proffered evidence to go to the jury, she must find that the proponent of the proffered evidence has introduced evidence sufficient to sustain a finding of the existence of the preliminary fact. The court may ***instruct the jury*** to determine whether the preliminary fact exists and to disregard the proffered evidence if the jury finds that the preliminary fact does not exist. Such an instruction may be desirable if the trier of fact would otherwise be confused, but with most questions of conditional relevancy the instruction will be unnecessary, since a rational jury will disregard these types of evidence anyway unless they believe in the existence of the foundational fact. If the judge allows the introduction of evidence and then subsequently determines that a jury could not reasonably find that the preliminary fact exists, she must instruct the jury to disregard that evidence.

2) **Examples of Preliminary Facts Decided by Jury**

a) **Agency**

If plaintiff sues defendant upon an alleged contract, evidence of negotiations with a third party is inadmissible because it is irrelevant unless the third party is shown to be defendant's agent. However, the evidence of the negotiations with the third party is admissible if there is evidence sufficient to sustain a finding of the agency.

b) **Authenticity of a Document**

If there is a dispute about whether a note was signed by the defendant (as opposed to a forger), the authenticity of the document is to be left for the jury. In a sense this is merely an issue of relevancy, since the note, if forged, is irrelevant to the liability of the defendant.

c) **Credibility**

When a conviction of a crime is offered to attack the credibility of a witness, the judge must admit the evidence and allow the jury to determine the witness's credibility if there is evidence sufficient to identify the witness as the person convicted.

d) **Personal Knowledge**

The question of whether a witness had personal knowledge can go to the jury if there is sufficient evidence to sustain a finding that the witness had personal knowledge.

b. **Preliminary Facts Decided by Judge**

1) **Facts Affecting Competency of Evidence**

The question of the existence or nonexistence of all preliminary facts other than those of conditional relevance must be determined by the court. In most cases, the questions which must be decided by the judge involve the competency of the evidence or the existence of a privilege. These questions are withheld from the jury because it is felt that, once the jury hears the disputed evidence, the damage will have been done and the instruction to disregard the evidence, if the preliminary fact is not found, will be ineffective.

2) **Requirements for Privilege**

Preliminary facts to establish the existence of a privilege must be determined by the court. This must be so, or else a privilege might be ignored merely because there was sufficient evidence (and this might not be a great deal) for a jury to find it did not exist. Whether or not the jury believed that the facts giving rise to the privilege existed, they would still have heard the privileged evidence, subject only perhaps to a most unrealistic instruction to disregard it if they found the privilege to exist.

3) **Requirements for Hearsay Exceptions**

All preliminary fact questions involving the standards of trustworthiness of alleged exceptions to the hearsay rule must also be determined by the court. For example, the court must decide whether a statement offered as a dying declaration was made under a sense of impending death, or whether a purported business record was made in the regular course of business. The reason for this is that, otherwise, the jury will hear the hearsay evidence where the judge's finding is not that it fell within an exception to the hearsay rule, but only that there was enough evidence for the jury to so find. The jurors, however, once they have heard the hearsay evidence, might ignore the judge's instruction to disregard it unless they found the preliminary fact.

4) **Others**

The above two cases are the most important where the judge must first determine the existence of a foundational fact. However, there are several other major categories.

a) The judge must determine whether a witness is disqualified for *lack of mental capacity*.

b) The judge must rule on the qualifications of a witness as *an expert*.

c) If a conviction of a crime is offered to attack credibility and the disputed preliminary fact is whether a *pardon* has been granted to the witness so convicted (the pardon rendering the impeaching conviction inadmissible), the judge must make the determination.

d) The judge must determine whether a witness is sufficiently acquainted with a person whose sanity is in question in order for him to be *qualified to express an opinion* as to that person's sanity.

e) The judge is required to determine the preliminary facts necessary to warrant reception of *secondary evidence of a writing* (e.g., whether original writing was lost or destroyed).

f) The judge is required to determine the *voluntariness of a confession* before he allows the jury to hear it. This is a rule of constitutional law. The theory is that otherwise the jury might hear involuntary confessions but rely on them anyway because the jury felt that they were nonetheless trustworthy.

5) Procedure for Preliminary Fact Determinations by Judge

    a) What Evidence May Be Considered
    Federal Rule 104(a) permits the trial judge to consider any (nonprivileged) *relevant evidence,* even though not otherwise admissible under the rules of evidence. Thus, the trial judge may consider affidavits or hearsay in ruling on preliminary fact questions. Most state courts, however, hold that the rules of evidence apply in preliminary fact determinations as much as in any other phase of the trial; thus, only admissible evidence may be considered.

    b) Presence of Jury
    Whether the jury should be excused during the preliminary fact determination is generally within the discretion of the trial judge. However, because of the potential for prejudice to the accused in a criminal trial, the jury *must* be excused during hearings on the admissibility of the accused's confession, or whenever the accused testifies during the preliminary fact hearing and requests that the jury be excused. [Fed. R. Evid. 104(c)]

c. Testimony by Accused Does Not Waive Privilege Against Self-Incrimination
An accused may testify as to any preliminary matter (e.g., circumstances surrounding allegedly illegal search) without subjecting herself to having to testify generally at the trial. Furthermore, while testifying upon a preliminary matter, an accused is not subject to cross-examination on other issues in the case. [Fed. R. Evid. 104(d)]

d. Judicial Power to Comment upon Evidence
The trial judge is expected to marshal or summarize the evidence when necessary. However, in most state courts, the trial judge may not comment upon the weight of the evidence or the credibility of witnesses. In federal court, the trial judge has traditionally been permitted to comment on the weight of the evidence and the credibility of witnesses.

e. Power to Call Witnesses
The judge may call witnesses upon her own initiative and may interrogate any witnesses who testify, but may not demonstrate partisanship for one side of the controversy.

f. Rulings
A trial judge has an obligation to rule promptly on counsel's evidentiary objections and, when requested to do so by counsel, to state the grounds for her rulings.

g. Instructions on Limited Admissibility of Evidence
When evidence that is admissible as to one party or for one purpose, but inadmissible as to another party or for another purpose, is admitted, the trial judge, on timely request, must restrict the evidence to its proper scope and instruct the jury accordingly, e.g., "Ladies and gentlemen of the jury, the testimony that you have just heard is receivable against the defendant Bushmat only and will in no way be considered by you as bearing on the guilt or innocence of the co-defendant Lishniss." [Fed. R. Evid. 105]

REAL PROPERTY

REAL PROPERTY

TABLE OF CONTENTS

REAL PROPERTY

I. ESTATES IN LAND

A. IN GENERAL

"Estates in land" are ***possessory interests*** in land. These interests may be ***presently*** possessory (present estates), or they may become possessory in the ***future*** (future interests). They may be "freeholds," which give possession under some legal title or right to hold (e.g., fees or life estates), or they may be "nonfreeholds," which give mere possession (i.e., leases). Estates in land may be of potentially infinite duration, as in the case of a fee simple, or they may be of limited duration, as in the case of an estate for years. But whatever their characteristics, "estates in land" must be distinguished from ***nonpossessory*** interests such as easements, profits, covenants, and servitudes.

This section of the outline will examine various estates in land. It divides the interests into two classes: present interests and future interests. However, some future interests (those following defeasible fees) will be considered with the present interests to which they are attached.

B. PRESENT POSSESSORY ESTATES

1. Fee Simple Absolute

An estate in fee simple absolute is the largest estate permitted by law. It invests the holder of the fee with full possessory rights, now and in the future. The holder can sell it, divide it, or devise it; and if she dies intestate, her heirs will inherit it. The fee simple has an indefinite and potentially infinite duration. The common law rule requiring technical words of inheritance ("and his heirs") has been abolished by statute in nearly all jurisdictions. Typically, such statutes provide: "A fee simple title is presumed to be intended to pass by a grant of real property unless it appears from the grant that a lesser estate was intended."

Example: A conveyance from "O to A" is presumed to pass a fee simple interest if O owned one. At common law, absent the words of inheritance, even a conveyance "to A in fee simple" would convey only a life estate to A.

2. Defeasible Fees

Defeasible fees are fee simple estates of ***potentially*** infinite duration that can be terminated by the happening of a specified event. Because defeasible fees can result in forfeitures, courts will construe, where possible, a purported limitation as a mere declaration of the grantor's purpose or motive for making the grant (i.e., as precatory language). (*See* b.1)a), *infra.*)

a. Fee Simple Determinable (and Possibility of Reverter)

A fee simple determinable, also called a determinable fee, is an estate that ***automatically terminates*** on the happening of a stated event and goes back to the grantor. (It must be distinguished from the fee simple subject to a condition subsequent, where the grantor must take affirmative steps to terminate the estate of the grantee if the stated event occurs.) It is created by the use of durational, adverbial language, such as "for so long as," "while," "during," or "until." A fee simple determinable can be conveyed by the owner thereof, but his grantee takes the land subject to the termination of the estate by the happening of the event.

Example: O conveys land "to A for so long as no alcoholic beverages are consumed on the premises." This gives A a fee simple because the estate may last forever if no one ever quaffs a brew. If A conveys his fee simple determinable estate to B, B will own the "for so long as" estate. If A does not convey his estate, on A's death it will pass by will or intestacy to his successors, and so on. If, however, someone ever consumes an alcoholic beverage on the premises, the estate will automatically come to an end according to its own terms; and O will immediately and automatically become the owner of the fee simple, without taking any steps to terminate A's interest.

1) Correlative Future Interest in Grantor—Possibility of Reverter
Because the grantee's estate may end upon the happening of the stated event, there is a possibility that the land may revert back to the grantor. The interest that is left in a grantor who conveys an estate in fee simple determinable is called a "possibility of reverter." It is a future interest because it becomes possessory only upon the occurrence of the stated event.

a) Possibility of Reverter Need Not Be Expressly Retained
At common law and in nearly all states today, the grantor does not have to expressly retain a possibility of reverter. It arises *automatically* in the grantor as a consequence of his conveying a fee simple determinable estate, with its built-in time limitation.

b) Transferability of Possibility of Reverter
At early common law, the possibility of reverter could not be transferred inter vivos or devised by will. An attempted transfer of the interest was invalid; but the possibility of reverter was not extinguished by the attempted transfer and would still descend to the heirs of the owner. Today, in most jurisdictions, the possibility of reverter can be transferred inter vivos or devised by will, and descends to the owner's heirs if she dies intestate.

2) Correlative Future Interest in Third Party—Executory Interest
A possibility of reverter arises only in the grantor, not in a third party. Technically, there is no correlative future interest in a third party with a fee simple determinable. However, a fee simple subject to an executory interest (*see* below) includes a grant with the same features as above but with a future interest in a third party. (*See* C.3., *infra*.)

b. Fee Simple Subject to Condition Subsequent (and Right of Entry)
A fee simple subject to a condition subsequent is created when the grantor retains the power to terminate the estate of the grantee upon the happening of a specified event. Upon the happening of the event stated in the conveyance, the estate of the grantee *continues until the grantor exercises her power of termination* (right of entry) by bringing suit or making reentry. The following words are usually held to create conditions subsequent: "upon condition that," "provided that," "but if," and "if it happens that."

Example: O, owning Blackacre in fee simple, conveys it "to A and his heirs, on the express condition that the premises are never to be used by A for the sale of liquor, and in the event that they are so used, then O or her heirs may enter and terminate the estate hereby conveyed." A has a fee simple subject to a condition subsequent. O has a right of entry. If the condition is broken, O has a power to terminate the estate of A by asserting her *right of entry*.

1) **Correlative Future Interest in Grantor—Right of Entry**

A right of entry (also known as "right of reentry" or "power of termination") is the future interest retained by the transferor who conveys an estate on condition subsequent. It is necessary to *expressly* reserve the right of entry in the grantor; this retained interest does not automatically arise as in the case of a fee simple determinable and possibility of reverter.

a) **Failure to Reserve Right of Entry**

Courts often hold that words of condition, standing alone, create only covenants, easements, or trusts, or are mere precatory terms.

Example: O conveys land "to A and his heirs, provided that liquor is not sold on the premises." O has not used words indicating the estate will terminate if liquor is sold on the premises. Nor has O retained a right to reenter. Because the grant does not clearly state an intent of the grantor to retain a discretionary power to reenter the land if the land ceased to be used for the stated purpose, a court may construe the deed as creating a covenant not to sell liquor or even as giving A a fee simple absolute.

b) **Waiver of Right of Entry**

Because the grantor can elect whether or not to terminate the grantee's estate, she may waive her right or power to enforce a forfeiture by express agreement or by her conduct. (Such is not the case with a fee simple determinable, where the forfeiture is automatic.)

(1) **Inaction by Itself Not a Waiver**

The general rule is that when there is a breach of the condition and the grantor simply does nothing about it, the power of termination is not waived. (*See also* V.D.2., *infra*.) However, where there is any element of *detrimental reliance* by the fee holder, many courts treat inaction as a waiver on an estoppel or laches theory.

c) **Transferability of Right of Entry**

At common law, a right of entry was *not devisable or transferable inter vivos* to a third person. The right of entry did, however, descend to the heirs of the grantor on her death. Today, in most jurisdictions, a right of entry is still *not* alienable inter vivos. (Indeed, in a handful of states, an attempted transfer destroys it.) But in most states, rights of entry are devisable; and in all states, they descend to the owner's heirs.

2) **Correlative Future Interest in Third Party—Executory Interest**

A right of entry can be created only in favor of the grantor and her heirs. If a similar interest is created in favor of a third party, the interest is called an executory interest (e.g., "if the property is ever used for other than church purposes, then to B and his heirs"). Unlike a right of entry, an executory interest is subject to the **Rule Against Perpetuities**. (*See* E., *infra.*)

3) Compare—Fee Simple Determinable

This estate is distinguished from a determinable fee in that the breach of the condition does **not** itself terminate the estate and immediately revest the fee in the grantor or her successor. The estate continues in the grantee or his successor unless or until the grantor or her successor affirmatively elects to terminate it.

a) Construction of Ambiguous Language

The general policy of courts is to avoid forfeiture of estates. Thus, a conveyance that contains both durational language and a power of termination may be construed as creating a *fee simple subject to a condition subsequent*, because the forfeiture is *optional* at the grantor's election rather than automatic.

Example: O conveys land "to A so long as liquor is not sold on the premises, and if liquor is sold, O has a right to reenter." The words "so long as" point to a fee simple determinable. The retained right of entry points to a fee simple subject to a condition subsequent. The court can classify the language to create either estate, but the fee simple subject to a condition subsequent is preferred.

c. Fee Simple Subject to an Executory Interest

A fee simple subject to an executory interest is an estate that, upon the happening of a stated event, is *automatically divested in favor of a third person* rather than the grantor.

Examples: 1) O conveys land "to Church; provided, however, that if the premises shall ever cease to be used for church purposes, title shall pass to the American Heart Association." Church has a fee simple subject to an executory interest in favor of the Heart Association. O does not have a right of entry because no such interest was reserved in the conveyance. The Heart Association's interest is not a right of entry because that future interest can be reserved only in favor of a grantor. The Heart Association's future interest is not a remainder because it divests a fee simple. Therefore, it is an executory interest.

Note: Executory interests are subject to the Rule Against Perpetuities, but the Heart Association's interest is valid because of the "charity-to-charity" exception to the Rule. (*See* E.1.e.1), *infra.*)

2) O conveys land "to Church for so long as the premises are used for church purposes, and if they shall ever cease to be so used, then and in that event to the American Red Cross." Church has a fee simple determinable subject to an executory interest in favor of the Red Cross. O has no possibility of reverter because he has not retained any interest; he

has conveyed away his entire estate in the property. The future interest in the Red Cross cannot be a possibility of reverter because that interest arises only in a grantor, and the Red Cross is a grantee. It is an executory interest and not a remainder because it divests a fee simple. (Further discussion of these points will come later.)

Note: Were it not for the "charity-to-charity" exception to the Rule Against Perpetuities, the executory interest in favor of the Red Cross would violate the Rule.

d. Limitations on Possibilities of Reverter and Rights of Entry
In a few states, statutes limit the permissible duration of possibilities of reverter and rights of entry to a certain number of years (usually 30) in order to foster marketability of title. Other statutes (usually called "marketable title acts") require the rerecording of various future interests (including possibilities of reverter and rights of entry) every 20 to 40 years or they become unenforceable.

e. Conditions and Limitations Violating Public Policy
Conditions and limitations that are designed to prevent the acquisition or retention of an interest in land generally are struck down if they are contrary to public policy. Striking such a condition will result in an interest different from that intended by the grantor. (*See also* F., *infra.*)

1) Restraints on Marriage
If the purpose of the condition or limitation is to *penalize* marriage, it likely will be struck down. On the other hand, if the purpose is to *give support* until marriage, when the new spouse's obligation of support arises, the condition or limitation generally is upheld.

Example: O conveys land "to A, but if she marries, to B." Absent any evidence as to O's motive, the condition subsequent will be struck down, leaving A with a fee simple absolute.

Compare: O conveys land "to A for her support until she marries." Because O intends to give A support only until the burden of support shifts to A's spouse, A's fee simple determinable is valid.

2) Provisions Involving Separation or Divorce
Conditions and limitations meant to *encourage* separation or divorce are invalid. On the other hand, conditions and limitations meant to *give support* in the event of separation or divorce generally are valid.

Example: O conveys land "to A, provided that he divorces his current spouse within one year; if he does not, to B." Absent any evidence as to O's motive, the condition subsequent will be struck down, leaving A with a fee simple absolute.

3. Fee Tail
The fee tail, typically created by the words "to A and the heirs of his body," limited inheritance to *lineal descendants* of the grantee. If no lineal descendants survived at the grantee's

death, the property either reverted to the grantor or her successors or passed to a designated remainderman. Today, most United States jurisdictions have abolished the fee tail and have enacted statutes under which any attempt to create a fee tail results in the creation of a fee simple.

4. Life Estate

An estate for life is an estate that is not terminable at any fixed or computable period of time, but cannot last longer than the life or lives of one or more persons. It may arise by operation of law or may be created by an act or agreement of the parties.

a. Life Estates by Marital Right (Legal Life Estates)

Such estates arise under *dower* and *curtesy*, the common law interests of wife and husband, respectively, in real property of which the other spouse was seized during marriage (including property acquired before marriage). At common law, a surviving wife's dower right entitled her to a life estate in an undivided one-third of her husband's lands. A surviving husband's right of curtesy gave him a life estate in all of his wife's lands if issue were born. For exam purposes, it is important to remember that a conveyance by a husband to a bona fide purchaser does not defeat dower unless the wife joins in the conveyance. Likewise, a husband's creditors cannot defeat a wife's dower rights. Most states have abolished both dower and curtesy and have instead given the surviving spouse a statutory right to take a portion of the deceased spouse's estate. Community property states do not recognize either dower or curtesy.

b. Conventional Life Estate

1) For Life of Grantee

The usual life estate is measured by the life of the grantee and is called simply a life estate. It may be indefeasible (so that it will end *only* when the life tenant dies), or it *may be made defeasible* in the same ways that fee estates can be defeasible (e.g., determinable, subject to a condition subsequent, subject to an executory interest). In such a case, the estate may end *before* the life tenant dies if the limiting condition occurs. (*See* Example 5), below.)

Examples: 1) O conveys "to A for life." In this case, A has an estate in the land for as long as he lives. On his death, the land reverts to O, the grantor.

2) "To A for life, then to B." This is a life estate because it is measured by the life of A and is not terminable at a fixed period of time.

3) "To A for life, but in no event for more than 10 years." This is an estate for years and not a life estate because the estate in A will end in 10 years (i.e., a fixed time period).

4) "To A for 10 years if he lives so long." This is also an estate for years and not a life estate because the estate in A will end in 10 years.

5) "To A for life or until she remarries." This is a life estate subject to a limitation, but nevertheless a life estate. The estate in A will not end at any fixed or computable time period. It can be termed a "life estate determinable," and is analogous to the fee simple determinable discussed above.

6) "To B and C after the life of A." A has an implied life estate.

2) Life Estate Pur Autre Vie (Life of Another)

A life estate pur autre vie is a life estate measured by the life of someone other than the life tenant. Such an estate can be created *directly* by the grantor, e.g., "to A for the life of B." A's estate ends when B dies. It can also be created *indirectly*, as where the grantor conveys "to B for life," and B later conveys his interest to A. A owns an estate measured by B's life; it ends when B dies.

a) Inheritability

At common law, if A died before B, the property was regarded as without an owner until B died. Today, statutes provide that such estates are devisable and inheritable if no special occupant is named in the original grant. (A "special occupant" is a person named by the grantor to take the balance of the term, if any.)

c. Rights and Duties of Life Tenant—Doctrine of Waste

A tenant for life is entitled to all the ordinary uses and profits of the land; but he cannot lawfully do any act that would injure the interests of the person who owns the remainder or the reversion. If he does, the future interest holder may sue for *damages and/or to enjoin* such acts.

1) Affirmative (Voluntary) Waste—Natural Resources

As a general rule, a life tenant may not consume or exploit natural resources on the property (e.g., timber, minerals, oil). *Exceptions* to this rule allow exploitation in the following circumstances:

(i) In reasonable amounts where necessary *for repair and maintenance* of the land;

(ii) When the life tenant is *expressly given the right to exploit* such resources in the grant;

(iii) When *prior to the grant, the land was used in exploitation* of such natural resources, so that in granting the life estate the grantor most likely intended the life tenant to have the right to exploit (*but see* "open mines doctrine," below); and

(iv) In many states, where the *land is suitable only for such exploitation* (e.g., a mine).

Note: There is a vague "reasonableness" limit on the amount of oil or coal a life tenant can remove from the property.

a)   **Open Mines Doctrine**

If mining (extraction of minerals) was done on the land before the life estate began, the life tenant may continue to mine the property—but is limited to the mines *already open*. The life tenant may not open any new mines. There is a trend away from this limitation, applying instead the rule in (iii), above, to all natural resources, including minerals.

2)   **Permissive Waste**

Absent a contrary provision in the instrument creating the life estate, a life tenant has a duty to make repairs to the property to keep it from being damaged by the weather, and to pay certain carrying charges (e.g., mortgage interest, property taxes, and special assessments for public improvements). However, this duty is limited *to the extent of the income or profits derived from the land* (or if there is no actual income or profit, to the extent of the reasonable rental value of the land). Failure to make required repairs or pay required carrying charges constitutes permissive waste. A future interest holder who expends funds in satisfaction of the life tenant's obligations (e.g., pays the property taxes to avoid a tax foreclosure sale) is entitled to reimbursement.

a)   **Obligation to Repair**

A life tenant is obligated to preserve the land and structures in a *reasonable state of repair* (to the limited extent stated above). But the tenant is under no obligation to make permanent improvements on the land, no matter how wise it might seem to do so.

b)   **Obligation to Pay Interest on Encumbrances**

A life tenant is obligated to pay interest on any encumbrances on the land (to the limited extent stated above). However, he does not have to pay anything on the principal of the debt; reversioners or remaindermen must pay the principal in order to protect their interests.

The foregoing applies to encumbrances on the entire fee simple estate. Of course, a life tenant could place a mortgage on the life estate alone, and would then be liable for both principal and interest payments.

c)   **Obligation to Pay Taxes**

The life tenant is obligated to pay *all ordinary taxes* on the land (to the limited extent stated above).

d)   **Special Assessments for Public Improvements**

If the life of a public improvement on the land is shorter than the expected duration of the life estate, the life tenant is obligated to pay all of the assessment (to the limited extent stated above). However, if the improvement is likely to outlast the life estate (e.g., curbing, sewers, water mains, a change in grade of a street), taxes and assessments are *apportioned* equitably between the life tenant and the holders of all future interests.

(1)   **Apportionment of Costs**

Costs are usually apportioned by using the ratio produced by the market value of the life estate over the market value of the property.

e) **No Obligation to Insure Premises**
The life tenant is under no obligation to insure the premises for the benefit of a remainderman. However, both the life tenant and the remainderman have an insurable interest.

f) **No Liability for Third Party's Torts**
Under the modern view, life tenants are not responsible to remaindermen (as they were at common law) for damages caused by third-party tortfeasors. The life tenant's action against such third parties is limited to the damages to the life estate.

3) **Ameliorative Waste**
Ameliorative waste consists of acts that economically benefit the property. Ameliorative waste occurs when the use of the property is substantially changed, but the change increases the value of the property. At common law, any change to existing buildings or other improvements was always actionable waste, even if it improved the value of the property. Under modern authorities, however, a life tenant can substantially alter or even demolish existing buildings if:

(i) The market value of the future (or other nonpossessory) interests is not diminished; and *either*

(ii) The remaindermen do not object; *or*

(iii) A substantial and permanent change in the neighborhood conditions has deprived the property in its current form of reasonable productivity or usefulness.

Example: A holds a life estate in Blackacre, and B holds the remainder. The premises consist of an old and somewhat shabby apartment building that is nearly fully rented and produces a consistent income. The surrounding neighborhood includes many similar buildings. A proposes to demolish the building and construct a new shopping center on the land, which will produce much higher income. B objects to the change and brings an action to enjoin the demolition. B will prevail even though A's proposed changes would increase the value of the property. Because the existing building is economically productive and consistent with the neighborhood, A's commission of waste would not be justified.

a) **Compare—Leasehold Tenant**
Leasehold tenants are treated differently from life tenants. Most leasehold tenants remain liable for ameliorative waste even if the neighborhood has changed and the market value of the premises is increased. (*See* II.C.1.a.3), *infra.*)

b) **Compare—Worthless Property**
Under modern authority, a life tenant may ask for a judicial sale in a partition

proceeding if it appears that the land is practically worthless in its present state. The proceeds are put in trust with income to the life tenant.

d. Renunciation of Life Estates
A life tenant who receives the estate by will or intestacy may renounce it, perhaps because owning it would be burdensome. If this occurs, the courts generally ***accelerate*** the future interest that follows the life estate, allowing it to become possessory immediately.

5. Estates for Years, Periodic Estates, Estates at Will, Tenancies at Sufferance
These nonfreehold present estates in land are considered in the Landlord and Tenant section of this outline (*see* II.A., *infra*).

C. FUTURE INTERESTS
A future interest is an estate that does not entitle the owner thereof to possession immediately, but will or may give the owner possession in the future. A future interest is a ***present***, legally protected right in property; it is not an expectancy.

Examples: 1) O conveys land "to A for life, and on A's death to B in fee simple." A has a present possessory life estate. B has a future interest. (B's future interest is an indefeasibly vested remainder.) Upon the termination of A's possessory life estate, B's remainder in fee simple will become a present possessory estate in fee simple.

2) O conveys land "to A for life, and on A's death to B in fee simple if B survives A." A has a present possessory life estate. B has a future interest. (It is a contingent remainder.) Upon the termination of A's life estate, B's remainder in fee simple ***may*** become a present possessory estate in fee simple. B must survive A in order to take. (In this example, O also has a future interest. He has not conveyed away the interest represented by the contingency that B may predecease A. If B does predecease A, on the termination of A's life estate title to the land will ***revert*** to O. O's retained future interest is called a reversion.)

3) After the conveyance "to A for life, and on A's death to B," B can transfer his remainder interest to another person. Alternatively, if B dies during A's lifetime, his vested remainder will pass to the devisees under his will or (if B left no will) to his intestate heirs.

1. Reversionary Interests—Future Interests in Transferor

a. Possibilities of Reverter and Rights of Entry
These future interests are discussed above in connection with the present estates to which they are attached.

b. Reversions
A person owning an estate in real property can create and transfer a lesser estate (in the durational sense). The residue left in the grantor, which ***arises by operation of law***, is a reversion.

Examples: 1) O, owning land in fee simple, conveys it (i) "to A for life," or (ii) "to A for 99 years." In each case, O has a reversion in fee simple. She (or her successors) will be entitled to present possession of the land when the granted estate terminates.

2) O, owning a life estate in land, leases it "to A for 20 years." O has a reversion in a life estate. If O is still alive when A's lease expires, title will revert to O for life. What happens if, 10 years after this transfer, O dies? A's lease will come to an end, for he was given a lease by one holding only a life estate. O cannot convey a greater interest than she has.

3) O, owning land in fee simple, conveys it "to A for life, and on A's death to B if B survives A." A has a life estate, B has a contingent remainder, and O has a reversion that will take in present possession at A's death if B predeceases A.

Reversions are transferable, devisable by will, and descendible by inheritance. The holder of a reversion may sue a possessory owner for waste and may recover against third-party wrongdoers for damages to the property (to the extent of the injury to the reversion).

c. **All Reversionary Interests Are "Vested"**
Although a reversionary interest becomes possessory in the future, it is a vested interest, not a contingent interest, because both the owner and the event upon which it will become possessory are certain. This is true even if the reversionary interest is determinable or defeasible. Because it is a vested interest, a reversionary interest is *not subject to the Rule Against Perpetuities*.

2. **Remainders**
A remainder is a future interest created in a transferee that is *capable of taking* in present possession and enjoyment (i.e., capable of becoming a present interest) *upon the natural termination of the preceding estates* created in the same disposition. Unlike a reversion, which arises by operation of law from the fact that the transferor has not made a complete disposition of his interest, a remainder *must be expressly created in the instrument creating the intermediate possessory estate*. At common law, the only preceding estates that could support a remainder were life estates and fee tails. Because nearly all American jurisdictions have abolished the fee tail estate, a safe rule of thumb is that remainders *always follow life estates*. (*Note:* According to the Restatement of Property, under modern law, a remainder can also follow a term of years. However, there is very little case law on the point, and it is so rare that it is extremely unlikely to be tested.)

Examples: 1) "To A for life, and on A's death to B and his heirs." A has a present possessory life estate. B has a remainder in fee simple. It is a remainder because upon the expiration of A's life estate (natural termination of the preceding estate), B will be entitled to present possession and enjoyment of the property. The term "remainder" derives from the consequence that when A's life estate comes to an end, title "remains away" from the transferor instead of reverting back to him.

2) On Monday, O conveys Blackacre "to A for life." On Wednesday, O conveys "all of my right, title, and interest in Blackacre" to B. B holds a

reversion, not a remainder. B's future interest was not created in the same disposition that gave A a life estate. The Monday conveyance gave A a life estate and raised a reversion in O. The Wednesday conveyance transferred O's reversion to B. "Once a reversion, always a reversion."

A remainder cannot "cut short" or divest a preceding estate prior to its normal expiration. Therefore, a remainder can **never follow a fee simple**, which has a potentially infinite duration. Future interests that cut short a preceding estate or follow a gap after it are called executory interests. (*See* 3., *infra*.)

a. Indefeasibly Vested Remainder

An indefeasibly vested remainder is a remainder that:

(i) Can be created in and held only by an **ascertained person or persons** in being;

(ii) **Must be certain to become possessory on termination of the prior estates** (i.e., there is no condition that may operate to prevent the remainder from someday becoming a present interest);

(iii) **Must not be subject to being defeated or divested** (compare the vested remainder subject to total divestment, c., *infra*); and

(iv) **Must not be subject to being diminished in size** (compare the vested remainder subject to open, b., *infra*).

Examples: 1) "To A for life, and on A's death to B." A has a life estate; B has an indefeasibly vested remainder which is certain to take in possession on the termination of A's life estate.

What if B dies in A's lifetime? There is no stated condition that B survive A in order to take, and the courts do not imply such a condition. B's indefeasibly vested remainder passes by will or intestacy to his successors, who own an indefeasibly vested remainder.

2) "To A for life, then to A's first-born son in fee." At the time of this disposition, A has no children. The state of title: life estate in A, contingent remainder in the first son to be born to A, reversion in fee simple in the transferor. (The reversion will take in present possession if A never has a son.) The remainder is not vested because it is not created in an ascertained person in being. Also, it is subject to the condition that A have a child.

Two years later A has a son, John. The state of title: life estate in A, indefeasibly vested remainder in fee simple in John.

b. Vested Remainder Subject to Open

This is a vested remainder created in a class of persons (e.g., "children," "brothers and sisters") that is certain to take on the termination of the preceding estates, but is **subject to diminution** by reason of other persons becoming entitled to share in the remainder. It is also called a "vested remainder subject to partial divestment."

Examples: 1) "To A for life, and on A's death to her children in equal shares." If at the time of this disposition A has no children, the state of title is: life estate in A; contingent remainder in the unborn children of A; reversion in fee in the transferor, which will take in possession if A never has any children.

Suppose two years later a child, Bob, is born to A. The state of title is: life estate in A, vested remainder subject to open in Bob. Bob's remainder is vested because he is in existence and ascertained and his taking is not subject to any contingency. But it is vested subject to open because A may have more children.

Two years later another child, Ray, is born to A. Bob's remainder has been partially divested in favor of Ray, who also meets the description "children of A." Bob and Ray now hold the vested remainder as tenants in common (each with an undivided one-half share) *subject to open*—i.e., their vested remainders will be partially divested if more children are born to A.

Two years later Bob dies; shortly thereafter, A dies. Bob's successors (by will or intestacy) and Ray are entitled to present possession and enjoyment of the property. Bob's share of the remainder was subject to partial divestment, but it was not subject to being totally defeated. No condition of survival was attached to Bob's interest. Bob (or his successors) was certain to take; the only question was the size of his share.

2) Gift by will "to my wife, Rowena, for life, and on her death to *my* children in equal shares." T is survived by Rowena and by three children. At first blush this looks like a vested remainder subject to open because it is a remainder to someone's children. In reality, though, it is *indefeasibly vested*. T, being dead, can have no more children. (Slight qualification of answer: If Rowena is pregnant with T's child at T's death, the posthumous child, if born alive, will share in the gift.)

1)   Divesting Interests Are Executory Interests

Once the remainder vests in one existing member of the class, the divesting interest in the unborn members of the class is called an executory interest.

2)   Effect on Marketability of Title

Note that where there are outstanding interests in the unborn children, the vested remainderman and the life tenant cannot jointly convey good title.

Example: O "to A for life, remainder to B's children." C wants to buy the land, and desires to know if he can get good title if he purchases from A and all of B's living children. The answer is no, as long as B is alive, because it is possible for B to have more children (no matter what B's age). Thus, there would be outstanding interests in the unborn children of B, and C would not get good title.

c.   **Vested Remainder Subject to Total Divestment**

A vested remainder subject to total divestment arises when the remainderman is in existence and ascertained and his interest is not subject to any condition precedent, but his right to possession and enjoyment is subject to being defeated by the happening of some *condition subsequent*.

Examples: 1) "To A for life, remainder to B and his heirs, but if at B's death he is not survived by issue, to C and his heirs." Here, B has a vested remainder in fee simple, but his fee simple interest is subject to being divested if at his death he is not survived by issue. (C has a shifting executory interest.)

2) "To A for life, then to B for life." A has a life estate. B has a vested remainder in a life estate subject to total divestment. The transferor has a reversion in fee. B's remainder is vested even though (as a practical matter) he must survive A in order to take. But this practical requirement does not make B's remainder contingent. The only condition to B's taking is the natural termination of A's life estate, and this "condition" is inherent in any remainder life estate. There is no other condition precedent. However, B's remainder life estate is not indefeasibly vested, for it will be *defeated if he dies in A's lifetime*. Therefore, it is a vested remainder subject to total divestment.

3) "To A for life, and on A's death to B; but if B predeceases A, on A's death to C." A has a life estate. B has a vested remainder subject to total divestment. Although B's taking is *contingent on his surviving A*, that contingency is expressed as a condition subsequent—meaning that B's remainder is vested subject to total divestment. (C has a shifting executory interest.)

d.   **Contingent Remainder**

There are two ways to create a contingent remainder.

1)   **Subject to Condition Precedent**

A remainder will be classified as contingent if its taking in possession is subject to a condition precedent ("contingent as to *event*").

Examples: 1) "To A for life, and on A's death to B if B survives A." A has a life estate; B has a contingent remainder in fee simple. The transferor has a reversion, which will become a possessory estate on the termination of A's life estate if B predeceases A. Here, B's taking is subject to a contingency, stated as a condition precedent, that he must survive A in order to take.

Compare this with Example 3) in the preceding section. In that example, B's taking is also subject to a contingency: he must survive A in order to take. Thus in substance, this example and Example 3) are quite similar. But in classifying future interests, the general rule is that *it is form and not substance that counts*. In Example 3), the contingency of survival is expressed as a *condition subsequent*; therefore, B's remainder is vested subject to total divestment. But in this example, the contingency of survival is expressed as a **condition precedent**; therefore, B's remainder is a contingent remainder.

2) "To A for life, and on A's death to B if B marries C." Here, B is an ascertained person, but there is a condition precedent to B's taking: he must marry C. If B marries C in A's lifetime, his remainder will become indefeasibly vested.

3) O conveys "to A for life, then to B and his heirs if B survives A; if B does not survive A, then to C and his heirs." Each remainder is contingent because each is subject to a condition precedent. They are mutually exclusive and exhaustive; i.e., only one can come into possession, and when it does the other can never do so. These are called **alternative contingent remainders**.

Compare: O conveys "to A for life, then to B and his heirs, but if B marries C, then to D and his heirs." Here B, an ascertained person, takes a vested remainder because it is not limited on a condition precedent. B's remainder is ready to come into possession whenever A dies. But the marriage condition is subsequent—B's marriage to C will forfeit his estate. D's interest is called an executory interest.

2)   Unborn or Unascertained Persons
A remainder is contingent if it is created in favor of unborn or unascertained persons ("contingent as to **person**"), because until the remainderman is ascertained, there is no one ready to take possession should the preceding estate come to an end.

Examples: 1) "To A for life, and on A's death, per stirpes to such of A's descendants as survive her." At the time of this disposition, A is in poor health and she has two adult children (B and C) who are very healthy. State of title: A has a life estate; there is a contingent remainder in such of A's descendants as survive A; the transferor has a reversion (for A may not be survived by any descendants).

While the odds are in B and C's favor that they will take the remainder upon A's death, they are not named as the remaindermen. The remainder is in such of A's descendants as survive A, and we will not be able to identify the remaindermen until A dies and we can see which of A's descendants survived her.

2) O transfers securities in trust "to pay the income to A for life, and on A's death to distribute the trust corpus to A's heirs." There is a contingent remainder in A's heirs. It is true that A's heirs will be determined the moment A dies and A's life estate terminates. But at the time O makes the transfer, the remaindermen are not ascertained, for "*nemo est haeres viventis*" (no one is heir of the living).

The persons who turn out to be A's heirs will not be ascertained until A dies.

3) Destructibility of Contingent Remainders

At common law, a contingent remainder had to vest prior to or upon termination of the preceding freehold estate or it was destroyed.

Examples: 1) O conveyed "to A for life, then to the heirs of B." If A predeceased B, there were no heirs of B to take possession so the remainder was destroyed and O or his estate retook possession.

2) O conveyed "to A for life, then to B if she reaches age 21." If A died before B reached 21, the remainder was destroyed. (Note that whenever a grantor created a contingent remainder, he retained a reversion, which was normally defeasible.)

Analysis: Why are the interests in the above examples remainders and not executory interests? In each instance it is possible that the future interest will take effect at the natural expiration of A's life estate (as remainders do), or that it will take effect following a gap after A's estate (as executory interests do). The rule is that if an interest may operate as either a remainder or an executory interest (depending on the circumstances at A's death), it is a remainder. Thus, at common law, if such a remainder was then called upon to act as an executory interest, it could not do so and was destroyed.

a) Rule Abolished

Today, the rule of destructibility has been abolished in all but a few states. Thus, in the two examples given above, on A's death, O's *reversion* would take over, and would then give way to a springing executory interest on B's death in the first example, and on B's attaining age 21 in the second. (Note that the contingent remainders are not destroyed when the preceding estate ends, but instead become executory interests because they will divest the transferor's estate.)

b) Related Doctrine of Merger

Whenever the same person acquires all of the existing interests in land, present and future, a merger occurs. That person then holds a fee simple absolute. For example, suppose O conveys by deed "to A for life." O now has a reversion. Subsequently, by a later deed, O conveys his reversion interest to A. A will have a fee simple absolute by merger. (A similar result would follow if A conveyed her life estate to O.) Moreover, the common law held (as an aspect of the destructibility doctrine) that if a person acquired all of the interests in land *except* a contingent remainder, the merger would occur anyway, and the contingent remainder would be destroyed! Contingent remainders were considered to be such flimsy, ephemeral interests that they would not keep the merger from occurring. Note that this is still the rule in those few states retaining the common law rule of destructibility.

Example: In Example 1), above (O "to A for life, then to the heirs of B"), title stands as a life estate in A, a contingent remainder in the as yet unascertained heirs of B, and a reversion (if B is still alive at the death of A) in O. If O then purchased A's interest, O would hold a life estate pur autre vie (for the life of A) and a reversion. At common law, O's two interests on either side of the contingent remainder *merged*, wiping out the contingent remainder and giving O a fee simple.

(1) Compare—Interests Created Simultaneously
If a life estate and the next vested interest were created simultaneously (by the same instrument), there would be no merger at that time because that would defeat the grantor's obvious intent to create a contingent remainder. However, if the life tenant subsequently conveyed his interest to the holder of the next vested estate, the contingent remainder would then be destroyed.

e. Rule in Shelley's Case (Rule Against Remainders in Grantee's Heirs)
At common law, where a freehold estate (usually a life estate) was given to A (by will or inter vivos transfer), and in the same instrument a *remainder was limited to the "heirs" or to the "heirs of the body" of A*, and the freehold estate and the remainder were both legal or both equitable, the purported remainder in the heirs was not recognized, and A took both the freehold estate and the remainder. The Rule operated (regardless of the grantor's intent) to convert what would otherwise have been a contingent remainder in the heirs into a remainder in the ancestor.

Examples: 1) O grants or devises land "to A for life, and then to the heirs of A." Apart from the Rule in Shelley's Case, the title would be: life estate in A, contingent remainder in fee simple in A's heirs. But by virtue of the Rule, the title is: life estate in A, vested remainder in A in fee simple. (Here, the law of merger causes A's life estate to merge with his remainder so that A gets a present estate in fee simple.)

2) O "to A for life, then to B for life, then to the heirs of A." A has a life estate, and the Rule in Shelley's Case transforms the contingent remainder in the heirs of A into a vested remainder in fee simple in A. But merger does not occur because of the intervening *vested* remainder limited to B.

3) O "to A for life, then to B for life, then to the heirs of B." The Rule in Shelley's Case operates, as does merger, and B has a vested remainder in fee simple.

4) O "to A for life, then one day after A's death to the heirs of A." The Rule in Shelley's Case does not operate because the interest limited to the heirs of A is not a remainder (it can never take over immediately at the termination of the prior freehold estate), but rather is an executory interest.

Compare: O conveys land "to A and his heirs." A takes a fee simple—not by operation of the Rule in Shelley's Case, but because the words "and his heirs" are words of limitation denoting that a fee simple estate has been conveyed. (*See* I.B.1., *supra.*) (It is a common student error to conclude, in this case, that "A takes a fee simple because of the Rule in Shelley's Case." This rule is triggered **only** by the attempted creation of a remainder in the grantee's heirs.)

Note: This Rule has been **abolished in most states today**, but arises occasionally where a conveyance was executed prior to abolition of the Rule.

f. **Doctrine of Worthier Title (Rule Against Remainders in Grantor's Heirs)**

Under the Doctrine of Worthier Title ("DOWT"), a remainder limited to the grantor's heirs is invalid, and the grantor retains a reversion in the property. This doctrine is still applied to inter vivos transfers in a majority of states, but most states treat it only as a *rule of construction* (i.e., it does not apply if the grantor has clearly manifested an intent to create a future interest in his heirs).

Example: O deeds property "to A for life, and on A's death to my heirs at law," or ". . . and on A's death to my next of kin." In most states, the disposition gives A a life estate and presumptively leaves a reversion in fee simple in O. The burden of establishing that O really intended to create a remainder in his heirs (or next of kin) would be on the parties so contending. The litigation would arise after O's death, and would be between (i) the persons designated as O's heirs under the state's intestacy laws, claiming that they take on A's death by remainder; and (ii) the devisees under O's will, contending that O died owning a reversion.

In a state that has abolished the doctrine, the state of title is: life estate in A; contingent remainder in O's heirs; reversion in O.

Compare: 1) O deeds property "to A for life, and on A's death to my children in equal shares." On O's death, his children, X and Y, are O's sole heirs. DOWT does not apply. The doctrine applies only when there is a disposition, following a life estate, to the transferor's *"heirs"* or *"next of kin,"* or words of like effect.

2) O deeds property "to A for life, and on A's death to the heirs born to my wife Martha and me." DOWT does not apply; the disposition creates a life estate in A and a vested remainder subject to open in the children of O and Martha. Although O used the term "heirs," it is clear from the context that he was not using the term in its technical sense, but was referring to his children by his wife Martha.

3. **Executory Interests**

Here is a good shorthand rule for classifying executory interests. Remember that there are two and only two future interests that can be created in a transferee: remainders and executory interests. *If it is not a remainder because the preceding estate is not a life estate, then it must be an executory interest.* Thus, an executory interest is any future interest in a transferee that does not have the characteristics of a remainder, i.e., it is not capable of taking on the natural termination of the preceding life estate. More specifically, an executory interest is an interest that *divests* the interest of another.

a. **Shifting Executory Interest—Divests a Transferee**

A shifting executory interest is one that divests the interest of another transferee; i.e., it cuts short a prior estate created by the same conveyance.

Examples: 1) "To A and her heirs; but if B returns from Canada, then and in that event to B and his heirs." A has a fee simple subject to an executory interest. Because the future interest is created in a transferee, it has to be either a remainder or an executory interest. B's future interest is not a remainder because it does not follow the natural termination of the preceding estate (here, A's fee simple estate). If B's interest does take in present possession, it will divest A's fee simple, and title will *shift* to B.

2) O conveys "to A for life, remainder to B and his heirs, *but if B predeceases A*, to C and his heirs." C's interest does not await the expiration of B's vested remainder, but instead may cut it short.

b. **Springing Executory Interest—"Follows a Gap" or Divests a Transferor**

A springing executory interest is an interest that follows a gap in possession or divests the estate of the transferor.

Examples: 1) O conveys property "to A when and if A marries B." State of title: fee simple subject to an executory interest in O; springing executory interest in fee simple in A. A's interest is not a remainder because if A's future interest becomes a present interest (if A marries B), it will divest O's fee simple. Because it *divests the estate of a transferor*, it is a springing executory interest.

2) O conveys property "to A for life, and one year after A's death to B." A has a life estate. O has a reversion. B has a springing executory interest in fee simple. B's interest cannot be a remainder because of the one-year gap; it is not capable of taking on the natural termination of the preceding estate (A's life estate). It is therefore an executory interest. It is a springing executory interest because it *springs out of the transferor's reversion*.

c. **Executory Interest Follows a Fee**

A *remainder cannot follow a fee simple interest* of any kind. Therefore, any interest that follows a fee and is held by a third person is an executory interest.

Examples: 1) O conveys land "to Church for so long as the premises are used for church purposes, and if they shall ever cease to be so used, then and in that event to the American Red Cross." Church has a fee simple determinable subject to an executory interest; the Red Cross has an executory interest that is valid under the charity-to-charity exception to the Rule Against Perpetuities.

2) O conveys "to Church; provided, however, that if the premises shall ever cease to be used for church purposes, then and in that event to the American Red Cross." Church has a fee simple subject to an executory interest; the Red Cross has an executory interest that is valid under the charity-to-charity exception to the Rule Against Perpetuities.

d. **Differences Between Executory Interests and Remainders**

It is important to be able to distinguish between executory interests and remainders for the following reasons: (i) executory interests are not destructible, while contingent remainders are still destructible in a few jurisdictions; (ii) executory interests are not considered vested, whereas contingent remainders can become vested; and (iii) the Rule in Shelley's Case does not apply to executory interests, but it does apply to remainders limited to the heirs of the grantee.

4. **Importance of Classifying Interests "In Order"**

Future interests are classified clause by clause—which will often mean that the label appended to the first future interest created in a disposition will determine the label to be appended to a second future interest created in the same disposition. For instance, if the first future interest is a contingent remainder, subsequent future interests must also be contingent remainders. Similarly, if the first future interest is a vested remainder subject to divestment, the following future interests will be executory interests.

Examples: 1) O conveys land "to A for life, and on A's death to B if B survives A; but if B does not survive A, on A's death to C." A has a life estate. B has a contingent remainder because B's taking is subject to a contingency (expressed in condition precedent form) that B must survive A in order to take. C has an alternative contingent remainder.

Because the contingency of B's survival is expressed both as a condition precedent and (in the next clause) as a condition subsequent, why is B's remainder classified as contingent rather than as vested subject to total divestment? The explanation is that interests are classified "in order." Looking first at the clause giving an interest to B, here the contingency is expressed as a condition precedent; therefore, B's remainder is contingent. Then, having classified B's interest, we turn to C's interest. But because B's interest has already been determined to be a contingent remainder, C's interest is necessarily an alternative contingent remainder.

2) O conveys land "to A for life, and on A's death to B. But if B predeceases A, on A's death to C." Watch this one carefully, for the answer turns on the principle that we classify interests "in order." First of all, A has a life estate. Next we classify B's interest. It is a remainder, for it is capable of taking on the natural termination of the preceding estate (A's life estate). It is a vested remainder in fee simple because B is an ascertained person and there is *no condition precedent* to B's taking other than the termination of A's life estate. Having classified it as a vested remainder, we read on ("but if") and see that B's estate will be defeated if he predeceases A. Therefore, it is a vested remainder subject to total divestment upon the happening of this condition, which is expressed in *condition subsequent* form.

Having classified B's remainder as vested subject to total divestment, we turn to C's interest. It cannot be a remainder, for a remainder follows the natural termination of the preceding estate—B's estate, which is a vested remainder in fee simple. But *no remainder can follow a fee simple*, for a fee simple is an estate of potentially infinite duration. If C does take, it will cut short B's vested remainder in fee simple some time short of infinity. Therefore, C's interest is an executory interest—a *shifting executory interest*, because it divests a transferee.

But isn't C's interest capable of taking on the natural termination of A's life estate (if B predeceases A)? Yes, but that does not affect our classification. A remainder is a future interest capable of taking on the termination of the *preceding* estate, and here the preceding estate is B's.

Suppose, some years after this disposition, B dies during A's lifetime. What is the state of title? The answer: life estate in A, indefeasibly vested *remainder* in C. Now that B's estate is out of the way, the preceding estate is A's life estate, and so now we can change the label and call C's interest a remainder.

5. **Transferability of Remainders and Executory Interests**

   a. **Vested Remainders Are Transferable, Devisable, and Descendible**
   At common law and in all jurisdictions today, vested remainders are fully transferable during life, devisable by will, and descendible by inheritance. This is true of all types of vested remainders: indefeasibly vested, vested subject to open, and vested subject to total divestment.

   b. **Contingent Remainders and Executory Interests Are Transferable Inter Vivos**
   At common law, contingent remainders and executory interests were not assignable. While this is still the rule in a few states, most American courts hold that these interests are freely transferable.

   c. **Contingent Remainders and Executory Interests Are Usually Devisable and Descendible**
   Whereas the rule at common law was that contingent remainders and executory interests were not transferable inter vivos, it has always been held that these interests are devisable and descendible—*unless*, of course, the holder's *survival is a condition* to the interest's taking.
   Example: "To A for life, and on A's death to B; but if B does not survive A, on A's death to C." State of title: life estate in A, vested remainder subject to total divestment in B, and shifting executory interest in C. Suppose B dies in A's lifetime, leaving a will that devises "all my property" to Mrs. B. B's remainder interest does not pass under his will because, by the terms of the disposition, that interest failed when B died in A's lifetime.

   d. **Any Transferable Future Interest Is Reachable by Creditors**
   The rule followed in nearly all states is this: If a future interest can, under the laws of the state, be transferred voluntarily by its owner, it is also subject to involuntary transfer; i.e., it can be reached by the owner's creditors by appropriate process.

   e. **Practical Ability to Transfer Marketable Title**
   Technically, most states consider all types of future interests transferable, but in practice those interests held by unborn or unascertained persons are not transferable because courts will not appoint a guardian for purposes of conveying land. (*See* VI.A.3.a.1)b), *infra*.)

6. **Class Gifts**
   A "class" is a group of persons having a common characteristic. Typically, they stand in the same relation to each other or to some other person (e.g., children, grandchildren,

descendants, nephews and nieces). In a gift to a class, the share of each member of the class is determined by the number of persons in the class.

a. Definitional Problems

1) Dispositions to "Children"
A gift to a person's "children" generally includes that person's children from all marriages as well as adopted and nonmarital children. That person's stepchildren and grandchildren are generally not included in the class.

2) Dispositions to "Heirs"
A disposition to the "heirs" of someone presumptively includes those persons who would take the named person's estate according to the laws of descent and distribution if she were to die without a will.

3) Dispositions to "Issue" or "Descendants"
The terms "issue" and "descendants" refer to the lineal offspring of the designated person, whatever the degree of relationship (children, grandchildren, great-grandchildren, etc.). As a general principle, the issue or descendants take per stirpes.

4) Class Members in Gestation
Persons in gestation at the time set for distribution are included in a class. The common law presumption is that a child born within 10 lunar months or 280 calendar days after the necessary point in time was in gestation at that time.

b. When the Class Closes—The Rule of Convenience
When a gift is made to a group of persons generically described as a class, such as to someone's "children," there is the possibility that other persons may be born who meet the class description. This raises the question, when does the class "close"; i.e., when is the maximum membership of the class determined, such that persons born thereafter are excluded from sharing in the gift? In resolving this problem, the common law courts developed the rule of convenience. This is a rule of construction, not a rule of law. It is applicable in the absence of an expression of intent to include all persons who meet the class description regardless of when they are born. Under the rule, a *class closes when some member of the class can call for a distribution of her share of the class gift*. It is presumed that the ordinary transferor intends to include all members of the class, whenever born, *provided* that this would *not cause any undue inconvenience*. Thus, the rule of convenience is based on a policy of including as many persons in the class as possible, consistent with permitting a distribution of the property at the first opportunity without the necessity of a future rebate.

1) Outright Gift—Class Closes at Time Gift Is Made
When a *will* makes an outright gift to a class, if any class members are alive at the testator's death, the class closes as of the *date of the testator's death*.

Example: T's will devises property "to the children of my good friend, John Brown." John has three children (A, B, and C) at the time of T's death; another child (D) is born two years later. The class closes at T's death; A, B, and C share the gift. D is excluded by the rule of convenience.

Here, additional members of the class are included up to the time of T's death because there is no inconvenience in doing so. But we close the class at T's death because it is assumed that T would want an immediate distribution, rather than postponing distribution until John Brown's death, which is the only time we will be sure that John Brown will have no more children. If we were to include D, we would also have to include E, F, and G, who might be born later. Moreover, if we distributed one-third shares to A, B, and C at T's death, but required them to make rebates if more children should be born later to their father, John, all sorts of practical problems would arise. To avoid these problems, there is a strong constructional preference to close the class at T's death.

a) **No Class Members Alive at Testator's Death—Class Stays Open**
If there are no members of the class living at the testator's death, all afterborn persons who come within the class designation are included. Thus, if T had bequeathed $100,000 "to the children of John," and John had no children living at T's death or born within the period of gestation thereafter, then all of John's children, whenever born, are included, regardless of any possible inconvenience in keeping the class open this long.

2) **Postponed Gift—Class Closes at Time Fixed for Distribution**
When possession and enjoyment of a gift are postponed, as where the gift follows a life estate, the class remains open until the time fixed for distribution (e.g., death of the life tenant).

Example: T's will creates a trust to pay the income to W for life, and on W's death to pay the principal to the children of John. At the time T executes his will, John has two children (A and B). After the will is executed but before T dies, another child (C) is born to John. After T's death but during W's lifetime, another child (D) is born to John. W dies; two years later John has another child (E).

The class closes at W's death; A, B, C, and D each take a one-fourth share. E is excluded by the rule of convenience. There was no inconvenience in leaving the class open until W's death, for the time had not yet come to distribute the corpus. But when W dies, it is time to make a distribution; the class is closed in order to determine the minimum shares going to each class member.

3) **Dispositions Subject to Condition of Reaching Given Age**
When there is a gift to a class conditioned upon the members attaining a certain age, the class closes when (i) the preceding estate, if any, terminates, and (ii) the first class member reaches the specified age. That class member's minimum share should be determined and distributed to her when she reaches the specified age.

Examples: 1) T's will devises his residuary estate "to the children of John who live to attain the age of 21." At T's death, John has three children: A (age 22), B (age 16), and C (age 10). The class closes at T's death. A is entitled to immediate distribution of her share, and the minimum size of that share must be fixed as of T's death, at one-third. If B lives to attain age 21, but C dies before attaining that age, on C's death, A and B's shares will be increased to one-half.

Two years after T's death, another child (D) is born to John. D is excluded by the rule of convenience. The class was closed at T's death in order to determine the minimum size of A's share so that this share could be distributed to her.

Suppose none of John's children is 21 at T's death. The class remains open until a child of John reaches the designated age, at which time the class closes.

2) T's will devises his residuary estate "to Wanda for life, and on Wanda's death to such of John's children as live to attain the age of 21." Here, the class will close, and the remaindermen who share in the disposition will be determined, when two things occur: (i) Wanda dies; **and** (ii) a child of John reaches age 21. If at T's death one of John's children is over age 21, it does not matter; the class remains open until Wanda's life estate terminates. Likewise, if at Wanda's death no child of John has attained age 21, the class remains open until one of John's children reaches that age. If at Wanda's death a child has attained age 21, the class will close at that time.

4) Rule of Convenience Is a Rule of Construction Only

The rule of convenience is a rule of construction only. If the transferor explicitly sets forth the time when membership of the class is to be determined, or if he provides that all members of the class, whenever born, are to share in the gift, then his directions will govern. However, courts have a strong preference for application of the rule of convenience unless there is a fairly clear indication that it is not to govern.

7. Survival

As a general rule, all future interests can pass at death by will or inheritance; i.e., they are descendible and devisable. This is true **unless** the interest's taking is subject to an expressed or implied contingency of survival. Note that under some anti-lapse statutes, a gift will be saved for the party's descendants even if there is an express survival contingency. (*See* VI.F.3., *infra.*)

Examples: 1) T's will devises his residuary estate "to my sister Sue for life, and on Sue's death to her children in equal shares." At the time of T's death, Sue has three children: A, B, and C. C dies, then Sue dies survived by A and B. The remainder is shared by A, B, and the estate of C (i.e., the estate takes under C's will or by intestacy), each with one-third shares. *Analysis:* A, B, and C had vested remainders subject to open, but their interests were not in terms conditioned on surviving the life beneficiary—and the law does not imply such a condition of survival. On C's death, his vested remainder subject to open passes via his will or by intestacy. (*Note:* This example does **not** invoke the lapsed gift doctrine of Wills law, for C was alive at the testator's death.)

2) "To A for life, and on A's death to B if B is then living; but if B is not then living, to C." C dies, then B dies, then A dies. Who takes? Answer: The takers under C's will or by intestacy. B and C were given alternative contingent

remainders. B's remainder was contingent on his surviving A, and B did not meet the condition; his estate was defeated. C's remainder was contingent on B's not surviving A; it was not in terms contingent on C's surviving A, and the law does not imply such a condition.

a. Express Words of Survival

In each of the following examples, the italicized language imposes a condition precedent that the remaindermen must survive the life tenant in order to take.

Examples: 1) "To A for life, remainder to his ***surviving children***."

2) "To A for life, and should he ***die leaving children***, to such children."

3) "To A for life, and after the death of A, remainder to the children of A ***then living***."

An express condition of survival is sometimes stated ambiguously. For example, it is unclear in 1), above, to what event the word "surviving" relates. The word "surviving" might relate to surviving A or to surviving the grantor. Unless the language or circumstances establish that the transferor had a different intention, the ambiguity is resolved by construing the word "surviving" as referring to the distribution date (A's death) because that is the more natural meaning of the language. [Restatement (Third) of Property (Wills & Don. Trans.) §15.4]

b. Implied Contingency of Survival—Gifts to "Issue," "Descendants," or "Heirs"

Gifts to a person's "issue," "descendants," or "heirs" imply a condition of surviving the named ancestor.

D. TRUSTS

An express trust involves the holding of title to property by a trustee, who has an equitable fiduciary duty to deal with it for the benefit of other persons (the beneficiaries).

1. Private Trust Concepts and Parties

a. Settlor

The settlor is the person who ***creates the trust*** by manifesting an intent to do so. While a trust of personal property may be expressed orally, the Statute of Frauds requires a writing to create a trust of real property. The settlor must own the property at the time the trust is created and must intend to make the trust effective immediately.

b. Trustee

The trustee ***holds legal title to the property***, but must act under the instructions of the settlor who created the trust. The trustee has a fiduciary duty to use the highest care and skill for the beneficiaries. If the trustee has no duties at all, the trust will fail, and legal title will vest immediately in the beneficiaries. However, if the trustee dies, resigns, or refuses to serve, the trust will not fail; a court of equity will appoint a substitute trustee.

c. Beneficiaries

The beneficiaries are the ***persons for whose benefit the trust is created and held***; they hold ***equitable title*** to the property. Every private trust must have at least one beneficiary, and the beneficiaries must be definitely identifiable by the time their interest comes into enjoyment and, in all events, within the period of the Rule Against Perpetuities. Acceptance of the benefits of the trust is normally presumed, but a beneficiary may renounce his rights under the trust within a reasonable time after learning of its creation. A trust may be for a class of beneficiaries (e.g., "all the living descendants of Mary Jones"), provided that the class is small enough to be "reasonably definite."

d. Res
The res is *the property that is the subject of the trust*. If there is no res, the trust fails. The res may be real property or personal property (tangible or intangible), and it may be either a present interest or a future interest (vested or contingent). The trust res must be segregated from other property of the settlor, but this does not preclude a trust of a fractional share interest, such as a trust of "an undivided one-half interest in Blackacre," where the settlor owns all of Blackacre.

e. Application of Rule Against Perpetuities
The Rule Against Perpetuities (*see* E., *infra*) applies to the equitable future interests of the beneficiaries in a private trust just as it does to "legal" future interests.
Example: O conveys land to T "in trust for the benefit of A so long as the existing house on the land remains standing, and then for the benefit of the then living descendants of A." The equitable interest of the descendants of A is void because it is not certain to vest or fail within 21 years after the life of any person living at the time the trust is created.

2. Creation of Trusts

a. Inter Vivos Conveyance
An inter vivos trust can be created by the settlor's conveyance of the trust res to the trustee while the settlor is alive. For real property, this must be done by a writing to satisfy the Statute of Frauds; this is usually accomplished by delivery of a deed.

b. Inter Vivos Declaration
The settlor may declare that he is now holding certain property (previously held outright by the settlor) in trust for certain beneficiaries. No deed or delivery is necessary, but if the res is real property, the declaration must be in writing and signed by the settlor.

c. Testamentary Conveyance
The settlor may create the trust by language in his will, and may also transfer the res to the trustee by a devise in the will. The trust will come into existence only upon the death of the settlor.

d. Pour-Over into Existing Trust
The settlor may create an inter vivos trust before death. The settlor's will may then bequeath property to the trust—"pouring it over" into the trust.

3. Charitable Trusts

a. Beneficiaries
A charitable trust, unlike the private trusts described above, must have an *indefinite*

group of beneficiaries. The beneficiaries must be reasonably numerous and not individually identified. The trust may be for the benefit of an established charity (e.g., the American Red Cross) or for a group of persons (e.g., the victims of Hurricane Sandy).

b. **Application of Rule Against Perpetuities**

The Rule Against Perpetuities does not apply to trusts that are *entirely charitable*. Such trusts may have infinite life. This is true even if the trust benefits two charities, one with a present interest and the other with a future interest that would normally violate the Rule Against Perpetuities. Note, however, that if either the first or second interest is noncharitable, the exemption from the Rule Against Perpetuities does not apply and the second gift is void.

Examples: 1) O conveys land to T in trust "for the benefit of the victims of Hurricane Sandy, and when all houses destroyed by the hurricane have been rebuilt, then for the benefit of the American Red Cross." The interest of the Red Cross may not vest until more than 21 years after the death of any person living when the trust is created, but it is still a valid interest.

2) O conveys land to T in trust "for the benefit of my son John, whose house was destroyed by Hurricane Sandy, and when his house has been rebuilt, then for the benefit of the American Red Cross." The interest of the Red Cross may not vest until more than 21 years after the death of any person living when the trust is created, and it is void.

c. **Cy Pres Doctrine**

If the purposes of a charitable trust are impossible to fulfill, are illegal, or have been completely fulfilled, a court may redirect the trust to a different purpose that is "as near as may be" (a translation of the Latin "cy pres") to the settlor's original intent.

d. **Enforcement of Charitable Trusts**

Charitable trusts may be enforced by an action of the attorney general of the state. Under the Uniform Trust Code ("UTC"), enacted by the majority of states, the settlor and qualified beneficiaries also have standing to enforce a charitable trust. [UTC §§110, 405(c)]

E.   **THE RULE AGAINST PERPETUITIES**

The Rule Against Perpetuities may be stated as follows: "No interest in property is valid unless it must vest, if at all, not later than 21 years after one or more lives in being at the creation of the interest." The Rule might be more easily understood if it had been expressed as an affirmative proposition: "An interest is void if there is any possibility, however remote, that the interest may vest more than 21 years after some life in being at the creation of the interest." This paraphrase of the Rule properly places the emphasis on the *possibility* of remote vesting, the test by which the invalidity of an interest is shown. If a situation can be imagined in which the interest might not vest within the perpetuities period, the interest is void. This is the result even though the circumstances that might bring about the remote vesting are unlikely to occur or are unrealistic. (All kinds of unlikely things are considered capable of happening under the Rule.) The Rule applies to the following legal and equitable future interests in personal or real property:

(i)   Contingent remainders;

(ii) Executory interests;

(iii) Class gifts (even if vested remainders);

(iv) Options and rights of first refusal; and

(v)   Powers of appointment.

1.   **Analysis of the Rule**

   a.   **When the Perpetuities Period Begins to Run**
   The validity of interests under the Rule is determined *at the time the interests are created*, taking into account the facts then existing. The "lives in being plus 21 years" period begins to run, and the measuring lives used to show the validity of an interest must be in existence, at that time.

      1)   **Wills—Date of Testator's Death**
      The perpetuities period in the case of a will begins to run on the date of the testator's death.

      2)   **Revocable Trusts—Date Trust Becomes Irrevocable**
      In the case of revocable trusts, the perpetuities period begins to run on the date the trust becomes irrevocable. This will be at the settlor's death unless the settlor amends the trust, making it irrevocable, during his lifetime.

      3)   **Irrevocable Trusts—Date Trust Is Created**
      The perpetuities period for irrevocable trusts begins to run on the date the trust is created.

      4)   **Deeds—Date Deed Is Delivered with Intent to Pass Title**
      In the case of a deed, the perpetuities period begins to run on the date the deed is delivered with the intent to pass title.

   b.   **"Must Vest"**
   To be valid under the Rule, it must be shown that the interest created in the transferee must vest, regardless of what might happen, within lives in being plus 21 years. An interest becomes "vested" for purposes of the Rule when: (i) it becomes a present possessory estate, or (ii) it becomes an indefeasibly vested remainder or a vested remainder subject to total divestment. Remember that the Rule is applicable only to future interests created in third persons; consequently, the Rule generally applies only to contingent remainders, executory interests, and vested remainders subject to open.
   Examples: 1) "To A for life, then to A's children for their lives, and on the death of the last survivor of A's children, to B in fee simple." At the time of this disposition, A has two very young children and is quite capable of having more children in the future. (i) A has a present possessory life estate. A's present children have vested remainders in life estates that are subject to open in favor of any future children born to A. There is

a contingent remainder in a life estate in A's unborn children—but this interest is valid under the Rule because the children's life estates will vest at their birth, which will be in A's lifetime. B has an indefeasibly vested remainder in fee simple. (ii) B's interest is valid under the Rule even though it may be years before B (or her successors) is entitled to present possession and enjoyment of the property, and even though B (or her successors) may not succeed to present possession and enjoyment until the death of some person not now in being (i.e., a future-born child of A may be the last survivor of A's children). Despite all this, B's interest is valid under the Rule because it is an *indefeasibly vested remainder from the time of its creation*.

2) "To A for life, then to B; but if at B's death she is not survived by children, then in that event to C." (i) A has a present possessory life estate. B has a vested remainder subject to total divestment in fee simple. C has a shifting executory interest in fee simple. (ii) C's interest is valid under the Rule. B's is the relevant life that can be used to show that C's interest will vest within the perpetuities period. If B dies in A's lifetime not survived by children, C's interest will become an indefeasibly vested remainder. If B survives A and thereafter dies not survived by children, C's executory interest will become a present possessory estate. Of course, B may die in A's lifetime (or after A's death) leaving children surviving her, in which case C's interest is extinguished. But that does not matter; the Rule requires that an interest must vest, *if it does vest* ("if at all"), within lives in being plus 21 years.

3) "To A for life, and on her death to such of her children as attain the age of 35." At the time this disposition takes effect, A is a 60-year-old woman who has had a hysterectomy. She has two children, ages 30 and 25. Under the common law Rule, here is what might happen: A *might* give birth to a child (defying medical science in the process). (*See also* V.D.2., *infra.*) Then A's other two children might die before attaining age 35; then A might die before the afterborn attained his 14th birthday. (Key: 35 minus 21 is 14.) The afterborn child lives on to attain age 35. If these events were to occur, the remainder to such of A's children as attain age 35 would vest remotely. Because these events *might* occur, the remainder violates the Rule; it is stricken.

1) **"Wait and See" Rule**

A majority of states have modified the "must vest, if at all" rule above. Under the modified approach, these states suspend judgment as to whether the interest in question is good or void. Potentially, they wait until the end of the perpetuities period. If the interest in question *actually* vests during the period, it is good; if it does not vest or fail during that period, it is void. Until the end of the perpetuities period, it is impossible to know for sure whether the interest is good or not.

Example: Consider Example 3), above: "To A for life, and on her death to such of her children as attain the age of 35." Under the "wait and see" approach, the courts would inquire as to whether *in fact* any child of A reaches the age of 35 within 21 years after A's death. If one or more of A's children does so, the remainder is valid; if none does so, the remainder is void.

c. **"If at All"**

This simply means that the interest does not have to vest within the perpetuities period in order to be valid; after all, many contingent remainders never vest because the condition precedent to their taking is not satisfied.

Examples: 1) "To A for life, and on A's death to B if B is then living." A has a life estate, B has a contingent remainder, and the transferor has a reversion. B may never take, for she may predecease A. But if B does take ("if at all"), her interest will vest—here, will become a possessory estate—on A's death, when we will know whether B has survived A. In this case, B is "her own life in being," for the condition precedent to B's taking must occur, if it does occur, within B's lifetime. B's interest is valid under the Rule.

2) "To A in fee, but on the express condition that if marijuana is ever smoked on the premises during B's lifetime or within 21 years after B's death, then and in that event to B in fee." A has a fee simple subject to an executory interest; B has an executory interest in fee simple. B's interest might not take, for marijuana might not be smoked on the premises during B's lifetime or within 21 years thereafter. But if B's interest does take, by the terms of the disposition it must take during B's lifetime or within 21 years thereafter. B's interest is valid under the Rule.

d. **"Lives in Being"**

The law allows any lives to be used to show the validity or invalidity of an interest, but no lives are of any help unless they are somehow ***connected with the vesting of an interest***. The measuring lives need not be given a beneficial interest in the property, and they need not even be expressly referred to in the instrument, but there must be some connection that insures vesting or failure of the interest within the perpetuities period.

Examples: 1) "To A for life, then to such of A's children as attain the age of 21." Here, the relevant measuring life is A. All of A's children are going to attain age 21, ***if at all***, within 21 years after A's death. (This includes a child in the mother's womb at A's death, for the perpetuities period includes any period of gestation actually involved.)

2) T's will devises her residuary estate "to such of my nephews and nieces as attain the age of 21." At the time of T's death, she has two brothers and six nephews and nieces, all of whom are under age 21. Is the gift valid under the Rule? The answer: It depends. Specifically, it depends on whether T's parents are living. The ***relevant measuring lives*** are T's brothers and sisters, because all of T's nephews and nieces will attain age 21, if at all, within 21 years after their parents' deaths. If T's parents are dead, her two brothers are all the brothers she is ever going to have; and T's nephews and nieces will be the children of these brothers. The disposition is valid.

But if T's parents are alive, they *might* have another child (call him Excelsior), a brother or sister of T not alive at T's death. Then T's two brothers and six nephews and nieces who were alive at T's death might die. Then Excelsior might have a child who lives to attain age 21—more than 21 years after any life in being. Because this might happen, the disposition is invalid under the Rule.

1) Who Can Be Used as Measuring Lives

In all the examples in this chapter, the measuring lives used to show the validity or invalidity of interests are referred to or are indirectly involved in the disposition itself. It is a common drafting practice to use a *"perpetuities saving clause"* (i) to make sure that the Rule has not been accidentally violated, for the Rule is difficult to master; and (ii) sometimes to extend the duration of trusts to the maximum extent permitted under the Rule. The clause reads something like this: "Notwithstanding anything herein to the contrary, any trust created hereunder shall terminate, if it has not previously terminated, 21 years after the death of the survivor of the following named persons: _____; and the remaining principal and undistributed income of such trusts shall be distributed to . . . ."

In the blanks are inserted the names of the persons to be used as "artificial" measuring lives. Most commonly, the descendants then living of the transferor are specifically named. Alternatively, the clause might provide, "after the death of the survivor of all my descendants who shall be living at the time of my death"— this clause works in a will but does not work in an irrevocable trust. A few more aggressive draftsmen will name 10 healthy babies born in some local hospital on the day the instrument is executed—the probability is that this will permit the trust to run for 100 years.

2) Reasonable Number of Human Lives Can Be Used

Animals and organizations cannot be used as measuring lives; only humans can be used as measuring lives. Also, the number of measuring lives must be reasonable.

Examples: 1) "The trust will terminate 21 years after the death of the survivor of all persons listed in the Manhattan telephone directory." Clearly impermissible.

2) "The trust will terminate 21 years after the death of the survivor of all the descendants of Queen Victoria who are alive at the time of my death." This "royal lives" clause was widely used in England shortly after the turn of the century, and the English courts grudgingly sustained it. If the name of some currently famous person were used in this fashion, it is highly questionable whether American courts would sustain the disposition.

e. Interests Exempt from Rule

1) Gift Over to Second Charity

A charitable trust may last forever (i.e., neither the Rule Against Perpetuities nor any analogous rule applies). However, like any other gift, a gift for charitable purposes is void for remoteness if it is contingent upon the happening of an event that may not occur within the perpetuity period. The only exception to this rule is that if there is a gift to Charity A, followed by a gift over to Charity B upon a possibly remote event, the gift over is valid. Remember, this is the charity-to-charity exception. The Rule Against Perpetuities applies to dispositions over from a *charity to an individual* on a remote condition, *and* to dispositions over from an *individual to a charity* on a remote condition.

Examples: 1) "To the Georgetown YMCA for so long as the premises are used for YMCA purposes; and when they shall cease to be so used, then and in that event to the American Cancer Society." The YMCA has a fee simple subject to an executory interest; the Cancer Society has a shifting executory interest. The gift over to the Cancer Society is valid under the charity-to-charity exception to the Rule.

2) "To the Georgetown YMCA for so long as the premises are used for YMCA purposes; and when they shall cease to be so used, then and in that event to John Hancock, his heirs, successors, and assigns." Classifying the interests without regard to the Rule, the YMCA would have a fee simple subject to an executory interest; Hancock would have a shifting executory interest—which is stricken because it violates the Rule. The YMCA has a fee simple determinable, and the transferor has a possibility of reverter.

3) "To John Hancock, his heirs, successors, and assigns, provided that no marijuana is ever smoked on the premises; and if marijuana is ever smoked on the premises, to the Georgetown YMCA." Classifying interests without regard to the Rule, Hancock would have a fee simple subject to an executory interest; the YMCA would have a shifting executory interest—which is stricken because it violates the Rule. Thus, Hancock has a fee simple absolute.

2) Vested Interests

A vested remainder in an individual is not subject to the Rule. Thus, a devise "to A for life, then to A's children for life, then to B in fee simple" is wholly valid. B has a presently vested remainder. It may vest in *possession* long after lives in being if A leaves some surviving children born after the testator's death, but the remainder to B is presently vested in interest, and that is what counts.

a) Compare—Class Gifts Are Subject to Rule

Vested remainders in a class, however, are subject to the Rule *so long as the class remains open*.

3) Reversionary Interests

Reversions, possibilities of reverter, and rights of entry are all vested in interest and hence are *not subject to the Rule Against Perpetuities*. (Even so, in many states, there are statutes expressly limiting the duration of possibilities of reverter or rights of entry.)

a) **Compare—Executory Interests Are Subject to Rule**
Possibilities of reverter and rights of entry, which are exempt from the Rule, must be carefully distinguished from executory interests, which are subject to the Rule. Remember that executory interests are created in *transferees*; possibilities of reverter and rights of entry are created only in the *grantor* (or the *testator's heirs* if a will is involved). An understanding of this distinction has frequently been tested by the bar examiners.

Example: O conveys Blackacre "to School so long as it is used for educational purposes, and when it is no longer so used, to A." A has an executory interest that violates the Rule because it may vest in possession many years after all lives in being are dead. Because any interest that violates the Rule is void and is stricken from the instrument, this leaves a determinable fee in the school and a possibility of reverter in O. O can now, by a second deed, transfer her possibility of reverter to A (if possibilities of reverter have been made transferable by statute in the jurisdiction). To get a possibility of reverter in A, two pieces of paper are required: one creating the possibility of reverter in O; the second transferring it to A.

f. **Consequence of Violating the Rule—Interest Is Stricken**
An interest that violates the Rule is void and is stricken (subject to the possible application of a perpetuities reform statute). However, all other interests created in the instrument of transfer that are valid under the Rule are given effect.

1) **Exception—"Infectious Invalidity"**
There is an important exception to the preceding statement. Under the principle of "infectious invalidity," if the invalid gift is an essential part of the transferor's dispositive scheme, such that to strike this interest and give effect to the remaining interests would be to subvert the transferor's intent—if it is determined that the transferor would prefer that the entire disposition fail—then the entire disposition is void.

Example: Irrevocable Trust A directs the trustee "to pay the income to my brother's children for life, and on the death of my brother's last surviving child, to pay the principal to the issue of my brother's children." The gift to "the issue of my brother's children" is void because the brother might have a child born *after the creation of the trust* (who would thus not be a life in being). That child might not die within 21 years after the death of the last child living at the time the trust was created. After the invalid interest is stricken, the brother's children have a life estate in the income, and the settlor has a reversion in the principal. However, Trust B provides that if any provision of Trust A is invalid, any income and principal from Trust A should be held in trust for the benefit of the brother's children and their issue. By striking out all the gifts in Trust A, valid and invalid, and by giving effect to Trust B, the settlor's presumed intent to benefit his brother's children and their issue may be substantially carried out. [New England Trust Co. v. Sanger, 149 N.E.2d 598 (Mass. 1958)]

2. The Rule in Operation—Common Pitfall Cases

a. Executory Interest Following Defeasible Fee Violates the Rule

An executory interest that follows a defeasible fee, with no limit on the time within which it must vest, violates the Rule Against Perpetuities and is stricken. The effect on the remaining fee estate depends on whether the estate is determinable or subject to a condition subsequent. If the defeasible fee is phrased in durational terms (e.g., "for so long as," "until"), the estate will still terminate upon the happening of the stated event and the grantor will have a possibility of reverter. In contrast, if the fee is subject to a condition subsequent, the condition is also stricken and the estate becomes a fee simple absolute.

Examples: 1) "To John Brown for so long as no marijuana is smoked on the premises; and if marijuana is ever smoked on the premises, then to Candy Barr." (i) John Brown has a fee simple subject to an executory interest; Candy Barr has an executory interest in fee simple. (ii) Candy's interest violates the Rule. Things may stay quiet for generations, long beyond 21 years after the deaths of John and Candy (the only relevant lives in this case). Then someone might light up, triggering the executory interest. Because this *might* happen, the executory interest might vest (i.e., might become a possessory estate) long after lives in being plus 21 years. Candy's interest violates the Rule, and it is stricken. This leaves a fee simple determinable in John Brown, and a possibility of reverter in the transferor. The possibility of reverter is valid; retained interests in the transferor are not subject to the Rule.

What if marijuana is smoked on the premises within five years after the transfer, well within lives in being plus 21 years, meaning that in actuality there was no remote vesting? It does not matter. Under the Rule we do not "wait and see." (*But see* 1.b.1), *supra.*) It is *what might happen* that counts, viewing the facts as they exist *at the time the interest is created*. What actually happens is irrelevant.

2) "To John Brown; provided, however, that if marijuana is ever smoked on the premises, then to Candy Barr." (i) John Brown has a fee simple subject to an executory interest; Candy Barr has an executory interest in fee simple. (ii) Candy's interest violates the Rule, under the analysis given in Example 1). Again we strike Candy's interest—leaving John Brown with a fee simple absolute. (Contrast this with the result in Example 1), where the transferor had a possibility of reverter. This is the result of two different forms of expressing the gift to John Brown. Whenever a fee simple determinable is created ("so long as"), the transferor automatically has a possibility of reverter. But when a fee on a condition subsequent is created, the transferor does not have a right of entry unless the right of entry is expressly raised.)

b. Age Contingency Beyond Age Twenty-One in Open Class

A gift to an open class conditioned upon the members surviving to an age beyond 21 violates the Rule Against Perpetuities.

Example: "To A for life, then to such of A's children as live to attain the age of 25." At the time of this disposition, A has two children: X (age 12) and Y (age nine). (i) A has a life estate; there is a contingent remainder in A's children who live to attain age 25, and a reversion in the transferor (for none of A's children may ever reach age 25). (ii) The remainder to A's children violates the Rule. After this transfer, A *might have another child* (Z); before this afterborn child (who cannot be used as a life in being) attains age four, A, X, and Y might die; then Z might live on to age 25, at which time the remainder to A's children would vest in Z. But if this were to happen (and it might), the remainder would vest beyond lives in being plus 21 years. Because the interest might vest remotely, it is stricken.

c. The Fertile Octogenarian

A woman is *conclusively presumed* to be capable of bearing children regardless of her age or medical condition.

Example: Suppose, in the preceding example, X and Y were age 24 and 22, respectively, and A was a 60-year-old woman who has undergone a hysterectomy. Under the "remote possibilities" test, it is *possible* for a woman, of whatever age and medical condition, to bear children. Thus, A might have another child, Z. The remainder to A's children violates the Rule.

d. The Unborn Widow or Widower

The problem is that the term "widow" (and "widower"), like "heir," is a technical word with a technical meaning: You do not know who a person's widow (or widower) is until he dies and you can determine to whom he was married at his death.

Example: "To A for life, then to his widow for life; and on the death of A's widow, to such of A's descendants as are then living." (i) A has a life estate; there is a contingent remainder in a life estate in his widow; there is a contingent remainder in fee simple in A's descendants; and the transferor has a reversion. (ii) The remainder in the descendants violates the Rule. Although A is now happily married, he might divorce his wife (or she might die), and A might marry someone who was not alive at the time the interest was created. A might have a child by this widow; then everyone now on the scene might die; the *widow might live for more than 21 years after the death of all lives in being*, then die—leaving the afterborn child or children as "A's descendants then living."

Compare: "To A for life, then to his widow for life; and on the death of A's widow, to A's children." (i) A has a life estate; there is a contingent remainder in a life estate in his widow; A's present children have vested remainders in fee simple that are subject to open in favor of any future children born to A, and A's unborn children have a contingent remainder in fee simple. (ii) The remainder in A's children is valid under the Rule because their interests will vest (and the class will close) within A's lifetime. The difference here is that the children's interest was not contingent on their surviving A's widow, and the law does not imply such a condition.

e. **The Administrative Contingency**
A gift that is conditioned on an administrative contingency (e.g., admission of will to probate) violates the Rule. The key question is "under the facts as they existed at the time of the gift, what might happen?"

Example: Disposition of residuary estate "per stirpes to such of my descendants as are living at the time my will is admitted to probate." Alternatively, a will of a German national written during World War II: "to such of my relations in Germany as are living at the time World War II is officially declared at an end." Under the "what might happen" approach of the common law Rule, wills are not probated, wars do not come to an end, decrees of distribution are never entered, etc. Moreover, because no person's lifetime is connected to the condition attached to this type of gift, we cannot use a life in being; we must use the "period in gross" of 21 years. And because the will "might not" be probated within 21 years, the gift is void.

The fact that the testator's will is in fact probated three weeks after her death does not matter. We do not wait and see. (*But see* 1.b.1), *supra*.) Rather, looking from the time of the testator's death, and taking into account facts as they existed at that time, the question is what might happen.

f. **Options and Rights of First Refusal**

1) **Options**
An option is a contract, supported by consideration, that creates in the optionee a right to purchase the property on terms provided in the option. (*See* Contracts and Sales outline.) Options are typically considered to be *assignable* unless the parties provide otherwise and, thus, are subject to the Rule Against Perpetuities (*but see* b), *infra*). If an option is structured so that it *might* be exercised later than the end of the Rule's period, it is usually held void.

Examples: 1) A is a subdivision developer and contracts with B to give B an option to purchase a lot in the subdivision "to be exercised within 60 days after the City Council grants approval for the filing of a subdivision plat." While the parties may expect this to occur soon, it is *possible* that it will not occur within 21 years after any life in being at the creation of the option. Hence, the option may be held void.

2) O conveys "to A and her heirs an option to purchase Blackacre for $25,000." This option is not limited to A's life, but can be exercised by A's heirs and their heirs long after A's death. Thus, the option is void.

a) **Reasonable Time Limit May Be Inferred**
A significant minority of courts, in applying the Rule to these interests, will construe the option as lasting only for a reasonable time, which is invariably less than 21 years, and thus will uphold it. Under this view, the option in Example 1), above, would be sustained on the ground that the parties

intended it to expire if the City Council failed to act within a reasonable time, less than 21 years. Similarly, if the parties to the option are natural persons, some courts construe the option as lasting only for their lifetimes; hence, it is valid under the Rule. Furthermore, the Uniform Statutory Rule Against Perpetuities (4.d., *infra*) excludes options in commercial transactions from the Rule's application.

b) Options Connected to Leaseholds

Options commonly arise in lease agreements (the consideration for the lease also acts as the consideration for the option). If a tenant under a lease has an option to purchase the leased premises during the lease term, the Rule is not applied, no matter how long the term. If a tenant assigns the leasehold, the option generally is considered a running covenant, exercisable by the assignee in the absence of contrary intent. However, a tenant may attempt to transfer the option to some other party, thereby separating it from the leasehold estate. While some courts do not permit the option to be transferred separately, most courts hold that the transferability of the option depends on the original parties' intent when they entered into the lease and option agreement. If the court finds that the option has been separated from the leasehold estate, so that it is no longer exercisable by the tenant, the option becomes subject to the Rule Against Perpetuities.

2) Rights of First Refusal

A right of first refusal (or "preemptive right") gives the holder the right to purchase the property if the seller receives a third party's offer to purchase, usually on the same terms as that offer. In contrast to options, rights of first refusal in many states are presumed to be personal to the holder and thus *not assignable* unless the instrument indicates otherwise. [Malone v. Flattery, 797 N.W.2d 624 (Iowa 2011)] Nonassignable rights of first refusal are *usually not subject to the Rule Against Perpetuities*, but rather are governed by the Rule Against Restraints on Alienation (*see* F.5.b., *infra*). In some states, however, rights of first refusal are subject to the Rule Against Perpetuities in the same manner as options.

3. Application of the Rule to Class Gifts

a. "Bad-as-to-One, Bad-as-to-All" Rule

The general principle that the Rule does not invalidate interests that "vest" within the perpetuities period *does not apply to vested remainders subject to open*. The class gift rule, sometimes called the "all-or-nothing" rule, requires that:

(i) The *class must close* within the perpetuities period; and

(ii) All conditions precedent for *every* member of the class must be satisfied, if at all, within the perpetuities period.

If it is possible that a disposition might vest remotely with respect to any member of the class, the *entire class gift is invalid*.

Examples: 1) "To A for life, then to such of A's children as live to attain the age of 35." At the time of this disposition, A has two children: X (age 38) and

Y (age 33). (i) A has a life estate. X has a vested remainder subject to open. There is a contingent remainder in such of A's other children as live to attain the age of 35. (ii) The remainder to A's children violates the Rule; the transferor has a reversion in fee. While X's remainder is vested subject to open, it is not vested for purposes of the Rule. Here is what might happen: A might have another child (Z); before Z attains age 14, A, X, and Y might die, etc. The *gift with respect to any afterborn child of A clearly violates the Rule*; under the "bad-as-to-one, bad-as-to-all" class gift rule, *the entire class gift is void*.

Why does the "class closing" rule not save the gift? Because X is already age 35, doesn't this mean that the class will close on the life tenant's death? The answer is: yes it does, but this does not help. Although we will close the class at that point, the class as closed might include the afterborn Z, who might be under age 14 at that time; and it still might be more than lives in being plus 21 years before Z's interest might vest.

2) "To A for life, then to A's children for their lives, and on the death of the last survivor of A's children, to A's grandchildren in fee." At the time this disposition takes effect, A is alive and has two children and three grandchildren. A has a life estate, the two children have vested remainders subject to open in a life estate, and the three grandchildren have vested remainders subject to open in fee. The remainder to A's grandchildren is void because every member of the class will not be ascertained until the death of the survivor of A's children; and that surviving child might be born to A after the date of this disposition. Then all of A's children and grandchildren who are lives in being might die and 21 years after their deaths, this afterborn child might give birth to a child (GC-4); although GC-4's interest would vest at birth, under the hypothesized facts it would vest remotely.

b. **Class Closing Rules May Save Disposition**
In some cases, the "rule of convenience" applicable to class gifts can be relied on to save a gift from the Rule.

Example: "To A for life, and on her death to A's grandchildren in fee." At the time of this disposition, A has two children and three grandchildren. A has a life estate and the grandchildren have vested remainders subject to open. As in the preceding example, A might have an afterborn child who might produce afterborn grandchildren—but there is one difference. Under the "rule of convenience" the *class will be closed at the time any member of the class can demand a distribution*—here the death of A, a life in being. Consequently, all members of the class who will be permitted to share in the remainder will be determined on A's death.

c. **"Gift to Subclass" Exception**
Separate gifts vest at different times. Each gift to a subclass may be treated as a separate gift under the Rule.

Example: "To pay the income to A for life, then to A's children for their lives, and as each child of A dies, to distribute the corpus to such child's issue then living, per stirpes." A has two children at the time of this disposition. In this case, the remainder to issue has been made by a gift to subclasses; as each child dies his issue are to take the share on which he was receiving income. With respect to A's two children now alive, the class of "issue then living" will be determined on their deaths; the gift is good. If A should have another child after the date of this disposition, the ***remainder to such afterborn child's issue is void*** because it might vest beyond the lives in being plus 21 years.

d. Per Capita Gift Exception

When there is a separate gift of a fixed sum to each class member, each gift is tested separately under the Rule.

Example: T's will bequeaths "$1,000 each to such of A's grandchildren as live to attain the age of 21, whether alive at my death or born thereafter." At T's death, A has two children and five grandchildren. Here, we have a per capita gift to each member of the class; there is no problem of knowing within the perpetuities period the number of class members who share in an aggregate gift, and thus the size of each share. Here, the amount to be received by each member is ascertainable without reference to the number of persons in the class. The bequest is valid for all grandchildren by A's two children who were alive at T's death. (This includes all future-born grandchildren as well as the five now on the scene, for all such grandchildren will reach 21, if at all, within 21 years after their parent's death.)

However, the ***bequest is void for any grandchildren by a child born to A after T's death***. Such an afterborn child cannot be used as a life in being.

4. Perpetuities Reform Legislation

Most states have enacted one of the following types of statutes designed to eliminate some of the harsh results of the common law Rule Against Perpetuities:

a.   A ***"wait and see"*** statute, under which the validity of an interest following one or more life estates is determined on the basis of facts existing at the end of the life estate rather than at the creation of the interest (*see* 1.b.1), *supra*);

b.   A ***cy pres*** approach, borrowed from Trusts law, under which an invalid interest is reformed to comply with the Rule and carry out the grantor's intent as nearly as possible;

c.   A statute dealing with ***specific perpetuities problems*** (e.g., age contingencies reduced to age 21, women over age 55 presumed incapable of childbearing, gift to widow presumed to mean the person who was the spouse on the date the gift was created); or

d.   The ***Uniform Statutory Rule Against Perpetuities***, which provides an alternative 90-year vesting period. The Uniform Rule takes a "wait and see" approach in determining whether an interest actually vests within 90 years.

5. Technique for Analysis of Perpetuities Problems
In applying the Rule Against Perpetuities, these three steps should be followed:

a. Determine What Interests Are Created
First, determine what interests are created, applying the proper future interests labels, as though there were no Rule Against Perpetuities.

b. Apply the Rule
Determine the measuring life or lives that can be used to show either that the interest must vest within lives in being plus 21 years *or* that the interest might not vest within that period. At this step, assume that there is no such thing as a perpetuities reform statute, for the statute is not brought into play unless there is a perpetuities problem.

c. Apply Reform Statute
If the particular jurisdiction has a perpetuities reform statute that is triggered by the perpetuities violation, apply the statute to reform or save the gift.

F. THE RULE AGAINST RESTRAINTS ON ALIENATION
As a general rule, any restriction on the transferability of a legal (as distinguished from an equitable) interest in property is void: The restriction violates the common law Rule Against Restraints on Alienation. "Restraint on alienation" means an express restriction on the transferability of property. Like the Rule Against Perpetuities, this is a rule of public policy that is designed to prevent property from being tied up and taken out of commerce.

1. Types of Restraints on Alienation
There are three types of restraints on alienation: (i) *disabling* restraints, under which any attempted transfer is ineffective; (ii) *forfeiture* restraints, under which an attempted transfer results in a forfeiture of the interest; and (iii) *promissory* restraints, under which an attempted transfer breaches a covenant. A disabling restraint on *any* legal interest is *void*.

Examples: 1) Property is transferred to A in fee simple, with the added proviso that "neither A nor any of her children shall have the right to transfer the land or any interest therein." Under this restriction, if given effect (*it is not*), any attempted transfer would simply be ineffective. This is a *disabling restraint*.

2) Property is transferred to A in fee simple, with the added proviso that "if A shall attempt to transfer the land or any interest therein during her lifetime, her estate shall cease, and title therein shall vest in B." This is a *forfeiture restraint*.

3) Property is transferred to A in fee simple, with the added proviso that "A hereby covenants that she will not transfer the land or any interest therein without [the transferor's] prior written consent." Under this *promissory restraint*, if given effect, the remedy is injunction or damages for breach of contract.

2. Restraints on a Fee Simple

a. Total Restraints
Any total restraint on a fee simple—either forfeiture, disabling, or promissory—is *void*. The grantee may ignore the restraint and freely transfer the property.

b. Partial Restraints

A partial restraint is one that purports to restrict the power to transfer to specific persons, or by a specific method, or until a specific time.

1) Reasonable Restraints Doctrine

Although absolute restraints on fee simple estates are void, a forfeiture or promissory restraint *for a limited time* and *for a reasonable purpose* may be upheld.

Example: A owns and resides in a house. He conveys a one-half interest in the house to his brother, B, including in the deed a covenant that "during their joint lifetimes, each party promises not to convey his interest to any other person without the consent of the other party." This promissory restraint is limited to the joint lifetimes of the parties and is a reasonable way to ensure that neither party will be faced with the prospect of residing with a stranger. The restraint would probably be upheld.

2) Discriminatory Restraints

Restraints prohibiting the transfer or use of property to or by a person of a specified racial, religious, or ethnic group are *not enforceable*.

a) Fourteenth Amendment

Judicial enforcement of a covenant forbidding use of property by persons of a particular race is *discriminatory state action* forbidden by the Fourteenth Amendment to the United States Constitution. [Shelley v. Kraemer, 334 U.S. 1 (1948)]

Example: O conveys Blackacre "to A and his heirs, and A promises that Blackacre will never be used or occupied by nonwhite persons." Thereafter A sells to B, a black man, who moves onto Blackacre. O sues for an injunction prohibiting B from using Blackacre, and sues A for damages for having sold to B. Injunction and damages are judicial remedies ordinarily available for breach of a covenant. The court cannot grant O either an injunction or damages, because such judicial action would be state action interfering with B's right to enjoy property free of racial discrimination. [Barrows v. Jackson, 346 U.S. 249 (1953)]

b) Fair Housing Act

Discriminatory restrictions may also violate the Fair Housing Act of 1968. Recording a deed with a racial restriction is prohibited by the Act. [42 U.S.C. §3604(c)]

3. Restraints on a Life Estate

a. Legal Life Estate

Forfeiture and promissory restraints on life estates are *valid*. A life estate is inalienable as a practical matter because few would be willing to pay full value for an estate of uncertain duration; thus, little is lost by giving effect to the transferor's intention to restrict the estate's transferability. (However, *disabling* restraints on legal life estates are *void*.)

b. Equitable Life Estate

The rule applicable to restrictions on equitable interests (i.e., those held in trust) is the exact opposite of the rule applicable to legal interests. Spendthrift clauses, which are true disabling restraints, are given effect in the great majority of American jurisdictions. (*See* Trusts outline.)

4. Restraints on Future Interests

Restraints on *vested* future interests generally are valid only to the extent that restraints on present interests of the same type are valid. *Disabling* restraints on all future interests are *void*.

a. Vested Remainders in Fee Simple

Any *total* restraint on a vested remainder in fee simple—either forfeiture, disabling, or promissory—is *void* (*see* 2.a., *supra*). *Partial forfeiture and promissory* restraints on vested remainders in fee simple *may be upheld* if reasonable (*see* 2.b.1), *supra*).

b. Vested Remainders for Life

Forfeiture and promissory restraints on vested remainders for life are *valid* (*see* 3.a., *supra*).

c. Contingent Remainders

The law is unsettled as to the validity of forfeiture and promissory restraints on contingent remainders. Thus, this issue is not likely to be tested.

5. Other Valid Restraints on Alienation

a. Reasonable Restrictions in Commercial Transactions

The courts tend to uphold restrictions on transferability that arise in the context of a commercial transaction on the theory that the restriction appears in an agreement entered into by the parties, it is a product of their bargaining, and presumably serves a useful purpose in facilitating the parties' objectives. Thus, restrictions on transferability that are part of a bargained-for agreement, as distinguished from a donative transaction, are valid.

Examples: 1) O borrows money from M Bank and gives the bank a mortgage on land. The mortgage provides that the land shall not be transferable by O without M's consent, and that if the land is transferred without consent, the entire indebtedness shall be accelerated and shall become immediately due and payable. This "due on sale" restriction on transferability is reasonable because M has an interest in approving who shall be the transferee of the land in which it has a security interest.

2) A, B, C, and D each own 25% of the stock in a closely held corporation. The articles of incorporation provide that no shareholder shall transfer her stock without the consent of a majority of the other shareholders. This restriction on transferability is valid because, due to the closely held nature of the business, the shareholders have a legitimate concern over the identity of their associates.

b. **Options and Rights of First Refusal**
The right to have the first opportunity to purchase real estate when it becomes available, or the right to meet any offer, is valid if *reasonable* (e.g., by specifying fair market value or other reasonable price). [Restatement (Third) of Property: Servitudes §3.4]

c. **Restrictions on Transferability of Leaseholds**
A provision in a lease prohibiting the lessee's assignment or subletting of her leasehold interest without the consent of the landlord is given effect in all jurisdictions. (*See* II.E.3., *infra*.)

G. CONCURRENT ESTATES

Any of the estates in land previously discussed can be held concurrently by several persons. These persons all have the right to the enjoyment and possession of the land at the same time. Three of the chief forms of concurrent ownership in land are discussed here: joint tenancy, tenancy by the entirety, and tenancy in common.

1. **Joint Tenancy**
A joint tenancy can be created between two or more co-tenants. Its distinguishing feature is the *right of survivorship*. Conceptually, when one joint tenant dies, the property is freed from his concurrent interest; the survivor or survivors retain an undivided right in the property, which is no longer subject to the interest of the deceased co-tenant. The survivors do not succeed to the decedent's interest; they hold free of it.

a. **Creation**

1) **Four Unities Required**
At common law, four unities are required to create a joint tenancy:

a) Unity of *time* (interests vested at the same time);

b) Unity of *title* (interests acquired by the same instrument);

c) Unity of *interest* (interests of the same *type* and *duration*); and

d) Unity of *possession* (interests give identical rights to enjoyment).

2) **Modern Law**
The above requirements have been eroded in some jurisdictions; e.g., by statute in some states, an owner can create a joint tenancy in herself and another by a single deed (she need not use a "strawman" conveyance), even though the unities of "time" and "title" are not satisfied. Similarly, as indicated below, a number of transactions are no longer found to sever a joint tenancy despite the seeming absence of continued unities.

3) **Express Language Required**
Under modern law, *joint tenancies are disfavored*. Hence, there must be a clear expression of intent to create this estate, or it will not be recognized. The usual language required is "to A and B as *joint tenants with right of survivorship*." Today, when two or more persons take property by a single conveyance, a tenancy

in common, not a joint tenancy, is presumed. A joint tenancy results only when an intention to create a right of survivorship is clearly expressed.

b. Severance

A joint tenancy can be terminated by a suit for *partition*, which can be brought by any joint tenant. It may also be terminated by various acts by any joint tenant.

1) Inter Vivos Conveyance by One Joint Tenant

An inter vivos conveyance by one joint tenant of her undivided interest destroys the joint tenancy so that the transferee takes the interest as a tenant in common and not as a joint tenant. This rule applies to both *voluntary and involuntary* conveyances (even secret conveyances).

a) When More than Two Joint Tenants

When property is held in joint tenancy by three or more joint tenants, a conveyance by one of them destroys the joint tenancy *only as to the conveyor's interest*. The other joint tenants continue to hold in joint tenancy as between themselves, while the grantee holds her interest as a tenant in common with them.

b) Transactions that May Not Result in Severance

(1) Judgment Liens

In most jurisdictions, when a plaintiff obtains a money judgment against a defendant, that judgment becomes a lien on the defendant's real estate in the county where the judgment is docketed. (This is automatic in some states; in others, the lien must be recorded in the real estate records.) The lien then "runs with the land," burdening it until the judgment is paid or until the lien expires under a statute of limitations (e.g., 10 years). Suppose such a lien is obtained against one of several joint tenants but not against the others. Does it sever the joint tenancy, converting it into a tenancy in common? The majority view is that it does not; a lien is not considered a sufficiently substantial "conveyance" to destroy the unities of time and title. However, if the plaintiff who obtained the judgment then proceeds to enforce it by *foreclosure* (often termed a "judgment sale"), the sheriff's deed issued to the buyer at that sale *will sever* the joint tenancy. That follows from the fact that the sheriff's deed conveys the defendant's full title.

Example: A and B own land as joint tenants with right of survivorship. P sues A on a tort claim, and obtains and records a judgment. If A dies at that point, B owns the entire land (by virtue of the right of survivorship), and P has a lien on nothing. However, assume that P has a judgment sale, and a sheriff's deed is issued to X, who buys at the sale. Then A dies. B and X each own a one-half interest in the land as tenants in common.

(2) Mortgages

In the majority of states, a mortgage is regarded as a lien on title, and one joint tenant's execution of a mortgage on her interest does not by itself cause a severance. (Rather, the severance occurs only if the mortgage is foreclosed and the property sold.) But in the minority of states, which regard a mortgage as a transfer of title, the transfer destroys the unity of title and severs the joint tenancy.

Example: A, B, and C are joint tenants. A mortgages her interest to Lender, who records. Thereafter, A dies and Lender seeks to enforce her mortgage on an undivided one-third interest in the property. In a state following the "lien theory" of mortgages, Lender loses. A's mortgage did not sever the joint tenancy. Lender's rights were lost when A died prior to foreclosure. A's interest evaporated, and with it Lender's security interest.

(3) Leases

Theoretically, when one joint tenant leases her interest in jointly held property, the lease destroys the unities of interest and possession and thereby should effect a severance (which is the view taken by some states). But other states hold that the joint tenancy is not destroyed, and is merely temporarily suspended (for the length of the lease).

(a) Death of Lessor

There is a split among the states following the latter view, on what happens if the lessor/joint tenant dies before the end of the lease. Some courts hold that because the lessor's own right to possession would cease on her death, so must the right of any lessee (i.e., the lessor could not convey more than she had). Others hold that the lease operates as a "temporary severance," and the remaining joint tenant's survivorship rights are therefore postponed until the end of the lease.

2) Contract to Convey by One Joint Tenant

In most states, a severance also results where one joint tenant executes a valid contract to convey her interest to another, even though no actual transfer of title has yet been made. The contract to convey is enforceable in equity, and hence is treated as an effective transfer of an equitable interest. Thus, if the vendor dies before the title is transferred, the purchaser is entitled to a deed from the vendor's estate and becomes a tenant in common with the original joint tenant or tenants.

a) Compare—Executory Contract by All Joint Tenants

There is a split as to whether an executory contract to sell, entered into by all the joint tenants, will terminate the joint tenancy. Suppose that on January 1, A and B, joint tenants, contract with X to sell and deliver title to Blackacre to X on February 1. A dies on January 15. Two questions arise: (i) On February 1, is B entitled to the full sales proceeds as surviving joint tenant, or is A's estate entitled to one-half (on the theory that the January 1 contract worked an equitable conversion, which created in the vendors a contract right to receive money that was held in tenancy in common)? And, (ii) will X have to obtain a deed not only from B but also from A's administrator on the theory that the retained legal title (for security purposes) was held in tenancy in common?

(1) Common Law View—Joint Tenancy Continues
The common law view, still followed by many courts, is that a joint tenancy continues in both the right to the proceeds and the retained legal title, meaning that B gets the full sales proceeds and can give good title.

(2) Other Courts—Tenancy in Common
Other jurisdictions, however, proceed on the doctrine of equitable conversion and hold that the executory contract converts A and B's land ownership rights to a mere contract right to receive the purchase price (which they hold as tenants in common because of the statutory presumption favoring such tenancies). Further, the legal title to the land, retained for security purposes, is also held to be in tenancy in common.

3) Testamentary Disposition by One Joint Tenant Has No Effect
A joint tenancy is not terminated where a joint tenant executes a will devising her interest to another or dies with such a will in effect. The reason is that a will is ambulatory (effective only at death) and hence is inoperative as to joint tenancy property, because at the instant of death the decedent's rights in the property evaporate. (The result would be contra if all joint tenants had agreed that the decedent could devise her interest; but in such a case, the agreement itself would cause the severance.)

a) Compare—"Secret" Deeds
As indicated above, an inter vivos conveyance severs a joint tenancy. This is true even though the deed is kept "secret" and the interest transferred is to take effect only upon the death of the grantor. However, if the grantee does not know about the deed, the grantee's acceptance *after* the death of the grantor does not relate back to defeat the right of survivorship. (*See* VI.C.4.b., *infra*.)

4) Effect of One Joint Tenant's Murdering Another
Some states have passed statutes under which the felonious and intentional killing of one joint tenant by another joint tenant operates as a severance. In other states, the surviving joint tenant holds the ill-gained portion on a constructive trust for the decedent's estate. Thus, the homicidal survivor keeps her original share but does not profit from her felony.

2. Tenancy by the Entirety
A tenancy by the entirety is a marital estate akin to a joint tenancy between spouses. It is not recognized in community property states, but in some common law jurisdictions, it arises presumptively in any conveyance made to a married couple.

a. Right of Survivorship
The estate carries a right of survivorship, which operates in the same manner as the right of survivorship incident to a joint tenancy.

b. Severance Limited

The major distinction between a joint tenancy and a tenancy by the entirety concerns severance. A tenancy by the entirety cannot be terminated by involuntary partition. It can be terminated only by: (i) the death of either spouse (leaving the survivor sole owner of the fee); (ii) divorce (in most states leaving the parties as tenants in common with no right of survivorship); (iii) mutual agreement; or (iv) execution by a joint creditor of *both* spouses (a creditor of one or the other cannot execute).

c. Individual Spouse Cannot Convey or Encumber

In most states, an individual spouse may not convey or encumber tenancy by the entirety property. A deed or mortgage executed by only one spouse is ineffective. Likewise, the creditors of one spouse may not attach a lien to tenancy by the entirety property. One exception to this rule is federal tax liens; an individual's interest in tenancy by the entirety property is subject to federal tax liens.

3. Tenancy in Common

A tenancy in common is a concurrent estate with no right of survivorship. Each owner has a distinct, undivided interest in the property. This interest is freely alienable by inter vivos and testamentary transfer, is inheritable, and is subject to claims of the tenant's creditors. The only "unity" involved is possession: Each tenant is entitled to possession of the whole estate. Today, by statute, multiple grantees are presumed to take as tenants in common. The same is true where multiple transferees take by descent.

4. Incidents of Co-Ownership

a. Possession

Each co-tenant has the right to possess all portions of the property; no co-tenant has the right to exclusive possession of any part. A co-tenant out of possession cannot bring a possessory action unless there has been an "ouster" by the tenant in possession. A claim of right to exclusive possession can constitute an ouster.

b. Rents and Profits

In most jurisdictions (but not all), a co-tenant in possession has the right to retain profits gained by her use of the property. A co-tenant in possession need not share such profits with co-tenants out of possession, nor reimburse them for the rental value of her use of the land, unless there has been an ouster or an agreement to the contrary. However, a co-tenant out of possession has a right to share in *rents from third parties* and in *profits* derived from a use of the land that reduces its value (e.g., removal of minerals, etc.).

c. Effect of One Concurrent Owner's Encumbering the Property

A joint tenant or tenant in common may place a mortgage on her interest, but may not, of course, encumber the other co-tenant's interest. If a tenancy in common is involved, the mortgagee can foreclose only on the mortgaging co-tenant's interest. Likewise, if a joint tenancy is involved and the mortgage itself does not sever the joint tenancy (*see* 1.b.1)b)(2), *supra*), the mortgagee can foreclose on the mortgagor/co-tenant's interest and the foreclosure sale itself will cause a severance. But in the case of a joint tenancy, the mortgagee runs the risk that the mortgaging co-tenant will die before foreclosure, extinguishing the mortgagee's interest. The same principles apply to judgment liens obtained against an individual co-tenant.

Example: A and B are joint tenants with right of survivorship. A injures P in an accident, and P sues A, obtaining a personal injury judgment against A for $1,000. This judgment is, by statute, a lien on A's one-half interest in the land, but it does not cause a severance. If A dies before the lien is foreclosed and is survived by B, B owns the land free and clear of the lien. But if P forecloses the lien before A's death, the foreclosure sale will cause a severance, and the buyer at the sale will own a one-half interest in the land as a tenant in common with B.

d. Ouster
Under the unity of possession, each co-tenant is entitled to possess and enjoy the whole of the property subject to the equal right of her co-tenant. If one tenant *wrongfully excludes* another co-tenant from possession of the whole or any part of the whole of the premises, there is an ouster. The ousted co-tenant is entitled to receive his share of the fair rental value of the property for the time he was wrongfully deprived of possession.

e. Remedy of Partition
A joint tenant or tenant in common has a right to judicial partition, either *in kind* (division of the tract into parcels) or *by sale and division of the proceeds* (in accordance with the ownership interests as modified by permitted recoupments for improvements, repairs, taxes, and the like). Although partition in kind is generally preferred, partition by sale and division of the proceeds is permitted when a fair and equitable physical division of the property cannot be made. [Nordhausen v. Christner, 338 N.W.2d 754 (Neb. 1983)]

Examples: 1) A and B own a single-family home as joint tenants. A brings an appropriate action to partition the land. Because physical division of the home is not feasible, the court will order a sale of the home and division of the proceeds equally between A and B.

2) A owns a three-fourths interest and B owns a one-fourth interest in a four-acre undeveloped parcel of land as tenants in common. The applicable zoning ordinance requires that a buildable lot contain at least two acres. A seeks to partition the land into a three-acre lot for himself and a one-acre lot for B. B argues that the land should be sold and the proceeds divided between A and B according to their respective shares. B will prevail, because the zoning ordinance makes it impossible to divide the land fairly.

1) Restraint on Partition by Co-Tenants
Although in general, a co-tenant has the right to demand a partition by judicial sale at any time, courts give effect to a provision prohibiting partition by any one co-tenant, provided that the restriction is to *last for only a reasonable time*. The restriction is not considered to be an invalid restraint on alienation because (i) any co-tenant can transfer her interest to a third person at any time, and (ii) the restraint can be eliminated if the co-tenants join in a deed to a third person, thereby terminating the co-tenancy relationship.

f. Expenses for Preservation of Property—Contribution
Under certain circumstances, equity courts will compel contribution between concurrent owners.

1) **Repairs—Contribution May Be Compelled for Necessary Repairs**
A co-tenant who pays more than her pro rata share of the cost of necessary repairs is entitled to contribution from the other co-tenants in actions for accounting or partition. Although the courts are split on whether a co-tenant who makes necessary repairs can maintain an independent action for contribution against the other co-tenants, the majority view is that she can compel contribution, provided she has notified the other co-tenants of the need for repairs. Moreover, several decisions authorize contribution even without such notice.

The common law view was that because no co-tenant has a duty to make necessary repairs, a co-tenant who makes such repairs cannot bring an action to compel contribution from the other co-tenants. This is now the minority view.

2) **Improvements—No Contribution or Setoff**
Generally, there is no right of contribution for the cost of improvements, nor can they be set off in an action for accounting. Only in an action for partition can the value of improvements be recouped.

3) **Taxes and Mortgages—Contribution Can Be Compelled**
Each co-tenant has a duty to pay her share of taxes and payments due on mortgages on the entire property. A tenant who is not in sole possession can pay the taxes and mortgage payments and then compel contribution from the other co-tenants. However, a co-tenant in sole possession will receive reimbursement only for the amount that exceeds the rental value of the property.

g. **Duty of Fair Dealing Among Co-Tenants**
A confidential relationship exists among co-tenants. Accordingly, the acquisition by one co-tenant of any outstanding title or lien that might affect the estate held by all the co-tenants is deemed to be an acquisition on behalf of all the other co-tenants as well. Thus, when one co-tenant purchases or otherwise acquires a lienholder's (mortgagee's) claim against the co-tenancy property, she must give the other co-tenants a reasonable time to pay their share and acquire a proportionate interest. Courts carefully scrutinize the fairness of transactions between co-tenants. Lastly, it is difficult for one co-tenant to *adversely possess* against other co-tenants. (*See* V.B.4.b., *infra*.)

Example: A and B own land as co-tenants. Neither pays the annual property taxes. The county conducts a tax sale and A buys the property for $10,000. If B is willing to pay A $5,000, many courts will compel A to put the property in co-tenancy again.

II. LANDLORD AND TENANT

A. **NATURE OF LEASEHOLD**
A leasehold is an estate in land. The tenant has a present possessory interest in the leased premises, and the landlord has a future interest (reversion). Certain rights and liabilities flow from this property relationship between landlord and tenant. The three major types of leasehold estates

are *tenancies for years*, *periodic tenancies*, and *tenancies at will*. There is a fourth category called *tenancies at sufferance*.

1. Tenancies for Years

a. Fixed Period of Time

A tenancy for years is one that is to continue for a fixed period of time. It may be for *more or less* than a year (e.g., 10 days or 10 years); it may be determinable (similar to a fee simple determinable) or on condition subsequent. The termination date of a tenancy for years is usually certain. As a result, the tenancy expires at the end of the stated period *without either party giving notice to the other*. Even if the date of termination is uncertain (e.g., L leases the premises to T "until the end of the war"), *most courts* hold that if the parties have attempted to state some period of duration, the lease creates a tenancy for years.

b. Creation

Tenancies for years are normally created by written leases. In most states, the Statute of Frauds requires that a lease creating a tenancy for more than one year be memorialized in writing. In addition, most states have statutes that restrict the number of years for which a leasehold estate may be created (e.g., 51 years for farm property and 99 years for urban property). When the lease term exceeds the statutory maximum, most courts hold that the lease is *entirely* void. Likewise, where the lease contains an *option to renew* for a period beyond the permitted maximum, most courts hold the entire lease void.

c. Termination

A tenancy for years ends *automatically* on its termination date.

1) Breach of Covenants

In most tenancy for years leases, the landlord reserves the right to terminate if the tenant breaches any of the leasehold covenants. This reserved power is called the landlord's *right of entry*.

a) Failure to Pay Rent

In many jurisdictions, if the tenant fails to pay the promised rent, the landlord has the right to terminate the lease *even in the absence of a reserved right of entry*.

2) Surrender

A tenancy for years also terminates upon surrender. Surrender consists of the tenant giving up his leasehold interest to the landlord and the landlord accepting. Usually the same *formalities* are required for the surrender of a leasehold as are necessary for its creation. Thus, a writing is necessary for the surrender of a leasehold if the unexpired term is more than one year.

2. Periodic Tenancies

A periodic tenancy is a tenancy that continues from year to year or for successive fractions of a year (e.g., weekly or monthly) until terminated by proper notice by either party. The beginning date must be certain, but the *termination date is always uncertain* until notice is given.

All conditions and terms of the tenancy are carried over from one period to the next unless there is a lease provision to the contrary. Periodic tenancies do not violate the rules limiting the length of leaseholds because each party retains the power to terminate upon giving notice.

a. Creation
Periodic tenancies can be created in three ways:

1) By Express Agreement
Periodic tenancies can be created by express agreement (e.g., "Landlord leases to Tenant from month to month").

2) By Implication
A periodic tenancy will be implied if the lease has no set termination but does provide for the payment of rent at specific periods.

Example: "Landlord leases to Tenant at a rent of $1,000 *payable monthly* in advance." The reservation of monthly rent will give rise to a periodic tenancy from *month to month*.

Note: If the lease reserves an annual rent, payable monthly (e.g., "$12,000 per annum, payable $1,000 on the first day of every month commencing January 1"), the majority view is that the periodic tenancy is from *year to year*.

3) By Operation of Law
A periodic tenancy may arise even without an express or implied agreement between the parties.

a) Tenant Holds Over
If a tenant for years remains in possession after the termination of his tenancy period, the landlord may elect to treat the tenant as a periodic tenant on the same terms as the original lease. (*See* 5.b., *infra*.)

b) Lease Invalid
If a lease is invalid (e.g., because of failure to satisfy the Statute of Frauds) and the tenant nonetheless goes into possession, the tenant's periodic payment of rent will convert what would otherwise be a tenancy at will into a periodic tenancy. The period of the tenancy coincides with the period for which the rent is paid.

b. Termination—Notice Required
A periodic tenancy is *automatically renewed*, from period to period, until proper notice of termination is given by either party. Many jurisdictions have statutorily prescribed the notice required to terminate a periodic tenancy. In general, the guidelines are as follows:

(i) The tenancy must end at the *end of a "natural" lease period*.

(ii) For a tenancy from year to year, the common law rule is that *six months' notice* is required, but the modern view is *one month's notice* for all but farm and grazing land. [*See* Restatement (Second) of Property, Land. & Ten. §1.5)

(iii) For tenancies less than one year in duration, a *full period in advance* of the period in question is required by way of notice (e.g., for a month-to-month periodic tenancy, one full month's notice is required).

In general, the notice required to terminate a periodic tenancy must be in *writing* and must actually be *delivered* to the party in question or deposited at his residence in a manner similar to that required for service of process.

3. Tenancies at Will

A tenancy at will is an estate in land that is terminable at the will of either the landlord or the tenant. To be a tenancy at will, both the landlord and the tenant must have the right to terminate the lease at will.

(i) If the lease gives *only the landlord* the right to terminate at will, a *similar right* will generally be *implied in favor of the tenant* so that the lease creates a tenancy at will.

(ii) If the lease is only at the will of the *tenant* (e.g., "for so long as the tenant wishes"), courts usually *do not imply a right to terminate in favor of the landlord*. Rather, most courts interpret the conveyance as creating a life estate or fee simple, either of which is terminable by the tenant. (If the Statute of Frauds is not satisfied, the conveyance is a tenancy at will.)

a. Creation

A tenancy at will generally arises from a specific understanding between the parties that *either party may terminate* the tenancy at any time. Note that unless the parties *expressly agree* to a tenancy at will, the payment of regular rent (e.g., monthly, quarterly, etc.) will cause a court to treat the tenancy as a periodic tenancy. Thus, tenancies at will are quite rare. Although a tenancy at will can also arise when the lease is for an indefinite period (one that does not satisfy the requirements for creating a tenancy for years), or when a tenant goes into possession under a lease that does not satisfy the requisite formalities (usually the Statute of Frauds), rent payments will usually convert it to a periodic tenancy.

b. Termination

A tenancy at will may be terminated by *either party*. At common law, no notice was required to terminate a tenancy at will. But the majority of states now require that a party give the other notice of termination and a reasonable time to quit the premises. A tenancy at will also terminates by *operation of law* if:

1) Either party *dies*;

2) The tenant commits *waste*;

3) The tenant attempts to *assign* his tenancy;

4) The *landlord transfers his interest* in the property; or

5) The *landlord executes a term lease* to a third person.

4. Tenancies at Sufferance

A tenancy at sufferance (sometimes called "occupancy at sufferance") arises when a tenant *wrongfully* remains in possession after the expiration of a lawful tenancy (e.g., after the stipulated date for the termination of a tenancy for years; or after the landlord has exercised a power of termination). Such a tenant is a wrongdoer and is *liable for rent*. The tenancy at sufferance lasts only until the landlord takes steps to evict the tenant. No notice is required to end the tenancy, and authorities are divided as to whether this is even an estate in land.

5. The Hold-Over Doctrine

When a tenant continues in possession after the termination of his right to possession, the landlord has two choices of action:

a. Eviction

The landlord may treat the hold-over tenant as a trespasser and evict him under an unlawful detainer statute.

b. Creation of Periodic Tenancy

The landlord may, in his sole discretion, bind the tenant to a new periodic tenancy.

1) Terms

The terms and conditions of the expired tenancy (e.g., rent, covenants, etc.) apply to the new tenancy. In *commercial leases*, if the original lease term was for *one year or more*, a year-to-year tenancy results from holding over. If the original term was for *less than one year*, the periodic term is determined by the manner in which the rent was due and payable under the prior tenancy. In *residential* leases, however, most courts would rule the tenant a month-to-month tenant (or a week-to-week tenant if the tenant was a roomer paying weekly rent), irrespective of the term of the original lease.

Example: A nonresidential tenant was holding under a six-month term tenancy with rent payable monthly. The tenant holds over and the landlord binds him to a new tenancy. The new periodic tenancy is a month-to-month tenancy.

2) Altered Terms

If the landlord notifies the tenant before termination of the tenancy that occupancy after termination will be at an increased rent, the tenant will be held to have acquiesced to the new terms if he does not surrender. The tenant will be held to the new terms *even if he objects* to the increased rent, provided that the rent increase is reasonable.

c. What Does Not Constitute Holding Over

The landlord cannot bind the tenant to a new tenancy under the hold-over doctrine if: (i) the tenant remains in possession for only a *few hours* after termination of the lease, or leaves a few articles of personal property on the premises; (ii) the delay is *not the tenant's fault* (e.g., because of severe illness); or (iii) it is a *seasonal lease* (e.g., summer cottage).

d.   Double Rent Jeopardy
Many state statutes provide that if a tenant *willfully* remains in possession after his term expires and after the landlord makes a *written demand for possession*, the landlord may collect double rent for the time the tenant in fact remains in possession.

e.   Forcible Entry Statutes
Most states by statute prohibit forcible entry, i.e., entry against the will of the possessor. Under such statutes, a landlord must not use force or self-help to remove a hold-over tenant. Some states also bar the landlord from more subtle methods of regaining possession, e.g., changing the locks and locking out the tenant.

The statutes allow the landlord to *evict* a tenant who has remained in possession after his right to possession has terminated. The sole issue is "who has the right to possession"; questions of title must be litigated in ejectment actions rather than in eviction actions.

B.   LEASES
A lease is a contract containing the promises of the parties. It governs the relationship between the landlord and tenant over the term of the lease.

1.   Common Law—Lease Covenants Independent
At common law, covenants in a lease were independent of each other; i.e., one party's performance of his promise did not depend on the other party's performance of his promise. Thus, if one party breached a covenant, the other party could recover *damages*, but still had to perform his promises and *could not terminate* the landlord-tenant relationship.
Example: L leases an office space to T for five years. T covenants to pay $1,250 per month, and L covenants to paint the office once each year. At the beginning of the second year, L refuses to paint the office. At common law, T could recover damages from L (the decrease in fair rental value or the cost of painting), but T could not terminate the lease or refuse to pay his rent because of L's breach.

2.   Modern Trend—Lease Covenants Dependent
Exceptions to the common law rule developed over time. For example, a tenant may be excused from his covenant to pay rent if the landlord actually or constructively *evicts* the tenant (*see* D.2., *infra*) or breaches the *implied warranty of habitability* (*see* D.3., *infra*). Similarly, in nearly all states a landlord may terminate the lease if the tenant breaches his covenant to *pay rent* (*see* C.4.a., *infra*). Modern courts are also likely to construe other covenants as dependent and excuse one party's performance (after proper notice and time to cure) when the other party's breach relates to a *material* part of the lease (e.g., the Uniform Residential Landlord and Tenant Act, which has been adopted in nearly half the states, codifies this rule for residential tenancies [URLTA §§4.101, 4.201]).
Example: L leases a retail space to T for four years to be used as a furniture store. T

covenants to pay $350 per month, and L covenants not to lease any other space in the building "for use as a furniture store." During the third year, L leases the adjoining retail space to a rug store. If T sells rugs and would suffer financial loss as a result of the competition, L's breach would be considered material, allowing T to terminate the lease. [Kulawitz v. Pacific Woodenware & Paper Co., 155 P.2d 24 (Cal. 1944)]

Compare: In the example in 1., above, L's breach of a covenant to paint likely would not be considered material.

C. TENANT DUTIES AND LANDLORD REMEDIES

1. Tenant's Duty to Repair (Doctrine of Waste)
A tenant cannot damage—commit waste on—the leased premises. The rules governing waste in the leasehold context are very much like those governing waste in the context of the life estate.

a. Types of Waste

1) Voluntary (Affirmative) Waste
A tenant is liable to the landlord for voluntary waste. Voluntary waste results when the tenant intentionally or negligently damages the premises. It also includes exploiting minerals on the property unless the property was previously so used, or unless the lease provides that the tenant may do so.

2) Permissive Waste
Unless the lease provides otherwise, the tenant has no duty to the landlord to make any *substantial* repairs (i.e., to keep the premises in good repair). However, the tenant has a duty to make *ordinary* repairs to keep the property in the same condition as at the commencement of the lease term, excluding ordinary wear and tear (unless the tenant *covenanted* to repair ordinary wear and tear; *see* c.2), *infra*). For example, it is the tenant's duty to repair broken windows or a leaking roof and to take such other steps as are needed to prevent damage from the elements (i.e., keep the premises "wind and water tight"). If the tenant fails to do so, he is liable to the landlord for any resulting damage, but not for the cost of repair. Under the URLTA, residential tenants have additional duties: (i) not to cause housing code violations; (ii) to keep the premises clean and free of vermin; and (iii) to use plumbing, appliances, etc., in a reasonable manner. Note that even when the burden of repair is on the landlord, the tenant does have a duty to report deficiencies promptly to the landlord.

3) Ameliorative Waste
A tenant is under an obligation to return the premises in the same nature and character as received. Therefore, a tenant is not permitted to make substantial alterations to leased structures even if the alteration increases the value of the property.

a) Liability—Cost of Restoration
The tenant is liable for the cost of restoration should he commit ameliorative waste.

b) Modern Exception—Value of Premises Decreasing
When, through the passage of time, the demised premises have been

significantly reduced in value, courts will permit a change in the character of the premises as long as:

(1) The change *increases the value* of the premises;

(2) The change *is performed by a long-term tenant* (e.g., 25 years); and

(3) The change *reflects a change* in the nature and character of the neighborhood.

b. Destruction of the Premises Without Fault

If the leased premises are destroyed (e.g., by fire) without the fault of either the landlord or the tenant, no waste is involved. In this situation, the common law held that the lease continues in effect. In the absence of lease language, neither party has a duty to restore the premises, but the tenant has a duty to continue paying the rent.

1) Majority View—Tenant Can Terminate Lease

In most states, statutes or case law now give the tenant an option to terminate the lease if the premises are destroyed without the tenant's fault, even in the presence of an explicit covenant to repair (*see* below).

c. Tenant's Liability for Covenants to Repair

In *residential* leases, even if the tenant covenants to repair, the landlord will usually be obligated to repair (except for damages caused by the tenant) under the "implied warranty of habitability" (*see* D.3., *infra*), because the landlord's obligations under that warranty are usually held not to be waivable. However, in *nonresidential* leases, the tenant's covenant to repair is enforceable, and a landlord's claim that the tenant breached the covenant will be assessed by comparing the property's condition when the lease terminates with its condition when the lease commenced.

1) Rebuilding After Structural Damage or Casualty Destruction

A covenant requiring the tenant to repair is *not* usually construed by the modern cases to include rebuilding of structural damage or destruction due to a casualty, structural defects, or a third party's acts, unless the covenant *expressly includes* these types of repairs.

Example: L leases greenhouses to T, and the lease contains a covenant by T to "maintain said (greenhouses); and, upon expiration of the term hereof surrender in as good a condition as it shall be when lessee takes possession thereof." The greenhouses are destroyed by fire, and L sues T for the cost of rebuilding them. *Held:* "Maintain" or "repair" does not include an obligation to rebuild after destruction by fire. [Washington Hydroculture, Inc. v. Payne, 635 P.2d 138 (Wash. 1981)]

2) Repairing Ordinary Wear and Tear

A covenant requiring the tenant to repair is usually construed to *include* even repair of ordinary wear and tear *if* the covenant in the lease makes no specific mention of ordinary wear and tear. However, repair covenants frequently *exclude* repair of ordinary wear and tear, and such an exclusion is enforceable.

Example: L leases a restaurant to T. T covenants to "maintain, repair and keep in good order the interior of the building." The covenant does not contain the usual exclusion for ordinary wear and tear. Thus, T is held liable for all needed repairs, including tears in booths and chairs, worn flooring, and a damaged ceiling. [Santillanes v. Property Management Services, Inc., 716 P.2d 1360 (Idaho 1986)]

2. Duty to Not Use Premises for Illegal Purpose
If the tenant uses the premises for an illegal purpose, and the landlord is not a party to the illegal use, the landlord may terminate the lease or obtain damages and injunctive relief.

a. Occasional Unlawful Conduct Does Not Breach Duty
Occasional unlawful conduct of the tenant does not breach this duty. The duty is breached only when the illegal conduct is continuous (e.g., if the tenant operates a gambling ring out of the leased premises).

b. Landlord Remedies—Terminate Lease, Recover Damages
If the conduct is continuous, the landlord may terminate the lease and recover the damages. If the conduct has first been stopped by a public authority, the landlord may terminate and recover damages, but only if she acts within a reasonable time after the use has been stopped. Alternatively, the landlord faced with unlawful tenant conduct may keep the lease in force and seek injunctive or monetary relief.

3. Duty to Pay Rent
At common law, rent is due at the end of the leasehold term. However, leases usually contain a provision making the rent payable at some other time (e.g., "monthly in advance").

a. When Rent Accrues
At common law, rent is not apportionable; i.e., it does not accrue from day to day, but rather accrues all at once at the end of the term. However, most states today have statutes that provide that if a leasehold terminates before the term originally agreed on, the tenant must pay a *proportionate amount* of the agreed rent.

b. Rent Deposits
Landlords often require a deposit by the tenant at the outset of the lease. If the money is considered a *security deposit*, the landlord will not be permitted to retain it beyond the extent of his recoverable damages. But if the deposit is denominated a *"bonus"* or a future rent payment (e.g., the last month's rent), then most courts permit the landlord to retain it after the tenant has been evicted.

1) Restrictions on Security Deposits
Most states restrict the amount of security deposits to one month's rent, require landlords to pay interest on security deposits, and allow statutory or punitive damages for a landlord's improper refusal to return a security deposit.

2) Choice of Law
Landlords cannot avoid strict state laws regarding security deposits or other rules related to leases by using a choice of law provision in a lease to select the law of another state. The law of the state in which the property is located generally applies to leases, even when a provision to the contrary appears in the lease.

c. **Termination of Rent Liability—Surrender**

If a tenant effectively conveys back (surrenders) his leasehold to the landlord, the tenant's liability for future rent ends. Normally, this occurs when there is an agreement between the landlord and tenant that the tenant's interest in the demised premises will end. If the unexpired term of the lease is more than one year, the surrender must be memorialized in writing to satisfy the Statute of Frauds.

4. **Landlord Remedies**

a. **Tenant on Premises But Fails to Pay Rent—Evict or Sue for Rent**

At common law, a breach, such as failure to pay rent, resulted only in a cause of action for money damages; a breach by either party did not give rise to a right to terminate the lease. Most leases, however, grant the nonbreaching party the right to terminate. Furthermore, nearly all states have enacted an ***unlawful detainer statute***, which permits the landlord to evict a defaulting tenant. These statutes provide for a quick hearing, but severely limit the issues that may be raised. Under most statutes, the only issue properly before the court is the landlord's right to rent and possession. The tenant cannot raise counterclaims.

1) **Distress—Landlord's Lien**

In some states (especially in nonresidential leases), a landlord who does not receive rent when due can assert a lien on the personal property found on the leased premises. This applies to property owned by sublessees as well as by the original tenant.

b. **Tenant Abandons**

If the tenant ***unjustifiably*** abandons the property, the landlord has several options depending on the jurisdiction: they may terminate the lease (accept surrender), do nothing (the common law rule), or they may repossess and/or relet.

1) **Terminate Lease—Accept Implicit Offer of Surrender**

Courts treat an abandonment of property by a tenant as an implied offer to terminate the lease. The landlord may choose to: (i) accept that offer to terminate the lease (known as "accepting surrender"), and free the tenant of future liability for rent; or (ii) reject the offer. When determining whether a landlord has accepted or rejected this offer, the courts look to the landlord's conduct after the abandonment. If the landlord accepts the offer of surrender, the tenant is liable only for rent accrued and for damages caused by the abandonment.

2) **Landlord Does Nothing—Tenant Liable for Rent Currently Due (Common Law)**

Under the common law view, a landlord has no duty to mitigate damages and can let the premises lie idle if the abandoning tenant does not tender an acceptable substituting tenant. However, the landlord cannot sue for rent due in the future because the tenant still might pay rent when due. In other words, under this view, the landlord cannot use anticipatory repudiation to sue for the entire amount owed on the balance of the lease—even when the tenant unequivocally indicates that he considers the lease terminated. The common law view is now a minority view. The majority view recognizes anticipatory repudiation by the tenant but also requires the landlord to make reasonable efforts to mitigate damages by reletting to a new tenant (*see* below). Thus, in most states, a landlord's failure to attempt to relet the premises would be a breach of the duty to mitigate, and the landlord's damages would be reduced accordingly.

3) Landlord Repossesses—Tenant's Liability Depends on Surrender

Under the majority view, which requires the landlord to mitigate damages, the landlord must repossess the premises and attempt to relet them. The tenant's liability will depend on whether that repossession constitutes acceptance of a surrender of the premises. If surrender is not found, the tenant remains liable for the difference between the promised rent and the fair rental value of the property (or, if the landlord is able to relet, between the promised rent and the rent received from the reletting). However, if the landlord's reletting or use of the premises is for her own profit (as opposed to on behalf of the tenant), it constitutes acceptance of surrender and the abandoning tenant is free from any rent liability accruing after abandonment. As noted above, if the landlord does not attempt to relet, any recovery against the tenant will be reduced accordingly.

a) Acts that Constitute Acceptance of Surrender

If the landlord resumes possession of the demised premises for herself, this conduct usually constitutes acceptance of the surrender, and the tenant will be relieved of any further liability.

b) Acts that Do Not Constitute Acceptance of Surrender

The fact that the landlord enters the premises after abandonment to make repairs, receives back the keys, or offers to attempt to relet the premises on behalf of the tenant, does not by itself constitute an acceptance of the offered surrender. Note that if the landlord has a duty to mitigate damages, she must repossess the premises; thus, doing so does not constitute acceptance of the tenant's surrender so as to relieve the tenant of liability for future rent. In that case, the tenant would be liable for past due rent as well as the difference between the future rent under the lease and the fair market or relet rental value.

D. LANDLORD DUTIES AND TENANT REMEDIES

At common law, a landlord had *no duty to repair or maintain* the premises. This rule has been modified for residential tenancies in most states by statute (e.g., the URLTA) and the implied warranty of habitability. Moreover, the lease itself commonly prescribes landlord liability to the tenant in several areas. If a lease does not expressly prescribe landlord duties, some duties will be implied.

1. Duty to Deliver Possession of Premises

a. Landlord Duty—Must Deliver Actual Possession

Statutes in most states require the landlord to put the tenant in actual possession of the premises at the beginning of the leasehold term. In a minority of states, the landlord's obligation is merely to give the tenant the legal right to possession. The difference can be important if the leased premises are occupied by a prior, hold-over tenant who has not moved out. Under the majority view, the landlord is in breach if she has not evicted the hold-over tenant by the beginning of the new tenant's term. Under the minority view, it is up to the new tenant to bring eviction proceedings against the hold-over tenant.

b. **Tenant Remedy—Damages**

In states following the majority rule, a tenant is entitled to damages against a landlord in breach of the duty to deliver possession. If, e.g., the tenant had to find more expensive housing during the interim or suffered business losses as a consequence of the landlord's breach, he may recover for these items.

2. **Quiet Enjoyment**

There is implied in every lease a covenant that neither the landlord nor someone with paramount title (e.g., a prior mortgagee of the landlord who forecloses) will interfere with the tenant's quiet enjoyment and possession of the premises. The covenant of quiet enjoyment may be breached in any one of three ways: actual eviction, partial actual eviction, or constructive eviction.

a. **Actual Eviction**

Actual eviction occurs when the landlord, a paramount title holder, or a hold-over tenant excludes the tenant from the *entire* leased premises. Actual eviction *terminates* the tenant's obligation to pay rent.

b. **Partial Actual Eviction**

Partial actual eviction occurs when the tenant is physically excluded from only *part* of the leased premises. (The part from which the tenant is excluded need not be a substantial part of the premises for breach to occur.) The tenant's remedies for breach will differ depending on whether the partial eviction was caused by the landlord or by one with paramount title.

1) **Partial Eviction by Landlord—Entire Rent Obligation Relieved**

Partial eviction by the landlord relieves the tenant of the obligation to pay rent for the *entire* premises, even though the tenant continues in possession of the remainder of the premises.

2) **Partial Eviction by Third Person—Rent Apportioned**

Partial eviction by a third person with paramount title results in an apportionment of rent; i.e., the tenant is liable for the reasonable rental value of the portion that he continues to possess.

c. **Constructive Eviction**

Constructive eviction occurs when a landlord's breach of duty renders the premises untenantable (i.e., unsuitable for occupancy). To establish a claim for constructive eviction, the tenant must prove:

(i) The *landlord*, or persons acting for him, breached a duty to the tenant (acts of neighbors or strangers will not suffice);

(ii) The breach *substantially and materially deprived* the tenant of her use and enjoyment of the premises (e.g., flooding, absence of heat in winter, loss of elevator service in a warehouse);

(iii) The tenant gave the landlord *notice and a reasonable time to repair*; and

(iv) After such reasonable time, the tenant *vacated the premises*.

A tenant who has been constructively evicted may *terminate the lease* (i.e., is relieved of her duty to pay rent from the date of abandonment) and may also seek *damages*. Constructive eviction is often raised as a defense in a landlord's suit for damages or rent.

3. **Implied Warranty of Habitability**

More than half the states have now adopted by court decision or statute the implied warranty of habitability for residential tenancies; it is clearly a growing trend. (It is rarely applied to nonresidential cases, unlike constructive eviction.) The standards are more favorable to tenants than in constructive eviction, and the range of remedies is much broader.

a. **Standard—Reasonably Suitable for Human Residence**

The standard usually applied is the local housing code if one exists; if there is none, the court asks whether the conditions are reasonably suitable for human residence.

b. **Remedies**

The following remedies have been adopted by various courts for violation of the implied warranty (although few courts have adopted all):

1) Tenant may move out and *terminate lease* (as in a constructive eviction).

2) Tenant may *make repairs* directly, and *offset the cost* against future rent obligations. (Some states limit this remedy by statute to a fixed amount, such as one month's rent, or to only one occasion each year.)

3) Tenant may reduce or *abate rent* to an amount equal to the fair rental value in view of the defects in the property. (In many jurisdictions, the tenant may withhold all rent until the court determines the amount of this fair rental value, and may then pay it without risk of the landlord's terminating the lease for rent delinquency.)

4) Tenant may remain in possession, pay full rent, and seek *damages* against the landlord.

4. **Retaliatory Eviction**

If a tenant exercises the legal right to report housing or building code violations or other rights provided by statute (e.g., a residential landlord-tenant act), the landlord is not permitted to terminate the tenant's lease in retaliation. The landlord is also barred from penalizing the tenant in other ways, such as raising the rent or reducing tenant services. This protection is recognized by residential landlord-tenant acts in nearly half the states. These statutes usually *presume* a retaliatory motive if the landlord acts within, say, 90 to 180 days after the tenant exercises his rights. In other states, the same conclusion is reached by judicial construction of the eviction and code statutes. The protection generally applies to tenants under both periodic leases when the landlord gives notice to terminate and fixed-term leases when the landlord refuses to renew. To overcome the presumption, the landlord must show a valid, nonretaliatory reason for his actions.

5. **Discrimination**

The *Civil Rights Act* bars racial or ethnic discrimination in the sale or rental of all property.

The *Fair Housing Act* bars discrimination based on race, ethnicity, religion, national origin, gender, and disability in the sale or rental of a dwelling. Discrimination against families with children is also barred except in senior citizen housing. The Act does not apply to religious organizations, private clubs, and owners who have no more than three single-family dwellings or who have an owner-occupied apartment with no more than four units. [42 U.S.C. §§3603(b), 3607]

a. Advertisements
The Fair Housing Act also makes it unlawul to express in a notice or advertisement a preference based on race, color, religion, sex, disability, familial status, or national origin.

b. Representations of Availability of Dwelling
Under the Fair Housing Act, it is also unlawful to falsely represent to anyone because of race, color, religion, sex, disability, familial status, or national origin that a dwelling is not available for inspection, sale, or rental.

c. Reasonable Accommodations
When the Fair Housing Act applies, landlords must permit disabled tenants to make reasonable modifications to existing premises to accommodate their disabilities at the tenants' own expense. Landlords must also make reasonable accommodations in rules, policies, and services when necessary to afford a disabled person an equal opportunity to use a dwelling.

Example: A landlord of an apartment building with 100 "first-come, first-served" parking spaces must provide a designated space by the door to the building for a disabled tenant who cannot walk long distances and cannot usually find an open space near the door. [Jankowski Lee & Associates v. Cisneros, 91 F.3d 891 (7th Cir. 1996)]

E. ASSIGNMENTS AND SUBLEASES
Absent an express restriction in the lease, a tenant may freely transfer his leasehold interest, in whole or in part. If he makes a *complete transfer of the entire remaining term*, he has made an *assignment*. If he *retains any part* of the remaining term, the transfer is a *sublease*.

Example: L leases property to T for a 10-year term. One month later, T transfers his interest to T1 for nine years, retaining the right to retake the premises (reversion) after nine years. The effect of his transfer is to create a sublease between T (sublessor) and T1 (sublessee).

If, on the other hand, T had transferred to T1 for the remaining period of the lease, reserving no rights, the transfer would constitute an assignment of the lease from T (assignor) to T1 (assignee). (*Note:* It is not controlling that the parties denominate the transfer an "assignment" or "sublease." The court still examines what interest, if any, is retained by T to determine the nature of the transaction.)

1. Consequences of Assignment
The label given to a transfer—an assignment or sublease—determines whether the landlord can proceed directly against the transferee or only against the transferor. To be an assignment, the transfer must be on the same terms as the original lease *except that the tenant*

may reserve a right of termination (reentry) for breach of the terms of the original lease that has been assigned; e.g., "to A for the balance of the leasehold term. However, should A fail to make the rental payments to the landlord, the right to reenter and reclaim the premises is reserved." If the transfer is an assignment, the assignee stands in the shoes of the original tenant in a direct relationship with the landlord. The assignee and the landlord are in *"privity of estate,"* and each is liable to the other on all covenants in the lease that "run with the land."

a. **Covenants that Run with the Land**

A covenant "runs" if the original parties to the lease so intend, and if the covenant *"touches and concerns"* the leased land; i.e., it benefits the landlord and burdens the tenant (or vice versa) with respect to their interests in the property. (These requirements are discussed in detail at IV.D., *infra*.) Covenants held to run with the land (unless the parties specify otherwise) include: covenants to *do or not do a physical act* (e.g., to repair, to conduct a business on the land in a specified manner, to supply heat); covenants to *pay money* (e.g., rent, taxes, etc.); and covenants regarding the *duration* of the lease (e.g., termination clauses).

b. **Rent Covenant Runs with the Land**

Because the covenant to pay rent runs with the land, an assignee owes the rent *directly* to the landlord. He does not owe rent for the period before the assignment, but only for the time that he is in "privity of estate," i.e., from the time of assignment until the end of the lease or until the assignee himself reassigns.

1) **Reassignment by Assignee—Privity of Estate with Landlord Ends**

If the assignee reassigns the leasehold interest, his privity of estate with the landlord ends, and he is not liable for the subsequent assignee's failure to pay rent. However, if the first assignee specifically promised the landlord that he would be liable for the rent for the remainder of the lease term, he may be obligated to pay based on *privity of contract*, even though his reassignment ended the privity of estate.

a) **Effect of Assignee Assuming Rent Obligation**

If the assignee made no promise to the landlord but did promise the original tenant that he would pay all future rent, the landlord may be able to sue the assignee as a *third-party beneficiary* of the contract between the original tenant and the assignee.

2) **Original Tenant Remains Liable**

After assignment, the original tenant is no longer in privity of estate with the landlord. However, if (as is likely) the tenant promised to pay rent in his lease with the landlord, he can still be held liable on his original contractual obligation to pay, i.e., on privity of contract. This allows the landlord to sue the original tenant where the assignee has disappeared, is judgment-proof, etc.

Example: L rents to T for three years at $9,400 per year. After one year, T assigns to T1. T1 pays the rent for one year, and then assigns to T2. T2 fails to pay rent. L can collect from T or T2 but not from T1 (unless T1 made some *promise* on the basis of which L can sue him).

2. Consequences of Sublease

In a sublease, the sublessee is considered the tenant of the original lessee, and usually pays rent directly to the original lessee, who in turn pays rent to the landlord under the main lease.

a. Liability of Sublessee for Rent and Other Covenants

The sublessee is liable to the original lessee for whatever rent the two of them agreed to in the sublease. However, the sublessee is ***not personally liable to the landlord*** for rent or for the performance of any other covenants made by the original lessee in the main lease. The reason is that the sublessee has no contractual relationship with the landlord (no privity of contract), and does not hold the tenant's full estate in the land (no privity of estate); therefore, the covenants in the main lease do not "run with the land" to bind the sublessee.

1) Termination for Breach of Covenants

Even though the sublessee is not personally liable to the landlord, the landlord can still terminate the main lease for nonpayment of rent or, if so stated in the lease, breach of other tenant covenants. If this occurs, the sublease will automatically terminate at the same time.

b. Assumption by Sublessee

It is possible for the sublessee to assume the rent covenant and other covenants in the main lease. An assumption is not implied, but must be expressed. If this occurs, the sublessee is bound by the assumption agreement and becomes personally liable to the landlord on the covenants assumed. The landlord is considered a third-party beneficiary of the assumption agreement.

c. Rights of Sublessee

The sublessee can enforce all covenants made by the original lessee in the sublease, but has no direct right to enforce any covenants made by the landlord in the main lease. However, it is likely (although there is very little case law on point) that a sublessee in a residential lease would be permitted to enforce the implied warranty of habitability against the landlord.

3. Covenants Against Assignment or Sublease

a. Strictly Construed Against Landlord

Many leases contain covenants on the part of the tenant not to assign or sublease without the consent of the landlord. These are strictly construed against the landlord. Thus, a covenant prohibiting assignment does not prohibit subleasing and vice versa.

b. Waiver of Covenant

Even if the lease has a valid covenant against assignment, the covenant may be held waived if the landlord knows of the assignment and does not object. This often occurs when the landlord knowingly accepts rent from the assignee.

c. Continuing Waiver

If the landlord grants consent to one transfer, the Rule in *Dumpor's Case* provides that he waives his right to avoid future transfers unless he expressly reserves the right to do so. Reservation of right must take place at the time of granting consent.

d. Transfer in Violation of Lease Not Void

If a tenant transfers (assigns or sublets) in violation of a prohibition in the lease against transfers, the transfer is not void. However, the landlord usually may terminate the lease under either the lease terms or a statute. Alternatively, he may sue for damages if he can prove any.

e. Reasonableness

In a minority of states, the landlord may not unreasonably withhold consent to transfers by the tenant. The majority imposes no such limitation.

4. Assignments by Landlords

a. Right to Assign

A landlord may assign the rents and reversion interest that he owns. This is usually done by an ordinary deed from the landlord to the new owner of the building. Unless required by the lease (which is very unlikely), the consent of the tenants is not required.

b. Rights of Assignee Against Tenants

Once the tenants are given reasonable evidence that the assignment has occurred, they are legally obligated to recognize and pay rent to the new owner as their landlord. This is called *attornment*. The benefits of all other tenant covenants (e.g., to repair, to pay taxes) also run with the landlord's estate and benefit the new landlord, provided that they touch and concern the land.

c. Liabilities of Assignee to Tenants

The assignee is liable to the tenants for performance of all covenants made by the original landlord in the lease, provided that those covenants touch and concern the land. The burdens of those covenants run with the landlord's estate and become the burdens of the new landlord. The *original landlord also remains liable* on all of the covenants he made in the lease.

Example: L leases to T, and in the lease covenants to repair and maintain the premises. L then sells the building to L2, subject to the lease. Because a covenant to repair and maintain touches and concerns the land, L2 is personally liable to T if L2 fails to perform the covenant. L also remains liable.

F. CONDEMNATION OF LEASEHOLDS

1. Entire Leasehold Taken by Eminent Domain—Rent Liability Extinguished

If all of the leased land is condemned for the full balance of the lease term, the tenant's liability for rent is extinguished because both the leasehold and the reversion have merged in the condemnor and there is no longer a leasehold estate. Absent a lease provision to the contrary, the lessee is entitled to compensation for the taking of the leasehold estate.

2. Temporary or Partial Taking—Tenant Entitled to Compensation Only

If the taking is temporary (i.e., for a period less than the remaining term), or if only a portion of the leased property is condemned, the tenant is *not* discharged from the rent obligation but is entitled to compensation (i.e., a share of the condemnation award) for the taking.

G. TORT LIABILITY OF LANDLORD AND TENANT

1. Landlord's Liability

At common law, subject to a few exceptions, a landlord had **no duty** to make the premises safe. Today there are six exceptions to this rule:

a. Concealed Dangerous Condition (Latent Defect)

If, at the time the lease is entered into, the landlord knows (or should know) of a dangerous condition that the tenant could not discover upon reasonable inspection, the landlord has a **duty to disclose** the dangerous condition. Failure to disclose results in liability for any injury resulting from the condition.

Once disclosure is made, if the tenant accepts the premises, she is considered to have assumed the risk of injuries to herself or her guests (e.g., family members, invitees, licensees); the landlord is no longer liable.

b. Common Areas

The landlord has a duty to exercise **reasonable care** over common areas, such as halls, walks, elevators, etc., that remain under his control. The landlord is liable for any injury resulting from a dangerous condition that could reasonably have been discovered and made safe. This duty is the same as the duty an owner-occupier owes his guests (*see* Multistate Torts outline).

c. Public Use

A landlord is liable for injuries to members of the public if, at the time of the lease, he: (i) knows or should know of a dangerous condition, (ii) has reason to believe that the tenant may admit the public before repairing the condition (e.g., because of short lease term), and (iii) fails to repair the condition. The landlord's liability extends only to people who enter the premises for the purpose for which the public is invited. Note that the tenant's promise to repair does not relieve the landlord of liability if the landlord has reason to suspect that the tenant will admit the public before making the repair.

d. Furnished Short-Term Residence

When a furnished house or apartment is leased for a short term (i.e., three months or less) for immediate occupancy, many jurisdictions hold that the landlord is liable if the premises are defective and cause injury to a tenant.

e. Negligent Repairs by Landlord

Even if a landlord has no duty to make repairs, a landlord who actually attempts to repair is liable if an injury results because the repairs are done **negligently**, or because they give a **deceptive appearance of safety**. [Restatement (Second) of Property: Landlord & Tenant §17.7]

Example: L leases an apartment to T. Without obligation, L agrees to repair sagging, rotted boards in the kitchen floor. The work appears to be done correctly, but in fact is structurally unsound. T relies on the deceptive appearance of safety thereby created and walks on the floor. L is subject to liability for injuries to T when the floor collapses.

f. Landlord Contracts to Repair

If a landlord covenants to repair, most courts hold that he is liable in tort for an injury to the tenant or the tenant's guests resulting from his failure to repair or negligent repair.

2. Modern Trend—General Duty of Reasonable Care

Increasingly, the courts are simply holding that landlords have a *general duty of reasonable care* with respect to residential tenants, and that they will be held liable for personal injuries of tenants and their guests resulting from the landlord's *ordinary negligence*, without regard to the exceptions discussed above. This duty is ordinarily not imposed until the landlord has *notice* of a particular defect and a reasonable opportunity to repair it.

a. Defects Arising After Tenant Takes Possession

A landlord will generally be held to have notice of defects that existed before the tenant took possession. However, the landlord will *not be liable* for defects arising after the tenant takes possession *unless* there is evidence that the landlord actually knew or should have known of them.

b. Legal Duty to Repair

If the landlord has a statutory duty to repair (e.g., under the housing code), he may be liable to the tenant or the tenant's guests for injuries resulting from his failure to repair. Some courts hold that violation of the housing code (or similar statute) is negligence per se, but most courts hold that it is merely *evidence of negligence*, which the jury may or may not find conclusive. The same analysis probably applies to a violation of the implied warranty of habitability, but there are very few cases on point.

c. Security

Some cases have held landlords liable for injuries inflicted on tenants by third-party criminals, where the landlord failed to comply with *housing code* provisions dealing with security, or failed to maintain *ordinary security* measures (e.g., working locks on apartment doors), or where he *advertised extraordinary security* measures (e.g., television surveillance, doormen, security patrols) and then failed to provide them.

3. Tenant's Liability

The tenant, as occupier of the premises, may be liable in tort to third persons for dangerous conditions or activities on the leased property. The duty of care owed by the tenant as an occupier of land is discussed in the Multistate Torts outline.

III. FIXTURES

A. IN GENERAL

A "fixture" is a chattel that has been so affixed to land that it has ceased being personal property and has become part of the realty. For example, S and B contract to sell and buy a house. Before vacating, S removes a "built-in" refrigerator. B claims that the item was "part of the house." Is the refrigerator a "fixture"? If so, B is entitled to its return or appropriate compensation.

It is important in dealing with "fixture" problems to distinguish between *common ownership* cases and *divided ownership* cases. Courts treat them differently even though they often purport to apply the same tests. "Common ownership" cases are those in which the person who brings the chattel onto the land owns both the chattel and the realty (e.g., X installs a furnace in her own home). "Divided ownership" cases are either ones where the person who owns and installs the chattel does not own the land (e.g., T installs a furnace in her rented home, which belongs to L); or the person owns the land but does not own the chattel (e.g., it is subject to a security interest held by the seller).

B. CHATTELS INCORPORATED INTO STRUCTURE ALWAYS BECOME FIXTURES

In both common ownership and divided ownership cases, where the items become incorporated into the realty so that they lose their identity, they become part of the realty. Examples include bricks built into a building or concrete poured into a foundation. Similarly, where identification is possible, but removal would occasion considerable loss or destruction, the items are considered fixtures, e.g., heating pipes embedded in the wall or floor of a house.

C. COMMON OWNERSHIP CASES

1. Annexor's Intent Controls in Common Ownership Cases

In all common ownership cases where a chattel is not incorporated into a structure, whether an item is a "fixture" (i.e., part of the realty) depends upon the *objective intention* of the party who made the "annexation." This intention is determined by considering:

(i) The *nature of the article* (i.e., how essential the item is to normal use of the premises);

(ii) The *manner in which it is attached* to the realty (the more substantially attached, the more likely it was intended to be permanent);

(iii) The *amount of damage* that would be caused by its removal; and

(iv) The *adaptation* of the item to the use of the realty (e.g., custom window treatments, wall-to-wall carpet).

a. Constructive Annexation

In some cases, an article of personal property is considered a fixture even though it is not physically annexed to the real estate at all. This is because it is so *uniquely adapted* to the real estate that it makes no sense to separate it. Examples include the keys to the doors of a house; curtain rods that have been cut and sized to the brackets on the walls of a house, even if the rods themselves are not presently installed; and a carpet that has been cut to fit an unusually shaped room, even if the carpet is not nailed or glued in place.

b. Vendor-Purchaser Cases

The typical situation is where the owner of land affixes chattels to the land and subsequently conveys the land without expressly providing whether the chattels are to pass with the realty. The intention test works fairly well. The question boils down to whether an owner bringing the disputed chattel to the realty would intend that it become part of the realty. Or to put it another way, *whether a reasonable purchaser would expect* that the disputed item was part of the realty.

c. Mortgagor-Mortgagee Cases

The intention test is universally applied to determine whether the owner (mortgagor) intended the chattels to become "part of the realty." Where the mortgagor has made the annexation *prior* to the giving of the mortgage, the question is what the "reasonably objective" lender expects to come within the security of her lien. However, where the annexation is made *after* the giving of the mortgage, the same considerations arguably should *not* apply because each item that is "added" to the lien of the mortgage represents a *windfall* to the mortgagee should foreclosure occur. Nevertheless, courts universally apply the same intention test regardless of when the annexation was made. (Courts also usually apply the intention test where items are annexed by one in possession of land under an *executory contract* to purchase.)

2. Effect of Fixture Classification

a. Conveyance
If a chattel has been categorized as a fixture, it is part of the real estate. A conveyance of the real estate, in the absence of any specific agreement to the contrary, passes the fixture with it. The fixture, as part of the realty, passes to the new owner of the real estate.

b. Mortgage
To the extent that the owner of the real estate mortgages the realty, in the absence of an agreement to the contrary, the mortgage attaches to all fixtures on the real estate.

c. Agreement to Contrary
Even though the concept of fixtures may apply and a chattel becomes a fixture, an agreement between a buyer and seller (similarly, between a mortgagor and mortgagee) can cause a severance of title. For example, a buyer and seller may agree that the seller will retain the right to remove fixtures. Similarly, a mortgagor and mortgagee can agree that the mortgage lien shall not attach to specified fixtures. The effect of such an agreement is to de-annex, so far as relevant, the chattel from the realty and reconvert the fixture into a chattel.

D. DIVIDED OWNERSHIP CASES
In divided ownership cases, unlike the ones just discussed, the chattel is owned and brought to the realty by someone who is not the landowner (e.g., by a tenant, a licensee, or a trespasser). The question is whether the ownership of the chattel has passed to the landowner. *Accession* is the term used to describe the intent of the annexor to make the chattels a permanent part of the real estate, and courts often say that the intention test (C.1., *supra*) is to be applied in these cases too. But the exceptions disprove the rule.

1. Landlord-Tenant
Early English law favored the landlord. However, American law created a *trade fixtures* exception under which tradesmen-tenants could remove an item used in their trade or business, that otherwise would have been a "fixture," unless its removal would cause substantial damage to the premises. Later, this exception was expanded to include *all tenants generally*. Some courts have treated the trade fixtures exception as consistent with the annexor's-intention test; i.e., a tenant's annexations are removable because "it was not the intention of the tenant to make them permanent annexations to the freehold and thereby donations to the owner of it."

a. Agreement
An agreement between the landlord and tenant is controlling on whether the chattel annexed to the premises was intended to become a fixture. To the extent that the

landlord and tenant specifically agree that such annexation is not to be deemed a fixture, the agreement controls.

b. No Intent If Removal Does Not Cause Damage
In the absence of an express agreement to the contrary, a tenant may remove a chattel that he has attached to the demised premises as long as the removal does not leave unrepaired damage to the premises or cause the virtual destruction of the chattel. In other words, the tenant will *not* have manifested an intention to permanently improve the freehold (and the concept of fixtures will be inapplicable) as long as the removal of the chattel does not substantially damage the premises or destroy the chattel.

c. Removal Must Occur Before End of Lease Term
Generally, a tenant must remove his annexed chattels before the termination of his tenancy or they become the property of the landlord. If the duration of the tenancy is indefinite (e.g., tenancy at will), the removal must occur within a reasonable time after the tenancy terminates. Similarly, a tenant has a reasonable time for removal if he holds over during unsuccessful negotiations for a new lease.

d. Tenant Has Duty to Repair Damages Resulting from Removal
Tenants are responsible for repairing damages caused by removal of "fixtures."

2. Life Tenant and Remainderman
Generally, the same rules apply here as in the landlord-tenant cases—with one key distinction. The personal representative of a life tenant may remove the annexed chattel within a reasonable time *after* the life tenant's death.

3. Licensee and Landowner
Licenses to bring items onto land usually contain agreements respecting removal. In the absence of an agreement, licensees are permitted to remove the items subject to a duty to repair damages caused thereby.

4. Trespasser and Landowner
Trespassers (e.g., adverse possessors before the running of the statute of limitations) normally lose their annexations whether installed in good faith or not. Moreover, the trespasser can be held liable for the reasonable rental value of the property on which she annexed the item for the period that she illegally occupied the land.

a. Trespasser's Recovery Limited to Value Added to Land
Some courts allow a good faith trespasser to recover for the improvement, but the recovery is measured by the value added to the land, not the cost to construct the improvement.

IV. RIGHTS IN THE LAND OF ANOTHER—EASEMENTS, PROFITS, COVENANTS, AND SERVITUDES

A. IN GENERAL
Easements, profits, covenants, and servitudes are *nonpossessory* interests in land. They create a

right to *use land possessed by someone else*. For example, A, the owner of Blackacre, grants to B, the owner of an adjacent parcel, Whiteacre, the right to use a path over Blackacre connecting Whiteacre to a public road. An easement has been created, giving B the right to use—but *not* to possess—the pathway over Blackacre. Easements, profits, covenants, and servitudes have many similarities in operation, coverage, creation, and termination. They also have important differences, mainly in the requirements that must be met for their enforcement.

B. EASEMENTS

1. Introduction

The holder of an easement has the *right to use* a tract of land (called the servient tenement) for a special purpose, but has *no right to possess and enjoy* the tract of land. The owner of the servient tenement continues to have the right of full possession and enjoyment subject only to the limitation that he cannot interfere with the right of special use created in the easement holder. Typically, easements are created in order to give their holder the right of access across a tract of land, e.g., the privilege of laying utility lines, or installing sewer pipes and the like. Easements are either affirmative or negative, appurtenant or in gross.

a. Types of Easements

1) Affirmative Easements

Affirmative easements entitle the holder *to enter upon the servient tenement and make an affirmative use of it* for such purposes as laying and maintaining utility lines, draining waters, and polluting the air over the servient estate. The *right-of-way* easement is another instance of an affirmative easement. Thus, an affirmative easement privileges the holder of the benefit to make a use of the servient estate that, absent the easement, would be an unlawful trespass or nuisance.

2) Negative Easements

A negative easement does not grant to its owner the right to enter upon the servient tenement. It does, however, entitle the privilege holder to compel the possessor of the servient tenement to *refrain from engaging in activity* upon the servient tenement that, were it not for the existence of the easement, he would be privileged to do. Courts historically recognized negative easements only for light, air, subjacent or lateral support, and for the flow of an artificial stream. Today, a negative easement is simply a restrictive covenant. (*See* D.1.e.1), *infra*.)

Example: A owns Lot 6. By written instrument, he stipulates to B that he will not build any structure upon Lot 6 within 35 feet of the lot line. B has acquired a negative easement in Lot 6.

b. Easement Appurtenant

An easement is deemed appurtenant when the right of special use benefits the holder of the easement in his physical use or enjoyment of another tract of land. For an easement appurtenant to exist, there must be *two tracts* of land. One is called the *dominant tenement*, which has the benefit of the easement. The second tract is the *servient tenement*, which is subject to the easement right. One consequence of appurtenance is that the benefit passes with transfers of the benefited land, regardless of whether the easement is mentioned in the conveyance.

Example: A owns Lot 6 and B owns Lot 7, which are adjoining tracts of land. By a written instrument, B grants to A the right to cross B's tract (Lot 7). A's use and enjoyment of Lot 6 is benefited by virtue of the acquisition of the right to use Lot 7 for this special purpose. The right is an easement appurtenant. B remains the owner of Lot 7. A has only a right to use Lot 7 for a special purpose, i.e., the right to cross the tract.

1)   Use and Enjoyment

In an easement appurtenant, the benefits to be realized by the easement must be directly beneficial to the possessor of the ***dominant tenement*** in his physical use and enjoyment of that tract of land. It is not sufficient that the easement makes use of the land more profitable.

Example: A owns Lot 6 and B owns adjacent Lot 7. A grants to B the right to use part of Lot 6 to mine coal. The right is not an easement appurtenant because the benefit granted is not related to B's physical use and enjoyment of Lot 7.

2)   Benefit Attached to Possession

The benefit of an easement appurtenant becomes an incident of the possession of the dominant tenement. All who possess or subsequently succeed to title to the dominant tenement become, by virtue of the fact of possession, entitled to the benefit of the easement. There can be no conveyance of the easement right apart from possession of the dominant tenement, except that the easement holder may convey the easement to the owner of the servient tenement in order to extinguish the easement (*see* 4.b., *infra*).

3)   Transfer of Dominant and Servient Estates

Both the dominant and servient parcels can be transferred. As discussed above, if the dominant parcel is transferred, the benefit of the easement goes with it automatically—even if it is not mentioned in the deed—and becomes the property of the new owner. If the servient parcel is transferred, its new owner takes it ***subject to*** the burden of the easement, ***unless*** she is a bona fide purchaser (*see* VI.E.3., *infra*) with no notice of the easement. There are three ways the person who acquires the servient land might have notice of the easement: (i) actual knowledge, (ii) notice from the visible appearance of the easement on the land, and (iii) notice from the fact that the document creating the easement is recorded in the public records. Everyone who buys land is expected to inspect the land physically and to examine the public records.

Example: A owns Lot 6 and grants B (the owner of Lot 7) an easement for a driveway across Lot 6 to benefit adjacent Lot 7. The easement is not recorded. Then A sells Lot 6 to X. The tire tracks of the driveway are plainly visible at the time of the sale. X is therefore not a bona fide purchaser, and takes Lot 6 subject to the easement.

c.   Easement in Gross

An easement in gross is created where the holder of the easement interest acquires a right of special use in the servient tenement independent of his ownership or possession of another tract of land. In an easement in gross, the easement holder is not benefited in his use and enjoyment of a possessory estate by virtue of the acquisition of that privilege. There is no dominant tenement. An easement in gross passes entirely apart from any transfer of land.

Example: A owns Lot 6. By a written instrument, she grants to B the right to build a pipeline across Lot 6. B receives the privilege independent of his ownership or possession of a separate tract of land. B has acquired an easement in gross.

Easements in gross can be either personal (e.g., O gives friend right to swim and boat on lake) or commercial (e.g., utility or railroad track easements). Generally, an easement in gross is transferable only if the easement is for a commercial or economic purpose.

d. Judicial Preference for Easements Appurtenant

If an easement interest is created and its owner holds a corporeal (possessory) estate that is or could be benefited in physical use or enjoyment by the acquisition of the privilege, the easement will be deemed appurtenant. This is true even though the deed creating the easement makes no reference to a dominant tenement.

Example: A conveys to "B, her heirs, successors, and assigns, the right to use a strip 20 feet wide on the north edge of Blackacre for ingress and egress to Whiteacre." Because there is ambiguity as to whether the benefit was intended to attach to B's land, Whiteacre, or to B personally, a court will apply the constructional preference and hold that the benefit was intended to be appurtenant, with the consequence that any conveyance of Whiteacre by B will carry with it the right to use the strip across Blackacre.

2. Creation of Easements

The basic methods of creating an easement are: express grant or reservation, implication, and prescription.

a. Express Grant

Because an easement is an interest in land, the Statute of Frauds applies. Therefore, any easement must be memorialized *in a writing* that is signed by the grantor (the holder of the servient tenement) unless its duration is brief enough (commonly one year or less) to be outside the coverage of a particular state's Statute of Frauds. An easement can be created by conveyance. A grant of an easement must comply with all the formal requisites of a deed. An easement is presumed to be of perpetual duration unless the grant specifically limits the interest (e.g., for life, for 10 years).

b. Express Reservation

An easement by reservation arises when the owner (of a present possessory interest) of a tract of land conveys title but reserves the right to continue to use the tract for a special purpose after the conveyance. In effect, the grantor passes title to the land but reserves unto himself an easement interest. Note that, under the majority view, the easement can be reserved *only for the grantor*; an attempt by the grantor to reserve an easement for anyone else is void. (There is a growing trend to permit reservations in third parties, but it remains a minority view.)

Example: G owns Lot 6 and Lot 7, which are adjacent. G sells Lot 7 to B. Later, when G is about to sell Lot 6 to A, B asks G to reserve an easement over Lot 6 in favor of B. G agrees to do so, and executes a deed of Lot 6 to A that contains the following language: "Reserving an easement for a driveway in favor of Lot 7, which is owned by B." The reservation clause is void and no easement is created.

c. Implication

An easement by implication is created by ***operation of law*** rather than by written instrument. It is an exception to the Statute of Frauds. There are only three types of implied easements: (i) an intended easement based on a use that existed when the dominant and servient estates were severed, (ii) an easement implied from a recorded subdivision plat or profit a prendre, and (iii) an easement by necessity.

1) Easement Implied from Existing Use ("Quasi-Easement")

An easement may be implied if, prior to the time the tract is divided, a use exists on the "servient part" that is reasonably necessary for the enjoyment of the "dominant part" and a court determines that the parties intended the use to continue after division of the property. It is sometimes called a "quasi-easement" before the tract is divided because an owner cannot hold an easement on his own land.

a) Existing Use at Time Tract Divided

For a use to give rise to an easement, it must be apparent and continuous at the time the tract is divided. "Apparent" means that a grantee could discover the existence of the use upon reasonable inspection. A nonvisible use may still be "apparent" if surface connections or the like would put a reasonable person on notice of its existence.

b) Reasonable Necessity

Whether a use is reasonably necessary to the enjoyment of the dominant parcel depends on many factors, including the cost and difficulty of the alternatives and whether the price paid reflects the expected continued use of the servient portion of the tract.

c) Grant or Reservation

An easement implied in favor of the grantee is said to be created by implied grant, while an easement implied in favor of the grantor is said to be created by implied reservation.

2) Easements Implied Without Any Existing Use

In two limited situations, easements are implied in a conveyance even though there is no preexisting use.

a) Subdivision Plat

When lots are sold in a subdivision with reference to a recorded plat or map that also shows streets leading to the lots, buyers of the lots have implied easements to use the streets in order to gain access to their lots. These easements continue to exist even if the **public** easements held by the city or county in the streets are later vacated.

b) Profit a Prendre

When a landowner grants a profit a prendre to a person to remove a valuable product of the soil (e.g., grass, asphalt, ore, etc.), the holder of the profit also has an implied easement to pass over the surface of the land and to use it as reasonably necessary to extract the product.

3) Easement by Necessity

When the owner of a tract of land sells a part of the tract and by this division deprives one lot of access to a public road or utility line, a right-of-way by absolute necessity is created by implied grant or reservation over the lot with access to the public road or utility line. The owner of the servient parcel has the right to locate the easement, provided the location is reasonably convenient. An easement by necessity terminates when the necessity ceases.

d. Prescription

Acquiring an easement by prescription is analogous to acquiring property by adverse possession. (*See* V., *infra*.) Many of the requirements are the same: To acquire a prescriptive easement, the use must be **open and notorious, adverse, and continuous and uninterrupted for the statutory period**. Note that the public at large can acquire an easement in private land if members of the public use the land in a way that meets the requirements for prescription.

1) Open and Notorious

The user must not attempt to conceal his use. Underground or other nonvisible uses, such as pipes and electric lines, are considered open and notorious if the use could be discovered (e.g., through surface connections) upon inspection.

2) Adverse

The use must not be with the owner's permission. Unlike adverse possession, the use **need not be exclusive**. The user of a common driveway, e.g., may acquire a prescriptive easement even though the owner uses it too.

3) Continuous Use

Continuous adverse use does not mean constant use. A continuous claim of right with periodic acts that put the owner on notice of the claimed easement fulfills the requirement. Note that tacking is permitted for prescriptive easements, just as for adverse possession (*see* V.B.5.b., *infra*).

4) When Prescriptive Easements Cannot Be Acquired

Negative easements cannot arise by prescription, nor generally may easements in public lands. An easement by necessity cannot give rise to an easement by prescription. However, if the necessity ends, so does the easement, and the use is adverse from that point forward.

3. Scope

Courts enforcing easements are often called upon to interpret the arrangement in order to determine the *scope* and *intended beneficiaries* of the interest. The key to interpretation employed in all these cases is the *reasonable intent of the original parties*. What would the parties reasonably have provided had they contemplated the situation now before the court? What result would reasonably serve the purposes of the arrangement?

a. General Rules of Construction

If, as typically happens, the language used is general (e.g., "a right-of-way over Blackacre"), the following rules of construction usually apply: (i) ambiguities are resolved in favor of the grantee (unless the conveyance is gratuitous); (ii) subsequent conduct of the parties respecting the arrangement is relevant; (iii) the parties are assumed to have intended a scope that would reasonably serve the purposes of the grant and to have foreseen reasonable changes in the use of the dominant estate. The rule of reasonableness will be applied only to the extent that the governing language is general. If the location or scope of the permitted use is spelled out in detail, the specifics will govern, and reasonable interpretation will be excluded.

Examples: 1) In 1890, A, the owner of Blackacre, granted to B, the owner of Whiteacre, a "right-of-way" over Blackacre for purposes of ingress and egress to Whiteacre from the public highway running along the western boundary of Blackacre. At the time of the grant, there were only horses and buggies, no automobiles. Applying a "rule of reasonableness" to the general language creating the right-of-way, a court would probably find that the right-of-way could today be used for cars. If, however, the use of cars would impose a *substantially* greater burden on Blackacre, the court would probably find against this use on grounds that it was outside the scope reasonably contemplated by A and B.

2) If, in the example just given, the right-of-way was specifically dedicated ("only to the use of horses and carriages"), automobile use would be excluded. Similarly, if the right-of-way was specifically located (e.g., "over the southern 10 feet of Blackacre"), the rule of reasonableness could not be invoked to change or enlarge the location.

b. Absence of Location

If an easement is created but not specifically located on the servient tenement, an easement of sufficient width, height, and direction to make the intended use reasonably convenient will be implied. The owner of the servient tenement may select the location of the easement so long as her selection is reasonable.

c. Changes in Use

In the absence of specific limitations in the deed creating an easement, the courts will assume that the easement is intended by the parties to meet both present and future reasonable needs of the dominant tenement.

Examples: 1) A roadway easement of unspecified width was created in 1920, when cars were only six feet wide. Today, however, cars are considerably wider. Because the original roadway easement was not specifically limited in width, the easement will expand in size to accommodate the changing and expanding needs of the owner of the dominant tenement.

2) But a basic change in the nature of the use is not allowed. Thus, a telephone or power line may not be added on the roadway. (Many courts are more liberal in allowing such additions if the roadway easement is public rather than private.)

d. Easements by Necessity or Implication
In the case of easements by necessity, the *extent of the necessity determines the scope* of the easement. Because there is no underlying written instrument to interpret, courts will look instead to the circumstances giving rise to the easement. Similarly, with other implied easements, the *quasi-easement* will provide the starting point for the court's construction of the scope of the easement. Modifications in the easement will be enforced to the extent that they are necessary for reasonably foreseeable changes in the use of the dominant parcel.

e. Use of Servient Estate
Absent an express restriction in the original agreement, the owner of the servient estate may use her land in any way she wishes so long as her conduct does not interfere with performance of the easement, profit, covenant, or servitude.

Example: A grants to B Water Company the right to lay water pipes in a specified five-foot right-of-way. A is not by this grant necessarily precluded from granting similar rights in the same right-of-way to a competing company, so long as the second grant does not interfere with the use made by B, the original grantee. A may also build over the right-of-way so long as the structure does not unreasonably interfere with B's use.

1) Duty to Repair
If the holder of the benefit is the only party making use of the easement, that party has the duty to make repairs (e.g., fill in potholes on a right-of-way) and, absent a special agreement, the servient owner has no duty to do so. If the easement is nonexclusive and *both* the holder of the benefit and the servient owner are making use of the easement, the court will *apportion* the repair costs between them on the basis of their relative use.

f. Intended Beneficiaries—Subdivision of Dominant Parcel
When an easement is created for the benefit of a landowner, and the landowner later subdivides the parcel, there is a question whether each subdivision grantee will succeed to the original benefit. The answer will turn on whether the extension of the benefit to each of the subdivided parcels will burden the servient estate to a greater extent than was contemplated by the original parties. Absent any other evidence on intent, a court will not find an intent to allow an extension if extending the benefit to each parcel in the subdivision will unreasonably overburden the servient estate. Weighing all the circumstances, a court could find subdivision into four lots reasonable, but subdivision into 50 lots unreasonable; it is determined on a case-by-case basis.

Example: A, the owner of Blackacre, grants to B, the owner of Whiteacre, a right-of-way easement of ingress and egress over Blackacre. B then subdivides Whiteacre into 150 lots. If A and B had not contemplated the subdivision of Whiteacre, and if use of the right-of-way by all 150 lot owners would substantially interfere with A's use of Blackacre (in a way that B's use alone would not), a court would probably not find an intent that the benefit of the right-of-way easement attach to each of the 150 parcels.

g. Effect of Use Outside Scope of Easement

When the owner of an easement uses it in a way that exceeds its legal scope, the easement is said to be *surcharged*. The remedy of the servient landowner is an *injunction* of the excess use, and possibly damages if the servient land has been harmed. However, the excess use *does not terminate* the easement or give the servient landowner a power of termination.

4. Termination of Easements

An easement, like any other property interest, may be created to last in perpetuity or for a limited period of time. To the extent the parties to its original creation provide for the natural termination of the interest, such limitations will control.

a. Stated Conditions

If the parties to the original creation of an easement set forth specific conditions upon the happening of which the easement right will terminate, the conditions will be recognized. On this basis, the following conditions are valid: an easement granted "so long as repairs are maintained," an easement granted "so long as X is the holder of the dominant tenement," an easement granted "until the dominant tenement is used for commercial purposes," etc.

b. Unity of Ownership

By definition, an easement is the right to use the lands of another for a special purpose. On this basis, the ownership of the easement and of the servient tenement must be in different persons. If ownership of the two comes together in one person, the easement is extinguished.

1) Complete Unity Required

For an easement to be extinguished by merger of dominant and servient tenements, the duration of the servient tenement must be *equal to or longer than* the duration of the dominant tenement (and therefore the easement) with which it is combined.

Examples: 1) A owns the servient tenement in fee simple. B owns the dominant tenement in fee simple, and B's dominant tenement has, appurtenant to it, an access easement across the servient tenement. A conveys a 10-year term tenancy in the servient tenement to B. The duration of the conveyed interest in the servient estate is *shorter* than the duration of the dominant estate (and therefore the easement) with which it is combined. Thus, the easement is not extinguished by merger.

2) A owns the servient tenement in fee simple. B holds a 10-year term tenancy in the dominant tenement, and B's fixed-term tenancy estate has, appurtenant to it, an access easement across the servient tenement. A conveys the fee simple servient tenement to B (or B conveys the 10-year term tenancy in the dominant tenement to A; it doesn't matter). The duration of the servient estate is *longer* than

the duration of the dominant estate (and therefore the easement) with which it is combined. Thus, the easement is extinguished by merger.

2) No Revival

If complete unity of title is acquired, the easement is extinguished. Even though there may be later separation, the easement will not be automatically revived.

Example: A owns Lot 6, the servient tenement. B owns adjacent Lot 7. A grants to B the privilege of crossing Lot 6, i.e., grants an easement appurtenant to B. Assume A conveys Lot 6 to B in fee simple. The easement would be extinguished because B then holds both the easement and title to the servient tenement. If, thereafter, B conveys Lot 6 to C, the easement is not revived. Of course, it could be created anew.

c. Release

An easement may be terminated by a release given by the owner of the easement interest to the owner of the servient tenement. A release requires the ***concurrence of both owners*** and is, in effect, a conveyance. The release must be executed with all the formalities that are required for the valid creation of an easement.

1) Easement Appurtenant

The basic characteristic of an easement appurtenant is that it becomes, for the purpose of succession, an incident of possession of the dominant tenement. This basic characteristic requires that the easement interest not be conveyed independently of a conveyance of the dominant tenement. However, an easement appurtenant may be conveyed to the owner of the servient tenement without a conveyance (to the same grantee) of the dominant tenement. This is an exception to the general alienability characteristics of an easement appurtenant (*see* 1.b., *supra*).

2) Easement in Gross

The basic characteristic of an easement in gross is that unless it is for a commercial purpose, it is inalienable. However, an easement in gross can be released; i.e., can be conveyed to the owner of the servient tenement. This is an exception to the general characteristics of an easement in gross.

3) Statute of Frauds

The Statute of Frauds requires that every conveyance of an interest in land that has a duration long enough to bring into play a particular state's Statute of Frauds (typically one year) must be evidenced by a writing. This writing requirement is also applicable to a release of an easement interest. If the easement interest that is being conveyed has a duration of greater than one year, a writing is required in order to satisfy the Statute of Frauds. An oral release is ineffective, although it may become effective by estoppel.

d. Abandonment

It has become an established rule that an easement can be extinguished without conveyance where the owner of the privilege demonstrates by physical action an intention to *permanently* abandon the easement. To work as an abandonment, the owner must have manifested an intention never to make use of the easement again.

Example: A owns Lot 6 and B owns Lot 7, which are immediately adjacent. A grants to B an easement across Lot 6. This easement is specifically located on the servient tenement and is a walkway. Subsequently, B constructs a house on Lot 7 that completely blocks his access to the walkway. By the physical action of constructing the house in such a way that access to the walkway (i.e., the easement) is denied, B has physically indicated an intent not to use the easement again. The easement is extinguished by abandonment.

1) **Physical Act Required**

An abandonment of an easement occurs when the easement holder physically manifests an intention to permanently abandon the easement. Such physical action brings about a termination of the easement by operation of law and therefore no writing is required; i.e., the Statute of Frauds need not be complied with.

2) **Mere Words Insufficient**

The oral expressions of the owner of the easement that he does not intend to use the easement again (i.e., he wishes to abandon it), by themselves, are insufficient to constitute an abandonment of the easement. For words alone to operate as a termination, such expression will only be effective if it qualifies as a release; i.e., the Statute of Frauds must be complied with. Note, however, that oral expressions may be sufficient if *accompanied by a long period of nonuse* (*see* 3), *infra*.

3) **Mere Nonuse Insufficient**

An easement is not terminated merely because it is not used for a long period by its owner. To terminate the easement, the nonuse must be combined with other evidence of intent to abandon it. Nonuse itself is not considered sufficient evidence of that intent.

e. **Estoppel**

While the assertions of the holder of the easement are insufficient to work a termination unless there is valid compliance with the requirements of a release, an easement may be extinguished by virtue of the reasonable reliance and change of position of the owner of the servient tenement, based on assertions or conduct of the easement holder.

Example: The owner of a right-of-way tells the owner of the servient tenement that the owner of the servient tenement may build a building on the servient tenement in such a way as to make the right-of-way no longer usable, and the servient owner does in fact build the building. There will be an extinguishment of the easement by estoppel.

For an easement to be extinguished by estoppel, three requirements must be satisfied. Namely, there must be (i) some *conduct or assertion* by the owner of the easement, (ii) a *reasonable reliance* by the owner of the servient tenement, (iii) coupled with a *change of position*. Even though there is an assertion by the easement holder, if the owner of the servient tenement does not change her position based upon the assertion, the easement will not be terminated.

f. Prescription

An easement may be extinguished, as well as created, by prescription. Long continued possession and enjoyment of the servient tenement in a way that would indicate to the public that no easement right existed will end the easement right. Such long continued use works as a statute of limitations precluding the whole world, including the easement holder, from asserting that his privilege exists.

The termination of an easement by prescription is fixed by analogy to the creation of an easement by prescription. The owner of the servient tenement must so *interfere with the easement* as to create a cause of action in favor of the easement holder. The interference must be open, notorious, continuous, and nonpermissive for the statutory period (e.g., 20 years).

g. Necessity

Easements created by necessity *expire as soon as the necessity ends*.

Example: A, the owner of a tract of land, sells a portion of it that has no access to a highway except over the remaining lands of A. B, the purchaser, acquires by necessity a right-of-way over the remaining lands of A. Some years later, a highway is built so that B no longer needs the right-of-way across A's property. The easement ends because the necessity has disappeared.

h. Condemnation

Condemnation of the servient estate will extinguish the nonpossessory interest. Courts are split, however, on whether the holder of the benefit is entitled to compensation for the value lost.

i. Destruction of Servient Estate

If the easement is in a structure (e.g., a staircase), involuntary destruction of the structure (e.g., by fire or flood) will extinguish the easement. Voluntary destruction (e.g., tearing down a building to erect a new one) will not, however, terminate the easement.

5. Compare—Licenses

Licenses, like affirmative easements, privilege their holder to go upon the land of another (the licensor). Unlike an affirmative easement, the license is *not an interest in land*. It is merely a *privilege*, revocable at the will of the licensor. (Although licenses may acquire some of the characteristics of easements through estoppel or by being coupled with an interest.) The Statute of Frauds does not apply to licenses, and licensees are not entitled to compensation if the land is taken by eminent domain. Licenses are quite common; examples of licensees include delivery persons, plumbers, party guests, etc.

a. Assignability

An essential characteristic of a license is that it is *personal to the licensee* and therefore *not alienable*. The holder of a license privilege cannot convey such right. In fact, most courts have held that the license privilege is so closely tied to the individual parties that it is revoked, by operation of law, upon an attempted transfer by the licensee.

b. Revocation and Termination

Another essential characteristic of a license is that it is revocable by nature. It may be revoked at any time by a manifestation of the licensor's intent to end it. This manifestation may be by a formal notice of revocation or it may consist of conduct that obstructs the licensee's continued use. Similarly, the licensee can surrender the privilege whenever he desires to do so. A license ends by operation of law upon the death of the licensor. In addition, a conveyance of the servient tenement by the licensor terminates the licensee's privilege.

1) Public Amusement Cases
Tickets issued by theaters, race courses, and other places of amusement have given rise to some controversy. The traditional rule is that such tickets create a license. Once describing the tickets as granting a license, the essential characteristic of a license applies; i.e., it is revocable by nature. On this basis, the licensor may terminate the licensee's privilege at will.

2) Breach of Contract
A license may be granted pursuant to an express or implied contract between the licensor and licensee. On this basis, the termination of the licensee's privilege may constitute a breach of contract. While many courts may grant a cause of action for money damages for a revocation of a license in breach of contract, they continue to sustain the licensor's right to terminate the licensee's privilege to continue to remain on the servient tenement.

Example: A pays a $70 greens fee to play 18 holes of golf on B's property. After A has played only nine holes, B terminates A's right to be on B's property. Because A acquired a license and it is revocable by its very nature, B's action is not, in property terms, wrongful. However, A may have a cause of action against B to recoup part or all of A's $70.

c. Failure to Create an Easement
The Statute of Frauds requires that any conveyance of an interest in land (including an easement interest) of duration greater than one year must be memorialized in writing to be enforceable. If a party attempts to create an easement orally, the result is the creation of a license, i.e., a revocable privilege. Note, however, that if an oral attempt to create an easement is subsequently "executed," to the extent that it would be inequitable to permit its revocation (e.g., the licensee has expended substantial funds in reliance on the license), the licensor may be estopped to revoke the license.

d. Irrevocable Licenses

1) Estoppel Theory
If a licensee invests substantial amounts of money or labor in reliance on a license, the licensor may be estopped to revoke the license, and the license will thus become the equivalent of an affirmative easement.

Example: A orally licenses B to come onto Blackacre to excavate a drainage ditch connected to B's parcel, Whiteacre. B does so at substantial expense. A will probably be estopped to revoke the license and prevent B from using the ditch.

Under the majority view, such irrevocable licenses or easements by estoppel last until the owner receives sufficient benefit to reimburse himself for the expenditures made in reliance on the license. A minority of courts treat easements by estoppel like any other affirmative easements and give them a potentially infinite duration.

2) License Coupled with an Interest
If a license is coupled with an interest, it will be irrevocable as long as the interest lasts.

a) Vendee of a Chattel
The purchaser of a chattel located upon the seller's land is, in the absence of an express stipulation to the contrary, given the privilege to enter upon the seller's land for the purpose of removing the chattel. The purchaser's right is irrevocable. He must, however, enter at reasonable times and in a reasonable manner.

Example: A, the owner of Blackacre, sells 100 crates of oranges stored in a shed on Blackacre and at the same time licenses B to come onto Blackacre to remove the crates of oranges. B has an irrevocable license to enter Blackacre and remove the crates within a reasonable time.

b) Termination of Tenancy
If a tenant's right to possess land has been lawfully terminated, the tenant may still reenter the land at reasonable times and in a reasonable manner for the purpose of removing his chattels. This is an irrevocable privilege.

c) Inspection for Waste
The owner of a future interest in land (e.g., a landlord, holder of a reversionary interest, or remainderman) is privileged to enter upon the land, at reasonable times and in a reasonable manner, for the purpose of determining whether waste is being committed by the holder of the present possessory estate.

C. PROFITS
Like an easement, a profit (profit a prendre) is a *nonpossessory* interest in land. The holder of the profit is entitled to enter upon the servient tenement and take the soil or a substance of the soil (e.g., minerals, timber, oil, or game). Also, like an easement, a profit may be appurtenant or in gross. In contrast to easements, however, there is a constructional preference for profits in gross rather than appurtenant.

1. Creation
Profits are created in the same way as easements.

2. Alienability
A profit appurtenant follows the ownership of the dominant tenement. A profit in gross may be assigned or transferred by the holder.

3. Exclusive and Nonexclusive Profits Distinguished
When an owner grants the *sole right* to take a resource from her land, the grantee takes an

exclusive profit and is solely entitled to the resources, even to the exclusion of the owner of the servient estate. By contrast, when a profit is nonexclusive, the owner of the servient estate may grant similar rights to others or may take the resources herself. Ordinarily, profits (like easements) are construed as nonexclusive.

4. Scope

The extent and nature of the profit is determined by the words of the ***express grant*** (if there was a grant), or by ***the nature of the use*** (if the profit was acquired by prescription). Note that implied in every profit is an easement entitling the profit holder to enter the servient estate to remove the resource.

Example: A, the owner of Blackacre, grants B the right to come onto Blackacre to carry off gravel from a pit on Blackacre. B has a profit with respect to the gravel and also the benefit of an implied affirmative easement to go onto Blackacre by reasonable means to remove the gravel.

a. Apportionment of Profits Appurtenant

Courts treat the subdivision of land with a profit appurtenant just as they treat the subdivision of land with an easement appurtenant. The ***benefit of the profit*** will attach to each parcel in a subdivision ***only*** if the burden on the servient estate is not as a result ***overly increased***.

Example: A, the owner of Blackacre, grants B, the owner of adjacent Whiteacre, the right to remove rock from Blackacre. If the profit was to take the rock for purposes of maintaining a boat launch on Whiteacre, then an increase in use from one to 50 boat launches when Whiteacre is subdivided will probably be viewed as overburdensome to Blackacre.

If, however, the profit was to take rock for purposes of reinforcing Whiteacre's coastline to prevent erosion, apportionment would likely be allowed because subdivision would not increase the number of acres to be reinforced and consequently would not impose a greater burden on Blackacre.

b. Apportionment of Profits in Gross

Because profits are freely alienable, a question frequently arises as to whether the holder of a profit can convey it to several people. If a profit is ***exclusive***, the holder may transfer the profit to as many transferees as he likes. Likewise, if the grant of the profit specifies a limit on the profit (less than all), the right can be transferred to multiple transferees. If, however, the profit is ***nonexclusive*** and not limited as to amount, it is generally not divisible. Undue burden to the servient estate is again the benchmark, however, and a nonexclusive profit may be assigned to a single person or to several persons jointly if the multiple assignees work together and take no more resources than would have been taken by the original benefit holder.

5. Termination

Profits are terminated in the same way as easements. In addition, ***misuse*** of a profit, unduly increasing the burden (typically through an improper apportionment), will be held to ***surcharge*** the servient estate. The result of surcharge in this case is to extinguish the profit. (Contrast this with the result when the benefit of an ***affirmative easement*** is misused:

Improper or excessive use increasing the burden on the servient estate is *enjoinable* but, in most jurisdictions, does not extinguish the easement; *see* B.3.g., *supra*.)

D. COVENANTS RUNNING WITH THE LAND AT LAW (REAL COVENANTS)

A real covenant, normally found in deeds, is a *written promise* to do something on the land (e.g., maintain a fence) or a promise not to do something on the land (e.g., conduct commercial business). Real covenants run with the land at law, which means that subsequent owners of the land may enforce or be burdened by the covenant. To run with the land, however, the benefit and burden of the covenant must be analyzed separately to determine whether they meet the requirements for running.

1. Requirements for Burden to Run

If all requirements are met for the burden to run, the successor in interest to the burdened estate will be bound by the arrangement entered into by her predecessor as effectively as if she had herself expressly agreed to be bound.

a. Intent

The covenanting parties must have intended that successors in interest to the covenantor be bound by the terms of the covenant. The requisite intent may be inferred from circumstances surrounding creation of the covenant, or it may be evidenced by language in the conveyance creating the covenant (e.g., "this covenant runs with the land," or "grantee covenants for herself, her heirs, successors, and assigns").

b. Notice

Under the common law, a subsequent purchaser of land that was subject to a covenant took the land burdened by the covenant, whether or not she had notice. However, under American recording statutes (*see* VI.E., *infra*), if the covenant is not recorded, a bona fide purchaser who has no notice of the covenant and who records her own deed *will take free* of the covenant. Hence, as a practical matter, if the subsequent purchaser pays value and records (as will nearly always be true), she is not bound by covenants of which she has no actual or constructive notice.

c. Horizontal Privity

This requirement rests on the relationship between the *original covenanting parties*. Specifically, horizontal privity requires that, at the time the promisor entered into the covenant with the promisee, the two shared *some interest in the land independent of the covenant* (e.g., grantor-grantee, landlord-tenant, mortgagor-mortgagee).

Examples: 1) A and B are neighboring landowners, neither having any rights in the other's land. For good consideration, A promises B, "for herself, her heirs, successors, and assigns," that A's parcel "will never be used for other than residential purposes." The horizontal privity requirement is *not* met, and successors in interest to A will *not* be bound because at the time A made this covenant, she and B shared no interest in land independent of the covenant.

2) A, the owner of Blackacre in fee, promised B, the holder of a right-of-way easement over Blackacre, "always to keep the right-of-way free of snow or other impediment to B's use of the right-of-way." Horizontal

privity is met because, at the time the covenant was made, A owned the parcel in fee and B held the benefit of an easement in it.

3) A, the owner of Blackacre and Whiteacre, deeds Whiteacre to B, promising "not to use Blackacre for other than residential purposes." Horizontal privity exists here by virtue of the grantor-grantee relationship between A and B.

d. Vertical Privity

To be bound, the successor in interest to the covenanting party must hold the *entire durational interest* held by the covenantor at the time she made the covenant.

Example: A, who owns Blackacre and Whiteacre in fee simple absolute, sells Whiteacre to B and, in the deed, covenants for herself, her heirs, successors, and assigns to contribute one-half the expense of maintaining a common driveway between Blackacre and Whiteacre. A then transfers Blackacre to C "for life," retaining a reversionary interest for herself. B *cannot* enforce the covenant against C because C does not possess the entire interest (fee simple absolute) held by her predecessor in interest, A, at the time A made the promise.

e. Touch and Concern

The covenant must be of the type that "touches and concerns" the land. The phrase "touch and concern the land" is not susceptible to easy definition. It generally means that the effect of the covenant is to make the land itself more useful or valuable to the benefited party. The covenant must affect the legal relationship of the parties as landowners and not merely as members of the community at large. Therefore, as a general matter, for the burden of a covenant to run, performance of the burden must diminish the landowner's rights, privileges, and powers in connection with her enjoyment of the land.

1) Negative Covenants

For the burden of a negative covenant to touch and concern the land, the covenant must restrict the holder of the servient estate in his *use of that parcel* of land.

Examples: 1) A, who owned Blackacre and Whiteacre, covenanted with B, the grantee of Whiteacre, that she would not erect a building of over two stories on Blackacre. The burden of the covenant touches and concerns Blackacre because it diminishes A's rights in connection with her enjoyment of Blackacre.

2) A, who owned Blackacre and Whiteacre, covenanted with B, the grantee of Whiteacre, that she would never operate a shoe store within a radius of one mile of Whiteacre. The covenant does not touch and concern Blackacre because its performance is unconnected to the enjoyment of Blackacre.

2) Affirmative Covenants

For the burden of an affirmative covenant to touch and concern the land, the covenant must require the holder of the servient estate *to do something*, increasing her obligations in connection with enjoyment of the land.

Examples: 1) A, who owned Blackacre and Whiteacre, covenanted with B, the grantee of Whiteacre, to keep the building on Blackacre in good repair. The covenant touches and concerns Blackacre because it increases A's obligations in connection with her enjoyment of Blackacre.

2) A owned Blackacre and Whiteacre, which were several miles apart. A covenanted with B, the grantee of Whiteacre, to keep the building on Whiteacre in good repair. The covenant does not touch and concern Blackacre because its performance is unconnected to the use and enjoyment of Blackacre.

3) A, the grantee of a parcel in a residential subdivision, covenants to pay an annual fee to a homeowners' association for the maintenance of common ways, parks, and other facilities in the subdivision. At one time, it was thought that such covenants, because physically unconnected to the land, did not touch and concern. The prevailing view today is that the burden will run because the fees are a charge on the land, increasing A's obligations in connection with the use and enjoyment of it. (*See* 4.a., *infra.*)

2. Requirements for Benefit to Run

If all requirements for the benefit to run are met, the successor in interest to the promisee will be allowed to enjoy the benefit (i.e., enforce the covenant).

a. Intent

The covenanting parties must have intended that the successors in interest to the covenantee be able to enforce the covenant. Surrounding evidence of intent, as well as language in the instrument of conveyance, is admissible.

b. Vertical Privity

The benefit of a covenant runs to the assignees of the original estate or of any lesser estate (e.g., a life estate). The owner of *any* succeeding possessory estate can enforce the benefit at law. In the majority of states today, horizontal privity is not required for the benefit to run. As a consequence, if horizontal privity is missing, the benefit may run to the successor in interest to the covenantee even though the burden is not enforceable against the successor in interest of the covenantor.

Example: A, who owns Blackacre, covenants with her neighbor, B, who owns Whiteacre, that "A, her successors, and assigns will keep the building on Blackacre in good repair." Horizontal privity is missing. B then conveys Whiteacre, the dominant estate, to C. C can enforce the benefit of the affirmative covenant against A because horizontal privity is not needed for the benefit to run. If, however, A conveys Blackacre to D, neither B nor C could enforce the covenant against D, for horizontal privity is required for the burden to run.

c. Touch and Concern

For the benefit of a covenant to touch and concern the land, the promised performance must benefit the covenantee and her successors *in their use and enjoyment of the benefited land*.

Examples: 1) A, who owns Blackacre and Whiteacre, covenants with B, the grantee of Whiteacre, not to erect a building over two stories on Blackacre. The benefit of the covenant touches and concerns Whiteacre because, by securing B's view, it increases his enjoyment of Whiteacre.

2) A, who owns Blackacre and Whiteacre, covenants with B, the grantee of Whiteacre, to keep the building on Blackacre freshly painted and in good repair. The benefit of the covenant touches and concerns Whiteacre because, by assuring the view of an attractive house, it increases the value of Whiteacre.

Compare: A, who owns Blackacre, covenants with B, a supermarket operator owning no adjacent land, to erect and maintain on Blackacre a billboard advertising B's supermarkets. The benefit of the covenant does *not* touch and concern because it is not connected to and does not operate to increase B's enjoyment of any piece of land.

3.   Modern Status of Running of Burden and Benefit

   a.   Horizontal and Vertical Privity
   The Restatement of Property provides that horizontal privity is not required for running of the burden, and further discards the requirement of vertical privity for running of both the burden and the benefit. Instead, the Restatement draws a distinction between *affirmative* and *negative* covenants. Negative covenants are treated like easements, which run to successors because they are interests in land. The burdens and benefits of affirmative covenants run to persons who succeed to an *estate of the same duration* as owned by the original parties, including in most cases an adverse possessor. But affirmative covenants do not run to persons who hold lesser estates than those held by the original parties to the covenant. Special rules are set forth for when affirmative burdens run to lessees and life tenants, and when they can enforce the benefits. [Restatement (Third) of Property: Servitudes §§5.2 - 5.5]

   b.   Touch and Concern
   The Restatement of Property also supersedes the touch and concern requirement by providing that real covenants are *presumed valid* unless they are illegal, unconstitutional, or violate public policy. [Restatement (Third) of Property: Servitudes §§3.1, 3.2]

4.   Specific Situations Involving Real Covenants

   a.   Promises to Pay Money
   The majority rule is that if the money is to be used in a way connected with the land, the burden will run with the land. The most common example is a covenant to pay a homeowners' association an annual fee for maintenance of common ways, parks, etc., in a subdivision.

   b.   Covenants Not to Compete
   Covenants not to compete have created several problems. Clearly, the burden of the

covenant—restricting the use to which the land may be put—"touches and concerns" the land. However, the benefited land, while "commercially enhanced," is not affected in its physical use. Thus, some courts have refused to permit the benefit of such covenants to run with the land.

    c.   Racially Restrictive Covenants

    If a covenant purports to prohibit an owner from transferring land to persons of a given race, no court (state or federal) is permitted to enforce the covenant. To do so would involve the court in a violation of the Equal Protection Clause of the Fourteenth Amendment (*see* I.F.2.b.2), *supra*).

5.   Remedies—Damages

A breach of a real covenant generally is remedied by an award of money damages. If equitable relief, such as an injunction, is sought, the promise may be enforced as an equitable servitude (*see* E., *infra*). Note that a real covenant gives rise to personal liability only. The damages are collectible out of the defendant's general assets.

6.   Termination

As with all other nonpossessory interests in land, a real covenant may be terminated by: (i) the holder of the benefit executing a *release in writing*; (ii) *merger* (fee simple title to both the benefited and burdened land comes into the hands of a single owner); and (iii) *condemnation* of the burdened property (*See* B.4.b., c., h., *supra*.)

F. EQUITABLE SERVITUDES

If a plaintiff wants an injunction or specific performance, he may show that the covenant qualifies as an equitable servitude. An equitable servitude is a covenant that, *regardless* of whether it runs with the land at law, equity will enforce against the assignees of the burdened land who have *notice* of the covenant. The usual remedy is an injunction against violation of the covenant.

1.   Creation

Generally, equitable servitudes are created by covenants contained *in a writing* that satisfies the Statute of Frauds. As with real covenants, acceptance of a deed signed only by the grantor is sufficient to bind the grantee as promisor. There is *one exception* to the writing requirement: Negative equitable servitudes may be implied from a common scheme for development of a residential subdivision.

    a.   Servitudes Implied from Common Scheme

    When a developer subdivides land into several parcels and some of the deeds contain negative covenants but some do not, negative covenants or equitable servitudes binding *all* the parcels in the subdivision may be implied under the doctrine of "reciprocal negative servitudes." The doctrine applies only to negative covenants and equitable servitudes and not to affirmative covenants. Two requirements must be met before reciprocal negative covenants and servitudes will be implied: (i) a common scheme for development, and (ii) notice of the covenants.

    Example: A subdivides her parcel into lots 1 through 50. She conveys lots 1 through 45 by deeds containing express covenants by the respective grantees that they will use their lots only for residential purposes. A orally assures the 45 grantees that *all* 50 lots will be used for residential purposes. Some time later, after the 45 lots have been developed as residences, A conveys lot 46 to an oil company, which plans to operate a service station on it. The deed to lot 46 contains no express residential restriction. A court will nonetheless imply a negative covenant, prohibiting use for other than residential purposes on lot 46 because both requirements have been met for an implied reciprocal negative servitude. First, there was a *common scheme*, here evidenced by A's statements to the first 45 buyers. Second, the oil company was on *inquiry notice* of the negative covenant because of the uniform residential character of the other lots in the subdivision development.

1) Common Scheme

Reciprocal negative covenants will be implied only if at the time that sales of parcels in the subdivision began, the developer had a plan that all parcels in the subdivision be developed within the terms of the negative covenant. If the scheme arises after some lots are sold, it cannot impose burdens on the lots previously sold without the express covenants. The developer's common scheme may be evidenced by a *recorded plat*, by a *general pattern* of prior restrictions, or by *oral representations*, typically in the form of statements to early buyers that all parcels in the development will be restricted by the same covenants that appear in their deeds. On the basis of this scheme, it is inferred that purchasers bought their lots relying on the fact that they would be able to enforce subsequently created equitable servitudes similar to the restrictions imposed in their deeds.

2) Notice

To be bound by the terms of a covenant that does not appear in his deed, a grantee must, at the time he acquired his parcel, have had notice of the covenants contained in the deeds of other buyers in the subdivision. The requisite notice may be acquired through *actual notice* (direct knowledge of the covenants in the prior deeds); *inquiry notice* (the neighborhood appears to conform to common restrictions); or *record notice* (if the prior deeds are in the grantee's chain of title he will, under the recording acts, have constructive notice of their contents).

2. Enforcement

For successors of the original promisee and promisor to enforce an equitable servitude, certain requirements must be met.

a. Requirements for Burden to Run

1) Intent

The covenanting parties must have intended that the servitude be enforceable by and against assignees. No technical words are required to express this intent. In fact, the intent may be ascertained from the purpose of the covenant and the surrounding circumstances.

2) Notice

A subsequent purchaser of land burdened by a covenant is not bound by it in equity unless she had actual or constructive notice of it when she acquired the land. This rule is part of the law of equitable servitudes, and exists apart from the recording acts.

3) Touch and Concern
This is the same requirement as applies to real covenants (*see* D.1.e., *supra*).

b. Requirements for Benefit to Run
The benefit of the equitable servitude will run with the land (and thus to successors in interest of the original parties) if the original parties so *intended* and the servitude *touches and concerns* the benefited property.

c. Privity Not Required
The majority of courts enforce the servitude not as an in personam right against the owner of the servient tenement, but as an equitable property interest in the land itself. There is, therefore, no need for privity of estate.

Examples: 1) A acquires title to Blackacre by adverse possession. Even though he is not in privity of estate with the original owner, he is subject to the equitable servitude because the servitude is an interest in the land.

2) A and B are neighboring landowners, neither having any rights in the other's land. A promises B, "for herself, her heirs, successors, and assigns," that A's parcel "will never be used for other than residential purposes." B records the agreement. A sells Blackacre to C. The burden created by this promise would *not run at law* as a negative covenant because horizontal privity is missing. However, under an equitable servitude theory, the burden *will run,* and an injunction will issue against other than residential uses.

3) Same as above, but A transfers only a life estate to C. Again, the burden would not run at law because of the absence of vertical privity. The burden would, however, be enforceable as an equitable servitude.

d. Implied Beneficiaries of Covenants—General Scheme
If a covenant in a subdivision deed is silent as to who holds its benefit, any neighbor in the subdivision will be entitled to enforce the covenant if a general scheme or plan is found to have existed at the time he purchased his lot.

Example: A subdivides her parcel into Lots 1 through 10. She conveys Lot 1 to B, who covenants to use the lot for residential purposes only. A then conveys Lot 2 to C, who makes a similar covenant. Thereafter, A conveys the balance of the lots to other grantees by deeds containing the residential restriction. Can C enforce the restrictions against B? Can B enforce against C?

Subsequent purchaser versus prior purchaser (C v. B): In most jurisdictions, C (the later grantee) can enforce the restriction against B if the court finds a common plan of residential restrictions at the very outset of A's sales. (Evidence would be the similar covenant restrictions in all the deeds.) The rationale is that B's promise was made for the benefit of the land at that time retained by A, the grantor. Such land, Lots 2 through

10, became the dominant estate. When A thereafter conveyed Lot 2 to C, the benefit of B's promise passed to C with the land.

Prior purchaser versus subsequent purchaser (B v. C): In most jurisdictions, B could likewise enforce the restriction against C, even though A made no covenant in her deed to B that A's retained land would be subject to the residential restrictions.

There are two theories on which a prior purchaser can enforce a restriction in a subsequent deed from a common grantor. One theory is that B is a third-party beneficiary of C's promise to A. The other theory is that an implied reciprocal servitude attached to A's retained land at the moment she deeded Lot 1 to B. Under this theory, B is enforcing an ***implied*** servitude on Lot 2 and ***not*** the express covenant later made by C.

3. Equitable Defenses to Enforcement

A court in equity is not bound to enforce a servitude if it cannot in good conscience do so.

a. Unclean Hands

A court will not enforce a servitude if the person seeking enforcement is violating a similar restriction on his own land. This defense will apply as long as the plaintiff's violation is of the same general nature.

b. Acquiescence

If a benefited party acquiesces in a violation of the servitude by one burdened party, he may be deemed to have abandoned the servitude as to other burdened parties. (Equitable servitudes, like easements, may be abandoned.) Note that this defense will not apply if the prior violation occurred in a location so distant from the complainant that it did not really affect his property.

c. Estoppel

If the benefited party has acted in such a way that a reasonable person would believe that the covenant was abandoned or waived, and the burdened party acts in reliance thereon, the benefited party will be estopped to enforce the covenant. Similarly, if the benefited party fails to bring suit against a violator within a reasonable time, the action may be barred by ***laches***.

d. Changed Neighborhood Conditions

Changed neighborhood conditions may also operate to end an equitable servitude. If the neighborhood has changed significantly since the time the servitude was created, with the result that it would be inequitable to enforce the restriction, injunctive relief will be withheld. (Many courts, however, will allow the holder of the benefit to bring an action at law for damages.)

Example: A, the owner of Blackacre and Whiteacre, adjacent parcels in an undeveloped area, sells Blackacre to B, extracting a promise that Blackacre "will always be used only for residential purposes." Fifteen years later, the neighborhood has developed as a commercial and industrial center. If B or her successors in interest to Blackacre now wish to use the parcel for a store, an injunction will probably ***not*** issue. A may, however, recover from B or her successors any damages that she may suffer from termination of the residential restriction.

1) Zoning

Zoning plays an important role in determining whether changed conditions will be allowed as a defense to enforcement of an equitable servitude. Zoning that is inconsistent with the private restriction imposed by the equitable servitude will not of itself bar the injunction, but it will provide good evidence that neighborhood conditions have changed sufficiently to make the injunction unjust. Thus, in the example above, the position of B or her successors would be fortified by a showing that the area in which Blackacre is situated is presently zoned for commercial uses.

2) Concept of the "Entering Wedge"

The concept of the "entering wedge" also plays an important role in changed condition cases. If the equitable servitude is part of a general plan of restrictions in a subdivision, and if the parcel in question is located somewhere at the *outer edge* of the subdivision, changed conditions outside of the subdivision will not bar the injunction if it is shown that lifting the restriction on one parcel will produce changed conditions for surrounding parcels, requiring that their restrictions also be lifted, and so on (the "domino effect"). Thus, in the example above, if removing the restriction and allowing commercial development of Blackacre would produce changed conditions for the neighboring, similarly restricted parcel—Whitcacre— with the consequence that its servitude could not be equitably enforced, the injunction against commercial use on Blackacre will probably be allowed, notwithstanding the changed conditions.

4. Termination

Like other nonpossessory interests in land, an equitable servitude may be terminated by a *written release* from the benefit holder(s), *merger* of the benefited and burdened estates, or *condemnation* of the burdened property. (*See* B.4.b., c., h., *supra*.)

F. RELATIONSHIP OF COVENANTS TO ZONING ORDINANCES

Both restrictive covenants and zoning ordinances (*see* IX.C., *infra*) may affect legally permissible uses of land. Both must be complied with, and neither provides any excuse for violating the other. For example, if the zoning permits both residential and commercial use but an applicable covenant allows only residential use, the covenant will control.

These two forms of land use restrictions are enforced differently. As discussed above, covenants (if they meet the relevant requirements) can be enforced by nearby property owners at law or in equity. Zoning, on the other hand, is not subject to enforcement by private suit, but can be enforced only by local governmental officials.

G. PARTY WALLS AND COMMON DRIVEWAYS

Often, a single wall or driveway will be built partly on the property of each of two adjoining landowners. Absent an agreement between the owners to the contrary, courts will treat the wall as belonging to each owner to the extent that it rests upon her land. Courts will also imply mutual cross-easements of support, with the result that each party has the right to use the wall or driveway, and neither party can unilaterally destroy it.

1. **Creation**

While a *written agreement* is required by the Statute of Frauds for the express creation of a party wall or common driveway agreement, an "irrevocable license" can arise if there has been detrimental reliance on a parol agreement. Party walls and common driveways can also result from *implication* or *prescription*.

2. **Running of Covenants**

If party wall or common driveway owners agree to be mutually responsible for maintaining the wall or driveway, the burdens and benefits of these covenants will run to successive owners of each parcel. The *cross-easements for support* satisfy the requirement of horizontal privity because they are mutual interests in the same property. Each promise touches and concerns the adjoining parcels, and the grantee will be charged with notice of the covenant because of the visibility of the common wall or driveway.

V. ADVERSE POSSESSION

A. IN GENERAL

Title to real property may be acquired by adverse possession. (Easements may also be acquired by prescription.) Gaining title by adverse possession results from the operation of the statute of limitations for ejectment, or recovery of real property. If an owner does not, within the statutory period, take legal action to eject a possessor who claims adversely to the owner, the owner is thereafter barred from bringing suit for ejectment. Moreover, title to the property vests in the possessor.

B. REQUIREMENTS

To establish title by adverse possession, the possessor must show (i) an *actual entry* giving *exclusive possession* that is (ii) *open and notorious*, (iii) *adverse* (hostile), and (iv) *continuous* throughout the statutory period.

1. **Running of Statute**

The statute of limitations begins to run when the claimant goes adversely into possession of the true owner's land (i.e., the point at which the true owner could first bring suit). The filing of suit by the true owner is not sufficient to stop the period from running; the suit must be pursued to judgment. However, if the true owner files suit before the statutory period (e.g., 20 years) runs out and the judgment is rendered after the statutory period, the judgment will relate back to the time that the complaint was filed.

2. **Actual and Exclusive Possession**

   a. **Actual Possession Gives Notice**

   The requirement of actual possession is designed to give the true owner notice that a trespass is occurring. It is also designed to give her notice of the *extent* of the adverse possessor's claim. As a general rule, the adverse possessor will gain title only to the land that she actually occupies.

      1) **Constructive Possession of Part**

      Actual possession of a portion of a unitary tract of land is sufficient adverse possession as to give title to the whole of the tract of land after the statutory period, as long as there is a **reasonable proportion** between the portion actually possessed and the whole of the unitary tract, and the possessor has color of title to the whole tract. Color of title is a document that purports to give title, but for reasons not apparent from its face does not. Usually, the proportion will be held reasonable if possession of the portion was sufficient to put the owner or community on notice of the fact of possession.

b. **Exclusive Possession—No Sharing with Owner**

"Exclusive" merely means that the possessor is not sharing with the true owner or the public at large. This requirement does not prevent two or more individuals from working **together** to obtain title by adverse possession. If they do so, they will obtain the title as tenants in common.

Example: A and B are next door neighbors. They decide to plant a vegetable garden on the vacant lot behind both of their homes. A and B share expenses and profits from the garden. If all other elements for adverse possession are present, at the end of the statutory period, A and B will own the lot as tenants in common.

3. **Open and Notorious Possession**

Possession is open and notorious when it is the kind of use the usual owner would make of the land. The adverse possessor's occupation must be **sufficiently apparent** to put the true owner on **notice** that a trespass is occurring.

Examples: 1) Water Company runs a pipe under Owner's land, and there is no indication of the pipe's existence from the surface of the land. Water Company cannot gain title by adverse possession because there is nothing to put Owner on notice of the trespass.

2) A's use of B's farmland for an occasional family picnic will not satisfy the open and notorious requirement because picnicking is not necessarily an act consistent with the ownership of farmland.

4. **Hostile**

The possessor's occupation of the property must be hostile (adverse). This means merely that the possessor does **not have the true owner's permission** to be on the land. It does not mean anger or animosity. The state of mind of the adverse possessor is irrelevant. By the large majority view, it does not matter whether the possessor believes she is on her own land, knows she is trespassing on someone else's land, or has no idea who owns the land.

a. **If Possession Starts Permissively—Must Communicate Hostility**

If the possessor enters with permission of the true owner (e.g., under a lease or license), the possession does not become adverse until the possessor makes clear to the true owner the fact that she is claiming "hostilely." This can be done by explicit notification, by refusing to permit the true owner to come onto the land, or by other acts inconsistent with the original permission.

b. **Co-Tenants—Ouster Required**

Possession by one co-tenant is not ordinarily adverse to her co-tenants because each co-tenant has a right to the possession of all the property. Thus, sole possession or use by one co-tenant is not adverse, unless there is a clear repudiation of the co-tenancy; e.g., one co-tenant ousts the others or makes an explicit declaration that he is claiming exclusive dominion over the property.

c. If Grantor Stays in Possession—Permission Presumed

If a grantor remains in possession of land after her conveyance, she is presumed to be there with the permission of her grantee. Only the grantor's open repudiation of the conveyance will start the limitation period running against the grantee. Likewise, if the tenant remains in possession after the expiration of her lease, she is presumed to have the permission of the landlord.

d. Compare—Boundary Line Agreements

There is a separate but related doctrine that may be helpful here. It operates where a boundary line (usually a fence) is fixed by agreement of the adjoining landowners, but later turns out not to be the "true" line. Most courts will fix ownership *as per the agreed line*, provided it is shown that: (i) there was original *uncertainty* as to the true line; (ii) the agreed line was *established* (i.e., agreed upon); and (iii) there has been *lengthy acquiescence* in the agreed line by the adjoining owners and/or their successors.

1) Establishment Requirement

The establishment requirement can be implied by acquiescence. A past dispute is not necessary to show uncertainty, although it can be good evidence of it. But a showing of original uncertainty is required; otherwise, in a court's view, a parol transfer of land would result.

5. Continuous Possession

The adverse claimant's possession must be continuous throughout the statutory period. Continuous possession requires only the degree of occupancy and use that the average owner would make of the property.

a. Intermittent Periods of Occupancy Not Sufficient

Intermittent periods of occupancy generally are not sufficient. However, constant use by the claimant is not required so long as the possession is of the type that the usual owner would make of the property. For example, the fact that the adverse possessor is using the land for the intermittent grazing of cattle will probably not defeat continuity if the land is *normally* used in this manner.

b. Tacking Permitted

There need not be continuous possession by the same person. Ordinarily, an adverse possessor can take advantage of the periods of adverse possession by her predecessor. Separate periods of adverse possession may be "tacked" together to make up the full statutory period with the result that the final adverse possessor gets title, provided there is privity between the successive adverse holders.

1) "Privity"

Privity is satisfied if the subsequent possessor takes by descent, by devise, or by deed purporting to convey title. Tacking is not permitted where one adverse claimant ousts a preceding adverse claimant or where one adverse claimant abandons and a new adverse claimant then goes into possession.

    2) **Formalities on Transfer**
Even an oral transfer of possession is sufficient to satisfy the privity requirement.

    Example: A received a deed describing Blackacre, but by mistake built a house on an adjacent parcel, Whiteacre. A, after pointing the house out to B and orally agreeing to sell the house and land to her, conveyed to B, by a deed copied from her own deed, describing the property as Blackacre. The true owner of Whiteacre argues that there was no privity between A and B because the deed made no reference to Whiteacre, the land actually possessed. Nonetheless, the agreed oral transfer of actual possession is sufficient to permit tacking.

  6. **Payment of Property Taxes Generally Not Required**
Only a minority of states require the adverse possessor to pay taxes on the property. However, in all states, payment of property taxes is good evidence of a claim of right.

C. DISABILITY

  1. **Effect of Disabilities—Statute Does Not Begin to Run**
The statute of limitations does not begin to run for adverse possession (or easements by prescription) if the true owner was under some disability to sue *when the cause of action first accrued* (i.e., the inception of the adverse possession). Typical disabilities are: minority, imprisonment, and insanity.

    Example: O, the true owner, is five years old when A goes into adverse possession. The statute will not begin to run until O reaches the age of majority.

    Compare: O, the true owner, is declared insane six months after A begins using a pathway adversely. The statute *has* begun to run because O's disability arose *after* A's adverse use began.

  2. **No Tacking of Disabilities**
Only a disability of the *owner* existing at the time the cause of action arose is considered. Thus, disabilities of successors in interest or subsequent additional disabilities of the owner have no effect on the statute.

    Examples: 1) O is a minor at the time A goes into adverse possession of O's land. One year before O reaches the age of majority, O is declared insane (a subsequent disability). The statute begins to run from the date O reaches the age of majority, whether she is then sane or insane.

                 2) O, the true owner, is insane when A begins an adverse use. Ten years later, O dies intestate and the land goes to her heir, H, who is then 10 years old. The statute of limitations begins to run upon O's death despite H's minority. H's minority is a "supervening" disability and cannot be tacked to O's.

3.   **Maximum Tolling Periods**
In some states, the maximum tolling period is 20 years; thus, the maximum period of the
statute of limitations would be the regular statute of limitations period plus the maximum
20-year tolling period.

D.   ADVERSE POSSESSION AND FUTURE INTERESTS
The statute of limitations does not run against the holder of a future interest (e.g., a remainder)
until that interest becomes possessory. Until the prior present estate terminates, the holder of
the future interest has no right to possession, and thus no cause of action against a wrongful
possessor.

Examples: 1) O devises Blackacre to A for life and then to B. Thereafter, X goes into possession and possesses adversely for the statutory period. X has acquired A's life estate
by adverse possession, but has not acquired any interests against B. Of course, if
following A's death, X or her successor stays in possession for the statutory period,
X will have acquired B's rights also.

2) X enters into adverse possession of Blackacre. Four years later, O devises
Blackacre to A for life and then to B. X continues her adverse possession for seven
more years. The statute of limitations is 10 years. In this case, X has acquired the
whole title by adverse possession. An adverse possession begun against the owner
of the fee simple absolute cannot be interrupted by a subsequent division of the
estate.

1.   **Possibility of Reverter—Statute of Limitations Runs on Happening of Event**
In a conveyance "to A for so long as" some event occurs or fails to occur, on the happening
of the event the fee simple determinable automatically comes to an end and the grantor (or
his successors) is entitled to present possession. At that point, the grantor has a cause of
action to recover possession of the property. If he does not bring the action within the period
specified by the applicable statute of limitations (and if A or her successors have the requisite
open, notorious, continuous, and adverse possession), his action will be barred.

2.   **Right of Entry—Happening of Event *Does Not* Trigger Statute of Limitations**
In the case of a right of entry, on the happening of the stated event the grantor (or his successors) has only a right to reenter the property, a power to terminate the grantee's estate.
Until the grantor asserts his right of entry, no cause of action arises because the grantee's
continued possession of the land is proper: her fee simple estate has not been terminated.
Thus (in most states), the statute of limitations does not operate to bar assertion of a right of
entry even though the condition triggering the right of entry has been breached.

a.   **Grantor Must Act Within Reasonable Time to Avoid Laches**
However, to avoid the title problems that might otherwise be presented, most courts
hold that the holder of the right of entry must bring his action within a reasonable time
after the event occurs. If he fails to do so, his action is barred by laches. As for what
constitutes a reasonable time, many courts look to the statute of limitations governing
actions for possession of real property.

E.   EFFECT OF COVENANTS IN TRUE OWNER'S DEED
The exact nature of the title obtained depends on the possessor's activities on the land. For

example, assume there is a recorded restrictive covenant limiting use of the land to a single-family residence. If the possessor uses the land in violation of that covenant for the limitations period, she takes title free of the covenant. But if she complies with the covenant, she takes title subject to it, and it remains enforceable against her (at least in an equitable action).

F. LAND THAT CANNOT BE ADVERSELY POSSESSED
The statute of limitations does not run against government-owned land (federal, state, or local) or land registered under a Torrens system.

VI. CONVEYANCING

A. LAND SALE CONTRACTS
Most transfers of land are preceded by contracts of sale. These normally contemplate escrows (delivery of deed to a third person to be held until purchase price paid) before closing (exchange of purchase price and deed).

1. Statute of Frauds Applicable
To be enforceable, a land contract must be memorialized in a writing that is signed by the party to be charged. The writing need not be a formal contract; a memorandum suffices— e.g., escrow instructions or e-mails can be contracts of sale. The Statute of Frauds requires that the writing contain all "essential terms" of the contract. These are: (i) a *description* of the property (*see* B.3., *infra*), (ii) identification of *the parties* to the contract, and (iii) the *price* and manner of payment (if agreed upon). Incidental matters (e.g., prorating of taxes, furnishing of deeds, title insurance, etc.) can be determined by custom; they need not appear in the writing nor even have been agreed upon.

a. Doctrine of Part Performance
A court may give specific performance of a contract (though not damages) despite the absence of a writing if additional facts are present.

1) Theories to Support the Doctrine

a) Evidentiary Theory
Courts state that if acts done by a party can be explained only by reference to an agreement, these acts unequivocally establish the existence of an oral contract.

b) Hardship or Estoppel Theory
If acts done by a party in reliance on the contract would result in hardship to such an extent that it would be a fraud on that party were the contract not specifically enforced, the other party will be estopped from asserting the Statute of Frauds as a defense.

2) Acts of Part Performance
In most states, two of the following are required:

(i) *Possession* of the land by the purchaser;

(ii)   Making of substantial *improvements*; and/or

(iii) *Payment* of all or part of the purchase price by the purchaser.

Some state courts will go beyond this list and will accept as "part performance" other types of detrimental reliance by the purchaser, such as performance of services or sale of other land.

3)   Can Seller Obtain Specific Performance Based on Buyer's Acts?

a)   Evidentiary Theory
Under the evidentiary theory, it is immaterial who performed the acts constituting the part performance. Because they refer unequivocally to a contract, the seller may obtain specific performance based on the buyer's acts.

b)   Hardship or Estoppel Theory
Under the hardship or estoppel theory, however, the *plaintiff* must be the one whose action would result in hardship if the Statute of Frauds were invoked. Consequently, the seller normally *cannot* rely on the buyer's acts. Even so, make sure that you ascertain whether the *seller* has done anything that would cause him a hardship if the Statute of Frauds were successfully asserted by the buyer.

2.   Doctrine of Equitable Conversion
Under the doctrine of equitable conversion, once a contract is signed and each party is entitled to specific performance, equity regards the purchaser as the owner of the *real property*. The seller's interest, which consists of the right to the proceeds of sale, is considered to be *personal property*. The bare legal title that remains in the seller is considered to be held in trust for the purchaser as security for the debt owed the seller. But note that possession follows the legal title; so even though the buyer is regarded as owning the property, the seller is entitled to possession until the closing.

a.   Risk of Loss
If the property is destroyed (without fault of either party) before the date set for closing, the majority rule is that, because the buyer is deemed the owner of the property, the *risk of loss is on the buyer*. Thus, the buyer must pay the contract price despite a loss due to fire or other casualty, unless the contract provides otherwise. Some states, however, have adopted the Uniform Vendor and Purchaser Risk Act, which places the risk on the *seller* unless the buyer has either legal title or possession of the property at the time of the loss.

1)   Casualty Insurance
Suppose the buyer has the risk of loss, as is true under the majority view, but the seller has fire or casualty insurance that covers the loss. In the event of loss, allowing the seller to recover the full purchase price on the contract and to collect the insurance proceeds would be unjust enrichment. Hence, the courts require the seller to give the buyer credit, against the purchase price, in the amount of the insurance proceeds.

b. Passage of Title on Death

The doctrine of equitable conversion also affects the passage of title when a party to a contract of sale dies before the contract has been completed. In general, it holds that a deceased seller's interest passes as personal property and a deceased buyer's interest as real property.

1) Death of Seller

If the seller dies, the "bare" legal title passes to the takers of his real property, but they must give up the title to the buyer when the contract closes. When the purchase price is paid, the money passes as personal property to those who take the seller's personal property. Note that if the property is *specifically* devised, the specific devisee may take the proceeds of the sale. (*See* F.1.b., *infra*.)

2) Death of Buyer

If the buyer dies, the takers of his real property can demand a conveyance of the land at the closing of the contract. Moreover, under the traditional common law rule, they are entitled to exoneration out of the personal property estate (*see* F.2., *infra*). Thus, the takers of his personal property will have to pay the purchase price out of their share of the buyer's estate. However, a majority of states have enacted statutes abolishing the doctrine of exoneration, and in those states the takers of the real property will take it subject to the vendor's lien for the purchase price. In these states, as a practical matter, the takers of the real property will have to pay the price unless the testator specifically provided to the contrary.

3. Marketable Title

There is an implied covenant in *every* land sale contract that at closing the seller will provide the buyer with a title that is "marketable."

a. "Marketability" Defined—Title Reasonably Free from Doubt

Marketable title is title reasonably free from doubt, i.e., title that a reasonably prudent buyer would be willing to accept. It need not be a "perfect" title, but the title must be free from questions that might present an unreasonable risk of litigation. Generally, this means an unencumbered fee simple with good record title.

1) Defects in Record Chain of Title

Title may be unmarketable because of a defect in the chain of title. Examples include: a significant *variation in the description* of the land from one deed to the next, a deed in the chain that was *defectively executed* and thus fails to meet the requirements for recordation, and evidence that a prior grantor *lacked capacity* to convey the property. Many courts hold that an ancient lien or mortgage on the record will not render title unmarketable if the seller has proof of its satisfaction or the statute of limitations on the claim would have run under any possible circumstance, including tolling for disabilities.

a) Adverse Possession

Historically, a title acquired by adverse possession was not considered marketable because the purchaser might be later forced to defend in court the facts that gave rise to the adverse possession against the record owner. On the bar exam, *title acquired by adverse possession is unmarketable*, despite the fact that most modern cases are contra. Most of the modern cases hold adverse possession titles to be marketable if: (i) the possession has been for a very lengthy period; (ii) the risk that the record owner will sue appears to be very remote; and (iii) the probability of the record owner's success in such a suit appears to be minimal. Because the bar examiners have yet to recognize this line of cases, the modern view should be considered only as a fallback position on the bar exam.

b) **Future Interest Held by Unborn or Unascertained Parties**
Even though most states consider all types of future interests to be transferable, it is often impossible for the owners of the present and future interests, acting together, to transfer a marketable fee simple absolute title. This is because the future interests are often held by persons who are unborn or unascertainable.

Example: "To A for life, and upon A's death to A's eldest surviving daughter." Assume that at the time of this conveyance A has one daughter, B. State of title: A has a life estate, and B has a contingent remainder. A and B together can transfer the land to a purchaser, such as C, but the title is not marketable. It may turn out that, upon A's death, B will have predeceased A, and some other daughter (perhaps not even yet born when A and B transferred to C) will be "A's eldest surviving daughter." Because that daughter did not join in the conveyance to C, she is not bound by it, and she owns the land. On the other hand, if B does turn out to be A's eldest surviving daughter (which cannot be determined until A's death), then C's title will become a marketable fee simple at that time.

While most courts will appoint a guardian ad litem to represent unborn or unascertained persons in *litigation*, the majority will not appoint such a guardian for purposes of *conveying* the land.

2) **Encumbrances**
Generally, mortgages, liens, easements, and covenants render title unmarketable unless the buyer waives them.

a) **Mortgages and Liens**
A seller has the right to satisfy a mortgage or lien *at the closing* with the proceeds from the sale. Therefore, as long as the purchase price is sufficient and this is accomplished simultaneously with the transfer of title (usually through the use of escrows), the buyer cannot claim that the title is unmarketable; the closing will result in a marketable title.

b) **Easements**
An easement that reduces the value of the property (e.g., an easement of way for the benefit of a neighbor) renders title unmarketable. The majority of courts, however, have held that a beneficial easement (e.g., utility easement

to service property) or one that was visible or known to the buyer does not constitute an encumbrance. Some courts go so far as to hold that the buyer is deemed to have agreed to take subject to any easement that was notorious or known to the buyer when she entered into the contract.

c) Covenants
Restrictive covenants render title unmarketable.

d) Encroachments
A significant encroachment constitutes a title defect, regardless of whether an adjacent landowner is encroaching on the seller's land or vice versa. However, the encroachment will not render title unmarketable if: (i) it is very slight (only a few inches) and does not inconvenience the owner on whose land it encroaches; (ii) the owner encroached upon has indicated that he will not sue on it; or (iii) it has existed for so long (many decades) that it has become legal by adverse possession, provided that the state recognizes adverse possession titles as being marketable (*see* 1)a), *supra*).

3) Zoning Restrictions
Generally, zoning restrictions do not affect the marketability of title; they are not considered encumbrances. An ***existing violation*** of a zoning ordinance, however, does render title unmarketable.

4) Waiver
Any of the above mentioned title defects can be waived in the contract of sale.

b. Quitclaim Deed—No Effect
The fact that a contract calls for a quitclaim deed, which does not contain any covenants for title, does not affect the implied covenant to provide marketable title (unless so provided in the contract).

c. Time of Marketability
If, as is usual, the seller has agreed to furnish title "at date of closing," the buyer cannot rescind prior to that date on grounds that the seller's title is not marketable.

1) Installment Land Contract
Similarly, where an installment land contract is used, the seller's obligation is to furnish marketable title ***when delivery is to occur***, e.g., when the buyer has made his final payment. Therefore, a buyer cannot withhold payments or seek other remedies (e.g., rescission) on grounds that the seller's title is unmarketable prior to the date of promised delivery. The buyer might get rescissionary relief before the date of delivery by showing that the seller cannot possibly cure the defects in time. Or, under compelling circumstances, a court might require the seller to quiet title during the contract period.

d. Remedy If Title Not Marketable
If the buyer determines that the seller's title is unmarketable, he must notify the seller and give a reasonable time to cure the defects, even if this requires extension of the

closing date. The notice must specify the nature of the defects. If the seller fails to cure the defects, the buyer may pursue several remedies.

1) Rescission, Damages, Specific Performance
In the absence of a contractual stipulation to the contrary, if title is not marketable, the buyer can rescind, sue for damages for breach, get specific performance with an abatement of the purchase price, or, in some jurisdictions, require the seller to quiet title. The seller cannot sue successfully for damages or specific performance.

2) Merger
If the buyer permits the closing to occur, the contract is said to merge with the deed (i.e., it disappears) and, in the absence of fraud, the seller is ***no longer liable*** on the implied covenant of marketable title. However, the buyer may have an action for violation of promises made in the deed, if any (*see* D., *infra*). *Note:* The merger rule does not apply to most nontitle matters, such as covenants regarding the physical condition of the property. [Campbell v. Rawls, 381 So. 2d 744 (Fla. 1980)]

4. Time of Performance

a. Presumption—Time Not of the Essence
In general, the courts assume that time is not "of the essence" in real estate contracts. This means that the closing date stated in the contract is not absolutely binding in equity, and that a party, even though late in tendering her own performance, can still enforce the contract if she tenders within a reasonable time after the date. (A month or two is typically considered a reasonable time.)

b. When Presumption Overcome
Time will be considered "of the essence" if:

1) The ***contract*** so states; or

2) The ***circumstances*** indicate it was the parties' intention; e.g., the land is rapidly fluctuating in value or a party must move from out of town and has no other place to go; or

3) One party gives the other ***notice*** that she desires to make time of the essence, and does so within a reasonable time prior to the date designated for closing.

c. Effect of Time of the Essence Construction
If time is of the essence, a party who fails to tender performance on the date set for closing is in total breach and loses her right to enforce the contract.

d. Liability When Time Not of the Essence
Even if time is not of the essence, a party who is late in tendering performance is liable in damages for the incidental losses she has caused, such as additional mortgage interest, taxes, etc.

5. **Tender of Performance**

In general, the buyer's obligation to pay the purchase price and the seller's obligation to convey the title are deemed to be *concurrent conditions*. This means that neither party is in breach of the contract until the other party tenders her performance, even if the date designated for the closing has passed.

a. **When Party's Tender Excused**

A party's tender is unnecessary and is excused if the party has repudiated the contract, or if it is impossible for the other party to perform (e.g., if the seller does not have marketable title and cannot get it).

b. **Neither Party Tenders Performance**

If neither party tenders performance, the closing date is automatically extended indefinitely until one of them does so.

c. **Buyer Finds Seller's Title Unmarketable**

If the buyer determines that the seller's title is unmarketable, the buyer must give the seller a reasonable time to cure title defects.

d. **Condition Precedent Unsatisfied**

Most contacts for the sale of residential property contain mortgage contingency clauses, which provide that if the buyer is unable to obtain a mortgage, the contract is voidable. These, and similar clauses, creation conditions precedent to the parties' performance of the contract at closing. A buyer must make a good faith effort to satisfy the condition precedent (e.g., file a timely mortgage application, respond to all of a lending company's requests for documents). A buyer's refusal to complete the transaction for any reason other than a good faith failure to satisfy the condition precedent will be a breach of contract.

6. **Remedies for Breach of the Sales Contract**

a. **Damages**

The usual measure of damages is the difference between the contract price and the market value of the land on the date of the breach. Incidental damages, such as title examination and moving or storage costs, can also be recovered.

1) **Liquidated Damages**

Sales contracts usually require the buyer to deposit "earnest money" with the seller, and provide that if the buyer defaults in performance, the seller may retain this money as liquidated damages. The courts routinely uphold the seller's retention of the deposit if the amount appears to be reasonable in light of the seller's anticipated and actual damages. Many courts will uphold a retention of a deposit of up to 10% of the sales price without further inquiry into its reasonableness. Even without a liquidated damages clause, courts may uphold retention of the deposit, on the ground that giving restitution of the funds to the buyer would unjustly reward a party in breach.

b. **Specific Performance**

1) Buyer's Remedy

A court of equity will order a seller to convey the title if the buyer tenders the purchase price. The remedy at law (damages) is deemed inadequate because the buyer is getting land and land is unique.

If the seller cannot give marketable title, but the buyer wishes to proceed with the transaction, she can usually get specific performance with an ***abatement of the purchase price*** in an amount reflecting the title defect.

2) Seller's Remedy

Somewhat illogically, the courts also generally will give a specific performance decree for the seller if the buyer is in breach. This is sometimes explained as necessary to have "mutuality of remedy." A few courts in recent years have refused to award specific performance to sellers if the property is not unique (e.g., if a developer is selling a house in a large subdivision of similar houses).

c. Special Rules for Unmarketable Title

If the seller's title is unmarketable for reasons that do not indicate the seller's bad faith (i.e., he did not realize that his title was defective when he signed the contract), about half of the courts limit the buyer's recovery of damages to incidental out-of-pocket costs (title examination, etc.) and return of the buyer's earnest money deposit. The other half of the courts give the buyer the standard measure of contract damages mentioned above.

7. Seller's Liability for Defects on Property

a. Warranty of Fitness or Quality—New Construction Only

The common law rule is that contracts of sale and deeds of real property, unlike conveyances of personal property, carry no implied warranties of quality or fitness for the purpose intended. One exception is a contract for the sale of a residential building under construction or to be constructed, on the ground that the buyer has no opportunity to inspect. Most courts extend the implied warranty of fitness or quality to the sale of any ***new house by the builder***. The warranty implied is that the new house is designed and constructed in a reasonably workmanlike manner and suitable for human habitation. Courts are split, however, on whether a subsequent purchaser can recover from the original builder because of the lack of privity. [*See* Speight v. Walters, 744 N.W.2d 108 (Iowa 2008); Conway v. Cutler Group, Inc., 2014 WL 4064261 (Pa. 2014)]

b. Negligence of Builder

A person who contracts for construction may always sue a builder for negligence in performing a building contract. Moreover, many courts now permit the ultimate vendee (e.g., a subdivision buyer) to sue the builder despite the fact that the seller hired the builder and the buyer thus lacks "privity."

c. Liability for Sale of Existing Land and Buildings

A seller of existing land and buildings (not new construction) may be liable to the purchaser for defects in the improvements (e.g., a leaky roof or basement, termite infestation, a nonfunctioning septic system) on any of several different theories.

1) **Misrepresentation (Fraud)**

This theory requires proof that the seller made a *false statement of fact* (oral or written) to the buyer, that the buyer *relied* on the statement, and that it *materially affected* the value of the property. The seller must either have known that the statement was false, or have made it negligently (without taking reasonable care to determine its truth).

2) **Active Concealment**

The seller is liable as above, even without making any statement, if the seller took steps to conceal a defect in the property (e.g., paneling over a wall to conceal cracks).

3) **Failure to Disclose**

A majority of states now hold sellers liable for failure to disclose defects if the following factors are present:

   (i) The seller *knows or has reason to know* of the defect;

   (ii) The defect is *not obvious* or apparent, and the seller realizes that the buyer is unlikely to discover it by ordinary inspection; *and*

   (iii) The defect is *serious* and would probably cause the buyer to reconsider the purchase if it were known.

These decisions are more likely to impose liability on the seller if the property is a personal residence, if the defect is dangerous, and if the seller personally created the defect or previously attempted to repair it and failed to do so.

d. **Disclaimers of Liability**

Sellers sometimes attempt to avoid liability for property defects by inserting clauses in sales contracts exculpating the seller.

1) **"As Is" Clauses**

A general clause, such as "property sold as is" or "with all defects," is *not* sufficient to overcome a seller's liability for fraud, concealment, or (in the states that recognize it) failure to disclose.

2) **Specific Disclaimers**

If the exculpatory clause identifies and disclaims liability for specific types of defects (e.g., "seller is not liable for leaks in the roof"), it is likely to be upheld.

8. **Real Estate Brokers**

Most real estate sales contracts are negotiated by real estate brokers. The broker who obtains the "listing" from the seller is the *seller's agent*. Other agents who participate in the sale (e.g., through a multiple listing service) are also the seller's agents, unless they specifically agree to serve as the buyer's agent. While these agents owe a fiduciary duty to the seller, they also have a duty to the buyer to disclose material information about the property if they have actual knowledge of it. Traditionally, the agent's commission was earned when she found a buyer who was "ready, willing, and able" to purchase the property, even if the buyer later backed out of the contract. But the growing trend of the cases is to award the commission only if the sale actually closes, or if it fails to close because of the seller's fault.

a. Exclusive Listing Agreements

A seller may enter into an exclusive listing agreement with a real estate broker. Under such an agreement, the broker's best efforts to sell the property is deemed the consideration for the broker's commission. "Best efforts" under this type of agreement includes expenditure of time, effort, or money. If the property is sold by the seller or another agent during the period covered by such an agreement, the seller may be bound to pay a commission even though the purchaser was not obtained by the broker. Note that some courts distinguish between exclusive agency agreements, which prohibit listing the property with other brokers during the time of the listing, and exclusive right-to-sell agreements, which additionally preclude the seller from selling the property without paying the commission. [*See* 23 Williston on Contracts §62:20 (4th ed.)]

9. Title Insurance

A title insurance policy insures that a good record title of the property exists as of the policy's date and agrees to defend the record title if litigated. The insurance can be taken out by either the owner of the property or the mortgage lender. An ***owner's policy*** protects only the person who owns the policy (i.e., the property owner ***or*** the mortgage lender) and does not run with the land to subsequent purchasers. In contrast, a ***lender's policy*** follows any assignment of the mortgage loan.

B. DEEDS—FORM AND CONTENT

Transfer of title to an interest in real property occasionally occurs through operation of law; but in most circumstances, transfer can be accomplished only by a deed that satisfies various formalities required by statute.

1. Formalities

a. Statute of Frauds

The Statute of Frauds requires that a deed be in ***writing*** and signed by the grantor.

b. Description of Land and Parties

A deed must identify the land. The description need not be formal, and it may incorporate extrinsic information, but it ***must be unambiguous***. The parties (grantor and grantee) must also be identified. This may be done by name, or by describing them in some other way (e.g., "I grant this land to my eldest daughter," or "I convey this land to the present members of the law review at State University"). If the deed is delivered with the identity of the grantee left blank, the courts will presume that the person taking delivery has authority to fill in the name of the grantee, and if she does so, the deed is valid. But if the land description is left blank, no such authority is presumed, and the deed is void unless the grantee was explicitly given authority to fill in the description, and did so.

c. Words of Intent

The deed must evidence an intention to transfer realty, but technical words are unnecessary. The word "grant" by itself is sufficient in many states.

d. Consideration Not Required

The deed need not recite any consideration, nor must any consideration pass in order to make a deed valid. A deed may validly convey real property by *inter vivos gift* so long as the following requirements are met: (i) donative intent, (ii) delivery, and (iii) acceptance (*see* C., *infra*).

e. Seal Is Unnecessary

A seal is unnecessary.

f. Attestation and Acknowledgment Generally Unnecessary

Attestation by witnesses is generally unnecessary, as is an acknowledgment. *But note:* Either or both might be required for the deed to be recorded.

g. Signature

A deed must be signed by the grantor. The grantor may designate an agent to sign on the grantor's behalf, but if the signing is not done in the grantor's presence, the Statute of Frauds generally requires that the agent's authority be written. In the case of deeds by corporations, statutes usually provide for execution by two officers of the corporation and the affixing of the corporation's seal. If the deed represents a conveyance of all or a substantial part of the corporation's assets, a resolution of the board of directors approving the transfer may be necessary. The *grantee's signature is not necessary* even if the deed contains covenants on her part. Her acceptance of the deed (called a "deed poll" when signed only by the grantor) is sufficient to make the covenants enforceable.

1) Spouse's Signature

In a minority of states, when a grantor wishes to sell her primary residence, her spouse must sign the deed, even if the spouse is not an owner, because the spouse has "homestead" rights as the spouse of the owner. Homestead rights must be waived by the holder of the rights for good title to be conveyed.

2) Trustee's Signature

When real property is held in trust, the trustee must sign a deed conveying the property. The beneficiary's signature is not generally required.

2. Defective Deeds and Fraudulent Conveyances

a. Void and Voidable Deeds

A deed that is defective may be either void or voidable. "Void" implies that the deed will be set aside by the court even if the property has passed to a bona fide purchaser. "Voidable" implies that the deed will be set aside only if the property has *not* passed to a bona fide purchaser.

1) Void Deeds

Deeds considered void include those that are forged, were never delivered, were issued to a nonexistent grantee (e.g., a grantee who is in fact dead at the time of delivery, or a corporation that has not yet been legally formed), or were obtained by fraud in the factum (i.e., the grantor was deceived and did not realize that he was executing a deed).

2) Voidable Deeds
Deeds considered voidable include those executed by persons younger than the age of majority or who otherwise lack capacity (e.g., because of insanity), and deeds obtained through fraud in the inducement, duress, undue influence, mistake, and breach of fiduciary duty.

b. Fraudulent Conveyances
Even when a deed complies with the required formalities mentioned above, it may be set aside by the grantor's creditors if it is a fraudulent conveyance. Under the Uniform Fraudulent Transfer Act, which nearly all states have adopted, a conveyance is fraudulent if it was made: (i) with actual intent to hinder, delay, or defraud any creditor of the grantor; or (ii) without receiving a reasonably equivalent value in exchange for the transfer, and the debtor was insolvent or became insolvent as a result of the transfer. However, the deed will not be set aside as against any grantee who took in good faith and paid reasonably equivalent value.

3. Description of Land Conveyed
In *land contracts and deeds*, property may be described in various ways; i.e., by reference to a government survey, by metes and bounds, by courses and angles, by references to a recorded plat, by reference to adjacent properties, by the name of the property, or by a street and number system.

a. Sufficient Description Provides a Good Lead
A description is sufficient if it provides a good lead as to the identity of the property sought to be conveyed.

Example: A conveyance of "all my land," or "all my land in Alameda County," provides a sufficient lead. The intention of the grantor is clear and the meaning of this intention can be proved without difficulty (by checking the land records of Alameda County).

b. Insufficient Description—Title Remains in Grantor
If the description is too indefinite, title remains in the grantor, subject to the possibility of a suit for reformation of the deed.

Example: A conveyance of "one acre off the western end of my 30-acre tract" (the 30-acre tract being adequately described) would probably fail for uncertainty. "Off the western end" is too vague to ascertain *which* acre, and the admission of parol evidence here would be considered a violation of the Statute of Frauds.

c. Parol Evidence Admissible to Clear Up Ambiguity
The general rule is that parol evidence is admissible to explain or supplement a written description or to clear up an ambiguity. If there is a *patent ambiguity*—one appearing on the face of the deed—parol evidence is normally admissible to ascertain the parties' intent. For example, one part of the deed states that it is conveying "Blackacre" but later it purports to convey an interest in "Whiteacre." Parol evidence is admissible to show which property the grantor intended to convey. Where the ambiguity is *latent*—not apparent on the face of the deed—parol evidence is generally admissible. For example, if A grants to B "my house in San Francisco," parol evidence is admissible to show which house A owns.

1) **Compare—Inadequate Description**

If, however, A grants to B "my house in San Francisco," and it turns out that A owns *three* houses in that city, the conveyance would probably fail for lack of adequate description. (*But note:* If there is an underlying original agreement in which there was no mistake or ambiguity, and the only mistake was in the *writing* of the instrument, relief might be available by way of *reformation* of the deed.)

d. **Rules of Construction**

Where there is a mistake or inconsistency in the description (as where the deed leaves in doubt the exact location of a property line, or measurements give two different locations for the line), the following rules of construction are applied to carry out the parties' probable intent. (These are not "rules of law" and will not be applied where there is clear evidence showing a contrary intent.)

1) Natural monuments prevail over other methods of description; i.e., artificial monuments, courses and distances, surfaces, acreage, or general descriptions (e.g., a call from "Point X to the old oak tree," prevails over a call from "Point X south 100 feet").

2) Artificial monuments (e.g., stakes, buildings, etc.) prevail over all but natural monuments.

3) Courses (e.g., angles) prevail over distances (e.g., "west 90 degrees to Main St." prevails over "west 100 feet to Main St.").

4) All of the foregoing prevail over general descriptions such as name (e.g., "Walker's Island") or quantity (e.g., "being 300 acres").

e. **Land Bounded by Right-of-Way**

1) **Title Presumed to Extend to Center of Right-of-Way**

If land is described as being bounded by a street, highway, or other right-of-way, or if the land conveyed is otherwise described but actually is bounded by such, there is a rebuttable presumption that the title of the grantee extends to the center of the right-of-way (assuming that the grantor owns to the center), or to the full width of it if the grantor retains no adjoining land. This presumption accords with (i) the presumed intention of the parties, and (ii) the public policy that disfavors a grantor's retention of thin strips of land.

a) **Evidence to Rebut Presumption**

In many jurisdictions, a description such as "running *along* the street" has been held sufficient to rebut the presumption that the grantee took title to the center. (This is to be distinguished from the language "*bounded* on the west by the highway" to which the presumption applies.)

But when the monument involved is a *body of water*, more definite language is necessary to rebut the presumption that the grantee takes title to the center. This is because, unlike streets, there are no public rights in most bodies of water abutting on land (except possible navigation easements), and because a grantee of land adjoining water normally expects a right of access to the water.

b) Measuring from Monument

Notwithstanding the general rule, and unless a contrary intention is expressed, measurements *"from"* a right-of-way are presumed to start from the *side* and not the center. Again, this is based on the parties' presumed intent.

2) Variable Boundary Line Cases

a) Slow Change in Course Changes Property Rights

The *slow and imperceptible* change in course of a river or stream serving as a boundary operates to change the legal boundary. Where land is described as abutting upon a body of water, any slow and imperceptible deposit of soil ("accretion") belongs to the owner of the abutting land (the riparian owner). Where accretion builds up in an irregular pattern over the lands of several adjacent property owners, courts determine title to it in a "just and equitable manner," either by (i) merely extending the property lines out into the water with each landowner getting the property that falls within the lines as extended; or (ii) dividing up the newly formed land in proportion to the owners' interests in the adjoining lands. Similarly, slow erosion of a stream's bank results in the owner losing title to the affected area.

b) Avulsion Does Not Change Property Rights

A *sudden*, perceptible change of a watercourse ("avulsion") does not change property rights. Thus, if a river changes course suddenly, boundaries remain where they were, even if someone who formerly had river access now finds himself landlocked.

c) Encroachment of Water Does Not Change Fixed Boundary Lines

According to the majority view, where property is encroached upon by a body of water (e.g., lake enlarges), previously fixed boundary lines do not change and ownership rights are not affected. Indeed, the boundary lines can still be proven even though the land is completely under water.

f. Reformation of Deeds

Reformation is an equitable action in which the court rewrites the deed to make it conform to the intention of the parties. It will be granted if the deed does not express what the parties agreed to, either because of their *mutual mistake* or a *scrivener's* (drafter's) *error*. It will also be granted for *unilateral mistake*, but only if the party who is not mistaken induced the mistake by *misrepresentation* or some other inequitable conduct. If the property has passed to a bona fide purchaser who relied on the original language of the deed, the court will not reform it.

4. Closing Documents

Most real estate closings require more than the exchange of a deed. They are complex events involving the signing of numerous documents and sometimes last minute negotiations (usually over whether a particular fixture will remain part of the property or whether the seller will pay to repair a portion of the property that was damaged between the contract date and the closing date). Below are a few of the most critical closing documents.

a. Closing Disclosure

Various federal laws and regulations require residential mortgage lenders to provide specific information to mortgagors at least ***three business days*** prior to closing. The required information has been consolidated into a single form called the "Closing Disclosure." The mortgagee must clearly provide the following information in the Closing Disclosure:

(i) Mortgage amount;

(ii) Interest rate;

(iii) Monthly payment;

(iv) Whether any of those amounts can change during the life of the loan;

(v) Whether the mortgage has a prepayment penalty or balloon payment;

(vi) Estimated monthly taxes, insurance, and assessments;

(vii) Total closing costs to the buyer; and

(viii) Cash required for the buyer to complete the closing.

Failure by the mortgagee to properly provide the Closing Disclosure can result in an opportunity for the mortgagor to cancel the mortgage or to recover damages.

b. Notification of Defects

The majority of states now require a seller of residential property to provide a form to the buyer at closing, notifying the buyer of any physical defects of which the seller is aware. In most states, the seller must provide this form even when selling the property "as is." This form generally includes a list of possible defects (e.g., roof leaks, foundation cracks, termites), each of which the seller must certify do not exist, or disclose information about. A seller who fails to disclose a known defect that must be disclosed in this form will be liable for the defect after closing.

c. Environmental Report

An owner of real property must generally pay to cure any environmental damage (e.g., soil contaminated by leaked gasoline) to the property, even if the damage occurred before the owner owned the property. As a result, buyers of commercial real estate often ask sellers to guarantee that the property complies with environmental laws. Sellers want to avoid making these guarantees, and the parties must ultimately negotiate an environmental report, to be signed by both parties at closing, that identifies which environmental guarantees the seller makes.

C. DELIVERY AND ACCEPTANCE

1. Delivery—In General

A deed is not effective to transfer an interest in realty unless it has been delivered. Physical transfer of a deed is not necessary for a valid delivery. Nor does physical transfer alone establish delivery (although it might raise a presumption thereof). Rather, "delivery" refers to the **grantor's intent**; it is satisfied by **words or conduct** evidencing the grantor's intention that the deed have **some present operative effect**; i.e., that **title** pass immediately and irrevocably, even though the right of possession may be postponed until some future time.

Examples: 1) O drafts an instrument conveying Blackacre to A and hands the instrument to A "for safekeeping." Although handed to the named grantee, this is not a valid delivery. There is no evidence that O intended the instrument to have any **present** operative effect.

2) O drafts an instrument conveying Blackacre to A. O attempts to give the instrument to A personally but is unable to find A; nevertheless, O quits possession of Blackacre and thereafter treats A as the owner thereof. Nearly all courts would hold that there has been a sufficient delivery.

Under some circumstances (i.e., when a third party is involved), conditional delivery is permissible. This type of delivery becomes effective only upon the occurrence of a condition, but the transfer then **relates back** to the time of the conditional delivery. The grantor has only limited rights to revoke prior to the occurrence of the condition. (*See* further discussion of conditional deliveries, 3., *infra*.)

a.   Manual Delivery
The delivery requirement will be satisfied where the grantor physically or manually delivers the deed to the grantee. Manual delivery may be accomplished by means of the mails, by the grantor's agent or messenger, or by physical transfer by the grantor's attorney in the grantor's presence.

b.   Presumptions Relating to Delivery
As a matter of theory, a deed may be delivered by words without an act of physical transfer. Delivery is presumed if the deed is: (i) **handed** to the grantee, or (ii) **acknowledged** by the grantor before a notary and **recorded**. Unless there is some clear expression of intent that the grantor envisioned the passage of title to the grantee without physical delivery, the continued possession of the deed by the grantor raises a presumption of nondelivery and therefore no passage of title. Conversely, possession by a grantee of a properly executed deed raises a presumption that the delivery requirement has been satisfied. Note, however, that the presumptions involved are rebuttable.

c.   Delivery Cannot Be Canceled
Title passes to the grantee upon effective delivery. Therefore, returning the deed to the grantor has no effect; it constitutes neither a cancellation nor a reconveyance.

d.   Parol Evidence

1)   Admissible to Prove Grantor's Intent
The **majority rule** is that any type of parol evidence, including conduct or statements made by the grantor **before or after** the alleged delivery, is admissible to prove her intent.

2)   Not Admissible to Show Delivery to Grantee Was Conditional
If a deed is **unconditional on its face** and is given **directly to the grantee**, in most

jurisdictions parol evidence is not admissible to show that the delivery was subject to a condition.

Example: O delivers an absolute deed of Blackacre to A, but *tells* A that the deed is effective only if A pays off the encumbrance on the property, or only if O does not return from the hospital. Under the above rule, even if A never pays off the encumbrance or if O returns from the hospital, A is the owner of Blackacre and O cannot claim that there was no valid delivery. *Rationale:* The rule is designed to avoid unsettling of land titles which appear to be in the grantee's name, and to protect both innocent third parties and grantees from testimony fabricated by grantors.

3) Admissible to Show No Delivery Intended

But while parol evidence is not admitted to prove that a delivery was subject to an oral condition, parol evidence *is* admissible to prove that the grantor did not intend the deed to have any present effect at all.

Example: O tells A, "I want you to have Blackacre when I die, and I'm giving you this deed to Blackacre so that you can have it *at that time*." Most courts would hold that O's statements are admissible, and that despite the unconditional nature of the deed itself, they show that O did not intend the deed to have any present effect.

a) Deed Intended as Mortgage

Parol evidence is *always* admissible to show that a deed absolute on its face was intended by the parties to be a mortgage; i.e., there was no intent to convey title outright. (*See* VII.A.4., *infra.*)

b) Transfer of Deed to Bona Fide Purchaser

Suppose O gives A a deed for examination by A's attorney (deed not intended to be effective at this point). A wrongfully records it and sells to B, a bona fide purchaser ("BFP"). On these facts, O would prevail against B unless estopped to assert lack of delivery (*see* below). In other words, absent estoppel, a subsequent BFP is not protected; if there was no delivery, the BFP's grantor had no power to convey.

(1) Estoppel in Favor of Innocent Purchaser

Even though the grantor is allowed to show that no delivery at all was intended as against the grantee, he often is estopped to assert lack of delivery against an innocent purchaser.

Example: O gives A a deed but does not intend the deed to be presently effective. A shows the deed to an innocent purchaser, B, who buys the land in reliance thereon. B will prevail in litigation with O, the original grantor, if it appears that O *negligently permitted* A to have possession of the deed. *Rationale:* As between two innocent parties, the one who contributed most directly to the loss must bear the burden of it, and in many cases O must be deemed responsible for entrusting A with a deed absolute on its face. The same result occurs where the grantee records the deed and an innocent purchaser relies on the recordation.

4) Comment
Obviously, the above rules give the courts flexibility to find either delivery or nondelivery in many situations. It is also evident that there exists a theoretical inconsistency in admitting parol evidence to show that no delivery was intended, but not to show that delivery was "conditional." This inconsistency has been criticized by numerous commentators.

2. Retention of Interest by Grantor or Conditional Delivery
Problems arise when the grantor attempts to retain an interest in the property (e.g., a life estate) or when he attempts to make the passage of title dependent upon the happening of a condition or event other than delivery.

a. No Delivery—Title Does Not Pass
If the grantor executes a deed but fails to deliver it during his lifetime, no conveyance of title takes place. Without adequate delivery, the title does not pass to the intended grantee.

b. No Recording—Title Passes
If the grantor executes and delivers a deed but fails to have it recorded, title passes. Therefore, an agreement between the grantor and grantee to the effect that the deed will not be recorded until some event takes place in the future does not affect the passage of title.

c. Express Condition of Death of Grantor Creates Future Interest
When a deed, otherwise properly executed and delivered, contains an express provision that the title will not pass until the grantor's death, the effect is to create a present possessory life estate in the grantor and a future estate in the grantee. Note, however, that this result follows only when the deed expressly contains such a provision.

d. Conditions Not Contained in Deed
If a deed is absolute on its face, but is delivered to the grantee with an *oral* condition (e.g., "title is not to pass until I return from the Orient"), the traditional view was that the condition dropped out and the delivery became absolute. A growing minority of cases enforces the condition. Where the condition is the grantor's death, the deed is usually held "testamentary" and therefore void (unless executed with testamentary formalities).

e. Test—Relinquishment of Control
To make an effective delivery, the grantor must relinquish absolute and unconditional control.

3. Where Grantor Gives Deed to Third Party
In this situation, the rules are quite different; *conditional delivery is permissible*. Three situations should be distinguished: (i) where the grantor gives the deed to a third party, there

being *no conditions* appended; (ii) where the grantor in a *commercial* context gives such a deed to a third party, there being conditions appended; and (iii) where the situation is the same as in (ii), but the transaction is *donative*.

a.   **Transfer to Third Party with No Conditions**
     If O (the grantor) gives B a deed naming A as grantee and instructs B to give the deed to A, has a delivery occurred? Most courts say yes. Because O indicated an intent to make the deed presently operative, A has a right to the deed and O should not be able to get it back. However, if O told B to retain the deed and give it to A upon O's later instructions, no delivery would have occurred.

     When there are no specific instructions regarding delivery, the question is one of O's intent. If B is A's attorney, delivery seems clear. But if B is O's attorney, a court might infer that B was merely O's *agent* and that O thus retained the power to recall the deed. (A few courts hold that B is to be treated as O's agent *in all circumstances*, even if O manifests a clear intention of present effectiveness, and consequently no delivery occurs.)

b.   **Transfer to Third Party with Conditions (Commercial Transaction)**
     Suppose that O gives B a deed naming A as grantee and tells B to transfer the deed to A when A has paid $5,000 on O's account on or before September 1. This is the *true escrow* situation—the true conditional delivery. Under the circumstances outlined below, a valid conditional delivery has occurred. The deed has a present operative effect in that title will transfer automatically upon the occurrence of the condition. O will retain title only if the condition does not occur.

     1)   **Parol Evidence Admissible to Show Conditions**
          Even though a deed is unconditional, the general rule is that parol evidence is admissible to show the conditions and terms upon which a deed was deposited with the escrow. (This is contrary to the rule excluding parol evidence where transfer is directly to the grantee.) If the escrow custodian has violated parol conditions, there will be no valid delivery. Once the condition occurs, whether parol or not, title automatically vests in the grantee and the escrow holds the deed as the grantee's agent.

     2)   **Grantor's Right to Recover Deed**

          a)   **Majority View—Can Recover Only If No Written Contract**
               Under the majority view, if the grantor seeks to recover the deed prior to the occurrence of the condition, the grantee can object only if there is an enforceable written contract to convey. (On the other hand, once the condition occurs, title passes even in the absence of an enforceable contract.)

               (1)   The requirement of a written contract is based on the Statute of Frauds consideration that oral contracts to convey realty should not become enforceable simply because the deed has been deposited with a third party.

(2) Ordinarily, the contract to convey will be a buy-sell land contract. However, written escrow instructions are often a sufficient memorandum of the contract to satisfy the Statute of Frauds.

b) Minority View—No Right to Recover
A strong minority prohibits revocation even in the absence of an enforceable underlying contract. Deposit of the deed with a third party on stated conditions is seen to obviate most possibilities of fraud.

3) Breach of Escrow Conditions—Title Does Not Pass
When the grantee wrongfully acquires the deed from the escrow holder prior to performance of the conditions of the escrow, title does not pass. Therefore, even though the grantee is in possession of the deed, she cannot convey any interest in the land to a subsequent transferee, even a BFP.

a) Estoppel Cases
A *few* cases have held that where the escrow holder was chosen by the grantor, the grantor is bound by the escrow holder's acts and is estopped to deny a valid delivery and passage of title to the grantee. Thus, an innocent purchaser (BFP) from the grantee may acquire good title. An important factor is whether the grantor has allowed the grantee to take possession of the property prior to completion of the conditions of the escrow. If the grantor has remained in possession, the purchaser may be held to have notice of the grantor's interest and cannot be a BFP.

4) Relation-Back Doctrine
In an escrow transaction, title does not pass to the grantee until performance of the named conditions. However, where justice requires, the title of the grantee will "relate back" to the *time of the deposit of the deed in escrow*. Generally, the relation-back doctrine will be applied if:

(i) The *grantor dies* (doctrine applied to avoid the rule that title must pass before death if instrument is not a will);

(ii) The grantor *becomes incompetent* (doctrine applied to avoid the rule that an incompetent cannot convey title); or

(iii) A *creditor* of the grantor (who is not a BFP or mortgagee) *attaches the grantor's title* (doctrine applied to cut off the creditor's claim).

a) Not Applied If Intervening Party Is BFP or Mortgagee
The relation-back doctrine is not applied where the intervening third party is a BFP or mortgagee. However, if the sales contract is recorded, there can be no intervening BFPs because its recordation gives constructive notice.

b) Not Applied in Favor of Escrow Grantee with Knowledge
The relation-back doctrine will not be applied in favor of an escrow grantee who, at the time she performs the terms and conditions of the escrow, has

actual or constructive knowledge of prior equities of other persons (e.g., that the grantor conveyed to another). But if the escrow grantee has performed part of the conditions when she acquires such knowledge, she will be protected against all but BFPs or mortgagees.

c. Transfer to Third Party with Conditions (Donative Transactions)

If the grantor gives a deed to a third party with instructions to turn it over to the named donee only when certain conditions occur, is there a valid delivery or can the grantor change her mind and demand the deed back before the conditions occur?

1) Condition Unrelated to Grantor's Death

When O gives to B a deed naming A as grantee, and instructs B to give it to A "when A marries," etc., no "true" escrow will exist unless there is an underlying contract of sale (which is extremely unlikely in a donative transaction such as this). Hence, O can retrieve the deed from B upon request. Nevertheless, if O does not do so, and B actually delivers the deed to A after the condition is satisfied, the delivery will be effective to convey title to A as of that date.

2) Where Condition Is Grantor's Death

When O executes a deed to A and hands the deed to B with instructions to give it to A upon the death of O, most courts hold that the grantor **cannot** get her deed back because her intent was to presently convey a future interest to the grantee (either a remainder, with a life estate reserved in the grantor, or an executory interest). Note that this analysis also makes the gift inter vivos, not testamentary, and thus not in conflict with the Statute of Wills. *Caution:* In dealing with death cases, make sure that it was the grantor's intent that the deed be operative immediately to convey a future interest.

a) Limitation—No Delivery If Conditioned on Survival

When O's instructions to B are to deliver the deed to A only if A survives O, it is generally held that there is no valid delivery because it was O's intent to retain title and possession until her death.

4. Acceptance

a. Usually Presumed

There must be an acceptance by the grantee in order to complete a conveyance. In most states, acceptance is presumed if the conveyance is beneficial to the grantee (whether or not the grantee knows of it). In other states, acceptance is presumed only where the grantee is shown to have knowledge of the grant and fails to indicate rejection of it. Acceptance is presumed in all states if the grantee is an infant or an incompetent.

b. Usually "Relates Back"

Acceptance (presumed or otherwise) usually "relates back" to the date of "delivery" of the deed in escrow. However, many courts refuse to "relate back" an acceptance where it would defeat the rights of *intervening third parties* such as BFPs, attaching creditors of the grantor, or surviving joint tenants. A few states will not even "relate back" an acceptance if doing so defeats the devisees of the grantor.

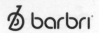

5. **Dedication**

Land may be transferred to a public body (e.g., a city or county) by dedication. An *offer* of dedication may be made by written or oral statement, submission of a map or plat showing the dedication, or opening the land to public use. An *acceptance* by the public agency is necessary. This may be accomplished by a formal resolution, approval of the map or plat, or actual assumption of maintenance or construction of improvements by the agency.

D. COVENANTS FOR TITLE AND ESTOPPEL BY DEED

There are three types of deeds characteristically used to convey property interests other than leaseholds: the *general warranty* deed (also known as "covenant and warranty deed"), the *special warranty* deed (usually statutory), and the *quitclaim* deed. The major difference between these deeds is the scope of assurances (covenants for title) they give to the grantee and the grantee's successors regarding the title being conveyed. The general warranty deed normally contains six covenants for title (*see* 1.a.1) - 6), *infra*). The special warranty deed contains fewer and more limited assurances. The quitclaim deed contains no assurances; it releases to the grantee whatever interest the grantor happens to own. Covenants for title must be distinguished from covenants for other than title (i.e., covenants running with the land used for private land regulation).

1. **Covenants for Title in a General Warranty Deed**

In this day of recording acts and title insurance, covenants for title are not much relied upon for title assurance. A general warranty deed is one in which the grantor covenants against title defects created both by himself and by *all prior titleholders*. In a special warranty deed, however, the grantor covenants only that he himself did not create title defects; he represents nothing about what prior owners might have done. General warranty deeds are a rarity in a number of states where many conveyances are made with statutory form special warranty deeds.

a. **Usual Covenants**

A grantor may give any or all of the following covenants, which are classified as the "usual covenants for title." A deed containing such covenants is called a "general warranty deed."

1) **Covenant of Seisin**

The covenant of seisin is a covenant that the grantor has the estate or interest that she purports to convey. Both title and possession at the time of the grant are necessary to satisfy the covenant.

2) **Covenant of Right to Convey**

The covenant of the right to convey is a covenant that the grantor has the power and authority to make the grant. Title alone will ordinarily satisfy this covenant, as will proof that the grantor was acting as the authorized agent of the titleholder.

3) **Covenant Against Encumbrances**

The covenant against encumbrances is a covenant assuring that there are neither visible encumbrances (easements, profits, etc.) nor invisible encumbrances (mortgages, etc.) against the title or interest conveyed.

4) **Covenant for Quiet Enjoyment**

The covenant for quiet enjoyment is a covenant that the grantee will not be disturbed in her possession or enjoyment of the property by a third party's *lawful* claim of title.

5) Covenant of Warranty
The covenant of warranty is a covenant wherein the grantor agrees to defend on behalf of the grantee any lawful or reasonable claims of title by a third party, and to compensate the grantee for any loss sustained by the claim of superior title. This covenant is generally considered to be similar to the covenant for quiet enjoyment.

6) Covenant for Further Assurances
The covenant for further assurances is a covenant to perform whatever acts are reasonably necessary to perfect the title conveyed if it turns out to be imperfect.

7) No Implied Warranties or Covenants
In the absence of a statute, no covenants of title are implied in deeds. Moreover, the implied (or express) covenant of marketable title found in contracts of sale of real estate is no longer assertable once a deed has been delivered, unless fraud or mistake is shown.

b. Breach of Covenants
Three of the covenants (seisin, right to convey, against encumbrances) are *present covenants* and are breached, if at all, *at the time of conveyance*. Quiet enjoyment, warranty, and further assurances are *future covenants* and are breached *only upon interference with the possession* of the grantee or her successors. This distinction is important in that it determines when the statute of limitations begins running and whether a remote grantee of the covenantor can sue.

1) Covenants of Seisin and Right to Convey
The covenants of seisin and right to convey are breached at the time of conveyance *if the grantor is not the owner* of the interest she purports to convey (or has not been authorized to so convey). If there is a breach, the grantee has a cause of action against which the statute of limitations begins to run at the time of conveyance. If the grantee reconveys, the general rule is that the subsequent grantee has *no right of action* against the covenantor. In a few jurisdictions, it is implied that the original grantee assigned the cause of action to the subsequent grantee, thus permitting suit against the original grantor-covenantor. (The latter is probably the better rule because the subsequent grantee most likely paid the original grantee the market value.)

Example: O conveys Blackacre to A by a deed containing a covenant of seisin. O purports to convey a fee simple, but in fact X was the owner of Blackacre. Soon thereafter, A conveys to B. Under the usual view, A, but not B, may recover from O. In a few jurisdictions, it is implied that A assigned her cause of action to B.

2) Covenant Against Encumbrances
The covenant against encumbrances is breached and a cause of action arises at the time of conveyance if the property is encumbered. Most jurisdictions hold that the covenant is breached even if the grantee knew of the encumbrance, whether it

be an encumbrance on title (*e.g.*, a mortgage) or a physical encumbrance (*e.g.*, an easement or servitude), but others hold there is no breach if the grantee knew of a physical encumbrance.

These jurisdictions charge grantees with constructive notice of visible physical encumbrances (*e.g.*, right-of-way). Several cases go so far as to hold that a covenant against encumbrances is not breached where the encumbrance ("visible" or not) is a benefit to the land involved (*e.g.*, an easement for a sewer or for an adjacent street). As with the covenants of seisin and right to convey, this covenant *cannot* be enforced by a remote grantee in the majority of states.

3) Covenants for Quiet Enjoyment, Warranty, and Further Assurances

Covenants for quiet enjoyment, warranty, and further assurances are not breached until a ***third party interferes with the possession*** of the grantee or her successors. (*But note:* A covenant for quiet enjoyment or of warranty is not breached by the covenantor's refusal to defend title against a ***wrongful*** claim or eviction by a third party.)

a) Covenant Runs to Successive Grantees

These covenants are viewed as "continuous"; *i.e.*, they can be breached a number of times. Their benefit "runs" with the grantee's estate (***unlike*** the present covenants discussed above).

Example: O conveys to A by a deed containing a covenant of warranty. A thereafter conveys to B and B to C, and then C is evicted by a third party with title that was paramount when O conveyed to A. C can successfully sue O.

b) Requirement of Notice

The covenantor is not liable on her covenant of warranty or of further assurances unless the party seeking to hold her liable gives her notice of the claim against the title she conveyed.

c) Any Disturbance of Possession

Most courts hold that any disturbance of possession suffices to constitute a breach. Thus, if the covenantee cannot obtain complete possession or pays off an adverse, paramount claim in order to retain possession, this is a sufficient disturbance of possession. *Compare:* A disturbance of the covenantee's possession is not required as a prerequisite to recovery for breach of covenants of seisin, right to convey, or against encumbrances.

c. Damages and Remote Grantees

Suppose successive conveyances from O to A to B to C, each conveyance containing full covenants. C is evicted by X, who was the true owner when O conveyed to A. C may sue O, A, or B because each gave a covenant of warranty the benefit of which "ran" with the land. But what is the measure of C's recovery? Is it the consideration the defendant (*i.e.*, O, A, or B) received? Is it the consideration C paid (an indemnity theory) so that if C was a donee, she gets nothing?

Many states permit C to recover to the extent of the *consideration received* by the defendant-covenantor (even though it exceeds the consideration paid by C). Under this view, defendant-shopping is advisable (to sue whomever received most). The defendant who is held liable then has a cause of action against any prior covenantor, until ultimately O is held liable. In other states, C can recover only the *actual consideration she paid* (but not to exceed the amount received by the defendant-covenantor).

2. **Statutory Special Warranty Deed**

Statutes in many states provide that (unless expressly negated) the use of the word "grant" in a conveyance creates *by implication* the following two limited assurances against *acts of the grantor* (not her predecessors): (i) that prior to the time of the execution of such conveyance, the *grantor has not conveyed the same estate* or any interest therein to any person other than the grantee; and (ii) that the estate conveyed is free from encumbrances made *by the grantor.*

3. **Quitclaim Deeds**

A quitclaim deed is basically a *release of whatever interest*, if any, the grantor has in the property. Hence, the use of covenants warranting the grantor's title is basically inconsistent with this type of deed; i.e., if the deed contains warranties, it is not a quitclaim deed.

4. **Estoppel by Deed**

If a grantor purports to convey an estate in property that she does not then own, her *subsequent acquisition of title to the property will automatically inure to the benefit of the grantee*. In other words, the grantor impliedly covenants that she will convey title immediately upon its acquisition.

Example: On Day 1, A, who does not own Blackacre, purports to convey Blackacre to B by general warranty deed. On Day 1, B has no interest in Blackacre. On Day 3, A acquires Blackacre from O. That interest automatically passes to B, so that on Day 3 B owns Blackacre. A's warranties will prevent her from denying ownership when she executed the deed on Day 1.

a. **Applies to Warranty Deeds**

The doctrine is most frequently applied where the conveyance is by warranty deed. Regardless of covenants for title, many courts hold that if the deed expressly purports to convey a fee simple or other *particular estate*, the grantee is entitled to that estate if later acquired by the grantor. In most states, however, the doctrine will not be applied when the conveyance is by a quitclaim deed.

b. **Rights of Subsequent Purchasers**

The majority of courts hold that title inures to the benefit of the grantee only *as against the grantor* (who is estopped to deny that she acquired title on behalf of the grantee). This is a personal estoppel only. Consequently, if the grantor transfers her after-acquired title to an innocent purchaser for value, the BFP gets good title. (There is no basis for invoking an estoppel against an innocent purchaser without notice.)

1) **Effect of Recordation by Original Grantee**

If the original grantee records the deed she receives from the grantor, the question arises as to whether this recordation imparts sufficient notice of the grantee's interest, so as to prevent a subsequent purchaser from being a BFP. This depends on the subsequent grantee's **burden of searching the title**. (*See* E.4., *infra*.)

c. Remedies of Grantee
In jurisdictions following the estoppel rationale, the original grantee, at her election, may **accept title** to the land **or sue for damages for breach of covenants** for title. However, if an innocent purchaser of the after-acquired title is involved, the grantee has no rights against the BFP.

E. RECORDING
At common law, in nearly all cases priority was given to the grantee *first in time*. Thus, if O conveyed Blackacre to A and then made an identical conveyance to B, A prevailed over B on the theory that after the first conveyance O had no interest left to convey.

1. Recording Acts—In General
Statutes known as "recording acts" require a grantee to make some sort of recordation so as to give "notice to the world" that title to certain property has already been conveyed, and thus to put subsequent purchasers on guard. These statutes are in effect in some form in every state. Basically, recording acts set up a system by which any instrument affecting title to property located in a certain county can be recorded in that county. These acts seek to protect all subsequent BFPs from secret, unrecorded interests of others.

a. Purpose of Recordation—Notice
Recordation is not essential to the validity of a deed, as between the grantor and grantee. However, if a grantee does not record her instrument, she may lose out against a subsequent BFP. By recording, the grantee gives constructive (or "record") **notice to everyone**. Hence, as stated earlier, proper recording prevents anyone from becoming a subsequent BFP.

b. Requirements for Recordation

1) What Can Be Recorded—Instrument Affecting an Interest in Land
Practically every kind of **deed, mortgage, contract to convey**, or other instrument creating or affecting an interest in land can be recorded. *Note:* A judgment or decree affecting title to property can also be recorded. And, even before judgment, where a *lawsuit is pending that may affect title* to property, any party to the action can record a *lis pendens* (notice of pending action), which will effectively put third parties on notice of all claims pending in the lawsuit.

2) Grantor Must Acknowledge Deed
Most recording statutes provide that, in order to be recorded, a deed must be acknowledged by the grantor before a notary public. This requirement offers some protection against forgery. Problems may arise if the recorder records a deed that has not been acknowledged or has been improperly acknowledged.

c. Mechanics of Recording

1) Filing Copy
The grantee or her agent normally presents the deed to the county recorder, who

photographs it and files the copy in the official records. These records are kept chronologically.

2) Indexing
The recorder also indexes the deed to permit title searches. The usual indexes are the grantor-grantee and grantee-grantor indexes, which are arranged by reference to the parties to the conveyance. Tract indexes, which index the property by location, exist in some urban localities.

2. Types of Recording Acts
There are three major types of recording acts, classified as "notice," "race-notice," and "race" statutes. Note that the burden is on the subsequent taker to prove that he qualifies for protection under the statute.

a. Notice Statutes
Under a notice statute, a subsequent BFP (i.e., a person who gives valuable consideration and has no notice of the prior instrument) prevails over a prior grantee who failed to record. The important fact under a notice statute is that the subsequent purchaser *had no actual or constructive notice* at the time of the conveyance. Constructive notice includes both record notice and inquiry notice (*see* 3.b.3), *infra*). A typical notice statute provides:

A conveyance of an interest in land, other than a lease for less than one year, shall not be valid against any subsequent purchaser for value, *without notice thereof*, unless the conveyance is recorded.

Note also that the subsequent BFP is protected, regardless of whether she records at all.

Example: On January 1, O conveys Blackacre to A. A does not record. On January 15, O conveys Blackacre to B, who gives valuable consideration and has no notice of the deed from O to A. B prevails over A.

> *What if A records before B?* Suppose in the example above that A recorded on January 18, and B never recorded. This is *irrelevant* under a "notice" statute, because B had no notice *at the time of her conveyance* from O. B is protected against a *prior* purchaser even though B does not record her deed (this is the difference between "notice" and "race-notice" statutes). Of course, if B does not record, she runs the risk that a subsequent purchaser will prevail over her, just as she prevailed over A.

b. Race-Notice Statutes
Under a race-notice statute, a subsequent BFP is protected only if she records *before* the prior grantee. *Rationale:* The best evidence of which deed was *delivered* first is to determine who recorded first. To obviate questions about the time of delivery and to add an inducement to record promptly, race-notice statutes impose on the BFP the additional requirement that she record first. A typical race-notice statute provides:

Any conveyance of an interest in land, other than a lease for less than one year, shall not be valid against any subsequent purchaser for value, *without notice thereof*, whose conveyance is *first recorded*.

Example: On January 1, O conveys Blackacre to A. A does not record. On January 15, O conveys Blackacre to B. On January 18, A records. On January 20, B records. A prevails over B because B did not record first.

c.   Race Statutes

Under a pure race statute, whoever records first wins. Actual notice is irrelevant. The rationale is that actual notice depends upon extrinsic evidence, which may be unreliable. *Very few states* have race statutes.

Example: On January 1, O conveys Blackacre to A. A does not record. On January 15, O conveys Blackacre to B. B *knows* of the deed to A. B records. Then A records. B prevails over A because she recorded first. It is immaterial that she had actual notice of A's interest.

3.   Who Is Protected by Recording Acts

Only *bona fide purchasers* ("BFPs") are entitled to prevail against a prior transferee under "notice" and "race-notice" statutes. To attain this status, a person must satisfy three requirements (each of which is discussed in detail below). The person must:

(i)   Be a *purchaser* (or mortgagee or creditor if the statute so allows; *see* below);

(ii)   Take *without notice* (actual, constructive, or inquiry) of the prior instrument; and

(iii)   Pay *valuable consideration*.

Note: If these requirements are not met, the person is not protected by the recording acts, so that the common law rule of first in time prevails.

Example: O, the owner of Blackacre, executes a contract of sale of the land to A on Monday. A immediately *records the contract*. On Tuesday, O deeds the land to B. B pays valuable consideration for the land, but is not a BFP because B is held to have constructive notice of A's rights. *Result:* A is entitled to enforce the contract against B, paying B the rest of the price and compelling B to deliver a deed to A. (If A had failed to record the contract, and B had no other notice of it, B would have taken free of A's contract rights. A would have an action in damages against O for breach of contract, but would not have a claim for specific performance against B.)

a.   Purchasers

All recording acts protect purchasers (of the fee or any lesser estate).

1)   Donees, Heirs, and Devisees Not Protected

Donees, heirs, and devisees are not protected because they do not give value for their interests.

Example: O, the owner of Blackacre, conveys it to A on Monday. A fails to record. O dies on Tuesday and his heirs/devisees succeed to his property interests. Even though O's heirs/devisees may be unaware of the prior conveyance of Blackacre to A, A prevails.

2) Purchaser from Donee, Heir, or Devisee

A person who buys land from the donee, heir, or devisee of the record owner is protected against a prior unrecorded conveyance from the record owner.

Example: O conveys Blackacre to A, who does not record. O dies, leaving H as her heir. (H does not prevail over A because he is not a purchaser.) H conveys to B, a BFP, who records. B prevails over A in nearly all jurisdictions.

An heir who purchases the interests of her co-heirs, without notice of the prior unrecorded conveyance, is entitled to the same protection as any other purchaser to the extent of her purchase.

3) Mortgagees

Mortgagees for value are treated as "purchasers," either expressly by the recording act or by judicial classification.

Example: O, the owner of a parcel in State X known as Blackacre, deeds the parcel to A on Monday, but A fails to record the deed. On Tuesday, O executes a mortgage to Bank. State X has a race-notice recording statute. Bank is a good faith purchaser for value, and immediately records its mortgage. *Result:* Bank has a valid mortgage on the land, while the title to the land is held by A. (If Bank had not been a BFP, or had failed to record, A would hold the title free of Bank's mortgage.)

4) Judgment Creditors

In nearly all states, a plaintiff who obtains a money judgment can obtain, by statute, a judgment lien on the defendant's real estate. A typical statute reads as follows:

Any judgment properly filed shall, for 10 years from filing, be a lien on the real property then owned or subsequently acquired by any person against whom the judgment is rendered.

Is a plaintiff who obtains a judgment lien under such a statute protected by the recording acts from a prior unrecorded conveyance made by the defendant? The cases are split, but the majority holds that the judgment lienor is ***not*** protected. These courts usually reason either (i) the plaintiff is not a BFP because he did not pay value for the judgment, or (ii) the judgment attaches only to property "owned" by the defendant, and not to property the defendant has previously conveyed away, even if that conveyance was not recorded.

Example: On January 1, O grants a mortgage on Blackacre to A. A does not record the mortgage. On January 15, B, who had previously sued O on a tort claim, obtains and properly files a judgment against O. B has no knowledge of the mortgage from O to A. Which lien has priority, A's mortgage or B's judgment lien? By the majority view, A has priority despite A's failure to record the mortgage. B is not protected by the recording act.

5) Transferees from Bona Fide Purchaser—Shelter Rule
A person who takes from a BFP will prevail against any interest that the trans-feror-BFP would have prevailed against. This is true even where the transferee had *actual knowledge* of the prior unrecorded interest.

Example: O conveys to A, who fails to record. O then conveys to B, a BFP, who records. B then conveys to C, who has actual knowledge of the O to A deed. C prevails over A. (And this is true whether C is a donee or purchaser.)

a) Rationale
If the rule were otherwise, a BFP might not be able to convey an interest in the land. The transferee is not protected for her own sake, but rather for the sake of the BFP from whom she received title.

b) Exception—No "Shipping Through"
This rule will not help someone who *previously* held title and had notice of the unrecorded interest. In the example above, if O repurchased from B, O would have notice of A's interest and could not claim the benefit of the "shelter rule."

6) Purchaser Under Installment Land Contract
In most states, a purchaser who has paid only part of the purchase price under an installment land contract (*see* VII.A.3., *infra*) is protected by the recording acts only to the extent of payment made. In a dispute between the contract purchaser and a prior claimant, the court may:

(i)   Award the contract purchaser a share of the property as a tenant in common equal to the proportion of *payments made*;

(ii)   Award the land to the prior claimant, but give the contract purchaser a lien on the property to the extent of the *amount paid* [Westpark, Inc. v. Seaton Land Co., 171 A.2d 736 (Md. 1961)]; or

(iii)   Award the land to the contract purchaser, but give the prior claimant a lien on the property to the extent of the *balance still owed* [Sparks v. Taylor, 90 S.W. 485 (Tex. 1906)].

Example: O conveys Blackacre to A, who does not record. O then conveys Blackacre to B as a gift. B, knowing nothing of the O-A convey-ance, records her deed. B then sells Blackacre to C for $100,000 via an installment land contract. C is to make four payments of $25,000. C makes the first payment and records his deed. A learns of the B-C conveyance and files suit against C to quiet title. *Result:* The court may (i) award C a one-fourth interest in Blackacre as a tenant in common; (ii) award Blackacre to A, but order A to pay C $25,000; or (iii) award Blackacre to C, but order C to pay the remaining $75,000 to A.

a) **Exception—Shelter Rule**
If B in the example above were a BFP, the shelter rule would apply and C would be fully protected even though C had notice of the O-A conveyance partway through C's payments.

b. **Without Notice**
"Without notice" means that the purchaser had no actual, record, or inquiry notice of the prior conveyance at the time she paid the consideration and received her interest in the land. While *no one has a legal duty to perform a title search*, a subsequent purchaser will be charged with the notice that such a search *would* provide, whether or not she actually searches. However, the fact that the purchaser obtains knowledge of the adverse claim after the conveyance but before she records it is immaterial; she only has to be "without notice" *at the time of the conveyance*.

1) **Actual Notice**
The subsequent purchaser must show that she did not actually know of any prior unrecorded conveyance. Actual notice includes knowledge obtained from any source (e.g., newspaper, word-of-mouth, etc.).

2) **Record Notice—Chain of Title**
The fact that a deed has been recorded does not always mean that a purchaser will be charged with notice of it. A subsequent purchaser will be held to have record notice only if the deed in question is recorded "in the chain of title," which means that it is recorded in a fashion that a searcher could reasonably find it. There are several situations in which a deed might be recorded, but very difficult or impossible for a search to locate.

a) **"Wild Deeds"**
A "wild deed" is a recorded deed that is not connected to the chain of title. It does not give constructive notice because the subsequent BFP cannot feasibly find it.

Example: O owns Blackacre, which she contracts to sell to A. The contract is not recorded, and O remains in possession. A thereupon conveys Blackacre by deed to B, and B records. O then conveys Blackacre by deed to C. Did B's recordation charge C with constructive notice of B's claim to equitable title to Blackacre derived through A? *No.* C is not charged with notice because there was no way for him to find the A-B deed. Nothing related it to O. It was not in O's chain of title; it was a "wild deed."

Compare: If the jurisdiction maintained a tract index, it would not be hard to find that A-B deed. It would be indexed under Blackacre's block and lot number. But it is impossible to find in a grantor-grantee index without looking at the descriptions of all the recorded properties.

b) **Deeds Recorded Late**
A deed recorded after the grantor therein is shown by the record to have

parted with title through another (subsequent) instrument is not constructive notice in most states.

Example: O conveys to A on May 1. O conveys to B, a donee, on May 15. B records on June 1. A records on June 15. B conveys to C on July 1. C has no actual notice of the O-A deed.

B v. A: As between A and B, A would win because B (a donee) was not a BFP.

C v. A: In *notice* statute jurisdictions, most courts hold that C will prevail over A because the O-A deed was recorded "late" and is not in C's chain of title; i.e., the search burden is too great if C is required to search "down" the grantor index to the present time for each grantor in the chain.

In several *race-notice* jurisdictions, however, A's recordation is treated as giving constructive notice to any purchaser *subsequent to* such recordation. In these states, the title searcher must search to the present date under the name of each person who ever owned the property in order to pick up deeds recorded late.

(1) Exception—Shelter Rule

If B in the example above were a BFP, C would win in any event, for she would "shelter" under B. This result would be the same even if C had actual knowledge of the O-A deed; otherwise B's power to transfer would be restricted.

(2) Lis Pendens Protection

What can A do to protect herself when she records her deed and finds the O-B deed on record? She can bring suit against B to expunge B's deed and file a lis pendens (litigation pending) notice under B's name, so any purchaser from B will have notice of A's claim.

c) Deeds Recorded Before Grantor Obtained Title

There is a split of authority on whether a recorded deed, obtained from a grantor who had no title at that time but who afterwards obtains title, is constructive notice to a subsequent purchaser from the same grantor.

Example: Suppose that on June 1, O owns Blackacre, but on that same day, A conveys Blackacre by warranty deed to B who promptly records. On July 2, O conveys Blackacre to A, and this deed is also promptly recorded. On August 3, A conveys Blackacre to C, a BFP who has no actual notice of the prior A-B deed.

Majority view: Most courts protect C over B on the theory that a deed from A that was recorded prior to the time title came to A is not in the chain of title and so does not give C constructive notice of B's claim to Blackacre. *Rationale:* It would put an excessive burden on the title searcher to have to search the index under each grantor's name *prior* to the date the grantor acquired title.

Minority view: However, a minority of courts protect B over C on the basis that as soon as A acquired title from O, it transferred automatically to B by virtue of A's earlier deed to B. Therefore, A had nothing to transfer to C. (*Criticism:* The minority view sharply increases the costs of title search.)

d) Deed in Chain Referring to Instrument Outside Chain

If a recorded document in the chain of title refers to another instrument, such reference may be sufficient to impart constructive notice of the other instrument, even if it is unrecorded or is not itself in the chain of title.

Example: O mortgages Blackacre to A, who does not record. Later, O sells Blackacre to B by deed which recites that title is subject to A's mortgage. This deed is recorded. B then sells to C. C takes subject to A's mortgage, even though it was never recorded, because of the reference to it in the OB deed.

e) Restrictive Covenants—Deeds from Common Grantor

(1) Subdivision Restrictions

Suppose that O, a subdivider, is developing a residential subdivision. She sells lot #1 to A, and the deed provides that lot #1 is restricted to residential use. The deed also provides that "O on behalf of herself, her heirs, and assigns promises to use her remaining lots (#2, #3, etc.) for residential purposes only." A records the deed. O then sells lot #2 to B. The deed to B contains no restrictions. B wishes to erect a gas station. Is B bound by the restrictions in the OA deed of which he had no actual notice? The courts are split.

(a) Some charge B with reading *all* deeds given by a common grantor, not just the deeds to his particular tract. Hence, B has constructive notice and is bound by the restriction.

(b) However, the *better view* is contra; i.e., because the burden of title search would be excessive, deeds to other lots given by a common grantor are not in B's chain of title. (But if B has actual or inquiry notice of the restriction, it may be enforced as an equitable servitude; *see* IV.E., *supra*.)

(2) Adjacent Lots

Suppose that O owns lot #1 and lot #2. She grants lot #2 to A with an easement of way over lot #1. The deed to A is indexed as a deed to lot #2; no mention is made of lot #1. Subsequently, O conveys lot #1 to B without mentioning the easement. As with subdivision restrictions, the courts are split as to whether B is required to read O's deeds of adjoining lots.

f) Marketable Title Acts

In some states, a ***search cut-off date*** is established by statute; e.g., defects of title reaching back farther than 40 years are barred (a title searcher need only check the chain of title back 40 years). The exact cut-off point varies from state to state.

3) Inquiry Notice

Inquiry notice means that if the subsequent grantee is bound to make reasonable inquiry, she will be held to have knowledge of any facts that such inquiry ***would have revealed*** (even though she made none).

a) Generally No Inquiry from Quitclaim Deed

In a ***majority*** of states, quitclaim grantees are treated the same as warranty deed grantees under the recording system; i.e., they are not charged with inquiry notice from the mere fact that a quitclaim deed was used.

b) Inquiry from References in Recorded Instruments

If a recorded instrument makes reference to an unrecorded transaction, the grantee is bound to make inquiry to discover the nature and character of the unrecorded transaction.

Example: O grants an easement in Blackacre to A, who does not record. O thereafter conveys the fee to B and in the deed states that the property is "subject to an easement." B records. C purchases Blackacre from B without any knowledge of the easement. The reference to the easement in the OB deed creates a ***duty to inquire*** concerning the easement. If a reasonable inquiry would have informed C of the easement, she has notice of it even though the deed of the easement was never recorded. (Remember the grantee is charged with constructive knowledge of the fruits of a reasonable inquiry even though she made no inquiry.) Thus, C will take subject to A's unrecorded interest in Blackacre.

c) Inquiry from Unrecorded Instruments in Chain of Title

Suppose O, the record owner, conveys a life estate to A by a deed that is not recorded. Thereafter, A purports to convey a fee simple to B, a purchaser for valuable consideration, without actual notice that A merely has a life estate. O would prevail over B with respect to the remainder interest because when a grantor's deed is unrecorded, the grantee is expected—at her peril—to demand a viewing of her grantor's title documents at the time of the purchase and insist that they be recorded.

d) Inquiry from Possession

A title search is not complete without an examination of possession. If the possession is unexplained by the record, the subsequent purchaser is obligated to make inquiry. The subsequent purchaser is charged with knowledge of whatever an inspection of the property would have disclosed ***and*** anything that would have been disclosed by inquiring of the possessor.

Example: O, the owner of Blackacre, conveys it to A, who fails to record. However, A goes into possession of Blackacre. Thereafter, O executes an identical conveyance of Blackacre to B, who purchases for valuable consideration and without actual notice of the prior unrecorded conveyance to A. A majority of states hold that B is placed on constructive notice of A's interest. An examination of possession would have revealed A's presence, and A's possession is inconsistent with O's ownership.

Similarly, the physical appearance of the land may give notice of an adverse interest. For example, tire tracks passing over the land to an adjacent parcel may give notice of an easement.

c. Valuable Consideration

A person is protected by the recording statute only from the time that valuable consideration was given. Thus, if a deed was delivered before the consideration was paid, the purchaser will not prevail over deeds recorded before the consideration was given. Valuable consideration must be more than merely nominal. A person who claims to be a BFP must prove that *real* consideration was paid.

1) Test—Substantial Pecuniary Value

The test is different from that of contract law, where any consideration suffices to support a contract. Here, the claimant must show that he is not a donee but a purchaser. The consideration need not be adequate, nor the market value of the property, but it must be of substantial pecuniary value. ("Love and affection" is not valuable consideration.)

2) Property Received as Security for Antecedent Debts Is Insufficient

One who receives a deed or mortgage only as security for a preexisting debt has not given valuable consideration.

Example: O becomes indebted to A. O conveys Blackacre to B, who does not record. O then gives A a mortgage on Blackacre to secure the indebtedness, and A records. A did not give valuable consideration, and B prevails over A.

4. Title Search

Suppose O has contracted to sell Blackacre to A. Prior to closing, A, the buyer, will have a title search performed to assure herself that O really owns Blackacre and to determine if there are any encumbrances on O's title. How will A's title searcher(s) proceed?

a. Tract Index Search

In a tract index jurisdiction, the job is comparatively easy. The searcher looks at the page indexed by block and/or lot describing Blackacre and at a glance can see prior recorded instruments conveying, mortgaging, or otherwise dealing with Blackacre.

b. Grantor and Grantee Index Search

The search is much more complicated in a grantor and grantee index jurisdiction.

Examples:

1) V owned Blackacre in 1935. In 1965, V conveyed Blackacre to W. In 1990, W conveyed Blackacre to X. In 1995, X gave B Bank a mortgage on the property. In 2005, X conveyed Blackacre to O. O contracts to sell the land to A. A's title searcher will look in the **grantee** index under O's name from the present back to 2005, when she finds the deed from X, then under X's name from 2005 to 1990, when she finds the deed from W to X, then under W's name from 1990 to 1965, then under V's name from 1965 backward. The searcher will then look in the **grantor** index under V's name from 1935 to 1965, under W's name from 1965 to 1990, under X's name from 1990 to 2005, and under O's name from 2005 to the present. In this manner, she will pick up the mortgage to B Bank, which was recorded in 1995 in the grantor index under X's name.

2)

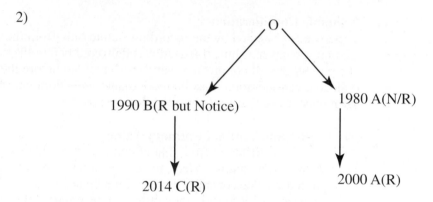

1980 O conveys to A.

1990 O executes an identical conveyance of Blackacre to B. B pays valuable consideration, but B has actual knowledge of the prior unrecorded conveyance to A. B records.

2000 A records.

2014 B conveys his interest in Blackacre to C, who purchases without notice of the conveyance to A and who pays valuable consideration.

In searching the title, C will first look in the grantee index under B's name to discover if his seller, B, ever acquired title. He will find that B acquired title in 1990 from O. Next, he will look in the grantor index under B's name to discover if B made any prior conveyances, and then will look in the grantee index once again, this time under O's name, to discover if O ever acquired title. C will find that O acquired title in 1970. Then he will look in the grantor index under O's name to discover if O made a conveyance prior to his conveyance to B. Under the majority rule, C is required to look under O's name in the grantor index only through 1990. C will find no conveyances. In 1990, C will find the recorded conveyance to B and he need look no further. On this basis, C will not find the recorded conveyance to A because A recorded after 1990. A's recording is "out of the chain of title," and therefore C is not charged with notice.

Under a **pure notice or race-notice statute**, as between A and B, A will prevail because B, having knowledge of A's unrecorded conveyance, is not a protected party. However, as between A and C, many courts hold that C should prevail because A's recording is out of the chain of title. The cases are split. Because notice is irrelevant under **pure race** statutes, B would prevail over A because B recorded first. Once it is established that B prevails over A, C obviously takes good title.

c. **Other Instruments and Events Affecting Title**

The title searcher's job may be complicated by marriages and divorces (e.g., a woman's name may have changed between her appearance as grantee and her reappearance as grantor) and by the fact that a number of interests in the land may be filed and indexed elsewhere than in the recording office (e.g., judgment liens may appear in the trial court's judgment docket, and tax liens may be filed only in the tax assessor's office). Similarly, discovering whether land has passed by will or intestacy rather than by conveyance may require a search of probate records.

5. **Effect of Recordation**

Proper recordation gives all prospective subsequent grantees constructive notice of the existence and contents of the recorded instruments; i.e., there can be no subsequent BFPs. Recordation also raises **presumptions** that the instrument has been validly delivered and that it is authentic. These presumptions are rebuttable, not conclusive.

a. **Does Not Validate Invalid Deed**

As stated earlier, recordation is not necessary for a valid conveyance. Nor does recordation validate an invalid conveyance, such as a forged or undelivered deed.

b. **Does Not Protect Against Interests Arising by Operation of Law**

Furthermore, recordation does not protect a subsequent purchaser against interests that arise by operation of law, rather than from a recordable document (e.g., dower rights; prescriptive and implied easements; title by adverse possession). Because there is no instrument to record in order to perfect such interests, the recording acts do not apply, and subsequent purchasers take subject to the interests. (*Remember:* If the recording act is inapplicable, the common law priority rules apply.)

Example: O is the record owner of Blackacre. X adversely possesses Blackacre for the period of the statute of limitations. O then conveys Blackacre to A, a BFP. Even though X's interest has never been recorded, X prevails against A.

1) **Exception**

A court **may** protect a subsequent BFP from an unrecorded **implied easement** that is **not visible** upon inspection of the premises (e.g., an underground sewer).

c. **Recorder's Mistakes**

An instrument is considered recorded from and after the time it is filed at the recorder's office, irrespective of whether it is actually listed on the indexes. If the recorder's office has made an error in recording, the subsequent purchaser has an action against the recorder's office. There is a strong minority view that protects the searcher.

d. Effect of Recording Unacknowledged Instrument

As discussed above, the recording acts require that before an instrument can be recorded, it must be acknowledged by the grantor before a notary. What happens if the recorder, by oversight, records a deed that has not been acknowledged or has been defectively acknowledged?

1) No Acknowledgment—No Constructive Notice

Because an unacknowledged deed does not qualify for recordation, it does not give constructive notice to subsequent purchasers. Hence, unless the subsequent purchaser has other notice of the earlier deed, the subsequent purchaser will prevail.

Example: O conveys Blackacre to A by a deed that is not acknowledged, but the recorder nevertheless records it. Later, O conveys to B by an acknowledged deed, which B records. B prevails over A unless B had ***actual*** notice of the deed from O to A (which she might have if she searched the title records) or ***inquiry*** notice (as she would have if A was in possession of Blackacre).

2) Compare—Defective Acknowledgment

When a recorded instrument has been acknowledged, but the acknowledgment is defective for some reason ***not apparent on the face*** of the instrument, the better view is that the recordation does impart constructive notice. *Rationale:* A hidden defect in the acknowledgment should not be allowed to destroy the constructive notice that the document otherwise clearly imparts. Purchasers should be entitled to rely on what ***appears*** to be a perfectly recorded document.

Example: A deed bears what appears to be a valid acknowledgment but is in fact invalid because the notary was disqualified to act or because the grantor did not appear personally in front of the notary to acknowledge her signature, as required by law.

F. CONVEYANCE BY WILL

A will is a conveyance that is prepared and executed by the property owner during life, but which does not "speak" or operate until the date of the owner's death. Thus, a will is "ambulatory," meaning that it can be revoked or modified so long as the testator is alive. Some special situations arise when there is a change in the status of the property or beneficiaries between the time the will is executed and the testator's death.

1. Ademption

If property is specifically devised or bequeathed in the testator's will, but the testator no longer owns that property at the time of death, the gift is adeemed. This means that the gift *fails* and is not replaced by other property. The reason that the property is no longer owned by the testator generally does not matter; i.e., it does not matter whether the testator sold the property or it was accidentally destroyed.

Example: T owns Blackacre and executes a will devising "Blackacre to my daughter Mary." Prior to his death, T sells Blackacre to A and deposits the proceeds of the sale in a bank account. Upon T's death, Mary is not entitled to Blackacre or to its proceeds. Note that if the will had provided for T's executor to sell Blackacre and distribute the proceeds to Mary, she would be entitled to the proceeds even though the sale occurred before T's death.

a. Not Applicable to General Devises
Ademption does not apply unless the gift mentioned specific property. A specific devise or legacy is one that can be satisfied only by the delivery of a particular item; it cannot be satisfied by money. Thus, a bequest of "$10,000," or even of "$10,000 to be paid out of the sale of my IBM stock" cannot be adeemed.

b. Not Applicable to Land Under Executory Contract
If the testator enters into an enforceable contract of sale of property after making a specific devise of it by will, the doctrine of *equitable conversion* holds that the testator's interest is converted into personal property. Logically, an ademption has occurred, and the proceeds of sale when the closing occurs should not pass to the specific devisee of the property. The traditional case law agrees, but the Uniform Probate Code and statutes in many states have reversed this result. Then, when property subject to a specific devise is placed under contract of sale before the decedent's death, the proceeds of the sale will pass to the specific devisee. [*See* UPC §2-606]

Example: T owns Blackacre and executes a will devising "Blackacre to my daughter Mary." Prior to his death, T enters into a contract to sell Blackacre to A. After T's death the contract is completed, and A pays the purchase price for the land. Mary is entitled to the purchase price in substitution of the land itself.

1) No Ademption If Decedent Incompetent When Contract Formed
If the decedent is unable to enter into the contract, and instead it is entered into by a guardian, attorney in fact, or other representative, courts usually do not apply the equitable doctrine, and they allow the proceeds of the sale to pass to the specific devisee.

c. Other Proceeds Not Subject to Ademption
When property is damaged or destroyed before the testator's death but the casualty insurance proceeds are not paid until after the testator's death, ademption does not usually apply. The beneficiary of the specific bequest takes the insurance proceeds. Similarly, ademption usually does not apply to property condemned by the government when the taking was before death but the condemnation award was paid after death.

d. Partial Ademption
If the testator specifically devises property and then sells or gives away a part of that property, only that portion is adeemed; the remainder passes to the devisee.

2. Exoneration
At common law and in some states today, if a testator makes a specific devise of real estate that is subject to a mortgage or other lien, the devisee is entitled to have the land "exonerated" by the payment of the lien from the testator's residuary estate. Thus, the property will pass to the devisee free of encumbrances. However, a majority of states have, by statute, abolished the exoneration doctrine. In these states, the property will pass to the devisee

subject to a preexisting mortgage or other lien unless the will expressly provides for a payoff of the lien. [*See* UPC §2-607]

3. **Lapse and Anti-Lapse Statutes**

A lapse occurs when the beneficiary of a gift in a will *dies before the testator*. Under the common law, if a lapse occurred, the gift was *void*. However, nearly all states now have statutes that prevent lapse by permitting the gift to pass to the predeceasing beneficiary's living descendants under certain circumstances. These statutes vary as to the scope of beneficiaries covered.

a. **Degree of Relationship to Testator**

Many of the anti-lapse statutes apply only when the named beneficiary is a descendant of the testator. Others apply if the beneficiary is more remotely related, such as a descendant of the testator's grandparent. Others apply to any relative, and still others apply to any beneficiary at all.

1) **Descendants Are Substituted**

The anti-lapse statute does not save the gift for the predeceasing beneficiary's estate; rather it substitutes the beneficiary's descendants for the beneficiary. Thus, property will never pass under the anti-lapse statute to a predeceasing beneficiary's spouse. The property passes to the beneficiary's descendants under the method of distribution (e.g., per stirpes, per capita) used by the state's intestate succession (inheritance) statute.

b. **Application to Class Gifts**

Ordinarily, if a gift is made by will to a class (e.g., "to my children," or "to the descendants of my brother Bob"), and some members of the class die before the testator, the gift is simply given to the surviving members of the class. However, if class members within the coverage of an anti-lapse statute predecease the testator leaving surviving issue, the statute will apply, and the issue will take the deceased class member's share of the gift.

c. **Anti-Lapse Statute Does Not Apply If Contrary Will Provision**

The anti-lapse statute does not apply if there is a contrary will provision—e.g., if the gift is contingent on the beneficiary's surviving the testator.

VII. SECURITY INTERESTS IN REAL ESTATE

A. **TYPES OF SECURITY INTERESTS**

A security interest in real estate operates to secure some other obligation, usually a promise to repay a loan, which is represented by a promissory note. If the loan is not paid when due, the holder of the security interest can either take title to the real estate or have it sold and use the proceeds to pay the debt with accrued interest and any legal and court costs. Of the six types of security interests, the first three are most important.

1. **Mortgage**

The debtor/notemaker is usually the mortgagor; he gives the mortgage (along with the note) to the lender, who is the mortgagee. But note that the debtor and mortgagor can be different people (e.g., a mother agrees to place a mortgage on her house to secure a loan to her daughter). Most states require that a lender realize on the real estate to satisfy the debt only by having a judicial (court-ordered) foreclosure sale conducted by the sheriff.

2. **Deed of Trust**

The debtor/notemaker is the trustor. The trustor gives the deed of trust to a third-party trustee, who is usually closely connected with the lender (e.g., the lender's lawyer, affiliated corporation, or officer). In the event of default, the lender (termed the beneficiary) instructs the trustee to proceed with foreclosing the deed of trust by sale. Many states allow the sale to be either judicial (as with a mortgage) or nonjudicial, under a "power of sale" clause that authorizes the trustee to advertise, give appropriate notices, and conduct the sale personally.

3. **Installment Land Contract**

In an installment land contract, the debtor is the purchaser of the land who signs a contract with the vendor, agreeing to make regular installment payments until the full contract price (including accruing interest) has been paid. Only at that time will the vendor give a deed transferring legal title to the purchaser. In case of default, the contract may contain a forfeiture clause providing that the vendor may cancel the contract, retain all money paid to date, and retake possession of the land. However, the defaulting purchaser may be entitled to restitution to the extent his payments exceed the vendor's damages. (*See* F., *infra*.)

4. **Absolute Deed—Equitable Mortgage**

A landowner needing to raise money may "sell" the land to a person who will pay cash and may give the "buyer" an absolute deed rather than a mortgage. This may seem to be safer than a mortgage loan to the creditor and may seem to have tax advantages. However, if the court concludes, by clear and convincing evidence, that the deed was really given for security purposes, they will treat it as an "equitable" mortgage and require that the creditor *foreclose* it by judicial action, like any other mortgage. This result will be indicated by the following factors: (i) the existence of a *debt or promise of payment* by the deed's grantor; (ii) the grantee's *promise to return the land* if the debt is paid; (iii) the fact that the amount advanced to the grantor/debtor was much *lower than the value of the property*; (iv) the degree of the grantor's *financial distress*; and (v) the parties' *prior negotiations*.

5. **Sale-Leaseback**

A landowner needing to raise money may sell her land to another for cash and may then lease the land back for a long period of time. As in the case of the absolute deed, the grantor/lessee may attack such a transaction later as a disguised mortgage. Factors that will lead the court to such a result are: (i) the fact that the regular rent payments on the lease are virtually identical to payments that would be due on a mortgage loan; (ii) the existence of an option to repurchase by the grantor/lessee; and (iii) the fact that the repurchase option could be exercised for much less than the probable value of the property at that time, so that the repurchase would be very likely to occur.

6. **Equitable Vendor's Lien**

In addition to an installment land contract (3., *supra*) and a purchase money mortgage (E.2.b.3), *infra*, a seller may finance the buyer's purchase of the land by an equitable vendor's lien. The lien does not result from an agreement, but rather arises by implication of law when the seller transfers title to the buyer and the purchase price or a portion of the purchase price remains unpaid.

B. TRANSFERS BY MORTGAGEE AND MORTGAGOR
All parties to a mortgage or deed of trust can transfer their interests. Ordinarily, the mortgagor transfers by deeding the property, while the mortgagee usually transfers by indorsing the note and executing a separate assignment of the mortgage. The note and mortgage must pass to *the same person* for the transfer to be complete.

1. Transfer by Mortgagee

a. Transfer of Mortgage Without Note
The case law is divided, with some states holding that the transfer of the mortgage automatically transfers the note as well, unless the mortgagee-transferor expressly reserves the rights to the note (which there would rarely be any reason for the mortgagee to do). In these states, the transferee of the mortgage can then file an equitable action and compel a transfer of the note as well. Other states hold that, because the note is the principal evidence of the debt, a transfer of the mortgage without the note is a nullity and is void.

b. Transfer of Note Without Mortgage
The *note can be transferred without the mortgage*, but the mortgage will automatically follow the properly transferred note, unless the mortgagee-transferor expressly reserves the rights to the mortgage (which there would rarely be any reason for the mortgagee to do). No separate written assignment of the mortgage is necessary, although it is customary for the transferee to obtain and record an assignment of the mortgage.

1) Methods of Transferring the Note
The note may be transferred either by indorsing it and delivering it to the transferee, or by a separate document of assignment. Only if the former method is used can the transferee become a holder in due course under UCC Article 3.

a) Holder in Due Course Status
To be a holder in due course of the note, the following requirements must be met:

(1) The note must be *negotiable in form*, which means that it must be payable "to bearer" or "to the order of" the named payee. It must contain a promise to pay a fixed amount of money (although an adjustable interest rate is permitted), and no other promises, except that it may contain an acceleration clause and an attorneys' fee clause.

(2) The original note must be *indorsed* (i.e., signed) by the named payee. Indorsement on a photocopy or some other document is not acceptable.

(3) The original note must be *delivered* to the transferee. Delivery of a photocopy is not acceptable.

(4) The transferee must take the note in *good faith* and must pay *value* for it. ("Value" implies an amount that is more than nominal, although it need not be as great as the note's fair market value.) The transferee *must not have any notice* that the note is overdue or has been dishonored, or that the maker has any defense to the duty to pay it.

b) **Benefits of Holder in Due Course Status**

A holder in due course will take the note free of any personal defenses that the maker might raise. "Personal defenses" include failure of consideration, fraud in the inducement, waiver, estoppel, and payment. The holder in due course is, however, still subject to "real" defenses that the maker might raise. These include infancy, other incapacity, duress, illegality, fraud in the execution, forgery, discharge in insolvency, and any other insolvency.

2) **Effect of Payment to Original Mortgagee After Transfer of Note**

Under the version of the UCC enacted in a large majority of states, if the original payee transfers possession of a negotiable instrument, a payment to the original payee will not count, and the holder of the instrument can still demand payment. [*See* UCC §3-602 (1995)] However, many notes secured by mortgages on real property are not negotiable in form (e.g., because their promise to pay is conditional or they are not payable to "bearer" or "order"). If the original mortgagee transfers possession of a ***nonnegotiable*** note, the mortgagor's payment to the original mortgagee ***is effective*** against the transferee ***until the mortgagor receives notice*** of the transfer. [Restatement (Third) of Property: Mortgages §5.5]

Example: A borrows $50,000 from B and gives B a nonnegotiable note for that amount, secured by a mortgage on Blackacre. One year later, B assigns the note and mortgage to C, transferring actual possession of the note to C. Two years thereafter, A, who does not realize that B no longer holds the note, pays $50,000 plus interest to B. This payment is effective against C. C's recourse is against B.

2. **Transfer by Mortgagor—Grantee Takes Subject to Mortgage**

If the mortgagor sells the property and conveys a deed, the grantee takes subject to the mortgage, which remains on the land. Unless there is a specific clause in the mortgage, the mortgagee has no power to object to the transfer.

a. **Assumption**

Often the grantee signs an assumption agreement, promising to pay the mortgage loan. If she does so, she becomes ***primarily*** liable to the lender (usually considered a third-party beneficiary), while the ***original*** mortgagor becomes secondarily liable as a ***surety***. Note, however, that the mortgagee may opt to sue either the grantee or the original mortgagor on the debt. If the mortgagee and grantee modify the obligation, the original mortgagor is completely discharged of liability.

b. **Nonassuming Grantee**

A grantee who does not sign an assumption agreement does not become personally liable on the loan. Instead, the original mortgagor remains primarily and personally liable. However, if the grantee does not pay, the mortgage may be foreclosed, thus wiping out the grantee's investment in the land.

c. **Due-on-Sale Clauses**

Most modern mortgages contain "due-on-sale" clauses, which purport to allow the lender to demand full payment of the loan if the mortgagor transfers any interest in the property without the lender's consent. Such clauses are designed to both: (i) protect the lender from sale by the mortgagor to a poor credit risk or to a person likely to commit waste; and (ii) allow the lender to raise the interest rate or charge an "assumption fee" when the property is sold. Federal law preempts state law and makes due-on-sale clauses enforceable for all types of institutional mortgage lenders on all types of real estate. The preemption does not apply to isolated mortgage loans made by private parties.

C. DEFENSES AND DISCHARGE OF THE MORTGAGE

1. Defenses to Underlying Obligation

Because a mortgage is granted to secure an obligation, if the obligation is unenforceable so is the mortgage. Therefore, defenses in an action on the underlying obligation are defenses against an action on the mortgage, including: (i) failure of consideration, (ii) duress, (iii) mistake, or (iv) fraud.

2. Consumer Protection Defenses to Foreclosure

Rules and regulations designed to protect consumers from unfair lending practices became extremely common after the 2008 foreclosure crisis. These rules provide mortgagors defenses in foreclosure proceedings.

a. Consumer Rights When Mortgage Is Signed

The Dodd-Frank Wall Street Reform and Consumer Protection Act ("Dodd-Frank Act") requires residential mortgage lenders to determine a mortgagor's ability to repay before extending a loan. The terms of the loan must be understandable and not unfair, deceptive, or abusive. The Act also prohibits a lender from steering mortgagors to transactions not in their interest in an effort to increase the lender's compensation. [15 U.S.C. §§1639b, 1639c] The mortgagor can assert violations of the ability to repay or anti-steering provisions as a defense in a foreclosure proceeding. [15 U.S.C. §1640(k)]

b. Consumer Rights During Foreclosure Process

After a mortgagor has defaulted on a mortgage, the mortgagee must, in good faith, consider a request made by the mortgagor for a modification of the mortgage or other alternative to foreclosure. The mortgagee cannot file an action to foreclose in court while such a request is pending, and if the request is made after the action is filed, the mortgagee cannot proceed to foreclosure sale until the request is resolved. [24 C.F.R. §203.606]

c. Choice of Law

The law of the state in which the property is located governs mortgages. So, while a mortgagee might be tempted to include a choice of law clause in a mortgage that selects the law of a state that has less stringent foreclosure consumer protection laws, such clauses are generally void.

3. Discharge of the Mortgage

A mortgagee's right to foreclose is precluded by anything amounting to a discharge of the mortgage, such as payment of the debt secured, merger of the legal and equitable interests, or the acceptance by the mortgagee of a deed in lieu of foreclosure tendered by the mortgagor.

a. Payment

Generally, full payment of the note discharges the mortgage lien. The agreement in the note, however, will normally govern whether the mortgagor may prepay the obligation.

If the note or mortgage does not provide for prepayment, the mortgagor has **no right to prepayment**. The mortgage may also provide for a prepayment fee or a total prohibition of prepayment for part or all of the mortgage term. *Note:* The Dodd-Frank Act prohibits prepayment penalties on certain loans (e.g., adjustable rate, interest-only). [15 U.S.C. §1639c(c)]

b. **Merger**

A mortgage lien vests the mortgagee with either an equitable interest (lien theory) or a legal interest (title theory), while the mortgagor retains the other interest (*see* D.1., *infra*). If the mortgagee subsequently acquires the mortgagor's interest, the mortgage is said to merge with the title, and the mortgagor's personal liability on the underlying debt is discharged up to the value of the land.

c. **Deed in Lieu of Foreclosure**

The mortgagor may also tender to the mortgagee a deed in lieu of foreclosure. In effect, the mortgagor simply turns over her equity of redemption (*see* E.1.a., *infra*) to the mortgagee. Acceptance of a deed in lieu of foreclosure permits the mortgagee to take immediate possession without the formalities of a foreclosure sale. Although it is common to negotiate a complete release from the debt, the parties also have the option to negotiate a mortgagor's agreement to remain liable on some portion of the debt. Mortgagors cannot be compelled to tender such a deed, and mortgagees have the right to refuse the deed and proceed to foreclosure.

D. **POSSESSION BEFORE FORECLOSURE**

When a mortgagor defaults on his debt, the mortgagee can sue on the debt or foreclose on the mortgage. A mortgagee may wish to take possession of the property, or begin receiving the rents from the property, before foreclosure. This is especially important in states where foreclosure is a lengthy process.

1. **Theories of Title**

The mortgagee may have a right to take possession before foreclosure, depending on the theory the state follows.

a. **The Lien Theory**

According to the lien theory, the mortgagee is considered the holder of a **security interest only** and the mortgagor is deemed the owner of the land until foreclosure. A majority of the states follow this theory, which provides that the mortgagee may not have possession before foreclosure.

b. **The Title Theory**

Under the title theory, legal **title is in the mortgagee** until the mortgage has been satisfied or foreclosed. A minority of states follow this theory, which provides that the mortgagee is entitled to possession upon demand at any time. In practice, this means that as soon as a default occurs, the mortgagee can take possession.

c. **The Intermediate Theory**

The intermediate theory is a compromise position in which legal **title is in the mortgagor until default**, and upon default, legal title is in the mortgagee. Only a handful of states follow this theory, which provides that the mortgagee may demand possession when a default occurs. There is little practical difference between this theory and the title theory.

2. Mortgagor Consent and Abandonment

All states agree that the mortgagee may take possession if the mortgagor gives consent to do so, or if the mortgagor abandons the property.

3. Risks of Mortgagee in Possession

The mortgagee who takes possession prior to foreclosure can intercept the rents, prevent waste, make repairs, and lease out vacant space. However, despite these advantages, most mortgagees do not wish to take possession because of the liability risks it presents. These risks include a very strict duty to account for all rents received, a duty to manage the property in a careful and prudent manner, and potential liability in tort to anyone injured on the property.

4. Receiverships

Instead of becoming a "mortgagee in possession," most mortgagees attempt to intercept the rents before foreclosure by getting a receiver appointed by the court to manage the property. Courts will generally appoint receivers for rental property upon a showing of some combination of three factors: (i) that waste is occurring, (ii) that the value of the property is inadequate to secure the debt, and (iii) that the mortgagor is insolvent.

E. FORECLOSURE

Foreclosure is a process by which the mortgagor's interest in the property is terminated. The property is generally sold to satisfy the debt in whole or in part (foreclosure by sale). Almost all states *require* foreclosure by sale. All states allow *judicial sale*, while about one-half also allow nonjudicial sale under a *power of sale*. The nonjudicial sale is often permitted with deeds of trust but not with mortgages. Foreclosure sales are conducted by auction, with the highest bidder taking the property. The lender may bid at the sale, and in many cases the lender is the sole bidder. (*Note:* For convenience, the discussion below speaks of mortgagors and mortgagees, but the same principles apply to deed-of-trust trustors and beneficiaries.)

1. Redemption

a. Redemption in Equity

At any time *prior to the foreclosure sale*, the mortgagor has the right to redeem the land or free it of the mortgage by paying off the amount due, together with any accrued interest. If the mortgagor has defaulted on a mortgage or note that contains an "acceleration clause" permitting the mortgagee to declare the full balance due in the event of default, the full balance must be paid in order to redeem. A mortgagor's right to redeem her own mortgage cannot be waived in the mortgage itself; this is known as "clogging the equity of redemption" and is prohibited. However, the right can be waived later for consideration.

b. Statutory Redemption

About half the states give the mortgagor (and sometimes junior lienors) a statutory right to redeem for some fixed period after the foreclosure sale has occurred; this period is usually six months or one year. The amount to be paid is usually the foreclosure sale price, rather than the amount of the original debt. Be careful to distinguish equitable redemption, which is universally recognized (but only up to the date of the sale), from statutory redemption, which is only recognized by about half the states and applies only *after* foreclosure has occurred.

2. Priorities

Generally, the priority of a mortgage is determined by the time it was placed on the property. When a mortgage is foreclosed, the buyer at the sale will take title as it existed when the mortgage was placed on the property. Thus, foreclosure will terminate interests junior to the mortgage being foreclosed but will not affect senior interests.

a. Effect of Foreclosure on Various Interests

1) Junior Interests Destroyed by Foreclosure

Foreclosure destroys all interests junior to the mortgage being foreclosed. In other words, junior mortgages, liens, leases, easements, and all other types of interests will be wiped out. If a lien senior to that of the mortgagee is in default, the junior mortgagee has the right to pay it off (i.e., redeem it) in order to avoid being wiped out by its foreclosure. Thus, those with interests subordinate to those of the foreclosing party are *necessary parties* to the foreclosure action. Failure to include a necessary party results in the preservation of that party's interest despite foreclosure and sale.

2) Senior Interests Not Affected

Foreclosure does not affect any interest senior to the mortgage being foreclosed. *The buyer at the sale takes subject to such interest.* She does not become personally liable on such senior interests, but she will be forced to pay them in order to prevent their foreclosure in the future.

b. Modification of Priority

As noted above, priorities among mortgages on the same real estate are normally determined simply by *chronology*: the earliest mortgage placed on the property is first in priority, the next mortgage is second, and so on. However, the chronological priority may be changed in the following ways:

1) Failure to Record

If the first mortgagee fails to record, and the second mortgagee records, gives value, and takes without notice of the first, the second mortgagee will have priority over the first by virtue of the normal operation of the recording acts.

2) Subordination Agreement

A first mortgagee may enter into an agreement with a junior mortgagee, subordinating its priority to the junior mortgagee. Such agreements are generally enforced. However, a broad promise to subordinate to any mortgage (or a vaguely described mortgage) to be placed on the property in the future may be considered too inequitable to enforce.

3) Purchase Money Mortgages

A purchase money mortgage ("PMM") is a mortgage given to:

(i)   The vendor of the property as a part of the purchase price; or

(ii)   A third-party lender who is lending the funds to allow the buyer to purchase the property.

A PMM, whether recorded or not, has priority over mortgages, liens, and other claims against the mortgagor that arise ***prior*** to the mortgagor's acquisition of title. However, PMM priority is subject to being defeated by ***subsequent*** mortgages or liens by operation of the recording acts or may be altered through a subordination agreement. [Restatement (Third) of Property: Mortgages §7.2; Slodov v. United States, 436 U.S. 238 (1978)]

Example: A properly records a judgment lien against O (which will attach to any after-acquired property of O). O finances the purchase of Blackacre with a $250,000 loan from B. B does not record its mortgage. A few months later, O borrows $10,000 from C in exchange for a mortgage on Blackacre. C records her mortgage. B's PMM has priority over A's lien because the lien arose before O acquired title to Blackacre (i.e., the general priority rule governing PMMs), but it is junior to C's mortgage under any recording act because C had no notice of B's interest and recorded first.

a)   **Vendor PMM vs. Third-Party PMM**
As between two PMMs, one to the vendor and one to a third-party lender, the vendor's mortgage is usually given priority over the third-party lender's. Because both PMMs arise from the same transaction, neither is treated as "subsequent" under the Restatement. Thus, the recording acts do not apply unless ***only one*** party has notice of the other. However, some jurisdictions that do not follow the Restatement allow the recording acts to determine priority between all PMMs.

b)   **Third-Party PMM vs. Third-Party PMM**
If two PMMs are given to two third-party lenders, their priority is deter-mined by the chronological order in which the mortgages were placed on the property, the recording act, and a subordination agreement (if any). Note that in these cases, the recording acts are often of no use because two purchase money mortgagees will almost always know of each other's existence and, thus, have notice.

4)   **Modification of Senior Mortgage**
Suppose there are two mortgages on the land. The landowner enters into a modification agreement with the senior mortgagee, raising its interest rate or otherwise making it more burdensome. The junior mortgage will be given ***priority over the modification***. For example, if the first mortgage debt is larger because of the modification, the second mortgage gains priority over the increase in the debt.

5)   **Optional Future Advances**
In general, a mortgage may obligate the lender to make further advances of funds after the mortgage is executed, and such advances will have the same priority as the original mortgage. However, if a junior mortgage is placed on the property and the senior lender later makes an "optional" advance while having

notice of the junior lien, the advance will lose priority to the junior lien. An optional advance is one that the senior lender is not contractually bound to make. Numerous states have reversed this rule by statute, but it remains the majority view.

6) Subrogation

A mortgage taken out for the purpose of ***refinancing*** a preexisting senior mortgage takes the priority position of the senior mortgage.

Example: Bank A holds a $100,000 senior mortgage on a tract of land owned by O. Bank B holds a $50,000 second mortgage on the same land. Bank C loans O $100,000, secured by a new mortgage, which O immediately uses to pay off Bank A's mortgage. Bank C now has the senior mortgage, and Bank B still has the junior mortgage. Note that Bank B has not been harmed: Bank C's mortgage simply replaced Bank A's.

3. Proceeds of Sale

The proceeds of the foreclosure sale are used first to pay expenses of the sale, attorneys' fees, and court costs; then to pay the principal and accrued interest on the ***loan that was foreclosed***; next to pay off any ***junior liens*** or other junior interests in the order of their priority; and finally, any remaining proceeds are distributed to the ***mortgagor***. In many cases, there is no surplus remaining after the principal debt is paid off.

4. Deficiency Judgments

If the proceeds of the sale are insufficient to satisfy the mortgage debt, the mortgagee can bring a personal action against the mortgagor/debtor for the deficiency. However, a number of states limit the deficiency that can be recovered to the difference between the debt and the property's fair market value when the fair market value is higher than the foreclosure price. Other states prohibit deficiency judgments entirely on PMMs and on deeds of trust that are foreclosed by power of sale.

Examples: 1) Assume that land has a fair market value of $50,000 and is subject to three mortgages executed by its owner, whose name is MR. The mortgages have priorities and secure outstanding debts in the amounts shown below, which are owed to three different creditors, ME1, ME2, and ME3:

Assume that Mortgage 1 is foreclosed, and the bid at the sale is $50,000 (the fair value of the land). How will the funds be distributed?

In an actual case, the funds would first be used to pay any attorneys' fees and expenses of the foreclosure, and then to any accrued interest on Mortgage 1. However, we will assume that these items are zero.

The $50,000 in funds from the sale will then be used to pay off the mortgages in the order of their priority. Thus, $30,000 is applied to fully pay off Mortgage 1. Then, $15,000 is applied to fully pay off Mortgage 2. There is a remaining balance from the foreclosure sale of $5,000, which is applied toward payment of Mortgage 3. Because this is not enough to discharge Mortgage 3 fully, ME3 is left with a deficiency of $5,000, and may sue MR for a personal judgment in this amount unless state anti-deficiency statutes prohibit it.

2) Assume the same facts as above, except that the bid at the sale is $60,000 rather than $50,000. This will allow full payment of Mortgage 1 ($30,000), Mortgage 2 ($15,000), and Mortgage 3 ($10,000), and will leave a surplus of $5,000. Assuming there are no further liens or encumbrances on the property, this $5,000 will be paid over to MR, the mortgagor.

3) Now assume the same facts as in the original problem, except that it is Mortgage 2 that is being foreclosed. Mortgage 1 exists, but it is either not in default or its holder has not yet taken action to foreclose it.

Recall from the outline above that ***foreclosure does not affect any interest senior to the mortgage being foreclosed***. Thus, foreclosure of Mortgage 2 will not affect Mortgage 1, which will continue to exist on the property in the hands of the foreclosure sale purchaser. Such a purchaser will not be personally liable to pay Mortgage 1 off, but as a practical matter, if Mortgage 1 is not paid, sooner or later ME1 will foreclose it. Hence, the buyer at the foreclosure sale of Mortgage 2 will have a strong economic incentive to pay Mortgage 1; otherwise, she will be subjected to the foreclosure action of ME1, and may well lose much or all of her investment in the property.

What will a wise bidder at the foreclosure sale on Mortgage 2 bid? The maximum is $20,000, which is the fair value of the land ($50,000) minus the amount the successful bidder will subsequently have to pay to discharge Mortgage 1 ($30,000).

If the bid at the foreclosure sale of Mortgage 2 is $20,000, how will the money be distributed? None of it will go to ME1, because he still has his mortgage on the property. $15,000 of the funds will be applied to fully pay off Mortgage 2, and $5,000 will remain to be applied against the $10,000 balance owed on Mortgage 3 (which is, of course, wiped out by the foreclosure of Mortgage 2). ME3 will still have a $5,000 deficiency, as in the first example above.

5. Marshaling

When a property is being foreclosed upon by a mortgagee whose mortgage interest covers multiple parcels, the holder of a junior interest may ask the court for an order to marshal assets.

a. Two-Funds Rule

An order of marshaling means that the foreclosing mortgagee of multiple parcels must proceed against parcels on which *no subordinate interests* exist before those on which subordinate interests exist. [*See* Restatement (Third) of Property (Mortgages) §8.6(a)(1)]

Example: O borrows $150,000 from Bank1, giving Bank1 a promissory note for that amount, secured by a mortgage on both Blackacre and Whiteacre. Subsequently, O borrows an additional sum from Bank2, giving a mortgage on Blackacre alone to secure repayment of that debt. O defaults in payment on the note secured by the first mortgage, and Bank1 initiates a foreclosure proceeding on Blackacre and Whiteacre. At Bank2's request, Bank1 will be required to foreclose first on Whiteacre and may foreclose on Blackacre only if the proceeds of the foreclosure on Whiteacre are insufficient to fully discharge the debt owed to Bank1.

b. Order for Parcels with Subordinate Interests

As among parcels on which subordinate interests exist, those with subordinate *interests created more recently are foreclosed upon first*. [*See* Restatement (Third) of Property (Mortgages) §8.6(a)(2)]

c. Does Not Affect Priorities

Marshaling merely affects the order of foreclosure, and does not prevent the mortgagee from taking action as to any of the parcels if all are needed to satisfy the obligation. Marshaling also does not alter existing priorities among mortgages, or between mortgages and other interests in the property.

F. INSTALLMENT LAND CONTRACTS

Installment contracts may provide for forfeiture rather than foreclosure as the vendor's remedy in the event of default. However, because forfeiture is often a harsh remedy, the courts have tended to resist enforcing forfeiture clauses and in doing so have developed the following theories:

1. Equity of Redemption

Several states allow the contract purchaser who is in default to pay off the accelerated full balance of the contract and to keep the land. In other words, they grant the purchaser a grace period. This is roughly analogous to the equity of redemption in mortgage law. A few states have statutory schedules of grace periods, which often provide for a longer time if a greater percentage of the total price has been paid.

2. **Restitution**

A number of decisions allow actions by the vendor for forfeiture of the land but require her to refund to the purchaser any amount by which his payments exceed the vendor's damages. The court may measure these damages by the property's fair rental value while the purchaser was in possession or by any drop in market value since the contract was executed.

3. **Treat as a Mortgage**

A few states, by statute or case law, now treat installment contracts like mortgages, at least for purposes of the vendor's remedies. In effect, the vendor must foreclose the contract by judicial sale in order to realize on the real estate, and she cannot simply reclaim the land.

4. **Waiver**

Many cases hold that where a vendor has established a pattern of accepting late payments from the purchaser, she cannot suddenly insist on strict on-time payment and declare a forfeiture if such payment is not forthcoming. Such a pattern is said to constitute a waiver of strict performance. To reinstate strict performance, the vendor must send the purchaser a notice of her intention to do so and must allow a reasonable time for the purchaser to make up any late payments and to get back "on stream."

5. **Election of Remedies**

It is commonly held that the vendor who elects to pursue a forfeiture cannot also bring an action for damages or for specific performance. The vendor must choose only one remedy and forgo all others.

VIII.   RIGHTS INCIDENTAL TO OWNERSHIP OF LAND (NATURAL RIGHTS)

A.   IN GENERAL

The owner of real property has the exclusive right to use and possess the surface, the airspace, and the soil of the property. This right is subject to restrictions in the chain of title (e.g., easements and covenants), to the law of nuisance, and to any valid laws or regulations that restrict the use of the land (e.g., zoning ordinances).

B.   RIGHT TO LATERAL AND SUBJACENT SUPPORT OF LAND

1. **Right to Lateral Support**

Ownership of land carries with it the right to have the land supported in its *natural state* by adjoining land. This normally means a right to have one's land undisturbed by withdrawal of support (e.g., by excavations on adjoining land).

a. **Support of Land in Natural State**

A landowner is *strictly liable* if his excavation causes adjacent land to subside (i.e., slip or cave in). Thus, he will be liable even if he used the utmost care.

b. **Support of Buildings on Land**

If land is improved by buildings and an adjacent landowner's excavation causes subsidence, the adjacent landowner will be *strictly liable* for damages to the land and buildings caused by the excavation only if it is shown that the land would have collapsed in its natural state (i.e., that it would have collapsed in the absence of the buildings and improvements). Even if the land would not have collapsed in its natural state (i.e., the collapse would not have occurred except for the weight of the buildings), the excavating landowner is liable for loss or damage to the land and buildings if his excavation is found to have been done **negligently**. (Tort rules apply here.)

2. **Right to Subjacent Support**

When a landowner conveys to a grantee the right to take minerals from beneath the land, the grantor retains the right to have the surface supported unless the conveyance expressly includes authority to destroy the surface if "reasonably necessary" to extract the mineral.

a. **Support of Land and Buildings**

This right of support extends not only to the land in its natural state but also to all buildings existing on the date when the subjacent estate is severed from the surface. However, the underground occupant is liable for damages to subsequently erected buildings only if he was **negligent**.

b. **Interference with Underground Waters**

Note that an underground occupant is liable for negligently damaging springs and wells, whereas an adjoining landowner is not liable for interfering with underground percolating waters.

C. **WATER RIGHTS**

Different rules apply depending on whether the water rights claimed involve (i) water in watercourses (e.g., streams, rivers, and lakes, including underground watercourses); (ii) ground or percolating water (e.g., water normally pumped or drawn from wells); or (iii) surface water (e.g., rainfall, seepage). Exam questions normally concern who has priority to use the water from watercourses and from the ground, and to what extent a landowner may obstruct or divert the flow of surface water.

1. **Watercourses**

There are two major systems for allocation of water in watercourses: (i) the **riparian doctrine** (generally applied in the eastern states where water is or was relatively abundant), and (ii) the **prior appropriation doctrine** (generally used in the 17 western states where water is relatively scarce).

a. **Riparian Doctrine**

Under the riparian doctrine, water does not belong to the public generally or to the state (with certain exceptions) but rather to the "riparian" proprietors who own land bordering on the watercourse. All of these landowners have "riparian rights" and none can use the water so as to deprive the others of these rights.

1) **What Land Is Riparian**

Under the **majority rule**, all tracts held under unity of ownership are riparian if the tracts are contiguous and **any** of them front on the water. Thus, if a riparian owner purchases a parcel which is contiguous to the riparian parcel, riparian rights attach to the newly acquired parcel. The **minority rule** limits riparian rights to the smallest tract of land ever owned abutting the water. Under this view, if a back portion of a riparian tract is sold, it becomes nonriparian and can never regain riparian rights.

a) Riparian Owner

Riparian owners include the fee owner of the abutting land and, to the extent of their title, lessees and easement owners of such land.

b) Doctrine Applies Only to Riparian Parcel

The riparian doctrine permits use of water only in connection with activities carried out on the riparian parcel. Riparian rights cannot be conveyed for the use of nonriparian land nor can they be lost by nonuse.

2) Nature of Riparian Right

a) Natural Flow Theory

Under the "natural flow" theory, a riparian owner is entitled to the water in the bordering stream or lake subject to the limitation that *he may not substantially or materially diminish its quantity, quality, or velocity*. Thus, a downstream owner can enjoin an upstream owner's use even though the downstream owner has plenty of water for his own use. No state appears to adhere strictly to this theory because it operates to limit beneficial upstream use and leads to "waste" of the resource.

b) Reasonable Use Theory

Under the more common theory, all riparian owners share the right of "reasonable use." The general idea is that the right of each riparian owner to use the stream (e.g., to divert for irrigation, to pollute, etc.) is subject to a like reasonable right in other riparian owners. *Each riparian owner must submit to reasonable use* by other riparian owners, and a downstream owner cannot enjoin such use by an upstream owner unless it substantially interferes with the needs of those who have a like right (i.e., unless actual damage is shown).

(1) Factors to Consider

In determining whether an owner's use of water is "reasonable," courts generally balance the utility of the use against the gravity of the harm. (Note the analogy to nuisance law.) Six factors are helpful in this balancing process: (i) the *purpose* of the questioned use; (ii) the *destination* to which the water is taken for use; (iii) the *extent* of the use; (iv) the *pollution* of water by use; (v) whether the use involves an *alteration* in the manner of flow; and (vi) *miscellaneous* types of conduct that may give rise to litigation. (These factors may be remembered more easily by using the acronym MAPPED.)

c) Natural vs. Artificial Use

Under either of the above theories, water use is categorized as "natural" or "artificial." Natural uses include those necessary for the daily sustenance of human beings (e.g., household consumption, gardening, minimal number of livestock). All other uses, including irrigation and manufacturing, are artificial. ***Natural uses prevail over artificial.*** Upper riparians can take all that they need for natural uses. However, they cannot take for artificial purposes unless there is enough water for the domestic wants of all.

b. Prior Appropriation Doctrine

Under the prior appropriation doctrine, the water belongs initially to the state, but the right to divert and use it can be acquired by an individual whether or not he is a riparian owner. Initially, individual rights were established by actual use; thus, each appropriator acquired a vested property right "to divert a given quantity of water, at given times from a given place, to use at a given place for a given purpose."

1) Factors to Note for Bar Exam

Present day acquisition and governance of rights under this doctrine are largely dealt with under complex state-administered permit systems that are too detailed for coverage here. However, it is sufficient for bar examination purposes to note that: (i) appropriative rights were originally determined simply by priority of beneficial use; (ii) if there is a decrease in stream flow, priority is accorded in terms of time of appropriation (i.e., the junior appropriators in descending order of priority must suffer); (iii) in many states, an appropriative right can be severed from the land it serviced when acquired and transferred (i.e., can be sold to another for use on other land), provided no injury is caused to existing uses; and (iv) an appropriative right (unlike a riparian one) can be lost by abandonment (intent and nonuse).

c. Accretion and Avulsion

A watercourse may affect a property's boundary line through accretion or avulsion. (*See* VI.B.3.e.2), *supra.*)

2. Groundwater

If water comes from an underground watercourse (e.g., a defined stream or river), the riparian or prior appropriation doctrines apply. However, the presumption is that underground water is percolating (i.e., the water moves through the ground diffusely and is usually withdrawn by wells from the underground water table). There are four different rules for determining rights in underground water.

a. Absolute Ownership Doctrine

The absolute ownership doctrine is followed by only a few states. The owner of the land overlying the source basin may extract as much water as she wishes and use it for whatever purpose she desires (including export). There is no firmly established system for allocation among overlying owners.

b. Reasonable Use Doctrine

The reasonable use doctrine, followed by many eastern states, allows the surface owner to make "reasonable use" of the groundwater. This rule differs from the absolute ownership rule mainly with respect to exporting water off site: Exporting is allowed only to the extent that it does not harm other owners who have rights in the same aquifer. On the other hand, virtually all beneficial uses of water ***on the land*** are considered reasonable and are allowed.

c.   Correlative Rights Doctrine

In some states, the owners of overlying land own the underground water basin as joint tenants, and each is allowed a reasonable amount for her own use.

    d.   Appropriative Rights Doctrine

In many western states, the prior appropriation doctrine applies to groundwater as well as watercourses. Priority of use determines appropriative rights. In most western states, rights to percolating water are now determined by a state water board which controls annual yield, prohibits water waste, etc.

    e.   Restatement Approach

A few states follow the Restatement approach, which is based on principles of nuisance law. This approach allows the surface owner to pump groundwater for a beneficial purpose unless the withdrawal: (i) unreasonably causes harm to neighboring landowners through lowering of the water table; (ii) exceeds the pumper's reasonable share of the annual supply or total store of groundwater; or (iii) directly and substantially affects surface waters and unreasonably causes harm to a surface water user. [Restatement (Second) of Torts §858]

3.   Surface Waters

Diffused surface waters are those that have no channel but pass over the surface of the land. The source may be rainfall, melting snow, seepage, etc. A landowner can use surface waters within her boundaries for any purpose she desires. Problems concern the right of a lower owner to restrict a flow that would naturally cross his land (e.g., by dikes) and the right of an upper owner to alter or divert a natural flow onto other lands (e.g., by drains, channels, or sloughs). The acting landowner's liability to other landowners depends upon which doctrine the state follows.

    a.   Natural Flow Theory

Under the natural flow theory, followed by many states, a landowner cannot refuse to take natural drainage, cannot divert surface water onto the land of another, and cannot alter the rate or manner of natural flow where such actions would injure others above or below him. Because this theory imposes substantial impediments on development (e.g., no paving, large roofs, culverts, etc.), most states have "softened" the rule to permit *reasonable* changes in natural flow. And a few states have held the doctrine inapplicable to urban property (because development would otherwise be hindered).

    b.   Common Enemy Theory

Under the common enemy theory, followed by many states, surface water is a common enemy and any owner can build dikes or change drainage to get rid of it. However, many courts have modified the doctrine and have held landowners to a standard of ordinary care to avoid unnecessary and negligent injury to the land of others.

    c.   Reasonable Use Theory

The growing trend is to apply the reasonable use doctrine which, as in nuisance and watercourse cases, requires balancing the utility of the use against the gravity of the harm. Judicial mitigation of both the natural flow and common enemy doctrines often results in an approximation of the reasonable use theory.

d.   Compare—Capture of Surface Water
    A landowner can capture (e.g., by dam, rain barrels) as much surface water as he wishes. It can be diverted to any purpose on or off the land. Owners below have no cause of action unless the diversion is malicious.

D.   RIGHTS IN AIRSPACE

The right to the airspace above a parcel is not exclusive, but the owner is entitled to freedom from excessive noise and transit by aircraft. If flights are so low as to be unreasonably disturbing, they constitute a trespass or (if the airport is government-owned) a taking by inverse condemnation.

E.   RIGHT TO EXCLUDE—REMEDIES OF POSSESSOR

1.   Trespass

If the land is invaded by a *tangible* physical object that interferes with the right of exclusive possession, there is a trespass.

2.   Private Nuisance

If the land is invaded by *intangibles* (e.g., odors or noises) that substantially and unreasonably interfere with a private individual's use or enjoyment of her property, the possessor may bring an action for private nuisance.

    a.   Compare—Public Nuisance
    Public nuisance is an invasion by intangibles that unreasonably interfere with the health, safety, or property rights of the *public*—i.e., a broad segment of the community, rather than one or a few individuals.

3.   Continuing Trespass

If the land is repeatedly invaded by a trespasser (e.g., the invader repeatedly swings a crane over the property), the possessor may sue for either trespass or nuisance.

4.   Law or Equity

If the possessor wants to force the invader to stop the invasion of the property, the remedy is an injunction in equity. If the possessor wants damages, the remedy is an action at law.

    a.   Ejectment
    The remedy at common law to remove a trespasser from the property is ejectment.

    b.   Unlawful Detainer
    In the landlord-tenant situation, the landlord may force the tenant to vacate the premises by the statutory remedy of unlawful detainer. (In some states, the term used to describe this action is forcible detainer or summary ejectment.) The action may be joined with a demand for money damages in rent due.

IX.   COOPERATIVES, CONDOMINIUMS, AND ZONING

A.   COOPERATIVES

In the most common form of housing cooperative, title to the land and buildings is held by a corporation that leases the individual apartments to its shareholders. Thus, the residents in a cooperative are both tenants of the cooperative (by virtue of their occupancy leases) and owners of the cooperative (by virtue of their stock interests). Stock interests in the cooperative are not transferable apart from the occupancy lease to which they are attached.

1. Restriction on Transfer of Interests

Because the members of a cooperative are tenants, the cooperative may retain the same controls over assignment and sublease of the apartments as may be exercised by any other landlord.

2. Mortgages

Permanent financing is provided through a blanket mortgage on the entire property owned by the cooperative corporation (land and buildings). This mortgage has priority over the occupancy leases. Failure to meet the payments on the blanket mortgage may result in the termination of the leases through foreclosure of the mortgage. Thus, each cooperative tenant is vitally concerned that the other tenants pay their shares of the blanket mortgage.

3. Maintenance Expenses

Ordinarily, cooperative tenants are not personally liable on the note or bond of the blanket mortgage. However, under their occupancy leases, each tenant is liable for her proportionate share of all of the expenses of the cooperative (including payments on the mortgage as well as other operating expenses).

B. CONDOMINIUMS

In a condominium, each owner owns the interior of her individual unit plus an undivided interest in the exterior and common elements.

1. Restriction on Transfer of Interests

Because condominium unit ownership is treated as fee ownership, the ordinary rules against restraints on alienation apply. A few jurisdictions (e.g., New York) by statute allow reasonable restraints on transfer of condominium units.

2. Mortgages

Each unit owner finances the purchase of her unit by a separate mortgage on her unit. Consequently, unit owners need not be as concerned about defaults by others as they must be in a cooperative.

3. Maintenance Expenses

Each unit owner is personally liable on her own mortgage and each pays her own taxes (unlike the cooperative situation, but like any other homeowner). In addition, each unit owner is liable to contribute her proportionate share to the common expenses of maintaining the common elements, including insurance thereon.

4. Homeowners' Associations

A homeowners' association (sometimes called a condominium association) oversees the common elements of a condominium property. The common elements include the exterior of the building, common staircases, landscaping, the front gate, etc. The association is usually a legal entity, such as a corporation or LLC.

a. **Membership**

The owner of each condominium is a member of the homeowners' association. The members vote to elect a board. The board either oversees the common elements directly or hires a management company to oversee them.

b. **Fees**

Each condominium unit owner must pay regular (e.g., monthly) fees to the homeowners' association which are used by the association to maintain the common elements. If the monthly fees are insufficient to pay necessary expenses (e.g., a major repair to the roof of the building is needed), the association may impose an additional one-time fee (sometimes called a special assessment) that each member must pay.

c. **Association Rules**

Most homeowners' associations pass charters and bylaws that place requirements or restrictions on each owner's use of her property. For example, bylaws might prevent the ownership of a pet larger than 20 pounds or require balconies to be kept free of trash. These rules are binding on the members and may be enforced either by individual members or by the association itself.

C. ZONING

The state may enact statutes to reasonably control the use of land for the protection of the *health, safety, morals, and welfare* of its citizens. Zoning is the division of a jurisdiction into districts in which certain uses and developments are permitted or prohibited. The zoning power is based on the state's police power and is limited by the Due Process Clause of the Fourteenth Amendment. Other limitations are imposed by the Equal Protection Clause of the Fourteenth Amendment and the "no taking without just compensation" clause of the Fifth Amendment. (*See* Multistate Constitutional Law outline.) Cities and counties can exercise zoning power only if authorized to do so by state *enabling acts*. Ordinances that do not conform to such acts are "ultra vires" (beyond the authority of the local body) and void.

1. **Cumulative Zoning**

There are two types of zoning ordinances: cumulative and noncumulative. A cumulative zoning ordinance creates a hierarchy of uses of land (e.g., a single-family home is a higher use than an apartment building, which is a higher use than a strip mall, which is a higher use than a factory). Under a cumulative zoning ordinance, land that is zoned for a particular use may be used for the stated purpose *or for any higher use*. Under a noncumulative zoning ordinance, land may be used only for the purpose for which it is zoned.

Example: Town zones a strip of vacant land as commercial land. A, who owns land in the strip, wants to build a single-family home there. B, who also owns land in the strip, wants to build a factory. If the ordinance is cumulative, A can build the home, but if it is noncumulative, he cannot build the home. B cannot build the factory, regardless of whether the ordinance is cumulative or noncumulative.

2. **Nonconforming Use**

A use that exists at the time of passage of a zoning ordinance and that does not conform cannot be eliminated at once. Generally, the nonconforming use may continue indefinitely, but any change in the use (e.g., tearing down an old building and replacing it with a new one) must comply with the zoning ordinance. Some statutes provide for ***amortization***—i.e., the gradual elimination of nonconforming uses (e.g., the use must end in 10 years).

3. Special Use Permits

Some unusual uses (e.g., hospitals, funeral homes, etc.) require issuance of a special permit even though the zoning of the particular district (e.g., commercial) allows that type of use.

4. Variance

A variance from the literal restrictions of a zoning ordinance may be granted by administrative action. The property owner must show that the ordinance imposes a unique hardship on him and that the variance will not be contrary to the public welfare.

TORTS

TORTS

TABLE OF CONTENTS

TORTS

I. INTENTIONAL TORTS

A. PRIMA FACIE CASE
To establish a prima facie case for intentional tort liability, it is generally necessary that plaintiff prove the following:

(i)   *Act* by defendant;

(ii) *Intent*; and

(iii) *Causation*.

1.   Act by Defendant
The "act" requirement for intentional tort liability refers to a ***volitional movement*** on defendant's part.

Examples: 1) Chauncey tripped and was falling. To break the fall, Chauncey stretched out his hand, which struck Darby. Even though the movement was reflexive, it nonetheless was one dictated by the mind, and hence will be characterized as volitional.

2) Lulu suffered an epileptic attack. During the course of it, she struck Darby. This is not a volitional act.

3) Chauncey pushed Lulu into Darby. Chauncey has committed a volitional act; Lulu has not.

2.   Intent
The requisite intent for this type of tort liability may be either specific or general.

a.   Specific Intent
An actor "intends" the consequences of his conduct if his ***purpose*** in acting is to bring about these consequences.

b.   General Intent
An actor "intends" the consequences of his conduct if he ***knows with substantial certainty*** that these consequences will result.

Example: D, five years old, pulls a chair out from under P as she is sitting down. Even if D did not desire that she hit the ground, if he knew with substantial certainty that she was trying to sit and would hit the ground, he will have the intent necessary for battery. [Garratt v. Dailey, 279 P.2d 1091 (Wash. 1955)]

c.   Actor Need Not Intend Injury
The intent of the actor that is relevant for purposes of intentional torts is the intent to bring about the consequences that are the basis of the tort. Thus, a person may be liable even for an unintended injury if he intended to bring about such "basis of the tort" consequences.

> *Example:* A intends to push B and does so. B falls and breaks his arm. This conduct gives rise to a cause of action for battery. The "consequences" that are the basis of this tort are harmful or offensive contact to the plaintiff's person. In this case, the actor intended to bring about harmful or offensive contact to B. Hence, he will be liable even though it was not intended that B break his arm.

d. Transferred Intent

1) General Rule

The transferred intent doctrine applies where the defendant intends to commit a tort against one person but instead (i) commits a different tort against that person, (ii) commits the same tort as intended but against a different person, or (iii) commits a different tort against a different person. In such cases, the *intent to commit a tort against one person is transferred to the other tort or to the injured person* for purposes of establishing a prima facie case.

Example: A swings at B, intending only to frighten him. A's blow lands on C. A's intent to commit assault on B is transferred to C, and A's act constitutes a battery on C.

2) Limitations on Use of Transferred Intent

Transferred intent may be invoked only where the tort intended and the tort that results are both within the following list:

a) Assault;

b) Battery;

c) False imprisonment;

d) Trespass to land; and

e) Trespass to chattels.

e. Motive Distinguished

Motive impels a person to act to achieve a result. *Intent* denotes the purpose to use a particular means to effect that result. *Only the intent is relevant* for purposes of establishing the prima facie case. Thus, for example, even though defendant acts without a hostile motive or desire to do any harm, or even where he is seeking to aid the plaintiff, he may be liable.

Note: Evil motive is not an essential element of most torts, but *malice* or ulterior purpose is an essential element of some (e.g., malicious prosecution, abuse of process). Further, malice may sometimes negate a privilege that the defendant might have, and it may permit the recovery of *punitive damages*.

f. Minors and Incompetents Can Have Requisite Intent

Under the majority view, both minors and incompetents will be *liable* for their intentional torts; i.e., they are held to possess the requisite intent.

3. Causation

The result giving rise to liability must have been legally caused by the defendant's act or something set in motion thereby. The causation requirement will be satisfied where the *conduct of defendant is a substantial factor* in bringing about the injury.

Note: Ordinarily, causation will not be at issue in intentional torts cases because it is usually obvious that the defendant's conduct was a substantial factor in causing the harm.

B. PRIMA FACIE CASE—INTENTIONAL TORTS TO THE PERSON

1. Battery

a. Prima Facie Case

To establish a prima facie case for battery, the following elements must be proved:

1) An act by the defendant which brings about *harmful* or *offensive contact* to the plaintiff's person;

2) *Intent* on the part of the defendant to bring about harmful or offensive contact to the plaintiff's person; and

3) *Causation.*

b. Harmful or Offensive Contact

Contact is harmful if it causes actual injury, pain, or disfigurement. Contact is offensive if it would be considered offensive by a *reasonable person* of ordinary sensibilities. Contact is deemed "offensive" if the plaintiff has not expressly or impliedly consented to it (*see* D.1., *infra*).

c. Meaning of "Plaintiff's Person"

For purposes of a battery, anything *connected* to the plaintiff's person is viewed as part of the plaintiff's person.

Example: Chauncey grabbed Lulu's purse, which was hanging from her shoulder. He may be liable for a battery. (He would also be liable if he had grabbed an article of clothing she was wearing, a cane she was holding, etc.)

d. Causation

The defendant is liable not only for "direct" contact, but also for "indirect" contact; i.e., it will be sufficient if he *sets in motion a force* that brings about harmful or offensive contact to the plaintiff's person.

Examples: 1) Chauncey, intending to set a trap, dug a hole in the road upon which Lulu was going to walk. Lulu fell in. Causation exists.

2) Horace struck a glass door so that the breaking glass cut Bowater. Causation exists.

e. Apprehension Not Necessary

A person may recover for battery even though he is not conscious of the harmful or offensive contact when it occurs (e.g., unauthorized surgery performed on unconscious patient).

f. Transferred Intent
The doctrine of transferred intent *applies* in battery cases. Hence, a defendant acting with the intent to commit an assault who causes harmful or offensive contact to the plaintiff has committed a battery.

g. Actual Damages Not Required
It is not necessary to sustain a prima facie case for battery that plaintiff prove actual damages. Plaintiff can recover at least *nominal damages* even though he suffered no severe actual damage. In a majority of jurisdictions, *punitive damages* may be recovered where defendant acted with *malice*.

2. Assault

a. Prima Facie Case
To establish a prima facie case for assault, the following elements must be proved:

1) An act by the defendant creating a *reasonable apprehension* in plaintiff of *immediate harmful* or *offensive contact* to plaintiff's person;

2) *Intent* on the part of the defendant to bring about in the plaintiff apprehension of immediate harmful or offensive contact with the plaintiff's person; and

3) *Causation*.

b. Construction of "Apprehension"

1) Requirement of Reasonableness
The apprehension of harmful or offensive contact must be a reasonable one. Courts generally will not protect a plaintiff against exaggerated fears of contact (unless defendant knows of the unreasonable fear and uses it to put plaintiff in apprehension).

a) Fear, Intimidation, etc., Distinguished
Apprehension is not the same as fear or intimidation. Note that "apprehension" here is used in the sense of *expectation*. Thus, one may reasonably apprehend an immediate contact although he believes he can defend himself or otherwise avoid it.

b) Knowledge of Act Required
Obviously, for there to be an apprehension, the plaintiff must have been aware of the threat from the defendant's act. Contrast this with battery (above), in which the plaintiff need not be aware of the contact at the time thereof.

c) Knowledge of Defendant's Identity Not Required
In contrast, it is not necessary that the plaintiff know who the defendant is at the time of the act; i.e., one only need apprehend an immediate harmful or

offensive contact, not the identity of the person who is directing this unpermitted force at him.

d) Defendant's Apparent Ability to Act Is Sufficient

A person may be placed in reasonable apprehension of immediate harmful or offensive contact even though the defendant is *not actually capable* of causing injury to the plaintiff's person. For such apprehension to be reasonable, however, it is necessary that the defendant have the apparent ability to bring about such contact.

Example: Jan points an unloaded gun at Myron. Myron does not know that the gun is not loaded. Myron's apprehension of immediate harmful or offensive contact is reasonable.

e) Effect of Words

(1) Overt Act Required

Some overt act is necessary. Words alone, however violent, generally do not constitute an assault because they cannot create a reasonable apprehension of immediate harmful or offensive contact. A different result might occur when such words are accompanied by some overt act, e.g., a clenching of the fist. Moreover, *words may negate an assault* by making unreasonable any apprehension of immediate contact, even though the defendant commits a hostile act.

Example: James shakes a clenched fist while talking to Myron, and says, "If I weren't such a good guy, I'd hit you." There is no reasonable apprehension of harmful or offensive contact.

(2) Conditional Threat Is Sufficient

Note that if the words and act combine to form a conditional threat, an assault will result.

Example: Robber points a gun at Plaintiff and says, "Your money or your life." Robber is liable for an assault.

2) Requirement of Immediacy

The apprehension must be of immediate harmful or offensive contact. Threats of future contact are insufficient. Similarly, there is no assault if the defendant is too far away to do any harm or is merely preparing for a future harmful act.

c. Causation

Plaintiff's apprehension must have been legally caused by the defendant's act or something set in motion thereby, either directly or indirectly.

d. Transferred Intent

The doctrine of transferred intent *applies* to assault cases. Hence, a defendant acting with the intent to commit a battery who causes the plaintiff to reasonably apprehend immediate harmful or offensive contact has committed an assault.

e. No Requirement of Damages

It is not necessary to prove actual damages to sustain a prima facie case for assault. If the case is otherwise made out, plaintiff can recover **nominal damages**. Most states allow **punitive damages** to be awarded where defendant's actions have been malicious.

3. False Imprisonment

a. Prima Facie Case
To establish a prima facie case for false imprisonment, the following elements must be proved:

1) An act or omission to act on the part of the defendant that **confines** or **restrains** the plaintiff to a **bounded** area;

2) **Intent** on the part of the defendant to confine or restrain the plaintiff to a bounded area; and

3) **Causation**.

b. Sufficient Methods of Confinement or Restraint
Actionable confinement or restraint may result in a variety of ways. The following should be noted:

1) Physical Barriers
Defendant may falsely imprison plaintiff by confining him through the use of physical barriers.

2) Physical Force
False imprisonment will result where plaintiff is restrained by the use of physical force directed at **him** or a member of his **immediate family**. An action may also lie if the force is directed against **plaintiff's property**.
Example: Lulu remained in a building because her purse had been confiscated by Chauncey. She could have left the building but that would have necessitated leaving the purse behind. False imprisonment could result if the purse was wrongfully withheld.

3) Direct Threats of Force
Direct threats of force by the defendant to the plaintiff's person or property or against persons of the plaintiff's immediate family can constitute false imprisonment.

4) Indirect Threats of Force
False imprisonment can also arise from indirect threats of force, i.e., acts or words that **reasonably** imply that the defendant will use force against plaintiff's person or property or persons of plaintiff's immediate family.

5) Failure to Provide Means of Escape
Where plaintiff has lawfully come under defendant's control and it would be impossible to leave without defendant's assistance (and it was understood between the parties that such assistance would be forthcoming), the withholding of such assistance with the intent to detain plaintiff will make defendant liable. In short,

the courts impose an ***affirmative duty*** on the defendant to take steps to release the plaintiff. If defendant intentionally breaches this duty, this is sufficient for false imprisonment. But, of course, it must first be established that defendant owes such a duty.

Examples: 1) Jailer refused to release a prisoner at the end of his jail sentence. Jailer may be liable for false imprisonment.

2) Plaintiff is imprisoned for failing to produce corporate records. Defendant has the records but is under no legal duty to produce them and refuses to do so. There is no false imprisonment.

6)   Invalid Use of Legal Authority

The invalid use of legal authority amounts to false imprisonment if it results in a confinement of plaintiff.

a)   False Arrests

An action for false imprisonment does ***not*** lie for an arrest or a detention made by virtue of legal process duly issued by a court or official having jurisdiction to issue it. However, where an arrest by a police officer or private citizen for a criminal offense ***without a warrant*** is unlawful (i.e., not privileged), it may constitute false imprisonment.

(1)   When Arrests Are Privileged

(a)   Felony Arrests Without Warrant

A felony arrest without a warrant by a ***police officer*** (or a private citizen acting at the officer's direction) is valid if the officer has ***reasonable grounds*** to believe that a felony has been committed and that the person arrested has committed it. Such an arrest by a ***private person*** will be privileged only if a felony has ***in fact*** been committed and the private person has reasonable grounds for believing that the person arrested has committed it.

(b)   Misdemeanor Arrests Without Warrant

Both police officers and private citizens are privileged for misdemeanor arrests without a warrant if the misdemeanor was a ***breach of the peace*** and was committed in the presence of the arresting party. (Note that in most states, police officers have a broader statutory privilege of arrest for ***any*** misdemeanor committed in their presence.)

(c)   Arrests to Prevent a Crime Without a Warrant

Where a felony or breach of the peace is in the process of being, or reasonably appears about to be, committed, both police officers and private citizens are privileged to make an arrest.

(2)   Amount of Force Allowable

(a) Felony Arrest

For felony arrests, both police officers and private citizens may use that degree of force reasonably necessary to make the arrest; however, deadly force is permissible only when the suspect poses a threat of serious harm to the arresting party or others.

(b) Misdemeanor Arrest

For misdemeanor arrests, both police officers and private citizens are privileged to use only that degree of force necessary to effect the arrest, but never deadly force.

b) "Shoplifting" Detentions Are Privileged

What if a shopkeeper suspects someone of shoplifting and detains that individual to ascertain whether this is the case? He may be liable for false imprisonment. But if he does nothing and permits the suspect to simply leave the premises, the merchandise and all possibilities of proving theft will be lost. Hence, by statute in some states and case law in others, shopkeepers have been given a privilege to detain for investigation. For the privilege to apply, the following conditions must be satisfied:

(1) There must be a *reasonable belief* as to the fact of theft;

(2) The detention must be conducted in a *reasonable manner* and only nondeadly force can be used; and

(3) The detention must be only for a *reasonable period of time* and only for the purpose of making an investigation.

c. Insufficient Forms of Confinement or Restraint

As stated above, restraints or confinements produced by requiring the plaintiff to choose between injury to his person or property and his freedom of motion are generally actionable. However, a cause of action will not be sustained for all forms of restraint or confinement.

1) Moral Pressure

A cause of action will not be sustained if a person remains in the area merely because he is responding to the exertion of moral pressure.

2) Future Threats

Similarly, a cause of action will not be sustained if a person remains in the area in response to future threats against person or property.

d. No Need to Resist

Plaintiff is not under any obligation to resist physical force that is being applied to confine him. Similarly, where there is a threat of force, he is not obligated to test the threat where the defendant has the apparent ability to carry it out.

e. Time of Confinement

It is *immaterial*, except as to the extent of damages, how short the time period of the confinement is.

f.   Awareness of Imprisonment

Most American cases hold that awareness of confinement is a necessary element of the tort. The Restatement provides an exception to this requirement where the person confined is actually injured by the confinement (e.g., an infant locked in a bank vault for several days).

g.   What Is a Bounded Area?

For an area to be "bounded," the plaintiff's freedom of movement in *all directions* must be limited; e.g., merely blocking plaintiff's access to a portion of a park does not constitute false imprisonment. The area will *not* be characterized as "bounded" if there is a *reasonable means of escape* of which plaintiff is aware.

h.   Causation

Plaintiff's confinement must have been legally caused by the defendant's act or something set in motion thereby, either directly or indirectly.

i.   Transferred Intent

The doctrine of transferred intent *applies* to false imprisonment.

j.   No Requirement of Damages

It is not necessary to prove actual damages to sustain a prima facie case for false imprisonment. Again, if defendant's conduct was motivated by malice, plaintiff may also be entitled to punitive damages.

k.   False Imprisonment and Malicious Prosecution Distinguished

One who participates in, procures, or instigates an unlawful arrest without proper authority may be liable for false arrest. Note that merely giving information to the police about the commission of a crime, leaving to the police the decision whether to make an arrest, does not constitute false imprisonment, as long as one stops short of instigating the arrest. Whether the defendant instigated the arrest or merely furnished information to the police is a question for the trier of fact. Where information only is given, there may be liability for malicious prosecution (*see* II.E.1., *infra*), if not for false imprisonment.

4.   Intentional Infliction of Emotional Distress

a.   Prima Facie Case

To establish a prima facie case for intentional infliction of emotional distress, the following elements must be proved:

1)   An act by defendant amounting to *extreme* and *outrageous conduct*;

2)   Intent on the part of defendant to cause plaintiff to suffer *severe* emotional distress, or *recklessness* as to the effect of defendant's conduct;

3)   *Causation*; and

4)   *Damages—severe* emotional distress.

b. Extreme and Outrageous Conduct

1) Some Courts Reluctant to Recognize Tort
This tort covers those situations where the defendant intentionally "shocks" the plaintiff but there is *no physical injury* or threat thereof. Some states have been reluctant to recognize this as a cause of action because of the difficulty of proving "shock" (and the ease with which it could be falsified), the speculative nature of the damage, and fear of a flood of litigation.

2) Liability Limited by Requiring Proof of Outrageous Conduct
To protect against potential abuses, the courts will limit liability for this tort to those situations where "outrageous conduct" on the part of the defendant is proved. "Outrageous conduct" is *conduct that transcends all bounds of decency* tolerated by society. In the absence of such conduct by the defendant, it is generally held that an average person of ordinary sensibilities would not suffer the kind of severe mental injury that is contemplated by the tort.

3) Examples of Outrageous Conduct

a) Extreme Business Conduct
Certain extreme methods of business conduct may be construed as outrageous conduct, e.g., use of extreme methods of collection, if repeated, may be actionable.

b) Misuse of Authority
Misuse of authority in some circumstances may be actionable, e.g., school authorities threatening and bullying pupils.

c) Offensive or Insulting Language
Generally, offensive or insulting language will *not* be characterized as "outrageous conduct." This result could change if there is a *special relationship* between plaintiff and defendant or a *sensitivity* on plaintiff's part of which defendant is aware. (*See* below.)

4) Special Relationship Situations
Common carriers and *innkeepers* owe special duties to their patrons that will be a basis for liability even when the act is something less than outrageous, e.g., bus driver making insulting remarks to passenger.

5) Known Sensitivity
If defendant knows that plaintiff is more sensitive and thus more susceptible to emotional distress than the average person, liability will follow if the defendant uses extreme and outrageous conduct intentionally to cause such distress and succeeds. These rules may also apply where defendant's conduct is directed at individuals in certain groups such as children, pregnant women, and elderly people.

c. Intent
Defendant will be liable not only for intentional conduct but also for *reckless* conduct, i.e., acting in reckless disregard of a high probability that emotional distress will result.

d. Causation
The defendant's conduct must have proximately caused the plaintiff's emotional distress.

1) Intent/Causation Requirements in Bystander Cases
When the defendant intentionally causes severe, *physical* harm to a third person and the plaintiff suffers severe *emotional* distress because of her relationship to the injured person, the elements of intent and causation may be harder to prove. To establish these elements in such cases, the plaintiff is generally required to show the following:

(i)   The plaintiff was *present* when the injury occurred to the other person;

(ii)   The plaintiff was a *close relative* of the injured person; and

(iii)   The *defendant knew* that the plaintiff was present and a close relative of the injured person.

Note: The plaintiff does not need to establish presence or a family relationship if she shows that the defendant had a *design or purpose* to cause severe distress to plaintiff.

Example: Defendant called Susan and threatened to kill Mike, with whom Defendant knew Susan was living. Defendant then made good his threat. Liability will attach when Susan suffers severe emotional distress by showing that Defendant's *purpose* was to cause her severe distress, even though she was not a relative of Mike and was not present when he was murdered.

2) Special Liability for Mishandling Corpses
In an analogous situation, many courts have allowed recovery where the mental distress resulted from the intentional or reckless mishandling of a relative's corpse. Although this cause of action is almost always for emotional distress arising from action directed toward another (the corpse), the courts have created a special category of liability for such conduct.

e. Actual Damages Required
Actual damages are required (nominal damages will not suffice). But it is *not* necessary to prove *physical injuries* to recover. It is, however, necessary to establish *severe* emotional distress (*i.e.*, more than a reasonable person could be expected to endure). Punitive damages are allowable where defendant's conduct was improperly motivated.

C. PRIMA FACIE CASE—INTENTIONAL TORTS TO PROPERTY

1. Trespass to Land

a. Prima Facie Case
To establish a prima facie case for trespass to land, the following elements must be proved:

1) An act of *physical invasion* of plaintiff's real property by defendant;

2) *Intent* on defendant's part to bring about a physical invasion of plaintiff's real property; and

3) *Causation*.

b. Physical Invasion of Plaintiff's Land

1) What Constitutes "Physical Invasion"?
The interest protected by this tort is the interest in exclusive possession of realty. Hence, all that is necessary to satisfy this element is that there be a physical invasion of plaintiff's land.

a) Defendant Need Not Enter onto Land
It is not necessary that the defendant personally come onto the land; e.g., trespass exists where defendant floods plaintiff's land, throws rocks onto it, or chases third persons onto it.

b) Lawful Right of Entry Expires
A trespass to land may also exist where defendant remains on plaintiff's land after an otherwise lawful right of entry has lapsed.

2) If No Physical Object Enters Land
If no physical object has entered onto plaintiff's land, e.g., damage resulted from blasting concussions, the courts generally do not treat the controversy as a trespass case. Rather, they treat it as a *nuisance* case or as a case of *strict liability* if ultrahazardous activities are involved.

3) What Constitutes "Land"?
The trespass may occur on the surface of the land, below the surface, or above it.

Courts generally construe plaintiff's "land" to include air space and subsurface space to the height or depth plaintiff can make beneficial use of such space. Thus, for example, one could commit a trespass by stringing wires over the land, flying an airplane at low altitudes over it, tunneling under it, etc.

c. Intent Required
Mistake as to the lawfulness of the entry is *no defense* as long as defendant intended the entry upon that particular piece of land. Intent to trespass is not required—*intent to enter onto the land* is sufficient.

Example: Relying on boundary markers fixed by a reputable surveyor, Farmer clears land for cultivation that he believes to be his. In fact, the survey was in error and Farmer cleared a portion of Neighbor's land. Farmer is liable to Neighbor for trespass to land.

d. Who May Bring Action?
An action for trespass may be maintained by *anyone in actual or constructive possession* of the land. This is so even if that possession is without title. If no one is in possession, the *true owner* is presumed in possession and may maintain the action.

If the action is maintained by a *lessee*, some decisions allow him to recover only to the extent that the trespass damages the leasehold interest. Other cases allow a full recovery for all damage done to the property, but require the lessee to account to the lessor for excess over damages to the leasehold.

e. Causation
The physical invasion of plaintiff's property must have been legally caused by the defendant's act or something set in motion thereby.

f. Transferred Intent
The doctrine of transferred intent *applies* to trespass to land.

g. No Requirement of Damages
As with most other intentional torts, damage is presumed; i.e., actual injury to the land is *not* an essential element of the cause of action.

Example: Tom intentionally bounced a tennis ball against the side of a building owned by Owen. Although no damage was done to Owen's building, Tom is liable for trespass. In contrast, if Tom had accidentally but negligently hit Owen's building with the ball, Tom would not be liable unless Owen established damages as part of the negligence prima facie case.

2. Trespass to Chattels

a. Prima Facie Case
To establish a prima facie case of trespass to chattels, the following elements must be proved:

1) An act by defendant *interfering with plaintiff's right of possession* in the chattel;

2) *Intent to perform the act* bringing about the interference with plaintiff's right of possession;

3) *Causation*; and

4) *Damages*.

b. Act by Defendant
Trespass to chattels is designed to protect a person against interferences with his *right to possess* his chattels. Hence, any act of interference will suffice. These generally take two forms:

1) **Intermeddling**
An intermeddling is conduct by defendant that in some way serves to directly damage plaintiff's chattels, e.g., denting plaintiff's car, striking plaintiff's dog.

2) **Dispossession**
A dispossession is conduct on defendant's part serving to dispossess plaintiff of his lawful right of possession.

c. **Intent Required**

Mistake as to the lawfulness of defendant's actions (e.g., a mistaken belief that defendant owns the chattel) is *no defense* to an action for trespass to chattels. Again, as with trespass to land, the intent to trespass is not required—*intent to do the act of interference* with the chattel is sufficient.

d. **Who May Bring Trespass to Chattels Action?**

Anyone with possession or the immediate *right to possession* may maintain an action for trespass to chattels.

e. **Causation**

The interference with plaintiff's possessory interests in the chattel must have been caused by defendant's act or something set in motion thereby.

f. **Actual Damages Required**

As a general rule, nominal damages will not be awarded for trespass to chattels; i.e., in the absence of any actual damages, an action will not lie. However, if the trespass amounts to a dispossession, the loss of possession itself is deemed to be an actual harm.

g. **Transferred Intent**

The doctrine of transferred intent *applies* to trespass to chattels.

h. **Trespass to Chattels and Conversion Distinguished**

As discussed below, conversion grants relief for interferences with a chattel so serious in nature, or so serious in consequences, as to warrant requiring the defendant to pay its full value in damages. For those interferences not so serious in nature or consequences, trespass to chattels is the appropriate action.

3. **Conversion**

a. **Prima Facie Case**

To establish a prima facie case for conversion, the following elements must be proved:

1) An act by defendant *interfering* with plaintiff's right of possession in the chattel;

2) *Intent* to perform the act bringing about the interference with plaintiff's right of possession;

3) *Causation*; and

4) *Damages*—an interference that is serious enough in nature or consequences to warrant that the defendant *pay the full value* of the chattel.

b. **Acts of Conversion**

One can act in such a way as to seriously invade another's chattel interest in a variety of ways. These include:

1) Wrongful acquisition, e.g., theft, embezzlement.

2) Wrongful transfer, e.g., selling, misdelivering, pledging.

3) Wrongful detention, e.g., refusing to return to owner.

4) Substantially changing.

5) Severely damaging or destroying.

6) Misusing the chattel.

c.   Mere Intent to Perform Act Required
The only intent required is the intent to perform the act that interferes with the plaintiff's right of possession. Even if the conduct is wholly innocent, liability may attach where the interference is serious in nature.

1)   Bona Fide Purchaser May Be Liable
Under this principle, even a bona fide purchaser of chattel may become a converter if the chattel had been stolen from the true owner.

2)   Accidental Conduct Insufficient
Accidentally causing damage to or loss of another's chattel does not amount to conversion unless the actor was using the chattel without permission when the accident occurred. (Note that the actor may be liable in negligence for accidental damage.)

d.   Seriousness of Interference or Consequence
Usually, where the interference with possessory rights is insubstantial (e.g., where a person momentarily takes another person's property or merely moves it for her own convenience), the actor is not viewed as asserting sufficient interference for conversion (although it may suffice for trespass to chattels). However, such interference with the possessory rights of another in the chattel, if serious enough, may amount to conversion. Thus, for example, if this person *refuses to return* the chattel when asked, or *alters* it, she may be liable for conversion because her action so seriously interferes with another's chattel rights that it amounts to a claim of dominion and control on the actor's part. No specific rule can be stated for these situations; however, the *longer the withholding period* and the *more extensive the use* of the chattel during this time, the more likely it is that conversion has resulted.

e.   Special Situation of Bailees Receiving Stolen Property
A bailee receiving goods from a thief without notice of the improper taking may return the goods to the thief without liability to the real owner. However, if the bailee has notice and the real owner makes a demand for his goods, the bailee is liable for conversion if she returns the goods to the thief.

f.   Subject Matter of Conversion
Property subject to conversion is limited to tangible *personal property* and *intangibles* that have been *reduced to physical form* (e.g., a promissory note), and documents in which title to a chattel is merged (e.g., a bill of lading or a warehouse receipt). Intangibles such as a bakery route, customer lists, or the goodwill of a business may not be the subject of conversion. Neither may real property be converted.

g. Who May Bring Action for Conversion?
Anyone with *possession* or the *immediate right to possession* may maintain an action for conversion. Possession is viewed as sufficient title against a wrongdoer. However, if the person in possession is not the true owner, she is accountable to the true owner for any recovery to the extent of the owner's interest.

h. Causation
The interference with plaintiff's chattel interests must have been legally caused by the defendant's act or something set in motion thereby.

i. Remedies
The basic conversion remedies are:

1) Damages
The plaintiff is entitled to damages for the *fair market value* of the chattel. This value is generally computed as of the *time and place of conversion*. The defendant is given title upon satisfaction of the judgment so that, in effect, there is a forced sale of the chattel. Note that even if the defendant wishes to return the item, the plaintiff is not obligated to take it back once it has been converted.

2) Replevin
If the plaintiff wishes to have the chattel returned, he may get it by availing himself of the remedy of replevin.

D. DEFENSES TO THE INTENTIONAL TORTS

1. Consent
A defendant is not liable for an otherwise tortious act if the plaintiff consented to the defendant's act. Consent may be given expressly; it may also be implied from custom, conduct, or words, or by law.

a. Express (Actual) Consent
Express (actual) consent exists where the plaintiff has expressly shown a willingness to submit to defendant's conduct.

1) Consent by Mistake
Where a plaintiff expressly consents by mistake, the consent is still a valid defense unless the defendant caused the mistake or knows of the mistake and takes advantage of it.

2) Consent Induced by Fraud
If the expressly given consent has been induced by fraud, the consent generally is *not a defense*. The fraud must, however, go to an essential matter; if it is only with respect to a collateral matter, the consent remains effective.

Examples: 1) Charles expressly consents to balance an apple on his head for Roberta to attempt to shoot it off from 50 yards. She told him she was a professional trick-shot artist, which was not true. Fraud goes to an essential matter; consent is ineffective.

2) Same as above, except that Roberta was in fact a professional trick-shot artist. However, she gave him a $10 bill she knew to be counterfeit. This is a collateral matter; consent is effective.

3) Consent Obtained by Duress
Consent obtained by duress may be held *invalid*. Note, however, that threats of future action or of some future economic deprivation do not constitute legal duress sufficient to invalidate the express consent.

b. Implied Consent
Plaintiff's consent may also be implied in a given case. There are two basic kinds of implied consent, apparent consent and consent implied by law.

1) Apparent Consent
Apparent consent is that which a *reasonable person would infer* from plaintiff's conduct. Thus, for example, somebody who voluntarily engages in a body contact sport impliedly consents to the normal contacts inherent in playing it.

a) Inferred from Usage and Custom
Such consent may also be inferred as a matter of usage or custom. Thus, for example, a person is presumed to consent to the ordinary contacts of daily life, e.g., minor bumping in a crowd.

2) Consent Implied by Law
In some situations, consent may be implied by law where action is necessary to save a person's life or some other important interest in person or property. Thus, for example, consent will be implied in an *emergency* situation where the plaintiff is incapable of consenting and a reasonable person would conclude that some contact is necessary to prevent death or serious bodily harm, e.g., a surgical operation where a person is unconscious after an automobile accident.

c. Capacity Required
Incompetents, drunken persons, and very young children are deemed incapable of consent to tortious conduct. Consent of parent or guardian is necessary to constitute a defense in such a case.

d. Criminal Acts
For purposes of tort liability, the *majority* view is that a person *cannot consent* to a criminal act. A minority and the Restatement of Torts take the contrary position and view consent to a criminal act as a valid defense in a civil action for an intentional tort.

1) Modern Trend
The modern tendency has been to differentiate between illegal acts that are *breaches of the peace*, e.g., a street fight (consent ineffective), and those that are not a breach of the peace, e.g., an act of prostitution (consent effective).

2) Consent Invalid Where Law Seeks to Protect Members of Victim's Class
Where the act is made criminal to protect a limited class against its own lack of

judgment (e.g., statutory rape), consent is not a good defense in an action by a member of that class.

e. Exceeding Consent Given

If the defendant goes beyond the act consented to and does something substantially different, he is *liable*; e.g., consent to perform a tonsillectomy is not consent to perform an appendectomy (unless, of course, an emergency situation is present).

2. Self-Defense

When a person has reasonable grounds to believe that he is being, or is about to be, attacked, he may use such force as is reasonably necessary for protection against the potential injury.

a. When Is Defense Available?

1) Reasonable Belief

The actor need only have a reasonable belief as to the other party's actions; i.e., apparent necessity, not actual necessity, is sufficient. Hence, reasonable mistake as to the existence of the danger does not vitiate the defense.

2) Retaliation Not Allowed

Self-defense is limited to the right to use force to prevent the commission of a tort. Thus, one may never use force in retaliation (where there is no longer any threat of injury).

3) Retreat Not Necessary

A substantial majority of the courts hold that one need not attempt to escape, but may stand his ground (and even use deadly force when necessary to prevent death or serious bodily harm to himself). A growing modern trend would impose a duty to retreat before using deadly force where this can be done safely *unless* the actor is in his own home.

4) Not Available to Aggressor

The initial aggressor is not privileged to defend himself against the other party's reasonable use of force in self-defense. However, if the other uses deadly force against an aggressor who had only used nondeadly force, the aggressor may defend himself with deadly force.

b. How Much Force May Be Used?

One may use only that force that *reasonably* appears to be *necessary to prevent the harm*. One may not use force likely to cause death or serious bodily injury unless he reasonably believes that he is in danger of serious bodily injury. If more force than necessary is used, the actor loses the privilege of self-defense.

c. Extends to Third-Party Injuries

If, in the course of reasonably defending himself, one *accidentally* injures a bystander, he is nevertheless protected by the defense. (He might, however, be liable to the bystander on a negligence theory if his conduct warranted it.) If the actor *deliberately* injures a bystander in trying to protect himself, he probably cannot raise the privilege of self-defense.

3. **Defense of Others**

a. **When Is Defense Available?**
The actor need only have a *reasonable belief* that the person being aided would have the right of self-defense. Thus, even if the person aided has no defense (e.g., if he were the initial aggressor), his defender is not liable as long as he reasonably believed that the person aided could have used force to protect himself.

b. **How Much Force May Be Used?**
The defender, assuming he is justified, may use as much force as he could have used in self-defense if the injury were threatened to him (*see* above).

4. **Defense of Property**

a. **When Is Defense Available?**
Generally, one may use reasonable force to prevent the commission of a tort against her property.

1) **Request to Desist Usually Required**
A request to desist must precede the use of force, unless the circumstances make it clear that the request would be futile or dangerous.

2) **Effect of Mistake**
Reasonable mistake is allowed as to the property owner's right to use force in defense of property where the mistake involves whether an intrusion has occurred or whether a request to desist is required. However, mistake is not allowed where the entrant has a privilege to enter the property that supersedes the defense of property right (*see* 4), below). In such a case the property owner is liable for mistakenly using force against a privileged entrant unless the entrant himself intentionally or negligently caused the mistake (e.g., by refusing to tell the property owner the reason for the intrusion).

3) **Limited to Preventing Commission of Tort**
Defense of property is limited to *preventing the commission of a tort* against the defendant's property. Thus, once the defendant has been permanently dispossessed of the property and the commission of the tort is complete, she may not use force to recapture it. However, where one is in *"hot pursuit"* of someone who wrongfully dispossessed her of her property, the defense still operates because the other is viewed as still in the process of committing the tort against the property.

4) **Superseded by Other Privileges**
Whenever an actor has a privilege to enter upon the land of another because of necessity, right of reentry, right to enter upon another's land to recapture chattels, etc. (discussed below), that privilege supersedes the privilege of the land possessor to defend her property.

b. **How Much Force May Be Used?**
One may use *reasonable* force to defend property. However, she may *not* use force that

will cause death or serious bodily harm. (Of course, if the invasion of property also entails a serious threat of bodily harm to the owner, she may then invoke the defense of self-defense and use deadly force.) Further, one may not use indirect deadly force such as a trap, spring gun, or vicious dog when such force could not lawfully be directly used, e.g., against a mere trespasser.

5. Reentry onto Land

a. Common Law Privilege
In former years, it was held that a person who had been ***tortiously dispossessed*** from her land (by fraud or force) could use ***reasonable force*** to regain possession if she acted promptly upon discovering the dispossession. (Note that this did not apply to a tenant merely overstaying her lease.)

b. Privilege Abolished in Most States
Most states today do not allow resort to "self-help"; one who has been wrongfully excluded from possession of real property may bring an ***ejectment*** action or other summary procedure to recover possession. Hence, the owner who uses force to retake possession is liable for whatever injury she inflicts.

6. Recapture of Chattels

a. When Is Defense Available?
The basic rule is the same as that for land: where another's possession began lawfully (e.g., a conditional sale), one may use only peaceful means to recover the chattel. ***Force*** may be used to recapture a chattel only when in ***"hot pursuit"*** of one who has obtained possession wrongfully, e.g., by theft.

1) Timely Demand Required
A demand to return the chattel must precede the use of force, unless the circumstances make it clear that the demand would be futile or dangerous.

2) Recovery Only from Wrongdoer
The recapture may only be from a tortfeasor or some third person who knows or should know that the chattels were tortiously obtained. If the chattels have come to rest in the hands of an innocent party, this will cut off the actor's privilege to use force to effect recapture.

b. How Much Force May Be Used?
Reasonable force, ***not*** including force sufficient to cause death or serious bodily harm, may be used to recapture chattels.

c. Entry upon Land to Remove Chattel

1) On Wrongdoer's Land
Where chattels are located on the land of the wrongdoer, the owner is privileged to enter upon the land and reclaim them at a ***reasonable time*** and in a ***reasonable manner***. It is generally required that there be a demand for the return of the chattels before any such entry.

2) On Land of Innocent Party

Similarly, when the chattels are on the land of an innocent party, the owner may enter and reclaim her chattel at a ***reasonable time*** and in a ***peaceful manner*** when the landowner has been given ***notice*** of the presence of the chattel and refuses to return it. In this case, the chattel owner will be liable for any actual damage caused by entry.

3) On Land Through Owner's Fault

If the chattels are on the land of another through the owner's fault, there is ***no privilege*** to enter upon the land. They may be recovered only through legal process.

d. Shopkeeper's Privilege

Shopkeepers may have a privilege to reasonably detain individuals whom they reasonably believe to be in possession of "shoplifted" goods. (*See* B.3.b.6)b), *supra.*)

7. Privilege of Arrest

Depending on the facts of the particular case, one may have a privilege to make an arrest of a third person.

a. Invasion of Land

The privilege of arrest carries with it the privilege to enter another's land for the purpose of effecting the arrest.

b. Subsequent Misconduct

Although the arrest itself may be privileged, the actor may still be liable for subsequent misconduct, e.g., failing to bring the arrested party before a magistrate, unduly detaining the party in jail, etc.

c. Mistake

One who makes an arrest under the mistaken belief that it is privileged may be liable for false imprisonment. (*See* B.3.b.6)a), *supra.*)

8. Necessity

A person may interfere with the real or personal property of another where the interference is reasonably and apparently necessary to avoid threatened injury from a natural or other force and where the threatened injury is substantially more serious than the invasion that is undertaken to avert it.

a. Public Necessity

Where the act is for the public good (e.g., shooting a rabid dog), the defense is absolute.

b. Private Necessity

Where the act is solely to benefit a limited number of people (e.g., the actor ties up his boat to another's dock in a storm), the defense is qualified; i.e., the actor must pay for any injury he causes. *Exception:* The defense is absolute if the act is to benefit the owner of the land.

9. Discipline

A parent or teacher may use reasonable force in disciplining children, taking into account the age and sex of the child and the seriousness of the behavior.

II. HARM TO ECONOMIC AND DIGNITARY INTERESTS

In contrast to the intentional torts, the torts in this section involve less tangible harms to a person's relational interests with other persons in society.

Depending on the tort involved, the level of fault required for the prima facie case may range from intent to strict liability.

A. DEFAMATION

1. Prima Facie Case

To establish a prima facie case for defamation, the following elements must be proved:

(i) *Defamatory language* on the part of the defendant;

(ii) The defamatory language must be *"of or concerning" the plaintiff*—i.e., it must identify the plaintiff to a reasonable reader, listener, or viewer;

(iii) *Publication* of the defamatory language by the defendant to a third person; and

(iv) *Damage to the reputation* of the plaintiff.

Where the defamation refers to a public figure or involves a matter of public concern, two additional elements must be proved as part of the prima facie case:

(v) *Falsity* of the defamatory language; and

(vi) *Fault* on defendant's part.

2. Defamatory Language

Defamatory language is language that tends to adversely affect one's reputation. This may result from impeaching the individual's honesty, integrity, virtue, sanity, or the like.

a. Inducement and Innuendo

If the statement standing alone is defamatory, it is defamatory "on its face." However, a statement is also actionable if the defamatory meaning becomes apparent only by adding extrinsic facts. The plaintiff pleads and proves such additional facts as inducement and establishes the defamatory meaning by innuendo. Inducement and innuendo identify to the courts and the parties that extrinsic facts are being introduced to the court by the plaintiff to establish the first element of a prima facie case.

Example: Defendant publishes an erroneous report that Plaintiff has given birth to twins. This is defamatory because Plaintiff pleads and establishes that she had been married only one month.

b. Methods of Defamation
Not all defamation consists of direct remarks. Pictures, satire, drama, etc., may convey an actionable defamatory meaning.

c. Statements of Opinion
While a statement of fact may always be defamatory, a statement of opinion is actionable only if it appears to be based on specific facts, **and** an express allegation of those facts would be defamatory.
Example: The statement "I don't think Robert can be trusted with a key to the cash register" implies personal knowledge of dishonest conduct by Robert, and thus may be actionable.

1) Distinguishing Fact and Opinion
Whether a published statement is one of "fact" or "opinion" depends on the circumstances surrounding the publication and the nature of the words used. Generally, the broader the language used, the less likely that it will be reasonably interpreted as a statement of fact or an opinion based on specific facts.

d. Who May Be Defamed?

1) Individual
Any *living* person may be defamed. Defamation of a deceased person is not actionable.

2) Corporation, Unincorporated Association, and Partnership
In a limited sense, a corporation, unincorporated association, or partnership may also be defamed, e.g., by remarks as to its financial condition, honesty, integrity, etc.

3. "Of or Concerning" the Plaintiff
The plaintiff must establish that a *reasonable* reader, listener, or viewer would understand that the defamatory statement referred to the plaintiff.

a. Colloquium
A statement may be actionable even though no clear reference to the plaintiff is contained on the face of the statement. In such a case, however, the plaintiff is required to introduce additional extrinsic facts that would lead a reasonable reader, listener, or viewer to perceive the defamatory statement as referring to the plaintiff. Pleading and proving such extrinsic facts to show that the plaintiff was, in fact, intended is called "colloquium."

b. Group Defamation
A significant issue is presented with respect to this prima facie case element when the defamatory language refers to a group without identifying any particular individual within that group. In such cases, the following rules operate:

1) All Members of Small Group
Where the defamatory language refers to all members of a small group, each

member may establish that the defamatory statement was made of and concerning him by alleging that he is a member of the group.

2) All Members of Large Group
If, however, the defamatory statement refers to all members of a large group, no member of that group may establish this element of the cause of action.

3) Some Members of Small Group
Where the defamatory language refers to some members of a small group, plaintiff can recover if a reasonable person would view the statement as referring to the plaintiff.

4. Publication
A statement is not actionable until there has been a "publication." The publication requirement is satisfied when there is a *communication to a third person who understood it*.

Example: Libby saw a defamatory statement about Jeffrey printed in Russian. The publication requirement is not met unless it is shown that Libby understood the foreign words.

The communication to the third person may be made either *intentionally or negligently*.

a. Only Intent to Publish Required
Once publication is established, it is no defense that defendant had no idea that she was defaming plaintiff because she neither knew nor had reason to know that plaintiff existed (use of fictional name), nor knew that the publication was defamatory. It is the intent to publish, not the intent to defame, that is the requisite intent.

Example: Defendant published a false statement that Plaintiff had given birth to twins. If Defendant neither knew nor had reason to know that Plaintiff had been married only one month, Defendant is nonetheless liable.

b. Repetition
Each repetition of the defamatory statement is a separate publication for which the plaintiff may recover damages.

c. "Single Publication" Rule—Statute of Limitations
However, as to publication of a defamatory statement in a number of copies of the same newspaper, magazine, or book, most American courts have adopted the "single publication" rule. Under this rule, all copies of a newspaper, magazine, or book edition are treated as only one publication. The publication is deemed to occur when the finished product is released by the publisher for sale (a matter which is, obviously, most important for the running of the statute of limitations). Damages are still calculated on the total effect of the story on all of the readers.

d. Who May Be Liable?

1) Primary Publisher
Each individual who takes part in making the publication is charged with the publication as a primary publisher; e.g., a newspaper or TV station carrying a defamatory message would be viewed as a primary publisher and held responsible

for that message to the same extent as the author or speaker. Note, however, that an Internet service provider is *not* treated as a publisher when a user of its service posts defamatory content.

2) Republisher

A republisher (i.e., one who repeats a defamatory statement) will be held *liable* on the same general basis as a primary publisher. This is so even if the repeater states the source or makes it clear that she does not believe the defamation.

Note: Where there has been a republication, the original defamer's liability may be increased to encompass any new harm caused by the repetition if the republication was either (i) intended by the original defamer or (ii) reasonably foreseeable to her.

3) Secondary Publishers

One who is responsible only for disseminating materials that might contain defamatory matter (e.g., a vendor of newspapers, a player of a tape) is viewed as a secondary publisher. Such individuals are liable only *if they know or should know* of the defamatory content.

5. Damage to Plaintiff's Reputation

In ascertaining whether this element of the plaintiff's prima facie case has been satisfied, it may be necessary to distinguish between libel and slander. As will be seen below, the burden of proof as to damages (to plaintiff's reputation) may depend on this distinction.

a. General and Special Damages

1) General or Presumed Damages

General damages are presumed by law and need not be proved by the plaintiff. They are intended to compensate the plaintiff for the general injury to her reputation caused by the defamation.

Note: Constitutional free speech and press considerations may restrict an award of presumed damages when the defamation involves matters of "public concern." [Dun & Bradstreet, Inc. v. Greenmoss Builders, Inc., 472 U.S. 749 (1985)] (*See* 7.d.3), *infra.*)

2) Special Damages

Special damages in a defamation law context means that the plaintiff must specifically prove that she suffered *pecuniary loss* as a result of the defamatory statement's effect on her reputation, and are not proved merely by evidence of actual injury—such as the loss of friends, humiliation, or wounded feelings. The loss of a job, a prospective gift or inheritance, an advantageous business relationship, or customers are pecuniary losses such as those contemplated by the special damages requirement.

b. Libel

1) Definition

Libel is a defamatory statement recorded in *writing or* some *other permanent form*. A libel may also be recorded by radio or television in some circumstances. (*See* below.)

2) Damages Rules for Libel

a) General Damages Presumed
In most jurisdictions, general damages are ***presumed by law*** for all libels; i.e., special damages need not be established.

b) Libel Distinction—Minority Position
A substantial minority of courts distinguish between libel per se and libel per quod in determining whether a libel is actionable without proof of special damages.

(1) Libel Per Se—Presumed Damages
These courts take the position that injury to the reputation of the plaintiff is presumed by law only if the statement is libelous and defamatory on its face (libel per se). Thus, such libels are actionable without pleading or proving special damages.

(2) Libel Per Quod—Special Damages Usually Required
The libelous statement that is not defamatory on its face, but that requires reference to extrinsic facts to establish its defamatory content, is characterized as libel per quod by these courts. These courts generally require special damages to be pleaded and proved for such libels.

c. Slander

1) Definition
Slander is ***spoken defamation***. It is to be distinguished from libel in that the defamation is in less permanent and less physical form.

a) Characterization of Repetitions
Where the original defamation is libel, any repetition, even if oral, is also libel. On the other hand, the written repetition of a slander will be characterized as libel.

b) Radio and Television Broadcasts Generally Libel
Most courts today treat defamation in radio and television broadcasts as libel, regardless of whether it was scripted. [*See* Restatement (Third) of Torts §568A]

2) Damages Rules for Slander

a) Special Damages Usually Required
In slander, injury to reputation is ***not presumed***. Thus, ordinary slander is not actionable in the absence of pleading and proof of special damages.

b) **Slander Per Se—Injury Presumed**
If, however, the spoken defamation falls within one of four categories, characterized as slander per se, an injury to reputation is presumed without proof of special damages. These four categories are:

(1) **Business or Profession**
A defamatory statement adversely reflecting on plaintiff's abilities in his business, trade, or profession is actionable without pleading or proof of special damages. Statements that the plaintiff is dishonest or lacks the basic skill to perform his profession or carry out his office are examples of this slander per se category. The statement must, however, directly relate to plaintiff's profession, trade, or business.
Example: Statement about an engineer stating "he is a terrorist" is not directly related to his trade.

(2) **Loathsome Disease**
A defamatory statement that the plaintiff is presently suffering from a loathsome and communicable disease is actionable without pleading or proof of special damages. Historically, this slander per se category has been limited to venereal disease and leprosy.

(3) **Crime Involving Moral Turpitude**
A defamatory statement that the plaintiff is or was guilty of a crime involving moral turpitude is actionable without pleading or proof of special damages. Because common law crimes generally are deemed to involve moral turpitude (e.g., assault, larceny, perjury), this category of slander per se incorporates a large number of statements. Thus, the allegation that a married man has a mistress implies that he is guilty of the crimes of fornication and adultery. The Restatement extends this category to all crimes punishable by imprisonment.

(4) **Unchastity of a Woman**
A defamatory statement imputing unchaste behavior to a woman is actionable without pleading or proof of special damages. The Restatement applies this category to men as well.

d. **"Per Se"**
"Per se" means defamatory on its face when used in libel actions and means slander within one of the four categories when used in slander actions.

6. **Falsity**
At common law, a defamatory statement was presumed to be false. The Supreme Court, however, has rejected this presumption in all cases in which the plaintiff is constitutionally required to prove some type of fault (*see* below). In these cases, the plaintiff must prove as an element of the prima facie case that the statement was false. [Philadelphia Newspapers, Inc. v. Hepps, 475 U.S. 767 (1986)]

a. **Exam Approach**
Even where the statement is true, it may nonetheless give rise to liability if it is uttered

under circumstances sufficient to constitute intentional infliction of severe emotional distress or invasion of the right to privacy; hence, consider these torts as well when your exam question presents potentially defamatory statements. However, where the plaintiff is a public figure or the matter is one of public concern, and recovery for defamation would be barred on First Amendment grounds, he will not be allowed to rely on these other tort theories. [Snyder v. Phelps, 562 U.S. 443 (2011)]

7. Fault on Defendant's Part

Although at common law defamation liability could be strict, a number of Supreme Court decisions based on the First Amendment now impose a fault requirement in cases involving public figures or matters of public concern. The degree of fault to be established depends on the type of plaintiff, i.e., whether he is a public official or public figure as compared with a private person involved in a matter of public concern.

a. Public Officials—Actual Malice Required

A public official may not recover for defamatory words relating to his official conduct in the absence of "clear and convincing" proof that the statement was made with "actual malice." (*See* below.) [New York Times v. Sullivan, 376 U.S. 254 (1964)]

b. Public Figures—Actual Malice Required

The rule of *New York Times v. Sullivan* has been extended to cover litigation where the plaintiff is a public figure. [Associated Press v. Walker, 388 U.S. 130 (1967); Curtis Publishing Co. v. Butts, 388 U.S. 130 (1967)]

1) What Constitutes a Public Figure?

A person may be deemed a "public figure" on one of two grounds: (i) where he has achieved *such pervasive fame or notoriety* that he becomes a public figure for all purposes and contexts (e.g., celebrity sports figure); or (ii) where he voluntarily assumes a *central role* in a particular *public controversy* (e.g., prominent community activist) and thereby becomes a "public figure" for that limited range of issues. [Gertz v. Robert Welch, Inc., 418 U.S. 323 (1974)]

In *Gertz*, the Court indicated that it might be possible for a person to become a public figure through no purposeful action of his own, but considered such instances to be "exceedingly rare." Subsequent cases support this interpretation. [Time, Inc. v. Firestone, 424 U.S. 448 (1976); Hutchinson v. Proxmire, 443 U.S. 111 (1979); Wolston v. Reader's Digest Association, 443 U.S. 157 (1979)]

c. What Is Actual Malice?

1) Test

Actual malice was defined by the Supreme Court in *New York Times v. Sullivan* as:

a) *Knowledge* that the statement was false, *or*

b) *Reckless disregard* as to its truth or falsity.

2) What Constitutes "Knowledge or Reckless Falsity"?

It must be shown that the defendant was subjectively aware that the statement he published was false or that he was subjectively reckless in making the statement. [New York Times v. Sullivan, *supra*]

a) Reckless Conduct—Subjective Standard

"Reckless" conduct is *not* measured by a reasonable person standard or by whether a reasonable person would have investigated before publishing. There must be a showing that the defendant in fact (subjectively) *entertained serious doubts* as to the truthfulness of his publication.

b) Spite, etc., Not Enough

It is not enough that the defendant is shown to have acted with spite, hatred, ill will, or intent to injure the plaintiff.

3) Alteration of Quotation as Actual Malice

A journalist deliberately altering a quotation attributed to a public figure can be found to have "knowledge of falsity" if it can be established that the alteration results in a *material change in the meaning conveyed by the statement*. [Masson v. New Yorker Magazine, 501 U.S. 496 (1991)]

d. Private Persons Need Not Prove Actual Malice

Where the defamatory statement relates to a *nonpublic* person, there is less concern for freedom of speech and press. In addition, private individuals are more vulnerable to injury from defamation because they usually do not have the same opportunities for rebuttal as do public persons. Accordingly, defamation actions brought by private individuals are subject to constitutional limitations only when the defamatory statement involves a matter of "public concern." And even in those cases, the limitations are not as great as those established for public officials and public figures. [Gertz v. Robert Welch, Inc., *supra*]

1) Matters of Public Concern—At Least Negligence Required

When the defamatory statement involves a matter of public concern, *Gertz* imposes two restrictions on private plaintiffs: (i) it prohibits liability without fault, and (ii) it restricts the recovery of presumed or punitive damages.

a) No Liability Without Fault

Where the statement published is such that its defamatory potential was *apparent* to a reasonably prudent person, the plaintiff must show that the defendant permitted the false statement to appear, if not through actual malice, at least through *negligence* as to its truth or falsity.

(1) The Supreme Court has left open the question of what the fault standard would be where the statement published involved *no* apparent defamatory potential (i.e., factual misstatements that are innocent on their face and require proof of extrinsic facts to be defamatory, such as libel per quod).

b) Damages Limited to "Actual Injury"

Assuming the defendant was in fact negligent in ascertaining the truth of what it published—but still it had no actual knowledge of the falsity, nor was it guilty of reckless disregard for the truth—damages can be recovered but are limited to the *"actual injury"* sustained by the plaintiff; i.e., presumed damages are prohibited.

(1) "Actual Injury"

The Supreme Court has deliberately chosen not to define this term, but has stated that it is *not limited to out-of-pocket loss*. It may include impairment of reputation and standing in the community, personal humiliation, and mental anguish and suffering (i.e., an injury to reputation not resulting in special damages may still be actionable). The important point is that there must be *competent evidence* of "actual" injury (no presumed damages), although there need be no evidence that assigns an actual dollar value to the injury.

(2) Presumed Damages or Punitive Damages Allowable Where Actual Malice Found

It follows that if the plaintiff cannot prove "actual injury," he cannot recover any damages, *unless* he can show that the publication was made with knowledge of its falsity or with reckless disregard for the truth. There is no constitutional protection for publications made with "knowledge or reckless falsity," and hence, the plaintiff is entitled to whatever recovery is permitted under state law in such cases (i.e., "presumed" or general damages and even punitive damages in appropriate cases). Note that this approach is simply a restatement of the general rule in torts that damages must be proved in negligence actions (*see infra,* III.E.) but usually are not required where the defendant is more culpable, such as for intentional torts.

2) Matters of Purely Private Concern—No Constitutional Limitations

When the defamatory statement involves a matter of purely private concern, the constitutional limitations established by *Gertz* do *not* apply; only the four elements of the common law prima facie case are required. Thus, presumed and punitive damages might be recoverable even if actual malice is not established. Note, though, that many states now require proof of negligence as a matter of state law even for defamation on matters of private concern.

3) What Is a Matter of Public Concern?

To determine whether the matter is a public or private concern, the courts will look to the content, form, and context of the publication. [Dun & Bradstreet, Inc. v. Greenmoss Builders, Inc., *supra*]

Example: In *Dun & Bradstreet,* the Court determined that a credit agency's erroneous report of plaintiff's bankruptcy, distributed to five subscribers, was speech solely in the private interest of the speaker and its specific business audience. The content (the bankruptcy of a small business), the form (a credit agency report), and the context (a communication to only five subscribers) established that a matter of public concern was not involved.

8. Defenses to Defamation

a. Consent
As with all torts, consent is a complete defense to a defamation action. (The rules relating to consent discussed under intentional torts, *supra,* also apply here.)

b. Truth
In cases of purely private concern where plaintiff is not required to prove falsity (*see* A.6., *supra*), defendant may establish the truth of the statement as a complete defense.

c. Absolute Privilege
Under certain circumstances, the speaker is not liable for defamatory statements because he enjoys an absolute privilege. Such absolute privileges are *not* affected by a showing of malice, abuse, or excessive provocation, as in the case of qualified privileges (*see* below). Absolute privilege exists in the following cases:

1) Judicial Proceedings
All statements made by the judge, jurors, counsel, witnesses, or parties in judicial proceedings are absolutely privileged. The privilege attaches to *all* aspects of the proceedings, e.g., statements made in open court, pretrial hearing, deposition, or in any of the pleadings or other papers in the case.

There is a requirement that the statement bear some *reasonable relationship* to the proceedings.

2) Legislative Proceedings
All remarks made by either federal or state legislators in their official capacity during legislative proceedings are likewise absolutely privileged.

There is *no requirement of a reasonable relationship* to any matter at hand.

3) Executive Proceedings
A governmental executive official is absolutely privileged with respect to any statement made by her while exercising the functions of her office.

There is a requirement that the statement have some *reasonable relationship* to the executive matter or proceeding in which she is acting.

4) "Compelled" Broadcast or Publication
A radio or TV station compelled to allow a speaker the use of the air, a newspaper compelled to print public notices, etc., is absolutely privileged in an action based on the content of the compelled publication. [Farmers Educational Cooperative v. WDAY, 360 U.S. 525 (1959)]

Example: Radio station gave time to one candidate for public office and hence came under obligation to extend similar treatment to other candidates for the same office. Station had no right to censor these later speeches. Thus, no liability attaches for defamation they might contain.

5) Communications Between Spouses
Communications from one spouse to another are generally treated as being absolutely privileged.

Note: Some states have dealt with communications between spouses on the basis that there is no publication. This is not the preferred view.

d. Qualified Privilege
In certain situations, a speaker may say something defamatory without being liable because of the existence of a qualified privilege.

1) Qualified Privilege Situations
Included within the category of qualified privilege situations are the following:

a) Reports of Public Proceedings
There is a qualified privilege for reports of public hearings or meetings. This includes judicial, legislative, or executive proceedings as well as other proceedings of sufficient public interest, e.g., political convention, trade association meeting, etc.

The privilege *excuses accurate reports* of statements that were false when made, but it *does not excuse inaccuracies* in the reporting of statements.

b) Public Interest

(1) Publication to One Acting in Public Interest
Statements made to those who are to take official action of some kind are qualifiedly privileged.
Example: Statements made to a parole board about a prisoner by one who opposed the grant of parole are privileged.

(2) Fair Comment and Criticism
One is permitted to make remarks that disparage another's acts in the course of a critique of public interest, e.g., book reviews, articles on public institutions, etc. The matter commented upon must be of *general public interest*.

Note: Obviously, the "qualified privilege" areas of subsections a) and b) have generally been preempted by the constitutional requirements imposed by *New York Times v. Sullivan* and its progeny, *supra*.

c) Interest of Publisher
Where defendant's statement is made to defend her own actions, property, or reputation, it may be privileged.
Example: A statement by a debtor explaining to a collection agency her reason for not paying a bill is qualifiedly privileged even if defamatory statements are contained therein.

d) Interest of Recipient

A qualified privilege is recognized when the recipient has an interest in the information and it is reasonable for the defendant to make the publication, i.e., when she is not a mere intermeddler.

Examples: 1) A statement by a credit bureau to a customer is qualifiedly privileged.

2) A statement made by a former employer to a prospective employer about a job applicant is qualifiedly privileged.

e) Common Interest of Publisher and Recipient

Where there is a common interest between the publisher and the recipient, there is a qualified privilege.

Example: A statement by one board member of a charitable foundation, relating to the foundation's business, to another board member is qualifiedly privileged.

2) Loss of Qualified Privilege Through Abuse

A qualified privilege exists only if exercised in a reasonable manner and for a proper purpose. Thus, even though the facts might otherwise give rise to a qualified privilege situation, the actor may have lost this privilege by virtue of his conduct. There are two basic ways in which this generally occurs:

a) Statement Not Within Scope of Privilege

The allegedly protected statement must fall within the scope of the privilege. Hence, the privilege does not encompass the publication of irrelevant defamatory matter unconnected with the public or private interest entitled to protection.

Similarly, the privilege does not cover publication to any person whose hearing or reading of the statement could not reasonably be believed to be necessary for the furtherance of that interest.

b) Actual Malice

A qualified privilege will be lost if it is shown that the speaker acted with actual malice, i.e., (i) *knowledge* that it was untrue or (ii) a *reckless disregard* as to its truth or falsity.

Note: At common law, many courts held that malice in the sense of ill will of defendant toward plaintiff would result in loss of the qualified privilege. Most courts no longer apply common law malice here, however. As long as the defendant is using a proper occasion for a qualified privilege in a proper way, she will not lose this privilege simply because she bears ill will toward the plaintiff.

3) Qualified Privilege—Burden of Proof

The *defendant bears the burden* of proving that a privilege exists. If the privilege is qualified, the plaintiff then bears the burden of proving that the privilege has been lost through excessive publication or actual malice.

9. Mitigating Factors

Several matters, while not defenses to an action, may be considered by the trier of fact on the issue of damages. These include:

a. No Actual Malice

Malice may be inferred from some statements, but if the jury is shown that there was no actual malice, such evidence is admissible to mitigate damages. To this end, defendant may prove the source of her information and grounds for her belief.

b. Retraction

Unless made immediately after publication so as to negate the defamatory effect of a statement, retraction does not undo the wrong. But the court may consider it to show *lack of actual malice* in mitigation of damages. A failure to retract after a request to do so is often allowed as evidence to the opposite effect.

c. Anger

Anger of the speaker may be a mitigating circumstance *if provoked* by the plaintiff.

B. INVASION OF RIGHT TO PRIVACY

The right to protection against unreasonable interferences with an individual's solitude is well recognized. The tort of invasion of privacy as it has developed, however, includes protection of "personality" as well as protection against interference with solitude. In all, the tort includes the following four kinds of wrongs:

(i) *Appropriation* by defendant of plaintiff's picture or name for defendant's *commercial advantage*;

(ii) *Intrusion* by the defendant upon plaintiff's *affairs* or *seclusion*;

(iii) Publication by the defendant of facts placing the plaintiff in a *false light*; and

(iv) Public disclosures of *private facts* about the plaintiff by the defendant.

1. Appropriation of Plaintiff's Picture or Name

a. Prima Facie Case

To establish a prima facie case for invasion of privacy—appropriation of plaintiff's picture or name—only one element need be proved:

1) *Unauthorized use* by defendant of plaintiff's picture or name for defendant's *commercial advantage*.

b. Limited to Advertisement or Promotion of Product or Services

Liability is generally limited to the use of plaintiff's picture or name in connection with the promotion or advertisement of a product or service, e.g., use of plaintiff's picture to advertise an automobile.

The mere fact that defendant is using plaintiff's picture or name for his own personal profit may not, by itself, be sufficient. Thus, for example, the use of a personality's name in a magazine story, even if motivated by profit, may not be actionable.

2. **Intrusion on Plaintiff's Affairs or Seclusion**

   a. **Prima Facie Case**
   To establish a prima facie case for invasion of privacy—intrusion on the plaintiff's affairs or seclusion—the following elements must be proved:

     1) *Act of prying or intruding* on the affairs or seclusion of the plaintiff by the defendant;

     2) The intrusion is something that would be *highly offensive to a reasonable person*; and

     3) The thing to which there is an intrusion or prying is *"private."*

   b. **Invasion of Plaintiff's Private Affairs or Seclusion**
   For liability to attach, there must be an invasion of the plaintiff's private affairs or seclusion; e.g., defendant puts a microphone in plaintiff's bedroom.

   c. **Intrusion Highly Offensive to a Reasonable Person**
   For liability to attach, the intrusion by defendant must be something that would be highly offensive to a reasonable person.

   d. **Intrusion Must Be into Something "Private"**
   For liability to attach, the intrusion by defendant must be into something within the plaintiff's own private domain. Thus, for example, taking pictures of a person in a public place is not actionable.

3. **Publication of Facts Placing Plaintiff in False Light**

   a. **Prima Facie Case**
   To establish a prima facie case for invasion of privacy—publication by defendant of facts placing plaintiff in a false light—the following elements must be proved:

     1) Publication of *facts* about plaintiff by defendant placing plaintiff in a *false light* in the public eye;

     2) The "false light" is something that would be *highly offensive to a reasonable person* under the circumstances; and

     3) *Actual malice* on the part of defendant where the published matter is in the *public interest*.

   b. **Publication or Public Disclosure**
   For liability to attach, there must be *publicity* concerning the "false light" facts; this requires *more* than "publication" in the defamation sense.

c. **What Is "False Light"?**
A fact will be deemed to present plaintiff in a false light if it attributes to him:

(i)   Views that he does not hold, or

(ii)   Actions that he did not take.

Note: This element involves falsity and, as such, may also involve defamation if the falsity affects reputation.

d. **Highly Offensive to Reasonable Person**
To be actionable, this "false light" must be something that would be highly offensive to a reasonable person under the circumstances.

e. **Actual Malice Necessary Where Matter of Public Interest**
In *Time, Inc. v. Hill*, 385 U.S. 374 (1967), a case involving this particular invasion of privacy branch, the Supreme Court held that the First Amendment prohibits recovery for invasion of privacy in cases where the published matter is of public interest, unless the plaintiff establishes that the defendant acted with actual malice (i.e., knowledge of falsity or reckless disregard for the truth).

After *Gertz* and *Dun & Bradstreet* (discussed *supra* under Defamation), the Supreme Court may be expected to give the states a slightly larger scope in which to protect privacy where a public figure is not involved. Thus, where the public interest in the information is not overriding and where the risks to the privacy interests of the private person are clear on the face of the material to a reasonably prudent publisher, the Supreme Court may choose in the future to permit an action in privacy without proof of actual malice. However, at least in public figure cases, the *Time, Inc. v. Hill* requirement of actual malice still holds. [*See* Hustler Magazine, Inc. v. Falwell, 485 U.S. 46 (1988)]

4. **Public Disclosure of Private Facts About Plaintiff**

a. **Prima Facie Case**
To establish a prima facie case for invasion of privacy—public disclosure of private facts about plaintiff—the following elements must be proved:

1)   Publication or public disclosure by defendant of ***private*** information about the plaintiff; and

2)   The matter made public is such that its disclosure would be ***highly offensive to a reasonable person***.

b. **Publication or Public Disclosure**
For liability to attach, there must be publicity concerning a private fact; i.e., the disclosure must be a public disclosure, not a private one.

c. **Facts Must Be Private**
The facts disclosed must be "private." For example, there is no liability for matters of public record, since these facts are not private.

d. **Disclosure Highly Offensive to Reasonable Person**
To be actionable, the disclosure of private facts must be such that a reasonable person would find it highly offensive.
Example: Barbara showed, in a public exhibition, a movie of Sandy's cesarean operation. This may be actionable.

e. **Facts May Be True**
Liability may attach under this privacy branch if the elements of a prima facie case are satisfied even though the factual statement about the plaintiff is true.

f. **Constitutional Privilege**
The rationale of *Time, Inc. v. Hill* appears to encompass this branch of the invasion of privacy tort as well. In other words, if the matter is one of *legitimate public interest*, the publication is privileged if made without actual malice.

1) **Effect of Passage of Time**
The mere passage of time does not preclude the "public interest" characterization of a publication. Hence, it has frequently been held that the life of one *formerly* in the public eye has become public property, even though that person is no longer in the public eye.
Example: A magazine published the life history of a former child prodigy. This may be construed to be a matter in the public interest.

2) **Absolute Privilege with Regard to Matters of Public Record**
Where the matters republished are taken from official public records, there is an absolute constitutional privilege (e.g., rape victim's name obtained from police records or court proceedings used in newspaper article).

5. **Causation**
The invasion of plaintiff's interest in privacy must have been *proximately caused* by defendant's conduct.

6. **Proof of Special Damages Unnecessary**
In an action for invasion of right to privacy, the plaintiff need not plead and prove special damages, provided the elements of a prima facie case are present. In other words, emotional distress and mental anguish *are* sufficient damages.

7. **Basis of Liability**
The basis for liability in a privacy action may rest upon an *intentional* or *negligent* invasion. It also appears that *strict liability* may be a sufficient basis (as in defamation).

8. **Defenses to Invasions of Privacy**

a. **Consent**
Consent is a defense to an action for invasion of the right to privacy. Some states, by statute, require that the consent be in writing. Here, as in all consent defense situations, the defendant may nonetheless be liable if the consent granted has been exceeded.
Example: Plaintiff consents to be interviewed, and a picture taken during the interview is used in conjunction with an advertisement for a product. Liability may attach.

Note that mistake, even if reasonable, as to whether consent was given (which in fact it was not) is **not** a valid defense.

b. Defamation Defenses

Those defenses to actions for defamation that are based on **absolute and qualified privileges** appear applicable to those invasion of right to privacy actions predicated on publication grounds, i.e., "false light" and "public disclosure of private facts" actions. Thus, for example, one may have an absolute privilege to comment as a participant in judicial proceedings or a qualified privilege to report public proceedings.

Note: Truth is **not** a good defense to most invasion of privacy actions. Similarly, inadvertence, good faith, and lack of malice generally are **not** good defenses.

9. Right of Privacy—Miscellaneous

a. Right Is Personal

The right of privacy is a personal right and does not extend to members of a family. The right of privacy does not survive the death of plaintiff and is not assignable.

b. Not Applicable to Corporations

Only individuals may avail themselves of a right to privacy action; it does not apply to corporations.

C. MISREPRESENTATION

1. Intentional Misrepresentation (Fraud, Deceit)

a. Prima Facie Case

To establish a prima facie case of intentional misrepresentation, fraud, or deceit, the following elements must be proved:

1) **Misrepresentation** made by defendant;

2) **Scienter**;

3) An **intent to induce** plaintiff's **reliance** on the misrepresentation;

4) **Causation** (i.e., actual reliance on the misrepresentation);

5) **Justifiable reliance** by plaintiff on the misrepresentation; and

6) **Damages**.

b. The Misrepresentation

Usually, there is a requirement that the false representation be of a **material past or present fact**. In certain cases, however, a misrepresentation of opinion may be actionable. (This is really a justifiable reliance question. *See* below.)

1) No General Duty to Disclose

No general duty to disclose a material fact or opinion to one is imposed upon another. Thus, simple failure to disclose a material fact or opinion does not generally satisfy the first element of this cause of action. A few general *exceptions* exist, however:

a) Defendant stands in such a *fiduciary relationship* to plaintiff as would call for a duty of disclosure.

b) Defendant selling real property knows that plaintiff is unaware of, and cannot reasonably discover, material information about the transaction (e.g., builder does not tell buyer that the house was built on a landfill).

c) Where defendant speaks and her *utterance deceives plaintiff,* she will be under a duty to inform plaintiff of the true facts.

2) Active Concealment Actionable

Where a person actively conceals a material fact, she is under a duty to disclose this fact, and failure to do so satisfies the first element of a prima facie case (e.g., salesperson turns back odometer on an automobile).

c. Scienter

To establish a prima facie case, plaintiff must prove that defendant made the representation knowing it to be false or, alternatively, that it was made with reckless disregard as to its truth or falsity. This element of the prima facie case is often given the technical name of "scienter."

Example: A corporation's president stated falsely that last year's profits were $100,000 without having looked at a profit and loss statement. Scienter is present.

Note: If scienter is not present, defendant may still be liable for negligent misrepresentation (discussed below).

d. Intent to Induce Reliance

The defendant must have intended to induce plaintiff or a class of persons to which plaintiff belongs to act or refrain from acting in reliance on the misrepresentation.

1) Continuous Deception Exception

An exception exists where the misrepresentation is a "continuous deception," e.g., mislabeling of product by manufacturer, misrepresentation in negotiable instrument. In such cases, it is not necessary that the reliance of a particular plaintiff be intended. Anyone into whose possession the product or instrument has come may bring an action.

2) Third-Party Reliance Problem

One recurring problem is where the defendant communicates directly to one person and another relies upon the misrepresentation. In such cases, the defendant is viewed as intending to deceive the person who relies upon the misrepresentation *if the defendant could reasonably foresee that the plaintiff will have such reliance.*

Example: Chauncey sends an intentionally false profit statement to a stockbroker, and a customer of the stockbroker relies on this statement to his detriment. Liability exists.

e.   Causation

Plaintiff must prove that the misrepresentation played a substantial part in inducing him to act as he did. In short, plaintiff must prove "actual reliance."

f.   Justifiable Reliance

1)   Reliance on Fact Almost Always Justified

Even though it may have been intended by defendant that plaintiff rely on the representation, plaintiff must nonetheless prove that such reliance was "justified." As a practical matter, the reliance of plaintiff on representations of fact is almost always justified. Only where the facts are obviously false is such reliance not justified.

a)   No Obligation to Investigate

Courts do not impose an obligation on plaintiff to reasonably investigate the veracity of defendant's representation of fact. This is so even though it would be easy for plaintiff to do this. If, however, plaintiff does in fact investigate, he may not rely on representations by defendant inconsistent with the facts reasonably ascertainable from such investigation.

2)   Reliance on Opinion Usually Not Justifiable

As a general matter, reliance on false statements of opinion, value, or quality will be viewed as unjustified. Some exceptions to this general rule do exist, however.

a)   Superior Knowledge of Defendant

If the defendant making a false representation of opinion has a superior knowledge of the subject matter, then reliance by a person without such knowledge may be viewed as justified.

b)   Statements of Law

Statements of law are treated as statements of opinion if they are merely predictions as to the legal consequences of facts; they may not be justifiably relied upon unless the statement is made by a lawyer to a layperson, in which case the "superior knowledge" rule operates. On the other hand, a statement of law that includes an express or implied misrepresentation of fact is actionable.

Example: Defendant falsely states that the house she is offering for sale conforms to the city plumbing and electrical requirements. Liability exists.

c)   Statements of Future Events

Statements of future events are viewed as statements of opinion and may not be justifiably relied upon. An exception exists if the statement of future events may be characterized as a statement of "present intent," which is viewed as a statement of fact.

Example: Defendant promises to pay plaintiff $50 per month installments for the next two years. This may be viewed as a statement of "fact." (Characterization of statements of future events as "present intent" statements is generally limited to those cases where the defendant has control over the future event, as in this example.)

g. **Damages**

In an action for intentional misrepresentation, plaintiff may recover *only* if he has suffered *actual pecuniary loss* as a result of the reliance on the false statement. Most courts use a contract measure of damages—plaintiff may recover the "benefit of the bargain," i.e., the value of the property as represented less the value of the property as it actually is.

2. **Negligent Misrepresentation**

a. **Prima Facie Case**

The prima facie case for negligent misrepresentation is similar to that for intentional misrepresentation. The following elements must be proved:

1) *Misrepresentation* made by defendant in a *business or professional capacity*;

2) *Breach of duty* toward *particular plaintiff*;

3) *Causation*;

4) *Justifiable reliance* by plaintiff upon the misrepresentation; and

5) *Damages*.

b. **Liability Confined to Commercial Transactions**

The ambit of liability for negligent misrepresentation is much more confined than that for deceit. Generally, the action is confined to only those misrepresentations made in a commercial setting, i.e., made by the defendant in a business or professional capacity.

c. **Duty Owed Only to Particular Plaintiff Whose Reliance Contemplated**

Liability attaches for a negligent misrepresentation only if reliance by the particular plaintiff could be contemplated. In other words, defendant is under a duty of care only to those persons to whom the representation was made or to specific persons who defendant *knew* would rely on it. Foreseeability that the statement will be communicated to third persons may be sufficient to impose liability for deceit (above), but it does *not* suffice for negligent misrepresentation in most states.

Example: Chauncey sends a negligently prepared profit statement to a stockbroker, and a customer of the stockbroker relies upon this statement to her detriment. Liability does not exist. (*Compare* example in section 1.d.2), *supra*.)

d.   **Other Elements**

The elements of causation, justifiable reliance, and damages are analyzed the same as under intentional misrepresentation.

D. INTERFERENCE WITH BUSINESS RELATIONS

To establish a prima facie case for interference with contract or prospective economic advantage, the following elements must be proved:

(i) Existence of a *valid contractual relationship* between plaintiff and a third party or a *valid business expectancy* of plaintiff;

(ii) *Defendant's knowledge* of the relationship or expectancy;

(iii) *Intentional interference* by defendant that induces a breach or termination of the relationship or expectancy; and

(iv) *Damage* to plaintiff.

1. Not Limited to Existing Contracts

Plaintiff has a cause of action not only for interference with existing contracts but also for interference with probable future business relationships for which plaintiff has a reasonable expectation of financial benefit.

Example: A real estate broker may have a cause of action against one who improperly diverts potential buyers of the property that the broker was selling.

2. Intent Required

Defendant must have *intended* to interfere with the existing or prospective contractual relationships of plaintiff. Most courts do not permit recovery for negligent interference with contract in the absence of some independent tort, such as negligent misrepresentation (*supra*).

3. Damages

Plaintiff must prove actual damage from the interference, but may also recover mental distress damages and punitive damages in appropriate cases.

4. Privileges

An interferor's conduct may be privileged where it is a proper attempt to obtain business for the interferor or protect its interests.

Example: A bank collecting on an existing promissory note is privileged to induce the debtor to pay it off, even if that will cause the debtor to fail to satisfy obligations owing to other parties.

Several factors will determine whether a privilege exists:

a. Type of Business Relationship Involved

Interference with a prospective business relationship that the plaintiff is pursuing is more likely to be privileged than interference with the plaintiff's existing contract with a third party.

b. **Means of Persuasion Used**
Interference using legitimate and commercially acceptable means of persuasion is more likely to be privileged than interference using illegal or threatening tactics.

c. **Whether Defendant Is a Competitor of Plaintiff**
Interference with the plaintiff's prospective business relationships is likely to be privileged if the defendant is a competitor of the plaintiff pursuing those same prospective customers.

d. **Defendant's Relationship with the Third Party**
Interference may be privileged if the defendant has responsibility for, or a financial interest in, the third party, or if the third party has sought the business advice of the defendant.

E. WRONGFUL INSTITUTION OF LEGAL PROCEEDINGS

1. Malicious Prosecution

a. **Prima Facie Case**
To establish a prima facie case for malicious prosecution, the following elements must be proved:

1) *Institution of criminal proceedings* against plaintiff;

2) Termination *favorable to plaintiff*;

3) *Absence of probable cause* for prosecution;

4) *Improper purpose* of defendant (i.e., malice); and

5) *Damages*.

b. **Institution of Criminal Proceedings**
For liability to attach for malicious prosecution, the defendant must have initiated a *criminal* proceeding against the plaintiff, such as by filing a police report to procure the plaintiff's arrest. The "initiation" of the proceeding can be by warrant, arrest, indictment, etc.

1) **Defendant Must Initiate Proceedings**
Remember, the defendant must have initiated the proceedings himself. Simply giving the full story to the prosecutor, whereupon the prosecutor decides to prosecute, is not sufficient for a later malicious prosecution action against the informer in most states.

2) **Prosecuting Attorneys Privileged**
Prosecuting attorneys are absolutely privileged and cannot be sued for malicious prosecution (even when they act in bad faith and without probable cause).

c. Termination of Proceedings in Plaintiff's Favor
The plaintiff may bring such an action only if the prior proceedings were terminated in her favor; e.g., she was acquitted, the case was dismissed, charges were dropped, etc. The termination must demonstrate the *innocence* of the accused.

d. Absence of Probable Cause for Prior Proceedings
To recover, the plaintiff must establish that the defendant initiated the prior proceedings without probable cause. She may do so by showing *either* (i) that there were insufficient facts for a reasonable person to believe that plaintiff was guilty; *or* (ii) that the defendant did not actually believe the plaintiff to be guilty.

1) Effect of Indictment
Note that indictment by a grand jury is prima facie evidence of probable cause. However, failure of a grand jury to indict is *not* evidence that there was no probable cause.

2) Prior Action Based on Advice
If defendant instituted the prior proceedings on advice of counsel after full disclosure of the facts, this establishes probable cause.

e. Improper Purpose in Bringing Suit
For purposes of malicious prosecution, the malice or improper purpose element of the prima facie case is satisfied when it is shown that defendant's primary purpose in instituting the prior action was something other than bringing a person to justice.

f. Damages
Damages must be *proved*. Plaintiff may recover damages for all harms that are the proximate result of defendant's wrong, e.g., expenses in defending criminal suit, embarrassment, etc. Punitive damages are often awarded, since defendant's improper purpose is, of course, already proved to establish the case.

g. False Arrest Distinguished
In a false arrest situation, the false arrest itself is illegal, e.g., made without a valid warrant. In a malicious prosecution situation, the arrest itself is carried out in a lawful manner, but is pursuant to a maliciously instituted prosecution.

2. Wrongful Civil Proceedings
Most jurisdictions have extended the malicious prosecution action to encompass wrongfully instituted civil cases. The same general rules govern as apply in malicious prosecution. However, lack of probable cause is harder to show in civil actions because reasonable people would more readily file a doubtful case where the only consequences to the person sued are civil.

3. Abuse of Process
It is a tort to use any form of process—civil or criminal—to bring about a result other than that for which the form of process was intended; e.g., defendant garnished an account to force plaintiff to sign a lease. The prima facie elements of the action are (i) the wrongful use of the process for an ulterior purpose, and (ii) some definite act or threat against plaintiff to accomplish the ulterior purpose.

a. **Malicious Prosecution Distinguished**

If the defendant uses the particular machinery of the law for the immediate purpose for which it was designed, he is not liable for abuse of process notwithstanding any malicious intent. Abuse of process is not the wrongful institution of the action or proceeding, but rather the improper use of process in connection therewith. Hence, the merits of the action itself are of no relevance. In contrast to malicious prosecution, therefore, neither want of probable cause nor favorable termination are elements of the tort.

III. NEGLIGENCE

A. PRIMA FACIE CASE

To establish a prima facie case for negligence, the following elements must be proved:

1. The existence of a *duty* on the part of the defendant *to conform to a specific standard of conduct* for the protection of the plaintiff against an unreasonable risk of injury;

2. *Breach* of that duty by the defendant;

3. That the breach of duty by the defendant was the *actual and proximate cause* of the plaintiff's injury; and

4. *Damage* to the plaintiff's person or property.

B. THE DUTY OF CARE

1. **Introduction—General Duty of Care**

A general duty of care is imposed on all human activity. When a person engages in an activity, he is under a legal duty to act as an *ordinary, prudent, reasonable person*. It is presumed that an ordinary, prudent, reasonable person will take precautions against creating unreasonable risks of injury to other persons. Thus, if the defendant's conduct creates an unreasonable risk of injury to persons in the position of the plaintiff, the general duty of care extends from the defendant to the plaintiff. No duty is imposed on a person to take precautions against events that cannot reasonably be foreseen. Therefore, if at the time of the negligent conduct, no foreseeable risk of injury to a person in the position of the plaintiff is created by the defendant's act, the general duty of care does not extend from the defendant to the plaintiff.

In addition, certain other factors such as the status of the parties (e.g., owners or occupiers of land) or statutes may limit or extend this general duty.

2. **To Whom Is the Duty of Care Owed?**

a. **General Rule—Foreseeable Plaintiffs**

A duty of care is owed only to foreseeable plaintiffs.

b. **The "Unforeseeable" Plaintiff Problem**

1)   The Problem
The "unforeseeable" plaintiff problem arises when defendant breaches a duty to one plaintiff (P1) and also causes injury thereby to a second plaintiff (P2) to whom a foreseeable risk of injury might or might not have been created at the time of the original negligent act.

Example: An employee of Defendant negligently aided a passenger boarding the train, causing the passenger to drop a package. The package exploded, causing a scale a substantial distance away to fall upon a second passenger. Is the second passenger a foreseeable plaintiff?

2)   The Solution(s)
Defendant's liability to P2 will depend upon whether the Andrews or Cardozo view in *Palsgraf* is adopted. [Palsgraf v. Long Island Railroad, 248 N.Y. 339 (1928)] Most courts considering this issue have followed the Cardozo view.

a)   Andrews View
According to the Andrews view in *Palsgraf,* the second plaintiff (P2) may establish the existence of a duty extending from the defendant to her by showing that the defendant has breached a duty he owed P1. In short, defendant owes a duty of care to ***anyone*** who suffers injuries as a proximate result of his breach of duty to ***someone***.

b)   Cardozo View
According to the Cardozo view in *Palsgraf,* the second plaintiff (P2) can recover only if she can establish that a reasonable person would have foreseen a risk of injury to her in the circumstances, i.e., that she was located in a foreseeable ***"zone of danger."***

c.   Specific Situations

1)   Rescuers
A rescuer is a foreseeable plaintiff as long as the rescue is not reckless; hence, defendant is liable if he negligently puts himself or a third person in peril and plaintiff is injured in attempting a rescue. Note, however, that the "firefighter's rule" (*infra*, 3.d.2)c)(2)(c)) may bar firefighters and police officers, on public policy or assumption of risk grounds, from recovering for injuries caused by the risks of a rescue.

2)   Prenatal Injuries
Prenatal injuries are actionable; i.e., a duty of care is owed toward a fetus. The fetus must have been ***viable*** at the time of injury. (Most states also permit a wrongful death action (*see* VII.C.2., *infra*) if the fetus dies from the injuries.)

a)   "Wrongful Life" Action Not Recognized
In most states, the failure to diagnose a congenital defect of the fetus or to properly perform a contraceptive procedure does ***not*** permit the unwanted child to recover damages for "wrongful life," even if the child is born handicapped.

b) **Compare—"Wrongful Birth" and "Wrongful Pregnancy"**
The child's parents, however, *do* have an action: either for failure to diagnose the defect ("wrongful birth") or for failure to properly perform a contraceptive procedure ("wrongful pregnancy"). The mother can recover damages for the unwanted labor (medical expenses and pain and suffering). If the child has a defect, parents may recover the additional medical expenses to care for the child and, in some states, damages for emotional distress. If the child is born healthy in a wrongful pregnancy case, most cases do *not* permit the parents to recover child-rearing expenses, just damages for the unwanted labor.

3) **Intended Beneficiaries of Economic Transactions**
A third party for whose economic benefit a legal or business transaction is made (e.g., the beneficiary of a will) is owed a duty of care if the defendant could reasonably foresee harm to that party if the transaction is done negligently. Note that this is an exception to the general rule that one who suffers *only* economic loss as a result of another's negligence cannot recover damages in a tort action (*see also* V.C.5., *infra*).

3. **What Is Applicable Standard of Care?**

   a. **Basic Standard—The Reasonable Person**
   Defendant's conduct is measured against the reasonable, ordinary, prudent person. This reasonable person has the following characteristics, measured by an *objective* standard:

   1) **Physical Characteristics—Same as Defendant's**
   Notwithstanding application of the objective standard, the "reasonable person" is considered to have the *same physical characteristics as the defendant*. However, a person is expected to know his physical handicaps and is under a duty to exercise the care of a person with such knowledge; e.g., it may be negligent for an epileptic to drive a car.

   2) **Average Mental Ability**
   Defendant must act as would a person with average mental ability. Unlike the rule as to physical characteristics, *individual mental handicaps are not considered*; i.e., low IQ is no excuse. Likewise, insanity is no defense, and the defendant is held to the standard of a reasonable person under the circumstances.

   3) **Same Knowledge as Average Member of Community**
   Defendant is deemed to have knowledge of things known by the average member of the community, e.g., that fire is hot. Again, the individual shortcomings of the particular defendant are *not* considered. On the other hand, a defendant with knowledge superior to that of the average person is required to use that knowledge.

   b. **Particular Standards of Conduct**
   Some persons are held to a standard of conduct different from that of the ordinary person.

1) Professionals

A person who is a professional or has special skills (e.g., doctor, lawyer, airplane mechanic, etc.) is required to possess and exercise the knowledge and skill of a member of the profession or occupation in good standing. For doctors, most courts will apply a national standard of care to evaluate their conduct.

The professional must also use such superior judgment, skill, and knowledge as he actually possesses. Thus, a specialist might be held liable where a general practitioner would not.

a) Duty to Disclose Risks of Treatment

A doctor proposing a course of treatment or a surgical procedure has a duty to provide the patient with enough information about its risks to enable the patient to make an *informed consent* to the treatment. If an undisclosed risk was serious enough that a reasonable person in the patient's position would have withheld consent to the treatment, the doctor has breached this duty.

Example: Patient consents to an operation not necessary to save his life. Patient is not informed that there is a 40% probability of paralysis in such operations, and paralysis results. Since a reasonable person would not have consented to the operation had the risks been disclosed, Doctor has breached his duty of disclosure.

2) Children

A majority of courts take the view that a child is required to conform to the standard of care of a child of *like age, education, intelligence, and experience*. This permits a *subjective* evaluation of these factors.

a) Minimum Age for Capacity To Be Negligent

There is a minimum age for which it is meaningful to speak of a child being capable of conforming his conduct to a standard of care. Most courts, however, do not fix this age at any arbitrary figure. Each case is dealt with in terms of whether there is evidence that the individual child—plaintiff or defendant—has the experience, intelligence, maturity, training, or capacity to conform his conduct to a standard of care. It is unlikely, nonetheless, that a court would view a child *below the age of five* as having the capacity to be negligent. Or, to put it another way, it is unlikely that a court would impose a legal duty to avoid injuries to others or himself upon a child who is under five.

b) Children Engaged in Adult Activities

Where a child engages in a potentially dangerous activity that is normally one that only adults engage in, most cases hold that he will be required to conform to the same standard of care as an adult in such an activity, e.g., driving an automobile, flying an airplane, driving a motorboat.

3) Common Carriers and Innkeepers

Common carriers and innkeepers are required to exercise a very high degree of care toward their passengers and guests; i.e., they are *liable for slight negligence*.

4) Automobile Driver to Guest

In most jurisdictions today, the duty owed by the driver of an automobile to a rider is one of ordinary care.

a) Guest Statutes

A few states have guest statutes. Under these statutes, the driver's only duty to a nonpaying rider is to **refrain from gross or wanton and willful misconduct**. Note that guest statutes do not apply to "passengers," i.e., riders who contribute toward the expense of the ride; they are owed a duty of ordinary care.

5) Bailment Duties

In a bailment relationship, the bailor transfers physical possession of an item of personal property to the bailee without a transfer of title. The bailee acquires the right to possess the property in accordance with the terms of the bailment. A bailment obligates the bailee to return the item of personal property to the bailor or otherwise dispose of it according to the bailment terms.

Example: When the owner of a computer delivers it to a technician to be repaired, the technician becomes a bailee of the computer and the owner is the bailor.

a) Duties Owed by Bailee

(1) Sole Benefit of Bailor Bailment

If the bailment is for the sole benefit of the bailor (e.g., the bailor asks his neighbor (the bailee) to take in the bailor's mail while he is on vacation), the bailee is liable only for **gross negligence**.

(2) Sole Benefit of Bailee Bailment

If the bailment is for the sole benefit of the bailee (e.g., the bailor gratuitously loans her lawnmower to the bailee), the bailee is liable even for **slight negligence.**

(3) Mutual Benefit Bailments

If the bailment is for the mutual benefit of the bailor and bailee (typically a bailment for hire such as in the computer example above), the bailee must exercise **ordinary due care**.

(4) Modern Trend

Today the trend is away from such classifications and toward a rule that considers whether the bailee exercised ordinary care under all the circumstances. These circumstances include, e.g., value of the goods, type of bailment, custom of a trade, etc.

b) Duties Owed by Bailor

(1) Sole Benefit of Bailee Bailments

If the bailment is for the sole benefit of the bailee (e.g., the bailor gratuitously loans her lawnmower to the bailee), the bailor need only inform the bailee of known dangerous defects in the chattel. There is no duty with regard to unknown defects.

(2) Bailments for Hire
If the bailment is for hire (e.g., the bailor loans her lawnmower to the bailee for a fee), the bailor owes a duty to inform the bailee of defects known to him, or of which he would have known by the exercise of reasonable diligence.

c. Standard of Care in Emergency Situations
The existence of an emergency, presenting little time for reflection, may be considered as among the circumstances under which the defendant acted; i.e., he must act as the reasonable person would under the same emergency. The emergency may *not* be considered, however, if it is of the defendant's own making.

d. Standard of Care Owed by Owners and/or Occupiers of Land
In this section, duty problems are resolved by application of special rules that have been developed imposing duties on individuals because of their relationship to property. In some cases, the duty of the owner or occupier depends on whether the injury occurred on or off his premises; in others it depends on the legal status of the plaintiff with regard to the property, i.e., trespasser, licensee, or invitee.

1) Duty of Possessor to Those Off the Premises

a) Natural Conditions
The general rule is that a landowner owes *no duty* to protect one outside the premises from natural conditions on the land.
Example: One is not liable for bugs that live in trees on one's land but that "visit" the neighbors from time to time.

Note: An exception exists for decaying trees next to sidewalks or streets in urban areas.

b) Artificial Conditions
As a general rule, there is also *no duty* owing for artificial conditions. Two major *exceptions* exist, however.

(1) Unreasonably Dangerous Conditions
A landowner is liable for damage caused by unreasonably dangerous artificial conditions or structures abutting adjacent land.
Example: While one would not be liable for natural collections of ice on the sidewalk, he might be liable for negligently permitting water to drain off his roof and form ice on the sidewalk.

(2) Duty to Protect Passersby
A landowner also has a duty to *take due precautions* to protect persons

passing by from dangerous conditions, e.g., by erecting a barricade to keep people from falling into an excavation at the edge of the property.

c)   Conduct of Persons on Property
An owner of land has a duty to exercise reasonable care with respect to his own activities on the land and to control the conduct of others on his property so as to avoid unreasonable risk of harm to others outside the property.

2)   Duties of Possessor to Those on the Premises
Under the traditional rule followed in many jurisdictions, the nature of a duty owed by an owner or occupier of land to those on the premises for dangerous conditions on the land depends on the legal status of the plaintiff with regard to the property, i.e., trespasser, licensee, or invitee. Note, though, that close to half the states have abolished the distinction between licensees and invitees and simply apply a reasonable person standard to dangerous conditions on the land. A few of these states have gone even further and abolished the trespasser distinction as well.

a)   Duty Owed to a Trespasser

(1)   Definition of Trespasser
A trespasser is one who comes onto the land without permission or privilege.

(2)   Duty Owed Undiscovered Trespassers
A landowner owes *no duty* to an undiscovered trespasser. He has no duty to inspect in order to ascertain whether persons are coming onto his property.

(3)   Duty Owed Discovered Trespassers
Once a landowner discovers the presence of a trespasser, he is under a duty to exercise ordinary care to *warn* the trespasser of, or to *make safe*, *artificial conditions* known to the landowner that involve a *risk of death or serious bodily harm* and that the trespasser is unlikely to discover. There is no duty owed for natural conditions and less dangerous artificial conditions.

The owner or occupier also has a duty to exercise reasonable care in the exercise of *"active operations"* on the property.

(a)   When Is a Trespasser "Discovered"?
A trespasser is discovered, of course, when she is actually noticed on the property by the owner or occupier. But in addition, a trespasser is viewed as discovered if the owner or occupier is notified by information sufficient for a reasonable person to conclude that someone is on the property.

(4)   Duty Owed Anticipated Trespassers
The majority of states now treat anticipated trespassers on generally the

same basis as discovered trespassers in terms of the duty owed them by the landowner.

(a) When Is a Trespasser "Anticipated"?

An "anticipated trespasser" situation arises where the landowner knows or should reasonably know of the presence of trespassers who constantly cross over a section of his land. (Although note that if the owner has posted "no trespassing" signs, this might serve to convert these "anticipated" trespassers into "undiscovered" trespassers.)

(5) "Attractive Nuisance" Doctrine

Most courts impose upon a landowner the duty to exercise *ordinary care* to avoid a reasonably foreseeable risk of harm to children caused by artificial conditions on his property. Under the general rule, to assess this special duty upon the owner or occupier of land with regard to children on his property, the plaintiff must show the following:

(i) There is a dangerous condition present on the land of which the owner is or should be aware;

(ii) The owner knows or should know that young persons frequent the vicinity of this dangerous condition;

(iii) The condition is likely to cause injury, i.e., is dangerous, because of the child's inability to appreciate the risk; and

(iv) The expense of remedying the situation is slight compared with the magnitude of the risk.

(a) What Is a Dangerous Condition?

As noted above, a dangerous condition exists where something on the land is likely to cause injury to children because of their inability to appreciate the risk. This usually is an artificial condition, but in some circumstances a natural condition might suffice.

1] Where Applied

The attractive nuisance doctrine has been applied to abandoned automobiles, lumber piles, sand bins, and elevators. Bodies of water are generally not dangerous conditions because the dangers are viewed as obvious and well-known. If, however, a body of water contains elements of unusual danger to children, it may be characterized as a dangerous condition, e.g., logs or plants floating in the water, or a thick scum that appears to be a path on the water.

(b) Foreseeability of Harm Is True Basis of Liability

Under the traditional "attractive nuisance" doctrine, it was necessary for the child/plaintiff to establish that she was lured onto the property by the attractive nuisance/dangerous condition. This no longer is the case. Most jurisdictions have substantially revised their attractive nuisance doctrines to bring them within general negligence concepts. Foreseeability of harm to a child is the true basis of liability and the element of attraction is important only insofar as it indicates that the presence of children should have been anticipated by the landowner.

(6) Duty of Easement and License Holders to Trespassers
While employees and independent contractors acting on behalf of the landowner have the status of the landowner, persons with an easement or license to use the land do not; they must exercise reasonable care to protect the trespasser.

Example: Power Company obtains an easement from Leonard to run high-tension wires across Leonard's land. Because of Power Company's negligent failure to maintain the wires, one of them falls and injures Plaintiff, an undiscovered trespasser on Leonard's land. Power Company is liable to Plaintiff.

b) Duty Owed to a Licensee

(1) Definition of Licensee
A licensee is one who enters on the land with the landowner's permission, express or implied, for her *own purpose or business* rather than for the landowner's benefit.

(2) Duty Owed
The owner or occupier owes a licensee a *duty to warn of or make safe* a dangerous condition *known* to the owner or occupier that creates an unreasonable risk of harm to the licensee and that the licensee is unlikely to discover.

(a) No Duty to Inspect
The owner or occupier has *no duty* to a licensee *to inspect* for defects *nor to repair* known defects.

(b) Duty of Care for Active Operations
The owner or occupier also has a duty to *exercise reasonable care* in the conduct of "active operations" for the protection of the licensee whom he knows to be on the property.

(3) Social Guests Are Licensees
The social guest is a licensee. Performance of minor services for the host does not make the guest an invitee.

c) Duty Owed to an Invitee

(1) Definition of Invitee

An invitee is a person who enters onto the premises in response to an express or implied invitation of the landowner. Basically, there are two classes of invitees:

(a) Those who enter as members of the public for a purpose for which the land is **held open to the public,** e.g., museums, churches, airports; and

(b) Those who enter for a purpose **connected with the business** or other interests of the landowner or occupier, e.g., store customers and persons accompanying them, employees, persons making deliveries, etc.

(2) Characterization of Privileged Entrants

There may be a problem of characterization regarding persons entering the premises in exercise of a privilege, e.g., police, firefighters, census takers, etc. In some situations, they are characterized as licensees, in others as invitees. The following rules should be noted:

(a) An entrant serving some **purpose of the possessor** generally is treated as an invitee, e.g., garbage collectors, mail carriers, etc.

(b) One who comes **under normal circumstances during working hours** generally is treated as an invitee, e.g., census takers, health inspectors, etc.

(c) Under the **"firefighter's rule,"** police officers and firefighters are generally treated like licensees rather than invitees, based on public policy or assumption of risk grounds. They cannot recover for a landowner's failure to inspect or repair dangerous conditions that are an inherent risk of their law enforcement or firefighting activity.

(3) Scope of Invitation

A person loses her status as an invitee if she exceeds the scope of the invitation—if she goes into a portion of the premises where her invitation cannot reasonably be said to extend. (Note that the invitation normally does extend to the entrance and steps of a building.)

Example: Gas station customer, buying gas, loses status as invitee when she leaves pumps and falls into grease pit inside station. (Reversion to licensee, perhaps even trespasser, status.)

(4) Duty Owed

The landowner owes an invitee a general duty to use reasonable and ordinary care in keeping the property reasonably safe for the benefit of the invitee. This general duty includes the **duties owed to licensees** (to warn of or make safe nonobvious, dangerous conditions known to the landowner and to use ordinary care in active operations on the property) *plus* a *duty to make reasonable inspections* to discover dangerous conditions and, thereafter, make them safe.

(a) Warning May Suffice
The requirement to "make safe" dangerous conditions usually is satisfied if a reasonable warning has been given.

(b) Obviousness of Danger
A duty to warn usually does not exist where the dangerous condition is so obvious that the invitee should reasonably have been aware of it. "Obviousness" is determined by all of the surrounding circumstances.
Example: A banana peel visible on the floor of a supermarket might not be considered obvious if a shopper's attention would likely be diverted by shelf displays.

d) Users of Recreational Land
In almost all states, a different standard applies by statute to users of recreational land. If an owner or occupier of open land permits the public to use the land for recreational purposes *without charging a fee*, the landowner is not liable for injuries suffered by a recreational user unless the landowner *willfully and maliciously* failed to guard against or warn of a dangerous condition or activity.
Example: The owner of a large tract of undeveloped rural land who permits the general public to use a pond on the land for swimming and fishing would be covered by this type of statute, whereas the owner of a swimming pool who permits his house guests to swim whenever they visit would not be covered by the statute (he would owe his guests the usual duties owed to licensees).

3) Duties of a Lessor of Realty

a) General Duty Rule
Ordinarily, tort liability in regard to conditions on the property is an *incident of occupation and control*. Thus, when the owner leases the entire premises to another, the lessee, coming into occupation and control, becomes burdened with the duty to maintain the premises in such a way as to avoid unreasonable risk of harm to others. Similarly, where the owner leases *portions* of the premises to tenants, the owner continues to be subject to liability as a landowner for unreasonably dangerous conditions in those portions of the premises such as corridors, entry lobby, elevators, etc., used in common by all tenants, or by third persons, and over which the owner has retained occupation and control.

b) Exceptions
This basic duty, however, is subject to certain exceptions and extensions, as set forth below.

(1) Duty of Lessor to Lessee

The lessor is obligated to give *warning* to the lessee of *existing defects* in the premises of which the lessor is aware, or has reason to know, and which he knows the lessee is not likely to discover on reasonable inspection.

(2) Effect of Lessor's Covenant to Repair

If the lessor has covenanted to make repairs and reserves the right to enter the leased premises for the purpose of inspecting for defects and repairing them, he is subject to *liability for unreasonably dangerous conditions*.

(3) Effect of Voluntary Repairs by Lessor

If the lessor, though under no obligation to make repairs, does so, he is subject to liability if he does so *negligently*, failing to cure the defect; it is not necessary that his negligent repairs make the condition worse.

(4) Effect of Admission of the Public

If the lessor leases the premises knowing that the lessee intends to admit the public, the lessor is subject to *liability for unreasonably dangerous conditions existing at the time he transfers possession* where the nature of the defect and length and nature of the lease indicate that the tenant will not repair (e.g., lessor rents convention hall to tenant for three-day period). This liability continues until the defect is actually remedied. A mere warning to the lessee concerning the defect is *not* sufficient.

(The duty of care of tenants and lessors is also covered in the Real Property outline.)

c) Tenant Remains Liable to Invitees and Licensees

Keep in mind that the potential liability of the lessor for dangerous conditions on the premises does not relieve the tenant, as occupier of the land, of liability for injuries to third persons from the dangerous conditions within the tenant's control.

4) Duties of Vendor of Realty

The vendor, at the time of transfer of possession to the vendee, has the *duty to disclose* concealed, unreasonably dangerous conditions of which the vendor knows or has reason to know, and of which he knows the vendee is ignorant and is not likely to discover on reasonable inspection. The vendor's responsibility continues until the vendee should have, in the exercise of reasonable care in inspection and maintenance, discovered and remedied the defect.

e. Statutory Standards of Care

1) When Statutory Standard Applicable

The precise standard of care in a common law negligence case may be established by proving the applicability to that case of a statute providing for criminal penalties (including fines). If this is done, a clearly stated specific duty imposed by the statute will replace the more general common law duty of due care. In proving the availability of the statutory standard, plaintiff must show the following:

a) Plaintiff Within Protected Class

The plaintiff must show that she is in the class intended to be protected by the statute.

Example: A statute requiring a landowner to keep a building in safe condition is meant to protect only those rightfully on the premises and not trespassers.

b) Particular Harm to Be Avoided

The plaintiff must show that the statute was designed to prevent the type of harm that the plaintiff suffered.

Example: Violation of a Sunday closing law is not evidence of negligence in the case of an accident in a store on Sunday.

2) Excuse for Violation

Violation of some statutes may be excused:

a) Where **compliance would cause more danger** than violation; e.g., defendant drives onto wrong side of road to avoid hitting children who dart into his path; or

b) Where **compliance would be beyond defendant's control**, e.g., blind pedestrian crosses against light.

3) Effect of Establishing Violation of Statute

Most courts still adhere to the rule that violation of a statute is "negligence per se." This means that plaintiff will have established a **conclusive presumption of duty and breach of duty.** (Plaintiff still must establish causation and damages to complete the prima facie case for negligence.)

A significant **minority** of courts, however, are unwilling to go this far. They hold either that (i) a rebuttable presumption as to duty and breach thereof arises, or (ii) the statutory violation is only prima facie evidence of negligence.

4) Effect of Compliance with Statute

Even though the violation of an applicable criminal statute may be negligence, compliance with it will **not necessarily establish due care**. If there are unusual circumstances or increased danger beyond the minimum that the statute was designed to meet, it may be found that there is negligence in not doing more.

5) Violation of a Civil Remedy Statute

Where the statute in question provides for a civil remedy, plaintiff will sue directly under the statute; i.e., it is not a common law negligence case.

f. **Duty Regarding Negligent Infliction of Emotional Distress**

A duty to avoid negligent infliction of emotional distress may be breached when the defendant creates a foreseeable risk of physical injury to the plaintiff. The plaintiff usually must satisfy two requirements to prevail: (i) plaintiff must be within the "zone of danger"; and (ii) plaintiff must suffer physical symptoms from the distress.

1) **Plaintiff Must Be Within the "Zone of Danger"**

The plaintiff usually must show that her distress has been caused by a threat of physical impact; i.e., she was within the "zone of danger."

Example: Driver negligently ran a red light and skidded to a stop inches away from Pedestrian, who was properly crossing the street in a crosswalk. Pedestrian's shock from nearly being run over caused her to suffer a heart attack. Pedestrian can recover for negligent infliction of emotional distress because she was in the zone of danger.

2) **Plaintiff Must Suffer Physical Symptoms from the Distress**

For the plaintiff to recover damages, most courts usually require that the defendant's conduct cause the plaintiff emotional distress that manifests itself in **physical symptoms** (e.g., a nervous breakdown, miscarriage, or heart attack, but note that severe shock to the nervous system that causes physical symptoms will satisfy this requirement). A growing minority of states have dropped the requirement of physical symptoms.

3) **Special Situations Where Requirements Not Always Necessary**

a) **Bystander Not in Zone of Danger Seeing Injury to Another**

Traditionally, a bystander outside the "zone of danger" of physical injury who sees the defendant negligently injuring another could not recover damages for her own distress. A majority of states now allow recovery in these cases as long as (i) the plaintiff and the person injured by the defendant are **closely related**, (ii) **the plaintiff was present** at the scene of the injury, and (iii) the plaintiff **personally observed or perceived** the event. Many of these states also drop the requirement of physical symptoms in this situation.

Example: Mother sees her child struck by negligently driven automobile on the other side of the street and goes into shock. Most courts would allow recovery.

b) **Special Relationship Between Plaintiff and Defendant**

The defendant may be liable for directly causing the plaintiff severe emotional distress when a duty arises from the relationship between the plaintiff and the defendant, such that the defendant's negligence has great potential to cause emotional distress. Many states drop the requirement of physical symptoms in this situation as well.

Example: Doctor negligently confused Patient's file with another and told Patient he had a terminal illness. Patient, who in fact did not have the illness, was shocked and became nauseated as a result. Patient can recover for negligent infliction of emotional distress. Although there was no threat of physical impact from

Doctor's negligence, negligently providing a false diagnosis of a terminal illness creates a foreseeable risk of severe emotional distress to the patient.

c) Other Situations

The plaintiff may be able to recover without proving the two requirements for this tort in other special situations where the defendant's negligence creates a great likelihood of emotional distress. These include a defendant providing an erroneous report that a relative of the plaintiff has died or a defendant mishandling a relative's corpse.

g. Affirmative Duties to Act

1) General Rule—No Duty to Act

As a general matter, no legal duty is imposed on any person to affirmatively act for the benefit of others. This general rule is, however, subject to exception, as indicated below.

2) Assumption of Duty to Act by Acting

One who gratuitously acts for the benefit of another, although under no duty to do so in the first instance, is then under a duty to act like an ordinary, prudent, reasonable person and continue the assistance.

Example: Defendant, under no duty to aid Plaintiff who has been injured, picks her up and carries her into a room. He then leaves her there unattended for seven hours and Plaintiff's condition is worsened. Defendant, having acted, may be considered to have breached his duty to act reasonably.

a) "Good Samaritan" Statutes

A number of states have enacted statutes exempting licensed doctors, nurses, etc., who voluntarily and gratuitously render emergency treatment, from liability for ordinary negligence. Liability still exists, however, for gross negligence.

3) Peril Due to Defendant's Conduct

One whose conduct (whether negligent or innocent) places another in a position of peril is under a duty to use reasonable care to aid or assist that person.

4) Special Relationship Between Parties

A defendant having a special relationship to the plaintiff (e.g., parent-child, employer-employee) may be liable for failure to act if the plaintiff is in peril.

a) Duty of Common Carriers

Common carriers are under a duty to use reasonable care to aid or assist passengers.

b) Duty of Places of Public Accommodation

Innkeepers, restaurateurs, shopkeepers, and others who gather the public for profit have a duty to use reasonable care to aid or assist their patrons and to prevent injury to them from third persons.

5) Role of Contract in Creating Duty

a) Nonfeasance—No Duty
In general, for mere nonfeasance, there is no tort duty of care, regardless of whether the defendant promises to undertake action gratuitously or for consideration. Liability for breach of contract extends only to parties in privity.

b) Misfeasance—Due Care Required
However, for misfeasance, failure to perform with due care contractual obligations owed to one may give rise to violation of a legal duty.

Example: Pursuant to a contract with the building owner, Defendant inspected and repaired the elevator, and did so carelessly. The elevator operator is injured as a result. Defendant is liable to the operator.

6) Duty to Prevent Harm from Third Persons
Generally, there is no duty to prevent a third person from injuring another. In some situations, however, such an affirmative duty might be imposed. In such cases, it must appear that the defendant had the *actual ability* and *authority* to control the third person's action. Thus, for example, bailors may be liable for the acts of their bailees, parents may be liable for the acts of their children, employers may be liable for the acts of their employees, etc.

It is generally required for imposition of such a duty that the defendant *knows* or *should know* that the third person is likely to commit such acts as would require the exercise of control by the defendant.

C. BREACH OF DUTY
Where the defendant's conduct falls short of that level required by the applicable standard of care owed to the plaintiff, she has breached her duty. Whether the duty of care is breached in an individual case is a question for the trier of fact. Evidence may be offered to establish the standard by which defendant's conduct is to be measured, e.g., custom or usage, applicability of a statute, etc.

1. Custom or Usage
Custom or usage may be introduced to establish the standard of care in a given case. However, customary methods of conduct do not furnish a test that is conclusive for controlling the question of whether certain conduct amounted to negligence.

2. Violation of Statute
As we have seen above, the existence of a duty owed to plaintiff and breach thereof may be established by proof that defendant violated an applicable statute.

3. Res Ipsa Loquitur
The circumstantial evidence doctrine of res ipsa loquitur ("the thing speaks for itself") deals

with those situations where the fact that a particular injury occurred may itself establish or tend to establish a breach of duty owed. Where the facts are such as to strongly indicate that plaintiff's injuries resulted from defendant's negligence, the trier of fact may be permitted to infer defendant's liability. Res ipsa loquitur requires the plaintiff to show the following:

a.   Inference of Negligence
Plaintiff must establish that the accident causing his injury is the type that would not normally occur unless someone was negligent.
Example: A windowpane fell from a second story window in Defendant's building, landing on Plaintiff. Res ipsa loquitur may apply.

b.   Negligence Attributable to Defendant
Plaintiff must establish evidence connecting defendant with the negligence in order to support a finding of liability, i.e., evidence that this type of accident ordinarily happens because of the negligence of someone in defendant's position. This requirement often can be satisfied by showing that the instrumentality that caused the injury was in the exclusive control of defendant, although actual possession of the instrumentality is not necessary.

1)   Multiple Defendants Problem
Where more than one person may have been in control of the instrumentality, res ipsa loquitur generally may *not* be used to establish a prima facie case of negligence against any individual party.
Example: Plaintiff left the operating room with an injury to part of her body that was healthy prior to entering the operating room. The injury was not in the zone of the original operation. Under the traditional rule, res ipsa loquitur may not be available to establish that any individual in that room was negligent. This is so despite the fact that, clearly, someone was negligent. However, many courts today take a different approach in such cases where defendants have control of the evidence, requiring each defendant to establish that his negligence did not cause the injury. [*See, e.g.,* Ybarra v. Spangard, 25 Cal. 2d 486 (1944)]

Compare: The doctrine would be available in all states where a particular defendant had the power of control over the site of the injury. For example, Plaintiff sues Surgeon after a sponge was left in his body at the site of the surgery. Even though Surgeon left it to her assistants to remove the sponges and close up the wound, her responsibility and power of control over the surgery itself allows Plaintiff to use res ipsa loquitur against her.

c.   Plaintiff's Freedom from Negligence
Plaintiff must also establish that the injury was not attributable to him, but may do so by his own testimony.

d.   Effect of Res Ipsa Loquitur

1)   No Directed Verdict for Defendant
The doctrine, where applicable, does not change the burden of proof, nor does it

create a presumption of negligence. Where the res ipsa element has been proved, the plaintiff has made a prima facie case and no directed verdict may be given for the defendant.

2) Effect of Defendant's Evidence of Due Care

However, the effect of defendant's evidence that due care was exercised has the same effect in a res ipsa case as in all other cases. If the jury rejects the defendant's evidence and draws the permissible inference of negligence, it will find for the plaintiff. If defendant's evidence overcomes the permissible inference that may be drawn from the res ipsa proof, the jury may find for the defendant. Such a finding for the defendant may result even where defendant rests without offering evidence on the issue if the jury elects not to infer negligence.

D. CAUSATION

1. Actual Cause (Causation in Fact)

Before the defendant's conduct can be considered a proximate cause of plaintiff's injury, it must first be a *cause in fact* of the injury. Several tests exist:

a. "But For" Test

An act or omission to act is the cause in fact of an injury when the injury would not have occurred *but for* the act.

Example: Failure to provide a fire escape is a cause of death of one who is thereby unable to flee a fire, but it is not a cause of death of one who suffocated in bed.

1) Concurrent Causes

The "but for" test applies where several acts combine to cause the injury, but none of the acts standing alone would have been sufficient (e.g., two negligently driven cars collide, injuring a passenger). But for any of the acts, the injury would not have occurred.

b. Additional Tests

Under certain circumstances, the "but for" test is inadequate to determine causation in fact. The courts must rely upon other tests.

1) Joint Causes—Substantial Factor Test

Where several causes commingle and bring about an injury—and any one alone would have been sufficient to cause the injury—it is sufficient if defendant's conduct was a "substantial factor" in causing the injury.

Example: Two fires meet and burn a farm. Either fire alone would have done the damage without the other. Under the "but for" test, neither was the "cause," since, looking at either fire alone, the loss would have occurred without it. Rather than reach this result, the courts consider as causes all those things that were a "substantial factor" in causing injury.

2) Alternative Causes Approach

a) Burden of Proof Shifts to Defendants

A problem of causation exists where two or more persons have been negligent, but uncertainty exists as to which one caused plaintiff's injury. Under the alternative causes approach, plaintiff must prove that harm has been caused to him by one of them (with uncertainty as to which one). The burden of proof then shifts to defendants, and each must show that his negligence is not the actual cause.

Example: Alex and Basil both negligently fire shotguns in Clara's direction. Clara is hit by one pellet, but she cannot tell which gun fired the shot. Under the alternative causes approach, Alex and Basil will have to prove that the pellet was not theirs. If unable to do this, they may both be liable. [Summers v. Tice, 33 Cal. 2d 80 (1948)]

b) Applied in Enterprise Liability Cases

This concept has been extended in some cases to encompass industry groups.

Example: Daughters of women who took the anti-miscarriage drug diethylstilbestrol ("DES") contracted cancer as a result of the drug manufacturer's negligence. However, because the cancer appeared many years after the DES was ingested, it was usually impossible to determine which manufacturer of DES had supplied the drug taken by any particular plaintiff. Several courts have required all producers of DES unable to prove their noninvolvement to pay in proportion to their percentage of the market share. [*See* Sindell v. Abbott Laboratories, 26 Cal. 3d 588, *cert. denied*, 449 U.S. 912 (1980)]

2. Proximate Cause (Legal Causation)

In addition to being a cause in fact, the defendant's conduct must also be a proximate cause of the injury. Not all injuries "actually" caused by defendant will be deemed to have been proximately caused by his acts. Thus, the doctrine of proximate causation is a *limitation of liability* and deals with liability or nonliability for unforeseeable or unusual consequences of one's acts.

a. General Rule of Liability

The general rule of proximate cause is that the defendant is liable for all harmful results that are *the normal incidents of and within the increased risk caused by* his acts. In other words, if one of the reasons that make defendant's act negligent is a greater risk of a particular harmful result occurring, and that harmful result does occur, defendant generally is liable. This test is based on *foreseeability*.

b. Direct Cause Cases

A direct cause case is one where the facts present an *uninterrupted chain* of events from the time of the defendant's negligent act to the time of plaintiff's injury. In short, there is no external intervening force of any kind.

1) Foreseeable Harmful Results—Defendant Liable

If a particular harmful result was at all foreseeable from defendant's negligent conduct, the unusual manner in which the injury occurred or the unusual timing of cause and effect is irrelevant to defendant's liability.

Example: D is driving her sports car down a busy street at a high rate of speed when a pedestrian steps out into the crosswalk in front of her. D has no time to stop, so she swerves to one side. Her car hits a parked truck and bounces to the other side of the street, where it hits another parked vehicle, propelling it into the street and breaking the pedestrian's leg. D is liable despite the unusual way in which she caused the injury to the pedestrian.

2) Unforeseeable Harmful Results—Defendant Not Liable

In the rare case where defendant's negligent conduct creates a risk of a harmful result, but an entirely different and totally unforeseeable type of harmful result occurs, most courts hold that defendant is not liable for that harm.

Example: D, a cabdriver, is driving too fast on a busy elevated highway, threatening P, his passenger, with injury. Without warning, the section of highway that D is on collapses because its support beams had deteriorated with age. P is seriously injured. Even if D's negligent conduct was an actual cause of P's injury (because the cab would not have been on that section of the highway but for D's speeding), courts would not hold D liable for the injury to P.

c. Indirect Cause Cases

An indirect cause case is one where the facts indicate that a force came into motion *after* the time of defendant's negligent act and combined with the negligent act to cause injury to plaintiff. In short, indirect cause cases are those where *intervening forces* are present. Whether an intervening force will cut off defendant's liability for plaintiff's injury is determined by foreseeability.

1) Foreseeable Results Caused by Foreseeable Intervening Forces—Defendant Liable

Where defendant's negligence caused a foreseeable harmful response or reaction from an intervening force or created a foreseeable risk that an intervening force would harm plaintiff, defendant is liable for the harm caused.

a) Common Foreseeable Intervening Forces

Intervening forces that are normal responses or reactions to the situation created by defendant's negligent act *are almost always foreseeable*.

The following are common intervening forces that are almost always foreseeable.

(1) Subsequent Medical Malpractice

The original tortfeasor is usually liable for the aggravation of plaintiff's condition caused by the malpractice of plaintiff's treating physician.

(2) Negligence of Rescuers

Generally, rescuers are viewed as foreseeable intervening forces, and so the original tortfeasor usually is liable for their negligence.

(3) Efforts to Protect Person or Property
Defendant usually is liable for negligent efforts on the part of persons
to protect life or property of themselves or third persons endangered by
defendant's negligence.

(4) "Reaction" Forces
Where defendant's actions cause another to "react" (e.g., negligently
firing a gun at another's feet), liability generally attaches for any harm
inflicted by the "reacting" person on another.

(5) Subsequent Disease
The original tortfeasor usually is liable for diseases caused in part by the
weakened condition in which defendant has placed the plaintiff by negligently injuring her; e.g., injury caused by defendant weakens plaintiff,
making her susceptible to pneumonia.

(6) Subsequent Accident
Where the plaintiff suffers a subsequent injury following her original
injury, and the original injury was a substantial factor in causing the
second accident, the original tortfeasor is usually liable for damages
arising from the second accident. For example, as a result of defendant's
negligence, plaintiff's leg is broken. Walking on crutches, plaintiff falls
and breaks her other leg.

b) Independent Intervening Forces
Independent intervening forces also operate on the situation created by defendant's negligence but are independent actions rather than natural responses or
reactions to the situation. Independent intervening forces may be foreseeable
where *defendant's negligence increased the risk that these forces would
cause harm* to the plaintiff.

The following are common fact situations involving independent intervening
forces:

(1) Negligent Acts of Third Persons
Defendant is liable for harm caused by the negligence of third persons
where such negligence was a foreseeable risk created by defendant's
conduct.
Example: D negligently blocked a sidewalk, forcing P to walk in the
                 roadway, where he is struck by a negligently driven car. D
                 is liable to P.

(2) Criminal Acts and Intentional Torts of Third Persons
If defendant's negligence created a foreseeable risk that a third person
would commit a crime or intentional tort, defendant's liability will not be
cut off by the crime or tort.
Example: D, a parking lot attendant, negligently left the keys in P's
                 car and the doors unlocked when he parked it, allowing a
                 thief to steal it. D is liable to P.

(3) Acts of God

Acts of God will not cut off defendant's liability if they are foreseeable.

Example: D, a roofer, negligently left a hammer on P's roof at the end of the day. P is struck by the hammer when a strong wind blows it off the roof. D is liable to P.

2) Foreseeable Results Caused by Unforeseeable Intervening Forces—Defendant Usually Liable

The problem: Defendant is negligent because his conduct threatens a result of a particular kind that will injure plaintiff. This result is ultimately produced by an ***unforeseeable*** intervening force. Most courts would generally find liability here because they give greater weight to foreseeability of result than to foreseeability of the intervening force. An exception exists, however, where the intervening force is an unforeseeable ***crime*** or ***intentional tort*** of a third party; it will be deemed a "superseding force" that cuts off defendant's liability (*see* discussion below).

Examples: 1) Defendant failed to clean residue out of an oil barge, leaving it full of explosive gas. Negligence, of course, exists since an explosion resulting in harm to any person in the vicinity was foreseeable from any one of several possible sources. An unforeseeable bolt of lightning struck the barge, exploding the gas and injuring workers on the premises. Defendant is liable.

             2) Same facts as above example, except that an arsonist caused the explosion. Most courts would not hold Defendant liable here. They think it unfair to make him responsible for such malevolent conduct. The important point here is that an unforeseeable intervening force may still relieve the defendant of liability if it is an unforeseeable crime or intentional tort of a third party.

3) Unforeseeable Results Caused by Foreseeable Intervening Forces—Defendant Not Liable

Most intervening forces that produce unforeseeable results are considered to be unforeseeable intervening forces (*see* below). Similarly, most results caused by foreseeable intervening forces are treated as foreseeable results. In the rare case where a foreseeable intervening force causes a totally unforeseeable result, most courts would not hold the defendant liable.

Example: D, a cabdriver, was driving recklessly during a violent windstorm that was blowing large branches and other debris onto the road, creating a risk to P, his passenger, that D would not be able to stop the cab in time to avoid an accident. D slammed on his brakes to avoid a large branch in the road, causing his cab to swerve sideways onto the shoulder of the road. Before he could proceed, another branch crashed onto the roof of the cab, breaking a window and causing P to be cut by flying glass. D is not liable to P even though his negligent driving was the actual (but for) cause of P's injury and the wind that was blowing the branches down was a foreseeable intervening force.

4) **Unforeseeable Results Caused by Unforeseeable Intervening Forces—Defendant Not Liable**

As a general rule, intervening forces that produce unforeseeable results (i.e., results that were not within the increased risk created by defendant's negligence) will be deemed to be unforeseeable and *superseding*. A superseding force is one that serves to *break the causal connection* between defendant's initial negligent act and the ultimate injury, and itself becomes a direct, immediate cause of the injury. Thus, defendant will be relieved of liability for the consequences of his antecedent conduct.

Example: D negligently blocks a road, forcing P to take an alternate road. Another driver negligently collides with P on this road, injuring him. Even though D is an actual (but for) cause of P's injury, the other driver's conduct is an unforeseeable intervening force because D's negligence did not increase the risk of its occurrence. Thus, the other driver is a superseding force that cuts off D's liability for his original negligent act.

d. **Unforeseeable Extent or Severity of Harm—Defendant Liable**

In both direct cause and indirect cause cases, the fact that the extent or severity of the harm was not foreseeable does not relieve defendant of liability; i.e., the tortfeasor takes his victim as he finds him. This is also known as the "eggshell-skull plaintiff" rule. Thus, where defendant's negligence causes an aggravation of plaintiff's existing physical or mental illness, defendant is liable for the damages caused by the aggravation.

Example: A car negligently driven by D collides with a car driven by P. P suffers a slight concussion, which was foreseeable, and also suffers a relapse of an existing mental illness, which was not foreseeable. D is liable for all of P's damages.

E. **DAMAGES**

Damage is an essential element of plaintiff's prima facie case for negligence. This means *actual* harm or injury. Unlike the situation for some of the intentional torts, damage will not be presumed. Thus, nominal damages are not available in an action in negligence; some proof of harm must be offered.

1. **Damages Recoverable in the Action**

a. **Personal Injury**

Plaintiff is to be compensated for *all* his damages (past, present, and prospective), both special and general. This includes fair and adequate compensation for *economic damages*, such as medical expenses and lost earnings, and *noneconomic damages*, such as pain and suffering. Plaintiff is also entitled to compensation for impaired future earning capacity, discounted to present value so as to avoid an excess award; i.e., plaintiff receives an amount that, if securely invested, would produce the income that the jury wishes him to have.

1) **Foreseeability Irrelevant**

As noted above in the proximate cause section, it is generally not necessary to foresee the extent of the harm. In other words, a tortfeasor takes the victim as he finds him.

2) **Emotional Distress Damages**

Plaintiff's noneconomic damages include damages for any emotional distress suffered as a result of the physical injury.

Example: Plaintiff was struck by a piece of metal when the engine blew on a defectively manufactured lawnmower. The piece of metal lodged in his spine at an inoperable location, significantly increasing his risk of future paralysis. In plaintiff's products liability action against the manufacturer of the lawnmower, plaintiff can recover damages not only for his physical injury but also for the emotional distress he suffers from his knowledge of the risk of paralysis, because it arises out of the physical injury caused by the defective product.

b. **Property Damage**

The measure of damages for property damage is the reasonable ***cost of repair***, or, if the property has been almost or completely destroyed, its ***fair market value*** at the time of the accident. Courts generally do not permit recovery of emotional distress damages for negligent harm to property.

c. **Punitive Damages**

Punitive damages generally are not available in negligence cases. However, if the defendant's conduct was "wanton and willful," reckless, or malicious, most jurisdictions permit recovery of punitive damages.

d. **Nonrecoverable Items**

Certain items are not recoverable as damages in negligence actions. These include:

1) Interest from date of damage in personal injury action; and

2) Attorneys' fees.

2. **Duty to Mitigate Damages**

As in all cases, the plaintiff has a duty to take reasonable steps to mitigate damages—in property damage cases to preserve and safeguard the property, and in personal injury cases to seek appropriate treatment to effect a cure or healing and to prevent aggravation. Failure to mitigate precludes recovery of any additional damages caused by aggravation of the injury.

3. **Collateral Source Rule**

As a general rule, damages are not reduced or mitigated by reason of benefits received by plaintiff from other sources, e.g., health insurance, sick pay from employer. Hence, at trial, defendants may not introduce evidence relating to any such financial aid from other sources. A growing number of states have made exceptions to this rule in certain types of actions (e.g., medical malpractice actions), allowing defendants to introduce evidence of insurance awards or disability benefits.

Note: These damages rules also are generally applicable to actions based on intentional torts.

F. DEFENSES TO NEGLIGENCE

1. Contributory Negligence

a. Standard of Care for Contributory Negligence

1) General Rule
The standard of care required is the same as that for ordinary negligence.

2) Rescuers
A plaintiff may take extraordinary risks when attempting a rescue without being considered contributorily negligent. The emergency situation is one of the factors taken into account when evaluating the plaintiff's conduct.

3) Remaining in Danger
It may be contributorily negligent to fail to remove oneself from danger, e.g., remaining in a car with a drunk driver.

4) Violation of Statute by Plaintiff
Plaintiff's contributory negligence may be established by his violation of a statute under the same rules that govern whether a statute can establish defendant's negligence (*see* B.3.e., *supra*).

5) As Defense to Violation of Statute by Defendant
Contributory negligence is ordinarily a defense to negligence proved by defendant's violation of an applicable statute. But where the defendant's negligence arose from violation of a statute designed to protect this particular class of plaintiffs from their own incapacity and lack of judgment, then plaintiff's contributory negligence is *not* a defense.

Example: D is exceeding the speed limit in a school zone when a child on his way to school darts into the street without looking. Because of her speed, D is unable to stop and hits the child. Any contributory negligence on the child's part is not a defense to D's violation of the statute, because the statute was designed to protect children on their way to school.

b. Avoidable Consequences Distinguished
As we have seen, plaintiff owes a duty to mitigate damages to person or property after the damage is inflicted. If he does not properly do this, then damages will be reduced. Failure to do this, however, is an avoidable consequence, not contributory negligence.

c. No Defense to Intentional Torts
Contributory negligence is never a defense to an action for an intentional tort or for willful or wanton misconduct.

d. Effect of Contributory Negligence
At common law, plaintiff's contributory negligence completely barred his right to recover. This was so even though the degree of defendant's negligence was much greater than that of plaintiff.

The severe consequences of strict application of contributory negligence rules initially caused courts to develop "escape" doctrines, such as *last clear chance* (below). More recently, however, most jurisdictions have rejected entirely the "all or nothing" approach of contributory negligence in favor of a *comparative negligence* system (discussed *infra*).

e. Last Clear Chance

The doctrine of last clear chance, sometimes called "the humanitarian doctrine," permits the plaintiff to recover *despite* his own contributory negligence. Under this rule, the person with the last clear chance to avoid an accident who fails to do so is liable for negligence. (In effect, last clear chance is plaintiff's rebuttal against the defense of contributory negligence.)

Example: Bowater negligently parked his car on the railroad tracks. The train engineer saw him in time to stop but failed to do so. The engineer had the last clear chance, and thus the railroad will be liable for the accident.

1) "Helpless" vs. "Inattentive" Peril

Many cases distinguish between "helpless" and "inattentive" peril situations in applying last clear chance rules.

a) Helpless Peril

Helpless peril exists where plaintiff, through his contributory negligence, puts himself in a position of actual peril from which he cannot extricate himself. In many states, defendant is liable under these circumstances if she had either *actual* knowledge of plaintiff's predicament or if she *should have known* of plaintiff's predicament. Other states require actual knowledge.

b) Inattentive Peril

Inattentive peril exists where plaintiff, through his own negligence, is in a position of actual peril from which he could extricate himself if he were attentive. Almost all courts require *actual* knowledge of plaintiff's predicament on defendant's part.

2) Prior Negligence Cases

For last clear chance to operate, defendant must have been able to avoid harming plaintiff *at the time of the accident*. In short, defendant must have had the "last clear chance" to avoid the accident. Hence, if defendant's only negligence had occurred earlier, e.g., she negligently failed to have the steering wheel fixed, the courts will not apply last clear chance.

f. Imputed Contributory Negligence

Driver and Passenger are involved in an automobile accident with Cyclist. Driver is negligent; Cyclist is also negligent. Passenger, who is injured, brings an action against Cyclist. Cyclist argues that liability should be denied because of Driver's negligence to the same extent as if Passenger had been negligent himself. This is the concept of "imputed contributory negligence."

1) General Rule—Plaintiff May Proceed Against Both Negligent Parties

As a general rule, a plaintiff's action for his damages is *not* barred by imputed contributory negligence. He may proceed against both negligent parties as joint tortfeasors to the extent that each is a legal cause of the harm.

2) **When Contributory Negligence Is Imputed**
Contributory negligence will be imputed *only* where the plaintiff and the negligent person stand in such a relationship to each other that the courts find it proper to charge plaintiff with that person's negligence, i.e., where plaintiff would be found *vicariously* liable for the negligent person's conduct if a third party had brought the action. (*See also* Vicarious Liability, VII.A., *infra*.)

3) **Common Fact Situations**
The following situations should be noted for bar examination purposes:

a) **Employer and Employee**
The contributory negligence of the employee or agent acting within the scope of employment will be imputed to the employer or principal when the latter is a plaintiff suing a third person.

b) **Partners and Joint Venturers**
The contributory negligence of one partner or joint venturer will be imputed to the other when the other is a plaintiff suing a third person.

c) **Husband and Wife**
The contributory negligence of one spouse will *not* be imputed to the other when the other is a plaintiff suing a third person.

d) **Parent and Child**
The contributory negligence of the parent or guardian is *not* imputed to the child, nor is the contributory negligence of the child imputed to the parent in actions against a third party.

Note: As to sections c) and d) above, note that in a spouse's action for loss of the other spouse's services, or a parent's action for loss of a child's services or recovery of his medical expenses, the contributory negligence of the injured spouse or child *will* bar recovery by the other spouse or by the parent. This is not because negligence is imputed, but because the loss of services action is derivative and cannot succeed unless the main action succeeds (*see* VII.D.3., *infra*). This result would also be obtained in a wrongful death action.

e) **Automobile Owner and Driver**
Unless the automobile owner would be vicariously liable for the driver's negligence (because, e.g., the driver was an employee within the scope of employment), the contributory negligence of the driver will *not* be imputed to her. (Remember, in situations where the owner is a passenger, she may be liable for her *own negligence* in not preventing the accident.)

2. **Assumption of Risk**
The plaintiff may be denied recovery if he assumed the risk of any damage caused by the

defendant's acts. This assumption may be expressed or implied. To have assumed risk, either expressly or impliedly, the plaintiff must have **known of the risk** and **voluntarily** assumed it. It is irrelevant that plaintiff's choice is unreasonable.

a. Implied Assumption of Risk

Implied assumption of risk situations are harder to resolve as, of course, the fact issues are difficult to prove.

1) Knowledge of Risk

Plaintiff must have known of the risk. Knowledge may be implied where the risk is one that the average person would clearly appreciate, e.g., risk of being hit by a foul ball in a baseball game.

2) Voluntary Assumption

The plaintiff must voluntarily go ahead in the face of the risk. However, plaintiff may not be said to have assumed the risk where there is no available alternative to proceeding in the face of the risk, e.g., the only exit from a building is unsafe.

3) Certain Risks May Not Be Assumed

Because of public policy considerations, the courts uniformly hold that some risks may not be assumed. These include:

a) Common carriers and public utilities are not permitted to limit their liability for personal injury by a disclaimer on, e.g., a ticket, a posted sign, etc.

b) When a statute is enacted to protect a class, members of that class will not be deemed to have assumed any risk.
   Example: When a statute imposes safety regulations on an employer, the employee is held not to have assumed the risk where the statute is violated.

c) Risks will not be assumed in situations involving fraud, force, or an emergency. Thus, for example, one could take action to save his person or property without assuming a risk unless his actions involve an unreasonable risk out of proportion to the value of those rights.

b. Express Assumption of Risk

The risk may be assumed by express agreement. Such exculpatory clauses in a contract, intended to insulate one of the parties from liability resulting from his own negligence, are closely scrutinized but are generally enforceable. (Note that it is more difficult to uphold such an exculpatory clause in an adhesion contract.)

c. No Defense to Intentional Torts

Assumption of risk is not a defense to intentional torts. It is, however, a defense to wanton or reckless conduct.

3. Comparative Negligence

The vast **majority** of states now permit a contributorily negligent plaintiff to recover a percentage of his damages under some type of **comparative negligence** system. In every case where contributory negligence is shown, the trier of fact weighs plaintiff's negligence against that of defendant and reduces plaintiff's damages accordingly.

Example: Defendant negligently drove through a stop sign and collided with Plaintiff, who was contributorily negligent by driving inattentively. Plaintiff suffers damages of $100,000. If a jury finds that Plaintiff was 30% negligent and Defendant was 70% negligent, Plaintiff will recover $70,000.

a. Types of Comparative Negligence

1) "Partial" Comparative Negligence

Most comparative negligence jurisdictions will still bar the plaintiff's recovery if his negligence passes a threshold level. In some of these states, a plaintiff will be barred if his negligence was *more serious* than that of the defendant (i.e., the plaintiff will recover nothing if he was more than 50% at fault). In the other states, a plaintiff will be barred from recovering if his negligence was *at least as serious* as that of the defendant (i.e., the plaintiff will recover nothing if he was 50% or more at fault).

a) Multiple Defendants

If several defendants have contributed to plaintiff's injury, most of these states use a "combined comparison" approach to determine the threshold level (i.e., plaintiff's negligence is compared with the total negligence of all the defendants combined).

2) "Pure" Comparative Negligence

The "pure" variety of comparative negligence, adopted in a third of the comparative negligence states, allows recovery no matter how great plaintiff's negligence is (e.g., if plaintiff is 90% at fault and defendant 10%, plaintiff may still recover 10% of his damages). On the MBE, pure comparative negligence is the applicable rule unless the question specifies otherwise.

b. Comparative Negligence Illustrations

1) Partial Comparative Negligence Jurisdiction—Single Defendant

Plaintiff is 30% negligent and Defendant is 70% negligent in causing the accident. Each party suffers $100,000 in damages. Plaintiff will recover $70,000 from Defendant—$100,000 minus 30% ($30,000). Defendant will recover nothing from Plaintiff because Defendant was more than 50% at fault.

2) Partial Comparative Negligence Jurisdiction—Multiple Defendants

Plaintiff is 40% negligent in causing the accident and suffers $100,000 in damages. D1 is 35% negligent and D2 is 25% negligent. Plaintiff can recover $60,000 from either D1 or D2 under joint and several liability rules (*infra*, VII.B.1.). Note that if D1 or D2 also suffered damages, each of them would have a claim against the other two negligent parties because each one's negligence is less than the total negligence of the other two.

3) Pure Comparative Negligence Jurisdiction

Same facts as in illustration 1). Plaintiff has a right to recover $70,000 from

Defendant, and Defendant has a right to recover $30,000 from Plaintiff. Defendant's damages will be offset against Plaintiff's damages, and Plaintiff will have a net recovery of $40,000.

c. Effect on Other Doctrines

1) Last Clear Chance
Last clear chance is *not* used in most comparative negligence jurisdictions.

2) Assumption of Risk

a) Implied Assumption of Risk
Most comparative negligence jurisdictions have abolished entirely the defense of implied assumption of risk. In these jurisdictions, traditional assumption of risk situations must be broken down into two categories:

(1) When the defendant has only a *limited duty* to the plaintiff because of plaintiff's knowledge of the risks (e.g., being hit by a foul ball at a baseball game), a court may protect the defendant simply by holding that the defendant did not breach his limited duty of care. The defendant will still be liable for reckless conduct.

(2) More common is the situation that is a *variant of contributory negligence,* in that defendant's initial breach of duty to plaintiff is superseded by plaintiff's assumption of a risk (e.g., builder is negligent in not barricading torn-up sidewalk, but pedestrian chooses to use it despite availability of reasonable alternate route). Here, the *reasonableness* of plaintiff's conduct is relevant: If the plaintiff has behaved unreasonably, plaintiff is contributorily negligent and damages will be apportioned under the state's comparative negligence statute.

b) Express Assumption of Risk
Most comparative negligence jurisdictions retain the defense of express assumption of risk.

3) Wanton and Willful Conduct
In most comparative negligence jurisdictions, plaintiff's negligence *will* be taken into account even though the defendant's conduct was "wanton and willful" or "reckless." However, plaintiff's negligence is still not a defense to intentional tortious conduct by the defendant.

IV. LIABILITY WITHOUT FAULT (STRICT LIABILITY)

A. PRIMA FACIE CASE
To establish a prima facie case for strict liability, the following elements must be shown:

1. The nature of the defendant's activity imposes an *absolute duty* to *make safe*;

2.   The dangerous aspect of the activity is the *actual* and *proximate cause* of the plaintiff's injury; and

3.   The plaintiff suffered *damage* to person or property.

B.   LIABILITY FOR ANIMALS

1.   Trespassing Animals
The owner is strictly liable for the damage done by the trespass of his animals (other than household pets) as long as it was *reasonably foreseeable*.

2.   Personal Injuries

a.   Wild Animals—Strict Liability
The owner is strictly liable for injuries caused by wild animals (e.g., lion or bear), even those kept as pets.

b.   Domestic Animals—Knowledge Required
The owner of a domestic animal (including farm animals) is *not* strictly liable for injuries it causes. Such liability does, however, attach if the owner has knowledge of that particular animal's dangerous propensities (i.e., propensities more dangerous than normal for that species). This rule applies even if the animal has never actually injured anyone. Some states have "dog bite" statutes, applicable only to dogs, which impose strict liability in personal injury actions even without prior knowledge of dangerous characteristics.

c.   Persons Protected

1)   Licensees and Invitees—Landowner Strictly Liable
Strict liability for injuries inflicted by wild animals or abnormally dangerous domestic animals kept by the landowner on his land will usually be imposed where the person injured came onto the land as an invitee or licensee.

a)   Public Duty Exception
An exception is recognized where the landowner is under a *public duty to keep the animals* (e.g., as a public zookeeper); in such cases, negligence must be shown.

2)   Trespassers Must Prove Negligence
Strict liability in such cases generally is *not* imposed in favor of undiscovered trespassers against landowners. Trespassers cannot recover for injuries inflicted by the landowner's wild animals or abnormally dangerous domestic animals in the absence of *negligence*, e.g., as where the landowner knows that trespassers are on the land and fails to warn them of the animal.

a)   Compare—Intentional Use of Vicious Watchdogs
A landowner who protects his property from intruders by keeping a vicious watchdog that he knows is likely to cause *serious bodily harm* may be liable even to trespassers for injuries caused by the animal. This liability is based on

intentional tort principles: Because the landowner is not entitled to use deadly force in person to protect only property, he also may not use such force indirectly. (*See* I.D.4.b., *supra*.)

C. ABNORMALLY DANGEROUS ACTIVITIES

1. Definition
An activity may be characterized as abnormally dangerous if it involves a substantial risk of serious harm to person or property even when reasonable care is exercised. Whether an activity is abnormally dangerous is a question of law that the court can decide on a motion for directed verdict.

2. Test
The courts generally impose two requirements for finding an activity to be abnormally dangerous:

(i) The activity must create a foreseeable risk of *serious harm even when reasonable care is exercised* by all actors; and

(ii) The activity is *not a matter of common usage* in the community.

Example: In *Rylands v. Fletcher,* 3 H.L. 330 (1868), the House of Lords held a mill owner strictly liable when a neighbor's mines were flooded by water escaping from the mill owner's reservoir. This was considered an abnormal use in "mining country."

Common examples of abnormally dangerous activities include blasting, manufacturing explosives, crop dusting, and fumigating.

3. Products Liability
There may be strict liability imposed for damage caused by products, depending on the theory used by a court in resolving such problems. (*See* V.D., *infra*.)

D. EXTENT OF LIABILITY

1. Defendant Liable Only to Foreseeable Plaintiffs
In most states, the defendant is liable only to *"foreseeable plaintiffs"*—persons to whom a reasonable person would have foreseen a risk of harm under the circumstances. Generally, strict liability is not imposed on a defendant's blasting that hurled rock onto a person so far away that no reasonable person would have foreseen a danger. (Note, however, that some courts find liability for all blasting harm because of the intrinsic danger of defendant's activity.)

2. Harm Must Result from "Normally Dangerous Propensity"
The harm must result from the kind of danger to be anticipated from the dangerous animal or abnormally dangerous activity; i.e., it must flow from the "normally dangerous propensity" of the condition or thing involved.
Example: D's toothless pet leopard escapes from its cage without fault on D's part and wanders into a park, causing P to break her arm while trying to flee. D is strictly liable to P.

> *Compare:* D's dynamite truck blows a tire without warning and hits Pedestrian. D is not strictly liable to Pedestrian. However, if the truck then crashed and exploded, and the explosion injured Bystander, D would be strictly liable to Bystander.

3. Proximate Cause
The majority view is that the same rules of direct and indirect causation govern in strict liability as they do in negligence—defendant's liability can be cut off by unforeseeable intervening forces. In fact, the courts tend to hold more intervening forces "unforeseeable."

4. Defenses

a. Contributory Negligence States
In contributory negligence states, plaintiff's contributory negligence is *no* defense if the plaintiff simply failed to realize the danger or guard against its existence (unknowing contributory negligence). It *is* a defense, however, if plaintiff *knew* of the danger and his unreasonable conduct was the very cause of the harm from the wild animal or abnormally dangerous activity. Courts call this conduct "knowing" contributory negligence or a type of assumption of risk. Furthermore, assumption of risk of any type is a good defense to strict liability in contributory negligence states.

> *Example:* P knowingly and unreasonably tries to pass D's dynamite truck on a sharp curve, causing it to turn over and explode. Regardless of whether P's conduct is called contributory negligence or assumption of risk, P cannot recover.

b. Comparative Negligence States
Most comparative negligence states will now simply apply the same comparative negligence rules that they apply to negligence cases.

V. PRODUCTS LIABILITY

A. BASIC PRINCIPLES
In this context, "products liability" is the generic phrase used to describe the liability of a supplier of a product to one injured by the product.

1. Theories of Liability
Plaintiffs in products liability cases may have one of five possible theories of liability available to them:

(i) *Intent*;

(ii) *Negligence*;

(iii) *Strict liability*;

(iv) *Implied warranties of merchantability and fitness for a particular purpose*; and

(v) *Representation theories (express warranty and misrepresentation)*.

In an exam question, always consider a defendant's potential liability under each of the theories unless the call of the question indicates the theory that the plaintiff is using.

2. **Existence of a Defect**

To find liability under any products liability theory, plaintiff must show that the product was "defective" when the product left defendant's control.

a. **Types of Defects**

1) **Manufacturing Defects**

When a product emerges from a manufacturing process not only different from the other products, but also more dangerous than if it had been made the way it should have been, the product may be so "unreasonably dangerous" as to be defective because of the manufacturing process.

2) **Design Defects**

When all the products of a line are made identically according to manufacturing specifications, but have dangerous propensities because of their mechanical features or packaging, the entire line may be found to be defective because of poor design.

a) **Inadequate Warnings**

Inadequate warnings can be analyzed as a type of design defect. A product must have clear and complete warnings of any dangers that may not be apparent to users. For prescription drugs and medical devices, warnings need not be supplied to the patient; a warning to the prescribing physician usually will suffice (the "learned intermediary" rule).

b. **Proving a Defect**

In most jurisdictions, a product can be the basis for a products liability action if it is in a "defective condition unreasonably dangerous" to users.

1) **Manufacturing Defects**

For a manufacturing defect, the plaintiff will prevail if the product was *dangerous beyond the expectation of the ordinary consumer* because of a departure from its intended design.

a) **Defective Food Products**

Defects in food products are treated the same as manufacturing defects—the "consumer expectation" approach is used.

2) **Design Defects**

For design defects, the plaintiff usually must show a reasonable alternative design, i.e., that a *less dangerous modification or alternative was economically feasible*.

The factors that the courts consider under the "feasible alternative" approach are the following:

(i) Usefulness and desirability of the product;

(ii)   Availability of safer alternative products;

(iii) The dangers of the product that have been identified by the time of trial;

(iv)   Likelihood and probable seriousness of injury;

(v)   Obviousness of the danger;

(vi)   Normal public expectation of danger (especially for established products);

(vii) Avoidability of injury by care in use of product (including role of instructions and warnings); and

(viii) Feasibility of eliminating the danger without seriously impairing the product's function or making it unduly expensive.

Examples: 1) Although people often cut themselves on sharp knives, knives are of great utility. Since there is no way to avoid the harm without destroying the utility of the product, and the danger is apparent to users, the product is not ***unreasonably*** dangerous and the supplier would not be liable for injuries.

2) A power lawnmower that is marketed with no guard over the opening from which cut grass is blown may be unreasonably dangerous even though the product carries several warnings that hands and feet should be kept away from the opening and that rocks may be ejected from the opening. While the product's danger is within the expectations of the user, a court will ***compare the harm caused*** by the product with what it would ***cost*** to put a guard on the opening and consider whether the guard would impair the machine's operation in order to determine whether the product is "defective."

a)   Effect of Government Safety Standards
A product is deemed to be defective in design or warnings if it fails to comply with applicable government safety standards. On the other hand, a product's ***compliance*** with applicable government safety standards (including labeling requirements) is evidence—but not conclusive—that the product is ***not*** defective. [Restatement (Third) of Torts—Products Liability §4] Note also that federal labeling requirements ***do not preempt*** state products liability law on defective warnings. [Wyeth v. Levine, 555 U.S. 555 (2009)—product may comply with FDA labeling requirements but still be defective due to inadequate warnings]

c.   Common Defect Problems

1)   Misuse
Some products may be safe if used as intended, but may involve serious dangers if used in other ways. Courts have required suppliers to ***anticipate reasonably foreseeable uses*** even if they are "misuses" of the product.

Examples: 1) Although a screwdriver is intended only for turning screws, a manufacturer must anticipate that screwdrivers are commonly used to pry up lids of cans and must make screwdrivers reasonably safe for that use as well as for their intended use.

2) Liquid furniture polish provided for home use may be fit for its intended use, but the manufacturer must anticipate that it will be used around small children who may play with the bottle and spill or drink its contents. Thus, the manufacturer may have to design a product that is either safe when drunk or that has a childproof top. A simple warning of danger may not suffice in most states under the "feasible alternative" approach if a childproof top would cost little to install.

2) Scientifically Unknowable Risks

Occasionally, totally unpredictable hazards of a product do not become apparent until after the product has been marketed. This situation arises most frequently with new drugs that yield unpredictable side effects. Even though these drugs might be dangerous beyond consumer expectations, courts have generally refused to find the drugs unreasonably dangerous where it was impossible to anticipate the problem and make the product safer or provide warnings.

3) Allergies

Some products affect different users differently—the problem of allergic reaction. If the allergic group is significant in number, the product is defective unless adequate warnings are conveyed. The modern trend requires such *warnings* whenever the manufacturer knows that there is a danger of allergic reaction, even though the number affected may be very small.

3. No Requirement of Contractual Privity Between Plaintiff and Defendant

Whether the parties to the suit are in privity with each other is generally irrelevant under current law except for some of the warranty theories of liability.

a. Defined

The parties are in privity when a contractual relationship exists between them, such as a *direct sale* by the defendant retailer to the plaintiff buyer or the buyer's agent.

b. Vertical Privity Absent

Privity does not exist where the injured plaintiff, usually the buyer, is in the direct distribution chain but is suing a remote party—the wholesaler or the manufacturer—rather than the retailer who sold the product to the plaintiff.

c. Horizontal Privity Absent

Privity is also absent where the defendant, usually the retailer, is in the direct distribution chain with the buyer, but the plaintiff injured by the product is not the buyer, but rather the buyer's friend, neighbor, or a complete stranger.

B. LIABILITY BASED ON INTENT

A defendant will be liable to anyone injured by an unsafe product if the defendant intended the consequences or knew that they were substantially certain to occur. Liability based on an intentional tort is *not very common* in products liability cases.

1. **Tort Involved**
    If the requisite intent on the part of the defendant is established, the intentional tort on which the cause of action most likely will be based is *battery*.

2. **Privity Not Required**
    The presence or absence of privity is irrelevant where liability is based on an intentional tort.

3. **Damages**
    In addition to compensatory damages, punitive damages are available in a products liability case based on intent, to the same extent as with intentional torts in general.

4. **Defenses**
    The usual defenses available in intentional torts cases, such as consent, would be applicable. Negligence defenses, such as contributory negligence and assumption of risk, are not applicable.

C. LIABILITY BASED ON NEGLIGENCE

1. **Prima Facie Case**
    To establish a prima facie case for negligence in a products liability case, the following elements must be proved:

    a. The existence of a *legal duty* owed by the defendant to that particular plaintiff;

    b. *Breach* of that duty;

    c. *Actual* and *proximate cause*; and

    d. *Damages*.

2. **Defendant with Duty of Care to Plaintiff**

    a. **Product Supplier**
        Anyone who supplies a product to another owes a duty of care, including a casual seller (e.g., the owner of a used car selling it to a friend). The usual case, however, involves a defendant who is a commercial supplier of products. "Suppliers" include: the manufacturer of a chattel or a component part thereof, assembler, wholesaler, retailer, or even a used car dealer who sells reconditioned or rebuilt cars. Those who repair a product owe a general duty of care, but are not usually "suppliers" for purposes of products liability cases.

        1) **Labeling Another's Product**
            A retailer who *labels* a product as the retailer's own or assembles a product from components manufactured by others is liable for the negligence of the actual manufacturer, even though the retailer is not personally negligent.

b. Privity Not Required

Since the case of *MacPherson v. Buick,* 217 N.Y. 382 (1916), and its extensions, absence of privity is ***not*** a defense. The duty of due care is owed to ***any foreseeable plaintiff***—user, consumer, or bystander (such as a pedestrian injured when struck by an automobile with defective brakes).

3. Breach of Duty

To prove breach of duty, the plaintiff must show (i) ***negligent conduct*** by the defendant leading to (ii) the supplying of a ***"defective product"*** by the defendant.

a. Negligence

The defendant's conduct must fall below the standard of care expected of a reasonable person under like circumstances, considering such superior skill or training as defendant has or purports to have.

1) Proof of Negligence in Manufacturing Defect Case

a) Liability of Manufacturer

To show negligence in a manufacturing defect case, the plaintiff may invoke ***res ipsa loquitur*** against the manufacturer if the error is something that does not usually occur without the negligence of the manufacturer.

b) Liability of Dealer

Retailers and wholesalers owe a duty of due care to their customers and foreseeable victims. But the majority view is that a dealer who buys from a reputable supplier or manufacturer with no reason to anticipate that the product is dangerous need make only a cursory inspection of the goods to avoid liability for manufacturing defects.

2) Proof of Negligence in Design Defect Case

To establish that a manufacturer's negligence has resulted in a design defect, the plaintiff must show that those designing the product ***knew or should have known*** of enough facts to put a reasonable manufacturer on notice about the dangers of marketing the product as designed. Negligence is ***not*** shown if the danger of the product becomes apparent to the reasonable manufacturer only after the product has reached the public. A dealer has the same limited duty for design defects as for manufacturing defects (above).

b. Defective Product

The analysis of whether a product is so "unreasonably dangerous" as to be defective, discussed *supra,* applies equally to products liability actions based on negligence and to those based on strict tort liability.

4. Causation

The standard negligence analysis for both actual causation and proximate cause applies to products liability cases based on negligence.

a. Intermediary's Negligence

An intermediary's negligent failure to discover a defect is ***not*** a superseding cause, and the defendant whose original negligence created the defect will be held liable along with the intermediary. But when the intermediary's conduct becomes something more than ordinary foreseeable negligence, it becomes a superseding cause.

Example: P buys a defective product from Retailer who bought it from D. D would still be liable to P if Retailer had negligently failed to notice a serious defect attributable to D. But if Retailer had in fact discovered the defect but failed to warn P of it, D would not be liable.

5. Nature of Damages Recoverable

A plaintiff may recover for personal injury and property damages as under the usual negligence analysis. However, if the plaintiff suffers *only* economic loss (the product does not work as well as expected or requires repairs), most courts do not permit recovery under a negligence theory, requiring the plaintiff to bring an action for breach of warranty to recover such damages.

6. Defenses

The standard negligence defenses are applicable to any products liability case predicated on negligence. Thus, in comparative negligence states, plaintiff's contributory negligence may be used to reduce his recovery in an action against a negligent supplier of defective chattels.

D. LIABILITY BASED ON STRICT TORT LIABILITY

For those products liability cases where negligence on the part of the supplier would be difficult to prove, plaintiffs formerly attempted to bring their claims under traditional breach of warranty law as an alternative to using a negligence theory. Gradually, courts began to discard the privity requirement in warranty cases so that an increasing number of victims could recover without proof of negligence. This development has led to strict liability in tort for products liability cases.

1. Prima Facie Case

To establish a prima facie case in products liability based on strict liability in tort, the following elements must be proved:

a. The defendant is a *commercial supplier*;

b. The defendant produced or sold a *defective product*;

c. The defective product was the *actual* and *proximate cause* of the plaintiff's injury; and

d. The plaintiff suffered *damages* to person or property.

2. Defendant Must Be "Commercial Supplier"

Plaintiff must prove that defendant is a *commercial* supplier of the product in question, as distinguished from a casual seller (e.g., a homemaker who sells a jar of jam to a neighbor). Thus, strict liability applies when the defendant is a manufacturer (including the manufacturer of a defective component part), retailer, assembler, or wholesaler.

Examples: 1) A theater may be held strictly liable for selling rotten candy. Even though the theater is not in the primary business of selling candy and similar products, it is a retail supplier of those products.

2) If the boiler in use on a shoe manufacturer's land explodes, the shoe manufacturer's liability is *not* analyzed in terms of products liability because the manufacturer is not a commercial supplier of boilers.

Most courts have expanded strict liability to include mass producers of new homes, commercial lessors of products (e.g., car rental agencies), and sellers of used products that have been reconditioned or rebuilt.

    a.   **Distinction Between Product and Service**

        Strict liability is imposed only on one who supplies a product, as opposed to one primarily performing a service. Restaurants are treated as suppliers of products, while most courts treat a transfusion of infected blood (e.g., that gives the recipient hepatitis) as the rendition of a service.

        Example: If an airplane crashes due to defective piloting of the plane, a passenger must prove negligence in order to sue the airline company. However, if the passenger sues the manufacturer for a defect in the plane itself, strict liability in tort may be used.

3.   Product Not Substantially Altered

To hold the commercial supplier strictly liable for a product defect, the product must be expected to, and must in fact, reach the user or consumer without substantial change in the condition in which it is supplied.

4.   Privity Not Required

As with liability based on negligence, a majority of courts extend this liability to *any supplier in the chain of distribution* and extend the protection not only to buyers, but also to members of the buyer's family, guests, friends, and employees of the buyer, and foreseeable bystanders.

5.   Production or Sale of Defective Product

For a strict liability action, the plaintiff need not prove that the defendant was at fault in selling or producing a defective product—only that the product in fact is "defective" (*see* A.2.b., *supra*). As with products liability based on negligence, the two main categories of defects are manufacturing defects and design defects. The only difference in analysis is that the element of *negligence need not be proved* in a strict liability case. Thus, in contrast to a negligence action, a retailer in a strict liability action may be liable for a manufacturing or design defect simply because it was a commercial supplier of a defective product—*even if it had no opportunity to inspect the manufacturer's product before selling it*.

6.   Causation

    a.   **Actual Cause**

        To prove actual cause, the plaintiff must trace the harm suffered to a defect in the product that existed *when the product left the defendant's control*. However, if the defect is difficult to trace (such as if the product is destroyed), the plaintiff may rely on an inference that this type of product failure ordinarily would occur only as a result of a product defect. If the plaintiff claims that one of the defective conditions was the lack of an adequate warning, plaintiff is entitled to a presumption that an adequate warning would have been read and heeded.

b.   Proximate Cause
The same concepts of proximate cause governing general negligence and strict liability actions are applicable to strict liability actions for defective products. As with products liability cases based on negligence, the negligent failure of an intermediary to discover the defect does not cut off the supplier's strict liability.

7.   Nature of Damages Recoverable
The types of damages recoverable in strict liability actions for defective products are the same as those recoverable in negligence actions, namely personal injury and property damages. Once again, most states *deny* recovery under strict liability when the sole claim is for *economic loss*.

8.   Defenses

a.   Contributory Negligence States
According to Restatement (Second) section 402A, ordinary contributory negligence is not a defense in a strict products liability action where the plaintiff merely *failed to discover the defect or guard against its existence*, or where plaintiff's misuse was reasonably foreseeable (*supra*, A.2.c.1)). On the other hand, other types of unreasonable conduct, such as voluntarily and unreasonably encountering a known risk (i.e., assumption of risk), are defenses.

b.   Comparative Negligence States
As with other strict liability actions, most comparative negligence states apply their comparative negligence rules to strict products liability actions. [*See* Restatement (Third) of Torts—Products Liability §17]

c.   Disclaimers of Liability Ineffective
Disclaimers of liability are *irrelevant* in negligence or strict liability cases if personal injury or property damage has occurred.

E.   IMPLIED WARRANTIES OF MERCHANTABILITY AND FITNESS

1.   Proof of Fault Unnecessary
If a product fails to live up to the standards imposed by an implied warranty, the warranty is breached and the defendant will be liable. Plaintiff need not prove any fault on defendant's part.

2.   Scope of Coverage
The Uniform Commercial Code ("UCC") provisions apply to the *sale of goods* under Article 2 and the *lease of goods* under Article 2A.

3.   Implied Warranty of Merchantability
When a merchant who deals in a certain kind of goods sells such goods, there is an implied warranty that they are *merchantable*. [UCC §2-314] "Merchantable" means that the goods are of a quality equal to that *generally acceptable* among those who deal in similar goods and are *generally fit for the ordinary purposes* for which such goods are used.

4. Implied Warranty of Fitness for Particular Purpose

An implied warranty of fitness for a particular purpose arises when the seller knows or has reason to know:

(i) The particular purpose for which the goods are required; *and*

(ii) That the buyer is relying on the seller's skill or judgment to select or furnish suitable goods.

[UCC §2-315] Usually the seller will be a merchant of the type of goods in question, but this is not essential.

5. Privity

a. Vertical Privity No Longer Required

Although, in the early period of warranty law, courts held strictly to the requirement of complete privity between the plaintiff and defendant, a trend developed with courts finding the needed privity between remote parties on various fictions and theories—e.g., the warranty ran with the goods, or the retailer was the manufacturer's agent. As a result, most courts no longer require vertical privity between the buyer and the manufacturer in implied warranty actions.

b. UCC Alternatives on Horizontal Privity

Although UCC section 2-318 is silent on the issue of vertical privity, it offers the states three alternative versions on the issue of horizontal privity: Alternative A extends implied warranty protection to a *buyer's family*, *household*, *and guests* who suffer personal injury; Alternative B extends protection to any natural person who suffers personal injury; and Alternative C covers any person who suffers any injury. *Most states have adopted Alternative A*, the narrowest modification of the privity requirement.

6. Effect of Disclaimers

Disclaimers of liability for breach of implied warranty *must be specific* and are narrowly construed. [UCC §2-316] Contractual limitations on *personal injury* damages resulting from a breach of warranty for consumer goods are prima facie *unconscionable*. [UCC §2-719]

7. Causation

Issues of actual cause and proximate cause are treated as in an ordinary negligence case.

8. Damages

In addition to personal injury and property damages, purely *economic losses* are recoverable in implied warranty actions.

9. Defenses

a. Assumption of Risk

UCC section 2-715 indicates that when the plaintiff assumes the risk by using a product while knowing of the breach of warranty, any resulting injuries are not proximately caused by the breach.

b.   **Contributory Negligence**
Courts in contributory negligence jurisdictions have adopted an approach similar to that used in strict liability in tort—that unreasonable failure to discover the defect does not bar recovery but that unreasonable conduct *after* discovery does bar recovery.

c.   **Comparative Negligence**
So also, courts in comparative negligence jurisdictions use comparative fault notions in warranty cases to reduce the damage award in the same way as in strict liability cases.

d.   **Notice of Breach**
UCC section 2-607 requires the buyer to give the seller notice *within a reasonable time* after the buyer discovers or should have discovered the breach. Most courts have held that the requirement applies even in personal injury cases and where there is no privity between the parties.

F.   **REPRESENTATION THEORIES (EXPRESS WARRANTY AND MISREPRESENTATION OF FACT)**
The two theories discussed in this section differ from those previously discussed because they involve some affirmative representation by the defendant beyond the act of distributing a product. When the product does not live up to the representation, both contract and tort problems are created.

1.   **Express Warranty**
An express warranty arises where a seller or supplier makes any affirmation of fact or promise to the buyer relating to the goods that becomes part of the "basis of the bargain." [UCC §2-313]

a.   **Scope of Coverage**
As with implied warranties, Article 2A of the UCC extends express warranties to leases.

b.   **Privity Not Required**
Although UCC section 2-318 declares that its privity alternatives apply to express as well as implied warranties, most courts have held privity to be irrelevant in express warranty cases.

c.   **"Basis of the Bargain"**
If the buyer is suing, the warranty must have been "part of the basis of the bargain." This is probably less difficult to show than a buyer's subjective "reliance" on the representation. If someone not in privity is permitted to sue, this remote person need *not* have known about the affirmation as long as it became part of the basis of the bargain for someone else in the chain of distribution.

d.   **Basis of Liability—Breach of Warranty**
As with implied warranties, the plaintiff need *not* show that the breach occurred through the fault of the defendant, but only that a breach of the warranty did in fact occur.
Example: The defendant advertises its hand lotion as "completely safe" and "harmless." Even if there is nothing wrong with the product itself, a

buyer who suffers an allergic reaction may bring a successful warranty action.

e. Effect of Disclaimers
UCC section 2-316 provides that a disclaimer will be effective only to the extent that it can be read consistently with any express warranties made. This has the effect of making it practically impossible to disclaim an express warranty.

f. Causation, Damages, and Defenses
These elements are analyzed the same as under implied warranties, *supra*.

2. Misrepresentation of Fact
Liability for misrepresentation may arise when a representation by the seller about a product induces reliance by the buyer. In products cases, liability for misrepresentation is usually based on strict liability, but may also arise for intentional and negligent misrepresentations.

a. Defendant's State of Mind

1) Strict Liability
As long as the defendant is a seller engaged in the business of selling such products, there is no need to show fault on the defendant's part. The plaintiff need only show that the representation proved false, without regard to the defendant's state of mind.

2) Intentional Misrepresentation
For intentional misrepresentations, the plaintiff must show that the misrepresentation was made *knowingly* or with *reckless* disregard for the facts.

3) Negligent Misrepresentation
For negligence liability, knowledge of the misrepresentation on the part of the defendant need not be proved. The plaintiff need only show that a reasonable person should have known such representations to be false when making them.

b. Material Fact Required
The misrepresentation must be of a material fact, i.e., a fact concerning the quality, nature, or appropriate use of the product on which a normal buyer may be expected to rely. "Puffing" and statements of opinion are not sufficient.

c. Intent to Induce Reliance of Particular Buyer
The defendant must have intended to induce the reliance of the buyer, or a class of persons to which the buyer belongs, in a particular transaction. Evidence of a representation made to the public by label, advertisement, or otherwise is sufficient to show an intent to induce reliance by anyone into whose hands the product may come.

d. Justifiable Reliance
There is no liability if the misrepresentation is not known or does not influence the transaction. Reliance may be found if the representation was a *substantial factor* in inducing the purchase, even though not the sole inducement.

1) Reliance Need Not Be Victim's
As with express warranties, ***privity is irrelevant*** for misrepresentation and the required reliance may be shown to be that of a prior purchaser who passed the product on to the victim.

Example: D, a manufacturer of automobiles, advertises that its cars contain "shatterproof" glass. H reads this advertisement and, partly in reliance on it, buys one of D's cars. While H's friend, F, is driving the car, a stone is thrown through the windshield, shattering the glass. F, hurt by flying glass, has a strict liability action against D for misrepresentation even though F is not in privity with D and knows nothing of the "shatterproof" representation.

e. Actual Cause
Reliance by the purchaser serves to show actual cause.

f. Proximate Cause and Damages
Both elements are analyzed in the same manner as for products liability cases based on negligence or strict liability, *supra*. If the plaintiff can show that the misrepresentation was intentional, some courts will allow punitive damages to be claimed.

g. Defenses

1) Assumption of Risk
If the plaintiff is entitled to rely on the representation, a defense of assumption of risk does not apply.

Example: D markets a mace pen to be used against attackers. The product's label says that it instantly renders attackers helpless when sprayed in their faces. When holdup men demanded money from P, P shot his mace pen in their faces but it had no effect—except that the attackers got angry and shot P. D's claim that P assumed the risk of injury by not complying with the attackers' demands fails, since P reasonably relied on the product to achieve its stated results.

2) Contributory Negligence (Fault)
Whether contributory negligence is a defense depends on the type of misrepresentation. For negligent misrepresentations, contributory negligence is a valid defense. In strict liability actions, the plaintiff's unreasonable behavior is analyzed as in other strict liability actions for defective products, *supra*. If the plaintiff can show that the defendant's misrepresentation was intentional, contributory negligence would be no defense.

VI. NUISANCE

A. BASIS OF LIABILITY
Nuisance is ***not*** a separate tort in itself, subject to rules of its own. Nuisances are types of harm—the invasion of either private property rights or public rights by conduct that is tortious because

it falls into the usual categories of tort liability. In other words, the defendant's conduct may have been intentional or negligent or subjected to liability on a strict liability basis. As a practical matter, nuisances generally are *intentional* interferences because defendant has been made aware that his conduct is interfering with plaintiff's use of her land. (If strict liability is the basis for redressing a nuisance, courts sometimes refer to this as an "absolute" nuisance or "nuisance per se.")

B. PRIVATE NUISANCE

Private nuisance is a *substantial, unreasonable interference* with another private individual's *use or enjoyment* of property he actually possesses or to which he has a right of immediate possession.

1. Substantial Interference

The interference with plaintiff's right in his land must be substantial. This means that it must be *offensive, inconvenient, or annoying to an average person in the community*. It will not be characterized as substantial if it is merely the result of plaintiff's hypersensitivity or specialized use of his own property.

2. Unreasonable Interference

For a nuisance based on intent or negligence, the interference with plaintiff's use of his land must be unreasonable. To be characterized as unreasonable, the severity of the inflicted *injury must outweigh the utility* of defendant's conduct. In balancing these respective interests, courts take into account that every person is entitled to use his own land in a reasonable way, considering the neighborhood, land values, and existence of any alternative courses of conduct open to defendant.

3. Trespass to Land Distinguished

Trespass to land is to be distinguished from private nuisance. In the former, there is an interference with the landowner's *exclusive possession* by a physical invasion of the land; in the latter, there is an interference with *use or enjoyment*.

C. PUBLIC NUISANCE

Public nuisance is an act that unreasonably interferes with the *health, safety, or property rights of the community*, e.g., blocking a highway or using a building to commit criminal activities such as prostitution, bookmaking, etc. Recovery is available for public nuisance only if a private party has suffered some unique damage not suffered by the public at large.

Example: Pedestrians generally are inconvenienced by having to walk around an obstruction maintained by defendant on the sidewalk. Plaintiff, however, has tripped and fallen. This unique damage permits plaintiff to recover for the public nuisance.

D. REMEDIES

1. Damages

For a private nuisance, or for a public nuisance where plaintiff has suffered some unique damage, the usual remedy is damages.

2. Injunctive Relief

Where the *legal remedy* of damages is *unavailable or inadequate*, injunctive relief may be granted. The legal remedy may be inadequate for a variety of reasons, e.g., the nuisance is a continuing wrong, the nuisance is of the kind that will cause irreparable injury, etc. In deciding whether an injunction should issue, the courts take into consideration the relative hardships that will result to the parties from the grant or denial of the injunction. Hardships will not be balanced, however, where defendant's conduct was willful.

3. Abatement by Self-Help

a. Abatement of Private Nuisance
One has the privilege to enter upon defendant's land and personally abate the nuisance after notice to defendant and defendant's refusal to act. The force used may be only that necessary to accomplish the abatement, and the plaintiff is liable for additional harm done.

b. Abatement of Public Nuisance
One who has suffered some unique damage has a similar privilege to abate a public nuisance by self-help. In the absence of such unique damage, however, a public nuisance may be abated or enjoined only by public authority.

E. DEFENSES

1. Legislative Authority
Conduct consistent with what a zoning ordinance or other legislative license permits is relevant but not conclusive evidence that the use is not a nuisance.

2. Conduct of Others
No one actor is liable for all the damage caused by the concurrence of his acts and others.
Example: Ten steel mills are polluting a stream. Each steel mill is responsible only for the pollution it causes.

3. Contributory Negligence
Contributory negligence is not ordinarily a defense to the tort of nuisance. However, when a nuisance is based on a negligence theory, one may not avert the consequences of his own contributory negligence by affixing to the negligence of the wrongdoer the label of a nuisance. In such a case, a plaintiff, though pleading nuisance, may have to show his freedom from contributory negligence.

4. "Coming to the Nuisance"
The problem: Has plaintiff assumed the risk, thereby being barred from recovery by the fact that he has "come to the nuisance," by purchasing land and moving in next to the nuisance after it is already in existence or operation? The prevailing rule is that, in the absence of a prescriptive right, the defendant may not condemn surrounding premises to endure the nuisance; i.e., the ***purchaser is entitled to reasonable use or enjoyment of his land*** to the same extent as any other owner as long as he buys in good faith and not for the sole purpose of a harassing lawsuit.

VII. GENERAL CONSIDERATIONS FOR ALL TORT CASES

A. VICARIOUS LIABILITY

Vicarious liability is liability that is derivatively imposed. In short, this means that one person commits a tortious act against a third party, and another person is liable to the third party for this act. This may be so even though the other person has played no part in it, has done nothing whatever to aid or encourage it, or indeed has done everything possible to prevent it. This liability rests upon a special relationship between the tortfeasor and the person to whom his tortious conduct is ultimately imputed.

The basic situations that you should note for bar examination purposes are set out below.

1. Doctrine of Respondeat Superior

A master/employer will be vicariously liable for tortious acts committed by her servant/employee if the tortious acts occur *within the scope of the employment relationship*.

a. Frolic and Detour

An employee on a delivery or on a business trip for his employer may commit a tort while deviating from the employer's business to run a personal errand. If the deviation was minor in time and geographic area, the employee will still be considered to be acting within the scope of employment rather than on a "frolic" of his own (for which the employer would not be liable).

b. Intentional Torts

It is usually held that intentional tortious conduct by employees is *not* within the scope of employment. In some circumstances, however, courts find intentional tortious conduct to be within the ambit of this relationship, such as when:

1) Force is authorized in the employment, e.g., bouncer.

2) Friction is generated by the employment, e.g., bill collector.

3) The employee is furthering the business of the employer, e.g., removing customers from the premises because they are rowdy.

c. Liability for Own Negligence

Employers may be liable for their *own negligence* by negligently selecting or supervising their employees. This is *not* vicarious liability, however.

2. Independent Contractor Situations

In general, a principal will *not* be vicariously liable for tortious acts of her agent if the latter is an independent contractor. Two *broad exceptions* exist, however:

(i) The independent contractor is engaged in *inherently dangerous activities*, e.g., excavating next to a public sidewalk, blasting.

(ii) The duty, because of *public policy* considerations, is simply nondelegable, e.g., the duty of a business to keep its premises safe for customers.

a. **Liability for Own Negligence**

An employer may be liable for her ***own negligence*** in selecting or supervising the independent contractor (e.g., hospital liable for contracting with unqualified and incompetent physician who negligently treats hospital's patient). (This is ***not*** vicarious liability.)

3. **Partners and Joint Venturers**

Each member of a partnership or joint venture is vicariously liable for the tortious conduct of another member committed in the scope and course of the affairs of the partnership or joint venture.

a. **What Is a Joint Venture?**

A joint venture, although similar to a partnership, is for a more limited time period and more limited purpose. It is generally an undertaking to execute a small number of acts or objectives. A joint venture exists when two or more people enter into an activity if two elements are present:

1) **Common Purpose**

The test is not precise, but it would appear that the majority of courts would now look for a "business purpose." The sharing of expenses between individuals is often highly persuasive.

Examples: 1) Two roommates were driving to a store to get decorating materials for their apartment when an accident occurred. *Held:* Joint venture.

2) Two parents were driving child to hospital. *Held:* No joint venture.

2) **Mutual Right of Control**

It is not crucial that the party does or does not give directions; it is sufficient if there is an understanding between the parties that each has a right to have her desires respected on the same basis as the others.

4. **Automobile Owner for Driver**

The general rule is that an automobile owner is ***not vicariously liable*** for the tortious conduct of another driving his automobile. However, many states by statute or judicial precedent have adopted the "***family car***" doctrine, by which the owner is liable for tortious conduct of ***immediate family or household members*** who are driving with the owner's express or implied permission. A number of states have now gone further by enacting "***permissive use***" statutes imposing liability for damage caused by ***anyone*** driving with such consent.

a. **Liability for Owner's Negligence**

Remember that the owner may be liable for her ***own negligence*** in entrusting the car to a driver. Some states have also imposed liability upon the owner if she was present in the car at the time of the accident, upon the theory that she could have prevented the negligent driving, and hence was negligent herself in not doing so. (This is not vicarious liability.)

5. Bailor for Bailee

Under the general rule, the bailor is *not vicariously liable* for the tortious conduct of his bailee. As above, the bailor may be liable for her *own negligence* in entrusting the bailed object. (This is not vicarious liability.)

6. Parent for Child

A parent is *not vicariously liable* for the tortious conduct of the child at common law. Note, however, that most states, by statute, make parents liable for the willful and intentional torts of their minor children up to a certain dollar amount (e.g., $5,000).

a. Child Acting as Agent for Parents

Courts may impose vicarious liability if the child commits a tort while acting as the agent for the parents.

Example: Parent vicariously liable if child is in an accident while running an errand for his mother, or driving his sister to school, but not while on a date.

b. Parent Liable for Own Negligence

The parent may be held liable for her *own negligence* in allowing the child to do something, e.g., use a dangerous object without proper instruction. Further, if the parent is apprised of the child's conduct on past occasions showing a tendency to injure another's person or property, she may be liable for not using due care in exercising control to mitigate such conduct, e.g., by allowing the child to play with other children he has a history of attacking.

7. Tavernkeepers

At common law, no liability was imposed on vendors of intoxicating beverages for injuries resulting from the vendee's intoxication, whether the injuries were sustained by the vendee or by a third person as a result of the vendee's conduct. Many states, to avoid this common law rule, have enacted *"Dramshop Acts."* Such acts usually create a *cause of action in favor of any third person injured* by the intoxicated vendee. Several courts have imposed liability on tavernkeepers even in the absence of a Dramshop Act. This liability is based on ordinary negligence principles (the foreseeable risk of serving a minor or obviously intoxicated adult) rather than vicarious liability.

B. PARTIES—MULTIPLE DEFENDANT ISSUES

1. Joint and Several Liability

When two or more tortious acts combine to proximately cause an *indivisible* injury to a plaintiff, each tortfeasor is jointly and severally liable for that injury. This means that *each is liable* to the plaintiff for the *entire damage* incurred. Joint and several liability applies even though each tortfeasor acted entirely independently. However, if the actions are independent, plaintiff's injury is divisible, and it is possible to identify the portion of injuries caused by each defendant (e.g., Car 1 breaks plaintiff's leg, and Car 2 breaks plaintiff's arm), then each will only be liable for the identifiable portion.

a. Tortfeasors Acting in Concert

When two or more tortfeasors act in concert (i.e., by agreement) and injure plaintiff, then each will be jointly and severally liable for the entire injury. This is so even though the injury is divisible and one could identify what each tortfeasor has done alone.

b. Statutory Limitations
Many states have limited the joint liability doctrine by statute in cases based on fault. Two of the most common types of statutes abolish joint liability either (i) for those tortfeasors judged to be less at fault than the plaintiff, or (ii) for all tortfeasors with regard to noneconomic damages (e.g., pain and suffering). The liability of a tortfeasor in these situations is proportional to his fault.

2. Satisfaction and Release

a. Satisfaction
If plaintiff recovers full payment from one tortfeasor, either by settlement or payment of a judgment, there is a "satisfaction." She may not recover further against any other joint tortfeasor. Until there is a satisfaction, however, she may proceed against other jointly liable parties.

b. Release
A release is a surrender of plaintiff's cause of action against the party to whom the release is given. In most states, a release of one tortfeasor does *not* discharge other tortfeasors unless expressly provided in the release agreement. Rather, the claim against the others is reduced to the extent of the amount stipulated in the agreement or the amount of consideration paid, whichever is greater.

3. Contribution and Indemnity

a. Contribution
As stated above, where joint and several tort liability exists, it permits plaintiff to recover the entire judgment amount from any tortfeasor. The rule of contribution, adopted in some form in most states, allows any tortfeasor required to pay more than his share of damages to have a claim against the other jointly liable parties for the excess. Thus, contribution is a device whereby responsibility is *apportioned* among those who are at fault.

1) Methods of Apportionment

a) Comparative Contribution
Most states have a comparative contribution system (discussed below), whereby contribution is imposed *in proportion to the relative fault* of the various tortfeasors.

b) Equal Shares
A minority of states require all tortfeasors to pay *equal shares* regardless of their respective degrees of fault.

2) Contribution Tortfeasor Must Have Liability
The tortfeasor from whom contribution is sought must be originally liable to the plaintiff. If the contribution tortfeasor has a defense that would bar liability, such as intra-family tort immunity, he is not liable for contribution.

3) Not Applicable to Intentional Torts
Contribution is not allowed in favor of those who committed intentional torts. This is so even though each of the tortfeasors was equally culpable.

b. Indemnity
Indemnity involves *shifting the entire loss* between or among tortfeasors, in contrast to apportioning it as in contribution. Indemnity is available in the following circumstances:

1) Right to Indemnity by Contract
Contracts in which one person promises to indemnify another against consequences of his own negligence are generally upheld. The right to indemnification will not be read into an agreement unless there is evidence that the right was clearly intended.

2) Vicarious Liability
When one is held for damages caused by another simply because of his relationship to that person (e.g., employer for employee's torts, landowner with nondelegable duty breached by an independent contractor, etc.), this party may seek indemnification from the person whose conduct actually caused the damage.

3) Indemnity Under Strict Products Liability
Each supplier of a defective product, where strict liability rules apply, is liable to an injured customer, but each supplier has a right of indemnification against all previous suppliers in the distribution chain. The manufacturer is ultimately liable if the product was defective when it left its control.

4) Identifiable Difference in Degree of Fault
A number of jurisdictions extend the principle of indemnity to allow one joint tortfeasor to recover against a co-joint tortfeasor where there is a considerable difference in degree of fault. In other words, he who is least at fault may be able to recover indemnification from the "more wrongful" tortfeasor.

a) Examples
The most common examples of such indemnification are:

(1) Retailers Who Negligently Rely on Product's Condition
Retailers who negligently fail to discover a product's defect may receive indemnification from the manufacturer who negligently manufactured it.

(2) Where Liability Imposed Under Secondary Duty
One whose liability is based on a secondary duty may recover indemnification from the person who had a primary duty.
Example: Municipal corporation under duty to keep streets safe may recover from a person who creates the unsafe condition causing an accident.

(3) Active/Passive Negligence Doctrine
Some jurisdictions allow a joint tortfeasor who is passively negligent to recover indemnification from a joint tortfeasor who is actively negligent.

Example: Charles parked his car in a no-parking zone, blocking the view of drivers approaching the intersection. Bowater, driving at 70 m.p.h., hits a pedestrian who could not be seen until it was too late to stop. If the pedestrian sues Charles and recovers, Charles may seek full reimbursement from Bowater by way of indemnification.

b) Effect of Comparative Negligence System

Most states with comparative negligence systems *reject* indemnity in degree of fault situations, instead applying a general comparative contribution system and apportioning damages based upon relative fault (*see* discussion below). These states continue to permit indemnity where indemnity rules are not based on differences in degree of fault, e.g., vicarious liability cases.

c. Comparative Contribution

A *majority* of states have now adopted a comparative contribution system based on the *relative fault* of the various tortfeasors. Comparative contribution changes the traditional method of apportionment in contribution cases (*supra*) and supplants indemnification rules based on identifiable differences in degree of fault. In both situations, nonpaying tortfeasors are required to contribute only in proportion to their relative fault.

Example: Plaintiff suffers $100,000 in damages from the combined negligence of D1 and D2. The jury determines that D1 is 80% at fault and D2 is 20% at fault. Applying joint and several liability rules, plaintiff recovers all $100,000 of her damages from D2. Under comparative contribution, D2 can recover $80,000 from D1.

C. SURVIVAL AND WRONGFUL DEATH

1. Survival of Tort Actions

At common law, a tort action abated at the death of either the tortfeasor or the victim. Most states have changed this by statute, i.e., the "survival acts." Thus, a victim's cause of action will survive to permit recovery of all damages from the time of injury to the time of death. In the majority of states, these acts apply to both torts to *property* and torts resulting in *personal injury*.

a. Torts that Expire on Victim's Death

Exceptions exist in most jurisdictions for those torts that invade an *intangible personal interest,* e.g., defamation, malicious prosecution, etc. These torts are felt to be so personal as to expire upon the victim's death.

2. Wrongful Death

Every state has now enacted some form of wrongful death act.

a. Who May Bring Action?

In some jurisdictions, the personal representative is the proper party to bring the action; in others, the surviving spouse or next of kin herself might be the proper party.

b. Measure of Recovery

The measure of recovery in wrongful death actions under most statutes is for the pecuniary injury resulting to the spouse and next of kin. Basically, this allows recovery for loss of support, loss of companionship, etc. It does *not* allow any recovery for decedent's pain and suffering; those damages would be an element of a personal injury survival action (*see* above) brought on behalf of the decedent.

1) Deaths of Children, Elderly People
Even though the actual loss of support may be very small where decedent is a child or elderly person, most states, nonetheless, allow recovery. Usually, the judgment is quite modest.

2) Rights of Creditors
Creditors of the decedent have no claim against the amount awarded.

c. Effect of Defenses

1) Defenses Against Deceased
Recovery is allowed *only* to the extent that the deceased could have recovered in the action if he had lived. Thus, for example, his contributory negligence would reduce or bar a wrongful death recovery in comparative negligence states.

2) Defenses Against Beneficiary
Defenses against potential beneficiaries do not bar the action. However, that particular beneficiary's recovery will be reduced or barred under the state's comparative negligence rules. The total damage award assessed by the jury will be reduced by the amount withheld from the beneficiary.

D. TORTIOUS INTERFERENCES WITH FAMILY RELATIONSHIPS

1. Husband-Wife
In most jurisdictions, both husbands and wives may recover damages for loss of their spouse's consortium or services because of injuries to the spouse from defendant's tortious conduct, whether intentional, negligent, or based on strict liability.

Example: Chauncey hits Husband on the head with a lead pipe, leaving him in a coma for several months and permanently disabled. Wife can recover from Chauncey for loss of consortium and services.

2. Parent-Child

a. Parent's Actions
A parent may maintain an action for loss of the child's services and consortium when the child is injured as a result of defendant's tortious conduct, whether such conduct is intentional, negligent, or based on strict liability.

b. Child's Action
A child has *no* action in most jurisdictions against one who tortiously injures his parent.

3. Nature of Action for Family Relationship Interference
The action for interference with family relationships is *derivative.* Recovery in the derivative action depends on the potential success of the injured family member's own action. Thus,

any defense that could be raised against the injured family member, e.g., her own contributory negligence, can also be raised in the derivative action for interference with family relationships.

Furthermore, a defense against a family member seeking such a derivative recovery may also be raised in this action.

Example: Husband and Wife, while driving, collide with Chauncey's car. Wife is severely injured; Husband and Chauncey are both negligent. Husband's recovery in his derivative action for loss of Wife's consortium and services will be reduced or barred by his own contributory negligence.

E. TORT IMMUNITIES

1. Intra-Family Tort Immunities

a. Injury to Person
Under the traditional view, one member of a family unit (i.e., husband, wife, or unemancipated child) could *not* sue another in tort for personal injury. This view has undergone substantial change in most states.

1) Husband-Wife Immunity Abolished
Most states have abolished interspousal immunity. Either spouse may now maintain a tort action against the other.

2) Parent-Child Immunity Limited
A slight majority of states have abolished parent-child immunity; however, these states generally grant parents broad discretion in the parent's exercise of parental authority or supervision. The remaining states retain parent-child immunity but do not apply it in cases of *intentional* tortious conduct and, in many of these states, in *automobile accident* cases (at least to the extent of insurance coverage).

b. Injury to Property
A suit for property damage may usually be maintained by any family member against any other family member. In short, to the extent that intra-family tort immunity exists, it applies to personal, not property, injuries.

2. Governmental Tort Immunity
Under the doctrine of sovereign immunity, governmental units were traditionally not subject to tort actions unless they had consented to the suit. Now, by statute and judicial decision, that immunity is considerably limited. Note, however, that a waiver of sovereign immunity does not create any new tort duties; it only waives immunity for existing statutory or common law duties of care.

a. Federal Government
By virtue of the Federal Tort Claims Act, Title 28 U.S.C., the United States has *waived immunity* for tortious acts. Under its provisions, the federal government may now be held liable to the same extent as a private individual. However, the Act spells out several situations where this immunity will still attach:

1) United States Still Immune for Certain Enumerated Torts

Immunity still attaches for (i) assault, (ii) battery, (iii) false imprisonment, (iv) false arrest, (v) malicious prosecution, (vi) abuse of process, (vii) libel and slander, (viii) misrepresentation and deceit, and (ix) interference with contract rights.

2) Discretionary Acts Distinguished from Ministerial Acts

The immunity is not waived for acts characterized as "discretionary," as distinguished from those acts termed "ministerial." In general, discretionary activity is that which takes place at the *planning or decisionmaking level*, while ministerial acts are performed at the *operational level* of government (e.g., repairing traffic signals, driving a vehicle).

3) Government Contractors

A government contractor may assert the federal government's immunity defense in a products liability case if the contractor conformed to reasonable, precise specifications approved by the government and warned the government about any known dangers in the product.

b. State Governments

Most states have substantially waived their immunity from tort actions to the same extent as the federal government. Thus, immunity still attaches for discretionary acts and for legislative and judicial decisionmaking.

Note: Where federal or state sovereign immunity still attaches, it also, as a general rule, covers not only "the government" but the various federal and state agencies as well, e.g., schools, hospitals, etc.

c. Municipalities

About half of the states have abolished municipal tort immunity by statute or judicial decision to the same extent that they have waived their own immunity. Hence, immunity is abolished for everything but discretionary acts and policy decisions.

1) Immunity Abolished—Public Duty Rule Limitation

Where municipal immunity has been abolished, many courts apply the "public duty" doctrine to limit the scope of government liability. A duty that is owed to the public at large, such as the duty of police to protect citizens, is not owed to any particular citizen, and no liability exists for failure to provide police protection in the absence of a *special relationship* between the municipality and the citizen that gives rise to a special duty. A special relationship can be shown by: (i) an assumption by the municipality, through promises or actions, of an affirmative duty to act on behalf of the party who was injured; (ii) knowledge on the part of the municipality's agents that inaction could lead to harm; (iii) some form of direct contact between the municipality's agents and the injured party; and (iv) that party's justifiable reliance on the municipality's affirmative undertaking.

2) Immunity Retained—Limited to Governmental Functions

Where municipal immunity still exists in its traditional form, the courts have sought in many instances to avoid its consequences. This has primarily been accomplished by differentiating between "governmental" and "proprietary" functions of the municipality. Immunity attaches to the former but not to the latter.

a) Governmental Functions

Certain functions historically have been construed such that they could only be performed adequately by the government, and thus they are held to be "governmental" in character, e.g., police, fire, courts, etc. As stated above, ***tort immunity attaches*** to those functions.

b) Proprietary Functions

If the municipality is performing a function that might as well have been provided by a private corporation, the function is construed as a "proprietary" one (e.g., utility companies, maintaining airport parking lot, etc.). ***No tort immunity*** attaches here.

The inference that a function is "proprietary" is strengthened where the city collects ***revenues*** by virtue of providing the service.

d. Immunity of Public Officials

In addition to the immunity conferred on the government entity, government officials may also have immunity from tort liability. Immunity applies to a public officer carrying out his official duties where they involve ***discretionary*** acts (*supra*) done without malice or improper purpose. On the other hand, for acts that are construed as ***ministerial*** (which generally involve lower-level officials), no tort immunity applies.

3. Charitable Immunity

The majority of jurisdictions have abrogated the common law rule of charitable immunity either by statute or decision. Even where such immunity still exists, it is riddled with exceptions.